Fodor's

FLORIDA

Welcome to Florida

With its accessible and varied pleasures, Florida is a favorite of many. Drawn to the colonial charm of St. Augustine, Miami's pulsing nightlife, the glitz of Palm Beach, or the quiet expanse of the Everglades, almost all visitors find something to love here. From the powdery white beaches of the Panhandle to the vibrant coral reefs of the Florida Keys, the ocean is always calling—for sailing, fishing, diving, swimming, and other water sports. Stray off the path a few miles, and you might glimpse a bit of the Florida of old, including cigar makers and mermaids.

TOP REASONS TO GO

★ **Miami:** A vibrant, multicultural metropolis that buzzes both day and night.

★ **Beaches:** Surf-pounded on the Atlantic coast, powdery and pure white on the Gulf.

★ **Key West:** Quirky, fun, and tacky, it's both family-friendly and decidedly not.

★ **Golf:** Oceanfront and inland, some of the country's finest links are found here.

★ **Theme parks:** The state has some of the biggest and best, not all of them Disney.

★ **Family fun:** From shelling in Sanibel to meeting astronauts at Kennedy Space Center.

Contents

Fodor's Features

Contents

MAPS

Chapter 1

EXPERIENCE FLORIDA

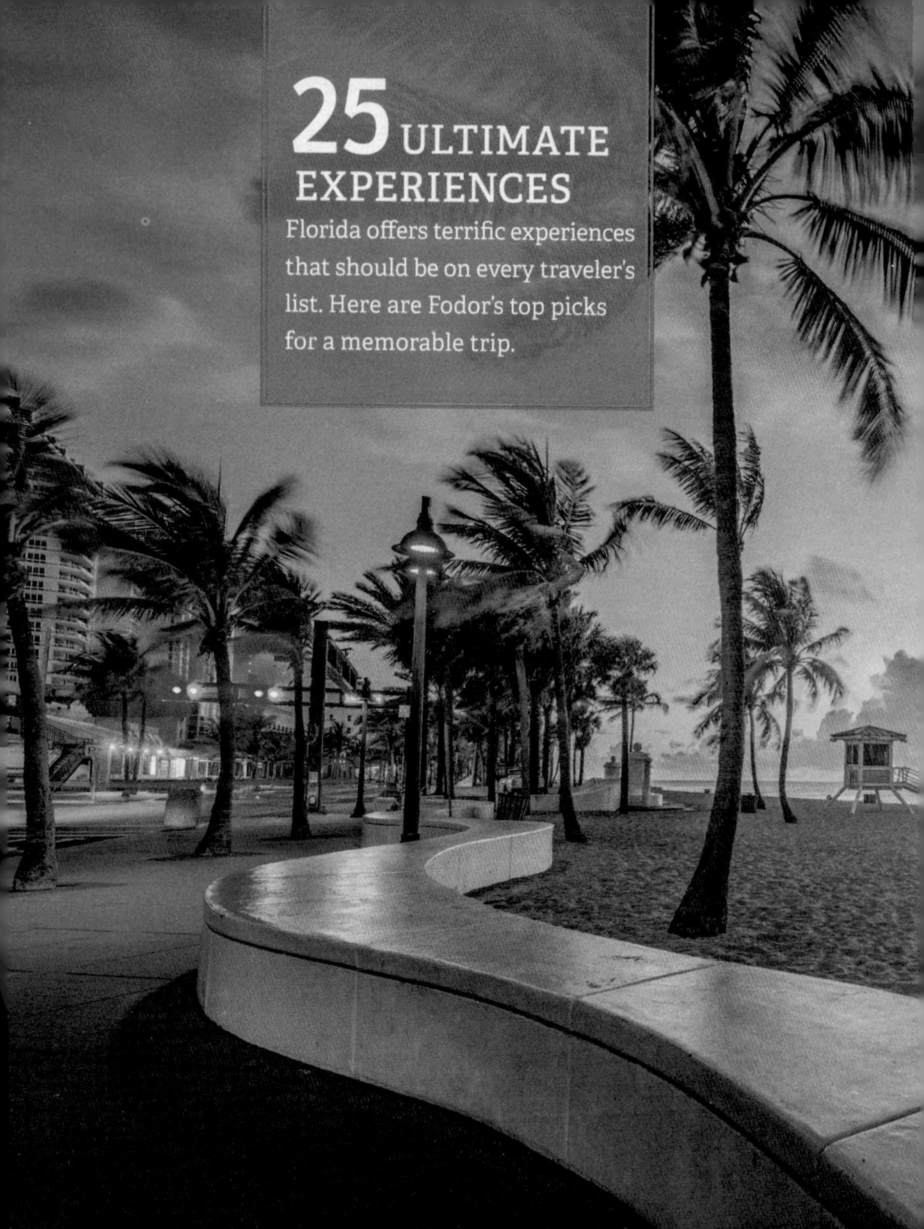

25 ULTIMATE EXPERIENCES
Florida offers terrific experiences that should be on every traveler's list. Here are Fodor's top picks for a memorable trip.

1 Hit the Beaches

Florida's many stretches of sand are just as varied as the state itself. Collect seashells on Sanibel Island, bar hop on South Beach, or snorkel in Key West. If a quieter coastline appeals, head to Blowing Rocks Preserve or South Walton. *(Ch. 3, 5, 6, 7, 8, 9, 13, 14)*

2 Admire Art Deco

Check out Miami's iconic 1920s architecture—the largest collection of art deco buildings in the world, with 800-plus preserved, pastel beauties—at the Art Deco Museum. *(Ch. 3)*

3 Snorkel and Dive in the Keys

Swim past a shipwreck and the U.S.'s only living coral reef at John Pennekamp Coral Reef State Park in Key Largo. *(Ch. 5)*

4 Photograph the Wynwood Walls

Graffiti artists around the globe create murals for this hip outdoor gallery, with over 80,000 square feet of colorful walls to explore. *(Ch. 3)*

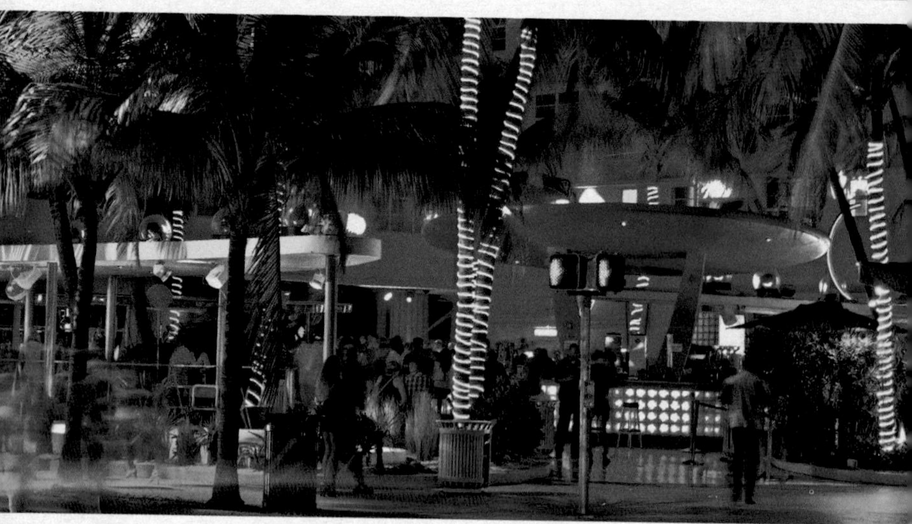

5 Party in Miami

Alternate between dancing and people-watching at the late-night lounges that helped earn South Beach its party-heavy rep. *(Ch. 3)*

6 Zip Through the Everglades

To really experience this national park, tour the swamp on an airboat and keep your eyes peeled for gators. *(Ch. 4)*

7 Shop at Boutiques

Miami's Design District, Fort Lauderdale's Las Olas Boulevard, and Palm Beach's Worth Avenue are a shopper's paradise. *(Ch. 3, 6, 7)*

8 Experience Cuban Culture

Little Havana's main drag, Calle Ocho, is where to find Miami's best Cuban restaurants and bars. Don't leave without trying a Cuban sandwich. *(Ch. 3)*

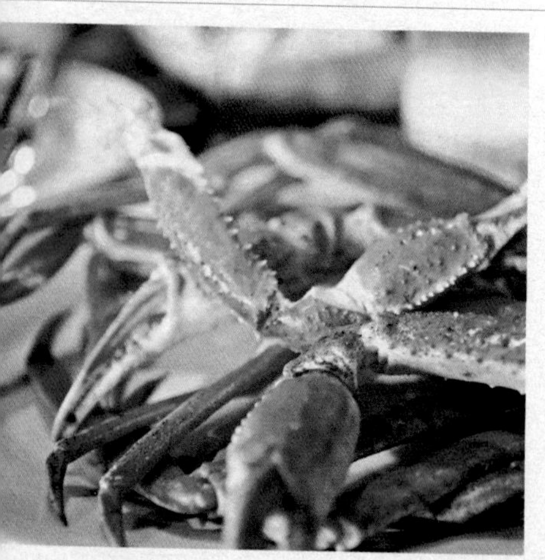

9 Eat Fresh Seafood

It's practically required on your visit to Florida to eat a fresh catch of the day baked, broiled, or blackened with Cajun spice. *(Ch. 3, 4, 5, 6, 7)*

10 Visit Ernest Hemingway's Home

The legendary American author's Key West home looks nearly the same as it did in the '30s—six-toed cats (descendants of his pet, Snow White) and all. *(Ch. 5)*

11 Catch a Sports Game

Cheering for the team is a huge part of Florida culture. Take your pick: the Miami Dolphins, Florida Gators, or FSU Seminoles are top teams. *(Ch. 3, 13, 14)*

12 Get Pampered in Palm Beach

In this glam town, you can stay at luxe resorts like The Breakers, shop at chic boutiques, play golf at the PGA National Resort, and gawk at palatial mansions. *(Ch. 7)*

13 Feel the Magic at Universal

Thrill-seekers flock to the cinema-centric Universal Studios and sister park Islands of Adventure, home of the magical Wizarding World of Harry Potter. *(Ch. 12)*

14 Swim with Manatees

One-sixth of Florida's sea cows make their way to Crystal River's warm, spring-fed waters each winter—the only place in the U.S. where you can legally swim with them. *(Ch. 8)*

15 Paddleboard on Coastal Dune Lakes

Of the Panhandle's white-sand beaches, South Walton's are some of the only in the world—along with New Zealand and Australia—with coastal dune lakes. *(Ch. 14)*

16 Witness a Rocket Launch

NASA's working spaceflight facility in Cape Canaveral's Kennedy Space Center is located just 45 minutes from Orlando and features the closest public-viewing points to the rocket launches. *(Ch. 13)*

17 Sample Craft Beer

Florida's craft beer scene is on the rise, with more than 200 breweries sprouting up statewide. Head to Cigar City in Tampa or hit the Ale Trail in Jacksonville. *(Ch. 8, 10, 13, 14)*

18 Explore Tampa Bay

Walk along the waterfront at the Riverwalk, ride rollercoasters at Busch Gardens, or dine and shop at hot spot Oxford Exchange before heading to Clearwater Beach. *(Ch. 8)*

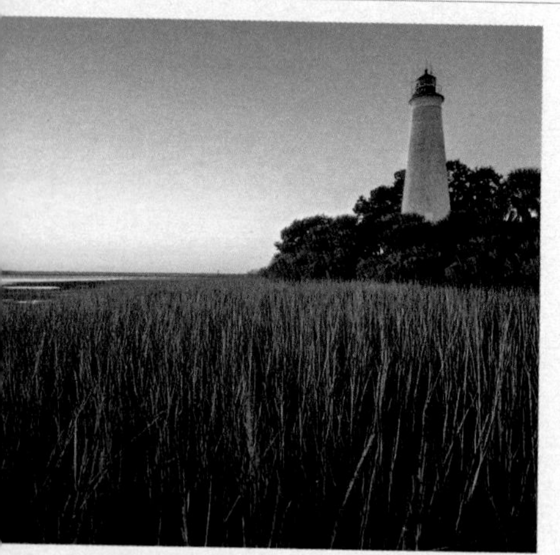

19 Find "Old Florida"

To see Florida as it was before the theme parks and high rises, head to the Northwest to dig into Apalachicola oysters at family-run restaurants or dive into Wakulla Springs. *(Ch. 14)*

20 Gawk at the Dalí Museum

What started as a private collection in St. Petersburg has expanded into one of the largest displays of Dalí's work outside of Europe. *(Ch. 8)*

21 Step Right Up to The Ringling

You could spend an entire day exploring the waterfront estate in Sarasota where circus star John Ringling built his museum, modeled after Florence's Uffizi Gallery. *(Ch. 8)*

22 Collect Shells on Sanibel

Hundreds of thousands of shells are swept to shore by the Gulf here, where shelling is so popular that locals created a term for collectors' stance: the "Sanibel stoop." *(Ch. 9)*

23 Race to Daytona

The World Center of Racing's DAYTONA 500 takes place every February. Get in on the excitement by riding shotgun with a pro around the famous track. *(Ch. 13)*

24 Soak Up History in St. Augustine

The star attraction, Castillo de San Marcos—a waterfront Spanish fortress made of coquina shells—was built more than 350 years ago. *(Ch. 13)*

25 Be a Kid at Walt Disney World

Mickey, the princesses, and even Star Wars characters come to life at the 40-square-mile resort—home to four theme parks, including the legendary Magic Kingdom. *(Ch. 11)*

WHAT'S WHERE

1 Miami and Miami Beach. Greater Miami is hot—and we're not just talking about the weather. Art deco buildings and balmy beaches set the scene. Vacations here are as much about lifestyle as locale, so prepare for power shopping, club-hopping, and decadent dining.

2 The Everglades. Covering more than 1.5 million acres, the fabled "River of Grass" is the state's greatest natural treasure. Biscayne National Park (95% of which is underwater) runs a close second. It's the largest marine park in the United States.

3 The Florida Keys. This slender necklace of landfalls, strung together by a 113-mile highway, marks the southern edge of the continental United States. It's nirvana for anglers, divers, literature lovers, and Jimmy Buffett wannabes.

4 Fort Lauderdale with Broward County. The town *Where the Boys Are* has grown up. The beaches that first attracted college kids are now complemented by luxe lodgings and upscale entertainment options.

5 Palm Beach with the Treasure Coast. This area scores points for diversity. Palm Beach and environs are famous for their golden sand and glitzy residents, whereas the Treasure Coast has unspoiled natural delights.

6 The Tampa Bay Area. Tampa's Busch Gardens and Ybor City are only part of the area's appeal. Culture vultures flock to St. Petersburg and Sarasota for concerts and museums, and eco-adventurers veer north to the Nature Coast.

7 The Lower Gulf Coast. Blessed with beaches, this was the last bit of coast to be settled. But as Naples's manicured golf greens and Fort Myers's mansions-cum-museums prove, it is far from uncivilized.

8 Orlando and Environs. Theme parks are what draw most visitors to the area, yet downtown Orlando, Kissimmee, and Winter Park have enough sights, shops, and restaurants to make them destinations in their own right.

9 Walt Disney World. The granddaddy of attractions, Disney is four theme parks in one—Magic Kingdom, Animal Kingdom, Epcot, and Hollywood Studios. Plus it has a pair of water parks and Disney Springs (an entertainment, dining, and shopping area).

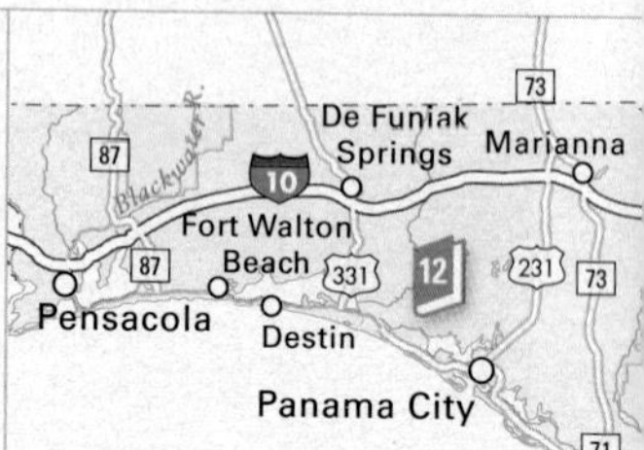

10 Universal Orlando. The movies are brought to life at Universal Studios, while Islands of Adventure delivers gravity-defying rides and special-effects surprises. Each has its own Wizarding World of Harry Potter (Diagon Alley and Hogsmeade, respectively). And there's Volcano Bay water park.

11 Northeast Florida. Though time rewinds in historic St. Augustine, it's on fast-forward in Daytona Beach and the Space Coast, where horse-drawn carriages are replaced by race cars and rocket ships.

12 Northwest Florida. Southern gentility and a slow pace make Northwest Florida (also called the Panhandle) a charming place—but it's the green Gulf waters and sugar-white sand that keep devotees coming back.

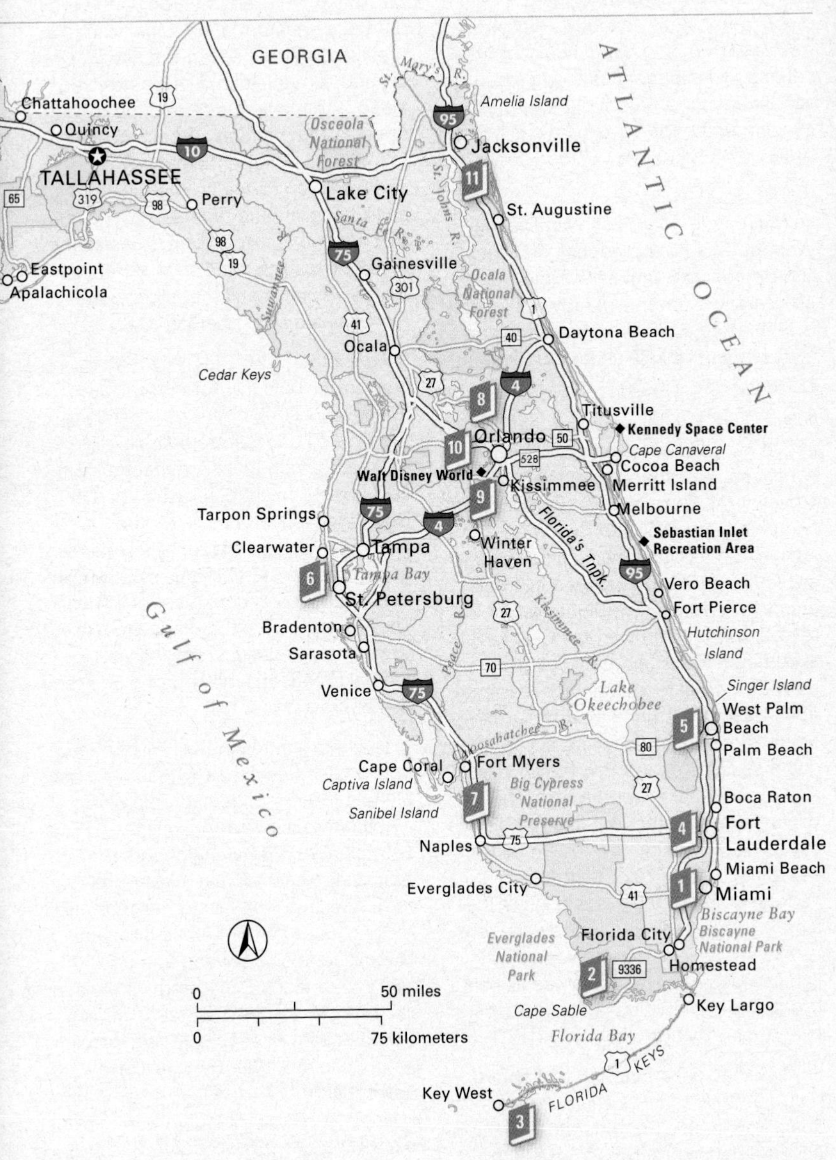
GEORGIA
ATLANTIC OCEAN
Gulf of Mexico
Chattahoochee
Quincy
TALLAHASSEE
Perry
Eastpoint
Apalachicola
Osceola National Forest
Lake City
Jacksonville
Amelia Island
St. Mary's R.
St. Augustine
St. Johns R.
Santa Fe R.
Gainesville
Ocala National Forest
Suwannee
Daytona Beach
Ocala
Cedar Keys
Titusville
Kennedy Space Center
Orlando
Cape Canaveral
Cocoa Beach
Walt Disney World
Kissimmee
Merritt Island
Melbourne
Tarpon Springs
Sebastian Inlet Recreation Area
Clearwater
Tampa
Winter Haven
Florida's Tnpk.
Tampa Bay
St. Petersburg
Vero Beach
Fort Pierce
Bradenton
Sarasota
Hutchinson Island
Kissimmee R.
Peace R.
Venice
Lake Okeechobee
Singer Island
West Palm Beach
Palm Beach
Caloosahatchee R.
Cape Coral
Fort Myers
Captiva Island
Big Cypress National Preserve
Sanibel Island
Boca Raton
Fort Lauderdale
Naples
Miami Beach
Everglades City
Miami
Biscayne Bay
Biscayne National Park
Everglades National Park
Florida City
Homestead
Cape Sable
Key Largo
Florida Bay
FLORIDA KEYS
Key West
0
50 miles
0
75 kilometers
1
2
3
4
5
6
7
8
9
10
11
1
4
10
19
27
40
41
50
65
70
75
80
95
98
301
319
528
9336

Florida Today

The Sunshine State continues to evolve as a tourist destination to meet the growing demands of today's globalized traveler. From new high-end accommodations and experiences to improved access and infrastructure, Florida is keeping at the top of its game as one of America's superlative vacation spots.

MORE LUXURY

From Orlando's timeless Walt Disney World to Miami's burgeoning Mid-Beach and expanding Sunny Isles Beach to Key West's charming Old Town, Florida is embracing a new luxury mantra and has plenty of new five-star residents to prove it.

Walt Disney World is proving that its secret recipe of fairy tales and imagination isn't just for tykes and tots. The arrival of the Four Seasons Resort Orlando at Walt Disney World Resort—and its over-the-top, near half-billion-dollar excess—has indeed ushered in a new era of five-star Disney. Eight Disney resorts have recently added Club Level accommodations and Club Level lounges with several food and wine presentations. Disney's Grand Floridian Resort & Spa has debuted pricey villa accommodations, and Disney's Polynesian Villas & Bungalows offers over-the-top, Tahitian-style overwater villas (with the price tag to match). Its next luxury hotel isn't set to debut until 2022, with the name and theme still under wraps. Nevertheless, you can treat yourself to experiences like VIP escorts, where you jump the line for each ride and go across all parks in a single day (and travel between parks in some pretty hot wheels).

Just as they did during the real estate boom of 2006, cranes and bulldozers are again dominating South Florida's most coveted neighborhoods, from South Beach to Sunny Isles Beach, to make way for super-high-end residential and hotel developments. But Miami's Mid-Beach area may be undergoing the most dramatic transformation. Significant progress has been made in the new Faena District, a multiblock quarter stretching along Collins Avenue from 32nd to 35th streets, with historic art deco buildings reimagined by Argentinean developer and icon Alan Faena (to the tune of over a billion dollars). In the heart of the district lies the apex of Miami's onslaught of luxury resorts, the Faena Hotel Miami Beach, which is still the talk of South Florida years after opening.

In November 2016 Downtown Miami welcomed its highly futuristic, Hong Kong–style $1.05-billion new resident: the Brickell City Centre complex, an 11-acre, high-tech, Arquitectonica-designed micro-city in the heart of Downtown encompassing more than 5.4 million square feet of retail and restaurant space, hotel rooms, office buildings, and two condominium buildings. The Design District continues to expand with ultrahigh-design retail spaces for the big brands that are moving into the neighborhood monthly.

In the northern reaches of Miami Beach, Sunny Isles Beach has witnessed a new high-rise frenzy underscored by the 47-story Mansions at Acqualina and The Estates at Acqualina, neighbors of the Acqualina Resort & Spa. Never one to forgo the limelight, South Beach is also making waves with the half-billion-dollar collaboration between hotel and real estate titans Barry Sternlicht and Richard LeFrak: the 1 Hotel & Homes South Beach—a seductive, two-block-long, beachfront enclave, inclusive of 156 oceanfront residences—sits in the beach's Art Deco District on the former site of the Gansevoort South Beach.

Down in Key West, the opening of The Marker Key West heralded Old Town's first new-build since 1996. The arrival of the luxury 96-room resort has spawned a number of renovations and rebuilds, including the multimillion-dollar transformation of the Hyatt Key West to the Hyatt Centric Key West, a flagship for the Hyatt's new stylish lifestyle brand. The Florida Keys recently welcomed its first all-inclusive resort, Bungalows Key Largo, a luxury waterfront oasis.

IMPROVED ACCESS

It's easier than ever to reach Florida by plane thanks to new flight routes and expanded airports. For example, Fort Lauderdale–Hollywood International Airport (FLL) is in the midst of a major expansion and renovation. So far, a new larger runway has been added, which permits jumbo-sized aircraft to utilize the airport, opening FLL to new destinations (e.g., Emirates serves Fort Lauderdale directly from Dubai on a Boeing 777-200LR). In 2018 Orlando International Airport (MCO) completed a highly anticipated, $1.1-billion expansion and is now expanding again one mile south of the main terminal. This new facility will serve as the Orlando station for Virgin Trains USA (formerly Brightline).

To improve access between cities, Florida-based Virgin Trains USA has opened and is the first privately funded U.S. high-speed railway. Ultimately, state-of-the-art trains will travel from Miami to Orlando in three hours at speeds of up to 125 mph. Phase One, which opened in summer 2017, provides intercity express train service connecting Miami, Fort Lauderdale, and West Palm Beach in style and comfort. New stations have been constructed in the downtown areas of these three cities to provide service from one city center to the next (as opposed to using their often out-of-the-way Amtrak stations).

RESPONSE TO CURRENT ISSUES

Florida has been quick to respond to several of the negative issues that have overshadowed travel to the Sunshine State in the recent past. In response to increased threats of gun violence and terrorism, Walt Disney World has now added walk-through metal detectors at the entrance of its four theme parks, while Universal Orlando and SeaWorld Orlando are using wand-style metal detectors. Hearing the call of animal rights activists and protestors, SeaWorld Orlando has phased out its orca shows, while Ringling Bros. and Barnum & Bailey Circus in Sarasota shut down in May 2017. (The company's elephants, retired in 2016, are now living at the Ringling Bros. conservation center in rural Florida).

And while Florida is known for mosquitoes and Miami-Dade County was listed as a Zika cautionary area in 2016, no local mosquito-borne Zika virus transmission has been reported. Since the Zika issue changes frequently, we recommend expectant mothers and future mothers to review the CDC website and its special up-to-date Florida section.

14 Things to Eat and Drink in Florida

CUBAN SANDWICH
It's said the first *cubano* was invented in 1905 in Tampa's Ybor City, but the classic sandwich is also widespread (and well loved) in South Florida. The historic hoagies are made with two flaky pieces of Cuban bread topped with ham, roast pork, Swiss cheese, yellow mustard, and pickles.

STONE CRAB
Stone crab season runs from October through May, when you'll find claws served at seafood spots throughout South Florida (one of the best is Joe's Stone Crab in Miami). Claws are presented in similar style to peel-and-eat shrimp, with crackers to help break through to the meaty flesh.

MOJITO
Warm weather begs for cold, summertime cocktails, so it's no surprise the classic Cuban mojito is referred to as one of Miami's unofficial drinks. The recipe is easy: a blend of white rum, fresh mint sprigs, sugar, and a splash of club soda. Head to Ball & Chain in Miami's Little Havana for a traditional take.

KEY LIME PIE
Florida's official state pie was first baked in the 1860s in Key West, where local Key limes add to the dessert's characteristic tangy taste. The original recipe has three main ingredients—Key lime, egg yolks, and sweetened condensed milk.

PASTELITOS
Step into any Cuban bakery in Miami and you'll spot these turnover-like pastries proudly displayed (and quickly devoured). The puff pastry sweets are as critical to breakfast here as croissants in Paris, with flavors ranging from savory ham to sweet guava and cream cheese. Order one of the flaky confections at family run shops like La Rosa Bakery in Miami.

ORANGE JUICE
The state's official beverage skyrocketed into a multimillion dollar industry during the Second World War. You'll often spot citrus stands just off the highway.

ROCK LOBSTER
Rock Lobster Rock (or spiny) lobster is Florida's answer to the more traditional type you'd find up in Maine. The best way to eat the tender tail meat is grilled and drizzled with rich garlic butter. Head to The Stoned Crab in Key West and order the Baked Half, served in Florida shrimp sauce.

CONCH FRITTERS
Deep-fried conch fritters may have started further south in the Bahamas, but this popular appetizer dish

Key Lime Pie

(typically served alongside tartar sauce) has become a favorite in Florida, especially in the Conch Republic of Key West.

CAFECITO

Cuban coffee, or cafecito, is what locals in Miami drink as an afternoon pick-me-up. The strong, espresso-based drink packs a powerful punch thanks to the heavy-handed sugar whipped in. You'll find dedicated cafecito windows, or *ventanillas*, around town, especially in Little Havana.

GATOR TAIL

Just as frog legs have become synonymous with France, gator has become a Florida specialty. Bite-sized, deep-fried pieces are served up as nugget-style snacks in the Everglades at Swamp Water Café (a memorable ending to an airboat ride). Tastes like chicken.

CROQUETAS

Considered Miami's official snack, meat- and cheese-stuffed Cuban croquetas are sold everywhere from fine dining restaurants to drive-through fast food joints and even gas stations. Order the breaded, fried food rolls in classic *jamón* (ham) or a variation like goat cheese and guava jam.

GULF OYSTERS

Slurp down raw Florida oysters right from the source in the Apalachicola Bay, where 90 percent of the state's shellfish are produced. Grouper is also huge here.

BLACKENED MAHI-MAHI

Mahi-mahi are often caught along the northeast coast near Jacksonville and served blackened with Cajun spices.

CEVICHE

South Florida's tie to South America. Peruvian-style ceviche is typically made with raw whitefish, lime juice, limo pepper and cilantro.

Best Beaches in South Florida

SOUTH BEACH
The legend of beautiful people is very much a reality on the sands parallel to deco-drenched Ocean Drive and upscale Collins Avenue, lined with luxe boutiques. Pose for pics at the iconic pastel-colored lifeguard stands or take a tour of the city's most historic buildings. *(Ch. 3)*

FORT LAUDERDALE BEACH
The Spring Break hotspot plays host to a reinvented, more upscale beachfront; however, the buzzy board-walk and iconic beach bars remain. Stroll and shop along Las Olas or people-watch along the beachfront promenade. *(Ch. 6)*

JOHN PENNEKAMP CORAL REEF STATE PARK
Florida's best bet for diving and snorkeling, this state park adjacent to the Florida Keys National Marine Sanctuary encompasses 78 square miles of ecological treasures. The beaches here do attract families, but the real draw is the underwater world. *(Ch. 5)*

DELRAY MUNICIPAL BEACH
This super-popular stretch of sand dotted with trade-mark royal blue umbrellas intersects trendy Atlantic Avenue in the alluring Village by the Sea; delicious nosh and cute boutiques are a short stroll from the waves. *(Ch. 7)*

HOLLYWOOD BEACH
In between Miami and Fort Lauderdale, this laid-back, family-friendly stretch of sand is the star of Broward County, where you can stroll along the 2½ -mile "Broadwalk," promenade and enjoy beachfront restaurants and bars. *(Ch. 6)*

BAHIA HONDA STATE PARK
Though the Florida Keys aren't renowned for beauti-ful sand beaches (most are man-made), this is an exception. The 524-acre park has three superb, white sand beaches, including the mile-long, Atlantic-facing Sandspur Beach. Fish off the old sea walls of the bridge or set off on a snorkel trip to the Looe Key National Marine Sanctuary. *(Ch. 5)*

HAULOVER BEACH PARK
Long known for its clothing-optional stretch of sand (between lifeguard stands 12 and 16), the park, which sits north of Miami Beach, also offers plenty of family-friendly attractions. Food trucks pull up to the Bill Bird Marina on Tuesday nights, and the park often hosts kite-making workshops. *(Ch. 3)*

Bahia Honda State Park

MID-BEACH

This stretch of coastline (which starts at 24th and Collins) sits just a few blocks north of South Beach's nonstop nightlife. Miami Modern buildings sprout across the historic neighborhood, where a few famous faces like Fontainebleau have received billion-dollar revamps in recent years. The area's revival doesn't end there; Argentinean hotelier Alan Faena has made it his mission to breathe new life into this part of Miami Beach, constructing condos and cultural institutions that are as fantastical as his flagship high-rise hotel, Faena. *(Ch. 3)*

BILL BAGGS CAPE FLORIDA STATE PARK

If you're looking to avoid the throngs of tourists sunbathing on South Beach, head to this park in Key Biscayne. Stroll along the shore to the beach's landmark lighthouse—the oldest standing building in the county. *(Ch. 3)*

BLOWING ROCKS PRESERVE

The dramatic cliffs hovering over the water in Hobe Sound have helped Blowing Rocks earn its distinct name. When high tide or storms hit, the surf sends water splashing nearly 50 feet in the air. The beauty here is in the backdrop; the rugged, exposed rocky coastline looks like it's been transplanted from a Greek island, yet this wild strip of mangrove wetlands, turtle nesting beaches, and practically perfect dunes lies less than an hour's drive from major cities like Palm Beach. *(Ch. 7)*

PALM BEACH

The shores of this tony beach town are favored by locals and visitors alike. With Worth Avenue's clock tower nearby, the beach is central to the town's best sights, and a beautiful spot to watch the sun set. *(Ch. 7)*

Best Central and North Florida Beaches

FORT DE SOTO BEACH

A winner of "America's Best Beach", the 1,136-acre park is spread over five islands on the Gulf of Mexico and features 7 miles of beach, two fishing piers, and a 4-mile hiking trail. The beaches are super packed on weekends but splendidly quiet on weekdays. *(Ch. 8)*

SIESTA KEY BEACH

Boasting the finest quartz sand in the world, the island's 40-acre beach park is exceptionally wide and long, providing ample space for families, romantics, and Sunday's Drum Circle Celebration. *(Ch. 8)*

PANAMA CITY BEACH

The former "Spring Break Capital of the World" is home to 27 miles of sand dotted with lively beach bars and Pier Park, home to stores, restaurants, and family-friendly attractions. *(Ch. 14)*

BOWMAN'S BEACH, SANIBEL ISLAND

On Sanibel's secluded northwest end, this beach doubles as a shell hunter's paradise and a beach wanderer's great escape. For the former, the likelihood of leaving with a bag full of gorgeous shells is high. For the latter, the chance of serene, inspiring vistas is guaranteed. *(Ch. 9)*

CALADESI ISLAND STATE PARK

Accessible only by ferry from Honeymoon Island State Recreation Area, Caladesi Island State Park—one of the sole untouched islands on Florida's Gulf Coast—offers pure white beaches, beautiful sunsets, and scenic kayaking adventures through mangrove forests. *(Ch. 8)*

CLEARWATER BEACH

At what is arguably the state's best beach for families, kids and parents alike love Clearwater Beach's white sand and shallow, clear warm water. In the evenings the scene transforms into a sunset celebration complete with musicians and artists. *(Ch. 8)*

PENSACOLA BEACH

Hugging the Gulf of Mexico along the western tip of Florida, Pensacola Beach is about as beautiful as it gets with its crystal-clear water, powdery white sand, and secluded shores. Snorkel or kayak through the Gulf Islands National Seashore—the longest protected stretch in the country. *(Ch. 14)*

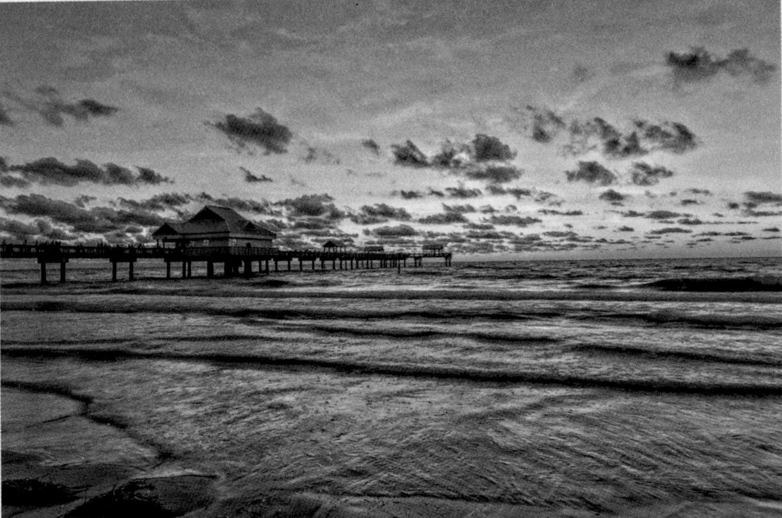

Clearwater Beach

GRAYTON BEACH STATE PARK, SOUTH WALTON

With its twisted scrub oaks and magnolias, the 400-acre Grayton Beach State Park has more of a Southern feel than the rest of the state. The area is part of South Walton, an under-the-radar collection of 16 beach communities in the Panhandle. Spend the day strolling the impressive sand dunes and swimming in what's been ranked one of the U.S.'s most beautiful beaches thanks to the picture-perfect shade of emerald-green water. This is one of the only areas in the world with coastal dune lakes. Grab a paddleboard to see them from the water. *(Ch. 14)*

FERNANDINA BEACH, AMELIA ISLAND

Located near Jacksonville on Amelia Island, Fernandina Beach invites a stroll back in time through its 50-block Historic District, dotted with Victorian-era homes-turned-bed and breakfasts, before you head to the picturesque beaches. *(Ch. 13)*

ST. GEORGE ISLAND

You won't find chain stores or high-rise hotels on the 28-mile barrier island sitting off North Florida's Gulf Coast. This is why the island's practically untouched shores, covered in sandy coves and sweeping dunes, make for great shelling and wildlife spotting—and offer prime views of the pristine water from cozy seaside cottages. *(Ch. 14)*

DESTIN

Known for its blue-green waters and sugarlike sand beaches made of Appalachian quartz crystals, this city on the Emerald Coast is great for fishing, paddleboarding, and setting up on the sand. *(Ch. 14)*

An Art Lover's Guide to Miami

ART BASEL

The event around which the Miami Beach art (and social) calendars revolve is this not-to-be-missed art fair, which takes place each December. More than 250 galleries from around the world showcase everything from installations to films, and along with the pricey art comes swanky parties.

VIZCAYA MUSEUM AND GARDENS

This European-style villa is an urban oasis where formal gardens meet the edge of Biscayne Bay. Built about 100 years ago, it has survived Miami's hurricanes, economic troubles, and redevelopment. Check out the decorative art spanning the Renaissance to rococo periods.

ART DECO AND MIMO ARCHITECTURE

In Miami, even the buildings are art. The art deco structures on Ocean Drive and Collins Ave, with their pastels and geometric shapes, put South Beach on the map in the '30s and '40s. In North Beach you'll see another iconic style–Miami Modern (MiMo), featuring futuristic, asymmetrical shapes.

THE BASS MUSEUM OF ART

Housed in an art deco gem from the '30s, the museum, renovated and expanded in 2017, spotlights contemporary art and its relationship to culture, design, fashion, and architecture. See whimsical contemporary pieces alongside historical works in the permanent collection.

PÉREZ ART MUSEUM MIAMI

Overlooking Biscayne Bay, PAMM's indoor-outdoor venue with hanging gardens, trusses, and steel frames, is a stunning home to international art of the 20th and 21st centuries. The museum is celebrated for sparking much of city's electric arts environment.

WYNWOOD ARTS DISTRICT

Once an unremarkable group of warehouses, this now trendy area is an international destination for edgy graffiti and galleries. Check out the Wynwood Walls, an outdoor museum of street art. Your visit will be unique: murals can disappear as quickly as they appear.

MUSEUM OF CONTEMPORARY ART

MOCA, an intimate museum in North Miami, is home to provocative contemporary art. Its stark gallery spaces are ideal for exhibitions that require time and space to fully understand. Stop by for Jazz at MOCA on the last Friday night of each month.

THE PATRICIA & PHILLIP FROST ART MUSEUM

Florida International University's free art museum boasts thousands of objects ranging from pre-Colombian era artifacts and American printmaking from the '70s to contemporary works. Note that it's off the beaten path in West Miami.

LITTLE HAITI AND LITTLE RIVER GALLERIES

Several top-notch galleries—Emerson-Dorsch, Nina Johnson, Mindy Solomon Gallery, Pan American Art Projects—have moved from Wynwood to the neighborhoods of Little Haiti and Little River, so it's no wonder the up-and-coming areas are being referred to as the "new Wynwood."

DESIGN DISTRICT

The Design District is a haven for ultra-high-end fashion houses and boutiques. If you can make it past Louis Vuitton, Hermès, and Saint Laurent, you'll find several notable galleries. The Institute of Contemporary Art, Miami (ICA) is the latest add to the city's museums; many pieces in its permanent collection and its major funders were once part of MOCA.

What to Read and Watch

FLORIDA BY LAUREN GROFF

This collection of short stories depicts Florida with equal doses fascination and horror, dream world and harsh reality. The state is a recurring character, and the diverse settings, cast of characters, and moods give a full and complex impression of the state.

SWAMPLANDIA! BY KAREN RUSSELL

The story of a young girl growing up in the Florida Everglades among her family's bizarre gator-wrestling entertainment park, *Swamplandia!* earned Russell the Pulitzer Prize. It has the right amount of fantasy to illustrate the swampy, untamed Everglades.

RAZOR GIRL BY CARL HIAASEN

A con artist works with detectives to find a redneck reality TV star in Hiaasen's most recent novel, but there's plenty more of his Florida-centric work to choose from (*Bad Monkey, Tourist Season,* and *Skin Tight,* to name a few).

THEIR EYES WERE WATCHING GOD BY ZORA NEALE HURSTON

Hurston's most-read novel journeys through Reconstruction-era, rural Florida. Through the lens of African American female narrator Janie Crawford, you'll see vivid depictions of small towns, migrant worker communities, and historical events.

TO HAVE AND HAVE NOT BY ERNEST HEMINGWAY

A desperate Key West fishing captain is forced into the illegal smuggling business during the Great Depression in Hemingway's book. It touches on the economic disparity in the Keys during that decade, and the close but complicated relationship with Cuba.

MOONLIGHT

A film in three chapters, *Moonlight* explores violence, identity, and sexuality for two young black males growing up in the Miami area. For a quiet film, it was met with loud praise—the Oscar for best picture. It was the first movie with an all-black cast (and first LGBTQ-themed movie) to win.

THE FLORIDA PROJECT

An indie film that's both heartbreaking and joyous, *Florida Project* follows a young, struggling mother and her hellion daughter through their days living in a pay-per-week motel in the shadow of Disney World.

BLOODLINE

Taking place on Islamorada in the Florida Keys, this Netflix show begins when a bad-seed brother returns home to stir up trouble. A small family inn serves as the epicenter for so much drama it could be a soap opera—full of family secrets, drug trafficking, and speedboat chases.

SPRING BREAKERS

A dark, highly hyperbolized representation of the wild college trips often associated with Florida, this movie loosely follows a group of teenage girls who go to great lengths to get to St. Petersburg for spring break.

FLIPPER

This feel-good flick stars a young Elijah Wood, who strikes up a friendship with a dolphin while spending the summer at his uncle's marina on Florida's Gold Coast.

MIAMI VICE

A team of undercover detectives takes on the shady drug world in South Florida in the 1980s. The show's loud fashion and music, neon lights, palm trees, alligators, and yachts could get anyone into a South Beach mood.

Chapter 2

TRAVEL SMART FLORIDA

Updated by
Galena Mosovich
and Jill Martin

★ CAPITAL
Tallahassee

POPULATION
21,299,325

LANGUAGE
English

$ CURRENCY
US dollar

DRIVING
On the right side

AREA CODES
South Florida: 305, 561, 786, 754, 954; Lower Gulf Coast: 239; Tampa Bay area: 727, 813, 941; Orlando and Environs: 321, 407; Northeast Florida: 352, 386, 904; Northwest Florida: 850

⚠ EMERGENCIES
911

ELECTRICITY
120-240 v/60 cycles; plugs have two or three rectangular prongs

TIME
Eastern Standard Time (same as New York); 3 hours ahead of Los Angeles

WEB RESOURCES
www.visitflorida.org

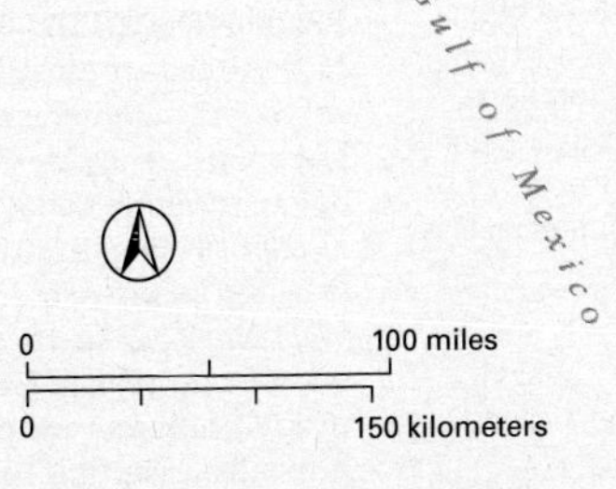

What You Need to Know Before You Visit Florida

FLORIDA COULD BE SEVERAL STATES.
If you drove from the western stretch of the Panhandle to the state's southern tip in Key West, you'd have traveled more than 800 miles. It's no wonder the state varies so widely in climate, geography, and demography. This massive peninsula's many distinct regions include the Southeast, Southwest, The Keys, Central, Northeast, and the Northwest (aka the Panhandle)—and all have different vibes. Generally, the northern and central regions are more conservative than the coastal communities and the land more akin to Southern Georgia, while the Southeast is by far the most diverse and progressive and the terrain more tropical.

HURRICANE SEASON SPANS HALF THE YEAR.
Florida's annual hurricane season spans from June 1 to November 30. Storms can form within a matter of days, sometimes dissipating or rapidly morphing into monsters. Big storms are more likely in August and September. If you're in or near a storm's projected path, fly out or drive away as soon as possible, regardless of whether you're in an evacuation zone.

RENTING A CAR IS ESSENTIAL.
Even Florida's urban hubs are sprawling, so a car is the preferred method of transportation. It's also the best way to string a few towns together on a road trip. While a new express train service (formerly Brightline, now called Virgin Trains USA) transports passengers from Miami to Fort Lauderdale to West Palm Beach and has grand plans to expand to Orlando and Tampa in the future, public transit unfortunately isn't an efficient mode in most of the state. Ride sharing services like Uber and Lyft also operate in most areas.

WINTER IS THE BUSIEST AND MOST EXPENSIVE SEASON.
Rates from December to April are high across the board since most try to escape their own winters, avoid the risk of a hurricane, and plan around school breaks. Winter is also the time to visit the Everglades, as temperatures, mosquito activity, and water levels are all lower (making wildlife easier to spot). Northern Florida, conversely, receives the greatest influx of visitors from Memorial Day to Labor Day.

BE PREPARED FOR HUMIDITY AND SUMMER RAIN.
Florida is rightly called the Sunshine State—areas like Tampa Bay report 361 days of sunshine a year! But it could also be dubbed the Humid State. From June through September, 90% humidity levels aren't uncommon, nor are accompanying thunderstorms. In fact, more than half of the state's rain falls during these months.

TAKE THE SUN SERIOUSLY.
Sunburn and heat exhaustion are concerns, even in winter. So hit the beach or play outdoor sports before 10 am or after 3 pm. Even on overcast days, ultraviolet rays shine through the haze, so use a sunscreen with an SPF of at least 15, and have children wear a waterproof SPF of at least 30 or higher.

SOME SUNSCREENS ARE BANNED.
Before you buy sunscreen make sure your choice doesn't have oxybenzone or octinoxate. These two chemicals, known to cause coral bleaching, will be banned in Key West starting in 2021.

PROTECT YOURSELF FROM MOSQUITOES.
Mosquitoes are most active in the wet summer months but are present year-round due to the state's climate. Even if the bugs aren't infected by diseases like West Nile or Zika (there was an outbreak in Miami in 2016), humans and pets are still susceptible to their

itchy bites. Pack a repellent or lemon eucalyptus oil to ward off the pests, and wear long sleeves, pants, and socks when spending time in nature. Also, avoid the outdoors at dawn and dusk.

RESPECT THE WILDLIFE.
Much of Florida's wildlife is protected or endangered due to overpopulation and development. While there are plenty of opportunities to commune with nature during your adventures (Everglades National Park to the west of Miami, for example, comprises 1.5 million acres of tropical and subtropical wetlands with one of the world's most diverse ecosystems), they should always come in the form of watching and appreciating from afar.

TOURING BY BOAT HAS ITS PERKS.
A boat ride can help you fully understand the majestic characteristics that make the state so popular. Fort Lauderdale, for example, has long been dubbed the "Venice of America" because of its many waterways, and seeing the city through this lens makes you feel like a local. In Central and North Florida, touring natural springs by glass-bottomed boat will help you spot manatees, who enjoy cruising slowly through the aquamarine waters.

PLAN AHEAD FOR THE THEME PARKS.
Make sure your trip is long enough to fit in all desired attractions and parks (Magic Kingdom alone features six lands and 40 attractions!). Select a hotel as close as possible to the park you're visiting, and purchase park tickets in advance so you can look for discounts and consider upgrading to fast passes that reduce wait times. Packing the most comfortable shoes you own will go a long way. Food inside the parks can be expensive, so read up on the food policy before you go. Some allow you to bring snacks, and refillable water bottles are usually allowed. Once you're inside the park, use free mobile apps such as the My Disney Experience, which provide navigation tools, purchasing capabilities, and tips for making your visit stress-free.

WHEN CHOOSING A BEACH, CONSIDER THE ATLANTIC OCEAN VERSUS THE GULF OF MEXICO.
Not sure which beach to pick? East Coast (Atlantic) beaches can be narrow and crowded or wide and empty depending on the location, while West Coast (Gulf) beaches are sprawling, peaceful respites. East Coast beaches can be havens for parties; Gulf beaches are usually sleepier and more casual. East Coast beaches tend to have oceanfront hotels and high rises that are just steps from the water; on the Gulf side, developments and other buildings are set back from the shoreline. East Coast beaches can be inundated with seaweed for lengthy periods; Gulf beaches can at times be overwhelmed by toxic red tide.

CHECK BEACH CONDITIONS FOR RED TIDE.
A harmful algae bloom that discolors the water and causes eye and respiratory irritations in humans, red tide isn't new to Florida, but scientists believe nutrient runoff from agricultural activities and the release of Lake Okeechobee's dirty water into the Gulf has increased the intensity of the blooms. Check for blooms from August to December, when the beaches and waterways of Southwest Florida struggle with the harmful algae.

ACCOUNT FOR RESORT TAXES.
Florida has no state personal income tax, instead heavily relying on tourism revenues. The state sales tax in Florida is 6% (with the exception of most groceries and medicine); when combined with local taxes, the total sales tax rate is as high as 8%. Hotel taxes, often called "resort taxes," vary.

Palm Beach County's resort tax is 6%, for a combined total of 13% with state sales tax (7%). In Greater Fort Lauderdale the resort tax is 5%, for a combined total of 11%. In Miami Beach visitors pay 7% sales tax, 3% Miami resort tax, plus 3% Miami Beach resort tax, for a total of 13%.

Getting Here and Around

Air Travel

Average flying time to Florida's international airports is 3 hours from New York, 4 hours from Chicago, 2¾ hours from Dallas, 4½–5½ hours from Los Angeles, and 8–8½ hours from London.

From–To	Miles	Hours +/-
Pensacola–Panama City	100	2
Tallahassee–Panama City	100	2
Tallahassee–Jacksonville	165	3
Jacksonville–St. Augustine	40	0:45
Cape/Port Canaveral–Orlando	60	1
Orlando–Tampa	85	1:30
Fort Lauderdale–Miami	30	0:45
Miami–Naples	125	2:15
Miami–Key Largo	65	1
Miami–Palm Beach	70	1:45
Key Largo–Key West	100	2

AIRPORTS

Florida has 66 airports in total, with about 20 being commercial; the busiest are Orlando International Airport (MCO), Miami International Airport (MIA), Tampa (TPA), and Fort Lauderdale–Hollywood International Airport (FLL). Flying to alternative airports can save you both time and money. Fort Lauderdale is close to Miami, Palm Beach International (PBI) is close to Fort Lauderdale, and Sarasota Bradenton International (SRQ) is close to Tampa. FLL is a 30-minute drive from MIA. And what you might lose in driving time between Sarasota and downtown Tampa you'll make up for in spades with shorter security lines and fewer in-terminal navigation woes at SRQ.

GROUND TRANSPORTATION

SuperShuttle service operates from several Florida airports: Fort Lauderdale, Miami, Orlando, Sarasota Bradenton, St. Petersburg–Clearwater, Tampa, and the Palm Beaches. That said, most airports offer some type of shuttle or bus service. In some cities airport cab fares are a single flat rate; in others, flat-rate fares vary by zone; and in others still, the fare is determined by the meter.

Car Travel

Three major interstates lead to Florida. Interstate 95 begins in Maine, runs south through the Mid-Atlantic states, and enters Florida just north of Jacksonville. It continues south past Daytona Beach, the Space Coast, Vero Beach, Palm Beach, and Fort Lauderdale, ending just south of Miami.

Interstate 75 begins in Michigan at the Canadian border and runs south, ending in Miami. Despite its interstate status, the Interstate 75 stretch between Naples and just west of Fort Lauderdale levies a toll each way per car.

California and most Southern and Southwestern states are connected to Florida by Interstate 10, which moves east from Los Angeles through Arizona, New Mexico, Texas, Louisiana, Mississippi, and Alabama. It enters Florida at Pensacola and runs straight across the northern part of the state, ending in Jacksonville.

SUNPASS

To save time and money while on the road, you may want to purchase a SunPass for your personal or rental vehicle. It provides a discount on most tolls, and you'll be able to sail past collection booths without stopping. You also can use SunPass to pay for parking at Orlando, Tampa, Palm Beach, Miami, and Fort Lauderdale airports. (SunPass now interfaces with North Carolina's Quick Pass and Georgia's Peach Pass.) With SunPass—transponders can be purchased for $4.99 to $25, at drugstores, supermarkets, or tourism welcome centers—you can charge up with a credit card and reload as needed. For more info, check out 🌐 *www.sunpass.com*.

RENTAL CARS

Unless you're going to plant yourself at a beach or theme-park resort, you really need a vehicle to get around in Florida. Rental rates, which are loaded with taxes, fees, and other costs, sometimes can start around $35 a day/$160 a week, plus the aforementioned add-ons. In Florida you must be 21 to rent a car, must have a credit card, and need to know rates are higher if you're under 25.

RIDE-SHARING SERVICES

Services like Uber and Lyft have revolutionized the way people get around while traveling. Download their respective apps and add your payment method before you go out of town. This will make using the tools a lot smoother when you're in an unfamiliar place. Rates vary depending on the type of car you select, whether it's a private ride or a carpool, and how far you're going.

RULES OF THE ROAD

Speed limits are generally 60 mph on state highways, 30 mph within city limits and residential areas, and 70 mph on interstates, some Orlando-area toll roads, and Florida's Turnpike. The driver will be held responsible for passengers under the age of 18 who aren't wearing seat belts, and all front-seat passengers are required to wear seat belts.

Florida's Alcohol/Controlled Substance DUI Law is one of the toughest in the United States. A blood-alcohol level of 0.08 or higher can have serious repercussions even for a first-time offender.

Cruise Travel

Many major cruise lines make Florida a point of embarkation for itineraries to the Caribbean and Mexico. Occasionally a cruise line actually offers an itinerary in which Florida is a port of call, most often Key West or Port Canaveral, and sometimes Fort Lauderdale's Port Everglades.

The port of Miami has the world's largest year-round fleet. It also handles more megaships—vessels capable of transporting more than 2,000 people at a time—than any other port in the world.

Port Everglades, 30 miles north of Miami in Fort Lauderdale, is also a cruise-ship mecca. Port Canaveral, 60 miles west of Orlando, is the home port for some Disney Cruise Line vessels but increasingly other cruise lines as well, including Carnival and Royal Caribbean. Other ships sail from Jacksonville or Tampa.

Train Travel

A new high-speed train line, Virgin Trains USA (formerly called Brightline), began service in 2018. It connects Downtown Miami to Fort Lauderdale and West Palm Beach in 30 and 60 minutes, respectively. Future expansion plans include Orlando.

Before You Go

Passport

American travelers never need a passport to travel domestically. Non-American travelers always need a valid passport to visit Florida. Passengers on cruises that depart from and return to the same U.S. port aren't currently required to carry a passport, but it's always a good idea to bring one if your ship travels through Caribbean waters in the unlikely event that you must fly out of a Caribbean airport during your trip.

Visa

For international travelers, a tourism visa is required for traveling to Florida and the rest of the United States.

Immunizations

No specific immunizations or vaccinations are required for visits to Florida.

When to Go

HIGH SEASON $$$$

High season in South Florida spans December to April. Snowbirds migrate down then to escape frosty weather back home, and festivalgoers flock in because major events are held this time of year to avoid summer's heat and high humidity. High season in North Florida is from May to September.

LOW SEASON $

You'll find the lowest rates in the summer months from June to September, but you'll trade savings for scorching summer temperatures and the unpredicability of hurricane season.

VALUE SEASON $$

In addition to good rates, shoulder season in April and May as well as October and November create some of the fairest beach conditions across the state. Most kids are still in school, so you'll miss the family crowds that head here for spring break and summer vacation.

Health and Safety

Stepped-up policing against thieves preying on tourists in rental cars has helped address what was once a serious issue in Florida. Still, visitors should be wary when driving in unfamiliar neighborhoods and leaving the airport. Don't leave valuables unattended while you walk the beach or go for a dip. And never leave handbags, cameras, etc., in your vehicle. Try to use ATMs only during the day or in brightly lighted, well-traveled locales.

If you're visiting Florida during the June through November hurricane season and a storm is imminent, be sure to follow safety orders and evacuation instructions.

While you're frolicking on the beach, steer clear of what look like blue bubbles on the sand. These are Portuguese men-of-war, and their tentacles can cause an allergic reaction. Also be careful of other large jellyfish, some of which can sting.

If you walk across a grassy area on the way to the beach, you'll probably encounter the tiny, light-brown, incredibly prickly sand spurs. If you get stuck with one, just pull it out.

What to Pack for Florida

CASUAL CLOTHING
Dress is relaxed throughout the state—sundresses, sandals, or shorts are appropriate. Even beach gear is accepted at a lot of places, but just make sure you've got a proper outfit on (shirt, shorts, and shoes). Clothes should be breathable or better yet, made of fabric that will drip-dry, since you will be facing a hot and humid climate.

A NICER "RESORT CHIC" OUTFIT FOR NIGHTS OUT
A very small number of restaurants request that men wear jackets and ties but most don't. Where there are dress codes, they tend to be fully adhered to. Take note that the strictest places are golf and tennis clubs. Women should be fine with a dress or a nice top and dark jeans.

A SWEATER OR LIGHT JACKET
Even in summer, ocean breezes can be cool, so it's good to have a lightweight sweater or jacket. You should be prepared for air-conditioning in overdrive anywhere you go. Northern Florida is much cooler in winter than southern Florida (when the mercury can drop to, say, 50), so pack a heavy sweater or more.

PRACTICAL SHOES
You'll need your flip-flops for the beach, but also pack a pair of comfortable walking shoes. Florida's non-beach destinations (think the Everglades and Orlando's theme parks) are no place to go with open toes.

SUN PROTECTION
Sunglasses, a hat, and sunscreen are essential for protecting yourself against Florida's strong sun and UV rays, even in overcast conditions. Consider waterproof sunscreens with an SPF of 15 or higher for the most protection. And to protect marine life and coral reefs, choose one without harmful chemicals such as oxybenzone and octinoxate.

A CHANGE OF CLOTHES FOR YOUR BEACH BAG
There's nothing worse than a car ride in a wet bathing suit. Avoid it by packing underwear and a casual outfit (shorts or a sundress) that's easy to change into in your beach bag. Don't forget a plastic bag for your wet bathing suit. Note that you can generally swim year-round in peninsular Florida from about New Smyrna Beach south on the Atlantic Coast and from Tarpon Springs south on the Gulf Coast.

RAIN GEAR
Be prepared for sudden storms all over in summer, and note that plastic raincoats are uncomfortable in the high humidity. Often, storms are quick, often in the afternoons, and the sun comes back in no time.

INSECT REPELLENT
Mosquitoes are always present in Florida, but especially so in the wet summer months. Pack a DEET-based bug spray for the most effective protection.

PORTABLE SPEAKER
The perfect addition to your beach time? Music. Pack waterproof speakers that s ync to your phone via Bluetooth.

WATERPROOF PHONE CASE
Whether you want to snap photos while snorkeling or simply protect your device from kids splashing by the pool, pack a waterproof phone case to protect your electronics.

Essentials

 Lodging

In general, peak seasons are during Christmas/New Year's holidays and late January through Easter in the state's southern half, during the summer along the Panhandle and around Jacksonville and St. Augustine, and both time frames in Orlando and Central Florida. Holiday weekends at any point during the year are packed; if you're considering home or condo rentals, minimum-stay requirements are longer during these periods, too. Fall is the slowest season, with only a few exceptions (Key West is jam-packed for the 10-day Fantasy Fest at Halloween). Rates are low and availability is high, but this is also prime time for hurricanes.

Children are generally welcome throughout Florida, except for some Key West B&Bs and inns; however, the buck stops at spring-breakers. While many hotels allow them—and some even cater to them—most rental agencies won't lease units to anyone under 25 without a guardian present.

Pets, although allowed at many hotels (one upscale chain, Kimpton, with properties in Miami, Palm Beach, and Vero Beach, celebrates its pet-friendliness with treats in the lobby and doggie beds for rooms), often carry an extra flat-rate fee for cleaning and de-allergen treatments, and are not a sure thing. Inquire ahead if Fido is coming with you.

APARTMENT AND HOUSE RENTALS

The state's allure for visiting snowbirds (Northerners "flocking" to Florida in winter) has caused private home and condo rentals to boom in popularity, at times affording better options for vacationers, particularly families who want to have some extra space and cooking facilities. In some destinations, home and condo rentals are more readily available than hotels. Fort Myers, for example, doesn't have many luxury hotel properties downtown. Everything aside from beach towels is provided during a stay, but some things to consider are that sizable down payments must be made at booking (15% to 50%), and the full balance is often due before arrival. Check for any cleaning fees (usually not more than $150). If being on the beach is of utmost importance, carefully screen properties that tout "water views," because they might actually be of bays, canals, or lakes rather than of the Gulf of Mexico or the Atlantic.

Finding a great rental agency can help you weed out the junk. Target offices that specialize in the area you want to visit, and have a personal conversation with a representative as soon as possible. Be honest about your budget and expectations. For example, let the rental agent know if having the living room couch pull double-duty as a bed is not OK. Although websites listing rentals directly from homeowners are growing in popularity, there's a higher chance of coming across Pinocchios advertising "gourmet" kitchens that have one or two nice gadgets but fixtures or appliances from 1982. To protect yourself, talk extensively with owners in advance, see if there's a system in place for accountability should something go wrong, and make sure there's a 24-hour phone number for emergencies.

BED-AND-BREAKFASTS

Small inns and guesthouses in Florida range from modest, cozy places with home-style breakfasts and owners who treat you like family, to elegantly furnished Victorian houses with four-course breakfasts and rates to match. Since most B&Bs are small, they rely on various agencies and organizations to get the word out and coordinate reservations.

HOTELS AND RESORTS

Wherever you look in Florida you'll find lots of plain, inexpensive motels and luxurious resorts, independents alongside national chains, and an ever-growing number of modern properties as well as quite a few classics. All hotels listed have a private bath unless otherwise noted.

Hotel reviews have been shortened. For full reviews, visit Fodors.com.

Dining

Smoking is banned statewide in most enclosed indoor workplaces, including restaurants. Exemptions are permitted for stand-alone bars where food takes a backseat to libations.

One caution: raw oysters pose a potential danger for people with chronic illness of the liver, stomach, or blood, or who have immune disorders. All Florida restaurants that serve raw oysters must post a notice in plain view warning of the risks associated with their consumption.

Restaurant reviews have been shortened. For full reviews, visit Fodors.com.

FLORIBBEAN FOOD

A true marriage of Floridian, Caribbean, and Latin cultures yields the stylized cuisine known as "Floribbean" (think freshly caught fish with tropical fruit salsa.) A trip to the Tampa area or South Florida, however, isn't quite complete without a taste of Cuban food. The cuisine is heavy, including dishes like *lechon asado* (roasted pork) that are served in garlic-based sauces. The two most typical dishes are *arroz con frijoles* (the staple side dish of rice and black beans) and *arroz con pollo* (chicken in sticky yellow rice).

Key West is famous for its Key lime pie (also served elsewhere throughout the state) and conch fritters. Stone-crab claws, a South Florida delicacy, can be savored during the official season from October 15 through May 15.

MEALS AND MEALTIMES

Unless otherwise noted, you can assume that the restaurants we recommend are open daily for lunch and dinner.

RESERVATIONS AND DRESS

We discuss reservations only when they're essential (there's no other way you'll ever get a table) or when they're not accepted. It's always smart to make reservations when you can, particularly if your party is large or if it's high season. It's critical to do so at popular restaurants (book as far ahead as possible, often 30 days, and reconfirm on arrival).

We mention dress only when men are required to wear a jacket or a jacket and tie. Expect places with dress codes to truly adhere to them.

Tipping

Tip airport valets or hotel bellhops $1 to $3 per bag (there typically is also a charge to check bags outside the terminal, but this isn't a tip). Maids often get $1 to $2 per night per guest, more at high-end resorts or if you require special services. Room-service waiters still hope to receive a 15% tip despite hefty room-service charges and service fees, which often don't go to the waiters. A door attendant or parking valet hopes to get $1 to $3. Waiters generally count on 15% to 20% (on the before-tax amount) or more, depending on your demands for special service. Bartenders get $1 or $2 per round of drinks. Golf caddies get 15% of the greens fee.

Great Itineraries

3 Days: Miami

DAY 1 (FRIDAY)

Fly into Miami International Airport as early as possible on Friday morning to maximize the day at the beach or your hotel's pristine pool. Staying directly on the beach is the right move, because you'll want to avoid traffic and other delays that might eat up your R&R time. Grab lunch from the outdoor counters at La Sandwicherie or My Ceviche in South Beach and have lunch on the sand a couple blocks away. While you're in the neighborhood, go in search of art deco, Miami Modern (MiMo), and Mediterranean Revival gems on a walking tour with the Miami Design Preservation League (MDPL) through the historic architectural district. The MDPL also maintains a museum dedicated to the subject on Ocean Drive and 10th Street. Pop by The Wolfsonian-FIU's iconic 1930s building for a dive into a unique collection of objects defining the modern area of world history. Later, dinner at Macchialina, a hip independent Italian eatery, will fuel you for the rest of the weekend. If you're not wiped out, join in the nightlife that makes Miami so famous: pick from Sugar, a swanky rooftop bar amidst the high rises of Brickell, Blackbird Ordinary for dancing with a younger set Downtown in Brickell, or LIV at the Fontainebleau for the quintessential nightclub experience on Mid Beach.

DAY 2 (SATURDAY)

Grab a late breakfast at Joe's Stone Crab (a Miami institution that's open only October–July). You can take it away for a picnic to South Pointe Park, where cruise ships and other boats go in and out of Government Cut at the confluence of the Atlantic Ocean and Biscayne Bay. Head over to the Miami Beach Marina and hitch a boat ride with Ocean Force Adventures. You'll cruise into Biscayne Bay and Biscayne National Park for an awe-inspiring glimpse of a protected saltwater world that's home to four distinct ecosystems and 500 species of wildlife (fish, birds, turtles, plants, etc.), while marveling at a cluster of wood houses from the 1930s in Stiltsville. Then head to Coconut Grove by car to take a walk back to 1891 under the old trees of a tropical hammock overlooking the bay. The Barnacle Historic State Park is a five-acre slice of the past, and you shouldn't miss the preserved bungalow known as the oldest house in Miami-Dade County still standing in its original location. Here, you'll find a peaceful place to catch your breath. Drive to Little Havana for a late-late lunch at El Exquisito, where authentic Cuban fare awaits in the Calle Ocho community. Exploring the area will result in a deeper understanding of the Cuban exile experience and its influence on Miami culture from the 1960s till now. While there are some kitschy tourist traps, you'll find legitimate tributes to the heritage at Cubaocho Museum & Performing Arts Center, Tower Theater, and Domino Park. Happy hour and live music at Ball & Chain continues the history lesson: Ball & Chain originally opened in 1935 and evolved along with the neighborhood. Expertly crafted mojitos and salsa dancing will bring you full circle at this vivacious bar and restaurant. To cap off the night, visit Azucar Ice Cream Company next door for artisanal ice cream and sorbet flavors inspired by Cuban-American culture.

DAY 3 (SUNDAY)

Your last day in Miami starts with an extraordinary brunch at Zuma in the Epic Hotel on the Miami River. The modern Japanese izakaya's brunch from 11:30 a.m. to 2:30 p.m. features all of the signature dishes from the kitchen, sushi bar, and robata grill in an all-you-can-eat situation known as baikingu in Japanese. But this isn't your typical buffet—it's super-premium and sophisticated ($95–$395 per person). From here, head to the Pérez Art Museum Miami (PAMM) for modern and contemporary works of art inside an impressive building on Biscayne Bay. Its neighbor in Museum Park, the Phillip and Patricia Frost Museum of Science, stands as another great option if a three-story aquarium with a gigantic oculus is more your speed. Before you venture back to the airport, take a drive through the Wynwood Arts District to see Wynwood Walls, the world's largest outdoor graffiti museum, and a swath of ephemeral murals by international street artists on literally every street. Grab a snack before the airport at Zak the Baker, Wynwood's favorite kosher bakery and café with sweets (chocolate babka!) that will make the airport security line less sour.

2 to 3 Days: Gold Coast and Treasure Coast

The opulent mansions of Palm Beach's Ocean Boulevard give you a glimpse of how the top of the 1% lives. For exclusive boutique shopping, art gallery browsing, and glittery sightseeing, sybarites should wander down "The Avenue" (that's Worth Avenue to non–Palm Beachers). The sporty set will find dozens of places to tee up (hardly surprising given that the PGA is based here), along with tennis courts, polo clubs, and even a croquet center. Those who'd like to see more of the Gold Coast can continue traveling south through Boca Raton to Fort Lauderdale (known as the Yachting Capital of the World). But to balance the highbrow with the low-key, turn northward for a tour of the Treasure Coast. You can also look for the sea turtles that lay their own little treasures in the sands from May through October.

Tips

Now that one-way airfares are commonplace, vacationers visiting multiple destinations can fly into and out of different airports. Rent a car in between, picking it up at your point of arrival and leaving it at your point of departure. If you do these itineraries as an entire vacation, your best bet is to fly into and out of Miami and rent a car from there.

2 to 3 Days: Florida Keys

Some dream of "sailing away to Key Largo," others of "wasting away again in Margaritaville." In any case, almost everybody equates the Florida Keys with relaxation. And they live up to their reputation, thanks to offbeat attractions and that fabled come-as-you-are, do-as-you-please vibe. Key West, alternately known as the Conch Republic, is a good place to get initiated. The Old Town has a funky, laid-back feel. So take a leisurely walk; pay your regards to "Papa" (Hemingway, that is); then rent a moped to tour the rest of the island. Clear waters and abundant marine life make underwater activities another must. After scoping out the parrot fish, you can always head back into town and join local "Parrotheads" in a Jimmy Buffett sing-along. When retracing your route to the mainland, plan a last pit stop at Bahia Honda State Park (it has ranger-led activities plus the Keys' best beach) or John Pennekamp Coral Reef State Park, which offers unparalleled snorkeling and scuba-diving opportunities.

Great Itineraries

Northern Florida in One Week

As much as South Florida centers on the present and future, northern Florida is more about the past. From America's oldest city—the circa-1565 St. Augustine—to the lost-in-time seaside communities along the 250-mile coastline of the Florida Panhandle, northern Florida embraces the architecture, simplicity, and pace of yesteryear. Beyond dedicated party towns, don't expect much in terms of nightlife or glitz. Do expect stunning, wide expanses of white-sand beach, day-caught seafood served up in no-frills settings, regions rich in marine life, excellent fishing, a family-friendly atmosphere and plenty of fun-in-the-sun.

ST. AUGUSTINE

1 or 2 days. Start your journey through northern Florida in the nation's oldest city, which was founded by the Spanish in 1565. To explore the state's Spanish past, visit Castillo de San Marcos (its colonial-era fortress), the Colonial Quarter (a 2-acre living history museum of Florida life in the 16th, 17th, and 18th centuries), or stroll the streets of the Old City that grew up around the colonial quarter, giving you a chance to experience life in the past lane. A whole city block of historic houses built between 1790 and 1910 has been turned into the Dow Museum. But St. Augustine's future isn't all in the past. Peruse the many boutiques and indulge at the prolific restaurants that line the town center, stay in one of the many charming bed-and-breakfasts, and discover why St. Augustine rivals Savannah and Charleston as one of America's most charming cities. To the east is Anastasia Island, a state park with a stunning beach. ⇨ *Chapter 13.*

AMELIA ISLAND AND VICINITY

2 days. Head northeast beyond Jacksonville to reach prestigious Amelia Island, home to world-class beach resorts and wide swaths of family-friendly beaches. By day simply enjoy some fun-in-the-sun or beachcomb nearby undeveloped beaches for sand dollars and seashells. At night, search for nesting sea turtles. You can stay in one of Amelia Island's posh resorts, or for a similar experience that doesn't require such deep pockets, enjoy the beach action slightly south along one of the four quieter communities of Jacksonville Beaches, specifically Atlantic Beach or Ponte Vedra Beach. Jacksonville itself is an underrated vacation destination full of charm with a lively arts scene that often turns up on lists of the best places to live in the United States. Take a short detour into Jacksonville one day to visit the Museum of Contemporary Art Jacksonville or the Jacksonville Zoo and Gardens, two of the area's world-class attractions. ⇨ *Chapter 13.*

TALLAHASSEE

1 day. Drive west toward the Panhandle to get a true taste of the Old South in Spanish moss–draped Tallahassee, visiting one or two of the region's 71 plantations, such as Goodwood Museum and Gardens. Then get a dose of Old Florida at Edward Ball Wakulla Springs State Park, protected since the 1930s and famous as the jungle setting of the original Tarzan films, which today houses the largest and deepest freshwater spring in the world and plenty of manatees, alligators, and turtles, plus more than 180 species of birds. ⇨ *Chapter 14.*

PANAMA CITY BEACH

1 or 2 days. Continue past the state capital to the 250-mile-plus belt known as Panhandle's Emerald Coast, heralded

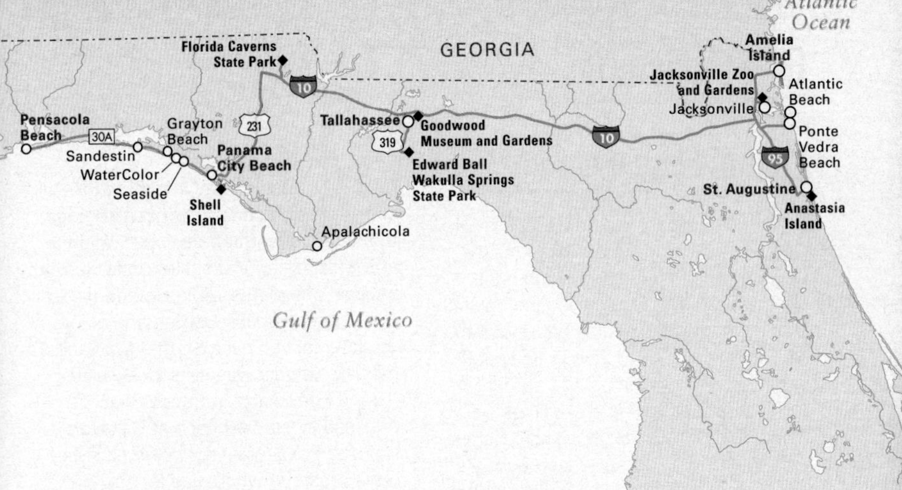

for its powdery white-sand beaches and sparkling water. If you take the coastal route, U.S. 98, along the way you may want to plan a stop in Apalachicola, a friendly and charming fishing town that's become a major regional tourist draw. Off the beach, this area feels more southern than South Florida. Sun-worship and indulge in Gulf-to-table seafood in Panama City Beach, enjoying enhanced nightlife options that go beyond the typical spring break options. Take a boat tour out to St. Andrews State Park to tour protected Shell Island, one of the few places in the world where you can swim with dolphins in the wild. ⇨ *Chapter 14.*

PENSACOLA BEACH

1 or 2 days. From Panama City Beach to Pensacola, take a relaxing drive along scenic Route 30A, passing nostalgia-inducing communities like WaterColor and Seaside, with an optional stop in glorious Grayton Beach, where kayaking ranks high on the agenda—or have lunch in the Panhandle's poshest subcity, Sandestin. At Pensacola Beach—one of the longest barrier islands in the world—enjoy such pursuits as fishing, boating, water sports, or simply relaxing and soaking in the laid-back beach vibe. Time and interest permitting, take a half-day trip up to Florida Caverns State Park, one of the state's lesser-known treasures, where rangers lead insightful cave tours. ⇨ *Chapter 14.*

Tips

- Begin this itinerary by flying into Jacksonville airport. You'll need to rent a car for the duration of the journey, dropping off the vehicle in Pensacola and returning home from Pensacola airport.
- The Panhandle runs on central time, meaning it's one hour behind the rest of Florida, which is in the eastern time zone.
- Unlike South and Central Florida, summer is high season for most of northern Florida.
- Northern Florida can be cold in winter. In Pensacola January temperatures on average fluctuate between 42 and 60 degrees.

Great Itineraries

Central Florida in One Week

Theme parks, nature, and beaches—oh my! Central Florida lures in the masses with the prospect of thrilling rides, handshakes with Mickey Mouse, overall Disney magic, and simply basking in the frivolity of childhood, though its appeal spans far beyond man-made attractions. In fact, Central Florida also stakes claim to the state's most exceptional natural riches, including some of the country's superlative beaches (with accolades to prove it) and unparalleled nature encounters, such as swimming with manatees in the wild and bird-watching at Merritt Island National Wildlife Refuge.

ORLANDO

2 or 3 days. You could easily spend a week at Walt Disney World alone. But unless you're a die-hard theme park devotee, a few days is sufficient. Spend a few days park-hopping at Walt Disney World between The Magic Kingdom, Epcot, Disney's Hollywood Studios, and Disney's Animal Kingdom. Smaller kids may enjoy a quieter time at nearby Legoland, some 50 miles from Orlando. For more intense thrills, allow a day or two for movie magic at Universal Studios or heart-pumping rides at Islands of Adventure, where Harry Potter now reigns and draws crowds by the millions. If you are theme parked–out after two days (or never really liked them to begin with), survey the collection of modern paintings at the Orlando Museum of Art, stroll through the 50-acre Harry P. Leu Gardens, or visit Orlando's serene sister city, Winter Park. Boaters can take advantage of the area's numerous lakes, and golfers can link up on courses designed by the sport's biggest stars. ⇨ *Chapters 10, 11, and 12.*

CAPE CANAVERAL

1 day. Head east from Orlando to discover one of Florida's best central coast treasures. Spend the day bird-watching at Merritt Island National Wildlife Refuge, have an out-of-this-world experience at the Kennedy Space Center (and enjoy the interactive Space Shuttle *Challenger* exhibit), catch a wave like local surfing legend Kelly Slater in Cocoa Beach, or blissfully hit the beach at Canaveral National Seashore—a 24-mile undeveloped preserve where you lounge in the shelter of dunes, not the shadow of high-rises. Adrenaline junkies may want to reset their GPS for Daytona Beach. Its International Speedway, which has hosted NASCAR's Daytona 500 every February since 1959, is a must-see for stock-car enthusiasts (and the plain ol' race-car curious). ⇨ *Chapter 13.*

TAMPA

1 day. If you crave more theme park fun, scream through the hair-raising rides at Busch Gardens and admire the 2,000-animal zoo, intricately woven throughout the park. The more sports-minded may want to catch one of Tampa Bay's myriad sporting events (the city has professional baseball, football, and hockey teams). Shoppers will love Oxford Exchange, at once a restaurant, bookstore, coffeehouse, and boutique. Don't forget to check out the Riverwalk, a pedestrian way lined with parks, museums, and entertainment. Beach-lovers who didn't get enough sand and surf in Cape Canaveral may want to head over to Clearwater Beach to find some of Central Florida's best sandy shores. At night dine and imbibe in the Spanish-inflected Ybor City entertainment district. ⇨ *Chapter 8.*

ST. PETERSBURG

2 days. Indulge in the culture and beaches of this sophisticated city, home to the riveting, world-class Salvador Dalí

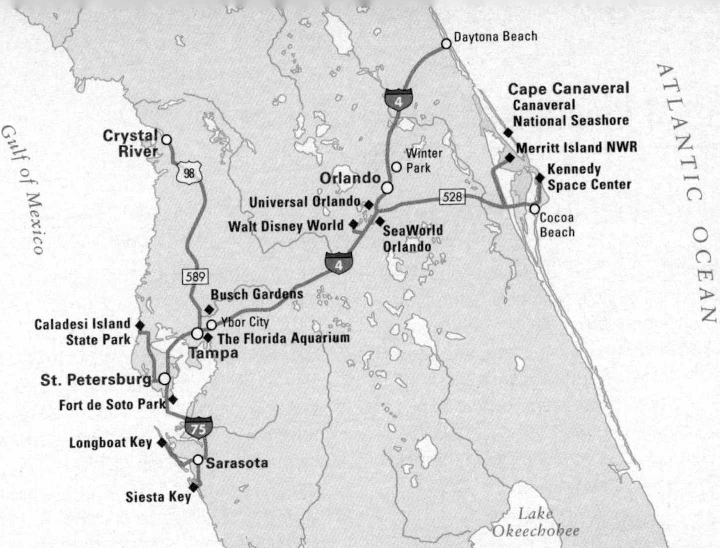

Museum, multiple art galleries, and a quaint, historic downtown. Hit the beach at Caladesi Island State Park to the west of the city or Fort De Soto Park at the mouth of Tampa Bay, both winners of the national "America's Best Beach" competition. Or explore the colorful waterfront community of Gulfport and its Art Village, which is full of locally owned boutiques, galleries, and eclectic eateries. Beer lovers will want to set aside time to explore the city's burgeoning craft beer scene. ⇨ *Chapter 8.*

SARASOTA

1 day. Drive south to Sarasota to appreciate Florida's thriving arts scene and stay overnight on one of the western barrier islands, namely Longboat Key or Siesta Key, the latter home to the finest quartz sand in the world and one of America's best beaches. In Sarasota visit the John and Mable Ringling Museum of Art to learn all about the history of the Ringling circus and enjoy John Ringling's mind-blowingly expansive art collection. The museum encompasses the entire Ringling estate and offers something for guests of all ages and interests. ⇨ *Chapter 8.*

Tips

- Fly into and out of Orlando or Tampa, but you'll definitely need to rent a car.
- In Orlando a park-hopper pass will save you money and permit entry into multiple theme parks in a single day.
- While within Disney World leave your rental car in the hotel parking lot. Complimentary Disney buses transport you around this magical land.
- The beaches around Tampa Bay and St. Petersburg are best on weekdays, when you are likely to have miles of sand all to yourself.

CRYSTAL RIVER

1/2 day. As a half-day trip, nature lovers should proceed north to Crystal River, less than two hours north of St. Petersburg, where you can snorkel with the manatees that congregate in the warm waters from November through March. It's one of the few places on the planet where you can legally interact with them in natural waters. ⇨ *Chapter 8.*

Great Itineraries

South Florida in One Week

Beautiful beaches and even more beautiful people, pulsing nightlife, striking architecture, fancy yachts, old money, new money, exotic wildlife, and stunning marine life—South Florida's got it all. One week is hardly enough to explore the region in detail, but it's enough for a sampler platter of this wildly popular vacation destination.

FORT LAUDERDALE

1 day. Whether you fly into Miami or right into Fort Lauderdale, make the Yachting Capital of the World and the Venice of America your first stop; it's only an hour from the Miami airport. Known for its expansive beaches, show-stopping resort hotels, exploding food scene, and burgeoning cultural scene, Fort Lauderdale has a lot to like, so it may be hard to get your fill in a single day. Take to the waterways to appreciate this coastal beauty. Stroll picture-perfect Las Olas Boulevard, browsing the boutiques and enjoying the eclectic eateries lining Fort Lauderdale's principal thoroughfare. ⇨ *Chapter 6.*

PALM BEACHES

1 day. Less than two hours north of Fort Lauderdale, the opulent mansions of Palm Beach's Ocean Boulevard give you a glimpse of how the richer half lives. For exclusive boutique shopping, art gallery browsing, and glittery sightseeing, sybarites should wander down "The Avenue" (that's Worth Avenue to non–Palm Beachers). The sporty set will find dozens of places to tee up in the Palm Beaches (hardly surprising given that the PGA is based here), along with tennis courts, polo clubs, even a croquet center. Although there's also a less expensive side to Palm Beach, the area's famous hotels are significantly cheaper after Easter weekend, when the high season ends and the city feels like a different place entirely. ⇨ *Chapter 7.*

TREASURE COAST

1 day. To balance the highbrow with the low-key, head northward for a tour of the Treasure Coast, from Stuart to Sebastian. The region is notable for its outdoor activities and Old Florida ambience. This region was named for the booty spilled by a fleet of Spanish galleons shipwrecked here in 1715, though these days you're more likely to discover manatees and golden surfing opportunities than actual gold. You can also look for the sea turtles that lay their own little treasures in the sands March through October. As you drive north, you may want to stop in Jupiter, especially if you're a dog lover, to see one of the state's most dog-friendly beaches. ⇨ *Chapter 7.*

MIAMI

2 or 3 days. Greater Miami lays claim to the country's most celebrated strand—South Beach—and lingering there tops most tourist itineraries. Once you've checked out the candy-color art deco architecture, take time off to ogle the parade of stylish people along Lincoln Road Mall, Ocean Drive, or at the bars, restaurants, and sleek swimming pools within the ever-growing number of trendy hotels in both South Beach and Mid-Beach. Do some credit card damage up in the posh beachfront city of Bal Harbour or inland in the see-and-be-seen Design District. Later merengue over to Calle Ocho, the center of Miami's Cuban community, and pay a visit to bohemian Coconut Grove or the Wynwood Arts District for some more culture. ⇨ *Chapter 3.*

THE EVERGLADES

1/2 day. Miami is the only U.S. city with two national parks and a national preserve in its backyard, deeming it a convenient base for eco-excursions. Especially if you stay three days, keep your car long enough to take a day trip to the Everglades. The easiest access point is Shark Valley, where you can bike along a trail teeming with alligators and herons. Alternatively, get a spectacular view of Florida's coral reefs from a glass-bottom boat in Biscayne National Park; and then spot some rare wood storks in Big Cypress Swamp, which is best explored via Alligator Alley (Interstate 75). ⇨ *Chapter 4.*

THE KEYS

2 or 3 days. Head south from the Florida mainland to the überrelaxing island chain, planning a pit stop at John Pennekamp Coral Reef State Park in Key Largo (which offers unparalleled snorkeling and scuba diving) or at Bahia Honda State Park farther south (it has ranger-led activities plus the Keys' best beach). Then plant yourself at the most famous key of all, Key West, where a come-as-you-are, do-as-you-please vibe rules. The Old Town has a funky, laid-back feel, with prolific nods to Ernest Hemingway. If you haven't imbibed too much at one of the renowned watering holes, rent a moped to tour the rest of the island. Clear waters and abundant marine life make underwater activities another must. ⇨ *Chapter 5.*

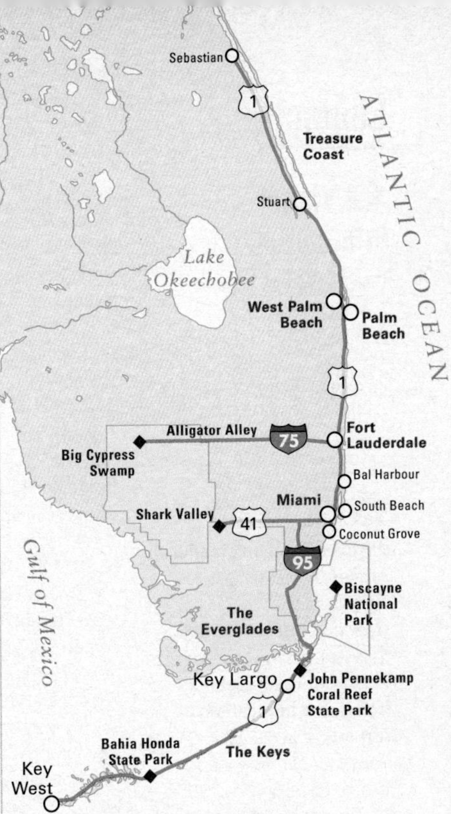

Tips

- You can fly into either Miami International Airport or Fort Lauderdale–Hollywood International Airport; pick whichever is cheaper.
- You'll definitely need a rental car to get between most destinations in South Florida, but expensive parking, pedestrian-friendly streets, and taxis make a car unnecessary in both South Beach and Key West.
- If you have time, drive from Miami to Key West, but flights back can be quick and cheap; check the drop-off charge for a one-way rental.

Contacts

Visitor Information

Visit Florida. ✉ *Visit Florida—Corporate Office, 2540 W. Executive Center Cir., Tallahassee* ☎ *850/488–5607* 🌐 *www.visitflorida.com.*

Air Travel

Daytona Beach International Airport (*DAB*). ✉ *700 Catalina Dr., Daytona Beach* ☎ *386/248–8030* 🌐 *www.flydaytonafirst.com.* **Fort Lauderdale–Hollywood International Airport** (*FLL*). ✉ *100 Terminal Dr., Fort Lauderdale* ☎ *866/435–9355* ✉ *ContactFLL@broward.org* 🌐 *www.broward.org/airport.* **Jacksonville International Airport** (*JAX*). ✉ *2400 Yankee Clipper Dr., Jacksonville* ☎ *904/741–4902* 🌐 *www.flyjax.com.* **Key West International Airport** (*EYW*). ✉ *3491 S. Roosevelt Blvd., Key West* ☎ *305/809–5200* 🌐 *eyw.com.* **Miami International Airport** (*MIA*). ✉ *Miami International Airport, 2100 N.W. 42nd Ave., Miami* ☎ *305/876–7000, 800/825–5642 International* 🌐 *www.iflymia.com.* **Northwest Florida Beaches International Airport** (*ECP*). ✉ *6300 W. Bay Pkwy., Panama City* ☎ *850/763–6751* 🌐 *www.iflybeaches.com.* **Orlando International Airport** (*MCO*). ✉ *1 Jeff Fuqua Blvd., Orlando* ☎ *407/825–2001* 🌐 *www.orlandoairports.net.* **Palm Beach International Airport** (*PBI*). ✉ *Palm Beach International Airport, 1000 Palm Beach International Airport, West Palm Beach* ☎ *561/471–7400* 🌐 *www.pbia.org.* **Sarasota Bradenton International Airport** (*SRQ*). ✉ *6000 Airport Circle, Bradenton* ☎ *941/359–5200* 🌐 *www.srq-airport.com.* **Southwest Florida International Airport** (*RSW*). ✉ *11000 Terminal Access Rd., Fort Myers* ☎ *239/590–4800* 🌐 *www.flylcpa.com.* **St. Petersburg–Clearwater International Airport** (*PIE*). ✉ *14700 Terminal Blvd., Clearwater* ☎ *727/453–7800* 🌐 *www.fly2pie.com.* **Tampa International Airport** (*TPA*). ✉ *4100 George J. Bean Pkwy., Tampa* ☎ *813/870–8700* 🌐 *www.tampaairport.com.*

SHUTTLE SERVICE SuperShuttle. ☎ *800/258–3826* 🌐 *www.supershuttle.com.*

Car Travel

Avis. ☎ *973/496–3500* 🌐 *www.avis.com.* **Budget.** ✉ *6 Sylvan Way, Parsippany* ☎ *800/218–7992* 🌐 *www.budget.com.* **Hertz.** ☎ *800/654–3131* 🌐 *www.hertz.com.* **Sunshine Rent A Car.** ✉ *321 W. State Rd. 84, Fort Lauderdale* ☎ *888/786–7446, 954/467–8100* 🌐 *www.sunshinerentacar.com.*

Train Travel

Virgin Trains USA (*Formerly Brightline*).

Ferry Travel

Key West Express. ✉ *1200 Main St., Fort Myers Beach* ☎ *239/463–5733* 🌐 *www.keywestexpress.net.*

Lodging

American Realty of Captiva. ✉ *11526 Andy Rose La., Captiva* ☎ *800/547–0127* 🌐 *www.captiva-island.com.* **Endless Vacation Rentals.** ☎ *877/782–9387* 🌐 *www.evrentals.com.* **Interhome.** ☎ *954/791–8282, 800/882–6864* 🌐 *www.interhomeusa.com.* **Sand Key Realty.** ✉ *790 S. Gulfview Blvd., Clearwater Beach* ☎ *800/257–7332, 727/443–0032* 🌐 *www.sandkey.com.* **Suncoast Vacation Rentals.** ✉ *224 Franklin Blvd., St. George Island* ☎ *800/341–2021* 🌐 *www.uncommonflorida.com.* **Wyndham Vacation Rentals.** ✉ *14 Sylvan Way, Parsippany* ☎ *800/467–3529* 🌐 *www.wyndhamvacationrentals.com.*

Chapter 3

MIAMI AND MIAMI BEACH

Updated by
Paul Rubio

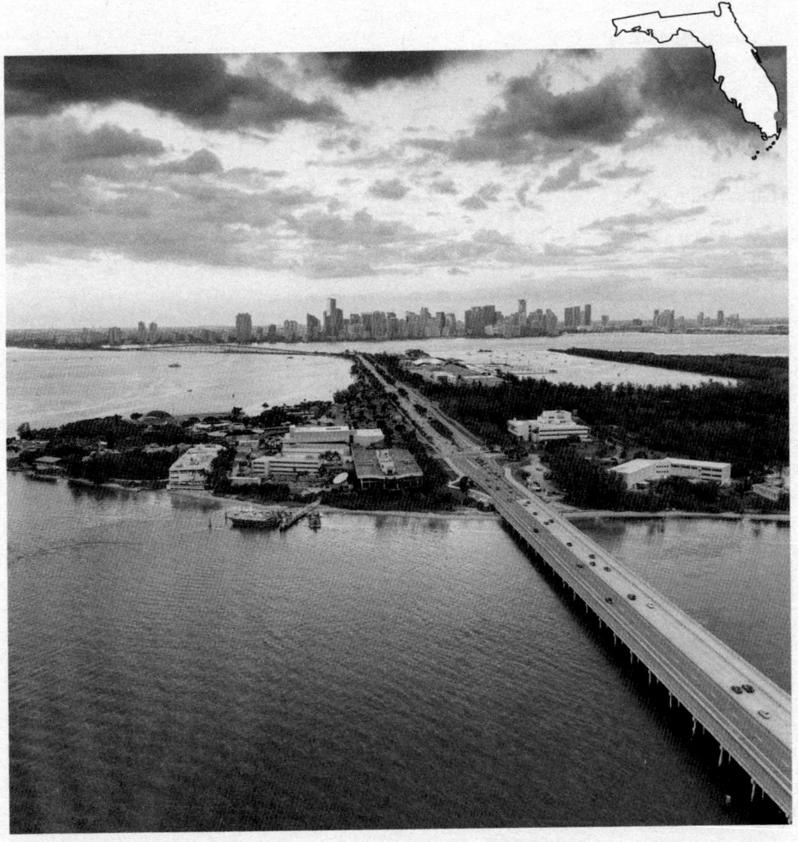

Sights ★★★★★ | Restaurants ★★★★★ | Hotels ★★★★★ | Shopping ★★★★★ | Nightlife ★★★★★

WELCOME TO MIAMI AND MIAMI BEACH

TOP REASONS TO GO

★ **The beach:** Miami Beach has been rated as one of the 10 best beaches in the world. White sand, warm water, and bronzed bodies everywhere provide just the right mix of relaxation and people-watching.

★ **Dining delights:** Miami's eclectic residents have transformed the city into a museum of epicurean wonders, ranging from Cuban and Asian fare to fusion haute cuisine.

★ **Wee-hour parties:** A 24-hour liquor license means clubs stay open until 5 am, and after-parties go until noon the following day.

★ **Picture-perfect people:** Miami is a watering hole for the vain and beautiful of South America, Europe, and the Northeast. Watch them—or join them—as they strut their stuff and flaunt their tans on the white beds of renowned art deco hotels.

★ **Art Deco District:** Iconic pastels and neon lights accessorize the architecture that first put South Beach on the map in the 1930s.

1 **Downtown.** Labyrinth of high rises and cool lounges.

2 **Coconut Grove.** Known for bohemian shops and live music.

3 **Coral Gables.** Dine and shop on family-friendly Miracle Mile.

4 **Key Biscayne.** Explore parks and beaches.

5 **Wynwood.** Trendy, creative area with colorful murals.

6 **Midtown.** Experience yuppie life and fab restaurants.

7 **Design District/Buena Vista.** Browse design rooms and haute boutiques.

8 **Little Haiti/Upper East Side.** Emerging arts scene and Haitian food.

9 **Little Havana.** The heart and soul of Cuba's exile community.

10 **South Beach.** People-watch, admire art deco, and party 'til dawn.

11 **Mid-Beach.** Blooming hotel scene beyond SoBe.

12 **Fisher and Belle Isle.** Exclusive private island.

13 **North Beach.** Quieter end of the beach with luxe hotels.

14 **Aventura.** Known for high end shopping and golf.

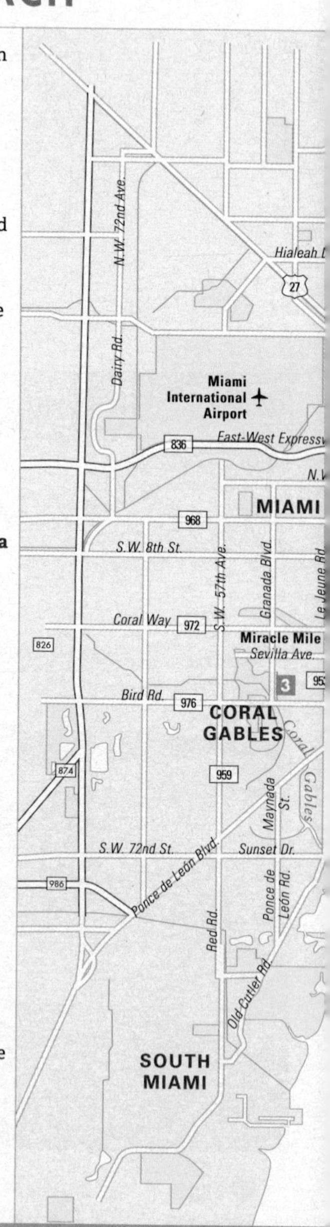

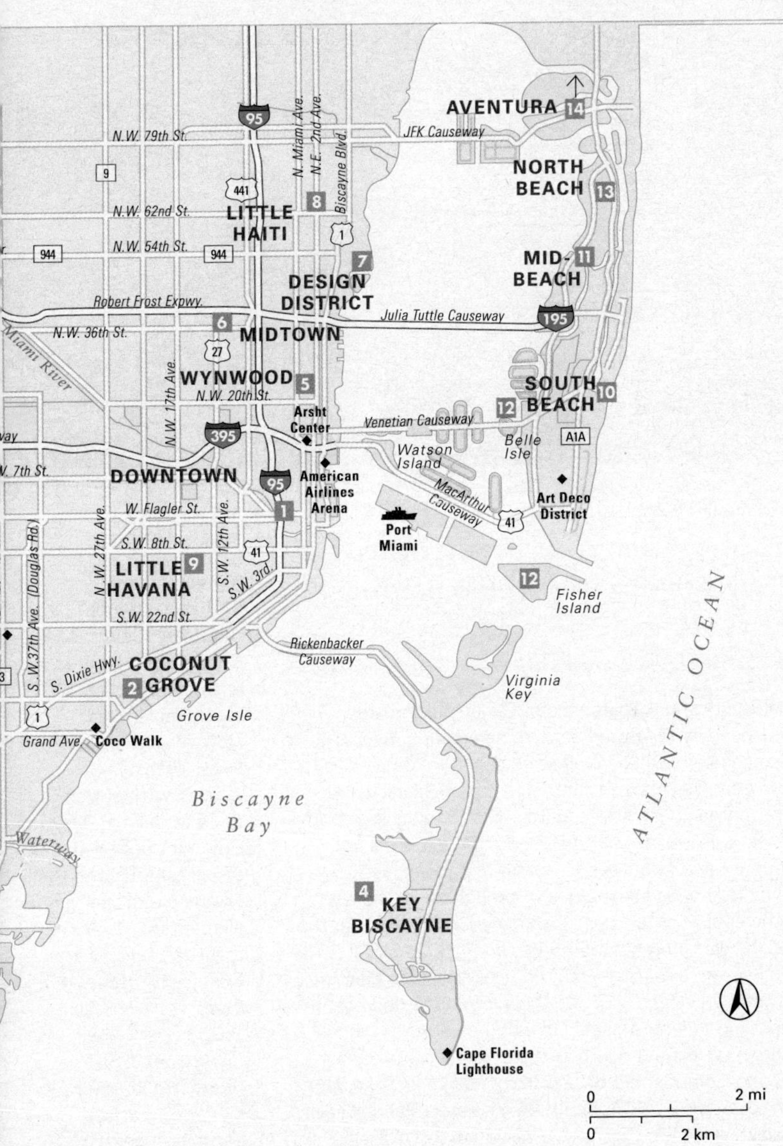

AVENTURA
14
JFK Causeway
N.W. 79th St.
95
N. Miami Ave.
N.E. 2nd Ave.
Biscayne Blvd.
9
441
NORTH
BEACH
13
N.W. 62nd St.
LITTLE
HAITI
8
1
N.W. 54th St.
944
944
7
MID-
BEACH
11
DESIGN
DISTRICT
Robert Frost Expwy.
Julia Tuttle Causeway
195
6
N.W. 36th St.
MIDTOWN
Miami River
27
N.W. 17th Ave.
WYNWOOD
5
SOUTH
BEACH
10
N.W. 20th St.
Arsht
Center
12
Venetian Causeway
395
Belle
Isle
A1A
Watson
Island
7th St.
DOWNTOWN
American
Airlines
Arena
95
MacArthur
Causeway
Art Deco
District
W. Flagler St.
1
41
Port
Miami
S.W. 8th St.
S.W. 12th Ave.
N.W. 27th Ave.
S.W. 37th Ave. (Douglas Rd.)
41
LITTLE
HAVANA
9
S.W. 3rd
12
Fisher
Island
S.W. 22nd St.
ATLANTIC OCEAN
Rickenbacker
Causeway
S. Dixie Hwy.
COCONUT
GROVE
2
Virginia
Key
1
Grove Isle
Grand Ave.
Coco Walk
Biscayne
Bay
Waterway
4
KEY
BISCAYNE
Cape Florida
Lighthouse
0
2 mi
0
2 km

CUBAN FOOD

If the tropical vibe has you hankering for Cuban food, you've come to the right place. Miami is the top spot in the country to enjoy authentic Cuban cooking.

The flavors and preparations of Cuban cuisine are influenced by the island nation's natural bounty (yuca, sugarcane, guava), as well as its rich immigrant history, from near (Caribbean countries) and far (Spanish and African traditions). Chefs in Miami tend to stick with the classic versions of beloved dishes, though you'll find some variation from restaurant to restaurant, as recipes have often been passed down through generations of home cooks. For a true Cuban experience, try either the popular **Versailles** (✉ *3555 S.W. 8th St.* ☎ *305/444–0240* 🌐 *www.versaillesrestaurant.com*) or classic **La Carreta** (✉ *3632 S.W. 8th St.* ☎ *305/444–7501*) in Little Havana, appealing to families seeking a home-cooked, Cuban-style meal. For a modern interpretation of Cuban eats, head to Coral Gable's **Havana Harry's** (✉ *4612 S. Le Jeune Rd.* ☎ *305/661–2622*). South Beach eatery **Puerto Sagua Restaurant** (✉ *700 Collins Ave.* ☎ *305/673–1115*) is the beach's favorite Cuban hole-in-the-wall, open daily from 7 am to 2 am.

THE CUBAN SANDWICH

A great *cubano* (Cuban sandwich) requires pillowy Cuban bread layered with ham, garlic-citrus-marinated slow-roasted pork, Swiss cheese, and pickles, with butter and/or mustard. The sandwich is grilled in a press until the cheese melts and the elements are fused together. Try one at **Enriqueta's Sandwich Shop** (✉ *186 N.E. 29 St.* ☎ *305/573–4681*) in Wynwood, or **Exquisito Restaurant** (✉ *1510 S.W. 8th St.* ☎ *305/643–0227*) in Little Havana.

Key Cuban Dishes

ARROZ CON POLLO

This chicken-and-rice dish is Cuban comfort food. Found throughout Latin America, the Cuban version is typically seasoned with garlic, paprika, and onions, then colored golden or reddish with saffron or achiote (a seed paste), and enlivened with a splash of beer near the end of cooking. Green peas and sliced, roasted red peppers are standard toppings.

BISTEC DE PALOMILLA

This thinly sliced sirloin steak is marinated in lime juice and garlic and fried with onions. The steak is often served with *chimichurri* sauce, an olive oil, garlic, and cilantro sauce that sometimes comes with bread. Also try *ropa vieja,* a slow-cooked, shredded flank steak in a garlic-tomato sauce.

DESSERTS

Treat yourself to a slice of *tres leches* cake. The "three milks" come from the sweetened condensed milk, evaporated milk, and heavy cream that are poured over the cake until it's an irresistible gooey mess. Also, don't miss the *pastelitos,* Cuban fruit-filled turnovers. Traditional flavors include plain guava, guava with cream cheese, and cream cheese with coconut.

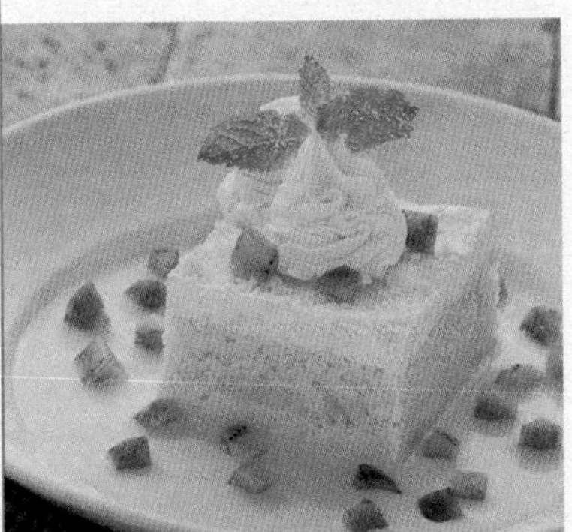

DRINKS

Sip *guarapo,* a fresh sugarcane juice that isn't really as sweet as you might think, or enjoy a *batido,* a Cuban-style milk shake made with tropical fruits like mango, *piña* (pineapple), or *mamey*. For a real twist, try the *batido de trigo*—a wheat shake that will remind you of sugar-glazed cereal.

FRITAS

If you're in the mood for an inexpensive, casual Cuban meal, have a *frita*—a hamburger with Cuban flair. It's made with ground beef that's mixed with chopped chorizo, spiced with pepper, paprika, and salt, topped with sautéed onions and shoestring potato fries, and then served on a bun slathered with a tomato-based ketchup-like sauce.

LECHÓN ASADO

Fresh ham or an entire suckling pig marinated in *mojo criollo* (parsley, garlic, sour orange, and olive oil) is roasted until tender and served with white rice, black beans, and *tostones* (fried plantains) or yuca, a starchy tuber with a mild nut taste that's often sliced into fat sticks and deep-fried like fries.

Three-quarters of a century after the art deco movement, Miami remains one of the world's trendiest and flashiest hot spots. Luckily for visitors, South Beach is no longer the only place to stand and pose in Miami. North of Downtown, the growing Wynwood and Design districts are home to Miami's hipster and fashionista movements, and the South Beach "scene" continues to extend both north and west, with the addition of new venues north of 20th Street, south of 5th Street, and along the bay on West Avenue.

Visit Miami today and it's hard to believe that 100 years ago it was a mosquito-infested swampland, with an Indian trading post on the Miami River. Then hotel builder Henry Flagler brought his railroad to the outpost known as Fort Dallas. Other visionaries—Carl Fisher, Julia Tuttle, William Brickell, and John Sewell, among others—set out to tame the unruly wilderness. Hotels were erected, bridges were built, the port was dredged, and electricity arrived. The narrow strip of mangrove coast was transformed into Miami Beach—and the tourists started to come. They haven't stopped since!

Greater Miami is many destinations in one. At its best it offers an unparalleled multicultural experience: melodic Latin and Caribbean tongues, international cuisines and cultural events, and an unmistakable joie de vivre—all against a beautiful beach backdrop. In Little Havana the air is tantalizing with the perfume of strong Cuban coffee. In Coconut Grove, Caribbean steel drums ring out during the Miami/Bahamas Goombay Festival. Anytime in colorful Miami Beach, restless crowds wait for entry to the hottest new clubs.

Many visitors don't know that Miami and Miami Beach are really separate cities. Miami, on the mainland, is South Florida's commercial hub. Miami Beach, on 17 islands in Biscayne Bay, is sometimes considered America's Riviera, luring refugees from winter with its warm sunshine; sandy beaches; graceful, shady palms; and tireless nightlife. The natives know well that there's more to Greater Miami than the bustle of South

Beach and its Art Deco Historic District. In addition to well-known places such as Ocean Drive and Lincoln Road, the less-reported spots—like the burgeoning Design District in Miami, the historic buildings of Coral Gables, and the secluded beaches of Key Biscayne—are great insider destinations.

Planning

When to Go

Miami and Miami Beach are year-round destinations. Most people come from November through April, when the weather is close to perfect; hotels, restaurants, and attractions are busiest; and each weekend holds a festival or event. High season kicks off in December with Art Basel Miami Beach, and hotel rates don't come down until after the college kids have left after spring break in late March.

It's hot and steamy May through September, but nighttime temperatures are usually pleasant. Also, summer is a good time for the budget traveler. Many hotels lower their rates considerably, and many restaurants offer discounts—especially during Miami Spice in August and September, when a slew of top restaurants offer special tasting menus at a steep discount.

FESTIVALS AND ANNUAL EVENTS

Art Basel Miami Beach

ARTS FESTIVALS | The most prestigious art show in the United States is held every December, with plenty of fabulous parties to go along with the pricey art. This is a who's who of the art world where collectors, emerging artists, renowned artists, curators, gallerists, and art aficionados convene alongside novices, trendsetters, and glitterati. Although the main exhibition is held at the Miami Beach Convention Center, dozens of smaller exhibitions are set up on the beach, Downtown, and in the Wynwood District at galleries, event spaces, and in hotel lobbies. The exquisite art and sensational people-watching more than soften the blow of exorbitant hotel prices, heavy traffic, and long waits. ■ **TIP→ Plan ahead to make the most of Art Basel, which includes purchasing tickets or securing your name on guest lists in advance.** 🌐 *www.artbasel.com.*

Art Deco Weekend

ARTS FESTIVALS | This annual weekend of all things art deco was started by the Miami Preservation League in the 1970s to draw attention to and celebrate Miami Beach's Art Deco Historic District. Tours, lectures, film screenings, and dozens of other 1930s-themed events are on tap over this January weekend. Festivities—many of them free—begin on Friday, followed by a car show and street fair (with over 140 vendors) on Saturday and Sunday. More than a quarter of a million people join in the action, which centers on Ocean Drive between 5th and 15th streets. 🌐 *www.artdecoweekend.com.*

Carnaval Miami

CULTURAL FESTIVALS | The Caribbean and Latin America know how to celebrate Carnival in style, so it's only natural their tropical stepsister does, too! Each year, Miami's pre-Lentan celebrations in February and/or March climax during Carnaval Miami. One of the main celebrations is held every year on Calle 8. The wild and fun street festival in the heart of Little Havana is the last blowout before Lent begins. This Sunday street party attracts over a million people, who dance in the streets and enjoy more than two dozen stages of DJs and live music. 🌐 *www.carnavalmiami.com.*

South Beach Wine and Food Festival

FESTIVALS | The Food Network and Cooking Channel's star-studded four-day weekend each February showcases the flavors and ingenuity of the country's top chefs and wine and spirits producers.

Personalities like Anne Burrell, Guy Fieri, and Bobby Flay headline brunches, lunches, dinners, and seminars across Miami Beach. The festival attracts more than 60,000 attendees annually. To avoid disappointment, book your choice events far in advance. ☎ *877/762–3933 for ticketed events* 🌐 *www.sobefest.com.*

The White Party

FESTIVALS | The White Party began in 1985 as a pioneering fund-raiser for AIDS research and awareness. Nowadays, Thanksgiving weekend is one of the most anticipated weekends of the year in the LGBTQ community thanks to the White Party (and another reason not to have that extra scoop of stuffing). On Saturday evening, thousands of gay men, women, and their friends get decked out in white and party the night away under the stars to the sounds of world-famous DJs and recording artists. The event remains a charitable event to support Care-Resource, a nonprofit, community-based AIDS service organization. 🌐 *www.whiteparty.org.*

Winter Music Conference

MUSIC FESTIVALS | Since 1985, the largest DJ showcase in the world has rocked Miami every March, when South Beach truly turns into one big ol' party with more than 100,000 attendees. The latest and greatest in electronic music (to the tune of 2,000 performers and 400 events) diffuses through the lobbies and pools of Miami's most iconic hotels, public spaces, and local event arenas. 🌐 *www.wintermusicconference.com.*

Getting Here and Around

You'll need a car to visit many attractions and points of interest. If possible, avoid driving during the rush hours of 7–9 am and 5–7 pm—the hour just after and right before the peak times also can be slow going. During rainy weather, be especially cautious of flooding in South Beach and Key Biscayne.

AIR TRAVEL

Miami is serviced by Miami International Airport (MIA), 8 miles northwest of Downtown, and Fort Lauderdale–Hollywood International Airport (FLL), 26 miles northeast. Many discount carriers, like Spirit Airlines, Southwest Airlines, and JetBlue, fly into FLL, making it a smart bargain if you're renting a car. Otherwise, look for flights to MIA, which has undergone an extensive face-lift, improving facilities, common spaces, and the overall aesthetic of the airport.

CAR TRAVEL

Interstate 95 is the major expressway connecting South Florida with points north; State Road 836 is the major east–west expressway and connects to Florida's Turnpike, State Road 826, and Interstate 95. Seven causeways link Miami and Miami Beach, with Interstate 195 and Interstate 395 offering the most convenient routes; the Rickenbacker Causeway extends to Key Biscayne from Interstate 95 and U.S. 1. The high-speed lanes on the left-hand side of Interstate 95—often separated by confusing orange poles—require a prepaid toll pass called a Sunpass, available in most drug and grocery stores, or it can be ordered by mail before your trip. It is available with all rental cars (but you are billed for the tolls and associated fees later).

PUBLIC TRANSPORTATION

Some sights are accessible via the public transportation system, run by the **Metro-Dade Transit Agency,** which maintains 800 Metrobuses on 95 routes; the 25-mile Metrorail elevated rapid-transit system; and the Metromover, an elevated light-rail system. Those planning to use public transportation should get an EASY Ticket available at any Metrorail station and most supermarkets, or download the EASY PAY MIAMI app to buy daily passes. Fares are discounted, and transfer fees are nominal. The bus stops for the **Metrobus** are marked with blue-and-green signs with a bus logo and route information. The fare is $2.25 (exact change only if paying cash). Cash-paying customers must pay for another ride if transferring. Elevated **Metrorail** trains run from Downtown Miami north to Hialeah and south along U.S. 1 to Dadeland. The system operates daily 5 am–midnight. The fare is $2.25 and accessible only by EASY Ticket or the EASY PAY MIAMI app (no cash). The free **Metromover** resembles an airport shuttle and runs on three loops around Downtown Miami, linking major hotels, office buildings, and shopping areas. The system spans about 4½ miles, including the 1-mile Omni Loop, the 1-mile Brickell Loop, and the smaller Inner-Loop. **Tri-Rail,** South Florida's commuter-train system, stops at 18 stations north of MIA along a 71-mile route. There's a Metrorail transfer station two stops north of MIA. Prices range from $2.50 to $6.90 for a one-way ticket.

CONTACTS Metro-Dade Transit Agency. ☎ *305/891–3131* 🌐 *www.miamidade.gov/transit/.* **Tri-Rail.** ☎ *800/874–7245* 🌐 *www.tri-rail.com.*

TAXI TRAVEL

These days, most use Uber or Lyft to get around Miami, but old-school taxis still exist. Except in South Beach, it's difficult to hail a cab on the street; in most cases you'll need to call a cab company or have a hotel doorman hail one for you. Taxi drivers in Miami are notorious for bad customer service and not having credit card machines in their vehicles. If using a regular taxi, note that fares run $4.50 for the first 1/6 of a mile and $0.40 for every additional 1/6 of a mile. Waiting time is $0.40 per minute. Flat-rate fares are also available from the airport to a variety of zones (including Miami Beach) for $35. Expect a $2 surcharge on rides leaving from MIA or the Port of Miami. For those heading from MIA to Downtown, the 15-minute, 7-mile trip costs around $21. Some but not all cabs accept credit cards, so ask when you get in.

TAXI COMPANIES Central Cab. ☎ *305/532–5555* 🌐 *www.centralcab.com.* **Uber.** 🌐 *www.uber.com.* **Yellow Cab.** ☎ *305/444–4444.*

TRAIN TRAVEL

New high-speed train service via Virgin Trains USA (formerly called Brightline) began in summer 2018, connecting Downtown Miami, Fort Lauderdale, and West Palm Beach. The trip from Downtown Miami to Fort Lauderdale takes about 30 minutes; it's another 40 minutes to West Palm Beach.

Amtrak provides service from 500 destinations to the Greater Miami area. The trains make several stops along the way; north–south service stops in the major Florida cities of Jacksonville, Orlando, Tampa, West Palm Beach, and Fort Lauderdale, but stations are not always conveniently located. The Auto Train (where you bring your car along) travels from Lorton, Virginia, just outside Washington, D.C., to Sanford, Florida, just outside Orlando. From there it's less than a four-hour drive to Miami. Fares vary, but expect to pay between around $275 and $350 for a basic sleeper seat and car passage each way. ■ **TIP→ You must be traveling with an automobile to purchase a ticket on the Auto Train.**

CONTACTS Virgin Trains USA (*Formerly Brightline*).

Sights

If you'd arrived here 50 years ago with a guidebook in hand, chances are you'd be thumbing through listings looking for alligator wrestlers and you-pick strawberry fields or citrus groves. Things have changed. While Disney sidetracked families in Orlando, Miami was developing a unique culture and attitude that's equal parts beach town/big business, Latino/Caribbean meets European/American—all of which fuels a great art and food scene, as well as exuberant nightlife and myriad festivals.

To find your way around Greater Miami, learn how the numbering system works (or better yet, use your phone's GPS). Miami is laid out on a grid with four quadrants—northeast, northwest, southeast, and southwest—that meet at Miami Avenue and Flagler Street. Miami Avenue separates east from west, and Flagler Street separates north from south. Avenues and courts run north–south; streets, terraces, and ways run east–west. Roads run diagonally, northwest–southeast. But other districts—Miami Beach, Coral Gables, and Hialeah—may or may not follow this system, and along the curve of Biscayne Bay the symmetrical grid shifts diagonally. If you do get lost, make sure you're in a safe neighborhood or public place when you seek guidance; cabdrivers and cops are good resources.

Restaurants

Miami's restaurant scene has exploded in the past few years, with new restaurants springing up left and right every month. The melting pot of residents and visitors has brought an array of sophisticated, tasty cuisine. Little Havana is still king for Cuban fare, and Miami Beach is swept up in a trend of fusion cuisine, which combines Asian, French, American, and Latin cooking with sumptuous—and pricey—results. Locals spend the most time in Downtown Miami, Wynwood, and the Design District, where the city's ongoing foodie and cocktail revolution is most pronounced. Since Miami dining is a part of the trendy nightlife scene, most dinners don't start until 8 or 9 pm, and may go well into the night. To avoid a long wait among the late-night partiers at hot spots, come before 7 pm or make reservations. Attire is usually casual-chic, but patrons like to dress to impress. Don't be surprised to see large tables of women in skimpy dresses—this is common in Miami. Prices tend to be extra inflated in tourist hot spots like Lincoln Road, but if you venture off the beaten path you can find better food for more reasonable prices. When you get your bill, check whether a gratuity is already included; most restaurants add between 18% and 22% (ostensibly for the convenience of, and protection from, the many Latin American and European tourists who are used to this practice in their homelands), but supplement it depending on your opinion of the service.

Restaurant reviews have been shortened. For full information, visit Fodors.com.

What It Costs

	$	$$	$$$	$$$$
RESTAURANTS	under $15	$15–$20	$21–$30	over $30

Hotels

Room rates in Miami tend to swing wildly. In high season, which is January through May, expect to pay at least $250 per night, even at value-oriented hotels. In fact, it's common nowadays for rates to begin around $500 at Miami's top hotels. In summer, however, prices can be as much as 50% lower than the dizzying winter rates. You can also find great deals between Easter and Memorial Day, which is actually a delightful time in Miami. Business travelers tend to stay in Downtown Miami, and most vacationers stay on Miami Beach, as close as possible to the water. South Beach is no longer the "in" place to stay. Mid-Beach and Downtown have taken the hotel scene by storm in the past few years and become home to some of the region's most avant-garde and luxurious properties to date. If money is no object, stay in one of the glamorous hotels lining Collins Avenue between 15th and 23rd streets or between 29th and 44th streets. Otherwise, stay on the quiet beaches farther north, or in one of the small boutique hotels on Ocean Drive, Collins, or Washington avenues between 10th and 15th streets. Two important considerations that affect price are balcony and view. If you're willing to have a room without an ocean view, you can sometimes get a much lower price than the standard rate, even at an oceanfront hotel.

Hotel reviews have been shortened. For full information, visit Fodors.com.

What It Costs

	$	$$	$$$	$$$$
HOTELS	under $200	$200–$300	$301–$400	over $400

Nightlife

One of Greater Miami's most popular pursuits is barhopping. Bars range from intimate enclaves to showy see-and-be-seen lounges to loud, raucous frat parties. There's a New York–style flair to some of the newer lounges, which are increasingly catering to the Manhattan party crowd who escape to Miami and Miami Beach for long weekends. No doubt, Miami's pulse pounds with nonstop nightlife that reflects the area's potent cultural mix. On sultry, humid nights with the huge full moon rising out of the ocean and fragrant night-blooming jasmine intoxicating the senses, who can resist Cuban salsa with some disco and hip-hop thrown in for good measure? When this place throws a party, hips shake, fingers snap, bodies touch. It's no wonder many clubs are still rocking at 5 am. If you're looking for a relatively nonfrenetic evening, your best bet is one of the chic hotel bars on Collins Avenue, or a lounge away from Miami Beach in Wynwood, the Design District, or Downtown.

The *Miami Herald* (🌐 *www.miamiherald.com*) is a good source for information on what to do in town. The Weekend section of the newspaper, included in the Friday edition, has an annotated guide to everything from plays and galleries to concerts and nightclubs. The "Ticket" column details the week's entertainment highlights. Or you can pick up the *Miami New Times* (🌐 *www.miaminewtimes.com*), the city's largest free alternative newspaper, published each Thursday. It lists nightclubs, concerts, and special events; reviews plays and movies; and provides in-depth coverage of the local music scene. *MIAMI* (🌐 *www.modernluxury.com/miami*) and *Ocean Drive* (🌐 *www.oceandrive.com*), Miami's model-strewn, upscale fashion and lifestyle magazines squeeze club, bar, restaurant, and events listings in with fashion spreads, reviews, and personality profiles. Paparazzi photos of local party people and celebrities give you a taste of Greater Miami nightlife before you even dress up to paint the town.

The Spanish-language *El Nuevo Herald* (🌐 *www.elnuevoherald.com*), published by the *Miami Herald,* has extensive information on Spanish-language arts and entertainment, including dining reviews, concert previews, and nightclub highlights.

Shopping

Beyond its fun-in-the-sun offerings, Miami has evolved into a world-class shopping destination. People fly to Miami from all over the world just to shop. The city teems with sophisticated malls—from multistory, indoor climate-controlled temples of consumerism to sun-kissed, open-air retail enclaves—and bustling avenues and streets, lined at once with affordable chain stores, haute couture boutiques, and one-off, "only in Miami"–type shops.

Following the incredible success of the Bal Harbour Shops in the highest of the high-end market (Chanel, Alexander McQueen, ETRO), the Design District and Downtown have followed suit. Beyond fabulous designer furniture showrooms, the Design District's tenants now include Hermès, Dior Homme, Rolex, and Prada. Downtown's mega Brickell City Centre is the latest arena for high-end retail, with a number of European brands making their U.S. debuts in the chic open-air mall.

Beyond clothiers and big-name retailers, Greater Miami has all manner of merchandise to tempt even the casual browser. For consumers on a mission to find certain items—art deco antiques or cigars, for instance—the city streets burst with a rewarding collection of specialty shops.

Stroll through Spanish-speaking neighborhoods where shops sell clothing, cigars, and other goods from all over Latin America, or even head to Little Haiti for rare vinyl records.

Activities

Sun, sand, and crystal-clear water mixed with an almost nonexistent winter and a cosmopolitan clientele make Miami and Miami Beach ideal for year-round sunbathing and outdoor activities. Whether the priority is showing off a toned body, jumping on a Jet Ski, or relaxing in a tranquil natural environment, there's a beach tailor-made to please. But tanning and water sports are only part of this sun-drenched picture. Greater Miami has championship golf courses and tennis courts, miles of bike trails along placid canals and through subtropical forests, and skater-friendly concrete paths amidst the urban jungle. For those who like their sports of the spectator variety, the city offers up a bonanza of pro teams for every season.

Visitor Information

For additional information about Miami and Miami Beach, contact the city's visitor bureaus.

CONTACTS City of Coral Gables. ✉ *Coral Gables City Hall, 405 Biltmore Way, Coral Gables* ☎ *305/446–6800* 🌐 *www.coralgables.com.* **Coconut Grove Business Improvement District.** ✉ *3390 Mary St., Suite 130, Coconut Grove* ☎ *305/461–5506* 🌐 *www.coconutgrove.com.* **Greater Miami Convention & Visitors Bureau.** ✉ *701 Brickell Ave., Suite 2700* ☎ *305/539–3000, 800/933–8448 in U.S.* 🌐 *www.miamiandbeaches.com.* **Key Biscayne Chamber of Commerce and Visitors Center.** ✉ *88 W. McIntyre St., Suite 100, Key Biscayne* ☎ *305/361–5207* 🌐 *www.keybiscaynechamber.org.* **Visit Miami Beach.** ✉ *Visitor Center, 530 17th St., Miami Beach* ☎ *305/672–1270* 🌐 *www.miamibeachguest.com.*

Downtown

Downtown Miami dazzles from a distance. America's third-largest skyline is fluid, thanks to the sheer number of sparkling glass high-rises between Biscayne Boulevard and the Miami River. Business is the key to Downtown Miami's daytime bustle. Nevertheless, the influx of massive, modern, and once-affordable condos has lured a young and trendy demographic to the areas in and around Downtown, giving Miami much more of a "city" feel come nightfall. In fact, Downtown has become a nighttime hot spot in recent years, inciting a cultural revolution that has fostered burgeoning areas north in Wynwood, Midtown, and the Design District, and south along Brickell Avenue. The pedestrian streets here tend to be very restaurant-centric, complemented by lounges and nightclubs.

The free, 4½-mile, elevated commuter system known as the Metromover runs inner and outer loops through Downtown and to nearby neighborhoods south and north. Many attractions are conveniently located within a few blocks of a station.

Sights

Adrienne Arsht Center

ARTS VENUE | Culture vultures and other artsy types are drawn to this stunning performing arts center, which includes the 2,400-seat Ziff Ballet Opera House, the 2,200-seat John S. and James L. Knight Concert Hall, the black-box Carnival Studio Theater, and the outdoor Parker and Vann Thomson Plaza for the Arts. Throughout the year, you'll find top-notch performances by local and national touring groups, including Broadway hits like *Wicked* and *Jersey Boys,* intimate music concerts, and showstopping ballet. Think of it as a sliver of savoir faire to temper Miami's often-over-the-top vibe. The massive development was designed by architect César Pelli. Complimentary one-hour tours of the Arsht Center, highlighting the architecture and its public art, are offered every Saturday and Monday at noon. Arrive early for your performance to dine at BRAVA By Brad Kilgore, a top Miami restaurant located within the Arsht center. ✉ *1300 Biscayne Blvd., at N.E. 13th St., Downtown* ☎ *305/949–6722 box office* 🌐 *www.arshtcenter.org.*

Bayside Marketplace

MARKET | **FAMILY** | The Bayside Marketplace, a waterfront complex of entertainment, dining, and retail stores, was en vogue circa 1992 and remains popular due to its location near Port Miami. You'll find the area awash in cruise-ship passenger chaos on most days (it's definitely *not* a draw for locals but a place to kill time in between airport arrival and cruise embarkation), so expect plenty of souvenir shops, a Hard Rock Cafe, and stores like Gap and Sunglass Hut. Many boat tours leave from the marinas lining the festival marketplace. ✉ *401 Biscayne Blvd., Downtown* ☎ *305/577–3344* 🌐 *www.baysidemarketplace.com.*

Fredric Snitzer Gallery

MUSEUM | The gallery of this longtime figure in the Miami arts scene highlights emerging and mid-career artists, providing them that tipping point needed for national and international exposure and recognition. The newly relocated space maintains its warehouse roots, letting the art speak for itself amid the raw walls and ample natural light. Though a commercial gallery, the selection is highly curated. Rotating monthly exhibitions are usually thematic, with works by one of its represented artists including Hernan Bas, Alice Aycock, Enrique Martinez Celaya, Rafael Domenech, and Jon Pylypchuk. For the art novice, the team, including Snitzer himself, are readily available and willing to share their knowledge. ✉ *1540 N.E. Miami Ct., Downtown* ☎ *305/448–8976* 🌐 *www.snitzer.com.*

Freedom Tower

BUILDING | In the 1960s this ornate Spanish-baroque structure was the Cuban Refugee Center, processing more than 500,000 Cubans who entered the United States after fleeing Fidel Castro's regime. Built in 1925 for the *Miami Daily News,* it was inspired by the Giralda, an 800-year-old bell tower in Seville, Spain. Preservationists were pleased to see the tower's exterior restored in 1988. Today it is owned by Miami Dade College (MDC), functioning as a cultural and educational center; it's also home to the MDC Museum of Art + Design, which showcases a broad collection of contemporary Latin art, as well as works in the genres of minimalism and pop art. ✉ *600 Biscayne Blvd., at N.E. 6th St., Downtown* ☎ *305/237–7700* 🌐 *www.mdcmoad.org* 🎫 *$12* 🕑 *Closed Mon.–Tues.*

★ HistoryMiami Museum

MUSEUM | **FAMILY** | Discover a treasure trove of colorful stories about the region's history. Exhibits celebrate the

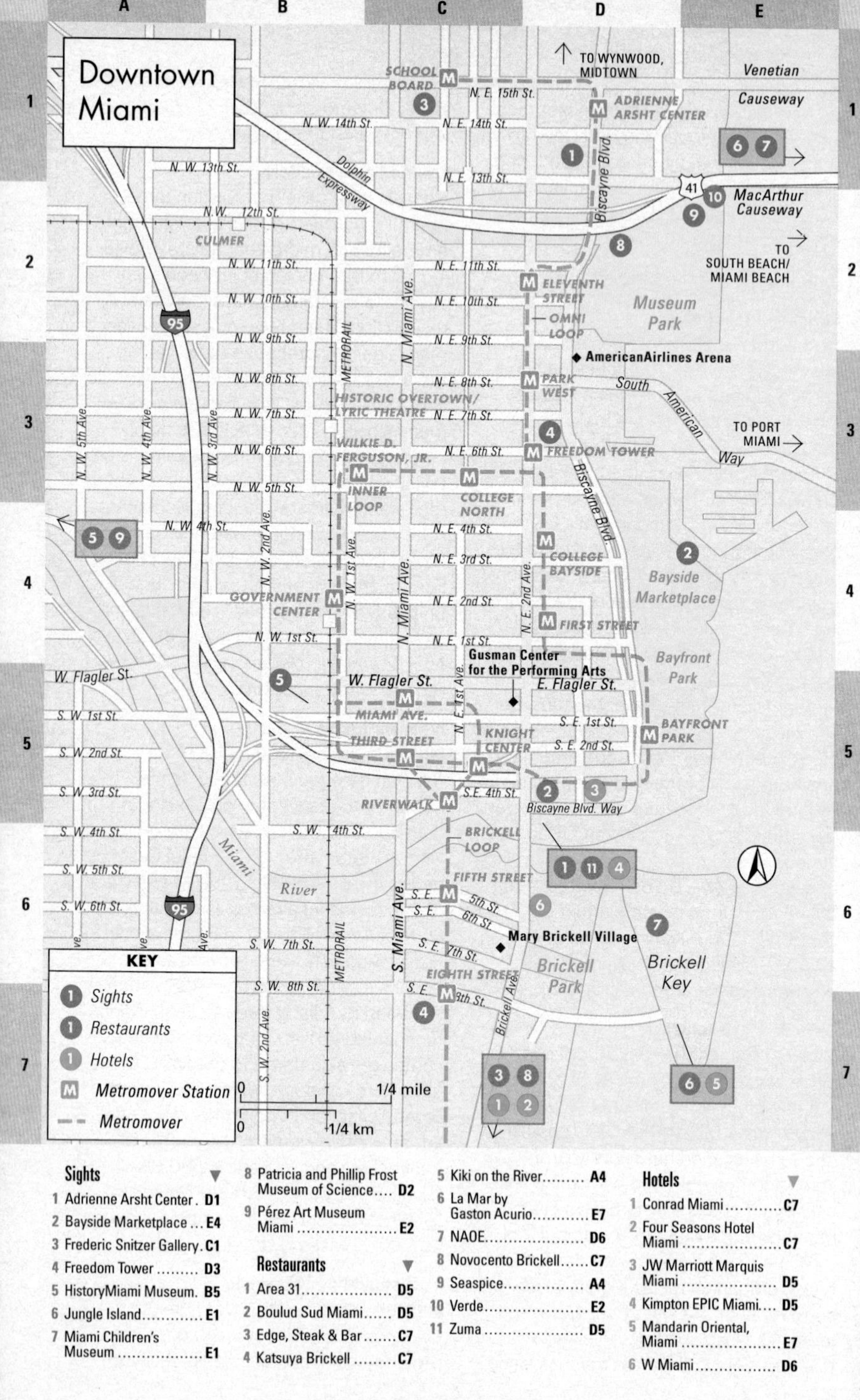

Sights

1 Adrienne Arsht Center . **D1**
2 Bayside Marketplace ... **E4**
3 Frederic Snitzer Gallery. **C1**
4 Freedom Tower **D3**
5 HistoryMiami Museum. **B5**
6 Jungle Island............ **E1**
7 Miami Children's Museum **E1**
8 Patricia and Phillip Frost Museum of Science.... **D2**
9 Pérez Art Museum Miami **E2**

Restaurants

1 Area 31.................. **D5**
2 Boulud Sud Miami...... **D5**
3 Edge, Steak & Bar....... **C7**
4 Katsuya Brickell **C7**
5 Kiki on the River......... **A4**
6 La Mar by Gaston Acurio............ **E7**
7 NAOE..................... **D6**
8 Novocento Brickell...... **C7**
9 Seaspice................. **A4**
10 Verde..................... **E2**
11 Zuma **D5**

Hotels

1 Conrad Miami............ **C7**
2 Four Seasons Hotel Miami **C7**
3 JW Marriott Marquis Miami **D5**
4 Kimpton EPIC Miami.... **D5**
5 Mandarin Oriental, Miami **E7**
6 W Miami................. **D6**

city's multicultural heritage, including an old Miami streetcar and unique items chronicling the migration of Cubans to Miami. Truth be told, the museum is not wildly popular with tourists; however, the museum's tours certainly are. You can take a wide range of walking, boat, coach, bike, gallery, and eco-history tours with varying prices, including culture walks through Little Haiti, informative and exciting Little Havana Arts and Culture Walks, and an evening of storytelling during the Moon Over Miami tour led by HistoryMiami historian Dr. Paul George, where you'll float through Downtown on the Miami River, learning all about Miami's early history circa the Tequesta Indians' days. ✉ *101 W. Flagler St., Downtown* ✥ *Between N.W. 1st and 2nd Aves.* ☎ *305/375–1492* 🌐 *www.historymiami.org* 🎫 *$10; tour costs vary* ⊗ *Closed Mon.*

Jungle Island

ZOO | FAMILY | This interactive zoological park is home to just about every unusual and endangered species you would want to see, including a rare albino alligator, a liger (lion and tiger mix), and myriad exotic birds. With an emphasis on the experiential versus mere observation, the park now offers several new attractions and activities, including private beaches, treetop zip-lining, aquatic activities, adventure trails, cultural activities, and enhanced VIP packages where you mingle with an array of furry and feathered friends. Jungle Island offers complimentary shuttle service to most Downtown Miami and South Beach hotels. ✉ *Watson Island, 1111 Parrot Jungle Trail, Downtown* ✥ *Off MacArthur Causeway (I–395)* ☎ *305/400–7000* 🌐 *www.jungleisland.com* 🎫 *$39.95, plus $10 parking.*

Miami Children's Museum

MUSEUM | FAMILY | This Arquitectonica-designed museum, both imaginative and geometric in appearance, is directly across the MacArthur Causeway from Jungle Island. Twelve galleries house hundreds of interactive, bilingual exhibits. Children can scan plastic groceries in the supermarket, scramble through a giant sand castle, climb a rock wall, learn about the Everglades, and combine rhythms in the world-music studio. ✉ *Watson Island, 980 MacArthur Causeway, Downtown* ✥ *Off I–395* ☎ *305/373–5437* 🌐 *www.miamichildrensmuseum.org* 🎫 *$20, parking $1/hr.*

★ Patricia and Phillip Frost Museum of Science

MUSEUM | FAMILY | Equal parts style and science, this hypermodern, $300 million-plus museum along Biscayne Bay is totally worth forgoing time at the beach. The high design museum transitions the indoors and outdoors over multiple levels and an impressive 250,000 square feet, crowned by a see-through, shark-filled, 500,000-gallon aquarium. Beyond exhibitions dedicated to oceans, engineering, and the Everglades, look forward to one of the most sophisticated planetariums in the country, which uses 16-million-color 8K projection. ✉ *1101 Biscayne Blvd., Downtown* ☎ *305/434–9600* 🌐 *www.frostscience.org* 🎫 *$30.*

★ Pérez Art Museum Miami (*PAMM*)

MUSEUM | FAMILY | This über-high-design architectural masterpiece on Biscayne Bay is a sight to behold. Double-story, cylindrical hanging gardens sway from high atop the museum, anchored to stylish wood trusses that help create this gotta-see-it-to-believe-it indoor-outdoor museum. Large sculptures, Asian-inspired gardens, sexy white benches, and steel frames envelop the property. Inside, the 120,000-square-foot space houses multicultural art from the 20th and 21st centuries. Most of the interior space is devoted to temporary exhibitions, which have included the likes of *Ai Weiwei: According to What?* and *Grids: A Selection of Paintings by Lynne Golob Gelfman.* Even if you aren't a "museum type," come check out this magnum opus over lunch at Verde at PAMM, the museum's sensational waterfront restaurant and bar. ■ **TIP→ Admission is free every first Thursday of the month and every second Saturday of the month.** ✉ *1103 Biscayne Blvd., Downtown* ☎ *305/375–3000* 🌐 *www.pamm.org* 🎟 *$16* ⏲ *Closed Wed.*

 Restaurants

Area 31

$$$$ | SEAFOOD | High atop the 16th floor of Downtown Miami's Kimpton Epic Hotel, memorable and sustainable ocean-to-table cuisine is prepared in the bustling, beautiful open kitchen. Look forward to a seafood-centric menu with innovative flavors and a hefty portion of ethos—all fruits of the sea here are certified by the Monterey Bay Aquarium's Seafood Watch. **Known for:** great raw bar; excellent bay-side views; artisanal cocktails. 💲 *Average main: $35* ✉ *Kimpton Epic Hotel, 270 Biscayne Blvd. Way, 16th fl., Downtown* ☎ *305/424–5234* 🌐 *www.area31restaurant.com.*

Boulud Sud Miami

$$$ | MEDITERRANEAN | One of America's most celebrated French chefs, Daniel Boulud brings his renowned cooking to the Miami scene with a menu that pays homage to a melange of Mediterranean cuisines, from France's Côte d'Azur to Turkey. Begin, for example, with mezze and octopus *a la plancha*; then feast on seared Mediterranean branzino with a side of patatas bravas. **Known for:** prix-fixe power-lunch menu; beautiful interiors; Hawaij spiced swordfish. 💲 *Average main: $29* ✉ *JW Marriott Marquis Miami, 255 Biscayne Blvd. Way, Downtown* ☎ *305/421–8800* 🌐 *www.bouludsud.com/miami.*

Edge, Steak & Bar

$$$$ | STEAKHOUSE | It's farm-to-table surf and turf at this elegantly understated restaurant in the Four Seasons Hotel Miami, where hefty portions of the finest cuts and freshest seafood headline the menu, prepared by renowned chef Aaron Brooks. For a more casual experience, enjoy your meal and the restaurant's artisanal cocktails under the skies on the alfresco terrace. **Known for:** charcuterie boards; Sunday brunch; five-course tasting menu. 💲 *Average main: $32* ✉ *Four Seasons Miami, 1435 Brickell Ave., Downtown* ☎ *305/381–3190* 🌐 *www.edgesteakandbar.com.*

★ Katsuya Brickell

$$$$ | JAPANESE FUSION | From the high design, photogenic Japanese-inspired interiors to the artistically presented dishes, trays, and cocktails, this restaurant by master sushi chef Katsuya Uechiis is the ultimate Instagram darling. Feast on sushi, sashimi, robata-grilled meats and veggies, and Katsuya legendary signatures like the Wagyu tenderloin, miso-marinated black cod, and baked crab hand rolls; wash it all down with top-tier sake or craft cocktails like the spicy-and-sweet Burning Mandarin. **Known for:** crispy rice with spicy tuna; cool lanterns and massive sake barrels; option of seating around sushi kitchen. 💲 *Average main: $41* ✉ *8 S.E. 8th St., Downtown* ☎ *305/859–0200* 🌐 *www.katsuyarestaurant.com/brickell.*

Kiki on the River

$$$$ | GREEK FUSION | In a contemporary waterfront garden setting along the Miami River, Kiki is a daily celebration of fabulous Greek food (hello, olive oil–braised octopus), steamy and sceney Miami nights, and an overall Greece-meets-the-tropics *joie de vivre*. Expect to people-watch, eat a lot, drink even more, and dance (especially if coming for the weekly Sunday Funday party). **Known for:** lobster pasta; tomato salad; great happy hour. 💲 *Average main; $38* ✉ *450 N.W. North River Dr., Downtown* ☎ *786/502–3243* 🌐 *www.kikiontheriver.com.*

La Mar by Gaston Acurio

$$$$ | PERUVIAN | FAMILY | Peruvian celebrity-chef Gaston Acurio dazzles with a sublime menu and an atmospheric, bay-side setting to match. Tour the far corners of

Peru through La Mar's signature *cebiches* (ceviche) and *tiraditos* (similar to crudo), freshly grilled skewers of street-style *anticuchos, causa* dishes (mashed potato topped with meat and vegetable toppings), and national libations, like the pisco sour. **Known for:** edgy interior design; alfresco dining; desserts served in dollhouses. *Average main: $35* ✉ *Mandarin Oriental, Miami, 500 Brickell Key Dr., Downtown* 🌐 *www.mandarinoriental.com/miami.*

NAOE

$$$$ | JAPANESE | By virtue of its petite size (eight patrons max) and strict seating times (at 6 and 9:30 nightly), the Japanese gem will forever remain intimate and original. Chef Kevin Cory prepares an *omakase* extravaganza a few feet from his patrons, using only the best Japanese ingredients and showcasing family treasures, like the renowned products of his centuries-old family *shoyu* (soy sauce) and sake brewery. **Known for:** freshest of fresh fish from Japan; authenticity in taste and delivery; $220-per-person price tag plus 20% gratuity. *Average main: $240* ✉ *661 Brickell Key Dr., Downtown* ☎ *305/947–6263* 🌐 *www.naoemiami.com* ⊙ *Closed Sun. No lunch.*

Novecento Brickell

$$$ | ARGENTINE | FAMILY | This popular Argentinian restaurant is the place to go for *empanadas* (tender chicken or spinach-and-cheese), simply grilled meats from the *parrilla* (including luscious grilled skirt steak with chimichurri sauce), and the innovative Ensalada Novecento (grilled skirt steak, french fries, baby mixed greens, and dijon vinaigrette). It's a power-lunch and happy-hour spot for Brickell's business crowd and frequented by families in the evening. **Known for:** daily bottomless sangria or bubbles for $20; range of Italian dishes; neighborhood hangout of Miami's Latin bourgeoisie. *Average main: $26* ✉ *1414 Brickell Ave., Downtown* ☎ *305/403–0900* 🌐 *www.novecento.com.*

Seaspice

$$$$ | CONTEMPORARY | Half the fun in dining at this sophisticated brasserie on the Miami River is watching stylish patrons arrive by yacht. Reserve a table outdoors on the patio for the best views of Downtown, and rest assured that a knowledgeable server will guide you through an eclectic menu highlighting fresh seafood, wood-fired casseroles, and refreshing cocktails. **Known for:** waterfront dining; impeccable service; octopus a la plancha. *Average main: $35* ✉ *422 N.W. North River Dr., Downtown* ☎ *305/440–4200* 🌐 *www.seaspicemiami.com.*

Verde

$$ | ECLECTIC | The slick, contemporary waterfront restaurant at Pérez Art Museum Miami (PAMM) offers seating both indoors and out, with chic decor and accessories true to its "green" name that blend seamlessly with the living walls and hanging gardens strewn across the museum's exterior. The exceptionally affordable, one-page menu features eclectic epicurean lunch plates that include shrimp tacos *al pastor*, tuna tartare, a house chopped salad (with green goddess dressing), and a gourmet cheeseburger with applewood-smoked bacon. **Known for:** fabulous bay views; light lunching; artisanal pizzas. *Average main: $18* ✉ *Pérez Art Museum Miami, 1103 Biscayne Blvd., Downtown* ☎ *305/375–3000* 🌐 *www.pamm.org/dining* ⊙ *Closed Wed. No dinner Fri.–Tues.*

Zuma

$$$$ | JAPANESE FUSION | This izakaya-style restaurant is known the world over for its sleek design, lounge atmosphere, and contemporary Japanese cuisine. On the ground floor of the Kimpton EPIC hotel, the Miami location promises excellent bay-side views, Zuma's signature menu items, such as roasted lobster with shizo-ponzu butter, and dishes exclusive to Miami (previous exclusives included the 24-ounce bone-in rib-eye.) **Known for:** incredible Sunday brunch; own line of sake; excellent sashimi. *Average main: $47 Kimpton EPIC Hotel, 270 Biscayne Boulevard Way, Downtown 305/577–0277 www.zumarestaurant.com.*

Hotels

Miami's skyline continues to grow by leaps and bounds. With Downtown experiencing a renaissance of sorts, the hotel scene here isn't just for business anymore. In fact, hotels that once relied solely on their Monday–Thursday traffic are now bustling on weekends, with a larger focus on cocktails around the rooftop pool and less on the business center. These hotels offer proximate access to Downtown's burgeoning food and cocktail scene, and historic sights, and are a short Uber ride away from Miami's beaches.

Conrad Miami

$$$$ | **HOTEL** | Occupying floors 16 to 26 of a 36-story skyscraper in Miami's burgeoning, business-centric city center, this hotel offers easy access to the best of Downtown and ubiquitous, jaw-dropping views of Biscayne Bay. Like many of its sister Downtown hotels, the lobby is located high in the sky—on the 25th floor to be exact. **Pros:** walking distance to most Downtown sights; great views from some bathrooms; rooftop tennis courts. **Cons:** poor views from some rooms; expensive parking; rooms lack personality. *Rooms from: $489 Espirito Santo Plaza, 1395 Brickell Ave., Downtown 305/503–6500 www.conradmiami.com 201 rooms No meals.*

Four Seasons Hotel Miami

$$$$ | **HOTEL** | A favorite of business travelers visiting Downtown's bustling Brickell Avenue, this plush sanctuary offers a respite from the nine-to-five mayhem—a soothing water wall greets you, the understated rooms impress you, and the seventh-floor, 2-acre-pool terrace relaxes you. **Pros:** sensational service; window-side daybeds; amazing gym and pool deck. **Cons:** no balconies; not near the beach; mostly a business crowd. *Rooms from: $599 1435 Brickell Ave., Downtown 305/358–3535 www.fourseasons.com/miami 221 rooms No meals.*

JW Marriott Marquis Miami

$$$$ | **HOTEL** | The Miami marriage of Marriott's JW and Marquis brands creates a truly high-tech, contemporary, and stylish business-minded hotel—from the three-story crystal chandelier in the entry to the smart and symmetric guest rooms, rife with electronic gadgets. **Pros:** entertainment and fitness amenities; amazing technology; pristine rooms. **Cons:** swimming pool receives limited sunshine; lots of conventioneers on weekdays; congestion at street entrance. *Rooms from: $499 255 Biscayne Blvd. Way, Downtown 305/421–8600 www.jwmarriottmarquismiami.com 313 rooms No meals.*

★ Kimpton EPIC Miami

$$$ | **HOTEL** | In the heart of Downtown, Kimpton's pet-friendly, artful EPIC Hotel has 411 guest rooms with spacious balconies (many of them overlook Biscayne Bay) and fabulous modern amenities to match the sophistication of the common areas, which include a supersexy rooftop pool. **Pros:** sprawling rooftop pool deck; balcony in every room; complimentary wine hour, coffee, and Wi-Fi. **Cons:** some rooms have inferior views; congested valet area; sometimes windy around pool area. *Rooms from: $375 270 Biscayne Blvd. Way, Downtown 305/424–5226 www.epichotel.com 411 rooms No meals.*

★ Mandarin Oriental, Miami

$$$$ | **HOTEL** | At the tip of prestigious Brickell Key in Biscayne Bay, the Mandarin Oriental feels as exclusive as it does glamorous, with luxurious rooms, exalted restaurants, and the city's top spa, all of which marry the brand's signature Asian style with Miami's bold tropical elegance.

Pros: impressive lobby; intimate vibe; top-notch spa. **Cons:** man-made beach; small infinity pool; traffic getting on/off Brickell Key. [$] *Rooms from: $579* ✉ *500 Brickell Key Dr., Downtown* ☎ *305/913–8288, 866/888–6780* 🌐 *www.mandarinoriental.com/miami* 🛏 *357 rooms* 🍽 *No meals.*

W Miami

$$$$ | HOTEL | Formerly the Viceroy, Miami's second W hotel cultivates a brash, supersophisticated Miami attitude, likely stemming from its whimsically decorated guest rooms, floor-to-ceiling marble bathrooms, and the Philippe Starck–designed 28,000-square-foot Iconbrickell Spa. Rooms are available in a host of categories, ranging from 440-square-foot "Wonderful" rooms to a 1,550-square-foot "Wow" suite that has a living room, dining room, and sweeping views of Biscayne Bay. Each room, though, is furnished with a private balcony, a W Signature bed with down comforter and pillows, safe, Wi-Fi, and TV. **Pros:** smart design elements; exceptional spa; great gym. **Cons:** serious traffic getting in and out of hotel entrance; the amazing 15th floor pool is for residents, not hotel guests; many rooms allow only two persons maximum. [$] *Rooms from: $659* ✉ *485 Brickell Ave., Downtown* ☎ *305/503–4400* 🌐 *www.wmiamihotel.com* 🛏 *168 rooms* 🍽 *No meals.*

Nightlife

★ Blackbird Ordinary

BARS/PUBS | With a vibe that's a bit speakeasy, a bit dive bar, a bit hipster hangout, and a bit Miami sophisticate, this local watering hole is hands down one of the coolest places in the city and appeals to a wide demographic. Mixology is a huge part of the Blackbird experience—be prepared for some awesome artisanal cocktails. There's something going on every night of the week, and the stylish outdoor space is great for cocktails under the stars, movie screenings, and live music. ✉ *729 S.W. 1st Ave., Downtown* ☎ *305/671–3307* 🌐 *www.blackbirdordinary.com.*

E11EVEN Miami

DANCE CLUBS | After a $40-million cash infusion, the former Gold Rush building has been transformed into an ultraclub with LED video walls, intelligent lighting, and a powerful sound system that pulses sports by day and beats by night, providing partygoers the 24/7 action they crave. Hospitality and VIP experiences are ample throughout the private lounges and second-level champagne room; however, the real action is in The Pit, featuring burlesque performances and intermittent Cirque du Soleil–style shows from a hydraulic-elevating stage. The fusion of theatrics and technology attracts an A-list clientele. Head up to the roof to find an intimate restaurant that serves tapas, as well as a live music lounge. ✉ *29 N.E. 11th St., Downtown* ☎ *305/829–2911* 🌐 *www.11miami.com.*

★ Komodo

CAFES—NIGHTLIFE | This swank, triple-story indoor/outdoor resto-lounge is the apex of the Downtown Miami scene, whether standing and posing at one of the three bars, dining in the floating birds nests of the 300-seat restaurant, or partying alongside celebs to DJ-led tunes inside the top-floor Komodo Lounge. The brains behind this hedonistic treehouse complex is David Grutman, the impresario behind Miami Beach's legendary LIV nightclub. ✉ *801 Brickell Ave., Downtown* ☎ *305/534–2211* 🌐 *www.komodomiami.com.*

★ Sugar

BARS/PUBS | This skyscraping rooftop bar, hands down the best in the city, is the essence of the new Downtown Miami: futuristic, worldly, and beyond sleek. It crowns the 40th floor of East, Miami, the luxury hotel tucked inside one of Miami's most ambitious multiuse endeavors: the billion-dollar-plus Brickell City Centre complex. The sunsets here are spectacular, as are the Southeast Asian bites and the exotic cocktails. ✉ *788 Brickell Plaza, Downtown* ☎ *305/805–4655* 🌐 *www.sugar-miami.com.*

Shopping

★ Acqua di Parma

PERFUME/COSMETICS | Downtown Miami's Brickell City Centre houses the one and only stand-alone store of this Italian fragrance and skin-care brand in the United States. But there's so much more than scents and fragrances for sample and sale in the 1,000-square-foot, marble-clad boutique; consumers can also purchase the brand's line of leather bags, travel accessories, and candles. Additionally, an in-store barbershop offers razor shaves with Acqua di Parma's coveted men's grooming products, the Collezione Barbiere. ✉ *Brickell City Centre, Level 1, 701 S. Miami Ave., Downtown* ☎ *786/220–8840* 🌐 *www.acquadiparma.com.*

★ Brickell City Centre

SHOPPING CENTERS/MALLS | A billion dollars in the making, this sleek, three-city-block, mixed-use complex in the heart of Downtown is rife with multiple levels of designer stores, restaurants, food halls, hotel rooms, and residences. The high-end retail rivals that in Bal Harbour and the Design District, solidifying Miami's status as a true shopping destination. The center is a grand fusion of indoor and outdoor space and futuristic architectural design, underscored by the striking, glass-and-steel Climate Ribbon, which controls the enclave's microclimate. ✉ *701 S. Miami Ave., Downtown* ☎ *786/704–0223* 🌐 *www.brickellcitycentre.com.*

Fabiana Filippi

CLOTHING | Although most cities have to settle for a simple rack or section of famed Umbria-based women's wear Fabiana Filippi at high-end department stores, Brickell City Centre houses the one and only stand-alone Filippi boutique in the United States. Browse through a vast range of the current collections that may include resort wear, skinny jeans, pullovers, silhouettes, knitwear, overcoats, and jersey joggers, depending on the season. ✉ *Brickell City Centre, Level 1, 701 S. Miami Ave., Downtown* ☎ *786/574–9621* 🌐 *www.fabianafilippi.com/us_en.*

Activities

HistoryMiami Public City Tours

TOUR—SPORTS | Cultural institution HistoryMiami Museum runs some fabulous walking tours of Little Havana (spiked with plenty of Cuban coffees and cigars, of course), Little Haiti, the Design District, and Wynwood. Most tours run one hour to 90 minutes and are led by HistoryMiami historian Dr. Paul George, the authority on all things Miami. ✉ *101 W. Flagler St., Downtown* ☎ *305/375–1492* 🌐 *www.historymiami.org* 🎫 *$30.*

Island Queen Cruises

SAILING | FAMILY | Experiences on the very touristy Island Queen Cruises run the gamut—sunset cruises, dance cruises, fishing cruises, speedboat rides, and their signature tours of Millionaires' Row, Miami's waterfront homes of the rich and famous. The *Island Queen, Island Lady,* and *Miami Lady* are three double-decker, 140-passenger tour boats docked at Bayside Marketplace that set sail daily for 90-minute narrated tours of the Port of Miami and Millionaires' Row. ✉ *401 Biscayne Blvd., Downtown* ☎ *844/295–8034* 🌐 *www.islandqueencruises.com* 🎫 *From $19.*

Miami Heat

BASKETBALL | FAMILY | The 2006, 2012, and 2013 NBA champs play at the 19,600-seat, waterfront AmericanAirlines Arena. The downtown venue features restaurants, a wide patio overlooking Biscayne Bay, and a silver sun-shaped special-effects scoreboard with rays holding wide-screen TVs. Home games are held November through April.

✉ *AmericanAirlines Arena, 601 Biscayne Blvd., Downtown* ☎ *800/745–3000 ticket hotline, 786/777–1000 arena* 🌐 *www.nba.com/heat/tickets* 🎫 *$11–$385.*

Coconut Grove

A former haven for writers and artists, Coconut Grove has never quite outgrown its image as a small village. You can still feel the bohemian roots of this artsy neighborhood, but it has grown increasingly mainstream and residential over the past 20 years. Posh estates mingle with rustic cottages, modest frame homes, and stark modern dwellings, often on the same block. If you're into horticulture, you'll be impressed by the Garden of Eden–like foliage that seems to grow everywhere without care. In truth, residents are determined to keep up the Grove's village-in-a-jungle look, so they lavish attention on exotic plantings even as they battle to protect any remaining native vegetation.

Sights

★ Vizcaya Museum and Gardens

HISTORIC SITE | FAMILY | Of the 10,000 people living in Miami between 1912 and 1916, about 1,000 of them were gainfully employed by Chicago industrialist James Deering to build this European-inspired residence. Once comprising 180 acres, this National Historic Landmark now occupies a 30-acre tract that includes a rockland hammock (native forest) and more than 10 acres of formal gardens with fountains overlooking Biscayne Bay. The house, open to the public, contains 70 rooms, 34 of which are filled with paintings, sculpture, antique furniture, and other fine and decorative arts. The collection spans 2,000 years and represents the Renaissance, baroque, rococo, and neoclassical periods. The 90-minute self-guided Discover Vizcaya Audio Tour is available in multiple languages for an additional $5. Moonlight tours, offered on evenings that are nearest the full moon, provide a magical look at the gardens; call for reservations. ✉ *3251 S. Miami Ave., Coconut Grove* ☎ *305/250–9133* 🌐 *www.vizcaya.org* 🎫 *$22* ⏲ *Closed Tues.*

Restaurants

Glass & Vine

$$$$ | MODERN AMERICAN | FAMILY | With a design that fuses the indoors and outdoors in the middle of Coconut Grove's residential Peacock Park, this charming, family-friendly restaurant by celebrity-chef Giorgio Rapicavoli (a champion on Food Network's *Chopped*) is as picturesque as it is unexpected. Parents can sit back and enjoy some incredible gourmet-style sharing plates (featuring local catch and produce) and the sensational wine selection, while the little ones are thoroughly entertained outside (there's even a playground). **Known for:** local fish tiradito; charred cauliflower appetizer; beautifully plated dishes. $ *Average main: $34* ✉ *2820 McFarlane Rd., Coconut Grove* ☎ *305/200–5268* 🌐 *www.glassandvine.com.*

GreenStreet Cafe

$$ | MEDITERRANEAN | A tried-and-true locals' hangout since it was founded in the early 1990s—with regulars including athletes, politicians, entrepreneurs, artists, and other prominent area names—this cozy café serves simple French-Mediterranean delights. Despite the restaurant's see-and-be-seen reputation, diners are encouraged to sit back and simply enjoy the experience with relaxed decor, good food, and friendly service. **Known for:** fruity cocktails; great breakfast; late-night lounging and noshing. $ *Average main: $19* ✉ *3468 Main Hwy., Coconut Grove* ☎ *305/444–0244* 🌐 *www.greenstreetcafe.net.*

Greater Miami
N.W. 79th St.
N.W. 62nd St.
LITTLE HAITI
Hialeah Dr.
N.W. 54th St.
N.W. 72nd Ave.
N.W. 39th St.
Robert Frost Expwy.
N.W. 36th St.
N.W. 28th St.
N.W. 20th St.
Dairy Rd.
Miami International Airport
Miami River
N.W. 17th Ave.
N.W. 2nd Ave.
N. Miami Ave.
N.E. 2nd Ave.
WYNWOOD ARTS D
East-West Expressway
N.W. 7th St.
N.W. 27th Ave.
MIAMI
W. Flagler St.
S.W. 12th Ave.
LITTLE HAVANA
S.W. 8th St.
Tamiami Trail
S.W. 13th St.
S.W. 3rd. Ave.
Brickell Ave.
Granada Blvd.
Le Jeune Rd.
Ponce de León Blvd.
S.W. 37th Ave. (Douglas Rd.)
S.W. 24th St.
S.W. 22nd St.
Coral Way
COCONUT GROVE
Sevilla Ave.
Rickenb
S.W. 57th Ave.
S. Dixie Hwy.
Bird Ave.
CocoWalk
Grand Ave.
Grove Isle
CORAL GABLES
Maynada St.
Coral Gables Waterway
Biscayne Bay
S.W. 72nd St.
Sunset Dr.
Cartagena Plaza
Ponce de León Blvd.
Ponce de León Rd.
Red Rd.
Old Cutler Rd.
SOUTH MIAMI
Matheson Hammock Park Beach

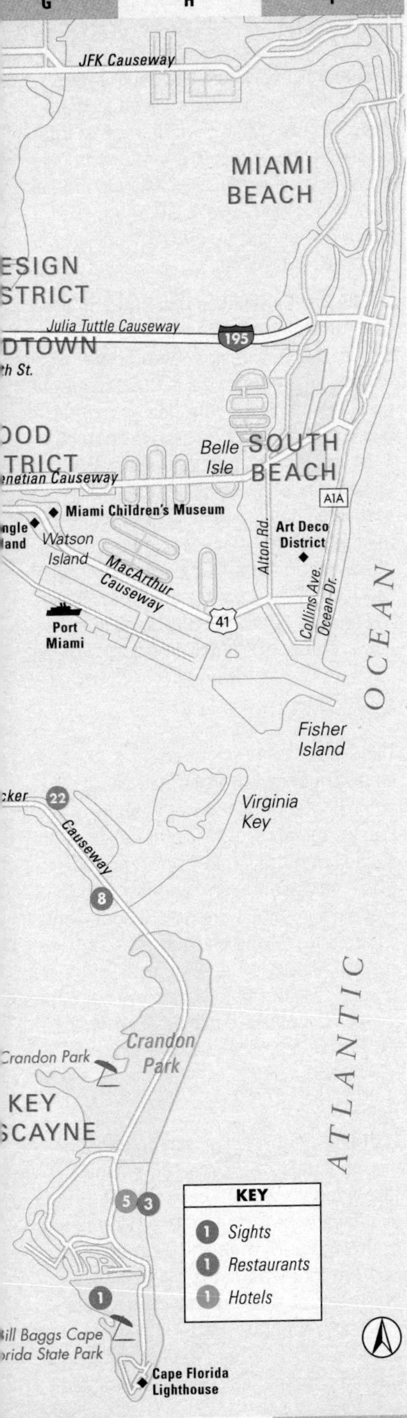

Sights

1 Bill Baggs Cape Florida State Park G9
2 The Biltmore............ B6
3 Cuban Memorial Boulevard................ E5
4 Domino Park............. E5
5 El Titan de Bronze F5
6 Fairchild Tropical Botanic Garden C8
7 Margulies Collection at the Warehouse F3
8 Miami Seaquarium G6
9 Rubell Family Collection................ F3
10 Venetian Pool C5
11 Vizcaya Museum and Gardens.................. E6
12 Wynwood Walls F3
13 Zoo Miami A8

Restaurants

1 Alter....................... F3
2 Azucar Ice Cream Company................. E5
3 Cantina Beach H8
4 Chez Le Bebe............ F2
5 eating house C5
6 El Exquisito Restaurant................ E5
7 El Palacio de los Jugos..................... D3
8 Glass & Vine............ D6
9 GreenStreet Cafe D6
10 Harry's Pizzeria........... F2
11 Havana Harry's........... C6
12 Joey's F3
13 KYU........................... F3
14 Los Piñarenos Fruteria.................... E5
15 Mandolin Aegean Bistro....................... F2
16 Michael's Genuine Food & Drink F2
17 Monty's Raw Bar D6
18 Ortanique on the Mile... C5
19 Panther Coffee F3
20 Peacock Garden Café............ D6
21 Plant Miami............... F3
22 Rusty Pelican............ G6
23 Sugarcane Raw Bar Grill........................ F3
24 Wynwood Kitchen & Bar...................... F3
25 Versailles D5

Hotels

1 The Biltmore............ B6
2 Hyatt Regency Coral Gables.............. C5
3 The Mayfair at Coconut Grove D6
4 The Ritz-Carlton Coconut Grove, Miami D6
5 The Ritz-Carlton Key Biscayne, Miami G8

Monty's Raw Bar

$$$ | **SEAFOOD** | **FAMILY** | Monty's has a Caribbean flair, thanks especially to live calypso and island music on the outdoor terrace. Consider it a fun, tropical-style, kid-friendly place where Mom and Dad can kick back in the early evening and enjoy a beer and the raw bar while the kids eat conch fritters and dance to the beats. **Known for:** palapa-topped outdoor seating; tropical cocktails; waterfront views. *Average main: $23* *Prime Marina Miami, 2550 S. Bayshore Dr., at Aviation Ave., Coconut Grove* *305/856–3992* *www.montysrawbar.com.*

Peacock Garden Café

$$ | **AMERICAN** | **FAMILY** | Reinstating the artsy and exciting vibe of Coconut Grove circa once-upon-a-time, this lovely spot offers an indoor-outdoor, teatime setting for light bites like salads, soups, and sandwiches. By day it's one of Miami's most serene lunch spots, as the lushly landscaped courtyard is lined with alfresco seating, drawing some of Miami's most fabulous ladies who lunch. **Known for:** old-school charm; idyllic setting for lunch; daily homemade soups. *Average main: $17* *2889 McFarlane Rd., Coconut Grove* *305/774–3332* *www.peacockspot.jaguarhg.com.*

Hotels

Although this area certainly can't replace the draw of Miami Beach or the business convenience of Downtown, about 20 minutes away, it's an exciting bohemian-chic neighborhood with a gorgeous waterfront.

The Mayfair at Coconut Grove

$$$ | **HOTEL** | Some 30 years strong, this five-story hotel still reflects Coconut Grove's bohemian roots, best exemplified by its eclectic exteriors: handcrafted wooden doors, one-of-a-kind decorative moldings, mosaic tiles inspired by Spain's Alhambra, and Gaudí-like ornaments adorning the rooftop pool deck. **Pros:** in the heart of walkable Coconut Grove; details in exterior design; rooftop pool. **Cons:** limited lighting within rooms; interior design looks dated; construction nearby. *Rooms from: $359* *3000 Florida Ave., Coconut Grove* *800/433–4555* *www.mayfairhotelandspa.com* *179 rooms* *No meals.*

★ The Ritz-Carlton Coconut Grove, Miami

$$$$ | **HOTEL** | In the heart of Coconut Grove, this business-oriented hotel was completely reimagined in 2018 to create an elegant and modern design masterpiece that rivals top leisure properties in Miami Beach and Downtown. **Pros:** elevated pool deck; fresh from renovation; in an easily walkable area. **Cons:** near residential area; not on beach; lots of conventioneers. *Rooms from: $577* *3300 S.W. 27th Ave., Coconut Grove* *305/644–4680* *www.ritzcarlton.com/coconutgrove* *115 rooms* *No meals.*

Shopping

The Griffin

SHOES/LUGGAGE/LEATHER GOODS | This small boutique packs a big punch with today's most coveted womens' shoe styles, with the latest from Aquazarra to Chloe to Valentino and Loeffler Randall. Walk around once, then do it again, and you're sure to find another style urging you to try it on. Need help pulling the trigger? The boutique's stocked bar eases the pain of pricey purchases. *3112 Commodore Plaza, Coconut Grove* *786/631–3522.*

Unika

CLOTHING | A longtime fashion resident of Coconut Grove (circa 1989), Unika takes shoppers from day to night, and all affairs in between, with a wide range of inventory for men and women. The contemporary boutique has an it-girl vibe, but the cool, relaxed one you'd actually want to be friends with. High–low pricing appeases all budgets; expect to uncover up-and-coming designer gems tucked within the racks of well-known brands. Bonus: the staff is great with styling for a head-to-toe look. ✉ *3432 Main Hwy., Coconut Grove* ☎ *305/445–4752.*

Coral Gables

You can easily spot Coral Gables from the window of a Miami-bound jetliner—just look for the massive orange tower of The Biltmore hotel rising from a lush green carpet of trees concealing the city's gracious homes. The canopy is as much a part of this planned city as its distinctive architecture, all attributed to the vision of George E. Merrick more than a century ago.

The story of this city began in 1911, when Merrick inherited 1,600 acres of citrus and avocado groves from his father. Through judicious investment he nearly doubled the tract to 3,000 acres by 1921. Merrick dreamed of building an American Venice here, complete with canals and homes. Working from this vision, he began designing a city based on centuries-old prototypes from Mediterranean countries. Unfortunately for Merrick, the devastating no-name hurricane of 1926, followed by the Great Depression, prevented him from fulfilling many of his plans. He died at 54, an employee of the post office. Today Coral Gables has a population of about 51,000. In its bustling downtown more than 150 multinational companies maintain headquarters or regional offices, and the University of Miami campus in the southern part of the Gables brings a youthful vibrancy to the area. A southern branch of the city extends down the shore of Biscayne Bay through neighborhoods threaded with canals.

Sights

The Biltmore

BUILDING | Bouncing back stunningly from its dark days as an army hospital, this hotel has become the jewel of Coral Gables—a dazzling architectural gem with a colorful past. First opened in 1926, it was a hot spot for the rich and glamorous of the Jazz Age until it was converted to an army–air force regional hospital in 1942. Until 1968 the Veterans Administration continued to operate the hospital after World War II. The Biltmore then lay vacant for nearly 20 years before it underwent extensive renovations and reopened as a luxury hotel in 1987. Its 16-story tower, like the Freedom Tower in Downtown Miami, is a replica of Seville's Giralda Tower. The magnificent pool is reportedly the largest hotel pool in the continental United States. ■**TIP→ Because it functions as a full-service hotel, your ticket in—if you aren't staying here—is to patronize one of the hotel's several restaurants or bars. Try to get a courtyard table for the Sunday champagne brunch, a local legend.** ✉ *1200 Anastasia Ave., Coral Gables* ✣ *Near De Soto Blvd.* ☎ *855/311–6903* 🌐 *www.biltmorehotel.com.*

Fairchild Tropical Botanic Garden

GARDEN | **FAMILY** | With 83 acres of lakes, sunken gardens, a 560-foot vine pergola, orchids, bellflowers, coral trees, bougainvillea, rare palms, and flowering trees, Fairchild is the largest tropical botanical garden in the continental United States. The tram tour highlights the best of South Florida and exotic flora; then you can set off exploring on your own. The 2-acre Simons Rainforest showcases tropical plants from around the world complete with a waterfall and stream. The conservatory is home to rare tropical plants, including the Burmese endemic *Amherstia nobilis,* flowering annually with orchidlike pink flowers. The Keys Coastal Habitat, created in a marsh and mangrove area in 1995 with assistance from the Tropical Audubon Society, provides food and shelter to resident and migratory birds. The excellent bookstore–gift shop carries books on gardening and horticulture, and the Garden Café serves sandwiches and, seasonally, smoothies made from the garden's own crop of tropical fruits. ✉ *10901 Old Cutler Rd., Coral Gables* ☎ *305/667–1651* 🌐 *www.fairchildgarden.org* 🎟 *$25.*

Venetian Pool

POOL | **FAMILY** | Sculpted from a rock quarry in 1923 and fed by artesian wells, this 820,000-gallon municipal pool had a major face-lift in 2018. It remains quite popular because of its themed architecture—a fantasy version of a waterfront Italian village—created by Denman Fink. The pool has earned a place on the National Register of Historic Places and showcases a nice collection of vintage photos depicting 1920s beauty pageants and swank soirées held long ago. Paul Whiteman played here, Johnny Weissmuller and Esther Williams swam here, and you should, too (note: children must be at least three years old and 38 inches tall). A snack bar, lockers, and showers make these historic splash grounds user-friendly as well, and there's free parking across De Soto Boulevard. ✉ *2701 De Soto Blvd., at Toledo St., Coral Gables* ☎ *305/460–5306* 🌐 *www.coralgables.com/venetian-pool* 🎟 *$20.*

Zoo Miami. Don't miss a visit to this top-notch zoo, 14 miles southwest of Coral Gables in the Miami suburbs. The only subtropical zoo in the continental United States, it has 320-plus acres that are home to more than 2,000 animals, including 40 endangered species, which roam on islands surrounded by moats. Amazon & Beyond encompasses 27 acres of simulated tropical rain forests showcasing 600 animals indigenous to the region, such as giant river otters, harpy eagles, anacondas, and jaguars. The Wings of Asia aviary has about 300 exotic birds representing 70 species flying free within the junglelike enclosure. Kids love visiting the meerkats and participating in the thrice-daily camel feedings at the Critter Connection exhibit. ✉ *12400 S.W. 152nd St. (1 Zoo Blvd.), Richmond Heights* ☎ *305/251–0400* 🌐 *www.zoomiami.org* 🎟 *$22.95; 45-min tram tour $6.50.*

Beaches

Matheson Hammock Park and Beach

BEACH—SIGHT | **FAMILY** | Kids love the gentle waves and warm (albeit often murky) waters of this beach in Coral Gables's suburbia, near Fairchild Tropical Botanic Garden. But the beach is only part of the draw—the park includes a boardwalk trail, a playground, and a golf course. Plus, the park is a prime spot for kiteboarding. The man-made lagoon, or "atoll pool," is perfect for inexperienced swimmers, and it's one of the best places in mainland Miami for a picnic. Most tourists don't make the trek here; this park caters more to locals who don't want to travel all the way to Miami Beach. The park also offers a full-service marina. **■ TIP→ With an emphasis on family fun, it's not the best place for singles. Amenities:** parking (fee); toilets. **Best for:** swimming. ✉ *9610 Old Cutler Rd., Coral Gables* ☎ *305/665–5475* 🌐 *www.miamidade.gov/parks/matheson-hammock.asp* 🎟 *$5 per vehicle weekdays, $7 weekends.*

Restaurants

eating house

$$$ | **ECLECTIC** | Check your calorie counter at the door when you enter this hip, small-plates restaurant, featuring an ever-changing menu that teems with extreme culinary innovation and unexpected flavor combinations. Save room for the famous "dirt cup" dessert, a "soil-filled" flowerpot, which is really crushed Oreos anchored by roots of pretzels, hazelnuts, and *tierra nueva* chocolate ice cream. **Known for:** chicken and waffles; intimate setting; foodie crowd. $ *Average main: $28* ✉ *804 Ponce de León Blvd., Coral Gables* ☎ *305/448–6524* 🌐 *www.eatinghousemiami.com* ⏲ *No lunch weekends.*

El Palacio de los Jugos

$ | **CUBAN** | **FAMILY** | To the northwest of Coral Gables proper, this small but boisterous indoor-outdoor market is one of the easiest and truest ways to see Miami's local Latin life in action. Besides the rows of fresh, tropical exotic fruits and vegetables—and the shakes you can make with any of them—Miami's original food hall has numerous counters where you can get a wide variety of Latin American food from *pan con lechón* (roast pork on Cuban bread) to fried pork rinds. **Known for:** fresh, cold coconut water in the shell; no-frills feel; picnic-style tables. *Average main: $8 ✉ 5721 W. Flagler St., Flagami, Coral Gables ☎ 305/264–1503 🌐 www.elpalaciodelosjugos.com/en* *No credit cards.*

Havana Harry's

$$ | **CUBAN** | **FAMILY** | When Cuban families want an affordable home-cooked meal with a twist but don't want to cook it themselves, they come to this big, unassuming restaurant. The fare is traditional Cuban: long, thin, panfried steaks known as *bistec palomilla,* roast chicken with citrus marinade, and fried pork chunks; most dishes come with white rice, black beans, and a choice of ripe or green plantains. **Known for:** mariquitas (plantain chips) with mojo; acclaimed flan; "tres leches overdose" dessert. *Average main: $17 ✉ 4612 Le Jeune Rd., Coral Gables ☎ 305/661–2622 🌐 www.havanaharrys.com.*

Ortanique on the Mile

$$$$ | **CARIBBEAN** | Cascading *ortaniques,* a Jamaican hybrid orange, are hand-painted on columns in this warm, welcoming, yellow dining room, setting an ideal stage for chef-partner Cindy Hutson's "cuisine of the sun." Food is vibrant in taste and color, imbued with island flavors, with dishes like the West Indian–style bouillabaisse and the daily fresh-catch ceviche. **Known for:** creative, tropical cocktails; passionate staff; excellent seafood. *Average main: $41 ✉ 278 Miracle Mile, Coral Gables ☎ 305/446–7710 🌐 www.ortaniquerestaurants.com* *No lunch weekends.*

Hotels

Beautiful Coral Gables is set around its beacon, the national landmark Biltmore hotel. The University of Miami is nearby.

The Biltmore

$$$$ | **HOTEL** | Built in 1926, this landmark hotel has had several incarnations over the years—including a stint as a hospital during World War II—but through it all, this grande dame has remained an opulent reminder of yesteryear, with its palatial lobby and grounds, enormous pool (largest in the Lower 48), and distinctive 315-foot tower, which rises above the canopy of trees shading Coral Gables. **Pros:** breathtaking history-steeped lobby; gorgeous pool; great golf. **Cons:** in the suburbs; a car is necessary to get around; nonrenovated rooms look tired. *Rooms from: $549 ✉ 1200 Anastasia Ave., Coral Gables ☎ 855/311–6903 🌐 www.biltmorehotel.com* *312 rooms* *No meals.*

Hyatt Regency Coral Gables

$$ | **HOTEL** | Within walking distance to the shops and businesses of Miami's most prestigious suburb and just 4 miles from Miami International Airport, this Moorish-inspired property mingles European charm with functionality. **Pros:** pet-friendly (for a fee); meets rigorous green standards; walking distance to several local restaurants. **Cons:** small bathrooms; bland design; no spa. *Rooms from: $259 ✉ 50 Alhambra Plaza, Coral Gables ☎ 305/441–1234 🌐 www.coralgables.regency.hyatt.com* *253 rooms* *No meals.*

Nightlife

The Bar

BARS/PUBS | One of the oldest bars in South Florida (est. 1946), the old Hofbrau has been reincarnated a few times and now goes by the name "The Bar." A massive American flag hangs on the wall of this locals' hangout, arguably the only cool nightlife in suburban Coral Gables. The Bar delivers DJ-led tunes Wednesday through Saturday night and karaoke on Tuesday night. Oh, and they have pretty awesome, farm-fresh bar food, too. ✉ *172 Giralda Ave., at Ponce de León Blvd., Coral Gables* ☎ *305/442–2730* 🌐 *www.gablesthebar.com.*

El Carajo

TAPAS BARS | The back of a Mobil gas station is perhaps the most unexpected location for a wine bar, yet for 30 years a passion for good food and drink has kept this family-run business among Miami's best-kept secrets. Tables are in the old-world-style wine cellar, stocked with bottles representing all parts of the globe (and at excellent prices). A waiter takes your order from the menu of exquisite cheeses and charcuterie, hot and cold tapas, paellas, and, of course, wine. ✉ *2465 S.W. 17th Ave., Coral Gables* ☎ *305/856–2424* 🌐 *www.el-carajo.com.*

Shopping

★ Books & Books, Inc.

BOOKS/STATIONERY | FAMILY | Greater Miami's only independent English-language bookshop specializes in contemporary and classical literature as well as in books on the arts, architecture, Florida, and Cuba. The Coral Gables store is the largest of seven South Florida stores. Here, you can sip 'n' read in the courtyard lounge or dine at the old-fashioned in-store café while browsing the photography gallery. Multiple rooms are filled with myriad genres, making for a fabulous afternoon of book shopping; plus there's an entire area dedicated to kids. There are book signings, literary events, poetry, and other readings, too. ✉ *265 Aragon Ave., Coral Gables* ☎ *305/442–4408* 🌐 *www.booksandbooks.com.*

Miracle Mile

SHOPPING NEIGHBORHOODS | The centerpiece of the downtown Coral Gables shopping district, lined with trees and busy with strolling shoppers, is home to a host of exclusive couturiers and bridal shops as well as some men's and women's boutiques, jewelry, and home-furnishings stores. The half-mile "mile" runs from Douglas Road to LeJeune Road and Aragon Avenue to Andalusia Avenue, but many of the Gables's best nonbridal shops are found on side streets, off the actual mile. In addition, the street itself teems with restaurants—more than two dozen—facilitating a fabulous afternoon of shopping and eating. **■ TIP→ If debating Miracle Mile versus Bal Harbour or the Design District, check out the others first.** ✉ *Miracle Mile (Coral Way), Coral Gables* ✥ *Douglas Rd. to LeJeune Rd., and Aragon Ave. to Andalusia Ave.* 🌐 *www.shopcoralgables.com.*

Nic Del Mar

CLOTHING | FAMILY | Attending one of Miami's famed pool parties practically requires a trip to this upscale swimwear boutique. From the teeny weeny to innovative one-pieces to sporty cuts, the varied suit selection includes Mara Hoffman, Acacia, and Zimmerman, many of which include matching children's styles for mini beach babes. Flowy cover-ups by the same labels and more can easily double as dinner dresses, while hats, totes, lotions, and even metallic temporary tattoos add a sun-kissed touch. Men's styles are also available. ✉ *475 Biltmore Way, Suite 105, Coral Gables* ☎ *305/442–8080* 🌐 *www.nicdelmar.com* ⏲ *Closed Sun.*

Ramon Puig Guayaberas

CLOTHING | This clothing shop sells custom-made Ramon Puig guayaberas, the natty four-pocket dress shirts favored by older Cuban men and hipsters alike. Ramon Puig is known as "the King of Guayaberas," and his shirts are top of the line as far as guayaberas go. Hundreds are available off the rack. There are styles for women, too. ✉ *5840 S.W. 8th St., Coral Gables* ☎ *855/ 482–9223* 🌐 *www.ramonpuig.com.*

Shops at Merrick Park

SHOPPING CENTERS/MALLS | At this open-air Mediterranean-style, tri-level, shopping-and-dining venue, Neiman Marcus and Nordstrom anchor over 100 specialty shops. Outposts by Jimmy Choo, Tiffany &Co., CH Carolina Herrera, and Gucci fulfill most high-fashion needs, and haute-decor shopping options include Brazilian contemporary-furniture designer Artefacto. ✉ *358 San Lorenzo Ave., Coral Gables* ☎ *305/529–0200* 🌐 *www.shopsatmerrickpark.com.*

Silvia Tcherassi

CLOTHING | The famed, Miami-based Colombian designer's signature boutique in the Shops at Merrick Park features ready-to-wear, feminine, and frilly dresses and separates accented with chiffon, toile, and sequins. You'll see plenty of Tcherassi's designs on Miami's Latin power players at events and A-list parties. A neighboring atelier at 270 San Lorenzo Avenue showcases the designer's bridal collection. ✉ *Shops at Merrick Park, 350 San Lorenzo Ave., No. 2140, Coral Gables* ☎ *305/461–0009* 🌐 *www.silviatcherassi.com.*

Activities

★ Biltmore Golf Course

GOLF | On the grounds of the historic Biltmore hotel, the championship Biltmore Golf Course was designed in 1925 by Scotsman Donald Ross, the "it" golf designer of the Roaring Twenties. Today, after an extensive renovation and expansion in 2018, the lush course looks better than ever and is easily accessible thanks to its advanced online booking system. There's a pro shop on-site, and golf instruction is available through the Biltmore Golf Academy or the more extensive on-site Golf Channel Academy. ✉ *The Biltmore, 1210 Anastasia Ave., Coral Gables* ☎ *305/460–5364* 🌐 *www.biltmorehotel.com/golf* *$122 for 9 holes, $200 for 18 holes* *18 holes, 7800 yards, par 71.*

Key Biscayne

Once upon a time, the two barrier islands that make up the village of Key Biscayne (Key Biscayne itself and Virginia Key) were outposts for fishermen and sailors, pirates and salvagers, soldiers and settlers. The 95-foot Cape Florida Lighthouse stood tall during Seminole Indian battles and hurricanes. Coconut plantations covered two-thirds of Key Biscayne, and there were plans as far back as the 1800s to develop the picturesque island as a resort for the wealthy. Fortunately, the state and county governments set much of the land aside for parks, and both keys are now home to top-ranked beaches and golf, tennis, softball, and picnicking facilities. The long and winding bike paths that run through the islands are favorites for in-line skaters and cyclists. Incorporated in 1991, the village of Key Biscayne is a hospitable community of about 13,200, even though Virginia Key remains undeveloped at the moment. These two playground islands are especially family-friendly.

Sights

Miami Seaquarium

ZOO | FAMILY | This classic family attraction promotes environmental education and raises conservation awareness yet stages shows with sea lions, dolphins, and other marine animals (including killer whales). Discovery Bay, an endangered-mangrove habitat, is home to sea turtles, alligators, herons, egrets, and ibis. You can also visit a shark pool, a tropical reef aquarium, and West Indian and Florida manatees. A popular interactive attraction is the Stingray Touch Tank, where you can touch and feed cow-nose rays and southern stingrays. Another big draw is the Dolphin Interaction program, including the quite intensive Dolphin Odyssey ($210) experience and the lighter shallow-water Dolphin Encounter ($150). ✉ *4400 Rickenbacker Causeway, Virginia Key* ☎ *305/361–5705* 🌐 *www.miamiseaquarium.com* 🎫 *$46.99, parking $10 (cash only).*

Beaches

★ Bill Baggs Cape Florida State Park

BEACH—SIGHT | **FAMILY** | Thanks to inviting beaches, sunsets, and a tranquil lighthouse, this park at Key Biscayne's southern tip is worth the drive. In fact, the 1-mile stretch of pure beachfront has been named several times in Dr. Beach's revered America's Top 10 Beaches list. It has 18 picnic pavilions available as daily rentals, two cafés that serve light lunches that include several Cuban specialties, and plenty of space to enjoy the umbrella and chair rentals. A stroll or ride along walking and bicycle paths provides wonderful views of Miami's dramatic skyline. From the southern end of the park you can see a handful of houses rising over the bay on wooden stilts, the remnants of Stiltsville, built in the 1940s and now protected by the Stiltsville Trust. The nonprofit group was established in 2003 to preserve the structures, because they showcase the park's rich history. Bill Baggs has bicycle rentals, a playground, fishing piers, and guided tours of the **Cape Florida Lighthouse,** South Florida's oldest structure. The lighthouse was erected in 1845 to replace an earlier one damaged in an 1836 Seminole attack, in which the keeper's helper was killed. Free tours are offered at the restored cottage and lighthouse at 10 am and 1 pm Thursday to Monday. Be there a half hour beforehand. **Amenities:** food and drink; lifeguards; parking (free); showers; toilets. **Best for:** solitude; sunset; walking. ✉ *1200 S. Crandon Blvd., Key Biscayne* ☎ *305/361–5811* 🌐 *www.floridastateparks.org/park/Cape-Florida* 🎫 *$8 per vehicle; $2 per pedestrian.*

Sail Away

If you can sail in Miami, do. Blue skies, calm seas, and a view of the city skyline make for a pleasurable outing—especially at twilight, when the fabled "moon over Miami" casts a soft glow on the water. Key Biscayne's calm waves and strong breezes are perfect for sailing and windsurfing, and although Dinner Key and the Coconut Grove waterfront remain the center of sailing in Greater Miami, sailboat moorings and rentals sit along other parts of the bay and up the Miami River, too.

Crandon Park Beach

BEACH—SIGHT | **FAMILY** | This relaxing oasis in northern Key Biscayne offers renowned tennis facilities, a great golf course, a family amusement center, and 2 miles of beach dotted with palm trees. The park is divided by Key Biscayne's main road, with tennis and golf on the bay side, the beaches on the ocean side. Families really enjoy the beaches here—the sand is soft, there are no riptides, there's a great view of the Atlantic, and parking is both inexpensive and plentiful. Nevertheless, on weekends be prepared for a long hike from your car to the beach. There are bathrooms, outdoor showers, plenty of picnic tables, and concession stands. The family-friendly park offers abundant options for those who find it challenging simply to sit and build sand castles. Kite-board rentals and lessons are offered from the northern-end water-sports concessions, as are kayak rentals. Eco-tours and nature trails showcase the myriad ecosystems of Key Biscayne including mangroves, coastal hammock, and sea-grass beds.

Bird-watching is great at the southern end of the park. **Amenities:** food and drink; lifeguards; parking (fee); showers; toilets; water sports. **Best for:** swimming; walking. ✉ *6747 Crandon Blvd., Key Biscayne* ☎ *305/361–5421* 🌐 *www.miamidade.gov/Parks/crandon.asp* 🎫 *$5 per vehicle weekdays, $7 weekends.*

Restaurants

Cantina Beach

$$$ | MEXICAN | Discover a small, sumptuous piece of coastal Mexico at this feet-in-the-sand Mexican restaurant at The Ritz-Carlton Key Biscayne, Miami. (Note: non–hotel guests are welcome.) Order the guacamole, prepared tableside, a few tequila-infused cocktails (like the sour black cherry Black Diamond margarita), and then move onto heartier plates of fajitas and enchiladas. **Known for:** top-shelf margaritas; ceviche; family-friendly setting. $ *Average main: $25* ✉ *The Ritz-Carlton Key Biscayne, Miami, 455 Grand Bay Dr., Key Biscayne* ☎ *305/365–4500* 🌐 *www.ritzcarlton.com/keybiscayne.*

Rusty Pelican

$$$$ | MODERN AMERICAN | Vistas of the bay and Miami skyline are sensational—whether you admire them through the floor-to-ceiling windows or from the expansive outdoor seating area, lined with alluring fire pits. The menu is split between tropically inspired small plates, ideal for sharing, and heartier entrées from land and sea. **Known for:** sunset views; crispy fried, whole local red snapper; protein-rich Rusty Pelican Board for Two. $ *Average main: $35* ✉ *3201 Rickenbacker Causeway, Key Biscayne* ☎ *305/361–3818* 🌐 *www.therustypelican.com.*

Hotels

There's probably no other place in Miami where slowness is lifted to a fine art. On Key Biscayne there are no pressures, there's no nightlife outside of the Ritz-Carlton's great live Latin music weekends, and the dining choices are essentially limited to the hotel (which has five dining options, including the languorous, Havana-style RUMBAR).

★ The Ritz-Carlton Key Biscayne, Miami

$$$$ | RESORT | FAMILY | In an ultra-laid-back setting on serene Key Biscayne, it's only natural to appreciate the Ritz hallmarks of pampering with luxurious rooms (renovated in 2017), attentive service, five on-property dining options, and ample recreational activities for the whole family. **Pros:** a world away from city life; feet-in-the-sand restaurants; an adults-only pool. **Cons:** outside noise may permeate thin, sliding glass doors; beach sometimes seaweed-strewn; limited nearby dining options off-property. $ *Rooms from: $599* ✉ *455 Grand Bay Dr., Key Biscayne* ☎ *305/365–4500* 🌐 *www.ritzcarlton.com/keybiscayne* 🛏 *402 rooms* 🍽 *No meals.*

Activities

Crandon Golf at Key Biscayne

GOLF | On the serene island of Key Biscayne, overlooking Biscayne Bay, this top-rated, championship municipal golf course is considered one of the state's most challenging par-72 courses. Enveloped by tropical foliage, mangroves, saltwater lakes, and bay-side waters, the course also happens to be the only one in North America with a subtropical lagoon. The Devlin/Von Hagge–designed course has a USGA rating of 75.4 and a slope rating of 129 and has received national awards from both *Golfweek* and *Golf Digest*. The course is located on the south side of Crandon Park. ✉ *Crandon Park, 6700 Crandon Blvd., Key Biscayne* ☎ *855/465–3305 for tee times* 🌐 *www.golfcrandon.com* 🎫 *$140* 🏌 *18 holes, 7400 yards, par 72.*

Key Cycling

BICYCLING | On an island where biking is a way of life, this Key Biscayne bike shop carries a wide range of amazing bikes in its showroom, as well as any kind of bike accessory imaginable. Out-of-towners can rent mountain or hybrid bikes for $20 for two hours, $25 for the day, and $100 for the week. ✉ *Galleria Shopping Center, 328 Crandon Blvd., Suite 121, Key Biscayne* ☎ *305/361–0061* 🌐 *www.keycycling.com.*

Wynwood

North of Downtown, the formerly downtrodden Wynwood neighborhood has arrived, with an impressive mix of one-of-a-kind shops and art galleries, public art displays, see-and-be-seen bars, slick restaurants, and plenty of eye-popping graffiti. Wynwood's trendiness has proven infectious, also taking root in proximate neighborhoods. One thing is still missing from the emerging landscape: a decent hotel. On a positive note, it's kept the Wynwood vibe more local and less touristy. The downside: you'll need a vehicle to get here, and though in close proximity to one another, you'll also need a vehicle to get to nearby Midtown and the Design District.

Between Interstate 95 and Northeast 1st Avenue from 29th to 22nd streets lies the centerpiece of the edgy Wynwood neighborhood—the funky and edgy **Wynwood Art District** (🌐 *www.wynwoodmiami.com*), which is peppered with galleries, art studios, and private collections accessible to the public. Though the neighborhood hasn't completely shed its dodgy past, artist-painted graffiti walls and reinvented urban warehouses have transformed the area from plain old grimy to supertrendy. The Wynwood Walls on Northwest 2nd Avenue between Northeast 25th and 26th streets are a cutting-edge enclave of modern urban murals. Nevertheless, these avant-garde graffiti displays by renowned artists are just the beginning; almost every street is colored with funky spray-paint art, making the neighborhood a photographer's dream. Wynwood's retail space is a hodgepodge of cheap garment stores, upscale boutiques, and contemporary galleries (some by appointment only). First-timers may want to visit during Wynwood's monthly gallery walk on the second Saturday evening of each month, when studios and galleries are all open at the same time.

Sights

Margulies Collection at the Warehouse

MUSEUM | Make sure a visit to Wynwood includes a stop at the Margulies Collection at the Warehouse. Martin Margulies's collection of vintage and contemporary photography, videos, and installation art in a 45,000-square-foot space makes for eye-popping viewing. Admission proceeds go to the Lotus Village, a local facility for homeless women and children. ✉ *591 N.W. 27th St., Wynwood* ✣ *Between N.W. 5th and 6th Aves.* ☎ *305/576–1051* 🌐 *www.margulieswarehouse.com* 🎫 *$10* ⏲ *Closed May–Dec.*

★ **Rubell Family Collection**

MUSEUM | Fans of edgy art will appreciate the Rubell Family Collection. Mera and Don Rubell have accumulated work by artists from the 1970s to the present, including Jeff Koons, Cindy Sherman, Damien Hirst, and Keith Haring. New, thematic and topical exhibitions debut annually during Art Basel in December. (For example, a previous exhibition *Still Human*delved into the impact of the digital revolution on the human condition.) Admission always includes a complimentary audio tour; however, true art lovers should opt for a complimentary guided tour of the collection, offered Wednesday through Saturday at 3 pm. The collection plans to move to a new,

Continued on page 89

A Stroll Down Deco Lane

by Susan MacCallum Whitcomb

> "It was an age of miracles, it was an age of art, it was an age of excess, and it was an age of satire."
>
> —F. Scott Fitzgerald, *Echoes of the Jazz Age*

The 1920s and '30s brought us flappers and gangsters, plunging stock prices and soaring skyscrapers, and plenty of headline-worthy news from the arts scene, from talking pictures and the jazz craze to fashions where pearls piled on and sequins dazzled. These decades between the two world wars also gave us an art style reflective of the changing times: art deco.

Distinguished by geometrical shapes and the use of industrial motifs that fused the decorative arts with modern technology, art deco became the architectural style of choice for train stations and big buildings across the country (think New york's Radio City Music Hall and Empire State Building).

Using a steel-and-concrete box as the foundation, architects dipped into art deco's grab bag of accessories, initially decorating facades with spheres, cylinders, and cubes. They later borrowed increasingly from industrial design, stripping elements used in ocean liners and automobiles to their streamlined essentials.

The style was also used in jewelry, furniture, textiles, and advertising. The fact that it employed inexpensive materials, such as stucco or terrazzo, helped art deco thrive during the Great Depression.

MIAMI BEACH'S ART DECO DISTRICT

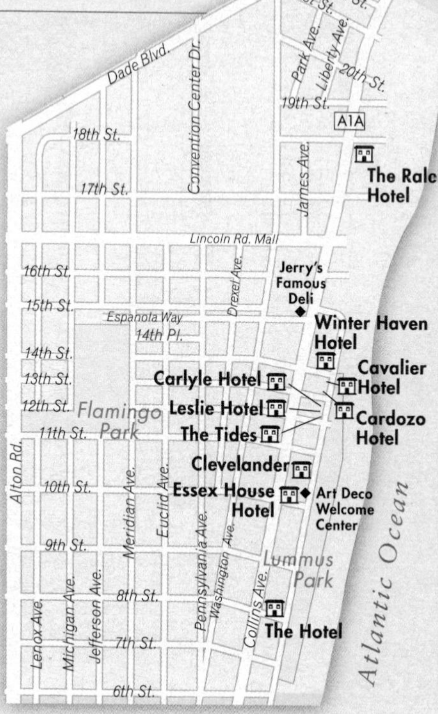

With its warm beaches and tropical surroundings, Miami Beach in the early 20th century was establishing itself as America's winter playground. During the roaring '20s luxurious hostelries resembling Venetian palaces, Spanish villages, and French châteaux sprouted up. In the 1930s, middle-class tourists started coming, and more hotels had to be built. Designers like Henry Hohauser chose art deco for its affordable yet distinctive design.

An antidote to the gloom of the Great Depression, the look was cheerful and tidy. And with the whimsical additions of portholes, colorful racing bands, and images of rolling ocean waves painted or etched on the walls, these South Beach properties created an oceanfront fantasy world for travelers.

Many of the candy-colored hotels have survived and been meticulously restored. They are among the more than 800 buildings of historical significance in South Beach's art deco district. Composing much of South Beach, the 1-square-mile district is bounded by Dade Boulevard on the north, the Atlantic Ocean on the east, 6th Street on the south, and Alton Road on the west.

Because the district as a whole was developed so rapidly and designed by like-minded architects—**Henry Hohauser, L. Murray Dixon, Albert Anis,** and their colleagues—it has amazing stylistic unity. Nevertheless, on this single street you can trace the evolution of period form from angular, vertically emphatic early deco to aerodynamically rounded Streamline Moderne. The relatively severe Cavalier and more curvaceous Cardozo are fine examples of the former and latter, respectively.

To explore the district, begin by loading up on literature in the **Art Deco Welcome Center** (✉ *1001 Ocean Dr.* ☎ *305/763–8026* 🌐 *www.mdpl.org*). If you want to view these historic properties on your own, just start walking. A four-block stroll north on Ocean Drive gets you up close to camera-ready classics: the **Clevelander** (1020), the **Tides** (1220), the **Leslie** (1244), the **Carlyle** (1250), the **Cardozo** (1300), the **Cavalier** (1320), and the **Winter Haven** (1400).

ARCHITECTURAL HIGHLIGHTS

Cavalier Hotel

FRIEZE DETAIL, CAVALIER HOTEL

The decorative stucco friezes outside the Cavalier Hotel at 1320 Ocean Drive are significant for more than aesthetic reasons. Roy France used them to add symmetry (adhering to the "Rule of Three") and accentuate the hotel's verticality by drawing the eye upward. The pattern he chose also reflected a fascination with ancient civilizations engendered by the recent rediscovery of King Tut's tomb and the Chichén Itzá temples.

The Raleigh Hotel

LOBBY FLOOR, THE RALEIGH HOTEL

Terrazzo—a compound of cement and stone chips that could be poured, then polished—is a hallmark of deco design. Terrazzo floors typically had a geometric pattern, like this one in the The Raleigh Hotel, a 1940 building by L Murray Dixon at 1775 Collins avenue.

Essex House Hotel

CORNER FACADE, ESSEX HOUSE HOTEL

Essex House Hotel, a 1938 gem that appears permanently anchored at 1001 Collins Avenue, is a stunning example of Maritime deco (also known as Nautical Moderne). Designed by Henry Hohauser to evoke an ocean liner, the hotel is rife with marine elements, from the rows of porthole-style windows and natty racing stripes to the towering smokestack-like sign. With a prow angled proudly into the street corner, it seems ready to steam out to sea.

The Hotel

NEON SPIRE, THE HOTEL

The name spelled vertically in eye-popping neon on the venue's iconic aluminum spire—Tiffany—bears evidence of the hotel's earlier incarnation. When the L. Murray Dixon–designed Tiffany Hotel was erected at 801 Collins Avenue in 1939, neon was still a novelty. Its use, coupled with the spire's rocket-like shape, combined to create a futuristic look influenced by the sci-fi themes then pervasive in popular culture.

Señor Frog's

ENTRANCE, SEÑOR FROG'S

Inspired by everything from car fenders to airplane noses, proponents of art deco's Streamline Moderne look began to soften buildings' hitherto boxy edges. But when Henry Hohauser designed Hoffman's Cafeteria in 1940 he took moderne to the max. The landmark at 1450 Collins Avenue (now Señor Frog's) has a sleek, splendidly curved facade. The restored interior echoes it through semicircular booths and rounded chair backs.

ARCHITECTURAL TERMS

The Rule of Three: Early deco designers often used architectural elements in multiples of three, creating tripartite facades with triple sets of windows, eyebrows, or banding.

Eyebrows: Small shelf-like ledges that protruded over exterior windows were used to simultaneously provide much-needed shade and serve as a counterpoint to a building's strong vertical lines.

Tropical Motifs: In keeping with the setting, premises were plastered, painted, or etched with seaside images. Palm trees, sunbursts, waves, flamingoes, and the like were particularly common.

Banding: Enhancing the illusion that these immobile structures were rapidly speeding objects, colorful horizontal bands (also called "racing stripes") were painted on exteriors or applied with tile.

Stripped Classic: The most austere version of art deco (sometimes dubbed Depression Moderne) was used for buildings commissioned by the Public Works Administration.

(top) Hotel Marlin; (left) Sherbrooke Hotel; (right) U.S. Post Office in Miami Beach.

Wynwood is famous for its walls covered by murals from famous contemporary artists, including these by Shepard Fairey.

larger home on the outskirts of Wynwood by 2020. *95 N.W. 29th St., Wynwood* *Between N. Miami and N.W. 1st Aves.* *305/573–6090* *www.rfc.museum* *$10* *Closed Sept.–Nov.*

★ Wynwood Walls

LOCAL INTEREST | Between Northeast 25th and 26th streets on Northwest 2nd Avenue, the Wynwood Walls are a cutting-edge enclave of modern urban murals, reflecting diversity in graffiti and street art. More than 50 well-known and lesser-known artists have transformed 80,000 square feet of warehouse walls into an outdoor museum of sorts (bring your camera). The popularity of the walls spawned the neighboring Wynwood Doors and Garden, an industrial space rife with metal roll-down gates also used as blank canvases, complemented by a garden with singular pieces of art and an eye-popping indoor gallery. *2520 N.W. 2nd Ave., Wynwood* *www.thewynwoodwalls.com.*

Restaurants

★ Alter

$$$$ | **ECLECTIC** | James Beard finalist and local superstar chef Bradley Kilgore is always changing the menu based on ingredient availability and then taking on the awesome task of transforming food into edible art. The best way to experience Kilgore's one-of-a-kind taste sensations is through the five- or seven-course tasting menu or, better yet, the wine-paired full chef's experience. **Known for:** interactive chef's counter; locavore patrons; tzatziki ice cream. *Average main: $34* *223 N.W. 23rd St., Wynwood* *305/573–5996* *www.altermiami.com.*

Joey's

$$ | **ITALIAN** | This small, modern Italian café offers a full line of flatbread pizzas, including the legendary *dolce e piccante* with figs, Gorgonzola, honey, and hot pepper—it's sweet-and-spicy goodness through and through. Joey's also serves the full gamut of Italian favorites in an intimate indoor space or on the buzzing patio. **Known for:** fresh burrata; true local feel; affordable wine selection. *Average main: $19* ✉ *2506 N.W. 2nd Ave., Wynwood* ☎ *305/438–0488* 🌐 *www.joeyswynwood.com* 🕒 *No dinner Mon.*

★ KYU

$$$$ | ECLECTIC | Foodies and locavores love this eco-minded restaurant in the heart of Wynwood, which plants five trees for every tree burned in its Japanese wood-fired grill. The Asian-inspired, small-plates menu wows through creative dishes such as the epic roasted cauliflower with goat cheese and shishito-herb vinaigrette and sizzling Thai fried-rice stone pot with king crab. **Known for:** living walls; apex of Wynwood atmosphere; flavor-rich small plates. *Average main: $32* ✉ *251 N.W. 25th St., Wynwood* ☎ *786/577–0150* 🌐 *www.kyurestaurants.com.*

★ Panther Coffee

$ | CAFÉ | The original location of the Miami-based specialty coffee roaster is smack in the center of the Wynwood Arts District (it has now expanded into Miami Beach and other South Florida neighborhoods), attracting a who's who of hipsters, artists, and even suburbanites to indulge in small-batch cups of joe and supermoist muffins and fresh-baked pastries. Baristas gingerly prepare every order, so expect to wait a little for your macchiato. **Known for:** cool clientele; strong coffee; fabulous people-watching. *Average main: $5* ✉ *2390 N.W. 2nd Ave., Wynwood* ☎ *305/677–3952* 🌐 *www.panthercoffee.com.*

★ Plant Miami

$$$$ | VEGETARIAN | Among Miami's new wave of plant-based, vegan restaurants, Plant Miami ranks tops in terms of both cuisine and design. While taking in the zen surrounds of The Sacred Space Miami, an indoor-meets-outdoor expansive wellness zone near the hubub of Wynwood, feast on hypercreative, hyperfresh dishes with global influences including those with an oh-so-Miami Latin flair (think Mexican-inspired jackfruit tacos *al pastor*, Cuban-inspired *sous vide* mushroom *ropa vieja*, and Argentinian-inspired cauliflower steak with chimichurri). **Known for:** gorgeous open kitchen; biodynamic and organic spirits; serene outdoor space with reflection pool. *Average main: $34* ✉ *The Sacred Space Miami, 105 N.E. 24th St., Wynwood* ☎ *305/814–5365* 🌐 *www.thesacredspacemiami.com/plant-miami.*

★ Wynwood Kitchen & Bar

$$$ | ECLECTIC | At the center of Miami's urban arts scene within the Wynwood Walls, Wynwood Kitchen & Bar offers an experience that includes both cultural and gastronomic excitement. Enjoy sharing-style, Latin-inspired small plates and artisanal cocktails while marveling at the powerful, hand-painted interiors and exterior murals by Shepard Fairey (of Obama *Hope* poster fame). **Known for:** ropa vieja empanadas; bacon-wrapped dates; graffiti art displays. *Average main: $22* ✉ *2550 N.W. 2nd Ave., Wynwood* ☎ *305/722–8959* 🌐 *www.wynwoodkitchenandbar.com.*

Nightlife

Cafeina Wynwood Lounge

BARS/PUBS | For those in the know, on any given Miami weekend, the evening either begins or ends at this seductive, design-driven lounge with a gorgeous patio and plenty of art on display. It's simply a great place to hang out and get a true feel for Miami's cultural revolution. It's open only Thursday–Saturday (5 pm to 3 am Thursday and Friday, 8 pm to 3 am Saturday). ✉ *297 N.W. 23rd St., Wynwood* ☎ *305/438–0792* 🌐 *www.cafeinamiami.com.*

Wood Tavern

BREWPUBS/BEER GARDENS | This is a neighborhood hangout where anything—and anyone—goes: suits mix with hoodies, fashionistas mingle with hipsters, musicians chill with groupies, but everyone in the crowd gives off a warm, welcoming vibe. The outdoor terrace is a block party scene with Latin bites served from grafitti-covered car countertops and bleacher-style stairs from which to people-watch or bob to the beats as the DJ jumps from Cypress Hill to Led Zepplin. The scene is a bit of a welcomed, artsy departure from the sultry nightlife typically associated with the Magic City (wine and cocktails are served in red plastic cups). ✉ *2531 N.W. 2nd Ave., Wynwood* ☎ *305/748–2828* 🌐 *www.woodtavern.com.*

Wynwood Brewing Company

BREWPUBS/BEER GARDENS | This family-owned craft brewery is hidden among the towering walls of graffiti arts of Wynwood. Communal tables and ever-changing pop-up galleries by neighborhood artists make the taproom cozy; however, a peek through the window behind the bar reveals there is much more to the establishment: 15 pristine silver vats are constantly brewing variations of blond ale, IPA, barrel-aged strong ales, seasonal offerings, and national Gold Medalist the Robust Porter. All staff members are designated "Beer Servers" under the Cicerone Certification Program, ensuring knowledgeable descriptions and recommendations to your liking. ✉ *565 N.W. 24 St., Wynwood* ☎ *305/982–8732* 🌐 *www.wynwoodbrewing.com.*

Shopping

Base

CLOTHING | This is the quintessential fun-and-funky Miami boutique experience. Stop here for men's eclectic clothing, shoes, jewelry, and accessories that mix Japanese design with Caribbean-inspired materials. Constantly evolving, this shop features an intriguing magazine section, a record section, groovy home accessories, and the latest in men's swimwear and sunglasses. The often-present house-label designer may help select your wardrobe's newest addition. ✉ *2215 N.W. 2nd Ave., Wynwood* ☎ *305/531–4982* 🌐 *www.baseworld.com.*

Midtown

Northeast of Wynwood, Midtown (🌐 *www.midtownmiami.com*) lies between Northeast 29th and 36th streets, from North Miami Avenue to Northeast 2nd Avenue. This subcity is anchored by a multitower residential complex with prolific retail space, often housing great dining and trusted shopping brands.

Restaurants

Sugarcane Raw Bar Grill

$$$$ | **JAPANESE FUSION** | The vibrant, supersexy, high-design restaurant perfectly captures Miami's Latin vibe while serving eclectic Latin American tapas and modern Japanese delights from three separate kitchens (*robata* grill, raw bar, and hot kitchen). Begin the Sugarcane experience in the alfresco lounge, engaging in a fabulous mix of standing, posing, flirting, and sipping on delicious cocktails, and then move on to a few of the some 60 small bites in the equally chic dining room. **Known for:** night crab sushi roll; crispy pig ear; great weekday happy hour. $ *Average main: $36* ✉ *3252 N.E. 1st Ave., Midtown* ☎ *786/369–0353* 🌐 *sugarcanerawbargrill.com.*

Nightlife

Lagniappe

GATHERING PLACES | Live musicians croon from the corner, with different bands each evening. Shelves house a selection of boutique-label wines with no corkage fee. Artisanal cheeses and meats are also available for the plucking and can be arranged into tapas-board displays. Once your selection is complete, take it back into the "living room" of worn sofas, antique lamps, and old-fashioned wall photos. Additional socializing can be found out in the "backyard" of mismatched seating and strung lighting. ✉ *3425 N.E. 2nd Ave., Midtown* ☎ *305/576–0108* 🌐 *www.lagniappe-house.com.*

Design District

North of Midtown, from about Northeast 38th to Northeast 42nd streets and across the other side of Interstate 195, the Design District (🌐 *www.miamidesigndistrict.net*) is yet another 18 blocks of clothiers, antiques shops, design stores, and bars and eateries. The real draws here are the interior design and furniture galleries as well as über-high-end shopping that's oh-so Rodeo Drive (and rivals Bal Harbour in North Beach).

Restaurants

★ Harry's Pizzeria

$$ | PIZZA | FAMILY | Harry's is a neighborhood spot with some seriously good pizza, as one would expect from Miami culinary darling Michael Schwartz and his team. The casual, friendly-yet-funky setting is inviting for all diner matchups, and seasonally inspired pizzas highlight locally sourced ingredients as unexpected, yet delicious, combinations as toppings for wood-fired, thin crusts. **Known for:** polenta fries; braised short rib pizza; warm chocolate chunk cookies. $ *Average main: $16* ✉ *3918 N. Miami Ave., Design District* ☎ *786/275–4963* 🌐 *www.harryspizzeria.com.*

★ Mandolin Aegean Bistro

$$$ | MODERN GREEK | A step inside this 1940s house-turned-bistro transports you to *ya-ya*'s home along the Aegean Sea. The Greek and Turkish cuisine is fresh and the service warm, matching its charming dining garden enlivened by an awning of trees, a rustic wooden canopy, and traditional village furnishings. **Known for:** signature Greek salad; bucolic courtyard; spectacular meze. $ *Average main: $29* ✉ *4312 N.E. 2nd Ave., Design District* ☎ *305/576–6066* 🌐 *www.mandolinmiami.com.*

★ Michael's Genuine Food & Drink

$$$ | ECLECTIC | Michael's is often cited as Miami's top tried-and-true restaurant, and it's not hard to see why: this indoor-outdoor bistro in Miami's Design District is an evergreen oasis for Miami dining sophisticates. Owner and chef Michael Schwartz aims for sophisticated eclectic cuisine with an emphasis on local and organic ingredients, and he gets it right (think crispy, sweet-and-spicy pork belly with kimchi and steamed mussels in coconut milk). **Known for:** house-smoked bacon cheddar burger; sceney alfresco dining area; Sunday brunch. $ *Average main: $27* ✉ *130 N.E. 40th St., Design District* ☎ *305/573–5550* 🌐 *www.michaelsgenuine.com.*

Shopping

Miami is synonymous with good design, and this ever-expanding visitor-friendly shopping district—officially from Northeast 38th to Northeast 42nd streets, between North Miami Avenue and Northeast 2nd Avenue (though unofficially beyond)—is an unprecedented melding of public space and the exclusive world of design. High-design buildings don the creativity of architects like Aranda & Lasch, Sou Fujimoto, and the Leong Leong firm. Throughout the district, there are more than 100 home design showrooms and galleries, including Bulthaup, Kartell, Ann Sacks, Poliform, and Luminaire Lab. Upscale retail outposts also grace the district. Cartier, Dolce & Gabbana, Fendi, Valentino, Giorgio Armani, Louis Vuitton, Prada, and Rolex sit next to design showrooms. Meanwhile, restaurants like Michael's Genuine Food & Drink and Mandolin Aegean Bistro also make this trendy neighborhood a hip place to dine. Unlike most showrooms, which are typically the beat of decorators alone, the Miami Design District's showrooms are open to the public and occupy windowed, street-level spaces. The area also has its own website: 🌐 *www.miamidesigndistrict.net.*

The Bazaar Project

ANTIQUES/COLLECTIBLES | Those looking for the rare and special need look no further than this boutique, curated by owner and Turkey-native Yeliz Titiz via her travels around the globe. Fashions, beauty, decor, and the wonderfully unusual exude the culture and craft akin to their respective regions. Highlights include whimsical housewares from Selab by Seletti, soaps by Haremlique, French wallpapers by Koziel, and intriguing jewelry by Titiz's own line, Sura. ✉ *4308 N.E. 2nd Ave., Design District* ☎ *786/703–6153* 🌐 *www.thebazaarprojectshop.com.*

COS

CLOTHING | This Scandinavian fashion label, famous throughout all of Europe, presents its one and only retail outpost in Miami's Design District in a chic, bi-level, 3,700-square-foot space. The brand is the most exclusive arm of H&M brands, which translates to wardrobe essentials with youthful sophistication at affordable prices (a rarity in the Design District). Shop options for men, women, and children. ✉ *Miami Design District, 3915 N.E. 1st Ave., Design District* ☎ *786/857–5923* 🌐 *www.cosstores.com.*

En Avance x Maison Francis Kurkdjian

CLOTHING | This Forall Studio–designed space commingles the Design District's first multibrand boutique and a French-fragrance luxury house. En Avance offers a feminine compilation of on-the-cusp designers like Protagonist and Anjuna. The owner's close connection with decorative artist Fornasetti brings to the store an extensive and exclusive selection of fashion-inspired furniture and accessories for the home. Style and beauty enthusiasts will also enjoy the table displays of lotions and potions by the iconic Maison Francis Kurkdjian. ✉ *151 N.E. 41st St., Suite 129, Design District* ☎ *305/576–0056* 🌐 *www.enavance.com.*

Galerah Mizrahi

SPECIALTY STORES | Shop for the most stylish handbags by designer Galerah Mizrahi at her only brick-and-mortar boutique in the world. (Other than here, her bags are sold exclusively at Barneys New York.) Browse through Mizrahi's namesake collection of quirky python clutches, shoulder bags, and wallets, sometimes even running into the designer herself. ✉ *Miami Design District, 151 N.E. 41st St., Suite 119, Design District* ☎ *301/787–5209* 🌐 *www.gelarehmizrahi.com* ⏲ *Closed Sun.*

Little Haiti

Once a small farming community, Little Haiti is the heart and soul of Haitian society in the United States. In fact, Miami's Little Haiti is the largest Haitian community outside of Haiti itself. Although people of different ethnic backgrounds have begun to move into the neighborhood, people here are still surprised to see tourists. Nevertheless, owners of shops and restaurants tend to be welcoming. Creole is commonly spoken, although some people—especially younger folks—also speak English. Its northern and southern boundaries are 85th Street and 42nd Street, respectively, with Interstate 95 to the west and Biscayne Boulevard to the east in its southern reaches, then Northeast 4th Court to the east (two blocks west of Biscayne Boulevard). The best section to visit is along North Miami Avenue from 54th to 59th streets.

Right outside Little Haiti's boundaries, running from 50th to 77th streets along Biscayne Boulevard, is the MiMo Biscayne Boulevard Historic District, known in short as the MiMo District. This strip is noted for its Miami modernist architecture and houses a number of boutiques and design galleries. Within this district and in the neighborhoods to the east—collectively known as Miami's Upper East Side—several new restaurants are beginning to open.

Restaurants

Chez Le Bebe

$$ | CARIBBEAN | Chez Le Bebe offers a short menu of Haitian home cooking—it's been going strong for over 30 years and has been featured on shows like the Travel Channel's *Bizarre Foods with Andrew Zimmern* and *The Layover with Anthony Bourdain*. Try the stewed goat (the specialty) or the tender and flavorful chicken, fish, oxtail, or fried pork; each plate comes with rice, beans, plantains, and salad, for around $15. **Known for:** authentic Haitian eats; no-frills atmosphere; hefty portions. *Average main: $15* *114 N.E. 54th St., Little Haiti* *305/751–7639* *No credit cards.*

Shopping

There's no shopping "scene" in Little Haiti—unless *botanicas* and voodoo supply shops are your thing. Nevertheless, farther east in Miami's Upper East Side lie several eclectic boutiques.

Fly Boutique

ANTIQUES/COLLECTIBLES | After 13 years on South Beach, this hip vintage clothing store moved to the up-and-coming MiMo District in Miami's Upper East Side. This resale boutique is where Miami hipsters flock for the latest arrival of used clothing. Glam designer pieces from the 1980s fly out at a premium price, but vintage camisoles and Levi's corduroys are still a resale deal. You'll find supercool art, furniture, luggage, and collectibles throughout the boutique. And be sure to look up—the eclectic lanterns are also for sale. *7235 Biscayne Blvd., Upper East Side* *305/604–8508* *www.flyboutiquevintage.com.*

Rebel

CLOTHING | Half new, half vintage consignment, the goods offered here make you feel as if you are raiding your stylish friend's closet. Racks are packed with all different types of styles and designers—from Lauren Moshi to Indah—requiring a little patience when sifting through. The store has a particularly strong collection of jeans, funky tees, and maxi dresses. *7648 Biscayne Blvd., Upper East Side* *786/803–8828.*

Sweat Records

MUSIC STORES | For a timeless version of an old-fashioned favorite,visit Sweat Records, one of Miami's last remaining record stores. Sweat sells a wide range of music—rock, pop, punk, electronic, hip-hop, and Latino—as well as turntables and vinyl accessories; there's also Miami's only vegan, organic coffee shop on the premises. *5505 N.E. 2nd Ave., Little Haiti* *786/693–9309* *www.sweatrecordsmiami.com.*

Little Havana

First settled en masse by Cubans in the early 1960s, after Cuba's Communist revolution, Little Havana is a predominantly working-class area and the core of Miami's Hispanic community. Spanish is the principal language, but don't be surprised if the cadence is less Cuban and more Salvadoran or Nicaraguan: the neighborhood is now home to people from all Latin American countries.

If you come to Little Havana expecting the Latino version of New Orleans's French Quarter, you're apt to be disappointed—it's not about the architecture here. Rather, it's a place to soak in the atmosphere. Little Havana is more about great, inexpensive food (not just Cuban; there's Vietnamese, Mexican, and Argentinean here as well), distinctive affordable Cuban-American art, cigars, and great coffee. It's not a prefab tourist destination—this is real life in Spanish-speaking Miami.

Sights

Cuban Memorial Boulevard

MEMORIAL | Four blocks in the heart of Little Havana are filled with monuments to Cuba's freedom fighters. South of Calle Ocho (8th Street), Southwest 13th Avenue becomes a ceiba tree–lined parkway known as Cuban Memorial Boulevard, divided at the center by a narrow grassy mall with a walking path through the various memorials. Among them is the *Eternal Torch of the Brigade 2506,* blazing with an endless flame and commemorating those who were killed in the failed Bay of Pigs invasion of 1961. Another is a bas-relief map of Cuba depicting each of its *municipios.* There's also a bronze statue in honor of Nestory (Tony) Izquierdo, who participated in the Bay of Pigs invasion and served in Nicaragua's Somozan forces. ✉ *S.W. 13th Ave., Little Havana* ⊕ *Between S.W. 8th and S.W. 12th Sts.*

★ **Domino Park**

CITY PARK | Watch a slice of Old Havana come to life in Miami's Little Havana. At Domino Park, officially known as Maximo Gomez Park, guayabera-clad seniors bask in the sun and play dominoes, while onlookers share neighborhood gossip and political opinions. **■ TIP→ There is a little office at the park with a window where you can get information on Little Havana; the office also stores the dominoes for the older gents who play regularly, but it's BYOD (bring your own dominoes) for everyone else.** ✉ *801 S.W. 15th Ave., Little Havana* ☎ *305/859–2717 park office.*

El Titan de Bronze

LOCAL INTEREST | A peek at the intently focused cigar rollers through the windows doesn't prepare you for the rich, pungent scent that jolts your senses as you step inside the store. Millions of stogies are deftly hand-rolled at this family-owned cigar factory and retail store each year. Visitors are welcome to watch the rolling action (and, of course, buy some cigars). ✉ *1071 S.W. 8th St., Little Havana* ☎ *305/860–1412* 🌐 *www.eltitancigars.com.*

Restaurants

★ **Azucar Ice Cream Company**

$ | **CAFÉ** | **FAMILY** | More crafty than churning, flavors at this Cuban ice-cream shop are inspired and derived from ingredients at nearby fruit stands, international grocery shops, and farmers' markets. The menu features creations that nod to the culturally rich, Little Havana location (*café con leche,* flan, and the signature Abuela Maria—made with Maria cookies, cream cheese, and guava) as well as seasonal specialties (like sweet creamed corn and egg nog). **Known for:** Abuela Maria ice cream; flan ice cream; one-of-a-kind frozen indulgences. $ *Average main: $6* ✉ *1503 S.W. 8th St., Little Havana* ☎ *305/381–0369* 🌐 *www.azucaricecream.com.*

El Exquisito Restaurant

$ | **LATIN AMERICAN** | For a true locals' spot and some substantial Cuban eats in the heart of Little Havana, pop into this local institution that's been popular since the 1970s. The unassuming Cuban café serves up delectable, authentic Cuban favorites, including a great *cubano* (a grilled Cuban sandwich layered with ham, garlic-and-citrus-marinated slow-roasted pork, Swiss cheese, and pickles) and succulent yuca with garlic sauce. **Known for:** chatty regulars; 75 cent Cuban coffee; quick serve to-go window. $ *Average main: $14* ✉ *1510 S.W. 8th St., Little Havana* ☎ *305/643–0227* 🌐 *www.elexquisitomiami.com* 💳 *No credit cards.*

Las Pinareños Fruteria

$ | **CUBAN** | If you're looking for something refreshing or a high-octane jolt while touring Little Havana, try this *fruteria* (fruit stand) that serves *coco frio* (fresh, cold coconut juice served in a whole coconut), mango juice, and other *jugos* (juices), as well as Cuban coffees and Cuban finger foods. You can order from the walk-up window and enjoy your drink at one of the tables inside the market. **Known for:** exotic juices; coco frio; friendly staff. *Average main: $7 ✉ 1334 S.W. 8th St., Little Havana ☎ 305/285–1135.*

★ Versailles

$$ | **CUBAN** | **FAMILY** | Miami visitors looking for that "Cuban food on Calle Ocho" experience, look no further: the storied eatery, where old émigrés opine daily about all things Cuban, is a stop on every political candidate's campaign trail, and it should be a stop for you as well. Order a heaping platter of *lechon asado* (roasted pork loin), *ropa vieja* (shredded beef), or *picadillo* (spicy ground beef), all served with rice, beans, and fried plantains. **Known for:** gossipy locals at takeout window; old-school Little Havana setting; guava-filled pastelitos. *Average main: $16 ✉ 3555 S.W. 8th St., Little Havana ☎ 305/444–0240 🌐 www.versaillesrestaurant.com.*

Nightlife

★ Ball & Chain

MUSIC CLUBS | Established in 1935 and steeped in legends of gambling, Prohibition protests, the rise of budding entertainers Billie Holiday and Chet Baker, and the development of Cuban-centric Calle Ocho, this storied nightlife spot has been reestablished under its original name. The high-vaulted ceilings, floral wallpaper, black-and-white photos, and palm-fringed outdoor lounge nod to its torrid history and the glamour of Old Havana. Live music flows freely, as do the Latin-inspired libations and tapas of traditional Cuban favorites. *✉ 1513 S.W. 8th St., Little Havana ☎ 305/643–7820 🌐 www.ballandchainmiami.com.*

Activities

Miami Marlins

BASEBALL/SOFTBALL | **FAMILY** | Miami's baseball team, formerly known as the Florida Marlins, then the Miami Marlins, then simply the Marlins, and now again as the Miami Marlins plays at the state-of-the-art Marlins Park—a 37,442-seat retractable-roof, air-conditioned baseball stadium on the grounds of Miami's famous Orange Bowl. Go see the team that came out of nowhere to beat the New York Yankees and win the 2003 World Series. Home games are April through early October. *✉ Marlins Park, 501 Marlins Way, Little Havana ☎ 305/480–1300 🌐 www.marlins.com $10–$395; parking from $20 and should be prepurchased online.*

South Beach

The hub of Miami Beach is South Beach (better known as SoBe), with its energetic Ocean Drive, Collins Avenue, and Washington Avenue. Here life unfolds 24 hours a day. Beautiful people pose in hotel lounges and sidewalk cafés, bronzed cyclists zoom past palm trees, and visitors flock to see the action. On Lincoln Road, café crowds spill onto the sidewalks, weekend markets draw all kinds of visitors and their dogs, and thanks to a few late-night lounges, the scene is just as alive at night. Farther north (in Mid-Beach and North Beach), the vibe is decidedly quieter and more sophisticated.

Sights

Art Deco Welcome Center and Museum

BUILDING | Run by the Miami Design Preservation League, the center provides information about the buildings in the district. An official Art Deco Museum opened within the center in October 2014, and a gift shop sells 1930s–'50s art deco memorabilia, posters, and books on Miami's history. Several tours also start here, including a self-guided audio tour and regular morning walking tours at 10:30 every day. On Thursdays a second tour takes place at 6:30 pm. ✉ *1001 Ocean Dr., South Beach* ☎ *305/672–2014, 305/531–3484 for tours* 🌐 *www.mdpl.org* 🎟 *Tours $25.*

★ The Bass

MUSEUM | Special exhibitions join a diverse collection of international contemporary art at this museum whose original 1930s art deco building was designed by Russell Pancoast and constructed entirely of Florida keystone (material with a coral base). A years-long, $12-million expansion by noted architects Arata Isozaki and David Gauld was completed in 2017, increasing internal space nearly 50% and adding four new galleries. The majority of exhibitions are temporary, but works on permanent display include *Chess Tables,* a sculpture by Jim Drain, and *Miami Mountain,* a sculpture by Ugo Rondinone. For free, docent-led tours of the temporary exhibitions, visit on Saturday and Sunday at 2 pm or 4 pm. ✉ *2100 Collins Ave., South Beach* ☎ *305/673–7530* 🌐 *www.thebass.org* 🎟 *$10* ⏲ *Closed Mon.–Tues.*

Española Way

NEIGHBORHOOD | There's a bohemian feel to this street lined with Mediterranean-revival buildings constructed in 1925 and inspired by New York's Greenwich Village. Al Capone's gambling syndicate ran its operations upstairs at what is now the Clay Hotel, a value-conscious boutique hotel. At a nightclub here in the 1930s, future bandleader Desi Arnaz strapped on a conga drum and started beating out a rumba rhythm. Visit this quaint pedestrian-only way nowadays and find a number of personality-driven restaurants and bars, and enjoy weekly programming, which includes the likes of salsa dancing, flamenco dancing, and opera performances. ✉ *Española Way, South Beach* ✣ *Between 14th and 15th Sts. from Washington to Pennslyvania Aves.* 🌐 *www.visitespanolaway.com.*

Holocaust Memorial

INFO CENTER | A bronze sculpture depicts refugees clinging to a giant bronze arm that reaches out of the ground and 42 feet into the air. Enter the surrounding courtyard to see a memorial wall and hear the music that seems to give voice to the 6 million Jews who died at the hands of the Nazis. It's easy to understand why Kenneth Treister's dramatic memorial is in Miami Beach: the city's community of Holocaust survivors was once the second largest in the country. ✉ *1933–1945 Meridian Ave., at Dade Blvd., South Beach* ☎ *305/538–1663* 🌐 *www.holocaustmemorialmiamibeach.org* 🎟 *Free.*

★ Lincoln Road Mall

BUILDING | FAMILY | This open-air pedestrian mall flaunts some of Miami's best people-watching. The eclectic interiors of myriad fabulous restaurants, colorful boutiques, art galleries, lounges, and cafés are often upstaged by the bustling outdoor scene. It's here among the prolific alfresco dining enclaves that you can pass the hours easily beholding the beautiful people. Indeed, Lincoln Road is fun, lively, and friendly for everyone—old, young, gay, and straight—and their dogs. A few of the shops on Lincoln Road are owner-operated boutiques carrying a smart variety of clothing, furnishings, jewelry, and decorative elements, but more often you'll find typical upscale chain stores.

Two landmarks worth checking out at the eastern end of Lincoln Road are the massive 1940s keystone building at 420 Lincoln Road, which has a 1945 Leo Birchanky mural in the lobby, and the 1921 mission-style Miami Beach Community Church, at Drexel Avenue. The Lincoln

A
B
C
D
E
F
1
2
3
4
5
6
7
8
9
Miami Beach and South Beach
KEY
Sights
Restaurants
Hotels
South Beach
Alton Rd.
Meridian Ave.
Dade Blvd.
Convention Center Dr.
Washington Ave.
Park Ave.
23rd St.
22nd St.
Collins Park
20th St.
19th St.
James Ave.
Collins Ave.
18th St.
17th St.
Lincoln Road Mall
16th St.
15th St.
Española Way
14th Pl.
14th St.
Flamingo Park
13th St.
12th St.
11th St.
10th St.
Alton Rd.
Meridian Ave.
Euclid Ave.
Pennsylvania Ave.
Washington Ave.
Collins Ave.
Lummus Park
9th St.
8th St.
7th St.
6th St.
5th St.
4th St.
3rd St.
2nd St.
1st St.
S Pointe Dr.
Lenox Ave.
Michigan Ave.
Jefferson Ave.
Ocean Dr.
Collins Ave.
Alton Rd.
Atlantic Ocean
826
N. Mia
95
N.E. 13
7th Ave.
Gratigny Rd.
N.W.
N.W. 103rd St.
N.W. 95th St.
N.E. 95th St.
N.W. 79th St.
441
N.W. 62nd St.
N. Miami Ave.
N.E. 2nd Ave.
DESIGN DISTRICT
N.W. 54th St.
N.W. 40th St.
Airport Expwy.
WYNWOOD
MIDTOW
27
DOWNTOWN MIAMI
S.W. 8th St.
LITTLE HAVANA
S.W. 22nd St.
COCONUT GROVE

Sights

1 Art Deco Welcome Center and Museum C6
2 The Bass..................C2
3 Española Way............C5
4 Holocaust Memorial.... B3
5 Lincoln Road Mall A4
6 World Erotic Art Museum (WEAM)..................C5

Restaurants

1 AQ Chop House by Il Mulino I2
2 Byblos.....................C4
3 Carpaccio Restaurant....I4
4 Cecconi's Miami Beach..I7
5 Chotto Matte A4
6 Dolce Italian..............C3
7 The Forge..................I7
8 Gianni's C5
9 Hakkasan Miami..........I7
10 Il Mulino New York-Sunny Isles Beach........I2
11 Jaya D2
12 Joe's Stone Crab........ B9
13 Juvia A4
14 Le Zoo......................I4
15 Lobster Bar Sea Grille.. B8
16 LT Steak and Seafood...C5
17 Macchialina............. A7
18 Makoto......................I4
19 Malibu Farm...............I6
20 Matador....................I7
21 Meat Market............ A4
22 NaiYaRa................. H8
23 News Cafe................C7
24 Prime 112................ B9
25 Pubbelly Noodle Bar ... H7
26 Pubbelly Sushi-South Beach H7
27 Red, the Steakhouse ... B9
28 Smith & Wollensky Miami Beach............ H9
29 Via Emilia 9 .... A4
30 Yardbird Southern Table & Bar.............. A4

Hotels

1 Acqualina Resort & Spa on the Beach............ I2
2 The Betsy–South Beach C5
3 Cadet Hotel...............C3
4 Carillon Miami Wellness Resort I5
5 Catalina Hotel & Beach Club...............C3
6 Circa 39 Hotel I7
7 COMO Metropolitan Miami Beach............ D2
8 The Confidante............I7
9 Crowne Plaza South Beach - Z Ocean Hotel............C5
10 Delano South Beach C4
11 Dream South Beach.....C5
12 Eden Roc Miami Beach..I6
13 Faena Hotel Miami Beach..............I7
14 Fisher Island Hotel and Resort........ H9
15 Fontainebleau Miami Beach..............I7
16 Gale South Beach C4
17 Hilton Bentley Miami/ South Beach C9
18 The Hotel of South Beach C7
19 Hotel Victor...............C5
20 Kimpton Angler's Hotel B7
21 Kimpton Surfcomber Miami D3
22 Loews Miami Beach Hotel...................... D4
23 The Miami Beach EDITION....................I7
24 Mondrian South Beach A5
25 National Hotel............C4
26 1 Hotel South Beach ... D2
27 The Palms Hotel & Spa ..I7
28 The Ritz-Carlton, Bal Harbour I4
29 Room Mate Lord Balfour............. B8
30 Royal Palm South Beach Miami C4
31 The St. Regis Bal Harbour Resort.......I4
32 The Setai Miami Beach............ D2
33 Shelborne South Beach D3
34 Shore Club............... D3
35 SLS South Beach....... D3
36 Soho Beach House.......I7
37 The Standard Spa, Miami Beach............ H8
38 W South Beach......... D2

Did You Know?

From sidewalk cafés, diners enjoy the bohemian atmosphere of Miami Beach's Española Way.

Theatre (541–545 Lincoln Rd.), at Pennsylvania Avenue, is a classical four-story art deco gem with friezes, which now houses H&M. ✉ *Lincoln Rd., South Beach* ✣ *Between Washington Ave. and Alton Rd.* 🌐 *www.lincolnroadmall.com.*

World Erotic Art Museum (WEAM)

MUSEUM | Late millionaire Naomi Wilzig's collection of some 4,000 erotic items is on display at this unique museum. Expect sexy art of varying quality—fertility statues from around the globe and historic Chinese *shunga* books (erotic art offered as gifts to new brides on the wedding night) share the space with some kitschy knickknacks. If this is your thing, an original phallic prop from Stanley Kubrick's *A Clockwork Orange* and an over-the-top Kama Sutra bed is worth the price of admission. Kids 17 and under are not admitted. ✉ *1205 Washington Ave., at 12th St., South Beach* ☎ *305/532–9336* 🌐 *www.weam.com* 🎫 *$15.*

Beaches

★ South Beach

BEACH—SIGHT | A 10-block stretch of white sandy beach hugging the turquoise waters along Ocean Drive—from 5th to 15th streets—is one of the most popular in America, known for drawing unabashedly model-like sunbathers and posers. With the influx of new luxe hotels and hot spots from 1st to 5th and 16th to 25th streets, the South Beach stand-and-pose scene is now bigger than ever and stretches yet another dozen-plus blocks. The beaches crowd quickly on the weekends with a blend of European tourists, young hipsters, and sun-drenched locals. Separating the sand from the traffic of Ocean Drive is palm-fringed **Lummus Park,** with its volleyball nets and chickee huts (huts made of palmetto thatch over a cypress frame) for shade. The beach at **12th Street** is popular with gays, in a section often marked with rainbow flags. Locals hang out on 3rd Street beach, in an area called **SoFi** (South of Fifth). **Amenities:** food and drink; lifeguards; parking (fee); showers; toilets. **Best for:** partiers; sunrise; swimming; walking. ✉ *Ocean Dr., South Beach* ✣ *From 5th to 15th Sts., then Collins Ave. to 25th St.*

Restaurants

★ Byblos

$$$ | MIDDLE EASTERN | Dynamic and delicious flavors of the Eastern Mediterranean merge over traditional and new-fashioned dishes at this photogenic local hot spot. Feast on *pides* (Turkish flat breads baked in a stone oven), Middle Eastern fried chicken (with tahini, za'atar, and house hot sauce) and *fattouche* (crunch salad) in between Instagram stories and Snapchats of the breezy, art deco surrounds and colorful interiors. **Known for:** creamed-spinach pide; yogurt-baked fluke; trendsetting crowd. $ *Average main: $28* ✉ *1545 Collins Ave., South Beach* ☎ *305/508–5041* 🌐 *www.byblos-miami.com.*

Chotto Matte

$$$ | JAPANESE FUSION | With bright graffiti walls, a buzzing bar, and an open-air roof, this trendy Japanese-Peruvian fusion restaurant has brought sophistication and edge to Lincoln Road. Order a pisco or Japanese whisky and settle in for flavor-packed Nikkei-style cuisine and some of the best sushi in town. **Known for:** excellent sharing menu; glow-in-the-dark bathrooms; flaming Holy Water cocktail. $ *Average main: $25* ✉ *1664 Lenox Ave., South Beach* ☎ *305/690-0743* 🌐 *www.chotto-matte.com/miami.*

Dolce Italian

$$$ | MODERN ITALIAN | Best known as a top contender on the Bravo TV show *Best New Restaurant,* Dolce Italian buzzes in the center of the South Beach action, doling out an irresistible ménage à trois: great food, great setting, and an easy-on-the-eyes crowd. Italian-born chef Paolo Dorigato's menu is packed with modern incarnations of Italian classics that would make *Nonna* proud. **Known for:** homemade mozzarella and pastas; Neopolitan-style pizzas; smart design. *Average main: $28* *Gale South Beach, 1690 Collins Ave., South Beach* *786/975–2550* *www.dolceitalianrestaurant.com/miami.*

Gianni's

$$$$ | **ITALIAN** | Set within the glitz and ostentation of Gianni Versace's former mansion, the Villa Casa Casuarina, this restaurant doles out pricey Italian-Mediterranean eats across the mansion's most prized nooks. It's more about the atmosphere here than the food, which includes caviar selections, filet mignon, and black-truffle risotto. **Known for:** haute dining; wow-factor surrounds; only-in-Miami experience. *Average main: $52* *The Villa Casa Casuarina, 1116 Ocean Dr., South Beach* *786/485–2200* *www.vmmiamibeach.com/gianni* *Closed Mon.*

Jaya

$$$$ | **ASIAN FUSION** | At the flagship restaurant of the Setai Miami Beach hotel, expect a pan-Asian extravaganza, representing the countries of Thailand, Vietnam, Singapore, Korea, India, China, and Japan, through dishes that range from sea bass tikka to Peking duck to lobster curry. Before or after dinner, be sure to enjoy a cocktail around the harmonious courtyard reflecting pool. **Known for:** beautiful interiors; kimchi fried rice; dim sum. *Average main: $41* *The Setai, 2001 Collins Ave., South Beach* *855/923–7899* *www.thesetaihotel.com/jaya.php.*

★ Joe's Stone Crab

$$$$ | **SEAFOOD** | In South Beach's decidedly new-money scene, the stately Joe's Stone Crab is an old-school testament to good food and good service. Stone crabs, served with legendary mustard sauce, crispy hash brown potatoes, and creamed spinach, remain the staple at South Beach's most-storied restaurant (which dates to 1913). **Known for:** the-best-of-the-best stone crab claws; Key lime pie; no reservations (arrive very early). *Average main: $46* *11 Washington Ave., South Beach* *305/673–0365, 305/673–4611 for takeout* *www.joesstonecrab.com* *Closed mid-May–mid-Oct. No lunch Sun. and Mon.*

★ Juvia

$$$$ | **JAPANESE FUSION** | High atop South Beach's design-driven 1111 Lincoln Road parking garage, rooftop Juvia commingles urban sophistication with South Beach seduction. Three renowned chefs unite to deliver an amazing eating experience that screams Japanese, Peruvian, and French all in the same breath, focusing largely on raw fish and seafood dishes. **Known for:** city and beach views; sunset cocktails on the terrace; bigeye tuna poke. *Average main: $35* *1111 Lincoln Rd., South Beach* *305/763–8272* *www.juviamiami.com* *No lunch weekdays.*

Lobster Bar Sea Grille—Miami Beach

$$$$ | **SEAFOOD** | As the name implies, lobster is the center of attention at this seafood-centric restaurant, where the Nova Scotian good stuff is perfectly prepared in a variety of ways: steamed and cracked, stuffed (with lobster stuffing), angry (in spicy, chili lobster sauce), flash-fried, or over lemon risotto. There's also a range of other fresh fruits of the sea and custom-aged prime steaks to be enjoyed in a seductive setting that at the same time recalls New York's Grand Central Station and a superyacht. **Known for:** jumbo lobster for two; shellfish towers; caviar selections. *Average main: $48* *404 Washington Ave., South Beach* *305/377–2675* *www.buckheadrestaurants.com/restaurant/lobster-bar-sea-grille-miami-beach.*

★ LT Steak and Seafood

$$$$ | **STEAKHOUSE** | Miami is filled with great steak houses, but this is arguably the best. Located in the glamorous art deco open lobby of Ocean Drive's Betsy Hotel, noted chef Laurent Tourondel (of

BLT Steak fame) presents a seasonally inspired menu that includes fresh seafood, sushi, the highest-quality cuts of USDA prime and certified Black Angus beef, and decadent sides (don't miss the hand-cut Parmesan truffle fries with truffle aioli). **Known for:** massive popovers; The Besty crabcake; cocktails inspired by literary greats. *Average main: $38 ✉ The Betsy Hotel—South Beach, 1440 Ocean Drive, South Beach ☎ 305/673–0044 🌐 www.thebetsyhotel.com/lt-restaurant.*

Macchialina

$$$ | **ITALIAN** | Framed by exposed-brick walls, decorated with daily specials on chalkboards, and packed with gregarious patrons, this local foodie hangout feels like a cozy, neighborhoody tavern. Owner and chef Michael Pirolo nails the concept of modern Italian cuisine through a small but special selection of antipasti (try the local burrata and creamy polenta with sausage) and daily homemade pastas (like tagliolini *al funghi* and spaghetti *con vongole).* **Known for:** Italian-imported salumi; house panna cotta; devoted local following. *Average main: $27 ✉ 820 Alton Rd., South Beach ☎ 305/534–2124 🌐 www.macchialina.com.*

Meat Market

$$$$ | **STEAKHOUSE** | Indeed, this is a meat market in every sense of the phrase, with great cuts of meat and plenty of sexy people passing by in skimpy clothes and enjoying fruity libations at the bar. Hard-core carnivores go wild over the 16-ounce center-cut prime New York steak, and pescatarians love the wood-grilled Scottish salmon, topped with red wine cherry butter. **Known for:** outdoor seating on Lincoln Road; great happy hour daily; strong cocktails. *Average main: $42 ✉ 915 Lincoln Rd., South Beach ☎ 305/532–0088 🌐 www.meatmarket.net.*

NaiYaRa

$$$ | **THAI** | Combine the pulse of Bangkok with the glitz of South Beach and undertones of Tokyo, and you get this hypercool, Thai-meets-Japanese restaurant with a sleek, retro-contemporary design in the heart of Miami's burgeoning Sunset Harbour area. The lovable and highly talented owner, Piyarat Potha Arreeratn (aka Chef Bee), guarantees a memorable night of fun, fruity and wild cocktails, and a diverse menu that spans classic Thai dishes perfected to more daring maki creations. **Known for:** Ab Zaab fried chicken dumplings; dynamic atmosphere; salmon-belly filled Naiyara roll. *Average main: $28 ✉ 1854 Bay Rd., South Beach ☎ 786/275–6005 🌐 www.naiyara.com.*

Cheap Eats on South Beach

Miami Beach is notoriously overpriced, but locals know that you don't always have to spend $30 for lunch or $45 for a dinner entrée here to have a good meal. **Pizza Rustica** (✉ *8th St. and Washington Ave. and 667 Lincoln Rd.*) serves up humongous slices overflowing with mozzarella, steak, olives, and barbecue chicken until 4 am. **La Sandwicherie** (✉ *14th St. between Collins and Washington Aves.*) is a South Beach classic that's been here since 1988, serving gourmet French sandwiches and salads.

News Café

$$ | **AMERICAN** | Twenty years strong, this 24-hour café attracts a late-night and early-morning crowd with diner-esque meals, drinks, periodicals, and the people parade on the sidewalk out front. Although service can be indifferent to the point of laissez-faire and the food is mediocre at best, News Café is just one of those places visitors love. **Known for:** post-drinking eats; people-watching; newspaper selection. *Average main:*

$15 ✉ 800 Ocean Dr., South Beach ☎ 305/538–6397 🌐 www.newscafe.com.

★ Prime 112

$$$$ | STEAKHOUSE | This wildly busy steak house is particularly prized for its highly marbleized prime beef, creamed corn with black truffles, lobster macaroni and cheese, and buzzing scene. While you stand at the bar awaiting your table—everyone has to wait, at least a little bit—you'll clamor for a drink with all facets of Miami's high society, from the city's top real estate developers and philanthropists to striking models and celebrities. **Known for:** reservations made by phone only; decadent side dishes; stellar service. *$ Average main: $53 ✉ 112 Ocean Dr., South Beach ☎ 305/532–8112 🌐 www.mylesrestaurantgroup.com.*

★ Pubbelly Noodle Bar

$$$ | ASIAN FUSION | This petite eatery, on a residential street in SoBe's western reaches, attracts the who's who of beach socialites, hipsters, and the occasional tourist coming to chow down on inventive Asian-Latin small plates, ramen noodle bowls, dumplings, and bao buns by executive chef–owner José Mendin. From uni pasta to short-rib tartare, the menu constantly pushes the envelope on inventive cuisine, and locals simply can't get enough. **Known for:** long waits; omakase tasting menu; lechon asado bao bun. *$ Average main: $28 ✉ 1418 20th St., South Beach ☎ 305/532–7555 🌐 pubbellyglobal.com/restaurants/pubbelly-noodle-bar.*

Pubbelly Sushi—South Beach

$$$$ | JAPANESE | At this contemporary, Japanese-inspired canteen by Miami's famed Pubbelly team, expect grade-A sashimi, meats from the *robata* (Japanese charcoal) grill, and flavor-rich Pubbelly Rolls like the bigeye tuna (spicy tuna over squares of crispy rice) and Navarro salmon (salmon, crab, melted mozzarella, and fried onions). Wash it all down with refreshing house sake cocktails like the Teasy Bear (green tea, honey, ginger, and sake). **Known for:** Sun.–Thurs. late-night happy hour (10 pm to closing); chocolate miso bread pudding; tuna pizza. *$ Average main: $31 ✉ 1424 20th St., South Beach ☎ 305/531–9282 🌐 www.pubbellysushi.us.*

Red, the Steakhouse

$$$$ | STEAKHOUSE | The carnivore glamour den seduces with its red-and-black dominatrix color scheme and overloads the senses with the divine smells and tastes of the extensive menu. Red boasts an equal number of seafood and more traditional meat offerings, each delicately prepared, meticulously presented, and gleefully consumed. **Known for:** tuna tartare; decadent, caloric side dishes; mussels diavolo. *$ Average main: $55 ✉ 119 Washington Ave., South Beach ☎ 305/534–3688 🌐 www.redthesteakhouse.com.*

Smith & Wollensky Miami Beach

$$$$ | STEAKHOUSE | Enjoy one of America's premier tried-and-true steak houses in one of Miami's best locations. Situated at the tip of South Pointe Park with fabulous views of Biscayne Bay, this waterfront outpost doles out the full range of signature cuts of 28-day, dry-aged beef and hefty sides, though the beach-conscious crowd skews toward the chilled shellfish platters and savory vegetable dishes. **Known for:** award-winning wine list; shellfish towers; 44-ounce rib eye, charred tableside. *$ Average main: $52 ✉ 1 Washington Ave., South Beach ☎ 305/673–2800 🌐 www.smithandwollensky.com/our-restaurants/miami-beach.*

★ Via Emilia 9

$$ | ITALIAN | If you're longing for a *true* taste of Italy's Emilia Romagna region and a respite from the overpriced SoBe dining scene, head to this adorable hole-in-the-wall restaurant off Alton Road, owned and operated by Italian chef Wendy Cacciatori and his lovely wife. The pastas and sauces are made fresh daily, using only the best ingredients imported from the chef's homeland supplemented with local produce. **Known for:** ravioli of the day; homemade flatbreads; variety of stuffed pastas. *Average main: $18* *1120 15th St., South Beach* *786/216–7150* *www.viaemilia9.com.*

Yardbird Southern Table & Bar

$$$ | SOUTHERN | There's a helluva lot of Southern lovin' from the lowcountry at this lively and funky South Beach spot, where Miami's A-list puts calorie-counting aside for decadent nights filled with comfort foods and innovative drinks. The family-style menu is divided between "small plates," "the bird," "plates," and "sides and snacks," but have no doubt "the bird" takes center stage (or plate) here: you'll rave about Llewellyn's fine fried chicken, which requires a 27-hour marination and slow-cooking process, for weeks to come. **Known for:** smoked brisket biscuits; peppered gnocchi pot pie; chicken 'n' watermelon 'n' waffles. *Average main: $27* *1600 Lenox Ave., South Beach* *305/538–5220* *www.runchickenrun.com.*

Hotels

If you are looking to experience the postcard image of Miami, look no further than South Beach. Most of the hotels along Ocean Drive, Collins Avenue, and Washington Avenue are housed in history-steeped art deco buildings, each one cooler than the next. From boutique hotels to high-rise structures, all South Beach hotels are in close proximity to the beach and never far from the action. Most hotels here cost a pretty penny and for good reason. They are more of an experience than a place to crash (think designer lobbies, some of the world's best pool scenes, and unparalleled people-watching).

★ 1 Hotel South Beach

$$$$ | RESORT | This snazzy eco-minded hotel delivers a picturesque, nature-inspired aesthetic throughout the common spaces and room interiors (think heavy use of repurposed wood, living walls, preserved moss, and glassware from recycled wine bottles) and offers a choice of four swimming pools (including the best rooftop one in Florida) and an excellent swath of beach. **Pros:** even basic level rooms are great; vibrant crowd; sustainability mantra. **Cons:** many rooms face street; constantly busy; balcony furniture a bit worn. *Rooms from: $499* *2341 Collins Ave., South Beach* *305/604–1000* *www.1hotels.com/south-beach* *426 rooms* *No meals.*

★ The Betsy—South Beach

$$$$ | HOTEL | After a massive expansion, the original Betsy Ross Hotel (christened the "Colonial" wing) has been joined with what was the neighboring, historic Carlton Hotel to create a retro-chic, art deco treasure that delivers the full-throttle South Beach experience with style, pizzazz, and a big-time cultural bonus: year-round programs include poetry readings, live jazz, and art shows. **Pros:** unbeatable location; superfashionable; great beach club. **Cons:** confusing hotel layout; great pet-friendly program but fee attached; pool sometimes crowded. *Rooms from: $477* *1440 Ocean Dr., South Beach* *844/539–2840* *www.thebetsyhotel.com* *130 rooms* *No meals.*

Cadet Hotel

$ | HOTEL | A former home to World War II air force cadets, this gem has been reimagined as an oasis in South Beach, offering the antithesis of the sometimes maddening jet-set scene, with 34 distinctive rooms exuding understated luxury. **Pros:** excellent service; lovely garden; historical value. **Cons:** tiny swimming pool; limited appeal for the party crowd; small bathrooms. *Rooms from: $169* *1701 James Ave., South Beach* *305/672–6688* *www.cadethotel.com* *34 rooms* *No meals.*

Catalina Hotel & Beach Club

$ | HOTEL | The Catalina is a fun, budget party spot in the heart of South Beach, attracting plenty of early twentysome-things who value freebies like a nightly drink hour, airport shuttles, fitness classes, two fun pools, and beach chairs over posh digs. **Pros:** cool crowd; free airport shuttle; good people-watching. **Cons:** service not a high priority; late-night debauchery; worn rooms. *$ Rooms from: $153 ✉ 1720–1756 Collins Ave., South Beach ☎ 877/762–3477 🌐 www.catalinahotel.com 190 rooms 🍴 No meals.*

COMO Metropolitan Miami Beach

$$$ | **RESORT** | The luxury COMO brand brings its Zen-glam swagger to South Beach, reinventing the art deco Traymore hotel into a 74-room, Paola Navone–designed boutique hotel that commingles brand signatures (excellent, health-driven cuisine, and myriad spa elements) with Miami panache. **Pros:** easy access to both South Beach and Mid-Beach; Como Shambhala toiletries; stylish "P" and "C" door magnets signal "Clean" or "Privacy". **Cons:** two people per room max; limited number of rooms with good views; small bathrooms. *$ Rooms from: $383 ✉ 2445 Collins Ave., South Beach ☎ 305/695–3600 🌐 www.comohotels.com/metropolitanmiamibeach 74 rooms 🍴 No meals.*

Crowne Plaza South Beach—Z Ocean Hotel

$$$ | **HOTEL** | This is definitely not your grandmother's Crowne Plaza: the lauded firm of Arquitectonica designed this glossy and bold all-suites hideaway, including 27 rooftop suites endowed with terraces, each complete with Jacuzzi, plush chaise lounges, and a view of the South Beach skyline. **Pros:** across street from beach; huge rooms; green, earth-friendly hotelwide initiatives. **Cons:** tiny gym; lack of privacy on rooftop suite decks; rooms could use refresh. *$ Rooms from: $304 ✉ 1437 Collins Ave., South Beach ☎ 305/672–4554 🌐 www.ihg.com 79 suites 🍴 No meals.*

Delano South Beach

$$$ | **HOTEL** | The hotel that single-handedly made South Beach cool again in the 1990s is still making waves across the beach as this Philippe Starck powerhouse immortalizes a glorious moment in South Beach's glamour revival. **Pros:** iconic design; lounging among the beautiful; trippy ornaments like the ladder-to-nowhere. **Cons:** pricey drinks; in need of a refresh; some smaller rooms. *$ Rooms from: $365 ✉ 1685 Collins Ave., South Beach ☎ 305/672–2000 🌐 www.morganshotelgroup.com/delano/delano-south-beach 208 rooms 🍴 No meals.*

Dream South Beach

$$ | **HOTEL** | This trendy boutique hotel, which is right in the center of the South Beach action, merges two refurbished, archetypal, 1939 art deco buildings into a single project of eclectic modernism, with whimsically decorated interiors that are at once trippy and cool. **Pros:** chef Ralph Pagaon's Naked Taco restaurant downstairs; heated rooftop pool; complimentary sparkling wine on arrival. **Cons:** limited natural light in some rooms; lack of bathroom privacy; not on the beach. *$ Rooms from: $209 ✉ 1111 Collins Ave., South Beach ☎ 305/673–4747 🌐 www.dreamhotels.com/southbeach 108 rooms 🍴 No meals.*

Gale South Beach

$$ | **HOTEL** | Though it's not directly on the beach—it's across the street—this boutique hotel offers fabulous, style- and value-conscious accommodations in the heart of South Beach with plenty of art deco history to boot. **Pros:** Regent Cocktail Club downstairs; Pizza Room Service button on guestroom phones; crisp, clean-lined rooms. **Cons:** smaller rooms; busy pool area; crowded hallways. *$ Rooms from: $299 ✉ 1690 Collins Ave., South Beach ☎ 305/673–0199 🌐 www.galehotel.com 87 rooms 🍴 No meals.*

Hilton Bentley Miami/South Beach

$$$ | **HOTEL** | **FAMILY** | Not to be confused with the budget Bentley Hotel down the street, the Hilton Bentley Miami is a contemporary, design-driven, and artsy boutique hotel in the emerging and trendy SoFi (South of Fifth) district, offering families just the right mix of South Beach flavor and wholesome fun while still providing couples a romantic base without any party madness. **Pros:** quiet location; rooms redeemable with points; family-friendly. **Cons:** small pool; small lobby; daily resort charge. *Rooms from: $389 101 Ocean Dr., South Beach 305/938–4600 www.hilton.com 109 rooms No meals.*

The Hotel of South Beach

$$ | **HOTEL** | This value-conscious art deco property inhabits the historic Tiffany building on Collins Avenue as well as a second building along Ocean Drive with interiors by fashion designer Todd Oldham. **Pros:** original terrazzo floors; room service from nearby News Café; rooftop pool deck. **Cons:** in need of a refresh; poor views from many rooms; no full dining restaurant. *Rooms from: $249 801 Collins Ave., South Beach 305/531–2222, www.thehotelofsouthbeach.com 73 rooms No meals.*

Hotel Victor

$$$ | **HOTEL** | At the sleek Hotel Victor, guest rooms are equipped with Yabu Pushelberg–designed interiors invoking a post-century beach cabana vibe, and a sexy infinity-edge pool overlooks Ocean Drive and the beach. **Pros:** late-night pool deck; complimentary bikes; complimentary fruit and water by pool. **Cons:** small rooms; noisy crowds at restaurants downstairs; no dedicated area on beach. *Rooms from: $329 1144 Ocean Dr., South Beach 305/908–1462 www.hotelvictorsouthbeach.com 91 rooms No meals.*

★ Kimpton Angler's Hotel

$$$ | **HOTEL** | This boutique hotel is an enclave of old and new South Beach: a contemporary, 85-room tower with a rooftop swimming pool (opened in summer 2018) neighbors a number of personality-driven villas (built in 1930 by architect Henry Maloney and renovated in 2018) and several modern low-rise units, together capturing the feel of a sophisticated private villa community. **Pros:** gardened private retreat; pet-friendly (no fee); daily complimentary wine hour. **Cons:** no gym; not directly on beach; most units have only showers. *Rooms from: $327 660 Washington Ave., South Beach 305/534–9600 www.anglershotelmiami.com 132 rooms No meals.*

Kimpton Surfcomber Miami, South Beach

$$ | **HOTEL** | As part of the hip Kimpton Hotel group, South Beach's legendary Surfcomber hotel reflects a vintage luxe aesthetic and an ocean-side freshness as well as a reasonable price point that packs the place with a young, sophisticated, yet unpretentious crowd. **Pros:** frozen spiked cappuccino at High Tide Bar; no pet fee; daily complimentary activities offered. **Cons:** small bathrooms; front desk often busy; last renovated in 2012. *Rooms from: $206 1717 Collins Ave., South Beach 305/532–7715 www.surfcomber.com 186 rooms No meals.*

Loews Miami Beach Hotel

$$$$ | **HOTEL** | **FAMILY** | This two-tower megahotel has 790 rooms (all redesigned in 2018 with a soothing, sea-inspired motif), top-tier amenities, a massive spa, a great pool, and direct beachfront access, making it a great choice for families, businesspeople, groups, and pet lovers. **Pros:** excellent on-site seafood restaurant; resort atmosphere; pets welcome. **Cons:** insanely large size; constantly crowded; pets desperate to go will need to wait several minutes to make it to the grass. *Rooms from: $459 1601 Collins Ave., South Beach 305/604–1601, 855/757–2061 for reservations www.*

loewshotels.com/miami-beach 🛏 *790 rooms* 🍽 *No meals.*

Mondrian South Beach

$$ | **HOTEL** | Located along the beach's lesser-known western perimeter and overlooking the bay, this hotel is a living and functioning work of art, an ingenious vision of provocateur Marcel Wanders. **Pros:** great pool scene; perfect sunsets; party vibe. **Cons:** could use a refresh; a short walk from most of the action; no direct beach access. *Rooms from: $299* ✉ *1100 West Ave., South Beach* ☎ *305/514–1500* 🌐 *www.meninhospitality.com/collection/hotels/mondrian-south-beach* 🛏 *335 rooms* 🍽 *No meals.*

National Hotel

$$ | **HOTEL** | The National Hotel is a glorious time capsule that honors its distinct art deco heritage (the building itself and wood pieces in the lobby date back to 1939 and new chocolate- and gold-hued furnishings look period-appropriate) while trying to keep up with SoBe's glossy newcomers (rotating art installations complement the throwback glamour). **Pros:** cabana suites; beautiful night lights around pool area; art deco Blues Bar. **Cons:** street noise on the weekends; gym located downstairs in back of house; no spa. *Rooms from: $255* ✉ *1677 Collins Ave., South Beach* ☎ *305/532–2311* 🌐 *www.nationalhotel.com* 🛏 *152 rooms* 🍽 *No meals.*

Room Mate Lord Balfour

$ | **HOTEL** | In South Beach's SoFi (South of Fifth) neighborhood, the boutique Lord Balfour hotel—part of Spain's Room Mate brand—is a great fit for young travelers who actually desire to go out and experience South Beach (as opposed to sitting at the resort all day) and still want to return to stylish digs. **Pros:** great European crowd; whimsical interior design; affordable pricing. **Cons:** small rooms and smaller bathrooms; occasional street noise from some rooms; no pool. *Rooms from: $175* ✉ *350 Ocean Dr., South Beach* ☎ *855/471–2739* 🌐 *www.room-matehotels.com/en/lordbalfour* 🛏 *64 rooms* 🍽 *No meals.*

★ **Royal Palm South Beach Miami**

$$$ | **RESORT** | The Royal Palm South Beach Miami, now part of Marriott's individualistic Tribute Portfolio, is a daily celebration of art deco, modernity, and design detail. **Pros:** design blending contemporary style with South Beach identity; photogenic pool areas; social lobby. **Cons:** small driveway for entering; older elevators; maintenance issues. *Rooms from: $321* ✉ *1545 Collins Ave., South Beach* ☎ *305/604–5700, 866/716–8147 reservations* 🌐 *www.royalpalmsouthbeach.com* 🛏 *393 rooms* 🍽 *No meals.*

★ **The Setai Miami Beach**

$$$$ | **RESORT** | This opulent, all-suites hotel feels like an Asian museum: serene and beautiful, with heavy granite furniture lifted by orange accents, warm candlelight, and the soft bubble of seemingly endless ponds complemented by three oceanfront infinity pools (heated to different temperatures) that further spill onto the beach's velvety sands. **Pros:** quiet and classy; beautiful grounds; both couple- and family-friendly. **Cons:** TVs are far from the beds; busy pool area; many rooms lack ocean views. *Rooms from: $878* ✉ *2001 Collins Ave., South Beach* ☎ *305/520–6111, 888/625–7500 reservations* 🌐 *www.thesetaihotel.com* 🛏 *130 suites* 🍽 *No meals.*

Shelborne South Beach

$$ | **RESORT** | The iconic Morris Lapidus–designed Shelborne hotel is a retro-chic art deco treasure with stylish yet functional rooms and plenty of oh-so-South Beach amenites, including the beach's most oversized poolside cabanas (which also happen to be air-conditioned); a slick pool deck; a private beach club; and a location that offers direct access to downy sands, art deco, and superlative shopping. **Pros:** Saturday morning meditation classes on the beach; in-house restaurant by Top Chef alums

Jeff McInnis and Janine Booth; Oasis Beer Garden features local brews in a beautiful outdoor space. **Cons:** entry-level rooms small; lack of balconies; some odd large spaces near lobby. *Rooms from: $259 1801 Collins Ave., South Beach 305/704–3668 www.shelborne.com 200 rooms No meals.*

Shore Club

$ | HOTEL | In terms of poolside lounging and people-watching, the Shore Club still ranks high in South Beach; the mod yet minimalist rooms aren't bad either (especially given the reasonable entry-level price point). **Pros:** complimentary beach chairs; multiple bars; direct beach access. **Cons:** old elevators; general wear and tear; thin walls. *Rooms from: $185 1901 Collins Ave., South Beach 305/695–3100 www.morganshotelgroup.com 309 rooms No meals.*

★ SLS South Beach

$$$$ | RESORT | Housed in a restored 1939 art deco building, the SLS Hotel South Beach exudes beachfront sophistication over a commingling of Latin and Asian inspiration in its common areas, which include headlining restaurants Bazaar by José Andrés, Katsuya South Beach, and Hyde Beach—an 8,000-square-foot masterpiece of pool, beach, and cabanas attracting glitterati and hotties daily. **Pros:** great in-house restaurants; masterful design; fun pool scene. **Cons:** some small rooms; no lobby per se; $40 per night resort fee. *Rooms from: $413 1701 Collins Ave., South Beach 305/674–1701 www.slshotels.com/southbeach 140 rooms No meals.*

★ W South Beach

$$$$ | HOTEL | Fun, fresh, and funky, the W South Beach flaunts some of the nicest rooms in South Beach—even the entry category evokes a wow factor—each with its own kitchen and balcony with ocean views. **Pros:** pool scene; giant Hello Kitty fountain; three in-house restaurants and bars. **Cons:** not a classic art deco building; crowded pool area; loud music at pool. *Rooms from: $494 2201 Collins Ave., South Beach 305/938–3000 www.wsouthbeach.com 248 rooms No meals.*

Nightlife

★ Blues Bar

BARS/PUBS | A highlight of any Miami art deco pub crawl is sipping classic cocktails over live music at the nifty wooden Blues Bar, one of many elements original to the iconic, circa 1939 National Hotel. The sights and sounds hark back to an era when you'd expect to watch Ginger Rogers and Fred Astaire dancing across the polished terrazzo floor. *National Hotel, 1677 Collins Ave., South Beach 305/532–2311 www.nationalhotel.com/food/blues.*

Lost Weekend

BARS/PUBS | Play pin ball, pool, or air hockey; chow down on bar grub; and order a few rounds from the full bar (which includes 150 different beer varieties) at this pool hall–resto–dive bar on quaint Española Way. Mingle with an eclectic crowd, from visiting yuppies to local drag queens to celebs on the down-low. It's so South Beach! *218 Española Way, South Beach 305/672–1707 www.sub-culture.org/lost-weekend-miami.*

Mac's Club Deuce Bar

BARS/PUBS | Smoky, dark, and delightfully unpolished, this complete dive bar is anything but what you'd expect from glitzy South Beach. The circa-1964 pool hall attracts a colorful crowd of clubbers, locals, celebs, and just about anyone else. Locals consider it a top spot for an inexpensive drink and cheap thrills. Visitors love it as a true locals' hangout. *222 14th St., at Collins Ave., South Beach 305/531–6200 www.macsclubdeuce.com.*

Nikki Beach Miami Beach

BARS/PUBS | Smack-dab on the beach, the full-service Nikki Beach Club is filled with more suburbanites and tourists

Cars whiz by the Avalon hotel and other art deco architecture on Ocean Drive, Miami South Beach.

than the in crowd but promises plenty of fun nevertheless. The Beach Club is typically a daytime affair, opening at 11 am and closing at 7 pm (though there are often special evening events, namely on Sundays). Visitors can get their food and drink in the tepees, hammocks, and beach beds (expect DJ-led tunes on weekends and rental fees all days). Sunday brunch at the club's restaurant is pretty spectacular with a true South Beach party atmosphere. ✉ *1 Ocean Dr., South Beach* ☎ *305/538–1111* 🌐 *www.nikkibeach.com.*

Onyx Bar

BARS/PUBS | Experience Villa Casa Casuarina, the 1930s-era oceanfront mansion that once belonged to late fashion designer Gianni Versace by grabbing a drink at this six-seat bar, a conversion of Versace's former kitchen. The drinks are as opulent as you'd expect from the locale, with gold-leafed accessories and over-the-top taste sensations. ✉ *1116 Ocean Dr., South Beach* ☎ *786/485–2200* 🌐 *www.vmmiamibeach.com.*

★ **Palace Bar**

BARS/PUBS | South Beach's gay heyday continues at this fierce oceanfront bar where folks gay, straight, and everything in between—everyone's welcome—come to revel in good times, cheap cocktails, and fierce drag performances. On weekdays the bar gets busiest in the early evening, but on weekends it's all about the drag brunch. It's a true showstopper—or car-stopper, shall we say: using Ocean Drive as a stage, drag queens direct oncoming traffic with street-side splits and acrobatic tricks in heels. ✉ *1052 Ocean Dr., South Beach* ☎ *305/531–7234* 🌐 *www.palacesouthbeach.com.*

★ **The Regent Cocktail Club**

BARS/PUBS | This classic cocktail bar exudes elegance and timelessness with strong masculine cocktails, dark furnishings, bartenders dressed to the nines, and the sounds of jazz legends in the background. It's a welcome respite from South Beach's more predictable nightlife scene. Despite some staples, many cocktails—each with bespoke ice cubes and garnishes—change daily and are posted on the house blackboard. ✉ *Gale South Beach, 1690 Collins Ave., South Beach* ☎ *786/975–2555* 🌐 *www.regentcocktailclub.com.*

Rose Bar

BARS/PUBS | Tucked away inside the art deco–imbued Delano South Beach, Rose Bar is a Miami mainstay and consistently delivers some of the beach's best mixology. Embodying Philippe Starck's original, iconic vision and design for the Delano South Beach, the bar features a rose-quartz bar top, velvet wall curtains, and striking chandeliers. ✉ *Delano Hotel, 1685 Collins Ave., South Beach* ☎ *305/674–5752* 🌐 *www.morganshotelgroup.com/delano/delano-south-beach.*

Score

DANCE CLUBS | Since the 1990s, Score has been the see-and-be-seen HQ of Miami's gay community, with plenty of global hotties coming from near and far to show off their designer threads and six-pack abs. DJs spin four nights a week but Planeta Macho Latin Tuesday is exceptionally popular, as is the circuit party–style throw-down every Saturday. Dress to impress (and then be ready to go shirtless and show off your abs). ✉ *1437 Washington Ave., South Beach* ☎ *305/535–1111* 🌐 *www.scorebar.net* ⏲ *Closed Mon. and Wed.*

Sweet Liberty

BARS/PUBS | This tropical-chic, come-as-you-are cocktail lounge and restaurant has won all kinds of national and local awards for its incredible spirit-forward cocktails and fresh-and-funky vibe. For something extra special, reserve the Bartender's Table, which operates like a chef's table, but here you're in the thick of the bar action, tasting libations. ✉ *237-B 20th St., South Beach* ☎ *305/763–8217* 🌐 *www.mysweetliberty.com.*

Twist

DANCE CLUBS | Twist is a gay institution in South Beach, having been the late-night go-to place for decades, filling to capacity around 2 am after the beach's fly-by-night bars and more established lounges begin to die down (though it's open daily from 1 pm to 5 am). There's never a cover here—not even on holidays or during gay-pride events—and there are a whopping seven different bars and dance floors spread over two levels and patios. ✉ *1057 Washington Ave., South Beach* ☎ *305/538–9478* 🌐 *www.twistsobe.com.*

Villa Azur

WINE BARS—NIGHTLIFE | St. Tropez meets South Beach at this sceney, French resto-lounge with prolific alfresco seating in a spacious, tree-lined courtyard and personality-driven relaxation areas indoors (replete with swaying chandeliers, white tufted couches, and whimsically accessorized library shelves). Although Veuve Clicquot is a staple among patrons, the tropical-inspired cocktails and the selection from the in-house wine cellar, La Cave d'Azur, also impress. ✉ *309 23rd St., South Beach* ☎ *305/763–8688* 🌐 *www.villaazurmiami.com.*

Watr at the Rooftop

BARS/PUBS | Come 7 pm Miami Beach's premier rooftop opens to the public as a full-service bar, restaurant, and lounge (before that it is exclusive to guests of the 1 Hotel South Beach). Up in the skies, expect tropically inspired drinks like pineapple and mint caipirinhas overlooking the twinkle of city lights, the sleek rooftop pool, and the lapping waves of the Atlantic Ocean. ✉ *1 Hotel South Beach, 2341 Collins Ave., South Beach* ☎ *305/604–6580* 🌐 *www.1hotels.com/south-beach.*

Shopping

★ Alchemist

CLOTHING | This boutique is synonymous with the pinnacle of design and fashion in the Magic City, so naturally it occupies a cutting-edge, glass-encased studio on the fifth floor of Lincoln Road's trendy Herzog and de Meuron–designed parking garage. The price tags skew high yet represent brands known for innovation and edge (like Adaptation, Es Vedra, Jacquemus, and Matsuda). ✉ *1111 Lincoln Rd., Carpark Level 5, South Beach* ☎ *305/531–4815* 🌐 *www.shopalchemist.com.*

Collins Avenue

SHOPPING NEIGHBORHOODS | Give your plastic a workout in South Beach shopping at the many high-profile tenants on this densely packed stretch of Collins between 5th and 8th streets, with stores like Steve Madden, The Webster, Ralph Lauren, and Intermix. Sprinkled among the upscale vendors are hair salons, spas, cafés, and such familiar stores as Gap and Sephora. ✉ *Collins Ave., South Beach* ✣ *Between 5th and 8th Sts.* 🌐 *www.lincolnroadmall.com/shopping/collins-avenue.*

Dog Bar

GIFTS/SOUVENIRS | Just north of Lincoln Road's main drag, this over-the-top pet boutique caters to enthusiastic animal owners with a variety of unique items for the superpampered pet. From luxurious, vegan "leather" designer dog purse/carriers to bling-bling-studded collars to chic poopy bag holders, Miami's "original pet boutique" carries pretty much every pet accessory imaginable. You'll also find plenty of gourmet food and treats, as well as a wide variety of fancy toys for dogs, large and small. ✉ *1684 Jefferson Ave., South Beach* ☎ *305/532–5654* 🌐 *www.dogbar.com.*

frankie. miami

CLOTHING | Expect high style and eye-catching garments at this boutique. The studiolike setting matches the highly edited collection of fashionista favorites (previous brands have included Beck & Bridge, Sam & Lavi, Iro, For Love & Lemons, and Loeffers). Co-owner Cheryl Herger also designs her own private-label line especially for frankie. miami. Skirts and dresses with interesting silhouettes, uniquely cut tops, and swimwear almost too good for just the pool are interspersed with easy-chic basics. ✉ *1891 Purdy Ave., South Beach* ☎ *786/479–4898* 🌐 *www.frankiemiami.com.*

Jessie

CLOTHING | A massive roster of established and young designer brands makes this one-stop boutique of clothing, swimwear, shoes, and accessories a favorite among those in the know. New daily arrivals draw from the latest celebrity looks and include designs by Alexis, Alice + Olivia, Chaser, Mara Hoffman, Karina Grimaldi, Rag & Bone, and many more. ✉ *1708 Alton Rd., South Beach* ☎ *305/604–7980* 🌐 *www.jessieboutique.com.*

★ Lincoln Road Mall

SHOPPING NEIGHBORHOODS | The eight-block-long pedestrian mall between Alton Road and Washington Avenue is home to more than 100 shops, art galleries, restaurants and cafés, and the renovated Colony Theatre. A see-and-be-seen theme is underscored by outdoor seating at every restaurant, where tourists and locals lounge and discuss the people (and pet) parade passing by. Due to high rents, you are more likely to see big corporate stores like Armani, H&M, and Victoria's Secret than original boutiques. Nevertheless, a few emporiums and stores with unique personalities, like Alchemist and Books & Books, remain, along with a number of top-notch restaurants like Juvia and Chotto Matte. ✉ *Lincoln Rd., South Beach* ✣ *Between Alton Rd. and Washington Ave.* 🌐 *www.lincolnroadmall.com.*

★ Romero Britto Fine Art Gallery

ANTIQUES/COLLECTIBLES | Though exhibited throughout galleries and museums in more than 100 countries, the vibrant, pop art creations by Brazilian artist Romero Britto have become most synonymous with Miami's playful spirit. His flagship gallery showcases original paintings and limited-edition sculptures for sale. Collectibles, fine art prints, and his signature interpretations in collaboration with some of America's most iconic characters and brands, including Disney and Coco-Cola, can be found at the Britto Concept store down the street at 532 Lincoln Road. ✉ *1102 Lincoln Rd., South Beach* ☎ *305/531–8821* 🌐 *www.britto.com.*

★ The Webster South Beach

CLOTHING | Occupying an entire circa-1939 art deco building, The Webster's flagship (and original) location is a tri-level, 20,000-square-foot, one-stop shop for fashionistas. This retail sanctuary carries ready-to-wear fashions by more than 100 top designers, plus in-store exclusive shirts, candles, books, and random trendy items you might need for your South Beach experience—a kind of haute Urban Outfitters for grown-ups. ✉ *1220 Collins Ave., South Beach* ☎ *305/674–7899* 🌐 *www.thewebster.us.*

Activities

Art Deco District Walking Tour

TOUR—SPORTS | **FAMILY** | Operated by the Miami Design Preservation League, this is a 90-minute guided walking tour that departs from the league's welcome center at Ocean Drive and 10th Street. It starts at 10:30 am daily, with an extra tour at 6:30 pm Thursday. Alternatively, you can go at your own pace with the league's self-guided iPod audio tour, which also takes roughly an hour and a half. ✉ *1001 Ocean Dr., South Beach* ☎ *305/763–8026* 🌐 *www.mdpl.org* 🎫 *$25 guided tour, $20 self-guided audio tour.*

★ Miami Beach Bicycle Center

BICYCLING | If you don't want to opt for the hassle of CitiBike or if you want wheels with some style on South Beach, rent a bike from this shop near Ocean Drive. They have all types of two-wheelers, from E-bikes to Carbon Road bikes and Fat Sand bikes, available by the hour, day, or week (and easily booked online). Prices are cheapest for single-speed beach cruisers at $5 per hour, $18 per day, or $80 for the week. All bike rentals include locks, helmets, and baskets. ✉ *746 5th St., South Beach* ☎ *305/674–0150* 🌐 *www.bikemiamibeach.com.*

★ South Beach Dive and Surf

SCUBA DIVING | Dedicated to all things ocean, this PADI five-star dive shop offers multiple diving and snorkeling trips weekly, as well as surfboard, paddleboard, and skateboard sales, rentals, and lessons. From a Discover Scuba course (for noncertified divers) to wreck and reef dives and even shark diving in Jupiter, tours here run the gamut. The dive shop itself is located in the heart of South Beach, but boats depart from marinas in Miami Beach and Key Largo, in the Florida Keys. ✉ *850 Washington Ave., South Beach* ☎ *305/531–6110* 🌐 *www.southbeachdivers.com.*

Mid-Beach

Where does South Beach end and Mid-Beach begin? North of 23rd Street, Collins Avenue curves its way to 44th Street, where it takes a sharp left turn after running into the Soho House Miami and then the Fontainebleau resort. The area between these two points—and up until 63rd Street—is officially Mid-Beach. The area has been experiencing a renaissance since the $1 billion re-debut of the Fontainebleau resort in 2008. Investors have followed suit with other major projects to revive the Mid-Beach area. Most recently, Argentinean developer Alan Faena completed the neighborhood's latest

$1 billion-plus mission: to restore the historic buildings along Collins Avenue from 32nd to 36th streets, creating new hotels, condos, and cultural institutions to collectively become the Miami Beach Faena District. And the results have been nothing short of amazing.

Restaurants

★ Cecconi's Miami Beach

$$$$ | **ITALIAN** | The wait for a table at this outpost of the iconic Italian restaurant is just as long as for its counterparts in West Hollywood and London. Expect heavy portions of atmosphere: It's a real scene of who's who and who's eating what, cast in a seductive, vintage-chic setting across the courtyard of the Soho Beach House Miami. **Known for:** light and succulent fish carpaccios; truffle pizza; beautiful lighting. *Average main: $35* ✉ *Soho Beach House Miami, 4385 Collins Ave., Mid-Beach* ☎ *786/507–7902* 🌐 *www.cecconismiamibeach.com.*

The Forge

$$$$ | **STEAKHOUSE** | Antiques, gilt-framed paintings, a chandelier from the Paris Opera House, and Tiffany stained-glass windows from New York's Trinity Church are the fitting background for some of Miami's best cuts. The tried-and-true menu also includes colossal shrimp cocktail, whole branzino, and the famous chocolate soufflé. **Known for:** expansive enomatic wine system; dramatic interiors; bone-in filet mignon. *Average main: $45* ✉ *432 Arthur Godfrey Rd., Mid-Beach* ☎ *305/538–8533* 🌐 *www.theforge.com* ⏲ *No lunch.*

★ Hakkasan Miami

$$$$ | **CANTONESE** | This stateside sibling of the Michelin-star London restaurant brings the haute-Chinese-food movement to South Florida, adding Pan-Asian flair to even quite simple and authentic Cantonese recipes, and producing an entire menu that can be classified as blow-your-mind delicious. Superb eats notwithstanding, another reason to experience Hakkasan is that it's arguably the sexiest, best-looking restaurant on Miami Beach. **Known for:** dim sum perfected; roasted silver cod with champagne and honey; high-design interiors including teak walls. *Average main: $52* ✉ *Fontainebleau Miami Beach, 4441 Collins Ave., 4th fl., Mid-Beach* ☎ *786/276–1388 after 4 pm, 877/326–7412 before 4 pm* 🌐 *www.hakkasan.com/locations/hakkasan-miami* ⏲ *No lunch weekdays.*

Malibu Farm

$$ | **MODERN AMERICAN** | Organic and locally sourced farm-to-table food is the focus at this airy beachfront restaurant, an outpost of the California location. Note that it's located at Eden Roc Miami Beach, but you don't have to be a hotel guest to enjoy the seafood, pizza, steak, and refreshing cocktails. **Known for:** views of the Atlantic; whole fish; fresh-pressed juices. *Average main: $20* ✉ *4525 Collins Ave., Mid-Beach* ☎ *305/674–5579* 🌐 *www.edenrochotelmiami.com.*

★ Matador

$$$ | **SPANISH** | In one of Miami's most captivating and seductive settings, this headline restaurant by celebrity-chef Jean-Georges Vongerichten fuses Spanish, Caribbean, and Latin American gastronomy while focusing on local products, resulting in a diverse collection of small and large plates. Indulge in tropically inspired plates like avocado pizza, Florida Keys shrimp in "Agua Diablo," and grilled Florida black-grouper tacos. **Known for:** "Light & Bright" beach-conscious options; the epic pineapple elixir cocktail served in a massive copper pineapple; stunning terrace for outdoor dining. *Average main: $29* ✉ *The Miami Beach EDITION, 2901 Collins Ave., Mid-Beach* ☎ *786/257–4600* 🌐 *www.matadorroom.com.*

 Hotels

The stretch of Miami Beach called Mid-Beach is undergoing a renaissance, as formerly run-down hotels are renovated and new hotels and condos are built. Most locals—and visitors—even prefer it to South Beach nowadays.

Circa 39 Hotel
$$ | **HOTEL** | Located in the heart of Mid-Beach, this stylish yet affordable boutique hotel houses 97 tropical-inspired rooms and a swimming pool and sundeck complete with cabanas and umbrella-shaded chaises that invite all-day lounging. **Pros:** lounge areas in the Wunder Garden; beach chairs provided; art deco fireplace. **Cons:** not on the beach side of Collins Avenue; bathrooms have showers only; no spa. *Rooms from: $299 3900 Collins Ave., Mid-Beach 305/538–4900 www.circa39.com 97 rooms No meals.*

★ The Confidante
$$$ | **RESORT** | Part of Hyatt's Unbound Collection, this hotel in Miami's burgeoning Mid-Beach district is a beachfront classic art deco building reinvented by Martin Brudnizki to channel a colorful, modern incarnation of 1950s Florida glamour, packed with all the trappings one would covet in a Miami beachfront experience. **Pros:** highly photogenic pool area; complimentary fitness classes; Hyatt points accepted for stays. **Cons:** day passes sometimes sold to nonguests; entry-level rooms are on the small side; dark hallways. *Rooms from: $369 4041 Collins Ave., Mid-Beach 304/424–1234 www.theconfidantehotel.com 363 rooms No meals.*

Eden Roc Miami Beach
$$$ | **RESORT** | This grand 1950s hotel designed by Morris Lapidus is a lesson in old-school glamour meets modern-day swagger after hundreds of millions in renovations and expansions over the past decade (including the addition of the hotel-within-a-hotel concept Nobu Hotel at Eden Roc). **Pros:** on-site Nobu and Malibu Farm restaurants; great pools; revival of golden age glamour. **Cons:** expensive parking; $35 charge for mini-refrigerator; some small bathrooms. *Rooms from: $330 4525 Collins Ave., Mid-Beach 786/801–6886 www.edenrochotel-miami.com 345 rooms No meals.*

★ Faena Hotel Miami Beach
$$$$ | **RESORT** | Hotelier Alan Faena delivers on the high expectations of his Miami debut with the jaw-dropping, larger-than-life principal hotel within his billion-dollar Faena Arts District in Miami Beach. **Pros:** incredible design; excellent service; spectacular beach club. **Cons:** pricey; construction in neighborhood; dark hallways. *Rooms from: $609 3201 Collins Ave., Mid-Beach 305/535–4697 www.faena.com/miami-beach 169 rooms No meals.*

★ Fontainebleau Miami Beach
$$$$ | **RESORT** | **FAMILY** | Vegas meets art deco at Miami's largest hotel, which has more than 1,500 rooms (in four separate towers, almost half of which are suites), 12 renowned restaurants and lounges, LIV nightclub, several pools with cabana islands, a state-of-the-art fitness center, and a 40,000-square-foot spa. **Pros:** expansive pool and beach areas; historic allure; great nightlife. **Cons:** lots of nonguests visiting grounds; massive size; loud, weekend parties outside. *Rooms from: $449 4441 Collins Ave., Mid-Beach 305/535–3283, 800/548–8886 www.fontainebleau.com 1504 rooms No meals.*

★ The Miami Beach EDITION
$$$$ | **RESORT** | At this reinvention of the 1955 landmark Seville Hotel by hospitality duo Ian Schrager and Marriott, historic glamour parallels modern relaxation from the palm-fringed marble lobby to the beachy guest rooms. **Pros:** excellent spa; hanging gardens in the alfresco area; great beachfront service. **Cons:** a bit pretentious; open bathroom setup in select rooms offers little privacy;

near a particularly rocky part of Miami Beach. 💲 *Rooms from: $559* ✉ *2901 Collins Ave., Mid-Beach* ☎ *786/257–4500* 🌐 *www.editionhotels.com/miami-beach* 🔑 *294 rooms* 🍴 *No meals.*

The Palms Hotel & Spa

$$ | **HOTEL** | If you're seeking a relaxed property away from the noise but close to both Mid-Beach and South Beach nightlife, you'll find an exceptional beach, an easy pace, and beautiful gardens with soaring palm trees and inviting hammocks here, with rooms as fabulous as the grounds. **Pros:** thatched chickee huts; direct beach access; beach yoga. **Cons:** standard rooms do not have balconies (but suites do); room decor a bit tired; not as "cool" as neighboring hotels. 💲 *Rooms from: $296* ✉ *3025 Collins Ave., Mid-Beach* ☎ *305/534–0505, 800/550–0505* 🌐 *www.thepalmshotel.com* 🔑 *251 rooms* 🍴 *No meals.*

Soho Beach House

$$$$ | **HOTEL** | The Soho Beach House is a throwback to swanky vibes of bygone decades, bedazzled in faded color palates, maritime setting, and circa-1930s avant-garde furnishings, luring both somebodies and wannabes to indulge in the amenity-rich, retro-chic rooms as long as they follow stringent house rules (no photos, no mobile phones, no suits, and one guest only). **Pros:** two pools; fabulous restaurant; full spa. **Cons:** members have priority for rooms; lots of pretentious patrons; house rules are a bit much. 💲 *Rooms from: $570* ✉ *4385 Collins Ave., Mid-Beach* ☎ *786/507–7900* 🌐 *www.sohobeachhouse.com* 🔑 *49 rooms* 🍴 *No meals.*

Nightlife

★ Basement Miami

GATHERING PLACES | This DJ-fueled, underground adult playground, below the Miami Beach EDITION hotel, features a micro version of the famed Studio 54, a four-lane bowling alley, and a very small ice skating rink. The 2,000-square-foot rink might be too tiny for Olympic-quality skaters, but it's a priceless visit if only for the memory of how you skated on your Miami Beach vacation. ✉ *The Miami Beach EDITION, 2901 Collins Ave., Mid-Beach* ☎ *786/257–4600* 🌐 *www.basementmiami.com.*

★ The Broken Shaker

BARS/PUBS | Popular with the cool crowd, this indoor-outdoor craft cocktail joint lures in droves to revel in creative mixology and fabulous people-watching. Everything here is perfectly Instagrammable, from the daring and beautifully presented drinks to the vintage-chic surrounds. It's no wonder the venue has been awarded national titles such as America's Best Bar. ✉ *Freehand Miami, 2727 Indian Creek Dr., Mid-Beach* ☎ *305/531–2727* 🌐 *www.freehandhotels.com/miami/broken-shaker.*

★ LIV

DANCE CLUBS | It's not hard to see why LIV often makes lists of the world's best clubs—if you can get in, that is (LIV is notorious for lengthy lines, so don't arrive fashionably late). Past the velvet ropes, the dance palladium impresses with its lavish decor, well-dressed international crowd, sensational light-and-sound system, and seductive bi-level club experience. **■ TIP→ Men beware: groups of guys entering LIV are often coerced into insanely priced bottle service.** ✉ *Fontainebleau Miami Beach, 4441 Collins Ave., Mid-Beach* ☎ *305/674–4680 for table reservations* 🌐 *www.livnightclub.com.*

Fisher and Belle Islands

A private island community near the southern tip of South Beach, Fisher Island is accessible only by the island's ferry service. The island is predominantly residential with a few hotel rooms on offer at Fisher Island Club Hotel and Resort. Belle Island is a small island connected to both the mainland and Miami Beach by road. It is a mile north of South Beach and just west over the Venetian Causeway.

Hotels

Fisher Island Hotel and Resort
$$$$ | **RESORT** | An exclusive private island, just south of Miami Beach but accessible only by ferry, Fisher Island houses an upscale residential community that includes a small inventory of overnight accommodations, including opulent cottages, villas, and junior suites, which surround the island's original 1920s-era Vanderbilt mansion. **Pros:** great private beaches; never crowded; varied on-island dining choices. **Cons:** not the warmest fellow guests; pretentious people; limited cell phone service. *Rooms from: $1,300* *1 Fisher Island Dr., Fisher Island* *305/535–6000* *www.fisherislandclub.com* *60 rooms* *No meals.*

The Standard Spa, Miami Beach
$$ | **RESORT** | An extension of André Balazs's trendy and hip—yet budget-conscious—brand, this shabby-chic boutique spa hotel is a mile from South Beach on an island just over the Venetian Causeway and boasts one of South Florida's most renowned spas, trendiest bars, and hottest pool scenes. **Pros:** free bike and kayak rentals; swank pool scene; great spa. **Cons:** slight trek to South Beach; small rooms with no views; nonguests visiting property spa and restaurants. *Rooms from: $224* *40 Island Ave., Belle Isle* *305/673–1717* *www.standardhotels.com/miami/properties/miami-beach* *105 rooms* *No meals.*

Nightlife

The Lido Bayside Grill
BARS/PUBS | By day, the colorful and chic waterfront alfresco restaurant is an idyllic place to kick back, sip cocktails, and watch bay-side boats and poolside hotties go by. In the evening, lights braided into the surrounding trees illuminate the terrace, sparking a seductive atmosphere. On weekdays from 4 to 7, the bar offers a locals-frequented happy hour. *The Standard Spa, Miami Beach, 40 Island Ave., Belle Isle* *786/245–0880* *www.standardhotels.com.*

North Beach

Though often referred to collectively as North Beach, there are several neighborhoods above Mid-Beach before reaching the Dade-Broward border. In Miami Beach proper, nearing the 63rd Street mark on Collins Avenue, Mid-Beach gives way to what is officially North Beach (until 87th Street), followed by Surfside (up until 95th Street).

Hotels

★ Carillon Miami Wellness Resort
$$$$ | **RESORT** | Formerly Canyon Ranch Miami, the Carillon Miami Wellness Resort carries the art deco building's original name but the physical and mental well-being motif of its predecessor—a 150-all-suites beachfront hotel, defined by a 70,000-square-foot wellness spa, including a rock-climbing wall, 54 treatment rooms, and 30 exercise classes daily. **Pros:** directly on the beach; spacious suites (minimum 720 square feet); incredible spa treatments. **Cons:** far from nightlife; rooms could be a bit more stylish; day visitors at spa and gym. *Rooms from: $495* *6801 Collins Ave., North Beach* *866/800–3858* *www.carillonhotel.com* *150 suites* *No meals.*

Bal Harbour

At 96th Street the town of Bal Harbour takes over Collins Avenue from Miami Beach. Bal Harbour is famous for its outdoor high-end shops, and if you take your shopping seriously, you may want to spend some considerable time in this area. The town runs a mere 10 blocks to the north before the bridge to another barrier island. After crossing the bridge, you'll first come to Haulover Beach Park, which is still technically in the village of Bal Harbour.

★ Haulover Beach Park

BEACH—SIGHT | This popular clothing-optional beach is embraced by naturists of all ages, shapes, and sizes; there are even sections primarily frequented by families, singles, and gays. Nevertheless, Haulover has more claims to fame than its casual attitude toward swimwear—it's also the best beach in the area for bodyboarding and surfing, as it gets what passes for impressive swells in these parts. Once you park in the North Lot, you'll walk through a short tunnel covered with trees and natural habitat until you emerge on the unpretentious beach, where nudity is rarely met by gawkers. There are volleyball nets, and plenty of beach chair and umbrella rentals to protect your birthday suit from too much exposure—to the sun, that is. The sections of beach requiring swimwear are popular, too, given the park's ample parking and relaxed atmosphere. Lifeguards stand watch. More-active types might want to check out the kite rentals, or charter-fishing excursions. **Amenities:** food and drink; lifeguards; parking (fee); showers; toilets. **Best for:** nudists; surfing; swimming; walking. ✉ *10800 Collins Ave., North Beach* ✥ *North of Bal Harbour* ☎ *305/947–3525* 🌐 *www.miamidade.gov/parks/haulover.asp* *Parking $5 per vehicle weekdays, $7 weekends.*

Carpaccio Restaurant

$$$$ | **MODERN ITALIAN** | As expected for its ritzy location, this upscale restaurant matches its high-fashion neighbors: waiters don bow ties and coattails, even for lunch hours, yet are approachable in their knowledge and attentiveness. Practically everything on the menu jumps out, though the handmade mozzarella antipasti, clam linguine, and namesake beef carpaccio are signature dishes, and an extensive list of wines from Italy, California, and other worldly regions perfectly complements a meal here. **Known for:** myriad carpaccios; ladies who lunch; well-heeled crowd. *Average main: $31* ✉ *Bal Harbour Shops, 9700 Collins Ave., Bal Harbour* ☎ *305/867–7777* 🌐 *www.carpaccioatbalharbour.com.*

Le Zoo

$$$$ | **FRENCH** | Restaurateur Stephen Starr imports a bona fide Parisian brasserie to the swanky Bal Harbour shops—inclusive of vintage decorations, furnishings, and an entire bar, all of which were shipped directly from France. Expect classics perfected, such as onion soup gratiné, steak frites and moules frites, and seafood *plateaux* (towers); a few delicious deviations like the escargots in hazelnut butter (rather than garlic butter); and plenty of excellent people-watching. **Known for:** Parisian flair; seafood towers; outdoor seating. *Average main: $42* ✉ *Bal Harbour Shops, 9700 Collins Ave., No. 135, North Beach* ☎ *305/602–9663* 🌐 *www.lezoo.com.*

★ Makoto

$$$$ | **JAPANESE** | Stephen Starr's Japanese headliner, executed by celebrity-chef and master of Edomae-style sushi Makoto Okuwa, offers two menus: one devoted solely to sushi, sashimi, and maki, the other to Japanese cold and hot dishes. Look forward to hyperfresh raw dishes, tempuras, meats, and vegetables grilled over Japanese charcoal (*robata*), rice and noodle dishes, and a variety of steaks and fish inspired by the Land of the Rising Sun. **Known for:** superfresh sushi; artistic presentation; well-dressed crowd. *Average main: $34* ✉ *Bal*

Harbour Shops, 9700 Collins Ave., Bal Harbour ☎ *305/864–8600* 🌐 *www.mako-to-restaurant.com.*

Hotels

The Ritz-Carlton Bal Harbour, Miami
$$$$ | RESORT | FAMILY | In one of South Florida's poshest neighborhoods, this property exudes contemporary beachfront luxury design with decadent mahogany-floor guest rooms featuring large terraces with panoramic views of the water and city, over-the-top bathrooms with 10-foot floor-to-ceiling windows, and LCD TVs built into the bathroom mirrors. **Pros:** proximity to Bal Harbour Shops; bathroom's soaking tubs have ocean views; great contemporary-art collection. **Cons:** narrow beach is a bit disappointing; quiet area; small lobby. $ *Rooms from: $518* ✉ *10295 Collins Ave., Bal Harbour* ☎ *305/455–5400* 🌐 *www.ritzcarlton.com/en/hotels/miami/bal-harbour* *187 rooms* *No meals.*

★ The St. Regis Bal Harbour Resort
$$$$ | RESORT | This posh resort (which cost over $1 billion to build) embodies the next level of ultraglamour and haute living along Miami's North Beach. **Pros:** beachfront setting; Sunday rosé brunch; large apartment-sized rooms. **Cons:** limited lounge space around main pool; limited privacy on balconies; high price tag. $ *Rooms from: $1,029* ✉ *9703 Collins Ave., Bal Harbour* ☎ *305/993–3300* 🌐 *www.stregisbalharbour.com* *216 rooms* *No meals.*

Shopping

★ Bal Harbour Shops
SHOPPING CENTERS/MALLS | Beverly Hills meets the South Florida sun at this swank collection of 100 high-end shops, boutiques, and department stores, which currently holds the title as the country's greatest revenue-earner per square foot. The open-air enclave includes Florida's largest Saks Fifth Avenue; an 8,100-square-foot, two-story flagship Salvatore Ferragamo store; and stores by Alexander McQueen, Valentino, and local juggernaut The Webster. Restaurants and cafés, in tropical garden settings, overflow with style-conscious diners. A $400 million expansion is currently under way to add 340,387 square feet of retail, including a Barneys New York flagship store and a Freds at Barneys restaurant. ✉ *9700 Collins Ave., Bal Harbour* ☎ *305/866–0311* 🌐 *www.balharbourshops.com.*

100% Capri
CLOTHING | This shop is one of only two stores by this Italian brand in the United States (the other is in Palm Beach). The collection is all pure linen (including the shopping bags). Designer Antonio Aiello sources and produces all pieces in Capri for an exciting interpretation that takes its wearers to exotic beach locales style-wise—and quite literally, given its clientele. You'll find clothing for women, men, and children, and even home goods with curated glass accessories brought over from Italy. ✉ *Bal Harbour Shops, 9700 Collins Ave., No. 236, Bal Harbour* ☎ *305/866–4117* 🌐 *www.100capri.com/en.*

★ The Webster Bal Harbour
CLOTHING | Complementing its sister store in South Beach, The Webster Bal Harbour houses high-level fashions aplenty for both men and women. Nearly every great contemporary luxury designer is represented (Chanel, Céline, Valentino, Givenchy, Proenza Schouler, Stella McCartney, etc.) as well as emerging runway darlings. Fashionably impatient? The store can snag ready-to-wear pieces from the latest shows. It also carries exclusive pieces, a real feat considering its influential mall neighbors, including a continuous flow of capsule collections in collaboration with the likes of Calvin Klein, Marc Jacobs, and Anthony Vaccarello, to name a few. ✉ *Bal Habour Shops, 9700 Collins Ave., No. 204,*

Bal Harbour ☎ 305/868–6544 🌐 www.thewebster.us/stores/bal-harbour.

Sunny Isles Beach

Beyond Haulover Beach (and on the same barrier island) is the town of Sunny Isles Beach. Once over the bridge, Collins Avenue bypasses several dozen street numbers, picking up again in the 150s; that's when you know you've arrived in the town of Sunny Isles Beach—an appealing, calm, and predominantly upscale choice for families looking for a beautiful beach, and where Russian may be heard as often as English. There's no nightlife to speak of in Sunny Isles, and yet the half-dozen mega-luxurious skyscraper hotels that have sprung up here in the past decade have created a niche-resort town from the demolished ashes of much older, affordable hotels.

Restaurants

AQ Chop House by Il Mulino

$$$$ | MODERN ITALIAN | This romantic Italian steak house commingles premium steaks and seafood with classic Italian favorites (and offers an excellent sushi menu, to boot). Consider starting with the grilled octopus, followed by the short rib ravioli, and then a buttery, 12-ounce filet mignon and washing it all down with artisanal cocktails like the AQ Smoked Negroni or the Black Cherry Old Fashioned. **Known for:** tequila-infused Spicy Passion cocktail; chophouse meatball appetizer; Caesar salad. *$ Average main: $41 ✉ Acqualina Resort & Spa on the Beach, 17875 Collins Ave., Sunny Isles Beach ☎ 305/466–9191 🌐 www.acqualinaresort.com/dining/aq-chop-house.*

Il Mulino New York—Sunny Isles Beach

$$$$ | ITALIAN | For decades Il Mulino New York has ranked among the top Italian restaurants in Gotham, so it's no surprise that this Miami outpost is similarly good. Start your food coma with the complimentary starters—fresh cuts of Parmesan cheese, four types of fresh bread, garlicky bruschetta, and spicy, fried zucchini whet the palate—and then move on to antipasti like calamari fritti followed by ever-changing risottos and other classic Italian dishes perfected. **Known for:** seafood risotto; excellent service; intimate setting. *$ Average main: $45 ✉ Acqualina Resort & Spa on the Beach, 17875 Collins Ave., Sunny Isles Beach ☎ 305/466–9191 🌐 www.ilmulino.com/miami.*

Hotels

★ Acqualina Resort & Spa on the Beach

$$$$ | RESORT | FAMILY | The grand dame of Sunny Isles Beach continues to raise the bar for Miami beachfront luxury, delivering a fantasy of modern Mediterranean opulence, with sumptuously appointed, striking gray- and silver-accented interiors and expansive facilities. **Pros:** excellent beach; in-room check-in; huge spa. **Cons:** no nightlife near hotel; hotel's towering height shades the beach by early afternoon; construction next door. *$ Rooms from: $846 ✉ 17875 Collins Ave., Sunny Isles Beach ☎ 305/918–8000 🌐 www.acqualinaresort.com 🛏 98 rooms 🍽 No meals.*

North Miami Beach

Don't let the name fool you. North Miami Beach actually isn't on the beach, but its southeastern end does abut Biscayne Bay. Beyond the popular Oleta River State Park on the bay, the city offers little in terms of touristic appeal.

Beaches

Oleta River State Park

BEACH—SIGHT | FAMILY | Tucked away in North Miami Beach, this urban park is a ready-made family getaway. Nature lovers will find it easy to embrace the 1,128 acres of subtropical beauty along Biscayne Bay. Swim in the calm bay waters and bicycle, canoe, kayak, and bask among egrets, manatees, bald eagles, and fiddler crabs. Dozens of picnic tables, along with 10 covered pavilions, dot the stunning natural habitat, which was restored with red mangroves to revitalize the ecosystem and draw endangered birds, like the roseate spoonbill. There's a playground for tots, a mangrove island accessible only by boat, 15 miles of mountain-bike trails, a half-mile exercise track, concessions, and outdoor showers. **Amenities:** food and drink; parking (fee); showers; toilets; water sports. **Best for:** solitude; sunrise; sunset; walking. ✉ *3400 N.E. 163rd St., North Miami Beach* ☎ *305/919–1844* 🌐 *www.floridastateparks.org/park/Oleta-River* 🎫 *$6 per vehicle; $2 per pedestrian.*

North Miami

This suburban city, north of Miami proper, is comprised predominantly of older homes in its western reaches—many derelict—but also some snazzy rebuilds in the sections around Biscayne Bay and U.S. 1. Several strip malls and restaurants line U.S. 1.

Aventura

West of Sunny Isles Beach and on the mainland are the high-rises of Aventura. This city is the heart and soul of South Florida's Jewish community as well as Miami's growing Russian community (along with Sunny Isles Beach). It is known for its high-end shopping opportunities, from the mega Aventura Mall to smaller boutiques in eclectic strip malls.

Restaurants

Bourbon Steak

$$$$ | **STEAKHOUSE** | Michael Mina's longstanding South Florida steak house is renowned for its seductive design, sophisticated clientele, outstanding wine list, phenomenal service, and, of course, exceptional food. Dinner begins with a skillet of fresh potato focaccia and flavor-dusted french fries as preludes to entrées like the Maine lobster potpie (with truffle cream) and any of the dozen varieties of butter-poached, wood-grilled steaks (from hormone-free prime cuts to American Wagyu). **Known for:** duck-fat fries with dipping sauces; perfectly cooked steaks; floor-to-ceiling glass wine cellar. $ *Average main: $65* ✉ *JW Marriott Miami Turnberry Resort & Spa, 19999 W. Country Club Dr., Aventura* ☎ *786/279–6600* 🌐 *www.michaelmina.net.*

Novecento Aventura

$$$ | **MODERN ARGENTINE** | **FAMILY** | At this lively Argentine bistro, empanadas, *picadas* (sharing platters of small bites), sizzling steaks (including a grilled beef tenderloin in a Malbec demi-glace), and homemade pastas (a nod to Argentina's Italian heritage) headline the menu. The dim lighting, seductive atmosphere, and early-19th-century black-and-white imagery recall a bona fide Buenos Aires bistro, helping patrons forget that they are, in fact, in suburban Aventura. **Known for:** homemade empanadas; great wine list; simply grilled meats from the parilla. $ *Average main: $24* ✉ *Town Center Aventura, 18831 N. Biscayne Blvd., Aventura* ☎ *305/466–0900* 🌐 *www.novecento.com.*

JW Marriott Turnberry Miami Resort and Spa

$$$$ | RESORT | FAMILY | After a head-to-toe makeover and expansion throughout 2018, golfers and families are once again flocking to this 300-acre tropical resort, now flaunting 625 jumbo-size rooms and suites (including 325 in the new 16-story Orchid Tower) and even more world-class amenities, including 36 holes of championship golf, prolific tennis courts, an on-site waterpark, the three-story âme Spa & Wellness Collective, and two renowned restaurants—Michael Mina's Bourbon Steak and Corsair restaurant. **Pros:** completely reimagined in 2018; free shuttle to Aventura Mall; situated between Miami and Fort Lauderdale. **Cons:** not on the beach; in residential area; $37 per day resort fee. *Rooms from: $529* *19999 W. Country Club Dr., Aventura* *305/932–6200* *www.jwturnberry.com* *625 rooms* *No meals.*

★ Aventura Mall

SHOPPING CENTERS/MALLS | This three-story megamall offers the ultimate in South Florida retail therapy and houses many global top performers including the most lucrative outposts of several U.S. chain stores, a supersize Nordstrom and Bloomingdale's, and 300 other shops like a two-story flagship Louis Vuitton, Façonnable, and Fendi, which together create the third-largest mall in the United States. Consider it a one-stop, shop-'til-you-drop retail mecca for locals, out-of-towners, and—frequently—celebrities. *19501 Biscayne Blvd., Aventura* *305/935–1110* *www.aventuramall.com.*

Miami Dolphins

FOOTBALL | The Miami Dolphins have one of the largest average attendance figures in the NFL. Come see the team that completed the NFL's only perfect season (circa 1972), ending in a Super Bowl win of Super Bowl VII. They also then won Super Bowl VIII. Home games are September through January at Hard Rock Stadium, which was upgraded to the tune of $350 million between 2015 and 2016 to become a more modern stadium. *Hard Rock Stadium, 2269 N.W. 199 St., Miami Gardens* *888/346–7849* *www.miamidolphins.com.*

Chapter 4

THE EVERGLADES

Updated by
Galena Mosovich

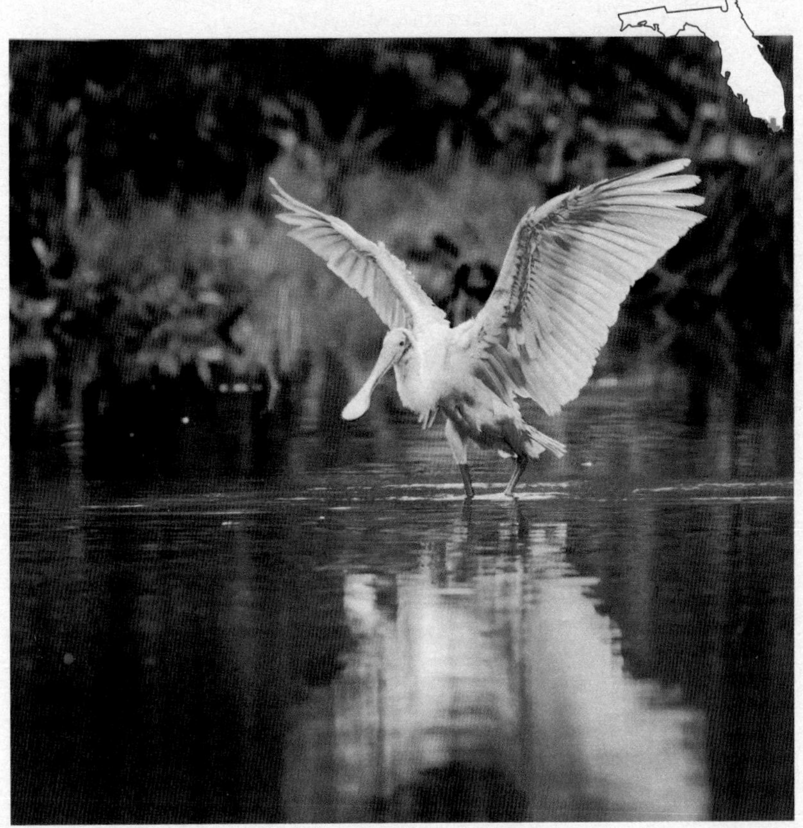

Sights	Restaurants	Hotels	Shopping	Nightlife
★★★★★	★★☆☆☆	★★☆☆☆	★☆☆☆☆	★☆☆☆☆

WELCOME TO THE EVERGLADES

TOP REASONS TO GO

★ **Serious fishing:** Cast for some of the world's most aggressive game fish—600 species in all—in the Everglades' backwaters.

★ **Abundant birdlife:** Check hundreds of birds off your list, including—if you're lucky—the rare Everglades snail kite.

★ **Cool kayaking:** Do a half-day trip in Big Cypress National Preserve, or grab a paddle for the ultimate 99-mile Wilderness Waterway.

★ **Swamp cuisine:** Want to chow down on alligator tail or frogs' legs? Or how about swamp cabbage, made from hearts of palm? Better yet, try stone crabs fresh from the traps.

★ **Gator spotting:** This is ground zero for alligator viewing in the United States, and odds are you'll leave having spotted your quota.

The southern third of the Florida peninsula is largely taken up by protected government land that includes Everglades National Park, Big Cypress National Preserve, and Biscayne National Park. Miami sits to the northeast, with Naples and Marco Island to the northwest. Land access to Everglades National Park is primarily by two roads. The park's main road traverses the southern Everglades from the gateway towns of Homestead and Florida City to the outpost of Flamingo on Florida Bay. To the north, Tamiami Trail (U.S. 41) cuts through the Everglades from Greater Miami on the east coast or from Naples on the west coast to the western park entrance near Everglades City at Route 29.

Gulf of Mexico

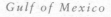

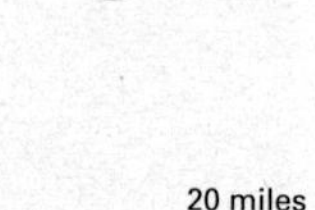

1 Everglades National Park. Alligators, Florida panthers, black bears, manatees, dolphins, bald eagles, and roseate spoonbills call this vast habitat home.

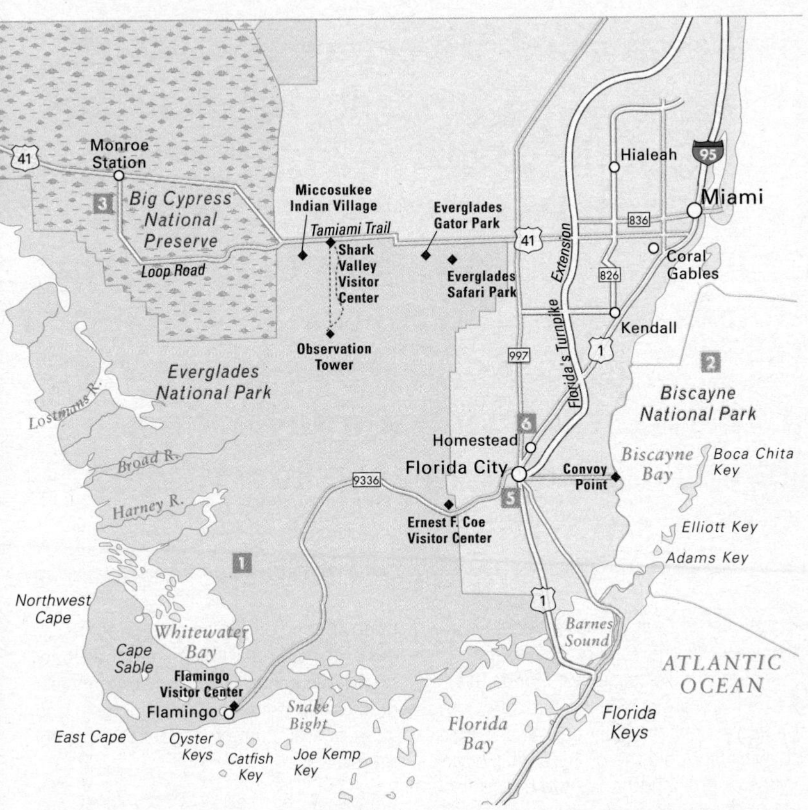

2 Biscayne National Park. Mostly underwater, this is where the string of coral reefs and islands that form the Florida Keys starts.

3 Big Cypress National Preserve. Neighbor to Everglades National Park, it's an outdoor lover's paradise.

4 Everglades City. In this small swamp town, the Ten Thousand Islands and fresh seafood await.

5 Florida City. The last suburb of Miami before reaching the Florida Keys, Florida City is home to Everglades National Park.

6 Homestead. A historic district is surrounded by a mix of modern living and farmland, including an exotic-fruit winery.

7 Tamiami Trail. This 100-year-old road is the path to Old Florida's wildest areas.

More than 1.5 million acres of South Florida's 4.3 million acres of subtropical, watery wilderness were given national park status and protection in 1947 with the creation of Everglades National Park. It's one of the country's largest national parks and is recognized by the world community as a Wetland of International Importance, an International Biosphere Reserve, and a World Heritage site. Visit if you want to spend the day biking, hiking, or boating in deep, raw wilderness with lots of wildlife.

To the east of Everglades National Park, Biscayne National Park brings forth a pristine and magical side of Florida. It's the nation's largest marine park and the largest national park boasting living coral reefs within the continental United States. A small portion of the park's 172,000 acres includes mainland coast and outlying islands, but 95 percent remains submerged. Of particular interest are the mangroves and their tangled masses of stiltlike roots that thicken shorelines. These "walking trees," as some locals call them, have curved prop roots arching down from trunks and aerial roots that drop from branches. The roots of these trees filter salt from water and create a coastal nursery that sustains marine life. You can see Miami's high-rise buildings from many of Biscayne's 44 islands, but the park is virtually undeveloped and large enough for escaping everything that Miami and the Upper Keys have become. To truly disconnect, grab scuba-diving or snorkeling gear and lose yourself in the wonders of the coral reefs.

On the northern edge of Everglades National Park lies Big Cypress National Preserve, one of South Florida's least developed watersheds. Established by Congress in 1974 to protect the Everglades, it comprises extensive tracts of prairie, marsh, pinelands, forested swamps and sloughs. Hunting is allowed, as is off-roading. Stop at the Oasis Visitor Center's boardwalk to see the alligators lounging underneath, and then drive Loop Road for a backwoods experience. If time and desire for watery adventure permit, kayak or canoe the Turner River.

Surrounding the parks and preserve are communities where you'll find useful outfitters: Everglades City, Florida City, and Homestead.

Planning

When to Go

Winter is the best, and busiest, time to visit the Everglades. Temperatures and mosquito activity are more tolerable, while low water levels concentrate the resident wildlife, and migratory birds settle in for the season. In late spring the weather turns hot and rainy, and tours and facilities are less crowded. Migratory birds depart, and you must look harder to see wildlife. Summer brings intense sun and afternoon rainstorms. Water levels rise and mosquitoes abound, making outdoor activity virtually unbearable, unless you protect yourself with netting. (Insect repellent is a necessity any time of year.)

Getting Here and Around

Miami International Airport (MIA) is 34 miles from Homestead and 47 miles from the eastern access to Everglades National Park. ⇨ *For MIA airline information, see the Travel Smart chapter.* Shuttles run between MIA and Homestead. Southwest Florida International Airport (RSW), in Fort Myers, a little over an hour's drive from Everglades City, is the closest major airport to the Everglades' western entrance.

Hotels

Accommodations near the parks range from inexpensive to moderate and offer off-season rates in summer, when rampant mosquito populations discourage spending time outdoors, especially at dusk. If you're devoting several days to exploring the east side of the Everglades, stay in park campgrounds; reasonably priced chain motels and RV parks about 11 miles away in Homestead and Florida City; in the Florida Keys; or in the Greater Miami–Fort Lauderdale area. Lodging and campgrounds are plentiful on the Gulf Coast (in Everglades City, Marco Island and Naples; the latter features upscale accommodations).

Restaurants

Dining in the Everglades area is dominated by mom-and-pop spots serving hearty home-style food, and small eateries specializing in fresh local fare such as alligator, fish, stone crab, frogs' legs, and Florida lobster. Native American–inspired restaurants serve these local favorites as well as catfish, Indian fry bread (a flour-and-water flatbread), and pumpkin bread. A flourishing Hispanic population around Homestead means authentic and inexpensive Latin cuisine, with an emphasis on Cuban and Mexican dishes. Restaurants in Everglades City, especially those along the river, specialize in fresh (often just hours out of the water) seafood including particularly succulent, sustainable stone crab. These mostly rustic places are ultracasual and often closed from late summer to fall. For finer dining, head for Marco Island or Naples.

Hotel and restaurant reviews have been shortened. For full information, visit Fodors.com.

What It Costs

$	$$	$$$	$$$$
RESTAURANTS			
under $15	$15–$20	$21–$30	over $30
HOTELS			
under $200	$200–$300	$301–$400	over $400

Continued on page 137

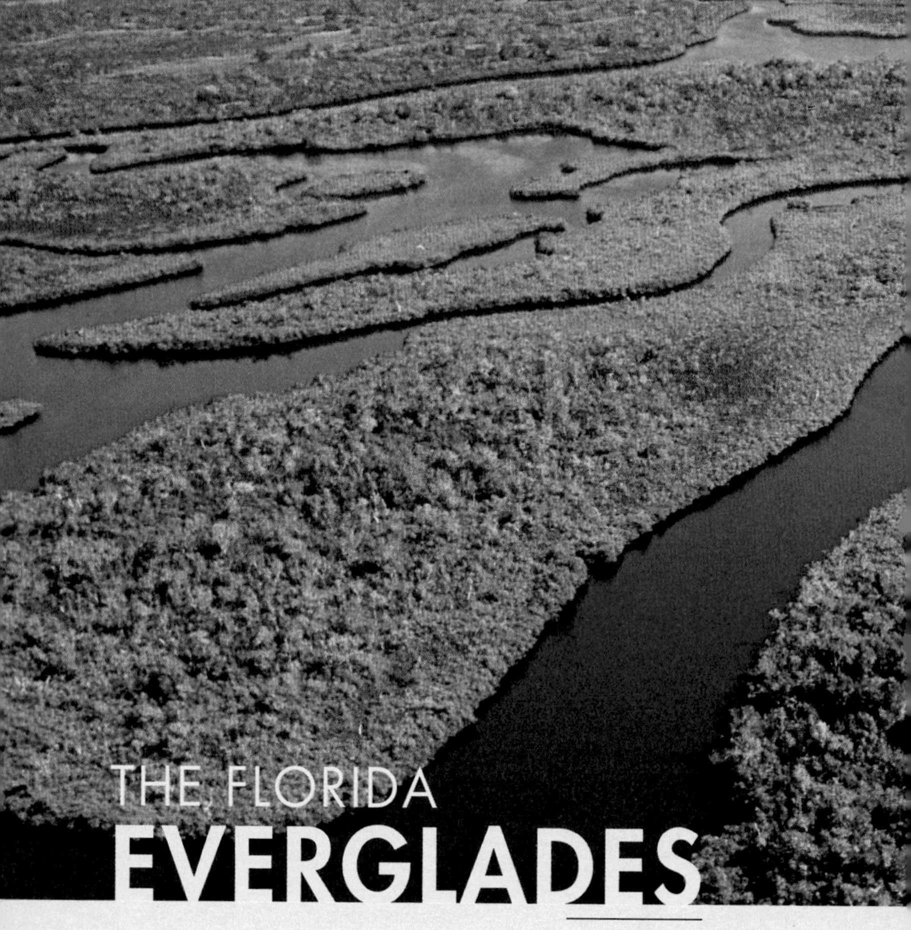

THE FLORIDA EVERGLADES

by Lynne Helm

Alternately described as elixir of life or swampland muck, the Florida Everglades is one of a kind—a 50-mi-wide "river of grass" that spreads across hundreds of thousands of acres. It moves at varying speeds depending on rainfall and other variables, sloping south from the Kissimmee River and Lake Okeechobee to estuaries of Biscayne Bay, Florida Bay, and the Ten Thousand Islands.

Today, apart from sheltering some 70 species on America's endangered list, the Everglades also embraces more than 7 million residents, 50 million annual tourists, 400,000 acres of sugarcane, and the world's largest concentration of golf courses.

Demands on the land threaten the Everglades' finely balanced ecosystem. Irrigation canals for agriculture and roadways disrupt natural water flow. Drainage for development leaves wildlife scurrying for new territory. Water runoff, laced with fertilizers, promotes unnatural growth of swamp vegetation. What remains is a miracle of sorts, given decades of these destructive forces.

Creation of the Everglades required unique conditions. South Florida's geology, linked with its warm, wet subtropical climate, is the perfect mix for a marshland ecosystem. Layers of porous, permeable limestone create water-bearing rock, soil, and aquifers, which in turn affects climate, weather, and hydrology.

This rock beneath the Everglades reflects Florida's geologic history—its crust was once part of the African region. Some scientists theorize that continental shifting merged North America with Africa, and then continental rifting later pulled North America away from the African continent but took part of northwest Africa with it—the part that is today's Florida. The Earth's tectonic plates continued to migrate, eventually placing Florida at its current location as a land mass jutting out into the ocean, with the Everglades at its tip.

EXPERIENCING THE ECOSYSTEMS

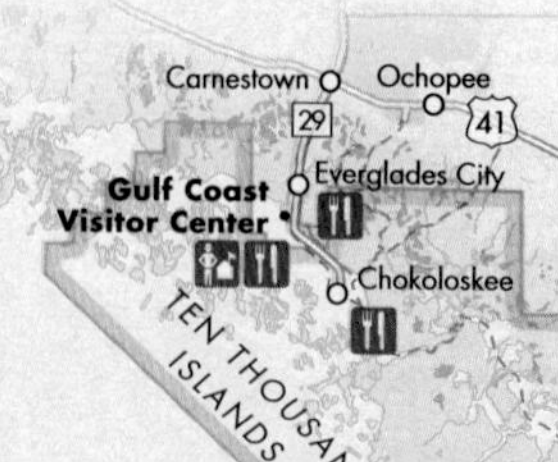

Eight distinct habitats exist within Everglades National Park, Big Cypress National Preserve, and Biscayne National Park.

ECOSYSTEMS	EASY WAY	MORE ACTIVE WAY
COASTAL PRAIRIE: An arid region of salt-tolerant vegetation lies between the tidal mud flats of Florida Bay and dry land. **Best place to see it: The Coastal Prairie Trail**	Take a guided boat tour of Florida Bay, leaving from Flamingo Marina.	Hike the Coastal Prairie Trail from Eco Pond to Clubhouse Beach.
CYPRESS: Capable of surviving in standing water, cypress trees often form dense clusters called "cypress domes" in natural water-filled depressions. **Best place to see it: Big Cypress National Preserve**	Drive U.S. 41 (also known as Tamiami Trail—pronounced Tammy-Amee), which cuts across Southern Florida, from Naples to Miami.	Hike (or drive) the scenic Loop Road, which begins off Tamiami Trail, running from the Loop Road Education Center to Monroe Station.
FRESH WATER MARL PRAIRIE: Bordering deeper sloughs are large prairies with marl (clay and calcium carbonate) sediments on limestone. Gators like to use their toothy snouts to dig holes in prairie mud. **Best place to see it: Pahayokee Overlook**	Drive there from the Ernest F. Coe Visitor Center.	Take a guided tour, either through the park service or from permitted, licensed guides. You also can set up camp at Long Pine Key.
FRESH WATER SLOUGH AND HARDWOOD HAMMOCK: Shark River Slough and Taylor Slough are the Everglades' two sloughs, or marshy rivers. Due to slight elevation amid sloughs, dense stands of hardwood trees appear as teardrop-shaped islands. **Best place to see it: The Observation Tower**	Take a two-hour guided tram tour from the Shark Valley Visitor Center to the tower and back.	Walk or bike (rentals available) the route to the tower via the tram road and (walkers only) Bobcat Boardwalk trail and Otter Cave Hammock Trail.
MANGROVE: Spread over South Florida's coastal channels and waterways, mangrove thrives where Everglades fresh water mixes with salt water. **Best place to see it: The Wilderness Waterway**	Picnic at the area near Long Pine Key, which is surrounded by mangrove, or take a water tour at Biscayne National Park.	Boat your way along the 99-mi Wilderness Waterway. It's six hours by motorized boat, seven days by canoe.
MARINE AND ESTUARINE: Corals, sponges, mollusks, seagrass, and algae thrive in the Florida Bay, where the fresh waters of the Everglades meet the salty seas. **Best place to see it: Florida Bay**	Take a boat tour from the Flamingo Visitor Center marina.	Canoe or kayak on White Water Bay along the Wilderness Waterway Canoe Trail.
PINELAND: A dominant plant in dry, rugged terrain, the Everglades' diverse pinelands consist of slash pine forest, saw palmettos, and more than 200 tropical plant varieties. **Best place to see it: Long Pine Key trails**	Drive to Long Pine Key, about 6 mi off the main road from Ernest F. Coe Visitor Center.	Hike or bike the 28 mi of Long Pine Key trails.

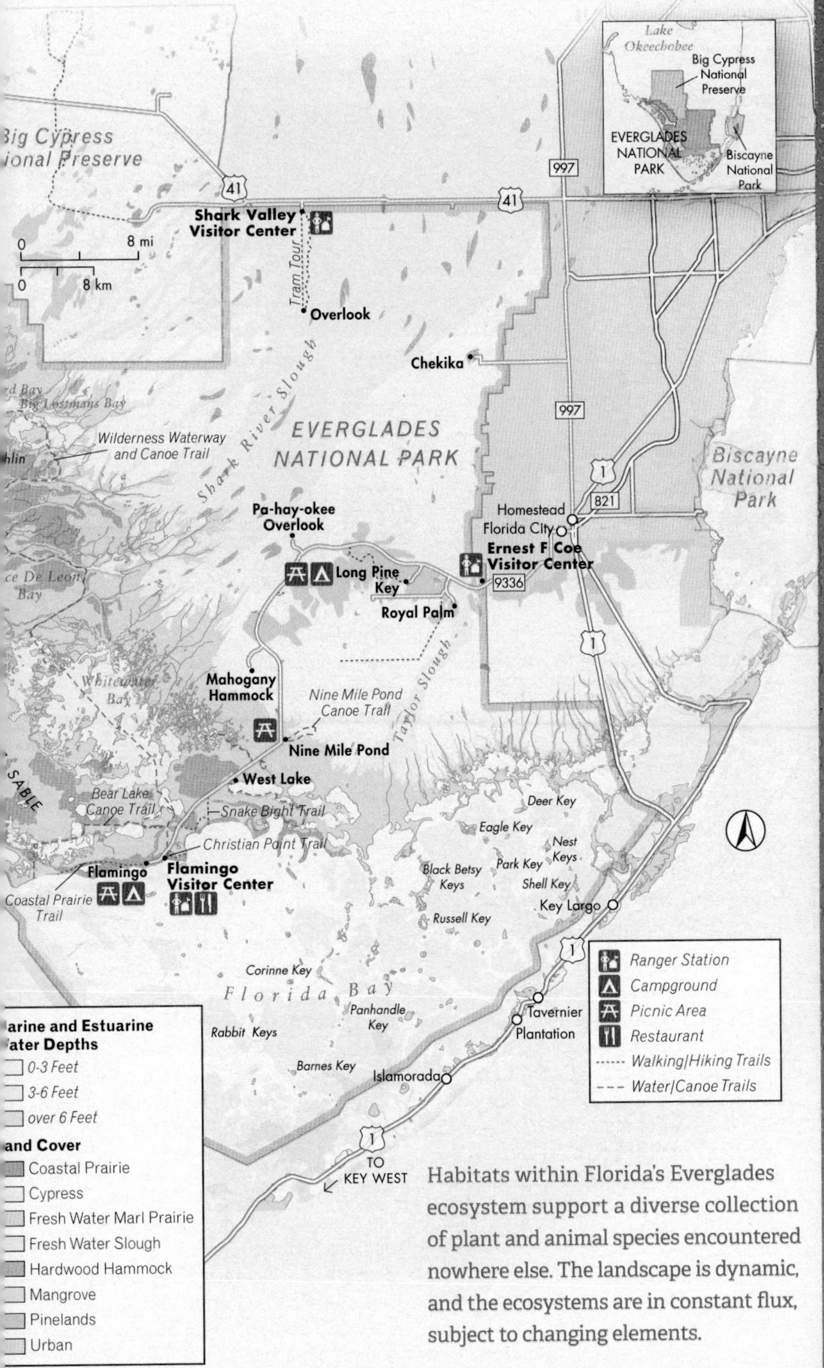

Habitats within Florida's Everglades ecosystem support a diverse collection of plant and animal species encountered nowhere else. The landscape is dynamic, and the ecosystems are in constant flux, subject to changing elements.

FLORA

❶ CABBAGE PALM

It's virtually impossible to visit the Everglades and not see a cabbage palm, Florida's official state tree. The cabbage palm (or sabal palm), graces assorted ecosystems and grows well in swamps. **Best place to see them:** At Loxahatchee National Wildlife Refuge (embracing the northern part of the Everglades, along Alligator Alley), throughout Everglades National Park, and at Big Cypress National Preserve.

❷ SAWGRASS

With spiny, serrated leaf blades resembling saws, sawgrass inspired the term "river of grass" for the Everglades. **Best place to see them:** Both Shark Valley and Pahayokee Overlook provide terrific vantage points for gazing over sawgrass prairie; you also can get an eyeful of sawgrass when crossing Alligator Alley, even when doing so at top speeds.

❸ MAHOGANY

Hardwood hammocks of the Everglades live in areas that rarely flood because of the slight elevation of the sloughs, where they're typically found. **Best place to see them:** Everglades National Park's Mahogany Hammock Trail (which has a boardwalk leading to the nation's largest living mahogany tree).

❹ MANGROVE

Mangrove forest ecosystems provide both food and protected nursery areas for fish, shellfish, and crustaceans. **Best place to see them:** Along Biscayne National Park shoreline, at Big Cypress National Preserve, and within Everglades National Park, especially around the Caple Sable area.

❺ GUMBO LIMBO

Sometimes called "tourist trees" because of peeling reddish bark (not unlike sunburns). **Best place to see them:** Everglades National Park's Gumbo Limbo Trail and assorted spots throughout the expansive Everglades.

FAUNA

❶ AMERICAN ALLIGATOR

In all likelihood, on your visit to the Everglades you'll see at least a gator or two. These carnivorous creatures can be found throughout the Everglades swampy wetlands.

Best place to see them: Loxahatchee National Wildlife Refuge (also sheltering the endangered Everglades snail kite) and within Everglades National Park at Shark Valley or Anhinga Trail. Sometimes (logically enough) gators hang out along Alligator Alley, basking in early morning or late-afternoon sun along four-lane I–75.

❷ AMERICAN CROCODILE

Crocs gravitate to fresh or brackish water, subsisting on birds, fish, snails, frogs, and small mammals.

Best place to see them: Within Everglades National Park, Big Cypress National Preserve, and protected grounds in or around Billie Swamp Safari.

❸ EASTERN CORAL SNAKE

This venomous snake burrows in underbrush, preying on lizards, frogs, and smaller snakes.

Best place to see them: Snakes typically shy away from people, but try Snake Bight or Eco Pond near Flamingo, where birds are also prevalent.

❹ FLORIDA PANTHER

Struggling for survival amid loss of habitat, these shy, tan-colored cats now number around 100, up from lows of near 30.

Best place to see them: Protected grounds of Billie Swamp Safari sometimes provide sightings during tours. Signage on roadway linking Tamiami Trail and Alligator Alley warns of panther crossings, but sightings are rare.

❺ GREEN TREE FROG

Typically bright green with white or yellow stripes, these nocturnal creatures thrive in swamps and brackish water.

Best place to see them: Within Everglades National Park, especially in or near water.

● =Extremely Common ● =Very Common ● =Somewhat Common ● =Rare

BIRDS

❶ ANHINGA

The lack of oil glands for waterproofing feathers helps this bird to dive as well as chase and spear fish with its pointed beak. The Anhinga is also often called a "water turkey" because of its long tail, or a "snake bird" because of its long neck.

Best place to see them: The Anhinga Trail, which also is known for attracting other wildlife to drink during especially dry winters.

❷ BLUE-WINGED TEAL

Although it's predominantly brown and gray, this bird's powder-blue wing patch becomes visible in flight. Next to the mallard, the blue-winged teal is North America's second most abundant duck, and thrives particularly well in the Everglades.

Best place to see them: Near ponds and marshy areas of Everglades National Park or Big Cypress National Preserve.

❸ GREAT BLUE HERON

This bird has a varied palate and enjoys feasting on everything from frogs, snakes, and mice to shrimp, aquatic insects, and sometimes even other birds! The all-white version, which at one time was considered a separate species, is quite common to the Everglades.

Best place to see them: Loxahatchee National Wildlife Refuge or Shark Valley in Everglades National Park.

❹ GREAT EGRET

Once decimated by plume hunters, these monogamous, long-legged white birds with S-shaped necks feed in wetlands, nest in trees, and hang out in colonies that often include heron or other egret species.

Best place to see them: Throughout Everglades National Park, along Alligator Alley, and sometimes even on the fringes of Greater Fort Lauderdale.

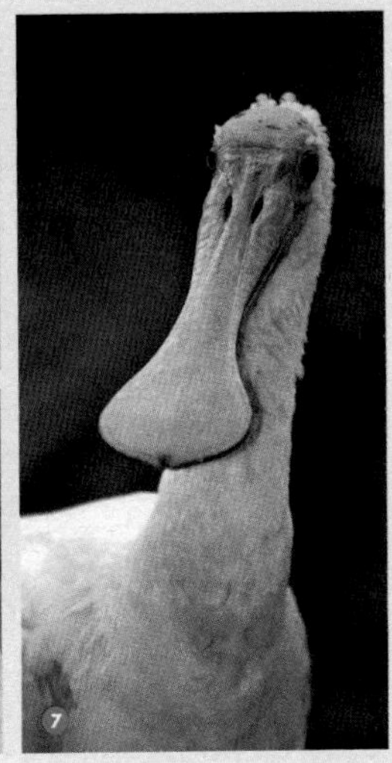

5 GREATER FLAMINGO

Flocking together and using long legs and webbed feet to stir shallow waters and mud flats, color comes a couple of years after hatching from ingesting shrimplike crustaceans along with fish, fly larvae, and plankton.

Best place to see them: Try Snake Bight or Eco Pond, near Flamingo Marina.

6 OSPREY

Making a big comeback from chemical pollutant endangerment, ospreys (sometimes confused with bald eagles) are distinguished by black eyestripes down their faces. Gripping pads on feet with curved claws help them pluck fish from water.

Best place to see them: Look near water, where they're fishing for lunch in the shallow areas. Try the coasts, bays, and ponds of Everglades National Park. They also gravitate to trees You can usually spot them from the Gulf Coast Visitor Center, or you can observe them via boating in the Ten Thousand Islands.

7 ROSEATE SPOONBILL

These gregarious pink-and-white birds gravitate toward mangroves, feeding on fish, insects, amphibians, and some plants. They have long, spoon-like bills, and their feathers can have a touch of red and yellow. These birds appear in the Everglades year-round.

Best place to see them: Sandy Key, southwest of Flamingo, is a spoonbill nocturnal roosting spot, but at sunrise these colorful birds head out over Eco Pond to favored day hangouts throughout Everglades National Park.

8 WOOD STORK

Recognizable by featherless heads and prominent bills, these birds submerge in water to scoop up hapless fish. They are most common in the early spring and often easiest to spot in the morning.

Best place to see them: Amid the Ten Thousand Island areas, Nine Mile Pond, Mrazek Pond, and in the mangroves at Paurotis Pond.

● =Extremely Common ● =Very Common ● =Somewhat Common ● =Rare

THE STORY OF THE EVERGLADES

Dreams of draining southern Florida took hold in the early 1800s, expanding in the early 1900s to convert large tracts from wetlands to agricultural acreage. By the 1920s, towns like Fort Lauderdale and Miami boomed, and the sugar industry—which came to be known as "Big Sugar"—established its first sugar mills. In 1947 Everglades National Park opened as a refuge for wildlife.

Meanwhile, the sugar industry grew. In its infancy, about 175,000 tons of raw sugar per year was produced from fields totaling about 50,000 acres. But once the U.S. embargo stopped sugar imports from Cuba in 1960 and laws restricting acreage were lifted, Big Sugar took off. Less than five years later, the industry produced 572,000 tons of sugar and occupied nearly a quarter of a million acres.

Fast-forward to 2008, to what was hailed as the biggest conservation deal in U.S. history since the creation of the national parks. A trailblazing restoration strategy hinged on creating a water flow-way between Lake Okeechobee and the Everglades by buying up and flooding 187,000 acres of land. The country's largest producers of cane sugar agreed to sell the necessary 187,000 acres to the state of Florida for $1.75 billion. Environmentalists cheered.

But within months, news broke of a scaled-back land acquisition plan: $1.34 billion to buy 180,000 acres. By spring 2009, the restoration plan had shrunk to $536,000 to buy 73,000 acres. With the purchase still in limbo, critics claim the state might overpay for acreage appraised at pre-recession values and proponents fear dwindling revenues may derail the plan altogether.

The Big Sugar land deal is part of a larger effort to preserve the Everglades. In 2010, two separate lawsuits charged the state, along with the United States Environmental Protection Agency, with stalling Everglades cleanup that was supposed to begin in 2006. "Glacial delay" is how one judge put it. The state must reduce phosphorus levels in water that flows to the Everglades or face fines and sanctions for violating the federal Clean Water Act. The fate of the Everglades remains in the balance.

Everglades National Park

45 miles southwest of Miami International Airport.

If you're heading across the southern portion of Florida on U.S. 41, from Miami to Naples, you'll breeze right through the Everglades. This mostly two-lane road, also known as Tamiami Trail, skirts the edge of Everglades National Park and cuts across the Big Cypress National Preserve. You'll also be near the park if you're en route from Miami to the Florida Keys on U.S. 1, which cuts through Homestead and Florida City—communities east of the main park entrance. Basically, if you're in South Florida, you can't escape at least fringes of the Everglades. With tourist strongholds like Miami, Naples, and the Florida Keys so close, travelers from all over the world typically make day trips to the park.

Everglades National Park has three main entry points: the park headquarters at Ernest F. Coe Visitor Center, southwest of Homestead and Florida City; the Shark Valley area, accessed by Tamiami Trail (U.S. 41); and the Gulf Coast Visitor Center, south of Everglades City to the west and closest to Naples.

Explore on your own or participate in ranger-led hikes, bicycle or bird-watching tours, and canoe trips. The variety of these excursions is greatest from mid-December through April, and some adventures (canoe trips, for instance) typically aren't offered in the sweltering summer months. Among the more popular activities are the Anhinga Amble, a 50-minute walk around the Taylor Slough (departs from the Royal Palm Visitor Center), and the Early Bird Special, a 90-minute walk centered on birdlife (departs from Flamingo Visitor Center). Check with the respective visitor centers for details.

PARK ESSENTIALS

Admission Fees The fee is $25 per vehicle; $20 per motorcycle; and $8 per pedestrian or cyclist. Payable online or at the gates, admission is good for seven consecutive days at all park entrances. Annual passes are $40.

Admission Hours Open daily, year-round. Both the main entrance near Florida City and Homestead and the Gulf Coast entrance are open 24/7. The Shark Valley entrance is open 8:30 am to 6 pm.

Ernest F. Coe Visitor Center to Flamingo Visitor Center

About 50 miles southwest of Miami.

The most utilized entrance to Everglades National Park is southwest of Homestead and Florida City. If you're traveling from Miami, take State Road 836/Dolphin Expressway West to State Road 826/Palmetto Expressway South to the Homestead Extension of Florida's Turnpike, U.S. 1, and Krome Avenue (State Road 997). Once you're in Homestead, go right (west) from U.S. 1 or Krome Avenue onto Palm Drive (State Road 9336/S.W. 344th Street) and follow signage to the park entrance.

This road runs 38 miles from the Ernest F. Coe Visitor Center to the Florida Bay at Flamingo, the southernmost headquarters of Everglades National Park. On the way it crosses a section of the park's eight distinct ecosystems: hardwood hammock, freshwater prairie, pinelands, freshwater slough, cypress, coastal prairie, mangrove, and marine-estuarine. Highlights include a dwarf cypress forest, the transition zone between sawgrass and mangrove forest, and a wealth of wading birds at Mrazek and Coot Bay ponds, where you can observe them feeding early in the morning or later in the afternoon. Flamingo sightings here are extremely rare. Boardwalks, looped

War on Pythons

The nonnative Burmese python population has flourished in the Everglades for a couple of decades, likely since Hurricane Andrew. Studies show that pythons dramatically reduce prey for native predators and this contributes to the decline of this delicate habitat. The dangerous constrictors are literally squeezing the life out of Everglades.

The South Florida Water Management District (SFWMD) incentivizes select members of the community to locate and remove invasive Burmese pythons in Miami-Dade, Broward, Collier, and Palm Beach counties. In other words, SFWMD is hand-picking hunters to locate and eliminate these apex predators for money. In 2018 the state-sponsored program eliminated more than 1,000 pythons after just 14 months—a huge success for Team Everglades.

The state's war on destructive and invasive species will likely continue, in increasingly creative and aggressive ways, to protect the wildlife of the Everglades. —Galena Mosovich

trails, several short spurs, and observation platforms help you stay dry. You can stop along the way to walk several short trails (each takes about 30 minutes): the wheelchair-accessible Anhinga Trail, which cuts through sawgrass marsh and allows you to see lots of wildlife (be on the lookout for alligators and the trail's namesake waterbirds: anhingas); the junglelike yet also wheelchair-accessible Gumbo-Limbo Trail; the Pinelands Trail, where you can see the park's limestone bedrock; the Pahayokee Overlook Trail, ending at an observation tower; and the Mahogany Hammock Trail, with its dense growth. ■ **TIP→ Before heading out on the trails, inquire about insect and weather conditions. Stocking up on bug repellent, sunscreen, and water is always a good idea. Even on sunny days, it's smart to bring rain gear.**

Sights

To explore this section of the park, follow Palm Drive (State Road 9336) from the main park entrance to Flamingo Visitor Center; you'll find plenty of opportunities to stop along the way and assorted activities to pursue in the Flamingo area. Other than campgrounds, there are no lodging options within the national park.

Ernest F. Coe Visitor Center

INFO CENTER | FAMILY | Get your park map here, 365 days a year, but don't just grab and go; this visitor center's interactive exhibits and films are well worth your time. The 15-minute film *River of Life,* updated frequently, provides a succinct park overview. A movie on hurricanes and a 35-minute wildlife film for children are available upon request. Learn about the Great Water Debate, the saga of how draining swampland for residential and agricultural development cuts off water-supply routes for precious wetlands in the ecosystem. Artists in Residence in Everglades' (AIRIE) Nest Gallery is also located at the visitor center. You'll also find a schedule of daily ranger-led activities, mainly walks and talks; information on the popular Nike missile site tour (harking back to the Cuban missile crisis era); and details about canoe rentals and boat tours at Flamingo. The visitor center is outside park gates, so you can stop in without paying park admission (and use the restrooms). Due to the remoteness of this location, visitors arriving via ride-sharing services

(Uber, Lyft) should plan for return transportation before starting their adventure. There's no public transportation to this site. ✉ *40001 State Rd. 9336, Homestead* ☎ *305/242–7700* 🎫 *Free.*

Flamingo Visitor Center

INFO CENTER | FAMILY | At the southernmost point of the park's main road to the Flamingo community, you'll find a visitor center, marina store (with beverages, snacks and a gift shop), public boat ramp, and campground with nearby hiking and nature trails. This is where you'll go for backcountry permits. Despite the name,you probably won't find any flamingos here. To try to get a glimpse of the flamboyant pink birds with toothpick legs, check out Snake Bight Trail, starting about 5 miles from the Flamingo outpost. But they are a rare sight indeed. Visitors can pitch tents or bring RVs to the campground, where amenities include solar-heated showers and electricity for RV sites. Be sure to make a reservation during winter, and note that during the summer wet season, portions of the campgrounds are closed due to flooding. ✉ *1 Flamingo Lodge Hwy., Homestead* ☎ *239/695–2945* 🌐 *www.nps.gov/ever/planyourvisit/flamdirections.htm.*

Royal Palm Information Station and Bookstore

INFO CENTER | FAMILY | Ideal for when there's limited time to experience the Everglades, this small center with a bookstore features ranger-led walks and talks. Visitors can also access the park's Pine Island Trails (Anhinga Trail, Gumbo Limbo Trail, Lone Pine Key Trails, Pineland Trail, Pahayokee Overlook, and Mahogany Hammock Trail) from Royal Palm. Two ranger-led programs, The Anhinga Amble (a 50-minute stroll brings you close to alligators, wading birds, and other wildlife) and Glades Glimpse (a 20-minute talk in the shade), are offered every day, year-round, including the summer months. As always, arm yourself with insect repellent. ✉ *Everglades National Park* ✥ *A little over a mile away from Ernest F. Coe Visitor Center* ☎ *305/242–7237* 🌐 *www.nps.gov/ever/planyourvisit/royal-palm.htm.*

Picnic Spots

Worthwhile spots to pull over for a picnic are **Paurotis Pond**, 24 miles from the main park entrance near Homestead (the actual pond is closed during nesting season) and **Nine Mile Pond**, less than 30 miles from the main visitor center.

Activities

BIRD-WATCHING

Some of the park region's best birding is in Everglades National Park, especially the Flamingo area.

CANOEING AND KAYAKING

The 99-mile inland **Wilderness Trail** between Flamingo and Everglades City is open to motorboats as well as canoes, although, depending on water levels, powerboats may have trouble navigating above Whitewater Bay. Flat-water canoeing and kayaking are best in winter, when temperatures are moderate, rainfall diminishes, and mosquitoes back off—a little, anyway. This activity is for the experienced and adventurous; most paddlers take eight days to complete the trail. But you can also do a day trip. The Flamingo area has well-marked water trails, but be sure to tell someone where you're going and when you expect to return. Getting lost is easy, and spending the night without proper gear can be unpleasant, if not dangerous. A company known as Guest Services, Inc. is the authorized concessioner for Flamingo, and they handle all reservations and rentals. 🌐 *flamingoeverglades.com*

Gulf Coast Visitor Center Entrance

To reach the park's western gateway, take U.S./Highway 41 (Tamiami Trail) west from Miami for about 90 miles, turn left (south) onto State Road 29, and travel another 3 miles through Everglades City to the Gulf Coast Ranger Station. From Naples on the Gulf Coast, take U.S./Highway 41 east for 37 miles, and turn right onto State Road 29.

Gulf Coast Visitor Center

INFO CENTER | FAMILY | The best place to start exploring Everglades National Park's watery western side is at this visitor center just south of Everglades City (5 miles south of U.S./Highway 41/Tamiami Trail), where rangers can give you the park lowdown and provide you with informational brochures and backcountry permits. A temporary Visitor Contact Station is in place until necessary repairs can be made to the Gulf Coast Visitor Center that was destroyed by Hurricane Irma in 2017. The Gulf Coast Visitor Center serves as the gateway for exploring the Ten Thousand Islands, a maze of mangrove islands and waterways that extends to Flamingo and Florida Bay and are accessible only by boat in this region. Naturalist-led boat trips are handled by Everglades National Park Boat Tours, the concessioner that also rents canoes and kayaks. ✉ *815 Oyster Bar Ln., Everglades City* ☎ *239/695–3311* 🌐 *www.nps.gov/ever/planyourvisit/gcdirections.htm.*

Activities

Everglades National Park Boat Tours

TOUR—SPORTS | FAMILY | This authorized concessioner frequently runs 90-minute trips through the Ten Thousand Islands National Wildlife Refuge. Adventure seekers often see dolphins, manatees, bald eagles, and roseate spoonbills in the saltwater portion of the Everglades.

Everglades Birding

The Tropical Audubon Society is where South Florida's most enthusiastic birders flock together to conserve local ecosystems while ensuring birds and their habitats are safe. This chapter of the National Audubon Society is extremely active year-round, and its birding field trips are fun and educational. Visit the website for the calendar of events and other valuable birding resources. 🌐 ***www.tropicalaudubon.org.***

Mangrove wilderness tours on smaller boats (up to six passengers) embark on shorter trips through the swampy, brackish areas. This is the best option to see alligators, bobcats, mangrove fox squirrels, and birds, including the mangrove cuckoo. ✉ *Gulf Coast Visitor Center, 905 S. Copeland Ave., Everglades City* ☎ *239/695–2591* 🌐 *www.evergladesnationalparkboattoursgulfcoast.com/index.php* 🎟 *Tours from $37.10 for Ten Thousand Islands Tour.*

★ Everglades Adventures

TOUR—SPORTS | This established year-round source for guided Everglades paddling tours and canoe and kayak rentals is located at the Ivey House Inn in Everglades City. Shuttles will deliver you to major launching areas like Turner River, where you'll meet the small group of adventure seekers on your excursion. Highlights include bird and gator sightings, mangrove forests, and spectacular sunsets, depending on the time of your tour. Every tour is led by a certified naturalist and spans about three to four hours. Longer adventures include equipment rental, guide, and meals. ✉ *The Ivey House & Everglades Adventures, 107 Camellia St. E., Everglades City*

☎ 877/567–0679, 239/695–3299 International 🌐 iveyhouse.com/everglades-adventures 🎫 Canoe rentals from $30 per day; kayak rentals from $50 per day.

Shark Valley Visitor Center

23½ miles west of Florida's Turnpike, off Tamiami Trail. Approximately an hour west of Miami.

You won't see sharks at Shark Valley. The name originates from the Shark River, also known as the River of Grass, that flows through the area. Several species of shark swim up this river from the coast (about 45 miles south of Shark Valley) to give birth, though not at this particular spot. Young sharks (called pups) are vulnerable to predators, but they're able to gain strength in waters of the slough before heading out to sea.

The Shark Valley entrance to Everglades National Park is on U.S./Highway 41 (Tamiami Trail), 25 miles west of Florida's Turnpike or 39 miles east of State Road 29.

Sights

To cover the most ground, hop aboard a two-hour tram tour with a naturalist guide. It stops halfway for a trip to the top of the 45-foot-tall Shark Valley Observation Tower via a sloping ramp.

Prefer to do the trail on foot? It takes nerve to walk the 15-mile loop in Shark Valley, because in the winter months alligators sunbathe along the road. Most, however, do move out of the way when they see you coming.

You can also ride a bicycle (the folks who operate the tram tours rent well-used bikes daily from 8:30 am to 4 pm for $9 per hour with helmets available). Near the bike-rental area, a short boardwalk trail meanders through sawgrass, and another courses through a tropical hardwood hammock.

Good Reads

- *The Everglades: River of Grass.* This 1947 classic by conservationist Marjory Stoneman Douglas is a must-read.
- *Everglades.* Jean Craighead George illustrates the park's natural history in a children's book.
- *Everglades: The Park Story.* Wildlife biologist William B. Robertson Jr. presents the park's flora, fauna, and history.
- *Swamplandia!* This story of a family's gator-wrestling theme park near Everglades City brings readers into the swamp.

Shark Valley Observation Tower
NATIONAL/STATE PARK | FAMILY | At the halfway point of the Shark Valley loop or tram tour, you can pause to navigate the Observation Tower, which is the highest accessible point in Everglades National Park. The viewing platform of this tower, first built in 1984, is nearly 50 feet from the ground. Once there, you'll find the River of Grass in all its glory, sprawling out as far as the eye can see. Observe waterbirds as well as alligators, and maybe even river otters crossing the road. The tower has a wheelchair-accessible ramp to the top. If you don't want to take the tram from the Shark Valley Visitor Center, you can either hike or bike in, but private cars are not allowed. ✉ *Shark Valley Tram Tours, 36000 S.W. 8th St., Miami* 🌐 *www.sharkvalleytramtours.com.*

Shark Valley Visitor Center
INFO CENTER | FAMILY | Inside a relatively modern white building is the Shark Valley Visitor Center. Go here for educational displays, a park video, and informational brochures. Books and other goods, such as hats, sunscreen, insect repellent, postcards are available, along with

Much skill is required to navigate boats through the shallow, muddy waters of the Everglades.

restrooms. Park rangers are also available, ready for your questions. ✉ *36000 S.W. 8th St., Miami* ✥ *23½ miles west of Florida's Turnpike, off Tamiami Trail* ☎ *305/221–8776* 🌐 *www.nps.gov/ever/planyourvisit/svdirections.htm.*

Activities

Buffalo Tiger Airboat Rides

BOATING | FAMILY | A former chief of Florida's Miccosukee tribe—Buffalo Tiger, who died in January 2015 at the age of 94—founded this Shark Valley tour operation, and his spirit carries on. Savvy guides narrate the trip to an old Miccosukee Indian camp on the north side of Tamiami Trail from the Native American perspective. Don't worry about airboat noise, they shut off the engines three times during informative talks and photo opportunities. The standard tours are 45 minutes, and longer private tours are available. Reservations are not required for standard tours, and credit cards are now accepted at this outpost, but it's cheaper to purchase online in advance. ✉ *29701 S.W. 8th St., West Miami-Dade* ☎ *305/559–5250* 🌐 *www.buffalotigersflevergladesairboattours.com/home.html* 🎫 *Standard tours from $24.75 per person. Private tours from $200 per group of 4.*

Shark Valley Bicycle Rentals

BICYCLING | FAMILY | You can gaze at gators while exercising on a bike rented from the Shark Valley Visitor Center (from the same authorized concessioner that operates the tram tours). Bike 15 miles of paved, level roadway (no hills or holes) to the Observation Tower and back while keeping an eye on the roadside reptile show. The single-speed bikes come with baskets and helmets, along with child seats for kids under 35 pounds. The fleet also includes a few 20-inch junior models. You'll need a driver's license or other ID for a deposit. Arm yourself with water, insect repellent, and sunscreen. ✉ *Shark Valley Visitor Center, 36000 S.W. 8th St., Shark Valley* ☎ *305/221–8455* 🌐 *www.sharkvalleytramtours.com/everglades-bicycle-tours* 🎫 *Bike rentals from $9/hour.*

Shark Valley Tram Tours
TOUR—SPORTS | **FAMILY** | Starting at the Shark Valley Visitor Center, these popular two-hour, narrated tours on bio-diesel trams follow a 15-mile loop into the interior, stopping at a wheelchair-accessible observation tower. Bring your own water. Reservations are recommended December through April. ✉ *Shark Valley Visitor Center, 36000 S.W. 8th St., Miami* ☎ *305/221–8455* 🌐 *www.sharkvalleytramtours.com* 🎫 *$25 for adults.*

Big Cypress National Preserve

Through the early 1960s, the world's largest cypress-logging operation prospered in Big Cypress Swamp until nearly all the trees were cut down. With the downfall of the industry, government entities began buying parcels of land, and now more than 729,000 acres of the swamp are included in this national preserve. *Big* refers to the swamp, which juts into the north edge of Everglades National Park like a puzzle piece. Its size and location make Big Cypress an important link in the region's hydrological system, where rainwater flows through the preserve, then south into the park, and eventually into Florida Bay. Its pattern of wet prairies, ponds, marshes, sloughs, and strands is a natural wildlife sanctuary, and thanks to a policy of balanced land use—"use without abuse"—the watery wilderness is devoted to recreation as well as to research and preservation. Bald cypress trees that may look dead are actually dormant, with green needles springing to life in the spring. The preserve allows—in limited areas—hiking, hunting, and off-road vehicles (airboat, swamp buggy, four-wheel drive) by permit. Compared with Everglades National Park, the preserve is less developed and hosts fewer visitors, and that makes it ideal for naturalists, birders, and hikers.

The Everglades with Kids

Although kids of all ages can enjoy the park, those six and older typically get the most out of the experience. Consider how much you as a supervising adult will enjoy keeping tabs on your little ones around so much water and so many teeth. Predators including alligators abound. Plus, some children are frightened by raw wilderness. Many of the tour/rentals have age restrictions.

Several scenic drives branch out from Tamiami Trail; a few lead to camping areas and roadside picnic spots. Aside from the Oasis Visitor Center, a popular springboard for viewing alligators, the newer Big Cypress Swamp Welcome Center features a platform for watching manatees. Both centers, along Tamiami Trail between Miami and Naples, feature a top-notch 25-minute film on Big Cypress.

PARK ESSENTIALS

Admission Fees It's free to visit the preserve.

Admission Hours The park is open 24/7, year-round. The Oasis Visitor Center and the Welcome Center are closed on December 25.

CONTACTS Big Cypress National Preserve. ☎ *239/695–2000* 🌐 *www.nps.gov/bicy/index.htm.*

Sights

Big Cypress Gallery
ARTS VENUE | **FAMILY** | Clyde Butcher's Big Cypress Gallery is a wonderful spot for finding a postcard, calendar, or a more serious piece of art. Butcher, a big guy with an even bigger beard, is known for

his stunning photography of landscapes and his knowledge of the 'glades. His ability to capture its magnetism through a large-format lens is unrivaled. Even if you can't afford his larger-scale stuff, you're warmly welcome to gaze at everything in the gallery. Out back, Butcher and his wife, Niki, also rent a bungalow ($295 per night, October–April) and a cottage ($350 per night, year-round). ■ **TIP→ Look into Butcher's private eco and photo swamp tours. After all, "to know the swamp, you have to get into the swamp," he says.** ✉ *52388 Tamiami Trail, Ochopee* ☎ *239/695–2428* 🌐 *clydebutcher.com/galleries.*

Big Cypress Swamp Welcome Center
INFO CENTER | FAMILY | The newer Big Cypress Swamp Welcome Center on the preserve's western side has abundant information and educational features, as well as restrooms, picnic facilities, and a 70-seat auditorium. An outdoor breezeway showcases an interactive Big Cypress watershed exhibit, illustrating Florida's water flow. It's a convenient place to stop when crossing from either coast. ■ **TIP→ Love manatees? The boardwalk overlooking the canal behind the welcome center can be a good spot for viewing the intriguing mammals. (Legend has it that they were once mistaken for mermaids by thirsty or love-starved sailors.)** ✉ *33000 Tamiami Trail E, Ochopee* ☎ *239/695–4757* 🌐 *www.nps.gov/bicy/planyourvisit/basicinfo.htm* 🎫 *Free.*

Oasis Visitor Center
INFO CENTER | FAMILY | The big attraction at the Oasis Visitor Center, on the east side of Big Cypress Preserve, is the observation deck for viewing fish, birds and other wildlife, such as gators. The native plants in a small butterfly garden attract winged wonders. Inside the visitor center, you'll find an exhibition gallery, the Florida National Parks association bookshop, and a theater showing an informative 25-minute film on the swamplands. (Leashed pets are allowed but not on the boardwalk deck.) The off-road vehicle permit office is also located at the Oasis Visitor Center. ✉ *52105 Tamiami Trail E, Ochopee* ☎ *239/695–1201* 🌐 *www.nps.gov/bicy/planyourvisit/oasis-visitor-center.htm* 🎫 *Free.*

Ochopee Post Office
BUILDING | FAMILY | The smallest post office in the United States is a former shed for irrigation pipes on the Tamiami Trail. Blink and you'll risk missing it. You can support this quaint and historical outpost by purchasing a postcard of the little shack and mailing it off to a history buff. You can also mail packages and buy money orders here. ✉ *United States Postal Service, 38000 Tamiami Trail E, Ochopee* ☎ *800/275–8777* ⏲ *Closed Sun.*

Restaurants

Joanie's Blue Crab Cafe
$$ | SEAFOOD | FAMILY | West of the nation's tiniest post office, you'll find this red barn of a place dishing out catfish, frogs' legs, gator, grouper, burgers, salads, and (no surprise here) an abundance of soft-shell crabs, crab cakes, and she-crab soup. Entrées are reasonably priced, and peanut butter pie makes for a solid finish. **Known for:** fresh seafood; live music; beer and wine only. 💲 *Average main: $15* ✉ *39395 Tamiami Trail E, Ochopee* ✥ *Less than a mile west of Ochopee Post Office* ☎ *239/695–2682* 🌐 *www.joaniesbluecrabcafe.com* ⏲ *Hours of operation vary seasonally; call to confirm.*

Activities

There are three types of trails—walking (including part of the extensive Florida National Scenic Trail), canoeing, and bicycling. All three trail types are easily accessed from the Tamiami Trail near the preserve visitor center, and one boardwalk trail departs from the center. Canoe and bike equipment can be rented from outfitters in Everglades City, 24 miles west, and Naples, 40 miles west.

Hikers can tackle the Florida National Scenic Trail, which begins in the preserve and is divided into segments of 6½ to 28 miles each. Two 5-mile trails, Concho Billy and Fire Prairie, can be accessed off Turner River Road, a few miles east. Turner River Road and Birdon Road form a 17-mile gravel loop drive that's excellent for birding. Bear Island has about 32 miles of scenic, flat, looped trails that are ideal for bicycling. Most trails are hard-packed lime rock, but a few miles are gravel. Cyclists share the road with off-road vehicles, most plentiful from mid-November through December.

To see the best variety of wildlife from your vehicle, follow 26-mile Loop Road, south of U.S. 41 and west of Shark Valley, where alligators, raccoons, and soft-shell turtles crawl around beside the gravel road, often swooped upon by swallowtail kites and brown-shouldered hawks. Stop at H. P. Williams Roadside Park, west of the Oasis, and walk along the boardwalk to spy gators, turtles, and garfish in the river waters.

RANGER PROGRAMS

From the Oasis Visitor Center you can get in on the seasonal ranger-led or self-guided activities, such as campfire and wildlife talks, hikes, slough slogs, and canoe excursions. The 8-mile Turner River Canoe Trail begins nearby and crosses through Everglades National Park before ending in Chokoloskee Bay, near Everglades City. Rangers lead four-hour canoe trips and two-hour swamp walks in season; call for days and times. Bring shoes and long pants for swamp walks and be prepared to wade at least knee-deep in water. Ranger program reservations are accepted up to 14 days in advance. The programs are free to the public.

Biscayne National Park

Occupying 172,000 acres along the southern portion of Biscayne Bay, south of Miami and north of the Florida Keys, Biscayne National Park is 95 percent submerged, its terrain ranges from 4 feet above sea level to 60 feet below. Contained within are four distinct zones, or ecosystems: Biscayne Bay, undeveloped upper Florida Keys, coral reefs, and coastal mangrove forest. Mangroves line the shores of the mainland much like they do elsewhere along South Florida's protected waters. Biscayne Bay serves as a lobster sanctuary and a nursery for fish, sponges, crabs, and other sea life. Manatees and sea turtles frequent its warm, shallow waters. The park hosts legions of boaters and landlubbers (novices) gazing in awe across the bay.

GETTING HERE

To reach Biscayne National Park from south of Homestead, take U.S. Highway and turn right on S.W. 344th Street (Palm Drive, the last light before the Florida Turnpike entrance). After about 4 miles, the road curves to the north near the Homestead Speedway. Turn right on S.W. 328th Street (North Canal Drive) heading east. Continue for 4 miles to the end of the road. The park entrance is on the left just before the entrance to Homestead Bayfront Marina. From the north, take Florida Turnpike south to Exit 6 (Speedway Boulevard). Turn left from exit ramp and continue south to S.W. 328th Street (North Canal Drive). Turn left on 328th Street and continue for 4 miles to the end of the road. The park entrance is on the left just before the entrance to Homestead Bayfront Marina.

PARK ESSENTIALS

Admission Fees There's no fee to enter Biscayne National Park, and you don't pay a fee to access the islands, but there's a $25 overnight camping fee for each stay at Elliott Key or Boca Chita Key. A solid selection of authorized park

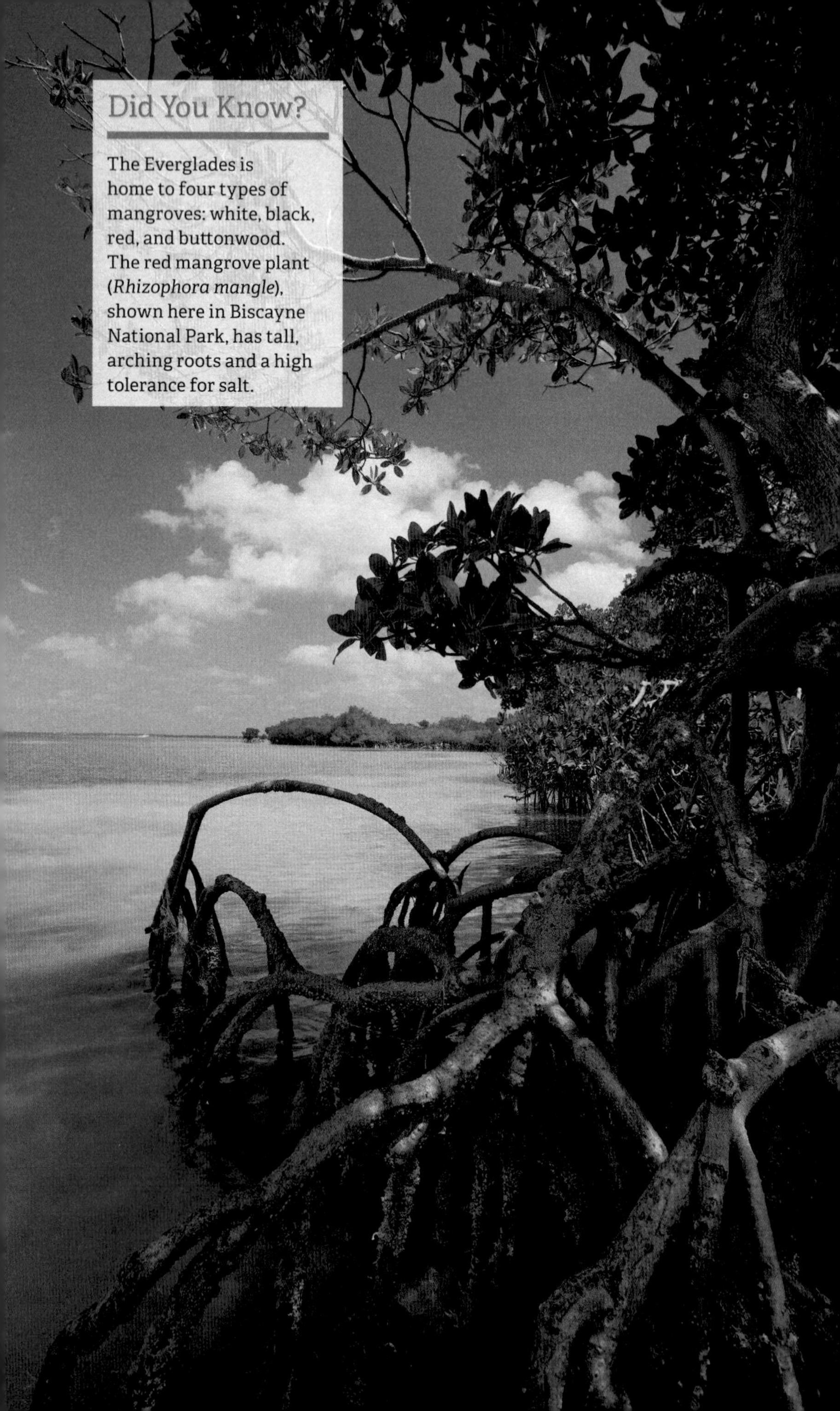

Did You Know?

The Everglades is home to four types of mangroves: white, black, red, and buttonwood. The red mangrove plant (*Rhizophora mangle*), shown here in Biscayne National Park, has tall, arching roots and a high tolerance for salt.

concessioners charge for day trips to the coral reefs and islands.

Admission Hours The park is open daily, year-round.

CONTACTS Biscayne National Park. ✉ *9700 S.W. 328th St., Sir Lancelot Jones Way, Homestead* ☎ *305/230–1144* 🌐 *www.nps.gov/bisc/index.htm.*

Sights

Biscayne is a hub for boating, diving, snorkeling, canoeing, birding, and, to some extent (if you have a private boat), camping. Elliott Key is the best place to hike; two trails tunnel through the island's tropical hardwood hammock.

Biscayne's corals range from soft, flagellant fans, plumes, and whips found chiefly in shallow patch reefs to the hard brain corals, elkhorn, and staghorn forms that can withstand depths and heavier shoreline wave action.

To the east, about 8 miles off the coast, 44 tiny keys stretch 18 nautical miles north to south, and are reached only by boat. No mainland commercial transportation operates to the islands, and only a handful are accessible: Elliott, Boca Chita, Adams, and Sands Keys (between Elliott and Boca Chita). The rest are wildlife refuges or have rocky shores or waters too shallow for boats. December through April, when the mosquito population is less aggressive, is the best time to explore. Bring insect repellent, sunscreen, and water.

Adams Key

ISLAND | FAMILY | A stone's throw from the western tip of Elliott Key and 9 miles southeast of Convoy Point, Adams Key is open for day use. It was once the site of the Cocolobo Club, a retreat known for hosting Presidents Harding, Hoover, Johnson, and Nixon, as well as other famous and infamous characters. Hurricane Andrew blew away what remained of club facilities in 1992. The island has picnic areas with grills, restrooms, dockage, and a short trail running along the shore through a hardwood hammock. Rangers live on-island. Access is by private boat, with no pets or overnight docking allowed. ✉ *Biscayne National Park* 🌐 *www.nps.gov/bisc/planyourvisit/adamskey.htm.*

Boca Chita Key

HISTORIC SITE | FAMILY | Ten miles northeast of Convoy Point and about 12 miles south of the Cape Florida Lighthouse on Key Biscayne, this island once was owned by the late Mark C. Honeywell, former president of Honeywell Company. It's on the National Register of Historic Places for its 10 historic structures and is the most visited island in the park. A half-mile hiking trail curves around the island's south side. Climb the 65-foot-high ornamental lighthouse (by ranger tour only) for a panoramic view of Miami, or check out the cannon from the HMS *Fowey*. There's no freshwater, access is by private boat only, and no pets are allowed. Only portable toilets are on-site, with no sinks or showers. A $25 fee for overnight docking (6 pm to 6 am) covers a campsite. ✉ *Biscayne National Park* 🌐 *www.nps.gov/bisc/planyourvisit/bocachita.htm.*

★ Dante Fascell Visitor Center

ARTS VENUE | FAMILY | Step out onto the wide veranda to soak up views of mangroves and Biscayne Bay at this Convoy Point visitor center. Inside, artistic vignettes and on-request videos, including the 11-minute *Spectrum of Life*, explore the park's four ecosystems, while the Touch Table gives both kids and adults a feel for bones, feathers, and coral. Facilities include the park's art gallery, canoe and tour concession, restrooms with showers, a ranger information area, gift shop with books, and vending machines. Various ranger programs take place daily during busy fall and winter seasons. Rangers give informal tours on Boca Chita Key, but these must be arranged in advance. A short trail and boardwalk lead to a jetty, and there are picnic tables and grills. This is the only area of the park accessible without a boat. You can snorkel from shore, but the water is shallow, with sea grass and a mud bottom. ✉ *9700 S.W. 328th St., Sir Lancelot Jones Way, Homestead* ☎ *305/230–1144* 🌐 *www.nps.gov/bisc/index.htm* 🎫 *Free.*

Elliott Key

ISLAND | **FAMILY** | The largest of the islands, 9 miles east of Convoy Point, Elliott Key has a mile-long hiking trail on the bay side at the north end of the campground. Another trail called Spite Highway runs approximately 6 miles down the center of the island. Boaters may dock at any of 36 slips; the fee for staying overnight includes use of a tent area for up to six people in two tents. Facilities include restrooms, picnic tables, fresh drinking water, cold (occasionally lukewarm) showers, grills, and a campground. Leashed pets are allowed in developed areas only, not on trails. A 30-foot-wide sandy shoreline about a mile north of the harbor on the west (bay) side of the key is the only one in the national park, and boaters like to anchor off here to swim. You can fish (check on license requirements) from the maintenance dock south of the harbor or from the shoreline outside of the swimming area. The beach, fun for families, is for day use only; it has picnic areas and a short trail that cuts through the hammock. Mosquitoes are always present. ✉ *Biscayne National Park* 🎫 *$25 overnight docking fee for campers.*

Activities

BIRD-WATCHING

More than 170 species of birds have been identified in and around the park. Expect to see flocks of brown pelicans patrolling the bay—suddenly rising, then plunging beak first to capture prey in the water. White ibis probe exposed mudflats for small fish and crustaceans. Although all the keys are excellent for birding, Jones Lagoon (south of Adams Key, between Old Rhodes Key and Totten Key) is outstanding. It's approachable only by nonmotorized craft.

DIVING AND SNORKELING

Diving is great year-round, but it's best in the summer, when calmer winds and seas result in clearer waters. Living tropical coral reefs are the highlight here; some are the size of a table, others are as large as a football field. Glass-bottom-boat rides, when operating, showcase this underwater wonderland, but you really should get in the water to fully appreciate it.

A diverse population of colorful fish—angelfish, gobies, grunts, parrot fish, pork fish, wrasses, and many more—hang out in the reefs. Shipwrecks from the 18th century are evidence of the area's international maritime heritage, and a Maritime Heritage Trail has been developed to link six of the major shipwrecks and underwater cultural sites, including the Fowey Rocks Lighthouse, built in

Biscayne National Park in One Day

Most visitors come to snorkel or dive. Divers should plan to spend the morning on the water and the afternoon exploring the visitor center. The opposite is true for snorkelers, as snorkel trips (and one-tank shallow-dive trips) depart in the afternoon. If you want to hike, turn to the trails at Elliott Key—just be sure to apply insect repellent (and sunscreen, too, no matter what time of year).

1878. Sites, including a 19th-century wooden sailing vessel, have been plotted with GPS coordinates and marked with mooring buoys.

Everglades City

36 miles southeast of Naples and 85 miles west of Miami.

Aside from a chain gas station or two, Everglades City retains its Old Florida authenticity. High-rises (other than an observation tower named for pioneer Ernest Hamilton) are nowhere to be found along this western gateway to Everglades National Park. Everglades City was developed in the late 19th century by Barron Collier, a wealthy advertising entrepreneur, who built it as a company town to house workers for his numerous projects, including construction of the Tamiami Trail. It grew and prospered until the Depression and World War II. Today the ramshackle town attracts adventure seekers heading to the park for the thrill of canoeing, fishing, and birdwatching. Airboat tours, though popular, are banned within the park because of the environmental damage they cause to the mangroves. The Everglades Seafood Festival, launched in 1970 and held the first full weekend of February, draws huge crowds for delights from the sea, music, and craft displays. At quieter times dining choices center on a handful of rustic eateries focused on seafood. The town is small, fishing-oriented, and unhurried, making it excellent for boating, bicycling, or just strolling around. You can pedal along the waterfront on a 2-mile strand out to Chokoloskee Island.

VISITOR INFORMATION

CONTACTS Everglades Area Chamber of Commerce Welcome Center. ✉ *32016 Tamiami Trail E* ☎ *239/695–3941*.

Sights

Collier-Seminole State Park

ARCHAEOLOGICAL SITE | FAMILY | At Collier-Seminole State Park, opportunities to try biking, birding, hiking, camping, and canoeing in Everglades territory are plentiful. This makes the 7,000-plus-acre park a prime introduction to the elusive mangrove swampland. The campground was recently renovated, and sites come complete with electricity, water, a grill, and a picnic table. Leashed pets are allowed. Alternatively, there are "primitive" campsites accessible by foot or canoe. Of historical interest, a Seminole War blockhouse has been recreated to hold the interpretative center, and one of the "walking dredges"—a towering black machine invented to carve the Tamiami Trail out of the muck—stands silent on the grounds. Kayaks and canoes can be launched into the Blackwater River here. Bring your own, or rent a canoe from the park. The Friends of Collier-Seminole State Park offers guided canoe trips from December to March; reservations are recommended. ✉ *20200 Tamiami Trail E, Naples* ☎ *239/394–3397* 🌐 *www.floridastateparks.org/parks-and-trails/collier-seminole-state-park* 🎫 *$5 per vehicle; $4 for solo driver; $2 for pedestrians or bikers; camping starts at $22 per night.*

Fakahatchee Strand Preserve State Park

NATIONAL/STATE PARK | FAMILY | The 2,000-foot-long boardwalk at Big Cypress Bend takes visitors fairly quickly through this swamp forest, providing an opportunity to see rare plants, nesting eagles, and Florida's largest swath of coexisting native royal palms—unique to Fakahatchee Strand—with bald cypress under the forest canopy. Fakahatchee Strand is also considered the orchid and bromeliad capital of the continent with 44 native orchids and 14 native bromeliads, many blooming most extravagantly in hotter months. It's particularly famed for ghost orchids (as seen in Susan

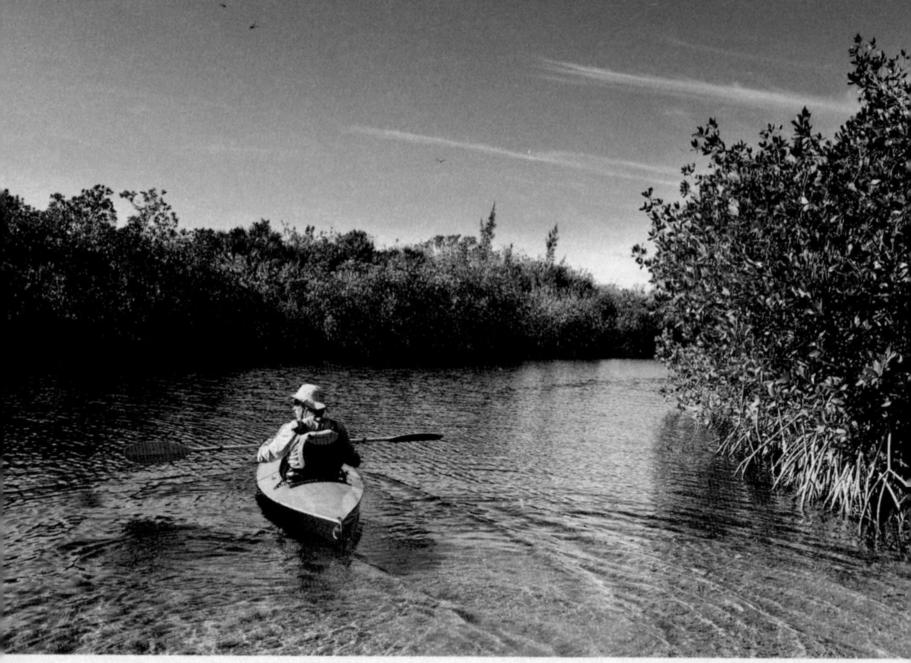

Native plants along the Turner River Canoe Trail hem in paddlers on both sides, and alligators lurk nearby.

Orlean's novel *The Orchid Thief*) that are visible on guided hikes. On your quest for ghost orchids, keep an eye out for white-tailed deer, black bears, bobcats, and the Florida panther. For park nature on parade, take the 6-mile stretch of the Janes Scenic Drive (between the visitor's center and East Main) that's still open to traffic; the rest of the drive is open only to hikers and bikers now. ✉ *137 Coastline Dr., Copeland* ☎ *239/695–4593* 🌐 *www.floridastateparks.org/parks-and-trails/fakahatchee-strand-preserve-state-park* 🎫 *$3 per vehicle. $2 per person for bicyclists and pedestrians.*

Museum of the Everglades

MUSEUM | **FAMILY** | At this Collier County museum, you can learn about early Native Americans, pioneers, entrepreneurs, and anglers who played pivotal roles in southwest Florida development. Exhibits of artifacts and photographs, as well as a short film chronicle, detail the tremendous feat of building the Tamiami Trail across mosquito-ridden, gator-infested Everglades wetlands. Permanent displays and monthly shows rotate works by local and regional artists in the Pauline Reeves Gallery. The small museum is housed in the 1927 Laundry Building, which was once used for washing linens from the Rod & Gun Club and the Everglades Inn until it closed during World War II. ✉ *105 W. Broadway* ☎ *239/695–0008* 🌐 *www.evergladesmuseum.org* 🎫 *Free.*

Restaurants

City Seafood

$$ | **SEAFOOD** | **FAMILY** | Gems from the sea are delivered fresh from the owners' boats to this rustic haven. Enjoy breakfast, lunch, or an early dinner inside, or sit outdoors to watch pelicans, gulls, tarpon, manatees, and the occasional gator play off the dock on the Barron River. **Known for:** sustainable stone crab in season; waterfront hangout; wrapping and shipping fresh seafood. 💲 *Average main: $15* ✉ *702 Begonia St.* ☎ *239/695–4700* 🌐 *www.cityseafood1.com.*

Havana Café

$$ | CUBAN | Cuban and Caribbean specialties are a welcome alternative to the typical seafood houses in the Everglades City area. This cheery eatery—3 miles south of Everglades City on Chokoloskee Island—has a dozen or so tables inside, and more seating on the porch amid plenty of greenery. Jump-start your day with *café con leche* and a pressed-egg sandwich, or try a Havana omelet. **Known for:** good café con leche for breakfast; Caribbean-style seafood dishes; Cuban specialties. *Average main: $18 191 Smallwood Dr., Chokoloskee 239/695–2214 havanacafeoftheeverglades.com Closed Apr.–Oct.*

Triad Seafood Market and Café

$$ | SEAFOOD | FAMILY | Along the Barron River, seafood houses, fishing boats, and crab traps populate one shoreline, while mangroves line the other. Some seafood houses added picnic tables and eventually grew into restaurants like the family-owned Triad Seafood Market & Café. **Known for:** coveted grouper sandwiches; screened porch for dining; all-you-can-eat stone crab feasts. *Average main: $15 401 W. School Dr. 239/695–0722 www.triadseafoodmarketcafe.com.*

Hotels

★ The Ivey House and Everglades Adventures

$ | B&B/INN | What was once a boardinghouse built for crews working on the Tamiami Trail in 1928 is now the top spot to stay in town for adventurers on assorted budgets. **Pros:** bed-and-breakfast style; charming; affordable. **Cons:** not on water; some small rooms; no pets. *Rooms from: $179 107 Camellia St. E 877/567–0679, 239/695–3299 International iveyhouse.com 18 rooms Breakfast.*

Activities

Wings Aero Tours

FLYING/SKYDIVING/SOARING | Wings' flightseeing tours of the Ten Thousand Islands National Wildlife Refuge, Fakahatchee Strand State Preserve, Big Cypress National Preserve, Everglades National Park, and Everglades City are available seasonally, November to May. Hop aboard an Alaskan bush plane to see sawgrass prairies, Native American shell mounds, alligators, manatees, dolphins, and wading birds from above. Captains provide passengers with headsets to keep you informed about the sights below. Flight tours can also be booked to see Marco Island and Key West, among other hot spots. *Everglades Airpark, 650 E.C. Airpark Rd. 239/695–3296 www.wingsaerotours.com From $150 per adult or $50 each for 3–4 adults.*

BOATING AND CANOEING

On the Gulf Coast, be sure to explore the nooks, crannies, and mangrove islands of Chokoloskee Bay and Ten Thousand Islands National Wildlife Refuge, as well as the rivers near Everglades City. The Turner River Canoe Trail, popular and populated even on Christmas as a pleasant day trip with almost guaranteed bird and alligator sightings, passes through mangrove tunnels, dwarf cypress, coastal prairie, and freshwater slough ecosystems of Everglades National Park and Big Cypress National Preserve.

Florida City

2 miles southwest of Homestead on U.S. 1.

Florida's Turnpike ends in Florida City, the southernmost town of Miami-Dade County's mainland. This is the point where thousands of vehicles spill onto U.S. 1 and eventually west to Everglades National Park, east to Biscayne National Park, or south to the Florida Keys.

As the last outpost before 18 miles of mangroves and water, this stretch of U.S. 1 is lined with fast-food eateries, service stations, hotels, bars, dive shops, and restaurants. Hotel rates increase significantly during NASCAR races at the nearby Homestead-Miami Speedway. Like Homestead, Florida City is rooted in agriculture, with expanses of farmland west of Krome Avenue and a huge farmers' market that ships produce nationwide.

GETTING HERE AND AROUND

SuperShuttle

This 24-hour service runs air-conditioned vans between Miami International Aiport (MIA) and PortMiami or wherever you'd like to go in the Miami-Dade County area; pickup is outside baggage claim. ✉ *Miami* ☎ *305/871–2000* 🌐 *miamisuper-shuttle.com.*

Sights

Tropical Everglades Visitor Center

INFO CENTER | Managed by the nonprofit Tropical Everglades Visitor Association, this pastel-pink information center with teal signage offers abundant printed material, plus tips from volunteer experts on exploring South Florida, especially Homestead, Florida City, and the Florida Keys. ✉ *160 U.S. 1* ☎ *305/245–9180* 🌐 *www.tropicaleverglades.com/index.php.*

Restaurants

Capri Restaurant

$$ | ITALIAN | FAMILY | This family-owned enterprise has been a magnet for affordable Italian-American classics since 1958. Eat pasta, crunchy-crust pizza, steak, prime rib, and a multitude of locally inspired desserts amid redbrick walls in the classic Capri dining room. **Known for:** affordable specials; family-friendly environment; full bar. *$ Average main: $20* ✉ *935 N. Krome Ave.* ☎ *305/247–1542* 🌐 *www.dinecapri.com* ⏱ *Dinner only on Sat. Closed Sun.*

Farmers' Market Restaurant

$ | SEAFOOD | This quaint eatery is inside the farmers' market on the edge of town, and it's big on serving fresh vegetables and seafood. A family of anglers runs the place, so fish and shellfish are only hours from the ocean. **Known for:** early hours for breakfast; seafood-centric menu; using fresh produce from the market. *$ Average main: $13* ✉ *300 S. Krome Ave., Ste. 17* ☎ *305/242–0008.*

Rosita's Mexican Restaurant

$ | MEXICAN | This delightful hole-in-the-wall Mexican spot boasts authenticity you can't get at the Tex-Mex chains. Breakfast, lunch, and dinner entrées, served all day, range from Mexican eggs, enchiladas, and taco salad to stewed beef and fried pork chops. **Known for:** authentic Mexican cuisine; a brisk take-out business; breakfast served all day. *$ Average main: $11* ✉ *199 W. Palm Dr., Homestead* ☎ *305/246–3114.*

Hotels

Best Western Gateway to the Keys

$ | HOTEL | For easy access to Everglades and Biscayne National Parks, as well as the Keys, you'll be well situated at this relatively modern, two-story motel close to Florida's Turnpike. **Pros:** conveniently located; free Wi-Fi and breakfast; attractive poolscape. **Cons:** traffic noise; books up fast in high season; no pets. *$ Rooms from: $120* ✉ *411 S. Krome Ave.* ☎ *305/246–5100* *114 rooms* *Breakfast* ☞ *A credit card with CHIP is required at check-in.*

Fairway Inn

$ | HOTEL | With a waterfall pool, this two-story motel has some of the area's lowest rates, and it's close to the Tropical Everglades Visitor Association, so you'll have easy access to tourism brochures and other information. **Pros:** affordable; conveniently located; nice pool. **Cons:**

plain, small rooms; no pets allowed; dated decor. $ *Rooms from: $75* ✉ *100 S.E. First Ave.* ☎ *305/248–4202, 888/340–4734 International* 🌐 *www.fairwayinnfl.com* *160 rooms* 🍴 *Breakfast.*

Travelodge by Wyndham

$ | **HOTEL** | This affordable hotel is close to Florida's Turnpike, Everglades and Biscayne National Parks, and Homestead-Miami Speedway. **Pros:** conveniently located; nice pool; complimentary breakfast. **Cons:** busy location; some small rooms; no pets allowed. $ *Rooms from: $70* ✉ *409 S.E. First Ave.* ☎ *305/482–1961, 877/257–2297 International* 🌐 *www.wyndhamhotels.com* *88 rooms* 🍴 *Breakfast.*

Shopping

Robert Is Here Fruit Stand and Farm

FOOD/CANDY | **FAMILY** | This historic fruit stand and farm sells more than 100 types of jams, jellies, honeys, and salad dressings along with farm-fresh veggies, juices, fabulous fresh-fruit milk shakes (try the papaya Key lime or guanabana), and dozens of tropical fruits. The list of rare finds includes carambola, lychee, egg fruit, monstera, sapodilla, dragonfruit, genipa, sugar apple, and tamarind. It all started as a tiny roadside stand back in 1960, when a pint-sized Robert sat at this spot hawking his father's bumper cucumber crop. Now with years of success and his own book (*Robert Is Here: Looking East for a Lifetime*), Robert remains on the scene daily with wife and kids; they ship nationwide and donate regularly to less fortunate families. An assortment of animals out back—goats, iguanas, and emus—along with a splash pool adds to the fun. Picnic tables, benches, and a waterfall with a koi pond provide serenity. Robert Is Here is open 8 am till 7 pm. ✉ *19200 S.W. 344th St., Homestead* ☎ *305/246–1592* 🌐 *www.robertishere.com.*

Homestead

40 miles southwest of Miami.

Homestead has established itself as a destination for tropical agritourism and ecotourism. At the confluence of Miami and the Keys, as well as Everglades and Biscayne National Parks, the area has the added dimension of shopping centers, residential development, hotel chains, and the Homestead-Miami Speedway. The historic downtown is a preservation-driven Main Street. Krome Avenue is lined with restaurants, an arts complex, antiques shops, and low-budget accommodations. West of Krome Avenue, miles of fields grow fresh fruits and vegetables. Some are harvested commercially, and others beckon with "U-pick" signs. Stands selling farm-fresh produce and nurseries that grow and sell orchids and tropical plants abound. In addition to its agricultural legacy, the town has an eclectic flavor, attributable to its population mix: descendants of pioneer Crackers, Hispanic growers and farm workers, professionals escaping the Miami mania, and retirees.

Sights

Coral Castle Museum

MUSEUM | **FAMILY** | Driven by unrequited love, Latvian immigrant Ed Leedskalnin (1887–1951) fashioned this attraction along Dixie Highway in the early 1900s out of massive slabs of coral rock, a feat he likened to building the pyramids. You can learn how he populated his fantasy world on his property with an imaginary wife and three children, studied astronomy, and created a simple home and elaborate courtyard without formal engineering education and with mostly handmade tools. Highlights of this National Register of Historic Places site, originally named Rock Gate, include a working sundial, a banquet table shaped like Florida, and other quirky coral sculptures. Fun fact:

Billy Idol wrote, recorded, and shot the video for his song "Sweet Sixteen" on the grounds of Coral Castle as a tribute to Ed. Candidly, among locals, it's known as a tourist trap. ✉ *28655 S. Dixie Hwy., Miami* ☎ *305/248–6345* 🌐 *coralcastle.com* 🎫 *$18.*

★ Fruit & Spice Park

GARDEN | **FAMILY** | You won't find this kind of botanical garden anywhere else in the United States. The tropical climate here helps it produce more than 500 varieties of fruit, nuts, and spices, as well as 75 varieties of bananas and 160 types of mango. The 37-acre park in Homestead's Redland historic agricultural district offers guided tram tours with experts several times a day, so visitors can make the most of their time on the property. You'll learn if what you're picking up off the ground to eat is, in fact, edible, and why some specimens may seem out of place for their designated region. You can sample fresh fruit at the gift shop, which also stocks canned and dried fruits plus cookbooks. The Mango Café is open for lunch daily and serves mango salsa, smoothies, and shakes along with salads, wraps, sandwiches, and its signature Mango Passion Cheesecake. Picnic in the garden at provided tables or on your own blankets. ✉ *24801 S.W. 187th Ave.* ☎ *305/247–5727* 🌐 *www.fruitandspice-park.com* 🎫 *$8.*

Schnebly Redland's Winery and Brewery

STORE/MALL | Homestead's fruit bounty is transformed into wine at this flourishing enterprise that started producing wines with lychee, mango, guava, and others as a way to eliminate waste from family groves each year. Over the course of a few decades, the Schnebly's tropical winery expanded to include a tasting room, a full-service restaurant, a lush plaza picnic area landscaped in coral rock, tropical plants, and waterfalls—plus a chickee hut inspired by the Seminole Indians. It's also home to popular beer brand Miami Brewing Company. ✉ *30205 S.W. 217th Ave.* ☎ *305/242–1224* 🌐 *www.schnebly-winery.com* 🎫 *Weekend tours $8 per person* ⏲ *Redlander Restaurant closed Mon.–Wed.*

Restaurants

Royal Palm Grill and Deli

$ | **AMERICAN** | **FAMILY** | You may have a déjà vu moment if you drive down Krome Avenue, where two Royal Palm Grills are just a hop-skip away from each other. This popular "breakfast all day, every day" enterprise has two locations, only a few blocks apart, to accommodate a steady stream of customers coming into the retro haven for everything from omelets and pancakes to biscuits and gravy, plus salads, steaks, and seafood. (Royal Palm's second location is at 436 N. **Known for:** early hours; breakfast all day; retro decor and vibe. 💲 *Average main: $10* ✉ *806 N. Krome Ave.* ☎ *305/246–5701* 🌐 *royalpalmhomestead.com.*

Shiver's BBQ

$$ | **BARBECUE** | **FAMILY** | Piggin' out since the 1950s, Shiver's BBQ is celebrated near and far for its slowly smoked pork, beef, and chicken in assorted forms of barbecue from baby back ribs to brisket. Be forewarned as you settle in at the communal tables, this spot is no place to cut calories. **Known for:** hickory-smoked barbecue; baby back ribs; takeout service. 💲 *Average main: $19* ✉ *28001 S. Dixie Hwy.* ☎ *305/248–2272* 🌐 *shiversbbq.com.*

Suvi Thai & Sushi Homestead

$$ | **ASIAN FUSION** | **FAMILY** | For fresh and light Asian fare near the Everglades, you can find Thai and Japanese favorites—from pad Thai and curries to traditional raw and cooked sushi rolls—at Suvi Thai & Sushi. If you want to go big here, try the sautéed Royal Thai Lobster or keep it simple with the Homestead Spicy Roll. **Known for:** lunch specials; family-friendly atmosphere; Asian favorites. 💲 *Average*

Are baby alligators more to your liking than their parents? You can pet one at Gator Park.

main: $20 ✉ 250 N. Homestead Blvd. ☎ 305/247–3500 🌐 suvimiami.com.

White Lion Cafe

$$ | AMERICAN | Although the antique shop within White Lion Cafe's cottage is now history, this 45-seat comfort-food haven, with a full bar, remains embellished with reminders of the past. From a 1950s-era wooden wall phone to a metal icebox and a Coca-Cola machine, you'll also find a mounted jackalope watching over a wide list of specials (Homestead crab cakes, burgers, fried chicken, and meatloaf). **Known for:** comfort food; lively bar scene; kitschy decor. [$] *Average main: $18 ✉ 146 N.W. 7th St. ☎ 305/248–1076 🌐 www.whitelioncafe.com ⏲ Closed Sun. and Mon.*

Hotels

The Hotel Redland

$ | HOTEL | Of downtown Homestead's smattering of mom-and-pop lodges, this historic inn is by far the most desirable. **Pros:** historic charm; conveniently located; excellent dining. **Cons:** traffic noise; small rooms; potentially haunted; dated website. [$] *Rooms from: $150 ✉ 5 S. Flagler Ave. ☎ 305/246–1904 🌐 www.cityhallbistromartinibar.com 13 rooms No meals.*

Activities

Homestead Bayfront Park

WATER SPORTS | FAMILY | Boaters, anglers, and beachgoers give unending praise to this recreational area adjacent to Biscayne National Park and the Florida Keys Marine Sanctuary. There's a natural atoll pool and beach, all within close proximity to coral reefs. The Herbert Hoover Marina can accommodate vessels up to 50 feet; it has a ramp, dock, bait-and-tackle shop, fuel station, ice station, and dry storage. The park also has a tropical restaurant called La Playa Grill, a playground, and a picnic pavilion with grills, showers, and restrooms. ✉ *Homestead Bayfront Park, 9698 S.W. 328th St. ☎ 305/230–3033 🌐 www.miamidade.gov/parks/*

homestead-bayfront.asp *$7 per car on weekends; $5 per car on weekdays.*

Homestead-Miami Speedway

AUTO RACING | FAMILY | Buzzing more than 300 days a year, the 600-acre speedway hosts racing, manufacturer testing, car-club events, driving schools, and ride-along programs. The motorsports facility has 65,000 grandstand seats, club seating, and two tracks—a 2.21-mile road course and a 1.5-mile oval. A packed schedule includes NASCAR events like Ford Championship Weekend. Parking includes space for 30,000 vehicles. *One Ralph Sanchez Speedway Blvd.* *305/230–5000, 866/409–7223 Ticket office* *www.homesteadmiamispeedway.com.*

Tamiami Trail

U.S. 41, between Naples and Miami.

There's a long stretch of U.S. 41 (originally known as the Tamiami Trail) that traverses the Everglades, Big Cypress National Preserve, and Fakahatchee Strand Preserve State Park, while connecting Florida's west coast to Miami. The road was conceived in 1915 to link Miami to Fort Myers and Tampa, but when it finally became a reality in 1928, it cut through the Everglades and altered the natural flow of water as well as the lives of the Miccosukee Indians who were trying mightily to make a living fishing, hunting, farming, and frogging here. The landscape is surprisingly varied, changing from hardwood hammocks to pinelands, then abruptly to tall cypress trees dripping with Spanish moss and back to sawgrass marsh. Slow down to take in the scenery and you'll likely be rewarded with glimpses of alligators sunning themselves along the banks of roadside canals and hundreds of waterbirds, especially in winter. The man-made portion of the landscape includes Native American villages, chickee huts, and airboats parked at roadside enterprises. Between Miami and Naples the road goes by several names, including Tamiami Trail, U.S. 41, Ninth Street in Naples, and, at the Miami end, Southwest 8th Street/Calle Ocho. **TIP→ Businesses along the trail estimate distance based on how far they are from Naples or the outskirts of Miami (from Krome Avenue or Florida's Turnpike).**

Sights

Everglades Safari Park

AMUSEMENT PARK/WATER PARK | FAMILY | A perennial favorite with tour operators, this family-run park has been in business since 1968 on a wild plot of land just 15 miles from overdeveloped West Miami. It has an arena for alligator wrestling shows with seating for up to 300 people. Before and after the show, get a closer look at both American alligators and American crocodiles on Gator Island, follow a jungle trail, walk through a small wildlife museum, or board an airboat for a 40-minute ride on the River of Grass (fee is included in park admission). The park also has a restaurant, a gift shop, and an observation platform overlooking the the lush vegetation in the surrounding Everglades. Smaller, private airboats can be chartered for tours lasting 40 minutes to two hours. Check online for discounts and count on free parking. *26700 S.W. 8th St., Miami* *305/226–6923* *www.evergladessafaripark.com* *$28.*

Gator Park

AMUSEMENT PARK/WATER PARK | FAMILY | At Gator Park, you can really get to know alligators, and even touch a baby gator during the park's wildlife show. You can also meet turtles, macaws, and peacocks. Native snakes also reside nearby, including the Blackpine, Brooks Kingsnake, Florida Kingsnake, and Red Ratsnake. The park, open rain or shine, also provides educational airboat tours through the River of Grass, as well as a gift shop and restaurant serving swamp fare like burgers, gator tail, and sausage. Tickets include admission, a group airboat ride, and an alligator wrestling show. Private tours are available. ✉ *24050 S.W. Eighth St., Miami* ☎ *305/559–2255, 800/559–2205 International* 🌐 *gatorpark.com* 🎫 *$19.99 online ($24.99 at the gate).*

Miccosukee Indian Village Museum
ARTS VENUE | FAMILY | Showcasing the skills and lifestyle of the Miccosukee Tribe of Florida, this cultural center offers craft demonstrations and insight into interaction with alligators. Narrated 30-minute airboat rides take you into the wilderness where natives hid after the Seminole Wars and Indian Removal Act of the mid-1800s. In modern times, many of the Miccosukee have relocated to this village on Tamiami Trail, but most still maintain their hammock farming and hunting camps. The museum shows two films on tribal culture and displays chickee hut structures and artifacts. Guided tours run throughout the day, and a gift shop stocks dolls, apparel, silver jewelry, beadwork, and other handicrafts. ✉ *Mile Marker 36, U.S. 41, Miami* ☎ *305/552–8365* 🌐 *www.miccosukee.com/indian-village-c/museum* 🎫 *Village entry $15; airboat rides $20.*

Restaurants

The Pit Bar-B-Q
$$ | BARBECUE | FAMILY | This old-fashioned roadside eatery on Tamiami Trail near Krome Avenue was opened in 1965 by the late Tommy Little, who wanted to provide easy access to cold drinks and rib-sticking fare for folks heading to and from the Everglades. Now spiffed up, the backwoods heritage vision remains a popular, affordable family option for lunch and dinner. **Known for:** huge pork sandwiches; Latin specialties; family-friendly atmosphere. $ *Average main: $15* ✉ *16400 S.W. 8th St., Miami* ☎ *305/226–2272* 🌐 *thepitbarbq.com/site.*

Crocs or Gators?

You can tell you're looking at a crocodile, not an alligator, if you can see its lower teeth sticking up over the upper lip when those powerful jaws are shut. Gators are much darker in color—a grayish black—compared with the lighter tan shades of crocodiles. Alligator snouts form a U-shape and are also much wider than their long, thin crocodilian counterparts (V-shape). South Florida is the only place in the world where the two coexist in the wild.

Hotels

Miccosukee Resort & Gaming
$ | RESORT | Like an oasis on the horizon of endless sawgrass, this nine-story resort on the edge of the Everglades can't help but attract attention—even if you're not a fan of 24-hour gaming action. **Pros:** casino; relatively modern; golf course. **Cons:** smoke-filled lobby; limited parking; stark contrast to its surroundings. $ *Rooms from: $169* ✉ *500 S.W. 177th Ave., Miami* ☎ *305/222–4600, 877/242–6464 International* 🌐 *www.miccosukee.com/resort* *302 rooms* *No meals.*

Activities

BOAT TOURS

Many Everglades-area tours operate only in season, roughly November through April.

Coopertown Airboat Tours
TOUR—SPORTS | FAMILY | Coopertown is the oldest airboat operator in the Everglades. The nearly 75-year-old business, which is attached to a restaurant with the same name, offers 35- to 40-minute tours that take you 9 miles into the fragile

ecosystem to see hammocks and alligator holes, red-shouldered hawks, and turtles. You can also book longer private charters with the company. ✉ *22700 S.W. 8th St., Miami* ☎ *305/226–6048* 🌐 *coopertownairboats.com* 🎫 *From $23.*

Everglades Alligator Farm

TOUR—SPORTS | **FAMILY** | More than 2,000 alligators live within the Everglades Alligator Farm. It's the oldest of its kind in South Florida and offers animal experiences, encounters, and airboat rides. Some are by reservation only, so check the website for details. It's a working farm—home of the late 14-foot "Grandpa" gator (now mounted for display)—and feedings for 500 hungry gators are at noon and 3 pm. ✉ *40351 S.W. 192nd Ave., Homestead* ☎ *305/247–2628* 🌐 *www.everglades.com* 🎫 *From $19.50 per person.*

Wooten's Everglades Airboat Tours

BOATING | **FAMILY** | This classic Florida roadside attraction is known as a one-stop-shop for Everglades adventures. They offer airboat tours through the Everglades, swamp buggy rides through the Big Cypress Swamp, educational sessions in the animal sanctuary, and live alligator shows. Some packages include an airboat ride, swamp buggy adventure, and sanctuary access. Rates change frequently, so check the website for individual prices and combo packages. ✉ *32330 Tamiami Trail E, Ochopee* ☎ *239/695–2781, 800/282–2781 International* 🌐 *www.wootenseverglades.com* 🎫 *Tours from $32.50; combo packages from $59.99; alligator show from $9.*

Chapter 5

THE FLORIDA KEYS

Updated by
Jill Martin

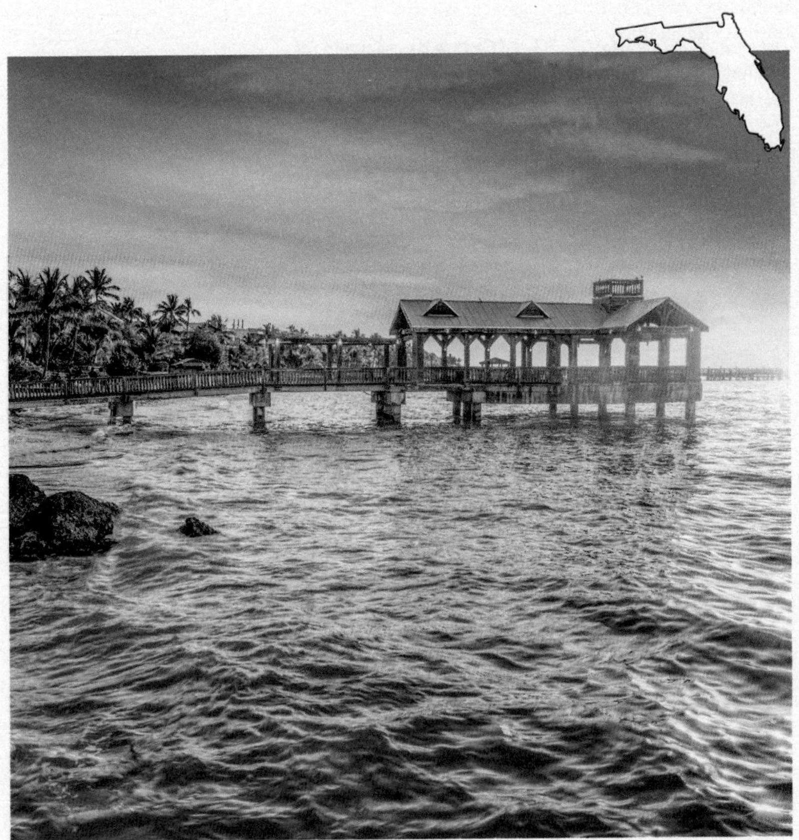

Sights ★★★★☆ | Restaurants ★★★☆☆ | Hotels ★★★☆☆ | Shopping ★★★☆☆ | Nightlife ★★★☆☆

WELCOME TO THE FLORIDA KEYS

TOP REASONS TO GO

★ **John Pennekamp Coral Reef State Park:** A perfect introduction to the Florida Keys, this nature reserve offers snorkeling, diving, camping, and kayaking. An underwater highlight is the massive Christ of the Deep statue.

★ **Viewing the Underwater World:** Whether you scuba dive, snorkel, or ride a glass-bottom boat, don't miss gazing at the coral reef and its colorful denizens.

★ **Sunset at Mallory Square:** Sure, it's touristy, but just once while you're here, you've got to witness the circuslike atmosphere of this nightly celebration.

★ **Duval crawl:** Shop, eat, drink, repeat. Key West's Duval Street and the nearby streets make a good day's worth of window-shopping and people-watching.

★ **Getting on the water:** From angling for trophy-size fish to zipping out to the Dry Tortugas, a boat trip is in your future. It's really the whole point of the Keys.

1 **Key Largo.** The first Key reachable by car, it's a prime spot for diving and snorkeling.

2 **Islamorada.** Sportfishing in deep offshore waters and backcountry reigns.

3 **Duck Key.** Come for a beautiful marina resort and boating.

4 **Grassy Key.** Known for natural wonders like Curry Hamock State Park.

5 **Marathon.** Most activity in the Middle Keys revolves around this bustling town.

6 **Bahia Honda Key.** One of the top beaches in Florida, with fine sand and clear water.

7 **Big Pine Key.** Laid-back community that's home to an impressive wildlife refuge.

8 **Little Torch Key.** A good jumping off point for divers headed to Looe Key Reef.

9 **Key West.** The ultimate in Keys craziness, this party town is for the open-minded.

10 **Dry Tortugas National Park.** Take a day trip to snorkel at these islands off Key West.

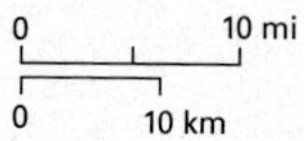

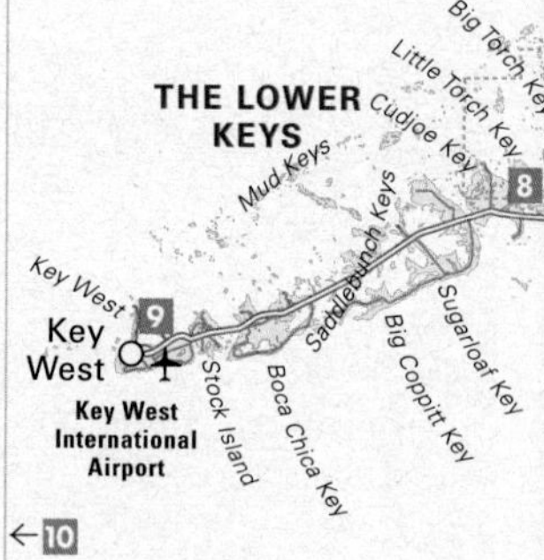

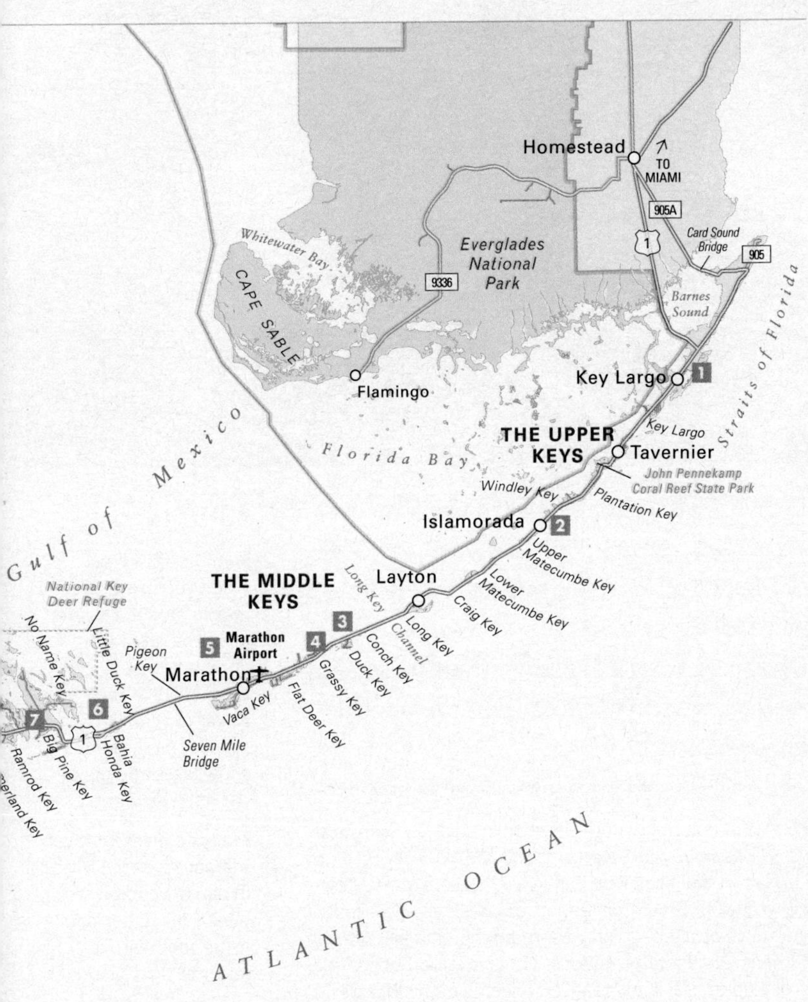
Homestead
TO MIAMI
905A
1
Card Sound Bridge
905
Whitewater Bay
Everglades National Park
9336
CAPE SABLE
Barnes Sound
Flamingo
Key Largo
1
Straits of Florida
Gulf of Mexico
Florida Bay
THE UPPER KEYS
Key Largo
Tavernier
John Pennekamp Coral Reef State Park
Windley Key
Plantation Key
Islamorada
2
Upper Matecumbe Key
THE MIDDLE KEYS
Long Key
Layton
Lower Matecumbe Key
Craig Key
Long Key Channel
National Key Deer Refuge
No Name Key
Little Duck Key
3
Long Key
Pigeon Key
5
Marathon Airport
4
Conch Key
Duck Key
Marathon
Grassy Key
Vaca Key
Flat Deer Key
6
7
1
Big Pine Key
Bahia Honda Key
Seven Mile Bridge
Ramrod Key
ATLANTIC OCEAN

SEAFOOD IN THE FLORIDA KEYS

Fish. It's what's for dinner in the Florida Keys. The Keys' runway between the Gulf of Mexico or Florida Bay and Atlantic warm waters means fish of many fin. Restaurants take full advantage by serving it fresh, whether you caught it or a local fisherman did.

Menus at colorful waterfront shacks such as **Snapper's** (✉ *139 Seaside Ave., Key Largo* ☎ *305/852–5956*) in Key Largo and **Half Shell Raw Bar** (✉ *231 Margaret St., Key West* ☎ *305/294–7496*) range from basic raw, broiled, grilled, or blackened fish to some Bahamian and New Orleans–style interpretations. Other seafood houses dress up their fish in creative styles, such as **Pierre's** (✉ *MM 81.5 BS, Islamorada* ☎ *305/664–3225* 🌐 *www.pierres-restaurant.com*) hogfish meunière, or yellowtail snapper with pear-ricotta pasta at **Café Marquesa** (✉ *600 Fleming St., Key West* ☎ *305/292–1244* 🌐 *www.marquesa.com*). Try a Keys-style breakfast of "grits and grunts"—fried fish and grits—at the **Stuffed Pig** (✉ *3520 Overseas Hwy., Marathon* ☎ *305/743–4059*).

BUILT-IN FISH

You know it's fresh when you see a fish market as soon as you open the restaurant door. It happens frequently in the Keys. You can even peruse the seafood showcases and pick the fish you want.

Many of the Keys' best restaurants are found in marina complexes, where the fishermen bring their catches straight from the sea. Try those in **Stock Island** (north of Key West) and at **Keys Fisheries Market & Marina** (✉ *MM 49 BS, end of 35th St., Marathon* ☎ *305/743–4353, 866/743–4353*).

CONCH

One of the tastiest legacies of the Keys' Bahamian heritage (and most mispronounced), conch (pronounced *konk*) shows up on nearly every menu in some shape or form. It's so prevalent in local diets that natives refer to themselves as Conchs. Conch fritters are the most popular culinary manifestations, followed by cracked (pounded, breaded, and fried) conch, and conch salad, a ceviche-style refresher. Since the harvesting of queen conch is now illegal, most of the islands' conch comes from the Bahamas.

FLORIDA LOBSTER

Where are the claws? Stop looking for them: Florida spiny lobsters don't have them. The sweet tail meat, however, makes up for the loss. Divers harvest these crustaceans from late July through March. Check with local dive shops on restrictions, and then get ready for a fresh feast. Restaurants serve them broiled with drawn butter or in dishes such as lobster Benedict, lobster spring rolls, lobster Reuben, and lobster tacos.

GROUPER

Once central to Florida's trademark seafood dish—fried grouper sandwich—its populations have been overfished in recent years, meaning that the state has exerted more control over bag regulations and occasionally closes grouper fishing on a temporary basis during the winter season. Some restaurants have gone antigrouper to try to bring back the abundance, but most grab it when they can. Black grouper is the most highly prized variety.

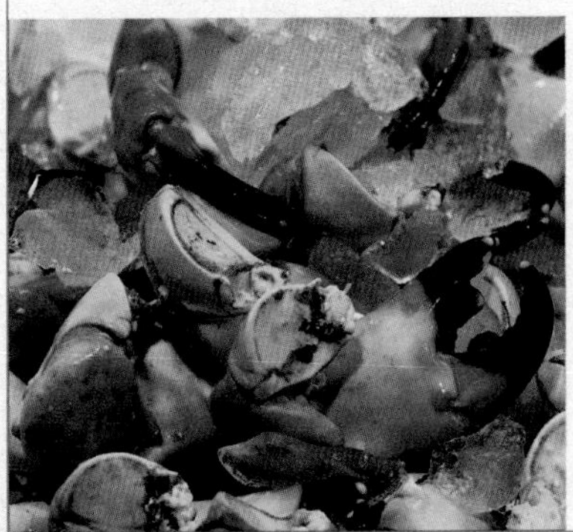

STONE CRAB

In season October 15 through May 15, it gets its name from its rock-hard shell. Fishermen take only one claw, which can regenerate in a sustainable manner. Connoisseurs prefer them chilled with tangy mustard sauce. Some restaurants give you a choice of hot claws and drawn butter, but this means the meat will be cooked twice, because it's usually boiled or steamed as soon as it's taken from its crab trap.

YELLOWTAIL SNAPPER

The preferred species of snappers, it's more plentiful in the Keys than in any other Florida waters. As pretty as it is tasty, its mild, sweet, and delicate meat lends itself to any number of preparations, and it's available pretty much year-round. Chefs top it with everything from key lime beurre blanc to mango chutney. **Ballyhoo's** in Key Largo (✉ *MM 97.8, in median* ☎ *305/852–0822*) serves it 10 different ways.

Your Keys experience begins on your 18-mile drive south on "The Stretch," a portion of U.S. 1 with a specially colored blue median that takes you from Florida City to Key Largo. The real magic starts at mile marker 113, where the Florida Keys Scenic Highway begins. As the only All-American Road in Florida, it is a destination unto itself, one that crosses 42 bridges over water, including the Seven Mile Bridge—with its stunning vistas—and ends in Key West. Look for crocodiles, alligators, and bald eagles along the way.

Key West has a Mardi Gras mood with Fantasy Festival, a Hemingway look-alike contest, and the occasional threat to secede from the Union. It's an island whose eclectic natives, known as "Conchs," mingle well with visitors (of the spring-break variety as well as those seeking to escape reality for a while) on this scenic, sometimes raucous 4x2-mile island paradise.

Although life elsewhere in the island chain isn't near as offbeat, it is as diverse. Overflowing bursts of bougainvillea, shimmering waters, and mangrove-lined islands can be admired throughout. The one thing most visitors don't admire much in the Keys are their beaches. They're not many, and they're not what you'd expect. The reason? The coral reef. It breaks up the waves and prevents sand from being dumped on the shores. That's why the beaches are mostly rough sand, as it's crushed coral. Think of it as a trade-off: the Keys have the only living coral reef in the United States, but that reef prevents miles of shimmering sands from ever arriving.

In season, a river of traffic gushes southwest on this highway. But that doesn't mean you can't enjoy the ride as you cruise along the islands. Gaze over the silvery blue-and-green Atlantic and its living coral reef, with Florida Bay, the Gulf of Mexico, and the backcountry on your right (the Keys extend southwest from the mainland). At a few points the ocean and Gulf are as much as 10 miles apart; in most places, however, they're from 1 to 4 miles apart, and on the narrowest landfill islands they're separated only by the road.

While the views can be mesmerizing, to appreciate the Keys you need to get off the highway, especially in more developed regions like Key Largo, Islamorada, and Marathon. Once you do, rent a boat, anchor, and then fish, swim, or marvel at the sun, sea, and sky. Or visit one of the many sandbars, which are popular places to float the day away. Ocean-side, dive or snorkel spectacular coral reefs or pursue grouper, blue marlin, mahimahi, and other deepwater game fish. Along Florida Bay's coastline, kayak to secluded islands through mangrove forests, or seek out the bonefish, snapper, snook, and tarpon that lurk in the shallow grass flats and mangrove roots of the backcountry.

MAJOR REGIONS

As the doorstep to the islands' coral reefs and blithe spirit, **the Upper Keys** introduce all that's sporting and sea-oriented about the Keys. They stretch from Key Largo, 56 miles south of Miami International Airport, to the Long Key Channel (MM 105–65). Centered on the town of Marathon, **the Middle Keys** hold most of the chain's historic and natural attractions outside of Key West. They go from Conch (pronounced *konk*) Key through Marathon to the south side of the Seven Mile Bridge, including Pigeon Key (MM 65–40). The Middle Keys make a fitting transition from the Upper Keys to the Lower Keys not only geographically but also mentally. Crossing Seven Mile Bridge prepares you for the slow pace and don't-give-a-damn attitude you'll find a little farther down the highway. Pressure drops another notch when you reach **the Lower Keys**, the most laid-back part of the region, where key-deer viewing and fishing reign supreme. The Lower Keys go from Little Duck Key west through Big Coppitt Key (MM 40–9). Finally, **Key West** lies 150 miles from Miami and encompasses MM 9–0.

Planning

When to Go

In high season, from mid-December through mid-April, traffic is inevitably heavy. From November to mid-December, crowds are thinner, the weather is superlative, and hotels and shops drastically reduce their prices. Summer is a second high season, especially among families, Europeans, bargain-seekers, and lobster divers.

Florida is rightly called the Sunshine State, but it could also be dubbed the "Humidity State." From June through September, 90% humidity levels are not uncommon. Thankfully, the weather in the Keys is more moderate than in mainland Florida. Temperatures can be 10°F cooler during the summer and up to 10°F warmer during the winter. The Keys also get substantially less rain than mainland Florida, mostly in quick downpours on summer afternoons. In hurricane season, June through November, the Keys get their fair share of warnings; pay heed, and evacuate earlier rather than later, when flights and automobile traffic get backed up.

Getting Here and Around

AIR TRAVEL

About 760,000 passengers use Key West International Airport (EYW) each year; its most recent renovation includes a beach where travelers can catch their last blast of rays after clearing security. Because direct flights to Key West are few, many prefer flying into Miami International Airport (MIA) or Fort Lauderdale–Hollywood International Airport (FLL) and driving the 110-mile Overseas Highway (aka U.S. 1).

BOAT AND FERRY TRAVEL

Key West Express operates air-conditioned ferries between the Key West Terminal (Caroline and Grinnell streets) and Marco Island and Fort Myers Beach. The trip takes at least four hours each way and costs $95 one way, from $125 round-trip (a $3 convenience fee is added to all online bookings). Ferries depart from Fort Myers Beach at 8:30 am and from Key West at 6 pm. The Marco Island ferry departs at 8:30 am (the return trip leaves Key West at 5 pm). A photo ID is required for each passenger. Advance reservations are recommended.

Boaters can travel to and through the Keys either along the Intracoastal Waterway (5-foot draft limitation) through Card, Barnes, and Blackwater sounds and into Florida Bay, or along the deeper Atlantic Ocean route through Hawk Channel, a buoyed passage. Refer to NOAA Nautical Charts Nos. 11451, 11445, and 11441. The Keys are full of marinas that welcome transient visitors, but they don't have enough slips for everyone. Make reservations in advance, and ask about channel and dockage depth—many marinas are quite shallow.

CONTACT Key West Express. ✉ *100 Grinnell St., Key West* ☎ *239/463–5733* 🌐 *www.keywestexpress.net.*

BUS TRAVEL

Keys Transportation provides private airport transfers to any destination in the Keys from either MIA or FLL. Prices start at $49 per person for transportation to Key Largo and get more expensive as you move south. Call or email for a price quote.

Greyhound Lines runs a special Keys shuttle twice a day (times depend on the day of the week) from Miami International Airport (departing from Concourse E, lower level) and stops throughout the Keys. Fares run from around $25 for Key Largo (✉ *MM 99.6*) or Islamorada (✉ *Burger King, MM 82*) to around $45 for Key West (✉ *3535 S. Roosevelt, Key West International Airport*).

Keys Shuttle runs scheduled service six times a day in 15-passenger vans between Miami and Fort Lauderdale airports and Key West with stops throughout the Keys for $60 to $90 per person sharing rides.

SuperShuttle charges $191 for up to two passengers for trips to the Upper Keys; to go farther, you must book an entire 11-person van, which costs $402. For a trip to the airport, place your request 24 hours in advance.

CONTACTS Greyhound. ☎ *800/231–2222* 🌐 *www.greyhound.com.* **Keys Shuttle.** ✉ *1333 Overseas Hwy., Marathon* ☎ *888/765–9997* 🌐 *www.keysshuttle.com.* **Keys Transportation.** ☎ *305/395–0299* 🌐 *www.keystransportation.com.* **SuperShuttle.** ☎ *800/258–3826* 🌐 *www.supershuttle.com.*

CAR TRAVEL

By car, from Miami International Airport, follow signs to Coral Gables and Key West, which puts you on LeJeune Road, then Route 836 west. Take the Homestead Extension of Florida's Turnpike south (toll road), which ends at Florida City and connects to the Overseas Highway (U.S. 1). Tolls from the airport run approximately $3. Payment is collected via SunPass, a prepaid toll program, or with Toll-By-Plate, a system that photographs each vehicle's license plate and mails a monthly bill for tolls, plus a $2.50 administrative fee, to the vehicle's registered owner.

Vacationers traveling in their own cars can obtain a mini-SunPass sticker via mail before their trip for $4.99 and receive the cost back in toll credits and discounts. The pass also is available at many major Florida retailers and turnpike service plazas. It works on all Florida toll roads and many bridges. For details on purchasing a mini-SunPass, call or visit the website.

For visitors renting cars in Florida, most major rental companies have programs allowing customers to use the Toll-By-Plate system. Tolls, plus varying service fees, are automatically charged to the credit card used to rent the vehicle (along with a hefty service charge in most cases). For details, including pricing options at participating rental-car agencies, check the program website. Under no circumstances should motorists attempt to stop in high-speed electronic tolling lanes. Travelers can contact Florida's Turnpike Enterprise for more information about the all-electronic tolling on Florida's Turnpike.

The alternative from Florida City is Card Sound Road (Route 905A), which has a (cash-only) bridge toll of $1. SunPass isn't accepted. Continue to the only stop sign and turn right on Route 905, which rejoins the Overseas Highway 31 miles south of Florida City.

Except in Key West, a car is essential for visiting the Keys.

CONTACTS Florida's Turnpike Enterprise. ☎ *800/749–7453* 🌐 *www.floridasturnpike.com.* **SunPass.** ☎ *888/865–5352* 🌐 *www.sunpass.com.*

THE MILE MARKER SYSTEM

Getting lost in the Keys is almost impossible once you understand the unique address system. Many addresses are simply given as a mile marker (MM) number. The markers are small, green, rectangular signs along the side of the Overseas Highway (U.S. 1). They begin with MM 126, 1 mile south of Florida City, and end with MM 0, in Key West. Keys residents use the abbreviation BS for the bay side of Overseas Highway and OS for the ocean side. From Marathon to Key West, residents may refer to the bay side as the Gulf side.

Hotels

Throughout the Keys, the types of accommodations are remarkably varied, from 1950s-style motels to cozy inns to luxurious resorts. Most are on or near the ocean, so water sports are popular. Key West's lodging portfolio includes historic cottages, restored Conch houses, and large resorts. Some larger properties throughout the Keys charge a mandatory daily resort fee, which can cover equipment rental, fitness-center use, and other services. You can expect another 12.5% (or more) in state and county taxes. Some guesthouses and inns don't welcome children, and many don't permit smoking.

Restaurants

Seafood rules in the Keys, which is full of chef-owned restaurants with not-too-fancy food. Many restaurants serve cuisine that reflects the proximity of the Bahamas and Caribbean (you'll see the term "Floribbean" on many menus). Tropical fruits figure prominently—especially on the beverage side of the menu. Florida spiny lobster should be local and fresh from August to March, and stone crabs from mid-October to mid-May. And don't dare leave the islands without sampling conch, be it in a fritter or in ceviche. Keep an eye out for authentic key lime pie—yellow custard in a graham-cracker crust. If it's green, just say "no." Note: Particularly in Key West and particularly during spring break, the more affordable and casual restaurants can get loud and downright rowdy, with young visitors often more interested in drinking than eating. Live music contributes to the decibel levels. If you're more of the quiet, intimate-dining type, avoid such overly exuberant scenes by eating early or choosing a restaurant where the bar isn't the main focus.

Hotel and restaurant reviews have been shortened. For full information, visit Fodors.com.

What It Costs			
$	$$	$$$	$$$$
RESTAURANTS			
under $15	$15–$20	$21–$30	over $30
HOTELS			
under $200	$200–$300	$301–$400	over $400

Visitor Information

There are several separate tourism offices in the Florida Keys, and you can use Visit Florida's website (🌐 *www.visitflorida.com*) for general information and referrals to local agencies. *See individual chapters for local visitor information centers.*

In addition to traditional tourist information, many divers will be interested in the Florida Keys National Marine Sanctuary, which has its headquarters in Key West and has another office in Key Largo.

CONTACT Florida Keys National Marine Sanctuary. ✉ *MM 95.23 BS* ☎ *305/809–4700* 🌐 *floridakeys.noaa.gov.*

Key Largo

56 miles south of Miami International Airport.

The first of the Upper Keys reachable by car, 30-mile-long Key Largo is the largest island in the chain. Key Largo—named Cayo Largo ("Long Key") by the Spanish—makes a great introduction to the region. This is the gateway to the Keys, and an evening of fresh seafood and views of the sunset on the water will get you in the right state of mind.

The history of Largo reads much like that of the rest of the Keys: a succession of native people, pirates, wreckers, and developers. The first settlement on Key Largo was named Planter, back in the days of pineapple, and later, key lime plantations. For a time it was a convenient shipping port, but when the railroad arrived Planter died on the vine. Today three communities—North Key Largo and Key Largo as well as the separately incorporated city of Tavernier—make up the whole of Key Largo.

What's there to do on Key Largo besides gaze at the sunset? Not much if you're not into diving or snorkeling. Nobody comes to Key Largo without visiting John Pennekamp Coral Reef State Park, one of the jewels of the state park system. Water-sports enthusiasts head to the adjacent Key Largo National Marine Sanctuary, which encompasses about 190 square miles of coral reefs, seagrass beds, and mangrove estuaries. If you've never tried diving, Key Largo is the perfect place to learn. Dozens of companies will be more than happy to show you the ropes.

Fishing is the other big draw, and world records are broken regularly in the waters around the Upper Keys. There are plenty of charter companies to help you find the big ones and teach you how to hook the elusive bonefish, sometimes known as the ghost fish.

On land, Key Largo provides all the conveniences of a major resort town, including restaurants that will cook your catch or prepare their own creations with inimitable style. You'll notice that some unusual specialties pop up on the menu, such as cracked conch, spiny lobster, and stone crab. Don't pass up a chance to try the local delicacies, especially the key lime pie.

Most businesses are lined up along U.S. 1, the four-lane highway that runs down the middle of the island. Cars whiz past at all hours—something to remember when you're booking a room. Most lodgings are on the highway, so you'll want to be as far back as possible. At MM 95, look for the mural painted in 2011 to commemorate the 100th anniversary of the railroad to the Keys.

GETTING HERE AND AROUND

Key Largo is 56 miles south of Miami International Airport, with its mile markers ranging from 106 to 91. The island runs northeast–southwest, with the Overseas Highway, divided by a median most of the way, running down the center. If the highway is your only glimpse of the island, you're likely to feel barraged by its tacky commercial side. Make a point of driving Route 905 in North Key Largo and down side streets to get a better feel for it.

VISITOR INFORMATION

In addition to traditional tourist information, many divers will be interested in the Florida Keys National Marine Sanctuary, which has an office in Key Largo.

CONTACTS Florida Keys National Marine Sanctuary. ✉ *MM 95.23 BS* ☎ *305/809–4700* 🌐 *floridakeys.noaa.gov.* **Key Largo Chamber of Commerce.** ✉ *MM 106 BS, 10600 Overseas Hwy.* ☎ *305/451–4747, 800/822–1088* 🌐 *www.keylargochamber.org.*

Sights

Dagny Johnson Key Largo Hammock Botanical State Park

LOCAL INTEREST | FAMILY | American crocodiles, mangrove cuckoos, white-crowned pigeons, Schaus swallowtail butterflies, mahogany mistletoe, wild cotton, and 100 other rare critters and plants inhabit these 2,400 acres, sandwiched between Crocodile Lake National Wildlife Refuge and the waters of Pennekamp Coral Reef State Park. The park is also a user-friendly place to explore the largest remaining stand of the vast West Indian tropical hardwood hammock and mangrove wetland that once covered most of the Keys. Interpretive signs describe many of the tropical tree species along a wide, 1-mile, paved road (2 miles round-trip) that invites walking and biking. A new, unpaved, extended loop trail can add 1–2 miles to your walk. There are also more than 6 additional miles of nature trails, most of which are accessible to both bikes and wheelchairs with a permit, easily obtainable from John Pennekamp State Park. Pets are welcome if on a leash no longer than 6 feet. You'll also find restrooms, information kiosks, and picnic tables. **■ TIP→ Rangers recommend not visiting when it's raining as the trees can drip poisonous sap.** ✉ *Rte. 905 OS, ½ mile north of Overseas Hwy., North Key Largo* ☎ *305/451–1202* 🌐 *www.floridastateparks.org/parks-and-trails/dagny-johnson-key-largo-hammock-botanical-state-park* 🎫 *$2.50 (exact change needed for the honor box).*

Dolphins Plus Bayside

ZOO | FAMILY | This educational program begins with a get-acquainted session beneath a tiki hut. After that, you slip into the water for some frolicking with your new dolphin pals. Options range from a shallow-water swim to a hands-on structured swim with a dolphin. You can also spend the day shadowing a trainer—it's $350 for a half day or a hefty $630 for a full day. ✉ *MM 101.9 BS, 101900 Overseas Hwy.* ☎ *305/451–4060, 866/860–7946* 🌐 *www.dolphinsplus.com* 🎫 *$10 admission only; interactive programs from $150.*

Dolphins Plus Marine Mammal Responder

COLLEGE | FAMILY | This nonprofit focuses on marine mammal conservation, and you can help it by participating in one of the educational offerings. One popular option is the Splash and Wade, a shallow-water program that begins with a one-hour briefing, after which you enter the water up to your waist to interact with the dolphins. Prefer to stay mostly dry? Opt to paint with a dolphin, or get a dolphin "kiss." For tactile interaction (fin tows, for example), sign up for the Interactive Swim, which is more expensive. ✉ *MM 99, 31 Corrine Pl.* ☎ *305/453–4321* 🌐 *www.dpmmr.org* 🎟 *Programs from $125.*

Florida Keys Wild Bird Center

COLLEGE | FAMILY | Have a nose-to-beak encounter with ospreys, hawks, herons, and other unreleasable birds at this bird rehabilitation center. The birds live in spacious screened enclosures along a boardwalk running through some of the best waterfront real estate in the Keys. Rehabilitated birds are set free, but about 30 have become permanent residents. Free birds—especially pelicans and egrets—come to visit every day for a free lunch from the center's staff. A short nature trail runs into the mangrove forest (bring bug spray May to October). Be sure to visit its interactive education center about 1½ miles south. ✉ *MM 93.6 BS, 93600 Overseas Hwy., Tavernier* ☎ *305/852–4486* 🌐 *www.keepthemflying.org* 🎟 *Free, donations accepted.*

Jacobs Aquatic Center

CITY PARK | FAMILY | Take the plunge at one of three swimming pools: an eight-lane, 25-meter lap pool with two diving boards; a 3- to 4-foot-deep pool accessible to people with mobility challenges; and an interactive children's play pool with a waterslide, pirate ship, waterfall, and sloping zero entry instead of steps. Because so few of the motels in Key Largo have pools, it remains a popular destination for visiting families. ✉ *Key Largo Community Park, 320 Laguna Ave., at St. Croix Pl.* ☎ *305/453–7946* 🌐 *www.jacobsaquaticcenter.org* 🎟 *$12 ($2 discount weekdays).*

Beaches

★ John Pennekamp Coral Reef State Park

BEACH—SIGHT | FAMILY | This state park is on everyone's list for easy access to the best diving and snorkeling in Florida. The underwater treasure encompasses 78 nautical square miles of coral reefs and sea-grass beds. It lies adjacent to the Florida Keys National Marine Sanctuary, which contains 40 of the 52 species of coral in the Atlantic Reef System and nearly 600 varieties of fish, from the colorful parrotfish to the demure cocoa damselfish. Whatever you do, get in the water. Snorkeling and diving trips ($30 and $75, respectively; equipment extra) and glass-bottom-boat rides to the reef ($24) are available, weather permitting. One of the most popular snorkel trips is to see *Christ of the Deep,* the 2-ton underwater statue of Jesus. The park also has nature trails, two man-made beaches, picnic shelters, a snack bar, and a campground. **Amenities:** food and drink; parking (fee); showers; toilets; water sports. **Best for:** snorkeling; swimming. ✉ *MM 102.5 OS, 102601 Overseas Hwy.* ☎ *305/451–1202 for park, 305/451–6300 for excursions* 🌐 *pennekamppark.com* 🎟 *$4 for 1 person in vehicle, $8 for 2–8 people, $2 for pedestrians and cyclists or extra people (plus a 50¢ per-person county surcharge).*

Restaurants

Alabama Jack's

$ | SEAFOOD | Calories be damned—the conch fritters here are heaven on a plate. Don't expect the traditional, golf-ball-size spheres of dough; these are unusual, mountainous, free-form creations of fried, loaded-with-flavor perfection. **Known for:** heavenly conch fritters; unique setting; live music. 💲 *Average main: $11* ✉ *58000 Card Sound Rd.* ☎ *305/248–8741.*

★ Buzzard's Roost Grill and Pub

$$$ | SEAFOOD | The views are nice at this waterfront restaurant, but the food is what gets your attention. Burgers, fish tacos, and seafood baskets are lunch faves. **Known for:** marina views; daily chef's specials; Sunday brunch with live steel drums. 💲 *Average main: $21*

Did You Know?

The bronze *Christ of the Deep* (also called *Christ of the Abyss*) statue of Jesus Christ underwater near John Pennekamp Coral Reef State Park is modeled after one in the Mediterranean Sea near where Italian Dario Gonzatti died while scuba diving.

✉ *Garden Cove Marina, 21 Garden Cove Dr.* ☎ *305/453–3746* 🌐 *www.buzzards-roostkeylargo.com.*

Chad's Deli & Bakery

$ | **AMERICAN** | It's a deli! It's a bakery! It's a pasta place! It's also where the locals go. **Known for:** homemade soups and chowders; eight varieties of supersized homemade cookies; huge portions. 💲 *Average main: $10* ✉ *MM 92.3 BS, 92330 Overseas Hwy., Tavernier* ☎ *305/853–5566* 🌐 *www.chadsdeli.com.*

The Fish House

$$$ | **SEAFOOD** | Restaurants not on the water have to produce the highest-quality food to survive in the Keys. Try fish Matecumbe style—baked with tomatoes, capers, olive oil, and lemon juice—or the buttery pan-sautéed preparation. **Known for:** smoked fish chunks and dip; excellent key lime pie; fresh-as-can-be seafood served fast. 💲 *Average main: $21* ✉ *MM 102.4 OS, 102341 Overseas Hwy.* ☎ *305/451–4665* 🌐 *www.fishhouse.com* ⏲ *Closed Sept.*

Harriette's Restaurant

$ | **AMERICAN** | If you're looking for comfort food—like melt-in-your-mouth biscuits the size of a salad plate or old-fashioned hotcakes with sausage or bacon—try this refreshing throwback for a hearty breakfast. At lunch, Harriette's shines in the burger department, and all the soups—from garlic tomato to chili—are homemade. **Known for:** always a wait but worth it; best muffins in Key Largo; tight dining space. 💲 *Average main: $8* ✉ *MM 95.7 BS, 95710 Overseas Hwy.* ☎ *305/852–8689* ⏲ *No dinner* ☞ *American Express not accepted.*

Jimmy Johnson's Big Chill

$$ | **SEAFOOD** | Owned by former NFL coach Jimmy Johnson, this waterfront establishment offers three entertaining experiences: the best sports bar in the Upper Keys; a main restaurant with all-glass dining room and a waterfront deck; and an enormous outdoor tiki bar with entertainment seven nights a week. There's even a pool and cabanas where (for an entrance fee) you can spend the day sunning. **Known for:** the place to watch a game; fantastic bay views; brick-oven chicken wings with rosemary. 💲 *Average main: $20* ✉ *MM 104 BS, 104000 Overseas Hwy.* ☎ *305/453–9066* 🌐 *www.jjsbigchill.com.*

Key Largo Conch House

$$ | **AMERICAN** | This family-owned restaurant in a Victorian-style home tucked into the trees is worth seeking out. Seven varieties of Benedicts, including conch, are brunch favorites, while lunch and dinner menus highlight local seafood like lionfish (when available) and yellowtail snapper. **Known for:** shrimp and grits; all-season outside dining; seafood tacos. 💲 *Average main: $16* ✉ *MM 100.2, 100211 Overseas Hwy.* ☎ *305/453–4844* 🌐 *www.keylargoconchhouse.com.*

Mrs. Mac's Kitchen

$$ | **SEAFOOD** | **FAMILY** | Locals pack the counters and booths at this tiny eatery, where license plates decorate the walls, to dine on everything from blackened prime rib to crab cakes. Every night is themed including Meatloaf Monday, Italian Wednesday, and Seafood Sensation (offered Friday and Saturday). **Known for:** a second location a half mile south with a full liquor bar; champagne breakfast; being a stop on the Florida Keys Food Tour. 💲 *Average main: $17* ✉ *MM 99.4 BS, 99336 Overseas Hwy.* ☎ *305/451–3722, 305/451–6227* 🌐 *www.mrsmacskitchen.com* ⏲ *Closed Sun.*

Sal's Ballyhoo's

$$$ | **SEAFOOD** | Occupying a 1930s Conch house with outdoor seating right alongside U.S. 1 under the sea-grape trees, this local favorite is all about the fish: yellowtail snapper, tuna, and mahimahi. Choose your favorite, then choose your preparation, such as the Hemingway, with a Parmesan crust, crabmeat, and key lime butter. **Known for:** spicy corn muffins; fish and fried-tomato sandwich;

grilled avocado appetizer. *Average main: $24* *MM 97.8 median, 97800 Overseas Hwy.* *305/852–0822* *www.ballyhoosrestaurant.com.*

Snapper's

$$ | **SEAFOOD** | In a lively, mangrove-ringed, waterfront setting, Snapper's has live music, Sunday brunch (including a build-your-own Bloody Mary bar), killer rum drinks, and seating alongside the fishing dock. "You hook 'em, we cook 'em" is the motto here—but you have to clean your own fish—and dinner is $14 for a single diner, $15 per person family-style meal with a mix of preparations when you provide the fish. **Known for:** grouper Oscar-style; fun and happening vibe; local crowd. *Average main: $17* *MM 94.5 OS, 139 Seaside Ave.* *305/852–5956* *www.snapperskeylargo.com.*

Sundowners

$$$ | **AMERICAN** | If it's a clear night and you can snag a reservation, this restaurant will treat you to a sherbet-hue sunset over Florida Bay. The food is also excellent: try the key lime seafood, a happy combo of sautéed shrimp, lobster, and crabmeat swimming in a tangy sauce spiked with Tabasco served over penne or rice. **Known for:** prime rib every Wednesday and Friday; Friday-night fish fry; choose your fish, choose your prepation. *Average main: $29* *MM 104 BS, 103900 Overseas Hwy.* *305/451–4502* *sundownerskeylargo.com.*

Hotels

Azul del Mar

$$ | **B&B/INN** | The dock points the way to many beautiful sunsets at this no-smoking, adults-only boutique hotel, which Karol Marsden (an ad exec) and her husband, Dominic (a travel photographer), have transformed from a run-down mom-and-pop place into a waterfront gem. **Pros:** quality bed linens and towels; good location; sophisticated design. **Cons:** small beach; high prices; minimum stays during holidays. *Rooms from: $299* *MM 104.3 BS, 104300 Overseas Hwy.* *305/451–0337, 888/253–2985* *www.azulkeylargo.com* *6 units* *No meals.*

★ Baker's Cay Resort Key Largo, Curio Collection by Hilton

$$$ | **RESORT** | **FAMILY** | Nestled within a "hardwood hammock" (localese for uplands habitat where hardwood trees such as live oak grow) near the southern border of Everglades National Park, this sparkling new, sprawling 13-acre resort is not to be missed. **Pros:** you never have to leave the resort; pretty pools with waterfalls; 21-slip marina for all your boating needs. **Cons:** some rooms overlook the parking lot; pools near the highway; expensive per-night resort fee. *Rooms from: $399* *MM 97 BS, 97000 Overseas Hwy.* *305/852–5553, 888/871–3437* *www.keylargoresort.com* *200 rooms* *No meals.*

Coconut Bay Resort & Bay Harbor Lodge

$ | **RESORT** | Some 200 feet of waterfront is the main attraction at these side-by-side sister properties that offer a choice between smaller rooms and larger separate cottages. **Pros:** temperature-controlled pool; owner Peg's homemade, amazing scones; free use of kayaks, paddleboat, and paddleboards. **Cons:** a bit dated; small sea-walled sand beach; bring your own charcoal for the barbecue grills. *Rooms from: $195* *MM 97.7 BS, 97702 Overseas Hwy.* *305/852–1625, 800/385–0986* *www.bayharborkeylargo.com* *21 units* *Free Breakfast.*

Coconut Palm Inn

$$ | **B&B/INN** | You'd never find this waterfront haven unless someone told you it was there, as it's tucked into a residential neighborhood beneath towering palms and native gumbo limbos. **Pros:** secluded and quiet; 100% smoke-free resort; sophisticated feel. **Cons:** front desk closes early each evening; no access to ice machine when staff leave; breakfast is ho-hum. *Rooms from: $299* *MM 92*

BS, 198 Harborview Dr., via Jo-Jean Way off Overseas Hwy., Tavernier ☎ 305/852–3017 🌐 www.coconutpalminn.com ⇨ 20 rooms 🍴 Free Breakfast.

★ Kona Kai Resort, Gallery & Botanic Gardens

$$ | RESORT | Brilliantly colored bougainvillea, coconut palm, and guava trees—and a botanical garden of other rare species—make this 2-acre adult hideaway one of the prettiest places to stay in the Keys. **Pros:** friendly staff; free use of sports equipment; spa-like pool area. **Cons:** expensive; some rooms are very close together. Ⓢ *Rooms from: $299 ✉ MM 97.8 BS, 97802 Overseas Hwy. ☎ 305/852–7200, 800/365–7829 🌐 www.konakairesort.com ⇨ 13 rooms 🍴 Free Breakfast.*

Marriott's Key Largo Bay Beach Resort

$$$ | RESORT | FAMILY | This 17-acre bay-side resort has plenty of diversions, from diving to a day spa. **Pros:** lots of activities; free covered parking; dive shop on property; free Wi-Fi. **Cons:** rooms facing highway can be noisy; thin walls; starting to show wear. Ⓢ *Rooms from: $359 ✉ MM 103.8 BS, 103800 Overseas Hwy. ☎ 305/453–0000, 866/849–3753 🌐 www.marriottkeylargo.com ⇨ 153 rooms 🍴 No meals.*

MB Resort at Key Largo

$$ | B&B/INN | With its sherbet-hue rooms and plantation-style furnishings, these tropical-style units range in size from simple lodge rooms to luxury two-bedroom suites. **Pros:** luxurious rooms; 10% discount to Snapper's restaurant next door; discounted ecotours from the dock. **Cons:** no beach; some find the music from next door bothersome; office closes at 8 pm. Ⓢ *Rooms from: $269 ✉ MM 94.5 OS, 147 Seaside Ave. ☎ 305/852–6200, 800/401–0057 🌐 www.mbatkeylargo.com ⇨ 14 rooms 🍴 Free Breakfast.*

The Pelican

$ | HOTEL | This 1950s throwback is reminiscent of the days when parents packed the kids into the station wagon and headed to no-frills seaside motels, complete with old-fashioned fishing off the dock. **Pros:** free use of kayaks and a canoe; well-maintained dock; reasonable rates. **Cons:** some rooms are small; basic accommodations and amenities; road noise with some units. Ⓢ *Rooms from: $159 ✉ MM 99.3, 99340 Overseas Hwy. ☎ 305/451–3576, 877/451–3576 🌐 www.hungrypelican.com ⇨ 21 units 🍴 Free Breakfast.*

★ Playa Largo Resort and Spa, Autograph Collection

$$$ | RESORT | At this luxurious 14-acre bay-front retreat, you'll find one of the nicest beaches in the Keys, as well as water sports galore, bocce, tennis, basketball, and a fitness center with inspiring pool views. **Pros:** comfortable rooms, most with balconies; excellent service; Playa Largo Kids Club. **Cons:** $41.93 per night resort fee; minimum stays may be required; luxury will cost you. Ⓢ *Rooms from: $399 ✉ 97450 Overseas Hwy. ☎ 305/853–1001 🌐 playalargoresort.com ⇨ 178 units 🍴 No meals ▭ No credit cards.*

Popp's Motel

$ | HOTEL | Stylized metal herons mark the entrance to this 67-year-old family-run motel. **Pros:** great beach; intimate feel; full kitchen in each unit. **Cons:** limited amenities; minimum stays in season; limited dock space. Ⓢ *Rooms from: $149 ✉ MM 95.5 BS, 95500 Overseas Hwy. ☎ 305/852–5201, 877/852–5201 🌐 www.poppsmotel.com ⇨ 9 units 🍴 No meals.*

Seafarer Resort and Beach

$ | HOTEL | FAMILY | If you're looking for modern and updated, this very basic, budget lodging isn't for you—this place is all about staying on the water for a song. **Pros:** kitchen units available; complimentary kayak use; cheap rates. **Cons:** can hear road noise in some rooms; some complaints about cleanliness. Ⓢ *Rooms from: $149 ✉ MM 97.6 BS,*

97684 Overseas Hwy. ☎ 305/852–5349 🌐 www.seafarerkeylargo.com 15 units 🍽 Free Breakfast.

Nightlife

The semiweekly *Keynoter* (Wednesday and Saturday), weekly *Reporter* (Thursday), and Friday through Sunday editions of the *Miami Herald* are the best sources of information on entertainment and nightlife. Daiquiri bars, tiki huts, and seaside shacks pretty well summarize Key Largo's bar scene.

Breezers Tiki Bar & Grille
BARS/PUBS | Mingle with locals over cocktails and catch amazing sunsets from the comfort of an enclosed, air-conditioned bar. Floor-to-ceiling doors can be opened on cool days and closed on hot days. It's located at Marriott's Key Largo Bay Beach Resort. ✉ *Marriott's Key Largo Bay Beach Resort, 103800 Overseas Hwy.* ☎ *305/453–0000.*

Caribbean Club
BARS/PUBS | Walls plastered with Bogart memorabilia remind customers that the classic 1948 Bogart–Bacall flick *Key Largo* has a connection with this worn watering hole. Although no food is served and the floors are bare concrete, this landmark draws boaters, curious visitors, and local barflies to its humble bar stools and pool tables. But the real magic is around back, where you can grab a seat on the deck and catch a postcard-perfect sunset. Live music draws revelers Thursday through Sunday. ✉ *MM 104 BS, 104080 Overseas Hwy.* ☎ *305/451–4466* 🌐 *caribbeanclubkl.com.*

Shopping

For the most part, shopping is sporadic in Key Largo, with a couple of shopping centers and fewer galleries than you find on the other big islands. If you're looking to buy scuba or snorkel equipment, you'll have plenty of choices.

★ Key Largo Chocolates
FOOD/CANDY | **FAMILY** | Specializing in key lime truffles made with quality Belgian chocolate, this is the only chocolate factory in the Florida Keys. But you'll find much more than just the finest white-, milk-, and dark-chocolate truffles; try the cupcakes, ice cream, and famous "chocodiles." The salted turtles, a fan favorite, are worth every calorie. Chocolate classes are also available for kids and adults, and a small gift area showcases local art, jewelry, hot sauces, and other goodies. Look for the bright-green-and-pink building. ✉ *MM 100 BS, 100471 Overseas Hwy.* ☎ *305/453–6613* 🌐 *www.keylargochocolates.com.*

Key Lime Products
LOCAL SPECIALTIES | Go into olfactory overload—you'll find yourself sniffing every single bar of soap and scented candle inside this key lime treasure trove. Take home some key lime juice (supereasy pie-making directions are right on the bottle), marmalade, candies, sauces, even key lime shampoo. Outside, you'll find a huge selection of wood carvings, pottery, unique patio furniture, and artwork. The fresh fish sandwiches and conch fritters served at the on-site Key Lime Cafe alone are worth the stop. ✉ *MM 95.2 BS, 95231 Overseas Hwy.* ☎ *305/853–0378, 800/870–1780* 🌐 *www.keylimeproducts.com.*

Randy's Florida Keys Gift Co.
GIFTS/SOUVENIRS | Since 1989, Randy's has been *the* place for unique gifts. Owner Randy and his wife, Lisa, aren't only fantastic at stocking the store with a plethora of items, they're also well respected in the community for their generosity and dedication. Stop in and say hello, then browse the aisles and loaded shelves filled with key lime candles, books, wood carvings, jewelry, clothing, T-shirts, and eclectic, tropical decor items. This friendly shop prides itself on carrying wares from local craftsmen, and there's something for every budget. ✉ *102421*

Overseas Hwy. ✣ On U.S. 1, next to the Sandal Factory Outlet ☎ 305/453–9229 ⊕ www.keysmermaid.com.

Shell World

GIFTS/SOUVENIRS | You can find lots of shops in the Keys that sell cheesy souvenirs—snow globes, alligator hats, and shell-encrusted anything. This is the granddaddy of them all. But this sprawling building in the median of Overseas Highway contains much more than the usual tourist trinkets—you'll find high-end clothing, jewelry, housewares, artwork, and a wide selection of keepsakes, from delightfully tacky to tasteful. ✉ *MM 97.5, 97600 Overseas Hwy.* ☎ *305/852–8245, 888/398–6233* ⊕ *www.shellworldflkeys.com.*

Activities

BOATING

Everglades Eco-Tours

BOATING | **FAMILY** | For over 30 years, Captain Sterling has operated Everglades and Florida Bay ecology tours and more expensive sunset cruises. With his expert guidance, you can see dolphins, manatees, and birds from the casual comfort of his pontoon boat, equipped with PVC chairs. Bring your own food and drinks; each tour has a maximum of six people. ✉ *Sundowners Restaurant, MM 104 BS , 103900 Overseas Hwy.* ☎ *305/853–5161, 888/224–6044* ⊕ *www.captainsterling.com* 🎫 *From $59.*

M.V. *Key Largo Princess*

BOATING | **FAMILY** | Two-hour glass-bottom-boat trips and more expensive sunset cruises on a luxury 70-foot motor yacht with a 280-square-foot glass viewing area depart from the Holiday Inn docks three times a day. **■ TIP→ Purchase tickets online to save big.** ✉ *Holiday Inn, MM 100 OS, 99701 Overseas Hwy.* ☎ *305/451–4655, 877/648–8129* ⊕ *www.keylargoprincess.com* 🎫 *$30.*

CANOEING AND KAYAKING

Sea kayaking continues to gain popularity in the Keys. You can paddle for a few hours or the whole day, on your own or with a guide. Some outfitters even offer overnight trips. The **Florida Keys Overseas Paddling Trail,** part of a statewide system, runs from Key Largo to Key West. You can paddle the entire distance, 110 miles on the Atlantic side, which takes 9 to 10 days. The trail also runs the chain's length on the bay side, which is a longer route.

Coral Reef Park Co.

CANOEING/ROWING/SKULLING | At John Pennekamp Coral Reef State Park, this operator has a fleet of canoes and kayaks for gliding around the 2½-mile mangrove trail or along the coast. Powerboat rentals are also available. ✉ *MM 102.5 OS, 102601 Overseas Hwy.* ☎ *305/451–6300* ⊕ *www.pennekamppark.com* 🎫 *Rentals from $20 per hr.*

Florida Bay Outfitters

CANOEING/ROWING/SKULLING | Rent canoes, sea kayaks, or Hobie Eclipses (the newest craze) from this company, which sets up self-guided trips on the Florida Keys Paddling Trail, helps with trip planning, and matches equipment to your skill level. It also runs myriad guided tours around Key Largo. Take a full-moon paddle or a one- to seven-day kayak tour to the Everglades, Lignumvitae Key, or Indian Key. ✉ *MM 104 BS, 104050 Overseas Hwy.* ☎ *305/451–3018* ⊕ *www.paddlefloridakeys.com* 🎫 *From $15.*

FISHING

Private charters and big "head" boats (so named because they charge "by the head") are great for anglers who don't have their own vessel.

Sailors Choice

FISHING | Fishing excursions depart twice daily (half-day trips are cash only), but the company also does private charters. The 65-foot boat leaves from the Holiday Inn docks. Rods, bait, and license are included. ✉ *Holiday Inn Resort &*

Marina, MM 100 OS, 99701 Overseas Hwy. ☎ 305/451–1802, 305/451–0041 🌐 www.sailorschoicefishingboat.com 🎫 From $45.

SCUBA DIVING AND SNORKELING

Much of what makes the Upper Keys a singular dive destination is variety. Places like Molasses Reef, which begins 3 feet below the surface and descends to 55 feet, have something for everyone from novice snorkelers to experienced divers. The *Spiegel Grove*, a 510-foot vessel, lies in 130 feet of water, but its upper regions are only 60 feet below the surface. On rough days, Key Largo Undersea Park's Emerald Lagoon is a popular spot. Expect to pay about $80 to $85 for a two-tank, two-site dive trip with tanks and weights, or $35 to $40 for a two-site snorkel outing. Get big discounts by booking multiple trips.

Amy Slate's Amoray Dive Resort

SCUBA DIVING | This outfit makes diving easy. Stroll down to the full-service dive shop (PADI, TDI, and BSAC certified), then onto a 45-foot catamaran. Certification courses are also offered. ✉ *MM 104.2 BS, 104250 Overseas Hwy. ☎ 305/451–3595, 800/426–6729 🌐 www.amoray.com 🎫 From $85.*

Conch Republic Divers

SCUBA DIVING | Book diving instruction as well as scuba and snorkeling tours of all the wrecks and reefs of the Upper Keys. Two-location dives are the standard, and you'll pay an extra $20 for tank and weights. ✉ *MM 90.8 BS, 90800 Overseas Hwy. ☎ 305/852–1655, 800/274–3483 🌐 www.conchrepublicdivers.com 🎫 From $80.*

Coral Reef Park Co.

SCUBA DIVING | At John Pennekamp Coral Reef State Park, this company gives 3½-hour scuba and 2½-hour snorkeling tours of the park. In addition to the great location and the dependability, it's also suited for water adventurers of all levels. ✉ *MM 102.5 OS, 102601 Overseas Hwy. ☎ 305/451–6300 🌐 www.pennekamppark.com 🎫 From $30.*

Horizon Divers

SCUBA DIVING | The company has customized diving and snorkeling trips that depart daily aboard a 45-foot catamaran. ✉ *105800 Overseas Hwy. ☎ 305/453–3535, 800/984–3483 🌐 www.horizondivers.com 🎫 From $50 for snorkeling, from $85 for diving.*

Island Ventures

SCUBA DIVING | If you like dry, British humor and no crowds, this is the operator for you. It specializes in small groups for snorkeling or dive trips, no more than 10 people per boat. Scuba trips are two tanks, two locations, and include tanks and weights; ride-alongs pay just $35. Choose morning or afternoon. ✉ *Jules Undersea Lodge, 51 Shoreland Dr. ☎ 305/451–4957 🌐 www.islandventure.com 🎫 Snorkel trips $45, diving $85.*

★ Quiescence Diving Services

SCUBA DIVING | This operator sets itself apart in two ways: it limits groups to six to ensure personal attention and offers both two-dive day and night dives, as well as twilight dives when sea creatures are most active. There are also organized snorkeling excursions. ✉ *MM 103.5 BS, 103680 Overseas Hwy. ☎ 305/451–2440 🌐 www.quiescence.com 🎫 Snorkel trips $55, diving from $89.*

Rainbow Reef Dive Center

SCUBA DIVING | The PADI five-star facility has been around since 1975 and offers day and night dives, a range of courses, and dive-lodging packages. Two-tank reef dives include tank and weight rental. There are also organized snorkeling trips with equipment. Two locations to choose from. ✉ *MM 100 OS, 522 Caribbean Dr. ☎ 305/451–1113, 800/451–1113 🌐 www.oceandivers.com 🎫 Snorkel trips from $35, diving from $80.*

Islamorada's warm waters attract large fish and the anglers and charter captains who want to catch them.

Islamorada

Islamorada is between MM 90.5 and 70.

Early settlers named this key after their schooner, *Island Home,* but to make it sound more romantic they translated it into Spanish: *Isla Morada.* The Chamber of Commerce prefers to use its literal translation, "Purple Island," which refers either to a purple-shelled snail that once inhabited these shores or to the brilliantly colored orchids and bougainvilleas.

Early maps show Islamorada as encompassing only Upper Matecumbe Key. But the incorporated "Village of Islands" is made up of a string of islands that the Overseas Highway crosses, including Plantation Key, Windley Key, Upper Matecumbe Key, Lower Matecumbe Key, Craig Key, and Fiesta Key. In addition, two state-park islands accessible only by boat—Indian Key and Lignumvitae Key—belong to the group.

Islamorada (locals pronounce it "*eye*-la-mor- *ah*-da") is one of the world's top fishing destinations. For nearly 100 years, seasoned anglers have fished these clear, warm waters teeming with trophy-worthy fish. There are numerous options for those in search of the big ones, including chartering a boat with its own crew or heading out on a vessel rented from one of the plethora of marinas along this 20-mile stretch of the Overseas Highway. More than 150 back-country guides and 400 offshore captains are at your service.

GETTING HERE AND AROUND

Most visitors arrive in Islamorada by car. If you're flying in to Miami International Airport or Key West International Airport, you can easily rent a car (reserve in advance) to make the drive.

TOURS

CONTACT Florida Keys Food Tours.
☎ *305/393–9183* 🌐 *www.flkeysfoodtours.com.*

VISITOR INFORMATION

CONTACT Islamorada Chamber of Commerce & Visitors Center. ✉ *MM 87.1 BS, 87100 Overseas Hwy.* ☎ *305/664–4503, 800/322–5397* 🌐 *www.islamoradachamber.com.*

Sights

Florida Keys Memorial/Hurricane Monument

MEMORIAL | On Monday, September 2, 1935, more than 400 people perished when the most intense hurricane to make landfall in the United States swept through this area of the Keys. Two years later, the Florida Keys Memorial was dedicated in their honor. Native coral rock, known as keystone, covers the 18-foot obelisk monument that marks the remains of more than 300 storm victims. A sculpted plaque of bending palms and waves graces the front (although many are bothered that the palms are bending in the wrong direction). In 1995, the memorial was placed on the National Register of Historic Places. ✉ *MM 81.8, in front of the public library, 81831 Old State Hwy. 4A, Upper Matecumbe Key* ✣ *Just south of the Cheeca Lodge entrance* 🎫 *Free.*

History of Diving Museum

MUSEUM | Adding to the region's reputation for world-class diving, this museum plunges into the history of man's thirst for undersea exploration. Among its 13 galleries of interactive and other interesting displays are a submarine and helmet re-created from the film *20,000 Leagues Under the Sea.* Vintage U.S. Navy equipment, diving helmets from around the world, and early scuba gear explore 4,000 years of diving history. For the grand finale, spend $3 for a mouthpiece and sing your favorite tune at the helium bar. There are extended hours (until 6:45 pm) on the third Wednesday of every month. ✉ *MM 83 BS, 82990 Overseas Hwy., Upper Matecumbe Key* ☎ *305/664–9737* 🌐 *www.divingmuseum.org* 🎫 *$12.*

Robbie's Marina

MARINA | FAMILY | Huge, prehistoric-looking denizens of the not-so-deep, silver-sided tarpon congregate around the docks at this marina on Lower Matecumbe Key. Children—and lots of adults—pay $4 for a bucket of sardines to feed them and $2.25 each for dock admission. Spend some time hanging out at this authentic Keys community, where you can grab a bite to eat indoors or out, shop at a slew of artisans' booths, or charter a boat, kayak, or other watercraft. ✉ *MM 77.5 BS, 77522 Overseas Hwy., Lower Matecumbe Key* ☎ *305/664–8070, 877/664–8498* 🌐 *www.robbies.com* 🎫 *Dock access $1.*

Theater of the Sea

ZOO | FAMILY | The second-oldest marine-mammal center in the world doesn't attempt to compete with more modern, more expensive parks. Even so, it's among the better attractions north of Key West, especially if you have kids in tow. In addition to marine-life exhibits and shows, you can make reservations for up-close-and-personal encounters like a swim with a dolphin or sea lion, or stingray and turtle feedings (which include general admission; reservations required). These are popular, so reserve in advance. Ride a "bottomless" boat to see what's below the waves and take a guided tour of the marine-life exhibits. Nonstop animal shows highlight conservation issues. You can stop for lunch at the grill, shop in the extensive gift shop, or sunbathe and swim at the private beach. This could easily be an all-day attraction. ✉ *MM 84.5 OS, 84721 Overseas Hwy., Windley Key* ☎ *305/664–2431* 🌐 *www.theaterofthesea.com* 🎫 *$35.95; interaction programs $45–$199.*

Restaurants

★ Chef Michael's

$$$ | SEAFOOD | This local favorite—whose motto is "Peace. Love. Hogfish."—has been making big waves since its opening in 2011 with chef Michael Ledwith at the helm. Seafood is selected fresh daily, then elegantly prepared with a splash of tropical flair. **Known for:** watermelon mint sangria; fresh catch "Juliette" with shrimp and scallops; intimate tropical dining. *Average main: $30 MM 81.7, 81671 Overseas Hwy., Upper Matecumbe Key 305/664–0640 www.foodtotalkabout.com No lunch Mon.–Sat.*

Green Turtle Inn

$$$ | SEAFOOD | This circa-1947 landmark inn and its vintage neon sign is a slice of Florida Keys history. Period photographs decorate the wood-paneled walls. **Known for:** excellent conch chowder; a piece of Florida Keys history; huge homemade sticky buns. *Average main: $24 MM 81.2 OS, 81219 Overseas Hwy., Upper Matecumbe Key 305/664–2006 www.greenturtlekeys.com Closed Mon.*

Hungry Tarpon

$$ | SEAFOOD | As part of the colorful, bustling Old Florida scene at Robbie's Marina, you know that the seafood here is fresh and top quality. The extensive menu seems as if it's bigger than the dining space, which consists of a few tables and counter seating indoors, plus tables out back under the mangrove trees. **Known for:** insanely good Bloody Marys with a beefstick straw; heart-of-the-action location; biscuits and gravy. *Average main: $19 MM 77.5 BS, 77522 Overseas Hwy., Lower Matecumbe Key 305/664–0535 www.hungrytarpon.com.*

Islamorada Fish Company

$$ | SEAFOOD | FAMILY | When a restaurant is owned by Bass Pro Shops, you know the seafood should be as fresh as you can get it. The restaurant, housed in an open-air, oversize tiki hut on Florida Bay, is the quintessential Keys experience, with menu highlights that include cracked conch beaten 'til tender and fried crispy, and fresh catch Portofino blackened perfectly and topped with Key West shrimp and a brandied lobster sauce. **Known for:** tourist hot spot; great views; afternoon fish and shark feedings in its private lagoon. *Average main: $18 MM 81.5 BS, 81532 Overseas Hwy., Windley Key 305/664–9271 restaurants.basspro.com/fishcompany/Islamorada.*

Kaiyo Grill & Sushi

$$$$ | JAPANESE | The decor—an inviting setting that includes colorful abstract mosaics and upholstered banquettes—almost steals the show, but the food is equally interesting. The menu, a fusion of East and West, offers sushi rolls that combine local ingredients with traditional Japanese tastes. **Known for:** drunken scallops; showstopping decor; dessert cupcakes that look like sushi. *Average main: $35 MM 81.5 OS, 81701 Overseas Hwy., Upper Matecumbe Key 305/664–5556 Closed Sun. and Mon. No lunch.*

Lorelei Restaurant & Cabana Bar

$$ | AMERICAN | While local anglers gather here for breakfast, lunch and dinner bring a mix of islanders and visitors for straightforward food and front-row seats to the sunset. Live music seven nights a week ensures a lively nighttime scene, and the menu staves off inebriation with burgers, barbecued baby back ribs, and Parmesan-crusted snapper. **Known for:** amazing sunset views; you catch it, they'll cook it; excellent tuna nachos. *Average main: $15 MM 82 BS, 81924 Overseas Hwy., Upper Matecumbe Key 305/664–2692 www.loreleicabanabar.com.*

Marker 88

$$$$ | SEAFOOD | A few yards from Florida Bay, on one of the Keys only natural beaches, this popular seafood restaurant has large picture windows that offer great sunset views, but most patrons choose to dine outside on the sand. Chef Bobby Stoky serves such irresistible entrées as onion-crusted mahimahi and house-smoked sea-salt-and-black-pepper-encrusted rib eye. **Known for:** a gathering place for locals and visitors; fantastic fresh fish sandwich; extensive wine list. *Average main: $34* *MM 88 BS, 88000 Overseas Hwy., Plantation Key* *305/852–9315* *www.marker88.info.*

Morada Bay Beach Café

$$$ | **ECLECTIC** | **FAMILY** | This bay-front restaurant wins high marks for its surprisingly stellar cuisine, tables in the sand, and tiki torches that bathe the evening in romance. Seafood takes center stage, but you can always get roasted organic chicken or prime rib. **Known for:** feet-in-the-sand dining; full-moon parties; intoxicating sunset views. *Average main: $27* *MM 81 BS, 81600 Overseas Hwy., Upper Matecumbe Key* *305/664–0604* *www.moradabay.com.*

★ **Pierre's**

$$$$ | **FRENCH** | One of the Keys' most elegant restaurants, Pierre's marries colonial style with modern food trends and lets you taste the world from its romantic verandas. French chocolate, Australian lamb, Hawaiian fish, Florida lobster—whatever is fresh and in season will be masterfully prepared and beautifully served. **Known for:** romantic spot for that special night out; seasonally changing menu; full-moon parties. *Average main: $43* *MM 81.5 BS, 81600 Overseas Hwy., Upper Matecumbe Key* *305/664–3225* *www.moradabay.com* *No lunch.*

Hotels

Amara Cay Resort

$$ | **RESORT** | Simple yet chic, Islamorada's newest resort is an oceanfront gem. **Pros:** free shuttle to local attractions; free use of kayaks, bikes, paddleboards; oceanfront zero-entry pool. **Cons:** pricey $30 daily resort fee; living areas of rooms lack seating. *Rooms from: $299* *MM 80 OS, 80001 Overseas Hwy.* *305/664–0073* *www.amaracayresort.com* *110 rooms* *No meals.*

★ **Casa Morada**

$$$ | **B&B/INN** | This relic from the 1950s has been restyled into a suave, design-forward, all-suites property with outdoor showers and Jacuzzis in some of the suites. **Pros:** private island connected by footbridge; adults only; complimentary use of bikes, kayaks, paddleboards, and snorkel gear. **Cons:** dinner off property; beach is small and inconsequential; minimum two-night stay on weekends. *Rooms from: $400* *MM 82 BS, 136 Madeira Rd., Upper Matecumbe Key* *305/664–0044, 888/881–3030* *www.casamorada.com* *16 suites* *Free Breakfast.*

★ **Cheeca Lodge & Spa**

$$$$ | **RESORT** | While Cheeca's 27 acres took a beating during Hurricane Irma, the grounds are looking better every month, and this legendary resort still packs in more amenities than any other we can think of. **Pros:** everything you need is on-site; new designer rooms; water-sports center on property. **Cons:** expensive rates; expensive resort fee; very busy. *Rooms from: $410* *MM 82 OS, 81801 Overseas Hwy., Upper Matecumbe Key* *305/664–4651, 800/327–2888* *www.cheeca.com* *123 rooms* *No meals.*

Drop Anchor Resort and Marina

$$ | **HOTEL** | Immaculately maintained, this place has the feel of an old friend's beach house, even though it's been completely redone since Hurricane Irma blew through town. **Pros:** bright and colorful; very clean; laid-back charm. **Cons:** noise from the highway; beach is for fishing, not swimming; simplicity isn't for everyone. *Rooms from: $200* *MM 85 OS, 84959 Overseas Hwy., Windley Key* *305/664–4863, 888/664–4863* *www.dropanchorresort.com* *18 suites* *No meals.*

The Islander Resort

$$ | **RESORT** | Guests here get to choose between a self-sufficient town home on the bay side or an oceanfront resort with on-site restaurants and oodles of amenities. **Pros:** spacious rooms; nice kitchens; eye-popping views. **Cons:** pricey; no dining at bay-side location. *Rooms from: $300* *MM 82.1 OS, 82200 Overseas Hwy., Upper Matecumbe Key* *305/664–0082* *www.islanderfloridakeys.com* *25 town homes at the bay-side property* *No meals.*

★ **The Moorings Village**

$$$$ | **HOTEL** | This tropical retreat is everything you imagine when you envision the laid-back Keys—from hammocks swaying between towering trees to manicured sand lapped by aqua-green waves. **Pros:** romantic setting; good dining options with room-charging privileges; beautiful views. **Cons:** no room service; $25 daily resort fee for activities; must cross the highway to walk or drive to its restaurants. *Rooms from: $800* *MM 81.6 OS, 123 Beach Rd., Upper Matecumbe Key* *305/664–4708* *www.themooringsvillage.com* *17 cottages* *No meals.*

Postcard Inn Beach Resort & Marina at Holiday Isle

$$ | **RESORT** | After an $11 million renovation that encompassed updating everything from the rooms to the public spaces, this iconic property (formerly known as the Holiday Isle Beach Resort) has found new life. **Pros:** large private beach; heated pools; on-site restaurants including Ciao Hound Italian Kitchen & Bar. **Cons:** rooms near tiki bar are noisy; minimum stay required during peak times; rooms without an oceanfront view overlook a parking lot. *Rooms from: $267* *MM 84 OS, 84001 Overseas Hwy., Plantation Key* *305/664–2321* *www.holidayisle.com* *145 rooms* *No meals.*

Ragged Edge Resort

$$ | **HOTEL** | **FAMILY** | Nicely tucked away in a residential area at the ocean's edge, this family-owned hotel draws returning guests who'd rather fish off the dock and grill up dinner than loll around on Egyptian cotton sheets. **Pros:** oceanfront setting; boat docks and ramp; cheap rates for Islamorada. **Cons:** dated decor; off the beaten path; not within walking distance to anything. *Rooms from: $209* *MM 86.5 OS, 243 Treasure Harbor Rd., Plantation Key* *305/852–5389, 800/436–2023* *www.ragged-edge.com* *10 units* *No meals.*

Shopping

Art galleries, upscale gift shops, and the mammoth World Wide Sportsman (if you want to look the part of a local fisherman, you must wear a shirt from here) make up the variety and superior style of Islamorada shopping.

Banyan Tree Garden and Boutique

HOUSEHOLD ITEMS/FURNITURE | Stroll and shop among the colorful orchids and lush plants at this outdoor garden and indoor boutique known for its tropical splendor, unique gifts, and free-spirited clothing. There is nothing quite like it in the area. *MM 81.2 OS, 81197 Overseas Hwy., Upper Matecumbe Key* *305/664–3433* *www.banyantreeboutique.com.*

Casa Mar Village

SHOPPING CENTERS/MALLS | Change is good, and in this case, it's fantastic. What was once a row of worn-down buildings is now a merry blend of gift shops and galleries with the added bonus of a place selling fresh-roasted coffee. By day, these colorful shops glisten at their canal-front location; by nightfall, they're lit up like a lovely Christmas town. The offerings include What the Fish Rolls & More restaurant; Casa Mar Seafood fish market; and Paddle the Florida Keys, where you can rent paddleboards and kayaks. *MM 90 OS, 90775 Old Hwy.,*

Kayak ready to be used on the beach in the Florida Keys

Upper Matecumbe Key 🌐 *www.casamar-village.com.*

Rain Barrel Artisan Village

CRAFTS | This is a natural and unhurried shopping showplace. Set in a tropical garden of shady trees, native shrubs, and orchids, the crafts village has shops selling the work of local and national artists, as well as resident artists who sell work from their own studios. Take a selfie with "Betsy," the giant Florida lobster, roadside. ✉ *MM 86.7 BS, 86700 Overseas Hwy., Plantation Key* ☎ *305/852–3084.*

Redbone Gallery

CRAFTS | This gallery stocks hand-stitched clothing, giftware, and jewelry, in addition to works of art by watercolorists C. D. Clarke, Christine Black, and Julie Joyce; and painters David Hall, Steven Left, Tim Borski, and Jorge Martinez. Proceeds benefit cystic fibrosis research. Find them in the Morada Way Arts and Cultural District. ✉ *MM 81.5 OS, 200 Morada Way, Upper Matecumbe Key* ☎ *305/664–2002* 🌐 *www.redbone.org.*

World Wide Sportsman

SPORTING GOODS | This two-level retail center sells upscale and everyday fishing equipment, resort clothing, sportfishing art, and other gifts. When you're tired of shopping, relax at the Zane Grey Long Key Lounge, located on the second level—but not before you step up and into *Pilar,* a replica of Hemingway's boat. ✉ *MM 81.5 BS, 81576 Overseas Hwy., Upper Matecumbe Key* ☎ *305/664–4615, 800/327–2880.*

Activities

BOATING

Keys Boat Rental

BOATING | You can rent both fishing and deck boats here (from 18 to 29 feet) by the day or the week. Free local delivery with seven-day rentals from each of its locations is available. ✉ *MM 85.9 BS and 99.7 OS, 85920 Overseas Hwy., Upper Matecumbe Key* ☎ *305/664–9404, 877/453–9463* 🌐 *www.keysboatrental.com* 🎫 *Rentals from $240 per day.*

Early Bird Fishing Charters

FISHING | Captain Ross knows these waters well, and he'll hook you up with whatever is in season—mahimahi, sailfish, tuna, and wahoo, to name a few—while you cruise on a comfy and stylish 43-foot custom Willis charter boat. The salon is air-conditioned for those hot summer days, and everything but booze and food is included. ✉ *Bud and Mary's Marina, MM 79.8 OS, 79851 Overseas Hwy.* ☎ *305/942–3618* 🌐 *www.fishearlybird.com* 🎫 *4 hrs $850; 6 hrs $1,100; 8 hrs $1,300.*

Nauti-Limo

BOATING | Captain Joe Fox has converted the design of a 1983 pink Caddy stretch limo into a less-than-luxurious but certainly curious watercraft. The seaworthy hybrid—complete with wheels—can sail with the top down if you're in the mood. Only in the Keys! One-hour and longer tours are available. New to the fleet is a 40-foot pirate ship, complete with plastic swords, that can hold about 14 people, available for two-hour rides. ✉ *Lorelei Restaurant & Yacht Club, MM 82 BS, 96 Madeira Rd., Upper Matecumbe Key* ☎ *305/942–3793* 🌐 *www.nautilimo.com* 🎫 *From $90.*

Robbie's Boat Rentals

BOATING | This full-service company will even give you a crash course on how not to crash your boat. The rental fleet includes an 18-foot skiff with a 90-horsepower outboard to a 21-foot deck boat with a 130-horsepower engine. Robbie's also rents snorkeling gear (there's good snorkeling nearby) and sells bait, drinks, and snacks. Want to hire a guide who knows the local waters and where the fish lurk? Robbie's offers offshore-fishing trips, patch-reef trips, and party-boat fishing. Backcountry flats trips are a specialty. ✉ *MM 77.5 BS, 77522 Overseas Hwy., Lower Matecumbe Key* ☎ *305/664–9814, 877/664–8498* 🌐 *www.robbies.com* 🎫 *From $185 per day.*

FISHING

Here in the self-proclaimed "Sportfishing Capital of the World," sailfish is the prime catch in the winter and mahimahi in the summer. Buchanan Bank just south of Islamorada is a good spot to try for tarpon in the spring. Blackfin tuna and amberjack are generally plentiful in the area, too. **■ TIP→ The Hump at Islamorada ranks highest among anglers' favorite fishing spots in Florida (declared Florida Monthly magazine's best for seven years in a row) due to the incredible offshore marine life.**

Captain Ted Wilson

FISHING | Go into the backcountry for bonefish, tarpon, redfish, snook, and shark aboard a 17-foot boat that accommodates up to three anglers. Choose half-day (four hours), three-quarter-day (six hours), or full-day (eight hours) trips, or evening tarpon fishing excursions. Rates are for one or two anglers. There's a $75 charge for an additional person. ✉ *Bud N' Mary's Marina, MM 79.9 OS, 79851 Overseas Hwy., Upper Matecumbe Key* ☎ *305/942–5224* 🌐 *www.captaintedwilson.com* 🎫 *Half-day and evening trips from $450.*

Florida Keys Fly Fish

FISHING | Like other top fly-fishing and light-tackle guides, Captain Geoff Colmes helps his clients land trophy fish in the waters around the Keys, from Islamorada to Flamingo in the Everglades. ✉ *105 Palm La., Upper Matecumbe Key* ☎ *305/393–1245* 🌐 *www.floridakeysflyfish.com* 🎫 *From $550.*

Florida Keys Outfitters

FISHING | Long before fly-fishing became popular, Sandy Moret was fishing the Keys for bonefish, tarpon, and redfish. Now he attracts anglers from around the world on a quest for the big catch. His weekend fly-fishing classes include classroom instruction, equipment, and daily lunch. Guided fishing trips can be done for a half day or full day. Packages combining fishing and accommodations

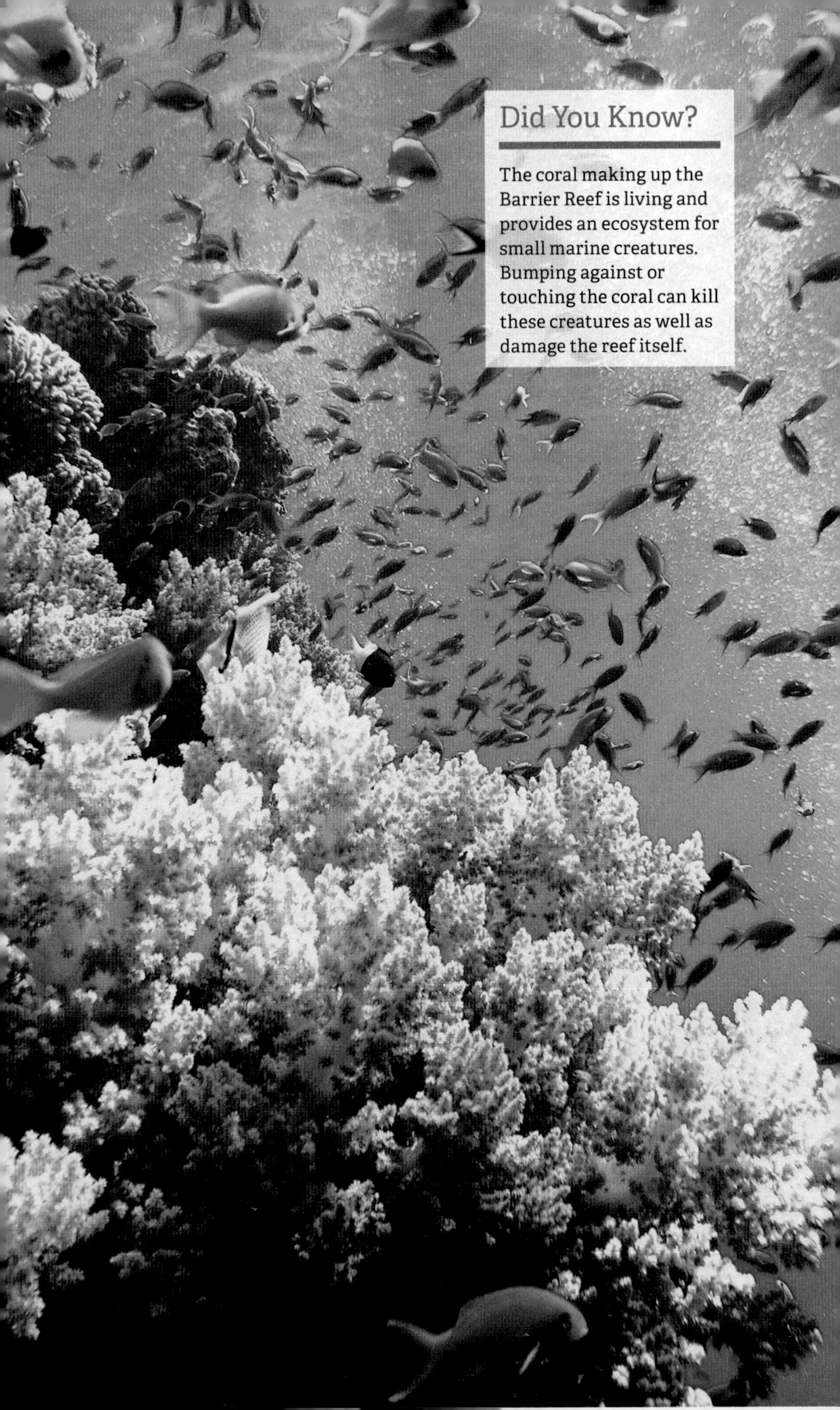

Did You Know?

The coral making up the Barrier Reef is living and provides an ecosystem for small marine creatures. Bumping against or touching the coral can kill these creatures as well as damage the reef itself.

at Islander Resort are available. ✉ *Green Turtle, MM 81.2, 81219 Overseas Hwy., Upper Matecumbe Key* ☎ *305/664–5423* 🌐 *www.floridakeysoutfitters.com* 🎫 *Half-day trips from $550.*

Miss Islamorada

FISHING | This 65-foot party boat offers full-day trips. Bring your lunch or buy one from the dockside deli. ✉ *Bud N' Mary's Marina, MM 79.8 OS, 79851 Overseas Hwy., Upper Matecumbe Key* ☎ *305/664–2461, 800/742–7945* 🌐 *www.budnmarys.com* 🎫 *$70.*

SCUBA DIVING AND SNORKELING

Florida Keys Dive Center

SCUBA DIVING | Dive from John Pennekamp Coral Reef State Park to Alligator Reef with this outfitter. The center has two 46-foot Coast Guard–approved dive boats, offers scuba training, and is one of the few Keys dive centers to offer nitrox and trimix (mixed-gas) diving. ✉ *MM 90.5 OS, 90451 Overseas Hwy., Plantation Key* ☎ *305/852–4599, 800/433–8946* 🌐 *www.floridakeysdivectr.com* 🎫 *Snorkeling from $38, diving from $84.*

Islamorada Dive Center

SCUBA DIVING | This one-stop dive shop has a resort, pool, restaurant, lessons, and twice-daily dive and snorkel trips and the newest fleet in the Keys. You can take a day trip with a two-tank dive or a one-tank night trip with their equipment or yours. Snorkel and spearfishing trips are also available. ✉ *MM 84 OS, 84001 Overseas Hwy., Windley Key* ☎ *305/664–3483, 800/327–7070* 🌐 *www.islamoradadivecenter.com* 🎫 *Snorkel trips from $45, diving from $85.*

San Pedro Underwater Archaeological Preserve State Park

SCUBA DIVING | About 1¼ nautical miles south of Indian Key is the San Pedro Underwater Archaeological Preserve State Park, which includes the remains of a Spanish treasure-fleet ship that sank in 1733. The state of Florida protects the site for divers; no spearfishing or souvenir collecting is allowed. Seven replica cannons and a plaque enhance what basically amounts to a 90-foot-long pile of ballast stones. Resting in only 18 feet of water, its ruins are visible to snorkelers as well as divers and attract a colorful array of fish. ✉ *MM 85.5 OS* ☎ *305/664–2540* 🌐 *www.floridastateparks.org/parks-and-trails/san-pedro-underwater-archaeological-preserve-state-park.*

WATER SPORTS

The Kayak Shack

WATER SPORTS | You can rent kayaks for trips to Indian (about 20 minutes one-way) and Lignumvitae (about 45 minutes one-way) keys, two favorite destinations for paddlers. Kayaks can be rented for a half day (and you'll need plenty of time to explore those mangrove canopies). The company also offers guided two-hour Jet Ski tours, including a snorkel trip to Indian Key or backcountry ecotours. It also rents stand-up paddleboards, including instruction, and canoes. ✉ *Robbie's Marina, MM 77.5 BS, 77522 Overseas Hwy., Lower Matecumbe Key* ☎ *305/664–4878* 🌐 *www.kayakthefloridakeys.com* 🎫 *From $40 for single, $55 for double; guided trips from $45.*

Duck Key

MM 61.

Duck Key holds one of the region's nicest marina resorts, Hawks Cay, plus a boating-oriented residential community.

Restaurants

Sixty-One Prime

$$$$ | **AMERICAN** | This fine-dining restaurant in Hawks Cay Resort serves steaks and seafood in an elegant setting. Chefs work with local farmers and fishermen to find what's fresh and in season, then create a menu that will wow your palate (and your wallet). **Known for:** naturally raised certified Black Angus beef; nightly

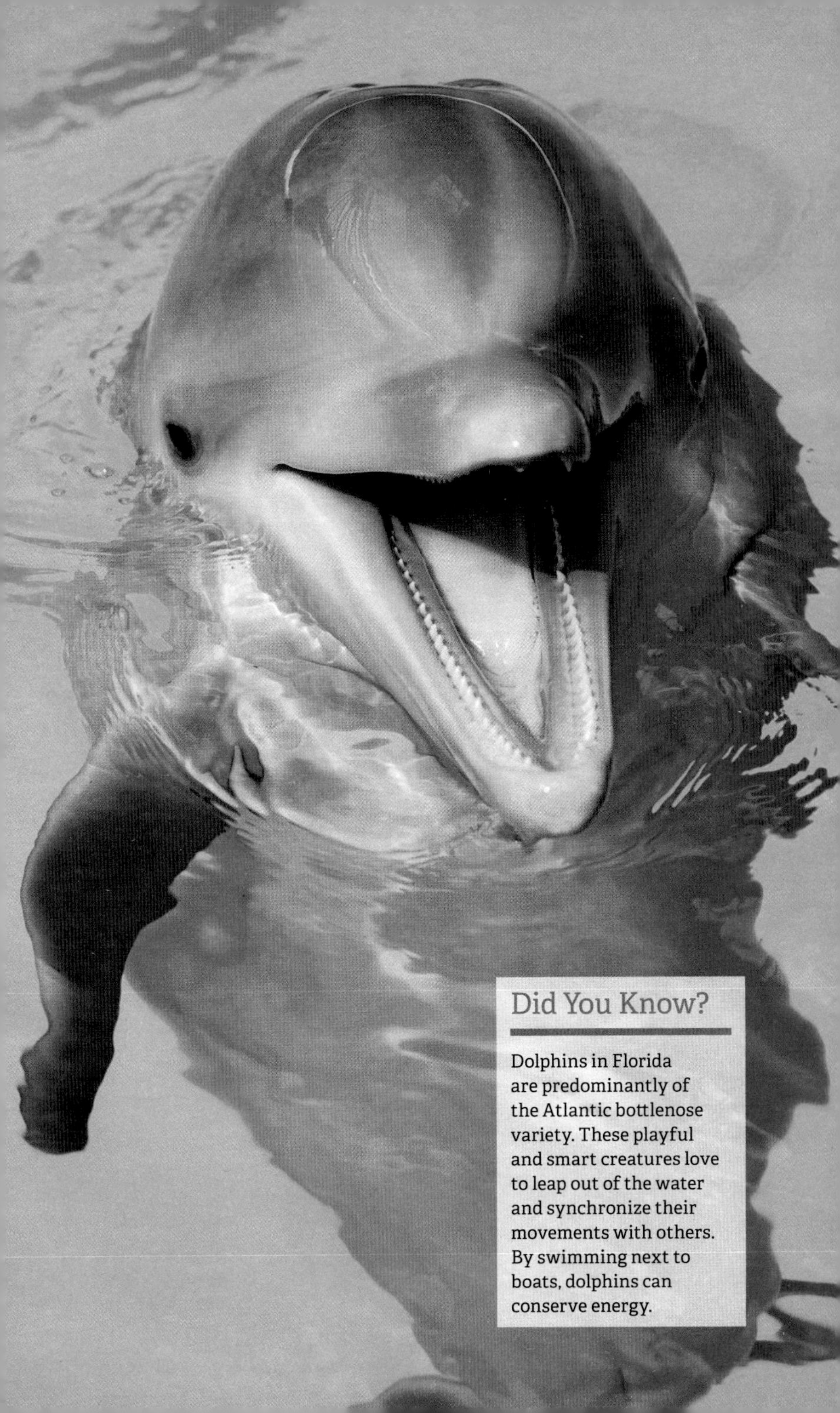

Did You Know?

Dolphins in Florida are predominantly of the Atlantic bottlenose variety. These playful and smart creatures love to leap out of the water and synchronize their movements with others. By swimming next to boats, dolphins can conserve energy.

changing menu; attentive service. *Average main: $36* *Hawks Cay Resort, 61 Hawks Cay Blvd.* *305/743–7000, 888/432–2242* *www.hawkscay.com* *No lunch.*

Hotels

★ Hawks Cay Resort

$$$ | RESORT | FAMILY | The 60-acre, Caribbean-style retreat with a full-service spa and two restaurants has plenty to keep the kids occupied (and adults happy). **Pros:** huge rooms; restful spa; full-service marina and dive shop. **Cons:** no real beach; far from Marathon's attractions; tram gets busy so either wait or walk far. *Rooms from: $315* *MM 61 OS, 61 Hawks Cay Blvd.* *305/743–7000, 888/432–2242* *www.hawkscay.com* *431 units* *No meals.*

Grassy Key

MM 60–57.

Local lore has it that this sleepy little key was named not for its vegetation—mostly native trees and shrubs—but for an early settler by the name of Grassy. A few families operating small fishing camps and roadside motels primarily inhabit the key. There's no marked definition between it and Marathon, so it feels sort of like a suburb of its much larger neighbor to the south. Grassy Key's sights tend toward the natural, including a worthwhile dolphin attraction and a small state park.

GETTING HERE AND AROUND

Most visitors arriving by air drive to this destination either from Miami International Airport or Key West International Airport. Rental cars are readily available at both, and in the long run, are the most convenient means of transportation for getting here and touring around the Keys.

Sights

Curry Hammock State Park

NATIONAL/STATE PARK | Looking for a slice of the Keys that's far removed from tiki bars? On the ocean and bay sides of Overseas Highway are 260 acres of upland hammock, wetlands, and mangroves. On the bay side, there's a trail through thick hardwoods to a rocky shoreline. The ocean side is more developed, with a sandy beach, a clean bathhouse, picnic tables, a playground, grills, and a 28-site campground, each with electric and water. Locals consider the paddling trails under canopies of arching mangroves one of the best kayaking spots in the Keys. Manatees frequent the area, and it's a great spot for bird-watching. Herons, egrets, ibis, plovers, and sanderlings are commonly spotted. Raptors are often seen in the park, especially during migration periods. *MM 57 OS, 56200 Overseas Hwy., Little Crawl Key* *305/289–2690* *www.floridastateparks.org/parks-and-trails/curry-hammock-state-park* *$4.50 for 1 person, $6 for 2, $0.50 per additional person* *Campsites are $43 per night.*

Dolphin Research Center

ZOO | FAMILY | The 1963 movie *Flipper* popularized the notion of humans interacting with dolphins, and Milton Santini, the film's creator, also opened this center, which is home to a colony of dolphins and sea lions. The nonprofit center has educational sessions and programs that allow you to greet the dolphins from dry land or play with them in their watery habitat. You can even paint a T-shirt with a dolphin—you pick the paint, the dolphin "designs" your shirt. The center also offers five-day programs for children and adults with disabilities. *MM 59 BS, 58901 Overseas Hwy.* *305/289–1121 information, 305/289–0002 reservations* *www.dolphins.org* *$28.*

Restaurants

Hideaway Café

$$$ | AMERICAN | It's easy to miss this café tucked between Grassy Key and Marathon, but when you find it (upstairs at Rainbow Bend Resort), you'll discover a favorite of locals who appreciate a well-planned menu, lovely ocean view, and quiet evening away from the crowds. For starters, dig into escargots à la Edison (sautéed with vegetables, pepper, cognac, and cream) before feasting on several specialties, such as a rarely found chateaubriand for one, or the seafood medley combining the catch of the day with scallops and shrimp. **Known for:** seclusion and quiet; amazing escargot; hand-cut steaks and fresh fish. *Average main: $30 ✉ Rainbow Bend Resort, MM 58 OS, 57784 Overseas Hwy. ☎ 305/289–1554 ⊕ www.hideawaycafe.com ⊙ No lunch.*

Marathon

MM 53–47.5.

New Englanders founded this former fishing village in the early 1800s. The community on Vaca Key subsequently served as a base for pirates, salvagers (also known as "wreckers"), spongers, and, later, Bahamian farmers who eked out a living growing cotton and other crops. More Bahamians arrived in the hope of finding work building the railroad. According to local lore, Marathon was renamed when a worker commented that it was a marathon task to position the tracks across the 6-mile-long island.

During the building of the railroad, Marathon developed a reputation for lawlessness that rivaled that of the Old West. It is said that to keep the rowdy workers from descending on Key West for their off-hours endeavors, residents would send boatloads of liquor up to Marathon. Needless to say, things have quieted down considerably since then.

Still, Marathon is a bustling town, at least compared with other communities in the Keys. As it leaves something to be desired in the charm department, Marathon may not be your first choice of places to stay, but water-sports types will find plenty to enjoy, and its historic and natural attractions merit a visit. Surprisingly good dining options abound, so you'll definitely want to stop for a bite even if you're just passing through on the way to Key West.

Throughout the year, Marathon hosts fishing tournaments (practically monthly), a huge seafood festival in March, and lighted boat parades around the holidays.

GETTING HERE AND AROUND

SuperShuttle charges $102 per passenger for trips from Miami International Airport to the Upper Keys. To go farther into the Keys, you must book an entire 11-person van, which costs about $280 to Marathon. For a trip to the airport, place your request 24 hours in advance. *See Getting Here and Around: Bus Travel.*

VISITOR INFORMATION

CONTACT Greater Marathon Chamber of Commerce and Visitor Center. *✉ MM 53.5 BS, 12222 Overseas Hwy. ☎ 305/743–5417, 800/262–7284 ⊕ www.floridakeysmarathon.com.*

Sights

Crane Point Museum, Nature Center, and Historic Site

MUSEUM | FAMILY | Tucked away from the highway behind a stand of trees, Crane Point—part of a 63-acre tract that contains the last-known undisturbed thatch-palm hammock—is delightfully undeveloped. This multiuse facility includes the **Museum of Natural History of the Florida Keys,** which has displays about local wildlife, a seashell exhibit, and a marine-life display that makes you feel like you're at the bottom of the sea. Kids love the replica 17th-century galleon and pirate dress-up room where they can play, and the re-created **Cracker House** filled with insects, sea-turtle exhibits, and children's activities. On the 1-mile indigenous loop trail, visit the **Laura Quinn Wild Bird Center** and the remnants of a Bahamian village, site of the restored **George Adderly House.** It is the oldest surviving example of Bahamian tabby (a concretelike material created from sand and seashells) construction outside Key West. A boardwalk crosses wetlands, rivers, and mangroves before ending at Adderly Village. From November to Easter, docent-led tours are available; bring good walking shoes and bug repellent during warm weather. ✉ *MM 50.5 BS, 5550 Overseas Hwy.* ☎ *305/743–9100* 🌐 *www.cranepoint.net* 🎫 *$14.95.*

Florida Keys Aquarium Encounters

LOCAL INTEREST | **FAMILY** | This isn't your typical large-city aquarium. It's more hands-on and personal, and it's all outdoors with several tiki huts to house the encounters and provide shade as you explore, rain or shine; plan to spend at least two to three hours here. You'll find a 200,000-gallon aquarium and plenty of marine encounters (extra cost), as well as guided tours, viewing areas, and a predator tank. The Coral Reef encounter ($95 snorkel, $130 regulator) lets you dive in a reef environment without hearing the theme from *Jaws* in your head (although you can see several sharks on the other side of the glass). Touch tanks are great for all ages and even have unique critters like slipper lobsters. Hungry? The on-site Eagle Ray Cafe serves up wings, fish tacos, salads, burgers, and more. Note that general admission is required, even if you're signed up for a marine encounter. ✉ *MM 53 BS, 11710 Overseas Hwy.* ☎ *305/407–3262* 🌐 *www.floridakeysaquariumencounters.com* 🎫 *$20.*

Pigeon Key

HISTORIC SITE | There's much to like about this 5-acre island under the Old Seven Mile Bridge. You might even recognize it from a season finale of the TV show *The Amazing Race*. You can reach it via a ferry that departs from their new gift shop location, a trailer at mile marker 47.5. Once there, tour the island on your own or join a guided tour to explore the buildings that formed the early-20th-century work camp for the Overseas Railroad that linked the mainland to Key West in 1912. Later the island became a fish camp, a state park, and then government-administration headquarters. Exhibits in a small museum recall the history of the Keys, the railroad, and railroad baron Henry M. Flagler. The ferry ride with tour lasts two hours; visitors can self-tour and catch the ferry back in a half hour. ■ **TIP→ Bring your own snorkel gear and dive flag and you can snorkel right from the shore.** Pack a picnic lunch, too. ✉ *MM 47.5 BS, between the Marriott and Hyatt Place, 2010 Overseas Hwy., Pigeon Key* ☎ *305/743–5999* 🌐 *pigeonkey.net* 🎫 *$12.*

Seven Mile Bridge

BRIDGE/TUNNEL | This is one of the most photographed images in the Keys. Actually measuring slightly less than 7 miles, it connects the Middle and Lower Keys and is believed to be the world's longest segmental bridge. It has 39 expansion joints separating its various concrete sections. Each April runners gather in Marathon for the annual Seven Mile Bridge Run. The expanse running parallel to Seven Mile Bridge is what remains of the **Old Seven Mile Bridge,** an engineering and architectural marvel in its day that's now on the National Register of Historic Places. Once proclaimed the Eighth Wonder of the World, it rested on a record 546 concrete piers. No cars are allowed on the old bridge today. ✉ *Marathon.*

The Turtle Hospital

COLLEGE | **FAMILY** | More than 100 injured sea turtles check in here every year. The

90-minute guided tours take you into recovery and surgical areas at the world's only state-certified veterinary hospital for sea turtles. In the "hospital bed" tanks, you can see recovering patients and others that are permanent residents due to their injuries. After the tour, you can feed some of the residents. Call ahead—space is limited and tours are sometimes canceled due to medical emergencies. The turtle ambulance out front makes for a memorable souvenir photo. ✉ *MM 48.5 BS, 2396 Overseas Hwy.* ☎ *305/743–2552* 🌐 *www.turtlehospital.org* 🎫 *$25.*

Beaches

Sombrero Beach

BEACH—SIGHT | **FAMILY** | No doubt one of the best beaches in the Keys, here you'll find pleasant, shaded picnic areas that overlook a coconut palm–lined grassy stretch and the Atlantic Ocean. Roped-off areas allow swimmers, boaters, and windsurfers to share the narrow cove. Facilities include barbecue grills, a large playground, a pier, a volleyball court, and a paved, lighted bike path off Overseas Highway. Sunday afternoons draw lots of local families toting coolers. The park is accessible for those with disabilities and allows leashed pets. Turn east at the traffic light in Marathon and follow signs to the end. **Amenities:** showers; toilets. **Best for:** swimming; windsurfing. ✉ *MM 50 OS, Sombrero Beach Rd.* ☎ *305/743–0033* 🎫 *Free.*

Restaurants

Fish Tales Market and Eatery

$ | **SEAFOOD** | This no-frills, roadside eatery has a loyal local following, an unfussy ambience, a couple of outside picnic tables, and friendly service. Signature dishes include snapper on grilled rye with coleslaw and melted Muenster cheese, a fried fish burrito, George's crab cake, and tomato-based conch chowder. **Known for:** luscious lobster bisque; fresh and affordable seafood and meat market; affordable dinner specials. 💲 *Average main: $10* ✉ *MM 52.5 OS, 11711 Overseas Hwy.* ☎ *305/743–9196, 888/662–4822* ⏱ *Closed Sun. No dinner Sat.*

Key Colony Inn

$$ | **ITALIAN** | The inviting aroma of an Italian kitchen pervades this family-owned favorite known for its Sunday brunch, served November through April. For lunch there are fish and steak entrées served with fries, salad, and bread in addition to Italian specialties. **Known for:** friendly and attentive service; Italian specialties; Sunday brunch. 💲 *Average main: $20* ✉ *MM 54 OS, 700 W. Ocean Dr., Key Colony Beach* ☎ *305/743–0100* 🌐 *www.kcinn.com.*

Keys Fisheries Market & Marina

$$ | **SEAFOOD** | **FAMILY** | You can't miss the enormous tiki bar on stilts, but the walk-up window on the ground floor is the heart of this warehouse turned restaurant. A huge lobster Reuben served on thick slices of toasted bread is the signature dish, and the adults-only upstairs tiki bar offers a sushi and raw bar for eat-in only. **Known for:** seafood market; marina views; fish-food dispensers (25¢) so you can feed the tarpon. 💲 *Average main: $16* ✉ *MM 49 BS, 3390 Gulfview Ave., at the end of 35th St.* ✥ *Turn onto 35th St. from Overseas Hwy.* ☎ *305/743–4353, 866/743–4353* 🌐 *www.keysfisheries.com.*

★ Lazy Days South

$$$ | **SEAFOOD** | Tucked into Marathon Marina a half mile north of the Seven Mile Bridge, this restaurant offers views just as spectacular as its highly lauded food. A spin-off of an Islamorada favorite, here you'll find a wide range of daily offerings from fried or sautéed conch and a coconut-fried fish du jour sandwich to seafood pastas and beef tips over rice. **Known for:** water views; delicious seafood entrées; hook and cook. 💲 *Average main: $22* ✉ *MM 47.3 OS, 725 11th St.* ☎ *305/289–0839* 🌐 *www.new.lazydayssouth.com.*

The Stuffed Pig

$ | **DINER** | With only nine tables and a counter inside, this breakfast-and-lunch place is always hopping. The kitchen whips up daily lunch specials like seafood platters or pulled pork with hand-cut fries, but the all-day breakfast is the main draw. **Known for:** pig's breakfast special; daily lunch specials; large portions. *Average main: $9 MM 49 BS, 3520 Overseas Hwy. 305/743–4059 www.thestuffedpig.com No credit cards No dinner.*

Sunset Grille & Raw Bar

$$$ | **SEAFOOD** | Treat yourself to a seafood lunch or dinner at this vaulted tiki hut at the foot of the Seven Mile Bridge. For lunch, try the Voodoo grouper sandwich topped with mango-guava mayo (and wear your swimsuit if you want to take a dip in the pool afterward). **Known for:** weekend pool parties and barbecues; pricey dinner specials; a swimming pool for patrons. *Average main: $22 MM 47 OS, 7 Knights Key Blvd. 305/396–7235 www.sunsetgrille7milebridge.com.*

Hotels

Glunz Ocean Beach Hotel & Resort

$$ | **RENTAL** | The Glunz family got it right when they purchased this former timeshare property and put a whole lot of love into renovating it to its full oceanfront potential. **Pros:** no resort fees, ever; nice private beach; excellent free Wi-Fi. **Cons:** small elevator; no interior corridors; not cheap. *Rooms from: $300 MM 53.5 OS, 351 E. Ocean Dr., Key Colony Beach 305/289–0525 www.GlunzOceanBeachHotel.com 46 units No meals.*

★ Tranquility Bay

$$$$ | **RESORT** | **FAMILY** | Ralph Lauren could have designed the rooms at this stylish, luxurious resort on a nice beach. **Pros:** secluded setting; tiki bar on the beach; main pool is nice and big. **Cons:** a bit sterile; no privacy on balconies; cramped building layout. *Rooms from: $425 MM 48.5 BS, 2600 Overseas Hwy. 305/289–0888, 866/643–5397 www.tranquilitybay.com 102 rooms No meals.*

Activities

BIKING

Tooling around on two wheels is a good way to see Marathon. There's easy cycling on a 1-mile off-road path that connects to the 2 miles of the Old Seven Mile Bridge leading to Pigeon Key.

Bike Marathon Bike Rentals

BICYCLING | "Have bikes, will deliver" could be the motto of this company, which gets beach cruisers to your hotel door, including a helmet, basket, and lock. It also rents kayaks. There's no physical location, but services are available Monday through Saturday 9–4 and Sunday 9–2. *Marathon 305/743–3204 www.bikemarathonbikerentals.com $45 per wk.*

BOATING

Sail, motor, or paddle: whatever your choice of modes, boating is what the Keys is all about. Brave the Atlantic waves and reefs or explore the backcountry islands on the Gulf side. If you don't have a lot of boating and chart-reading experience, it's a good idea to tap into local knowledge on a charter.

Captain Pip's

BOATING | This operator rents 18- to 24-foot outboards as well as snorkeling gear. Ask about multiday deals, or try one of the accommodation packages and walk right from your bay-front room to your boat. *MM 47.5 BS, 1410 Overseas Hwy. 305/743–4403, 800/707–1692 www.captainpips.com Rentals from $199 per day.*

Fish'n Fun

BOATING | Get out on the water on 19- to 26-foot powerboats. Rentals can be for a half or full day. The company also offers free delivery in the Middle Keys. ✉ *Duck Key Marina, MM 61 OS, 1149 Greenbriar Rd.* ☎ *305/743–2275, 800/471–3440* 🌐 *www.fishnfunrentals.com* 🎫 *From $175.*

FISHING

For recreational anglers, the deepwater fishing is superb in both bay and ocean. Marathon West Hump, one good spot, has depths ranging from 500 to more than 1,000 feet. Locals fish from a half dozen bridges, including Long Key Bridge, the Old Seven Mile Bridge, and both ends of Tom's Harbor. Barracuda, bonefish, and tarpon all frequent local waters. Party boats and private charters are available.

Marathon Lady

FISHING | Morning, afternoon, and night, fish for mahimahi, grouper, and other tasty catch aboard this 73-footer, which departs on half-day excursions from the Vaca Cut Bridge (MM 53), north of Marathon. Join the crew for night fishing ($55) from 6:30 to midnight from Memorial Day to Labor Day; it's especially beautiful on a full-moon night. ✉ *MM 53 OS, 11711 Overseas Hwy., at 117th St.* ☎ *305/743–5580* 🌐 *www.marathonlady.net* 🎫 *From $45.*

Sea Dog Charters

FISHING | Captain Jim Purcell, a deep-sea specialist for ESPN's *The American Outdoorsman,* provides one of the best values in Keys fishing. Next to the Seven Mile Grill, his company offers half- and full-day offshore, reef and wreck, and backcountry fishing trips, as well as fishing and snorkeling trips aboard 30- to 37-foot boats. The per-person cost for a half-day trip is the same regardless of whether your group fills the boat, and includes bait, light tackle, ice, coolers, and fishing licenses. If you prefer an all-day private charter on a 37-foot boat, he offers those, too, for up to six people. A fuel surcharge may apply. ✉ *MM 47.5 BS, 1248 Overseas Hwy.* ☎ *305/743–8255* 🌐 *www.seadogcharters.net* 🎫 *From $60.*

SCUBA DIVING AND SNORKELING

Local dive operations take you to Sombrero Reef and Lighthouse, the most popular down-under destination in these parts. For a shallow dive and some lobster nabbing, Coffins Patch, off Key Colony Beach, is a good choice. A number of wrecks such as *Thunderbolt* serve as artificial reefs. Many operations out of this area will also take you to Looe Key Reef.

Hall's Diving Center & Career Institute

SCUBA DIVING | The institute has been training divers for more than 40 years. Along with conventional twice-a-day snorkel and two-tank dive trips to the reefs at Sombrero Lighthouse and wrecks like the *Thunderbolt,* the company has more unusual offerings like rebreather, photography, and nitrox courses. ✉ *MM 48.5 BS, 1994 Overseas Hwy.* ☎ *305/743–5929, 800/331–4255* 🌐 *www.hallsdiving.com* 🎫 *From $45.*

Spirit Snorkeling

SCUBA DIVING | Join regularly scheduled snorkeling excursions to Sombrero Reef and Lighthouse Reef on this company's comfortable catamaran. It also offers sunset cruises and private charters. ✉ *MM 47.5 BS, 1410 Overseas Hwy., Slip No. 1* ☎ *305/289–0614* 🌐 *www.captainpips.com* 🎫 *From $30.*

Tildens Scuba Center

SCUBA DIVING | Since the mid-1980s, Tildens Scuba Center has been providing lessons, tours, gear rental, and daily snorkel, scuba, and Snuba adventures. Look for the huge, colorful angelfish sculpture outside the building. ✉ *MM 49.5 BS, 4650 Overseas Hwy.* ☎ *305/743–7255, 888/728–2235* 🎫 *From $60 for snorkel trips; from $70 for dive trips.*

Bahia Honda Key

MM 38.5–36.

All of Bahia Honda Key is devoted to its eponymous state park, which keeps it in a pristine state. Besides the park's outdoor activities, it offers an up-close view of the original railroad bridge.

★Bahia Honda State Park

NATIONAL/STATE PARK | **FAMILY** | Most first-time visitors to the region are dismayed by the lack of beaches—but then they discover Bahia Honda Key. The 524-acre park sprawls across both sides of the highway, giving it 2½ miles of fabulous sandy coastline. The snorkeling isn't bad, either; there's underwater life (soft coral, queen conchs, random little fish) just a few hundred feet offshore. Seasonal ranger-led nature programs take place at or depart from the Sand and Sea Nature Center. There are rental cabins, a campground, snack bar, gift shop, 19-slip marina, nature center, and facilities for renting kayaks and arranging snorkeling tours. Get a panoramic view of the island from what's left of the railroad—the Bahia Honda Bridge. ✉ *MM 37 OS, 36850 Overseas Hwy.* ☎ *305/872–2353* 🌐 *www.floridastateparks.org/park/Bahia-Honda* 🎫 *$4.50 for single-occupant vehicle, $8 for vehicle with 2–8 people, plus $0.50 per person up to 8.*

Sandspur Beach

BEACH—SIGHT | Bahia Honda Key State Beach contains three beaches in all—on both the Atlantic Ocean and the Gulf of Mexico. Sandspur Beach, the largest, is regularly declared the best beach in the Florida Keys, and you'll be hard-pressed to argue. The sand is baby-powder soft, and the aqua water is warm, clear, and shallow. With their mild currents, the beaches are great for swimming, even with small fry. **Amenities:** food and drink; showers; toilets; water sports. **Best for:** snorkeling; swimming. ✉ *MM 37 OS, 36850 Overseas Hwy.* ☎ *305/872–2353* 🌐 *www.floridastateparks.org/park/Bahia-Honda* 🎫 *$4.50 for single-occupant vehicle, $9 for vehicle with 2–8 people.*

Bahia Honda State Park Cabins

$ | **RENTAL** | Elsewhere you'd pay big bucks for the wonderful water views available at these cabins on Florida Bay. Each of three cabins has two, two-bedroom units with a full kitchen and bath and air-conditioning (but no television, radio, or phone). **Pros:** great bay-front views; beachfront camping; affordable rates. **Cons:** books up fast; area can be buggy. 💲 *Rooms from: $163* ✉ *MM 37 OS, 36850 Overseas Hwy.* ☎ *305/872–2353, 800/326–3521* 🌐 *www.reserveamerica.com* 🛏 *6 cabins* 🍽 *No meals.*

Bahia Honda Dive Shop

SCUBA DIVING | The concessionaire at Bahia Honda State Park manages a 19-slip marina; rents wet suits, snorkel equipment, and corrective masks; and operates twice-daily offshore-reef snorkel trips. Park visitors looking for other fun can rent kayaks and beach chairs. ✉ *MM 37 OS, 36850 Overseas Hwy.* ☎ *305/872–3210* 🌐 *www.bahiahondapark.com* ☞ *Kayak rentals from $10 per hr; snorkel tours from $30.*

Big Pine Key

MM 32–30.

Welcome to the Keys' most natural holdout, where wildlife refuges protect rare and endangered animals. Here you have left behind the commercialism of the Upper Keys for an authentic backcountry

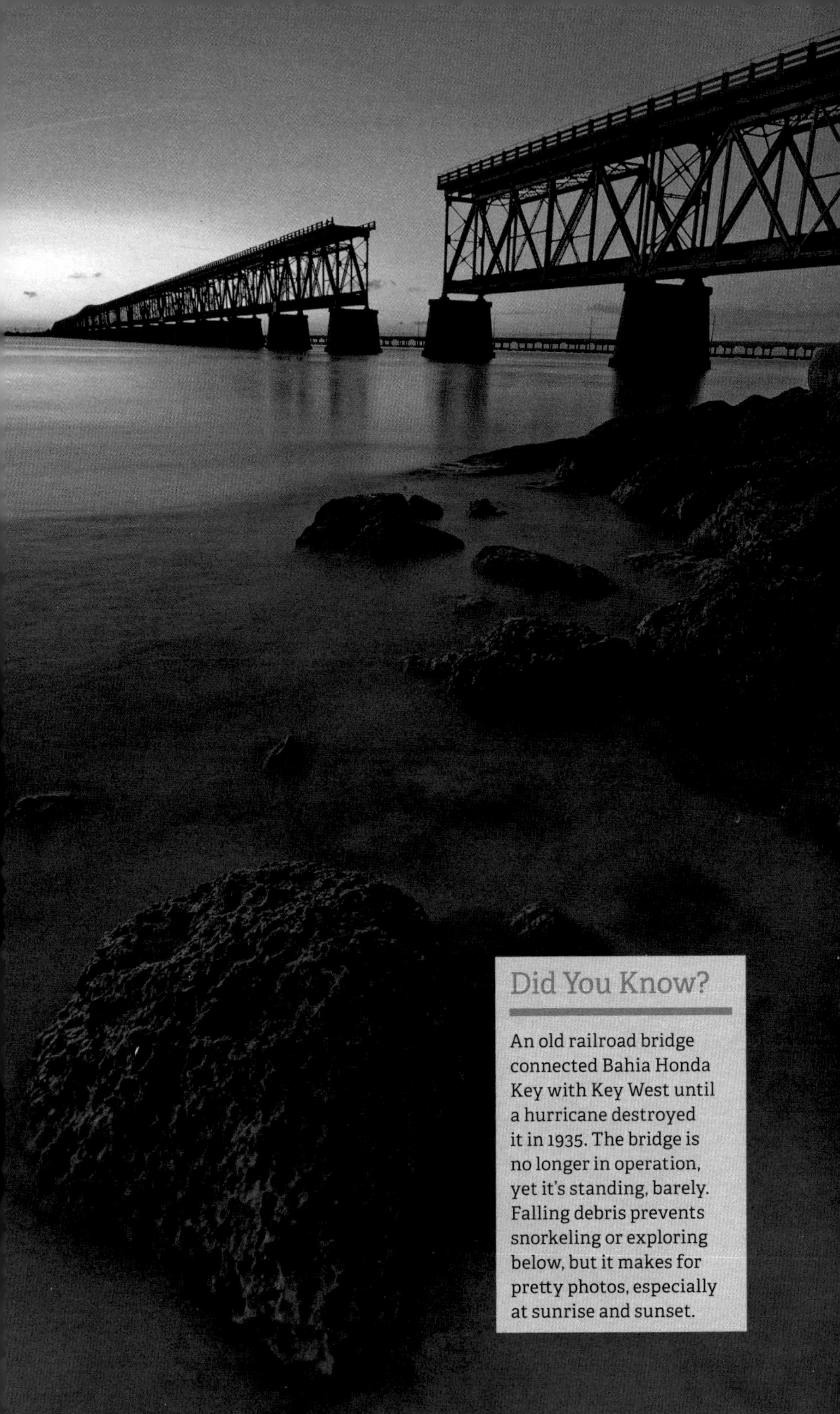

Did You Know?

An old railroad bridge connected Bahia Honda Key with Key West until a hurricane destroyed it in 1935. The bridge is no longer in operation, yet it's standing, barely. Falling debris prevents snorkeling or exploring below, but it makes for pretty photos, especially at sunrise and sunset.

atmosphere. How could things get more casual than Key Largo, you might wonder? Find out by exiting U.S. 1 to explore the habitat of the charmingly diminutive Key deer or cast a line from No Name Bridge. Tours explore the expansive waters of National Key Deer Refuge and Great White Heron National Wildlife Refuge, one of the first such refuges in the country. Along with Key West National Wildlife Refuge, it encompasses more than 200,000 acres of water and more than 8,000 acres of land on 49 small islands. Besides its namesake bird, the Great White Heron National Wildlife Refuge provides habitat for uncounted species of birds and three species of sea turtles. It is the only U.S. breeding site for the endangered hawksbill turtle.

GETTING HERE AND AROUND

Most people rent a car to get to Big Pine Key so they can also explore Key West and other parts of the chain.

VISITOR INFORMATION

CONTACT Big Pine and the Lower Keys Chamber of Commerce. *31020 Overseas Hwy.* *305/872–2411, 800/872–3722* *www.lowerkeyschamber.com.*

Sights

National Key Deer Refuge

NATURE PRESERVE | This 84,824-acre refuge was established in 1957 to protect the dwindling population of the Key deer, one of more than 22 animals and plants federally classified as endangered or threatened, including five that are found nowhere else on Earth. The Key deer, which stands about 30 inches at the shoulders and is a subspecies of the Virginia white-tailed deer, once roamed throughout the Lower and Middle Keys, but hunting, destruction of their habitat, and a growing human population caused their numbers to decline to 27 by 1957. The deer have made a comeback, increasing their numbers to approximately 750. The best place to see Key deer in the refuge is at the end of Key Deer Boulevard and on No Name Key, a sparsely populated island just east of Big Pine Key. Mornings and evenings are the best time to spot them. Deer may turn up along the road at any time of day, so drive slowly. They wander into nearby yards to nibble tender grass and bougainvillea blossom, but locals do not appreciate tourists driving into their neighborhoods after them. Feeding them is against the law and puts them in danger.

A quarry left over from railroad days, the **Blue Hole** is the largest body of freshwater in the Keys. From the observation platform and nearby walking trail, you might see the resident alligator, turtles, and other wildlife. There are two well-marked trails, recently revamped: the Jack Watson Nature Trail (0.6 mile), named after an environmentalist and the refuge's first warden; and the Fred Mannillo Nature Trail (0.2 mile), one of the most wheelchair-accessible places to see an unspoiled pine-rockland forest and wetlands. The visitor center has exhibits on Keys biology and ecology. The refuge also provides information on the Key West National Wildlife Refuge and the Great White Heron National Wildlife Refuge. Accessible only by water, both are popular with kayak outfitters. *Visitor Center–Headquarters, Big Pine Shopping Center, MM 30.5 BS, 28950 Watson Blvd.* *305/872–2239* *www.fws.gov/nationalkeydeer* *Free* *Visitor center closed Sun. and Mon.*

Restaurants

Good Food Conspiracy

$ | **VEGETARIAN** | Like good wine, this small natural-foods eatery and market surrenders its pleasures a little at a time. Step inside to the aroma of brewing coffee, and then pick up the scent of fresh strawberries or carrots blending into a smoothie, the green aroma of wheatgrass juice, followed by the earthy odor of hummus. **Known for:** vegetarian and vegan dishes; sandwiches and smoothies; organic items. *Average main: $10 ✉ MM 30.2 OS, 30150 Overseas Hwy. ☎ 305/872–3945 🌐 www.goodfoodconspiracy.com ⏲ No dinner Sun.*

No Name Pub

$$ | AMERICAN | This no-frills honky-tonk has been around since 1936, delighting inveterate locals and intrepid vacationers who come for the excellent pizza, cold beer, and *interesting* companionship. The decor, such as it is, amounts to the autographed dollar bills that cover every inch of the place. **Known for:** shrimp pizza and fish sandwich; local and tourist favorite; decor of dollar bills. *Average main: $15 ✉ MM 30 BS, 30813 Watson Blvd. ✣ From U.S. 1, turn west on Wilder Rd., left on South St., right on Ave. B, right on Watson Blvd. ☎ 305/872–9115 🌐 www.nonamepub.com.*

Hotels

Big Pine Key Fishing Lodge

$ | HOTEL | There's a congenial atmosphere at this lively, family-owned lodge-campground-marina—a happy mix of tent campers (who have the fabulous waterfront real estate), RVers (who look pretty permanent), and motel dwellers who like to mingle at the rooftop pool and challenge each other to a game of poker. **Pros:** local fishing crowd; nice pool; great price. **Cons:** RV park is too close to motel; deer will eat your food if you're camping; trees and trails recovering from Hurricane Irma. *Rooms from: $134 ✉ MM 33 OS, 33000 Overseas Hwy. ☎ 305/872–2351 🌐 www.bpkfl.com 16 rooms No meals ☞ To protect Key deer, no dogs allowed.*

Deer Run Bed & Breakfast

$$$ | B&B/INN | Although Hurricane Irma came ashore here in 2017, the owners of Deer Run have made lemonade from Irma's lemons with a new raised addition that sits adjacent to the main building and houses three guest rooms, all with ocean views, cathedral ceilings, king beds, private baths, small porches, and calming decor. **Pros:** quiet neighborhood; vegan, organic breakfasts; complimentary use of bikes, kayaks, beach towels, and state park passes. **Cons:** major deforestation and loss of mangroves from hurricane; a little hard to find; may be too secluded for some. *Rooms from: $375 ✉ MM 33 OS, 1997 Long Beach Dr. ☎ 305/872–2015 🌐 www.deerrunfloridabb.com 4 rooms Free Breakfast.*

Activities

BIKING

A good 10 miles of paved roads run from MM 30.3 BS, along Wilder Road, across the bridge to No Name Key, and along Key Deer Boulevard into the National Key Deer Refuge. Along the way you might see some Key deer. Stay off the trails that lead into wetlands, where fat tires can damage the environment.

Big Pine Bicycle Center

BICYCLING | Owner Marty Baird is an avid cyclist and enjoys sharing his knowledge of great places to ride. He's also skilled at selecting the right bike for the journey, and he knows his repairs, too. His old-fashioned single-speed, fat-tire cruisers rent by the half or full day. Helmets, baskets, and locks are included. *✉ MM 30.9 BS, 31 County Rd. ☎ 305/872–0130 🌐 www.bigpinebikes.com From $10.*

FISHING

Cast from No Name Key Bridge or hire a charter to take you into backcountry or deep waters for fishing year-round.

Captain Hook's Looe Key Reef Adventures and Strike Zone Charters

BOATING | Glass-bottom-boat excursions venture into the backcountry and Atlantic Ocean. The five-hour Out Island Excursion and Picnic emphasizes nature and Keys history; besides close encounters with birds, sea life, and vegetation, there's a fish cookout on an island. Snorkel and fishing equipment, food, and drinks are included. This is one of the few nature outings in the Keys with wheelchair access. Deep-sea charter rates for up to six people can be arranged for a half or full day. It also offers flats fishing in the Gulf of Mexico. Dive excursions head to the wreck of the 110-foot *Adolphus Busch,* and scuba and snorkel trips to Looe Key Reef, prime scuba and snorkeling territory, aboard glass-bottom boats. ✉ *MM 29.6 BS, 29675 Overseas Hwy.* ☎ *305/872–9863, 800/654–9560* 🌐 *www.captainhooks.com* 🎟 *From $38.*

KAYAKING

There's nothing like the vast expanse of pristine waters and mangrove islands preserved by national refuges from here to Key West. The mazelike terrain can be confusing, so it's wise to hire a guide at least the first time out.

Big Pine Kayak Adventures
KAYAKING | There's no excuse to skip a water adventure with this convenient kayak rental service, which delivers them to your lodging or anywhere between Seven Mile Bridge and Stock Island. The company, headed by *The Florida Keys Paddling Guide* author Bill Keogh, will rent you a kayak and then ferry you—called taxi-yakking—to remote islands with clear instructions on how to paddle back on your own. Rentals are by the half day or full day. Three-hour group kayak tours are the cheapest option and explore the mangrove forests of Great White Heron and Key Deer National Wildlife Refuges. More expensive four-hour custom tours transport you to exquisite backcountry areas teeming with wildlife. Kayak fishing charters are also popular. Paddleboard ecotours, rentals, and yoga are available. ✉ *Old Wooden Bridge Fishing Camp, 1791 Bogie Dr.* ✣ *From MM 30, turn right at traffic light, continue on Wilder Rd. toward No Name Key; the fishing camp is just before the bridge with a big yellow kayak on the sign out front* ☎ *305/872–7474* 🌐 *www.keyskayaktours.com* 🎟 *From $50.*

Little Torch Key

MM 29–10.

Little Torch Key and its neighbor islands, Ramrod Key and Summerland Key, are good jumping-off points for divers headed for Looe Key Reef. The islands also serve as a refuge for those who want to make forays into Key West but not stay in the thick of things.

The undeveloped backcountry at your door makes Little Torch Key an ideal location for fishing and kayaking. Nearby **Ramrod Key,** which also caters to divers bound for Looe Key, derives its name from a ship that wrecked on nearby reefs in the early 1800s.

Restaurants

Baby's Coffee
$ | **AMERICAN** | The aroma of rich, roasting coffee beans arrests you at the door of "the Southernmost Coffee Roaster in America." Buy beans by the pound or coffee by the cup, along with sandwiches and sweets. **Known for:** best coffee in the Keys; gluten-free, vegan, and vegetarian specialty foods; excellent service. 💲 *Average main: $8* ✉ *MM 15 OS, 3180 Overseas Hwy.* ☎ *305/744–9866, 800/523–2326* 🌐 *www.babyscoffee.com.*

Geiger Key Smokehouse Bar & Grill
$$ | **AMERICAN** | There's a strong hint of the Old Keys at this ocean-side marina restaurant, where local fisherman stop for breakfast before heading out to catch the big one, and everyone shows up on Sunday for the barbecue from 4 to 9. "On the backside of paradise," as the sign says, its tiki structures overlook quiet mangroves at an RV park marina. **Known for:** Sunday barbecue; casual atmosphere on the water; conch fritters loaded with

conch. $ *Average main: $16* ✉ *MM 10, 5 Geiger Key Rd., off Boca Chica Rd., Bay Point* ☎ *305/296–3553, 305/294–1230* 🌐 *www.geigerkeymarina.com.*

Mangrove Mama's Restaurant
$$ | **SEAFOOD** | This could be the prototype for a Keys restaurant, given its shanty appearance, lattice trim, and roving sort of indoor-outdoor floor plan. Then there's the seafood, from the ubiquitous fish sandwich (fried, grilled, broiled, or blackened) to lobster Reubens, crab cakes, and coconut shrimp. **Known for:** pizza; award-winning conch chowder; slow service. $ *Average main: $20* ✉ *MM 20 BS, Sugarloaf Key* ☎ *305/745–3030* 🌐 *www.mangrovemamasrestaurant.com.*

★ **My New Joint**
$ | **AMERICAN** | Atop the famed Square Grouper restaurant is a secret spot that locals love and smart travelers seek out for its tapas and well-stocked bar. Sit at a high-top table or on a sofa, and savor made-from-scratch small plates you won't soon forget, like salted caramel puffs or chicken lollipops. **Known for:** craft cocktails and 170 types of beer; cheese or chocolate fondue; raw bar. $ *Average main: $13* ✉ *22658 Overseas Hwy., 2nd fl. of Square Grouper restaurant, Sugarloaf Key* ☎ *305/745–8880* 🌐 *www.mynewjoint420lounge.com* ⏲ *Closed Sun. and Mon.*

★ **Square Grouper**
$$$ | **SEAFOOD** | In an unassuming warehouse-looking building on U.S. 1, chef-owner Lynn Bell is creating seafood magic. For starters, try the flash-fried conch with wasabi drizzle or homemade smoked-fish dip. **Known for:** everything made fresh, in-house; long lines in season; outstanding seafood. $ *Average main: $25* ✉ *MM 22.5 OS* ☎ *305/745–8880* 🌐 *www.squaregrouperbarandgrill.com* ⏲ *Closed Sun.; Mon. May–Dec.; and Sept.*

Hotels

★ **Little Palm Island Resort & Spa**
$$$$ | **RESORT** | This ultraluxurious tropical retreat set on a private island was devastated by Hurricane Irma but is scheduled to reopen in early 2020—check the website for updates. **Pros:** secluded setting; heavenly spa; easy wildlife viewing. **Cons:** expensive; might be too quiet for some; accessible only by boat or seaplane. $ *Rooms from: $1,590* ✉ *MM 28.5 OS, 28500 Overseas Hwy.* ☎ *305/872–2524, 800/343–8567* 🌐 *www.littlepalmisland.com* *30 suites* *Some meals* ☞ *No one under age 16 allowed on island.*

Looe Key Reef Resort & Center
$ | **HOTEL** | If your Keys vacation is all about diving, you won't mind the no-frills, basic motel rooms with dated furniture at this scuba-obsessed operation because it's the closest place to the stellar reef to stay. **Pros:** guests get discounts on dive and snorkel trips; inexpensive rates; casual Keys atmosphere. **Cons:** some reports of uncleanliness; unheated pool; close to the road. $ *Rooms from: $115* ✉ *MM 27.5 OS, 27340 Overseas Hwy., Ramrod Key* ☎ *305/872–2215, 877/816–3483* 🌐 *www.diveflakeys.com* *24 rooms* *No meals.*

Parmer's Resort
$ | **HOTEL** | Almost every room at this budget-friendly option has a view of South Pine Channel, with the lovely curl of Big Pine Key in the foreground. **Pros:** bright rooms; pretty setting; good value. **Cons:** a bit out of the way; housekeeping costs extra; little shade around the pool. $ *Rooms from: $159* ✉ *MM 28.7 BS, 565 Barry Ave.* ☎ *305/872–2157* 🌐 *www.parmersresort.com* *47 units* *Free Breakfast.*

Activities

SCUBA DIVING AND SNORKELING

This is the closest you can get on land to Looe Key Reef, and that's where local dive operators love to head.

In 1744 the HMS *Looe,* a British warship, ran aground and sank on one of the most beautiful coral reefs in the Keys. Today the key owes its name to the ill-fated ship. The 5.3-square-nautical-mile reef, part of the **Florida Keys National Marine Sanctuary,** has strands of elkhorn coral on its eastern margin, purple sea fans, and abundant sponges and sea urchins. On its seaward side, it drops almost vertically 50 to 90 feet. In its midst, **Shipwreck Trail** plots the location of nine historic wreck sites in 14 to 120 feet of water. Buoys mark the sites, and underwater signs tell the history of each site and what marine life to expect. Snorkelers and divers will find the sanctuary a quiet place to observe reef life—except in July, when the annual Underwater Music Festival pays homage to Looe Key's beauty and promotes reef awareness with six hours of music broadcast via underwater speakers. Dive shops, charters, and private boats transport about 500 divers and snorkelers to hear the spectacle, which includes classical, jazz, New Age, and Caribbean music, as well as a little Jimmy Buffett. There are even underwater Elvis impersonators.

Looe Key Reef Resort & Dive Center

SCUBA DIVING | This center, the closest dive shop to Looe Key Reef, offers two affordable trips daily, at 8 am and 12:45 pm (for divers, snorkelers, or bubble watchers). The maximum depth is 30 feet, so snorkelers and divers go on the same boat. Call to check for availability for wreck and night dives. The dive boat, a 45-foot catamaran, is docked at the full-service Looe Key Reef Resort. ✉ *Looe Key Reef Resort, MM 27.5 OS, 27340 Overseas Hwy., Ramrod Key* ☎ *305/872–2215, 877/816–3483* 🌐 *www.diveflakeys.com* 🎫 *From $40.*

WATER SPORTS

★ Reelax Charters

BOATING | For a guided tour, join Captain Andrea Paulson of Reelax Charters, who takes you to remote locations by boat, then hops in a kayak for a tour like no other. Charters carry up to six people at $85 per person and can include snorkeling and beaching on a secluded island in the Keys backcountry. ✉ *Sugarloaf Marina, MM 17 BS, 17015 Overseas Hwy., Sugarloaf Key* ☎ *305/304–1392* 🌐 *www.keyskayaking.com* 🎫 *From $255 per boat.*

Sugarloaf Marina

BOATING | Rates for one-person kayaks are based on an hourly or daily rental. Two-person kayaks are also available. Delivery is free for rentals of three days or more. The folks at the marina can also hook you up with an outfitter for a day of offshore or backcountry fishing. There's also a well-stocked ship store. ✉ *MM 17 BS, 17015 Overseas Hwy., Sugarloaf Key* ☎ *305/745–3135* 🌐 *www.sugarloafkeymarina.com* 🎫 *From $15 per hr.*

Key West

Situated 150 miles from Miami, 90 miles from Havana, and an immeasurable distance from sanity, this end-of-the-line community has never been like anywhere else. Even after it was connected to the rest of the country—by the railroad in 1912 and by the highway in 1938—it maintained a strong sense of detachment. The United States acquired Key West from Spain in 1821, along with the rest of Florida. The Spanish had named the island Cayo Hueso, or Bone Key, after the Native American skeletons they found on its shores. In 1823, President James Monroe sent Commodore David S. Porter to chase pirates away. For three decades, the primary industry in Key

West was wrecking—rescuing people and salvaging cargo from ships that foundered on the nearby reefs. According to some reports, when pickings were lean the wreckers hung out lights to lure ships aground. Their business declined after 1849, when the federal government began building lighthouses.

In 1845, the army began construction on Fort Taylor, which kept Key West on the Union side during the Civil War. After the fighting ended, an influx of Cubans unhappy with Spain's rule brought the cigar industry here. Fishing, shrimping, and sponge gathering became important industries, as did pineapple canning. Throughout much of the 19th century and into the 20th, Key West was Florida's wealthiest city per capita. But in 1929, the local economy began to unravel. Cigar making moved to Tampa, Hawaii dominated the pineapple industry, and the sponges succumbed to blight. Then the Depression hit, and within a few years half the population was on relief.

Tourism began to revive Key West, but that came to a halt when a hurricane knocked out the railroad bridge in 1935. To help the tourism industry recover from that crushing blow, the government offered incentives for islanders to turn their charming homes—many of them built by shipwrights— into guesthouses and inns. That wise foresight has left the town with more than 100 such lodgings, a hallmark of Key West vacationing today. In the 1950s, the discovery of "pink gold" in the Dry Tortugas boosted the economy of the entire region. Catching Key West shrimp required a fleet of up to 500 boats and flooded local restaurants with some of the sweetest shrimp alive. The town's artistic community found inspiration in the colorful fishing boats.

Key West reflects a diverse population: Conchs (natives, many of whom trace their ancestry to the Bahamas), freshwater Conchs (longtime residents who migrated from somewhere else years ago), Hispanics (primarily Cuban immigrants), recent refugees from the urban sprawl of mainland Florida, military personnel, and an assortment of vagabonds, drifters, and dropouts in search of refuge. The island was once a gay vacation hot spot, and it remains a decidedly gay-friendly destination. Some of the once-renowned gay guesthouses, however, no longer cater to an exclusively gay clientele. Key Westers pride themselves on their tolerance of all peoples, all sexual orientations, and even all animals. Most restaurants allow pets, and it's not surprising to see stray cats, dogs, and even chickens roaming freely through the dining rooms. The chicken issue is one that government officials periodically try to bring to an end, but the colorful fowl continue to strut and crow, particularly in the vicinity of Old Town's Bahamian Village.

As a tourist destination, Key West has a lot to sell—an average temperature of 79°F, 19th-century architecture, and a laid-back lifestyle. Yet much has been lost to those eager for a buck. Duval Street is starting to resemble a shopping mall with name-brand storefronts, garish T-shirt shops, and tattoo shops with sidewalk views of the inked action. Cruise ships dwarf the town's skyline and fill the streets with day-trippers gawking at the hippies with dogs in their bike baskets, gay couples walking down the street holding hands, and the oddball lot of locals, some of whom bark louder than the dogs.

GETTING HERE AND AROUND

AIR TRAVEL

You can fly directly to Key West on a limited number of flights, most of which connect at other Florida airports. But a lot of folks fly into Miami or Fort Lauderdale and drive down or take the bus.

BOAT TRAVEL

Key West Express operates air-conditioned ferries between the Key West Terminal (Caroline and Grinnell streets) and

Marco Island, and Fort Myers Beach. The trip from Fort Myers Beach takes at least four hours each way and costs $95 one way, $155 round-trip. Ferries depart from Fort Myers Beach at 8:30 am and from Key West at 6 pm. The Miami and Marco Island ferry costs $95 one way and $155 round-trip, and departs at 8:30 am. A photo ID is required for each passenger. Advance reservations are recommended and can save money.

BUS AND SHUTTLE TRAVEL TO KEY WEST

Greyhound Lines runs a special Keys Shuttle up to twice a day (depending on the day of the week) from Miami International Airport (departing from Concourse E, lower level) that stops throughout the Keys. Fares run about $45 (web fare) to $57 for Key West. Keys Shuttle runs scheduled service three times a day in 15-passenger vans between Miami Airport and Key West with stops throughout the Keys for $70 to $90 per person. SuperShuttle charges $102 per passenger for trips from Miami International Airport to the Upper Keys. To go farther into the Keys, you must book an entire 11-person van, which costs about $350 to Key West. You need to place your request for transportation back to the airport 24 hours in advance. Uber is also available throughout the Keys and from the airport. *For detailed information on these services, see Getting Here and Around: Bus Travel*

BUS TRAVEL AROUND KEY WEST

Between mile markers 4 and 0, Key West is the one place in the Keys where you could conceivably do without a car, especially if you plan on staying around Old Town. If you've driven the 106 miles down the chain, you're probably ready to abandon your car in the hotel parking lot anyway. Trolleys, buses, bikes, scooters, and feet are more suitable alternatives. When your feet tire, catch a rickshaw-style pedicab ride, which will run you about $1.50 a minute. But to explore the beaches, New Town, and Stock Island, you'll need a car or taxi.

The City of Key West Department of Transportation has six color-coded bus routes traversing the island from 5:30 am to 11:30 pm. Stops have signs with the international bus symbol. Schedules are available on buses and at hotels, visitor centers, shops, and online. The fare is $2 one way.

VISITOR INFORMATION

CONTACTS Greater Key West Chamber of Commerce. ✉ *510 Greene St., 1st fl.* ☎ *305/294–2587, 800/527–8539* 🌐 *www.keywestchamber.org.*

TOURS

Conch Tour Train

BUS TOURS | The Conch Tour Train is a 90-minute narrated tour of Key West, traveling 14 miles through Old Town and around the island. Board at Mallory Square or Angela Street and Duval Street depot every half hour from 9 to 4:30. Discount tickets are available online. ✉ *Key West* ☎ *305/294–5161, 888/916–8687* 🌐 *www.conchtourtrain.com* 🎟 *$31.45.*

Historic Florida Keys Foundation

WALKING TOURS | In addition to publishing several good guides on Key West, the foundation conducts tours of the City Cemetery on Tuesday and Thursday at 9:30 am. ✉ *Old City Hall, 510 Greene St.* ☎ *305/292–6718* 🌐 *www.historicfloridakeys.org* 🎟 *$15.*

Key West Promotions

WALKING TOURS | If you're not entirely a do-it-yourselfer, Key West Promotions offers a variety of pub tours, from the famous Duval Crawl to a chilling, haunted, and "spirited" adventure. ✉ *424 Greene St.* ☎ *305/294–7170* 🌐 *www.keywestwalkingtours.com.*

Lloyd's Original Tropical Bike Tour

BICYCLE TOURS | Explore the natural, noncommercial side of Key West at a leisurely pace, stopping on backstreets and in backyards of private homes to sample native fruits and view indigenous plants and trees with a 45-year Key West veteran. The behind-the-scenes tours run two hours and include a bike rental. ✉ *Moped Hospital, Truman Ave. and Simonton St.* ☎ *305/304–4700* 🌐 *www.lloydstropicalbiketour.com* 🎫 *$49.*

Old Town Trolley

BUS TOURS | FAMILY | Old Town Trolley operates trolley-style buses, departing from Mallory Square every 30 minutes from 9 to 4:30, for 90-minute narrated tours of Key West. The smaller trolleys go places the larger Conch Tour Train won't fit, and you can ride a second consecutive day for only $15. You may disembark at any of 13 stops and reboard a later trolley. You can save nearly $4 by booking online. It also offers package deals with Old Town attractions. ✉ *1 Whitehead St.* ☎ *305/296–6688, 855/623–8289* 🌐 *www.trolleytours.com* 🎫 *$38.80.*

Sights

OLD TOWN

The heart of Key West, the historic Old Town area runs from White Street to the waterfront. Beginning in 1822, wharves, warehouses, chandleries, ship-repair facilities, and eventually, in 1891, the U.S. Custom House, sprang up around the deep harbor to accommodate the navy's large ships and other sailing vessels. Wreckers, merchants, and sea captains built lavish houses near the bustling waterfront. A remarkable number of these fine Victorian and pre-Victorian structures have been restored to their original grandeur and now serve as homes, guesthouses, shops, restaurants, and museums. These, along with the dwellings of famous writers, artists, and politicians who've come to Key West over the past 175 years, are among the area's approximately 3,000 historic structures. Old Town also has the city's finest restaurants and hotels, lively street life, and popular nightspots.

Audubon House and Tropical Gardens

GARDEN | If you've ever seen an engraving by ornithologist John James Audubon, you'll understand why his name is synonymous with birds. See his works in this three-story house, which was built in the 1840s for Captain John Geiger and filled with period furniture. It now commemorates Audubon's 1832 stop in Key West while he was traveling through Florida to study birds. After an introduction by a docent, you can do a self-guided tour of the house and gardens. An art gallery sells lithographs of the artist's famed portraits. ✉ *205 Whitehead St.* ☎ *305/294–2116, 877/294–2470* 🌐 *www.audubonhouse.com* 🎫 *$14.*

★ Custom House

HISTORIC SITE | When Key West was designated a U.S. port of entry in the early 1820s, a customhouse was established. Salvaged cargoes from ships wrecked on the reefs were brought here, setting the stage for Key West to become—for a time—the richest city in Florida. The imposing redbrick-and-terra-cotta Richardsonian Romanesque–style building reopened as a museum and art gallery in 1999. Smaller galleries have long-term and changing exhibits about the history of Key West, including a Hemingway room and a permanent Henry Flagler exhibit that commemorates the arrival of Flagler's railroad to Key West in 1912. ✉ *281 Front St.* ☎ *305/295–6616* 🌐 *www.kwahs.com* 🎫 *$10.*

Dry Tortugas National Park and Historic Key West Bight Museum

HISTORIC SITE | FAMILY | If you can't see Ft. Jefferson in the Dry Tortugas in person, this is the next best thing. Opened in 2013 by the national park's official ferry commissioner, this free attraction located in Key West's historic seaport has an impressive (1:87) scale model of the fort; life-size figures including the fort's most famous prisoner, Dr. Samuel Mudd; and even a junior ranger station for the little ones with hands-on educational fun.

The exhibits are housed in a historic site as well, the old Thompson Fish House, where local fisherman would bring their daily catch for processing. History lingers on within these walls, but to get a whiff of the sea and days gone past, you'll have to walk the docks out front. ✉ *240 Margaret St.* ☎ *305/294–7009* 🌐 *www.drytortugas.com* 🎫 *Free.*

★ The Ernest Hemingway Home and Museum

HOUSE | Amusing anecdotes spice up the guided tours of Ernest Hemingway's home, built in 1801 by the town's most successful wrecker. While living here between 1931 and 1942, Hemingway wrote about 70% of his life's work, including classics like *For Whom the Bell Tolls*. Few of his belongings remain aside from some books, and there's little about his actual work, but photographs help you visualize his day-to-day life. The famous six-toed descendants of Hemingway's cats—many named for actors, artists, authors, and even a hurricane—have free rein of the property. Tours begin every 10 minutes and take 30 minutes; then you're free to explore on your own. Be sure to find out why there is a urinal in the garden! ✉ *907 Whitehead St.* ☎ *305/294–1136* 🌐 *www.hemingwayhome.com* 🎫 *$14.*

Fort Zachary Taylor Historic State Park

BEACH—SIGHT | Construction of the fort began in 1845 but was halted during the Civil War. Even though Florida seceded from the Union, Yankee forces used the fort as a base to block Confederate shipping. More than 1,500 Confederate vessels were detained in Key West's harbor. The fort, finally completed in 1866, was also used in the Spanish-American War. Take a 30-minute guided walking tour of the redbrick fort, a National Historic Landmark, at noon and 2, or self-guided tour anytime between 8 and 5. In February a celebration called Civil War Heritage Days includes costumed reenactments and demonstrations. From mid-January to mid-April the park serves as an open-air gallery for pieces created for Sculpture Key West. One of its most popular features is its man-made beach, a rest stop for migrating birds in the spring and fall; there are also picnic areas, hiking and biking trails, and a kayak launch. ✉ *Southard St., at end of street, through Truman Annex* ☎ *305/292–6713* 🌐 *www.floridastateparks.org/park/Fort-Taylor* 🎫 *$4 for single-occupant vehicles, $6 for 2–8 people in a vehicle, plus a 50¢ per person county surcharge.*

Harry S. Truman Little White House Museum

HOUSE | Renovations to this circa-1890 landmark have restored the home and gardens to the Truman era, down to the wallpaper pattern. A free photographic review of visiting dignitaries and presidents—John F. Kennedy, Jimmy Carter, and Bill Clinton are among the chief executives who passed through here—is on display in the back of the gift shop. Engaging 45-minute tours begin every 20 minutes until 4:30. They start with an excellent 10-minute video on the history of the property and Truman's visits. On the grounds of **Truman Annex,** a 103-acre former military parade grounds and barracks, the home served as a "winter White House" for presidents Truman, Eisenhower, and Kennedy. Entry is cheaper when purchased in advance online; tickets bought on-site add sales tax. ■ **TIP→ The house tour does require climbing steps. Visitors can do a free self-guided botanical tour of the grounds with a brochure from the museum store.** ✉ *111 Front St.* ☎ *305/294–9911* 🌐 *www.trumanlittlewhitehouse.com* 🎫 *$21.45.*

Historic Seaport at Key West Bight

HISTORIC SITE | What was once a funky—in some places even seedy—part of town is a 20-acre historic restoration of businesses, including waterfront restaurants, open-air bars, museums, clothing stores, and water-sports concessions. It's all linked by the 2-mile waterfront **Harborwalk,** which runs between Front

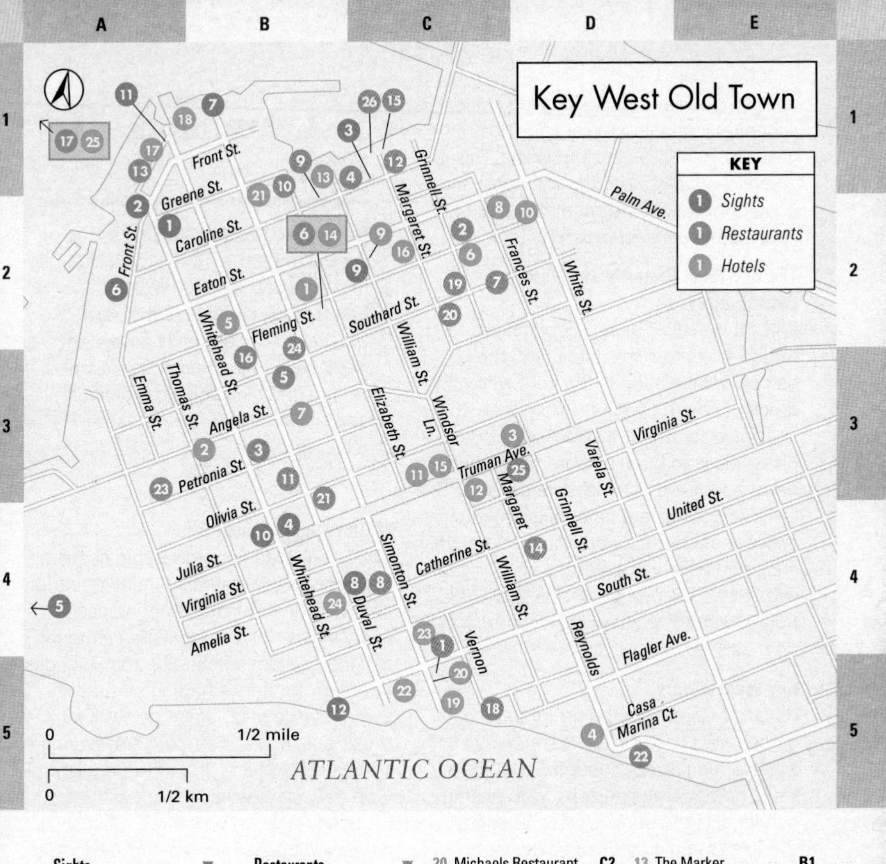

Sights

1 Audubon House and Tropical Gardens A2
2 Custom House........... A2
3 Dry Tortugas National Park and Historic Key West Bight Museum C1
4 The Ernest Hemingway Home and Museum B4
5 Fort Zachary Taylor Historic State Park A4
6 Harry S Truman Little White House Museum A2
7 Historic Seaport at Key West Bight............... B1
8 The Key West Butterfly and Nature Conservatory............. C4
9 Key West Library......... C2
10 Key West Lighthouse Museum and Keeper's Quarters B4
11 Mallory Square and Pier................... A1
12 The Southernmost Point....................... B5

Restaurants

1 Ambrosia C5
2 Azur Restaurant......... C2
3 Blue Heaven............ B3
4 B.O.'s Fish Wagon C1
5 The Café B3
6 Café Marquesa B2
7 Café Solé C2
8 Camille's Restaurant..... C4
9 Coffee Plantation B2
10 Conch Republic Seafood Company...... B1
11 Croissants de France... B3
12 Dante's Key West Restaurant and Pool Bar.................. C1
13 El Meson de Pepe A1
14 El Siboney D4
15 Half Shell Raw Bar C1
16 Jimmy Buffett's Margaritaville Cafe..... B3
17 Latitudes................ A1
18 Louie's Backyard C5
19 Mangia Mangia.......... C2
20 Michaels Restaurant.... C2
21 Nine One Five B4
22 Salute on the Beach.... D5
23 Santiago's Bodega A3
24 Sarabeth's B3
25 Seven Fish.............. D3
26 Turtle Kraals............. C1

Hotels

1 Ambrosia Key West.... B2
2 Angelina Guest House . B3
3 Azul Key West........... C3
4 Casa Marina, A Waldorf–Astoria Resort........... D5
5 Crowne Plaza La Concha Hotel and Spa B2
6 Eden House.............. C2
7 The Gardens Hotel...... B3
8 Heron House C2
9 Island City House Hotel C2
10 Island House D2
11 Key Lime Inn............. C3
12 La Pensione C3
13 The Marker.............. B1
14 Marquesa Hotel......... B2
15 Mermaid & the Alligator.................. C3
16 NYAH: Not Your Average Hotel............ C2
17 Ocean Key Resort & Spa A1
18 Pier House Resort and Spa.......... A1
19 The Reach, A Waldorf Astoria Resort............ C5
20 Santa Maria Suites...... C5
21 Simonton Court B2
22 Southernmost Beach Resort............ C5
23 Southwinds............... C4
24 Speakeasy Inn B4
25 Sunset Key A1

and Grinnell streets, passing big ships, schooners, sunset cruises, fishing charters, and glass-bottom boats. This is where the locals go for great music and good drinks. ✉ *100 Grinnell St.* 🌐 *www.keywesthistoricseaport.com.*

The Key West Butterfly and Nature Conservatory

GARDEN | FAMILY | This air-conditioned refuge for butterflies, birds, and the human spirit gladdens the soul with hundreds of colorful wings—more than 45 species of butterflies alone—in a lovely glass-encased bubble. Waterfalls, artistic benches, paved pathways, birds, and lush, flowering vegetation elevate this above most butterfly attractions. The gift shop and gallery are worth a visit on their own. ✉ *1316 Duval St.* ☎ *305/296–2988, 800/839–4647* 🌐 *www.keywestbutterfly.com* 🎫 *$12.*

Key West Library

LIBRARY | Check out the pretty palm garden next to the Key West Library at 700 Fleming Street, just off Duval. This leafy, outdoor reading area, with shaded benches, is the perfect place to escape the frenzy and crowds of downtown Key West. There's free Internet access in the library, too. ✉ *700 Fleming St.* ☎ *305/292–3595* 🌐 *www.keyslibraries.org* 🕐 *Closed Sun.*

Key West Lighthouse Museum and Keeper's Quarters

LIGHTHOUSE | For the best view in town, climb the 88 steps to the top of this 1847 lighthouse. The 92-foot structure has a Fresnel lens, which was installed in the 1860s at a cost of $1 million. The keeper lived in the adjacent 1887 clapboard house, which now exhibits vintage photographs, ship models, nautical charts, and artifacts from all along Key West's reefs. A kids' room is stocked with books and toys. ✉ *938 Whitehead St.* ☎ *305/294–0012* 🌐 *www.kwahs.com* 🎫 *$10.*

The Sunblock Ban

In order to protect the only living coral barrier reef in the continental United States, Key West will ban the sale of sunscreens with two harmful chemicals known to negatively impact marine life and cause coral bleaching: oxybenzone and octinoxate. The ban takes effect in 2021.

Mallory Square and Pier

LOCAL INTEREST | For cruise-ship passengers, this is the disembarkation point for an attack on Key West. For practically every visitor, it's the requisite venue for a nightly sunset celebration that includes street performers—human statues, sword swallowers, tightrope walkers, musicians, and more—plus craft vendors, conch-fritter fryers, and other regulars who defy classification. With all the activity, don't forget to watch the main show: a dazzling tropical sunset. ✉ *Mallory Sq.*

The Southernmost Point

HISTORIC SITE | Possibly the most photographed site in Key West (even though the actual geographic southernmost point in the continental United States lies across the bay on a naval base, where you see a satellite dish), this is a must-see. Have your picture taken next to the big striped buoy that's been marking the southernmost point in the continental United States since 1983. A plaque next to it honors Cubans who lost their lives trying to escape to America, and other signs tell Key West history. ✉ *Whitehead and South Sts.*

NEW TOWN

The Overseas Highway splits as it enters Key West, the two forks rejoining to encircle New Town, the area east of White Street to Cow Key Channel. The

See the typewriter Hemingway used at his home office in Key West. He lived here from 1931 to 1942.

southern fork runs along the shore as South Roosevelt Boulevard (Route A1A) and skirts Key West International Airport, while the northern fork runs along the north shore as North Roosevelt Boulevard and turns into Truman Avenue once it hits Old Town. Part of New Town was created with dredged fill. The island would have continued growing this way had the Army Corps of Engineers not determined in the early 1970s that it was detrimental to the nearby reef.

Fort East Martello Museum & Gardens

MUSEUM | This redbrick Civil War fort never saw a lick of action during the war. Today it serves as a museum, with historical exhibits about the 19th and 20th centuries. Among the latter are relics of the USS *Maine,* cigar factory and shipwrecking exhibits, and the citadel tower you can climb to the top. The museum, operated by the Key West Art and Historical Society, also has a collection of Stanley Papio's "junk art" sculptures inside and out, and a gallery of Cuban folk artist Mario Sanchez's chiseled and painted wooden carvings of historic Key West street scenes. ✉ *3501 S. Roosevelt Blvd.* ☎ *305/296–3913* 🌐 *www.kwahs.com* 🎫 *$10.*

Key West Tropical Forest & Botanical Garden

LOCAL INTEREST | Established in 1935, this unique habitat is the only frost-free botanical garden in the continental United States. You won't see fancy topiaries and exotic plants, but you'll see a unique ecosystem that naturally occurs in this area and the Caribbean. There are paved walkways that take you past butterfly gardens, mangroves, Cuban palms, lots of birds like herons and ibis, and ponds where you can spy turtles and fish. It's a nice respite from the sidewalks and shops, and offers a natural slice of Keys paradise. ✉ *5210 College Rd.* ☎ *305/296–1504* 🌐 *www.kwbgs.org* 🎫 *$7.*

Hemingway Was Here

In a town where Pulitzer Prize–winning writers are almost as common as coconuts, Ernest Hemingway stands out. Many bars and restaurants around the island claim that he ate or drank there.

Hemingway came to Key West in 1928 at the urging of writer John Dos Passos and rented a house with his second wife, Pauline Pfeiffer. They spent winters in the Keys and summers in Europe and Wyoming, occasionally taking African safaris. Along the way, they had two sons, Patrick and Gregory. In 1931, Pauline's wealthy uncle Gus gave the couple the house at 907 Whitehead Street. Now known as the Ernest Hemingway Home & Museum, it's Key West's number one tourist attraction. Renovations included the addition of a pool and a tropical garden.

In 1935, when the visitor bureau included the house in a tourist brochure, Hemingway promptly built the brick wall that surrounds it today. He wrote of the visitor bureau's offense in a 1935 essay for *Esquire*, saying, "The house at present occupied by your correspondent is listed as number eighteen in a compilation of the forty-eight things for a tourist to see in Key West. So there will be no difficulty in a tourist finding it or any other of the sights of the city, a map has been prepared by the local F.E.R.A. authorities to be presented to each arriving visitor. This is all very flattering to the easily bloated ego of your correspondent but very hard on production."

During his time in Key West, Hemingway penned some of his most important works, including *A Farewell to Arms*, *To Have and Have Not*, *Green Hills of Africa*, and *Death in the Afternoon*. His rigorous schedule consisted of writing almost every morning in his second-story studio above the pool, then promptly descending the stairs at midday. By afternoon and evening he was ready for drinking, fishing, swimming, boxing, and hanging around with the boys.

One close friend was Joe Russell, a craggy fisherman and owner of the rugged bar Sloppy Joe's, originally at 428 Greene Street but now at 201 Duval Street. Russell was the only one in town who would cash Hemingway's $1,000 royalty check. Russell and Charles Thompson introduced Hemingway to deep-sea fishing, which became fodder for his writing.

Hemingway stayed in Key West for 11 years before leaving Pauline for his third wife. Pauline and the boys stayed on in the house, which sold in 1951 for $80,000, 10 times its original cost.

Beaches

OLD TOWN

Dog Beach

BEACH—SIGHT | Next to Louie's Backyard restaurant, this tiny beach—the only one in Key West where dogs are allowed unleashed—has a shore that's a mix of sand and rocks. **Amenities:** none. **Best for:** walking. ✉ *Vernon and Waddell Sts.* *Free.*

Fort Zachary Taylor Beach

BEACH—SIGHT | **FAMILY** | The park's beach is the best and safest place to swim in Key West. There's an adjoining picnic area with barbecue grills and shade trees, a snack bar, and rental equipment,

Divers examine the intentionally scuttled 327-foot former U.S. Coast Guard cutter *Duane* in 120 feet of water off Key Largo.

including snorkeling gear. A café serves sandwiches and other munchies. Water shoes are recommended since the bottom is rocky here. **Amenities:** food and drink; showers; toilets; water sports. **Best for:** snorkeling; swimming. ✉ *End of Southard St., through Truman Annex* ☎ *305/292–6713* 🌐 *www.fortzacharytaylor.com* 🎫 *$4 for single-occupant vehicles, $6 for 2–8 people, plus $0.50 per person county surcharge.*

Higgs Beach–Astro City Playground

BEACH—SIGHT | **FAMILY** | This Monroe County park with its groomed pebbly sand is a popular sunbathing spot. A nearby grove of Australian pines provides shade, and the West Martello Tower provides shelter should a storm suddenly sweep in. Kayak and beach-chair rentals are available, as is a volleyball net. The beach also has the largest AIDS memorial in the country and a cultural exhibit commemorating the grave site of 295 enslaved Africans who died after being rescued from three South America–bound slave ships in 1860. An athletic trail with 10 fitness stations is also available. Hungry? Grab a bite to eat at the on-site restaurant, Salute. Across the street, **Astro City Playground** is popular with young children. **Amenities:** parking; toilets; water sports. **Best for:** snorkeling; swimming. ✉ *Atlantic Blvd. between White and Reynolds Sts.* 🎫 *Free.*

NEW TOWN

C. B. Harvey Memorial Rest Beach

BEACH—SIGHT | This beach and park were named after Cornelius Bradford Harvey, former Key West mayor and commissioner. Adjacent to Higgs Beach, it has half a dozen picnic areas across the street, dunes, a pier, and a wheelchair and bike path. **Amenities:** none. **Best for:** walking. ✉ *Atlantic Blvd., east side of White St. Pier* 🎫 *Free.*

Smathers Beach

BEACH—SIGHT | This wide beach has nearly 1 mile of nice white sand, plus beautiful coconut palms, picnic areas, and volleyball courts, all of which make it popular with the spring-break crowd. Trucks along the road rent rafts,

The Conch Republic

Beginning in the 1970s, pot smuggling became a source of income for islanders who knew how to dodge detection in the maze of waterways in the Keys. In 1982, the U.S. Border Patrol threw a roadblock across the Overseas Highway just south of Florida City to catch drug runners and undocumented aliens. Traffic backed up for miles as Border Patrol agents searched vehicles and demanded that the occupants prove U.S. citizenship. Officials in Key West, outraged at being treated like foreigners by the federal government, staged a protest and formed their own "nation," the so-called Conch Republic. They hoisted a flag and distributed mock border passes, visas, and Conch currency. The embarrassed Border Patrol dismantled its roadblock, and now an annual festival recalls the city's victory.

windsurfers, and other beach "toys." **Amenities:** food and drink; parking; toilets; water sports. **Best for:** partiers. ✉ *S. Roosevelt Blvd.* 🎫 *Free.*

Restaurants

Bring your appetite, a sense of daring, and a lack of preconceived notions about propriety. A meal in Key West can mean overlooking the crazies along Duval Street, watching roosters and pigeons battle for a scrap of food that may have escaped your fork, relishing the finest in what used to be the dining room of a 19th-century Victorian home, or gazing out at boats jockeying for position in the marina. And that's just the diversity of the setting. Seafood dominates local menus, but the treatment afforded that fish or crustacean can range from Cuban and New World to Asian and Continental.

OLD TOWN

Ambrosia

$$ | **JAPANESE** | Ask any savvy local where to get the best sushi on the island and you'll undoubtedly be pointed to this bright and airy dining room with a modern indoor waterfall literally steps from the Atlantic. Grab a seat at the sushi bar and watch owner and head sushi chef Masa (albeit not the famous chef from New York and Las Vegas) prepare an impressive array of sashimi delicacies. **Known for:** consistently good fish; great tempura and teriyaki bento lunch specials; the Ambrosia special, with a mix of sashimi, sushi, and rolls. 💲 *Average main: $20* ✉ *Santa Maria Resort, 1401 Simonton St.* ☎ *305/293–0304* 🌐 *www.ambrosiasushi.com* 🕒 *Closed 2 wks after Labor Day. No lunch weekends.*

Azur Restaurant

$$$ | **ECLECTIC** | In a contemporary setting with indoor and outdoor seating, welcoming staff serve original, eclectic dishes that stand out from those at the hordes of Key West restaurants. Key lime–stuffed French toast and yellowtail snapper Benedict make breakfast a pleasant wake-up call. **Known for:** homemade gnocchi; a nice variety of fish specials; daily brunch. 💲 *Average main: $26* ✉ *425 Grinnell St.* ☎ *305/292–2987* 🌐 *www.azurkeywest.com.*

Blue Heaven

$$$ | **CARIBBEAN** | The outdoor dining area here is often referred to as "the quintessential Keys experience," and it's hard

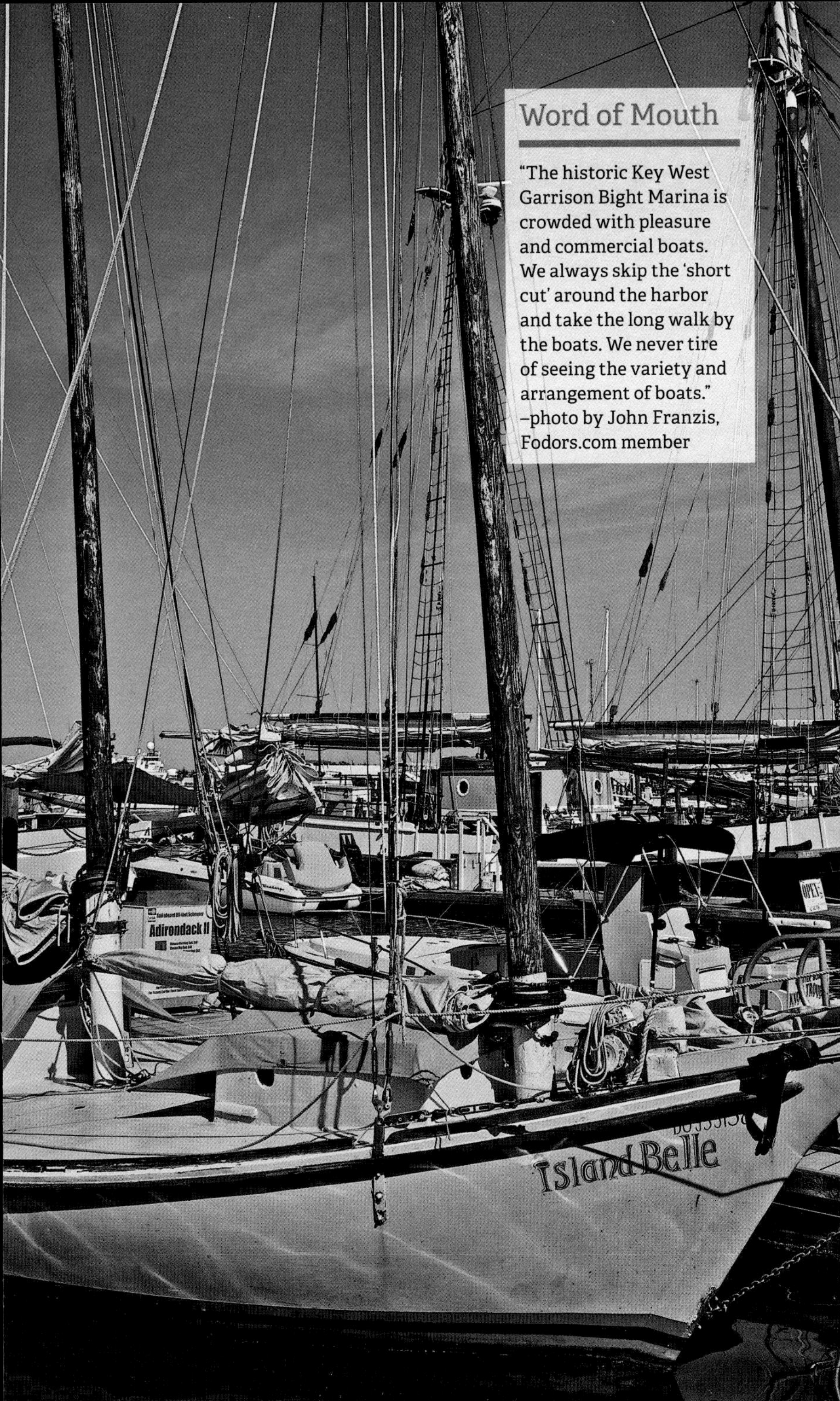

Word of Mouth

"The historic Key West Garrison Bight Marina is crowded with pleasure and commercial boats. We always skip the 'short cut' around the harbor and take the long walk by the boats. We never tire of seeing the variety and arrangement of boats." –photo by John Franzis, Fodors.com member

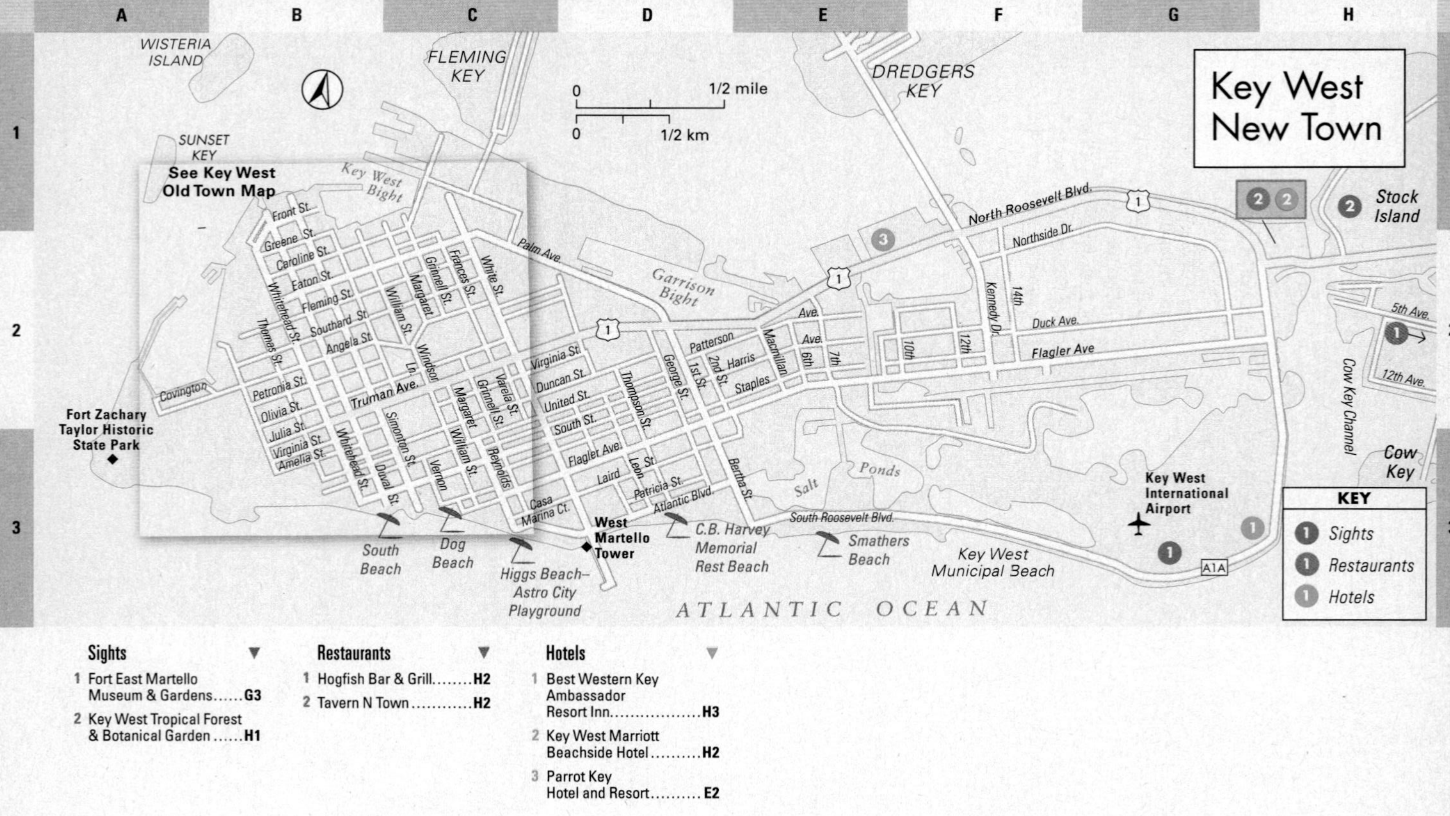

Sights

1 Fort East Martello Museum & Gardens...... **G3**

2 Key West Tropical Forest & Botanical Garden...... **H1**

Restaurants

1 Hogfish Bar & Grill........ **H2**

2 Tavern N Town............ **H2**

Hotels

1 Best Western Key Ambassador Resort Inn.................. **H3**

2 Key West Marriott Beachside Hotel.......... **H2**

3 Parrot Key Hotel and Resort.......... **E2**

to argue. There's much to like about this historic Caribbean-style restaurant where Hemingway refereed boxing matches and customers cheered for cockfights. **Known for:** shrimp and grits; lobster Benedict with key lime hollandaise; the wait for a table and lack of parking. *$ Average main: $24 ✉ 729 Thomas St. ☎ 305/296–8666 🌐 www.blueheavenkw.com ⏲ Closed after Labor Day for 6 wks.*

★ B.O.'s Fish Wagon

$$ | SEAFOOD | What started out as a fish house on wheels appears to have broken down on the corner of Caroline and William streets and is today the cornerstone for one of Key West's junkyard-chic dining institutions. Step up to the window and order a grouper sandwich fried or grilled and topped with key lime sauce. **Known for:** lots of Key West charm; Friday-night jam sessions; all seating on picnic tables in the yard. *$ Average main: $18 ✉ 801 Caroline St. ☎ 305/294–9272 🌐 bosfishwagon.com.*

The Café

$ | VEGETARIAN | You don't have to be a vegetarian to love this new-age café decorated with bright artwork and a corrugated-tin-fronted counter. Local favorites include homemade soup, veggie sandwiches and burgers (order them with a side of sweet-potato fries), grilled portobello mushroom salad, seafood, vegan specialties, stir-fry dinners, and grilled veggie pizzas. **Known for:** vegan options; homemade sangria; weekend brunch. *$ Average main: $11 ✉ 509 Southard St. ☎ 305/296–5515 🌐 www.thecafekw.com.*

★ Café Marquesa

$$$ | EUROPEAN | You'll find seven or more inspired entrées on a changing menu each night, including anything from yellowtail snapper to seared duck breast. End your meal on a sweet note with chocolate pot de crème and homemade ice cream—there's also a fine selection of wines and custom martinis. **Known for:** relaxed but elegant setting; good wine and martini lists; desserts worth ordering. *$ Average main: $30 ✉ 600 Fleming St. ☎ 305/292–1244 🌐 www.marquesa.com ⏲ No lunch.*

Café Solé

$$$ | FRENCH | This little corner of France hides behind a high wall in a residential neighborhood. Inside, French training intertwines with local ingredients, creating delicious takes on classics, including a must-try conch carpaccio and some of the best bouillabaisse that you'll find outside Marseilles. **Known for:** hogfish in several different preparations; intimate, romantic atmosphere; award-winning key lime pie. *$ Average main: $28 ✉ 1029 Southard St. ☎ 305/294–0230 🌐 www.cafesole.com.*

Camille's Restaurant

$$$ | MODERN AMERICAN | FAMILY | Break out the stretchy pants because everything on the menu at this affordable hot spot not only *sounds* scrumptious, it *is*. Start your day with a shrimp, lobster, or crab-cake Benedict—the latter was voted best in the Florida Keys. **Known for:** popularity with both locals and tourists; fresh seafood daily; BOGO menu from 3 pm to closing daily. *$ Average main: $21 ✉ 1202 Simonton St., at Catherine St. ☎ 305/296–4811.*

Coffee Plantation

$ | BAKERY | Get your morning (or afternoon) buzz, and hook up to the Internet in the comfort of a homelike setting in a circa-1890 Conch house. Sit inside or out and munch on sandwiches, wraps, and pastries, and sip a hot or cold espresso beverage. **Known for:** tropical macchiatos; Almond Joy lattes; homemade quiche of the day. *$ Average main: $3 ✉ 713 Caroline St. ☎ 305/295–9808 🌐 www.coffeeplantationkeywest.com ⏲ Closed Sun.*

Conch Republic Seafood Company

$$$ | SEAFOOD | FAMILY | Because of its location where the fast ferry docks, Conch Republic does a brisk business.

It's huge, open-air, on the water, and the menu is ambitious, offering more than just standard seafood fare. **Known for:** "Royal Reds" peel-and-eat shrimp; no reservations; live music most nights. 💲 *Average main: $25* ✉ *631 Greene St., at Elizabeth St.* ☎ *305/294–4403* 🌐 *www.conchrepublicseafood.com.*

Croissants de France

$ | **FRENCH** | Pop into the bakery for something sinfully sweet or spend some time people-watching at the sidewalk café next door. You can get breakfast or lunch at the café, and the bakery is open late. **Known for:** gluten-free buckwheat crepes; popularity with both locals and visitors; great coffee and croissants. 💲 *Average main: $14* ✉ *816 Duval St.* ☎ *305/294–2624* 🌐 *www.croissantsdefrance.com.*

Dante's Key West Restaurant and Pool Bar

$$ | **SEAFOOD** | With the motto "Come be an aquaholic," Dante's is as unique as Key West itself. Sun loungers, tiki bars, and tables with umbrellas and chairs surround a large free-form swimming pool. **Known for:** food and drink minimum at some key tables; popular happy hour; "Hook and Cook" (bring your fresh catch and they cook it for you). 💲 *Average main: $18* ✉ *Conch Harbor Marina, 951 Caroline St.* ☎ *305/423–2001* 🌐 *www.danteskeywest.com.*

El Meson de Pepe

$$ | **CUBAN** | If you want a taste of the island's Cuban heritage, this is the place to dine alfresco or in the dining room on refined Cuban classics. Begin with a megasize mojito while you browse the expansive menu offering *tostones rellenos* (green plantains with different traditional fillings), ceviche, and more. **Known for:** authentic plantain chips; Latin band during the nightly sunset celebration; touristy atmosphere. 💲 *Average main: $19* ✉ *Mallory Sq., 410 Wall St.* ☎ *305/295–2620* 🌐 *www.elmesondepepe.com.*

El Siboney

$ | **CUBAN** | Dining at this family-style restaurant is like going to Mom's for Sunday dinner—if your mother is Cuban. The dining room is noisy, and the food is traditional *cubano*. To make a good thing even better, the prices are very reasonable and the homemade sangria is *muy bueno*. **Known for:** memorable paella and traditional dishes; wine and beer only; cheaper than more touristy options close to Duval. 💲 *Average main: $11* ✉ *900 Catherine St.* ☎ *305/296–4184* 🌐 *www.elsiboneyrestaurant.com.*

Half Shell Raw Bar

$$ | **SEAFOOD** | **FAMILY** | Smack-dab on the docks, this legendary institution gets its name from the oysters, clams, and peel-and-eat shrimp that are a departure point for its seafood-based diet. It's not clever recipes or fine dining (or even air-conditioning) that packs 'em in; it's fried fish, po'boy sandwiches, and seafood combos. **Known for:** daily happy hour with food and drink deals; few non-seafood options; good people-watching spot. 💲 *Average main: $16* ✉ *Lands End Village at Historic Seaport, 231 Margaret St.* ☎ *305/294–7496* 🌐 *www.halfshellrawbar.com.*

Jimmy Buffett's Margaritaville Cafe

$$ | **AMERICAN** | If you must have your cheeseburger in paradise, it may as well be here. The first of Buffett's line of chain eateries, it belongs here more than anywhere else, but quite frankly it's more about the name, music, and attitude (and margaritas) than the food. **Known for:** pricey Caribbean bar food; good and spicy conch chowder; raucous party atmosphere almost all the time. 💲 *Average main: $18* ✉ *500 Duval St.* ☎ *305/292–1435* 🌐 *www.margaritaville.com.*

Latitudes

$$$ | **ECLECTIC** | For a special treat, take the short boat ride to lovely Sunset Key for lunch or dinner on the beach. Creativity and quality ingredients combine

for dishes that are bound to impress as much as the setting, like the fish tacos with chipotle aioli. **Known for:** amazing sunset views; sophisticated atmosphere and expensive food; lobster bisque. *Average main: $28 Sunset Key Guest Cottages, 245 Front St. 305/292–5300, 888/477–7786 www.sunsetkeycottages.com/latitudes-key-west Reservations are required to catch the ferry: no reservation, no ride.*

Louie's Backyard

$$$$ | **ECLECTIC** | Feast your eyes on a steal-your-breath-away view and beautifully presented dishes prepared by executive chef Doug Shook. Once you get over sticker shock on the seasonally changing menu, settle in on the outside deck and enjoy dishes like cracked conch with mango chutney, lamb chops with sun-dried tomato relish, and tamarind-glazed duck breast. **Known for:** fresh, pricey seafood and steaks; affordable lunch menu; late night drinks at Afterdeck Bar, directly on the water. *Average main: $36 700 Waddell Ave. 305/294–1061 www.louiesbackyard.com Closed Labor Day–mid-Sept. Café closed Sun. and Mon.*

Mangia Mangia

$$ | **ITALIAN** | This longtime favorite serves large portions of homemade pastas that can be matched with any of the homemade sauces. Tables are arranged in a brick garden hung with twinkling lights and in a cozy, casual dining room in an old house. **Known for:** extensive wine list with a nice range of prices; gluten-free and organic pastas; outdoor seating in the garden. *Average main: $18 900 Southard St. 305/294–2469 www.mangia-mangia.com No lunch.*

Michaels Restaurant

$$$$ | **AMERICAN** | White tablecloths, subdued lighting, and romantic music give Michaels the feel of an urban eatery, while garden seating reminds you that you are in the Keys. Chef-owner Michael Wilson flies in prime rib, cowboy steaks, and rib eyes from Allen Brothers in Chicago, which has supplied top-ranked steak houses for more than a century. **Known for:** elegant, romantic atmosphere; small plates available until 7:30 Sunday–Thursday; steak and seafood. *Average main: $32 532 Margaret St. 305/295–1300 www.michaels-keywest.com No lunch.*

Nine One Five

$$$$ | **ECLECTIC** | Twinkling lights draped along the lower- and upper-level outdoor porches of a 100-year-old Victorian home set an unstuffy and comfortable stage here. If you like to sample and sip, you'll appreciate the variety of smaller-plate selections and wines by the glass. **Known for:** fun place to people-watch; intimate and inviting atmosphere; light jazz during dinner. *Average main: $32 915 Duval St. 305/296–0669 www.915duval.com No lunch Mon. and Tues.*

Salute on the Beach

$$$ | **ITALIAN** | Sister restaurant to Blue Heaven, this colorful establishment sits on Higgs Beach, giving it one of the island's best lunch views—and a bit of sand and salt spray on a windy day. The intriguing menu is Italian with a Caribbean flair and will not disappoint. **Known for:** amazing water views; casual, inviting atmosphere; pricey slice of key lime pie. *Average main: $22 Higgs Beach, 1000 Atlantic Blvd. 305/292–1117 www.saluteonthebeach.com.*

★ Santiago's Bodega

$ | **TAPAS** | Picky palates will be satisfied at this funky, dark, and sensuous tapas restaurant, which is well off the main drag—it's a secret spot for local foodies in the know. Small plates include yellowfin tuna ceviche with hunks of avocado and mango, and filet mignon with creamy Gorgonzola butter. **Known for:** legendary bread pudding; homemade white or red sangria; a favorite with local chefs. *Average main: $14 Bahama Village, 207 Petronia St. 305/296–7691 www.santiagosbodega.com.*

Sarabeth's

$$ | **AMERICAN** | Named for the award-winning jam-maker and pastry chef Sarabeth Levine, who runs the kitchen, this restaurant serves all-day breakfast, best enjoyed in the picket-fenced front yard of this circa-1870 synagogue. Lemon ricotta pancakes, pumpkin waffles, and homemade jams make the meal. **Known for:** homemade granola and old-fashioned porridge; daily specials including meat loaf and mac and cheese; orange apricot bread pudding. *Average main: $20 ✉ 530 Simonton St., at Souhard St. ☎ 305/293–8181 🌐 www.sarabethskeywest.com ⏲ Closed Mon. and Tues.*

Seven Fish

$$$ | **SEAFOOD** | This local hot spot exudes a casual Key West vibe with an eclectic mix of dishes. The specialty is the local fish of the day (like snapper with creamy Thai curry). **Known for:** fresh seafood; busy spot requiring reservations; amazing foccacia bread. *Average main: $26 ✉ 921 Truman Ave. ☎ 305/296–2777 🌐 www.7fish.com ⏲ Closed Tues. No lunch.*

Turtle Kraals

$$ | **SEAFOOD** | **FAMILY** | Named for the kraals, or corrals, where sea turtles were once kept until they went to the cannery, this place calls to mind the island's history. The menu offers an assortment of marine cuisine that includes seafood enchiladas, mesquite-grilled fish of the day, and mango crab cakes. **Known for:** mesquite-grilled oysters with Parmesan and cilantro; Peruvian-style ceviche; great views of the harbor. *Average main: $16 ✉ 231 Margaret St. ☎ 305/294–2640 🌐 www.turtlekraals.com.*

NEW TOWN

Hogfish Bar & Grill

$$ | **SEAFOOD** | It's worth a drive to Stock Island, one of Florida's last surviving working waterfronts, just outside Key West, to indulge in the freshness you'll witness at this down-to-earth spot. Hogfish is the specialty, of course. **Known for:** pricey fish sandwiches; a taste of local life; fried grouper cheeks. *Average main: $17 ✉ 6810 Front St., Stock Island ☎ 305/293–4041 🌐 www.hogfishbar.com.*

Tavern N Town

$$$$ | **ECLECTIC** | This handsome and warm restaurant has an open kitchen that adds lovely aromas from the wood-fired oven. The dinner menu offers a variety of options, including small plates and full entrées. **Known for:** upscale atmosphere (and prices); popular happy hour; noisy when busy. *Average main: $33 ✉ Key West Marriott Beachside Resort, 3841 N. Roosevelt Blvd. ☎ 305/296–8100, 800/546–0885 🌐 www.taverntown.com ⏲ No lunch.*

Hotels

Historic cottages, restored century-old Conch houses, and large resorts are among the offerings in Key West, the majority charging between $100 and $300 a night. In high season, Christmas through Easter, you'll be hard-pressed to find a decent room for less than $200, and most places raise prices considerably during holidays and festivals. Many guesthouses and inns do not welcome children under 16, and most do not permit smoking indoors. Most tariffs include an expanded Continental breakfast and, often, an afternoon glass of wine or snack.

LODGING ALTERNATIVES

The Key West Lodging Association is an umbrella organization for dozens of local properties. Vacation Rentals Key West lists historic cottages, homes, and condominiums for rent. Rent Key West Vacations specializes in renting vacation homes and condos for a week or longer. Vacation Key West lists all kinds of properties throughout Key West. In addition to these local agencies, 🌐 *airbnb.com* and vrbo.com have many offerings in Key West.

CONTACTS Key West Vacations. *888/775–3993 www.keywestvacations.com.* **Lodging Association of Key West and the Florida Keys.** *800/492–1911 www.keywestinns.com.* **Rent Key West Vacations.** *1075 Duval St., Suite C11 305/294–0990, 800/833–7368 www.rentkeywest.com.* **Vacation Key West.** *100 Grinnell St., Key West Ferry Terminal 305/295–9500, 800/595–5397 www.vacationkw.com.*

OLD TOWN

Ambrosia Key West

$$$ | **B&B/INN** | If you desire personal attention, a casual atmosphere, and a dollop of style, stay at these twin inns spread out on nearly 2 acres. **Pros:** spacious rooms; breakfast served poolside; great location. **Cons:** on-street parking can be tough to come by; a little too spread out; high windows in some rooms let in the early morning light. *Rooms from: $385 615, 618, 622 Fleming St. 305/296–9838, 800/535–9838 www.ambrosiakeywest.com 20 rooms Free Breakfast.*

Angelina Guest House

$ | **B&B/INN** | In the heart of Old Town, this adults-only home away from home offers simple, clean, attractively priced accommodations. **Pros:** good value; nice garden; friendly staff. **Cons:** thin walls; basic rooms with no TVs; shared balcony and four of the rooms share a bathroom. *Rooms from: $159 302 Angela St. 305/294–4480, 888/303–4480 www.angelinaguesthouse.com 13 rooms Free Breakfast.*

Azul Key West

$$ | **B&B/INN** | The ultramodern—nearly minimalistic—redo of this classic circa-1903 Queen Anne mansion is a break from the sensory overload of Key West's other abundant Victorian guesthouses. **Pros:** lovely building; marble-floored baths; luxurious linens. **Cons:** on a busy street; modern isn't for everyone; two-night minimum stay, five nights in season. *Rooms from: $289 907 Truman Ave. 305/296–5152, 888/253–2985 www.azulhotels.us 11 rooms Free Breakfast.*

Casa Marina, A Waldorf-Astoria Resort

$$$ | **RESORT** | **FAMILY** | This luxurious property is on the largest private beach in Key West, and it has the same richly appointed lobby with beamed ceilings, polished pine floor, and original art as it did when it opened on New Year's Eve 1920. **Pros:** hugh beach; on-site dining, bars, and water sports; away from the crowds. **Cons:** long walk to central Old Town; expensive resort fee; spa is across the street in a separate building. *Rooms from: $399 1500 Reynolds St. 305/296–3535, 866/203–6392 www.casamarinaresort.com 311 rooms No meals.*

Crowne Plaza La Concha Hotel and Spa

$$$ | **HOTEL** | History and franchises can mix, as this 1920s-vintage hotel proves with its handsome atrium lobby and sleep-conducive rooms. **Pros:** location is everything; good on-site restaurant and wine bar; free Wi-Fi. **Cons:** high-traffic area; rooms are small, bathrooms are smaller; expensive valet-only parking. *Rooms from: $350 430 Duval St. 305/296–2991 www.laconchakeywest.com 178 rooms No meals.*

Eden House

$$ | **HOTEL** | From the vintage metal rockers on the streetside porch to the old neon hotel sign in the lobby, this 1920s rambling Key West mainstay hotel is high on character, low on gloss. **Pros:** free parking; hot tub is actually hot; daily happy hour around the pool. **Cons:** pricey for older rooms; brown towels take getting used to; parking is first-come, first-served. *Rooms from: $225 1015 Fleming St. 305/296–6868, 800/533–5397 www.edenhouse.com 44 rooms No meals.*

★ The Gardens Hotel

$$$$ | **HOTEL** | Built in 1875, this gloriously shaded, well-loved property was a labor of love from the get-go, and it covers a third of a city block in Old Town. **Pros:** luxurious bathrooms; secluded garden seating; free Wi-Fi. **Cons:** hard to get reservations; expensive; nightly secure parking fee. *Rooms from: $415 ✉ 526 Angela St. ☎ 305/294–2661, 800/526–2664 🌐 www.gardenshotel.com 23 rooms 🍴 Free Breakfast.*

Heron House

$$ | **B&B/INN** | Built in the 1850s, rooms at this hotel just off Duval (not to be confused with Heron House Court, although they are sister properties) are outfitted in rattan and tropical watercolors, and bathrooms are updated with a touch of granite. **Pros:** vintage charm; close enough to the action but quiet; friendly staff. **Cons:** early bird gets the hot food at breakfast; furnishings need updating; no designated parking lot. *Rooms from: $229 ✉ 512 Simonton St. ☎ 305/294–8477, 800/294–1644 🌐 www.heronhousehotels.com 23 rooms 🍴 Free Breakfast.*

Island City House Hotel

$$$ | **B&B/INN** | A private garden with brick walkways, tropical plants, and a canopy of palms sets this convivial guesthouse apart from the pack. **Pros:** lush gardens; knowledgeable staff; bike rentals on-site. **Cons:** spotty Wi-Fi service; front desk is staffed only 8 am–8 pm; no parking. *Rooms from: $320 ✉ 411 William St. ☎ 305/294–5702, 800/634–8230 🌐 www.islandcityhouse.com 24 suites 🍴 No meals.*

Island House

$$$$ | **HOTEL** | Geared specifically toward gay men, this hotel features a health club, a video lounge, a café and bar, and rooms in historic digs. **Pros:** lots of privacy; just the place to get that all-over tan; free happy hour for guests. **Cons:** no women allowed; three rooms share a bath; day passes bring visitors of every age, which is a pro or con depending on your mood. *Rooms from: $459 ✉ 1129 Fleming St. ☎ 305/294–6284, 800/890–6284 🌐 www.islandhousekeywest.com 34 rooms 🍴 No meals.*

Key Lime Inn

$$ | **B&B/INN** | This 1854 Grand Bahama–style house on the National Register of Historic Places succeeds by offering amiable service, a great location, and simple rooms with natural-wood furnishings. **Pros:** walking distance to clubs and bars; some rooms have private outdoor spaces; free Wi-Fi. **Cons:** over a mile to the sunset end of Duval Street; pool faces a busy street; $20 daily parking fee. *Rooms from: $259 ✉ 725 Truman Ave. ☎ 305/294–5229, 800/549–4430 🌐 www.keylimeinn.com 37 rooms 🍴 Free Breakfast.*

La Pensione

$$ | **B&B/INN** | Hospitality and period furnishings make this 1891 home, once owned by a cigar executive, a wonderful glimpse into Key West life in the late 19th century. **Pros:** pine-paneled walls; first-come, first-served parking included; some rooms have wraparound porches. **Cons:** street-facing rooms are noisy; rooms do not have TVs; rooms accommodate only two people. *Rooms from: $258 ✉ 809 Truman Ave. ☎ 305/292–9923, 800/893–1193 🌐 www.lapensione.com 9 rooms 🍴 Free Breakfast.*

The Marker

$$$ | **RESORT** | The Marker is one of Key West's newest hotels, and a welcome and luxurious addition to the waterfront in Old Town, with Conch-style architecture and an authentic Keys aesthetic. **Pros:** convenient Old Town location; on-site restaurant Cero Bodega; three saltwater pools, including one for adults only. **Cons:** hefty resort and parking fees nightly; "locals welcome" policy means pool loungers can be hard to come by; lots of walking if your room isn't near the amenities. *Rooms from: $400 ✉ 200 William St. ☎ 305/501–5193 🌐 www.*

themarkerkeywest.com 🛏 *96 rooms* 🍽 *No meals.*

★ Marquesa Hotel

$$$ | **HOTEL** | In a town that prides itself on its laid-back luxury, this complex of four restored 1884 houses stands out. **Pros:** room service; romantic atmosphere; turndown service. **Cons:** street-facing rooms can be noisy; expensive rates; no elevator. 💲 *Rooms from: $395* ✉ *600 Fleming St.* ☎ *305/292–1919, 800/869–4631* 🌐 *www.marquesa.com* 🛏 *27 rooms* 🍽 *No meals.*

Mermaid & the Alligator

$$ | **B&B/INN** | An enchanting combination of flora and fauna makes this 1904 Victorian house a welcoming retreat. **Pros:** hot plunge pool; massage pavilion; island-getaway feel. **Cons:** minimum stay required (length depends on season); dark public areas; plastic lawn chairs. 💲 *Rooms from: $278* ✉ *729 Truman Ave.* ☎ *305/294–1894, 800/773–1894* 🌐 *www.kwmermaid.com* 🛏 *9 rooms* 🍽 *Free Breakfast.*

NYAH: Not Your Average Hotel

$$$ | **B&B/INN** | From its charming white picket fence, it may look similar to other Victorian-style Key West B&Bs, but that's where the similarities end. **Pros:** central location; perfect for traveling with a group of friends; free daily happy hour. **Cons:** small rooms, even smaller closets; street parking only; no toiletries provided. 💲 *Rooms from: $349* ✉ *420 Margaret St.* ☎ *305/296–2131* 🌐 *www.nyahotels.com* 🛏 *36 rooms* 🍽 *Free Breakfast* ☞ *Age 18 and over only.*

★ Ocean Key Resort & Spa

$$$$ | **RESORT** | This full resort—relatively rare in Key West—has large, tropical-look rooms with private balconies and excellent amenities, including a pool and bar overlooking Sunset Pier and a Thai-inspired spa. **Pros:** well-trained staff; lively pool scene; fantastic location at the busy end of Duval. **Cons:** daily valet parking and resort fee; too bustling for some; rooms are starting to show their age. 💲 *Rooms from: $495* ✉ *Zero Duval St.* ☎ *305/296–7701, 800/328–9815* 🌐 *www.oceankey.com* 🛏 *100 rooms* 🍽 *No meals.*

Pier House Resort and Spa

$$$$ | **RESORT** | This upscale resort, near Mallory Square in the heart of Old Town, offers a wide range of amenities, including a beach and comfortable, traditionally furnished rooms. **Pros:** beautiful beach; free Wi-Fi; nice spa and restaurant. **Cons:** lots of conventions; poolside rooms are small; not really suitable for children under 16. 💲 *Rooms from: $470* ✉ *1 Duval St.* ☎ *305/296–4600, 800/327–8340* 🌐 *www.pierhouse.com* 🛏 *145 rooms* 🍽 *No meals.*

The Reach, A Waldorf Astoria Resort

$$$ | **RESORT** | Embracing Key West's only natural beach, this full-service, luxury resort offers sleek rooms, all with balconies and modern amenities as well as reciprocal privileges to its sister Casa Marina resort nearby. **Pros:** removed from Duval hubbub; great sunrise views; pullout sofas in most rooms. **Cons:** expensive resort fee; high rates; some say it lacks the grandeur you'd expect of a Waldorf property. 💲 *Rooms from: $399* ✉ *1435 Simonton St.* ☎ *305/296–5000, 888/318–4316* 🌐 *www.reachresort.com* 🛏 *150 rooms* 🍽 *No meals.*

★ Santa Maria Suites

$$$$ | **RESORT** | It's odd to call this a hidden gem when it sits on a prominent corner just one block off Duval, but you'd never know what luxury awaits behind its concrete facade, which creates total seclusion from the outside world. **Pros:** amenities galore; front desk concierge services; private parking lot. **Cons:** daily resort fee; poolside units must close curtains for privacy; only two-bedroom units available. 💲 *Rooms from: $549* ✉ *1401 Simonton St.* ☎ *866/726–8259, 305/296–5678* 🌐 *www.santamariasuites.com* 🛏 *35 suites* 🍽 *No meals.*

Simonton Court
$$$ | **B&B/INN** | A small world all its own, this adults-only maze of accommodations and four swimming pools makes you feel deliciously sequestered from Key West's crasser side but keeps you close enough to get there on foot. **Pros:** lots of privacy; well-appointed accommodations; friendly staff. **Cons:** minimum stay required in high season; off-street parking $25 nightly; some street noise in basic rooms. *Rooms from: $310* *320 Simonton St.* *305/294–6386, 800/944–2687* *www.simontoncourt.com* *29 rooms* *Free Breakfast.*

Southernmost Beach Resort
$$$ | **HOTEL** | Rooms at this hotel on the quiet end of Duval—a 20-minute walk from downtown—are modern and sophisticated, and it's far enough from the hubub that you can relax but close enough that you can participate if you wish. **Pros:** pool attracts a lively crowd; access to nearby properties and beach; free parking and Wi-Fi. **Cons:** can get crowded around the pool and public areas; expensive nightly resort fee; beach is across the street. *Rooms from: $359* *1319 Duval St.* *305/296–6577, 800/354–4455* *www.southernmostbeachresort.com* *118 rooms* *No meals.*

Southwinds
$$ | **B&B/INN** | Operated by the same company as the ultra-high-end Santa Maria Suites, this motel-style property, though still pretty basic, has been modestly upgraded and is a good value-oriented option in pricey Key West. **Pros:** early (2 pm) check-in may be available; clean and spacious rooms; free parking and Wi-Fi. **Cons:** bland decor; small pools; thin walls. *Rooms from: $200* *1321 Simonton St.* *305/296–2829, 877/879–2362* *www.keywestsouthwinds.com* *58 rooms* *Free Breakfast.*

Speakeasy Inn
$ | **B&B/INN** | During Prohibition, Raul Vasquez made this place popular by smuggling in rum from Cuba; today its reputation is for having reasonably priced rooms within walking distance of the beach. **Pros:** good location; all rooms have kitchenettes; first-come, first-served free parking. **Cons:** no pool; on busy Duval; rooms are fairly basic. *Rooms from: $189* *1117 Duval St.* *305/296–2680* *www.speakeasyinn.com* *7 suites* *Free Breakfast.*

★ Sunset Key
$$$$ | **RESORT** | This luxurious private island retreat with its own sandy beach feels completely cut off from the world, yet you're just minutes away from the action: a 10-minute ride from Mallory Square on the 24-hour free ferry. **Pros:** all units have kitchens; roomy verandas; free Wi-Fi. **Cons:** luxury doesn't come cheap; beach shore is rocky; launch runs only every 30 minutes. *Rooms from: $780* *245 Front St.* *305/292–5300, 888/477–7786* *www.sunsetkeycottages.com* *40 cottages* *Free Breakfast.*

NEW TOWN

Best Western Key Ambassador Resort Inn
$$ | **HOTEL** | You know what to expect from this chain hotel: well-maintained rooms, predictable service, and competitive prices. **Pros:** big pool area; popular tiki bar serves liquor and food; most rooms have screened-in balconies. **Cons:** roar of airplanes from nearby airport; lacks personality; far from Duval Street. *Rooms from: $300* *3755 S. Roosevelt Blvd., New Town* *305/296–3500, 800/432–4315* *www.keyambassador.com* *100 rooms* *Free Breakfast.*

Key West Marriott Beachside Hotel
$$$$ | **HOTEL** | **FAMILY** | This hotel vies for convention business with the biggest ballroom in Key West, but it also appeals to families with its spacious condo units decorated with impeccable good taste. **Pros:** private tanning beach; poolside cabanas; complimentary shuttle to Old Town and airport. **Cons:** no swimming at its beach; lots of conventions and conferences; cookie-cutter facade. *Rooms*

The Holidays Key West Style

On New Year's Eve, Key West celebrates the turning of the calendar page with three separate ceremonies that parody New York's dropping-of-the-ball drama. Here they let fall a 6-foot conch shell from Sloppy Joe's Bar, a pirate wench from the towering mast of a tall ship at the Historic Seaport, and a drag queen (elegantly decked out in a ball gown and riding an oversize red high-heel shoe) at Bourbon Street Pub. You wouldn't expect any less from America's most outrageous city.

Key West is one of the nation's biggest party towns, so the celebrations here take on a colorful hue. In keeping with Key West's rich maritime heritage, its monthlong Bight Before Christmas begins Thanksgiving Eve at Key West Bight. The Lighted Boat Parade creates a quintessential Florida spectacle with live music and decorated vessels of all shapes and sizes.

Some years, the Tennessee Williams Theatre hosts a Key West version of *The Nutcracker*. In this unorthodox retelling, the heroine sails to a coral reef and is submerged in a diving bell. (What? No sugarplum fairies?) Between Christmas and New Year's Day, the Holiday House and Garden Tour is another yuletide tradition.

from: $409 ✉ 3841 N. Roosevelt Blvd., New Town ☎ 305/296–8100, 800/546–0885 🌐 www.keywestmarriottbeachside.com ⇨ 93 rooms, 93 1-bedroom suites, 10 2-bedroom suites, 26 3-bedroom suites 🍽 No meals.

Parrot Key Hotel and Resort
$$$ | **HOTEL** | This revamped destination resort feels like an old-fashioned beach community with picket fences and rocking-chair porches. **Pros:** four pools; finely appointed units; access to marina and other facilities at three sister properties in Marathon. **Cons:** not in walking distance to Old Town; no transportation provided; hefty resort fee. [$] *Rooms from: $355 ✉ 2801 N. Roosevelt Blvd., New Town ☎ 305/809–2200 🌐 www.parrotkeyresort.com ⇨ 222 units 🍽 No meals.*

Nightlife

Rest up: much of what happens in Key West occurs after dark. Open your mind and take a stroll. Scruffy street performers strum next to dogs in sunglasses. Characters wearing parrots or iguanas try to sell you your photo with their pet. Brawls tumble out the doors of Sloppy Joe's. Drag queens strut across stages in Joan Rivers garb. Tattooed men lick whipped cream off women's body parts. And margaritas flow like a Jimmy Buffett tune.

Capt. Tony's Saloon
BARS/PUBS | When it was the original Sloppy Joe's in the mid-1930s, Hemingway was a regular. Later, a young Jimmy Buffett sang here and made this watering hole famous in his song "Last Mango in Paris." Captain Tony was even voted mayor of Key West. Yes, this place is a beloved landmark. Stop in and take a look at the "hanging tree" that grows through the roof, listen to live music seven nights a week, and play some pool. *✉ 428 Greene St. ☎ 305/294–1838 🌐 www.capttonyssaloon.com.*

Cowboy Bill's Honky Tonk Saloon
BARS/PUBS | Ride the mechanical bucking bull, listen to live bands croon cry-in-your-beer tunes, and grab some pretty decent chow at the indoor-outdoor spread

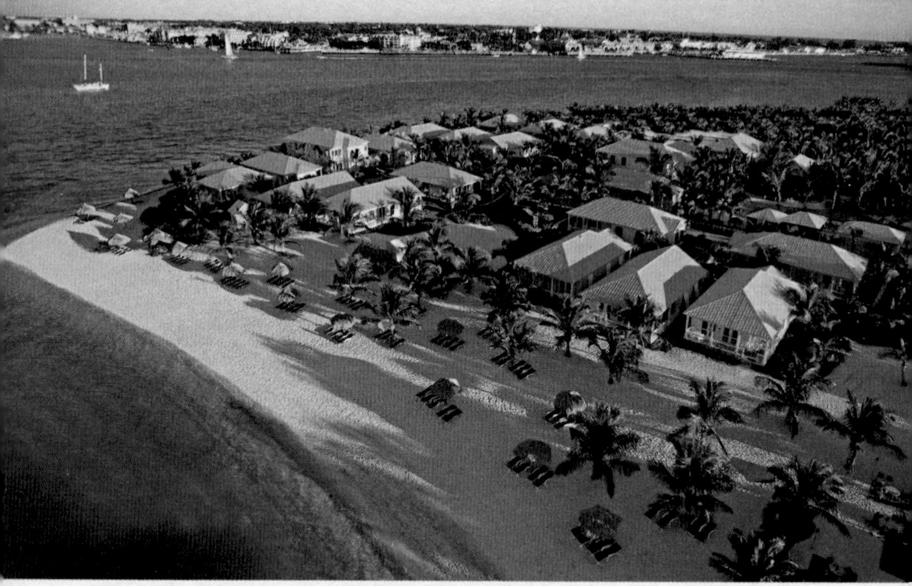

Sunset Key cottages are right on the water's edge, far away from the action of Old Town.

known as Cowboy Bill's Honky Tonk Saloon. There's live music from Tuesday through Saturday. Wednesday brings—we kid you not—sexy bull riding. ✉ *610½ Duval St.* ☎ *305/295–8219* 🌐 *www.cowboybillskw.com.*

Durty Harry's

BARS/PUBS | This megasize entertainment complex is home to eight different bars and clubs, both indoor and outdoor. Their motto is "Eight Famous Bars, One Awesome Night," and they're right. You'll find pizza, dancing, live music, Rick's Key West, and the infamous Red Garter strip club. ✉ *208 Duval St.* ☎ *305/296–5513* 🌐 *www.ricksbarkeywest.com.*

The Garden of Eden

BARS/PUBS | Perhaps one of Duval's more unusual and intriguing watering holes, The Garden of Eden sits atop the Bull & Whistle saloon and has a clothing-optional policy. Most drinkers are lookie-loos, but some actually bare it all, including the barmaids. ✉ *Bull & Whistle Bar, 224 Duval St.* ☎ *305/396–4565.*

Green Parrot Bar

BARS/PUBS | Pause for a libation in the open air and breathe in the spirit of Key West. Built in 1890 as a grocery store, this property has been many things to many people over the years. It's touted as the oldest bar in Key West and the sometimes-rowdy saloon has locals outnumbering out-of-towners, especially on nights when bands play. ✉ *601 Whitehead St., at Southard St.* ☎ *305/294–6133* 🌐 *www.greenparrot.com.*

Hog's Breath Saloon

BARS/PUBS | Belly up to the bar for a cold mug of the signature Hog's Breath Lager at this infamous joint, a must-stop on the Key West bar crawl. Live bands play daily 1 pm–2 am (except when the game's on TV). You never know who'll stop by and perhaps even jump on stage for an impromptu concert (can you say Kenny Chesney?). ✉ *400 Front St.* ☎ *305/296–4222* 🌐 *www.hogsbreath.com.*

Margaritaville Café

BARS/PUBS | A youngish, touristy crowd mixes with aging Parrot Heads. It's owned by former Key West resident and recording star Jimmy Buffett, who has been known to perform here. The drink of choice is, of course, a margarita, made with Jimmy's own brand of Margaritaville tequila. There's live music nightly, as well as lunch and dinner. ✉ *500 Duval St.* ☎ *305/292–1435* 🌐 *www.margaritaville-keywest.com.*

Pier House

BARS/PUBS | The party here begins at the Beach Bar with live entertainment daily to celebrate the sunset on the beach, then moves to the funky Chart Room. It's small and odd, but there are free hot dogs and peanuts, and its history is worth learning. ✉ *1 Duval St.* ☎ *305/296–4600, 800/327–8340* 🌐 *www.pierhouse.com.*

Schooner Wharf Bar

BARS/PUBS | This open-air waterfront bar and grill in the historic seaport district retains its funky Key West charm and hosts live entertainment daily. Its margaritas rank among Key West's best, as does the bar itself, voted Best Local's Bar six years in a row. For great views, head up to the second floor and be sure to order up some fresh seafood and fritters and Dark and Stormy cocktails. ✉ *202 William St.* ☎ *305/292–3302* 🌐 *www.schoonerwharf.com.*

Sloppy Joe's

BARS/PUBS | There's history and good times at the successor to a famous 1937 speakeasy named for its founder, Captain Joe Russell. Decorated with Hemingway memorabilia and marine flags, the bar is popular with travelers and is full and noisy all the time. A Sloppy Joe's T-shirt is a de rigueur Key West souvenir, and the gift shop sells them like crazy. Grab a seat (if you can) and be entertained by the bands and by the parade of people in constant motion. ✉ *201 Duval St.* ☎ *305/294–5717* 🌐 *www.sloppyjoes.com.*

Two Friends Patio Lounge

BARS/PUBS | Love karaoke? Get it out of your system at Two Friends Patio Lounge, where your performance gets a live Internet feed via the bar's Karaoke Cam. The singing starts at 8:30 pm most nights. The Bloody Marys are famous. ✉ *512 Front St.* ☎ *305/296–3124* 🌐 *www.twofriendskeywest.com.*

Shopping

On these streets, you'll find colorful local art of widely varying quality, key limes made into everything imaginable, and the raunchiest T-shirts in the civilized world. Browsing the boutiques—with frequent pub stops along the way—makes for an entertaining stroll down Duval Street. Cocktails certainly help the appreciation of some goods, such as the figurine of a naked man blowing bubbles out his backside or the swashbuckling pirate costumes that are no longer just for Halloween.

Alan S. Maltz Gallery

ART GALLERIES | The owner, declared the state's official wildlife photographer by the Wildlife Foundation of Florida, captures the state's nature and character in stunning portraits. Spend four figures for large-format images on canvas or save on small prints and closeouts. ✉ *1210 Duval St.* ☎ *305/294–0005* 🌐 *www.alanmaltz.com.*

Art@830

ART GALLERIES | This inviting gallery carries a little bit of everything, from pottery to paintings and jewelry to sculptures. Most outstanding is its selection of glass art, particularly the jellyfish lamps. Take time to admire all that is here. ✉ *830 Caroline St., Historic Seaport* ☎ *305/295–9595* 🌐 *www.art830.com.*

Bahama Village

SHOPPING CENTERS/MALLS | Where to start your shopping adventure? This cluster of spruced-up shops, restaurants, and vendors is responsible for the restoration of

Sloppy Joe's is one must-stop on most Key West visitors' bar-hop stroll, also known as the Duval Crawl.

the colorful historic district where Bahamians settled in the 19th century. The village lies roughly between Whitehead and Fort streets and Angela and Catherine streets. Hemingway frequented the bars, restaurants, and boxing rings in this part of town. ✉ *Between Whitehead and Fort Sts. and Angela and Catherine Sts.*

Cayo Hueso y Habana

GIFTS/SOUVENIRS | Part museum, part shopping center, this circa-1879 warehouse includes a hand-rolled-cigar shop, one-of-a-kind souvenirs, a Cuban restaurant, and exhibits that tell of the island's Cuban heritage. Outside, a memorial garden pays homage to the island's Cuban ancestors. ✉ *410 Wall St., Mallory Sq.* ☎ *305/293–7260.*

Fairvilla Megastore

SPECIALTY STORES | Don't leave town without a browse through the legendary shop. Although it's not really a clothing store, you'll find an astonishing array of fantasy wear, outlandish costumes (check out the pirate section), as well as other "adult" toys. (Some of the products may make you blush.) ✉ *520 Front St.* ☎ *305/292–0448* 🌐 *www.fairvilla.com.*

Fausto's Food Palace

FOOD/CANDY | Since 1926 Fausto's has been the spot to catch up on the week's gossip and to chill out in summer—it has groceries, organic foods, marvelous wines, a sushi chef on duty 8 am–3 pm, and box lunches and dinners-by-the-pound to go. There are two locations you can shop at in Key West (the other is at 1105 White Street) plus a recently opened online store. ✉ *522 Fleming St.* ☎ *305/296–5663* 🌐 *www.faustos.com.*

Gallery on Greene

ART GALLERIES | This is the largest gallery–exhibition space in Key West, and it showcases 37 museum-quality artists. It prides itself on being the leader in the field of representational fine art, painting, sculptures, and reproductions from the Florida Keys and Key West. You can see the love immediately from gallery curator Nancy Frank, who aims to please everyone, from the casual buyer to the established collector. ✉ *606 Greene St.* ☎ *305/294–1669* 🌐 *www.galleryongreene.com.*

Gingerbread Square Gallery

ART GALLERIES | The oldest private art gallery in Key West represents local and internationally acclaimed artists on an annually changing basis, in media ranging from paintings to art glass. ✉ *1207 Duval St.* ☎ *305/296–8900* 🌐 *www.gingerbreadsquaregallery.com.*

★ Kermit's Key West Lime Shoppe

FOOD/CANDY | You'll see Kermit himself standing on the corner every time a trolley passes, pie in hand. Besides pie, his shop carries a multitude of key lime products from barbecue sauce to jelly beans. His prefrozen pies, topped with a special long-lasting whipped cream instead of meringue, travels well. This is a must-stop shop while in Key West. The key lime pie is the best on the island; once you try it frozen on a stick, dipped in chocolate, you may consider quitting your job and moving here. Savor every bite on the outdoor patio-garden area, or come for breakfast or lunch at the on-site café. A smaller second location is on the corner of Duval and Front streets. ✉ *200 Elizabeth St., Historic Seaport* ☎ *305/296–0806, 800/376–0806* 🌐 *www.keylimeshop.com.*

Key West Island Bookstore

BOOKS/STATIONERY | This home away from home for the large Key West writers' community carries new, used, and rare titles. It specializes in Hemingway, Tennessee Williams, and South Florida mystery writers. ✉ *513 Fleming St.* ☎ *305/294–2904* 🌐 *www.keywestislandbooks.com.*

Key West Pottery

CERAMICS/GLASSWARE | You won't find any painted coconuts here, but you will find a collection of contemporary tropical ceramics. Wife-and-husband owners Kelly Lever and Adam Russell take real pride in this working studio that, in addition to their own creations, features artists from around the country. This is one of the island's few specialty galleries. ✉ *1203 Duval St.* ☎ *305/900–8303* 🌐 *www.keywestpottery.com.*

Kino Sandals

TEXTILES/SEWING | A pair of Kino sandals was once a public declaration that you'd been to Key West. The attraction? You can watch these inexpensive items being made. The factory has been churning out several styles since 1966. Walk up to the counter, grab a pair, try them on, and lay down some cash. It's that simple. ✉ *107 Fitzpatrick St.* ☎ *305/294–5044* 🌐 *www.kinosandalfactory.com.*

Lucky Street Gallery

ART GALLERIES | High-end contemporary paintings are the focus at this gallery that has been in business for over 30 years. There are also a few pieces of jewelry by internationally recognized Key West–based artists. Changing exhibits, artist receptions, and special events make this a lively venue. Although the location has changed, the passionate staff remain the same. ✉ *1204 White St.* ☎ *305/294–3973* 🌐 *www.luckystreetgallery.com.*

Peppers of Key West

FOOD/CANDY | If you like it hot, you'll love this collection of hundreds of sauces, salsas, and sweets guaranteed to heat you up. Take a seat at the tasting bar and see which products light your fire. ✉ *602 Greene St.* ☎ *305/295–9333, 800/597–2823* 🌐 *www.peppersofkeywest.com.*

Seam Shoppe

TEXTILES/SEWING | Take home a shopping bag full of scarlet hibiscus, fuchsia heliconias, blue parrotfish, and even pink flamingo fabric, selected from the city's widest selection of tropical-print fabrics. ✉ *1113 Truman Ave.* ☎ *305/296–9830* 🌐 *www.tropicalfabricsonline.com.*

Unlike the rest of the region, Key West isn't known primarily for outdoor pursuits. But everyone should devote at least half a day to relaxing on a boat tour, heading out on a fishing expedition, or pursuing some other adventure at sea. The ultimate excursion is a boat or seaplane trip to Dry Tortugas National Park for snorkeling and exploring Ft. Jefferson. Other excursions cater to nature lovers, scuba divers, and snorkelers, and folks who just want to get out in the water and enjoy the scenery and sunset. For those who prefer land-based recreation, biking is the way to go. Hiking is limited, but walking the streets of Old Town provides plenty of exercise.

BIKING

Key West was practically made for bicycles, but don't let that lull you into a false sense of security. Narrow and one-way streets along with car traffic result in several bike accidents a year. Some hotels rent or lend bikes to guests; others will refer you to a nearby shop and reserve a bike for you. Rentals usually start at about $12 a day, but some places also rent by the half day. ■ **TIP→ Lock up; bikes—and porch chairs!—are favorite targets for local thieves.**

A&M Rentals

BICYCLING | Rent beach cruisers with large baskets, scooters, and electric mini-cars. Look for the huge American flag on the roof, or call for free airport, ferry, or cruise-ship pickup. A second location is on South Street. ✉ *523 Truman Ave.* ☎ *305/294–0399* 🌐 *www.amscooterskeywest.com* 🎫 *Bicycles from $15, scooters from $35, electric cars from $139.*

Eaton Bikes

BICYCLING | Tandem, three-wheel, and children's bikes are available in addition to the standard beach cruisers and hybrid bikes. Delivery is free for all Key West rentals. ✉ *830 Eaton St.* ☎ *305/294–8188* 🌐 *www.eatonbikes.com* 🎫 *From $18 per day.*

Moped Hospital

BICYCLING | This outfit supplies balloon-tire bikes with yellow safety baskets for adults and kids, as well as scooters and even double-seater scooters. ✉ *601 Truman Ave.* ☎ *305/296–3344, 866/296–1625* 🌐 *www.mopedhospital.com* 🎫 *Bicycles from $12 per day, scooters from $35 per day.*

BOATING

Key West is surrounded by marinas, so it's easy to find what you're looking for, whether it's sailing with dolphins or paddling in the mangroves. In addition to its popular kayaking trips, Key West Eco-Tours offers sunset sails and private charters *(see Kayaking)*.

★ Classic Harbor Line

SAILING | The *Schooner America 2.0* is refined and elegant, and her comfortable seating makes her a favorite when she sails Key West each November–April. Two-hour sunset champagne cruises are an island highlight. Make reservations well in advance. These sailings are popular with locals and visitors. ✉ *202-R Williams St.* ☎ *305/293–7245* 🌐 *www.sail-keywest.com* 🎫 *Day sails from $55, sunset sails from $85.*

Dancing Dolphin Spirit Charters

BOATING | **FAMILY** | Victoria Impallomeni-Spencer, a wilderness guide and environmental marine science walking encyclopedia, invites up to six nature lovers—especially children—aboard the *Imp II*, a 25-foot Aquasport, for four- and seven-hour ecotours that frequently include encounters with wild dolphins. While island-hopping, you visit underwater gardens and reefs, natural shoreline, and mangrove habitats. For the "Dolphin Day for Humans" tour, you'll be pulled through the water, equipped with mask and snorkel, on a specially designed "dolphin water massage board" that simulates dolphin swimming motions. All equipment is supplied. Captain Victoria is known around these parts as the dolphin whisperer, as she's been guiding for over

40 years. ✉ *MM 5 OS, Murray's Marina, 5710 Overseas Hwy.* ☎ *305/304–7562, 305/745–9901* 🌐 *www.dancingdolphinspirits.com* 🎫 *From $600.*

FISHING

Any number of local fishing guides can take you to where the big ones are biting, either in the backcountry for snapper and snook or to the deep water for the marlins and shark that lured Hemingway here.

Key West Bait & Tackle

FISHING | Prepare to catch a big one with the live bait, frozen bait, and fishing equipment provided here. They even offer rod and reel rentals (starting at $15 for one day, $5 each additional day). Stop by their on-site Live Bait Lounge where you can sip $3.25 ice-cold beer while telling fish tales. ✉ *241 Margaret St.* ☎ *305/292–1961* 🌐 *www.keywestbaitandtackle.com.*

Key West Pro Guides

FISHING | This outfitter offers private charters, and you can choose four-, five-, six-, or eight-hour trips. Choose from flats, backcountry, reef, offshore fishing, and even specialty trips to the Dry Tortugas. Whatever your fishing (even spearfishing) pleasure, their captains will hook you up. ✉ *G–31 Miriam St.* ☎ *866/259–4205* 🌐 *www.keywestproguides.com* 🎫 *From $450.*

GOLF

Key West Golf Club

GOLF | Key West isn't a major golf destination, but there is one course on Stock Island designed by Rees Jones that will downright surprise you with its water challenges and tropical beauty. It's also the only "Caribbean" golf course in the United States, boasting 200 acres of unique Florida foliage and wildlife. Hole 8 is the famous "Mangrove Hole," which will give you stories to tell. It's a 143-yard par 3 that is played completely over a mass of mangroves with their gnarly roots and branches completely intertwined. Bring extra balls and book your tee time early in season. Nike rental clubs are available. ✉ *6450 E. College Rd.* ☎ *305/294–5232* 🌐 *www.keywestgolf.com* 🎫 *$55–$99* ⛳ *18 holes, 6500 yards, par 70.*

KAYAKING

Key West Eco-Tours

KAYAKING | Key West is surrounded by marinas, so it's easy to find a water-based activity or tour, whether it's sailing with dolphins or paddling in the mangroves. These sail-kayak-snorkel excursions take you into backcountry flats and mangrove forests without the crowds. The 4½-hour trip includes a light lunch, equipment, and even dry camera bags. Private sunset sails, backcountry boating adventures, kayak, and paddleboard tours are available, too. ✉ *Historic Seaport behind Turtle Kraals, 231 Margaret St.* ☎ *305/294–7245* 🌐 *www.keywestecotours.com* 🎫 *From $115.*

Lazy Dog

KAYAKING | Take a two-hour backcountry mangrove ecotour or a four-hour guided sea kayak–snorkel tour around the mangrove islands just east of Key West. Costs include transportation, bottled water, a snack, and supplies, including snorkeling gear. Paddleboard tours, PaddleYoga, and PaddleFit classes are also available, as are maps and rentals for self-touring. ✉ *5114 Overseas Hwy.* ☎ *305/295–9898* 🌐 *www.lazydog.com* 🎫 *From $50.*

SCUBA DIVING AND SNORKELING

The Florida Keys National Marine Sanctuary extends along Key West and beyond to the Dry Tortugas. Key West National Wildlife Refuge further protects the pristine waters. Most divers don't make it this far out in the Keys, but if you're looking for a day of diving as a break from the nonstop party in Old Town, expect to pay about $65 and upward for a two-tank dive. Serious divers can book dive trips to the Dry Tortugas. The USS *Vandenberg* is another popular dive spot, known for its world's-first underwater transformative art exhibit on an artificial reef.

Captain's Corner

SCUBA DIVING | This PADI-certified dive shop has classes in several languages and twice-daily snorkel and dive trips to reefs and wrecks aboard a 60-foot dive boat, the *Sea Eagle*. Use of weights, belts, masks, and fins is included. ✉ *125 Ann St.* ☎ *305/296–8865* 🌐 *www.captainscorner.com* 🎫 *From $45.*

Dive Key West

SCUBA DIVING | Operating over 40 years, Dive Key West is a full-service dive center that has charters, instruction, gear rental, sales, and repair. You can take either snorkel excursions or scuba trips with this outfit that is dedicated to coral reef education and preservation. ✉ *3128 N. Roosevelt Blvd.* ☎ *305/296–3823* 🌐 *www.divekeywest.com* 🎫 *Snorkeling from $69, scuba from $95.*

Snuba of Key West

SCUBA DIVING | **FAMILY** | If you've always wanted to dive but never found the time to get certified, Snuba is for you. You can dive safely using a regulator tethered to a floating air tank with a simple orientation. Ride out to the reef on a catamaran, then follow your guide underwater for a one-hour tour of the coral reefs. It's easy and fun. No prior diving or snorkeling experience is necessary, but you must know how to swim and be at least eight years old. The price includes beverages. ✉ *Garrison Bight Marina, Palm Ave. between Eaton St. and N. Roosevelt Blvd.* ☎ *305/292–4616* 🌐 *www.snubakeywest.com* 🎫 *From $109.*

STAND-UP PADDLEBOARDING

SUP Key West

KAYAKING | This ancient sport from Hawaii involves a surfboard and a paddle and has quickly become a favorite Florida water sport known as SUP (stand-up paddleboarding). SUP Key West gives lessons and morning, afternoon, or sunset tours of the estuaries. What's more, your tour guides are experts (one's even a PhD) in marine biology and ecology. Call ahead to make arrangements. ✉ *110 Grinnell St.* ☎ *305/240–1426* 🌐 *www.supkeywest.com* 🎫 *From $45.*

Excursion to Dry Tortugas National Park

70 miles southwest of Key West.

The Dry Tortugas lie in the central time zone. Key West Seaplane pilots like to tell their passengers that they land 15 minutes before they take off. If you can't do the time-consuming (and by air, at least, expensive) trip, the national park operates an interpretive center in the Historic Seaport at Old Key West Bight.

GETTING HERE AND AROUND

For now, the ferryboat *Yankee Freedom III* departs from a marina in Old Town and does day trips to Garden Key. Key West Seaplane Adventures has half- and full-day trips to the Dry Tortugas, where you can explore Ft. Jefferson, built in 1846, and snorkel on the beautiful protected reef. Departing from the Key West airport, the flights include soft drinks and snorkel equipment for $265 half day, $465 full day, plus there's a $10 park fee (cash only). If you want to explore the park's other keys, look into renting a boat or hiring a private charter. The Dry Tortugas National Park and Historic Key West Bight Museum at 240 Margaret Street is a way to experience it for free. *See Exploring in Key West.*

Key West Seaplane Adventures

TRANSPORTATION SITE (AIRPORT/BUS/FERRY/TRAIN) | The 35- to 40-minute trip to the Dry Tortugas skims above the trademark windowpane-clear waters of the Florida Keys. The seaplane perspective provides an awesome experience that could result in a stiff neck from craning to look out the window and down from 500 feet above. In the flats that edge Key West, you can spot stingrays, sea turtles, and sharks in the shallow water. In the area dubbed The Quicksands, water plunges to 30-foot depths and sand undulates in dunelike formations. Shipwrecks also festoon these waters; here's where Mel Fisher harvested treasure from the *Atocha* and *Margarita*. His 70-foot work ship, the *Arbutus*, deteriorated and eventually sank at the northern edge of the treasure sites. With its mast poking out above water, it's easy to spot and fun to photograph. From there, the water deepens from emerald hues to shades of deep blue as depths reach 70 feet. Seaplanes of Key West's most popular trip is the half-day option, where you spend about 2½ hours on Garden Key. The seaplanes leave during your stay, so be prepared to carry all of your possessions with you. The morning trip beats the ferries to the island, so you'll have it to yourself until the others arrive. Snorkeling equipment, soft drinks, and birding lists are supplied. ✉ *3471 S. Roosevelt Blvd., Key West* ☎ *305/615–7429* 🌐 *www.keywestseaplanecharters.com* 🎫 *From $342.*

Yankee Freedom III

TRANSPORTATION SITE (AIRPORT/BUS/FERRY/TRAIN) | The fast, sleek, 110-foot catamaran *Yankee Freedom III* travels to the Dry Tortugas in 2¼ hours. The time passes quickly on the roomy vessel equipped with four restrooms, three warm freshwater showers, and two bars. Stretch out on two decks that are both air-conditioned, with cushioned seating. There is also an open sundeck with sunny and shaded seating. Continental breakfast and lunch are included. On arrival, a naturalist leads a 45-minute guided tour, which is followed by lunch and a free afternoon for swimming, snorkeling (gear included), and exploring. The vessel is ADA-certified for visitors using wheelchairs. The Dry Tortugas lies in the central time zone. ✉ *Ticket booth, 240 Margaret St., Key West* ☎ *305/294–7009, 800/634–0939* 🌐 *www.drytortugas.com* 🎫 *$180; parking $19 in city garage* ☞ *Vessel departs from the Ferry Terminal at 100 Grinnell St. in the Historic Seaport.*

Sights

Dry Tortugas National Park

NATIONAL/STATE PARK | This park, 70 miles off the shores of Key West, consists of seven small islands. Tour the fort; then lay out your blanket on the sunny beach for a picnic before you head out to snorkel on the protected reef. Many people like to camp here ($15 per site for one of eight sites, plus a group site and overflow area; first-come, first-served), but note that there's no freshwater supply and you must carry off whatever you bring onto the island.

The typical visitor from Key West, however, makes it no farther than the waters of Garden Key. Home to 19th-century Ft. Jefferson, it is the destination for seaplane and fast ferry tours out of Key West. With 2½ to 6½ hours to spend on the island, visitors have time to tour the mammoth fort-prison and then cool off with mask and snorkel along the fort's moat wall.

History buffs might remember long-deactivated Ft. Jefferson, the largest brick building in the Western Hemisphere, as the prison that held Dr. Samuel Mudd, who unwittingly set John Wilkes Booth's leg after the assassination of Abraham Lincoln. Three other men were also held there for complicity in the assassination. Original construction on the fort began in 1846 and continued for 30 years, but was never completed because the invention of the rifled cannon made it obsolete. That's when it became a Civil War prison and later a wildlife refuge. In 1935 President Franklin Roosevelt declared it a national monument for its historic and natural value.

The brick fort acts as a gigantic, almost 16-acre reef. Around its moat walls, coral grows and schools of snapper, grouper, and wrasses hang out. To reach the offshore coral heads requires about 15 minutes of swimming over sea-grass beds. The reef formations blaze with the color and majesty of brain coral, swaying sea fans, and flitting tropical fish. It takes a bit of energy to swim the distance, but the water depth pretty much measures under 7 feet all the way, allowing for sandy spots to stop and rest. (Standing in sea-grass meadows and on coral is detrimental to marine life.)

Serious snorkelers and divers head out farther offshore to epic formations, including Palmata Patch, one of the few surviving concentrations of elkhorn coral in the Keys. Day-trippers congregate on the sandy beach to relax in the sun and enjoy picnics. Overnight tent campers have use of restroom facilities and achieve a total getaway from noise, lights, and civilization in general. Remember that no matter how you get here, the park's $15 admission fee must be paid in cash.

The park has signposted a self-guided tour that takes about 45 minutes. You should budget more time if you're into photography, because the scenic shots are hard to pass up. Ranger-guided tours are also available at certain times. Check in at the visitor center for a schedule. The small office also shows an orientation video, sells books and other educational materials, and, most importantly, provides a blast of air-conditioning on hot days.

Birders in the know bring binoculars to watch some 100,000 nesting sooty terns at their only U.S. nesting site, Bush Key, adjacent to Garden Key. Noddy terns also nest in the spring. During winter migrations, birds fill the airspace so thickly they literally fall from the sky to make their pit stops, birders say. Nearly 300 species have been spotted in the park's seven islands, including frigate birds, boobies, cormorants, and broad-winged hawks. Bush Key is closed to foot traffic during nesting season, January through September. ✉ *Key West* 🌐 *www.nps.gov/drto* 🎫 *$15.*

Chapter 6

FORT LAUDERDALE

Updated by
Galena Mosovich

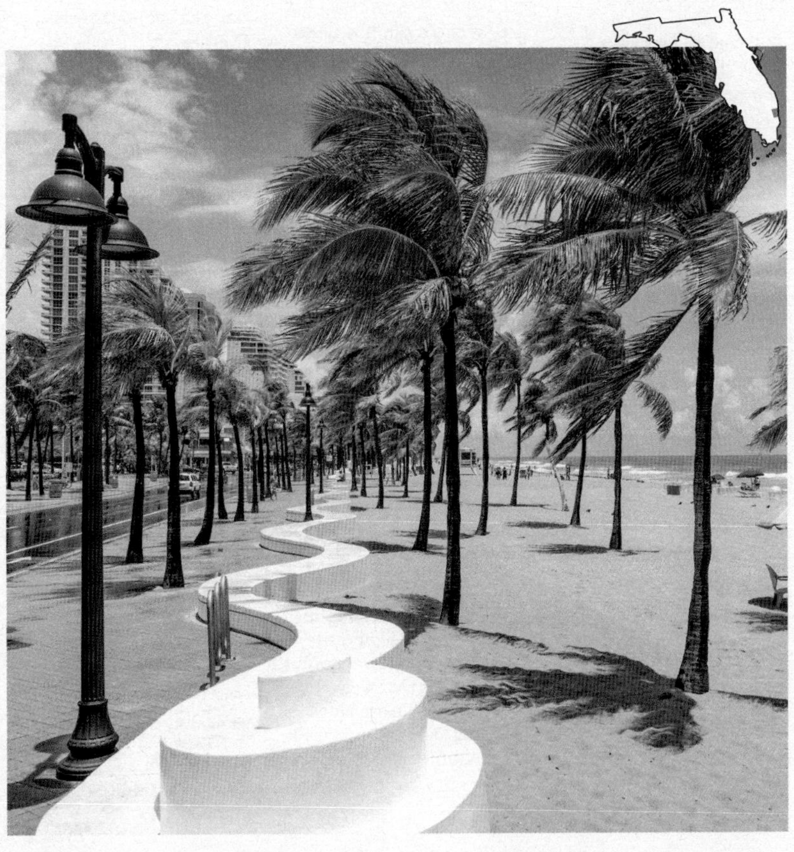

Sights	Restaurants	Hotels	Shopping	Nightlife
★★★★☆	★★★★☆	★★★★☆	★★★☆☆	★★★☆☆

WELCOME TO FORT LAUDERDALE

TOP REASONS TO GO

★ **Blue waves:** The cerulean waters of the Atlantic Ocean hugging Broward County's entire coast form a 23-mile stretch of picturesque beaches between Miami-Dade and Palm Beach counties.

★ **Inland waterways:** More than 300 miles of inland waterways, including downtown Fort Lauderdale's historic New River and Intracoastal, create what's known as the "Venice of America."

★ **Everglades adventures:** The untamed landscape of the Everglades—home to alligators, crocodiles, colorful birds, and other elusive wildlife—is a short trip from beachfront luxury.

★ **Emerging arts scene:** Experience the local contemporary art scene as it grows into a major force in the region.

★ **Cruise gateway:** A dozen supermodern terminals serve about 4 million cruisers and ferry guests a year at Port Everglades, one of the busiest cruise ports in the country.

Along Florida's Gold Coast, Fort Lauderdale and Broward County present a delightful middle ground between the posh Palm Beaches and the extravagance of Miami. From downtown Fort Lauderdale, it's about a four-hour drive to Orlando or Key West, but Broward's allure is undeniable. From oceanside to inland, the county's sprawling geography encompasses 31 communities with a resident population of 1.9 million.

1 Downtown and Las Olas. The eclectic hub of town is known for its arts and nightlife scenes and is complemented by Las Olas Boulevard's boutiques, sidewalk cafés, and restaurants.

2 Fort Lauderdale Beach. Fort Lauderdale's 23 miles of sparkling beaches are lined with restaurants and hotels.

3 Intracoastal and Inland Fort Lauderdale. Even if you're not on the beach, you're likely still near the water: waterways and canals that weave through town are big among the boating community.

4 Wilton Manors and Oakland Park. Wilton Manors is a progressive area with independent shops and nightlife venues.

5 Western Suburbs and Beyond. The suburbs are just as bustling, if not more, than the city center, but out west you're essentially on the edge of the Everglades.

6 Lauderdale-by-the-Sea. North of Fort Lauderdale on State Road A1A, old-school seaside charm draws families and cost-conscious travelers to a more low-rise, low-key beach alternative to Fort Lauderdale.

7 Pompano Beach. Explore shipwrecks and coral reefs on a scuba diving adventure off the shore of this beach town, just north of Lauderdale-by-the-Sea.

8 Deerfield Beach. The northernmost beach community in Broward County has uncrowded beaches and a wilderness area.

9 Hollywood. From the beachside Broadwalk to historic Young Circle (now ArtsPark), this South Broward destination provides grit and good times in a laid-back manner.

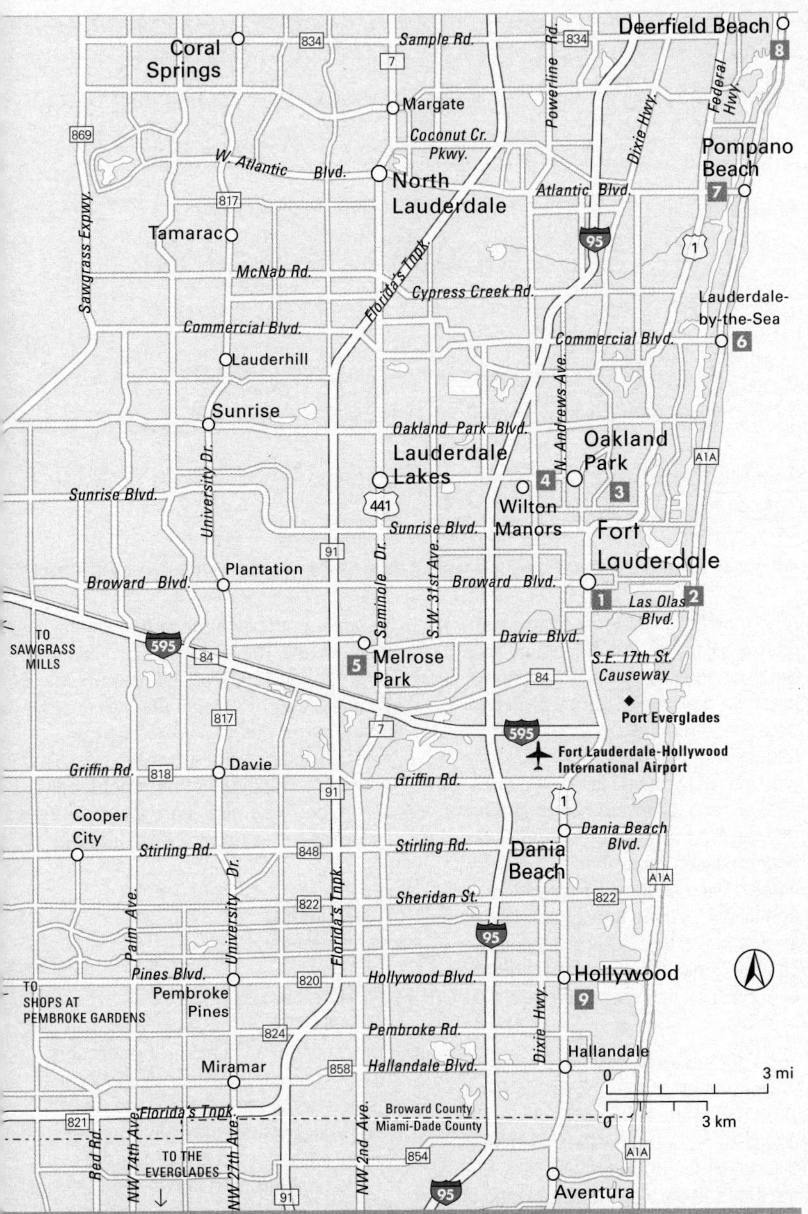
Deerfield Beach
Coral Springs
Sample Rd.
Margate
Coconut Cr. Pkwy.
W. Atlantic Blvd.
North Lauderdale
Pompano Beach
Atlantic Blvd.
Tamarac
McNab Rd.
Cypress Creek Rd.
Lauderdale-by-the-Sea
Commercial Blvd.
Lauderhill
Sunrise
Oakland Park Blvd.
Oakland Park
Lauderdale Lakes
Sunrise Blvd.
Wilton Manors
Fort Lauderdale
Plantation
Broward Blvd.
Las Olas Blvd.
TO SAWGRASS MILLS
Davie Blvd.
Melrose Park
S.E. 17th St. Causeway
Port Everglades
Fort Lauderdale-Hollywood International Airport
Griffin Rd.
Davie
Cooper City
Dania Beach Blvd.
Stirling Rd.
Dania Beach
Sheridan St.
Pines Blvd.
Hollywood Blvd.
Hollywood
TO SHOPS AT PEMBROKE GARDENS
Pembroke Pines
Pembroke Rd.
Miramar
Hallandale Blvd.
Hallandale
Florida's Tnpk.
Broward County
Miami-Dade County
TO THE EVERGLADES
Aventura
Sawgrass Expwy.
University Dr.
Seminole Dr.
S.W. 31st Ave.
N. Andrews Ave.
Powerline Rd.
Dixie Hwy.
Federal Hwy.
Palm Ave.
Red Rd.
NW 74th Ave.
NW 27th Ave.
NW 2nd Ave.
0 3 mi
0 3 km

It was only a matter of time before the sun-soaked streets of Fort Lauderdale faced an identity crisis. What was once a hotbed of dive bars, diners, and all-day beach parties is now a more upscale destination with a deeper focus on quality in the pursuit of leisure. The city has more notable eateries and world-class hotel brands than ever, and fortunately, the upscaling doesn't follow Miami's over-the-top lead. Fort Lauderdale is still a place where flip-flops are acceptable, if not encouraged.

Along the Strip and west to the Intracoastal, many of the midcentury-modern boutique properties are trying to preserve the neighborhood's vintage design aesthetic. Somehow Greater Fort Lauderdale gracefully melds disparate eras into nouveau nirvana, seasoned with a lot of sand. This could be the result of its massive territory: Broward County encompasses more than 1,100 square miles of land—ranging from dense residential enclaves to agricultural farms and subtropical wilds. But it's the county's beautiful beaches and some 3,000 hours of sunshine each year that make all this possible.

Fort Lauderdale was named for Major William Lauderdale, who built a fort in 1838 during the Second Seminole War. It was incorporated in 1911 with only 175 residents, but it grew quickly during the Florida boom of the 1920s, and it became a popular spring break destination in the 1960s. Today's population is more than 178,000, and the suburbs continue to grow. Of Broward County's 31 municipalities and unincorporated areas, Fort Lauderdale is the largest. And now showstopping hotels, a hot food scene, and a burgeoning cultural platform accompany the classic beach lifestyle.

Planning

When to Go

Peak season is Thanksgiving through April, when cultural events (performing arts, visual art displays, concerts, and other outdoor entertainment) go full throttle. Expect extreme heat and humidity along with rain in the summer.

Hurricanes come most notably in August and September. Tee times are harder to get on weekends year-round. Regardless of season, remember that Fort Lauderdale sunshine will burn even on a cloudy day.

ANNUAL FESTIVALS AND EVENTS

Fort Lauderdale International Boat Show (*FLIBS*)
FESTIVAL | FAMILY | The city hosts the world's largest in-water boat show in the fall. FLIBS has been the end-all, be-all of marine envy since 1960, with more than $2 billion in boats, yachts, superyachts, and accessories from every major manufacturer and builder worldwide. The city buzzes with parties to celebrate, while the official show takes place at several locations along the Intracoastal and A1A. Tickets are required. ✉ *Bahia Mar Yachting Center, 801 Seabreeze Blvd., Beachfront* ☎ *954/463–6762 Informa U.S. Boat Shows* 🌐 *www.flibs.com/en/home.html* 🎫 *From $33 per day/per person.*

Fort Lauderdale International Film Festival (*FLIFF*)
FILM FESTIVALS | Founded in 1986, this annual festival is a celebration of independent cinema, showcasing more than 100 American and international feature, documentary, and short films at various locations across Broward County. Cinema Paradiso in downtown Fort Lauderdale is the base camp. In addition to more than two weeks of screenings, seminars, events, and parties fill the calendar, but don't expect the pomp of a big-city film festival. With that said, the Florida Arts Council refers to FLIFF as the highest-rated film festival in the state of Florida and it's the only film festival in the South to receive four major grants from the Academy of Motion Picture Arts and Sciences. ✉ *Fort Lauderdale* ☎ *954/525–3456* 🌐 *www.fliff.com.*

Seminole Hard Rock Winterfest Boat Parade
FESTIVAL | FAMILY | Known as "the greatest show on H2O" and the largest one-day spectator event in Florida, the Seminole Hard Rock Winterfest Boat Parade's 12-mile route through Fort Lauderdale's main waterways draws about a million people every year. The theme and decorations change, as do the participating yachts and superyachts. If you can't make it, you can watch the event live on the Internet. ✉ *Fort Lauderdale* ☎ *954/767–0686* 🌐 *winterfestparade.com.*

Getting Here and Around

AIR TRAVEL

Fort Lauderdale–Hollywood International Airport (FLL) serves more than 32 million passengers a year with nonstop flights to over 100 U.S. and international cities. FLL is 3 miles south of downtown Fort Lauderdale—just off U.S. 1 (South Federal Highway) between Fort Lauderdale and Hollywood, and near Port Everglades and Fort Lauderdale Beach. Other options include **Miami International Airport (MIA),** which is about 32 miles southwest, and the far less chaotic **Palm Beach International Airport (PBI),** which is about 50 miles north.

AIRPORT INFORMATION Fort Lauderdale–Hollywood International Airport (*FLL*). ☎ *866/435–9355* 🌐 *www.broward.org.* **Miami International Airport** (*MIA*). ☎ *305/876-7000* 🌐 *www.iflymia.com.* **Palm Beach International Airport** (*PBI*). ☎ *561/471–7420* 🌐 *www.pbia.org.*

BUS TRAVEL

Broward County Transit (BCT) operates Bus Route 1 between the airport and its main terminal at Broward Boulevard and Northwest First Avenue in downtown Fort Lauderdale. Service from the airport (Rental Car Center, Stop 7) is every 20 to 30 minutes and begins at 5:29 am on weekdays, 6:04 am Saturday, and 6:44 am Sunday; the last bus leaves the airport at 11:36 pm on weekdays, 11:44 pm Saturday, and 9:44 pm Sunday. The one-way cash fare is $2 (exact change). ■ **TIP→ The Northwest First Avenue stop is**

in a sketchy part of town. Exercise caution there, day or night. Better yet, take an Uber, Lyft, or taxi to and from the airport. BCT also covers the county on fixed routes to four transfer terminals: Broward Central Terminal, West Regional Terminal, Lauderhill Mall Transfer Facility, and Northeast Transit Center. The fare for an all-day bus pass is $5 (exact change). Service starts around 4:30 am and continues to 12:40 am, except on Sunday.

BUS CONTACTS Broward County Transit (*BCT*). ☎ *954/357–8400* 🌐 *www.broward.org/BCT.*

CAR TRAVEL

Renting a car to get around Broward County is highly recommended. Traditional cabs are unreliable and expensive; ride-hailing apps such as Uber and Lyft are a cheaper, better option. Public transportation is not a realistic option for most travelers, but the Sun Trolley can be sufficient for some visitors who don't need or wish to explore beyond the downtown core and beaches.

By car, access to Broward County from north or south is via Florida's Turnpike, Interstate 95, U.S. 1, or U.S. 441. Interstate 75 (Alligator Alley, requiring a toll despite being part of the nation's interstate-highway system) connects Broward with Florida's west coast and runs parallel to State Road 84 within the county. East–west Interstate 595 runs from westernmost Broward County and connects Interstate 75 with Interstate 95 and U.S. 1, providing easy access to the airport and seaport. State Road A1A, designated a Florida Scenic Highway by the state's Department of Transportation, runs parallel to the beach.

TRAIN TRAVEL

Amtrak provides daily service to Fort Lauderdale and stops in Deerfield Beach and Hollywood.

All three of the region's airports link to Tri-Rail, a commuter train operating daily through Palm Beach, Broward, and Miami-Dade counties.

The modern, privately operated Virgin Trains USA (formerly Brightline) high-speed train service connects downtown Miami, Fort Lauderdale, and West Palm Beach. The trip from downtown Miami to Fort Lauderdale takes about 30 minutes; it's another 30 minutes to West Palm Beach.

CONTACTS Virgin Trains USA (*Formerly Brightline*).

Hotels

A collection of relatively young luxury beachfront hotels—the Atlantic Hotel & Spa, The Conrad, Four Seasons, The Gale, Hilton Fort Lauderdale Beach Resort, the Ritz-Carlton, the W, the Westin—that opened within the last decade are welcoming newcomers to the "Luxe Lauderdale" corridor. These seriously sophisticated places to stay are increasingly popular as smaller retro spots are disappearing. You can also find hotel chains along the Intracoastal Waterway. If you want to be *on* the beach, be sure to ask when booking your room, as many hotels on the inland waterways or on A1A advertise "waterfront" accommodations.

Restaurants

Greater Fort Lauderdale offers one of the best and most diverse dining scenes of any U.S. city its size. There are more than 4,000 eateries in Broward offering everything from new American and South American to Pan-Asian cuisines. Go beyond the basics, and you'll find an endless supply of hidden gems.

Hotel and restaurant reviews have been shortened. For full information, visit Fodors.com.

What It Costs

	$	$$	$$$	$$$$
RESTAURANTS	under $15	$15–$20	$21–$30	over $30
HOTELS	under $200	$200–$300	$301–$400	over $400

Fort Lauderdale

Like most of southeast Florida, Fort Lauderdale has long been revitalizing. Despite wariness of overdevelopment, city leaders have allowed a striking number of glittering high-rises and new hotels. Nostalgic locals and frequent visitors fret over the diminishing vision of sailboats bobbing in waters near downtown; however, Fort Lauderdale remains the yachting capital of the world, and the water toys don't seem to be going anywhere. Sharp demographic changes are also altering the face of Greater Fort Lauderdale with increasingly cosmopolitan communities. Young professionals and families are settling into Fort Lauderdale proper, whereas longtime residents are heading north for more space. Downtown Fort Lauderdale's burgeoning arts district, cafés, and nightlife venues continue to the main drag of Las Olas Boulevard, where boutiques and restaurants dot the pedestrian-friendly street. Farther east is the sparkling shoreline. There are myriad neighborhoods to the north and south of Las Olas Boulevard that all offer their own brand of charm.

GETTING HERE AND AROUND

The city's road system suffers from traffic overload. Interstate 595 connects the city and suburbs and provides a direct route to the Fort Lauderdale–Hollywood International Airport and Port Everglades, but lanes slow to a crawl during rush hours. The Intracoastal Waterway is the nautical equivalent of an interstate highway; it provides easy boating access to local hot spots as well as neighboring waterfront communities.

To bounce around for relatively cheap, catch a multicolored Sun Trolley. There are seven routes and each operates on its own schedule. Simply wave at the trolley driver: trolleys will stop for pickups anywhere along their route. Luggage is not allowed, so this isn't a viable option for airport transportation. The most popular routes—Las Olas/Beaches Link—is $1 per ride or $3 for a day pass (cash only); it even connects to the city's train station.

Yellow Cab covers most of Broward County, but it's very expensive. You can book by phone, text, app, or website, and all Yellow Cab vehicles accept major credit cards. The Uber and Lyft ride-sharing services give more attention to the passenger experience and charge cheaper rates, hence their significant presence in the area.

CONTACTS Sun Trolley. ☎ *954/876–5539* 🌐 *www.suntrolley.com.* **Yellow Cab Broward.** ☎ *954/777–7777* 🌐 *www.yellowcabbroward.com.*

TOURS

The labyrinthine waterways of Fort Lauderdale are home to thousands of privately owned vessels, but you don't need to be or know a boat owner to play on the water. To fully understand this city of canals (aka the "Venice of America"), you must see it from the water. Kick back on a boat tour or hop on a Water Taxi, Fort Lauderdale's floating trolley.

Carrie B Cruises

BOAT TOURS | Board the *Carrie B*, a 112-foot paddle wheeler, for a 90-minute sightseeing tour of the New River, Intracoastal Waterway, and Port Everglades. Cruises depart at 11 am, 1 pm, and 3 pm daily from October through April; Thursday–Monday between May and September. The cost is $23.95 plus tax. Book ahead online for discounts. ✉ *440*

N New River Dr. E ☎ *888/238–9805* 🌐 *www.carriebcruises.com.*

Jungle Queen Riverboats

BOAT TOURS | FAMILY | The kitschy *Jungle Queen* and *River Queen* riverboats cruise through the heart of Fort Lauderdale on the New River. It's an old-school experience that dates back to 1935, when the company launched its tours, and the touristy charm is a big part of the fun. There are several types of sightseeing tours that leave at various times of day—from morning cruises to dinner cruises with entertainment—and prices start at around $25 per person. Check the website for details and availability. ✉ *Bahia Mar Yachting Center, 801 Seabreeze Blvd.* ☎ *954/462–5596* 🌐 *www.junglequeen.com.*

★ **Water Taxi**

BOAT TOURS | FAMILY | At once a sightseeing tour and a mode of transportation, the Water Taxi is a smart way to experience most of Fort Lauderdale and Hollywood's waterways. There are 15 scheduled stops and on-demand whistle stops and the system has three connected routes: the Fort Lauderdale, the Margaritaville Express, and the Hollywood Local. The Fort Lauderdale and River routes run from around 10 am to 10 pm; the Margaritaville route starts at 9 am and runs every other hour. It's possible to cruise all day while taking in the sights. Captains and crew share fun facts and white lies about the city's history, as well as quirky tales about celebrity homes. A day pass is $28. Download the free Water Taxi Tracker app for accurate arrival times. ✉ *Fort Lauderdale* ☎ *954/467–6677* 🌐 *watertaxi.com.*

VISITOR INFORMATION

Greater Fort Lauderdale Convention and Visitors Bureau (*Hello Sunny*). ✉ *101 NE Third Ave., Suite 100* ☎ *954/765–4466* 🌐 *www.sunny.org.*

Downtown and Las Olas

The jewel of downtown is the Arts and Entertainment District, where Broadway shows, ballet, and theater take place at the Broward Center for the Performing Arts on the riverfront. A cluster of cultural entities are within a five-minute walk: the Museum of Discovery and Science, the Fort Lauderdale Historical Society, and the NSU Museum of Art. Restaurants, sidewalk cafés, bars, and nightclubs flourish along Las Olas's downtown extension, and its main presence brings a more upscale atmosphere. Riverwalk ties these two areas together with a 2-mile stretch along the New River's north and south banks, though the commercial success of this section has been tepid. Tropical gardens with benches and interpretive displays line the walk on the north, with boat landings on the south side.

Sights

★ **Flagler + Arts + Technology Village** (*FATVillage*)

ARTS VENUE | FAMILY | Inspired by Miami's Wynwood Arts District, Flagler + Arts + Technology Village (or FATVillage) encompasses several square blocks of a formerly blighted warehouse district in downtown Fort Lauderdale. It's now thriving with a slew of production studios, art studios, loft-style apartments, and a fabulous coffee shop. On the last Saturday of the month (except in December), FATVillage hosts an evening art walk, in which businesses display contemporary artworks by local talent and where food trucks gather. There are libations, of course, and the warehouse district erupts into a giant, culture-infused street party. Check out one of Fort Lauderdale's coolest coffee shops slash bars, Next Door at C&I Studios. It's nestled inside a creative agency's lofty space. Adorned with antique nods to the literary world, tufted couches, and an eerie 1972

Airstream trailer, Next Door serves the locally made Brew Urban Cafe. After dark, it turns into a cocktail bar with live music, film screenings, and networking. ✉ *FATVillage, 521 NW First Ave., Downtown* ☎ *954/760–5900* 🌐 *www.fatvillage.com.*

Fort Lauderdale Antique Car Museum

MUSEUM | FAMILY | To preseve the history of the Packard, a long-vanished luxury American car company, Arthur O. Stone and his wife, Shirley, set up a foundation and a showroom in downtown Fort Lauderdale. The collection includes about two dozen of the buggy-style Packards (all in pristine and working condition) made in the Midwest from 1909 to 1958. The collection includes everything from grease caps, spark plugs, and gearshift knobs to Texaco Oil signage, plus an enlarged automotive library. There's also a gallery saluting Franklin Delano Roosevelt and his family. ✉ *Fort Lauderdale Antique Car Museum, 1527 SW First Ave., Downtown* ☎ *954/779–7300* 🌐 *www.antiquecarmuseum.net* 🎫 *$10 minimum donation* ⏲ *By appointment only Sat.; closed Sun.*

Fort Lauderdale Fire and Safety Museum

MUSEUM | FAMILY | The museum is housed inside the historic building formerly known as Fire Station No. 3, which has been restored to its original Mediterranean beauty (circa 1927). The Sailboat Bend landmark was designed by architect Francis Abreu and retired from active duty in 2004; it now functions on the weekends as a historical, cultural, and educational facility with vintage equipment including a 1942 Chevrolet "Parade" fire engine. Legend has it the fire station is haunted by a young firefighter. ✉ *1022 W Las Olas Blvd., at SW 11th Ave., Downtown* ☎ *954/763–1005* 🌐 *www.fortlauderdalefiremuseum.com* 🎫 *Free; donations appreciated* ⏲ *Closed weekdays.*

Historic Stranahan House Museum

MUSEUM | FAMILY | The city's oldest surviving structure was once home to businessman Frank Stranahan, who arrived from Ohio in 1892. With his wife, Ivy, the city's first schoolteacher, he befriended and traded with Seminole Indians. In 1901 he built a store that would later become his home after serving as a post office, a general store, and a restaurant. The couple's tale is filled with ups and downs. Their home remains Fort Lauderdale's principal link to its brief history and has been on the National Register of Historic Places since 1973. Guided tours are about an hour long and are offered a few times a day; however, calling ahead for availability is a good idea. Self-guided tours of the museum are not allowed. ✉ *335 SE Sixth Ave., Downtown* ☎ *954/524–4736* 🌐 *www.stranahanhouse.org* 🎫 *$12* ⏲ *Closed holidays.*

★ Las Olas Boulevard

COMMERCIAL CENTER | FAMILY | What Lincoln Road is to South Beach, Las Olas Boulevard is to Fort Lauderdale. Regarded as the heart and soul of Broward County, Las Olas has historically been the premier street for restaurants, art galleries, museums, shopping, dining, and people-watching. Lined with high-rises in the downtown area and original boutiques and ethnic eateries along 10 blocks of the main stretch, it's also home to beautiful mansions and traditional Florida homes along the Intracoastal Waterway to the east, which typify the modern-day aesthetic of Fort Lauderdale. The ocean appears beyond the residential swath, and that's where you see that the name "Las Olas" (Spanish for "The Waves") begins to make more sense. It's a pedestrian-friendly thoroughfare, but it's not closed to vehicular traffic at any point. ✉ *E Las Olas Blvd., Downtown* 🌐 *www.lasolasboulevard.com.*

Museum of Discovery and Science and AutoNation IMAX Theater

COLLEGE | FAMILY | There are dozens of interactive exhibits here to entertain children—*and* adults—through the wonders

Fort Lauderdale
A
B
C
D
E
F
1
2
3
4
5
6
7
8
9
Lake Ridge
Victoria Park
Holiday Park
Flagler Village
Colee Hammock
Downtown
Florence Hardy Park
Rio Vista
Lauderdale Harbours
Poinciana Park
Harbordale
Las Olas Is
Nurmi Isle
New River
Tarpon R.
Stranahan River
N Federal Hwy.
S Federal Hwy.
E Sunrise Blvd.
E Broward Blvd.
N Andrews Ave.
S Andrews Ave.
NE 3rd Ave.
SE 3rd Ave.
SE 12th St.
KEY
Sights
Restaurants
Hotels
0
1/4 mi
0
1/4 km

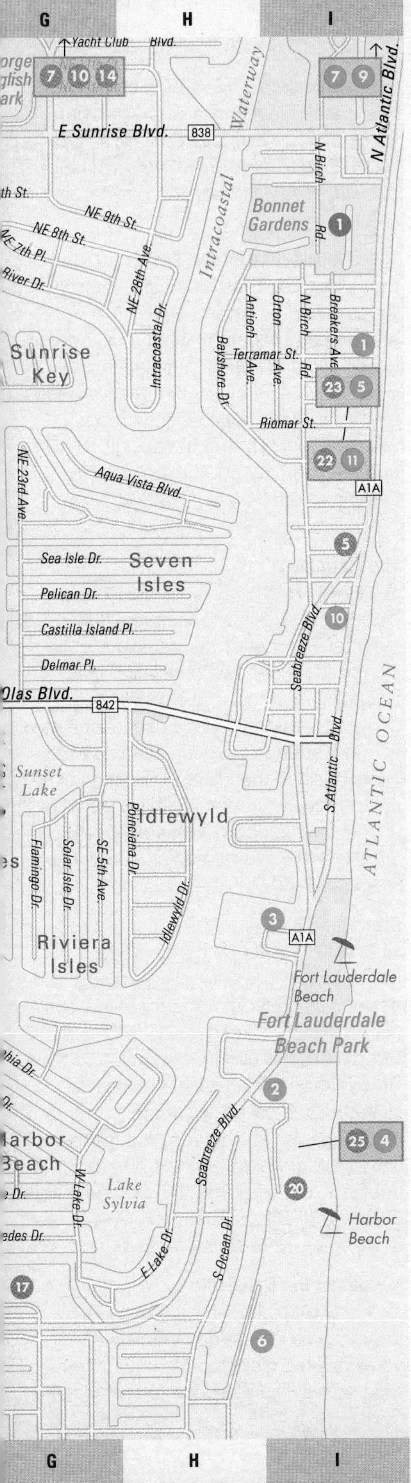

Sights

1 Bonnet House Museum and Gardens ... I2
2 Flagler + Arts + Technology Village A3
3 Fort Lauderdale Antique Car Museum... A8
4 Fort Lauderdale Fire and Safety Museum......... A5
5 Historic Stranahan House Museum......... B5
6 Las Olas Boulevard..... B5
7 Museum of Discovery and Science and AutoNation IMAX Theater........... A4
8 NSU Museum of Art Fort Lauderdale......... A5

Restaurants

1 American Social......... C5
2 Big City Tavern.......... B5
3 Canyon Southwest Cafe.......... F1
4 Casa D'Angelo Ristorante................. E1
5 Casablanca Cafe.......... I4
6 Coco Asian Bistro and Bar.................. C9
7 Eduardo de San Angel............... G1
8 The Floridian D5
9 Gran Forno Bakery D5
10 Kitchenetta G1
11 Lips D1
12 Lobster Bar Sea Grille.. B5
13 Luigi's Coal Oven Pizza. D5
14 Mai-Kai Restaurant and Polynesian Show....... G1
15 Old Fort Lauderdale Breakfast House A4
16 Old Heidelberg Restaurant............... A9
17 Pelican Landing......... G8
18 Rocco's Tacos and Tequila Bar D5
19 The Royal Pig Pub B5
20 Sea Level Restaurant and Ocean Bar................ I8
21 Southport Raw Bar..... D8
22 Steak 954 .... I3
23 S3.......................... I3
24 Stork's Cafe and Bakery D1
25 3030 Ocean............... I8
26 Timpano Italian Chophouse B5
27 Tom Jenkins' Barbecue............... B7
28 Wild Sea Oyster Bar and Grille C5

Hotels

1 The Atlantic Resort and Spa............ I2
2 B Ocean Resort........... I7
3 Bahia Mar Fort Lauderdale Beach Hotel, a DoubleTree by Hilton H6
4 Fort Lauderdale Marriott Harbor Beach Resort and Spa............ I8
5 Hilton Fort Lauderdale Beach Resort.............. I3
6 Lago Mar Resort and Club......... H9
7 Pelican Grand Beach Resort....................... I1
8 Pineapple Point.......... E4
9 Residence Inn Fort Lauderdale Intercoastal/ Il Lugano................... I1
10 The Ritz-Carlton, Fort Lauderdale I4
11 W Fort Lauderdale........ I3

of science and Florida's delicate ecosystem. The state-of-the-art 7-D theater takes guests on a virtual tour of aviation technology, while the Ecodiscovery Center comes with an Everglades Airboat Adventure ride, resident otters, and an interactive Florida storm center. The 300-seat AutoNation IMAX theater is part of the complex and shows mainstream and educational films, some in 3-D, on the biggest screen in South Florida with a rare high-tech laser projection system. ✉ *401 SW Second St., Downtown* ☎ *954/467–6637 Museum, 954/463–4629 IMAX* 🌐 *mods.org* 🎟 *Museum $17, IMAX tickets are extra and start at $9 per person.*

★ NSU Museum of Art Fort Lauderdale

ARTS VENUE | FAMILY | Led by visionary director and chief curator Bonnie Clearwater, the NSU Museum of Art's international exhibition programming ignites downtown Fort Lauderdale. The interior of the 83,000-square-foot modernist building, designed by architect Edward Larrabee Barnes in 1986, holds an impressive permanent collection of more than 7,000 works, including the country's largest collection of paintings by American realist William Glackens, and pivotal works by female and multicultural artists, avant-garde CoBrA artists, and a wide array of Latin American masters. **■ TIP→ The lobby-level Museum Café is a cool hangout with art-inspired gifts.** ✉ *1 E Las Olas Blvd., Downtown* ☎ *954/525–5500* 🌐 *nsuartmuseum.org* 🎟 *$12* ⏲ *Closed Mon.*

Restaurants

American Social

$$$ | MODERN AMERICAN | In the sports bar desert of South Florida, it's nice to know you can eat well while watching your team. American Social flaunts a seafood-mac-and-cheese skillet, shrimp-pesto flatbread, and a full spectrum of gourmet burgers with sides of parmesan-truffle fries or sweet-potato fries. **Known for:** upscale bar food; live sports on TV; craft beers and good cocktails. [$] *Average main: $25* ✉ *721 E Las Olas Blvd., Downtown* ☎ *954/715–1134* 🌐 *https://americansocialbar.com/las-olas/.*

★ Big City Tavern

$$$ | MODERN AMERICAN | FAMILY | A must-visit Las Olas landmark, Big City Tavern mingles Asian entrées like shrimp pad Thai with Italian four-cheese ravioli and an American grilled-chicken Cobb salad. The crispy flatbread changes every day. **Known for:** eclectic menu; weekend brunch; fun bar scene. [$] *Average main: $26* ✉ *609 E Las Olas Blvd., Downtown* ☎ *954/727–0307* 🌐 *www.bigcitylasolas.com.*

The Floridian

$$ | DINER | FAMILY | This classic 24-hour diner serves no-nonsense breakfast favorites (no matter the hour) like oversized omelets with biscuits, toast, or English muffins, and a choice of grits or sliced tomatoes. Good hangover eats abound, but don't expect anything exceptional besides the location and the low prices. **Known for:** breakfast anytime; low prices; always open. [$] *Average main: $15* ✉ *1410 E Las Olas Blvd., Downtown* ☎ *954/463–4041* 🌐 *thefloridiandiner.com.*

Gran Forno Bakery

$ | BAKERY | FAMILY | Most days, the Italian sandwiches, specialty breads, and pastries sell out before noon at this aptly named bakery ("large oven" in Italian). Customers line up in the morning to get Gran Forno's hot artisanal breads like ciabatta (800 loaves are made a day), returning later for the decadent desserts. **Known for:** great Italian-style breads; desserts; strong coffee. [$] *Average main: $14* ✉ *1235 E Las Olas Blvd., Downtown* ☎ *954/467–2244* 🌐 *granforno.com.*

★ Lobster Bar Sea Grille

$$$$ | SEAFOOD | Lobster Bar Sea Grille brought a much-needed infusion of sophisticated dining to the downtown food scene. The selection of seafood and fish is solid and ranges from Nova Scotian lobsters to Atlantic char from Iceland. **Known for:** fresh seafood and steaks; sophisticated atmosphere; lively happy hour. *Average main: $40 450 E Las Olas Blvd., Downtown 954/772–2675 buckheadrestaurants.com/restaurant/lobster-bar-sea-grille-ft-lauderdale.*

★ Luigi's Coal Oven Pizza
$$ | **PIZZA** | **FAMILY** | One of the best little pizza joints in South Florida, Luigi's Coal Oven Pizza has the full gamut of pizzas, phenomenal salads with fresh dressings, classics like eggplant parmigiana, and oven-baked chicken wings. For the Margherita Napoletana, the quality and flavors of the crust, cheese, and sauce are the result of Luigi's century-old recipe from Napoli. **Known for:** traditional Neopolitan-style pizza; intimate dining room; coal-fired oven. *Average main: $19 1415 E Las Olas Blvd., Downtown 954/522–8888 www.luigiscoaloven-pizza.com/index.html.*

★ Old Fort Lauderdale Breakfast House *(O-B House)*
$$$ | **AMERICAN** | Locals can't get enough of the O-B House's commitment to quality; you'll find only fresh and organic ingredients here. Try cheesy grits, mega-pancakes with real Vermont maple syrup, or the free-range-egg omelets with wild-caught mahimahi. **Known for:** organic ingredients; fun breakfast options; unique renovation of an old post office. *Average main: $21 333 Himmarshee St., Downtown 954/530–7520 www.o-bhouse.com No lunch Sun.*

Rocco's Tacos and Tequila Bar
$$ | **MODERN MEXICAN** | With pitchers of margaritas, Rocco's is more of a scene than a restaurant. In fact, Rocco's drink menu is even larger than its sizable food menu. **Known for:** 400 kinds of tequila; fresh guacamole; busy atmosphere. *Average main: $19 1313 E Las Olas Blvd., Downtown 954/524–9550 www.roccostacos.com.*

The Royal Pig Pub
$$$ | **CAJUN** | This gastropub revels in doling out hefty portions of Cajun comfort food and potent cocktails. It's one of Fort Lauderdale's busiest watering holes. **Known for:** busy bar; barbecue shrimp; weekend brunch. *Average main: $24 350 E Las Olas Blvd., Downtown 954/617–7447 www.royalpigpub.com.*

Timpano Italian Chophouse
$$$ | **ITALIAN** | Combine the likes of a high-end steak house with a typical trattoria, and you've got yourself a successful recipe for an Italian chophouse. Timpano's offerings include fresh pastas, flatbreads, and the full gamut of parmesans, marsalas, and fra diavolos. **Known for:** great salads; steakhouse favorites; live music in the Starlight Lounge. *Average main: $25 450 E Las Olas Blvd., Downtown 954/462–9119 timpanochophouse.net.*

Wild Sea Oyster Bar and Grille
$$$$ | **SEAFOOD** | In the heart of Las Olas, this oyster bar and grill keeps things simple with a small menu focused on a beautiful raw bar and ever-changing preparations of diverse catches from Florida, Hawaiian, and New England waters. **Known for:** worldly interpretations of seafood; raw bar; extensive wine list. *Average main: $43 Riverside Hotel, 620 E Las Olas Blvd., Downtown 954/467–2555 www.wildseaonlasolas.com.*

Hotels

Pineapple Point
$$ | **B&B/INN** | Tucked a few blocks behind Las Olas Boulevard in the residential neighborhood of Victoria Park, clothing-optional Pineapple Point is a magnificent maze of posh tropical cottages and dense foliage catering to the gay community and is nationally renowned for its stellar service. **Pros:** superior service; luxurious and tropical setting;

clothing is optional. **Cons:** difficult to find at first; cancellations or changes require 14-day notice; rates can get high during season. *Rooms from: $300 315 NE 16th Terr., Downtown 954/527–0094, 888/844–7295 www.pineapplepoint.com 25 rooms Breakfast.*

Nightlife

The majority of Fort Lauderdale nightlife takes place near downtown, beginning on Himmarshee Street (Second Street) and continuing on to the riverfront, and then to Las Olas Boulevard. The downtown area tends to draw a younger demographic somewhere between underage teens and late twenties. On Himmarshee Street, a dozen rowdy bars and clubs, ranging from the seedy to the sophisticated, entice a wide range of partygoers. Toward East Las Olas Boulevard, near the financial towers and boutique shops, upscale bars cater to the yuppie crowd.

★ Laser Wolf

BARS/PUBS | Far from the main drag of Fort Lauderdale's nightlife district, Laser Wolf celebrates the urban grit on the other side of the tracks as an artsy, hipster, craft-beer bar. It's located on the railroad tracks in a cool indoor-outdoor space and might be the most popular bar for locals because of its great drinks, music, and overall vibe. Motto: "No jerks. Yes beer." **TIP→ Drive or Uber it here. It's best not to walk from other bars off Las Olas and Himmarshee due to distance and safety concerns.** *901 Progresso Dr., No. 101, Downtown 954/667–9373 www.laserwolf.bar/home.html.*

ROK: BRG

BARS/PUBS | Downtown Fort Lauderdale loves this personality-driven burger bar and gastropub, as it gives the grown-ups something to enjoy in the teenage-infested nightlife district. The long and narrow venue, adorned with exposed-brick walls and flat-screen TVs, is great for watching sports and for mingling on weekends. Locals come here for the great cocktails and beer selection. The burgers are also locally famous. *208 SW Second St., Downtown 954/525–7656 rokbrgr.com/location/ft-lauderdale.*

Stache, 1920's Drinking Den + Coffee Bar

BARS/PUBS | Inspired by the Roaring Twenties, this speakeasy-style drinking den and nightclub infuses party-hard downtown Fort Lauderdale with some class and pizzazz. Expect awesome craft cocktails, inclusive of bespoke ice cubes for old-school drinks like Manhattans and Sidecars. Late-night on Friday and Saturday anticipate great music and a fun crowd. The 5,000-square-foot bar opens at 7 am on the weekdays to serve coffee. *109 SW Second Ave., Downtown 954/449–1025 stacheftl.com.*

★ Tap 42 Bar and Kitchen

BARS/PUBS | With 42 rotating draft beers from around the U.S., 50-plus bourbons, a few dozen original cocktails (including beer cocktails), and dozens of bottled craft beers, good times await. The drafts adorn a stylish wall constructed of pennies, which creates an interesting trompe l'oeil. The venue attracts large crowds of young professionals for nights of heavy drinking and high-calorie bar eats. *1411 S Andrews Ave., Downtown 954/463–4900 tap42.com/ft-lauderdale.*

Performing Arts

★ Broward Center for the Performing Arts

ARTS CENTERS | **FAMILY** | Fort Lauderdale's 2,700-seat architectural gem offers more than 500 events annually, including Broadway-style musicals, plays, dance, symphony, opera, rock, film, lectures, comedy, and children's theater. The theaters are state-of-the-art and dining venues are available, including the restaurant Marti's New River Bistro and the Intermezzo Lounge. An elevated walkway connects the centerpiece of the complex to a parking garage across the street. ✉ *201 SW Fifth Ave., Downtown* ☎ *954/462–0222* 🌐 *www.browardcenter.org.*

Savor Cinema

ARTS-ENTERTAINMENT OVERVIEW | FAMILY

Formerly called Cinema Paradiso, this arthouse theater operates out of a former church south of New River near the county courthouse. The space doubles as headquarters for the Fort Lauderdale International Film Festival (FLIFF), while still playing films year-round. FLIFF's website is the easiest way to see what's playing on any given evening at the cinema. ✉ *503 SE Sixth St., Downtown* ☎ *954/525–3456* 🌐 *www.fliff.com.*

Shopping

★ Las Olas Boulevard

ANTIQUES/COLLECTIBLES | FAMILY | Las Olas Boulevard is the epicenter of Fort Lauderdale's lifestyle. Not only are 50 of the city's best boutiques, dozens of top restaurants, and eclectic art galleries found along this landscaped street, but Las Olas links the growing downtown area with Fort Lauderdale's beautiful beaches. ✉ *E Las Olas Blvd., Downtown* ☎ *954/258–8382* 🌐 *lasolasboulevard.com.*

Fort Lauderdale Beach

If you want to stop for a bite to eat or a drink before or after visiting Bonnet House, consider **Casablanca Café** (✉ *3049 Alhambra St.*) or **Steak 954** (✉ *W Fort Lauderdale, 401 N Fort Lauderdale Beach Blvd.*).

Sights

★ Bonnet House Museum and Gardens

BUILDING | FAMILY | This 35-acre subtropical estate endures as a tribute to Old South Florida. Prior to its "modern" history, the grounds had already seen 4,000 years of activity when settler Hugh Taylor Birch purchased the site in 1895. Birch gave it to his daughter Helen as a wedding gift when she married Frederic Bartlett, and the newlyweds built a charming home for a winter residence in 1920. Years after Helen died, Frederic married his second wife, Evelyn, and the artistically gifted couple embarked on a mission to embellish the property with personal touches and surprises that are still evident today. This historic place is a must-see for its architecture, artwork, and horticulture. While admiring the fabulous gardens, look out for playful monkeys swinging from the trees. ✉ *Bonnet House Museum and Gardens, 900 N Birch Rd., Beachfront* ☎ *954/563–5393* 🌐 *www.bonnethouse.org* 🎫 *$20 for house tours or $10 for gardens only; $4 for tram tour* ⏲ *Closed Mon., holidays.*

Beaches

★ Fort Lauderdale Beach

BEACH—SIGHT | FAMILY | The same stretch of sand that once welcomed America's wild spring breakers is now miles of beachside sophistication. It remains gloriously open and uncluttered when compared to other major beaches along the Florida coastline; walkways line both sides of the road, and traffic is trimmed to two gently curving northbound lanes. Fort Lauderdale Beach unofficially begins between the B Ocean Resort (formerly the Sheraton Yankee Clipper) and the DoubleTree by Hilton Bahia Mar Resort, starting with the quiet **Fort Lauderdale Beach Park,** where picnic tables and palm trees rule. Going north, a younger crowd gravitates toward the section near Las Olas Boulevard. The beach is actually most crowded from here to **Beach Place,** home of Marriott's vacation rentals and touristy places like Hooters and Fat Tuesday (and a beach-themed CVS). An LGBTQ crew soaks up the sun along **Sebastian Street Beach,** just north of the Ritz-Carlton. Families with children enjoy hanging out between Seville Street and Vistamar Street, between the Westin Fort Lauderdale Beach and the Atlantic Resort and Spa. High-spirited dive bars dot the Strip and epitomize its "anything goes" attitude. **Amenities:** food and drink; lifeguards; parking (fee). **Best for:** partiers; sunrise; swimming; walking; windsurfing. ✉ *SR A1A, from Holiday Dr. to Sunrise Blvd., Beachfront.*

Harbor Beach

BEACH—SIGHT | **FAMILY** | The posh Harbor Beach community includes Fort Lauderdale's most opulent residences on the Intracoastal Waterway. Due east of this community, a stunning beach has adopted the name of its surroundings. The Harbor Beach section has some of the only private beaches in Fort Lauderdale, and most of this beach belongs to hotels like the Marriott Harbor Beach Resort and the Lago Mar Resort & Club. (To be clear: Only hotel guests have access.) Such status allows the hotels to provide guests with full-service amenities and dining options on their own slices of heaven. **Amenities:** water sports. **Best for:** solitude; swimming; walking. ✉ *S Ocean Ln. and Holiday Dr., Beachfront.*

Restaurants

Casablanca Cafe

$$$ | **ECLECTIC** | **FAMILY** | The menu at this piano bar and restaurant offers a global hodgepodge of American, Mediterranean, and Asian flavors, with a specific focus on eclectic preparations of Florida fish. The food isn't particularly good, but the atmosphere at this historic home is excellent. **Known for:** dining with ocean views; historic setting in Jova House; popular piano bar. $ *Average main: $28* ✉ *3049 Alhambra St., Beachfront* ☎ *954/764–3500* 🌐 *www.casablancacafeonline.com.*

Sea Level Restaurant and Ocean Bar

$$$ | **SEAFOOD** | **FAMILY** | You have to take the road less traveled to find Sea Level, a haven for fresh seafood. The indoor-outdoor restaurant literally overlooks the ocean from sea level at Marriott's Harbor Beach Resort and Spa, and its seasonal menu wows with daily specials and cocktails featuring ingredients from the chef's organic garden. **Known for:** the freshest seafood; outdoor dining; good cocktail menu. $ *Average main: $25* ✉ *Fort Lauderdale Marriott Harbor Beach Resort and Spa, 3030 Holiday Dr., Beachfront* ☎ *954/765–3041* 🌐 *www.marriott.com.*

Steak 954

$$$$ | **MODERN AMERICAN** | It's not just the steaks that impress at Stephen Starr's superstar spot inside the W Fort Lauderdale, the seafood selections shine, too. Order as many dishes as possible, like the lobster and crab-coconut ceviche, the red snapper tiradito, and the Colorado lamb chops. **Known for:** high-quality (and expensive) steaks and seafood; outdoor dining; Sunday brunch. $ *Average main: $55* ✉ *W Fort Lauderdale, 401 N Fort Lauderdale Beach Blvd., Beachfront* ☎ *954/414–8333* 🌐 *steak954.com.*

★ 3030 Ocean

$$$$ | **SEAFOOD** | 3030 Ocean's unpredictable menus are guided by award-winning chef Adrienne Grenier's perfectionist flair. Her interpretation of modern American seafood focuses on balancing complex flavors to enhance her fresh ingredients—without subtracting from their integrity. **Known for:** ever-changing menu; locally sourced seafood; consistently good food. $ *Average main: $45* ✉ *Fort Lauderdale Marriott Harbor Beach Resort and Spa, 3030 Holiday Dr., Beachfront* ☎ *954/765–3030* 🌐 *www.3030ocean.com.*

★ S3

$$$ | **FUSION** | S3 stands for the fabulous trio of sun, surf, and sand, paying homage to its prime beachfront location. The menu features a variety of Japanese-inspired raw dishes, sushi rolls, and dishes with a New American focus. **Known for:** eclectic Asian and American flavors; solid

Fort Lauderdale's picture-perfect beach is designated Blue Wave certified by the Clean Beaches Coalition.

selection of wine and cocktails; drawing both locals and visitors. *Average main: $29* *Hilton Fort Lauderdale Beach Resort, 505 N Fort Lauderdale Beach Blvd., Beachfront* *s3restaurant.com.*

Hotels

The Atlantic Resort and Spa
$$$ | **HOTEL** | **FAMILY** | This towering oceanfront hotel has fantastic views of the ocean from its beds (unless, of course, you select a city view). **Pros:** oceanfront property; en suite kitchenettes; pet-friendly. **Cons:** dated decor in the rooms; expensive parking; issues with service. *Rooms from: $320* *601 N Fort Lauderdale Beach Blvd., Beachfront* *954/516–1720* *www.atlantichotelfl.com* *104 rooms* *No meals.*

B Ocean Resort
$$ | **HOTEL** | This iconic riverboat-shaped landmark, once the Yankee Clipper, is chic yet functional, and the unobstructed ocean views and beach access set it apart from neighboring properties. **Pros:** retro mermaid show in swimming pool; proximity to beach; excellent gym. **Cons:** small rooms; low ceilings in lobby; some aspects need a refresh. *Rooms from: $200* *1140 Seabreeze Blvd., Beachfront* *954/564–1000* *www.bhotelsandresorts.com/b-ocean* *481 rooms* *No meals.*

Bahia Mar Fort Lauderdale Beach Hotel, A DoubleTree by Hilton
$$ | **HOTEL** | **FAMILY** | This nicely situated resort has identical rooms in both its marina building and its tower building; however, the latter offers superior views. **Pros:** crosswalk from hotel to beach; on-site yacht center; Water Taxi stop. **Cons:** busy location; small bathrooms; high rates during events. *Rooms from: $215* *801 Seabreeze Blvd., Beachfront* *954/764–2233* *www.bahiamarhotel.com* *296 rooms* *No meals.*

★ Fort Lauderdale Marriott Harbor Beach Resort and Spa
$$$$ | **RESORT** | **FAMILY** | Bill Marriott's personal choice for his annual four-week family vacation, the Marriott Harbor

Beach sits on a quarter-mile of private beach; it shines with the luxe personality of a top-notch island resort. **Pros:** private beachfront; all rooms have balconies; great eateries. **Cons:** Wi-Fi isn't free; expensive parking; large resort feel. *Rooms from: $450 3030 Holiday Dr., Beachfront 954/525–4000 www.marriott.com 650 rooms No meals.*

Hilton Fort Lauderdale Beach Resort
$$ | **HOTEL** | **FAMILY** | This oceanfront sparkler features tasteful, large suites and a fabulous sixth-floor pool deck. **Pros:** fun pool and adults-only lounge; most rooms have balconies; great spa. **Cons:** not pet-friendly; expensive valet parking; beach umbrellas not included in resort fee. *Rooms from: $300 505 N Fort Lauderdale Beach Blvd., Beachfront 954/414–2222 www3.hilton.com 374 rooms No meals.*

Lago Mar Resort and Club
$$$ | **RESORT** | **FAMILY** | The sprawling family-friendly Lago Mar retains its sparkle and authentic Florida feel thanks to committed owners. **Pros:** secluded setting; no resort fee; free valet and self-parking. **Cons:** not easy to find; far from restaurants and beach action; dated decor. *Rooms from: $375 1700 S Ocean La., Beachfront 954/523–6511 lagomar.com 204 rooms No meals.*

Pelican Grand Beach Resort
$$$ | **RESORT** | **FAMILY** | This bright yellow Key West–style Noble House property fuses a heritage seaside charm with understated luxury. **Pros:** incredible spa; directly on the beach; romantic restaurant. **Cons:** small fitness center; dated room decor; small property. *Rooms from: $350 2000 N Ocean Blvd., Beachfront 954/568–9431 www.pelicanbeach.com 159 rooms No meals.*

★ **The Ritz-Carlton, Fort Lauderdale**
$$$$ | **HOTEL** | Twenty-four dramatically tiered, glass-walled stories rise from the sea, forming a resort that's helping to revive a golden age of luxury travel. **Pros:** prime beach location; exceptional service; organic spa treatments. **Cons:** expensive valet parking; cancel at least 14 days in advance or get hit with a two-night penalty; extra-busy poolscape. *Rooms from: $750 1 N Fort Lauderdale Beach Blvd., Beachfront 954/465–2300 www.ritzcarlton.com/FortLauderdale 192 rooms No meals.*

W Fort Lauderdale
$$ | **HOTEL** | Fort Lauderdale's trendiest hotel has a glamorous poolscape, über-modern rooms and suites, and dramatic views from every direction. **Pros:** amazing pool; pet-friendly; great restaurant. **Cons:** party atmosphere not for everyone; can be hard to navigate the property; Wi-Fi isn't free. *Rooms from: $300 435 N Fort Lauderdale Beach Blvd., Beachfront 954/414–8200 www.marriott.com/hotels/travel/fllwh-w-fort-lauderdale 329 rooms No meals.*

Nightlife

Given its roots as a beachside party town, it's hard to believe that Fort Lauderdale Beach offers very few options in terms of nightlife. A few dive bars are at opposite ends of the main strip, near Sunrise Boulevard and Route A1A, as well as Las Olas Boulevard and A1A. On the main thoroughfare between Las Olas and Sunrise, a few high-end bars at the beach's showstopping hotels have become popular, namely those at the W Fort Lauderdale.

McSorley's Beach Pub
BARS/PUBS | This modern take on a classic Irish pub offers standard pub fun—from a jukebox to 35 beers on tap—but remains wildly popular thanks to its location right across from Fort Lauderdale Beach. Indeed, it's one of the few places on the beach to get an affordable drink and attracts its fair share of tourists and

locals. Upstairs, the pub has a second lounge that's far clubbier, as well as a rooftop terrace. ✉ *837 N Fort Lauderdale Beach Blvd., Beachfront* ☎ *954/565–4446* 🌐 *www.mcsorleysftl.com.*

The World Famous Parrot Lounge

BARS/PUBS | FAMILY | A venerable Fort Lauderdale hangout, this dive bar–sports bar is particularly popular with Philadelphia Eagles fans and folks reminiscing about the big hair and spray tans of '80s Fort Lauderdale (aka its heyday). This place is stuck in the past, but it's got great bartenders, wings, chicken fingers, poppers, and skins. 'Nuff said. ✉ *911 Sunrise La., Beachfront* ☎ *954/563–1493* 🌐 *www.parrotlounge.com.*

The Wreck Bar

BARS/PUBS | Travel back in time to the '50s at this "under the sea" dive bar and seafood eatery at B Ocean Resort, where huge aquariums and a porthole show off live mermaids, who perform in the pool on Friday and Saturday. ✉ *B Ocean Resort, 1140 Seabreeze Blvd., Beachfront* ☎ *954/524–5551* 🌐 *www.bhotelsandresorts.com/b-ocean/wreck-bar.*

Shopping

Most of Fort Lauderdale's upscale spas are located within elegant beachfront hotels, yet they remain open to the public. During low season (September and October), top spas offer $99 treatments during the "Spa Chic" promotion (🌐 *www.sunny.org/spachic*).

The Gallery at Beach Place

GIFTS/SOUVENIRS | FAMILY | Just north of Las Olas Boulevard on Route A1A, this shopping gallery is attached to the mammoth Marriott's BeachPlace Towers' timeshare property. Retail spaces are occupied by touristy shops that sell everything from sarongs to alligator heads, chain restaurants like Hooter's, bars serving frozen drinks, and a supersized CVS pharmacy, which sells everything you need for the beach. ■ **TIP→ Beach Place has covered parking, and usually has plenty of spaces, but you can pinch pennies by using a nearby municipal lot.** ✉ *17 S Fort Lauderdale Beach Blvd., Beachfront* ☎ *954/764–3460* 🌐 *www.galleryatbeachplace.com.*

★ The Ritz-Carlton Spa, Fort Lauderdale

SPA/BEAUTY | The Ritz-Carlton's expansive 8,500-foot hideaway is focused on tranquility and relaxation, from the layout of the treatment rooms to the magical hands of Fort Lauderdale's top therapists. Massage options run the gamut, including Swedish, aromatherapy, hot stone, couples, deep tissue, hydrotherapy, reflexology, Thai, and prenatal. Dermatologist-developed skin-care treatments, anti-cellulite and anti-aging treatments, facials, manicures, and pedicures are also on the menu. Go for the Intuitive Ocean treatment for an intense detoxification with help from the marine mud, seaweed, and sea salt. You'll feel a renewed sense of balance after the body scrub, wrap, and massage. ✉ *The Ritz-Carlton Spa, Fort Lauderdale, 1 N Fort Lauderdale Beach Blvd., Beachfront* ☎ *954/302–6490* 🌐 *www.ritzcarlton.com/en/hotels/florida/fort-lauderdale/spa.*

Spa Atlantic

SPA/BEAUTY | Spa Atlantic exudes a relaxed glamour and offers perfected core spa services. Many treatments are rooted in Asia, the Middle East, and the Mediterranean. Body treatments include a wide variety of massages, baths, body wraps, and body glows (exfoliation). Other beauty treatments offered include skin-care enhancements, anti-aging treatments, facials, manicures, pedicures, waxing, hair, and makeup. ✉ *The Atlantic Hotel and Spa, 601 N Fort Lauderdale Beach Blvd., Beachfront* ☎ *954/567–8085* 🌐 *www.atlantichotelfl.com/spa-atlantic.*

Did You Know?
More than 165 miles of canals and waterways earned Fort Lauderdale the nickname "the Venice of America."

Intracoastal and Inland Fort Lauderdale

Beaches

★ Hugh Taylor Birch State Park

BEACH—SIGHT | FAMILY | North of the bustling beachfront at Sunrise Boulevard, quieter sands run parallel to Hugh Taylor Birch State Park, an exquisite patch of Old Florida. The 180-acre subtropical oasis forms a barrier island between the Atlantic Ocean and the Intracoastal Waterway—surprisingly close to the urban core. Lush vegetation includes mangroves, and there are lovely nature trails through the hammock system. Visit the Birch House Museum, enjoy a picnic, play volleyball, or grab a canoe, kayak, or stand-up paddleboard. **Amenities:** toilets, water sports. **Best for:** solitude; walking. ✉ *3109 E Sunrise Blvd., Intracoastal and Inland* ☎ *954/564–4521* 🌐 *www.floridastateparks.org/parks-and-trails/hugh-taylor-birch-state-park* 🎫 *$6 for group in vehicle; $4 single driver or motorcycle; $2 per pedestrian or bicyclist.*

Restaurants

Canyon Southwest Cafe

$$$ | SOUTHWESTERN | Inside this magical enclave, a Southwestern fusion of Central and South American flavors and a twist of Asian influence is on the menu. Pair the fresh seafood or wild game with a robust selection of tequilas, a few mezcals, or a bottle from the decent wine list. **Known for:** locally sourced ingredients; long waits; large selection of tequilas. $ *Average main: $28* ✉ *1818 E Sunrise Blvd., Intracoastal and Inland* ✣ *At NE 18th Ave.* ☎ *954/765–1950* 🌐 *www.canyonfl.com* ⏲ *Closed Mon.*

★ Casa D'Angelo Ristorante

$$$$ | ITALIAN | Casa D'Angelo is always packed. The Tuscan-style fine-dining restaurant is beloved for its rustic and refined philosophy. **Known for:** everything made from scratch; grilled tiger prawns; extensive wine list. $ *Average main: $40* ✉ *1201 N Federal Hwy., No. 5A, Intracoastal and Inland* ☎ *954/564–1234* 🌐 *www.casa-d-angelo.com.*

★ Coco Asian Bistro and Bar

$$$ | ASIAN | The best of Thai and Japanese cooking unite in an unassuming Fort Lauderdale strip mall. Chef-owner Mike Ponluang's lobster pad Thai and classic curries are the go-to for loyal locals, as are sushi rolls and more traditional Japanese selections. **Known for:** extensive Pan-Asian menu; soothing, elegant atmosphere; good desserts. $ *Average main: $27* ✉ *Harbor Shops, 1841 Cordova Rd., Intracoastal and Inland* ☎ *954/525–3541* 🌐 *www.cocoasianbistro.com.*

Kitchenetta

$$$ | ITALIAN | FAMILY | Kitchenetta is a modern trattoria serving gourmet Italian-American favorites in an industrial-chic setting. The best things to come out of this family-owned kitchen include the spaghetti with Neopolitan-style stuffed artichokes (seasonal), gnocchi Gorgonzola, and the wood-fired mushroom pizza. **Known for:** family-sized portions; good pastas; special Sunday supper. $ *Average main: $25* ✉ *2850 N Federal Hwy., Intracoastal and Inland* ☎ *954/567–3333* 🌐 *www.kitchenetta.com* ⏲ *Closed Mon. No lunch.*

Old Heidelberg Restaurant

$$$ | GERMAN | FAMILY | Old Heidelberg is like a Bavarian mirage on State Road 84 with a killer list of German specialties and beers on tap. Classics like bratwurst, knockwurst, kielbasa, and spaetzle dovetail nicely with four types of Wiener schnitzel. **Known for:** kitschy decor; huge selection of German imports on tap; extensive menu of German favorites. $ *Average main: $25* ✉ *900 W State Road 84, Intracoastal and Inland* ☎ *954/463–6747* 🌐 *www.heidelbergfl.com* ⏲ *No lunch weekends.*

Lago Mar Resort and Club in Fort Lauderdale has its own private beach on the Atlantic Ocean.

Pelican Landing

$$ | **SEAFOOD** | **FAMILY** | Somehow Pelican Landing has managed to stay under the radar in spite of its high-quality seafood, burgers, and Caribbean dishes. The fish is caught daily, served simply blackened or grilled, and presented with sides. **Known for:** fresh seafood; casual atmosphere; sunset views. *Average main: $19* *Pier Sixty-Six Hotel & Marina, 2301 SE 17th St., Intracoastal and Inland* *At end of main dock* *954/524–3444* *www.pelican-landing.com.*

Southport Raw Bar

$$ | **SEAFOOD** | You can't go wrong at this unpretentious dive where seafood reigns. Feast on raw or steamed clams, raw oysters, and peel-and-eat shrimp. **Known for:** affordable prices; fresh seafood; open late on weekends. *Average main: $19* *1536 Cordova Rd., Intracoastal and Inland* *954/525–2526* *www.southportrawbar.com.*

Tom Jenkins' Barbecue

$ | **BARBECUE** | **FAMILY** | Big portions of dripping barbecue are dispensed at this chill spot for eat-in or take-out. Dinners come with two sides from a list that includes baked beans, collards, and mac and cheese. **Known for:** ample portions; very reasonable prices; good sides. *Average main: $12* *1236 S Federal Hwy., Intracoastal and Inland* *954/522–5046* *tomjenkinsbbq.net* *Closed Sun. and Mon.*

Hotels

Residence Inn Fort Lauderdale Intracoastal/Il Lugano

$ | **HOTEL** | This modern, clean hotel has studios and suites with fully equipped kitchens, private balconies with intracoastal views, plus amenities including a pool and fitness center. **Pros:** docking is available to guests; pet-friendly; bike rentals available. **Cons:** lacks character of other properties; business traveler vibes; not on the beach. *Rooms from: $154* *3333 NE 32nd Ave, Intracoastal and Inland* *954/564–4400* *www.marriott.com* *105 rooms* *Free Breakfast.*

Nightlife

Bars and pubs along Fort Lauderdale's Intracoastal cater to the city's large, transient boating community along with its young professional population. Heading inland along Sunrise Boulevard, the bars around Galleria Mall target singles.

Blue Martini Fort Lauderdale

BARS/PUBS | A hot spot for the wild set, Blue Martini's menu is filled with tons of unconventional martini creations. The drinks are usually very good and the scene is fun for everyone, even those who aren't single and looking to mingle. ✉ *The Galleria at Fort Lauderdale, 2432 E Sunrise Blvd., Intracoastal and Inland* ☎ *954/653–2583* 🌐 *fortlauderdale.bluemartinilounge.com.*

Shopping

The Galleria at Fort Lauderdale

SHOPPING CENTERS/MALLS | **FAMILY** | Fort Lauderdale's most sophisticated mall is just west of the Intracoastal Waterway. The split-level emporium comprises Neiman Marcus, Apple, H&M, Macy's, and dozens of specialty shops. You can chow down at The Capital Grille, Truluck's, P.F. Chang's China Bistro, or Seasons 52—or sip cocktails at Blue Martini. The mall itself is open Monday through Saturday 10–9, Sunday noon–6. The stand-alone restaurants and bars are open later. ✉ *2414 E Sunrise Blvd., Intracoastal and Inland* ☎ *954/564–1015* 🌐 *www.galleriamall-fl.com.*

Wilton Manors and Oakland Park

North of Fort Lauderdale, Wilton Manors is the hub of gay life in the greater Fort Lauderdale area and has several popular restaurants and bars. Oakland Park, immediately to the north, also has several restaurants that are worth a visit.

Restaurants

★ **Eduardo de San Angel**

$$$ | **MEXICAN** | Authentic chiles, spices, and herbs enhance classic seafood, meat, and poultry dishes at this inviting Mexican enclave known for its hospitality. The beloved restaurant has packed the house (which feels like a hacienda) for over 20 years, a testament to its excellent cuisine. **Known for:** upscale Mexican cuisine; exceptional service; cilantro soup. 💲 *Average main: $30* ✉ *2822 E Commercial Blvd., Oakland Park* ☎ *954/772–4731* 🌐 *eduardodesanangel.com* ⏲ *Closed Sun.*

Lips

$$$ | **AMERICAN** | The '90s are still alive and well at Lips. The hit restaurant and drag-show bar is a hot spot for groups celebrating birthdays, bachelorette parties, and other milestones requiring glitz and glamour. **Known for:** drag performances while you dine; Sunday brunch; raucous celebrations. 💲 *Average main: $23* ✉ *1421 E Oakland Park Blvd., Oakland Park* ☎ *954/567–0987* 🌐 *www.fladragshow.com* ⏲ *Closed Mon.*

Mai-Kai Restaurant and Polynesian Show

$$$$ | **SOUTH PACIFIC** | **FAMILY** | Touristy to some yet downright divine to others, Mai-Kai merges the South Pacific with South Florida. This torch-lit landmark is undeniably gimmicky, but it's the only place in town to drink tiki cocktails while watching Polynesian dances and fire shows. **Known for:** Peking duck; good wine list; long waits—reservations are essential. 💲 *Average main: $39* ✉ *3599 N Federal Hwy., Oakland Park* ☎ *954/563–3272* 🌐 *www.maikai.com* ⏲ *Closed Mon.*

Stork's Café and Bakery

$ | **CAFÉ** | Stork's Café stands out as a friendly coffeehouse and café for gourmet sandwiches and salads. In addition to brewing eight types of coffee, Stork's has excellent baked goods that range from croissants, tortes, cakes, and pies to "monster cookies," including gingersnap and snickerdoodle. **Known for:** great coffee; baked goods; extensive sandwich menu. *Average main: $14* *2505 NE 15th Ave., Wilton Manors* *954/567–3220* *storksbakery.com.*

Nightlife

The hub of Fort Lauderdale's gay nightlife is in Wilton Manors. Wilton Drive, aka "The Drive," has numerous bars, clubs, and lounges that cater to the LGBTQ community.

Georgie's Alibi Monkey Bar
BARS/PUBS | An anchor for the Wilton Manors gay community fills to capacity for cheap Long Island Iced Teas and stands out as a kind of gay "Cheers"—a chill neighborhood drinking hole with darts, pool, and friendly people. *2266 Wilton Dr., Wilton Manors* *954/565–2526* *www.alibiwiltonmanors.com.*

Rosie's Bar and Grill
BARS/PUBS | Rosie's is very lively, pumping out pop tunes and award-winning burgers. It's the go-to gay-friendly place for affordable drinks and great times. Sunday brunch, with its cast of alternating DJs, is wildly popular. *2449 Wilton Dr., Wilton Manors* *954/563–0123* *www.rosiesbng.com.*

Shopping

Living Green Fresh Market
SPECIALTY STORES | **FAMILY** | Living Green Fresh Market is a fabulous alternative to overpriced behemoths for the health-conscious in Oakland Park. This green shop and café is bursting with colorful, local, fresh produce, wild-caught fish, prepared foods, and other goods. The quality is top-notch yet the prices are affordable. You can grab breakfast or lunch and cross things off your grocery list, while knowing that each item has a ton of integrity. Plus there's fair-trade coffee. *1305 E Commercial Blvd., Oakland Park* *954/771–9770* *https://livinggreenfreshmarket.com.*

Western Suburbs and Beyond

West of Fort Lauderdale is an ever-evolving suburbia, where most of Broward's gated communities, golf courses, shopping outlets, casinos, and chain restaurants exist. As you reach the county's western side, the terrain takes on more characteristics of the Everglades, and you can see alligators sunning on canal banks with other exotic reptiles and birds.

Sights

Ah-Tah-Thi-Ki Museum
GARDEN | **FAMILY** | Beyond the western suburbs of Broward County and a couple of miles from Billie Swamp Safari is Ah-Tah-Thi-Ki Museum, which means "a place to learn, a place to remember" in the Seminole language. This Smithsonian Institution Affiliate documents the living history and culture of the Seminole Tribe of Florida through artifacts, exhibits, and experiential learning. There's a mile-long boardwalk above the swamplands (wheelchair-accessible) that leads you through the Big Cypress Seminole Indian Reservation. At the midpoint of the boardwalk, you can take a break at the re-created ceremonial grounds. *30290 Josie Billie Hwy., Clewiston* *877/902–1113* *www.ahtahthiki.com* *$10* *Closed holidays.*

Billie Swamp Safari
NATURE PRESERVE | **FAMILY** | Four different ecosystems in the "River of Grass" are preserved by the Seminole Tribe of Florida, and Billie Swamp Safari's daily tours can introduce you to the elusive wildlife that resides in each area—by airboat or swamp buggy. Sightings of deer, turtles, raccoons, wild hogs, hawks, eagles, and alligators are likely but

certainly not guaranteed. Animal exhibits, a petting zoo, and snake/critter shows provide a solid contingency plan. For the rugged adventurer, overnight camping in a native-style chickee hut (thatched-roof dwelling) is available. If a sleepover is too much, Twilight Expeditions offers a campfire with storytelling followed by a nighttime tour. Head to the Swamp Water Café to try Native American dishes like Indian fry bread with honey, Indian tacos, and bison burgers. Check the website for showtimes and tour schedules. ✉ *30000 Gator Tail Trail, Clewiston* ☎ *863/983–6101* 🌐 *www.billieswamp.com* 🎟 *Swamp Safari Day Package $50; Twilight Swamp Expedition $43* ⏲ *Closed Christmas Day.*

★ Butterfly World

GARDEN | FAMILY | More than 80 native and international butterfly species live inside the first butterfly house in the U.S. and the largest in the world. The 3-acre site inside Coconut Creek's Tradewinds Park has aviaries, observation decks, waterfalls, ponds, and tunnels. There are lots of birds, too: kids love the lorikeet aviary, where birds alight on every limb. ✉ *Butterfly World, 3600 W Sample Rd., Coconut Creek* ☎ *954/977–4400* 🌐 *www.butterflyworld.com* 🎟 *$29.95* ⏲ *Closed holidays* ☞ *A Tradewinds Park gate fee of $1.50 per person is in effect on weekends and holidays.*

Everglades Holiday Park

MARINA | FAMILY | Many episodes of Animal Planet's *Gator Boys* are filmed here, making this wetland "park" an extremely popular tourist attraction. Take an hour-long airboat tour, snap a selfie with a python, and catch alligators wrestling in the pit. ⚠ **The airboats tend to be supersized, and the overall experience can feel commercialized.** ✉ *21940 Griffin Rd.* ☎ *954/434–8111* 🌐 *www.evergladesholidaypark.com* 🎟 *$33.39 for 60-minute airboat ride (includes group photo).*

Flamingo Gardens

GARDEN | FAMILY | Wander through the aviary, arboretum, wildlife sanctuary, and Everglades museum inside the historic Wray Home at Davie's Flamingo Gardens. A half-hour guided tram ride winds through tropical fruit groves and wetlands, where the largest collection of Florida native wildlife lives (flamingos, alligators, bobcats, otters, panthers, and more). ✉ *Flamingo Gardens, 3750 S Flamingo Rd., Davie* ☎ *954/473–2955* 🌐 *www.flamingogardens.org* 🎟 *$19.95.*

Sawgrass Recreation Park

NATURE PRESERVE | FAMILY | Catch a good glimpse of plants and wildlife—from ospreys and alligators to turtles, snakes, and fish—on a 30-minute airboat ride through the Everglades. The fee covers admission to all nature exhibits as well as a visit to a model Seminole village. **■ TIP→ Nature truly comes alive at night. Sawgrass Recreation Park offers longer nighttime airboat rides on Wednesday and Saturday at 8 pm, reservations required.** ✉ *1006 U.S. 27, Weston* ☎ *888/424–7262, 954/389–0202* 🌐 *www.evergladestours.com* 🎟 *$22.95; Gator Night tours $40.*

Restaurants

Angelo Elia Pizza, Bar and Tapas

$$ | PIZZA | FAMILY | This casual Weston outpost is one of chef Angelo Elia's popular Tuscan-inspired restaurants in Broward County. Affordable small plates, salads, ceviches, and pizzas are neighborhood favorites. **Known for:** moderate prices; family-friendly atmosphere; housemade gelato. 💲 *Average main: $20* ✉ *Country Isles Shopping Center, 1370 Weston Rd., Weston* ☎ *954/306–0037* 🌐 *www.angeloeliapizza.com.*

★ Anthony's Coal Fired Pizza

$$ | PIZZA | FAMILY | Before this legendary South Florida pizzeria spread to more than 50 outposts across eight states, Anthony's original coal-fired oven was heating up Broward County in a big way. Its Miramar location packs the house with a simple menu of pizza made with fresh ingredients in an 800°F oven,

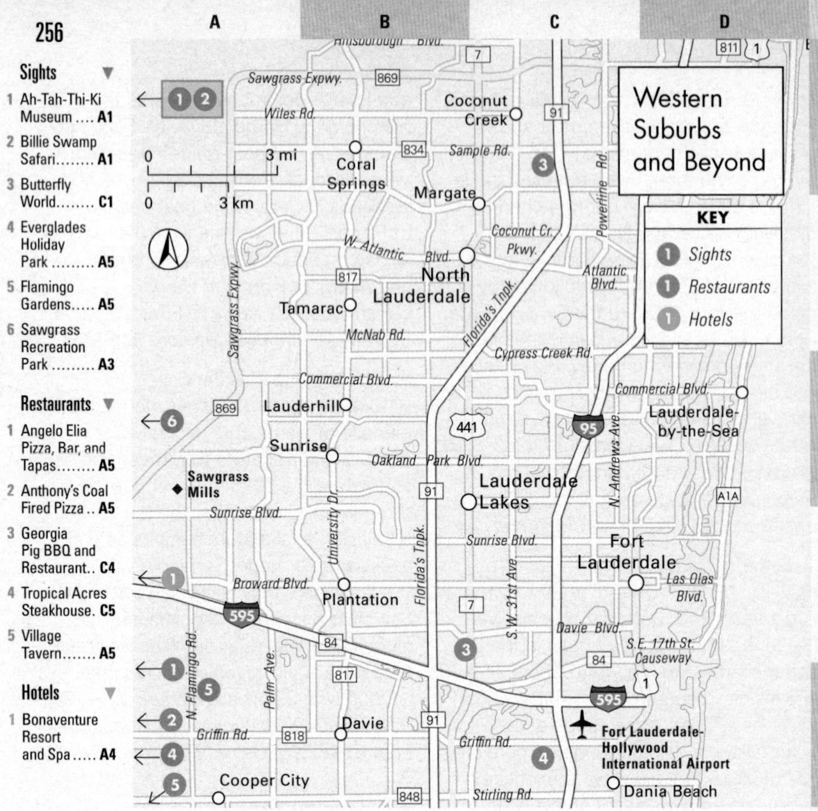

chicken wings, and salads. **Known for:** approachable menu with pizza and Italian favorites; casual, fun atmosphere; coal-fired oven. *Average main: $17 3111 SW 160th Ave., Hollywood 954/392–3811 acfp.com/location/miramar.*

Georgia Pig BBQ and Restaurant

$ | BARBECUE | FAMILY | When heading out to the area's western reaches, this postage-stamp-sized outpost can add down-home zing to your day—if you can find it, that is. Breakfast, which includes sausage gravy and biscuits, is served 7–11 am, but the big attraction is barbecue beef, pork, or chicken, on platters or in sandwiches for lunch and dinner. **Known for:** North Georgia–style barbecue sauce; chopped pork sandwiches; open-pit cooking. *Average main: $12 1285 S State Rd. 7 U.S. 441, just south of Davie Blvd. 954/587–4420 No credit cards Closed Sun.*

Tropical Acres Steakhouse

$$$ | STEAKHOUSE | FAMILY | This old-school, family-owned steak house hasn't changed much since it opened in 1949. Sizzling steaks are served from a fiery grill, and there are dozens of other entrées to choose from, such as Maine lobster, frogs' legs, rack of lamb, and boneless New York strip. **Known for:** nostalgia galore; family-friendly dining; popular happy hour. *Average main: $24 2500 Griffin Rd. 954/989–2500 www.tropicalacres.com Closed Sun. in July–Nov. No lunch.*

★ Village Tavern

$$ | CONTEMPORARY | FAMILY | Village Tavern is truly a neighborhood hub for those who love good food, good wine and cocktails, and great company. The bar scene is always fun, especially on Wine Wednesdays when all the wines (even the premium labels) are $5 per glass. **Known for:** fresh ingredients; busy bar scene; outdoor dining. *Average main: $19 Shops at Pembroke Gardens, 14555 SW 2nd St. 954/874–1001 www.villagetavern.com/locations/pembroke-pines-fl.*

Hotels

Bonaventure Resort and Spa

$ | **RESORT** | **FAMILY** | This suburban enclave targets conventions and business travelers as well as international vacationers who value golf, the Everglades, and shopping over beach proximity. **Pros:** lush landscaping; pampering spa; located near Sawgrass Mills, the outlet shopping mall. **Cons:** dated decor; 30-minute drive from airport; rental car necessary. *Rooms from: $120 250 Racquet Club Rd., Weston 954/228–9030 https://www.bonaventureresortandspa.com The semi-private Bonaventure Country Club is an 18-hole course designed by Joe Lee. 501 rooms No meals.*

Nightlife

Florida's cowboy country, Davie, offers country-western fun out in the 'burbs. In addition, South Florida's Native American tribes have long offered gambling on Indian Territory near Broward's western suburbs. These casinos offer Vegas-style slot machines and even blackjack. Hollywood's Seminole Hard Rock Hotel & Casino offers the most elegant of Broward's casino experiences. *See Nightlife in Hollywood.*

Round Up Nightclub and Restaurant

MUSIC CLUBS | Round Up is South Florida's hot country-music and nightclub venue in the heart of Broward's horse country. In addition to line dancing, the venue offers great libations, dance lessons, large-screen TVs, and theme nights coinciding with drink specials (Whiskey Wednesday, Beer Pong Thursday, Friday Ladies Night, and the like). Open Wedesday through Sunday from 6 pm to 4 am; closed Monday and Tuesday. **■ TIP→ Happy hour is a good bet, from 6 to 9.** *9020 W State Rd. 84, Davie 954/423–1990 www.roundupnightclub.com.*

Shopping

★ Sawgrass Mills

OUTLET/DISCOUNT STORES | **FAMILY** | This alligator-shaped megamall draws millions of shoppers a year to its collection of over 350 outlet stores. Sawgrass Mills also has more than 70 luxury brand outlets, including Burberry, Diane von Furstenberg, GUCCI, Jimmy Choo, Prada, Salvatore Ferragamo Company Store, Tory Burch, and Versace at the Colonnade Outlets at Sawgrass Mills. According to the mall, it's the second-largest attraction in Florida—second only to Walt Disney World. Although this may sound like an an exaggeration, prepare for insane crowds. *12801 W Sunrise Blvd., Sunrise 954/846–2350 https://www.simon.com/mall/sawgrass-mills.*

Activities

BIKING

Among the most popular routes are Route A1A and Bayview Drive, especially in early morning before traffic builds, and a seven-mile bike path that parallels State Road 84 and New River and leads to Markham Park, which has mountain-bike trails. **■ TIP→ Alligator alert: Do not dangle your legs from seawalls.**

AvMed Rides powered by Broward BCycle

BICYCLING | **FAMILY** | The big-city trend of bike sharing is alive and well in Broward County. With over 20 station locations in six cities, from as far south as Hallandale to as far north as Pompano Beach, bikes can be rented for as little as 30 minutes or as long as a week, and can be picked up and dropped off at any and all stations in Broward County. Most stations are found downtown and along the beach. This is an excellent green and health-conscious way to explore Fort Lauderdale. Download the BCycle app for up-to-date station availability. Please note that helmets are not provided at the kiosks. 🌐 *broward.bcycle.com.*

BIRD-WATCHING

Evergreen Cemetery

BIRD WATCHING | FAMILY | North of Fort Lauderdale's 17th Street Causeway sits an unexpected haven for bird-watchers. It's the city's oldest cemetery (established 1910), and the shade from its gumbo-limbo and strangler figs doubles as a place of repose for Bahama mockingbirds and other species flying through Broward. Warblers are big here, and there are occasional sightings of red-eyed vireos, northern water thrushes, and scarlet tanagers across 11 acres on Cliff Lake. ✉ *1300 SE 10th Ave., Intracoastal and Inland* ☎ *954/745–2140* 🌐 *www.fortlauderdale.gov/departments/parks-recreation/cemeteries.*

FISHING

Bahia Mar Yachting Center

BOATING | FAMILY | If you're interested in a saltwater charter, check out the offerings on the A Dock at the marina of the Bahia Mar Fort Lauderdale. Sportfishing and drift fishing bookings can be arranged. Snorkeling and diving outfitter Sea Experience also leaves from here, as does the famous *Jungle Queen* steamboat. In addition, the Water Taxi makes regular stops here. ✉ *801 Seabreeze Blvd., Beachfront* ☎ *954/627–6309* 🌐 *bahiamaryachtingcenter.com.*

RODEOS

Davie Pro Rodeo

RODEO | FAMILY | South Florida has a surprisingly established cowboy scene, concentrated in the western suburb of Davie. And for decades, the Bergeron Rodeo Grounds (also known as the Davie Pro Rodeo Arena) has hosted the area's riders and ropers. Throughout the year, the rodeo hosts national tours and festivals as well as the annual Southeastern Circuit Finals. Check the website for the exact dates of special events. ✉ *Bergeron Rodeo Grounds, 4271 Davie Rd., Davie* ☎ *954/680–8005* 🌐 *davieprorodeo.com.*

SCUBA DIVING AND SNORKELING

Lauderdale Diver

SCUBA DIVING | FAMILY | This dive center facilitates daily trips on a bevy of hardcore dive boats up and down Broward's shoreline (they don't have their own boats, but they work with a handful of preferred outfitters). A variety of snorkeling, reef-diving, and wreck-diving trips are offered as well as scuba-diving lessons. ✉ *1334 SE 17th St., Intracoastal and Inland* ☎ *954/467–2822* 🌐 *lauderdalediver.com.*

★ Sea Experience

SCUBA DIVING | FAMILY | The *Sea Experience I* leaves daily at 10:15 am and 2:15 pm for glass-bottom-boat-and-snorkeling combination trips through offshore reefs. Beginner and advanced scuba-diving experiences are available as well. ✉ *Bahia Mar Fort Lauderdale Beach–A DoubleTree by Hilton Hotel, 801 Seabreeze Blvd., Beachfront* ☎ *954/770–3483* 🌐 *www.seaxp.com.*

TENNIS

Jimmy Evert Tennis Center

LOCAL SPORTS | FAMILY | This grande dame of Fort Lauderdale's public tennis facilities is where legendary champ Chris Evert learned her two-handed backhand under the watchful eye of her now-retired father, Jimmy, the center's tennis pro for 37 years. There are 18 lighted clay courts and three hard courts. ✉ *Holiday Park, 701 NE 12th Ave., Intracoastal and Inland* ☎ *954/828–5378* 🌐 *www.fortlauderdale.gov/departments/parks-recreation/tennis-centers/jimmy-evert-tennis-center* 🎫 *$18 per day for non-residents.*

Lauderdale-by-the-Sea

Lauderdale-by-the-Sea is 5 miles north of Fort Lauderdale.

Just north of Fort Lauderdale proper, the low-rise family resort town of Lauderdale-by-the-Sea boasts shoreline access that's rapidly disappearing in neighboring beach towns. The closest and most convenient of the A1A cities to Fort Lauderdale proper embraces its quaint personality by welcoming guests to a different world, drawing a mix of Europeans and cost-conscious families who are looking for fewer frills and longer stays.

GETTING HERE AND AROUND

Lauderdale-by-the-Sea is just north of Fort Lauderdale. From Interstate 95, exit at Commercial Boulevard and head east past the Intracoastal Waterway. From U.S. 1 (Federal Highway), go east at Commercial Boulevard. If driving north on State Road A1A, simply continue north from Fort Lauderdale Beach.

ESSENTIALS

VISITOR INFORMATION Lauderdale-by-the-Sea Chamber of Commerce. ✉ *4201 N Ocean Dr., Lauderdale-by-the-Sea* ☎ *954/776–1000* 🌐 *www.lbts.com.*

Beaches

★ Lauderdale-by-the-Sea Beach
BEACH—SIGHT | **FAMILY** | Preferred by divers and snorkelers, this laid-back beach is a gateway to magnificent coral reefs. When you're not underwater, look up and you'll likely see a pelican flying by. It's a super-relaxing retreat from the buzz of Fort Lauderdale's busier beaches. That said, the southern part of the beach is crowded near the restaurants at the intersection of A1A and Commercial Boulevard. The no-frills hotels and small inns for families and vacationers visiting for a longer stay are typically filled with Europeans. Look for metered parking around Commercial Boulevard and A1A. **Amenities:** food and drink; lifeguards; parking (fee). **Best for:** family outings; snorkeling; swimming. ✉ *Commercial Blvd. at State Rd. A1A, Lauderdale-by-the-Sea.*

Restaurants

Aruba Beach Café
$$$ | **CARIBBEAN** | **FAMILY** | This casual beachfront eatery is arguably Lauderdale-by-the-Sea's most famous restaurant. Aruba Beach serves Caribbean-American cuisine with standouts like conch chowder and conch fritters. **Known for:** Bimini bread with Aruba glaze; nightly live music; Sunday breakfast buffet. $ *Average main: $22* ✉ *One Commercial Blvd., Lauderdale-by-the-Sea* ☎ *954/776–0001* 🌐 *www.arubabeachcafe.com.*

★ LaSpada's Original Hoagies
$ | **AMERICAN** | **FAMILY** | The crew at this seaside hole-in-the-wall puts on quite a show while assembling their sandwiches—locals rave that this indie chain has the best around. Fill up on the foot-long Monster (ham, turkey, roast beef, and cheese), Mama (turkey and Genoa salami), or hot meatballs marinara. **Known for:** the Monster, a foot-long sandwich with ham, turkey, roast beef, cheese; fresh bread; freshly sliced meats. $ *Average main: $12* ✉ *233 Commercial Blvd., Lauderdale-by-the-Sea* ☎ *954/776–7893* 🌐 *www.laspadashoagies.com*
☞ *There are four additional locations in Broward County.*

Hotels

★ Blue Seas Courtyard
$ | **B&B/INN** | **FAMILY** | Husband-and-wife team Cristie and Marc Furth have run this whimsical Mexican-themed motel in Lauderdale-by-the-Sea since 1971. **Pros:** south-of-the-border vibe; friendly owners; across the street from the beach. **Cons:** no ocean views; old bathtubs in some rooms; small setting. $ *Rooms*

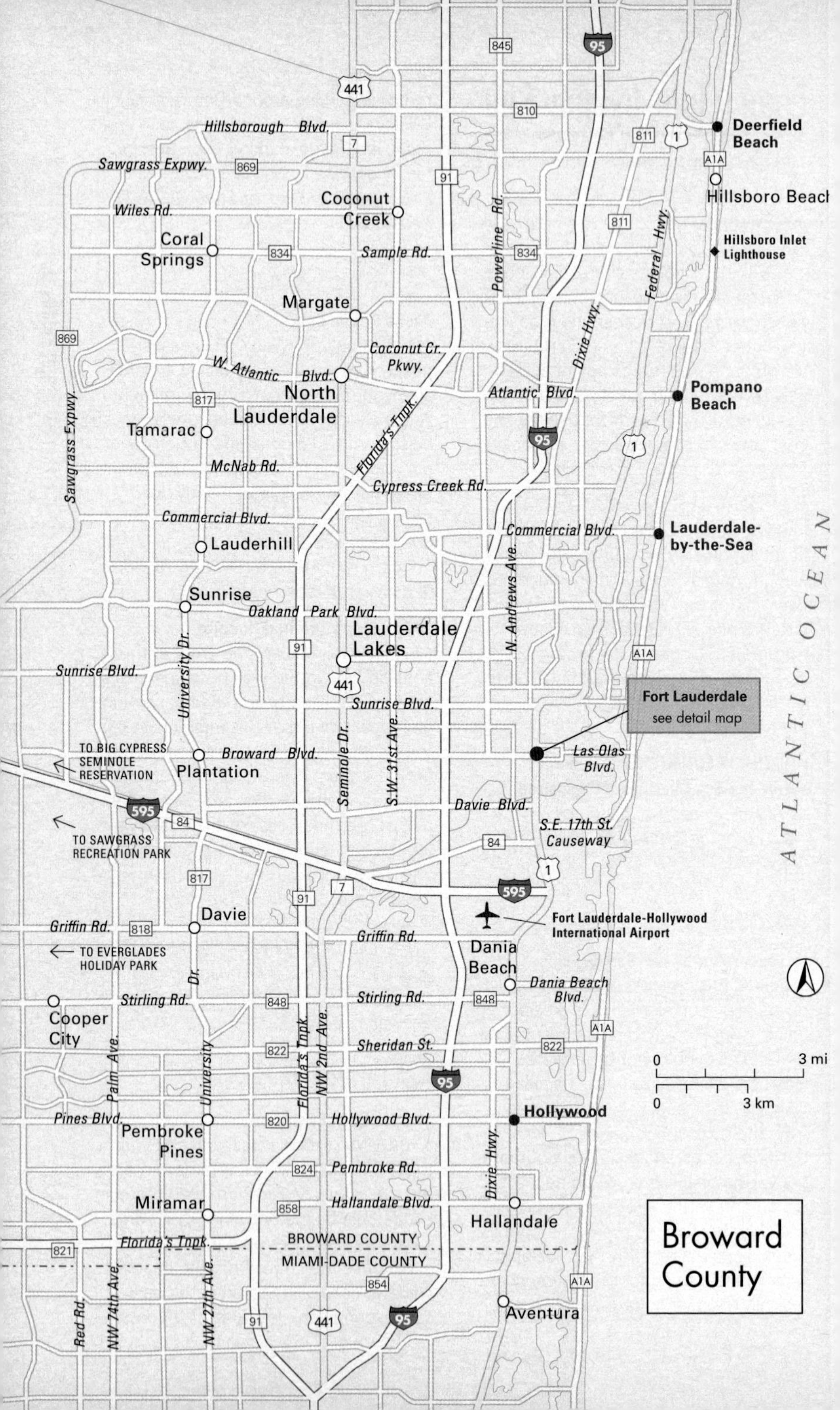

Broward County
Deerfield Beach
Hillsboro Beach
Hillsboro Inlet Lighthouse
Pompano Beach
Lauderdale-by-the-Sea
Fort Lauderdale
see detail map
Fort Lauderdale-Hollywood International Airport
Hollywood
Hallandale
Aventura
Dania Beach
Coconut Creek
Coral Springs
Margate
North Lauderdale
Tamarac
Lauderhill
Sunrise
Lauderdale Lakes
Plantation
Davie
Cooper City
Pembroke Pines
Miramar
ATLANTIC OCEAN
TO BIG CYPRESS SEMINOLE RESERVATION
TO SAWGRASS RECREATION PARK
TO EVERGLADES HOLIDAY PARK
BROWARD COUNTY
MIAMI-DADE COUNTY
Hillsborough Blvd.
Sawgrass Expwy.
Wiles Rd.
Sample Rd.
Coconut Cr. Pkwy.
W. Atlantic Blvd.
Atlantic Blvd.
McNab Rd.
Cypress Creek Rd.
Commercial Blvd.
Oakland Park Blvd.
Sunrise Blvd.
Broward Blvd.
Las Olas Blvd.
Davie Blvd.
S.E. 17th St. Causeway
Griffin Rd.
Stirling Rd.
Dania Beach Blvd.
Sheridan St.
Pines Blvd.
Hollywood Blvd.
Pembroke Rd.
Hallandale Blvd.
Florida's Tnpk.
Powerline Rd.
Dixie Hwy.
Federal Hwy.
N. Andrews Ave.
University Dr.
Seminole Dr.
S.W. 31st Ave.
NW 2nd Ave.
Palm Ave.
Red Rd.
NW 74th Ave.
NW 27th Ave.
0 3 mi
0 3 km

from: $178 ✉ 4525 El Mar Dr., Lauderdale-by-the-Sea ☎ 954/772–3336 🌐 www.blueseascourtyard.com 🛏 12 rooms 🍽 Breakfast.

High Noon Beach Resort

$ | B&B/INN | FAMILY | This highly rated family-run hotel sits on 300 feet of beachy paradise with plenty of cozy spots, two heated pools, and an atmosphere that keeps visitors coming back for more. **Pros:** directly on the beach; free Wi-Fi; great staff. **Cons:** 45-day notice of cancellation; no maid service on Sunday; no guarantee for room type. *$ Rooms from: $190 ✉ 4424 El Mar Dr., Lauderdale-by-the-Sea ☎ 954/776–1121 🌐 www.highnoonresort.com 🛏 41 rooms 🍽 Breakfast.*

Sea Lord Hotel and Suites

$ | B&B/INN | FAMILY | This gem is one of the nicest in Lauderdale-by-the-Sea. Many of the rooms have great ocean views, balconies, and full kitchens. **Pros:** gorgeous beach location; great staff; rooms with balconies and full kitchens. **Cons:** limited parking; aging decor; no fitness center. *$ Rooms from: $190 ✉ 4140 El Mar Dr., Lauderdale-by-the-Sea ☎ 954/776–1505, 800/344–4451 🌐 sealordhotel.com 🛏 47 rooms 🍽 Breakfast.*

Activities

Anglins Fishing Pier

FISHING | FAMILY | A longtime favorite for 24-hour fishing, it's a spot where you may catch snapper, snook, cobia, blue runner, and pompano. It's also the longest pier in South Florida. The on-site bait-and-tackle shop can advise newbies to advanced anglers. *✉ Two Commercial Blvd., Lauderdale-by-the-Sea ☎ 954/924–3613 🌐 www.boatlessfishing.com/anglins.htm.*

Pompano Beach

Pompano Beach is 3 miles north of Lauderdale-by-the-Sea.

The high-rise scene resumes as soon as Route A1A enters this town directly north of Lauderdale-by-the-Sea. Sportfishing is big in Pompano Beach, as its name implies, but there's more to beachside attractions than the popular Fisherman's Wharf. Behind a low coral-rock wall, Alsdorf Park (also called the 14th Street boat ramp) extends north and south of the wharf along the road and beach.

GETTING HERE AND AROUND

From Interstate 95, Pompano Beach exits include Sample Road, Copans Road, and Atlantic Boulevard.

Sights

There aren't many "sights" to see in Pompano Beach, but to the north, Route A1A traverses the so-called Hillsboro Mile (actually more than 2 miles), a millionaire's row featuring some of Broward's most beautiful and expensive homes. The road runs along a narrow strip of land between the Intracoastal Waterway and the Atlantic Ocean, with bougainvillea and oleander edging the way and yachts docked along the banks. Traffic often moves at a snail's pace, especially in winter, as vacationers (and sometimes even envious locals) gawk at the beauty.

Hillsboro Inlet Lighthouse

LIGHTHOUSE | FAMILY | About 2 miles north of Pompano Beach, you'll find a beautiful view across Hillsboro Inlet to a lighthouse, which is often called the brightest lighthouse in the Southeast and used by mariners as a landmark for decades. When at sea you can see its light from almost halfway to the Bahamas. Although the octagonal-pyramid, iron-skeletal tower lighthouse is on private property (inaccessible to the public), it's well worth a peek, even from afar. The Hillsboro Lighthouse Preservation Society offers tours about eight times a year (sometimes on holiday weekends), and these include a boat ride to and from the lighthouse. Visit the society's website for the current schedule and tips on viewing vantage points. Tours cost around $35 per person. ✉ *2801, 907 Hillsboro Mile, Hillsboro Beach* ☎ *954/942–2102* 🌐 *www.hillsborolighthouse.org.*

Restaurants

Cap's Place Island Restaurant
$$$ | SEAFOOD | FAMILY | On an island that was once a bootlegger's haunt, this ramshackle seafood spot reached by launch has served the famous as well as the infamous, including the likes of Winston Churchill, FDR, JFK, and Al Capone. Cap was Captain Theodore Knight, born in 1871, who, with partner-in-crime Al Hasis, floated a derelict barge to the area in the '20s. $ *Average main: $26* ✉ *Cap's Dock/Cap's Place, 2765 NE 28th Ct.* ☎ *954/941–0418* 🌐 *www.capsplace.com* ⏲ *Closed Mon. No lunch.*

Hotels

Cottages by the Ocean
$$ | RENTAL | FAMILY | For families favoring home-style comforts over resort-style bling, Cottages by the Ocean is one of five beach-area properties run by Beach Vacation Rentals. **Pros:** shops within walking distance; no resort fees (though there are cleaning fees); complimentary Wi-Fi. **Cons:** not directly on beach; no pool; slightly dated decor. $ *Rooms from: $214* ✉ *3309 SE Third St.* ☎ *954/283–1111* 🌐 *4rentbythebeach.com/properties/cottages-by-the-ocean* *6 rooms* *No meals.*

Activities

SS Copenhagen Shipwreck
SCUBA DIVING | The wreck of the SS *Copenhagen* lies in 15- to 30-foot depths just outside the second reef on the Pompano Ledge, 3.6 miles south of Hillsboro Inlet. The 325-foot-long steamer's final voyage, from Philadelphia to Havana, began May 20, 1900, ending six days later when the captain—attempting to avoid Gulf currents—crashed into a reef. In 2000, the missing bow section was identified a half mile to the south. The wreck, a haven for colorful fish and corals and a magnet for skin and scuba divers, became Florida's fifth Underwater Archaeological Preserve in 1994 and was listed on the National Register of Historic Places in 2001. Outfitters offer regular trips to the wreck site officially known as the SS Copenhagen State Underwater Archaeological Preserve. ✉ *Pompano Beach* 🌐 *museumsinthesea.com/copenhagen/index.htm.*

Deerfield Beach

Deerfield Beach is 2 miles north of Pompano Beach.

As posh Hillsboro Mile comes to an end, Route A1A spills out into Deerfield Beach, Broward's northernmost oceanside community.

GETTING HERE AND AROUND

From Interstate 95, take the Hillsboro Boulevard exit east. From A1A, continue north past Pompano Beach and Hillsboro Beach.

Sights

Deerfield Island Park
NATURE PRESERVE | FAMILY | You can reach this officially designated Urban Wilderness Area only by boat on the weekends. The coastal hammock island contains a mangrove swamp that provides a critical

habitat for manatees, gopher tortoises, gray foxes, raccoons, and armadillos. County-operated boat shuttles run on the hour from 10 am to 3 pm Saturday and Sunday. The last shuttle departs for the mainland at 4 pm. The ride is five minutes each way. Amenities within the 53.3-acre park include nature trails, a butterfly garden, kayaks and paddleboards, and picnic areas. Pets and fishing are prohibited on the island. ✉ *1720 Deerfield Island Park* ☎ *954/357–5100* 🌐 *www.broward.org/parks/deerfieldislandpark/pages/default.aspx* 🎫 *Free.*

Quiet Waters Park

AMUSEMENT PARK/WATER PARK | FAMILY | Its name belies what's in store for kids here. Splash Adventure is a high-tech water-play system with slides and tunnels, among other activities. There's also cable waterskiing and boat rentals on the lake inside this county park. You'll also find a campground with platform tents and tepees, as well as mountain biking trails and a skate park. Note that this space functions mostly as a public park for locals rather than as a tourist attraction. ✉ *401 S Powerline Rd.* ☎ *954/357–5100* 🌐 *www.broward.org/Parks/QuietWatersPark/Pages/Default.aspx* 🎫 *Park $1.50 weekends, free weekdays.*

Restaurants

★ Charm City Burger Company

$ | DINER | FAMILY | This fun-and-funky grease pit in Deerfield Beach is one of Broward County's favorite dives on the supercheap. Serving up massive beef burgers, chicken burgers, and veggie burgers piled high with unapologetically fattening toppings like candied bacon strips, haystack onion straws, hash browns, and blue cheese spread, this is the true diet Antichrist. $ *Average main: $8* ✉ *1136 E Hillsboro Blvd.* ☎ *954/531–0300* 🌐 *www.charmcityburgerco.com.*

The Whale's Rib Raw Bar

$$ | SEAFOOD | FAMILY | For a casual, almost funky, nautical experience near the beach, look no further than this raw bar featured on *Diners, Drive-Ins, and Dives*. If you want to blend in, order a fish special with whale fries—thinly sliced potatoes that look like hot potato chips. (People come from near and far for these famous fries!) Those with smaller appetites can choose from salads and raw-bar favorites like steamed Ipswich clams. $ *Average main: $19* ✉ *2031 NE Second St.* ☎ *954/421–8880* 🌐 *www.whalesrib.com.*

Hotels

Carriage House Resort Motel

$ | HOTEL | This tidy no-frills motel, accredited as an SSL (Superior Small Lodging), is less than a block from the ocean and comprises a two-story, colonial-style building with a second-story sundeck. **Pros:** friendly staff; bargain rates; complimentary Wi-Fi. **Cons:** nothing fancy; dated decor; road noise. $ *Rooms from: $100* ✉ *250 SE 20th Ave.* ☎ *954/427–7670* 🌐 *www.carriagehouseresort.com* 🛏 *30 rooms* 🍽 *No meals.*

Activities

SCUBA DIVING

Dixie Divers

DIVING/SNORKELING | FAMILY | Dixie Divers is among the area's most popular dive operators, offering daily dive and snorkel trips aboard the 48-foot *Lady-Go-Diver*. Certified divers and snorkelers can explore the marine life of nearby reefs and shipwrecks, including the SS *Copenhagen*. Dixie Divers also offers scuba courses of all levels. ✉ *455 S Federal Hwy.* ☎ *954/420–0009* 🌐 *www.dixiediver.com.*

Hollywood

Hollywood has had several face-lifts to shed its old-school image, but there's still something delightfully retro about the city. New shops, restaurants, and art galleries open at a persistent clip, and the city has continually spiffed up its boardwalk—a wide pedestrian walkway along the beach—where local joggers are as commonplace as sun-seeking snowbirds from the North.

GETTING HERE AND AROUND

From Interstate 95, exit east on Sheridan Street or Hollywood Boulevard for Hollywood, or Hallandale Beach Boulevard for either Hollywood or Hallandale.

ESSENTIALS

VISITOR INFORMATION Hollywood Community Redevelopment Agency. ✉ *1948 Harrison St.* ☎ *954/924–2980* 🌐 *www.hollywoodcra.org.*

Sights

★ Art and Culture Center/Hollywood
ARTS VENUE | FAMILY | The Art and Culture Center, which is southeast of Young Circle, has a great reputation for presenting übercool contemporary art exhibitions and providing the community with educational programming for adults and children. Check online for the latest exhibition schedule. ✉ *1650 Harrison St.* ☎ *954/921–3274* 🌐 *www.artandculturecenter.org* 🎫 *$7.*

ArtsPark at Young Circle
LOCAL INTEREST | FAMILY | In the center of downtown Hollywood, this 10-acre urban park has promenades and green spaces, public art, a huge playground for kids, a state-of-the-art amphitheater, and spaces for educational workshops like weekly glassblowing and jewelry making. There are food trucks and movie nights as well. ✉ *1 N Young Cir.* ☎ *954/921–3500* 🌐 *www.hollywoodfl.org/65/ArtsPark-at-Young-Circle.*

Design Center of the Americas (*DCOTA*)
LOCAL INTEREST | Though access is typically reserved strictly to those in the design biz, the Design Center of the Americas still permits visitors to browse the myriad showrooms, which parade the latest and greatest in home furnishings and interior design. Note, however, that this is purely for inspiration, as direct consumer sales are not permitted. ✉ *1855 Griffin Rd., Dania Beach* ☎ *954/920–7997* 🌐 *www.dcota.com* ⊗ *Closed weekends and major holidays.*

West Lake Park and Anne Kolb Nature Center
COLLEGE | FAMILY | Grab a canoe or kayak, or take a 40-minute guided boat tour at this lakeside park on the Intracoastal Waterway. At 1,500 acres, it's one of Florida's largest urban nature facilities. Extensive boardwalks traverse mangrove wetlands that shelter endangered and threatened species. A 65-foot observation tower showcases the entire park. At the **Anne Kolb Nature Center,** there's a 3,500-gallon aquarium. The center's exhibit hall also has interactive displays explaining the park's delicate ecosystem. ✉ *751 Sheridan St.* ☎ *954/357–5163* 🌐 *www.broward.org/Parks/WestLakePark/Pages/AnneKolbNatureCenter.aspx* 🎫 *Park: weekdays free, weekends and holidays $1.50.*

Beaches

★ Dr. Von D. Mizell-Eula Johnson State Park
BEACH—SIGHT | FAMILY | Formerly known as John U. Lloyd Beach State Park, this 310-acre park was renamed Dr. Von D. Mizell–Eula Johnson State Park in honor of the duo who led efforts to change the "colored beach" into a state park in 1973, creating appropriate access for all residents. Native sea grapes, gumbo-limbo trees, and other native plants offer shade. Nature trails and a marina are large draws; canoeing on Whiskey Creek is also popular. The beaches are

excellent, but beware of mosquitoes in summer. **Amenities:** ample trails; parking (fee); toilets. **Best for:** solitude; sunrise; water sports. ✉ *6503 N Ocean Dr., Dania Beach* ☎ *954/923–2833* 🌐 *www.floridastateparks.org/parks-and-trails/dr-von-d-mizell-eula-johnson-state-park* 🎫 *$6 per vehicle; $4 for lone driver.*

★ **Hollywood Beach and Broadwalk**
BEACH—SIGHT | **FAMILY** | The name might be Hollywood, but there's nothing hip or chic about **Hollywood North Beach Park,** which sits at the north end of Hollywood before the 2½-mile pedestrian Broadwalk begins. And this is a good thing. It's an easygoing place to enjoy the sun, sand, and sea. The year-round **Dog Beach of Hollywood,** between Pershing and Custer streets, allows canine companions to join the fun a few days a week. Walk along the **Broadwalk** for a throwback to the 1950s, with mom-and-pop stores and ice-cream parlors, where elderly couples go for long strolls and families build sand castles. The popular stretch has spiffy features like a pristine pedestrian walkway, a concrete bike path, a crushed-shell jogging path, an 18-inch decorative wall separating the Broadwalk from the sand, and places to shower off after a dip. Expect to hear French spoken throughout Hollywood since its beaches are a getaway for Québécois. **Amenities:** food and drink; lifeguards; parking (fee); showers; toilets. **Best for:** sunrise; swimming; walking. ✉ *101 S Broadwalk* 🌐 *www.hollywoodfl.org/1049/Hollywood-Beach* 🎫 *Parking in public lots: $3/hour weekdays and $4/hour weekends.*

Restaurants

★ **Jaxson's Ice Cream Parlor and Restaurant**
$$ | **AMERICAN** | **FAMILY** | This midcentury landmark whips up malts, shakes, and jumbo sundaes from ice cream that is made on-site daily. Owner Monroe Udell's trademarked Kitchen Sink—a small sink full of ice cream, topped by sparklers—is a real hoot for parties. **Known for:** license-plate decor; homemade ice cream; salads and sandwiches. 💲 *Average main: $15* ✉ *128 S Federal Hwy., Dania Beach* ☎ *954/923–4445* 🌐 *www.jaxsonsicecream.com.*

The LeTub Saloon
$$ | **AMERICAN** | Despite molasses-slow service and an abundance of insects at sundown, this eatery is beloved by locals, and management seemed genuinely appalled when hordes of trend-seeking city slickers started jamming bar stools and tables after *GQ* and Oprah declared its thick, juicy Angus burgers the best around. Once a Sunoco gas station, this quirky waterside saloon has an enduring affection for claw-foot bathtubs; lunch will run you around $16 (burger $12; small fries $3.50). **Known for:** late-night service; vintage setting; great burgers and Key lime pie. 💲 *Average main: $16* ✉ *1100 N Ocean Dr.* ☎ *954/921–9425* 🌐 *www.theletub.com.*

★ **Monkitail**
$$$$ | **JAPANESE** | Philadelphia-based chef and restaurateur Michael Schulson brings contemporary Japanese cuisine to the Diplomat Beach Resort's collection of popular restaurants. At Monkitail, superb ingredients and extremely fresh fish are complemented by the chef's precise techniques. **Known for:** superpremium ingredients; fantastic cocktails; traditional Japanese dishes. 💲 *Average main: $45* ✉ *The Diplomat Beach Resort Hollywood, Curio Collection by Hilton, 3555 S Ocean Dr.* ☎ *954/602–8755* 🌐 *www.monkitail.com* 🕒 *Closed Mon.–Tues.*

Taverna Opa
$$$ | **GREEK** | **FAMILY** | It's a Greek throwdown every night at this Hollywood institution. Expect a lively night of great eats (including authentic hot and cold meze, wood-fire-grilled meats and seafood), table-top dancing, and awkward moments (especially when suburban parents with two left feet decide to get in on the act), and lots of wine to make it

all okay. **Known for:** near Water Taxi stop; celebratory atmosphere; menu of Greek favorites. *Average main: $29* *410 N Ocean Dr.* *954/929–4010* *www.tavernaopa.com/locations/hollywood-fl.*

Hotels

★ The Diplomat Beach Resort

$$$ | RESORT | FAMILY | This colossal 39-story, contemporary, multitower resort property sits on a 50,000-square foot swath of Hollywood Beach's ocean and has a stunning new identity thanks to a $100 million renovation. **Pros:** coastal chic vibe; excellent dining; incredible ocean views. **Cons:** large complex; numerous conventioneers; expensive rates. *Rooms from: $400* *3555 S Ocean Dr.* *954/602–6000* *www.diplomatresort.com* *1,000 rooms* *No meals.*

★ Margaritaville Beach Resort

$$$ | RESORT | FAMILY | The funky boardwalk of Hollywood Beach has a tropical destination inspired by Jimmy Buffett's lifelong search for paradise. **Pros:** oceanfront location; fun water activities; daily live entertainment. **Cons:** the surrounding area isn't very upscale; touristy vibe; must be a Jimmy Buffett fan. *Rooms from: $370* *1111 N Ocean Dr.* *954/874–4444* *www.margaritavillehollywoodbeachresort.com* *349 rooms* *No meals.*

Seminole Hard Rock Hotel & Casino

$$$ | HOTEL | On the industrial flatlands of western Hollywood, the Seminole Hard Rock Hotel & Casino is a magnet for folks looking for Las Vegas–style entertainment (i.e., casinos that never close, clubbing, and hedonism). **Pros:** limitless entertainment; solid bars and restaurants; 24/7 gaming action. **Cons:** in an unsavory neighborhood; construction is under way on new hotel tower; rental car necessary. *Rooms from: $379* *One Seminole Way* *866/502–7529* *www.seminolehardrockhollywood.com* *500 rooms* *No meals.*

Nightlife

★ Seminole Hard Rock Hotel & Casino

CAFES—NIGHTLIFE | Seminole Hard Rock Hotel & Casino is a Vegas-inspired gaming and entertainment complex in a fairly forlorn area of Hollywood. Once inside the Hard Rock fortress, you'll feel the excitement immediately. In addition to the AAA Four Diamond hotel, there's a monster casino, a 5,500-seat performance venue (Hard Rock Event Center), plus dozens of restaurants, bars, and nightclubs. **TIP→ The Seminole Hard Rock Hotel & Casino is not to be confused with its neighbor, the Seminole Classic Casino.** *One Seminole Way* *866/502–7529* *www.seminolehardrockhollywood.com.*

Shopping

★ Shops at Pembroke Gardens

SHOPPING CENTERS/MALLS | FAMILY | The Shops at Pembroke Gardens is an outdoor oasis for consumers looking for a variety of shops, restaurants, salons, and spas. From shops like Ann Taylor and Sephora to local dining options like RA Sushi and Village Tavern, it's a popular hangout among locals and tourists. The wide range of retail options keeps this relatively upscale stretch accessible to shoppers on a budget. A small-scale farmers' market sets up in the center promenade on Sundays. *527 SW 145th Ter., Pembroke Pines* *954/450–1580* *www.pembrokegardens.com.*

Chapter 7

PALM BEACH AND THE TREASURE COAST

Updated by
Sara Liss

Sights	Restaurants	Hotels	Shopping	Nightlife
★★★★☆	★★★★☆	★★★★★	★★★★☆	★★☆☆☆

WELCOME TO PALM BEACH AND THE TREASURE COAST

TOP REASONS TO GO

★ **Exquisite resorts:** Two grandes dames, The Breakers and the Boca Raton Resort & Club, perpetually draw the rich, the famous, and anyone else who can afford the luxury. The Eau Palm Beach and Four Seasons sparkle with service fit for royalty.

★ **Beautiful beaches:** From Jupiter, where dogs run free, to Stuart's tubular waves, to the broad stretches of sand in Delray Beach and Boca Raton, swimmers, surfers, sunbathers—and sea turtles looking for a place to hatch their eggs—all find happiness.

★ **Top-notch golf:** The Champion Course and reenvisioned Fazio Course at PGA National Resort & Spa are world renowned; pros sharpen up at PGA Village.

★ **Horse around:** Wellington, with its popular polo season, is often called the winter equestrian capital of the world.

★ **Excellent fishing:** The Atlantic Ocean, teeming with kingfish, sailfish, and wahoo, is a treasure chest for anglers.

1 **Palm Beach.** Tony beach town with luxury resorts and shopping.

2 **West Palm Beach.** No beach, but a great arts scene.

3 **Lake Worth.** Stop for its charming, artsy center.

4 **Lantana.** Its famous Key Lime House overlooks the water.

5 **Boynton Beach.** A family favorite with access to coral reefs.

6 **Delray Beach.** Its lively downtown is blocks from the ocean.

7 **Boca Raton.** Modern mixes with historic buildings.

8 **Palm Beach Gardens.** Golfers love the PGA National Resort & Spa.

9 **Singer Island.** Easy access to snorkeling at Peanut Island.

10 **Juno Beach.** Famous for its sea turtles.

11 **Jupiter and Vicinity.** Calm respite with rugged coastline.

12 **Stuart and Jensen Beach.** Charming historic district and beach.

13 **Fort Pierce and Port St. Lucie.** Ample fishing and surfing.

14 **Vero Beach.** Cosmopolitan yet understated.

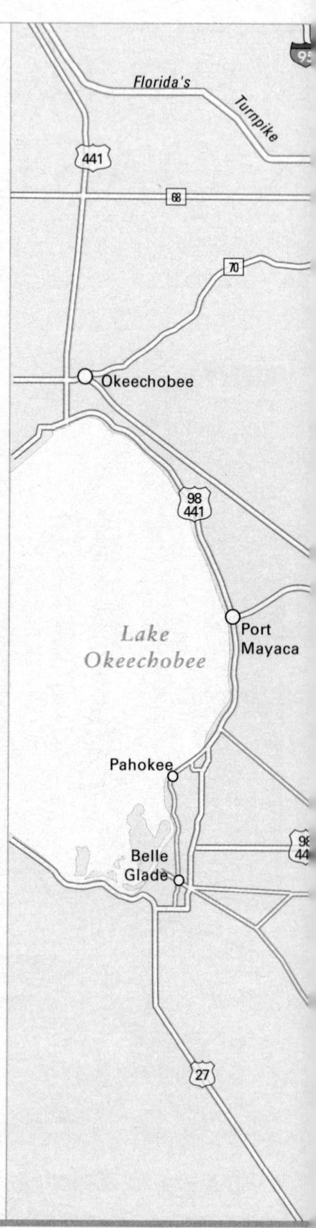

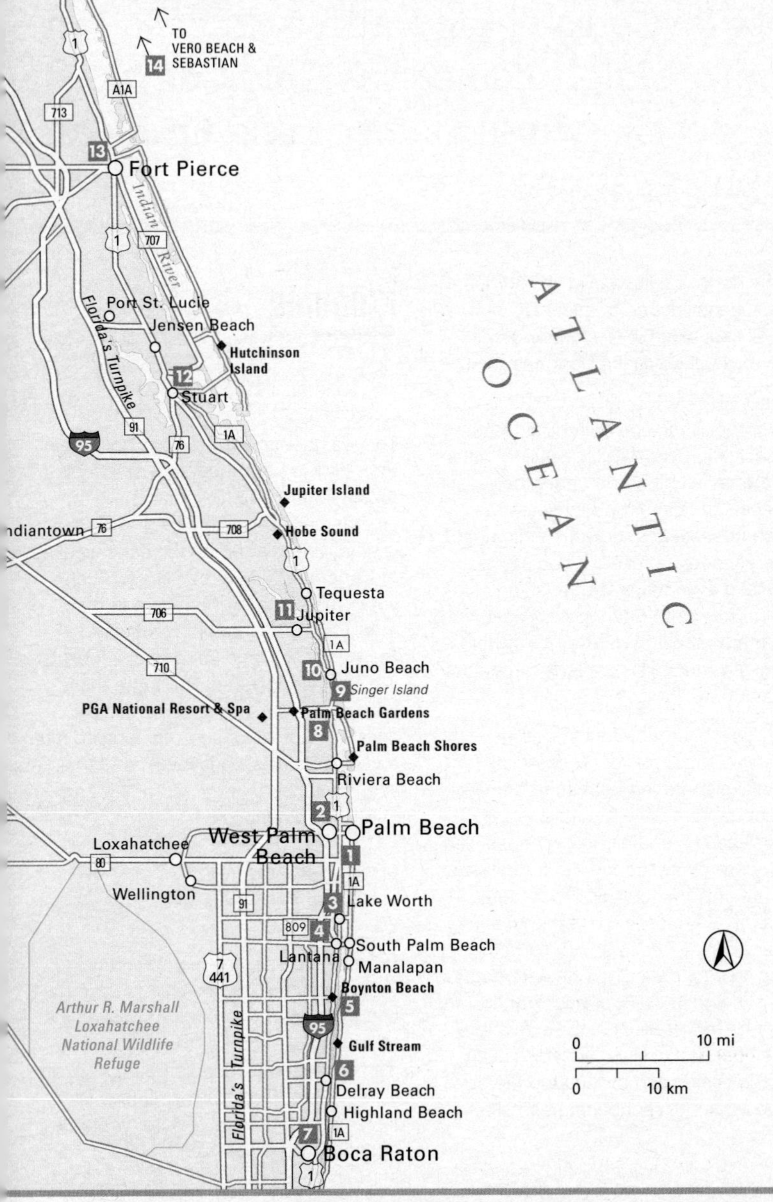
TO
VERO BEACH &
14 SEBASTIAN
A1A
713
1
13
Fort Pierce
Indian River
707
Port St. Lucie
Florida's Turnpike
Jensen Beach
Hutchinson Island
12
Stuart
91
95
76
1A
ATLANTIC OCEAN
Jupiter Island
Indiantown
76
708
Hobe Sound
Tequesta
706
11 Jupiter
1A
710
10 Juno Beach
9 Singer Island
PGA National Resort & Spa
Palm Beach Gardens
8
Palm Beach Shores
Riviera Beach
2
West Palm Beach
Palm Beach
1
Loxahatchee
80
1A
Wellington
91
3 Lake Worth
809
4
South Palm Beach
Lantana
Manalapan
7
441
Boynton Beach
5
Arthur R. Marshall Loxahatchee National Wildlife Refuge
95
Gulf Stream
Florida's Turnpike
6
Delray Beach
Highland Beach
7
1A
Boca Raton
0
10 mi
0
10 km

A golden stretch of the Atlantic shore, the Palm Beach area resists categorization, and for good reason: the territory stretching south to Boca Raton, appropriately coined the Gold Coast, defines old-world glamour and new-age sophistication.

To the north you'll uncover the comparatively undeveloped Treasure Coast—liberally sprinkled with seaside gems and wide-open spaces along the road awaiting your discovery.

Altogether, there's a delightful disparity between Palm Beach, pulsing with old-money wealth, and under-the-radar Hutchinson Island. Seductive as the gorgeous beaches, eclectic dining, and leisurely pursuits can be, you should also take advantage of flourishing commitments to historic preservation and the arts, as town after town yields intriguing museums, galleries, theaters, and gardens.

Palm Beach, proud of its status as America's first luxe resort destination and still glimmering with its trademark Mediterranean-revival mansions, manicured hedges, and highbrow shops, can rule supreme as the focal point for your sojourn any time of year. From there, head off in one of two directions: south toward Delray Beach and Boca Raton along an especially scenic estate-dotted route known as A1A, or back north to the beautiful barrier islands of the Treasure Coast. For rustic inland activities such as bass fishing and biking atop the dike around Lake Okeechobee, head west.

Planning

When to Go

The weather is optimal from November through May, but the trade-off is that roads, hotels, and restaurants are more crowded and prices higher. If the scene is what you're after, try the early weeks of December when the "season" isn't yet in full swing. But be warned that after Easter, the crowd relocates to the Hamptons, and Palm Beach feels like another universe. For some that's a blessing—and a great time to take advantage of lower summer lodging rates and dining deals—but you'll need to bring your tolerance for heat, humidity, and afternoon downpours.

Getting Here and Around

AIR TRAVEL

Palm Beach International Airport is in West Palm, but it's possible (and sometimes cheaper) to fly to Fort Lauderdale, Miami, or Orlando. Do rent a car if you plan on exploring. Scenic Route A1A, also called Ocean Boulevard or Ocean Drive, depending on where you are, ventures out onto the barrier islands. Interstate 95 runs parallel to U.S. 1, a main north–south thoroughfare in the region (also known as Federal Highway), but a few miles inland.

BUS TRAVEL

The county's bus service, Palm Tran, runs two routes (Nos. 44 and 40) that offer daily service connecting the airport, the Tri-Rail stop near it, and locations in central West Palm Beach. A network of 34 routes joins towns all across the area; it's $5 for a day pass. The free Downtown Trolley connects the West Palm Beach Amtrak station and the Tri-Rail stop in West Palm on its Green Line. Its Yellow Line makes continuous loops down Clematis Street, the city's main stretch of restaurants and watering holes interspersed with stores, and through City-Place, a shopping-dining-theater district, and to the Kravis Center. Hop on and off at any of the stops. The trolley's Yellow Line runs Sunday to Wednesday 11–9 and Thursday to Saturday 11–11. The trolley's Green Line, which stretches farther east, west, and south, and connects to Tri-Rail and Amtrak, runs weekdays 7–7, Saturday 9–7, and Sunday 11–7. A Blue Line, operating year-round, runs from downtown West Palm Beach to Northwood Village and the Palm Beach Outlets mall. Times are Thursday–Saturday, 11–10.

TAXI TRAVEL

Several taxi companies serve the area, including the Southeastern Florida Transportation Group. Also available are limousine services to Palm Beach or out of county. The ride-sharing services Uber (🌐 *www.uber.com*) and Lyft (🌐 *www.lyft.com*) are accessible as apps from your phone.

TRAIN TRAVEL

Amtrak stops daily in West Palm Beach. The station is at the same location as the Tri-Rail stop, so the same free shuttle, the Downtown Trolley, is available (via the trolley's Green Line).

Tri-Rail Commuter Service is a rail system with 18 stops altogether between West Palm Beach and Miami; tickets can be purchased at each stop, and a one-way trip from the first to the last point is $6.90 weekdays, $5 weekends. Three stations—West Palm Beach, Lake Worth, and Boca—have free shuttles to their downtowns, and taxis are on call at others.

A new high-speed train line, Virgin Trains USA (formerly called Brightline) began running in summer 2018. It connects downtown Miami to Fort Lauderdale and West Palm Beach in 30 and 60 minutes respectively.

Hotels

Palm Beach has a number of smaller hotels in addition to the famous Breakers. Lower-priced hotels and bed-and-breakfasts can be found in West Palm Beach, Palm Beach Gardens, and Lake Worth. Heading south, the ocean-side town of Manalapan has the Eau Palm Beach Resort & Spa. The Seagate Hotel & Spa sparkles in Delray Beach, and the posh Boca Beach Club lines the superlative swath of shoreline in Boca Raton. In the opposite direction there's the PGA National Resort & Spa, and on the opposite side of town on the ocean is the Marriott on Singer Island, a well-kept secret for spacious, sleek suites. Even farther north, Vero Beach has a collection of luxury boutique hotels, as well as more modest options along the Treasure Coast. To the west, towns close to Lake Okeechobee offer country-inn accommodations geared to bass-fishing pros.

Restaurants

Numerous elegant establishments offer upscale American, Continental, and international cuisine, but the area also is chock-full of casual waterfront spots serving affordable burgers and fresh seafood feasts. Snapper and grouper are especially popular here, along with the ubiquitous shrimp. Happy hours and early-bird menus, Florida hallmarks, typically entice the budget-minded with several dinner entrées at reduced prices offered during certain hours, usually before 5 or 6.

Hotel and restaurant reviews have been shortened. For full information, visit Fodors.com.

What It Costs

$	$$	$$$	$$$$
RESTAURANTS			
under $15	$15–$20	$21–$30	over $30
HOTELS			
under $200	$200–$300	$301–$400	over $400

Visitor Information

CONTACTS Discover the Palm Beaches. ✉ *1555 Palm Beach Lakes Blvd., Suite 800, West Palm Beach* ☎ *800/554–7256* 🌐 *www.thepalmbeaches.com.*

Palm Beach

70 miles north of Miami, off I–95.

Long reigning as the place where the crème de la crème go to shake off winter's chill, Palm Beach continues to be a seasonal hotbed of platinum-grade consumption. It's been the winter address for heirs of the iconic Rockefeller, Vanderbilt, Colgate, Post, Kellogg, and Kennedy families. Strict laws govern everything from building to landscaping, and not so much as a pool awning gets added without a town council nod. Only three bridges allow entry, and huge tour buses are a no-no.

All this fabled atmosphere started with Henry Morrison Flagler, Florida's premier developer, and cofounder, along with John D. Rockefeller, of Standard Oil. No sooner did Flagler bring the railroad to Florida in the 1890s than he erected the famed Royal Poinciana and Breakers hotels. Rail access sent real-estate prices soaring, and ever since, princely sums have been forked over for personal stationery engraved with 33480, the zip code of Palm Beach (which didn't actually get its status as an independent municipality until 1911). Setting the tone in this town of unparalleled Florida opulence is the ornate architectural work of Addison Mizner, who began designing homes and public buildings here in the 1920s and whose Moorish-Gothic Mediterranean-revival style has influenced virtually all landmarks.

GETTING HERE AND AROUND

Palm Beach is 70 miles north of Miami (a 90-minute trip with traffic). To access Palm Beach off Interstate 95, exit east at Southern Boulevard, Belvedere Road, or Okeechobee Boulevard. To drive from Palm Beach to Lake Worth, Lantana, Manalapan, and Boynton Beach, head south on Ocean Boulevard/Route A1A; Lake Worth is roughly 6 miles south, and Boynton is another 6. Similarly, to reach them from West Palm Beach, take U.S. 1 or Interstate 95. To travel between Palm Beach and Singer Island, you must cross over to West Palm before returning to the beach. Once there, go north on U.S. 1 and then cut over on Blue Heron Boulevard/Route 708. If coming straight from the airport or somewhere farther west, take Interstate 95 up to the same exit and proceed east. The main drag in Palm Beach Gardens is PGA Boulevard/Route 786, which is 4 miles north on U.S. 1 and Interstate 95; A1A merges with it as it exits the top part of Singer Island. Continue on A1A to reach Juno Beach and Jupiter.

Draped in European elegance, The Breakers in Palm Beach sits on 140 acres along the oceanfront.

Sights

Most streets around major attractions and commercial zones have free parking as well as metered spaces. If you can stake out a place between a Rolls-Royce and a Bentley, do so, but beware of the "Parking by Permit Only" signs, as a $50 ticket might take the shine off your spot. Better yet, if you plan to spend an entire afternoon strolling Worth Avenue, park in the Apollo lot behind Tiffany's midway off Worth on Hibiscus; some stores will validate your parking ticket.

Bethesda-by-the-Sea

HISTORIC SITE | This Gothic-style Episcopal church had a claim to fame upon its creation in 1926: it was built by the first Protestant congregation in southeast Florida. Church lecture tours, covering Bethesda's history, architecture, and more, are offered at 12:15 on the second and fourth Sunday each month from September to mid-May (excluding December) and at 11:15 on the fourth Sunday each month from end of May to August. Also notable are the annual Boar's Head and Yule Log festivals in January. Adjacent is the formal, ornamental Cluett Memorial Garden. ✉ *141 S. County Rd.* ☎ *561/655–4554* 🌐 *www.bbts.org* 🎫 *Free.*

★ The Breakers

HISTORIC SITE | Built by Henry Flagler in 1896 and rebuilt by his descendants after a 1925 fire, this magnificent Italian Renaissance–style resort helped launch Florida tourism with its Gilded Age opulence, attracting influential wealthy Northerners to the state. The hotel, still owned by Flagler's heirs, is a must-see even if you aren't staying here. Walk through the 200-foot-long lobby, which has soaring arched ceilings painted by 72 Italian artisans and hung with crystal chandeliers. Meet for a drink and a round of eclectic small plates at the HMF, one of the most beautiful bars in the state. **■ TIP→ Book a pampering spa treatment or dine at the popular oceanfront Seafood Bar that was renovated in 2016. The $30 parking fee is waived if you spend at least $30 anywhere in the hotel (just have your ticket**

validated). ✉ *1 S. County Rd.* ☎ *561/655–6611* 🌐 *www.thebreakers.com.*

El Solano

HOUSE | No Palm Beach mansion better represents the town's luminous legacy than the Spanish-style home built by Addison Mizner as his own residence in 1925. Mizner later sold El Solano to Harold Vanderbilt, and the property was long a favorite among socialites for parties and photo shoots. Vanderbilt held many a gala fund-raiser here. Beatle John Lennon and his wife, Yoko Ono, bought it less than a year before Lennon's death. It's still privately owned and not open to the public, but it's well worth a drive-by on any self-guided Palm Beach mansion tour. ✉ *720 S. Ocean Blvd.*

★ Henry Morrison Flagler Museum

HOUSE | The worldly sophistication of Florida's Gilded Age lives on at Whitehall, the plush 55-room "marble palace" Henry Flagler commissioned in 1901 for his third wife, Mary Lily Kenan. Architects John Carrère and Thomas Hastings were instructed to create the finest home imaginable—and they outdid themselves. Whitehall rivals the grandeur of European palaces and has an entrance hall with a baroque ceiling similar to Louis XIV's Versailles. Here you'll see original furnishings; a hidden staircase Flagler used to sneak from his bedroom to the billiards room; an art collection; a 1,200-pipe organ; and Florida East Coast Railway exhibits, along with Flagler's personal railcar, No. 91, showcased in an 8,000-square-foot Beaux Arts–style pavilion behind the mansion. Docent-led tours and audio tours are included with admission. The museum's Café des Beaux-Arts, open from Thanksgiving through mid-April, offers a Gilded Age–style early afternoon tea for $40 (11:30 am–2:30 pm); the price includes museum admission. ✉ *1 Whitehall Way* ☎ *561/655–2833* 🌐 *www.flaglermuseum.us* 🎫 *$18.*

Mar-a-Lago

HISTORIC SITE | Breakfast-food heiress Marjorie Merriweather Post commissioned a Hollywood set designer to create Ocean Boulevard's famed Mar-a-Lago, a 114-room, 110,000-square-foot Mediterranean-revival palace. Its 75-foot Italianate tower is visible from many areas of Palm Beach and from across the Intracoastal Waterway in West Palm Beach. Its notable owner, President Donald Trump, has turned it into a private membership club and has realized Marjorie Post's dream of turning the estate into a presidential retreat. Tourists have to enjoy the view from the car window or bicycle seat, but even the gates are impressive. ✉ *1100 S. Ocean Blvd.* ☎ *561/832–2600* 🌐 *www.maralagoclub.com.*

Society of the Four Arts

ARTS VENUE | **FAMILY** | Despite widespread misconceptions of its members-only exclusivity, this privately endowed institution—founded in 1936 to encourage appreciation of art, music, drama, and literature—is funded for public enjoyment. The Esther B. O'Keeffe gallery building artfully melds an exhibition hall that houses traveling exhibits with a 700-seat theater. A library designed by prominent Mizner-peer Maurice Fatio, a children's library, a botanical garden, and the Philip Hulitar Sculpture Garden round out the facilities and are open daily. A complete schedule of programming is available on the society's website. ✉ *2 Four Arts Plaza* ☎ *561/655–7227* 🌐 *www.fourarts.org* 🎫 *$5 gallery; special program costs vary.*

★ Worth Avenue

HISTORIC SITE | Called the Avenue by Palm Beachers, this half-mile-long street is synonymous with exclusive shopping. Nostalgia lovers recall an era when faces or names served as charge cards, purchases were delivered home before customers returned from lunch, and bills were sent directly to private accountants. Times have changed, but a stroll amid the Spanish-accented buildings, many designed by Addison Mizner, offers a tantalizing taste of the island's ongoing commitment to elegant consumerism. Explore the labyrinth of nine pedestrian "vias" off each side that wind past boutiques, tiny plazas, bubbling fountains, and bougainvillea-festooned balconies; this is where the smaller, unique shops are. The Worth Avenue Association holds historic walking tours on Wednesdays at 11 am during "the season" (December through April). The $10 fee benefits local nonprofit organizations. ✉ *Worth Ave.* ⊕ *Between Cocoanut Row and S. Ocean Blvd.* ☎ *561/659–6909* 🌐 *www.worth-avenue.com.*

Beaches

Phipps Ocean Park

BEACH—SIGHT | About 2 miles south of "Billionaire's Row" on Ocean Boulevard sits this public ocean-side park, with two metered parking lots separated by a fire station. There are four entry points to the beach, but the north side is better for beachgoers. At the southern entrance, there is a six-court tennis facility. The beach is narrow and has natural rock formations dotting the shoreline, making it ideal for snorkelers. There are picnic tables and grills on-site, as well as the Little Red Schoolhouse, an 1886 landmark that hosts educational workshops for local kids. If a long walk floats your boat, venture north to see the mega-mansions, but don't go too far inland, because private property starts at the high-tide line. Parking is metered, and time limits strictly enforced. There's a two-hour time limit for free parking—but read the meter carefully: it's valid only during certain hours at some spots. **Amenities:** lifeguards; parking (no fee); showers; toilets. **Best for:** solitude; walking. ✉ *2201 S. Ocean Blvd.* ☎ *561/227–6450 Ext. 8, 561/227–6450 tennis reservations* 🌐 *wpbparks.com/beaches/phipps-ocean-park-and-beach* 🎫 *Free.*

Town of Palm Beach Municipal Beach

BEACH—SIGHT | You know you're here if you see Palm Beach's younger generation frolicking on the sands and locals setting up chairs as the sun reflects off their gleaming white veneers. The Worth Avenue clock tower is within sight, but the gateways to the sand are actually on Chilean Avenue, Brazilian Avenue, and Gulfstream Road. It's definitely the most central and longest lifeguarded strip open to everyone and a popular choice for hotel guests from the Colony, Chesterfield, and Brazilian Court. Lifeguards are present from Brazilian Avenue down to Chilean Avenue. It's also BYOC (bring your own chair). You'll find no water-sports or food vendors here; however, casual eateries are a quick walk away. Metered spots line A1A. **Amenities:** lifeguards; showers. **Best for:** sunset; swimming. ✉ *S. Ocean Blvd.* ⊕ *From Brazilian Ave. to Gulfstream Rd.* ☎ *561/838–5483 beach patrol* 🌐 *www.thepalmbeaches.com/central-region/town-palm-beach-municipal-beach.*

Restaurants

Bice Ristorante

$$$$ | **ITALIAN** | The bougainvillea-laden trellises set the scene at the main entrance on Peruvian Way, off posh Worth Avenue. Even though it's a chain, this is a favorite of Palm Beach society, and both the restaurant and the bar become packed and noisy during high season. **Known for:** seafood risotto; homemade pizzaccia bread with basil, chives, and oregano; outdoor dining where you can watch the scene on Worth Avenue. $ *Average main: $35* ✉ *313½ Worth Ave.* ⊕ *Entrance is on Peruvian Ave.* ☎ *561/835–1600* 🌐 *www.palmbeach.bicegroup.com.*

Bistro Chez Jean-Pierre

$$$$ | **FRENCH** | With walls adorned by avant-garde contemporary art, this family-run bistro is where the Palm Beach old guard likes to let down its hair, all the

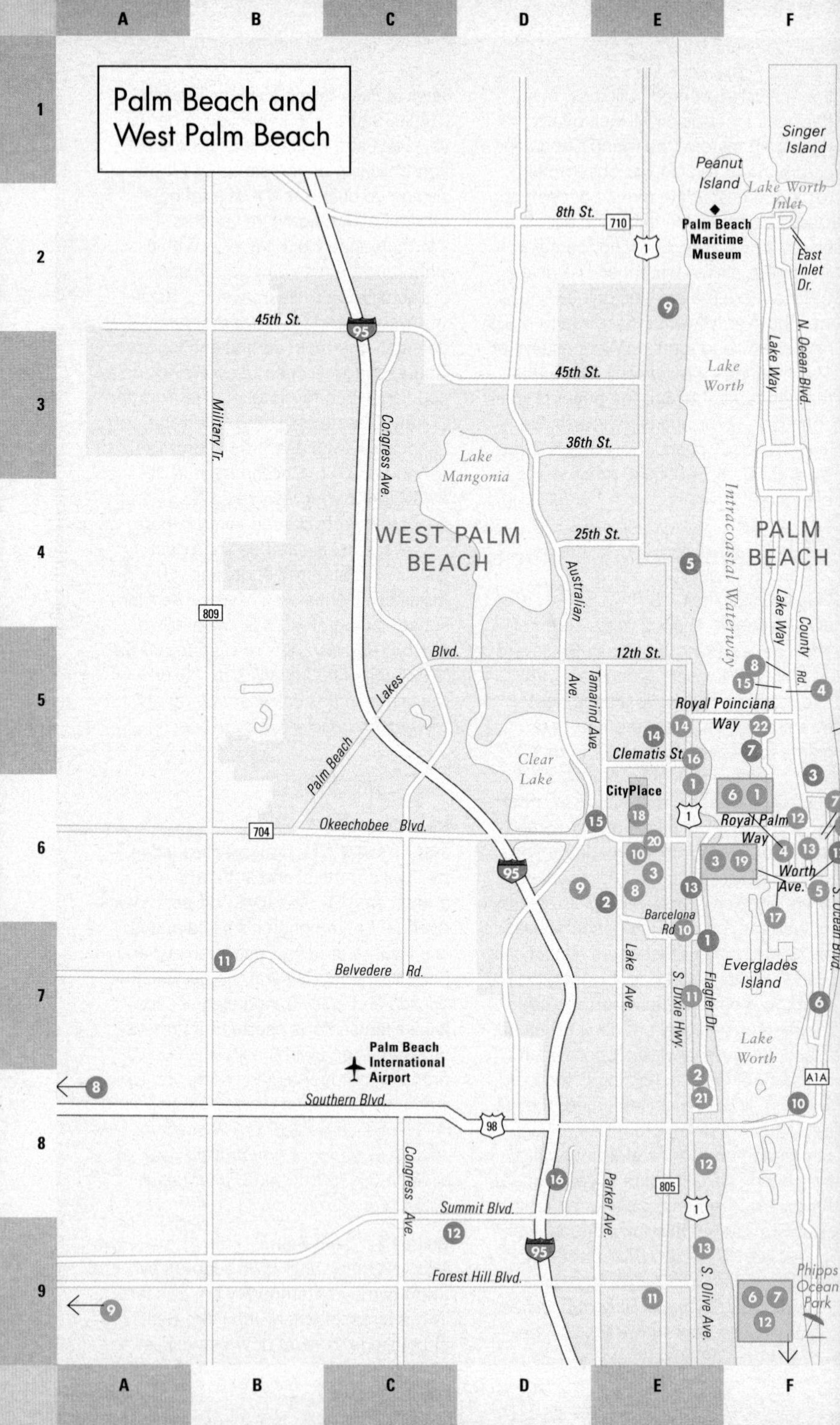
Palm Beach and West Palm Beach
Singer Island
Peanut Island
Lake Worth Inlet
Palm Beach Maritime Museum
East Inlet Dr.
8th St.
45th St.
36th St.
25th St.
12th St.
Lake Worth
Lake Way
N. Ocean Blvd.
Military Tr.
Congress Ave.
Lake Mangonia
WEST PALM BEACH
PALM BEACH
Intracoastal Waterway
Australian Ave.
County Rd.
Lakes Blvd.
Palm Beach
Tamarind Ave.
Royal Poinciana Way
Clematis St.
Clear Lake
CityPlace
Okeechobee Blvd.
Royal Palm Way
Worth Ave.
S. Ocean Blvd.
Barcelona Rd.
Lake Ave.
S. Dixie Hwy.
Flagler Dr.
Everglades Island
Belvedere Rd.
Palm Beach International Airport
Southern Blvd.
Congress Ave.
Parker Ave.
Summit Blvd.
Forest Hill Blvd.
S. Olive Ave.
Phipps Ocean Park
A B C D E F
1 2 3 4 5 6 7 8 9

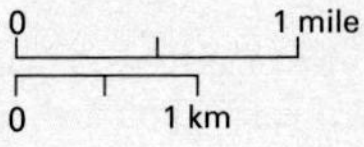

ATLANTIC OCEAN

Sights

1 Ann Norton Sculpture Gardens ... E7
2 Armory Art Center ... E6
3 Bethesda-by-the-Sea ... F6
4 The Breakers ... F5
5 Currie Park ... E4
6 El Solano ... F7
7 Henry Morrison Flagler Museum ... F5
8 Lion Country Safari ... A8
9 Manatee Lagoon ... E2
10 Mar-a-Lago ... F8
11 Mounts Botanical Garden ... B7
12 National Croquet Center ... C9
13 Norton Museum of Art ... E6
14 Richard and Pat Johnson Palm Beach County History Museum ... E5
15 Society of the Four Arts ... D6
16 South Florida Science Center and Aquarium ... D8
17 Worth Avenue ... F6

Restaurants

1 Avocado Grill ... E6
2 Belle and Maxwell's ... E8
3 Bice Ristorante ... F6
4 Bistro Chez Jean-Pierre ... F5
5 bûccan ... F6
6 Café Boulud ... F6
7 Café L'Europe ... F6
8 Echo ... F5
9 Grandview Public Market ... D6
10 Grato ... E6
11 Havana ... E9
12 Howley's ... E8
13 Marcello's La Sirena ... E9
14 Mediterranean Market & Deli ... E5
15 PB Catch ... F5
16 Pistache French Bistro ... E5
17 Pizza Al Fresco ... F6
18 The Regional Kitchen & Public House ... E6
19 Renato's ... F6
20 RH Rooftop Restaurant ... E6
21 Rhythm Cafe ... E8
22 Sant Ambroeus ... F5

Hotels

1 The Brazilian Court Hotel ... F6
2 The Breakers Palm Beach ... F5
3 Casa Grandview West Palm Beach ... E6
4 The Chesterfield Palm Beach ... F6
5 The Colony ... F6
6 Eau Palm Beach ... F9
7 Four Seasons Resort Palm Beach ... F9
8 Grandview Gardens Bed & Breakfast ... E6
9 Hampton Inn & Suites Wellington ... A9
10 Hilton West Palm Beach ... E6
11 Hotel Biba ... E7
12 The Tideline Resort & Spa ... F9

KEY
1 *Sights*
1 *Restaurants*
1 *Hotels*

4 2

The Mansions of Palm Beach

Whether you aspire to be a former president (Kennedy), a current one (Trump), or a rock legend (John Lennon, Rod Stewart, Jimmy Buffett—all onetime or current Palm Beach residents)—no trip to the island is complete without gawking at the megamansions lining its perfectly manicured streets.

No one is more associated with how the island took shape than Addison Mizner, architect extraordinaire and society darling of the 1920s. But what people may not know is that a "fab four" was really the force behind the residential streets as they appear today: Mizner, of course, plus Maurice Fatio, Marion Sims Wyeth, and John Volk.

The four architects dabbled in different genres, some more so than others, but the unmissable style is Mediterranean revival, a Palm Beach hallmark mix of stucco walls, Spanish red-tile roofs, Italianate towers, Moorish-Gothic carvings, and the uniquely Floridian use of coquina, a grayish porous limestone made of coral rock with fossil-like imprints of shells. As for Mizner himself, he had quite the repertoire of signature elements, including using differently sized and shaped windows on one facade, blue tile work inside and out, and tiered roof lines (instead of one straight-sloping panel across, having several sections overlap like scales on a fish).

The majority of preserved estates are clustered in three sections: along Worth Avenue; the few blocks of South County Road after crossing Worth and the streets shooting off it; and the 5-mile stretch of South Ocean Boulevard from Barton Avenue to near Phipps Ocean Park, where the condos begin cropping up.

If 10 miles of riding on a bike while cars zip around you isn't intimidating, the two-wheeled trip may be the best way to fully take in the beauty of the mansions and surrounding scenery. Many hotels have bicycles for guest use. Another option is the dependable Palm Beach Bicycle Trail Shop (☎ *561/659–4583* 🌐 *www.palmbeachbicycle.com*). Otherwise, driving is a good alternative. Just be mindful that Ocean Boulevard is a one-lane road and the only route on the island to cities like Lake Worth and Manalapan, so you can't go too slowly, especially at peak travel times.

If gossip is more your speed, in-the-know concierges rely on Leslie Diver's Island Living Tours (☎ *561/868–7944* 🌐 *www.islandlivingpb.com*); she's one of the town's leading experts on architecture *and* dish, both past and present.

Top 10 Self-Guided Stops: (1) Casa de Leoni (✉ *450 Worth Ave.*, Addison Mizner); (2) Villa des Cygnes (✉ *456 Worth Ave.*, Addison Mizner and Marion Sims Wyeth); (3) Horgacito (✉ *17 Golfview Road*, Marion Sims Wyeth); (4) (✉ *220 and 252 El Bravo Way*, John Volk); (5) (✉ *126 South Ocean Boulevard*, Marion Sims Wyeth); (6) El Solano (✉ *720 S. Ocean Blvd.*, Addison Mizner); (7) Casa Nana (✉ *780 S. Ocean Blvd.*, Addison Mizner); (8) ✉ *920 and 930 South Ocean Boulevard*, Maurice Fatio); (9) Mar-a-Lago (✉ *1100 S. Ocean Blvd.*, Joseph Urban); (10) Il Palmetto (✉ *1500 S. Ocean Blvd.*, Maurice Fatio).

—Dorothea Hunter Sönne

while partaking of sumptuous northern French cuisine along with an impressive wine selection. Forget calorie or cholesterol concerns, and indulge in scrambled eggs with caviar or house-made foie gras, or the best-selling Dover sole. **Known for:** Dover sole; foie gras prepared in-house; dessert soufflés. *Average main: $39 ✉ 132 N. County Rd. ☎ 561/833–1171 🌐 www.chezjean-pierre.com ⏲ Closed on Mon. from May–Nov. Closed Sun. No lunch.*

★ bûccan

$$$$ | ECLECTIC | An antidote to the sometimes stuffy and "jackets-encouraged" atmosphere of most restaurants on the island, chef-owner Clay Conley's ode to ecelectic American cuisine neatly straddles the line between fine dining and exciting gastropub. The restaurant attracts both old money and the younger set, with a buzzing bar-and-lounge scene and an open kitchen showcasing the culinary acrobatics on display. **Known for:** small sharing plates; hamachi tiradito; short rib empanadas. *Average main: $32 ✉ 350 S. County Rd. ☎ 561/833–3450 🌐 www.buccanpalmbeach.com ⏲ No lunch.*

★ Café Boulud

$$$$ | FRENCH | Palm Beach socialites just can't get enough of this prized restaurant by celebrated chef Daniel Boulud. This posh, French-American venue in the Brazilian Court hotel is casual yet elegant with a large and inviting bar that hosts a daily happy hour and a plush dining room that features a seashell-clad ceiling. **Known for:** house-cured charcuterie; Dover sole; an extensive wine list. *Average main: $38 ✉ The Brazilian Court Hotel & Beach Club, 301 Australian Ave. ☎ 561/655–6060 🌐 www.cafeboulud.com.*

Café L'Europe

$$$$ | INTERNATIONAL | Since 1980, the favorite spot of society's movers and shakers—and a few celebs—has remained a regular stop on foodie itineraries. Service and consistency are big reasons for its longevity. **Known for:** veal chops; romantic setting; champagne-and-caviar bar with extensive selections. *Average main: $47 ✉ 331 S. County Rd. ☎ 561/655–4020 🌐 www.cafeleurope.com ⏲ Closed Mon.*

Echo

$$$ | ASIAN | Palm Beach's window on Asia has a sleek sushi bar and floor-to-ceiling glass doors separating the interior from the popular terrace dining area. Chinese, Japanese, Thai, and Vietnamese selections are neatly categorized: Wind (small plates starting your journey), Water (seafood mains), Fire (open-flame wok creations), Earth (meat dishes), and Flavor (desserts, sweets). **Known for:** sushi and specialty rolls; fresh seafood; cocktails in the Dragonfly Lounge. *Average main: $30 ✉ 230-A Sunrise Ave. ☎ 561/802–4222 🌐 www.thebreakers.com/dining/echo ⏲ No lunch.*

PB Catch

$$$$ | SEAFOOD | As the name implies, it's all about fins and shells here, including the live ones that entertain diners in their tanks in the modern dining room. The menu includes a raw bar with a good selection of raw (or grilled) oysters, clams, and the chef's "seacuterie" platter, a build-your-own sampler of such choices as salmon pastrami, citrus-cured fluke, cured sea bass, or octopus torchon. **Known for:** in-house cured fish; shellfish tower from the raw bar; craft cocktails. *Average main: $35 ✉ 251 Sunrise Blvd. ☎ 561/655–5558 🌐 www.pbcatch.com.*

Pizza Al Fresco

$$ | PIZZA | The hidden-garden setting is the secret to the success of this European-style pizzeria, where you can dine under a canopy of century-old banyans in an intimate courtyard. Specialties are 12-inch hand-tossed brick-oven pizzas with such interesting toppings as prosciutto, arugula, and caviar. **Known for:** caviar-and-smoked-salmon pizza;

fresh salads; garden setting. $ *Average main: $19* ✉ *14 Via Mizner, at Worth Ave.* ✣ *Tucked in a courtyard off Worth Ave.* ☎ *561/832–0032* 🌐 *www.pizzaalfresco.com.*

Renato's

$$$$ | **ITALIAN** | Here, at one of the most romantic restaurants in Palm Beach, guests can dine Italiano. Sit in the beautiful courtyard, with stars above and twinkling lights on the bougainvillea, or in the intimate, low-lighted dining room flickering with candles and enhanced with fresh flowers and quiet classical music. **Known for:** fresh pasta dishes; homemade soups; romantic setting. $ *Average main: $37* ✉ *87 Via Mizner* ☎ *561/655–9752* 🌐 *www.renatospalmbeach.com* ⊗ *No lunch Sun.*

★ **Sant Ambroeus**

$$$ | **ITALIAN** | An outpost of the famed New York Italian spot, this chic café churns out crispy pizzas, delicate pasta dishes, and to-swoon-for desserts with polished service. The vibe is '60s era glam meets dreamy Milanese café, making it a hit with both socialites and shoppers who stop in for an espresso break in between jaunts to the boutiques at Royal Poinciana Plaza. **Known for:** heavenly cacio e pepe; opulent decor; gelato. $ *Average main: $24* ✉ *340 Royal Poinciana Way* ☎ *561/285–7990* 🌐 *www.santambroeus.com/restaurant-sant-ambroeus-palm-beach.*

Hotels

★ **The Brazilian Court Hotel**

$$$$ | **HOTEL** | This posh boutique hotel, stomping ground of Florida's well-heeled, is full of historic touches and creature comforts—from its yellow facade with dramatic white-draped entry to modern draws like the renowned spa and Daniel Boulud restaurant. **Pros:** stylish and hip local crowd; charming courtyard; free beach shuttle. **Cons:** small fitness center; nondescript pool; 10-minute ride to ocean and suggested 24-hour advance reservation for shuttle. $ *Rooms from: $609* ✉ *301 Australian Ave.* ☎ *561/655–7740* 🌐 *www.thebraziliancourt.com* *80 rooms* *No meals.*

★ **The Breakers Palm Beach**

$$$$ | **RESORT** | **FAMILY** | More than an opulent hotel, The Breakers is a legendary 140-acre self-contained jewel of a resort built in a Mediterranean style and loaded with amenities, from a 20,000-square-foot luxury spa and grandiose beach club with four pools and a half-mile private beach to 10 tennis courts, croquet courts, and two 18-hole golf courses. **Pros:** impeccable attention to detail; beautiful room views; extensive activities for families. **Cons:** big price tag; short drive to reach off-property attractions. $ *Rooms from: $699* ✉ *1 S. County Rd.* ☎ *561/655–6611, 888/273–2537* 🌐 *www.thebreakers.com* *538 rooms* *No meals.*

The Chesterfield Palm Beach

$$$$ | **HOTEL** | A distinctly upper-crust northern European feel pervades the peach stucco walls and elegant rooms here; the hotel sits just north of the western end of Worth Avenue, and high tea, a cigar parlor, and daily turndown service recall a bygone, more refined era. **Pros:** gracious, attentive staff; Leopard Lounge entertainment; free valet parking. **Cons:** long walk to beach; only one elevator; to some, can come off as a bit stuffy. $ *Rooms from: $495* ✉ *363 Cocoanut Row* ☎ *561/659–5800, 800/243–7871* 🌐 *www.chesterfieldpb.com* *52 rooms* *No meals.*

The Colony

$$$$ | **HOTEL** | This exuberant and undeniably charming hotel underwent a five-year, $18 million top-to-bottom renovation in 2015 that gave the British-colonial-style a much-needed face-lift. **Pros:** unbeatable location; gorgeous decor; pillow-top mattresses. **Cons:** lobby is small; elevators are tight. $ *Rooms from: $600* ✉ *155 Hammon Ave.* ☎ *561/655–5430,*

800/521–5525 ⊕ www.thecolonypalmbeach.com ⇆ 90 rooms ♨ No meals.

★ Eau Palm Beach

$$$$ | RESORT | FAMILY | In the coastal town of Manalapan (just south of Palm Beach), this sublime, glamorous destination resort (formerly the Ritz-Carlton) showcases a newer, younger face of luxury, including a 3,000-square-foot oceanfront terrace, two sleek pools, a huge fitness center, and a deluxe spa. **Pros:** magnificent aesthetic details throughout; indulgent pampering services; excellent on-site dining; kids love the cool cyberlounge just for them. **Cons:** golf course is off property; 15-minute drive to Palm Beach. *$ Rooms from: $560 ✉ 100 S. Ocean Blvd., Manalapan ☎ 561/533–6000, 800/241–3333 ⊕ www.eaupalmbeach.com ⇆ 309 rooms ♨ No meals.*

★ Four Seasons Resort Palm Beach

$$$$ | RESORT | FAMILY | Couples and families seeking relaxed seaside elegance in a luxe yet understated setting will love this manicured 6-acre oceanfront escape at the south end of Palm Beach, with serene, bright, airy rooms in a cream-colored palette and spacious marble-lined baths. **Pros:** Cabana Terrace Rooms have direct access to pool deck; all rooms have balconies; Michelin-starred chef heads Florie's restaurant; outstanding complimentary kids' program. **Cons:** 10-minute drive to downtown Palm Beach (but can walk to Lake Worth); pricey. *$ Rooms from: $739 ✉ 2800 S. Ocean Blvd. ☎ 561/582–2800, 800/432–2335 ⊕ www.fourseasons.com/palmbeach ⇆ 210 rooms ♨ No meals.*

The Tideline Resort & Spa

$$$ | RESORT | This Zenlike boutique hotel has a loyal following of young, hip travelers, who appreciate the updated rooms and the full-service spa. **Pros:** most rooms have beautiful views of the private beach; ultracontemporary vibe; luxury setting. **Cons:** a hike from shopping and nightlife; the infinity pool is across the driveway. *$ Rooms from: $340 ✉ 2842 S. Ocean Blvd. ☎ 561/540–6440, 888/344–4321 ⊕ www.tidelineresort.com ⇆ 134 rooms ♨ No meals.*

Nightlife

Palm Beach is teeming with restaurants that turn into late-night hot spots, plus hotel lobby bars perfect for tête-à-têtes.

★ bûccan

BARS/PUBS | At this hip Hamptons-esque scene, society darlings crowd the lounge, throwing back killer cocktails like the French Pearl (gin, Pernod, lemon juice, mint) and Buccan T (vodka, black tea, cranberry, citrus, basil, and agave nectar). *✉ 350 S. County Rd. ☎ 561/833–3450 ⊕ www.buccanpalmbeach.com.*

Café Boulud

BARS/PUBS | A sleek, redesigned dining room bar with bar bites from a special menu plus an extended happy hour draws locals and visitors alike. **■ TIP→ Dress to impress.** *✉ 301 Australian Ave. ☎ 561/655–6060 ⊕ www.cafeboulud.com/palmbeach.*

Cucina Palm Beach

BARS/PUBS | Though this spot is popular for lunch and dinner, it's even more popular later in the night. The younger, trendier set comes late to party, mingle, and dance into the wee hours. *✉ 257 Royal Poinciana Way ☎ 561/655–0770 ⊕ www.cucinapalmbeach.com.*

The Leopard Lounge

PIANO BARS/LOUNGES | In the Chesterfield hotel, this enclave feels like an exclusive club. The trademark ceiling and spotted floors of the renovated lounge are a nod to this hotel's historic roots, but the rest of the decor is new-age Palm Beach glam. Though it starts each evening as a restaurant, as the night progresses the Leopard is transformed into an old-fashioned club with live music for Palm Beach's old guard. The bartenders know how to pour a cocktail here. *✉ The Chesterfield Palm Beach, 363 Cocoanut*

Row ☎ *561/659–5800* 🌐 *www.chesterfieldpb.com.*

Shopping

As is the case throughout South Florida, many of the smaller boutiques in Palm Beach close in the summer, and most stores are closed on Sunday. Consignment stores in Palm Beach are definitely worth a look; you'll often find high-end designer clothing in impeccable condition.

Betteridge Jewelers

JEWELRY/ACCESSORIES | Jewelry is very important in Palm Beach, and for more than 119 years the diverse selection here has included investment pieces. Window-shopping is allowed. ✉ *236 Worth Ave.* ☎ *561/655–5850* 🌐 *www.betteridge.com.*

The Church Mouse

OUTLET/DISCOUNT STORES | Many high-end resale boutique owners grab their merchandise at this thrift store run by the Episcopal Church of Bethesda-by-the-Sea, in business since 1970. The mouse accepts cheese from October to June, Monday–Saturday, 10–4. The store's end-of-season sale draws crowds that line the block. You can feel good about your purchases here: proceeds go to regional nonprofits. ✉ *378 S. County Rd.* ☎ *561/659–2154* 🌐 *www.bbts.org/about-us/church-mouse/* ⏲ *closed Sun.*

★ Worth Avenue

SHOPPING NEIGHBORHOODS | One of the world's premier showcases for high-quality shopping runs half a mile from east to west across Palm Beach, from the beach to Lake Worth. The street has more than 200 shops (more than 40 of them sell jewelry), and many upscale chain stores (Gucci, Hermès, Saks Fifth Avenue, Neiman Marcus, Louis Vuitton, Chanel, Cartier, Tiffany & Co., and Tourneau) are represented—their merchandise appealing to the discerning tastes of the Palm Beach clientele. Don't miss walking around the vias, little courtyards lined with smaller boutiques; historic tours are available each month during "the season" from the Worth Avenue Association. ■ **TIP→ For those looking to go a little lighter on the pocketbook, just north of Worth Avenue, the six blocks of South County Road have interesting and somewhat less expensive stores.** ✉ *Worth Ave.* ✣ *Between Cocoanut Row and S. Ocean Blvd.* 🌐 *www.worth-avenue.com.*

Activities

Palm Beach Island has two good golf courses—The Breakers and the Palm Beach Par 3 Golf Course, but only the latter is open to the public. Not to worry, there are more on the mainland, as well as myriad other outdoor sports opportunities, including a new spring-training baseball stadium where two teams will play.

The Breakers Golf Courses

GOLF | The Breakers' historic par-70 Ocean Course, the oldest 18 holes in all of Florida, as well as its contemporary Breakers Rees Jones Course, are open exclusively to members and hotel guests. The Ocean Course, redesigned to bring back its "vintage" feel, is located on-site, on the grounds of the sprawling Breakers Palm Beach. The resort's sister course, designed by Rees Jones, is 10 miles west in West Palm Beach and replaces the former Breakers West course. A $210 greens fee for each includes range balls, cart, and bag storage; the John Webster Golf Academy at The Breakers offers private and group lessons. Discounts are given at the Ocean Course for afternoon starts, and for adults accompanied by kids, who play for free. ✉ *The Breakers Palm Beach, 1 S. County Rd.* ☎ *561/655–6611* 🌐 *www.thebreakers.com/golf* 🎫 *$210 for 18 holes, cart included* ⛳ *Ocean Course: 18 holes, 6177 yards, par 72; Breakers Rees Jones Course: 18 holes, 7100 yards, par 72.*

Island Living Tours

GUIDED TOURS | Book a private mansion-viewing excursion around Palm Beach, and hear the storied past of the island's upper crust. Owner Leslie Diver also hosts an Antique Row Tour and a Worth Avenue Shopping Tour. Vehicle tours are 90 minutes for the Best of Palm Beach and 2½ hours for a more extensive architecture and history tour. Costs are from $60 to $150 per person, depending on the vehicle used. Leslie also runs 90-minute bicycle tours through Palm Beach ($45, not including bike rental). One bicycle tour explores the Estate Section and historic Worth Avenue; another explores the island's lesser known North End. Call in advance for location and to reserve. ✉ *Palm Beach* ☎ *561/309–5790* 🌐 *www.islandlivingpb.com.*

Lake Trail

BICYCLING | **FAMILY** | This palm-fringed trail, about 4 miles long, skirts the backyards of mansions and the edge of Lake Worth. The start ("south trail" section) is just up from Royal Palm Way behind the Society of the Four Arts; follow the signs and you can't miss it. As you head north, the trail gets a little choppy around the Flagler Museum, so most people just enter where the "north trail" section begins at the very west end of Sunset Avenue. The path stops just short of the tip of the island, but people follow the quiet residential streets until they hit North Ocean Boulevard and the dock there with lovely views of Peanut Island and Singer Island, and then follow North Ocean Boulevard the 4 miles back for a change of scenery. ✉ *Parallel to Lake Way* ✣ *Behind Society of the Four Arts.*

★ Palm Beach Bicycle Trail Shop

BICYCLING | Open daily year-round, the shop rents bikes by the hour or day, and it's about a block from the north Lake Trail entrance. The shop has maps to help you navigate your way around the island, or you can download the main map from the shop's website. They are experts on the nearby, palm-fringed, 4-mile Lake Trail. ✉ *50 Cocoanut Row, Suite 117* ☎ *561/659–4583* 🌐 *www.palmbeachbicycle.com.*

★ Palm Beach Par 3 Golf Course

GOLF | This course has been named the best par-3 golf course in the United States by *Golf Digest* magazine. The 18-hole course—originally designed by Dick Wilson and Joe Lee in 1961—was redesigned in 2009 by Hall of Famer Raymond Floyd. The par-3 course includes six holes directly on the Atlantic Ocean, with some holes over 200 yards. The grounds are exquisitely landscaped, as one would expect in Palm Beach. A lavish clubhouse houses Al Fresco, an Italian restaurant. A cart is an extra $15, but walking is encouraged. Summer rates are greatly discounted. ✉ *2345 S. Ocean Blvd.* ☎ *561/547–0598* 🌐 *www.golfontheocean.com* 💵 *$50 for 18 holes* 🏌 *18 holes, 2458 yards, par 58.*

West Palm Beach

Long considered Palm Beach's less privileged stepsister, West Palm Beach has come into its own. Its $30 million Centennial Square waterfront complex at the eastern end of Clematis Street, with piers, a pavilion, and an amphitheater, has transformed West Palm into an attractive, easy-to-walk downtown area—not to mention there's the Downtown Trolley that connects the shopping-and-entertainment mecca City-Place with restaurant-and-lounge-lined Clematis Street. The Palm Beach Outlet Mall gives options to those looking for tony bargains. West Palm is especially well regarded for its arts scene, with unique museums and performance venues; a number of public art projects have appeared around the city.

The city's outskirts, vast flat stretches with strip malls and car dealerships, may not inspire but are worth driving through to reach attractions scattered around the southern and western reaches. Several sites are especially rewarding for children and other animal and nature lovers.

Sights

Ann Norton Sculpture Gardens

GARDEN | This landmarked complex is a testament to the creative genius of the late American sculptor Ann Weaver Norton (1905–82), who was the second wife of Norton Museum founder, industrialist Ralph H. Norton. A set of art galleries in the studio and main house where she lived is surrounded by 2 acres of gardens with 300 species of rare palm trees, eight brick megaliths, a monumental figure in Norwegian granite, and plantings designed to attract native birds. ✉ *253 Barcelona Rd., West Palm Beach* ☎ *561/832–5328* 🌐 *www.ansg.org* 🎫 *$10* ⏲ *Closed Mon.–Tues.*

Armory Art Center

COLLEGE | Built by the Works Progress Administration (WPA) in 1939, this art deco facility is now a nonprofit art school hosting rotating exhibitions and art classes throughout the year. The Armory Art Center became an institution for art instruction when the Norton Museum Gallery and School of Art dropped the latter part of its name in 1986 and discontinued art-instruction classes. ✉ *1700 Parker Ave., West Palm Beach* ☎ *561/832–1776* 🌐 *www.armoryart.org* 🎫 *Free.*

Currie Park

NATIONAL/STATE PARK | **FAMILY** | Frequent weekend festivals, including an annual celebration of seafood, take place at this scenic city park next to the Intracoastal Waterway. Sit on one of the piers and watch the yachts and fishing boats pass by. Put on your jogging shoes—the park is at the north end of a 6.3-mile waterfront biking-jogging-skating path. Tennis courts, a boat ramp, and a playground are here, along with the Maritime Museum. DivaDuck tours launch from this park. ✉ *N. Flagler Dr. at 23rd St., West Palm Beach* ☎ *561/804–4900* 🌐 *wpbparks.com/west-palm-beach-parks/currie-park.*

Lion Country Safari

AMUSEMENT PARK/WATER PARK | **FAMILY** | Drive your own vehicle along 4 miles of paved roads through a cageless zoo with free-roaming animals (chances are you'll have an ostrich nudging at your window) and then let loose in a 55-acre fun-land with bird feedings, games, and rides. A CD included with admission narrates the winding trek past white rhinos, zebras, and ostriches grouped into exhibits like Gir Forest that's modeled after a sanctuary in India and has native twisted-horned blackbuck antelope and water buffalo. (For obvious reasons, lions are fenced off, and no convertibles or pets are allowed.) Aside from dozens more up-close critter encounters after debarking, including a petting zoo, kids can go paddleboating, do a round of mini-golf, climb aboard carnival rides, or have a splash in a 4,000-square-foot aquatic playground (some extra fees apply). ✉ *2003 Lion Country Safari Rd., at Southern Blvd. W, West Palm Beach* ☎ *561/793–1084* 🌐 *www.lioncountrysafari.com* 🎫 *$35, $8 parking.*

★ **Manatee Lagoon**

LOCAL INTEREST | **FAMILY** | Once a casual spot next to the local electric plant's discharge waters, this center celebrating the manatee—South Florida's popular winter visitors—opened in 2016 at a spot where the peaceful creatures naturally congregate. The airy, two-story facility is surrounded by wraparound decks to accommodate sea-cow spotters from fall to spring. Educational, interactive displays tell the story of this once-endangered species. A long deck along the seawall leads to picnic pavilions from where you can watch the action at nearby Peanut Island and the Port of Palm Beach. Free admission makes it group-friendly; a live "manatee cam"

The Armory Art Center in West Palm Beach helps students of all ages create works of art in various mediums.

shows manatee counts before you go. The center offers weekend art classes for children but requires advance registration; check their calendar for details. ✉ *6000 N. Flagler Dr., West Palm Beach* ✣ *Entrance is on Flagler Dr., via 58th St. east of U.S. 1 and south of the Port of Palm Beach flyover* ☎ *561/626–2833* 🌐 *www.visitmanateelagoon.com* 🎫 *Free* ⏲ *Closed Mon.*

Mounts Botanical Garden

GARDEN | The oldest public green space in the county is, unbelievably, across the road from the West Palm Beach airport; but the planes are the last thing you notice while walking around and relaxing amid the nearly 14 acres of exotic trees, rain-forest flora, and butterfly and water gardens. The gift shop contains a selection of rare gardening books on tropical climes. Frequent plant sales are held here, and numerous plant societies with international ties hold meetings open to the public in the auditorium. Experts in tropical edible and ornamental plants are on staff. ✉ *531 N. Military Trail, West Palm Beach* ☎ *561/233–1757* 🌐 *www.mounts.org* 🎫 *$5 (suggested donation).*

National Croquet Center

SPORTS VENUE | The world's largest croquet complex, the 10-acre center is also the headquarters for the U.S. Croquet Association. Vast expanses of orderly lawns are the stage for fierce competitions. There's also a clubhouse with a pro shop and the Croquet Grille, with verandas for dining and viewing (armchair enthusiasts can enjoy the games for no charge). You don't have to be a member to try your hand out on the lawns, and on Saturday morning at 10 am, there's a free group lesson with an introduction to the game, and open play; call in advance to reserve a spot. ✉ *700 Florida Mango Rd., at Summit Blvd., West Palm Beach* ☎ *561/478–2300* 🌐 *www.croquetnational.com* 🎫 *Center free; full day of croquet $30.*

★ **Norton Museum of Art**

MUSEUM | Fresh off an expansion, the museum (constructed in 1941 by steel magnate Ralph H. Norton and his wife,

Elizabeth) has grown to become one of the most impressive in South Florida with an extensive collection of 19th- and 20th-century American and European paintings—including works by Picasso, Monet, Matisse, Pollock, Cassatt, and O'Keeffe—plus Chinese art, earlier European art, and photography. To accommodate a growing collection, the museum is undergoing an extensive expansion to include 12,000 additional square feet of gallery space in a new west wing, event spaces, and a great hall. A garden will also be incorporated into the space. **■ TIP→ The popular Art After Dark, Thursday from 5 to 9 pm, is a gathering spot for art lovers, with wine and music in the galleries.** ✉ *1451 S. Olive Ave., West Palm Beach* ☎ *561/832–5196* 🌐 *www.norton.org* 🎫 *Free* ⏲ *Closed Mon.*

Richard and Pat Johnson Palm Beach County History Museum

MUSEUM | A beautifully restored 1916 courthouse in downtown opened its doors in 2008 as the permanent home of the Historical Society of Palm Beach County's collection of artifacts and records dating back before the town's start—a highlight is furniture and decorative objects from Mizner Industries (a real treat since many of his mansions are not open to the public). ✉ *300 N. Dixie Hwy., West Palm Beach* ☎ *561/832–4164* 🌐 *www.historicalsocietypbc.org* 🎫 *Free* ⏲ *Closed Sun.*

South Florida Science Center and Aquarium

MUSEUM | **FAMILY** | Both fresh- and saltwater aquariums greet the curious at this interactive, family-friendly science museum. Permanent exhibits of Moon and Mars rocks and meteorites, a giant sphere with global animation projection for Earth sciences, and Everglades conservation exhibit teach while entertaining. A planetarium with daily themed shows and a conservation 9-hole mini-golf course designed by Jim Fazio and Gary Nicklaus are popular with all ages and carry separate admission charges. ✉ *4801 Dreher Trail N, West Palm Beach* ☎ *561/832–1988* 🌐 *www.sfsciencecenter.org* 🎫 *$16.95; planetarium $5; mini-golf $7.*

Avocado Grill

$$ | **ECLECTIC** | In downtown West Palm Beach's waterfront district, this hot spot is an alternative to the bar food, tacos, and burgers more common in the area. "Green" cuisine—seasonal salads, vegetarian dishes, and sustainably produced meats and seafood—is making waves at the avocado-themed restaurant. **Known for:** everything avocado, including wonderful guacamole; mushroom fricassee with cheddar grits; mixed seafood ceviche. 💲 *Average main: $19* ✉ *125 Datura St., West Palm Beach* ☎ *561/623–0822* 🌐 *www.avocadogrillwpb.com.*

Belle and Maxwell's

$$ | **AMERICAN** | Palm Beach ladies who lunch leave the island for an afternoon at Belle and Maxwell's, while young professionals loosen up after work at the wine bar, part of the bistro's expanded dining area. Tucked along Antique Row, it looks like a storybook tea party at lunch, with eclectic furnishings and decor and charming garden. **Known for:** classic chicken marsala; extensive list of lunch salads; homemade desserts. 💲 *Average main: $18* ✉ *3700 S. Dixie Hwy., West Palm Beach* ☎ *561/832–4449* 🌐 *www.belleandmaxwells.com* ⏲ *Closed Sun. No dinner Mon.*

Grandview Public Market

$ | **ECLECTIC** | **FAMILY** | This laid-back food hall and community-centric market complete with colorful murals has been a crowd pleaser since it opened in the summer of 2017. There's plenty to taste, with 12 vendors selling everything from tacos to fried chicken to rolled ice cream. **Known for:** coffee; live music; tacos. 💲 *Average main: $12* ✉ *1401 Clare Ave., West*

Palm Beach ☎ n/a 🌐 www.grandviewpublic.com.

★ Grato

$$$ | TUSCAN | FAMILY | A sprawling cavern of wood-fired pizzas, pastas, and cocktails, this sibling to popular bûccan quickly became a hit when it opened on the mainland. Soaring ceilings, concrete floors, dark wood, and an open kitchen provide a buzzy backdrop to dishes of nicely charred pies (made with organic flour) and homemade pastas. **Known for:** wood-fired pizzas; fresh pastas; busy bar scene. *$ Average main: $24 ✉ 1901 Dixie Hwy., West Palm Beach ☎ 561/404–1334 🌐 www.gratowpb.com.*

Havana

$$ | CUBAN | FAMILY | Decorated with vintage travel posters of its namesake city, this two-level restaurant serves authentic Cuban specialties on the cheap, including great Cubano (pressed roast pork) sandwiches, arroz con pollo, and *ropa vieja.* The friendly place attracts a late-night crowd at its popular walk-up window. Get strong Cuban coffee (often awarded the best in Palm Beach County), sugary fried churros, and fruit juices in exotic flavors like mamey, mango, papaya, guava, and guanabana. **Known for:** late-night food service; Cuban sandwiches; picadillo Cubano. *$ Average main: $15 ✉ 6801 S. Dixie Hwy., West Palm Beach ☎ 561/547–9799 🌐 www.havanacubanfood.com.*

Howley's

$ | AMERICAN | Since 1950, this diner's eat-in counter and "cooked in sight, it must be right" motto have made it a congenial setting for meeting old friends and making new ones. Nowadays, Howley's prides itself on its kitsch factor and old-school eats like turkey potpie and a traditional Thanksgiving feast, as well as its retro-redux dishes like potato-and-brisket burrito. **Known for:** kitschy setting; retro diner specialties; late-night dining. *$ Average main: $13 ✉ 4700 S. Dixie Hwy., West Palm Beach ☎ 561/833–5691 🌐 www.sub-culture.org/howleys/.*

Marcello's La Sirena

$$$$ | ITALIAN | A longtime favorite of locals, this sophisticated Italian restaurant is in an unexpected, nondescript location on Dixie Highway away from downtown and central hubs. But warm hospitality from a husband-and-wife team, along with smart service and delectable traditional dishes, await. **Known for:** fresh pasta dishes; award-winning wine list; great desserts. *$ Average main: $31 ✉ 6316 S. Dixie Hwy., West Palm Beach ☎ 561/585–3128 🌐 www.lasirenaonline.com ⊗ Closed Sun.*

★ Mediterranean Market & Deli

$ | MIDDLE EASTERN | This hole-in-the-wall Middle Eastern bakery, deli, and market is packed at lunchtime with regulars who are on a first-name basis with the gang behind the counter. From the nondescript parking lot the place doesn't look like much, but inside, delicious hot and cold Mediterranean treats await the takeout crowd. **Known for:** lamb salad; gyros; freshly baked pita bread. *$ Average main: $10 ✉ 327 5th St., West Palm Beach ☎ 561/659–7322 🌐 www.mediterraneanmarketanddeli.com ⊗ Closed Sun.*

Pistache French Bistro

$$$ | FRENCH | Although "the island" is no doubt a bastion of French cuisine, this cozy bistro across the bridge on the Clematis Street waterfront entices a lively crowd looking for an unpretentious good meal. The outdoor terrace can't be beat, and the fabulous modern French menu with twists such as roasted sliced duck with truffled polenta is a delight. **Known for:** fresh seafood; cheese and charcuterie; great desserts. *$ Average main: $27 ✉ 101 N. Clematis St., West Palm Beach ☎ 561/833–5090 🌐 www.pistachewpb.com.*

★ The Regional Kitchen & Public House

$$$ | SOUTHERN | *Top Chef* finalist and James Beard Award nominee Lindsay

Autry debuted her own Southern-inspired American cuisine in CityPlace to the acclaim of local critics. The menu of updated comfort food includes fried green tomatoes, creamy tomato pie, pimento cheese done table-side, and shrimp and grits. **Known for:** reinvented Southern classics; table-side pimento cheese; weekend brunch. *Average main: $24 CityPlace, 651 Okeechobee Blvd., West Palm Beach Directly across from the Convention Center 561/557–6460 www.eatregional.com.*

★ RH Rooftop Restaurant
$$ | **AMERICAN** | **FAMILY** | Atop the glossy Restoration Hardware store adjacent to CityPlace is this regal, glass-enclosed atrium outfitted with white couches, crystal chandeliers, lush greenery, and a tinkling fountain. It's proven a hit with the old guard and the stroller-pushers alike; everyone basks in the sun-filled room and tucks into seasonal comfort food (prime rib french dip, truffled grilled cheese) and lingers on exceptionally comfortable couches. **Known for:** lobster roll; beautiful atrium; brunch. *Average main: $17 560 Okeechobee Blvd., West Palm Beach 561/804–6826 www.restorationhardware.com/content/category.jsp?context=WestPalm.*

Rhythm Cafe
$$$ | **MODERN AMERICAN** | West Palm Beach's Rhythm Cafe is anything but Palm Beach formal (the decor includes a feathered pink flamingo perched on the terrazzo floor). Fun, funky, cheesy, campy, and cool all at once, the former 1950s-era drugstore-cum-restaurant on West Palm Beach's Antique Row features an ever-changing creative menu of homemade items with Italian, Greek, American, and Creole influences. **Known for:** "tapas-tizer" small plates; fresh fish; graham-cracker-crusted key lime chicken. *Average main: $24 3800 S. Dixie Hwy., West Palm Beach 561/833–3406 www.rhythmcafe.com No lunch.*

Hotels

Casa Grandview West Palm Beach
$$ | **B&B/INN** | In West Palm's charming Grandview Heights historic district—and just minutes away from both downtown and the beach—this warm and personalized B&B offers a wonderful respite from South Florida's big-hotel norm. **Pros:** daily dry cleaning of all linens; complimentary soft drinks, coffee, and snacks (and lots of them) in lobby; simple keyless entry (number code lock system). **Cons:** cottages and suites have seven-day minimum; free breakfast in B&B rooms only; art deco suites don't have air-conditioning. *Rooms from: $289 1410 Georgia Ave., West Palm Beach 561/655–8932 www.casagrandview.com 17 rooms Breakfast.*

Grandview Gardens Bed & Breakfast
$$ | **B&B/INN** | Defining the Florida B&B experience, this 1925 Mediterranean-revival home overlooks a serene courtyard pool and oozes loads of charm and personality, while the fabulous owners provide heavy doses of bespoke service. **Pros:** multilingual owners; outside private entrances to rooms; free bicycle use; innkeepers offer historic city tours. **Cons:** not close to the beach; in a residential area; rental car needed. *Rooms from: $225 1608 Lake Ave., West Palm Beach 561/833–9023 www.grandview-gardens.com 5 rooms, 2 cottages Breakfast.*

Hampton Inn & Suites Wellington
$$ | **HOTEL** | **FAMILY** | The only hotel near the polo fields in the equestrian mecca of Wellington—10 miles west of downtown Palm Beach—feels a bit like a tony clubhouse, with rich wood paneling, hunt prints, and elegant chandeliers; but inside the rooms are standard Hampton Inn fare. **Pros:** complimentary hot breakfast; free Wi-Fi; outdoor swimming pool; close to a large shopping center; near the county fairgrounds. **Cons:** no restaurant; Intracoastal Waterway is a 30-minute

drive, and beach is farther. *Rooms from: $250 2155 Wellington Green Dr., West Palm Beach 561/472–9696 hamptoninn3.hilton.com 122 rooms, 32 suites Breakfast.*

Hilton West Palm Beach

$$ | HOTEL | FAMILY | In downtown, the contemporary business hotel situated next door to the county convention center has a pool with cabanas many resorts would envy. **Pros:** walking distance to convention center, CityPlace, Kravis Center; resort-style pool; amenities geared toward business travelers. **Cons:** long ride to the beach; noise from downtown construction and trains. *Rooms from: $279 600 Okeechobee Blvd., West Palm Beach Adjacent to the Palm Beach County Convention Center 561/231–6000 www3.hilton.com 400 rooms No meals.*

Hotel Biba

$ | HOTEL | In the El Cid historic district, this 1940s-era motel has gotten a fun, stylish revamp from designer Barbara Hulanicki: each room has a vibrant mélange of colors, along with handcrafted mirrors, mosaic bathroom floors, and custom mahogany furnishings. **Pros:** cool, punchy design and luxe fixtures; popular wine bar; free continental breakfast with Cuban pastries. **Cons:** water pressure is weak; bathrooms are tiny; noisy when the bar is open late and trains run nearby; not all rooms have central air-conditioning. *Rooms from: $160 320 Belvedere Rd., West Palm Beach 561/832–0094 www.hotelbiba.com 43 rooms Breakfast.*

Nightlife

West Palm is known for its exuberant nightlife—Clematis Street and CityPlace are the prime party destinations. Downtown rocks every Thursday from 6 pm on with Clematis by Night (*www.wpb.org/clematis-by-night*), a celebration of music, dance, art, and food at Centennial Square.

Blue Martini

BARS/PUBS | The CityPlace outpost of this South Florida hot spot for thirty-, forty-, and fiftysomething adults gone wild has a menu filled with tons of innovative martini creations (42 to be exact), tasty tapas, and lots of cougars on the prowl, searching for a first, second, or even third husband. And the guys aren't complaining! The drinks are great and the scene is fun for everyone, even those who aren't single and looking to mingle. Expect DJs some nights, live music others. *CityPlace, 550 S. Rosemary Ave., #244, West Palm Beach 561/835–8601 www.bluemartinilounge.com.*

ER Bradley's Saloon

BARS/PUBS | People of all ages congregate to hang out and socialize at this kitschy open-air restaurant and bar to gaze at the Intracoastal Waterway; the mechanical bull is a hit on Saturdays. Live music's on tap five to seven nights a week. *104 Clematis St., West Palm Beach 561/833–3520 www.erbradleys.com.*

★ Rocco's Tacos and Tequila Bar

BARS/PUBS | In the last few years, Rocco's has taken root in numerous South Florida downtowns and become synonymous with wild nights of chips 'n' guac, margaritas, and intoxicating fun. This is more of a scene than just a restaurant, and when Rocco's in the house and pouring shots, get ready to party hearty. With pitchers of margaritas continuously flowing, the middle-aged crowd is boisterous and fun, recounting (and reliving) the days of spring break debauchery from their pre-professional years. Get your party started here with more than 220 choices of tequila. There's another branch at 5250 Town Center Circle in Boca Raton; at 110 Atlantic Avenue in Delray Beach; and in Palm Beach Gardens in PGA Commons at 5090 PGA Boulevard. *224 Clematis St., West Palm Beach 561/650–1001 www.roccostacos.com.*

Performing Arts

Palm Beach Dramaworks *(pbd)*
THEATER | Housed in an intimate venue with only 218 seats in downtown West Palm Beach, the modus operandi is "theater to think about," with plays by Pulitzer Prize winners on rotation. ✉ *201 Clematis St., West Palm Beach* ☎ *561/514–4042* 🌐 *www.palmbeachdramaworks.org.*

Palm Beach Opera
OPERA | Still going strong after nearly 60 years, three main-stage productions are offered during the season from January through April at the Kravis Center with English-language supertitles. There's an annual Children's Performance where all tickets are $5, plus a free outdoor concert at the Meyer Amphitheatre in downtown West Palm Beach. Tickets start at $25. ✉ *1800 S. Australian Ave., Suite 301, administrative office, West Palm Beach* ☎ *561/833–7888* 🌐 *www.pbopera.org.*

★ **Raymond F. Kravis Center for the Performing Arts**
ARTS CENTERS | This is the crown jewel amid a treasury of local arts attractions, and its marquee star is the 2,195-seat Dreyfoos Hall, a glass, copper, and marble showcase just steps from the restaurants and shops of CityPlace. The center also boasts the 289-seat Rinker Playhouse, 170-seat Persson Hall, and the Gosman Amphitheatre, which holds 1,400 total in seats and on the lawn. A packed year-round schedule features a blockbuster lineup of Broadway's biggest touring productions, concerts, dance, dramas, and musicals; the Miami City Ballet, Palm Beach Opera, and the Palm Beach Pops perform here. ✉ *701 Okeechobee Blvd., West Palm Beach* ☎ *561/832–7469 box office* 🌐 *www.kravis.org.*

Shopping

★ **Antique Row**
SHOPPING NEIGHBORHOODS | West Palm's U.S. 1, "South Dixie Highway," is the destination for those who are interested in interesting home decor. From thrift shops to the most exclusive stores, it is all here within 40 stores—museum-quality furniture, lighting, art, junk, fabric, frames, tile, and rugs. So if you're looking for an art deco, French-provincial, or Mizner pièce de résistance, big or small, schedule a few hours for an Antique Row stroll. You'll find bargains during the off-season (May to November). Antique Row runs north–south from Belvedere Road to Forest Hill Boulevard, although most stores are bunched between Belvedere Road and Southern Boulevard. ✉ *U.S. 1, between Belvedere Rd. and Forest Hill Blvd., West Palm Beach* 🌐 *www.westpalmbeachantiques.com.*

CityPlace
SHOPPING NEIGHBORHOODS | FAMILY | The 72-acre, four-block-by-four-block commercial and residential complex centered on Rosemary Avenue attracts people of all ages to restaurants like Italian-inspired Il Bellagio, bars like Blue Martini, a 20-screen AMC theater, the bowling alley and sports bar Revolutions, the Harriet Himmel Theater, and the Improv Comedy Club. In the courtyard, a 36,000-gallon water fountain and light show entertains, along with live bands on weekends. The dining, shopping, and entertainment are all family-friendly; at night, however, a lively crowd likes to hit the outdoor bars. Among CityPlace's stores are such popular national retailers as H&M, Tommy Bahama, and Restoration Hardware. Anushka Spa and Salon draws locals and visitors. ✉ *700 S. Rosemary Ave., West Palm Beach* ☎ *561/366–1000* 🌐 *www.cityplace.com.*

Clematis Street
SHOPPING NEIGHBORHOODS | FAMILY |
If lunching is just as important as

window-shopping, the renewed downtown West Palm around Clematis Street that runs west to east from South Rosemary Avenue to Flagler Drive is the spot for you. Centennial Park by the waterfront has an attractive design—and fountains where kids can cool off—which adds to the pleasure of browsing and resting at one of the many outdoor cafés. Hip national retailers such as Design Within Reach mix with local boutiques like third-generation Pioneer Linens, and both blend in with restaurants and bars. ✉ *Clematis St., West Palm Beach* ✣ *Between S. Rosemary Ave. and Flagler Dr.* 🌐 *www.westpalmbeach.com/clematis.*

Palm Beach Outlets

OUTLET/DISCOUNT STORES | An outlet mall worthy of Palm Beach finally opened in 2014 in West Palm Beach. It features more than 130 retailers, with big names among the usual suspects. Off Fifth (Saks Fifth Avenue's store), Nordstrom Rack, White House | Black Market, Brooks Brothers, DKNY, and Calvin Klein are interspersed with stores selling shoes, discounted home decor, sports gear, kids' fashions, and more. The mall has several restaurants as well as coffee shops and a food court. And it continues to expand, so check the website for an updated list of shops. **■ TIP→ The wine bar in Whole Foods Market is the "see and be seen" scene at this outdoor mall.** ✉ *1751 Palm Beach Lakes Blvd., West Palm Beach* ☎ *561/515–4400* 🌐 *www.palmbeachoutlets.com.*

Activities

DivaDuck Amphibious Tours

BOAT TOURS | FAMILY | Running 75 minutes, these duck tours go in and out of the water on USCG-inspected amphibious vessels around West Palm Beach and Palm Beach. The tours depart two or three times most days for $29 per person (adults); there are discounts for seniors and kids. ✉ *CityPlace, 600 S. Rosemary Ave., West Palm Beach* ✣ *Corner of Hibiscus St. and Rosemary Ave.* ☎ *877/844–4188* 🌐 *www.divaduck.com.*

Fitteam Ballpark of the Palm Beaches

BASEBALL/SOFTBALL | FAMILY | There's a lot to root for at the new-in-2017 state-of-the-art baseball stadium. It plays host to spring training for the Houston Astros and the Washington Nationals, along with farm team play and numerous tournaments in the summer on its many fields. Seating includes lawn, bleacher, field boxes, and suites, with full food service in the latter two. A full bar overlooks left field. With free (and plenty of) parking—as well as reasonably priced tickets—it's a value day out. Check the website to see the other teams coming to play in Florida's "Grapefruit League" against the home teams. The stadium complements Roger Dean Stadium in Jupiter, which hosts the spring games for the Miami Marlins and St. Louis Cardinals. Fields for lacrosse, football, and soccer are part of the massive complex and expected to draw those games; other community events are staged here. ✉ *5444 Haverhill Rd., West Palm Beach* ✣ *Best exit off I-95 is 45th St.; off Florida's Tpke. is Okeechobee Blvd.* ☎ *561/500-4487* 🌐 *www.ballparkpalmbeaches.com* 🎫 *From $17.*

★ International Polo Club Palm Beach

POLO | Attend matches and rub elbows with celebrities who make the pilgrimage out to Palm Beach polo country (the western suburb of Wellington) during the January–April season. The competition is not just among polo players. High society dresses in their best polo couture week after week, each outfit more fabulous than the next; they tailgate out of their Bentleys and Rollses. An annual highlight at the polo club is the U.S. Open Polo Championship at the end of season. **■ TIP→ One of the best ways to experience the polo scene is by enjoying a gourmet brunch on the veranda of the International Polo Club Pavilion; it'll cost you from $100 to $120 per person depending on the month,**

The posh Palm Beach area has its share of luxury villas on the water; many are Mediterranean in style.

but it's well worth it. ✉ *3667 120th Ave. S, Palm Beach* ☎ *561/204–5687* 🌐 *www.internationalpoloclub.com.*

Lake Worth

For years, tourists looked here mainly for inexpensive lodging and easy access to Palm Beach, since a bridge leads from the mainland to a barrier island with Lake Worth's beach. Now Lake Worth has grown into an arts community, with several blocks of restaurants, nightclubs, shops, and galleries, making this a worthy destination on its own.

Sights

Museum of Polo and Hall of Fame
MUSEUM | The history of the sport of kings is displayed in a time line here, with other exhibits focusing on polo ponies, star players, trophies, and a look at how mallets are made. It provides a great introduction to the surprisingly exciting, hoof-pounding sport that is played live on Sundays from January to April in nearby Wellington. ✉ *9011 Lake Worth Rd., Lake Worth* ☎ *561/969–3210* 🌐 *www.polomuseum.com* *Free (donations accepted)* *Closed Sun. Closed Sat. May–Dec.*

Beaches

Lake Worth Beach
BEACH—SIGHT | FAMILY | This public beach bustles with beachgoers of all ages thanks to the prolific family offerings. The waterfront retail promenade—the old-fashioned nongambling Lake Worth "casino"—has a Mulligan's Beach House Bar & Grill, a T-shirt store, a pizzeria, and a Kilwin's ice-cream shop. The beach also has a municipal Olympic-sized public swimming pool, a playground, a fishing pier—not to mention the pier's wildly popular daytime eatery, Benny's on the Beach (open for dinner weekends in season). Tideline Ocean Resort and Four Seasons guests are steps away from the action; Eau Palm Beach guests are a short bike ride away. **Amenities:** food and drink; lifeguards; parking (fee); showers;

toilets; water sports. **Best for:** sunset; swimming. ✉ *10 S. Ocean Blvd., at A1A and Lake Ave., Lake Worth* 🌐 *www.lakeworth.org* 🎫 *$1 to enter pier, $3 to enter and fish, $2 per hr for parking.*

Restaurants

Benny's on the Beach
$ | **AMERICAN** | Perched on the Lake Worth Pier, Benny's has a walk-up bar, a take-out window, and a full-service beach-themed restaurant serving casual fare at bargain prices. "Beach Bread" is a take on a waffle sandwich; the fresh seafood is from Florida waters. **Known for:** Florida seafood; beach brunch; afternoon drinks. 💲 *Average main: $12* ✉ *Lake Worth Beach, 10 S. Ocean Blvd., Lake Worth* ✣ *On Lake Worth Pier* ☎ *561/582–9001* 🌐 *www.bennysonthebeach.com.*

Paradiso
$$$$ | **ITALIAN** | Arguably downtown Lake Worth's fanciest restaurant, with sophisticated modern Northern Italian cuisine, this is a go-to place for a romantic evening. Waiters are on point and anticipate needs. **Known for:** whole branzino baked in a salt crust; extensive wine list; lighter lounge menu. 💲 *Average main: $42* ✉ *625 Lucerne Ave., Lake Worth* ☎ *561/547–2500* 🌐 *www.paradisolakeworth.com.*

Hotels

Sabal Palm House
$ | **B&B/INN** | Built in 1936, this romantic, two-story B&B is a short walk from Lake Worth's downtown shops, eateries, and the Intracoastal Waterway, and each room is decorated with antiques and inspired by a different artist, including Renoir, Dalí, Norman Rockwell, and Chagall. **Pros:** on quiet street; hands-on owners; chairs and totes with towels provided for use at nearby beach. **Cons:** no pool; peak times require a two-night minimum stay; no parking lot. 💲 *Rooms from: $159* ✉ *109 N. Golfview Rd., Lake Worth* ☎ *561/582–1090, 888/722–2572* 🌐 *www.sabalpalmhouse.com* *5 rooms, 2 suites* 🍽 *Breakfast.*

Activities

Palm Beach National Golf and Country Club
GOLF | Despite the name, this classic 18-hole course resides in Lake Worth, not in Palm Beach. It is, however, in Palm Beach County and prides itself on being "the most fun and friendly golf course" in Palm Beach County. The championship layout was designed by Joe Lee in the 1970s and is famous for its 3rd and 18th holes. The 3rd: a par-3 island hole with a sand bunker. The 18th: a short par 4 of 358 yards sandwiched between a wildlife preserve and water. Due to the challenging nature of the course, it's more popular with seasoned golfers. The Steve Haggerty Golf Academy is also based here. Summer rates are significantly discounted. ✉ *7500 St. Andrews Rd., Lake Worth* ☎ *561/965–3381* 🌐 *www.palmbeachnational.com* 🎫 *$94 for 18 holes* 🏌 *18 holes, 6734 yards, par 72.*

Lantana

Lantana—just a bit farther south from Palm Beach than Lake Worth—has inexpensive lodging and a bridge connecting the town to its own beach on a barrier island. Tucked between Lantana and Boynton Beach is **Manalapan,** a tiny but posh residential community.

Beaches

Town of Lantana Public Beach
BEACH—SIGHT | Ideal for quiet ambles, this sandy stretch is also noteworthy for a casual restaurant, the no-frills breezy Dune Deck Café, which is perched above the waterline and offers great views for an oceanfront breakfast or lunch. The beach's huge parking lot is directly adjacent to the Eau Palm Beach (meters take

credit cards), and diagonally across the street is a sizable strip mall with all sorts of conveniences, including boutiques and more eateries. Note: the beach is very narrow and large rocks loom in the water. Nevertheless, these are some of the clearest waters along the Florida coastline, and they make an idyllic background for long walks and great photos. **Amenities:** food and drink; lifeguards; parking (fee); showers; toilets. **Best for:** walking. ✉ *100 N. Ocean Blvd., Lantana* 🌐 *www.lantana.org* 🎫 *$1.50 per hr for parking.*

Restaurants

Jerk Oceano

$$ | **CONTEMPORARY** | Once strictly a pizza place—some say the best in the county—this tiny deck-fronted spot now serves eclectic American cuisine, with a once-a-week night of pizzas. Take cash and your patience along if you're going; everything is made to order, one order at a time. **Known for:** daily-changing menu; thin-crust made-to-order pizza; cash only. [$] *Average main: $16* ✉ *210 E. Ocean Ave., Lantana* ☎ *561/429–5550* 🌐 *www.pizzeriaoceano.com* 💳 *No credit cards* ⏲ *Closed Sun.*

Old Key Lime House

$$ | **SEAFOOD** | **FAMILY** | An informal seafood spot—serving crab cakes, fish sandwiches, and fillets—and a favorite of locals and tourists, is perched on the Intracoastal Waterway with spectacular views. Observation decks with separate bars wrap around the back where boats can dock; indoors is more family-oriented. **Known for:** unpretentious, casual atmosphere; fried and grilled fish; great Key lime pie. [$] *Average main: $20* ✉ *300 E. Ocean Ave., Lantana* ☎ *561/582–1889* 🌐 *www.oldkeylimehouse.com.*

Activities

Bar Jack Fishing

FISHING | Three deep-sea-fishing excursions aboard the *Lady K* deep-sea drift-fishing boat depart daily: 8–noon, 1–5, and 6:30–10:30. They don't take reservations; just show up 30 minutes before the boat is scheduled to leave. The cost of the trip includes fishing license, bait, and tackle. ✉ *314 E. Ocean Ave., Lantana* ☎ *561/588–7612* 🌐 *www.barjackfishing.com* 🎫 *From $40.*

Boynton Beach

In 1884 when fewer than 50 settlers lived in the area, Nathan Boynton, a Civil War veteran from Michigan, paid $25 for 500 acres with a mile-long stretch of beachfront thrown in. How things have changed, with today's population at about 118,000 and property values still on an upswing. Far enough from Palm Beach to remain low-key, Boynton Beach has two parts, the mainland and the barrier island—the town of Ocean Ridge—connected by two bridges.

Sights

Arthur R. Marshall Loxahatchee National Wildlife Refuge

NATURE PRESERVE | **FAMILY** | The most robust part of the northern Everglades, this 221-square-mile refuge is one of two huge water-retention areas accounting for much of the "River of Grass" outside the national park near Miami. Start at the visitor center, which has fantastic interactive exhibits and videos like *Night Sounds of the Everglades* and an airboat simulator. From there, you can take a marsh trail to a 20-foot-high observation tower, or stroll a half-mile boardwalk lined with educational signage through a dense cypress swamp. There are also guided nature walks (including some specifically for bird-watching), and there's great bass fishing (bring your own poles and bait) and a 5½-mile canoe and kayak trail loop (both can be rented from a kiosk by the fishing pier). ✉ *10216 Lee Rd., Boynton Beach* ✣ *Off U.S. 441 between Rte. 804* *and Rte. 806 ☎ 561/734–8303 🌐 www.fws.gov/refuge/arm_loxahatchee/ 🎟 $5 per vehicle; $1 per pedestrian or bicyclist.*

Restaurants

Banana Boat

$$ | **AMERICAN** | A mainstay for local boaters who cruise up and down the Intracoastal Waterway, Banana Boat is easily recognizable by the lighthouse on its roof. On weekends casual crowds clad in tank tops, flip-flops, and bikinis dance to live island music while downing frozen drinks (try the Dirty Banana or Hurricane Wilma) and nibbling on bar foods like burgers and ribs. **Known for:** frozen bar drinks; burgers and other pub grub; brunch on Sunday. *$ Average main: $18 ✉ 739 E. Ocean Ave., Boynton Beach ☎ 561/732–9400 🌐 www.bananaboatboynton.com.*

Delray Beach

15 miles south of West Palm Beach.

A onetime artists' retreat with a small settlement of Japanese farmers, Delray has grown into a sophisticated beach town. Delray's current popularity is caused in large part by the fact that it has the feel of an organic city rather than a planned development or subdivision—and it's completely walkable. Atlantic Avenue, which fell from a tony downtown to a dilapidated main drag, has been reinvented into a mile-plus-long stretch of palm-dotted sidewalks lined with stores, art galleries, and restaurants. Running east–west and ending at the beach, it's a happening place for a stroll, day or night. Another active pedestrian area, the Pineapple Grove Arts District, begins at Atlantic and stretches northward on Northeast 2nd Avenue about half a mile, and yet another active pedestrian way begins at the eastern edge of Atlantic Avenue and runs along the big, broad swimming beach that extends north to George Bush Boulevard and south to Casuarina Road.

GETTING HERE AND AROUND

To reach Delray Beach from Boynton Beach, drive 2 miles south on Interstate 95, U.S. 1, or Route A1A.

ESSENTIALS

VISITOR INFORMATION

Discover the Palm Beaches. *✉ 1555 Palm Beach Lakes Blvd., Suite 800, West Palm Beach ☎ 800/554–7256 🌐 www.thepalmbeaches.com.*

Colony Hotel

HOTEL—SIGHT | The chief landmark along Atlantic Avenue since 1926 is this sunny Mediterranean-revival-style building, which is a member of the National Trust's Historic Hotels of America. Walk through the lobby to the parking lot where original garages still stand—relics of the days when hotel guests would arrive via chauffeured cars and stay there the whole season. The bar is a locals' gathering spot. *✉ 525 E. Atlantic Ave. ☎ 561/276–4123 🌐 colonyflorida.com.*

Delray Beach Center for the Arts at Old School Square

ARTS VENUE | **FAMILY** | Instrumental in the revitalization of Delray Beach circa 1995, this cluster of galleries and event spaces was established in restored school buildings dating from 1913 and 1925. The **Cornell Museum of Art & American Culture** offers ever-changing exhibits on fine arts, crafts, and pop culture, plus a hands-on children's gallery. From November to April, the 323-seat **Crest Theatre** showcases national-touring Broadway musicals, cabaret concerts, dance performances, and lectures. *✉ 51 N. Swinton Ave. ☎ 561/243–7922 🌐 oldschoolsquare.org 🎟 $8 for museum ⏲ Closed Sun. and Mon.*

Zenlike landscapes inspire relaxation at the Morikami Museum and Japanese Gardens in Delray Beach.

★ Morikami Museum and Japanese Gardens

GARDEN | **FAMILY** | The boonies west of Delray Beach seems an odd place to encounter one of the region's most important cultural centers, but this is exactly where you can find a 200-acre cultural and recreational facility heralding the Yamato Colony of Japanese farmers that settled here in the early 20th century. A permanent exhibit details their history, and all together the museum's collection has more than 7,000 artifacts and works of art on rotating display. Traditional tea ceremonies are conducted monthly from October to June, along with educational classes on topics like calligraphy and sushi making (these require advance registration and come with a fee). The six main gardens are inspired by famous historic periods in Japanese garden design and have South Florida accents (think tropical bonsai), and the on-site Cornell Café serves light Asian fare at affordable prices and was recognized by the Food Network as being one of the country's best museum eateries. ✉ *4000 Morikami Park Rd.* ☎ *561/495–0233* 🌐 *www.morikami.org* *$15* ⏲ *Closed Mon.*

Beaches

★ Delray Municipal Beach

BEACH—SIGHT | If you're looking for a place to see and be seen, head for this wide expanse of sand, the heart of which is where Atlantic Avenue meets A1A, close to restaurants, bars, and quick-serve eateries. Singles, families, and water-sports enthusiasts alike love it here. Lounge chairs and umbrellas can be rented every day, and lifeguards man stations half a mile out in each direction. The most popular section of beach is south of Atlantic Avenue on A1A, where the street parking is found. There are also two metered lots with restrooms across from A1A at Sandoway Park and Anchor Park (bring quarters if parking here). On the beach by Anchor Park, north of Casuarina Road, are six volleyball nets and a kiosk that offers Hobie Wave rentals, surfing lessons, and snorkeling excursions to the 1903 SS *Inchulva* shipwreck half a mile offshore. The beach itself is open 24 hours, if you're at a nearby hotel and fancy a moonlight stroll. **Amenities:** food and drink; lifeguards; parking (fee); showers; toilets; water sports. **Best for:** partiers; swimming; windsurfing. *Rte. A1A and E. Atlantic Ave. www.mydelraybeach.com/departments/parks_and_recreation/delray_municipal_beach.php $1.50 per 1 hr parking.*

Restaurants

Blue Anchor

$$ | **BRITISH** | Yes, this pub was actually shipped from England, where it had stood for 150 years in London's historic Chancery Lane. There it was a watering hole for famed Englishmen, including Winston Churchill; here you may hear stories of lingering ghosts told over some suds. **Known for:** fish-and-chips; beer selection; late-night food spot. *Average main: $18 804 E. Atlantic Ave. 561/272-7272.*

★ City Oyster & Sushi Bar

$$$ | **SEAFOOD** | This trendy restaurant mingles the personalities and flavors of a New England oyster bar, a modern sushi eatery, an eclectic seafood grill, and an award-winning dessert bakery to create a can't-miss foodie haven in the heart of Delray's bustling Atlantic Avenue. Dishes like the oyster bisque, New Orleans–style shrimp and crab gumbo, tuna crudo, and lobster fried rice are simply sublime. **Known for:** large selection of oysters; excellent desserts; loud and busy, especially in high season. *Average main: $26 213 E. Atlantic Ave. 561/272-0220 www.cityoysterdelray.com.*

★ Max's Harvest

$$$ | **MODERN AMERICAN** | A few blocks off Atlantic Avenue in the artsy Pineapple Grove neighborhood, a tree-shaded, fenced-in courtyard welcomes foodies eager to dig into its "farm-to-fork" offerings. The menu encourages people to experiment with "to share," "start small," and "think big" plates. **Known for:** menu aimed at sharing; cocktails made from artisanal spirits; Sunday brunch. *Average main: $27 169 N.E. 2nd Ave. 561/381-9970 www.maxsharvest.com No lunch Mon.–Sat.*

★ The Office

$$$ | **AMERICAN** | Scenesters line the massive indoor-outdoor bar from noon until the wee hours at this cooler-than-thou retro library restaurant, but it's worth your time to stop here for the best burger in town. There's a whole selection, but the Prime CEO steals the show: Maytag bleu cheese and Gruyère with tomato-onion confit, arugula, and bacon. **Known for:** upscale comfort food; weekend brunch; alcoholic shakes. *Average main: $24 201 E. Atlantic Ave. 561/276-3600 www.theofficedelray.com.*

Hotels

Colony Hotel & Cabaña Club

$ | **HOTEL** | Not to be confused with the luxurious Colony in Palm Beach, this charming hotel in the heart of downtown Delray dates back to 1926; and although it's landlocked, it does have a cabana club 2 miles away for hotel guests only. **Pros:** pet-friendly; full breakfast buffet included with rooms; free use of cabanas, umbrellas, and hammocks. **Cons:** no pool at main hotel building; must walk to public beach for water-sports rentals. *Rooms from: $195 525 E. Atlantic Ave. 561/276-4123, 800/552-2363 www.thecolonyhotel.com 70 rooms Breakfast.*

Crane's Beach House Boutique Hotel & Luxury Villas

$$$ | **HOTEL** | A tropical oasis, this boutique hotel is a hidden jungle of lush exotic and tropical plants, only a block from the beach. **Pros:** private location within the city setting; short walk to the beach; free parking; property is smoke-free. **Cons:** pricey; no restaurants

on-site; no fitness or spa facilities. $ *Rooms from: $349* ✉ *82 Gleason St.* ☎ *866/372–7263, 561/278–1700* 🌐 *www.cranesbeachhouse.com* *28 rooms, 4 villas* 🍴 *No meals.*

Delray Beach Marriott

$$$$ | **HOTEL** | **FAMILY** | By far the largest hotel in Delray Beach, the Marriott has two towers on a stellar plot of land at the east end of Atlantic Avenue—it's the only hotel that directly overlooks the water, yet it is still within walking distance of restaurants, shopping, and nightlife. **Pros:** fantastic ocean views; pampering spa; two pools. **Cons:** chain-hotel feel; charge for parking; must rent beach chairs. $ *Rooms from: $499* ✉ *10 N. Ocean Blvd.* ☎ *561/274–3200* 🌐 *www.delraybeachmarriott.com* *269 rooms* 🍴 *No meals.*

★ **The Seagate Hotel & Spa**

$$$$ | **RESORT** | **FAMILY** | Those who crave 21st-century luxury in its full glory (ultraswank tilework and fixtures, marble vanities, seamless shower doors) will love this LEED-certified hotel that offers a subtle Zen-coastal motif throughout. **Pros:** two swimming pools; fabulous beach club; exceptionally knowledgeable concierge team. **Cons:** main building not directly on beach; daily resort fee; separate charge for parking. $ *Rooms from: $489* ✉ *1000 E. Atlantic Ave.* ☎ *561/665–4800, 877/577–3242* 🌐 *www.theseagatehotel.com* *154 rooms* 🍴 *No meals.*

★ **Sundy House**

$$ | **B&B/INN** | Just about everything in this bungalow-style B&B is executed to perfection—especially its tropical, verdant grounds, which are actually a nonprofit botanical garden (something anyone can check out during free weekday tours) with a natural, freshwater swimming pool where your feet glide along limestone rocks and mingle with fish. **Pros:** charming eclectic decor; each room is unique; renowned restaurant with popular indoor-outdoor bar and free breakfast; in quiet area off Atlantic Avenue. **Cons:** need to walk through garden to reach rooms (i.e., no covered walkways); beach shuttle requires roughly half-hour advance notice; no private beach facilities. $ *Rooms from: $299* ✉ *106 Swinton Ave.* ☎ *561/272–5678, 877/434–9601* 🌐 *www.sundyhouse.com* *11 rooms* 🍴 *Breakfast.*

Nightlife

Boston's on the Beach

MUSIC CLUBS | You'll find beer flowing and the ocean breeze blowing at this beach bar and eatery, a local watering hole since 1983. The walls are laden with paraphernalia from the Boston Bruins, New England Patriots, and Boston Red Sox, including a shrine to Ted Williams. Boston's can get loud and rowdy (or lively, depending on your taste) later at night. Groove to reggae on Monday, live blues bands on Tuesday, and other live music from rock to country on Friday, Saturday, and Sunday. ✉ *40 S. Ocean Blvd.* ☎ *561/278–3364* 🌐 *www.bostonsonthebeach.com.*

Dada

MUSIC CLUBS | Bands play in the living room of this historic house, though much of the action is outdoors on the lawn in fair weather, where huge trees and lanterns make it a fun stop for drinks or a group night out. It's a place where those who don't drink will also feel comfortable, however, and excellent gourmet nibbles are a huge bonus (a full dinner menu is available, too). A bohemian, younger crowd gathers later into the night. ✉ *52 N. Swinton Ave.* ☎ *561/330–3232* 🌐 *www.sub-culture.org/dada.*

Jellies Bar at the Atlantic Grille

BARS/PUBS | Within the Seagate Hotel, the fun and fabulous bar at the Atlantic Grille is known locally as Jellies Bar. The over-thirty set consistently floats over to this stunning bar to shimmy to live music Tuesday to Saturday; the namesake jellyfish tank never fails to entertain as well. ✉ *The Seagate Hotel & Spa, 1000 E. Atlantic Ave.* ☎ *561/665–4900* 🌐 *www.theatlanticgrille.com.*

Shopping

Atlantic Avenue and Pineapple Grove, both charming neighborhoods for shoppers, have maintained Delray Beach's small-town integrity. Atlantic Avenue is the main street, with art galleries, boutiques, restaurants, and bars lining it from just west of Swinton Avenue all the way east to the ocean. The now established Pineapple Grove Arts District is centered on the half-mile strip of Northeast 2nd Avenue that goes north from Atlantic; these areas are broadening as the downtown area expands south and east.

Furst

JEWELRY/ACCESSORIES | This studio-shop gives you the chance to watch designer Flavie Furst or her pupils at work—and then purchase their fine, handcrafted gold, gold-filled, and silver jewelry. The other half of this space is the Ronald Furst bespoke handbag store, selling unique bags, purses, and sacks. ✉ *123 N.E. 2nd Ave.* ☎ *561/272–6422* 🌐 *www.flaviefurst.com.*

Snappy Turtle

CLOTHING | Jack Rogers sandals and Trina Turk dresses mingle with other fun resort fashions and beachy gifts for the home and family at this family-run store. ✉ *1100 E. Atlantic Ave.* ☎ *888/762–7798* 🌐 *www.snappy-turtle.com.*

Activities

Delray Beach Tennis Center

TENNIS | Each year this complex hosts simultaneous professional tournaments where current stars like Ivo Karlovic and Marin Cilic along with legends like Andy Roddick, Ivan Lendl, and Michael Chang duke it out. Florida's own Chris Evert hosts the Pro-Celebrity Tennis Classic charity event here. The rest of the time, you can practice or learn on 14 clay courts and seven hard courts; private lessons and clinics are available, and it's open from 7:30 am to 9 pm weekdays and until 6 pm weekends. Since most hotels in the area do not have courts, tennis players visiting Delray Beach often come here to play. ✉ *201 W. Atlantic Ave.* ☎ *561/243–7360* 🌐 *www.delraytennis.com.*

Richwagen's Bike & Sport

BICYCLING | Rent bikes by the hour, day, or week (they come with locks, baskets, and helmets); Richwagen's also has copies of city maps on hand. A seven-speed cruiser rents for $60 per week, or $30 a day. They also rent bike trailers, child seats, and electric carts. The shop is closed Sunday. ✉ *298 N.E. 6th Ave.* ☎ *561/276–4234* 🌐 *www.delraybeachbicycles.com.*

Boca Raton

6 miles south of Delray Beach.

Less than an hour south of Palm Beach and anchoring the county's south end, upscale Boca Raton has much in common with its fabled cousin. Both reflect the unmistakable architectural influence of Addison Mizner, their principal developer in the mid-1920s. The meaning of the name Boca Raton (pronounced boca rah- *tone*) often arouses curiosity, with many folks mistakenly assuming it means "rat's mouth." Historians say the probable origin is Boca Ratones, an ancient Spanish geographical term for an inlet filled with jagged rocks or coral. Miami's Biscayne Bay had such an inlet, and in 1823 a mapmaker copying Miami terrain confused the more northern inlet, thus mistakenly labeling this area Boca Ratones. No matter what, you'll know you've arrived in the heart of downtown when you spot the historic town hall's gold dome on the main street, Federal

Highway. Much of the Boca landscape was heavily planned, and many of the bigger sights are clustered in the area around town hall and Lake Boca, a wide stretch of the Intracoastal Waterway between Palmetto Park Road and Camino Real (two main east–west streets at the southern end of town).

GETTING HERE AND AROUND

To get to Boca Raton from Delray Beach, drive south 6 miles on Interstate 95, Federal Highway (U.S. 1), or Route A1A.

ESSENTIALS

VISITOR INFORMATION

Discover the Palm Beaches. ✉ *1555 Palm Beach Lakes Blvd., Suite 800, West Palm Beach* ☎ *800/554–7256* 🌐 *www.thepalmbeaches.com.*

Sights

Boca Raton Museum of Art

ARTS VENUE | **FAMILY** | Changing-exhibition galleries on the first floor showcase internationally known artists—both past and present—at this museum in a spectacular building that's part of the Mizner Park shopping center; the permanent collection upstairs includes works by Picasso, Degas, Matisse, Klee, Modigliani, and Warhol, as well as notable African and pre-Columbian art. Daily tours are included with admission. In addition to the treasure hunts and sketchbooks you can pick up from the front desk, there's a roster of special programs that cater to kids, including studio workshops and gallery walks. Another fun feature is the cell phone audio guide—certain pieces of art have a corresponding number you dial to hear a detailed narration. ✉ *501 Plaza Real, Mizner Park* ☎ *561/392–2500* 🌐 *www.bocamuseum.org* 🎫 *$12* 🕑 *Closed Mon.*

Gumbo Limbo Nature Center

FISH HATCHERY | **FAMILY** | A big draw for kids, this stellar spot has four huge saltwater tanks brimming with sea life, from coral to stingrays to spiny lobsters, touch tanks, plus a sea turtle rehabilitation center. Nocturnal walks in spring and early summer, when staffers lead a quest to find nesting female turtles coming ashore to lay eggs, are popular; so are the hatching releases in August and September. (Call to purchase tickets in advance, as there are very limited spaces.) This is one of only a handful of centers that offer this. There is also a nature trail and butterfly garden, a ¼-mile boardwalk, and a 40-foot observation tower, where you're likely to see brown pelicans and osprey. ✉ *1801 N. Ocean Blvd.* ☎ *561/544–8605* 🌐 *www.gumbolimbo.org* 🎫 *Free ($5 suggested donation); turtle walks $15.*

Old Floresta

HISTORIC SITE | This residential area was developed by Addison Mizner starting in 1925 and is beautifully landscaped with palms and cycads. Its houses are mainly Mediterranean in style, many with balconies supported by exposed wood columns. Explore by driving northward on Paloma Avenue (Northwest 8th Avenue) from Palmetto Park Road, then weave in and out of the side streets. ✉ *Paloma Ave.* ✣ *North of W. Palmetto Park Rd.*

Beaches

Boca's three city beaches (South Beach, Red Reef Park, and Spanish River Park, south to north, respectively) are beautiful and hugely popular; but unless you're a resident or enter via bicycle, parking can be very expensive. Save your receipt if you care to go in and out, or park hop—most guards at the front gate will honor a same-day ticket from another location if you ask nicely. Another option is the county-run South Inlet Park that's walking distance from the Waterstone Resort (formerly the Boca Raton Bridge Hotel) at the southern end of Lake Boca; it has a metered lot for a fraction of the cost, but not quite the same charm as the others.

Red Reef Park

BEACH—SIGHT | **FAMILY** | The ocean with its namesake reef that you can wade up to is just one draw: a fishing zone on the Intracoastal Waterway across the street, a 9-hole golf course next door, and the Gumbo Limbo Environmental Education Center at the northern end of the park can easily make a day at the beach into so much more. But if pure old-fashioned fun in the sun is your focus, there are tons of picnic tables and grills, and two separate playgrounds. Pack snorkels and explore the reef at high tide when fish are most abundant. Swimmers, be warned: once lifeguards leave at 5, anglers flock to the shores and stay well past dark. **Amenities:** lifeguards; parking (fee); showers; toilets. **Best for:** snorkeling; swimming; walking. ✉ *1400 N. Rte. A1A* ☎ *561/393–7974, 561/393–7989 for beach conditions* 🌐 *www.mybocaparks.org/Red-Reef-Park* 🎫 *$16 parking (weekdays), $18 parking (weekends).*

South Beach Park

BEACH—SIGHT | Perched high up on a dune, a large open-air pavilion at the east end of Palmetto Park Road offers a panoramic view of what's in store below on the sand that stretches up the coast. Serious beachgoers need to pull into the main lot a quarter mile north on the east side of A1A, but if a short-but-sweet visit is what you're after, the 15 or so one-hour spots with meters in the circle driveway will do (and not cost you the normal $15 parking fee). During the day, pretty young things blanket the shore, and windsurfers practice tricks in the waves. Quiet quarters are farther north. **Amenities:** lifeguards; parking (fee); showers; toilets. **Best for:** sunset; swimming; walking; windsurfing. ✉ *400 N. Rte A1A* 🌐 *www.myboca.us/Facilities/Facility/Details/South-Beach-Park-56* 🎫 *$15 parking (weekdays), $17 parking (weekends).*

Spanish River Park

BEACH—SIGHT | At 76 acres and including extensive nature trails, this is by far one of the largest ocean parks in the southern half of Palm Beach County and a great pick for people who want more space and fewer crowds. Big groups, including family reunions, favor it because of the number of covered picnic areas for rent, but anyone can snag a free table (there are plenty) under the thick canopy of banyan trees. Even though the vast majority of the park is separated from the surf, you never actually have to cross A1A to reach the beach, because tunnels run under it at several locations. **Amenities:** lifeguards; parking (fee); showers; toilets. **Best for:** solitude; swimming; walking. ✉ *3001 N. Rte. A1A* ☎ *561/393–7815* 🌐 *www.myboca.us/Facilities/Facility/Details/Spanish-River-Park-55* 🎫 *$16 parking (weekdays), $18 parking (weekends).*

Restaurants

★ Casa D'Angelo Ristorante

$$$$ | **TUSCAN** | The lines are deservedly long at chef Angelo Elia's upscale Tuscan restaurant in Boca Raton. The outpost of his renowned Casa D'Angelo in Broward impresses with an outstanding selection of antipasti, carpaccios, pastas, and specialties from the wood-burning oven. **Known for:** wide range of antipasti; veal osso buco and scaloppine; extensive wine list. $ *Average main: $38* ✉ *171 E. Palmetto Park Rd.* ☎ *561/996–1234* 🌐 *www.casa-d-angelo.com* 🕒 *No lunch.*

Farmer's Table

$$$ | **MODERN AMERICAN** | Taking up the local-food mantle, the menu here includes inventive dishes following the seasons using locally sourced meats, seafood, and vegetables. Whenever possible, the foods are organic or sustainable. **Known for:** Buddha bowl with stir-fried vegetables and udon; good wine, cocktails, and beer; some vegan options. $ *Average main: $22* ✉ *Wyndham Boca Raton, 1901 N. Military Trail* ☎ *561/417–5836* 🌐 *www.farmerstableboca.com.*

Racks Downtown Eatery & Tavern
$$$ | **AMERICAN** | Whimsical indoor–outdoor decor and comfort food with a twist help define this popular eatery in tony Mizner Park. Instead of dinner rolls, pretzel bread and mustard get things started. **Known for:** menu made for sharing; raw bar; popular happy hour. Ⓢ *Average main: $23* ✉ *402 Plaza Real, Mizner Park* ☎ *561/395–1662* 🌐 *www.racksboca.com.*

Hotels

★ Boca Beach Club
$$$$ | **RESORT** | **FAMILY** | Dotted with turquoise lounge chairs, ruffled umbrellas, and white-sand beaches, this contemporary resort, part of the Waldorf-Astoria collection, looks as if it were carefully replicated from a retro-chic postcard. **Pros:** great location on the beach; kids' activity center. **Cons:** pricey; shuttle ride away from the main building; resort fee. Ⓢ *Rooms from: $542* ✉ *900 S. Ocean Blvd.* ☎ *888/564–1312* 🌐 *www.bocabeachclub.com* *212 rooms* *No meals.*

★ Boca Raton Resort & Club
$$$ | **RESORT** | **FAMILY** | Addison Mizner built this Mediterranean-style hotel in 1926, and additions over time have created a sprawling, sparkling resort, one of the most luxurious in all of South Florida and part of the Waldorf-Astoria collection. **Pros:** superexclusive—grounds are closed to the public; decor strikes the right balance between historic roots and modern comforts; plenty of activities. **Cons:** daily resort charge; conventions often crowd common areas. Ⓢ *Rooms from: $309* ✉ *501 E. Camino Real* ☎ *561/447–3000, 888/543–1277* 🌐 *www.bocaresort.com* *635 rooms* *No meals.*

Waterstone Resort & Marina
$$ | **HOTEL** | The former Bridge Hotel was transformed into a sleek, modern resort with a $20 million restoration in 2014. **Pros:** short walk to beach; pet-friendly; waterfront views throughout. **Cons:** parking fee; no quiet common space; some rooms noisy from nearby bridge traffic. Ⓢ *Rooms from: $289* ✉ *999 E. Camino Real* ☎ *561/368–9500* 🌐 *www.waterstoneboca.com* *139 rooms* *No meals.*

Shopping

Mizner Park
SHOPPING CENTERS/MALLS | This distinctive 30-acre shopping center off Federal Highway, one block north of Palmetto Park Road, intersperses apartments and town houses among its gardenlike commercial areas. Some three dozen retailers—including Lord & Taylor, which moved in as the only national department store east of Interstate 95 in Boca—line the central axis. It's peppered with fountains and green space, restaurants, galleries, a jazz club, a movie theater, the Boca Raton Museum of Art, and an amphitheater that hosts major concerts as well as community events. ✉ *327 Plaza Real* ☎ *561/362–0606* 🌐 *www.miznerpark.com.*

Royal Palm Place
SHOPPING CENTERS/MALLS | The retail enclave of Royal Palm is filled with independent boutiques selling fine jewelry and apparel. By day, stroll the walkable streets and have your pick of sidewalk cafés for a bite alongside Boca's ladies who lunch. Royal Palm Place assumes a different personality come nightfall, as its numerous restaurants and lounges attract throngs of patrons for great dining and fabulous libations. Parking here is free. ✉ *101 Plaza Real S* ☎ *561/392–8920* 🌐 *www.royalpalmplace.com.*

Town Center at Boca Raton
SHOPPING CENTERS/MALLS | Over on the west side of the interstate in Boca, this indoor megamall has over 220 stores, with anchor stores including Saks and Neiman Marcus and just about every

major high-end designer, including Kate Spade and Anne Fontaine. But not every shop here requires deep pockets. The Town Center at Boca Raton is also firmly rooted with a variety of more affordable national brands like Gap and Banana Republic. ✉ *6000 Glades Rd.* ☎ *561/368–6000* 🌐 *www.simon.com/mall/town-center-at-boca-raton.*

Activities

Force-E

SCUBA DIVING | This company, in business since the late 1970s, rents, sells, and repairs scuba and snorkeling equipment—and organizes about 80 dive trips a week from the Palm Beach Inlet to Port Everglades in Broward County. The PADI–affiliated five-star center has instruction for all levels and offers private charters, too. They have two other outposts besides this Boca Raton location—one north in Riviera Beach and one south in Pompano Beach. ✉ *2621 N. Federal Hwy.* ☎ *561/368–0555, 561/368–0555* 🌐 *www.force-e.com.*

Red Reef Park Executive Golf Course

GOLF | This executive golf course offers 9 holes with varying views of the Intracoastal and the Atlantic Ocean. The Joe Palloka and Charles Ankrom–designed course dates back to 1957. It was refreshed in 2001 through a multimillion-dollar renovation. The scenic holes are between 54 and 227 yards each—great for a quick round. Carts are available, but the short course begs to be walked. Park in the lot across the street from the main beach entrance, and put the greens fees receipt on the dash; that covers parking. ✉ *1221 N. Ocean Blvd.* ☎ *561/391–5014* 🌐 *www.mybocaparks.org/Red-Reef-Executive-Golf-Course* *$17 to walk; $27 to ride* *9 holes, 1357 yards, par 32.*

Palm Beach Gardens

13½ miles north of West Palm Beach.

About 15 minutes northwest of Palm Beach is this relaxed, upscale residential community known for its high-profile golf complex, the **PGA National Resort & Spa.** Although not on the beach, the town is less than a 15-minute drive from the ocean. Malls and dining are centered on the main street, PGA Boulevard, running east from the resort to U.S. 1.

Restaurants

Café Chardonnay

$$$$ | **AMERICAN** | A longtime local favorite, Café Chardonnay is charming, romantic, and has some of the most refined food in the suburban town of Palm Beach Gardens. Soft lighting, warm woods, white tablecloths, and cozy banquettes set the scene for a quiet lunch or romantic dinner. **Known for:** outstanding wine list; innovative specials; many locally sourced ingredients. *Average main: $34* ✉ *The Gardens Square Shoppes, 4533 PGA Blvd., Palm Beach Gardens* ☎ *561/627–2662* 🌐 *www.cafechardonnay.com* *No lunch weekends.*

★ **Coolinary Cafe**

$$$ | **AMERICAN** | It's tucked away in a strip mall and has only 50 seats inside (counting the bar) and a handful out on the sidewalk, but everything down to the condiments is made in-house here. Rabbit sausage and noodles or lamb meatball risotto are examples on the seasonal one-page menus the chef puts together daily. **Known for:** small, focused regular menu; fresh fish specials; long waits for dinner in season. *Average main: $22* ✉ *Donald Ross Village Plaza, 4650 Donald Ross Rd., Suite 110, Palm Beach Gardens* ☎ *561/249–6760* 🌐 *www.coolinarycafe.com* *Closed Sun.*

The Cooper

$$$ | **AMERICAN** | **FAMILY** | With a contemporary farm-to-table menu, and spacious dining rooms and bars, this spot in PGA Commons has plenty of local fans. Happy-hour crowds fill the patio bar-lounge area to sip the craft cocktails and nibble from a cheese or salumi board. **Known for:** wide-ranging American menu; extensive wine list; gluten-free options. *Average main: $23 PGA Commons, 4610 PGA Blvd., Palm Beach Gardens 561/622–0032 www.thecooperrestaurant.com.*

Ironwood Steak & Seafood

$$$$ | **STEAKHOUSE** | Located in the PGA National Resort & Spa, this eatery draws guests, locals, and tourists alike eager for a taste of its fired-up Vulcan-cooked steaks (Vulcan to meat eaters is like Titleist to golfers—the best equipment around). Wagyu and Angus beef cuts are featured. **Known for:** wide range of steaks; raw bar; extensive wine list. *Average main: $38 PGA National Resort & Spa, 400 Ave. of the Champions, Palm Beach Gardens 561/627–4852 www.pgaresort.com/restaurants/ironwood-grille.*

Spoto's Oyster Bar

$$$ | **SEAFOOD** | If you love oysters and other raw bar nibbles, head here, where black-and-white photographs of oyster fisherman adorn the walls. The polished tables give the eatery a clubby look. **Known for:** wide range of oysters and clams; fresh seafood; live music in the Blue Point Lounge. *Average main: $26 PGA Commons, 4560 PGA Blvd., Palm Beach Gardens 561/776–9448 spotos.com.*

Hotels

Hilton Garden Inn Palm Beach Gardens

$$ | **HOTEL** | A hidden find in Palm Beach Gardens, this hotel sits on a small lake next to a residential area but near two shopping malls and close to PGA golf courses. **Pros:** 24-hour free business center; walk to two different malls with shops, restaurants, and movie theaters. **Cons:** outdoor self-parking; no bell service; pool closes at dusk; 15 minutes from the beach. *Rooms from: $209 3505 Kyoto Gardens Dr., Palm Beach Gardens 561/694–5833, 561/694–5829 hiltongardeninn3.hilton.com 180 rooms No meals.*

★ PGA National Resort & Spa

$$$ | **RESORT** | This golfer's paradise (five championship courses and the site of the yearly Honda Classic pro-tour tournament) is a sleek modern playground with a gorgeous zero-entry lagoon pool, seven different places to eat, and a full-service spa with unique mineral-salt therapy pools. **Pros:** dream golf facilities; affordable rates for top-notch amenities; close to shopping malls. **Cons:** no beach shuttle; difficult to get around if you don't have a car; long drive to Palm Beach proper. *Rooms from: $348 400 Ave. of the Champions, Palm Beach Gardens 561/627–2000, 800/633–9150 www.pgaresort.com 339 rooms No meals.*

Shopping

Downtown at The Gardens

SHOPPING CENTERS/MALLS | **FAMILY** | This open-air pavilion down the street from The Gardens Mall has boutiques, chain stores, a grocery store, day spas, a 16-screen movie theater, and a lively restaurant and nighttime bar scene that includes the Dirty Martini and the Yard House, both of which stay open late. A carousel, children's barbershop, boutiques, and Cool Beans (an indoor playground), make this a family-friendly mall. *11701 Lake Victoria Gardens Ave., Palm Beach Gardens 561/340–1600 www.downtownatthegardens.com.*

★ The Gardens Mall

SHOPPING CENTERS/MALLS | **FAMILY** | One of the most refined big shopping malls in America, the 160-store Gardens Mall in northern Palm Beach County has stores like Chanel, Gucci, Louis Vuitton, and David Yurman, along with Saks Fifth Avenue and Nordstrom. There are also plenty of reasonably priced national retailers like H&M and Abercrombie & Fitch, Bloomingdale's, and Macy's. This beautiful mall has prolific seating pavilions, making it a great place to spend a humid summer afternoon. ✉ *3101 PGA Blvd., Palm Beach Gardens* ☎ *561/775–7750* 🌐 *www.thegardensmall.com.*

Activities

Spring-training fans travel to the area to see the Cardinals and Marlins tune up for their seasons at Roger Dean Stadium in Palm Beach Gardens, and to watch their AAA feeder teams in summer. Port St. Lucie and Vero Beach stadiums and more teams are only a short drive up Interstate 95.

★ PGA National Resort & Spa

GOLF | If you're the kind of traveler who takes along a set of clubs, you'll achieve nirvana on the greens of PGA National Resort & Spa. The five championship courses are open only to hotel guests and club members, which means you'll have to stay to play, but packages that include a room and a round of golf are reasonably priced. The Champion Course, redesigned by Jack Nicklaus and famous for its Bear Trap holes, is the site of the yearly Honda Classic pro tournament. The four other challenging courses are also legends in the golfing world: the Palmer, named for its architect, the legendary Arnold Palmer; the Fazio (formerly the Haig)) and the Squire, both from Tom and George Fazio; and the Karl Litten–designed Estates, the sole course not on the property (it is located 5 miles west of the PGA resort). Lessons are available at the David Leadbetter Golf Academy, and they also run a summertime kids' golf camp. ✉ *PGA National Resort & Spa, 1000 Ave. of the Champions, Palm Beach Gardens* ☎ *561/627–1800* 🌐 *www.pgaresort.com/golf/pga-national-golf* *$409 for 18 holes for Champion Course, Fazio Course, and Squire Course. $250 for 18 holes for Palmer Course and Estates Course.* *Champion Course: 18 holes, 7048 yards, par 72. Palmer Course: 18 holes, 7079 yards, par 72. Fazio Course: 18 holes, 6806 yards, par 72. Squire Course: 18 holes, 6465 yards, par 72. Estates Course: 18 holes, 6694 yards, par 72.*

Singer Island

6 miles north of West Palm Beach.

Across the inlet from the northern end of Palm Beach is Singer Island, which is actually a peninsula that's big enough to pass for a barrier island, rimmed with mom-and-pop motels and high-rises. Palm Beach Shores occupies its southern tip (where tiny Peanut Island is a stone's throw away); farther north are Riviera Beach and North Palm Beach, which also straddle the inlet and continue on the mainland.

Beaches

★ John D. MacArthur Beach State Park

BEACH—SIGHT | **FAMILY** | If getting far from rowdy crowds is your goal, this spot on the north end of Singer Island is a good choice. Encompassing 2 miles of beach and a lush subtropical coastal habitat, inside you'll find a great place for kayaking, snorkeling at natural reefs, bird-watching, fishing, and hiking. You might even get to see a few manatees. A 4,000-square-foot nature center has aquariums and displays on local flora and fauna, and there's a long roster of monthly activities, such as surfing clinics, art lessons, and live bluegrass music. Guided sea turtle walks are available at night in season, and daily nature walks depart at 10 am. Check the website for times and costs of activities. **Amenities:** parking (fee); showers; toilets; water sports. **Best for:** solitude; surfing; swimming; walking. ✉ *10900 Jack Nicklaus Dr., North Palm Beach* ☎ *561/624–6950* 🌐 *www.macarthurbeach.org* 🎫 *Parking $5, bicyclists and pedestrians $2.*

Peanut Island Park

BEACH—SIGHT | Partiers, families, and overnight campers all have a place to go on the 79 acres here. The island, in a wide section of the Intracoastal between Palm Beach Island and Singer Island with an open channel to the sea, is accessible only by private boat or water taxi, two of which set sail regularly from the Riviera Beach Municipal Marina (🌐 *peanutislandshuttleboat.com/*) and the Sailfish Marina (🌐 *www.sailfishmarina.com/water_taxi*). Fun-loving seafarers looking for an afternoon of Jimmy Buffett and picnics aboard pull up to the day docks or the huge sandbar on the north—float around in an inner tube, and it's spring break déjà vu. Walk along the 20-foot-wide paver-lined path encircling the island, and you'll hit a 170-foot fishing pier, a campground, the lifeguarded section to the south that is particularly popular with families because of its artificial reef. There are picnic tables and grills, but no concessions. A new ordinance means alcohol possession and consumption is restricted to permit areas. **Amenities:** lifeguards (summer only); showers; toilets. **Best for:** partiers; sunrise; swimming; walking. ✉ *6500 Peanut Island Rd., Riviera Beach* ☎ *561/845–4445* 🌐 *discover.pbcgov.org/parks/Locations/Peanut-Island.aspx* 🎫 *Beach free; water taxi $12; park stay $17.*

Hotels

Palm Beach Marriott Singer Island Beach Resort & Spa

$$$$ | **RESORT** | **FAMILY** | Families with a yen for the cosmopolitan but requiring the square footage and comforts of home revel in these one- and two-bedroom suites with spacious, marble-tiled, granite-topped kitchens. **Pros:** wide beach; genuinely warm service; plenty of kids' activities; sleek spa. **Cons:** no upscale dining nearby; unspectacular room views for an oceanside hotel. $ *Rooms from: $509* ✉ *3800 N. Ocean Dr., Singer Island, Riviera Beach* ☎ *561/340–1700, 877/239–5610* 🌐 *www.marriott.com* *202 suites* 🍽 *No meals.*

Sailfish Marina Resort

$ | **HOTEL** | A marina with deepwater slips—and prime location at the mouth to the Atlantic Ocean on the Intracoastal Waterway across from Peanut Island—lures boaters and anglers here to these rather basic rooms, studios, and efficiencies. **Pros:** inexpensive rates; great waterfront restaurant; has a water taxi; pretty grounds. **Cons:** no real lobby; not directly on beach; area attracts a party crowd and can be noisy; dated decor. $ *Rooms from: $150* ✉ *98 Lake Dr., Palm Beach Shores* ☎ *561/844–1724* 🌐 *www.sailfishmarina.com* *30 units* 🍽 *No meals.*

Activities

Sailfish Marina

FISHING | **FAMILY** | Book a full or half day of deep-sea fishing for up to six people with the seasoned captains and large fleet of 28- to 65-foot boats. A ship's store and restaurant are also on-site. ✉ *Sailfish Marina Resort, 98 Lake Dr., Palm Beach Shores* ☎ *561/844–1724* 🌐 *www.sailfishmarina.com.*

Juno Beach

12 miles north of West Palm Beach.

This small town east of Palm Beach Gardens has 2 miles of shoreline that becomes home to thousands of sea turtle hatchlings each year, making it one of the world's densest nesting sites. A 990-foot-long pier lures fishermen and beachgoers seeking a spectacular sunrise.

Sights

★ Loggerhead Park Marine Life Center of Juno Beach

NATURE PRESERVE | FAMILY | Located in a certified green building in Loggerhead Park—and established by Eleanor N. Fletcher, the "turtle lady of Juno Beach"—the center focuses on the conservation of sea turtles, using education, research, and rehabilitation. The education center houses displays of coastal natural history, detailing Florida's marine ecosystems and the life and plight of the various species of sea turtles found on Florida's shores. You can visit recovering turtles in their outdoor hospital tanks; volunteers are happy to tell you the turtles' heroic tales of survival. The center has regularly scheduled activities, such as Kid's Story Time and Junior Vet Lab, and most are free of charge. During peak nesting season, the center hosts night walks to experience turtle nesting in action. Given that the adjacent beach is part of the second-biggest nesting ground for loggerhead turtles in the world, your chances of seeing this natural phenomenon are pretty high (over 15,000 loggerheads nested here in 2017). *14200 U.S. 1 561/627–8280 www.marinelife.org Free.*

Beaches

Juno Beach Ocean Park

BEACH—SIGHT | FAMILY | An angler's dream, this beach has a 990-foot pier that's open daily, like the beach, from sunrise to sunset—but from November through February, pier gates open at 6 am and don't close until 10 pm on weeknights and midnight on weekends, making it an awesome place to catch a full sunrise and sunset (that is, if you don't mind paying the small admission fee). A concession stand on the pier sells fish food as well as such human favorites as burgers, sandwiches, and ice cream. Rods and tackle are rented here. Families adore this shoreline because of the amenities and vibrant atmosphere. There are plenty of kids building castles but also plenty of teens having socials and hanging out along the beach. Pets are not allowed here, but they are allowed on Jupiter Beach. **Amenities:** food and drink; lifeguards; parking (no fee); showers; toilets. **Best for:** sunrise; sunset; swimming. *14775 U.S. 1 561/799–0185 for pier discover.pbcgov.org/parks/Locations/Juno-Beach.aspx $4 to fish, $1 to enter pier; beach free.*

Jupiter and Vicinity

12 miles north of West Palm Beach.

Jupiter is one of the few towns in the region not fronted by an island but still quite close to the fantastic hotels, shopping, and dining of the Palm Beach area. The beaches here are on the mainland, and Route A1A runs for almost 4 miles along the beachfront dunes and beautiful homes.

Northeast across the Jupiter Inlet from Jupiter is the southern tip of Jupiter Island, which stretches about 15 miles to the St. Lucie Inlet. Here expansive and expensive estates often retreat from the road behind screens of vegetation, and the population dwindles the farther north you go. At the very north end, which adjoins tiny Hobe Sound in Martin County on the mainland, sea turtles come to nest.

GETTING HERE AND AROUND

If you're coming from the airport in West Palm Beach, take Interstate 95 to Route 706. Otherwise, Federal Highway (U.S. 1) and Route A1A are usually more convenient.

CONTACTS Discover the Palm Beaches. *1555 Palm Beach Lakes Blvd., Suite 800, West Palm Beach 800/554–7256 www.thepalmbeaches.com.*

Away from developed shorelines, Jupiter's Blowing Rocks Preserve is rugged and otherworldly.

Sights

★ Blowing Rocks Preserve

BEACH—SIGHT | FAMILY | Managed by the Nature Conservancy, this protected area on Jupiter Island is headlined by an almost otherworldly looking limestone shelf that fringes South Florida's most turquoise waters. Also protected within its 73 acres are plants native to beachfront dunes, coastal strand (the landward side of the dunes), mangrove swamps, and tropical hardwood forests. There are two short walking trails on the Intracoastal side of the preserve, as well as an education center and a butterfly garden. The best time to come and see the "blowing rocks" is when a storm is brewing: if high tides and strong offshore winds coincide, the sea blows spectacularly through the holes in the eroded outcropping. During a calm summer day, you can swim in crystal clear waters on the mile-long beach and climb around the rock formations at low tide. Park in one of the two lots, because police ticket cars on the road. ✉ *574 S. Beach Rd., CR 707, Hobe Sound* ☎ *561/744–6668* 🌐 *www.nature.org/blowingrocks* 🎫 *$2.*

★ Hobe Sound Nature Center

NATURE PRESERVE | FAMILY | Though located in the Hobe Sound National Wildlife Refuge, this nature center is an independent organization. The exhibit hall houses live baby alligators, crocodiles, a scary-looking tarantula, and more—and is a child's delight. Just off the center's entrance is a mile-long nature trail loop that snakes through three different kinds of habitats: coastal hammock, estuary beach, and sand pine scrub, which is one of Florida's most unusual and endangered plant communities and what composes much of the refuge's nearly 250 acres. **■ TIP→ Among the center's more popular events are the annual nighttime sea turtle walks, held between May and June; reservations are accepted as early as April 1.** ✉ *13640 S.E. U.S. 1, Hobe Sound* ☎ *772/546–2067* 🌐 *www.hobesoundnaturecenter.com* 🎫 *Free (donation requested)* 🕒 *Closed Sun.*

★ Jonathan Dickinson State Park
NATIONAL/STATE PARK | FAMILY | This serene state park provides a glimpse of predevelopment "real" Florida. A beautiful showcase of Florida inland habitat, the park teems with endangered gopher tortoises and manatees. From Hobe Mountain, an ancient dune topped with a tower, you are treated to a panoramic view of this park's more than 11,000 acres of varied terrain and the Intracoastal Waterway. The Loxahatchee River, named a National Wild and Scenic River, cuts through the park, and is home to plenty of charismatic manatees in winter and alligators year-round. Two-hour boat tours of the river depart daily. Kayak rentals are available, as is horseback riding (it was reintroduced after a 30-year absence). Among the amenities are a dozen newly redone cabins for rent, tent sites, bicycle and hiking trails, two established campgrounds and some primitive campgrounds, and a snack bar. Palmettos on the Loxahatchee is a new food-and-beverage garden with wine, beer, and local foods featured. Don't skip the Elsa Kimbell Environmental Education and Research Center, which has interactive displays, exhibits, and a short film on the natural history of the area. The park is also a fantastic birding location, with about 150 species to spot. ✉ *16450 S.E. U.S. 1, Hobe Sound* ☎ *772/546–2771* 🌐 *www.floridastateparks.org/jonathandickinson* 🎫 *Vehicles $6, bicyclists and pedestrians $2.*

★ Jupiter Inlet Lighthouse & Museum
MUSEUM | FAMILY | Designed by Civil War hero Lieutenant George Gordon Meade, this working brick lighthouse has been under the Coast Guard's purview since 1860. Tours of the 108-foot-tall landmark are held approximately every half hour and are included with admission. (Children must be at least 4 feet tall to go to the top.) The museum tells about efforts to restore this graceful spire to the way it looked from 1860 to 1918; its galleries and outdoor structures, including a pioneer home, also showcase local history dating back 5,000 years. ✉ *Lighthouse Park, 500 Capt. Armour's Way, Jupiter* ☎ *561/747–8380* 🌐 *www.jupiterlighthouse.org* 🎫 *$12* ⏲ *Closed Mon. May–Dec.*

Beaches

Carlin Park
BEACH—SIGHT | About ½ mile south of the Jupiter Beach Resort and Indiantown Road, the quiet beach here is just one draw; otherwise, the manicured park, which straddles A1A, is chock-full of activities and amenities, and it has the most free parking of any beach park in the area. Several picnic pavilions, including a few beachside, two bocce ball courts, six lighted tennis courts, a baseball diamond, a wood-chip-lined running path, and an amphitheater that hosts free concerts and Shakespeare productions are just some of the highlights. Locals also swear by the Lazy Loggerhead Café that's right off the seaside parking lot for a great casual breakfast and lunch. **Amenities:** food and drink; lifeguards; parking (no fee); showers; toilets. **Best for:** swimming; walking. ✉ *400 S. Rte. A1A, Jupiter* 🌐 *discover.pbcgov.org/parks/Locations/Carlin.aspx.*

Hobe Sound National Wildlife Refuge
BEACH—SIGHT | Nature lovers seeking to get as far as possible from the madding crowds will feel at peace at this refuge managed by the U.S. Fish & Wildlife Service. It's a haven for people who want some quiet while they walk around and photograph the gorgeous coastal sand dunes, where turtles nest and shells often wash ashore. The beach has been severely eroded by high tides and strong winds (surprisingly, surfing is allowed and many do partake). You can't actually venture within most of the 735 protected acres, so if hiking piques your interest, head to the refuge's main entrance a few miles away on Hobe Sound (*13640 S.E. U.S. 1 in Hobe Sound*) for a mile-long trek

close to the nature center, or to nearby Jonathan Dickinson State Park (*16450 S.E. U.S. 1 in Hobe Sound*). **Amenities:** parking (fee); toilets. **Best for:** solitude; surfing; walking. ✉ *198 N. Beach Rd., Jupiter Island* ⊕ *At end of N. Beach Rd.* ☎ *772/546–6141* 🌐 *www.fws.gov/hobesound* 🎫 *$5.*

Jupiter Beach

BEACH—SIGHT | Famous throughout all of Florida for a unique pooch-loving stance, the town of Jupiter's beach welcomes Yorkies, Labs, pugs—you name it—along its 2½-mile oceanfront. Dogs can frolic unleashed (once they're on the beach) or join you for a dip. Free parking spots line A1A in front of the sandy stretch, and there are multiple access points and continuously refilled dog-bag boxes (29 to be exact). The dog beach starts on Marcinski Road (Beach Marker No. 25) and continues north until Beach Marker No. 59. Before going, read through the guidelines posted on the Friends of Jupiter Beach website; the biggest things to note are be sure to clean up after your dog and steer clear of lifeguarded areas to the north and south. **■ TIP→ Dogs fare best early morning and late afternoon, when the sand isn't too hot for their paws.** **Amenities:** showers; toilets. **Best for:** walking. ✉ *2188 Marcinski Rd., Jupiter* ⊕ *Across the street from the parking lot* ☎ *561/748–8140* 🌐 *www.friendsofjupiterbeach.org.*

Restaurants

Guanabanas

$$ | **SEAFOOD** | Expect a wait for dinner, which is not necessarily a bad thing at this island paradise of a waterfront restaurant and bar. Take the wait time to explore the bridges and trails of the open-air tropical oasis, or grab a chair by the river to watch the sunset, listen to the live band, or nibble on some conch fritters at the large tiki bar until your table is ready. **Known for:** water views from the outdoor dining area; live music; weekend breakfast. $ *Average main: $18* ✉ *960 N. Rte. A1A, Jupiter* ☎ *561/747–8878* 🌐 *www.guanabanas.com.*

Little Moir's Food Shack

$$ | **SEAFOOD** | This local favorite is not much to look at and a bit tricky to find, but well worth the search. The fried-food standards you might expect at such a casual, small place that uses plastic utensils are not found on the menu; instead there are fried tuna rolls with basil, and panko-crusted fried oysters with spicy fruit salad. **Known for:** fresh fish; good beer selection; long lines during the season. $ *Average main: $17* ✉ *103 S. U.S. 1, Jupiter* ☎ *561/741–3626* 🌐 *www.littlemoirs.com/food-shack* ⊙ *Closed Sun.*

Sinclair's Ocean Grill

$$$$ | **SEAFOOD** | This upscale restaurant at the Jupiter Beach Resort & Spa has a slick, contemporary look and is a favorite of locals in the know. The menu has a daily selection of fresh fish, such as Atlantic black grouper over lemon crab salad, sesame-seared tuna, and mahimahi with fruit salsa. **Known for:** fresh fish; weekend brunch; drinks in Sinclair's Lounge. $ *Average main: $31* ✉ *Jupiter Beach Resort, 5 N. Rte. A1A, Jupiter* ☎ *561/746–2511* 🌐 *www.jupiterbeachresort.com.*

Taste Casual Dining

$$ | **AMERICAN** | Located in the center of historic Hobe Sound, this cozy dining spot with a pleasant, screened-in patio offers piano dinner music on Fridays. Locals like to hang out at the old, English-style wine bar; however, the food itself is the biggest draw here. **Known for:** fresh fish specials; slow-cooked prime rib; signature Gorgonzola salad. $ *Average main: $18* ✉ *11750 S.E. Dixie Hwy., Hobe Sound* ☎ *772/546–1129* 🌐 *www.tasteaculinaryadventure.50megs.com* ⊙ *May–Oct., closed Sun.*

★ **Jupiter Beach Resort & Spa**

$$$ | **RESORT** | **FAMILY** | Families love this nine-story hotel filled with rich Caribbean-style rooms containing mahogany sleigh beds and armoires; all rooms have balconies, and many have stunning views of the ocean and local landmarks like the Jupiter Lighthouse and Juno Pier. **Pros:** fantastic beachside pool area with hammocks and a fire pit; marble showers; great restaurant. **Cons:** $25 nightly resort fee; no covered parking; bathtubs in suites only. *Rooms from: $360 5 N. Rte. A1A, Jupiter 561/746–2511, 800/228–8810 www.jupiterbeachresort.com 168 rooms No meals.*

Wyndham Grand Jupiter at Harbourside Place

$$$ | **HOTEL** | This luxury waterfront hotel is in an upscale complex of business and retail development just minutes from the beach. **Pros:** convenient to plaza shops and restaurants; only minutes from the beach; boat docks and fitness center available. **Cons:** no covered walkway to restaurant; no green spaces; pricey. *Rooms from: $309 Harbourside Place, 122 Soundings Ave., Jupiter 561/273–6600 www.wyndhamgrandjupiter.com 179 rooms No meals.*

Abacoa Golf Club

GOLF | Built in 1999, the tagline for this Joe Lee–designed 18-hole course in Jupiter is "public golf at its finest." Most of the courses in this golfing community are private, but the range at Abacoa is on par with them and membership (nor deep pockets) *isn't* required. Since 2013, $1 million has been spent to renovate the facilities throughout the course and clubhouse. One of the course's more interesting features includes the several elevation changes throughout, which is a rarity in flat Florida. The course caters to golfers at all skill levels. The greens fee ranges from $45 to $110 (including cart), depending on time of year, time of day, and weekday versus weekend. *105 Barbados Dr., Jupiter 561/622–0036 www.abacoagolfclub.com $100 for 18 holes 18 holes, 7200 yards, par 72.*

Golf Club of Jupiter

GOLF | Locally owned and operated since 1981, this Lamar Smith–designed golf club features a public championship golf course—the "Jupiter" course—with 18 holes of varying difficulty. It has a course rating of 69.9 and a slope rating of 117 on Bermuda grass. There's a full-time golf pro on staff and an on-site bar and restaurant. *1800 S. Central Blvd., Jupiter 561/747–6262 www.golfclubofjupiter.com $59 for 18 holes 18 holes, 6275 yards, par 70.*

★ **Jonathan Dickinson State Park River Tours**

TOUR—SPORTS | **FAMILY** | Boat tours of the Loxahatchee River and guided horseback rides, along with canoe, kayak, bicycle, and boat rentals, are offered daily. The popular Wilderness Guided Boat Tour leaves four times daily at 9 and 11 am and 1 and 3 pm (for best wildlife photos take the 11 or 1 tour). The pontoon cruises for 90 minutes up the Loxahatchee in search of manatees, herons, osprey, alligators, and more. The skipper details the region's natural and cultural history; and from Thursday to Monday the boat also stops at the Trapper Nelson Interpretive Site for a tour of the home of a local legend, the so-called Wildman of the Loxahatchee. *Jonathan Dickinson State Park, 16450 S.E. U.S. 1, Hobe Sound 561/746–1466 www.jdstatepark.com/boat-tours $6 park admission; boat tours $20.*

Roger Dean Stadium

BASEBALL/SOFTBALL | It's a spring-training doubleheader: both the St. Louis Cardinals and the Miami Marlins call this 6,600-seat facility home base from February to April. The rest of the year two

Lake Okeechobee

Forty miles west of West Palm Beach, amid the farms and cattle pastures rimming the western edges of Palm Beach and Martin counties, is **Lake Okeechobee**, the second-largest freshwater lake completely within the United States. It's girdled by 120 miles of road yet remains shielded from sight for almost its entire circumference. (The best place to view it is in Port Mayaca on the north side—where you can get great sunset shots—and the Okeechobee docks on the northwest.) Lake Okeechobee—the Seminole's "Big Water" and the gateway of the great Everglades watershed—measures 730 square miles, at its longest roughly 33 miles north–south and 30 miles east–west, with an average natural depth of only 10 feet (flood control brings the figure up to 12 feet and deeper). Six major lock systems and 32 separate water-control structures manage the water and allow boaters to cross the state through its channels from the Atlantic Ocean to the Gulf of Mexico. Encircling the lake is a 34-foot-high grassy levee that locals call "the dike," and atop it, the Lake Okeechobee Scenic Trail, a segment of the Florida National Scenic Trail that's an easy, flat ride for bikers. Anglers have a field day here as well, with great bass and perch catches. **■TIP→ There's no shade, so wear a hat, sunscreen, and bug repellent (a must). Be sure to bring lots of bottled water, too, because restaurants and stores are few and far between.**

minor-league teams (Jupiter Hammerheads and Palm Beach Cardinals) share its turf. In the Abacoa area of Jupiter, the grounds are surrounded by a mix of restaurants and sports bars for pre- and postgame action. ✉ *4751 Main St., Jupiter* ☎ *561/775–1818* 🌐 *www.rogerdeanstadium.com* 🎫 *From $12.*

Stuart and Jensen Beach

10 miles north of Hobe Sound.

The compact town of Stuart lies on a peninsula that juts out into the St. Lucie River off the Indian River and has a remarkable amount of shoreline for its size. It scores huge points for its charming historic district and is the self-described "Sailfish Capital of the World." On the southern end, you'll find Port Salerno and its waterfront area, the Manatee Pocket, which are a skip away from the St. Lucie Inlet.

Immediately north of Stuart is down-to-earth Jensen Beach. Both Stuart and Jensen Beach straddle the Indian River and occupy Hutchinson Island, the barrier island that continues into the town of Fort Pierce. Between late April and August, hundreds, even thousands, of turtles come here to nest along the Atlantic beaches. Residents have taken pains to curb the runaway development that has created commercial crowding to the north and south, although some high-rises have popped up along the shore.

GETTING HERE AND AROUND

To get to Stuart and Jensen Beach from Jupiter and Hobe Sound, drive north on Federal Highway (U.S. 1). Route A1A crosses through downtown Stuart and is the sole main road throughout Hutchinson Island. Route 707 runs parallel on the mainland directly across the tidal lagoon.

Sights

Strict architectural and zoning standards guide civic-renewal projects in the heart of Stuart. Antiques stores, restaurants, and more than 50 specialty shops are rooted within the two-block area of Flagler Avenue and Osceola Street north of where A1A cuts across the peninsula (visit *www.stuartmainstreet.org* for more information). A self-guided walking-tour pamphlet is available at assorted locations to clue you in on this once-small fishing village's early days.

Elliott Museum

MUSEUM | FAMILY | Opened in March 2013, the museum's glittering, green-certified, 48,000-square-foot facility is double its previous size and houses a permanent collection along with traveling exhibits. The museum was founded in 1961 in honor of Sterling Elliott, an inventor of an early automated-addressing machine, the egg crate, and a four-wheel bicycle, and it celebrates history, art, and technology, much of it viewed through the lens of the automobile's effect on American society. There's an impressive array of antique cars, plus paintings, historic artifacts, and nostalgic goods like vintage baseball cards and toys. *825 N.E. Ocean Blvd., Jensen Beach* *772/225–1961* *elliott-museum.org* *$14.*

Florida Oceanographic Coastal Center

NATURE PRESERVE | FAMILY | This hydroland is the place to go for an interactive marine experience and live the center's mission "to inspire environmental stewardship of Florida's coastal ecosystems through education and research." Petting and feeding stingrays can be done at various times; in the morning, a sea turtle program introduces you to three full-time residents. Make sure to catch the "feeding frenzy" when keepers toss food into the 750,000-gallon lagoon tank and sharks, tarpon, and snook swarm the surface. Join a 1-mile guided walk through the coastal hardwood hammock and mangrove swamp habitats, or explore the trails on your own—you may see a dolphin or manatee swim by. *890 N.E. Ocean Blvd., Stuart* *772/225–0505* *www.floridaocean.org* *$12.*

Gilbert's Bar House of Refuge Museum

MUSEUM | Built in 1875 on Hutchinson Island, this is the only remaining example of 10 such structures that were erected by the U.S. Life-Saving Service (a predecessor of the Coast Guard) to aid stranded sailors. The displays here include antique lifesaving equipment, maps, artifacts from nearby wrecks, and boatbuilding tools. The museum is affiliated with the nearby Elliott Museum; package tickets are available. *301 S.E. MacArthur Blvd., Jensen Beach* *772/225–1875* *www.houseofrefuge-fl.org* *$8.*

Beaches

Bathtub Reef Beach

BEACH—SIGHT | FAMILY | Rough tides are often the norm in this stretch of the Atlantic Ocean, and frequently take away the beach, but a charming enclave at the southern end of Hutchinson Island—after the Marriott's beach and right by the Indian River Plantation luxury development—provides a perfect escape for families with young children and anyone who likes to snorkel. The waters are shallow and usually calm, and youngsters can walk up to the reef and see a dazzling assortment of fish. The parking lot is small, so get there early. Erosion is a problem, and sometimes lifeguards can't pull their hefty chairs out, leaving the beach unguarded (but it shouldn't deter you, because the sea isn't rough). **Amenities:** parking (no fee); lifeguards; toilets. **Best for:** snorkeling; swimming. *1585 S.E. MacArthur Blvd., Stuart* *772/320–3112* *www.martin.fl.us/BathtubReefBeach.*

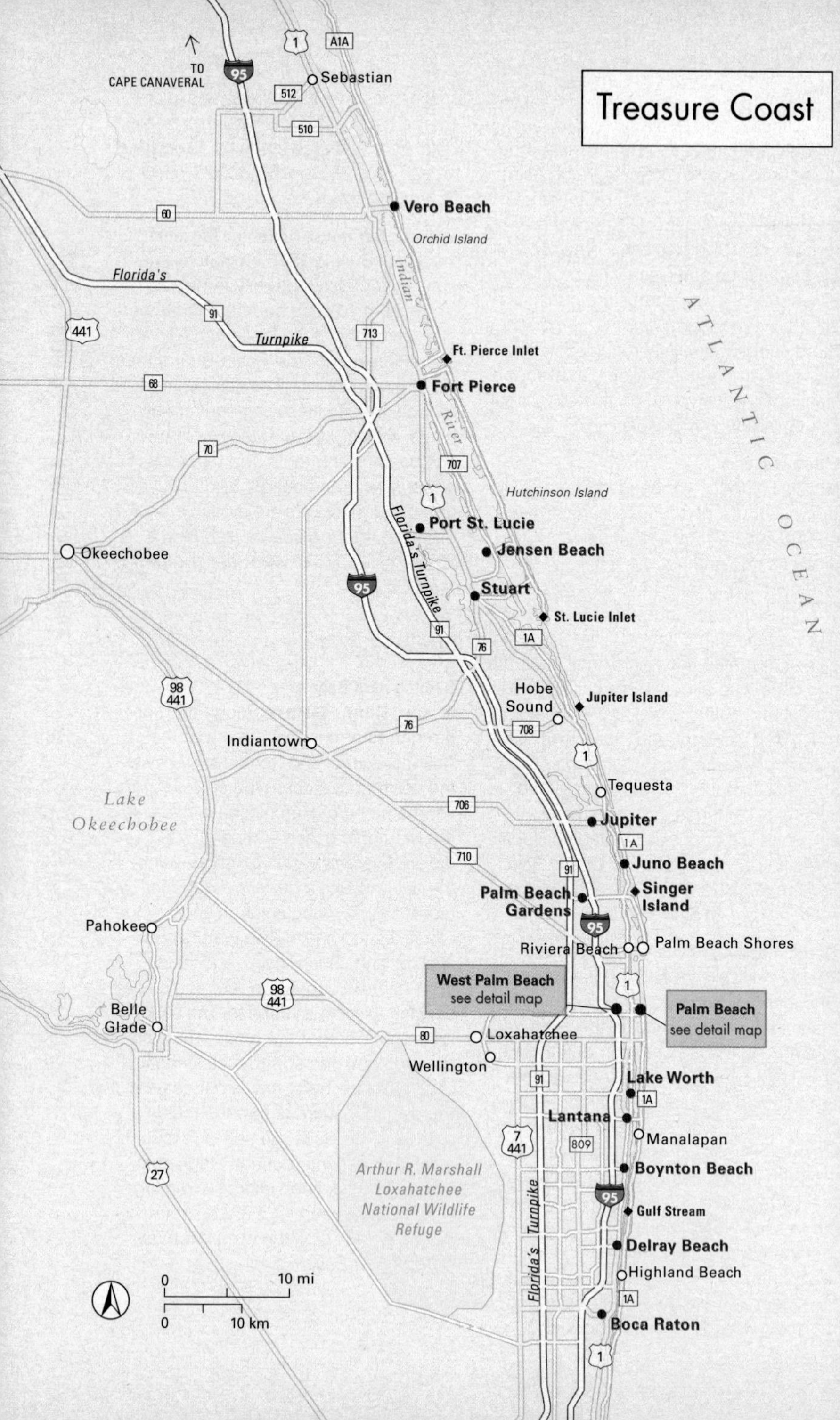
Treasure Coast
TO
CAPE CANAVERAL
Sebastian
Vero Beach
Orchid Island
Indian River
Florida's Turnpike
Ft. Pierce Inlet
Fort Pierce
Hutchinson Island
Port St. Lucie
Jensen Beach
Okeechobee
Stuart
St. Lucie Inlet
Hobe Sound
Jupiter Island
Indiantown
Tequesta
Jupiter
Lake Okeechobee
Juno Beach
Palm Beach Gardens
Singer Island
Pahokee
Riviera Beach
Palm Beach Shores
West Palm Beach
see detail map
Palm Beach
see detail map
Belle Glade
Loxahatchee
Wellington
Lake Worth
Lantana
Manalapan
Boynton Beach
Arthur R. Marshall Loxahatchee National Wildlife Refuge
Gulf Stream
Delray Beach
Highland Beach
Boca Raton
ATLANTIC OCEAN
0
10 mi
0
10 km

Florida's Sea Turtles: The Nesting Season 

From May to October, turtles nest all along the Florida coast. Female loggerhead, Kemp's ridley, and other species living in the Atlantic Ocean or Gulf of Mexico swim as much as 2,000 miles to the Florida shore. By night they drag their 100- to 400-pound bodies onto the beach to the dune line. Then each digs a hole with her flippers, drops in 100 or so eggs, covers them up, and returns to sea.

The babies hatch about 60 days later. Once they burst out of the sand, the hatchlings must get to sea rapidly or risk becoming dehydrated from the sun or being caught by crabs, birds, or other predators.

Instinctively, baby turtles head toward bright light, probably because for millions of years starlight or moonlight reflected on the waves was the brightest light around, serving to guide hatchlings to water. Many coastal towns enforce light restrictions during nesting months. Florida homeowners are asked to dim their lights on behalf of baby sea turtles.

At night, volunteers walk the beaches, searching for signs of turtle nests. Upon finding telltale scratches in the sand, they cordon off the sites, so beachgoers will leave the spots undisturbed. (It is illegal to disturb turtle nests.) Volunteers also keep watch over nests when babies are about to hatch, and assist disoriented hatchlings.

Several local organizations offer nightly turtle walks during nesting season. Most are in June and July, starting around 8 pm and sometimes lasting until midnight. Expect a $10 to $15 fee. Call in advance to confirm times and to reserve a spot—places usually take reservations as early as April. If you're in southern Palm Beach County, contact Boca Raton's **Gumbo Limbo Nature Center** (☎ *561/338–1473* 🌐 *www.gumbolimbo.org*). The **John D. MacArthur Beach State Park** (☎ *561/624–6952* 🌐 *www.macarthurbeach.org*) is convenient for Palm Beach–area visitors at the northern end of Singer Island. **Hobe Sound Nature Center** (☎ *772/546–2067* 🌐 *www.hobesoundnaturecenter.com*) is farther up. Treasure Coasters in or near Vero Beach can go to **Sebastian Inlet State Park** (☎ *321/984–4852* 🌐 *www.floridastateparks.org/sebastianinlet*).

Stuart Beach

BEACH—SIGHT | FAMILY | When the waves robustly roll in, the surfers are rolling in, too. Beginning surfers are especially keen on Stuart Beach because of its ever-vigilant lifeguards, and pros to the sport like the challenges that the choppy waters here bring. But the beach is equally popular with surf fishers. Families enjoy the snack bar known for its chicken fingers, the basketball courts, the large canopy-covered playground, and the three walkways interspersed throughout the area for easy ocean access. **Amenities:** food and drink; lifeguards; parking (no fee); showers; toilets. **Best for:** surfing; swimming. ✉ *889 N.E. Ocean Blvd., Stuart* 🌐 *www.stuartfla.com/stuart/article/stuart-beach.*

Restaurants

Conchy Joe's

$$$ | SEAFOOD | Like a hermit crab sliding into a new shell, Conchy Joe's moved up from West Palm Beach in 1983 to its current home, a 1920s rustic stilt house on the Indian River. It's full of antique fish mounts, gator hides, and snakeskins, and is a popular tourist spot—but the waterfront location, very casual vibe, and delicious seafood lures locals, too. **Known for:** conch chowder; grouper marsala; live reggae Thursday–Sunday. $ *Average main: $27 ✉ 3945 N.E. Indian River Dr., Jensen Beach ☎ 772/334–1130 🌐 www.conchyjoes.com.*

District Table and Bar

$$$ | **SOUTHERN** | Farm-fresh foods with a Southern accent are served up at this chef-owned restaurant with a theater kitchen, where comfort foods are taken to new levels. (Slow Foods, a group that celebrates local foods and artisans, has given the restaurant a "Snail of Approval.") **Known for:** farm-to-table menu; lively bar scene; everything homemade, including condiments and jams. $ *Average main: $23 ✉ 900 S.E. Indian St., Stuart ☎ 772/324–8357 🌐 www.districttableandbar.com ⏲ Closed Mon.*

11 Maple Street

$$$$ | **ECLECTIC** | This cozy spot is as good as it gets on the Treasure Coast. Soft music and a friendly staff set the mood in the antiques-filled dining room of this old house, which holds only 21 tables. **Known for:** nice selection of wines; good desserts; Old Florida setting in vintage house. $ *Average main: $42 ✉ 3224 N.E. Maple Ave., Jensen Beach ☎ 772/334–7714 🌐 www.elevenmaple.com ⏲ Closed Sun. and Mon. No lunch.*

Ian's Tropical Grill

$$$ | **SEAFOOD** | Tucked inside a small plaza, the restaurant has a small, cozy dining room and covered alfresco patio. The menu changes often, depending on what's fresh in the markets and from local farms, which are named. **Known for:** fresh Florida seafood; primarily locally sourced ingredients; inventive cocktails. $ *Average main: $25 ✉ 2875 S.E. Ocean Blvd., Stuart ☎ 772/334–4563 🌐 www.ianstropicalgrill.com ⏲ Closed Sun.*

Talk House

$$$ | **FRENCH** | Formerly known as Courtine's, Talk House changed hands in 2018 but kept much of the menu and staff. French and American influences are clear in the Swiss chef's dishes, from rack of lamb with Dijon mustard to grilled filet mignon stuffed with Roquefort and fresh spinach. **Known for:** refined Continental cuisine; elegant atmosphere; more casual bar menu. $ *Average main: $25 ✉ 514 N. Dixie Hwy., Stuart ☎ 772/692–3662 🌐 stuartstalkhouse.com ⏲ Closed Mon. No lunch.*

Hotels

Hutchinson Island Marriott Beach Resort & Marina

$$ | **RESORT** | **FAMILY** | With a 77-slip marina, a full water-sports program, a golf course, two pools, tons of tennis courts, and children's activities, this self-contained resort is excellent for families, most of whom prefer to stay in the tower directly on the ocean. **Pros:** attentive, warm staff; rooms are comfortable and casually chic; all rooms have balconies. **Cons:** only one sit-down indoor restaurant; common areas are a bit dated; no spa; daily resort fee. $ *Rooms from: $230 ✉ 555 N.E. Ocean Blvd., Stuart ☎ 772/225–3700, 800/775–5936 🌐 www.marriott.com/hotels/travel/pbiir-hutchinson-island-marriott-beach-resort-and-marina ⇨ 274 rooms 🍽 No meals.*

Pirate's Cove Resort & Marina

$ | **RESORT** | This cozy enclave on the banks of the Manatee Pocket with ocean access at the southern end of Stuart is the perfect place to set forth on a day at sea or wind down after one—it's relaxing and casual, and has amenities like a swimming-pool courtyard, restaurant, and fitness center. **Pros:** spacious tropical-themed rooms; great for boaters, with a 50-slip, full-service, deepwater marina; each room has a balcony overlooking the water; free Wi-Fi and parking. **Cons:** lounge gets noisy at night; decor and furnishings are pretty but not luxurious; pool is on the small side. *Rooms from: $150* ✉ *4307 S.E. Bayview St., Port Salerno* ☎ *772/287–2500* 🌐 *www.piratescoveresort.com* *50 rooms* *No meals.*

Shopping

More than 60 restaurants and shops with antiques, art, and fashion draw visitors downtown along Osceola Street.

B&A Flea Market

OUTDOOR/FLEA/GREEN MARKETS | A short drive from downtown and operating for more than two decades, the oldest and largest weekend-only flea market on the Treasure Coast has a street-bazaar feel, with shoppers happily scouting the 500 vendors for the practical and unusual. A produce market carries local tropical fruits and vegetables. If you have an open mind and love to shop garage sales, you'll do just fine here. ✉ *2885 S.E. U.S. 1, Stuart* ☎ *772/288–4915* 🌐 *www.bafleamarket.com* *Free.*

Activities

***Island Princess* Cruises**

BOAT TOURS | Cruise the Indian River and St. Lucie River as well as Jupiter Sound aboard the *Island Princess,* an 82-footer that docks at the Sailfish Marina in Stuart. In season, there are nature cruises and cruises that go through the St. Lucie River locks. Have lunch during their Jupiter Island cruise, embarking Tuesday and weekends year-round. The schedule, which changes often, is posted on the company's website. All ages are welcome, and advance reservations are required. ✉ *Sailfish Marina, 3585 S.E. St. Lucie Blvd., Stuart* ☎ *772/225–2100* 🌐 *www.islandprincesscruises.com* *Cruises from $28.*

Sailfish Marina of Stuart

FISHING | Nab a deep-sea charter here to land a sailfish, a popular sport fish that is prolific off the St. Lucie Inlet. This is the closest public marina to the St. Lucie Inlet. Recently expanded, it is home to *Island Princess* Cruises, which takes visitors to Vero Beach or Jupiter via the Intracoastal Waterway. ✉ *3565 S.E. St. Lucie Blvd., Stuart* ☎ *772/283–1122* 🌐 *www.sailfishmarinastuart.com.*

Fort Pierce and Port St. Lucie

11 miles north of Jensen Beach.

About an hour north of Palm Beach, Fort Pierce has a distinctive rural feel—but it has a surprising number of worthwhile attractions for a town of its size, including those easily seen while following Route 707 on the mainland (A1A on Hutchinson Island). The downtown is expanding, and sports new theater revivals, restaurants, and shops. A big draw is an inlet that offers fabulous fishing and excellent surfing. Nearby Port St. Lucie is largely landlocked southwest of Fort Pierce and is almost equidistant from there and Jensen Beach. It's not a big tourist area except for two sports facilities near Interstate 95: the St. Lucie Mets' training grounds, Tradition Field, and the PGA Village. If you want a hotel directly on the sand or crave more than simple, motel-like accommodations, stay elsewhere and drive up for the day.

GETTING HERE AND AROUND

You can reach Fort Pierce from Jensen Beach by driving 11 miles north on Federal Highway (U.S. 1), Route 707, or Route A1A. To get to Port St. Lucie, continue north on U.S. 1 and take Prima Vista Boulevard west. From Fort Pierce, Route 709 goes diagonally southwest to Port St. Lucie, and Interstate 95 is another choice.

ESSENTIALS

VISITOR INFORMATION St. Lucie County Tourist Development Council. ✉ *2300 Virginia Ave., Fort Pierce* ☎ *800/344–8443* 🌐 *www.visitstluciefla.com.*

Heathcote Botanical Gardens

GARDEN | Stroll through this 3½-acre green space, which includes a palm walk, a Japanese garden, and a collection of 100 bonsai trees. There is also a gift shop with whimsical and botanical knickknacks. Guided tours are available by appointment for an extra fee. ✉ *210 Savannah Rd., Fort Pierce* ☎ *772/464–0323* 🌐 *www.heathcotebotanicalgardens.org* 🎟 *$6* ⏲ *Closed Mon.*

National Navy UDT-SEAL Museum

MILITARY SITE | **FAMILY** | Commemorating the more than 3,000 troops who trained on these shores during World War II when this elite military unit got its start, there are weapons, vehicles, and equipment on view. Exhibits honor all frogmen and underwater demolition teams and depict their history. The museum houses the lifeboat from which SEALs saved the *Maersk Alabama* captain from Somali pirates in 2009. Kids get a thrill out of the helicopters and aircraft on the grounds. ✉ *3300 N. Rte. A1A, Fort Pierce* ☎ *772/595–5845* 🌐 *www.navysealmuseum.com* 🎟 *$15* ⏲ *Closed Mon.*

Savannas Recreation Area

NATURE PRESERVE | **FAMILY** | Once a reservoir, the 550 acres have been returned to their natural wetlands state. Today the wilderness area has campgrounds, interpretive trails, and a boat ramp, and the recreation area is open year-round. Canoe and kayak rentals are available Thursday through Monday. A dog park (open daily) is also on-site. Amenities include showers, toilets, and free Wi-Fi for campers. ✉ *1400 E. Midway Rd., Fort Pierce* ☎ *772/464–7855* 🌐 *www.stlucieco.gov/parks/savannas.htm* 🎟 *Free; $25.25 for campers (full service).*

Fort Pierce Inlet State Park

BEACH—SIGHT | Across the inlet at the northern side of Hutchinson Island, a fishing oasis lures beachgoers who can't wait to reel in snook, flounder, and bluefish, among others. The park is also known as a prime wave-riding locale, thanks to a reef that lies just outside the jetty. Summer is the busiest season by a long shot, but don't be fooled: it's a laid-back place to sun and surf. There are covered picnic tables but no concessions; however, from where anglers perch, a bunch of casual restaurants can be spotted on the other side of the inlet that are a quick drive away. Note that the area of Jack Island Preserve has been closed indefinitely. **Amenities:** lifeguards (summer only); parking (fee); showers; toilets. **Best for:** solitude; surfing; walking. ✉ *905 Shorewinds Dr., Fort Pierce* ☎ *772/468–3985* 🌐 *www.floridastateparks.org/parks-and-trails/fort-pierce-inlet-state-park* 🎟 *Vehicle $6, bicyclists and pedestrians $2.*

Dockside Inn

$ | **HOTEL** | This hotel is the best of the lodgings lining the scenic Fort Pierce Inlet on Seaway Drive (and that's not saying much); it's a practical base for fishing enthusiasts with nice touches like two pools and a waterfront restaurant. **Pros:** good value; overnight boat docking available; reasonable rates at marina; parking included. **Cons:** basic decor; some steps to climb; grounds are nothing too fancy but have great views. 💲 *Rooms from: $125* ✉ *1160 Seaway Dr., Fort Pierce* ☎ *772/468–3555, 800/286–1745* 🌐 *www.docksideinn.com* 🛏 *36 rooms* 🍴 *No meals.*

Activities

The region's premier dive site is actually on the National Register of Historic Places. The *Urca de Lima* was part of the storied treasure fleet bound for Spain that was destroyed by a hurricane in 1715. It's now part of an underwater archaeological preserve about 200 yards from shore, just north of the National Navy UDT-SEAL Museum and under 10 to 15 feet of water. The remains contain a flat-bottom, round-bellied ship and cannons that can be visited on an organized dive trip.

Dive Odyssea

SCUBA DIVING | This full-service dive shop offers kayak rentals, tank rentals, and scuba lessons. The shop can arrange a scuba charter in Jupiter or Palm Beach (two-tank dive trips typically start at $65), but Dive Odyssea no longer offers dive trips of its own. ✉ *Fort Pierce Inlet, 621 N. 2nd St., Fort Pierce* ☎ *772/460–1771* 🌐 *www.diveodyssea.com.*

First Data Field

BASEBALL/SOFTBALL | Out west by Interstate 95, this Port St. Lucie baseball stadium, formerly known as Tradition Field, is where the New York Mets train; it's also the home of the St. Lucie Mets minor-league team. ✉ *525 N.W. Peacock Blvd., Port St. Lucie* ☎ *772/871–2115* 🌐 *www.milb.com/st-lucie.*

PGA Village

GOLF | Owned and operated by the PGA of America, the national association of teaching pros, PGA Village is the winter home to many Northern instructors, along with permanent staff. The facility is a little off the beaten path and the clubhouse is basic, but serious golfers will appreciate the three championship courses by Pete Dye and Tom Fazio and the chance to sharpen their skills at the 35-acre PGA Center for Golf Learning and Performance, which has nine practice bunkers mimicking sands and slopes from around the globe. Between the Fazio-designed Wanamaker Course, the Ryder Course, and the Dye-designed Dye Course, there are 54 holes of championship golf at PGA Village. Also affiliated is the nearby St. Lucie Trail Golf Club, another Fazio design. Beginners can start out on the lesser known (and easier) 6-hole PGA Short Course. Holes are 35 to 60 yards each, and course play is free. ✉ *1916 Perfect Dr., Port St. Lucie* ☎ *772/467–1300, 800/800–4653* 🌐 *www.pgavillage.com* 🎫 *Wanamaker Course $131; Ryder Course $131; Dye Course $131; St. Lucie Trail Golf Club $89* 🏌 *Wanamaker Course: 18 holes, 7123 yards, par 72; Ryder Course: 18 holes, 7037 yards, par 72; Dye Course: 18 holes, 7279 yards, par 72; St. Lucie Golf Club Trail Course: 18 holes, 6901 yards, par 72.*

Vero Beach

12 miles north of Fort Pierce.

Tranquil and picturesque, this upscale Indian River County town has a strong commitment to the environment and culture, and it's also home to eclectic galleries and trendy restaurants. Downtown Vero is centered on the historic district on 14th Avenue, but much of the fun takes place across the Indian River (aka the Intracoastal Waterway) around Orchid Island's beaches. It was once home to the Dodgers Spring Training base, and there's still a strong affinity for baseball here, and it's kid-friendly, with the former Dodgertown Stadium hosting Little League tournaments, and plenty of parks around. Its western edges still are home to cattlemen and citrus growers, so there is a juxtaposition of country and gentry.

GETTING HERE AND AROUND

To get here, you have two basic options: Route A1A along the coast (not to be confused with Ocean Drive, an offshoot on Orchid Island), or either U.S. 1 or Route 605 (also called Old Dixie Highway) on the mainland. As you approach

Vero on the latter, you pass through an ungussied-up landscape of small farms and residential areas. On the beach route, part of the drive bisects an unusually undeveloped section of the Florida coast. If flying in, consider Orlando International Airport, which is larger and a smidge closer than Palm Beach International Airport.

VISITOR INFORMATION

CONTACTS Indian River County Chamber of Commerce. ✉ *1216 21st St.* ☎ *772/567–3491* 🌐 *www.indianriverchamber.com.*

Sights

Environmental Learning Center

NATURE PRESERVE | Off Wabasso Beach Road, the 64 acres here are almost completely surrounded by water. In addition to a 600-foot boardwalk through the mangrove shoreline and a 1-mile canoe trail, there are aquariums filled with Indian River creatures. Boat and kayak trips to see the historic Pelican Island rookery are on offer along with guided nature walks and touch-tank encounters. Call or check the center's website for times. ✉ *255 Live Oak Dr.* ☎ *772/589–5050* 🌐 *www.discoverelc.org* *$5* *Closed Mon.*

★ McKee Botanical Garden

GARDEN | On the National Register of Historic Places, the 18-acre plot is a tropical jungle garden—one of the most lush and serene around. This is *the* place to see spectacular water lilies, and the property's original 1932 Hall of Giants, a rustic wooden structure that has stained-glass and bronze bells, contains what is claimed to be the world's largest single-plank mahogany table at 35 feet long. There's a Seminole bamboo pavilion, a gift shop, and café (open for lunch Tuesday through Saturday, and Sunday in season), which serves especially tasty snacks and sandwiches. ✉ *350 U.S. 1* ☎ *772/794–0601* 🌐 *www.mckeegarden.org* *$12* *Closed Mon.*

Pelican Island National Wildlife Refuge

NATURE PRESERVE | Founded in 1903 by President Theodore Roosevelt as the country's first national wildlife refuge, the park encompasses the historic Pelican Island rookery itself—a small island in the Indian River lagoon and important nesting place for 16 species of birds such as endangered wood storks and, of course, brown pelicans—and the land surrounding it overlooking Sebastian. The rookery is a closed wilderness area, so there's no roaming alongside animal kingdom friends; however, there is an 18-foot observation tower across from it with direct views and more than 6 miles of nature trails in the refuge. Another way to explore is via guided kayak tours from the Florida Outdoor Center. Make sure to bring a camera—it's a photographer's dream. ✉ *Rte. A1A* ✢ *1 mile north of Treasure Shores Park. Take A1A and turn on Historic Jungle Trail* ☎ *772/581–5557* 🌐 *www.fws.gov/pelicanisland* *Free.*

Beaches

Most of the hotels in the Vero Beach area are clustered around South Beach Park or line Ocean Drive around Beachland Boulevard just north of Humiston Park. Humiston Park is smack-dab in the main commercial zone with restaurants galore, including the lauded Citrus Grillhouse at its southern tip.

Humiston Park

BEACH—SIGHT | Just south of the Driftwood Resort on Ocean Drive sits Humiston Park, one of the best beaches in town. Parking is free and plentiful, as there's a large lot on Easter Lily Lane and there are spots all over the surrounding business district. The shore is somewhat narrow and there isn't much shade, but the vibrant scene and other amenities make it a great choice for people who crave lots of activity. With lifeguards on call daily, there's a children's playground, plus a ton of hotels, restaurants, bars, and shops within walking distance.

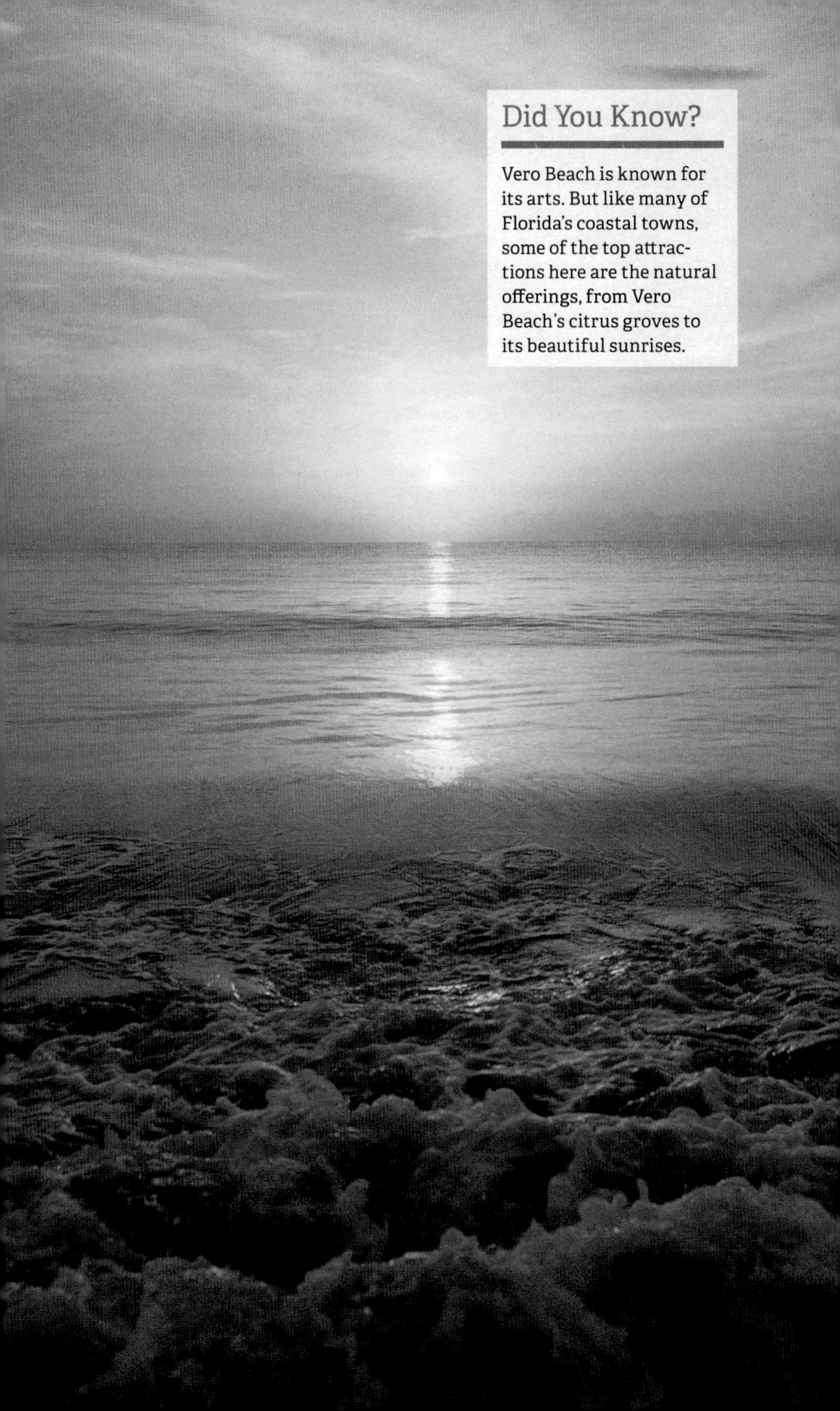

Did You Know?

Vero Beach is known for its arts. But like many of Florida's coastal towns, some of the top attractions here are the natural offerings, from Vero Beach's citrus groves to its beautiful sunrises.

Amenities: food and drink; lifeguards; showers; toilets. **Best for:** partiers; sunsets; swimming; walking. ✉ *3000 Ocean Dr., at Easter Lily La.* ☎ *772/231–5790.*

★ Sebastian Inlet State Park

BEACH—SIGHT | **FAMILY** | The 1,000-acre park, which runs from the tip of Orchid Island across the passage to the barrier island just north, is one of the Florida park system's biggest draws, especially because of the inlet's highly productive fishing waters. Views from either side of the tall bridge are spectacular, and a unique hallmark is that the gates never close—an amazing feature for die-hard anglers who know snook bite better at night. Two jetties are usually packed with fishers and spectators alike. The park has two entrances, the entrance in Vero Beach and the main entrance in Melbourne (*9700 Rte. A1A*). Within its grounds, you'll discover a wonderful two-story restaurant that overlooks the ocean, a fish and surfing shop (by the way, this place has some of the best waves in the state, but there are also calmer zones for relaxing swims), two museums, guided sea turtle walks in season, 51 campsites with water and electricity, and a marina with powerboat, kayak, and canoe rentals. **Amenities:** food and drink; parking (fee); showers; toilets; water sports. **Best for:** sunrise; sunset; surfing; walking. ✉ *14251 N. Rte. A1A* ☎ *321/984–4852* 🌐 *www.floridastateparks.org/parks-and-trails/sebastian-inlet-state-park* 🎫 *$8 vehicles with up to 8 people, $4 single drivers, $2 bicyclists and pedestrians.*

Wabasso Beach Park

BEACH—SIGHT | **FAMILY** | A favorite for local surfboarding teens and the families at the nearby Disney's Vero Beach Resort, the park is nestled in a residential area at the end of Wabasso Road, about 8 miles up from the action on Ocean Drive and 8 miles below the Sebastian Inlet. Aside from regular amenities like picnic tables, restrooms, and a dedicated parking lot (which really is the "park" here—there's not much green space—and it's quite small, so arrive early), the Disney crowd walks there for its lifeguards (the strip directly in front of the hotel is unguarded) and the local crowd appreciates its conveniences, like a pizzeria and a store that sells sundries, snacks, and beach supplies. **Amenities:** food and drink; lifeguards; parking (no fee); showers; toilets. **Best for:** surfing; swimming. ✉ *1820 Wabasso Rd.*

Restaurants

The Lemon Tree

$ | **DINER** | **FAMILY** | If Italy had old-school luncheonettes, this is what they'd look like: a storefront of yellow walls, dark-green booths, white linoleum tables, and cascading sconces of faux ivy leaves and hand-painted Tuscan serving pieces for artwork. It's self-described by the husband-and-wife owners (who are always at the front) as an "upscale diner," and locals swear by it for breakfast (served all day) and lunch. **Known for:** shrimp scampi; treats on the house; waits during the high season. 💲 *Average main: $11* ✉ *3125 Ocean Dr.* ☎ *772/231–0858* 🌐 *www.lemontreevero.com* 🕒 *No lunch or dinner Sun. No dinner June–Sept.*

Ocean Grill

$$$ | **SEAFOOD** | Opened in 1941, this family-owned Old Florida–style restaurant combines its ocean view with Tiffany-style lamps, wrought-iron chandeliers, and paintings of pirates. Count on at least three kinds of seafood any day on the menu, along with steaks, pork chops, soups, and salads. **Known for:** just OK food; great drinks; the Pusser's Painkiller. 💲 *Average main: $28* ✉ *1050 Beachland Blvd.* ☎ *772/231–5409* 🌐 *www.ocean-grill.com* 🕒 *Closed 2 wks around Labor Day. No lunch Sun.*

★ The Tides

$$$ | **ECLECTIC** | A charming cottage restaurant west of Ocean Drive prepares some of the best food around—not just in Vero Beach, but all of South Florida. The chefs, classically trained, give a nod to international fare with disparate dishes such as tuna tataki, Asian-inspired carpaccio with satay, penne *quattro formaggi,* and classic lobster bisque. **Known for:** fresh Florida fish; jumbo crab cakes with corn-and-pepper sauce; chef's table with wine pairings. *Average main: $29 3103 Cardinal Dr. 772/234–3966 www.tidesofvero.com No lunch.*

Hotels

★ Costa d'Este Beach Resort

$ | **RESORT** | This stylish, contemporary boutique hotel in the heart of Vero's bustling Ocean Drive area has a gorgeous infinity pool overlooking the ocean and a distinctly Miami Beach vibe—just like its famous owners, singer Gloria Estefan and producer Emilio Estefan, who bought the property in 2004. **Pros:** all rooms have balconies or secluded patios; huge Italian marble showers; complimentary signature mojitos on arrival. **Cons:** spa is on small side; rooms have only blackout shades; daily resort fee. *Rooms from: $139 3244 Ocean Dr. 772/562–9919 www.costadeste.com 94 rooms No meals.*

Disney's Vero Beach Resort

$$$ | **RESORT** | **FAMILY** | This oceanfront, family-oriented retreat tucked away in a residential stretch of Orchid Island has a retro Old Florida design and not too much Mickey Mouse, which is a welcome surprise for adults. **Pros:** a great pool with waterslide and kiddie splash pool; campfire circle; several dining options on property. **Cons:** far from shopping and dining options; minimal Disney-themed decor. *Rooms from: $365 9250 Island Grove Terr. 772/234–2000, 407/939–7540 www.disneybeachresorts.com/vero-beach-resort/ 181 rooms No meals.*

The Driftwood Resort

$ | **RESORT** | **FAMILY** | On the National Register of Historic Places, the two original buildings of this 1935 inn were built entirely from ocean-washed timbers with no blueprints; over time more buildings were added, and all are now decorated with such artifacts as ship's bells, Spanish tiles, a cannon from a 16th-century Spanish galleon, and plenty of wrought iron, which create a quirky, utterly charming landscape. **Pros:** central location and right on the beach; free Wi-Fi; laundry facilities; weekly treasure hunt is a blast. **Cons:** older property; rooms can be musty; no-frills furnishings. *Rooms from: $150 3150 Ocean Dr. 772/231–0550 www.verobeachdriftwood.com 100 rooms No meals.*

★ Vero Beach Hotel & Spa

$$ | **RESORT** | **FAMILY** | With a sophisticated, relaxed British West Indies feel, this luxurious five-story beachfront hotel at the north end of Ocean Drive is an inviting getaway and, arguably, the best on the Treasure Coast. **Pros:** beautiful pool; complimentary daily wine hour with hors d'oeuvres. **Cons:** separate charge for valet parking; some rooms overlook parking lot. *Rooms from: $299 3500 Ocean Dr. 772/231–5666 www.verobeachhotelandspa.com 102 rooms No meals.*

Shopping

The place to go when in Vero Beach is **Ocean Drive.** Crossing over to Orchid Island from the mainland, the Merrill P. Barber Bridge turns into Beachland Boulevard; its intersection with Ocean Drive is the heart of a commercial zone with a lively mix of upscale clothing stores, specialty shops, restaurants, and art galleries.

Just under 3 miles north of that roughly eight-block stretch on A1A is a charming outdoor plaza, the **Village Shops.** It's a delight to stroll between the brightly painted cottages that have more unique, high-end offerings.

Back on the mainland, take 21st Street westward and you'll come across a small, modern shopping plaza with some independent shops and national chains. Keep going west on 21st Street, and then park around 14th Avenue to explore a collection of art galleries and eateries in the historic downtown.

Exclusively Coastal

CRAFTS | Stop here for lovely handcrafted goods inspired by the sea, many by local artisans. Choose from jewelry, candles, gifts for kids, home decor items, and artwork. ✉ *3119 Ocean Dr.* ☎ *772/234–4790* 🌐 *exclusivelycoastal.com.*

Maison Beach

GIFTS/SOUVENIRS | Formerly called Christine, the owner changed the name of this cute shop and moved to Pelican Plaza. It still is *the* place to find gorgeous hostess and dining entertainment gifts like Mariposa napkin holders, Julia Knight bowls, and Michael Aram picture frames, along with trendy Mudpie household ware. ✉ *Pelican Plaza, 4895 Hwy. A1A* ☎ *772/492–0383* 🌐 *maisonbeach.myshopify.com.*

Sassy Boutique

CLOTHING | One of the chicest spots in town sells bright, punchy, and pretty women's designer fashions such as Tory Burch, Kate Spade New York, Kenneth Jay Lane, Stacia, and Nanette Lepore. ✉ *3375 Ocean Dr.* ☎ *772/234–3998* 🌐 *www.sassyboutique.com.*

Vero Beach Outlets

OUTLET/DISCOUNT STORES | Need some retail therapy? Just west of Interstate 95 off Route 60 is a discount shopping destination with 50 high-end brand-name stores, including Ann Taylor, Calvin Klein, Christopher & Banks, Dooney & Bourke, Polo Ralph Lauren, Restoration Hardware, and White House/Black Market. ✉ *1824 94th Dr.* ✥ *On Rte. 60, west of I–95 at Exit 147* ☎ *772/770–6097* 🌐 *www.verobeachoutlets.com.*

Activities

Sandridge Golf Club

GOLF | The Sandridge Golf Club features two public 18-hole courses designed by Ron Garl: the Dunes course, with 6 holes located on a sand ridge; and the Lakes course, named for—you guessed it—the ubiquitous lakes around the course. The Dunes course, opened in 1987, follows a history-steeped pathway once used during mining operations. The Lakes course, opened in 1992, is renowned for the very challenging, par-4 14th hole with an island green. There's a pro shop on-site offering lessons and clinics. Florida and Indian River County residents can get membership cards to book tee times eight days out—and get discounts for play. ✉ *5300 73rd St.* ☎ *772/770–5000* 🌐 *www.sandridgegc.com* 🎫 *$50 for 18 holes with cart* 🏌 *Dunes course: 18 holes, 6817 yards, par 72; Lakes course: 18 holes, 6181 yards, par 72.*

Chapter 8

THE TAMPA BAY AREA

8

Updated by
Tiffany Razzano

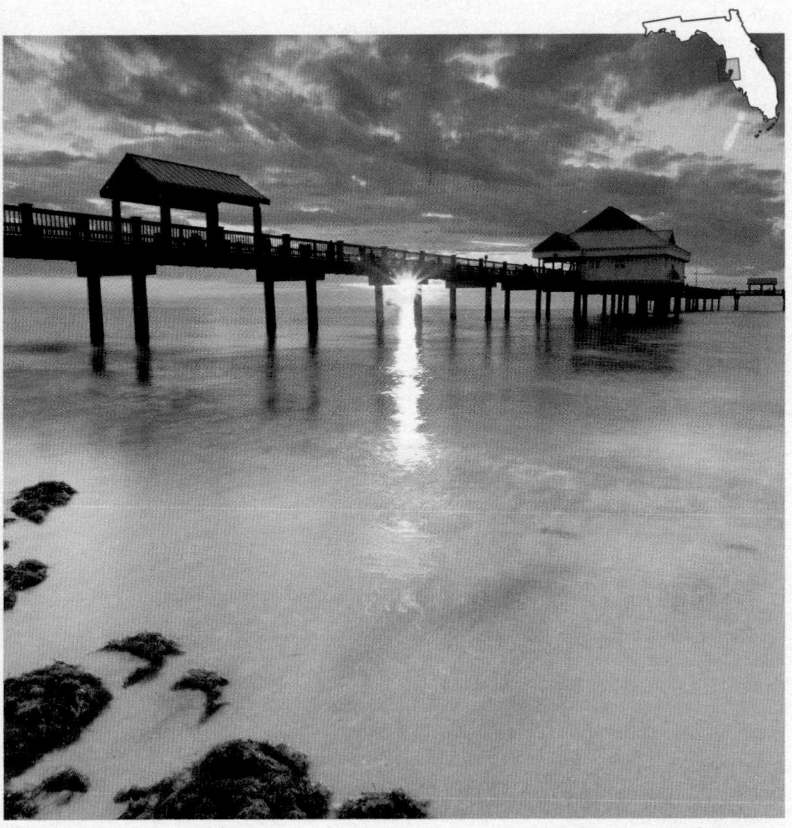

Sights	Restaurants	Hotels	Shopping	Nightlife
★★★★★	★★★★☆	★★★★☆	★★★★☆	★★★★☆

WELCOME TO THE TAMPA BAY AREA

TOP REASONS TO GO

★ **Art gone wild:** Whether you take the guided tour or chart your own course, experience the one-of-a-kind collection at the Salvador Dalí Museum, which is located in a gorgeous waterfront building in downtown St. Petersburg.

★ **Cuban roots:** You'll find great food and vibrant nightlife in historic Ybor City, just east of downtown Tampa.

★ **Beachcomber bonanza:** Caladesi Island State Park has some of the best shelling on the Gulf Coast, and its five-star sunsets are a great way to end the day.

★ **Culture fix:** If you love the arts, there's no finer offering in the Bay Area than at the Florida State University Ringling Center for the Cultural Arts in Sarasota.

1 **Tampa.** Waterfront metropolis with inviting shopping, a growing restaurant and craft brewery scene, and Busch Gardens.

2 **St. Petersburg.** The Sunshine City has a lively downtown and Dalí museum.

3 **Clearwater.** The beach here buzzes all spring and summer.

4 **Dunedin.** Come for the beautiful Caladesi Island State Park.

5 **Palm Harbor.** A championship golf course and craft brewery are big draws.

6 **Tarpon Springs.** In this highly Greek-influenced town, you'll find historic sponge docks and great beaches.

7 **Indian Shores.** Its bird sanctuary rose to fame as the cleanup site during the Gulf oil spill in 2010.

8 **Safety Harbor.** Home to a lovely resort built over natural mineral springs.

9 **Weeki Wachee.** Watching the "mermaids" perform at the springs is a classic piece of Florida culture.

10 **Homosassa Springs.** This area has a great state park with manatees.

11 **Crystal River.** One of the only places where you can legally swim with manatees.

12 **Bradenton.** A town with miles of beach plus golfing and a manatee aquarium.

13 **Sarasota.** White-sand beaches and cultural treasures await in this top beach town.

Cosme
Lake Tarpon
Palm Harbor
Curlew Rd.
DUNEDIN
Oldsmar
Safety Harbor
Waters
Sheldon Rd.
Carrollwood
Gunn Hwy.
Fletcher Ave.
Fowler Ave.
Busch Gardens
Temple Terrace
Busch Blvd.
Nebraska Ave.
Dale Mabry Hwy.
Hillsborough Ave.
Tampa International Airport
Ybor City
Adamo St.
(toll)
Kennedy Blvd.
Courtney Campbell Causeway
Gulf to Bay Blvd.
Old Tampa Bay
Rocky Point
St. Petersburg-Clearwater International Airport
Howard Frankland Bridge
TAMPA
South Crosstown Expwy.
Causeway Blvd.
BIG ISLAND
Gandy Bridge
West Shore Blvd.
Hillsborough Bay
78th St.
East Tampa
Alafia River
Gibsonton
MacDill Air Force Base
WEEDON I.
ROSS I.
Gadsden Point
Adamsville
Starkey Rd.
Belcher Rd.
Haines Rd.
48th St. N
74th Ave. N
62nd Ave. N
54th Ave. N
38th Ave. N
Tyrone Blvd.
Park St.
5th Ave. N
38th St. N
9th St. N
ST. PETERSBURG
Salvador Dalí Museum
Central
22nd Ave. S
Apollo Beach
Tamiami Rd.
Mangrove Point
Boyd Hill Nature Park
54th Ave. S
COQUINA KEY
Ruskin
Pinellas Point
Gulf City
Tierra Verde
Tampa Bay
Little Manatee River
Sun City
Valroy
Piney Point
Sunshine Skyway (toll)
MULLET KEY
TO BRADENTON & SARASOTA
Gillett
Parrish
611
19
598
597
586
580
41
583
301
92
574
60
275
75
4
693
699
1
2
3
4
5
6
8
12
13

If you seek a destination that's no one-trick pony, the Tampa Bay region is a spot you can't miss. Encompassing an area from Tarpon Springs to Tampa proper and all the way south to Sarasota, it's one of those unsung places as dynamic as it is appealing—and word has definitely started to spread about its charms. With its long list of attractions—from pristine beaches to world-class museums—it's easy to see why.

First and foremost, Tampa Bay's beaches are some of the best in the country. Whether you want coarse or fine sand, and whether you seek a mellow day of shelling or a raucous romp on a crowded stretch of waterfront, this place has it all. Of course, you can choose from a range of water activities, including charter fishing, parasailing, sunset cruises, kayaking, and more.

The region has its share of boutique districts spotted with shops and sidewalk cafés. Tampa's Hyde Park Village and downtown St. Petersburg's Beach Drive are among the top picks if you're looking to check out some upscale shops and dine alfresco while getting the most of the area's pleasant climate. Vibrant nightlife tops off Tampa Bay's list of assets. Ybor City attracts the club set, and barrier islands like St. Pete Beach offer loads of live music and barefoot dancing into the wee hours.

Tampa Bay has lots of family-friendly attractions, too. You can check out Busch Gardens, Adventure Island, and the Clearwater Marine Aquarium, to name a few. And art fanatics will find an astonishing array of attractions, including Sarasota's Ringling Museum of Art, St. Petersburg's enrapturing Salvador Dalí and Dale Chihuly collections (both permanent and housed in exquisite new digs), and Tampa's Museum of Art. Come prepared to explore and see for yourself what a compelling, unforgettable place the Tampa Bay area really is.

Planning

When to Go

Winter and spring are high season, and the amount of activity during this time is double that of the off-season. Beaches do stay pretty packed throughout the sweltering summer, which is known for massive, almost-daily afternoon thunderstorms. Summer daytime temperatures hover around or above 90°F. Luckily the mercury drops to the mid-70s at night, and the beaches have a consistent onshore breeze that starts just before sundown, which enabled civilization to survive here before air-conditioning arrived.

Getting Here and Around

AIR TRAVEL

Tampa International Airport, the area's largest and busiest airport, with 19 million passengers per year, is served by most major carriers and offers ground transportation to surrounding cities. Many of the large U.S. carriers also fly into and out of Sarasota–Bradenton International Airport. St. Petersburg–Clearwater International Airport, 9 miles west of downtown St. Petersburg, is much smaller than Tampa International and has limited service.

Airport Transfers: SuperShuttle is one of the easiest ways to get to and from the airport if you forgo a rental car. All you need to do is call or visit the SuperShuttle website to book travel—they'll pick you up and drop you off wherever you're staying at any hour. Basic service costs around $28.

Blue One Transportation provides service to and from Tampa International Airport for areas including Hillsborough (Tampa, Plant City), Pinellas (St. Petersburg, St. Pete Beach, Clearwater), and Polk (Lakeland) counties. Rates vary by pickup location, destination, and fuel costs.

AIRPORT Sarasota–Bradenton International Airport. ☎ *941/359–2770* 🌐 *www.srq-airport.com.* **St. Petersburg–Clearwater International Airport.** ☎ *727/453–7800* 🌐 *www.fly2pie.com.* **Tampa International Airport.** ☎ *813/870–8700* 🌐 *www.tampaairport.com.*

AIRPORT TRANSFERS Blue One Transportation. ☎ *813/282–7351* 🌐 *www.blueonetransportation.com.* **SuperShuttle.** ☎ *727/571–4220* 🌐 *www.supershuttle.com.*

BUS TRAVEL

Several transit lines serve Hillsborough (Tampa), Pinellas (St. Petersburg and Clearwater), Sarasota, and Manatee (Bradenton) counties, and if you are staying in a resort, they may meet your needs, but none is as convenient as a car.

CAR TRAVEL

Interstates 75 and 275 span the Bay Area from north to south. Coming from Orlando, you're likely to drive west into Tampa on Interstate 4. Along with Interstate 75, U.S. 41 (the Tamiami Trail) stretches the length of the region and links the business districts of many communities; avoid this route during rush hours (7–9 am and 4–6 pm).

Hotels

Many convention hotels in the Tampa Bay area double as family-friendly resorts—taking advantage of nearby beaches, marinas, spas, tennis courts, and golf links. Unlike Orlando and some other parts of Florida, however, the area has been bustling for more than a century, and its accommodations often reflect a sense of its history.

You'll find a turn-of-the-20th-century beachfront resort where Zelda and F. Scott Fitzgerald stayed, a massive all-wood building from the 1920s, plenty of art deco, and Spanish-style villas. But one thing they all have in common is a certain Gulf Coast charm.

Restaurants

Fresh Gulf seafood is plentiful—raw bars serving oysters, clams, and mussels are everywhere. Tampa's many Cuban and Spanish restaurants serve paella with seafood and chicken, *boliche criollo* (sausage-stuffed eye-round roast) with black beans and rice, *ropa vieja* (shredded flank steak in tomato sauce), and other treats. Tarpon Springs adds classic Greek specialties. In Sarasota the emphasis is on ritzier dining, though many restaurants offer extra-cheap early-bird menus.

Hotel and restaurant reviews have been shortened. For full information, visit Fodors.com.

What It Costs

$	$$	$$$	$$$$
RESTAURANTS			
under $15	$15–$20	$21–$30	over $30
HOTELS			
under $200	$200–$300	$301–$400	over $400

Tampa

84 miles southwest of Orlando via I–4.

Tampa, the west coast's business-and-commercial hub, has a sprinkling of high-rises and heavy traffic. A concentration of restaurants, nightlife, stores, and cultural events is amid the bustle. The city has really come into its own in recent years. The downtown Tampa waterfront features stunning views and excellent museums. Animal lovers flock here for attractions like Lowry Park Zoo, Busch Gardens, Big Cat Rescue, and Giraffe Ranch. Revelers will enjoy the strip of bars and clubs that constitutes Ybor City, a historic area with a heavy Cuban influence. The city also abounds with art museums, shops, and a wide array of restaurants. Downtown and Ybor City are both excellent spots to look for live music. Not too far out of town are some great golf courses and nature trails. Tampa is also a short drive from a long stretch of gorgeous Gulf Coast beaches.

GETTING AROUND

Downtown Tampa's Riverwalk, on Ashley Drive at the Hillsborough River, connects waterside entities such as the Florida Aquarium, the Channelside shopping-and-entertainment complex, and Marriott Waterside. The landscaped park is 6 acres and extends along the Garrison cruise-ship channel and along the Hillsborough River downtown. The walkway is being expanded as waterside development continues.

Hillsborough Area Regional Transit and TECO Line Street Cars replicate Tampa's first electric streetcars, transporting cruise-ship passengers to Ybor City and downtown Tampa.

Although downtown Tampa, the Channelside District, and Ybor City are easy to navigate without a car, you'll want to rent one if you plan on hitting the beaches or heading to Busch Gardens, Hyde Park, International Plaza, or any of the zoos.

BUS AND TROLLEY CONTACTS Hillsborough Area Regional Transit. ☎ *813/254–4278* 🌐 *www.gohart.org.* **TECO Line Street Cars.** ☎ *813/254–4278* 🌐 *www.tecoline-streetcar.org.*

VISITOR INFORMATION

CONTACTS Tampa Bay Beaches Chamber of Commerce. ✉ *6990 Gulf Blvd., St. Pete Beach* ☎ *727/360–6957* 🌐 *www.tampabaybeaches.com.* **Visit Tampa Bay.** ✉ *201 N. Franklin St.* ☎ *800/448–2672, 813/223–1111* 🌐 *www.visittampabay.com.* **Ybor City Chamber Visitor Information Center.** ✉ *1800 E. 9th Ave., Ybor City* ☎ *813/241–8838* 🌐 *www.ybor.org.*

Sights

★ Big Cat Rescue

NATURE PRESERVE | Suburban Citrus Park in North Tampa is probably the last place you'd expect to be able to get face-to-face with an 800-pound tiger. Yet at the end of a shaded road just yards off the Veterans' Expressway, you can do just that. This nonprofit, accredited sanctuary rescues and provides a permanent home for lions, tigers, ocelots, bobcats, cougars, and members of any other large-cat species you can imagine. Each and every one of these marvelous creatures has a unique story. Some arrived here after narrowly avoiding becoming an expensive coat. Others were kept as pets until the owners realized how pricey 15 pounds of meat per day (what it takes to feed some of these creatures) can be. They're all kept in large enclosures. A volunteer guide will lead you around the property and tell you the story of every cat you see. You'll also get an earful of little-known facts about these big cats, from the true origin of the white tiger to why some cats have white spots on the backs of their ears. Tours (no unescorted visits are allowed) are every day but Thursday, and special tours for children under 10 accompanied by an adult are offered on weekends. Night tours, feeding tours, and appointment-only private tours are also available. ✉ *12802 Easy St., Citrus Park* ☎ *813/920–4130* 🌐 *bigcatrescue.org* 🎫 *$37.*

★ Busch Gardens

AMUSEMENT PARK/WATER PARK | FAMILY | The Jungala exhibit at Busch Gardens brings Bengal tigers to center stage and puts them at eye level—allowing you to view them from underground caves and underwater windows. The big cats are just one of the reasons the theme park attracts some 4.5 million visitors each year. This is a world-class zoo, with more than 2,000 animals, and a live-entertainment venue that provides a full day (or more) of fun for the whole family. If you want to beat the crowds, start in the back of the park and work your way around clockwise.

The 335-acre adventure park's habitats offer views of some of the world's most endangered and exotic animals. For the best animal sightings, go to their habitats early, when it's cooler. You can experience up-close animal encounters on the Serengeti Plain, a 65-acre free-roaming habitat, home to reticulated giraffes, Grevy's zebras, white rhinos, bongos, impalas, and more. Myombe Reserve allows you to view lowland gorillas and chimpanzees in a lush, tropical-rain-forest environment. Down Under–themed Walkabout Way offers those ages five and up an opportunity to hand-feed kangaroos and wallabies (a cup of vittles is $5).

Interested in watching a tiger get a dental checkup? Then head over to the Animal Care and Nutrition Center, where you can observe veterinary care for many of the park's animals.

One of the park's newer thrill rides is Falcon's Fury, a 335-foot drop that is reportedly the tallest freestanding drop ride on the continent. It's the centerpiece of the park's Pantopia section, a colorful collection of rides, cafés, and retail space that replaced its Timbuktu section.

Many consider the seven roller coasters to be the biggest lure. On the wings of an African hawk, SheiKra—North America's first dive coaster—takes riders on a three-minute journey 200 feet up, then (gulp!) plunges 90 degrees straight down at 70 mph. The park's coaster lineup also includes steel giants Kumba, Scorpion, and Montu, and Sand Serpent, a five-story family coaster full of hairpin turns and breathtaking dips. When it's running, the Cheetah Hunt is an absolutely exhilarating 4,429-foot-high launch coaster. With three different launch points, this coaster takes you through the Serengeti and into a rocky gorge with a top speed of 60 mph.

Catering to the shorter set, the Sesame Street Safari of Fun is a 5-acre kids' playground with Sesame-themed rides, shows, and water adventures. The Air Grover Rollercoaster takes kids (and parents) on minidives and twisty turns over the Sahara, while Jungle Flyers gets them swinging and screeching. If you're looking to cool off, your best bets are Congo River Rapids, Stanleyville Falls (a flume ride), or Bert and Ernie's Water Hole—complete with bubblers, geysers, water jets, and dumping buckets. Character lunches are available (but you might want to wait until after your rides). ✉ *10165 N. Malcolm McKinley Dr., Central Tampa* ☎ *813/884–4386, 888/800–5447* 🌐 *www.buschgardens.com* 🎫 *from $79.99; parking $23.*

Florida Aquarium

ZOO | FAMILY | Although eels, sharks, and stingrays are the headliners, the Florida Aquarium is much more than a giant fishbowl. This architectural landmark features an 83-foot-high, multitier, glass dome; 250,000 square feet of air-conditioned exhibit space; and more than 20,000 aquatic plants and animals representing species native to Florida and the rest of the world—from black-tip sharks to leafy sea dragons.

Floor-to-ceiling interactive displays, behind-the-scenes tours, and in-water adventures allow kids to really get hands-on—and even get their feet wet. Adventurous types (certified divers age 15 and up) can dive with mild-mannered sharks and sea turtles or shallow-water swim with thousands of reef fish, eels and stingrays (for age six and up).

But you don't have to get wet to have an interactive experience: the *Ocean Commotion* exhibit offers virtual dolphins and whales and multimedia displays and presentations. The Coral Reef Gallery, the aquarium's premier exhibit, is a 500,000-gallon tank with viewing windows, an awesome 43-foot-wide panoramic opening, and a walk-through tunnel that gives the illusion of venturing into underwater depths. There you see a thicket of elkhorn coral teeming with tropical fish, and a dark cave reveals sea life you would normally see only on night dives. The *Journey to Madagascar* exhibit features ring-tailed lemurs, hissing cockroaches, and an Indian Ocean coral reef to showcase the nation's vast diversity of creatures and ecosystems.

If you have an extra 90 minutes, try the Wild Dolphin Adventure Cruise, which takes up to 130 passengers onto Tampa Bay in a 72-foot catamaran for an up-close look at bottlenose dolphins and other wildlife. The outdoor *Explore a Shore* exhibit, which gives younger kids a chance to release some energy, is an aquatic playground with a waterslide, water-jet sprays, and a climbable replica pirate ship. Last but not least, South African penguins make daily appearances in the Coral Reef Gallery. For an extra cost, you can get an up-close look at the daily lives of these penguins during the half-hour-long Penguins: Backstage Pass demonstration. ✉ *701 Channelside Dr., Downtown* ☎ *813/273–4000* 🌐 *www.flaquarium.org* 🎫 *Aquarium from $24.95; Aquarium/Dolphin Cruise combo $49.90; Penguins Backstage Pass combo $70; Dive with the Sharks $150; Shark Swim $100; parking $6.*

Florida Museum of Photographic Arts

MUSEUM | Housed in downtown Tampa's iconic Cube building, a mid-1980s structure known for its unique shape and large glass panels, the Florida Museum of Photographic Arts is the epicenter for the photographic arts in the region. With a series of rotating exhibits that runs the gamut, there's something for everyone, from historic images to contemporary works. ✉ *400 N. Ashley Dr., Downtown* ☎ *813/221–2222* 🌐 *fmopa.org* 🎫 *$10.*

★ Giraffe Ranch

FARM/RANCH | FAMILY | Rural Dade City is known mostly for its strawberries, but word is quickly spreading about something else that makes people flock here: giraffes. These graceful creatures are the headliners at this nearly 50-acre ranch. You can view them as part of a tour in a safari-style vehicle, on the back of a camel or flanked by a llama, or on a Segway; on any tour, you get to

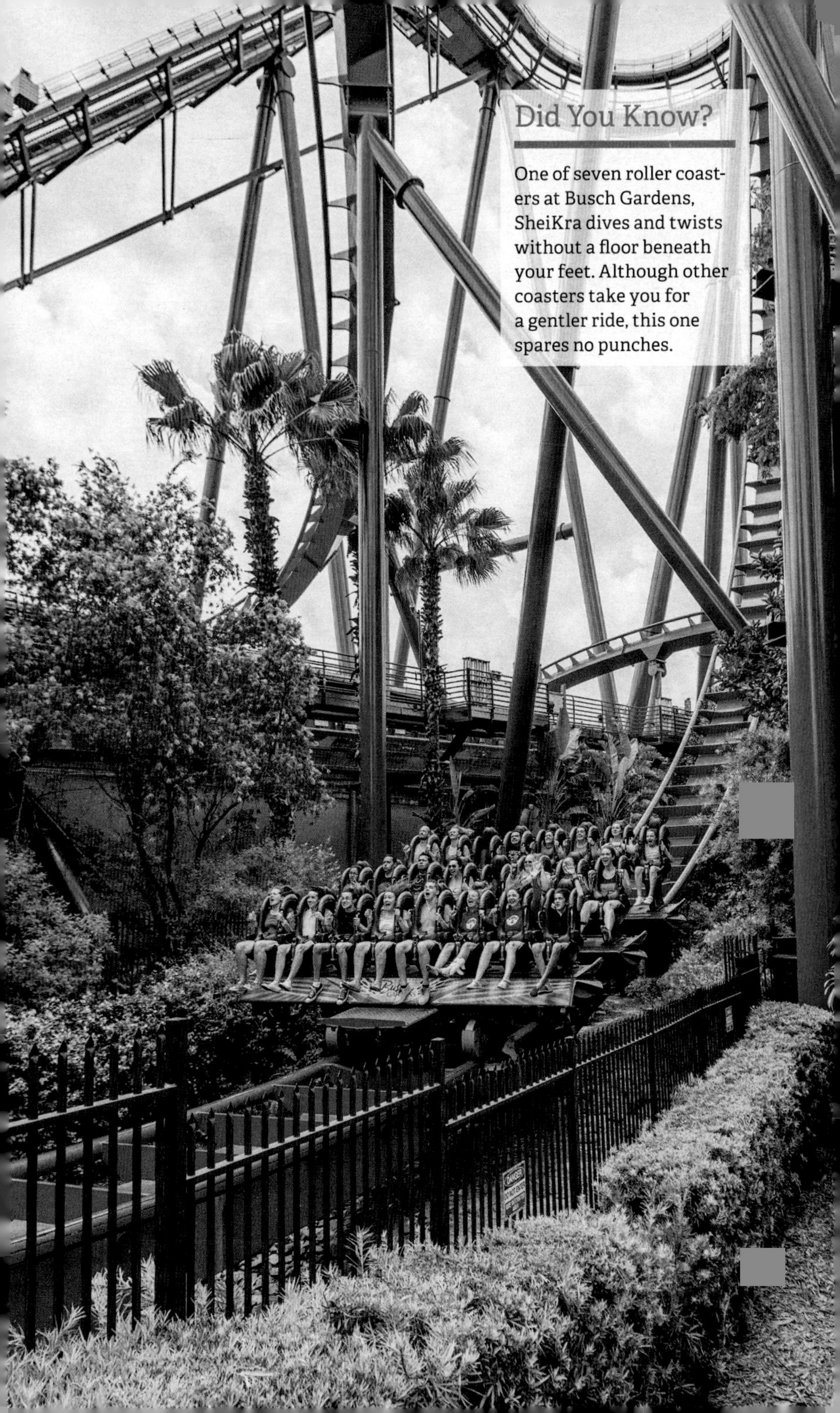

Did You Know?

One of seven roller coasters at Busch Gardens, SheiKra dives and twists without a floor beneath your feet. Although other coasters take you for a gentler ride, this one spares no punches.

hand-feed them cabbage leaves. You'll also see tons of zebras, a pair of pygmy hippos, a giant porcupine, ostriches, and many other animal species roaming the grounds. Near the ranch's welcome center and gift shop is a corral of enclosures where you can watch guinea pigs chomp on sweet-potato chunks, hold a baby goat, (for a little extra cash) feed a flock of resident lemurs or bongo cattle, or watch a group of otters. You can also feed and help bathe a pair of rhinos. The ranch's proprietors have encyclopedic knowledge of the animal kingdom, and the overall experience is meant to impart a sense of connection to the animal world—and the environment—on those who visit. Tours, which start at 11 am and 2 pm, take about one-and-a-half hours, and reservations are required. Credit cards are not accepted. ✉ *38650 Mickler Rd., Dade City* ☎ *813/482–3400* 🌐 *www.girafferanch.com* 🎫 *$99 for tour in safari van; $199 for tour by camelback; $199 by Segway; $199 for a llama trek.*

Glazer Children's Museum

MUSEUM | FAMILY | It's all about play here, and, with 53,000 square feet, more than a dozen themed areas, and more than 170 "interactives," there's plenty of opportunity for it. Areas designed to nurture imagination and strengthen confidence allow children and families to experience everything from flying an airplane to shopping for groceries. Kids can also create art, control the weather, navigate a mini–shipping channel, and "drive" a miniature (stationary) fire truck through Tampa. The Water's Journey Tree lets kids climb the tree to the second floor and mimics the water cycle. ✉ *110 W. Gasparilla Plaza, Downtown* ☎ *813/443–3861* 🌐 *glazermuseum.org* 🎫 *$15.*

Museum of Science & Industry

MUSEUM | FAMILY | At this state-of-the-art facility near the University of South Florida's main campus, you learn about Florida weather, anatomy, flight, and space by seeing *and* by doing. A booth in the exhibit *Disasterville* lets you experience what a hurricane and its 78-mph winds feel like, though crowds sometimes mean a long wait. Explore a lunar colony in *Mission: Moonbase*, a NASA-funded exhibit. The Sky Trail is a 36-foot high multilevel ropes course with a variety of fun and challenging elements. One of the museum's latest attractions is ConnectUs, which lets you explore new, innovative technologies not yet on the market. Idea Zone, MOSI's makerspace, lets you get creative through a variety of hands-on activities and tools.

The 23-seat Saunders Planetarium offers daily shows guided by astronomy experts helping you explore our vast universe. For adventurous spirits, there's a virtual reality simulator that lets you experience everything from spacewalks to run-ins with prehistoric creatures. ✉ *4801 E. Fowler Ave., North Tampa* ✥ *1 mile north of Busch Gardens* ☎ *813/987–6000, 800/995–MOSI* 🌐 *www.mosi.org* 🎫 *Adults 13 and older $12.95; children $7.95; under two years free.*

Tampa Bay History Center

MUSEUM | FAMILY | From the early civilizations that once flourished on its shores to the 2000 presidential vote recount, the Tampa Bay region has long had an integral role in Florida history and that of the country as a whole. The interactive exhibits here let you peer back in time at the people and events that helped shape the area. You'll learn about the Tocobaga and other people who lived in coastal areas and the Spanish explorers who encountered them. A new 8,500 square-foot space explores Tampa Bay's pirate lore with help from a massive replica pirate ship. You'll find a wealth of information and artifacts from the Seminole Wars, Ybor City's once-thriving cigar industry, and Florida crackers who, believe it or not, once drove their cattle in areas now saturated with busy roads and shopping centers. Exhibits also cover the sports teams that have called Tampa Bay home, not to mention the war heroes and politicians of the 20th and 21st centuries. Museumgoers looking for a bite to eat are in for a treat: the café here is a branch of none other than the Columbia, Tampa's most famous and historic restaurant. ✉ *801 Old Water St.* ☎ *813/228–0097* 🌐 *tampabayhistory-center.org* 🎫 *$14.95.*

Tampa Museum of Art

MUSEUM | Housed in an exquisitely designed building, the Tampa Museum of Art is emblematic of the city's efforts to revitalize the downtown riverfront. The facility overlooks Curtis Hixon Park, the towering minarets of the University of Tampa, and the Hillsborough River. The museum's 66,000 square feet of gallery space displays an impressive permanent collection of 20th- and 21st-century sculpture as well as Greek and Roman antiquities. Five additional galleries host traveling exhibits ranging from the classics to some of the most prominent artists working today. The building's external walls are lit at night with colorful LED lights, which are best viewed from Curtis Hixon Waterfront Park. ✉ *120 W. Gasparilla Plaza, Downtown* ☎ *813/274–8130* 🌐 *www.tampamuseum.org* 🎫 *$15.*

Tampa Riverwalk

TRAIL | Tampa's downtown riverfront has come into its own in recent years. The newly revitalized waterfront boasts numerous restaurants, breweries, shops, museums, and outdoors activities along a 2.6-mile stretch of the eastern bank of the Hillsborough River. The transformation has been amazing. Now, whether you're biking, walking, or roller blading, there are dozens of attractions along the pedestrian-friendly pathway, with something to pique all interests. Foodies will enjoy the many dining options, from **Sparkman Wharf** in Channelside to Tampa Heights' **Armature Works** and **The Hall on Franklin**. History buffs can soak in the stories behind Tampa's past as they walk the **Historic Monument Trail**. Meanwhile, outdoorsy types will love the open spaces and stunning waterfront views. ✉ *Armature Works, 1910 N. Ola Ave* ☎ *813/274–7723* 🌐 *thetampariverwalk.com.*

Ybor City

NEIGHBORHOOD | Tampa's Latin quarter is one of only a few National Historic Landmark districts in Florida. Bordered by Interstate 4 to the north, 22nd Street to the east, Adamo Drive to the south, and Nebraska Avenue to the West, it has antique-brick streets and wrought-iron balconies. Cubans brought their cigar-making industry to Ybor (pronounced *ee*-bore) City in 1886, and the smell of cigars—hand-rolled by Cuban immigrants—still wafts through the heart of this east Tampa area, along with the strong aroma of roasting coffee. These days the neighborhood makes for an interesting visit, as empty cigar factories and historic social clubs have been transformed into boutiques, art galleries, restaurants, and nightclubs. Nevertheless, it can also be seedy and rowdy at times. ✉ *Ybor City.*

Restaurants

Bella's Italian Café

$$ | **ITALIAN** | Although this popular SoHo (South Howard Avenue) eatery earned its wings by offering crowd-pleasing Italian classics, much of this mainstay's popularity stems from the creative takes on them. Carnivores are not slighted here, but it is often more delicious to go meatless. **Known for:** hearty Italian classics; homemade pasta; intimate dining environment. 💲 *Average main: $20* ✉ *1413 S. Howard Ave., Hyde Park* ☎ *813/254–3355* 🌐 *www.bellasitaliancafe.com.*

★ **Bern's Steak House**

$$$$ | **STEAKHOUSE** | With the air of an exclusive club, this is one of—if not *the*—finest steak houses in Florida. Rich mahogany paneling and ornate chandeliers define the legendary circa-1956

Bern's, where the chef ages his own beef, grows much of his own produce, and roasts his own coffee. **Known for:** colossal wine list; exclusive atmosphere; after dinner, a trip upstairs to the famous dessert room. *Average main: $36* *1208 S. Howard Ave., Hyde Park* *813/251–2421* *www.bernssteakhouse.com* *Jacket and tie.*

Bernini

$$$ | ITALIAN | Named for the 17th-century Italian baroque sculptor, this trendy restaurant is something of a gallery for copies of his works. In the former Bank of Ybor City building, it has a classy look and creative takes on Italian classics. **Known for:** trendy atmosphere; cioppino à la Cinzano; good drink specials. *Average main: $26* *1702 E. 7th Ave., Ybor City* *813/242–9555* *www.berniniofybor.com* *No lunch Sun.*

Café Dufrain

$$$ | MODERN AMERICAN | Dogs can tag along if you dine on the front patio at pet-friendly Café Dufrain, an eatery right on the Hillsborough River across from the Amalie Arena. Creative menu items, which vary by season, include teriyaki-glazed salmon and homemade dim-sum. **Known for:** internationally influenced American cuisine, such as a bánh mì–style chicken sandwich; excellent water and downtown views; large selection of craft beers and cocktails. *Average main: $24* *707 Harbour Post Dr., Downtown* *813/275–9701* *cafedufrain.com.*

Cappy's Pizza

$ | PIZZA | Chicago may be the first place you think of when you hear the words "deep-dish pizza," which is why the high-quality pies this local chain offers may surprise (and please) you. The menu at this family-friendly spot is pretty simple: choose either a Chicago- or New York–style crust, and select your toppings. **Known for:** the "Cappy" (pepperoni, ham, onions, green pepper, sausage, and mushrooms); bottled beer selection—grab one yourself from the cooler; real-deal vintage decor. *Average main: $14* *4910 N. Florida Ave., Seminole Heights* *813/238–1516* *cappyspizzaonline.com* *No credit cards* *No lunch.*

★ The Columbia Restaurant

$$$ | SPANISH | Make a date for some of the best Latin cuisine in Tampa. A fixture since 1905, this magnificent structure with an old-world air and spacious dining rooms takes up an entire city block and seems to feed the entire city—locals as well as visitors—throughout the week, but especially on weekends. **Known for:** paella à la Valenciana with seafood, chicken, and pork; 1905 salad with ham, olives, cheese, and garlic; delicious sangria. *Average main: $28* *2117 E. 7th Ave., Ybor City* *813/248–4961* *www.columbiarestaurant.com.*

Datz Tampa

$$ | ECLECTIC | Fans of a hearty meal will not be slighted here; the eclectic menu is mostly massive sandwiches and hefty plates (and printed on tabloid paper, an indication of how much it changes). The show-stealer here is the Cheesy Todd, a hamburger patty sandwiched between two deep-fried mounds of bacon-jalapeño mac-and-cheese. **Known for:** large portions; extensive beer and cocktail list; over-the-top sweets from Datz Dough. *Average main: $17* *2616 S. MacDill Ave., SoHo* *813/831–7000* *datztampa.com.*

Edison Food + Drink Lab

$$$$ | ECLECTIC | In the relatively short time this gastropub has been around, it has handily earned a spot at the table of Tampa culinary musts. The internationally influenced, creative menu changes almost every day as chef–owner Jeannie Pierola experiments with a revolving list of intriguing ingredients. **Known for:** grilled octopus appetizer; interesting cocktails; extensive wine list. *Average main: $35* *912 W. Kennedy Blvd., Downtown*

☎ *813/254–7111* 🌐 *edison-tampa.com* ⊙ *Closed Sun. No lunch Sat.*

Gourmet Pizza Company

$$$ | **PIZZA** | This unique pizza joint offers authentic handcrafted pizzas for all diets—veggie lovers and carnivores alike—without sacrificing taste. Choose from a bevy of inventive specialty pies (the Grape N' Gorg, the Gambini, the Shrimp Scampi) or build your own. **Known for:** mouthwatering vegan and gluten-free options; uniquely named pies; fun specialty toppings like peanut butter, guava, or crawfish. $ *Average main: $22* ✉ *610 S. Armenia Ave., Hyde Park* ☎ *813/258–1999* 🌐 *gourmetpizza-company.com.*

Kojak's House of Ribs

$ | **SOUTHERN** | Few barbecue joints can boast the staying power of this family-owned and-operated pit stop. Located along a shaded stretch in South Tampa, it debuted in 1978 and has since earned a following of sticky-fingered regulars who have turned it into one of the most popular barbecue stops in central Florida. **Known for:** barbecued-meat dishes, especially spareribs; great sangria; serene setting. $ *Average main: $13* ✉ *2808 W. Gandy Blvd., South Tampa* ☎ *813/837–3774* 🌐 *kojaksbbq.net* ⊙ *Closed Mon.*

La Segunda Central Bakery

$ | **CUBAN** | For more than a century, this family-owned Ybor City institution has been a go-to stop for authentic Cuban bread—crispy on the outside, and soft and chewy on the inside. La Segunda is the largest producer of Cuban bread in the world, each day baking 18,000 loaves for restaurants throughout Tampa and around the country. **Known for:** authentic Cuban bread; pastries like guava turnovers; café con leche. $ *Average main: $9* ✉ *2512 N. 15th St., Ybor City* ☎ *813/248–1531* 🌐 *lasegundabakery.com.*

Mel's Hot Dogs

$ | **HOT DOG** | Look for the red wiener-mobile parked on the north side of the highway near the theme park, and you'll find this 1950s-style diner that specializes in dogs and fries. It's a must after a long day of riding roller coasters and scoping out zebras at Busch Gardens. **Known for:** long list of hot dogs; crispy, gold fries; decent beer selection. $ *Average main: $9* ✉ *4136 E. Busch Blvd., Central Tampa* ☎ *813/985–8000* 🌐 *www.melshotdogs.com* ⊙ *Closed Sun.*

Mise en Place

$$$$ | **MODERN AMERICAN** | Known to locals as "Mise" (pronounced *meez*), this upscale, modern downtown space is a popular lunch spot for Tampa's political and social elite. At night, it transforms into an elegant, understated dining destination with an ever-changing, seasonal menu that offers adventurous yet meticulously crafted modern American cuisine. **Known for:** five-course "Get Blitzed" tasting menu of the week's highlights; lovingly assembled wine and cocktail list; staples like chicken liver pâté and rack of lamb. $ *Average main: $33* ✉ *442 W. Grand Central Ave., Suite 110, Downtown* ☎ *813/254–5373* 🌐 *www.miseonline.com* ⊙ *Closed Sun. and Mon. No lunch Sat.*

★ The Refinery

$$ | **MODERN AMERICAN** | Since opening in 2010, the Seminole Heights eatery has received five semifinalist nods from James Beard, including best new restaurant and best chef in the South—and it's easy to see why. With a focus on hyper-local cuisine, The Refinery changes its menu several times a week, resulting in innovative, inspired dishes made with whatever local produce, meats, and seafood happen to be available at the moment. **Known for:** local ingredients; innovative and ever-changing menu; quality food at affordable prices. $ *Average main: $20* ✉ *5910 N. Florida Ave., Seminole Heights* ☎ *813/234–3710* 🌐 *thetamparefinery.com* ⊙ *Brunch only on Sun.*

★ Ulele

$$$ | **ECLECTIC** | Named after a 16th-century Tocobagan princess, this hot spot from the same family behind the historic

Tampa
A
B
C
D
E
F
1
2
3
4
5
6
7
8
9
W. Hillsborough Ave.
600
92
N. Macdill Ave.
N. Gomez Ave.
N. Habana Ave.
N. Armenia Ave.
N. Howard Ave.
Wellswood
South Seminole Heights
W. Osborne. Ave.
N. Grady Ave.
N. Dale Mabry Hwy.
Al Lopez Field
W. Osborne E. Ave.
Plaza Terrace
Wishart Blvd.
N. Rome Ave.
Hillsborough River
N. Lynn N. Ave.
Drew Park
574
W. Dr. Martin Luther King Jr. Blvd.
West Virgina Ave.
Riverside Heights
N. Ridge Ave.
West Virginia Ave.
W. Indiana Ave.
Raymond James Stadium
Hillsborough Community College
W. Lake Ave.
W. Woodlawn. Ave.
W. Woodlawn N. Ave.
Tampa Heights
W. Collins St.
W. Fribley St.
W. Tampa Bay Blvd.
N. Himes Ave.
N. Glen Ave.
N. Lincoln Ave.
N. Matanzas Ave.
N. Macdill Ave.
Braddock St.
W. Dewey St.
W. Ivy St.
W. Aileen St.
N. Perry Ave.
N. Kinyon ve.
N. Oakdale Ave.
W. Braddock St.
Poplar Ave.
Myrtle N. Ave.
North Blvd.
W. Columbus Dr.
W. ColumbuS. Dr.
Macfarlane Park
W. St. Joseph St.
W. St. Louis S. St.
W. Francis Ave.
W. St. Conrad St.
W. Beach St.
W. Cherry St.
W. SpruceSt.
MacFarlane Park
W. Green St.
Carver City/ Lincoln Gardens
N. Gomez Ave.
N. Habana Ave.
N. Tampania Ave.
N. Howard Ave.
N. Albany Ave.
Old West Tampa
N. Rome Ave.
W. Palm
W. Spruce St.
W. Union St.
W. Main St.
W. Laurel St.
275
W. La Salle E. St.
W. Nassau St.
N. Tampania Ave.
North Hyde Park
W. Arch St.
N. WilloW. St.
Riverside Park
W. Cypress S. St.
W. CypresS. St.
W. Lemon t.
North Bon Air
W. Cass St.
W. Lemont.
W. CarmenSt.
N. Oregon t.
The University of Tampa
Oakford Park
W. Fig St.
W. North B St.
W. North A St.
W. Kennedy Blvd.
60
685
Swann Estates
Gray Gables
S. Armenia Ave.
W. Cleveland St.
S. Albany Ave.
S. Fremont Ave.
W. Platt St.
Bon Air
S. Dale E. Mabry Hwy.
S. Matanzas Ave.
W. Azeele E. St.
S. Audubon N. Ave.
S. Howard Ave.
S. Orleans Ave.
W. Horatio St.
South Blvd.
S. Clark Ave.
S. Grady Ave.
S. Church Ave.
S. Lincoln Ave.
W. DE. Leon N. St.
W. Swann Ave.
Parkland Estates
S. Glen Ave.
S. Himes Ave.
S. Macdill Ave.
S. Rome Ave.
South Dakota Ave.
S. Newport Ave.
S. Edison Ave.
Hyde Park
W. Inman Ave.
W. Morrison Ave.
S. Sterling Ave.
W. Watrous Ave.
Lee Roy Selmon Expwy. (TOLL)
Hillsborough Bay
Henderson Blvd.
Golfview
W. Neptune St.
W. Hills Ave.
Bayshore E. Blvd.
Palma Ceia West
Palma Ceia Golf and Country Club
0
1/2 mi
1/2 km

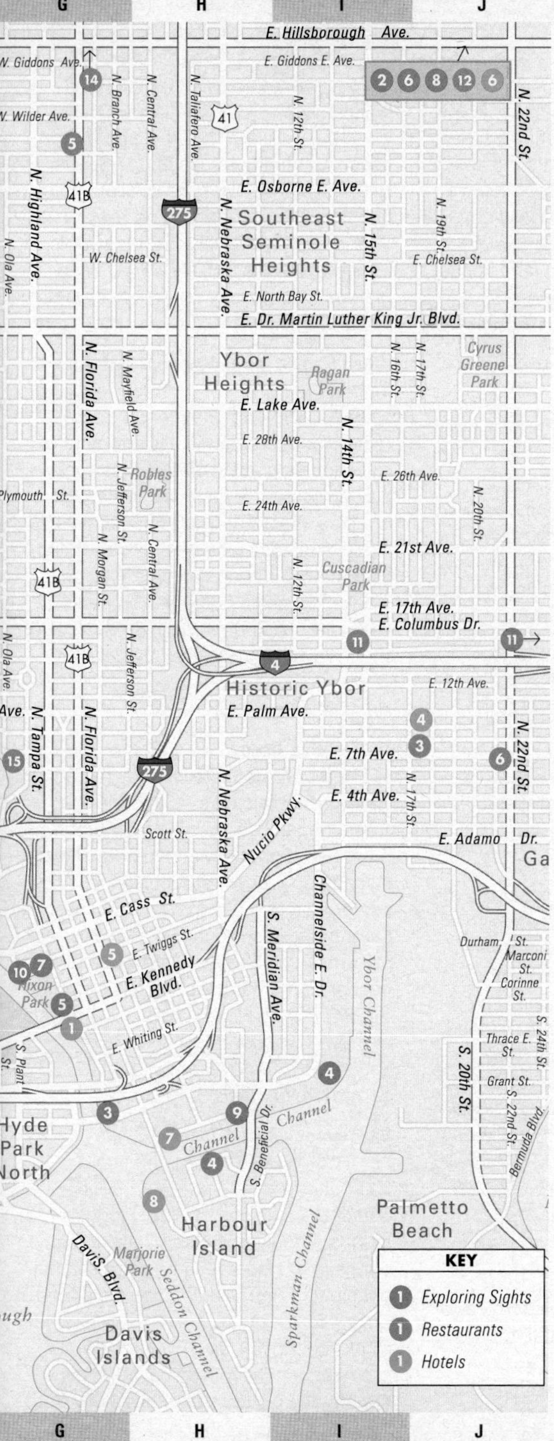

Sights

1 Big Cat Rescue........ A1
2 Busch Gardens........ J1
3 Tampa Riverwalk........ G8
4 Florida Aquarium........ I7
5 Florida Museum of Photographic Arts........ G7
6 Giraffe Ranch........ J1
7 Glazer Children's Museum........ G7
8 Museum of Science & Industry... J1
9 Tampa Bay History Center........ H8
10 Tampa Museum of Art........ G7
11 Ybor City........ J4

Restaurants

1 Bella's Italian Café........ D9
2 Bern's Steak House........ D9
3 Bernini........ J5
4 Café Dufrain........ H8
5 Cappy's Pizza........ G1
6 The Columbia Restaurant........ J5
7 Datz Tampa........ C9
8 Edison Food + Drink Lab........ F7
9 Gourmet Pizza Company........ D8
10 Kojak's House of Ribs........ C9
11 La Segunda Central Bakery........ I4
12 Mel's Hot Dogs........ J1
13 Mise en Place........ F7
14 The Refinery........ G1
15 Ulele........ G5

Hotels

1 Aloft Tampa Downtown........ G7
2 Epicurean........ D9
3 Grand Hyatt Tampa Bay........ A5
4 Hilton Garden Inn Tampa Ybor Historic District........ J5
5 Le Méridien Tampa........ G7
6 Saddlebrook Resort Tampa........ J1
7 Tampa Waterside Hotel & Marina........ H8
8 Westin Tampa Waterside........ H8

Columbia restaurant in Ybor City has become the go-to spot for Tampa diners in the know. The diverse menu focuses on locally available ingredients but has an easy-to-detect Southern accent. **Known for:** Florida pompano and seafood potpie; spectacular views of the Hillsborough River; creative cocktail menu and house-brewed beer. *Average main: $28 1810 N. Highland Ave. 813/999–4952 ulele.com.*

Hotels

Aloft Tampa Downtown
$$ | **HOTEL** | Right on the Hillsborough River, this high-rise used to be a bank but now offers sweeping downtown and water views close to some of Tampa's best restaurants and entertainment venues. **Pros:** right in the middle of everything; tech-friendly; excellent views. **Cons:** parking is valet only; no full-service restaurant; DJ on weekend nights can be loud for early birds on lower floors. *Rooms from: $224 100 W. Kennedy Blvd., Downtown 813/898–8000 alofttampadowntown.com 130 rooms No meals.*

★ Epicurean
$$$ | **HOTEL** | Brought to you in part by the people at Bern's Steak House (which happens to be across the street), this vibrant, cuisine-centric installment of Marriott's Autograph Collection is an absolute must for foodies, but it doesn't make nonfoodies feel left out. **Pros:** excellent service; great location; tons of amenities. **Cons:** can get pricey; exclusive vibe; not the best option for families. *Rooms from: $329 1207 S. Howard Ave., SoHo 813/999–8700, 855/829–2536 epicureanhotel.com 137 rooms No meals.*

Grand Hyatt Tampa Bay
$$ | **RESORT** | On the southwestern edge of Tampa, near the airport and overlooking the Courtney Campbell Causeway, the Grand Hyatt has a lot to offer—both in its guest rooms and on the property. **Pros:** extensive amenities; amazing views; world-class dining. **Cons:** far from beach; getting here can be tough due to traffic and awkward road layout; lots of business conventions and travelers. *Rooms from: $299 2900 Bayport Dr., West Tampa 813/874–1234 www.grandhyatttampabay.com 442 rooms No meals.*

Hilton Garden Inn Tampa Ybor Historic District
$ | **HOTEL** | Although its modern architecture and rooms make it seem out of place in this historic district, this chain hotel's location across from Centro Ybor is a plus. **Pros:** located in top cultural and nightlife district; free Wi-Fi; free parking. **Cons:** neighborhood can be rowdy on weekends; chain-hotel feel; limited amenities. *Rooms from: $186 1700 E. 9th Ave., Ybor City 813/769–9267 www.hiltongardeninn.com 95 rooms No meals.*

Le Méridien Tampa
$$ | **HOTEL** | A meticulous renovation transformed this historic, marble-lined former federal courthouse into Tampa's most talked-about boutique hotel. **Pros:** close to downtown attractions; fascinating for history buffs; lots of amenities. **Cons:** traffic in surrounding area can be a nightmare; all that marble makes for loud echoes in the hallways. *Rooms from: $269 601 N. Florida Ave., Downtown 813/221–9555, 877/782–0116 reservations lemeridientampa.com 130 rooms No meals.*

Saddlebrook Resort Tampa
$$ | **RESORT** | **FAMILY** | Situated about a half hour north of downtown Tampa, Saddlebrook is one of west Florida's top resorts, largely because it has so many things in one spot—36 holes of championship golf; the Saddlebrook Golf Academy; 45 clay, grass, and artificial-surface tennis courts; a Harry Hopman tennis program; a full-service spa; a fitness center; and a kids' club. **Pros:** away from

urban sprawl; great choice for the fitness minded; good for families. **Cons:** a bit isolated; very far from attractions; some rooms could use an update. *Rooms from: $249* ✉ *5700 Saddlebrook Way, Wesley Chapel* ☎ *813/973–1111, 800/729–8383* 🌐 *www.saddlebrook.com* *540 rooms* *No meals.*

Tampa Marriott Waterside Hotel & Marina

$$ | HOTEL | Across from the Tampa Convention Center, this downtown hotel was built for conventioneers but is also convenient to tourist spots such as the Florida Aquarium and the Ybor City and Hyde Park shopping and nightlife districts. **Pros:** great downtown location; near sights, dining, nightlife; direct access to Riverwalk. **Cons:** gridlock during rush hour; streets tough to maneuver; half the rooms overlook concrete-walled channel to Tampa Bay. *Rooms from: $234* ✉ *700 S. Florida Ave., Downtown* ☎ *888/268–1616 for reservations, 813/221–4900* 🌐 *www.marriott.com* *719 rooms* *No meals.*

Westin Tampa Waterside

$$ | HOTEL | Few folks think of the islands when visiting Tampa, but this 12-story hotel on a 177-acre man-made islet is a short drive from downtown Tampa and even closer to the cruise terminal. **Pros:** close to downtown; nice views; on the TECO streetcar line. **Cons:** lots of traffic in immediate area; chain-hotel feel; lots of business travelers. *Rooms from: $240* ✉ *725 S. Harbour Island Blvd., Harbour Island* ☎ *813/229–5000* 🌐 *westintampaharbourisland.com* *318 rooms* *No meals.*

Nightlife

When it comes to entertainment, there's never a dull moment in Tampa. Colorful Ybor City, a heavily Cuban-influenced area minutes from downtown, is a case in point. It has by far the biggest concentration of nightclubs (too many to list here), all situated along 7th and 8th avenues. Ybor comes alive at night and on weekends, when a diverse array of bars and clubs open their doors to throngs of partygoers. Whether it's bumping house music or some live rock and roll you seek, you'll find it here. Downtown Tampa is also becoming a formidable nightlife destination. When it comes to the arts—visual, musical, performing, or otherwise—Tampa is one of the South's leading spots.

Amalie Arena

MUSIC | Many major events take place at this conveniently located arena, which sits near downtown Tampa in the Channelside district. The Tampa Bay Lightning call this spot home, but the 670,000-square-foot venue hosts at least 150 special events each year—mostly musical ones. ✉ *401 Channelside Dr., Downtown* ☎ *813/301–6500* 🌐 *amaliearena.com.*

c. 1949

BARS/PUBS | This low-key bar supports the ever-growing Florida beer scene with more than 40 craft brews on tap and bottled, many of them hailing from the Tampa Bay area. There's also a decent wine selection and a handful of snacks on the menu. This old-timey venue is also a Lowry Park-area community mainstay, hosting numerous events each week, from trivia to yoga to music performances. The lush tropical outdoor courtyard hosts food trucks. ✉ *6905 N. Orleans Ave.* ☎ *813/990–8883* 🌐 *c1949.com.*

The Castle

MUSIC CLUBS | Everybody's welcome on the dance floor at this iconic Ybor City club that's catered to the alternative set for nearly three decades. Thursday through Saturday each week, DJs play a wide range of genres, including goth, new wave, electro, industrial, dark wave, and EBM (a type of alternative electronic dance music). In addition to embracing musical—and personal—diversity, this multilevel venue has several bars offering a good selection of single malt scotches, small batch bourbon, aged tequila, and beers from around the world, including several local craft brews. ✉ *2004 N. 16th St., Ybor City* ☎ *813/247–7547* 🌐 *castleybor.com*.

Cigar City Brewing Tasting Room
BARS/PUBS | Offering the fruits of the adjacent Cigar City brewery, the large tasting room here puts Tampa on the map for craft beer enthusiasts. On tap, it offers mainstay brews like Jai Alai IPA and Maduro Brown Ale as well as an interesting rotation of seasonal beers. It's a spot with friendly staff and generally good music. But beware: happy hour can be packed. Brewery tours are available Wednesday through Sunday at 12, 1:30, 4, and 5:30 pm for a nominal fee. ✉ *3924 W. Spruce St., Suite A, Central Tampa* ☎ *813/348–6363* 🌐 *cigarcitybrewing.com*.

Ella's Americana Folk Art Café
GATHERING PLACES | A Seminole Heights staple, the eclectic Ella's Americana Folk Art Café dons two hats: it's a favorite local eatery offering a creative twist on Southern comfort food and also a raucous juke joint hosting local, regional and national musical acts several nights of the week. The bar boasts more than 100 rare and small-batch bourbons and an extensive craft beer list, including many brewed locally. And don't miss their weekend brunch. Ella's switches up its menu for its award-winning Soul Food Sundays and breaks out their infamous Bloody Ella, complete with a smoked barbecue rib garnish. ✉ *5119 N. Nebraska Ave., Seminole Heights* ☎ *813/234–1000* 🌐 *ellasfolkartcafe.com*.

Gaspar's Grotto
BARS/PUBS | Spanish pirate Jose Gaspar was known for swashbuckling up and down Florida's west coast in the late 18th and early 19th century. His legend has inspired a massive, raucous street festival each winter. This Ybor City drinkery has adopted his name, and rightly so. Decked out in tons of pirate memorabilia, it's the cornerstone to any night spent barhopping on the Ybor strip. The sangria is a good choice, but the aged rums may be a better fit here. You'll also find a food menu that goes well beyond standard bar fare. ✉ *1805 E. 7th Ave., Ybor City* ☎ *813/248–5900* 🌐 *www.gasparsgrotto.com*.

Lowry Parcade
BARS/PUBS | Arcade bars may be all the rage these days, but Lowry Parcade set the stage in Tampa, opening in 2016 as the first bar to combine retro gaming with craft beer in the city. This haven for all things nerdy hosts numerous events from cookie cook-offs to pup-friendly meetups to indie markets. ✉ *1213 W. Waters Ave.* ☎ *813/915-9180* 🌐 *lowryparcade.com*.

Seminole Hard Rock Hotel & Casino
CASINOS | In addition to playing one of the hundreds of Vegas-style slot machines, gamers can get their kicks at the casino's poker tables and video-gaming machines. The lounge serves drinks 24 hours a day. Hard Rock Cafe, of course, has live music, dinner, and nightlife. There is a heavy smell of cigarette smoke here, as with most casinos. ✉ *5223 N. Orient Rd., East Tampa* ✣ *Off I–4 at N. Orient Rd. exit* ☎ *813/627–7625* 🌐 *www.seminolehardrock.com*.

Skippers Smokehouse
MUSIC CLUBS | A junkyard-style restaurant and oyster bar, Skippers is known for hosting Uncle John's Band (a long-running Grateful Dead cover act) every Thursday, and for having great smoked fish every night. Check their calendar for exceptional musical lineups on the weekends; it's closed on Mondays. ✉ *910 Skipper Rd., North Tampa* ☎ *813/971–0666* 🌐 *www.skipperssmokehouse.com*.

Tampa Theatre
THEATER | This renovated 1926 movie palace is a gorgeous throwback to Hollywood's golden age. A downtown icon, the Tampa Theatre boasts a charming indoor Mediterranean courtyard, replica

antique statuary, ornate architectural artistry, and a Mighty Wurlitzer theater organ that's still in use. Rescued from demolition in the late 1970s, the venue is not only a Tampa City landmark, it's also listed on the National Register of Historic Places. In addition to showcasing foreign, independent, and classic films on a daily basis, this cultural hot spot also hosts hundreds of community and educational events, concerts, and historic tours. ✉ *711 N. Franklin St., Downtown* ☎ *813/274–8286* 🌐 *www.tampatheatre.org.*

Shopping

Centro Ybor

SHOPPING CENTERS/MALLS | Ybor City's destination within a destination is this dining-and-entertainment palace. It has shops, bars, and restaurants, a 20-screen movie theater, and even a gourmet Popsicle shop. ✉ *1600 E. 8th Ave., Ybor City* 🌐 *www.centroybor.com.*

King Corona Cigar Factory

TOBACCO | If you are shopping for hand-rolled cigars, head to Ybor City, where a few hand-rollers practice their craft in small shops. This is one of the more popular places thanks to its plentiful outdoor seating, perfect if you want to grab some nibbles and a Cuban coffee. ✉ *1523 E. 7th Ave., Ybor City* ☎ *813/241–9109* 🌐 *www.kingcoronacigars.com.*

★ Oxford Exchange

BOOKS/STATIONERY | With fresh, simple but refined dining options, boutique shopping, coffee and tea stations, and community workspaces, it's impossible to pigeonhole this hip locale. So let's call it what it is: a lifestyle experience that shouldn't be missed. Housed in a turn-of-the-century building that was once used as a stable for the nearby Tampa Bay Hotel, this Hyde Park destination utilizes every nook and cranny of the renovated historic structure to create an atmosphere unlike anything else in the Tampa Bay area. Large and meandering, each corner of the building exudes its own elegant sense of space from a cerebral bookstore with great literary finds to a spacious and sunny courtyard for hosting the perfect brunch to low-key comfy seating great for grabbing a coffee and catching up with a friend. ✉ *420 W. Kennedy Blvd., Hyde Park* ☎ *813/253–0222* 🌐 *oxfordexchange.com.*

Squaresville

CLOTHING | From the mildly unusual to the downright bizarre this vintage store has it all—from the mid-20th century, that is. Among the finds are Cuban clothing, Elvis posters, and Bettie Page clocks. ✉ *3224 W. Bay to Bay Blvd., Hyde Park* ☎ *813/259–9944* 🌐 *www.squaresvilletampa.com* ⏲ *Closed Sun. and Mon.*

Bayshore Boulevard Trail

HIKING/WALKING | Considered the world's longest continuous sidewalk, this 4½-mile trail is a good spot for just standing still and taking it all in, with its spectacular views of downtown Tampa and the Hillsborough Bay area. Of course, you can also walk, talk, jog, bike, and in-line skate with locals. The trail is open from dawn to dusk daily. ✉ *Bayshore Blvd.* ☎ *813/274–8615.*

Canoe Escape

BOATING | This outfit in northeast Tampa arranges guided or self-guided trips from one hour to all-day duration on the upper Hillsborough River, abounding with alligators, ibises, hawks, and other wildlife. It also rents canoes and kayaks. ✉ *John B. Sargeant Park, 12702 U.S. 301, Thonotosassa* ☎ *813/986–2067* 🌐 *www.canoeescape.com.*

The Claw at USF

GOLF | Named for its many dog-legged fairways, this University of South Florida course is one of the most challenging public courses in the area. Live oaks as well as cypress and pine trees line the tight twists and turns of the fairways. This is one of the few places in Tampa Bay where you'll find deer grazing along the fairway (especially early in the morning) and gators sunning themselves next to the course's ponds. You'll also find a driving range and a golf shop. After you play, grab a beer at Rocky's Sports Grill, where you'll be able to catch the game on one of several flat- or plasma-screen TVs. ✉ *13801 N. 46th St., North Tampa* ☎ *813/632–6893* 🌐 *www.theclawatusf-golf.com* 💳 *From $20* 🏌 *18 holes, 6863 yards, par 71.*

George M. Steinbrenner Field

BASEBALL/SOFTBALL | Locals and tourists flock each March to see the New York Yankees play about 17 spring training games at this 11,000-seat facility. (Call or visit the website for tickets.) From April through September, the stadium belongs to a Yankee farm team, the Tampa Yankees, who play 70 games against the likes of the Daytona Cubs and the Sarasota Red Sox. ✉ *1 Steinbrenner Dr., Central Tampa* ✣ *Near the corner of Dale Mabry Hwy., off I–275 Exit 41B* ☎ *813/875–7753* 🌐 *www.steinbrenner-field.com.*

Saddlebrook Golf Club

GOLF | This expansive complex half an hour northeast of Tampa offers not one but two courses designed by Arnold Palmer. The Palmer Golf Course's hilly terrain contrasts with Tampa Bay's generally flat landscape, and it makes you think you're playing on a course somewhere in New England. With its Spanish moss–draped cypress hammocks, the Saddlebrook Golf Course has more of an Old Florida feel to it. As you make your way past this course's green ponds, keep an eye out for turtles—and gators. There's also a golf shop, driving range, on-site pros, and, if you're aching from a grueling day on the course, a luxury spa on the resort property. ✉ *Saddlebrook Resort, 5700 Saddlebrook Way, Wesley Chapel* ☎ *813/729–8383* 🌐 *www.saddlebrook.com* 💳 *From $46* 🏌 *Palmer Course: 18 holes, 6243 yards, par 71; Saddlebrook Course: 18 holes, 6480 yards, par 70.*

Tampa Bay Buccaneers

FOOTBALL | Seeing the National Football League play isn't easy without connections, though catching a Bucs home game is a little easier than most. Tickets can be found for some games at the box office, though it's a safer bet when you buy them online in advance. ✉ *Raymond James Stadium, 4201 N. Dale Mabry Hwy., Central Tampa* ☎ *813/879–2827* 🌐 *www.buccaneers.com.*

Tournament Players Club of Tampa Bay

GOLF | A stop along the PGA Champion's Tour, this public course sits about 15 miles north of Tampa. It was designed by Bobby Weed with consultation from Chi Chi Rodriguez and is laid out along natural wetlands, which means you can spot plenty of local wildlife as you play. The course was designed to be challenging while still giving novices a fair shake. Practice ahead of time at the driving, chipping, or putting range. There's a golf shop on-site as well as the Cuatro, where you can grab a sandwich and a cold one after your game. ✉ *5300 W. Lutz Fern Rd., Lutz* ☎ *813/949–0090* 🌐 *www.tpctampabay.com* 💳 *$95 to $225 (varies seasonally)* 🏌 *18 holes, 6898 yards, par 71.*

St. Petersburg

21 miles west of Tampa.

Nicknamed the Sunshine City, St. Pete is much more than a mass of land between the airport and the beaches. In recent years it's seen a fierce arts and cultural revival, which you can plainly see as you stroll through the city's lively downtown area. The Salvador Dalí Museum building is a testament to the great pride residents of the 'Burg take in their waterfront city. But the city has other arts-oriented attractions, including the Dale Chihuly

Collection, the Fine Arts Museum, and the burgeoning young artist hub known as the 600 Block, where eateries and bars attract crowds in the evening. Beach Drive offers some upscale options, whereas Central Avenue appeals more to night owls. The Grand Central District offers some unique vintage and antiques shopping. Gulfport is a stylishly low-key suburb southwest of St. Petersburg. The long strip of barrier islands lining St. Pete's west coast offer miles of gorgeous white beaches as well as dining, nightlife, and phenomenal sunsets. Nearby beach towns include St. Pete Beach, Treasure Island, Madeira Beach, and Redington Shores. No trip to this area is complete without a visit to the remote, pristine beaches of Fort De Soto.

GETTING HERE AND AROUND

Interstate 275 heads west from Tampa across Tampa Bay to St. Petersburg, swings south, and crosses the bay again on its way to Terra Ceia, near Bradenton. U.S. 19 is St. Petersburg's major north–south artery; traffic can be heavy, and there are many lights, so try to avoid it. Alternatives include 66th and 4th streets. One key thing to remember about St. Pete is that the roads form an easy-to-navigate grid: streets run north to south; avenues run east to west. Central Avenue connects downtown to the beaches.

Around St. Petersburg, Pinellas Suncoast Transit Authority serves Pinellas County. Look for buses that cover the beaches and downtown exclusively.

St. Petersburg Trolley will get you to key destinations throughout downtown St. Pete, and even offers free service between the Chamber of Commerce Visitor's Bureau and certain destinations.

CONTACTS Pinellas Suncoast Transit Authority. ☎ *727/540–1800* 🌐 *www.psta.net.* **St. Petersburg Trolley.** ☎ *727/821–5166* 🌐 *www.loopertrolley.com.*

TOURS

Dolphin Landings Tours

BOAT TOURS | This operation runs a four-hour shelling trip, a two-hour dolphin-sighting excursion powered mostly by sail, back-bay or party-boat fishing, and other outings to Egmont Key and Shell Key. It's not easy to spot from the road: the boats are docked behind a strip mall. ✉ *4737 Gulf Blvd., St. Pete Beach* ☎ *727/360–7411* 🌐 *www.dolphinlandings.com* 🎟 *From $35.*

Ghost Tours of St. Petersburg and Tampa Bay

SPECIAL-INTEREST | With candlelit tours along the Sunshine City's beautiful waterfront and downtown corridor, as well as other areas of the region, these walks combine local history with chilling tales of the city's most haunted spots. ✉ *181 4th Ave. NE, Downtown* ☎ *727/894–4678* 🌐 *www.ghosttour.net/stpetersburg* 🎟 *$20.*

VISITOR INFORMATION

CONTACTS Visit St. Petersburg-Clearwater. ✉ *8200 Bryan Dairy Rd., Suite 200, Largo* ☎ *727/464–7200,* 🌐 *www.visitstpete-clearwater.com.*

Downtown St. Petersburg

Sights

★ Chihuly Collection

MUSEUM | An electrifying, 10,000-square-foot Albert Alfonso–designed building is home to world-renowned glass sculptor Dale Chihuly's work. Here impossibly vibrant, larger-than-life pieces such as *Float Boat* and *Ruby Red Icicle* sit next to some of the famed sculptor's smaller and more under-the-radar works. You can tour the museum independently or with one of its volunteer docents (no added cost; tours are given hourly on the half hour during the week). Each display is perfectly lit against a shade of gray paint on the walls Chihuly himself handpicked, which adds to the drama of the designs.

Don't miss *Mille Fiore* (*Thousand Flowers*), a spectacular, whimsical glass montage mimicking a wildflower patch, critters and all. Check out the gift shop at the end if you'd like to take some of the magic home with you. Your admission includes access to Morean Arts Center's glassblowing studio, where you can watch resident artisans create a unique glass piece before your eyes. ✉ *720 Central Ave., Downtown* ☎ *727/896–4527* 🌐 *www.moreanartscenter.org/chihuly* 🎫 *$19.95.*

★ The Dalí Museum

MUSEUM | Inside and out, the waterfront Dalí Museum, which opened on 1/11/11 (Dalí is said to have been into numerology), is almost as remarkable as the Spanish surrealist's work. The state-of-the-art building has a surreal geodesic-like glass structure called the *Dalí Enigma*, as well as an outdoor labyrinth and a DNA-inspired spiral staircase leading up to the collection. All this before you've even seen the collection, which is one of the most comprehensive of its kind—courtesy of Ohio magnate A. Reynolds Morse, a friend of Dalí's.

Here you can scope out his early impressionistic works and see how the painter evolved into the visionary he's now seen to be. The mind-expanding paintings in this downtown headliner include *Eggs on a Plate Without a Plate, The Hallucinogenic Toreador,* and more than 90 other oils. You'll also discover more than 2,000 additional works including watercolors, drawings, sculptures, photographs, and objets d'art. The museum also hosts temporary collections from the likes of Pablo Picasso and Andy Warhol. Free hour-long tours are led by well-informed docents. ✉ *1 Dali Blvd.* ☎ *727/823–3767* 🌐 *www.thedali.org* 🎫 *$24.*

Florida Holocaust Museum

MUSEUM | The downtown Florida Holocaust Museum is one of the largest of its kind in the United States. It has the permanent *History, Heritage, and Hope* exhibit, an original boxcar, and an extensive collection of photographs, art, and artifacts. One compelling display includes portraits and biographies of Holocaust survivors. The museum, which also has a series of rotating exhibits, was conceived as a learning center for children, so many of the exhibits avoid overly graphic content; signs are posted outside galleries if the subject matter might be too intense for kids. ✉ *55 5th St. S* ☎ *727/820–0100* 🌐 *www.flholocaustmuseum.org* 🎫 *$16.*

Great Explorations

MUSEUM | **FAMILY** | "Don't touch" are words never spoken here. The museum is hands-on through and through, with an art studio, replica vet's office and grocery store, a "beach" with real sand, a touch tunnel, and other interactive play areas. Kids and grown-ups alike will marvel at Reefscape, a brilliantly colorful fabric and yarn interpretation of the underwater ecosystems surrounding Florida. ✉ *1925 4th St. N* ☎ *727/821–8992* 🌐 *greatex.org* 🎫 *$10.*

The James Museum of Western & Wildlife Art

MUSEUM | One of St. Petersburg's newest museums, the James Museum of Western & Wildlife Art has hundreds of paintings and sculptures that portray the history, culture, and lifestyles of the American West, Native Americans, and wildlife that spans the globe. Founded by philanthropists Tom and Mary James, the museum is divided into themed galleries—Early West, Native Life, Native Artists, Frontier, Wildlife and New West—in a cohesive and easy-to-navigate collection. Rotating special exhibits regularly bring new works to the museum. ✉ *150 Central Ave., Downtown* ☎ *727/892–4200* 🌐 *thejamesmuseum.org* 🎫 *$20.*

Museum of Fine Arts

MUSEUM | One of the city's cornerstones, this museum is a gorgeous Mediterranean Revival structure that houses outstanding collections of Asian, African, Native American, European, and American art. Major works here by American artists range from Hassam to O'Keeffe to Bellows and Morisot, but the museum is known for its collection of French artists, including Cézanne, Monet, Rodin, Gauguin, and Renoir. There are also photography exhibits that draw from a permanent collection of more than 14,000 works. Docents give narrated gallery tours. Special events abound on Thursday nights. A café offers visitors a lunch respite and a beautiful view of the bay. *✉ 255 Beach Dr. NE ☎ 727/896–2667 🌐 mfastpete.org 🎫 $20.*

St. Petersburg Museum of History

MUSEUM | Learn about the history of the Tampa Bay region, from the Tocobaga Indians to St. Pete's spring training history to America's first commercial airline, at the St. Petersburg Museum of History. Exhibits include those on Native American primitive shell tools and thousands of baseballs signed by the likes of Babe Ruth. There's also a full-size replica of the Benoist Airboat flown by pioneer aviator Tony Jannus. *✉ 335 2nd Ave. NE ☎ 727/894–1052 🌐 www.spmoh.com 🎫 $15.*

Sunken Gardens

GARDEN | FAMILY | A cool oasis amid St. Pete's urban clutter, this lush 4-acre plot was created from a lake that was drained in 1903. Explore the cascading waterfalls and koi ponds, and walk through the butterfly house and exotic gardens where more than 50,000 tropical plants and flowers from across the globe thrive amid groves of some of the area's most spectacular palm trees. The flock of wading flamingoes is a favorite here. *✉ 1825 4th St. N ☎ 727/551–3102 🌐 www.sunkengardens.org 🎫 $10.*

Restaurants

Bella Brava New World Trattoria

$$ | ITALIAN | This trendy eatery is one of the more sought-after places on equally trendy Beach Drive. It offers a fresh, imaginative approach to Italian fare. **Known for:** ravioli Genovese (stuffed with pine nuts and goat cheese); pasta brava (with wood-grilled chicken, cotto ham, peas, and Asiago cream); lively happy hour and people-watching scene. *$ Average main: $20 ✉ 204 Beach Dr. NE, Downtown ☎ 727/895–5515 🌐 bellabrava.com.*

Birch & Vine

$$$ | MODERN AMERICAN | Seasonal, locally sourced ingredients work equally well in both the surf and the turf columns at Birch & Vine, which has turned The Birchwood hotel lobby and patio into an evening dining destination for hungry diners in downtown St. Petersburg. Umbrella-covered patio tables face Beach Drive and North Straub Park to provide the best people-watching. **Known for:** maple cream sous vide scallops; blackberry-and-five spice duck; outdoor dining with views of downtown waterfront parks. *$ Average main: $28 ✉ The Birchwood, 340 Beach Dr. NE, Downtown ☎ 727/896–1080 🌐 www.thebirchwood.com/birch-vine-menu.*

Bodega

$ | LATIN AMERICAN | This charming eatery has carved a niche for itself in the bustling Edge District by serving up flavorful, rustic Latin American food that keeps customers coming back for more. From authentic Cuban sandwiches—a Tampa Bay area staple—to interesting veggie options, Bodega caters to all diets. **Known for:** authentic Cuban sandwiches; flavorful Latin American dishes; long lines most days of the week that move quickly. *$ Average main: $8 ✉ 1120 Central Ave. ☎ 727/623–0942 🌐 eatatbodega.com.*

Brick & Mortar Kitchen & Wine Bar

$$$ | MODERN AMERICAN | Gourmet cuisine meets a rustic, chic setting at this bustling New American restaurant. Small-plate favorites include the truffle Parmesan hand-cut fries, beef tenderloin carpaccio with homemade ravioli and slow-braised octopus. **Known for:**

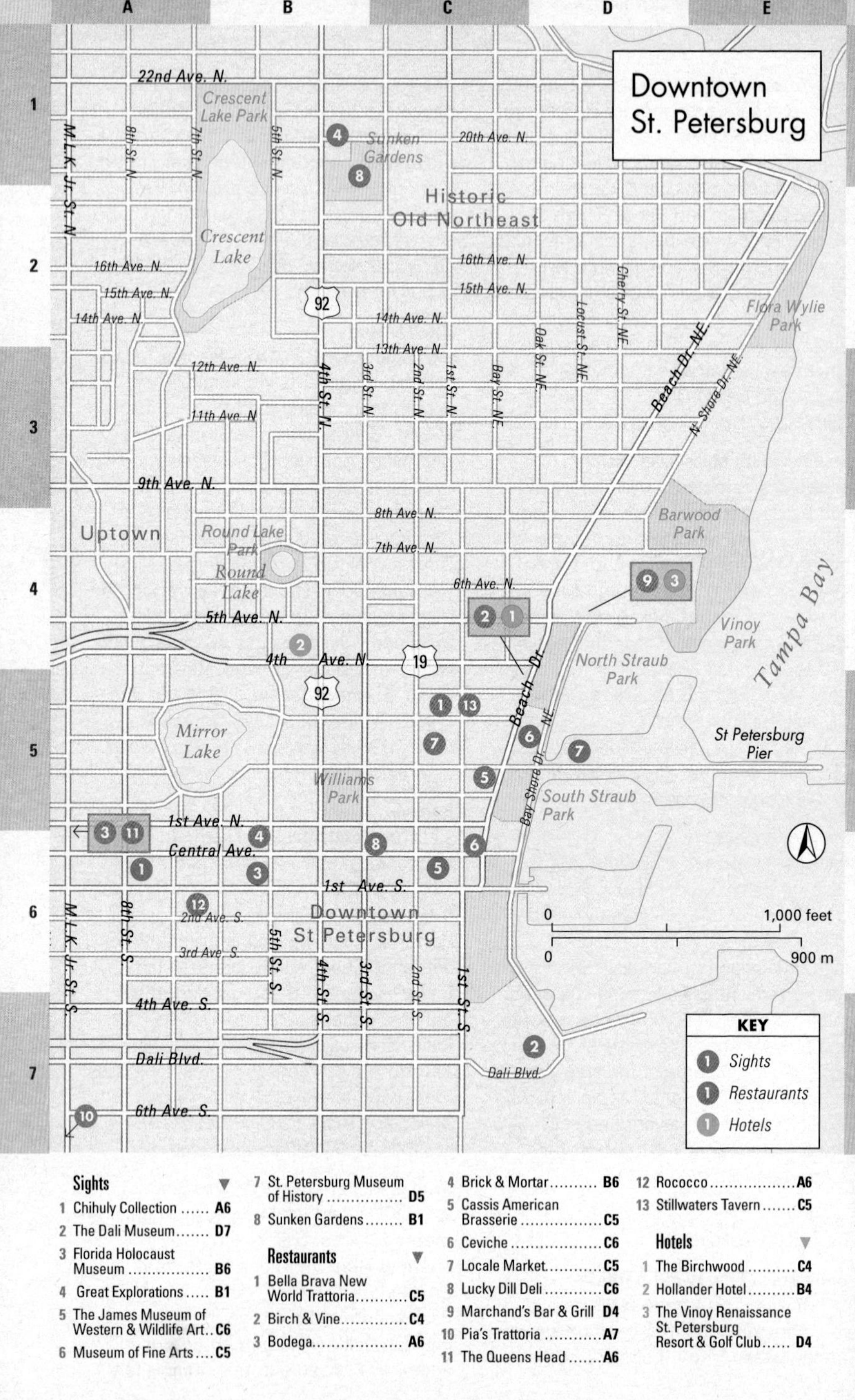

Sights

1 Chihuly Collection A6
2 The Dali Museum....... D7
3 Florida Holocaust Museum B6
4 Great Explorations B1
5 The James Museum of Western & Wildlife Art.. C6
6 Museum of Fine Arts C5
7 St. Petersburg Museum of History D5
8 Sunken Gardens........ B1

Restaurants

1 Bella Brava New World Trattoria.......... C5
2 Birch & Vine............. C4
3 Bodega................... A6
4 Brick & Mortar.......... B6
5 Cassis American Brasserie C5
6 Ceviche C6
7 Locale Market........... C5
8 Lucky Dill Deli C6
9 Marchand's Bar & Grill D4
10 Pia's Trattoria A7
11 The Queens Head A6
12 Rococco.................. A6
13 Stillwaters Tavern C5

Hotels

1 The Birchwood C4
2 Hollander Hotel.......... B4
3 The Vinoy Renaissance St. Petersburg Resort & Golf Club...... D4

innovative New American fare; variety of small and large plates; vast wine and craft beer selection. 💲 *Average main: $22* ✉ *539 Central Ave., Downtown* ☎ *727/822–6540* ⊗ *Closed Sun. and Mon.*

Cassis American Brasserie

$$$$ | **BRASSERIE** | If you drop in for a drink at one of the best places in St. Petersburg for happy hour, it's worth sticking around for the French-inspired cuisine for dinner. More casual options include a croque monsieur, but there are also entrées like bouillabaisse and Atlantic salmon, which is served with smashed peas, baby-carrot confit, and an orange-coriander glaze. **Known for:** European-inspired fare such as bouillabaisse; happy-hour deals, especially on good wine; dog-friendly outdoor dining (including a "mutt menu"). 💲 *Average main: $31* ✉ *170 Beach Dr. NE, Downtown* ☎ *727/827–2927* 🌐 *cassisstpete.com.*

Ceviche

$$$ | **TAPAS** | A choice romantic destination as well as an excellent launchpad for a night out, this tapas bar offers an astonishing spate of pleasant sensations for those with savvy taste buds. You can't go wrong with a huge order of seafood or chicken and pork paella. **Known for:** wide range of small plates; delicious sangria; live jazz, salsa, and flamenco music. 💲 *Average main: $25* ✉ *10 Beach Dr. NE, Downtown* ☎ *727/209–2299* 🌐 *www.ceviche.com.*

Locale Market

$$ | **CONTEMPORARY** | The brainchild of celebrity chefs Michael Mina and Don Pintabona, this unconventional farm-to-table food court in the new upscale Sundial St. Pete shopping and dining complex allows you to choose your own culinary adventure. Multiple stations are scattered throughout the two-story culinary fortress. **Known for:** robust turkey burger with avocado, pepperjack cheese, and aioli; brussels sprout halves roasted with apples and garlic; bakery/chocolate counter featuring a variety of cupcakes and pastries. 💲 *Average main: $15* ✉ *179 2nd Ave. N, Downtown* ☎ *727/523–6300* 🌐 *localegourmetmarket.com.*

Lucky Dill Deli

$ | **AMERICAN** | This New York–style deli serving breakfast, lunch, and early dinner is often packed. Favorites include Cuban sandwiches, pastrami sandwiches, and the "black and bleu" burger. **Known for:** good sandwiches for lunch; outdoor seating for prime people-watching; popular weekend brunch. 💲 *Average main: $10* ✉ *277 Central Ave.* ☎ *727/895–5859* 🌐 *luckydillofstpete.com.*

Marchand's Bar & Grill

$$$$ | **ECLECTIC** | Opened in 1925, this wonderful restaurant in the posh Renaissance Vinoy Resort has frescoed ceilings and a spectacular view of Tampa Bay. Upscale and special-occasion diners are drawn to Marchand's dynamic menu, which changes often and embraces a farm-to-table approach. **Known for:** Wednesday through Saturday sushi; 1925 early-bird menu; great happy hour. 💲 *Average main: $34* ✉ *Renaissance Vinoy Resort, 501 5th Ave. NE* ☎ *727/824–8072* 🌐 *www.marchandsbarandgrill.com.*

Pia's Trattoria

$$ | **ITALIAN** | Warm and intimate, Pia's Trattoria feels like a European hideaway along the waterfront. The rustic Italian eatery, a downtown Gulfport gem, serves up simple yet bold flavors. **Known for:** flavorful Italian dishes; inventive weekly specials; intimate feel perfect for couples. 💲 *Average main: $20* ✉ *3054 Beach Blvd. S., Gulfport* ☎ *727/327–2190* 🌐 *www.piastrattoria.com* ⊗ *No lunch Mon.*

The Queens Head

$$ | **BRITISH** | A staple of the hip Grand Central District, the Queens Head adds a creative flair to classic British fare. You'll find traditional dishes like fish and chips and steak and ale pie, but with a tasty, irreverent spin. **Known for:** fish and chips

and Bubble & Squeak; killer weekend brunch; bathrooms with cheeky UK tabloid headlines. *Average main: $20 2501 Central Ave., Grand Central District 727/498–8584 thequeenshead-bar.com Brunch on weekends only.*

Rococo

$$$$ | **STEAKHOUSE** | Yet another spot inspired by the St. Pete of yesteryear, this happening steak house sits in what was once a historic YWCA building. Possibly the only independent steak house in St. Petersburg, it gets its name from the late-baroque art movement (but displays the work of local artists on its walls). **Known for:** solid steak offerings; famous lobster bisque; variety of craft cocktails and beer. *Average main: $35 655 2nd Ave. S 727/822–0999 roco-costeak.com No lunch.*

Stillwaters Tavern

$$$ | **MODERN AMERICAN** | Equal parts happy-hour spot and go-to dinner locale, this trendy Beach Drive trattoria—from the folks who brought us Bella Brava—has something for everyone. Their take on fish-and-chips gets cheers, as does the catch of the day (whatever that might be), the falafel (served on a bed of hummus), and most of the menu's other diverse, often locally sourced options. **Known for:** catch of the day; craft cocktails; outdoor seating. *Average main: $22 224 Beach Dr. NE, Downtown 727/350–1019 stillwaterstavern.com.*

The Birchwood

$$ | **B&B/INN** | Few things are as emblematic of Beach Drive's renaissance as this boutique hotel, which like many of downtown St. Pete's best attractions, seamlessly blends old and new. **Pros:** highly sought-after location; exquisite furnishings; close to downtown attractions. **Cons:** service seems more like a B&B than a hotel and sometimes staff is MIA; not the best choice for families with kids; 20 minutes from the beach. *Rooms from: $215 340 Beach Dr. NE, Downtown 727/896–1080 thebirchwood.com 18 rooms No meals.*

★ Hollander Hotel

$ | **HOTEL** | This charming, chicly renovated 1933 hotel and restaurant on the edge of downtown has become a hub for visitors and Floridians alike and offers a less pricey alternative to the Vinoy. **Pros:** some rooms have refurbished vintage bathtubs; close to action; good for nightlife. **Cons:** smaller rooms; small bathrooms; some blight nearby. *Rooms from: $110 421 4th Ave. N, Downtown 727/873–7900 hollanderhotel.com 100 rooms No meals.*

★ The Vinoy Renaissance St. Petersburg Resort & Golf Club

$$$ | **RESORT** | Built in 1925 (making it roughly the same vintage as the Don CeSar), the Vinoy is a luxury resort in St. Petersburg's gorgeous Old Northeast. **Pros:** charming property; friendly service; close to downtown museums. **Cons:** pricey; small rooms; drive to the beach. *Rooms from: $385 501 5th Ave. NE 727/894–1000 www.vinoy-renaissanceresort.com 361 rooms No meals.*

Ale and the Witch

BREWPUBS/BEER GARDENS | Situated in the courtyard of an office building just off trendy Beach Drive, this establishment is a live-music hub—mostly jam bands—as well as the cornerstone of St. Petersburg's exploding craft beer scene. Fans of IPAs, saisons, stouts, you name it, will find their beer of choice somewhere amid the lengthy list of brews on tap. There's some seating inside, but all the action happens outside in the courtyard, where there are plenty of tables and a makeshift band shell. Patrons are welcome to grab food from one of the complex's several restaurants

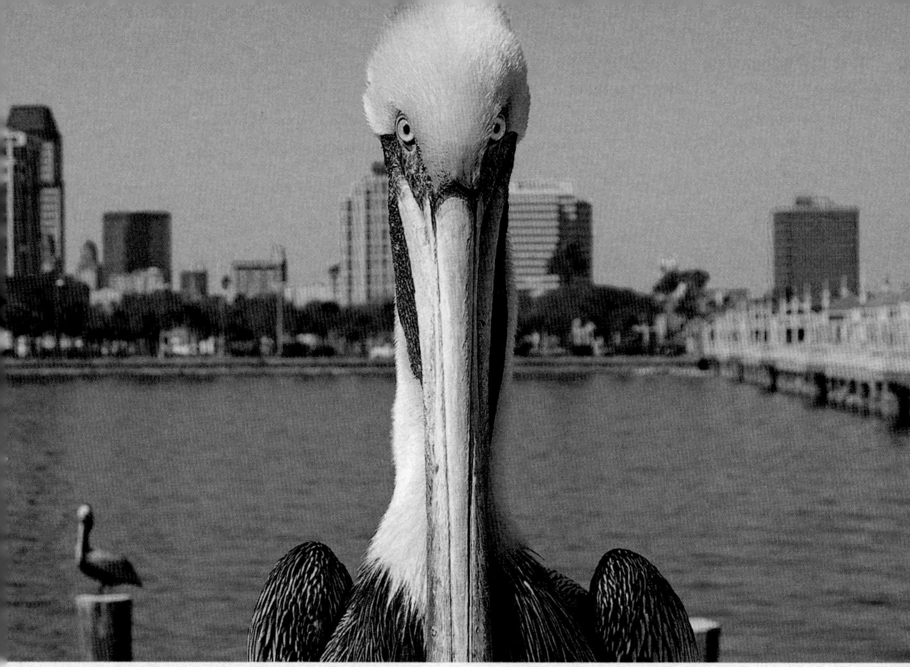

A St. Petersburg pelican stares down passersby on the wharf.—photo by Seymour Levy, Fodors.com member.

to go along with their brews. Although it's a late-night draw, kids and dogs are welcome. ✉ *111 2nd Ave. NE, Downtown* ☎ *727/821–2533* 🌐 *thealeandthewitch.com.*

Central Cigars

GATHERING PLACES | Located in the heart of downtown St. Petersburg, this homey cigar bar has one of the area's largest selections of cigars, from top brands from around the world to Central Cigars' own private-label brand. The lounge includes a full-liquor bar that also serves beer and wine, encouraging folks to enjoy their cigars with a drink in hand. ✉ *273 Central Ave., Downtown* ☎ *727/898–2442* 🌐 *centralcigars.com.*

Enigma

DANCE CLUBS | Part neighborhood watering hole, part energetic multideck nightclub, this welcoming Edge District venue caters to the LGBTQ crowd and straight allies. Enjoy daily drink specials and great happy hour deals from the time the bar opens until 9 pm. And no matter what day of the week it is, there's always something fun going on at the lively hot spot, from drag shows and karaoke to talent competitions and DJs playing the hottest music. ✉ *1110 Central Ave., Edge District* ☎ *727/235–0867* 🌐 *enigmastpete.com.*

Green Bench Brewing Company

BREWPUBS/BEER GARDENS | The name of this bar is a nod to the green benches that once lined Central Avenue, which retirees occupied in a bygone era. St. Pete has shaken its rap as a sleepy retirement town, and this brewery embodies the Sunshine City's recent emergence as a craft beer town. Barkeeps here serve brews made on-site as well as a few guest kegs. The interior has a lodgelike feel (as much as a bar can in Florida), but the real atmosphere lies outside, where Adirondack chairs and badminton sets are scattered across the lawn. It's also conveniently located a couple of blocks from Tropicana Field, so the place can get packed before and after the Rays play. ✉ *1133 Baum Ave.,*

Downtown ☎ *727/800–9836* 🌐 *greenbenchbrewing.com.*

Hofbrauhaus St. Petersburg

BREWPUBS/BEER GARDENS | This authentic German beer hall brings Munich's 400+ year beer-brewing—and drinking—legacy to downtown St. Petersburg. Hofbrauhaus imports classic Bavarian brews, based on the Duke of Bavaria's original recipes. Dine on traditional German fare while you're there and enjoy the music of the Bavarian Beer Band daily. ✉ *123 4th St. S, Downtown* ☎ *727/898–3333* 🌐 *hofbrauhausstpetersburg.com.*

The Mandarin Hide

BARS/PUBS | Perhaps the epitome of downtown St. Pete's bold transformation into a stylish nightlife destination, this place exudes a classy yet jubilant speakeasy vibe. Just as vintage as the decor is the drinks menu, which features numerous classic cocktails (made the old-fashioned way), tasty concoctions you'll find nowhere else, and craft beers. You'll find either live music or a DJ most nights. On weekends you can get a mean Bloody Mary when the bar opens early. ✉ *231 Central Ave., Downtown* ☎ *727/440–9231* 🌐 *www.mandarinhide.com* ⏲ *Closed Mon.*

Old Key West Bar & Grill

BARS/PUBS | Try a cocktail or grab a beer at this relaxed, Old Florida bar and grill, where kitschy decor, vintage photographs and artwork, and carefully placed knickknacks add to the charm. Live local music takes the stage several nights a week, and it's often the venue of other community events, from pub crawls to Pride celebrations. There's a full menu if you want a bite to eat, and a weekend brunch complete with an all-you-can-drink, build-your-own Bloody Mary bar. ✉ *2451 Central Ave., Grand Central District* ☎ *727/623–0969* 🌐 *oldkeywestbarandgrill.com.*

St. Pete Brewing Company

BREWPUBS/BEER GARDENS | A welcoming spot just off the main drag in downtown, this tasting room offers tons of craft beer options (the St. Pete Orange Wheat is a longtime local favorite). There's plenty of outdoor and indoor seating, and the clientele tends to be friendly. It's not far from St. Pete's dining and other nightlife. If you are looking to bring your dog, this is one of the best places to have a beer. ✉ *544 1st Ave. N, Downtown* ☎ *727/692–8809* 🌐 *stpetebrewingcompany.com.*

3 Daughters Brewing

BREWPUBS/BEER GARDENS | This local craft brewery and tasting room is something of an oasis within the Warehouse Arts District, but it's close enough to Central Avenue to be within easy walking distance from Tropicana Field and the restaurants of the Grand Central District (or drive/trolley ride from downtown). On tap in this converted industrial space is a spate of excellent creations made in-house (their Bimini Twist IPA is a favorite). There's live music some nights as well as a few game options. ✉ *222 22nd St. S, Warehouse Arts District* ☎ *727/495–6002* 🌐 *3dbrewing.com.*

Shopping

There's no need for a trip to the mall here. Few places in the Tampa Bay area offer so many eclectic shopping options as the St. Petersburg area. Downtown St. Petersburg's Beach Drive is sprinkled with tons of smart yet pricey boutiques. The Grand Central district has plenty of antiques and vintage clothing shops. Beach shopping hubs John's Pass Village and 8th Avenue offer souvenir shopping that goes well beyond the norm. Each of these is also packed with a range of enticing eateries, many with outdoor seating and live entertainment.

Epitomizing St. Petersburg's cultural rebirth, the block-long stretch of Central Avenue between 6th and 7th streets has loads of art galleries and indie shops, as well as dive bars frequented by tattooed hipsters. The central point is Crislip Arcade, where you'll find a vintage clothing shop (Ramblin' Rose), local art galleries (eve-N-odd and Olio, to name a couple), and a unique jewelry shop (Kathryn Cole). Local businesses line the street, including one that specializes in Moroccan imports (Treasures of Morocco), one that hawks a colorful array of vintage clothing and campy memorabilia (Star Booty), and a smoky bar specializing in craft beer and punk rock (Fubar). Local 662 and the State Theater are two music venues on this block that attract national indie music acts.

ARTpool Gallery

ANTIQUES/COLLECTIBLES | This local gallery/boutique offers scores of works by local artists and so much more. With one of the flashier storefronts in St. Pete's bustling Grand Central District, this sprawling store is a must for lovers of real-deal vintage clothing and accessories, not to mention furnishings and handmade crafts. There's a courtyard connecting the two buildings that constitute this creative megaplex. In the second building, where you can score everything from record albums to antique ashtrays and typewriters, there's a café with a diverse menu as well as wine and craft beer. Occasionally, owner Marina Williams opens her doors up for after-hours art-centric special events. ✉ *2030 Central Ave.* ☎ *727/324–3878* 🌐 *www.artpoolrules.com* ⏲ *Closed Sun. and Mon.*

Craftsman House Gallery

ART GALLERIES | In a lovingly renovated historic Craftsman-style bungalow, this spot offers a variety of wares from both local and national artists and craftspeople. The jewelry counter has some particularly intriguing finds. You'll also come across art made from glass, wood, and other media. Toward the back is a small café where you can order a wrap or bowl of soup and a craft beer or espresso drink, which you can take onto the large front porch as you watch the action along bustling Central Avenue. Occasionally, owner Jeff Schorr opens the gallery for house concerts by touring musicians. ✉ *2955 Central Ave.* ☎ *727/323–2787* 🌐 *craftsmanhousegallery.com.*

Downtown Gulfport

SHOPPING NEIGHBORHOODS | It's hard to believe that the low-key yet vibrant artist enclave of Gulfport was once a blighted fishing village. Now it's a colorful waterfront community and popular with the LGBT community. It's in between St. Pete Beach and St. Petersburg proper, and the area's main thoroughfare, Beach Boulevard, is home to a large number of locally owned boutiques, galleries, and eclectic eateries. An Art Walk occurs every first Friday and third Saturday of the month, and there's a farmers' market every Tuesday. Keep an eye out for cool local events, as there are many here. ✉ *Beach Blvd. at Shore Dr., Gulfport.*

Duncan McClellan Glass

ART GALLERIES | One of the better-known artists to call St. Petersburg home, Duncan McClellan set up this studio and gallery in a former fish-processing plant, helping spur a renaissance in what was until recently known as a gritty industrial district. The main draw is an enormous gallery featuring diverse works from a rotating cast of artists from around the globe, as well as glassblowing demonstrations. If you happen to be in town for the second Saturday evening of the month, this spot is the hub for a trendy monthly art walk through the area. There are regular hours from Tuesday through Saturday, but it's open by appointment only on Sunday and Monday. ✉ *2342 Emerson Ave. S* ☎ *855/436–4527* 🌐 *dmglass.com.*

Florida CraftArt

ART GALLERIES | Downtown St. Pete's bursting art revival is epitomized at this nonprofit, formerly known as Florida Craftsmen Gallery, that gives 125 artisans from throughout the state a chance to exhibit glassware, jewelry, furniture, and more. (Imagine a vivid coral reef seascape made entirely out of yarn. Stuff like that.) You can also book a walking tour of downtown St. Pete's colorful murals. The gallery is open seven days from 10 to 5:30 but stays open late for the famed Second Saturday Art Walk. ✉ *501 Central Ave.* ☎ *727/821–7391* 🌐 *www.floridacraftart.org.*

Haslam's

BOOKS/STATIONERY | One of the state's most notable bookstores, this family-owned emporium has been doing business in St. Petersburg's Grand Central District since the 1930s. Rumored to be haunted by the ghost of *On the Road* author Jack Kerouac (indeed, the renowned Beat Generation author used to frequent Haslam's before he died in St. Pete in 1969), the store carries some 300,000 volumes, from cutting-edge best sellers to ancient tomes. If you value a good book or simply like to browse, you could easily spend an afternoon here. ✉ *2025 Central Ave.* ☎ *727/822–8616* 🌐 *www.haslams.com.*

Sundial St. Pete

SHOPPING CENTERS/MALLS | With a gigantic (and functional) sundial in the middle of the plaza, this open-air collection of upscale shops occupies the space of former shopping and dining hub Baywalk. The renovation of the space created a more open atmosphere that has attracted a Ruth's Chris Steakhouse, a St. Pete branch of the restaurant Sea Salt, and celebrity chef Michael Mina's Locale Market. The shopping here is equally high-end, and retail here includes Diamonds Direct, Jackie Z Style Co., and White House Black Market, as well as local retailers like Florida Jean Company and My Favorite Art Place. If that's not enough, there's the Shave Cave, something of a masculine take on a salon, and its feminine counterpart Marilyn Monroe Glamour Room. At the back of the complex is a 19-screen Muvico theater with an IMAX theater. ✉ *153 2nd Ave. N, Downtown* ☎ *727/800–3201* 🌐 *sundialstpete.com.*

Wagon Wheel Flea Market

OUTDOOR/FLEA/GREEN MARKETS | You'll find whatever you're looking for—even if you didn't know you were looking for it—at this flea market just north of St. Petersburg in Pinellas Park. With more than 2,500 vendors, there's something for everyone, from fresh local produce to antiques and collectibles to artwork. In addition to shopping, there are several food vendors and places to grab a beer, plus live entertainment including Elvis impersonators, line dancing, karaoke, and more. ✉ *7801 Park Blvd., Pinellas Park* ☎ *727/544–5319* 🌐 *thewagonwheelfleamarket.com* ⏲ *Closed Mon., Tues., Thurs., and Fri.*

Activities

Pinellas Trail

BICYCLING | This 47-mile paved route spans Pinellas County, from near the southernmost point all the way north to Tarpon Springs. Along a former railway line, the trail runs adjacent to major thoroughfares, no more than 10 feet from the roadway, so you can access it from almost any point. The trail, also popular with in-line skaters, has spawned trailside businesses such as repair shops, breweries, and cafés. There are also many lovely rural areas to bike through and plenty of places to rent bikes. Be wary of traffic in downtown Clearwater and on the congested areas of the Pinellas Trail, which still needs more bridges for crossing over busy streets, and avoid the trail at night. To start, ride north from the route's south end in downtown St. Petersburg (1st Street South at Shore Boulevard). To ride south from the north end, park your car in downtown Tarpon Springs (East Tarpon Avenue at North Stafford Avenue). ☎ *727/582–2100 Pinellas County*

Parks & Conservation Department 🌐 *www.pinellascounty.org/trailgd.*

St. Pete Beach and Vicinity

Egmont Key

BEACH—SIGHT | In the middle of the mouth of Tampa Bay lies the small (350 acres), largely unspoiled but critically eroding island Egmont Key, now a state park, national wildlife refuge, national historic site, and bird sanctuary. On the island are the ruins of Ft. De Soto's sister fortification, Ft. Dade, built during the Spanish-American War to protect Tampa Bay. The primary inhabitants of the less-than-2-mile-long island are the threatened gopher tortoise and box turtles. The only way to get here is by boat—you can catch a ferry from Ft. De Soto, among other places. Nature lovers will find the trip well worth it—the beach here is excellent for shelling, secluded beach bathing, wildlife viewing, and snorkeling. Multiple ferry operators run trips here, including Hubbard's Marina, Dolphin Landings, and Island Boat Adventures. ✉ *Tierra Verde* ☎ *727/644–6235* 🌐 *www.floridastateparks.org/egmont-key-state-park.*

★ Fort De Soto Park

BEACH—SIGHT | FAMILY | Spread over five small islands, 1,136-acre Fort De Soto Park lies at the mouth of Tampa Bay. It has 7 miles of waterfront (much of it beach), two fishing piers, a 4-mile hiking, cycling, and skating trail, picnic-and-camping grounds, and a historic fort that kids of any age can explore. For those traveling with their canine family members, there is a long and popular dog beach just north of the main fishing pier. The fort for which it's named was built on the southern end of Mullet Key to protect sea lanes in the Gulf during the Spanish-American War. Roam the fort or wander the beaches of any of the islands within the park. Kayaks and beach cruisers are available for rental, and mementos can be found at a souvenir shop/grille on the park's north side. ✉ *3500 Pinellas Bayway S, Tierra Verde* ☎ *727/582–2267* 🌐 *www.pinellascounty.org/park/05_ft_desoto.htm* 🎫 *$5.*

Madeira Beach

BEACH—SIGHT | Known to locals as "Mad Beach," this lively barrier island town occupies the southern tip of Shell Key. The beachfront consists of a long stretch of soft, shell-strewn sand, and it's often crowded with families as well as clusters of twentysomething beachgoers. You can get to the beach via numerous public access points, but your best bet is to park at the municipal beach parking lot and head to the sand from there. It's easily accessible from Treasure Island, northern St. Petersburg, and Clearwater Beach. **Amenities:** food and drink; parking; showers; toilets. **Best for:** partiers; swimming; walking. ✉ *14400 Gulf Blvd., Madeira Beach.*

North Beach, Fort De Soto

BEACH—SIGHT | Pretty much anywhere you go in this county park can make you feel like you're hundreds of miles from civilization, but the beach on the northern tip of this island chain has perhaps the most remote feel. Sure, it gets pretty packed with weekend revelers and family reunions, but you can easily find your own space on this award-winning beach. It starts out wide at the entrance, and narrows as you go north, so it's perfect for those who enjoy a good stroll. There are some striking panoramic views of the park's undeveloped wetlands. Be warned that once you get past a certain point, the beach becomes clothing optional. **Amenities:** food and drink; parking; showers; toilets. **Best for:** solitude; sunset; swimming; walking. ✉ *3500 Pinellas Bayway, head right at the flag, Tierra Verde.*

★ Pass-a-Grille Beach

BEACH—SIGHT | **FAMILY** | At the southern tip of St. Pete Beach (past the Don Cesar), this is the epitome of Old Florida. One of the most popular beaches in the area, it skirts the west end of charming, historic Pass-a-Grille, a neighborhood that draws tourists and locals alike with its stylish yet low-key mom-and-pop motels and restaurants. There's a sunset celebration each night at a pavilion/snack shop on the stretch of beach between the ends of 9th and 10th avenues. On weekends check out the Art Mart, an open-air market showcasing the work of local artisans. **Amenities:** food and drink; parking; showers; toilets. **Best for:** sunset; windsurfing. ✉ *1000 Pass-a-Grille Way, St. Pete Beach.*

Redington Beach

BEACH—SIGHT | Sand Key, the landmass that is home to Madeira Beach at the south end and Belleaire Beach in the north, is spotted with public beach access points. This particular spot has a bigger parking area than the others, though it's not free. It's also within walking distance of the Redington Pier, one of the most popular areas for fishing. **Amenities:** food and drink; parking; toilets. **Best for:** solitude; swimming; walking. ✉ *160th Ave. at Gulf Blvd., Redington Beach.*

Shell Key

BEACH—SIGHT | If you want to find the most pristine beach possible without heading to some remote outpost, this is your best bet. Shuttles to this seemingly remote paradise run out of Pass-A-Grille and Dolphin Landings. You can catch them in the morning and early afternoon most days. If you do, expect some amazing snorkeling, shelling, and bird-watching. (You can also kayak or canoe here from a launch near Ft. De Soto.) Rustic overnight camping is allowed here in the part of the island not designated as a bird sanctuary. Watch for rip currents when swimming, as they can be pretty strong. **Amenities:** none. **Best for:** solitude; swimming; walking. ✉ *Shell Key Shuttle, 801 Pass-A-Grille Way, St. Pete Beach* ☎ *727/360–1348* 🌐 *shellkeyshuttle.com* 🎟 *$25.*

St. Petersburg Municipal Beach

BEACH—SIGHT | **FAMILY** | Though the beach is technically in the city of Treasure Island, the city of St. Petersburg owns and maintains this stretch. Due in part to a concession stand and playground, it's excellent for families. The beach here is very, very wide, near hotels, and great for beach volleyball. **Amenities:** food and drink; parking; showers; toilets. **Best for:** solitude; partiers; sunset; swimming. ✉ *11260 Gulf Blvd., Treasure Island.*

★ Sunset Beach

BEACH—SIGHT | **FAMILY** | A peninsula that's technically part of Treasure Island, this 2-mile-long outcrop is one of Tampa Bay's best-kept secrets. The northern end has a mixed crowd—from bikers to spring breakers, the middle portion is good for families (there's a pavilion and playground at around 78th and West Gulf Boulevard), and the southern tip attracts the LGBTQ crowd. Surfers hit up Sunset Beach on the rare occasion that the Gulf has some swells to offer. Once you turn onto West Gulf, you can find multiple paid parking lots. There are several pay lots starting to your right just south of 82nd Avenue. But if you would rather take advantage of the abundant street parking on the neighborhood's side streets, make sure you park legally—it's all too easy to unwittingly get a parking ticket here. **Amenities:** parking; toilets. **Best for:** partiers; solitude; sunset. ✉ *9000 West Gulf Blvd., Treasure Island.*

Treasure Island

BEACH—SIGHT | **FAMILY** | Large, wide swaths of sand that are sans crowd abound, but you can also find some good crowds, especially on weekends. The Sunday-evening drum circle, which happens around sunset just southwest of the Bilmar, makes for some interesting people-watching, as do the many festivals occurring here each month. It's also

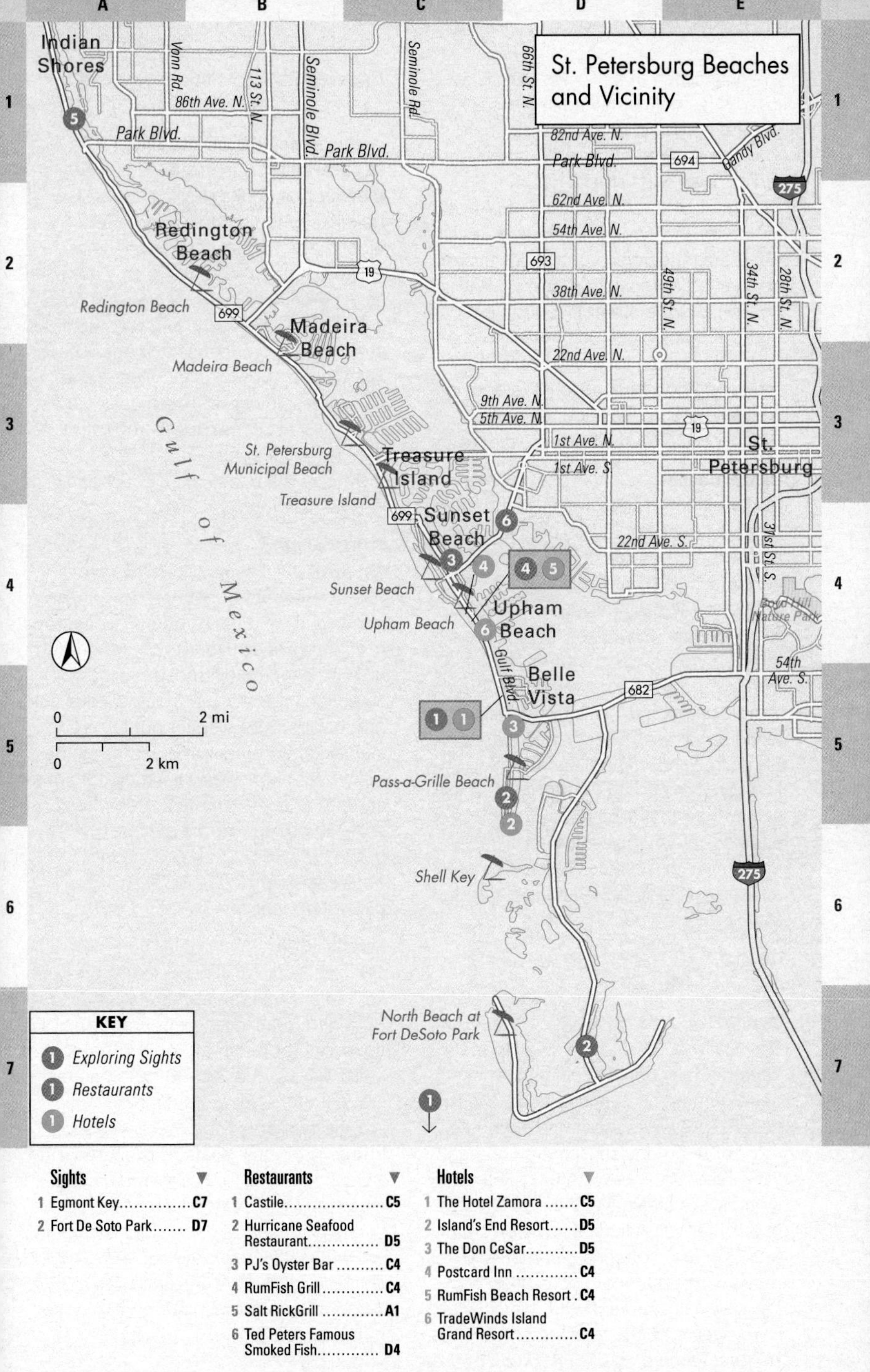

Sights

1 Egmont Key.............. **C7**

2 Fort De Soto Park....... **D7**

Restaurants

1 Castile..................... **C5**

2 Hurricane Seafood Restaurant............... **D5**

3 PJ's Oyster Bar **C4**

4 RumFish Grill............. **C4**

5 Salt RickGrill **A1**

6 Ted Peters Famous Smoked Fish............ **D4**

Hotels

1 The Hotel Zamora **C5**

2 Island's End Resort...... **D5**

3 The Don CeSar........... **D5**

4 Postcard Inn **C4**

5 RumFish Beach Resort . **C4**

6 TradeWinds Island Grand Resort............ **C4**

the only beach that allows alcohol, as long as it's not contained in glass. Plus, getting here is super easy—just head west on St. Petersburg's Central Avenue, which dead-ends smack-dab in the middle of T.I. (that's what the locals call it), where the iconic Thunderbird Beach Resort sign towers over the boulevard. Hang a left at the light. There's a Publix right across the street if you're up for an impromptu picnic or don't want to pay beach-bar prices for a beer. **Amenities:** food and drink; parking; showers; toilets. **Best for:** partiers; solitude; sunsets. ✉ *10400 Gulf Blvd., Treasure Island.*

Upham Beach

BEACH—SIGHT | **FAMILY** | One of the most notable things about this popular beach is the series of large objects that look like yellow school buses buried in the sand. These are actually designed to stabilize the shoreline (this beach is known for rapid erosion). The structures, called T-groins, may not please the eye, but that doesn't keep locals from flocking here. Upham is a wide beach with tons of natural landscaping, and it's near Postcard Inn and the TradeWinds. There's a snack bar that slings burgers and beer at its north end. **Amenities:** food and drink; showers; toilets. **Best for:** partiers; sunset; swimming; walking. ✉ *900 Gulf Way, St. Pete Beach.*

Restaurants

Castile

$$$ | **SPANISH** | Within the chic Hotel Zamora, this popular dining spot has been getting much praise from local and national press. As the name suggests, most of the menu's inspiration comes from Spain, but many items—all the creations of executive chef Ted Dorsey—have other influences. **Known for:** creative Spanish fusion offering a particularly deft touch with seafood; Caesar salad with Parmesan custard and white anchovies; lovely views. $ *Average main: $28* ✉ *Hotel Zamora, 3701 Gulf Blvd., St. Pete Beach* ☎ *727/456–8660* 🌐 *www.castilerestaurant.com.*

★ **Hurricane Seafood Restaurant**

$$ | **SEAFOOD** | Sunsets and Gulf views are the bait that hooks regulars as well as travelers who find their way to this somewhat hidden pit stop in historic Pass-A-Grille. Dating to 1977, it's mainly heralded as a watering hole where you can hoist a cold one while munching on one of the area's better grouper sandwiches. **Known for:** genuine grouper sandwiches and delicious crab cakes; spectacular views, especially at sunset; great tropical mixed drinks. $ *Average main: $15* ✉ *809 Gulf Way, St. Pete Beach* ☎ *727/360–9558* 🌐 *www.thehurricane.com.*

PJ's Oyster Bar

$$ | **SEAFOOD** | Follow the crowds to this off-the-beaten-path eatery, where numerous varieties of beer flow as freely as the rolls of paper towels mounted on wire hangers overhead. Seafood selections range from fried scallops and grouper to more elegant options such as blackened tuna, but oysters are the main event here. **Known for:** oysters and shrimp in many varieties; menu heavy on seafood; popular happy hour. $ *Average main: $17* ✉ *7490 Gulf Blvd., St. Pete Beach* ☎ *727/367–3309* 🌐 *www.pjsoysterbar.net.*

RumFish Grill

$$$ | **SEAFOOD** | **FAMILY** | Although the fish served at this upbeat restaurant at the RumFish Beach Resort by TradeWinds is deserving of much attention, the ones swimming in the 33,500-gallon aquarium lining the restaurant's back wall are the real draw. The menu consists primarily of local seafood prepared with a Caribbean touch. **Known for:** dishes featuring local seafood; adjacent sports bar with its own menu; alluring aquarium vistas. $ *Average main: $28* ✉ *6000 Gulf Blvd., St. Pete Beach* ☎ *727/329–1428* 🌐 *www.rumfishgrill.com* 🌐 *www.rumfishgrill.com.*

Salt Rock Grill

$$$ | **SEAFOOD** | Tourists and locals converge to enjoy a fun and lively waterfront atmosphere, but the rock-solid (if slightly less than imaginative) menu is the best reason to come. Don't believe the Caribbean fire-roasted lobster tails are "jumbo"—at 1¼ pounds they're on the small side, but they're twice-cooked, including a finish on the grill, and quite tasty. **Known for:** consistently fresh, local seafood; great waterfront views; upscale atmosphere. *Average main: $28 ✉ 19325 Gulf Blvd., Indian Shores ☎ 727/593–7625 🌐 www.saltrockgrill.com ⏲ No lunch Mon.–Sat.*

★ Ted Peters Famous Smoked Fish

$ | **SEAFOOD** | Picture this: flip-flop-wearing anglers and beach-towel-clad bathers lolling on picnic benches, sipping a beer, and devouring oak-smoked salmon, mullet, mahimahi, and mackerel. Dinner comes to the table with heaped helpings of potato salad and coleslaw. **Known for:** red oak–smoked fish; region's best burger; smoked fish spread. *Average main: $13 ✉ 1350 Pasadena Ave. S, South Pasadena ☎ 727/381–7931 🌐 tedpetersfish.com No credit cards ⏲ Closed Tues.*

Hotels

★ The Don CeSar

$$ | **RESORT** | Today the Pink Palace, as it's called thanks to its paint job, is a storied resort and Gulf Coast architectural landmark, with exterior and public areas oozing turn-of-the-20th-century elegance. **Pros:** romantic destination; great beach with cabanas and paddleboards available; tasty dining options, namely popular Maritana. **Cons:** small rooms; can be quite pricey; $25 daily resort fee adds to already-hefty tab. *Rooms from: $271 ✉ 3400 Gulf Blvd., St. Pete Beach ☎ 727/360–1881 🌐 www.doncesar.com 317 rooms No meals.*

The Hotel Zamora

$$$ | **HOTEL** | An excellent choice for a romantic getaway, this new hotel offers modern rooms with a flamenco twist—you may think you've been swept away to a luxurious Spanish villa. **Pros:** stylish, flamenco-inspired decor and furnishings; great restaurant; beautiful views of Gulf and Intracoastal. **Cons:** beach is across busy street; can get surprisingly pricey in high season; rooftop bar can close for private parties without much notice. *Rooms from: $319 ✉ 3701 Gulf Blvd., St. Pete Beach ☎ 727/456–8900 🌐 thehotelzamora.com 50 rooms No meals.*

Island's End Resort

$ | **HOTEL** | This converted 1950s-vintage motel has some of the area's best sunrise and sunset views and, like the rest of historic Pass-A-Grille, is totally friendly and totally Old Florida. **Pros:** good value; nice views; near restaurants and shops. **Cons:** access via a traffic-clogged road; parking can be tricky; not directly on the beach. *Rooms from: $180 ✉ 1 Pass-A-Grille Way, St. Pete Beach ☎ 727/360–5023 🌐 www.islandsend.com 6 cottages Breakfast.*

Postcard Inn

$ | **HOTEL** | Take a Waikiki surf shack from back in Duke's day, shake it up with a little midcentury Miami chic, and give it a clean modern twist—that's this ultrahip beachfront hotel to a T. This place was the toast of the beaches when it opened in 2010, and it's easy to see why. **Pros:** on the beach; walking distance to restaurants and nightlife; friendly staff. **Cons:** can be crowded; not for squares. *Rooms from: $119 ✉ 6300 Gulf Blvd., St. Pete Beach ☎ 727/367–2711, 800/237–8918 🌐 www.postcardinn.com 196 rooms Breakfast.*

RumFish Beach Resort by TradeWinds

$$$ | **RESORT** | **FAMILY** | Fresh off a redesign, this high-rise beachfront hotel (formerly Guy Harvey Outpost) offers good options for both dining and exploring. **Pros:** large rooms with kitchenettes; lots of resort

amenities; close to other beach attractions. **Cons:** layout can be confusing; $35 nightly resort fee; can be busy and noisy. *Rooms from: 6000 Gulf Blvd., St. Pete Beach 727/360–5551 www.tradewindsresorts.com 211 rooms No meals.*

TradeWinds Island Grand Resort

$$ | RESORT | FAMILY | The only resort on the beach offering its own fireworks display, the island-chic TradeWinds is very popular for beach weddings and is one of the few pet-friendly resorts in the area, with a play area and a room-service menu for dogs and cats. **Pros:** great beachfront location; close to restaurants; pet-friendly. **Cons:** large, sprawling complex; lots of conventions; pesky resort fee. *Rooms from: $239 5500 Gulf Blvd., St. Pete Beach 727/367–6461 www.tradewindsresort.com 687 rooms No meals.*

Nightlife

Daiquiri Shak

BARS/PUBS | If frozen DayGlo concoctions spinning around in washing machine–like mechanisms are your thing, this place should certainly be on your list. If not, this is still a good go-to weekend watering hole on Madeira Beach (technically, it's across the street from the beach). In addition to selections like the Grape Ape and the Voodoo Loveshake, there's a respectable selection of beer on tap and a full bar. Entertainment includes some excellent funk and rock bands Thursday through Sunday. The food menu includes loads of seafood, of course (oysters are a winner), and the late-night menu is served until 1:30 am. *14995 Gulf Blvd., Madeira Beach 727/393–2706 www.daiquirishak.com.*

Mad Beach Craft Brewing Company

BREWPUBS/BEER GARDENS | Until very recently, Tampa Bay's beach towns were something of a craft beer dead zone, even as the rest of the region teemed with such establishments. This spot, located in John's Pass, is a shining example of how things are changing. Most of the beers on tap are brewed on-site, though there are a few guest taps. Although there is plenty of space at the bar, the barroom is massive and styled after a German beer hall, large tables and all. There's foosball and indoor beanbag tossing if you're feeling competitive, live music many nights, and a menu featuring bar food. *12945 Village Blvd., Madeira Beach 727/362–0008 madbeachbrewing.com.*

Activities

Tampa Bay Rays

BASEBALL/SOFTBALL | Major League Baseball's Tampa Bay Rays completed an improbable worst-to-first turnaround when they topped the American League Eastern Division in 2008, and again in 2010. Then there was that dramatic end-of-season comeback in 2011, and the World Series near-miss in 2014. Tickets are available at the box office for most games, but you may have to rely on the classifieds sections of the *Tampa Bay Times* for popular games. Get here early; parking is often at a premium (pre-gaming at Ferg's or Green Bench is always a safe bet). *Tropicana Field, 1 Tropicana Dr., off I–175 727/825–3137 tampabay.rays.mlb.com.*

Clearwater

12 miles north of St. Petersburg via U.S. 19.

In Clearwater, residential areas are a buffer between the commercial zone that centers on U.S. 19 and the beach, which is moderately quiet during winter but buzzing with life during spring break and in the busy summer season. There's a quaint downtown area on the mainland, just east of the beach, with a theater and a couple of small eateries.

Clearwater's Bait House lures in those heading to the pier to fish. —photo by watland, Fodors.com member.

On the beach itself, which is part of the city of Clearwater, you'll find a nightly sunset celebration at Pier 60 and tons of options for dining and entertainment, not to mention the beautiful sand. Among this area's celebrity residents is Winter, the dolphin who was fitted with a prosthetic tail and depicted in the film *Dolphin Tale,* along with her friend Hope, her costar in the sequel.

GETTING HERE AND AROUND

Clearwater is due west of Tampa International Airport via State Road 60, and it's about 45 minutes north of St. Petersburg. If you want to fly directly to Clearwater instead of Tampa, though, St. Pete/Clearwater International Airport is another option. From St. Pete you can get here via U.S. 19, which is notorious for its congestion; Alternate U.S. 19; or County Road 1. If you're up for a scenic yet slower drive, Gulf Boulevard takes you all the way to Clearwater from St. Pete Beach—as does a beach trolley that runs along that route.

VISITOR INFORMATION

CONTACTS Clearwater Regional Chamber of Commerce. ☎ *727/461–0011* 🌐 *clearwaterflorida.org.*

Sights

Clearwater Marine Aquarium

ZOO | FAMILY | This aquarium gives you the opportunity to participate in the work of saving and caring for endangered marine species. Many of the sea turtles, dolphins, and other animals living at the aquarium were brought here to be rehabilitated from an injury or saved from danger. The dolphin exhibit has an open-air arena giving the dolphins plenty of room to jump during their shows. This aquarium is also home to Winter, a dolphin fitted with a prosthetic tail that was the subject of the 2011 film *Dolphin Tale* (and its 2014 sequel), as well as her friend Hope. The aquarium conducts tours of the bays and islands around Clearwater, including a daily cruise on a pontoon boat (you might just see a wild dolphin or two), and kayak tours of

Clearwater Harbor and St. Joseph Sound. ✉ *249 Windward Passage* ☎ *727/441–1790* 🌐 *seewinter.com* 🎫 *$21.95.*

Florida Botanical Gardens

GARDEN | FAMILY | Florida flora and fauna shine in more than a dozen gardens and natural areas at these botanical gardens, open to visitors for free nearly every day of the year. You can wander through areas devoted to native plants, cacti and succulents, and a butterfly garden. You never know what sort of wildlife you might encounter–alligators, birds, and turtles–in the Aquatic Habitat, made of a gorgeous retention pond and McKay's Creek. ✉ *12520 Ulmerton Rd., Largo* ☎ *727/582–2100* 🌐 *flbg.org.*

Pier 60

MARINA | FAMILY | This spot is the terminus of State Road 60 (hence the name), which runs under various names between Vero Beach on the east coast and Clearwater Beach on the west coast. Around 3:30 pm each day, weather permitting, the area surrounding the pier starts to liven up. Local artists and craftspeople populate their folding tables with beaded jewelry, handmade skin-care products, and beach landscape paintings. Jugglers, musicians, break-dancers, and fire breathers put on some lively shows for those in attendance. And the grand finale is the sun setting over the Gulf of Mexico. On weekends when the weather is mild, there are also free, family-friendly movie screenings. ✉ *10 Pier 60 Dr., Clearwater Beach* ☎ *727/434–6060* 🌐 *www.sunsetsatpier60.com.*

Beaches

★ Clearwater Beach

BEACH—SIGHT | On a narrow island between Clearwater Harbor and the Gulf is a stretch of sand with a widespread reputation for beach volleyball. Pier 60, which extends from shore here, is the site of a nightly sunset celebration, complete with musicians and artisans. It's one of the area's nicest and busiest beaches, especially on weekends and during spring break, but it's also one of the costliest in terms of parking fees, which can reach $2 per hour. **■ TIP→ Traffic can get pretty gnarly here and parking spots scarce, especially approaching sunset, so get here early or opt for public or on-foot transportation as much as possible. Amenities:** food and drink; showers; toilets. **Best for:** partiers; sunset; walking. ✉ *Western end of Rte. 60, 2 miles west of downtown Clearwater.*

Sand Key Park

BEACH—SIGHT | This is a mellow counterpart to often-crowded Clearwater Beach to the north. It has a lovely beach, plenty of green space, a playground, and a picnic area in an otherwise congested area. Parking is a flat $5. **Amenities:** food and drink; lifeguards; showers; toilets. **Best for:** solitude; sunset; swimming. ✉ *1060 Gulf Blvd.* ☎ *727/588–4852* 🎫 *$5.*

Restaurants

Bob Heilman's Beachcomber

$$$ | AMERICAN | The Heilman family has fed hungry diners since 1920, and although it's very popular with tourists, you'll also rub shoulders with devoted locals. Despite the frequent crowds, the service is fast and friendly. **Known for:** classic sautéed chicken with mashed potatoes, vegetables, and fresh bread; Gulf shrimp prepared several ways; good wine selection. $ *Average main: $28* ✉ *447 Mandalay Ave., Clearwater Beach* ☎ *727/442–4144* 🌐 *heilmans-beachcomber.com.*

Frenchy's Rockaway Grill

$$ | SEAFOOD | Quebec native Mike "Frenchy" Preston runs four eateries in the area, including the fabulous Rockaway Grill. Visitors and locals alike keep coming back for the grouper sandwiches that are moist and not battered into submission. **Known for:** she-crab soup, grouper sandwiches, and egg rolls; beachfront sunset vistas. $ *Average main: $15* ✉ *7 Rockaway St.* ☎ *727/446–4844* 🌐 *www.frenchysonline.com.*

Hotels

Hilton Clearwater Beach

$$$ | **HOTEL** | This marquee property has a look that is clean and modern without losing the Clearwater Beach vibe, and staying here may be a little less pricey than you might expect. **Pros:** on the beach; modern look; ample amenities. **Cons:** chain hotel feel; lots of conventions; resort fee. $ *Rooms from: $364* ✉ *400 Mandalay Ave., Clearwater Beach* ☎ *727/461–3222* 🌐 *www.hilton-clearwaterbeach.com* *428 rooms* *No meals.*

Hyatt Regency Clearwater Beach

$$$ | **RESORT** | One of the more recent additions to the Clearwater Beach skyline, this upscale resort towers above almost everything else in the immediate area, both in terms of height and luxury. **Pros:** gorgeous hotel; plenty of amenities, including a full-service spa; near the action. **Cons:** beach is across busy street; daily resort fee. $ *Rooms from: $359* ✉ *301 S. Gulfview Blvd.* ☎ *727/373–1234* 🌐 *www.hyatt.com/en-US/hotel/florida/hyatt-regency-clearwater-beach-resort-and-spa/pierc#* *287 rooms* *No meals.*

Sandpearl Resort

$$$ | **RESORT** | Two things set this expansive, luxurious Clearwater Beach resort apart from other upscale accommodations in the vicinity: it's not part of a major chain, and the property has deep local ties. **Pros:** on the beach; tons of amenities and dining options. **Cons:** resort fee; lots of conventions. $ *Rooms from: $344* ✉ *500 Mandalay Ave.* ☎ *727/441–2425* 🌐 *sandpearl.com* *253 rooms* *No meals.*

Sheraton Sand Key Resort

$$ | **RESORT** | Expect something special when you stay here, including a modern property and one of the few uncluttered beaches in the area. **Pros:** secluded beach; great views; no resort fee and parking is also free. **Cons:** near Clearwater Beach traffic; views come with a high price tag. $ *Rooms from: $204* ✉ *1160 Gulf Blvd., Clearwater Beach* ☎ *727/595–1611* 🌐 *sheratonsandkey.com* 🌐 *sheratonsandkey.com* *390 rooms* *No meals.*

Wyndham Grand Clearwater Beach

$$ | **RESORT** | **FAMILY** | The resort, which opened in 2017 near Pier 60, guarantees sweeping water views (of either the Gulf or the Intracoastal Waterway) from your balcony regardless of where your room is located. **Pros:** excellent views; good accommodations for families; brand-new resort. **Cons:** residential building on property; lots of beach traffic; busy with events and meetings. $ *Rooms from: $299* ✉ *100 Coronado Dr., Clearwater Beach* ☎ *727/281–9000* 🌐 *wyndhamgrandclearwater.com* *343 rooms* *No meals.*

Nightlife

Big Storm Brewing Co.

BREWPUBS/BEER GARDENS | The popular mid-Pinellas County brewery has more than 20 beers on tap. Favorites include the Wavemaker Amber Ale, the Arcus Southern Pale Ale and the Tropic Pressure Florida Ale. For those who don't drink, Big Storm Coffee & Creamery, serving craft coffee beverages, is a new addition to the brewery. (You definitely want to try their signature drink, Eye of the Storm, a French press coffee served with a shot of espresso.) Big Storm Creamery also serves up treats like hand-made ice cream, in flavors such as salted caramel pretzel and birthday cake. ✉ *12707 49th St. N* ☎ *727/201–4186* 🌐 *bigstormbrewery.com.*

Activities

FlowRider at Surf Style

SURFING | FAMILY | Surf Style, in the towering Hyatt, is a chain store that sells beach essentials like sarongs, sunblock, and souvenirs. But what sets this particularly enormous store apart is the FlowRider, an indoor pool that generates artificial waves suitable for surfing; for $20 per half hour, you and the kids can surf or learn to surf, something you can't usually do out in the Gulf. An instructor is on hand to show you the ropes. ✉ *Hyatt Regency Clearwater Beach, 311 S. Gulfview Blvd.* ☎ *888/787–3789 Ext. 175* 🌐 *flowrider.surfstyle.com* 🎟 *$30 for 30 mins.*

Philadelphia Phillies

BASEBALL/SOFTBALL | The Phillies get ready for the season with spring training here (late February to early April). The stadium also hosts the Phillies' farm team. Check out their minor-league team, the Clearwater Threshers, at Spectrum Field during the summer months. ✉ *Spectrum Field, 601 N. Old Coachman Rd.* ☎ *727/712–4300* 🌐 *philadelphia.phillies.mlb.com.*

Dunedin

CONTACTS Greater Dunedin Chamber of Commerce. ☎ *727/733–3197* 🌐 *www.dunedinfl.com.*

Beaches

★ Caladesi Island State Park

BEACH—SIGHT | Quiet, secluded, and still wild, this 3½-mile-long barrier island is one of the best shelling beaches on the Gulf Coast, second only to Sanibel. The park also has plenty of sights for birders—from common sandpipers to majestic blue herons to rare black skimmers—and miles of trails through scrub oaks, saw palmettos, and cacti (with tenants such as armadillos, rabbits, and raccoons). The landscape also features mangroves and dunes, and the gradual slope of the sea bottom makes this a good spot for novice swimmers and kids. You have to get to Caladesi Island by private boat (there's a 108-slip marina) or through its sister park, Honeymoon Island State Recreation Area, where you take the hourly ferry ride across to Caladesi; ferry rides cost $14 per person. You can also paddle yourself over in a kayak. **Amenities:** food and drink; showers; toilets. **Best for:** solitude; swimming. ✉ *Dunedin Causeway, Dunedin* ☎ *727/469–5918* 🌐 *floridastateparks.org/parks-and-trails/caladesi-island-state-park* 🎟 *$6 per boat; $2 per kayaker.*

Honeymoon Island State Park

BEACH—SIGHT | If you're seeking an almost completely undeveloped beach that's still easily accessible by car, this is one of your best bets. Northwest of Clearwater, this large state park offers some of the best shell hunting you'll find, as well as thousands of feet of serene beachfront. If you head north along the park road, you find extensive hiking trails, along which you'll see an astonishing array of birds. You can also catch a ferry to Caladesi Island from here. **Amenities:** food and drink; showers; toilets. **Best for:** solitude; swimming; walking. ✉ *1 Causeway Blvd., Dunedin* 🌐 *floridastateparks.org/honeymoonisland* 🎟 *$8 per vehicle; $4 per single-occupant vehicle.*

Restaurants

Bon Appétit

$$$ | EUROPEAN | Known for its creative fare, this waterfront restaurant has a menu that changes frequently, offering such entrées as broiled rack of lamb in herbed pecan crust, and red snapper on a bed of lobster hash. The creative grouper options, including grouper medallions, get well-deserved plaudits from many patrons. **Known for:** real Gulf grouper on the menu; live music Thursday through Sunday; gorgeous water views. $ *Average main: $27* ✉ *148 Marina Plaza,*

Dunedin ☎ 727/733–2151 🌐 www.bonappetitrestaurant.com.

★ **Casa Tina**

$$ | **MEXICAN** | At this colorful Dunedin institution, vegetarians can veg out on roasted chiles *rellenos* (cheese-stuffed peppers), enchiladas with vegetables, and a cactus salad that won't prick your tongue but will tickle your taste buds with theflavors of tender pieces of cactus, cilantro, tomatoes, onions, lime, and queso fresco. The chayote squash relleno also makes the grade. **Known for:** chayote squash relleno; duck sopas with cotija cheese and guava sauce; good margaritas and sangria. *Average main: $15 ✉ 365 Main St., Dunedin ☎ 727/734–9226 🌐 casatinas.com.*

The Living Room on Main

$$ | **MEDITERRANEAN** | Hand-picked antique furnishings add charm to this downtown Dunedin spot, which specializes in Mediterranean-inspired small plates and spectacular cocktails. For a little more sustenance, check out the sandwich menu—the seared tuna club with avocado and caper aioli, and the deconstructed egg salad sandwich make for some good options. **Known for:** creative small plates; excellent craft cocktails; vintage-inspired setting. *Average main: $17 ✉ 487 Main St., Dunedin ☎ 727/736–5202 🌐 thelivingroomonmain.com.*

Blur Nightclub

DANCE CLUBS | This lively downtown Dunedin nightclub caters to the LGBTQ crowd and anyone looking for a fun night out. Sports fans will enjoy game-day watch parties while music lovers can take the stage during karaoke or catch a live band perform. Meanwhile, drag queen bingo is a fun addition to the calendar. *✉ 325 Main St., Dunedin ☎ 727/736–2587 🌐 blurdunedin.com.*

Dunedin Brewery

BREWPUBS/BEER GARDENS | Tampa Bay is seen by many as a flourishing craft beer hub. If it weren't for Dunedin Brewery, that might not be the case. It was the first of its kind in the area and continues to offer delicious brews to throngs of patrons. It doesn't hurt that it offers live music many nights of the week, either. *✉ 937 Douglas Ave., Dunedin ☎ 727/736–0606 🌐 dunedinbrewery.com.*

7venth Sun Brewery

BREWPUBS/BEER GARDENS | Northern Pinellas County is a hotbed for craft brewing. This small tasting room features this brewery's offerings, largely Belgian-style, spirit barrel-aged sour beer as well as IPAs, and a handful of others. It's near downtown Dunedin's shopping, dining, and nightlife and isn't too far from the Pinellas Trail. *✉ 1012 Broadway, Dunedin ☎ 727/733–3013 🌐 www.7venthsun.com.*

Dunedin Golf Club

GOLF | Dunedin is Tampa Bay's little Scotland, the birthplace of golf, so it's only natural that one of the area's better courses is here. Designed by influential golf-course architect Donald Ross, this semiprivate, recently restored facility also has a driving range, a pro shop, and a clubhouse. The course itself offers numerous challenging holes with names like Isn't Easy, Calamity Jane, and Devil's Kick, with the twists and turns to match. Water hazards aren't too overwhelming here, except on the 14th hole, known as Round the Lake. *✉ 1050 Palm Blvd., Dunedin ☎ 727/733–2134 🌐 www.dunedingolfclub.com $47.99 18 holes, 6625 yards, par 72.*

Toronto Blue Jays

BASEBALL/SOFTBALL | The Jays play around 15 to 20 spring training games here, starting in February, which is why Dunedin is packed with Canadians this time of year. The team has trained here since its

1977 inception—and this consistency is not common for a major-league team. A farm team plays here in the summer. The training fields are located several miles away, at 1700 Solon Avenue. ✉ *Florida Auto Exchange Stadium, 373 Douglas Ave., north of Hwy. 580, Dunedin* ☎ *727/733–0429* 🌐 *toronto.bluejays.mlb.com.*

Palm Harbor

Suncoast Primate Sanctuary

ZOO | **FAMILY** | You may not be able to find monkeys in the wild in the Tampa Bay area (at least not naturally), but you can catch them bouncing around in their cages at this low-key facility. The alleged final home of Cheetah, the chimp who played Tarzan's sidekick for a couple of years in the 1930s, the sanctuary houses a whole slew of primates. One of the first you'll meet is Pongo, a massive Bornean orangutan; if he's in the right mood, he will greet you when you walk up. The sanctuary also hosts baboons, lemurs, spider monkeys, macaques—you name it—many of them former pets or onetime laboratory test subjects that aren't deemed able to make it in the wild. There are also a few reptiles (you can get a picture of yourself holding a baby alligator) and a colorful array of birds. You may find the colorful plastic toys in the primate enclosures odd, but they actually serve to enhance the animals' senses. ✉ *4600 Alt. U.S. 19, Palm Harbor* ☎ *727/943–5897* 🌐 *www.suncoastprimate.org* 🎫 *$15.*

Innisbrook Resort & Golf Club

$ | **RESORT** | A massive pool complex with a 15-foot waterfall, two winding waterslides, and a sandy waterfront are part of the allure of this sprawling resort, but it may be the 72 holes of golf, including the challenging Copperhead course, that are the real draw. **Pros:** good seasonal golf packages; varied dining options, namely Packard's Steakhouse; lots of family-friendly activities and amenities. **Cons:** far from attractions; surrounding environment is unattractive, traffic-strangled U.S. 19; $20 resort fee can add up. 💲 *Rooms from: $185* ✉ *36750 U.S. 19 N, Palm Harbor* ☎ *727/942–2000, 888/794–8627* 🌐 *www.innisbrookgolfresort.com* 🛏 *600 rooms* 🍽 *No meals.*

Stilt House Brewery

BREWPUBS/BEER GARDENS | If you happen to be riding on the Pinellas Trail between Clearwater and Tarpon Springs, this place is right on the trail. It's also right on Alternate U.S. 19, though it can be hard to spot from the road since it's in a small strip mall. Beers are brewed on-site (like the Norbert's Valkyrie Belgian Tripel or the Soul Candy Milk Stout), though there are also some guest taps. There's always a friendly crowd. Off to the side you'll notice a small room packed with vintage video games. ✉ *625 Alt. U.S. 19, Palm Harbor* ☎ *727/270–7373* 🌐 *www.stilthousebrewery.com.*

Activities

Innisbrook

GOLF | Considered one of the top 100 golf destinations in Florida, this resort is home to Larry Packard–designed Copperhead Course, which hosts the annual PGA Tour Valspar Championship. Open to resort guests as well as the public, the four courses here take full advantage of the fact that they're on the coast, with plenty of ponds and sand traps adding to the scenery as well as the challenge. Fairways here on the Copperhead Course consist of rolling hills lined with trees, which are prime for spotting blue herons, squirrels, and even an alligator or two.

The Island Course offers narrow fairways, some of which are lined by Lake Innisbrook, others by tall stands of pine and cypress trees. The North Course features tight fairways, numerous bunkers, and 11 water hazards, while the South Course has more of a links course–like layout. The Fox Squirrel Course is a quick 9-hole course available to guests only. ✉ *36750 U.S. Hwy. 19 N, Palm Harbor* ☎ *888/794–8627, 727/942–2000* 🌐 *innisbrookgolfresort.com* 🎫 *Copperhead Course, $280; Island Course, $240; North and South Courses, $190* 🏌 *Copperhead Course: 18 holes, 7209 yards, par 71; Island Course: 18 holes, 7194 yards, par 72; North Course: 18 holes, 6085 yards, par 70; South Course, 18 holes, 6642 yards, par 71; Fox Squirrel Course: 9 holes, 1236 yards, par 36 (resort guests only, closed during high season).*

Tarpon Springs

CONTACTS Tarpon Springs Chamber of Commerce. ☎ *727/937–6109* 🌐 *tarponspringschamber.com.*

Sights

The Sponge Docks

HISTORIC SITE | Paralleled by a busy boulevard lined with sponge shops and Greek restaurants, this several-blocks-long waterfront spot showcase's Tarpon Spring's Greek roots as well as the industry that first made the town thrive over a century ago. Stroll along the docks and you'll find an aquarium, tons of small boutiques, bakeries specializing in baklava and the like, and several boat tours of the surrounding waters. Pop into the Sponge Docks Museum to see a film about the much-sought-after creatures from the phylum *porifera* and how they helped the town prosper in the early 1900s. You'll come away converted to (and loaded up with) natural sponges. ✉ *Dodecanese Blvd., off Alt. U.S. 19, Tarpon Springs* 🌐 *www.spongedocks.net* 🎫 *Free.*

Beaches

Fred Howard Park Beach

BEACH—SIGHT | It comes in two parts: a shady mainland picnic area with barbecues and a white-sand beach island. The causeway is a popular hangout for windsurfers, and the entire area is great for birding. The beach itself is very relaxed and family-friendly, and you can find kayak rentals on the island's eastern side. **Amenities:** showers; toilets. **Best for:** sunset; swimming; windsurfing. ✉ *1700 Sunset Dr., Tarpon Springs* 🎫 *$5 flat fee to park.*

Sunset Beach

BEACH—SIGHT | As the name suggests, this beach park is known as one of the best places in North Pinellas County to watch the sunset. It's a small beach but a great place to barbecue. From April through November there's a weekly concert. **Amenities:** toilets. **Best for:** sunset; swimming. ✉ *1715 Gulf Rd., Tarpon Springs.*

Indian Shores

Seaside Seabird Sanctuary

NATURE PRESERVE | **FAMILY** | When pelicans and other birds become entangled in fishing lines, locals sometimes carry them to this nonprofit sanctuary dedicated to the rescue, repair, recuperation, and release of sick and injured birds. Formerly the Suncoast Seabird Sanctuary, this beachfront spot played a big role after the Gulf oil disaster in 2010. At times there are hundreds of land and sea birds in residence, including egrets, herons, gulls, terns, sandhill cranes, hawks, owls, and cormorants. ✉ *18328 Gulf Blvd., Indian Shores* ☎ *727/391–6211* 🌐 *www.seasideseabirdsanctuary.org.*

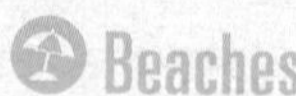

Indian Rocks Beach

BEACH—SIGHT | This beach community is a mellow alternative to the oft-crowded shorelines of Clearwater and St. Pete Beach along the Gulf Coast. This is a town in which the road narrows to two lanes and is lined with upscale residential condos instead of busy hotels. There are quite a few beach access points, though your best bet is a landscaped facility offering ample parking, nearby food and drink, and an occasional event. **Amenities:** food and drink; parking; showers; toilets. **Best for:** solitude; swimming; walking. ✉ *Indian Rocks Beach Nature Preserve, 1700 Gulf Blvd., Indian Rocks Beach* 🌐 *indian-rocks-beach.com.*

Safety Harbor

Gigglewaters

$ | **BURGER** | You've never experienced dinner and a movie quite like this. At Gigglewaters' intimate, speakeasy-like restaurant, diners can enjoy gourmet burgers, hot dogs, and craft cocktails while catching a classic flick in the one-screen, back-room movie theater. **Known for:** one-screen movie theater; white-truffle citrus popcorn; inspired craft cocktails. $ *Average main: $14* ✉ *737 Main St., Safety Harbor* ☎ *727/669–7077* 🌐 *gigglewaters.com.*

Safety Harbor Resort & Spa

$$ | **RESORT** | Built over natural mineral springs, this resort, which has been consistently expanded and renovated, has been drawing visitors since 1927. **Pros:** charm to spare; good choice for pampering; large spa with natural springs. **Cons:** far from beach; not ideal for families with children. $ *Rooms from: $209* ✉ *105 N. Bayshore Dr., Safety Harbor* ☎ *727/726–1161, 727/282–5707* 🌐 *www.safetyharborspa.com* *188 rooms* *No meals.*

Safety Harbor Art & Music Center

ARTS CENTERS | This funky little cultural center is a lively downtown Safety Harbor gathering place and a vibrant venue that brings together all sorts of artists and art lovers. Live music takes over the stage several evenings of each week, and there are not one, but two monthly open mics for literary folks. And these are just a smattering of the offbeat arts events offered. When you visit, don't forget to take a selfie with Ellie, the big pink elephant out front. ✉ *706 2nd St. N., Safety Harbor* ☎ *727/725–4018* 🌐 *safetyharborartandmusiccenter.com.*

Weeki Wachee

This Citrus County town north of Tampa and St. Petersburg is located in what's called the Nature Coast, and aptly so. Flora and fauna have been well preserved in this area, and West Indian manatees are showstoppers.

U.S. 19 and the Suncoast Parkway, a toll road, are the prime north–south routes through this rural region, and traffic flows freely once you've left the congestion of St. Petersburg, Clearwater, and Port Richey. In most cases, the Suncoast Parkway is a far quicker drive than U.S. 19, though you'll have to pay several dollars in tolls. If you're planning a day trip from the Bay Area, pack a picnic lunch before leaving, since most of the sights are outdoors.

Boyett's Grove & Citrus Attraction

FARM/RANCH | **FAMILY** | This kitschy roadside attraction exudes old Florida charm. Grab a snack at the old-fashioned

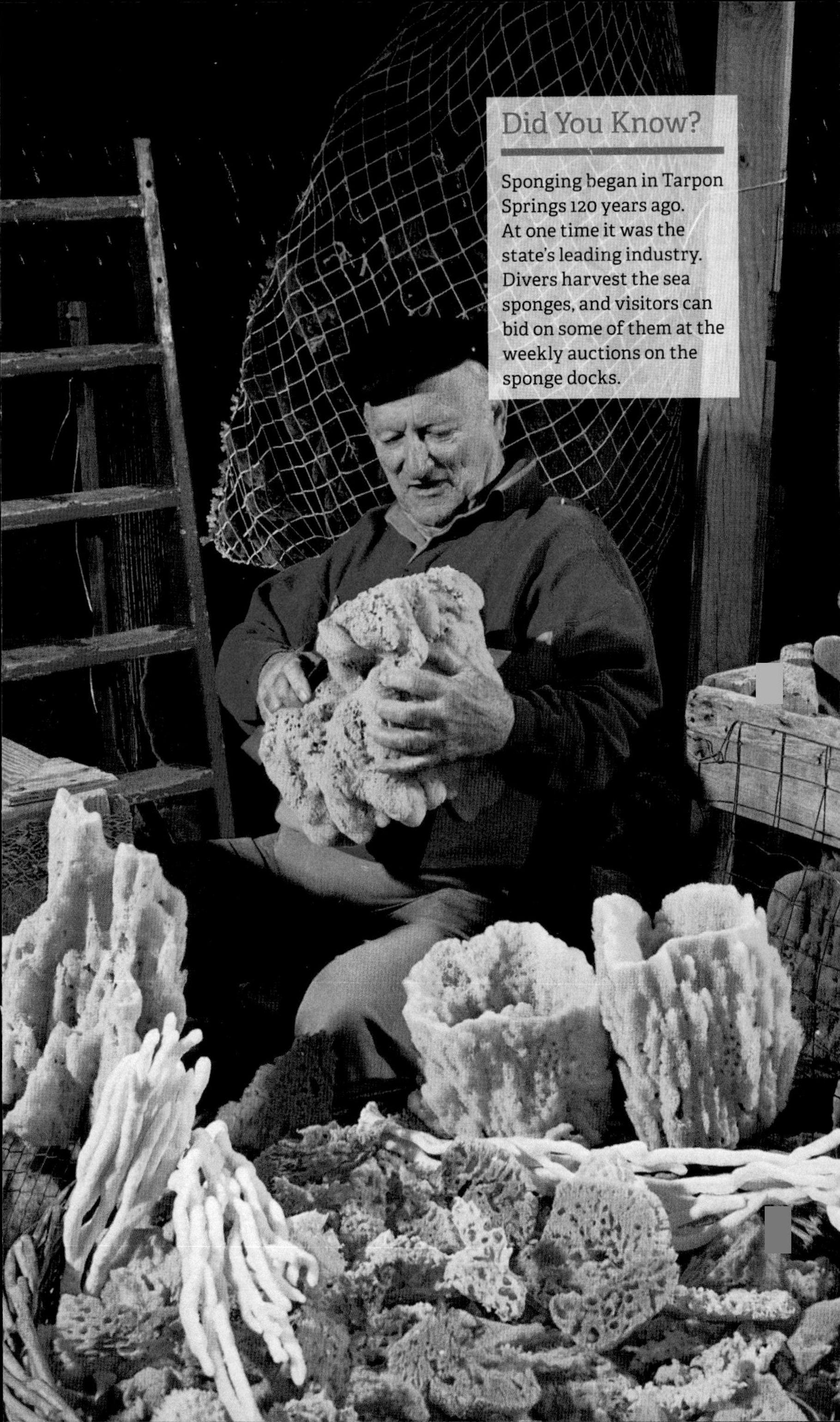

Did You Know?

Sponging began in Tarpon Springs 120 years ago. At one time it was the state's leading industry. Divers harvest the sea sponges, and visitors can bid on some of them at the weekly auctions on the sponge docks.

ice cream parlor after feeding animals in the wildlife park and kayaking down the Weeki Wachee River. Families will also enjoy exploring the dinosaur cave, and touring the aviary and aquariums. And, of course, Boyett's is a great spot to buy Florida citrus, including oranges, grapefruits, lemons, and limes. (Trees, too!) ✉ *4355 Spring Lake Highway, Brooksville* ☎ *352/796–2289* 🌐 *boyettsgrove.com.*

★ Weeki Wachee Springs

AMUSEMENT PARK/WATER PARK | **FAMILY** | At Weeki Wachee Springs, the spring flows at the remarkable rate of 170 million gallons a day with a constant temperature of 74°F. The spring has long been famous for its live "mermaids," clearly not the work of Mother Nature, as they wear bright costumes and put on an underwater choreography show that's been virtually unchanged since the park opened in 1947. The park is considered a classic piece of Florida history and culture. It also features snorkel tours and canoe trips on the river, and a wilderness boat ride gives an up-close look at raccoons, otters, egrets, and other semitropical Florida wetlands wildlife. In summer Buccaneer Bay water park opens for swimming, beaching, and riding its thrilling slides and flumes. ✉ *6131 Commercial Way* ✣ *At U.S. 19 and Rte. 50* ☎ *352/592–5656* 🌐 *weekiwachee.com* 🎟 *$13.*

Marker 48 Brewing

BREWPUBS/BEER GARDENS | One of the best breweries north of Pinellas and Hillsborough counties, this 6,000-square-foot facility in Hernando County has a large tasting room and beer garden. There's always something going on: live music every weekend, trivia, and karaoke during the week. Those interested in how the beer is made can tour the brewery on Saturday afternoons. ✉ *12147 Cortez Blvd., Brooksville* ☎ *352/606–2509* 🌐 *marker48.com.*

Homosassa Springs

65 miles north of St. Petersburg on U.S. 19.

A little more than an hour north of Clearwater, you'll come upon this small and friendly hub for water lovers. Along with a phenomenal manatee-centric state park, you'll find more than a handful of charming restaurants, some featuring live music in the evening. This and Crystal River provide you with the once-in-a-lifetime chance to swim with manatees, something best done in winter. Summer's scallop season is also a massive draw.

★ Ellie Schiller Homosassa Springs Wildlife State Park

NATURE PRESERVE | **FAMILY** | Here you can see many manatees and several species of fish through a floating glass observatory known as the Fish Bowl—except in this case the fish are outside the bowl and you are inside it. The park's wildlife walk trails lead you to excellent manatee, alligator, and other animal programs. Among the species are bobcats, a western cougar, white-tailed deer, a black bear, pelicans, herons, snowy egrets, river otters, whooping cranes, and even a hippopotamus named Lu, a keepsake from the park's days as an exotic-animal attraction. Boat cruises on Pepper Creek lead you to the Homosassa wildlife park (which takes its name from a Creek Indian word meaning "place where wild peppers grow"). ✉ *4150 S. Suncoast Blvd., U.S. 19* ☎ *352/628–5343* 🌐 *floridastateparks.org/parks-and-trails/ellie-schiller-homosassa-springs-wildlife-state-park* 🎟 *$13.*

Yulee Sugar Mill Ruins Historic State Park

ARCHAEOLOGICAL SITE | This state park has the remains of a circa-1851 sugar mill and other remnants of a 5,100-acre sugar plantation owned by Florida's

Did You Know?

Homosassa Springs' claim to fame may be its manatees, but it's also home to a great birding trail where you can spot flamingos.

first U.S. senator, David Levy Yulee. Interpretive panels spaced throughout the mill ruins describe early methods of the sugar-making process. ✉ *Rte. 490 (Yulee Dr.)* ✥ *3 miles off U.S. 19/98* ☎ *352/795–3817* 🌐 *floridastateparks.org/parks-and-trails/yulee-sugar-mill-ruins-historic-state-park* 🎟 *Free.*

Restaurants

Dan's Clam Stand

$ | **SEAFOOD** | Four reasons to go: the fried grouper sandwich, the clam "chowda," anything else seafood, and the beef burgers. The original location is about 2 miles east of Homosassa Springs State Wildlife Park. **Known for:** local favorite; clams and lobster; reasonable prices. $ *Average main: $10* ✉ *7364 Grover Cleveland Blvd.* ☎ *352/628–9588* ⏲ *Closed Sun.*

Museum Cafe

$ | **CUBAN** | A short trip west of Homosassa Springs State Wildlife Refuge, this tiny eatery is housed in the Olde Mill House Printing Museum. It's open only for lunch, but it's well worth making room in your itinerary for a visit here. **Known for:** Cuban sandwiches; occasional live blues shows; takeout for picnics. $ *Average main: $7* ✉ *10466 W. Yulee Dr.* ☎ *352/628–1081* ⏲ *No dinner.*

Hotels

Homosassa Riverside Resort

$ | **RESORT** | Five villas with multiple guest rooms fill this resort. **Pros:** on the river; plenty of activities; monkey island. **Cons:** out of the way; dated room decor. $ *Rooms from: $85* ✉ *5297 Cherokee Way* ☎ *352/628–2474, 800/442–2040* 🌐 *www.riversideresorts.com* 🛏 *57 rooms* 🍽 *No meals.*

Shopping

Howard's Flea Market

OUTDOOR/FLEA/GREEN MARKETS | **FAMILY** | Thousands of shoppers swarm to Howard's Flea Market each weekend seeking all kinds of treasures: antiques and collectibles, books, clothing, jewelry, art, produce, and home goods. The largest flea market in Citrus County, this shopper's paradise has 800 covered vendors on 55 acres. ✉ *6373 S. Suncoast Blvd.* ☎ *352/628–3532* 🌐 *howardsflea-market.com* ⏲ *Closed Mon.–Fri.*

Crystal River

6 miles north of Homosassa Springs on U.S. 19.

Situated along the peaceful Nature Coast, this area is *the* low-key getaway spot in one of the most pristine and beautiful areas in the state. It's also one of the few places on the planet where you can legally swim with manatees. The river's fed by a spring that's a constant 72°F, which is why manatees enjoy spending their winters here. Boating and snorkeling are popular, as is scalloping in the summer. This is a true paradise for nature lovers, and absolutely worth making room for in your vacation itinerary.

Sights

★ **Crystal River National Wildlife Refuge**

NATURE PRESERVE | This is a U.S. Fish and Wildlife Service sanctuary for the endangered manatee. Kings Bay, around which manatees congregate in winter (generally from November to March), feeds crystal clear water into the river at 72°F year-round. This is one of the sure-bet places to see manatees in winter since hundreds congregate near this 90-acre refuge. The small visitor center has displays about the manatee and other refuge inhabitants. If you want to get an even closer look at these gentle giants, several dive companies provide opportunities for you to swim among them—if you don't mind shelling out some extra cash, donning a wet suit, and adhering to some strict interaction guidelines. In warmer months, when most manatees scatter, the main spring is fun for a swim or scuba diving. ✉ *1502 S.E. Kings Bay Dr.* ☎ *352/563–2088* 🌐 *www.fws.gov/refuge/crystal_river* 🎫 *Free.*

Beaches

Fort Island Gulf Beach

BEACH—SIGHT | This is one of the most remote beaches you will find north of Ft. De Soto, the isolated beach south of St. Petersburg. One of the best parts of coming here is the drive. The beach sits as the terminus of Fort Island Trail, the same road where you'll find the Plantation Inn & Golf Resort. A 9-mile drive through the wetlands gets you here, offering sweeping views along the way (though the Crystal River nuclear plant looms to the north). The beach itself is raw and subdued, though there are picnic shelters, barbecues, and a fishing pier. Don't expect many frills, but if you need to relax after a long day of playing in the water, this is your place. **Amenities:** showers; toilets. **Best for:** solitude; sunset. ✉ *16000 W. Fort Island Trail* ☎ *352/527–7540* 🌐 *www.citrusbocc.com/commserv/parksrec/parks/ft-isl-beach/fib-park.jsp?parkid=18.*

Hotels

Plantation on Crystal River

$ | RESORT | On the shore of Kings Bay, this two-story plantation-style resort is on 232 acres near nature preserves and rivers. **Pros:** good location; perfect for nature lovers. **Cons:** lots of conventions; basic rooms. [$] *Rooms from: $119* ✉ *9301 W. Fort Island Trail* ☎ *352/795–4211* 🌐 *www.plantationinn.com* *196 rooms, 12 villas* *No meals.*

Activities

American Pro Diving Center

SCUBA DIVING | This is one of several local operators in the area conducting manatee tours of Crystal River National Wildlife Refuge or Homosassa River, something you can't legally do pretty much anywhere else in the country. ✉ *821 S.E. U.S. 19* ☎ *352/563–0041* 🌐 *www.americanprodiving.com* 🎫 *$68.*

Crystal Lodge Dive Center

SCUBA DIVING | This dive center is one of the more popular operators offering dives, swims, and snorkel trips to see manatees. ✉ *525 N.W. 7th Ave.* ☎ *352/795–6798* 🌐 *www.manatee-central.com* 🎫 *$35.*

Plantation Adventure Center

BOATING | An obvious choice if you're staying at the Plantation on Crystal River, this dive tour company stands on its own as a manatee tour operator. The guides bring you out to various spots along the river to interact with manatees, and tend to be longtime residents who know their subject well. Day trips to nearby Rainbow River, scenic cruises, and sunset/sunrise kayak tours are also available. If the weather is warm, that means no manatees, so plan accordingly. ✉ *Plantation on Crystal River, 9301 Fort Island Trail* ☎ *352/795–4211* 🌐 *www.plantationoncrystalriver.com* 🎫 *$65.*

Bradenton

49 miles south of Tampa.

In 1539 Hernando de Soto landed near this Manatee River city, which has some 20 miles of beaches. Bradenton is well situated for access to fishing, both fresh- and saltwater, and it also has its share of golf courses and historic sites dating to the mid-1800s. Orange groves and cattle ranches mix with farmlands between Bradenton's beaches and Interstate 75. Anna Maria Island, a nearby barrier island connected to Bradenton by a causeway, contains the towns of Anna Maria, Holmes Beach, and Bradenton Beach.

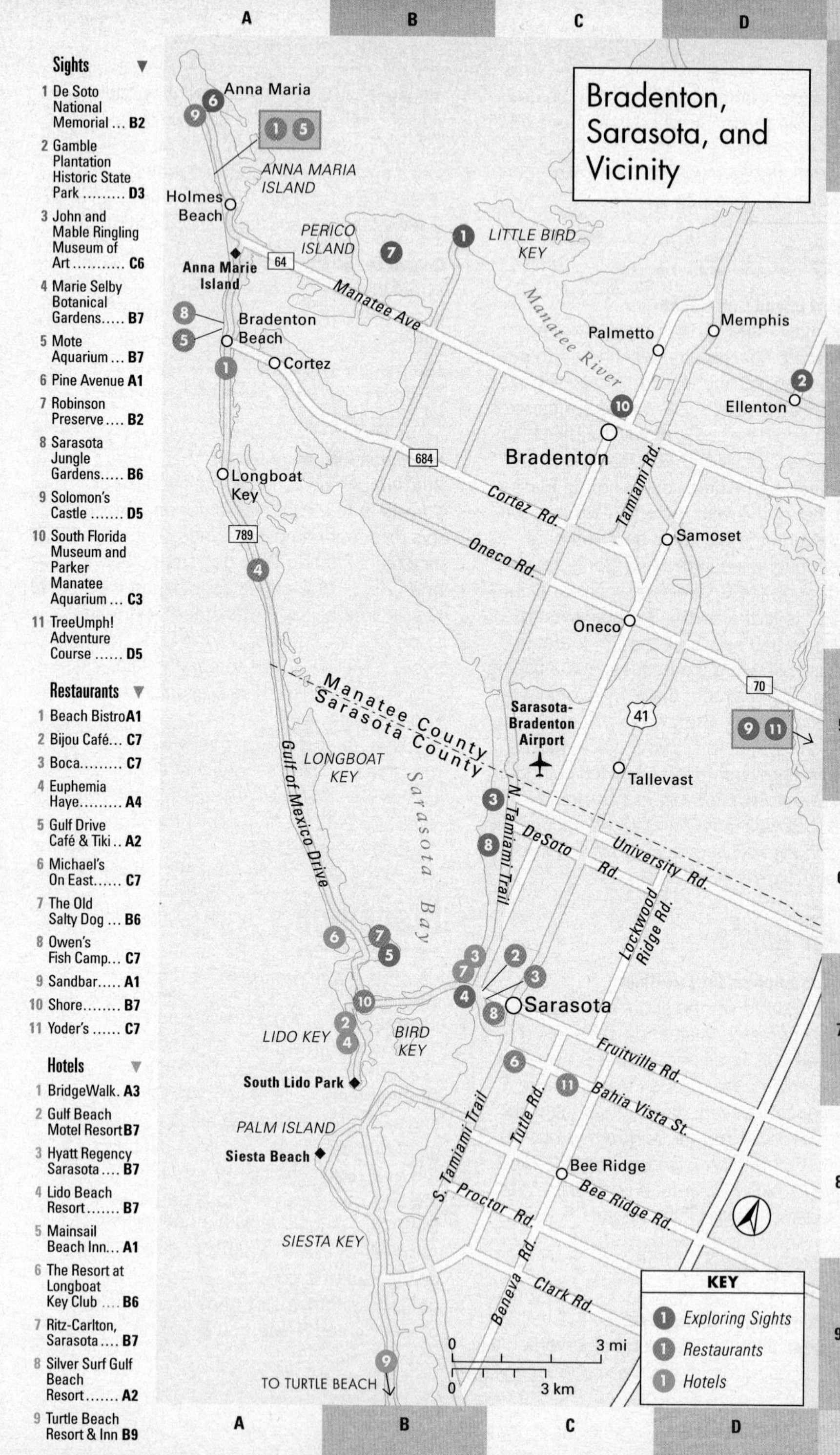

Bradenton, Sarasota, and Vicinity
Sights
1 De Soto National Memorial ... B2
2 Gamble Plantation Historic State Park D3
3 John and Mable Ringling Museum of Art C6
4 Marie Selby Botanical Gardens..... B7
5 Mote Aquarium ... B7
6 Pine Avenue A1
7 Robinson Preserve.... B2
8 Sarasota Jungle Gardens..... B6
9 Solomon's Castle D5
10 South Florida Museum and Parker Manatee Aquarium ... C3
11 TreeUmph! Adventure Course D5
Restaurants
1 Beach Bistro A1
2 Bijou Café... C7
3 Boca......... C7
4 Euphemia Haye......... A4
5 Gulf Drive Café & Tiki .. A2
6 Michael's On East...... C7
7 The Old Salty Dog ... B6
8 Owen's Fish Camp... C7
9 Sandbar..... A1
10 Shore........ B7
11 Yoder's C7
Hotels
1 BridgeWalk. A3
2 Gulf Beach Motel Resort B7
3 Hyatt Regency Sarasota B7
4 Lido Beach Resort....... B7
5 Mainsail Beach Inn... A1
6 The Resort at Longboat Key Club B6
7 Ritz-Carlton, Sarasota B7
8 Silver Surf Gulf Beach Resort....... A2
9 Turtle Beach Resort & Inn B9
Anna Maria
ANNA MARIA ISLAND
Holmes Beach
PERICO ISLAND
LITTLE BIRD KEY
Anna Marie Island
64
Manatee Ave
Manatee River
Palmetto
Memphis
Bradenton Beach
Cortez
Ellenton
684
Bradenton
Tamiami Rd.
Cortez Rd.
Longboat Key
Samoset
789
Oneco Rd.
Oneco
70
Manatee County
Sarasota County
Sarasota-Bradenton Airport
41
Tallevast
Gulf of Mexico Drive
LONGBOAT KEY
Sarasota Bay
N. Tamiami Trail
DeSoto Rd.
University Rd.
Lockwood Ridge Rd.
Sarasota
LIDO KEY
BIRD KEY
Fruitville Rd.
South Lido Park
Bahia Vista St.
PALM ISLAND
Siesta Beach
S. Tamiami Trail
Tutle Rd.
Bee Ridge
Proctor Rd.
Bee Ridge Rd.
SIESTA KEY
Beneva Rd.
Clark Rd.
KEY
Exploring Sights
Restaurants
Hotels
0
3 mi
0
3 km
TO TURTLE BEACH
A B C D
1 2 3 4 5 6 7 8 9

GETTING HERE AND AROUND

You can get to Bradenton via Interstate 75, Interstate 275, and U.S. 41/301. West Manatee Avenue gets you out to the beaches. Manatee County Area Transit (MCAT) has buses throughout Bradenton and the nearby towns of Palmetto and Ellenton, as well as connections to Sarasota attractions. Fares for local bus service range from $1.50 to $4 (for an all-day pass); exact change is required. A $40 monthly "M-Card" is available for unlimited rides on all MCAT routes. But if you want to get around efficiently—and want access to more places—you're best off renting a car.

CONTACTS Manatee County Area Transit. ☎ *941/749–7116* 🌐 *ridemcat.org.*

VISITOR INFORMATION

CONTACTS Bradenton Area Convention and Visitors Bureau. ☎ *941/729–9177* 🌐 *www.bradentongulfislands.com.*

Sights

De Soto National Memorial

ARCHAEOLOGICAL SITE | One of the first Spanish explorers to land in North America, Hernando de Soto came ashore with his men and 200 horses near what is now Bradenton in 1539; this federal park commemorates De Soto's expedition and the Native Americans he and his crew encountered. During the height of tourist season, from mid-December to late April, park staff and volunteers dress in period costumes at Camp Uzita, demonstrate the use of 16th-century weapons, and show how European explorers prepared and preserved food for their overland journeys. The season ends with a reenactment of the explorer's landing. The site also offers a film and short nature trail through the mangroves. ✉ *8300 De Soto Memorial Hwy.* ☎ *941/792–0458 Ext. 105* 🌐 *www.nps.gov/deso/index.htm* 🎫 *Free (donations accepted).*

Gamble Plantation Historic State Park

HISTORIC SITE | Built in the 1840s, this antebellum mansion 5 miles northeast of Bradenton was home to Major Robert Gamble and is the headquarters of an extensive sugar plantation. It is the only surviving plantation house in South Florida. The Confederate secretary of state took refuge here when the Confederacy fell to Union forces. Picnic tables are available. Guided tours of the house are available six times a day. ✉ *3708 Patten Ave., Ellenton* ☎ *941/723–4536* 🌐 *www.floridastateparks.org/parks-and-trails/judah-p-benjamin-confederate-memorial-gamble-plantation-historic-state-park* 🎫 *Free, tours $6* ⏲ *Museum/visitor center closed Tues. and Wed.*

Pine Avenue

NEIGHBORHOOD | Anna Maria Island's newly restored "Main Street" features numerous upscale mom-and-pop boutiques, including beach-appropriate clothiers, beach-inspired home decor stores, and antique furniture shops. You can also find shops offering items such as quality jewelry and infused olive oil. The Anna Maria City Pier, which overlooks the southern end of Tampa Bay, sits at the end of the street. If you're here in the morning, check out Anna Maria Donuts, which offers made-to-order custom donuts, some having sriracha sauce among their ingredients. ✉ *Pine Ave., Anna Maria* 🌐 *www.pineavenueinfo.com.*

Robinson Preserve

HOUSE | With miles of trails that wind through wetlands and mangroves to lookout towers and peaceful waterfront spots, this Manatee County park is a must for anyone who likes a quiet walk (or run) and sweeping views of the landscape and the wildlife that inhabit it. There's also a kayak launch here, which links into a network of trails for small watercraft. Toward the front of the property the historic Valentine House, which was moved from its original site in Palmetto and restored, now serves as a visitor center and offers a few wonders of its own, including reptiles and shells the kids will dig. ✉ *1704 99th St. NW* ☎ *941/742–5923* 🌐 *www.mymanatee.org/departments/parks___natural_resources/parks__preserves___beaches/robinson_preserve.*

Solomon's Castle

BUILDING | For a visit to the wild and weird side, particularly fun for children, head to this "castle" about 45 minutes east of Bradenton through orange groves and cattle farms. Artist and Renaissance man Howard Solomon began building the 12,000-square-foot always-in-progress work out of thousands of aluminum offset printing plates. Inside, you'll find tons of intrigues—everything from a knight assembled with Volkswagen parts to a chair fashioned out of 86 beer cans to an elephant made from seven oil drums. A restaurant serves sit-down lunches in a full-scale model of a Spanish galleon. ✉ *4533 Solomon Rd., Ona* ☎ *863/494–6077* 🌐 *www.solomonscastle.org* 🎫 *$12.50* ⏲ *Closed Aug. and Sept.*

South Florida Museum and Parker Manatee Aquarium

MUSEUM | **FAMILY** | Programs about manatees run four times daily, and the first-floor gallery features fossils that tell the story of prehistoric Florida. View changing exhibits in the East Gallery; glass cases and roll-out drawers on the second floor allow you to look at exhibits normally out of public view. At the Bishop Planetarium (with a domed theater screen), programs presented range from black holes to the origin of life itself. The aquarium focuses on manatee rehabilitation and was once home to Snooty, the oldest manatee in captivity until he died at the age of 69 in 2017. ✉ *201 10th St. W* ☎ *941/746–4131* 🌐 *www.southfloridamuseum.org* 🎫 *$19* ⏲ *Closed Mon.*

★ **TreeUmph! Adventure Course**

AMUSEMENT PARK/WATER PARK | Daredevils of all ages will love this collection of aerial ropes courses and zip lines. Those who partake will traverse swinging bridges, Tarzan ropes, treacherous hanging nets, and other obstacles suspended high in the air between the tall trees here, not to mention the many zip lines at the end of each set of obstacles. Adrenaline will flow more than once during this half-day adventure, but cautious parents need not worry; everyone is secured in a harness, and staff require everyone to demonstrate that they understand the park's many rules by watching a safety video and traversing a small demo course. There's a course that's just for small kids aged seven–12, but most can test their bravery on the five main courses, which get progressively more difficult (culminating in the ultratough Summit Course; most people don't get that far). At the end, everyone, regardless of whether they finished, can partake in a 650-foot-long zip line that starts at 60 feet high and offers spectacular views (the only way to get there is to climb a series of ladders). **■ TIP→ Check the weather before you go. If there's lightning within a small radius, staff has to ground you for at least half an hour, and the clock gets set back every time there's a nearby strike.** ✉ *21805 E. State Rd. 70* ☎ *941/322–2130, 855/322–2130* 🌐 *treeumph.com* 🎫 *$54.95* ⏲ *Closed Tues. and Wed.*

Beaches

Anna Maria Island, Bradenton's 7-mile barrier island to the west, has a number of worthwhile beaches, as does Longboat Key. Manatee Avenue connects the mainland to the island via the Palma Sola Causeway, adjacent to which is a long, sandy beach fronting Palma Sola Bay. There are boat ramps, a dock, and picnic tables.

Coquina Beach

BEACH—SIGHT | Singles and families flock to Coquina Beach, a wider swath of sand at the southern end of Anna Maria Island. Beach walkers love this stretch since it's

Did You Know?

Sometimes called "sea cows," manatees are aquatic relatives of elephants. They can weigh more than 1,500 pounds and live 50-plus years. There are more than 3,000 in Florida's coastal waters.

Anna Maria's longest beach, and it also attracts crowds of young revelers. **Amenities:** food and drink; showers; toilets. **Best for:** solitude; swimming; walking. ✉ *2650 Gulf Dr. S, Anna Maria* ☎ *941/742–5923.*

Cortez Beach

BEACH—SIGHT | Towering Australian pines greet you at the entrance of this popular beach park, a favorite among locals and visitors alike. **Amenities:** showers; toilets. **Best for:** solitude; swimming; walking. ✉ *Gulf Dr., Bradenton Beach* ✣ *Between 5th and 13th Aves.*

Greer Island Beach

BEACH—SIGHT | Just across the inlet on the northern tip of Longboat Key, Greer Island Beach is accessible by boat or by car via North Shore Boulevard (you can walk here at low tide, but be sure to leave before the tide comes in). You'll also hear this place referred to as Beer Can Island. The secluded peninsula has a wide beach and excellent shelling, but no facilities. **Amenities:** none. **Best for:** solitude; walking. ✉ *7500 Gulf of Mexico Dr., Longboat Key.*

Manatee Beach Park

BEACH—SIGHT | In the middle of Anna Maria Island, Manatee County Beach is popular with beachgoers of all ages. Paid parking is in the gravel lot next to the beach. **Amenities:** food and drink; parking (fee); showers; toilets. **Best for:** solitude; swimming; walking. ✉ *4000 S.R. 64, at Gulf Dr., Holmes Beach.*

Restaurants

Beach Bistro

$$$$ | **CONTEMPORARY** | The menu at this cozy beachfront spot offers such standards as a melt-in-your-mouth, herb-rubbed rack of lamb; seafood bouillabaisse; and duckling confit with peppercorn-and-cognac demi-glace. But the menu also includes a variety of specials and small plates. **Known for:** "One Helluva Soup" with plum tomatoes, cream, and blue cheese; beachfront dining with amazing sunset views; prix-fixe tasting menu. $ *Average main: $49* ✉ *6600 Gulf Dr., Holmes Beach* ☎ *941/778–6444* 🌐 *www.beachbistro.com* ⏲ *No lunch.*

★ Euphemia Haye

$$$$ | **STEAKHOUSE** | A lush tropical setting on the barrier island of Longboat Key, this is one of the most romantic restaurants around. Signature dishes include crisp roast duckling with bread stuffing, and flambéed prime peppered steak; the popular dessert display is a sweet ending. **Known for:** crispy roast duckling with bread stuffing and tangy, fruit-based sauce; upstairs dessert bar offers delicious, heaping portions; quaint, intimate atmosphere. $ *Average main: $40* ✉ *5540 Gulf of Mexico Dr., Longboat Key* ☎ *941/383–3633* 🌐 *www.euphemiahaye.com* ⏲ *No lunch.*

Gulf Drive Café & Tiki

$ | **AMERICAN** | Especially popular for breakfast (served all day), this unassuming landmark squats on the beach and serves cheap sit-down eats: mostly sandwiches, but also a wide array of entrées after 4 pm. The dinner menu at this beachfront spot, which is great for watching sunsets, features all the seafood options, from lobster mac-and-cheese to grilled or blackened mahimahi. **Known for:** Greek-inspired foods like lemon chicken topped with feta; baked Gulf grouper stuffed with crab cake; beachfront sunset vistas. $ *Average main: $14* ✉ *900 Gulf Dr. N, Bradenton Beach* ☎ *941/778–1919* 🌐 *gulfdrivetiki.com.*

Sandbar Restaurant

$$$ | **AMERICAN** | Though their ever-evolving menu features cutting-edge fare for the most sophisticated of palates, the margarita-and-coconut-shrimp crowd will thoroughly enjoy it here as well. Much of what you'll find on the menu at this beachfront spot is harvested nearby, whether it's herbs and vegetables from one of the gardens along Pine Avenue or fresh fish from nearby Cortez. **Known for:** unconventional, locally sourced ingredients like grouper cheeks and crab bellies; private-label wines; cocktails on the beach at sunset. *Average main: $22 100 Spring Ave., Anna Maria 941/778–0444 sandbar.groupersandwich.com.*

Hotels

BridgeWalk
$ | **RENTAL** | This circa-1947 Caribbean colonial-style property is across from the beach and a community within itself. **Pros:** great location; units are roomy; spa and restaurant on property. **Cons:** can be pricey; minimum stays required February–April; not all units have full kitchens. *Rooms from: $171 100 Bridge St., Bradenton Beach 941/779–2545, 866/779–2545 www.silverresorts.com 28 units Breakfast.*

Mainsail Beach Inn
$$$$ | **RENTAL** | If you're looking for upscale digs on low-key Anna Maria Island, you'll find them at this small, amenity-laden complex on the beach. **Pros:** on beach; upscale apartments; full of amenities. **Cons:** not for the thrifty; early (10 am) checkout. *Rooms from: $589 101 66th St., Holmes Beach 888/849–2642 mainsailbeachinn.com 12 condos No meals.*

The Resort at Longboat Key Club
$$$ | **RESORT** | This spectacularly landscaped property is one of the best places to play golf in the state, and among the top tennis resorts in the country. **Pros:** resort offers an impressive number of amenities; lovely grounds; all rooms have private balcony. **Cons:** facilities are for guests and members only; few off-site dining options nearby; daily $24 resort fee can add up. *Rooms from: $339 220 Sands Point Rd., Longboat Key 941/383–8821, 855/314–2619 www.longboatkeyclub.com 223 rooms No meals.*

Silver Surf Gulf Beach Resort
$ | **RESORT** | A sister to BridgeWalk, the Silver Surf has the air of a well-maintained 1960s motel with a modern twist, thanks to recent renovations to all of the studios and full apartments. **Pros:** location; freshly renovated rooms and exterior; good value for your money. **Cons:** while nice, the rooms are still pretty basic (this is not luxury). *Rooms from: $158 Anna Maria Island, 1301 Gulf Dr. N, Bradenton Beach 941/778–6626, 800/441–7873 www.silverresorts.com 26 rooms No meals.*

Activities

Buffalo Creek Golf Course
GOLF | The excellent county-owned course was designed by Ron Garl to resemble a Scottish links course, making it among the more challenging courses in the area. Still, novice golfers have a shot here. There are water hazards on several holes (not to mention a gator or two), and the terrain varies throughout. Some consider it to be the best public golf course in the Tampa Bay area. All greens were renovated in 2014. Players can choose to play the whole course or just a quick 9-hole game. The clubhouse offers cold beer at the end of the course. *8100 69th St. E., Palmetto 941/776–2611 www.golfmanatee.com 18 holes from $49, 9 holes $30 18 holes, 7005 yards, par 72.*

Sarasota

30 miles south of Tampa and St. Petersburg.

Sarasota is a year-round destination and home to some of Florida's most affluent residents. Circus magnate John Ringling and his wife, Mable, started the city on the road to becoming one of the state's hotbeds for the arts. Today sporting and cultural events can be enjoyed any time of the year, and there's a higher concentration of upscale shops, restaurants, and hotels here than in other parts of the Tampa Bay area. Across the water from Sarasota lie the barrier islands of Siesta Key and Lido Key, with myriad beaches, shops, hotels, condominiums, and houses.

GETTING HERE AND AROUND

Sarasota is accessible from Interstate 75, Interstate 275, and U.S. 41. The town's public transit company is Sarasota County Area Transit (SCAT). Fares for local bus service range from $1.25 to $4 (for an all-day pass); exact change is required. A $60 monthly "R-Card" is available for unlimited rides on all SCAT and Manatee County Area Transit (MCAT) routes. If you want to make it to the farther reaches of the area, though, renting a car is probably your best bet.

CONTACTS Sarasota County Area Transit (SCAT). ☎ *941/861–1234* 🌐 *www.scgov.net/scat.*

VISITOR INFORMATION

CONTACTS Visit Sarasota. ✉ *1777 Main St.* ☎ *941/955–0991* 🌐 *www.visitsarasota.com.*

★ **John and Mable Ringling Museum of Art**
ARTS VENUE | FAMILY | Administered by Florida State University, the museum encompasses the entire Ringling estate, far more than just the art museum; there's also the Tibbals Learning Center and Circus Museums as well as Ca' d'Zan Mansion, the original Ringling home, and its expansive gardens. The entire compound covers 20 waterfront acres and also has the Historic Asolo Theater, restaurants, and a research library.

The **Art Museum** was a dream long in the making for John Ringling (of Ringling Brothers fame). Finally finished in 1931 after setbacks including a land bust and the death of his wife, Mable, this enormous museum was originally built to house Ringling's mind-blowingly expansive art collection. You'll find works ranging from Indian doorways elaborately carved with Jain deities to opalescent baroque paintings from the likes of Rubens. There seems to be an endless number of rooms, themselves decorated in an appropriately gorgeous manner, housing these masterpieces. Contemporary art—both visiting and permanent exhibits—has dedicated space here, as do rotating exhibits from the museum's permanent photography collection. A newer wing, with its facade of jade-tinged terra-cotta, houses ancient and contemporary works of Asian art. The museum's exit opens out into an enormous courtyard, over which a towering replica statue of *David* presides, flanked by royal palms.

Circus magnate John Ringling's grand home, **Ca' d'Zan,** which was built along Sarasota Bay, was patterned after the Doge's Palace in Venice. This exquisite mansion of 32 rooms, 15 bathrooms, and a 61-foot Belvedere Tower was completed in 1925, and today is the crowning jewel at the site of the Ringling estate. Its 8,000-square-foot terrace overlooks the dock where Ringling's wife, Mable, moored her gondola. Mansion tours occur on the hour and last for a half hour. If you don't want a guided tour, show up on the half hour for a self-guided tour.

Allot some extra time to wander around in Mable Ringling's **Rose Garden,** a lush labyrinth surrounded by towering banyans and full of rare roses and haunting statues.

Don't let the name **Tibbals Learning Center** fool you. This Ringling estate attraction offers a colorful glimpse into a most wondrous element of a bygone era: the traveling circus. The center focuses on the history of the American circus and the collection of Howard Tibbals, master model builder, who spent 40 years building the world's largest miniature circus.

Ringling Mansion Sarasota

Perhaps the center's main attraction, this impressive to-scale replica of the circa 1920s and '30s Ringling Bros. and Barnum & Bailey Circus is an astonishingly accurate portrayal of a circus coming through town—the number of pancakes the circus cooks are flipping, the exact likenesses and costumes of the performers, the correct names of the animals marked on the miniature mess buckets—you name it. Tibbals's passion to re-create every exact detail continues in his on-site workshop, where kids can ask him questions and watch him carving animals and intricate wagons.

If you're looking for clown noses, ringmaster hats, and circus-themed T-shirts, don't leave before checking out the **Ringling Museum of Art Store.**

The **Historic Asolo Theater** is also on the estate grounds and is home to the Asolo Repertory Company. ✉ *5401 Bay Shore Rd.* ✥ *½ mile west of Sarasota-Bradenton Airport* ☎ *941/359–5700* 🌐 *www.ringling.org* 🎫 *$25 (art museum only free Mon.); $20 Ca d'Zan docent tours.*

Marie Selby Botanical Gardens

GARDEN | Orchids make up nearly a third of the 20,000 species of flowers and plants here. You can stroll through the Tropical Display House, home of orchids and colorful bromeliads gathered from rain forests, and wander the garden pathway past plantings of bamboo, ancient banyans, and mangrove forests along Little Sarasota Bay. Although spring sees the best blooms, the greenhouses make this an attraction for all seasons. The added bonus is a spectacular view of downtown. There are rotating exhibits of botanical art and photography in a 1934 restored Southern Colonial mansion. Enjoy lunch at the Local Coffee + Tea, a café in the historic Selby House. ✉ *900 S. Palm Ave.* ☎ *941/366–5731* 🌐 *www.selby.org* 🎫 *$20.*

Mote Aquarium

ZOO | **FAMILY** | A renowned research facility, the Mote is also a popular tourist attraction that draws families and others interested in its international array of ocean creatures. Its newest draw is a large outdoor habitat featuring a family of frolicking river otters. In the main building, 135,000-gallon shark tank lets you view various types of sharks from above and below the surface. Other tanks show off eels, rays, and other marine creatures native to the area. Touch tanks abound here for the little ones, and the not-so faint of heart can scope out a preserved giant squid; a rare find out in the wild. The expanded Seahorse Conservation Lab offers a glimpse into the unusual creatures' lives and how the aquarium is working to help them survive and thrive. Hugh and Buffett are the resident manatees and, though not as venerable as Snooty at the Parker Manatee Aquarium, they have lived here since 1996 as part of a research program. There's also a permanent sea-turtle exhibit. For an extra fee, **Sarasota Bay Explorers** offers boat tours from the museum's dock (reservations required), guided kayak tours through the mangroves, private tours, and a Nature Safari. ✉ *City Island, 1600 Ken Thompson Pkwy.* ☎ *941/388–4441* 🌐 *www.mote.org* 🎫 *$24.*

Sarasota Jungle Gardens

ZOO | **FAMILY** | One of Old Florida's charming, family-owned and-operated attractions, Sarasota Jungle Gardens fills 10 acres with native and exotic animals as well as tropical plants. The lush gardens date to 1939, and still have the small-world feel of yesterday's Florida. You'll find red-tailed hawks and great horned owls in the Wildlife Wonder show, American alligators and a variety of snakes in the reptile encounter, and an exotic bird show. Among more cuddly residents here are lemurs, monkeys, and prairie dogs. You can talk to trainers and get to know such plants as the rare Australian nut tree and the Peruvian apple cactus in the gardens. Also on-site are flocks of flamingos that guests can hand-feed, plus reptiles and a butterfly garden. ✉ *3701 Bay Shore Rd.* ☎ *941/355–5305* 🌐 *www.sarasotajunglegardens.com* 🎫 *$17.99.*

Beaches

★ Siesta Key Beach

BEACH—SIGHT | With 40 acres of nature trails, this park is popular; you'll find tons of amenities. This beach has fine, powdery quartz sand that squeaks under your feet, very much like the sand along the state's northwestern coast. Don't forget to bring a volleyball—or a tennis racket. **Amenities:** food and drink; lifeguards; toilets. **Best for:** partiers; sunset; swimming; walking. ✉ *946 Beach Rd., Siesta Key.*

South Lido County Park

BEACH—SIGHT | At the southern tip of the island, South Lido County Park has one of the best beaches in the region, but there are no lifeguards. The 100-acre park interacts with four significant bodies of water: the Gulf of Mexico, Big Pass, Sarasota Bay, and Brushy Bayou. The sugar-sand beach has plenty of early-morning sand dollars and is a popular place to fish. Picnic as the sun sets through the Australian pines into the water. Facilities include nature trails, canoe and kayak trails, restrooms, and picnic grounds. This park was purchased by John Ringling in 1920 as part of his ambitious plan to develop island properties. His plan collapsed with the great Florida land bust of 1926. Because of swift rip currents, swimming here is not recommended. **Amenities:** showers; toilets. **Best for:** solitude; walking. ✉ *2201 Ben Franklin Dr., Lido Key.*

Turtle Beach

BEACH—SIGHT | A 14-acre beach-park that's popular with families, Turtle has 2,600 linear feet of beach frontage and is more secluded than most Gulf beaches. Though narrower than most of the region's beaches, it's also much less crowded, so it doesn't feel so narrow. It's known for abundant sea turtles. It has covered picnic shelters, grills, and a volleyball court. Locals like the 40-site campground that is also open to visitors with advance reservations. Fittingly enough, this beach is near the übermellow Turtle

Beach Resort. **Amenities:** toilets. **Best for:** solitude; sunset; swimming; walking. *8862 Midnight Pass Rd., Siesta Key* *941/861–2267.*

Restaurants

★ Bijou Café

$$$ | **FRENCH** | This 1920s-era gas station–turned–restaurant has been expanded over the years so that it is now a 140-seat restaurant. The enchanting decor is what you might expect in a quaint, modern European café—think French windows and doors, sparkling glassware, bouquets of freshly picked flowers, and the soft glow of candlelight. **Known for:** contemporary takes on traditional dishes, heavy on the seafood; cheaper bar menu; pre- or post-show dining. *Average main: $30* *1287 1st St.* *941/366–8111* *www.bijoucafe.net* *Closed Sun. No lunch weekends.*

Boca

$$$ | **MODERN AMERICAN** | One of four locations, this regional chain fits right into downtown Sarasota's hopping dining and shopping scene. The menu is as locally inspired as it gets—from the catch of the day courtesy of local fishing boats, to the fresh herbs that literally grow on the walls here. **Known for:** locally sourced seafood; craft cocktails; prime downtown location. *Average main: $23* *19 S. Lemon Ave.* *941/256–3565* *bocasarasota.com.*

Michael's on East

$$$ | **AMERICAN** | Not only do the lounge and piano bar, with their extensive wines and vintage cocktails, lure the after-theater set, but inspired cuisine and superior service also entice. Dinner fare ranges from pompano sautéed with Gulf shrimp, tomatoes, and fresh herbs to pan-roasted chicken breast with anise-scented sweet potato purée. **Known for:** large menu of seafood and meat dishes; extensive wine list; supper club atmosphere with piano bar. *Average main: $29* *1212 East Ave. S* *941/366–0007* *bestfood.com* *Closed Sun. No lunch Sat.*

The Old Salty Dog

$$ | **AMERICAN** | A menu of steamer and raw-bar options has been added to the much-enjoyed old favorites, including quarter-pound hot dogs, fish-and-chips, wings, and burgers—and early birds can catch breakfast here, too. With views of New Pass between Longboat and Lido Keys, this is a popular stop for locals and visitors en route from Mote Aquarium and the adjoining bay-front park. **Known for:** oysters and raw bar; hot dogs, burgers, and sandwiches; outdoor dining and sunset views. *Average main: $15* *1601 Ken Thompson Pkwy., City Island* *941/388–4311* *www.theoldsaltydog.com.*

Owen's Fish Camp

$$ | **SOUTHERN** | Nestled in a banyan-shaded corner of the hip Burns Court district of downtown Sarasota, this spot dishes out quintessentially Southern fare (though the menu is not geographically limited) that is particularly heavy on the seafood options. You'll find everything from the shrimp-and-oyster po'boy with bacon to chicken-fried lobster tail, a popular appetizer. **Known for:** fresh oysters and locally caught seafood; casual, low-key setting; no reservations and occasionally long waits. *Average main: $16* *516 Burns Ct.* *941/951–6936* *owensfishcamp.com* *No lunch.*

Shore

$$$ | **MODERN AMERICAN** | If you're a sucker for midcentury modern flair, the aesthetic alone at this partially open-air St. Armand's Circle spot is a draw. But the menu here, whether you're in the mood for the St. Louis "Jenga" ribs or roasted cauliflower and quinoa, is the real draw, especially when paired with the right local brew served on tap. **Known for:** Maine lobster sliders; spareribs with a Mongolian glaze; chic atmosphere. *Average main: $24* *465 John Ringling*

Blvd., Suite 200 ☎ 941/296–0301 ⊙ dine-shore.com.

Yoder's

$ | **AMERICAN** | Lines for meals stretch well beyond the hostess podium here. Pies—Key lime, egg custard, banana cream, peanut butter, strawberry rhubarb, and others—are the main event at this family restaurant in the heart of Sarasota's Amish community. **Known for:** fresh-baked pies; comfort food; good breakfast. *Average main: $10 ✉ 3434 Bahia Vista ☎ 941/955–7771 ⊕ www.yodersrestaurant.com ⊙ Closed Sun.*

Hotels

Gulf Beach Motel Resort

$ | **RENTAL** | Lido Key's first motel, this beachfront condo complex has been designated a historic property. **Pros:** near shopping; most units have kitchens or kitchenettes; free Wi-Fi. **Cons:** decor is fairly basic; motel feel; limited amenities. *Rooms from: $149 ✉ 930 Ben Franklin Dr., Lido Key ☎ 941/388–2127, 800/232–2489 ⊕ www.gulfbeachsarasota.com 49 rooms No meals.*

Hyatt Regency Sarasota

$ | **HOTEL** | Popular among business travelers, the Hyatt Regency is contemporary in design and sits in the heart of the city across from the Van Wezel Performing Arts Hall. **Pros:** great location; stellar views. **Cons:** chain-hotel feel; not on the beach. *Rooms from: $195 ✉ 1000 Blvd. of the Arts ☎ 941/953–1234, 800/233–1234 ⊕ www.sarasota.hyatt.com 294 rooms Breakfast; No meals.*

Lido Beach Resort

$$ | **RENTAL** | Superb Gulf views can be found at this stylish beachfront resort. **Pros:** beachfront location; many rooms have kitchens. **Cons:** bland, somewhat dated furnishings; high per-night fee for pets. *Rooms from: $239 ✉ 700 Ben Franklin Dr., Lido Key ☎ 941/388–2161, 866/306–5457 ⊕ www.lidobeachresort.com 222 rooms No meals.*

Ritz-Carlton, Sarasota

$$$$ | **HOTEL** | With a style that developers like to say is circus magnate John Ringling's realized dream, The Ritz is appointed with fine artwork and fresh-cut flowers. **Pros:** Ritz-style glitz; lots of amenities; attentive staff. **Cons:** long distance to golf course; not on the beach. *Rooms from: $518 ✉ 1111 Ritz-Carlton Dr. ☎ 941/309–2000, ⊕ www.ritzcarlton.com/sarasota 296 rooms No meals.*

★ **Turtle Beach Resort & Inn**

$ | **HOTEL** | Reminiscent of a quieter time, many of the cottages at this friendly, affordable, family- and pet-friendly resort date to the 1940s, a romantic plus for yesteryear lovers. **Pros:** nice location; romantic setting; self-serve laundry and Wi-Fi included. **Cons:** far from the area's cultural attractions; amenities are lacking; not family-friendly. *Rooms from: $175 ✉ 9049 Midnight Pass Rd., Siesta Key ☎ 941/349–4554 ⊕ www.turtlebeachresort.com 7 rooms, 3 suites, 10 cottages No meals.*

Nightlife

Gator Club

DANCE CLUBS | A famous nightclub located in a beautifully restored, brick historic cornerstone building downtown, the Gator Club has live music and dancing 365 days a year. *✉ 1490 Main St. ☎ 941/366–5969 ⊕ www.thegatorclub.com.*

JDub's Brewing Company

BREWPUBS/BEER GARDENS | Sarasota is no exception to the Tampa Bay area's thriving craft beer scene. Though JDub's may be best known for the popular milk chocolate porter, the ever-rotating cast of options on tap include the Left on Lido Mosaic Pale Ale and the warm-weather appropriate Poolside Kolsch. The brewery/tasting room is well off the beaten path—it's situated in an industrial area a solid 15 minutes from the beach—but the atmosphere here is excellent. Out back, there's a dog-friendly area with yard games like bean bag toss. There are also food trucks most days out front. Brewery tours are available every day at 1 and 6 for $5 (which includes a free "flagship" beer). ✉ *1215 Mango Ave.* ☎ *941/955–2739* 🌐 *jdubsbrewing.com.*

Performing Arts

Asolo Repertory Theatre

THEATER | One of the best theaters in Sarasota stages productions year-round in varying venues, which include the Historic Asolo Theater on the Ringling estate. ✉ *5555 Tamiami Trail* ☎ *941/351–8000* 🌐 *www.asolorep.org.*

Burns Court Cinema

FILM | There aren't many places in the Tampa Bay area where you can catch indie and foreign films. Since it first opened on the edge of downtown Sarasota in 1993, this old-timey four-screen movie house has been one of the few. It's less than a block from Burns Square's many stylish yet low-key dining offerings, and, unlike your average corporate movie theater, admission doesn't cost an arm and a leg. Beer and wine are also available. ✉ *506 Burns Ct.* ☎ *941/955–3456* 🌐 *filmsociety.org.*

The Players Centre for Performing Arts

THEATER | A long-established community theater, having launched such actors as Montgomery Clift and Paul Reubens, this troupe performs comedies, special events, live concerts, and musicals. ✉ *838 N. Tamiami Trail, U.S. 41 at 9th St.* ☎ *941/365–2494* 🌐 *www.theplayers.org.*

Sarasota Opera

OPERA | Performing in a historic 1,122-seat downtown theater, the Sarasota Opera features internationally known artists singing the principal roles, supported by a professional chorus of young apprentices. The season typically lasts from February through March, though a few special events take place at the venue throughout the year. ✉ *61 N. Pineapple Ave.* ☎ *941/328–1300* 🌐 *sarasotaopera.org.*

Activities

Bobby Jones Golf Course

GOLF | This public 45-hole course is over a century old and caters to a range of golfers. The setting is lush and green, with plenty of live oak trees and water. The grounds here are so pleasant that many choose to walk their chosen course, of which there are three. The American Course is best for less experienced golfers or those who want to practice their short shot, and features a range of lakes and varied terrain. The British Course is slightly more challenging, offering longer fairways dotted with water hazards and sand bunkers. The Gillespie Executive Course is recommended for beginners or those lacking the time needed for a full 18 holes. A large ravine divides much of the course from several of its greens approaches. ✉ *1000 Circus Blvd.* ☎ *941/365–4653* 🌐 *www.bobbyjonesgolfclub.com* 🎫 *From $14.50 for 9 holes, from $25 for 18 holes* ⛳ *American Course: 18 holes, 6032 yards, par 71; British Course:18 holes, 6710 yards, par 72; Gillespie Executive Course: 9 holes, 1716 yards, par 30.*

Flying Fish Fleet

FISHING | Several boats can be chartered for deep-sea fishing by the day or half day, and there are daily group trips on a "party" fishing boat. ✉ *2 Marina Plaza, on the bay front at Marina Jack* ✣ *On the bay front at Marina Jack* ☎ *941/366–3373* 🌐 *www.flyingfishfleet.com* 🎫 *Group trips from $75 per person, charters from $700.*

Sarasota Bay Explorers

BOATING | Many visitors to the Mote Aquarium take the 105-minute boat trip onto Sarasota Bay. Conducted by Sarasota Bay Explorers, all boat trips are done in conjunction with the aquarium and leave from the aquarium's dock. The crew brings marine life on board, explains what it is, and throws it back to swim away. You are almost guaranteed to see bottlenose dolphins. Reservations are recommended. You can also charter the *Miss Explorer*, a 24-foot Sea Ray Sundeck, or take a nature tour. ✉ *Mote Aquarium, 1600 Ken Thompson Pkwy.* ☎ *941/388–4200* 🌐 *www.sarasotabayexplorers.com* 🎫 *Sea Life Encounter Cruise $29, Sunset Cruise $29, boat tour $27, Nature Safari $45, charters $345–$495.*

Siesta Sports Rentals

BICYCLING | Up for rent here are kayaks, stand-up paddleboards, bikes, beach chairs, scooters, and beach wheelchairs and strollers. Guided kayaking trips are also available. ✉ *6551 Midnight Pass Rd., Siesta Key* ☎ *941/346–1797* 🌐 *www.siestasportsrentals.com.*

Chapter 9

THE LOWER GULF COAST

Updated by
Jill Martin

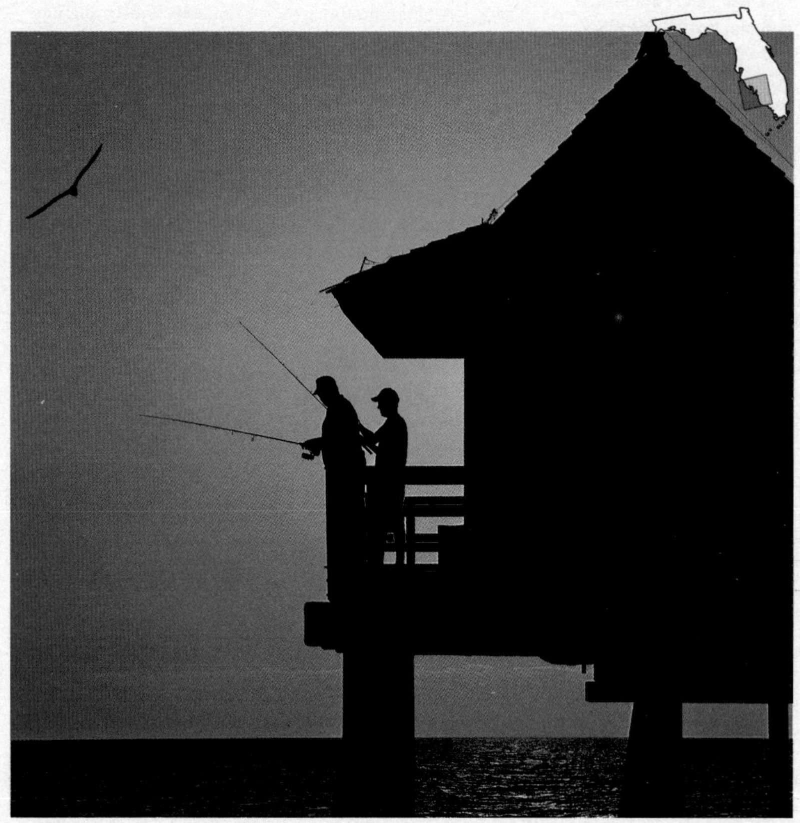

Sights	Restaurants	Hotels	Shopping	Nightlife
★★★★☆	★★★☆☆	★★★☆☆	★★★☆☆	★★★☆☆

WELCOME TO THE LOWER GULF COAST

TOP REASONS TO GO

★ **Heavenly beaches:** Whether you go to the beach to sun, swim, gather shells, or watch the sunset, the region's Gulf of Mexico beaches rank among the best.

★ **Edison and Ford Winter Estates:** A rare complex of two famous inventors' winter homes comes complete with botanical-research gardens, Edison's lab, and a museum.

★ **Island-hopping:** Rent a boat or jump aboard a charter for lunch, picnicking, beaching, or shelling on a subtropical island adrift from the mainland.

★ **Naples shopping:** Flex your buying power in downtown Naples's charming shopping districts or in lush outdoor centers around town.

★ **Watch for wildlife:** On the edge of Everglades National Park, the region protects vast tracts of fragile land and water where you can see alligators, manatees, dolphins, roseate spoonbills, and hundreds of other birds.

The Lower Gulf Coast of Florida, as its name suggests, occupies a stretch of coastline along southernmost west Florida, bordered by the Gulf of Mexico. It lies south of Tampa and Sarasota, directly on the other side of the state from West Palm Beach and Fort Lauderdale. In between the two coasts stretch heartland agricultural areas and Everglades wilderness. The region encompasses the major resort towns of Fort Myers, Fort Myers Beach, Sanibel Island, Naples, and Marco Island, along with a medley of suburban communities and smaller islands.

1 **Fort Myers.** Don't miss the Edison and Ford Winter Estates along royal palm–lined McGregor Boulevard. For museums, theater, and art, the up-and-coming downtown River District rules.

2 **Cape Coral, North Fort Myers, and Pine Island.** Hop on a buggie for a wildlife adventure and explore a variety of colorful communities.

3 **Gasparilla Island.** Fish for tarpon, enjoy the secluded beaches, or photograph the lighthouse on Boca Grande.

4 **Sanibel and Captiva islands.** Shells and wildlife refuges bring nature lovers to Sanibel and Captiva islands.

5 **Fort Myers Beach.** This area is known for its lively clubs and shrimp fleet. For true seclusion head to the area's unbridged island beaches.

6 **Estero/Bonita Springs.** Visit gardens, state historic sites, outlet malls, or catch an event at the arena.

7 **Naples.** Some of the region's best shopping and dining take up residence in historic buildings trimmed with blossoms and street sculptures in Old Naples.

8 **Marco Island.** Hit Marco Island for the boating lifestyle and funky fishing-village character.

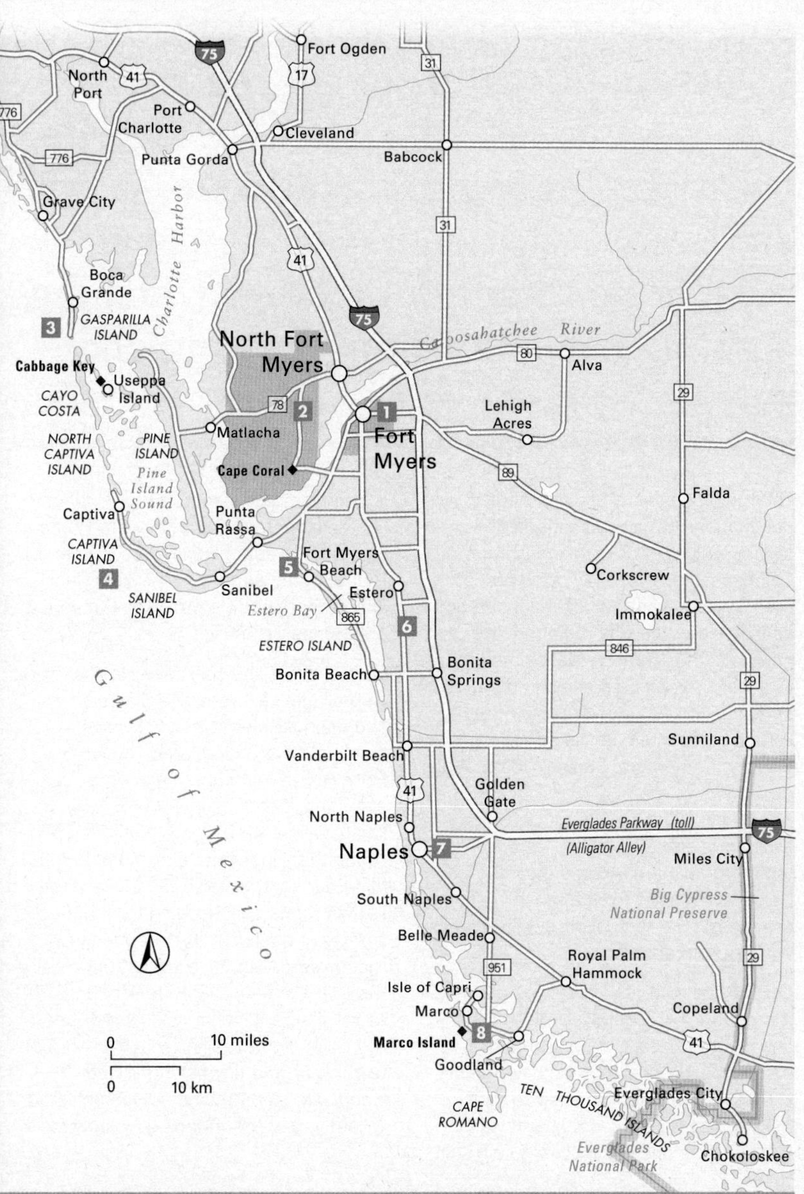
Fort Ogden
North Port
Port Charlotte
Cleveland
Punta Gorda
Babcock
Grave City
Charlotte Harbor
Boca Grande
GASPARILLA ISLAND
Caloosahatchee River
North Fort Myers
Alva
Cabbage Key
Useppa Island
CAYO COSTA
Matlacha
Lehigh Acres
Fort Myers
NORTH CAPTIVA ISLAND
PINE ISLAND
Cape Coral
Pine Island Sound
Falda
Captiva
Punta Rassa
CAPTIVA ISLAND
Fort Myers Beach
Corkscrew
Sanibel
Estero
Immokalee
SANIBEL ISLAND
Estero Bay
ESTERO ISLAND
Bonita Beach
Bonita Springs
Gulf of Mexico
Sunniland
Vanderbilt Beach
Golden Gate
North Naples
Everglades Parkway (toll)
(Alligator Alley)
Naples
Miles City
South Naples
Big Cypress National Preserve
Belle Meade
Royal Palm Hammock
Isle of Capri
Marco
Copeland
0 10 miles
0 10 km
Marco Island
Goodland
TEN THOUSAND ISLANDS
Everglades City
CAPE ROMANO
Everglades National Park
Chokoloskee

With its subtropical climate and beckoning family-friendly beaches known for their powdery sand, calm surf, and nary a freighter in sight, the Lower Gulf Coast, also referred to as the state's southwestern region, is a favorite vacation spot of Florida residents as well as visitors. Vacationers tend to spend most of their time outdoors—swimming, sunning, shelling, fishing, boating, and playing tennis or golf.

The region has several distinct travel destinations. Small and historic downtown Fort Myers rises inland along the Caloosahatchee River, and the rest of the town sprawls in all directions. It got its nickname, the City of Palms, from the hundreds of towering royal palms that inventor Thomas Edison planted between 1900 and 1917 along McGregor Boulevard, a historic residential street and site of his winter estate. Edison's idea caught on, and more than 2,000 royal palms now line 14-mile-long McGregor Boulevard. Museums and educational attractions are the draw here. Across the river, Cape Coral has evolved from a mostly residential community to a resort destination for water-sports enthusiasts.

Off the coast west of Fort Myers are more than 100 coastal islands in all shapes and sizes. Connected to the mainland by a 3-mile causeway, Sanibel is known for its superb shelling, fine fishing, beachfront resorts, and wildlife refuge. Here and on Captiva, to which it is connected by a short bridge, multimillion-dollar homes line both waterfronts. Just southwest of Fort Myers is Estero Island, home of busy Fort Myers Beach, and farther south, Lovers Key State Park and Bonita Beach.

Farther down the coast lies Naples, once a small fishing village and now a thriving and sophisticated enclave. It's like a smaller, more understated version of Palm Beach, with fine restaurants, chichi shopping areas, luxury resorts, and—locals will tell you—more golf holes per capita than anywhere else in the world. A half hour south basks Marco Island, best known for its beaches and fishing. See a maze of pristine miniature mangrove islands when you take a boat tour from the island's marinas into Ten Thousand Islands National Wildlife Refuge. Although high-rises line much of Marco's waterfront, the tiny fishing village of Goodland, an outpost of Old Florida, tries valiantly to stave off new development.

Planning

When to Go

In winter this is one of the warmest areas of the United States. Occasionally temperatures drop in December or January, but rarely below freezing. From February through April you may find it next to impossible to find a hotel room.

Numbers drop the rest of the year, but visitors within driving range, European tourists, and convention clientele still keep things busy. Temperatures and humidity spike, but discounted room rates make summer attractive. Summer is also rainy season, but most storms occur in the afternoon and last for a flash. Hurricane season runs from June through November.

Getting Here and Around

AIR TRAVEL

The area's primary airport is Southwest Florida International in Fort Myers, where many airlines offer flights; private pilots land at both RSW and Page Field, also in Fort Myers. Gulf Coast Airways to Key West and a couple of private charter services also land at Naples Municipal Airport, and North Captiva Island has a private airstrip.

AIRPORT TRANSFER CONTACTS Aaron Airport Transportation. ☎ *239/768–1898.* **Sanibel Taxi.** ☎ *239/472–4160, 888/527–7806* 🌐 *www.sanibeltaxi.com.*

AIRPORT CONTACTS Naples Municipal Airport. ✉ *160 Aviation Dr. N, Naples* ☎ *239/643–0733* 🌐 *www.flynaples.com.* **Southwest Florida International Airport** *(RSW).* ✉ *11000 Terminal Access Rd., Fort Myers* ☎ *239/590–4800* 🌐 *www.flylcpa.com.*

CAR TRAVEL

If you're driving, U.S. 41 (the Tamiami Trail) runs the length of the region. Sanibel Island is accessible from the mainland via the Sanibel Causeway (toll $6 round-trip). Captiva Island lies across a small pass from Sanibel's north end, accessible by bridge.

Be aware that the destination's popularity, especially during winter, means traffic congestion at peak times of day. Avoid driving when the locals are getting to and from work and visitors to and from the beach.

Hotels

Lodging in Fort Myers, the islands, and Naples can be pricey, but there are affordable options even during the busy winter season. If these destinations are too rich for your pocket, consider visiting in the off-season, when rates drop drastically, or look to Fort Myers Beach and Cape Coral for better rates. Beachfront properties tend to be more expensive; to spend less, look for properties away from the water. In high season—Christmastime and Presidents' Day through Easter—always reserve ahead for the top properties. Fall is the slowest season: rates are low and availability is high, but this is also hurricane season (June–November).

Restaurants

In this part of Florida, fresh seafood reigns supreme. Succulent native stone-crab claws, a particularly tasty treat, in season from mid-October through mid-May, are usually served hot with drawn butter or chilled with tangy mustard sauce. Supplies are typically steady, since claws regenerate in time for the next season. Other seafood specialties include fried grouper sandwiches and Sanibel pink shrimp. In Naples's highly hailed restaurants and sidewalk cafés, mingle with locals, winter visitors, and other travelers, and catch up on the latest culinary trends.

Hotel and restaurant reviews have been shortened. For full information, visit Fodors.com.

What It Costs

	$	$$	$$$	$$$$
RESTAURANTS	under $15	$15–$20	$21–$30	over $30
HOTELS	under $200	$200–$300	$301–$400	over $400

Tours

Captiva Cruises

BOAT TOURS | Shelling, dolphin, luncheon, beach, sunset, and history cruises run to and around the out islands of Cabbage Key, Useppa Island, Cayo Costa, and Gasparilla Island. Night sky cruises and excursions also go to historic Tarpon Lodge and Calusa Indian Mound Trail on Pine Island. Excursions are from $27.50, and there may be a charge for parking. ✉ *McCarthy's Marina, 11401 Andy Rosse La., Captiva* ☎ *239/472–5300* 🌐 *www.captivacruises.com* 🎫 *Tours from $27.50.*

Manatee and Eco River Tours

SPECIAL-INTEREST | **FAMILY** | To spot some sea cows in the Fort Myers area, hook up with Manatee and Eco River Tours. Open November 1–April 30, during the height of manatee-viewing season. You can even bring your pet. Reservations required. ✉ *16991 Rte. 31, Fort Myers* ☎ *239/693–1434* 🌐 *www.manateeandecorivertours.com* 🎫 *Tours from $15.*

Manatee Sightseeing Adventure

SPECIAL-INTEREST | **FAMILY** | See manatees in the wild all year. Tours depart at Port of the Islands. Discount tickets are available online. ✉ *525 Newport Dr., Naples* ☎ *239/642–8818, 239/398–0962* 🌐 *www.see-manatees.com* 🎫 *Admission $58.*

★ **Tarpon Bay Explorers**

SPECIAL-INTEREST | One of the best ways to see the J.N. "Ding" Darling National Wildlife Refuge is by taking a guided or self-guided nature tour. There are many options to choose depending on your activity level and desire—including a sea life cruise, open-air tram tours, and nature cruises, to name a few. Rentals of kayaks, canoes, stand-up paddleboards, bikes, and pontoon boats are right on-site. Charter boats are also available. ✉ *900 Tarpon Bay Rd., Sanibel* ☎ *239/472–8900* 🌐 *www.tarponbayexplorers.com* 🎫 *Tours from $13.*

Fort Myers

80 miles southeast of Sarasota, 125 miles west of Palm Beach.

In parts of Fort Myers, old Southern mansions and their modern-day counterparts peek out from behind stately palms and blossomy foliage. Views over the broad Caloosahatchee River, which borders the city's small but businesslike cluster of office buildings downtown, soften the look of the area. These days it's showing the effects of age and urban sprawl, but planners work at reviving what has been termed the River District at the heart of downtown. North of Fort Myers are small fishing communities and new retirement towns, including Boca Grande on Gasparilla Island; Englewood Beach on Manasota Key; and Port Charlotte, north of the Peace River.

GETTING HERE AND AROUND

The closest airport to Fort Myers is Southwest Florida International Airport (RSW), about 15 miles southeast of town. A taxi for up to three passengers costs about $25–$40; extra people are

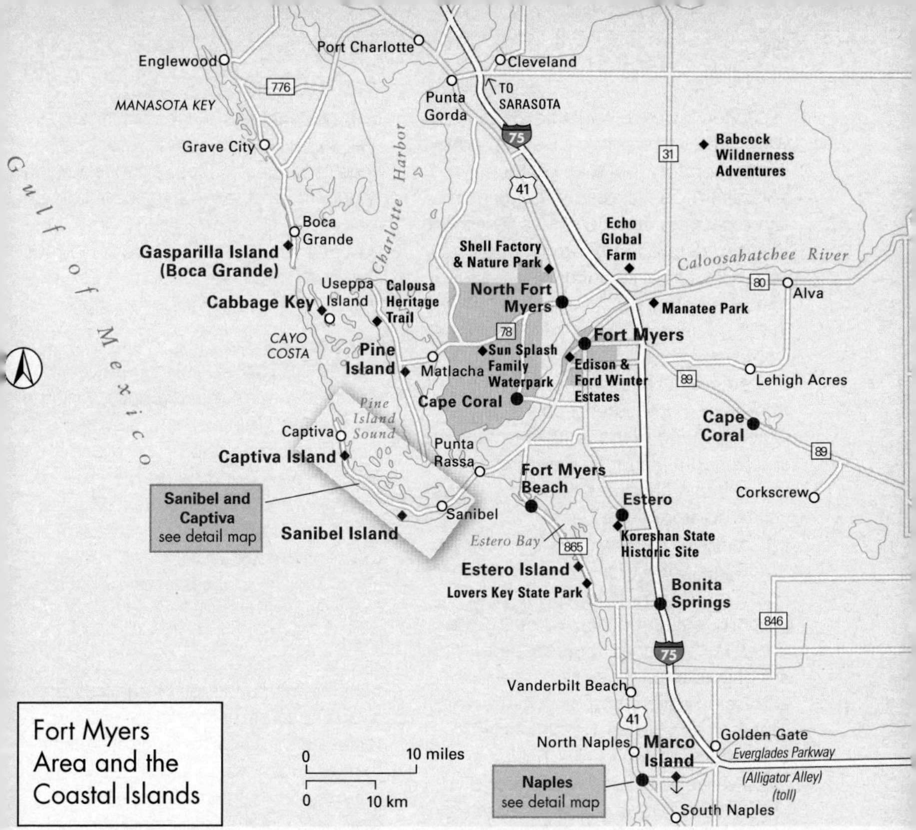

Fort Myers Area and the Coastal Islands

charged $10 each. LeeTran bus service serves most of the Fort Myers area.

If you're driving here from Florida's East Coast, consider Alligator Alley, a toll section of Interstate 75 that runs from Fort Lauderdale to Naples. Interstate 75 then runs north–south the length of the region. U.S. 41 (the Tamiami Trail, also called South Cleveland Avenue in Fort Myers) runs parallel to the interstate to the west and goes through downtown Naples and Fort Myers. McGregor Boulevard (Route 867) and Summerlin Road (Route 869), Fort Myers's main north–south city streets, head toward Sanibel and Captiva islands. San Carlos Boulevard (Route 865) runs southwest from Summerlin Road to Fort Myers Beach, and Pine Island–Bayshore Road (Route 78) leads from North Fort Myers through northern Cape Coral onto Pine Island.

BUS CONTACTS LeeTran. ☎ *239/275–8726, 239/533–8726* 🌐 *www.rideleetran.com.*

VISITOR INFORMATION

CONTACTS Lee County Visitor & Convention Bureau. ✉ *2201 2nd St., Suite 600* ☎ *239/338–3500, 800/237–6444* 🌐 *www.fortmyers-sanibel.com.*

Sights

★ Edison and Ford Winter Estates

HOUSE | Fort Myers's premier attraction pays homage to two of America's most ingenious inventors: Thomas A. Edison, who gave the world the stock ticker, the incandescent lamp, and the phonograph, among other inventions; and his friend and neighbor, automaker Henry Ford. Donated to the city by Edison's widow, his once 12-acre estate has been expanded into a remarkable 25 acres, with three homes, two caretaker cottages, a laboratory, botanical gardens, and a museum. The laboratory contains the same gadgets and gizmos as when Edison last stepped foot into it. Visitors can see many of his inventions, along with historic photographs and memorabilia, in the museum. Edison traveled south from New Jersey and devoted much of his time here to inventing things (there are 1,093 patents to his name), experimenting with rubber for friend and frequent visitor Harvey Firestone, and planting hundreds of plant species collected around the world. Next door to Edison's two identical homes is Ford's "Mangoes," the more modest seasonal home of Edison's fellow inventor. The property's oldest building, the Edison Caretaker's House, dates to 1860. Tours are guided or audio self-guided. One admission covers homes of both men; museum and laboratory-only tickets and botanical-garden tour tickets are also available. ✉ *2350 McGregor Blvd.* ☎ *239/334–7419* 🌐 *www.edisonfordwinterestates.org* 🎫 *Complete Estate Tour $25; other tours available.*

★ IMAG History and Science Center

MUSEUM | FAMILY | Kids can't wait to get their hands on the wonderful interactive exhibits at this lively museum–aquarium combo that explores technology, physics, weather, and other science topics. Check out the stingrays and other marine life in the aquariums, touch tanks, and the USS *Mohawk* artificial reef tank featured on Animal Planet's "Tanked!" Feed the fish, turtles, and swans in the outdoor lagoon; visit a tarantula, python, hissing cockroach, juvenile alligator, and other live critters in the Animal Lab; dig for dinosaur bones; watch a 3-D movie in the theater; take part in a hands-on Animal Encounter demonstration, and touch a cloud. Other highlights include the Mini Museum early childhood area, Backyard Nature, aquaponics area, Nano Lab, and Idea Lab engineering design center, as well as Build-Your-Own-Coaster and Science of Motion. History exhibits include underwater plane wrecks, a Columbian mammoth, and giant ground sloth, as well as a replica Cracker House. ✉ *2000 Cranford Ave.* ☎ *239/243–0043* 🌐 *www.theimag.org* 🎫 *$14* ⏲ *Closed Mon.*

Manatee Park

NATURE PRESERVE | FAMILY | Here you may glimpse Florida's most famous, yet often hard to spot, marine mammal. When Gulf waters drop to 68°F or below—usually from November to March—the sea cows congregate in these waters, which are warmed by the outflow of a towering nearby power plant. Pause at any of the three observation decks (the first nearest the outflow and last at the lagoon usually yield the most sightings, as does the fishing pier) and watch for bubbles. Hydrophones on the last deck allow you to eavesdrop on their songs. Periodically, one of these gentle giants—mature adults weigh an average of 1,000 pounds—will surface. Calusa Blueway Outfitters run the visitor center/gift shop and offer kayak and canoe rentals, as well as clinics and tours to paddle the canals and get a closer look. ✉ *10901 Palm Beach Blvd.* ✥ *1¼ miles east of I–75 Exit 141* ☎ *239/690–5030* 🌐 *www.leeparks.org* 🎫 *Free. Parking (cash only) May–Nov. $1 per hr, $5 daily; Dec.–Apr. $2 per hr, $5 daily* ⏲ *Concessions closed Apr.–Nov.*

Sidney & Berne Davis Art Center

ARTS VENUE | The River District has become a haven for independent galleries, and in 2003 Florida Arts, Inc., a nonprofit organization, stepped in to turn an abandoned post office from 1933 into a space for edgy, up-and-coming visual artists, musical acts, films, and theater. Even if your taste runs more to Broadway and Monet than M-Pact and Marcus Jansen, a visit is worthwhile for the neoclassical revival facade: eight towering coral-rock Ionic columns give way to swaths of intricately detailed window screens. The friendly staff is happy to answer questions about the building's history. Renovations of the upper floors have recently been completed. ■ **TIP→ Plan a trip around the first or third Friday every month for Art Walk or Music Walk; the center stays open late for the throngs of passersby.** ✉ *2301 1st St.* ☎ *239/333–1933* 🌐 *www.sbdac.com* 🎟 *$5 suggested donation.*

Restaurants

Bistro 41

$$$ | **AMERICAN** | Amid brightly painted, textured walls and a display kitchen, shoppers and businesspeople meet here for some of the town's most dependable and inventive cuisine. To experience the kitchen at its imaginative best, check the night's specials, which often include daringly done seafood. **Known for:** 41 Prime Dip sandwich; nightly specials; creative seafood dishes. $ *Average main: $26* ✉ *13499 S. Cleveland Ave.* ☎ *239/466–4141* 🌐 *www.bistro41.com.*

Cibo

$$$ | **ITALIAN** | Its flavor-bursting Italian food and its propensity for fresh, quality ingredients keep Cibo (pronounced *chee-bo*) at the head of the class for local Italian restaurants. In contrast to the sophisticated black-and-white setting, the menu comes in colors from the classic Caesar salad with shaved Grana Padano and spaghetti and meatballs to salmon piccata and veal porterhouse with porcini risotto. **Known for:** classic Italian dishes; excellent service; great wine list. $ *Average main: $28* ✉ *12901 McGregor Blvd.* ☎ *239/454–3700* 🌐 *www.cibofortmyers.com* ⏲ *No lunch.*

Il Pomodoro Cucina Italiana

$$ | **ITALIAN** | We may say *tomato* or *tomahtoe*, but in Italy, they say *pomodoro*. But there's much more than the use of fresh tomatoes to recommend this place to the locals who find their way off the beaten culinary path. **Known for:** rigatoni Bolognese; good pizza; chicken Sinatra. $ *Average main: $15* ✉ *9681 Gladiolus Dr.* ☎ *239/985–0080* 🌐 *www.ilpomodororestaurant.com* ⏲ *No lunch Sat. May–Dec., closed Sun.*

Philly Junction

$ | **AMERICAN** | From the bread (Amoroso rolls) to the corned beef, almost everything here comes from Philadelphia. Not only are the Philly cheesesteaks delicious and authentic, but the burgers and other sandwiches are excellent—and the prices are among the lowest around. **Known for:** authentic Philly cheesesteaks; good, inexpensive breakfast; closing by 8 pm. $ *Average main: $7* ✉ *4600 Summerlin Rd., C12* ☎ *239/936–6622* ⏲ *No dinner Sun.*

Saigon Paris Bistro

$$$ | **VIETNAMESE** | Irish omelets, Belgian waffles, crepes, steak au poivre, Vietnamese sea bass, Waldorf chicken salad: this eatery's extensive menu clearly travels farther abroad than its name implies. And it does so with utmost taste and flavor, as its faithful local clientele will attest. **Known for:** pho soup; two-for-one breakfast deals; international cuisine. $ *Average main: $21* ✉ *12995 S. Cleveland. Ave., Suite 118* ☎ *239/936–2233* 🌐 *www.saigonparisbistro.com* ⏲ *Closed Mon. June–Sept.*

Shrimp Shack

$$ | **SEAFOOD** | **FAMILY** | Seafood lovers, families, and retired snowbirds flock to this venue with its vivacious staff, bustle, and colorful, cartoonish wall murals. Southern-style deep frying prevails—whole-belly clams, grouper, shrimp, onion rings, hush puppies, and fried pork loins—though you can get certain selections broiled or blackened, and there's some New England flavor with seafood rolls at lunch. **Known for:** fried seafood; great burgers; online coupons for free kids' meals. $ *Average main: $15*

View 200 phonographs, an invention Thomas Edison patented in 1878, at his Fort Myers winter estate.

✉ *13361 Metro Pkwy.* ☎ *239/561–6817* 🌐 *www.shrimpshackusa.com.*

The Veranda

$$$$ | **SOUTHERN** | A favorite of business and government bigwigs at lunch, the Veranda serves imaginative Continental fare with a trace of a Southern accent for dinner. The restaurant is a combination of two turn-of-the-20th-century homes, with a two-sided central brick fireplace, and sconces and antique oil paintings on its pale-yellow walls. **Known for:** fried-green-tomato salad; courtyard dining; fresh seafood. *Average main: $34* ✉ *2122 2nd St.* ☎ *239/332–2065* 🌐 *www.verandarestaurant.com* *Closed Sun. No lunch Sat.*

Hotels

Baymont by Wyndham Fort Myers Airport

$ | **HOTEL** | A top option for its value and facilities, this spot is close to the airport and interstate, with complete business services, a basic gym, and a warm, cozy lobby. **Pros:** free airport shuttle; many dining options nearby; near local college and attractions. **Cons:** no frills; high-traffic area; busy for breakfast. *Rooms from: $160* ✉ *9401 Marketplace Rd.* ☎ *239/454–0040* 🌐 *www.baymontinns.com* *85 rooms* *Breakfast.*

Crowne Plaza Hotel Fort Myers at the Bell Tower Shops

$$ | **HOTEL** | Baseball fans often make this hotel their home base since spring training and other sports parks are just a few miles away; others love the sports bar downstairs and being a stroll from the Bell Tower Shops. **Pros:** free airport shuttle; complimentary transportation within a 3-mile radius; laundry facilities. **Cons:** showing signs of age; rooms a bit tight; meeting traffic crowds the lobby. *Rooms from: $210* ✉ *13051 Bell Tower Dr.* ☎ *239/482–2900* 🌐 *www.ihg.com* *225 rooms* *No meals.*

Hilton Garden Inn Fort Myers

$$ | **HOTEL** | This compact, prettily landscaped low-rise is near Fort Myers's

cultural and commercial areas, and a business clientele favors it for its convenience. **Pros:** near lots of shops and restaurants; enjoyable on-site restaurant; large rooms. **Cons:** chain feel; small pool; at busy intersection. *Rooms from: $210* *12600 University Dr.* *239/790–3500* *www.fortmyers.stayhgi.com* *126 rooms* *Breakfast.*

Hotel Indigo, Ft. Myers Downtown River District

$ | HOTEL | The only modern boutique hotel downtown, it attracts a cosmopolitan set that wants to be in the center of the River District's art, dining, and shopping scene—and just minutes from other attractions. **Pros:** sleek design; walking distance to restaurants and nightlife; rooftop bar. **Cons:** must drive to beach; no suites have full kitchens; pricey valet parking. *Rooms from: $199* *1520 Broadway* *239/337–3446* *www.hotelindigo.com* *67 rooms* *No meals.*

★ Sanibel Harbour Marriott Resort & Spa

$$$ | RESORT | FAMILY | Vacationing families and businesspeople who want luxury pick this sprawling resort complex that towers over the island-studded San Carlos Bay at the last mainland exit before the Sanibel Causeway. **Pros:** top-notch accommodations; full amenities; updated spa. **Cons:** daily parking fee; unspectacular beach; $25 daily resort fee. *Rooms from: $369* *17260 Harbour Pointe Dr.* *239/466–4000, 800/767–7777* *www.marriott.com* *347 rooms* *No meals.*

Nightlife

Buddha Rock Club

MUSIC CLUBS | A giant gold statue of his Zen-ness out front greets fans—a fun mix of frat boys, retirees, and young professionals—who crowd the casual, smoky bar and listen to hits from live bands and DJs. This is a local favorite. It's closed on Monday nights. *12701 McGregor Blvd.* *239/482–8565* *buddharockclub.com.*

Crü

TAPAS BARS | Trendsters in the mood for a drink and excellent global tapas crowd the lounge area of this cutting-edge restaurant. The lounge serves food until midnight on weekends. *13499 S. Cleveland Ave., Suite 241* *239/466–3663* *www.eatcru.com.*

Florida Rep

THEATER | In the restored circa-1915 Arcade Theatre downtown, this top professional company stages Tony- and Pulitzer-winning plays and musicals. There's also an adjacent, more intimate space for edgier works and a Lunchbox Theatre Series for children. *2267 1st St.* *239/332–4488* *www.floridarep.org.*

Laugh-In Comedy Cafe

COMEDY CLUBS | For more than 20 years, this is the place to watch top comedians perform every Friday and Saturday, in a no-smoking atmosphere. *College Plaza, 8595 College Pkwy., Suite 300* *239/479–5233* *www.laughincomedycafe.com.*

Stevie Tomato's Sports Page

BARS/PUBS | Five miles up on Interstate 75 from the buzzing Gulf Coast Town Center bars, this is a low-key spot to catch a game and feast on good food; earlier in the evening it's very family-friendly. Best bets are their baby back ribs, Chicago-style pizza, and Italian beef. *9510 Market Place Rd.* *239/939–7211* *stevietomato.com.*

Performing Arts

Barbara B. Mann Performing Arts Hall

ARTS CENTERS | Catch Broadway musicals, concerts, symphony performances, and comedy shows. *Florida SouthWestern State College, 8099 College Pkwy.* *239/481–4849, 800/440–7469* *www.bbmannpah.com.*

Broadway Palm Dinner Theatre

THEATER | Buffet dinners come along with some of Broadway's best musicals. There's also a 100-seat Off Broadway Palm Theatre that hosts smaller-scale comedies and musicals. ✉ *1380 Colonial Blvd.* ☎ *239/278–4422* 🌐 *www.broadwaypalm.com.*

Shopping

Bell Tower Shops

SHOPPING CENTERS/MALLS | This open-air shopping center has about 40 stylish boutiques and specialty shops, some of Fort Myers's best restaurants and bars, and 20 movie screens. ✉ *S. Cleveland Ave. at Daniels Pkwy.* ☎ *239/489–1221* 🌐 *www.thebelltowershops.com.*

Edison Mall

SHOPPING CENTERS/MALLS | The largest air-conditioned indoor mall in Fort Myers houses several major department stores and some 160 specialty shops. ✉ *4125 Cleveland Ave.* ☎ *239/939–1933* 🌐 *www.shopedisonmall.com.*

Fleamasters Fleamarket

OUTDOOR/FLEA/GREEN MARKETS | Just east of downtown, more than 900 vendors sell new and used goods Friday through Sunday 9–5. Its music hall hosts live entertainment. ✉ *4135 Dr. Martin Luther King Jr. Blvd.* ✣ *1.7 miles west of I–75 Exit 138* ☎ *239/334–7001* 🌐 *www.fleamall.com.*

Gulf Coast Town Center

SHOPPING CENTERS/MALLS | This megamall of stores and chain restaurants includes a 130,000-square-foot Bass Pro Shops, Ron Jon Surf Shop, Best Buy, Costco, Golf Galaxy, and movie theaters. ✉ *9903 Gulf Coast Main St.* ☎ *239/267–0783* 🌐 *www.gulfcoasttowncenter.com.*

Sanibel Outlets

OUTLET/DISCOUNT STORES | Its boardwalks are lined with outlets for Nike, Van Heusen, Maidenform, Coach, Under Armour, Calvin Klein, and Samsonite, among others. ✉ *20350 Summerlin Rd.* ☎ *888/471–3939* 🌐 *www.sanibeloutlets.com.*

Activities

BASEBALL

The region is a popular outpost for spring training teams, with two in Fort Myers.

Boston Red Sox

BASEBALL/SOFTBALL | The Sox settled into new digs in 2012 at JetBlue Park at Fenway South, a 10,823-capacity stadium and 106-acre training facility. The field itself is an exact duplicate of their famous home turf, with a Green Monster wall and manual scoreboard. ✉ *JetBlue Park, 11581 Daniels Pkwy.* ☎ *239/334–4700, 888/733–7696* 🌐 *boston.redsox.mlb.com.*

Minnesota Twins

BASEBALL/SOFTBALL | The team plays exhibition games in town during March and early April. From April through September, the Miracle (🌐 *www.miraclebaseball.com*), a Twins single-A affiliate, plays home games at Hammond Stadium. ✉ *Lee County Sports Complex, 14100 6 Mile Cypress Pkwy.* ☎ *800/338–9467* 🌐 *minnesota.twins.mlb.com.*

BIKING

One of the longest bike paths in Fort Myers is along Summerlin Road. It passes commercial areas and gets close to Sanibel through dwindling wide-open spaces. Linear Park, which runs parallel to Six Mile Cypress Parkway, offers more natural, less congested views. Trailhead Park is linked to the new John Yarbrough Linear Park to create a 30-mile pathway, the longest in Lee County.

Bike Route

BICYCLING | Since 1974, this is the place to come for a good selection of rentals. ✉ *8595 College Pkwy., Suite 200* ☎ *239/481–3376* 🌐 *www.thebikeroute.com* 🕓 *Closed Sun.*

BOATING AND SAILING

Southwest Florida Yachts

BOATING | Charter a sailboat or powerboat, or take lessons. With 30 years in the business, they can help you explore southwest Florida like a native. ✉ *6095 Silver King Blvd., Cape Coral* ☎ *239/656–1339, 800/257–2788* 🌐 *www.swfyachts.com.*

GOLF

Eastwood Golf Course

GOLF | Golfers love how this Robert von Hagge–and Bruce Devlin–designed course is in an area where there is little development, meaning no homes around the course, just plenty of water, trees, and wildlife (aka gators). The driving range and course are affordable, too, especially if you don't mind playing at unfavorable times (midday in summer, for example). Test your skills on the short par 4 on hole 7, where your second shot is over water. The 10th hole will have you shooting over water, too. ✉ *4600 Bruce Herd La.* ☎ *239/321–7487* 🌐 *www.cityftmyers.com/eastwood* 🎫 *From $45; rental clubs $15* ⛳ *18 holes, 6772 yards, par 72.*

Fort Myers Country Club

GOLF | Walk in the footsteps of Thomas Edison and Henry Ford when you play this course known as "The Fort" to its huge fan base. Located less than a mile from the winter estates of these famous inventors, this course is one of the oldest on Florida's west coast. In fact, it was designed in 1916 by Donald Ross and opened in 1917. Number 10 is a par 3 where you can hit anything from a 7 iron to a hybrid as the hole stretches out 203 yards. The Yuengling Open (formerly the Coors Light Open) is held here early each year. Next door is a lively restaurant and bar, The Edison. ✉ *3591 McGregor Blvd.* ☎ *239/321–7488* 🌐 *www.cityftmyers.com/countryclub* 🎫 *$45–$70* ⛳ *18 holes, 6400 yards, par 72.*

Shell Point Golf Club

GOLF | Newbies to heavy hitters enjoy the layout of this Gordon Lewis–designed course with its challenging fairways and share of water hazards—eight tees on every hole. The front nine play like a symphony, but the back nine can be rough and slow with the wind and their somewhat compacted layouts. If you're looking for a 19th hole where you can toast your one-under-par score, you won't find it here, as no alcohol is served. One nice feature at "The Shell" is that they offer Laser Link for accurate yardage to the pin. ✉ *17401 On Par Blvd.* ☎ *239/433–9790* 🌐 *www.shellpointgolf.com* 🎫 *$85* ⛳ *18 holes, 6880 yards, par 71.*

KAYAKING

Calusa Blueway Outfitters

KAYAKING | Paddling enthusiasts can rent kayaks or canoes to explore the Manatee Park environs daily from Thanksgiving to Easter and on weekends in the summer; clinics and guided tours are also available, but go in winter if spotting sea cows is your aim. ✉ *Manatee Park, 10901 Palm Beach Blvd.* ✥ *1¼ miles east of I–75 Exit 141* ☎ *239/481–4600* 🌐 *www.calusabluewayoutfitters.com.*

Cape Coral, Pine Island, and North Fort Myers

13 miles from downtown Fort Myers.

Cape Coral is determinedly trying to move from its pigeonhole as a residential community by attracting tourism with its downtown reconfiguration, the Resort at Marina Village, and destination restaurants at the Cape Harbour residential marina development.

GETTING HERE AND AROUND

Four bridges cross from Fort Myers to Cape Coral and North Fort Myers. Pine Island–Bayshore Road (Route 78) leads from North Fort Myers through northern

Cape Coral onto off-the-beaten path Pine Island, known for its art galleries, fishing, and exotic-fruit farms.

Sights

Babcock Wilderness Adventures

NATURE PRESERVE | FAMILY | To see what Florida looked like centuries ago, visit Babcock's Crescent B Ranch, northeast of Fort Myers. During the 90-minute swamp-buggy-style excursion you ride in a converted school bus through several ecosystems, including the unusual and fascinating Telegraph Cypress Swamp. Along the way an informative and typically amusing guide describes the area's social and natural history while you keep an eye peeled for alligators, wild pigs, all sorts of birds, Florida panthers, and other denizens of the wild. The tour also takes in the ranch's resident cattle and cougar in captivity. Reservations are needed for tours. An on-site restaurant serves "Cracker" chow in season. ✉ *8000 Rte. 31, Punta Gorda* ☎ *800/500–5583* 🌐 *www.babcockranchecotours.com* 🎟 *Ecotour $24; cost for other specialty tours varies* ✍ *Reservations essential.*

Calusa Heritage Trail

TRAIL | Affiliated with the University of Florida's natural history museum in Gainesville, this 0.7-mile interpretive walkway explores the site of an ancient Calusa village—more than 1,500 years old—with excellent signage, two intact shell mounds you can climb, the remains of a complex canal system, and ongoing archaeological research. Guided tours are given three times a week from January to April. Check the website for special tours and lecture events. ✉ *Randell Research Center, 13810 Waterfront Dr., Bokeelia, Pineland* ☎ *239/283–2157* 🌐 *www.flmnh.ufl.edu/rrc* 🎟 *$7 (suggested donation).*

ECHO Global Farm Tours & Nursery

GARDEN | FAMILY | ECHO is an international Christian nonprofit striving to end world hunger via creative farming. A 90-minute tour of its working farm is honestly fascinating; it takes you through seven simulated tropic-zone gardens and has you tasting leaves, walking through rain-forest habitat, visiting farm animals, stopping at a simulated Haitian school, witnessing urban gardens grown inside tires on rooftops, and learning about ECHO's mission. Although the group is religiously based, the tour guides are far from preachy, plus the organization's scope is all-inclusive, equipping and training people who deserve it no matter what their beliefs are. If you have time, spring for the Appropriate Technology Tour. It's held in a covered facility and runs slightly shorter than the basic Global Farm Tour, and you'll see simple contraptions that give ingenious solutions to everyday challenges in the developing world, like pressing seeds and making rope (spoiler alert—one involves a bicycle-powered saw). The ECHO Global Nursery and Gift Shop sells fruit trees and the same seeds ECHO distributes to impoverished farmers in 180 countries. ✉ *17391 Durrance Rd., North Fort Myers* ☎ *239/543–3246* 🌐 *www.echonet.org* 🎟 *$12.50.*

Shell Factory & Nature Park

AMUSEMENT PARK/WATER PARK | FAMILY | This entertainment complex, once just a quirky shopping destination and a survivor from Florida's roadside-attraction era, now contains eateries, an arcade, bumper boats, miniature golf, and a mining sluice where kids can pan for shells, fossils, and gemstones. Strolling the grounds is free, including seeing over $6 million worth of exhibits and displays, but some activities carry individual fees, and a separate admission is required to enter the Nature Park, which has the feel of a small zoo. There you can find llamas; a petting farm with sheep, pigs, and goats;

a walk-through aviary; an EcoLab; a touch center; and a gator slough. The Shell Factory hosts family-friendly events throughout the year, such as the Gumbo Fest in January. It's newest addition is the Soaring Eagle Zipline. ✉ *2787 N. Tamiami Trail, North Fort Myers* ☎ *239/995–2141* 🌐 *www.shellfactory.com* 🎟 *Shell Factory free; attractions starting at $2 each; Nature Park $13* ⏲ *Shell Factory daily 9–7; Nature Park daily 10–5.*

★ Sun Splash Family Waterpark
AMUSEMENT PARK/WATER PARK | FAMILY | Head here to cool off when summer swelters. Nearly two dozen wet and dry attractions include 10 thrill waterslides; the Sand Dollar Walk, where you step from one floating "sand dollar" to another; pint-sized Pro Racer flumes; a professional sand volleyball court; a family pool and Tot Spot; and a river-tube ride. Rates go down after 2 pm, plus the park offers Family Fun Night specials. ✉ *400 Santa Barbara Blvd., Cape Coral* ☎ *239/574–0558* 🌐 *www.sunsplashwaterpark.com* 🎟 *$17.95.*

Restaurants

Bert's Bar & Grill
$ | AMERICAN | Looking to hang out with the locals of Pine Island? Here you'll find cheap eats, live entertainment, a pool table, and a water view to boot. **Known for:** great views; grouper Reuben sandwiches; homemade Key lime pie. *$ Average main: $9* ✉ *4271 Pine Island Rd., Matlacha* ☎ *239/282–3232* 🌐 *www.bertsbar.com.*

Blue Dog Bar & Grill
$$ | SEAFOOD | FAMILY | Ask any resident where to go for local flavor, and they'll send you to the bright yellow building with a big dog in boots painted on the side. Even before entering the part restaurant, part community watering hole, you might catch a whiff of whatever the chef is slow cooking on the smoker. **Known for:** shrimp tacos with mango salsa; house-smoked fish dip; homemade Key lime pie. *$ Average main: $15* ✉ *4597 Pine Island Road, Matlacha* ☎ *239/558–4970* 🌐 *www.bluedogrestaurant.com.*

Rumrunners
$ | AMERICAN | Cape Coral's best casual cuisine is surprisingly affordable, considering the luxury condo development that rises around it and the size of the yachts that pull up to the docks. Caribbean in spirit, with lots of indoor and outdoor views of a mangrove-fringed waterway, it serves bistro specialties such as conch fritters, seafood potpie, bronzed salmon, and a warm chocolate bread pudding that is addictive. **Known for:** coconut fried shrimp; seafood potpie; Rumrunner cocktails. *$ Average main: $14* ✉ *Cape Harbour Marina, 5848 Cape Harbour*

Punta Gorda Day Trip

A half hour (23 miles) north of Fort Myers, the small, old town of Punta Gorda merits a day trip for its restaurants and historic sites. If you're driving to Boca Grande via U.S. 41, it also makes a nice stop along the way. On the mouth of the Peace River, where it empties into Charlotte Harbor, a new riverfront park, water views, and murals enliven the compact downtown historic district. Away from the downtown area, a classic-car museum, wildlife rehabilitation center, and waterfront shopping complex built into an old fish-packing plant fills out a day of sightseeing. Fishing and nature-watching tours also depart from the Fishermen's Village complex.

Dr., Cape Coral ✣ *Off Chiquita Blvd.* ☎ *239/542–0200* 🌐 *www.rumrunnersrestaurant.com.*

Siam Hut

$ | **THAI** | Lunch and dinner menus at this Cape Coral fixture let you design your own stir-fry, noodle, or fried-rice dish. Dinner specialties include fried crispy frogs' legs with garlic and black pepper, a sizzling shrimp platter, fried whole tilapia with curry sauce, salads, and pad Thai (rice noodles, egg, ground peanuts, vegetables, and choice of protein). **Known for:** duck royal with pineapple, tomato, and red curry; stir-fry dishes; special fried rice with meat and seafood. $ *Average main: $14* ✉ *4521 Del Prado Blvd., Cape Coral* ☎ *239/945–4247* 🌐 *www.siamhutcapecoral.com* ⏲ *Closed Sun. No lunch Sat.*

Casa Loma Motel

$ | **HOTEL** | Stay at this pretty little motel, 15 minutes from Fort Myers at the end of the Croton Canal, to be close to Cape Coral's attractions and escape the sticker shock of beachfront lodgings. **Pros:** kitchen facilities in rooms; free Wi-Fi; large sundeck with canal access. **Cons:** must drive to beach; on a busy street; decor a bit dated. $ *Rooms from: $119* ✉ *3608 Del Prado Blvd., Cape Coral* ☎ *239/549–6000, 877/227–2566* 🌐 *www.casalomamotel.com* *49 rooms* *No meals.*

Tarpon Lodge

$ | **B&B/INN** | A no-frills escape, this lodge, named for a local game fish, was built in 1926 on a sweep of green lawn with magnificent views out to sea. **Pros:** historic property; great restaurant; can dock boats overnight. **Cons:** some rooms are basic; far from other restaurants; quite far from beach by land. $ *Rooms from: $185* ✉ *13771 Waterfront Dr., Pineland* ☎ *239/283–3999* 🌐 *www.tarponlodge.com* *22 rooms* *Breakfast.*

The Westin Cape Coral Resort at Marina Village

$$$ | **RESORT** | Cape Coral's only luxury resort, this modern 19-story tower sits alongside a marina fringed with mangroves and caters to families and water-sports enthusiasts. **Pros:** designer touches; kids club; great kayaking. **Cons:** 45-minute ferry to beach; high-rise; far from everything. $ *Rooms from: $309* ✉ *5951 Silver King Blvd., Cape Coral* ☎ *239/541–5000,* 🌐 *www.westincapecoral.com* *264 units* *No meals.*

Gasparilla Island (Boca Grande)

43 miles northwest of Fort Myers.

Before roads to the Lower Gulf Coast were even talked about, wealthy northerners came by train to spend the winter at the Gasparilla Inn. The inn was completed in 1913 in Boca Grande on Gasparilla Island, named, legend has it, for a Spanish pirate who set up headquarters in these waters. Although condominiums and modern mansions occupy the rest of Gasparilla, much of the town of Boca Grande evokes another era. The mood is set by the Old Florida homes and tree-framed roadways. The island's calm is disrupted in the spring when anglers descend with a vengeance on Boca Grande Pass, considered among the best tarpon-fishing spots in the world.

GETTING HERE AND AROUND

Boca Grande is more than an hour's drive northwest of Fort Myers. Day-trippers can catch a charter boat or rent a boat, dock at a marina, and rent a bike or golf cart for a day of exploring and lunching. North of it stretches a long island, home to Don Pedro Island State Park and Palm Island Resort, both accessible only by boat. Also nearby is the off-the-beaten-path but car-accessible island

Did You Know?

Florida's Pine Island, about 30 minutes from Fort Myers, actively seeks to have its own charm and prohibits high-rise development. Visitors can enjoy viewing its mangroves, colorful galleries, and seafood houses.

of Manasota Key and its fishing resort community of Englewood Beach.

Sights

Gasparilla Island State Park and Port Boca Grande Lighthouse Museum
MUSEUM | The island's beaches are its greatest prize and lie within the state park at the south end. The long, narrow beach ends at Boca Grande Pass, famous for its deep waters and tarpon fishing. The pretty, two-story, circa-1890 lighthouse once marked the pass for mariners. In recent years it has been restored as a museum that explores the island's fishing and railroad heritage. The lighthouse is closed in August. ✉ *880 Belcher Rd., Boca Grande* ☎ *941/964–0060* 🌐 *www.floridastateparks.org* *$3 per vehicle; $3 suggested donation to lighthouse (exact change only).*

Restaurants

The Loose Caboose
$$$ | **AMERICAN** | Revered by many—including Katharine Hepburn in her time—for its homemade ice cream, this is also a good spot for comfort food and fresh seafood. Housed in the town's historic depot, it offers indoor and patio seating in an all-American setting. **Known for:** extremely rich (16% butterfat) ice cream; green tomatoes and crab cake appetizer; Caboose Thai shrimp. *$ Average main: $26* ✉ *433 W. 4th St., Boca Grande* ☎ *941/964–0440* 🌐 *www.loosecaboose.biz* *No dinner Wed. or Apr.–Dec.*

Hotels

The Boca Grande Resort
$$ | **RESORT** | Once known as Uncle Henry's, this marine-lodging-shopping complex north of downtown Boca Grande has undergone a serious upgrade and injection of character. **Pros:** intimate; top-notch restaurants; lots of character. **Cons:** distance from downtown; high-priced; no beach. *$ Rooms from: $219* ✉ *5800 Gasparilla Rd., Gasparilla Island* ☎ *941/964–4443* 🌐 *www.thebocagranderesort.com* *18 rooms* *No meals.*

Gasparilla Inn & Club
$$$ | **HOTEL** | Once the playground of social-register members such as the Vanderbilts and DuPonts, the gracious pale-yellow wooden hotel was built by shipping industrialists in the early 1900s. **Pros:** historic property; nicely renovated; plenty of activities. **Cons:** expensive rates; the quirks of a very old building; dress code. *$ Rooms from: $385* ✉ *500 Palm Ave., Boca Grande* ☎ *941/964–2201, 800/996–1913* 🌐 *www.gasparillainn.com* *160 units* *Some meals.*

Cabbage Key

5 miles south of Boca Grande.

Cabbage Key is the ultimate island-hopping escape in these parts. Some say Jimmy Buffett was inspired to write "Cheeseburger in Paradise" after a visit to its popular restaurant.

GETTING HERE AND AROUND

You'll need to take a boat—from Bokeelia or Pineland, on Pine Island, or from Captiva Island—to get to this island, which sits at mile marker 60 on the Intracoastal Waterway. Local operators offer day trips and luncheon cruises.

Hotels

Cabbage Key Inn
$ | **HOTEL** | Atop an ancient Calusa Indian shell mound and accessible only by boat, the friendly, somewhat quirky inn built by novelist and playwright Mary Roberts Rinehart in 1938 welcomes guests seeking quiet and isolation. **Pros:** plenty of solitude; Old Florida character; great shelling on nearby Cayo Costa. **Cons:**

two-night minimum stay; accessible only by boat or seaplane; limited amenities, some rooms have no TV. *Rooms from: $175* ✉ *Cabbage Key* ☎ *239/283–2278* 🌐 *www.cabbagekey.com* *14 units* *No meals.*

Sanibel and Captiva Islands

23 miles southwest of downtown Fort Myers.

Sanibel Island is famous as one of the world's best shelling grounds, a function of the unusual east–west orientation of the island's south end. Just as the tide is going out and after storms, the pickings can be superb, and shell seekers performing the telltale "Sanibel stoop" patrol every beach carrying bags of conchs, whelks, cockles, and other bivalves and gastropods. (Remember, it's unlawful to pick up live shells.) Away from the beach, flowery vegetation decorates small shopping complexes, pleasant resorts and condo complexes, mom-and-pop motels, and casual restaurants. But much of the two-lane road down the spine of the island is bordered by nature reserves that have made Sanibel as well known among bird-watchers as it is among seashell collectors.

Captiva Island, connected to the northern end of Sanibel by a bridge, is quirky and engaging. At the end of a twisty road lined with million-dollar mansions lies a delightful village of shops, eateries, and beaches.

GETTING HERE AND AROUND

Sanibel Island is approximately 23 miles southwest of downtown Fort Myers, and Captiva lies north of 12-mile-long Sanibel. If you're flying into Southwest Florida International Airport, an on-demand taxi for up to three passengers to Sanibel or Captiva costs about $60 to $68; additional passengers are charged $10 each. Sanibel Island is accessible from the mainland via the Sanibel Causeway (toll $6 round-trip). Captiva Island lies across a small pass from Sanibel's north end, accessible by bridge.

ESSENTIALS

VISITOR INFORMATION Sanibel and Captiva Islands Chamber of Commerce. ✉ *1159 Causeway Rd., Sanibel* ☎ *239/472–1080* 🌐 *www.sanibel-captiva.org.*

Sights

★ Bailey-Matthews National Shell Museum

MUSEUM | FAMILY | There have been big changes at the museum and it all starts before you even enter, with giant shell photos on the exterior of the building by nature photographer Henry Domke. Once inside there are more than 30 permanent and short-term exhibits. See a life-size display of native Calusa and how they used shells. From tiny to enormous, view local specimens and a variety from around the world. Play in the colorful kids' lab. Watch movies about how shells are formed and where to find them. Get a close-up look at mollusks in the 8-foot-long, live-viewing tank. The museum has two full-time marine biologists who lead daily tank talks and host daily guided beach walks. From colossal squids to Shelling 101, make this your first stop and you'll be giving your own talks on the beach. Don't miss the museum store, filled with upscale nautical gifts. Look for the addition of an Aquarium in early 2020. ✉ *3075 Sanibel–Captiva Rd., Sanibel* ☎ *239/395–2233, 888/679–6450* 🌐 *www.shellmuseum.org* *$15.*

Clinic for the Rehabilitation of Wildlife (CROW)

NATURE PRESERVE | In existence for more than 40 years, the clinic currently cares for more than 4,000 wildlife patients each year. The center offers a look inside the world of wildlife medicine through exhibits, videos, interactive displays, touch screens, and critter cams that feed live footage from four different animal spaces. Wildlife walks give a behind-the-scenes look and can be reserved for $25 per person. This is an excellent facility, but the displays may be too graphic for young visitors. ✉ *3883 Sanibel–Captiva Rd., Sanibel* ☎ *239/472–3644* 🌐 *www.crowclinic.org* 🎫 *$12.*

★ J. N. "Ding" Darling National Wildlife Refuge

NATURE PRESERVE | **FAMILY** | More than half of Sanibel is occupied by the subtly beautiful 6,300 acres of wetlands and jungly mangrove forests named after a conservation-minded Pulitzer prize–winning political cartoonist. The masses of roseate spoonbills and ibis and the winter flock of white pelicans here make for a good show even if you're not a die-hard bird-watcher. Birders have counted some 230 species, including herons, ospreys, and the timid mangrove cuckoo. Raccoons, otters, alligators, and a lone American crocodile also may be spotted. The 4-mile Wildlife Drive is the main way to explore the preserve; drive, walk, or bicycle along it, or ride a specially designed open-air tram with an onboard naturalist. QR-coded signs link to interactive YouTube videos and a new Discover Ding app combines social media, GPS, and trivia to make learning on-site fun. There are also a couple of short walking trails, including one to a Calusa shell mound. Or explore from the water via canoe or kayak (guided tours are available). The best time for bird-watching is in the early morning and about an hour before or after low tide; the observation tower along the road offers prime viewing. Interactive exhibits in the free visitor center, at the entrance to the refuge, demonstrate the refuge's various ecosystems and explain its status as a rest stop along a major bird-migration route. A new hands-on manatee exhibit was recently unveiled, too. Wildlife Drive is closed to vehicular traffic on Friday, but you can still kayak and do tours from the Tarpon Bay Recreation Area. ✉ *1 Wildlife Dr., Sanibel* ✣ *Off Sanibel–Captiva Rd. at MM 2* ☎ *239/472–1100 for refuge, 239/472–8900 kayaking and tours* 🌐 *www.fws.gov/dingdarling* 🎫 *$5 per car, $1 for pedestrians and bicyclists, tram $13.*

Sanibel–Captiva Conservation Foundation

NATURE PRESERVE | **FAMILY** | For a quiet walk to watch for inhabitants of Sanibel's interior wetlands, follow some or all of the 4½ miles of interlocking walking trails here and climb the observation tower. View information about wildlife research projects, a butterfly house, live turtles, snakes, and a marine touch tank at the nature center. In winter, guided walks and programs are available on and off property. ✉ *3333 Sanibel–Captiva Rd., Sanibel* ☎ *239/472–2329* 🌐 *www.sccf.org* 🎫 *$5; 17 and under are free.*

Sanibel Historical Museum & Village

MUSEUM | Charming buildings from the island's past include a general store, a one-room schoolhouse, a 1927 post office, a tearoom, a 1925 winter-vacation cottage, a 1898 fishing cottage, and the 1913 Rutland House Museum, containing old documents and photographs, artifacts, and period furnishings. All buildings are authentic and have been moved from their original locations to the museum grounds. ✉ *950 Dunlop Rd., Sanibel* ☎ *239/472–4648* 🌐 *www.sanibelmuseum.org* 🎫 *$10.*

Beaches

Red tide, an occasional natural beach occurrence that kills fish, also has negative effects on the human respiratory system. It causes scratchy throats, runny eyes and noses, and coughing. Although the effects aren't long-term, it's a good idea to avoid the beach when red tide is in the vicinity (look for posted signs).

Continued on page 410

SHELL-BENT ON SANIBEL ISLAND

by Chelle Koster Walton

Sanibel Island beachgoers are an unusual breed: they pray for storms; they muck around tidal pools rather than play in the waves; and instead of lifting their faces to the sun, they have their heads in the sand—almost literally—as they engage in the so-called "Sanibel Stoop."

Odd? Not when you consider that this is Florida's prime shelling location, thanks to the island's east-west bend (rather than the usual north-south orientation of most beaches along the coastline). The lay of the land means a treasure trove of shells—more than 400 species—wash up from the Caribbean.

These gifts from the sea draw collectors of all levels. Come winter, when the cold and storms kill the shellfish and push them ashore, a parade of stoopers forms on Sanibel's shores.

The reasons people shell are as varied as the shellers themselves. The hardcore compete and sell, whereas others collect simply for the fun of discovery, for displaying, for use in gardens, or for crafts. The typical Sanibel tourist who comes seeking shells is usually looking for souvenirs and gifts to take home.

WHERE TO SHELL

Shelling is good anywhere along Sanibel's gulf-front. Remote **Bowman's Beach** (*off Sanibel-Captiva Road at Bowman's Beach Rd.*) offers the least competition. Other public accesses include **Lighthouse Beach** (Periwinkle Way), **Tarpon Bay Beach** (Tarpon Bay Rd.), and **Turner Beach** (Sanibel-Captiva Rd.). If you want to ditch your car (and crowds), walk or bike using **resident access beaches** (along the Gulf drives). If you want to search with others and get a little guidance, you can join shelling cruises from Sanibel and Captiva islands to the un-bridged island of Cayo Costa. Cruises leave from both islands and usually include pickup from your hotel or condo. Most are done on a covered catamaran.

Captiva Island
Captiva
Turner Beach
Bowman's Beach
SANIBEL ISLAND
Sanibel
Lighthouse Beach
Tarpon Bay Beach

Cockle | Conch | Junonia

Lightning Whelk | Sand Dollar | Scallop

TYPES OF SHELLS

Cockles: The common Sanibel bivalve (hinged two-shelled mollusk), the heart cockle (named for its Valentine shape) is larger and more bowl-like than the scallop, which makes it a popular, colorful find for soap dishes, ashtrays, and catch-alls.

Conchs: Of the large family of conchs, fighting conchs are most commonly found on Sanibel. Contrary to its macho name, the fighting conch is one of the few vegetarian gastropods. While alive, the shell flames brilliant orange; it fades under tropical sunshine.

Junonias: These olive-shaped, spotted gastropods (single-shell mollusks) are Sanibel's signature, though somewhat rare, finds. People who hit upon one get their picture in the local paper. Resorts have been accused of planting them on their beaches for publicity.

Lightning Whelks: The lightning variety of whelk is "left-handed"—opening on the opposite side from most gastropods. Early islanders used them for tools. The animals lay their miniature shell eggs in papery egg-case chains on the beach.

Sand Dollars: Classified as an echinoderm not a mollusk, the thin sand dollar is brown and fuzzy while alive, studded with tiny tubes for breathing and moving. Unoccupied shells bleach to a beautiful white textured pattern, ideal for hanging on Christmas trees.

Scallops: No surprise that these pretty little bivalves have "scalloped" edges. They invented the word. Plentiful on Sanibel beaches, they come in a variety of colors and sizes.

SHELLING LIKE A PRO

Veteran shell-seekers go out before the sun rises so they can be the first on the beach after a storm or night of high tides. (Storms and cold fronts bring in the best catches.)

Most shellers use a bag to collect their finds. But once you're ready to pack shells for transit, wash them thoroughly to remove sand and debris. Then wrap fragile species such as sand dollars and sea urchins in tissue paper or cotton, then newspaper. Last, place your shells in a cardboard or plastic box. To display them, restore the shell's luster by brushing it with baby oil.

Sanibel shops sell books and supplies for identifying your finds and turning them into craft projects.

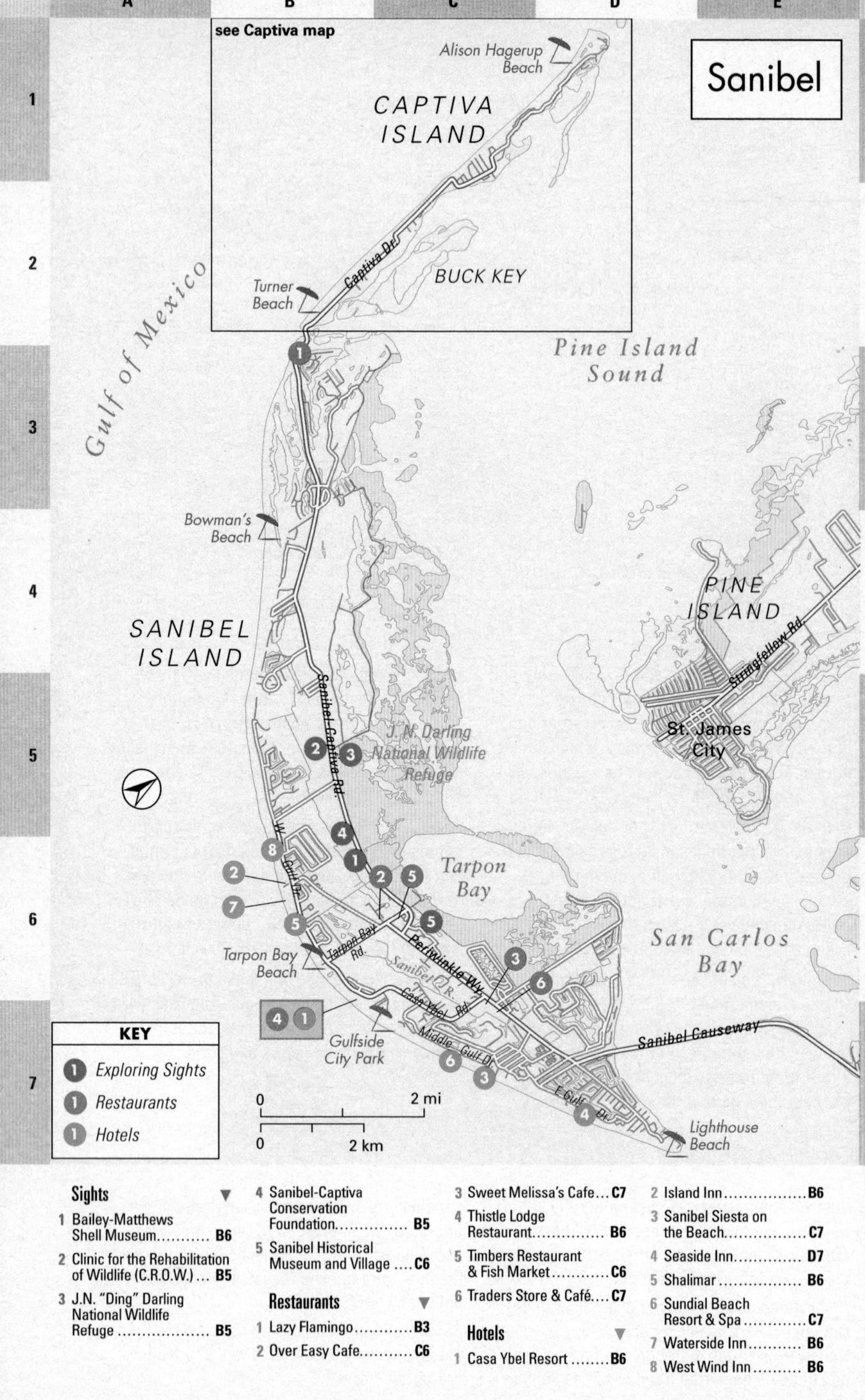
A
B
C
D
E
1
2
3
4
5
6
7
Sanibel
see Captiva map
Alison Hagerup Beach
CAPTIVA ISLAND
Captiva Dr.
BUCK KEY
Turner Beach
Gulf of Mexico
Pine Island Sound
Bowman's Beach
SANIBEL ISLAND
PINE ISLAND
Stringfellow Rd.
St. James City
Sanibel-Captiva Rd.
J. N. Darling National Wildlife Refuge
W. Gulf Dr.
Tarpon Bay
Tarpon Bay Rd.
Periwinkle Wy.
Tarpon Bay Beach
Sanibel-C.R.
Casa Ybel Rd.
San Carlos Bay
Middle Gulf Dr.
Gulfside City Park
Sanibel Causeway
E Gulf Dr.
Lighthouse Beach
KEY
Exploring Sights
Restaurants
Hotels
0
2 mi
0
2 km
Sights
1 Bailey-Matthews Shell Museum........... B6
2 Clinic for the Rehabilitation of Wildlife (C.R.O.W.) ... B5
3 J.N. "Ding" Darling National Wildlife Refuge B5
4 Sanibel-Captiva Conservation Foundation.............. B5
5 Sanibel Historical Museum and Village C6
Restaurants
1 Lazy Flamingo............B3
2 Over Easy Cafe........... C6
3 Sweet Melissa's Cafe... C7
4 Thistle Lodge Restaurant............... B6
5 Timbers Restaurant & Fish Market............ C6
6 Traders Store & Café.... C7
Hotels
1 Casa Ybel Resort B6
2 Island Inn................. B6
3 Sanibel Siesta on the Beach................. C7
4 Seaside Inn.............. D7
5 Shalimar B6
6 Sundial Beach Resort & Spa C7
7 Waterside Inn........... B6
8 West Wind Inn.......... B6

SANIBEL

★ Bowman's Beach

BEACH—SIGHT | **FAMILY** | This long, wide beach on Sanibel's northwest end is the island's most secluded strand, but it also has the most amenities. Park facilities include a playground, picnic tables, grills, bathrooms, and bike racks. It is famed for its shell collecting and spectacular sunsets at the north end—try to spot the green flash, said to occur just as the sun sinks below the horizon. For utmost seclusion, walk north from the two main access points where bridges cross an estuary to reach the beach. It's a long walk from the parking lot over the estuary to the beach, so pack accordingly and plan on a long stay. Tall Australian pines provide shade behind the white sands. Typically gentle waves are conducive to swimming and wading with kids. **Amenities:** parking (fee); showers; toilets. **Best for:** sunsets; swimming; walking. ✉ *Bowman Beach Rd., at Blind Pass, Sanibel* ☎ *239/472–3700* 🎫 *Parking $5 per hr.*

Gulfside Park Preserve

BEACH—SIGHT | **FAMILY** | The beach is quiet, safe from strong currents, and good for solitude, bird-watching, and shell-finding. There are restrooms, and long stretches to stroll. The white sand is slightly coarse and borders a park with shade, picnic tables, and a loop nature trail. Low-rise resorts and homes lie to the east and west of the parking lot accesses. **Amenities:** parking (fee); toilets. **Best for:** swimming; walking. ✉ *Algiers La., Sanibel* ✥ *Off Casa Ybel Rd.* ☎ *239/472–3700* 🎫 *Parking $5 per hr.*

Lighthouse Beach

BEACH—SIGHT | At Sanibel's eastern tip, the beach is guarded by the frequently photographed Sanibel Lighthouse, built in 1884, before the island was settled. The lighthouse is not currently open to the public, but there's talk of refurbishing the tower so visitors can climb to the top. The park rounds the island's east end for waterfront on both the Gulf and bay, where a fishing pier draws avid anglers. Shaded nature trails connect the two shores; the park is listed on the Great Florida Birding Trail because of its fall and spring migration fallouts. A pair of ospreys frequently perch on the lighthouse railing; look and listen for these local residents while you're there. **Amenities:** parking (fee); toilets. **Best for:** sunrise; walking; windsurfing. ✉ *East end of Periwinkle Way, Sanibel* ☎ *239/472–3700* 🎫 *Parking $5 per hr.*

Tarpon Bay Beach

BEACH—SIGHT | This centrally located beach is safer for swimming than beaches at the passes, where waters move swiftly. It is, however, one of the more populated beaches, lined with low-rise condos and resorts set back behind vegetation. Casa Ybel Resort lies east of the public access; other smaller resorts can be found along the stretch to the west. The parking lot is a five-minute walk from the beach, so drop off your gang and gear before you park (the lot is open daily from 7 am to 7 pm). At the beach, you can walk for miles in either direction on soft white sand studded with shells. **Amenities:** parking (fee); toilets. **Best for:** swimming; walking. ✉ *Tarpon Bay Rd. at Gulf Dr., off Sanibel–Capriva Rd., Sanibel* ✥ *Drive to the end of W. Gulf Dr. and east to Casa Ybel Rd.* ☎ *239/472–3700* 🎫 *Parking $5 per hr.*

CAPTIVA

Alison Hagerup Beach Park

BEACH—SIGHT | **FAMILY** | This park, once called Captiva Beach, is acclaimed as one of the nation's most romantic beaches for its fabulous sunsets—the best view on Sanibel and Captiva. Shells stud the white, wide sands. The parking lot is filled with potholes and is small, so arrive early, watch where you're driving, and bring an umbrella if you need shade. The beach can get crowded, especially in the busy winter and spring seasons. Facilities are limited to portable restrooms and a volleyball net, but stores and restaurants are nearby. South Seas Island Resort lines the north end of the beach. **Amenities:** parking (fee); toilets. **Best for:** sunsets; swimming; walking. ✉ *Captiva Dr., at the north end, Captiva* 🎫 *Parking 2 hrs $5, 4 hrs or more $20.*

Turner Beach

BEACH—SIGHT | Looking for some romance? This is a prime sunset-watching spot on the southern point of Captiva. Strong currents through Blind Pass make swimming tricky but shelling amazing, and parking is limited. Surfers head here when winds whip up the waves. The beach is narrower than in other parts of the island. No buildings sit on the beach, but 'Tween Waters Resort is across the road to the north of the public access, and Castaways Beach & Bay Cottages is beachfront across the bridge on the Sanibel side of Blind Pass. Restaurants are nearby. **Amenities:** parking (fee); toilets. **Best for:** sunsets; surfing; walking. ✉ *Captiva Dr., at Blind Pass, Captiva* 🎫 *Parking $5 per hr.*

Restaurants

SANIBEL

Lazy Flamingo

$ | **AMERICAN** | **FAMILY** | At two Sanibel locations, plus two more in neighboring Fort Myers and Pine Island Sound, this is a friendly neighborhood hangout enjoyed by locals and visitors alike. All these restaurants have a funky nautical look à la Key West and a popular following for their Dead Parrot Wings (Buffalo wings coated with tongue-scorching hot sauce), mesquite-grilled grouper sandwiches, burgers, and steamer pots. **Known for:** mesquite-grilled grouper; family-friendly atmosphere; fiery Dead Parrot Wings. [$] *Average main: $12* ✉ *6520C Pine Ave., Sanibel* ☎ *239/472–5353* 🌐 *www.lazyflamingo.com.*

Over Easy Café

$$ | **AMERICAN** | Locals head to this chicken-theme eatery mainly for breakfast and lunch, although it also serves dinner in season. Kick-start the day with the egg Reuben sandwich, veggie Benedict, pancakes, or omelets such as crab and asparagus or "meat-lovers." **Known for:** smoked salmon Benedict; all-day breakfast; egg Reuben sandwich. [$] *Average main: $16* ✉ *630-1 Tarpon Bay Rd., Sanibel* ☎ *239/472–2625* 🌐 *www.overeasycafesanibel.com* 🕑 *No dinner.*

★ Sweet Melissa's Cafe

$$$ | **MODERN AMERICAN** | You've seen them before, those people who take photos of their food: you'll become one of them when you eat here. Choose from full portions or small plates, but the latter are recommended so that you can savor more outstanding dishes in one sitting. **Known for:** imaginative cuisine; fish stew; impeccable service. [$] *Average main: $27* ✉ *1625 Periwinkle Way, Sanibel* ☎ *239/472–1956* 🌐 *www.sweetmelissascafe.com* 🕑 *No lunch weekends.*

★ Thistle Lodge Restaurant

$$$$ | **CONTEMPORARY** | Now this is romance: the lodge was built as a wedding gift from a husband to his wife and is now a gift to those lucky enough to dine here. The food is fresh, elegant, and flavorful with entrées that span everything from Parmesan-and-herb-crusted black grouper to Asian braised beef short ribs. **Known for:** romantic atmosphere; fresh seafood; Gulf views. [$] *Average main: $35* ✉ *Casa Ybel Resort, 2255 W. Gulf Dr., Sanibel* ☎ *239/472–9200* 🌐 *www.thistlelodge.com.*

Timbers Restaurant & Fish Market

$$$ | **SEAFOOD** | One of Sanibel's longest-running restaurants successfully satisfies visitors and residents with consistent quality and a full net of nightly catches and specials. The fish market inside the door is a sure sign

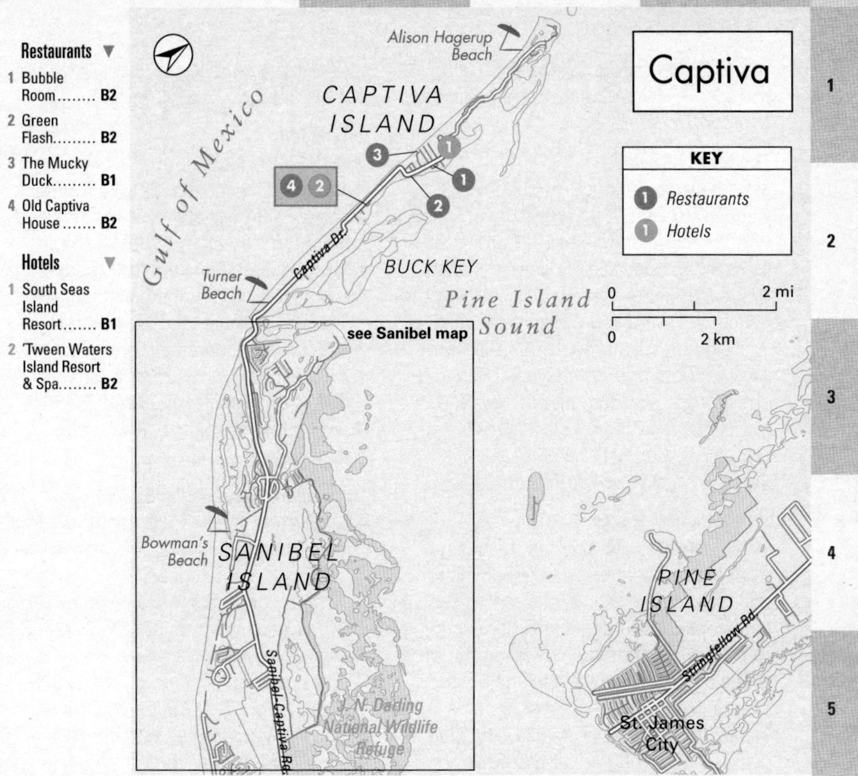

of freshness, and most of the dishes showcase seafood simply and flavorfully. **Known for:** crunchy grouper; seafood bisque; seafood market on-site. *Average main: $21* *703 Tarpon Bay Rd., Sanibel* *239/472–3128* *www.prawnbroker.com.*

★ Traders Store & Café

$$$ | **AMERICAN** | In the midst of a warehouse-size store, this bistro, accented with stunning Florida photography from Alan Maltz, is a favorite of locals. The marvelous sesame-seared tuna lunch salad with Asian slaw and wasabi vinaigrette exemplifies the creative fare. **Known for:** barbecue ribs; fresh fish dishes; comfortable atmosphere. *Average main: $26* *1551 Periwinkle Way, Sanibel* *239/472–7242* *www.traderssanibel.com.*

CAPTIVA

Bubble Room

$$$ | **AMERICAN** | **FAMILY** | This lively, kitschy visitors' favorite is fun for families and nostalgic types with fat wallets. Servers wear scout uniforms and funny headgear. **Known for:** mile-high slices of cake; kitschy decor; prime rib. *Average main: $25* *15001 Captiva Dr., Captiva* *239/472–5558* *www.bubbleroomrestaurant.com.*

Green Flash

$$$ | **SEAFOOD** | Good food and sweeping views of quiet waters and a mangrove island keep boaters and others coming back to this casual indoor-outdoor restaurant. Seafood dominates, but there's a bit of everything on the menu. **Known for:** shrimp bisque; Captiva steam pot (seafood); grouper tacos. *Average* main: $23 ✉ 15183 Captiva Dr., Captiva ☎ 239/472–3337 🌐 www.greenflashcaptiva.com.

The Mucky Duck

$$$ | **SEAFOOD** | A longtime fixture on Captiva's beach, it parodies British pubs with its name and sense of humor. Since 1975 it has consistently drawn crowds that occupy themselves with walking the beach and watching the sunset while waiting for their name to be called for a table indoors or out. **Known for:** fish-and-chips; fresh seafood; frozen Key lime pie. *$ Average main: $24 ✉ 11546 Andy Rosse La., Captiva ☎ 239/472–3434 🌐 www.muckyduck.com.*

★ Old Captiva House

$$$$ | **SEAFOOD** | Just across the street from the beach, this wonderfully historic and newly renovated restaurant is casual, comfortable, and considered by many to be the best fine-dining restaurant on Captiva Island. Entrées include seafood dishes like the blackened snapper with watermelon cucumber salad, and land dishes like pomegranate-glazed lamb chops.Tempting appetizers, creative salads, and tantalizing desserts round out the menu. **Known for:** romantic atmosphere; fresh seafood and sushi; good wine selection. *$ Average main: $32 ✉ 'Tween Waters Inn, 15951 Captiva Dr., Captiva ☎ 239/472–5161 🌐 oldcaptivahouse.com.*

Hotels

SANIBEL

★ Casa Ybel Resort

$$$$ | **RESORT** | **FAMILY** | Palm trees, quiet ponds, and gazebos set the mood at this resort on 23 acres of Gulf-facing grounds. **Pros:** on the beach; good restaurants; lots of recreational opportunities. **Cons:** spa treatments in-room only; minimum-stay requirement in some units; pricey. *$ Rooms from: $599 ✉ 2255 W. Gulf Dr., Sanibel ☎ 239/472–3145, 800/276–4753 🌐 www.casaybelresort.com 114 units No meals.*

Island Inn

$$$ | **RESORT** | Choose from your own cottage on the beach, or take your pick from six different styles of modernized hotel rooms at the most established inn on Sanibel. **Pros:** right on the beach; free breakfast; laundry facilities. **Cons:** minimum stays in season; furniture and bathrooms are dated in some units; small pool area. *$ Rooms from: $360 ✉ 3111 W. Gulf Dr., Sanibel ☎ 239/472–1561 🌐 www.islandinn.com 49 units Breakfast.*

★ Sanibel Siesta on the Beach

$$$ | **RENTAL** | **FAMILY** | You might want to move right in and never leave once you discover these luxurious two-bedroom/two-bath condos right on the sand. **Pros:** on the beach; swimming pool; free Wi-Fi. **Cons:** minimum stays; office closes early; limited parking. *$ Rooms from: $330 ✉ 1246 Fulgur St., Sanibel ☎ 239/472–4117 🌐 www.sanibelsiesta.com 67 units No meals.*

Seaside Inn

$$ | **HOTEL** | Tucked among the tropical greenery, this beachfront inn is a pleasant alternative to the area's larger resorts. **Pros:** intimate feel; lots of character; beautiful beachfront. **Cons:** no on-site restaurant; cramped parking lot; daily resort fee. *$ Rooms from: $299 ✉ 541 E. Gulf Dr., Sanibel ☎ 239/472–1400, 866/565–5092 🌐 www.seasideinn.com 42 units Breakfast.*

Shalimar

$$$ | **HOTEL** | Well-maintained grounds and an inviting beach appeal at this small property. **Pros:** on the beach; intimate feel; variety of accommodations. **Cons:** no restaurant on-site; no-frills plastic beach chairs; interiors on some units need updating. *$ Rooms from: $335 ✉ 2823 W. Gulf Dr., Sanibel ☎ 239/472–1353, 800/472–1353 🌐 www.shalimar.com 33 units No meals.*

Sundial Beach Resort and Spa
$$ | RESORT | FAMILY | With multimillion-dollar renovations, Sanibel's largest resort encompasses 400 privately owned studio, one-, two-, and three-bedroom low-rise condo units, about half of which are in its rental program. **Pros:** great beach; plenty of amenities; good on-site restaurants. **Cons:** conference crowds; packed pool area; pricey per-night resort fee. *Rooms from: $279 1451 Middle Gulf Dr., Sanibel 239/472–4151, 866/565–5093 www.sundialresort.com 184 units No meals.*

Waterside Inn
$$ | HOTEL | Palm trees, sea-grape trees, pastel cottages, and a tiki on the Gulf set the scene at this quiet beachside vacation spot. **Pros:** beachfront location; intimate feel; small pets allowed in most cottages. **Cons:** office closes at night; cottage interiors are worn; parking for only one car per unit. *Rooms from: $293 3033 W. Gulf Dr., Sanibel 239/472–1345, 800/741–6166 www.watersideinn.net 27 units No meals.*

West Wind Inn
$$$ | HOTEL | Families and couples flock to this resort for its upscale, West Gulf Drive location on the residential side of the island. **Pros:** on the beach; quiet side of the island; laundry facilities on-site. **Cons:** Wi-Fi can be sporadic; pool towels are small and wafer thin; updates have increased the nightly rate. *Rooms from: $340 3345 W. Gulf Dr., Sanibel 239/472–1541 www.westwindinn.com 103 rooms No meals.*

CAPTIVA

★ South Seas Island Resort
$$$ | RESORT | FAMILY | This full-service 330-acre resort feels as lush as its name suggests, and with 18 swimming pools (one with two tubular slides), private restaurants including Doc Ford's, shops, a full-service spa, a nature center stocked with live animals, a family interactive center, and a 9-hole beachfront golf course, it won't disappoint. **Pros:** full range of amenities; exclusive feel; car-free transportation. **Cons:** high rates in season; a bit isolated; spread out. *Rooms from: $339 5400 Plantation Rd., Captiva 239/472–5111, 888/222–7848 www.southseas.com 471 rooms No meals.*

'Tween Waters Island Resort & Spa
$$ | B&B/INN | Besides its great beach-to-bay location, this inn has historic value and in 2011 was listed in the National Register of Historic Places. **Pros:** great views; lots of water-sports options; free Wi-Fi. **Cons:** beach is across the road; pay to upgrade to premium Wi-Fi ; $19.99 resort fee if you don't book direct. *Rooms from: $280 Captiva Dr., Captiva 239/472–5161, 800/223–5865 www.tween-waters.com 138 units No meals.*

Shopping

Sanibel is known for its art galleries, shell shops, and one-of-a-kind boutiques; the several small open-air shopping complexes are inviting, with their tropical flowers and shady ficus trees.

SANIBEL

Periwinkle Place
SHOPPING CENTERS/MALLS | The largest complex of outdoor Sanibel shopping has 26 shops in a parklike setting on 7 acres. Fountains, gazebos, and a playground make it even more family-friendly. *2075 Periwinkle Way, Sanibel 734/769–2289 www.periwinkleplace.com.*

Seashells.com
LOCAL SPECIALTIES | Among the island's cache of shell shops, this one is favored by serious collectors and crafters because of its reasonable prices and the knowledgeable family that runs it. It's super easy to find, located right on the main drag. *905 Fitzhugh St., Sanibel 239/472–1603 www.seashells.com.*

She Sells Sea Shells

LOCAL SPECIALTIES | At She Sells Sea Shells, everything imaginable is made from shells, from mirrors to lamps to Christmas ornaments. The owner wrote the book on shell art, and you can buy it here. You can also purchase local shells, like the prized junonia and pick up a T-shirt at a fair price. ✉ *1157 Periwinkle Way, Sanibel* ☎ *239/472–6991* 🌐 *www.sanibelshellcrafts.com.*

CAPTIVA

★ Jungle Drums

ART GALLERIES | Expect the unexpected in wildlife art, where fish, sea turtles, and other creatures are depicted with utmost creativity and touches of whimsy. If you're looking for souvenirs above and beyond the usual, or unique jewelry, paintings, sculptures, and pottery—this is the place. ✉ *11532 Andy Rosse La., Captiva* ☎ *239/395–2266* 🌐 *www.jungle-drumsgallery.com* 🕑 *Closed Sun.*

Activities

BIKING

Everyone bikes around flat-as-a-pancake Sanibel and Captiva—on bikeways that edge the main highway in places, on the road through the wildlife refuge, and along side streets. Free maps are available at bicycle liveries.

Billy's Bikes

BICYCLING | Rent by the hour or the day from this Sanibel outfitter, which also rents motorized scooters and leads Segway tours. They even have beach gear like chairs, umbrellas, and bodyboards. ✉ *1470 Periwinkle Way, Sanibel* ☎ *239/472–5248* 🌐 *www.billysrentals.com.*

Yolo Watersports

BICYCLING | Everything you need to spend time at the beach is here. You'll find bikes and water-sports recreation rentals of all kinds (sailboats, WaveRunners, paddleboards), along with gear, apparel, accessories, and more. ✉ *11534 Andy Rosse La., Captiva* ☎ *239/472–1296* 🌐 *www.yolowatersports.com.*

CANOEING AND KAYAKING

Tarpon Bay Explorers

CANOEING/ROWING/SKULLING | One of the best ways to scout out the wildlife refuge is by paddle. Rent a canoe or kayak from the refuge's official concessionaire and explore at your leisure. The kayak water trail is easy to follow, simply paddle your way along 17 markers and see a bevy of birds and other wildlife. Guided tours by kayak or pontoon boat are also offered and worthwhile for visitors unfamiliar with the ecosystem. Their on-site touch tank gives a hands-on learning experience about local sea life. ✉ *900 Tarpon Bay Rd., Sanibel* ☎ *239/472–8900* 🌐 *www.tarponbayexplorers.com.*

FISHING

Local anglers head out to catch mackerel, pompano, grouper, snook, snapper, tarpon, and shark.

Sanibel Marina

FISHING | To find a charter captain on Sanibel, visit their on-site Ship Store or give them a call. ✉ *634 N. Yachtsman Dr., Sanibel* ☎ *239/472–2723* 🌐 *www.sanibelmarina.com.*

'Tween Waters Marina

FISHING | On Captiva, this is the place to look for guides. You can also rent kayaks, canoes, stand-up paddleboards, and other recreational watercrafts. ✉ *'Tween Waters Inn, 15951 Captiva Dr., Captiva* ☎ *239/472–5161* 🌐 *www.tween-waters.com/marina.*

GOLF

Dunes Golf & Tennis Club

GOLF | When your back nine are sanctioned as a wildlife preserve by the Audubon Cooperative Society—even if you play poorly—you're rewarded with lusher than lush fairways and more wildlife than you can shake a stick at. Bring your camera if you golf here, as it's not every day that bald eagles watch you play. Water hazards at every hole will have you losing more balls than usual, so bring plenty. Hole 10 is the toughest, which explains why most wish it were a par 5 instead of a par 4. Go for a long, straight tee shot and watch out for the water (and the gators). ✉ *949 Sandcastle Rd., Sanibel* ☎ *239/472–2535* 🌐 *www.dunesgolfsanibel.com* 🎫 *$125* ⛳ *18 holes, 5583 yards, par 70.*

Fort Myers Beach (Estero Island)

18 miles southwest of Fort Myers.

Crammed with motels, hotels, and restaurants, Estero Island is one of Fort Myers's more frenetic Gulf playgrounds. Dolphins frequently frolic in Estero Bay, part of the Intracoastal Waterway, and marinas provide a starting point for boating adventures, including sunset cruises, sightseeing cruises, and deep-sea fishing. At the southern tip, a bridge leads to Lovers Key State Park.

GETTING HERE AND AROUND

San Carlos Boulevard in Fort Myers leads to Fort Myers Beach's high bridge, Times Square, and Estero Boulevard, the island's main drag. Estero Island is 18 miles southwest of Fort Myers.

Beaches

Lovers Key State Park

BEACH—SIGHT | Once a little-known secret, this out-of-the-way park encompassing 1,616 acres on four barrier islands and several uninhabited islets is popular among beachgoers and birders. Bike, hike, walk, or paddle the park's trails (rentals available); go shelling on its 2½ miles of white-sand beach; take a boat tour; or have a beach picnic under the trees. Trams run regularly from 9 to 4:30 to deliver you and your gear to South Beach. The ride is short but often dusty. North Beach is a five-minute walk from the concession area and parking lot. Watch for osprey, bald eagles, herons, ibis, pelicans, and roseate spoonbills, or sign up for a free excursion to learn fishing and nature photography. On the park's bay side, across the road from the beach entrance, playgrounds and a picnic area cater to families, plus there are boat ramps, kayak rentals, and a bait shop. **Amenities:** food and drink; parking (fee); showers; toilets; water sports. **Best for:** swimming; walking. ✉ *8700 Estero Blvd., Fort Myers Beach* ☎ *239/463–4588* 🌐 *www.floridastateparks.org/loverskey* 🎫 *$4–$8 per vehicle, $2 for pedestrians and bicyclists.*

Lynn Hall Memorial Park

CITY PARK | FAMILY | At the 17-acre park in the commercial northern part of Estero Island, the wide, sandy shore slopes gradually into the usually tranquil and warm Gulf waters, providing safe swimming for children. And since houses, restaurants, condominiums, and hotels (including the Best Western Beach Resort and Pink Shell Resort north of the parking lot) line most of the beach, you're never far from civilization. There are picnic pavilions and barbecue grills, as well as playground equipment and a free fishing pier. The park is part of a pedestrian mall with a number of beach shops and restaurants steps away. The parking lot fills early on sunny days. **Amenities:** food and drink; parking (fee); showers; toilets; water sports. **Best for:** partiers; sunsets; walking. ✉ *Estero Blvd. at San Carlos Blvd., to Bowditch Point Park, Fort Myers Beach* ☎ *239/463–1116* 🌐 *www.leeparks.org* 🎫 *Parking $2 per hr.*

Restaurants

Doc Ford's Rum Bar & Grille

$$ | **MODERN AMERICAN** | For dependably well-prepared food with a water view, Doc Ford's is the top choice in Fort Myers Beach. A spin-off of a Sanibel Island original, its name and theme come from a murder-mystery series by local celebrity author Randy Wayne White. **Known for:** Yucatan shrimp, steamed with spicy Key lime butter; fish tacos; lively atmosphere. *Average main: $20* *708 Fisherman's Wharf, Fort Myers Beach* *239/765–9660* *www.docfordsfortmyersbeach.com.*

Matanzas Inn

$$$ | **SEAFOOD** | Watch boats coming and going whether you sit inside or out at this rustic Old Florida–style restaurant right on the docks alongside the Intracoastal Waterway. When the weather cooperates, enjoy the view from the shaded outdoor tables. **Known for:** pizza at Petey's Upper Deck; fresh seafood; slow, sometimes grumpy servers. *Average main: $24* *416 Crescent St., Fort Myers Beach* *239/463–3838* *www.matanzas.com.*

Parrot Key Caribbean Grill

$$$ | **SEAFOOD** | For something more contemporary than Fort Myers Beach's traditional shrimp and seafood houses, head to San Carlos Island on the east side of the high bridge where the shrimp boats dock. Parrot Key sits marina-side near the shrimp docks, offering a casual vibe that exudes merriment with its Floribbean cuisine and island music. **Known for:** Caribbean-inspired cuisine; seafood nachos; live music most nights. *Average main: $24* *2500 Main St., Fort Myers Beach* *239/463–3257* *www.myparrotkey.com.*

The Plaka

$ | **GREEK** | A casual long-timer and a favorite for a quick breakfast, filling lunch, and sunset dinner, Plaka—named after the historic neighborhood in Athens—has typical Greek fare. Expect standards like moussaka, pastitsio, gyros, and roast lamb, as well as burgers, sandwiches, fried seafood, and strip steak. **Known for:** gyro platters; pastitsio (Greek lasagna); sunset views. *Average main: $14* *1001 Estero Blvd., Fort Myers Beach* *239/463–4707.*

Hotels

DiamondHead

$$$$ | **RESORT** | **FAMILY** | This 12-story resort sits on the beach, and many of the suites, especially those on higher floors, have stunning views. **Pros:** on the beach; well-organized childlen's programs; kitchens in all units. **Cons:** heavy foot and car traffic; tiny fitness center; not the best value on the beach. *Rooms from: $429* *2000 Estero Blvd., Fort Myers Beach* *239/765–7654, 888/765–5002* *www.diamondheadfl.com* *121 suites* *No meals.*

Harbour House

$$ | **RENTAL** | This condo-hotel adds a degree of beach luxury with brightly painted and sea-motif studios and one- and two-bedroom condos, all privately owned and all with a balcony or lanai. **Pros:** close to lots of restaurants; roomy units; free covered parking. **Cons:** a walk to the beach; not great views from most rooms; no housekeeping service. *Rooms from: $245* *450 Old San Carlos Blvd., Fort Myers Beach* *239/463–0700, 866/998–9250* *www.harbourhouseattheinn.com* *34 units* *No meals.*

Lighthouse Resort Inn & Suites

$ | **HOTEL** | These pastel-painted buildings hold fairly basic but spacious rooms, standing tall and welcoming at the foot of the Fort Myers bridge, an ideal location for exploring. **Pros:** convenient location; on-site laundry; views of the area from balconies. **Cons:** can be noisy; may have to park across the street if under-building parking is full; some complaints of cleanliness. *Rooms from: $175* *1051 5th Ave., Fort Myers Beach* *239/463–9392* *www.lighthouseislandresort.com* *79 units* *No meals.*

Lovers Key Resort

$$ | **RENTAL** | Views can be stupendous from upper floors in this 14-story tower just north of Lovers Key State Park. **Pros:** excellent views; off the beaten path; spacious accommodations. **Cons:** not a true beach; far from shopping and restaurants; limited amenities. *Rooms from: $290* *8771 Estero Blvd., Fort Myers Beach* *239/765–1040, 877/798–4879* *www.loverskey.com* *100 units* *No meals.*

Outrigger Beach Resort

$ | **RESORT** | **FAMILY** | On a wide Gulf-side beach, this casual resort has rooms and efficiencies with configurations to suit different guests' needs, including some kitchenettes. **Pros:** beautiful beach; water-sports rentals; family-friendly vibe. **Cons:** can be noisy; crowded pool area; old-school feel. *Rooms from: $199* *6200 Estero Blvd., Fort Myers Beach* *239/463–3131, 800/657–5659* *www.outriggerfmb.com* *144 rooms* *No meals.*

Pierview Hotel & Suites

$$ | **HOTEL** | In the thick of things at Fort Myers Beach's so-called Times Square, this three-story property has pretty gingerbread trim outside and cheery florals inside. **Pros:** near all the action; right on the beach; affordable rates. **Cons:** old building; limited amenities; showing its age inside and out. *Rooms from: $220* *1160 Estero Blvd., Fort Myers Beach* *239/463–6158, 877/744–4592* *www.pierviewhotelfmb.com* *70 rooms* *No meals.*

Activities

BIKING

Fort Myers Beach has no designated trails, so most cyclists ride along the road.

Fun Rentals

BICYCLING | Bike rentals are available from anywhere between two hours and a week. Not your speed? Rent a Harley or a scooter instead. *1901 Estero Blvd., Fort Myers Beach* *239/463–8844* *www.funrentalsfmb.com.*

Lover's Key Adventures and Events

BICYCLING | This company rents one-speed bikes, kayaks, canoes, paddleboards, and concessions in Lovers Key State Park. *8700 Estero Blvd., Fort Myers Beach* *239/765–7788* *www.loverskeyadventures.com* *$20 for half day, $25 for full day.*

CANOEING

Lover's Key Adventures and Events

CANOEING/ROWING/SKULLING | Lovers Key State Park offers kayak, canoe, and paddleboard rentals and guided kayaking tours of its bird-filled estuary. Call ahead for a guided tour schedule. *8700 Estero Blvd., Fort Myers Beach* *239/765–7788* *www.loverskeyadventures.com* *Guided tours $60; rentals from $38 for 2 hrs.*

FISHING

Getaway Deep Sea Fishing

FISHING | Arrange anything from half-day party-boat charters to full-day excursions, fishing equipment included. *18400 San Carlos Blvd., Fort Myers Beach* *800/641–3088, 239/466–3600* *www.getawaymarina.com* *From $65.*

Estero/Bonita Springs

10 miles south of Fort Myers via U.S. 41.

Towns below Fort Myers have started to flow seamlessly into one another since the opening of Florida Gulf Coast University in San Carlos Park and as a result of the growth of Estero and Bonita Springs, which were agricultural communities until the 1990s. In recent years the area has become a shopping mecca of mega–outdoor malls mixing big-box stores, smaller chains, and restaurants. Bonita Beach, the closest beach to Interstate 75, has evolved from a fishing community into a strip of upscale homes and beach clubs built to provide access for residents of inland golf developments.

GETTING HERE AND AROUND

U.S. 41 (Tamiami Trail) runs right through the heart of these two adjacent communities. You can also reach them by exits 123 and 116 off Interstate 75.

Sights

Everglades Wonder Gardens

GARDEN | FAMILY | Opened in 1936 by two retired moonshiners from Detroit, the Everglades Wonder Gardens was one of the first roadside attractions in the state and remained little changed until 2013, when the family decided to close its doors—and thus a rich chapter of Florida tourism history—forever. In stepped Florida landscape photographer John Brady, who negotiated a lease with the founding family and transformed the old-style cramped zoological gardens (that once featured Florida panthers, black bears, crocodiles, alligators, and tame Florida deer) into a botanical garden by conserving the flora and fauna following contemporary standards. Now in focus are diverse gardens that include old-growth trees like kapok, banyan, candle nut, egg fruit, plumeria, jaboticaba, mahogany, cashew, avocado, and mango, as well as integrated animal exhibits with tortoises, turtles, smaller alligators, flamingos, and a butterfly garden. The original buildings have been preserved and made into a modern gallery that showcases Brady's photography. ✉ *27180 Old 41 Rd., Bonita Springs* ☎ *239/992–2591* 🌐 *www.evergladeswondergardens.com* 🎫 *$12.*

Koreshan State Historic Site

HISTORIC SITE | Tour one of Florida's quirkier chapters from the past. Named for a religious cult that was active at the turn of the 20th century, Koreshan preserves a dozen structures where the group practiced arts, worshipped a male-female divinity, and created its own branch of science called cosmogony, which claimed the universe existed within a giant hollow sphere. The cult foundered when leader Cyrus Reed Teed died in 1908, and in 1961 the four remaining members deeded the property to the state. Rangers and volunteers lead tours and demonstrations, and the grounds are lovely for picnicking and camping. Canoeists paddle the Estero River, fringed by a forest of exotic vegetation the Koreshans planted. ✉ *3800 Corkscrew Rd., at U.S. 41 (Tamiami Trail), Estero* ☎ *239/992–0311* 🌐 *www.floridastateparks.org/park/koreshan* 🎫 *$5 per vehicle with up to 8 passengers; $4 for single motorist; $2 per bicyclist, pedestrian, or extra passenger.*

Beaches

Barefoot Beach Preserve

BEACH—SIGHT | This one isn't exactly easy to find since it's accessible only by a quiet neighborhood road around the corner from buzzing Bonita Beach Park, but it's well worth the effort if you appreciate natural coastal habitats with fun interpretive programs. Shells here are bountiful, as are gopher tortoises that may park in shade of your car. Stop by the nature center to join a ranger-led walk through the trails and gardens, or take up a paddle and go kayaking. There's no towel-jockeying here along the wide-open space (the preserve as a whole is 342 acres), and refreshments and beach rentals provide ample comfort while you unwind in the pristine sands. **Amenities:** food and drink; parking (fee); showers; toilets; water sports. **Best for:** solitude; walking. ✉ *5901 Bonita Beach Rd., at Barefoot Beach Rd., Bonita Springs* ☎ *239/591–8596* 🌐 *www.collierparks.com* *Parking $8.*

Bonita Beach Park

BEACH—SIGHT | The joint is always jumping on this rowdy stretch of coast, the easiest by far to reach from the inland areas south of Fort Myers. Local favorite hangout Doc's Beach House, open from breakfast until the wee hours of the night, keeps bellies full and libations flowing. Other food and sports vendors camp out here, too, making it nearly impossible to resist an ice cream or a ride on a Jet Ski. Shaded pavilions between the parking lot and dunes are a great way to cool off from the sweltering heat—just don't sit too close to the picnickers barbecuing. **Amenities:** food and drink; parking (fee); showers; toilets; water sports. **Best for:** partiers; windsurfing. ✉ *27954 Hickory Blvd., at Bonita Beach Rd., Bonita Springs* ☎ *239/949–4615* 🌐 *www.leeparks.org* *Parking $2 per hr.*

Restaurants

★ Angelina's Ristorante

$$$$ | ITALIAN | Here it's all about the experience—one of the most indulgent, pampered meals you'll ever eat. Formally trained waitstaff attend to your every need in this temple of traditional Italian cuisine. **Known for:** phenomenal service; homemade pastas; sea salt baked snapper for two. *$ Average main: $36* ✉ *24041 U.S. 41, Bonita Springs* ☎ *239/390–3187* 🌐 *www.angelinasofbonitasprings.com* *No lunch.*

Doc's Beach House

$ | AMERICAN | FAMILY | Right next door to the public access point for Barefoot Beach, Doc's has fed hungry beachgoers for decades. Come barefoot and grab a quick libation or meal downstairs, outside on the beach, or in the courtyard. **Known for:** spicy conch chowder; unfancy seafood; dining right on the water. *$ Average main: $10* ✉ *27908 Hickory Blvd., Bonita Springs* ☎ *239/992–6444* 🌐 *www.docsbeachhouse.com* *No credit cards.*

Old 41 Restaurant

$ | AMERICAN | A mostly local clientele populates the cheery dining room with its Philadelphia allegiances, offering a great Philly cheesesteak. For breakfast, don't miss the incredible Texas French toast with homemade caramel and pecans, Carbon's malted Belgian waffles, or eggs and homemade hash with Boar's Head meat. **Known for:** slow-cooked turkey and roast beef; chipped beef for breakfast; no reservations (but a call-ahead wait list on weekends). *$ Average main: $7* ✉ *25091 Bernwood Dr., Bonita Springs* ☎ *239/948–4123* 🌐 *www.old41.com* *No dinner.*

Hotels

★ Hyatt Regency Coconut Point Resort & Spa

$$$$ | RESORT | FAMILY | This secluded luxury resort, with its marble-and-mahogany lobby and championship golf course, makes a lovely, tropical sanctuary for families who want a refined atmosphere. **Pros:** pampering spa; insane water park with lazy river and high-speed slides; private island beach. **Cons:** need water shuttle to reach the beach; expensive restaurants; fee to park. *$ Rooms from: $649* ✉ *5001 Coconut Rd., Bonita Springs* ☎ *239/444–1234, 800/554–9288* 🌐 *www.hyatt.com* *454 rooms* *No meals.*

Trianon Bonita Bay

$$ | HOTEL | Convenient to Bonita Springs' best shopping and dining, this branch of a refined downtown Naples favorite has a peaceful, sophisticated feel and a poolside–lakeside alfresco bar and grill. **Pros:** spacious rooms; intimate atmosphere; good value. **Cons:** sometimes less-than-friendly staff; far from beach; slightly stuffy. *Rooms from: $239* *3401 Bay Commons Dr., Bonita Springs* *239/948–4400, 800/859–3939* *www.trianonbonitabay.com* *100 rooms* *No meals.*

Shopping

Coconut Point

SHOPPING NEIGHBORHOODS | FAMILY | A 500-acre planned community is host to one of the area's largest shopping complexes with more than 140 stores including upscale boutiques, big-box retailers, and plenty of big-name restaurants. There's a boardwalk for a breather between impulse purchases, and a castle-themed kids' play area. *23106 Fashion Dr., Estero* *239/992–9966* *www.shopcoconutpoint.com.*

Miromar Outlets

OUTLET/DISCOUNT STORES | The complex includes Adidas, Guess, Michael Kors, Nike, Nautica, and more than 140 other stores and eateries, plus a free Playland for kids. *10801 Corkscrew Rd., at I–75 Exit 123, Estero* *Near Germain Arena* *239/948–3766* *www.miromaroutlets.com.*

Activities

BIRDING

The last leg of the Great Florida Birding Trail has more than 20 stops in the Lower Gulf Coast. Go to *www.floridabirdingtrail.com* for a complete list.

CANOEING

The meandering Estero River is pleasant for canoeing as it passes through Koreshan State Historic Site to the bay.

Estero River Outfitters

CANOEING/ROWING/SKULLING | Since 1977, this is the place to rent canoes, kayaks, paddleboards, and equipment. They're also a full-service tackle shop. *20991 Tamiami Trail S, Estero* *239/992–4050* *www.esteroriveroutfitters.com.*

Naples

21 miles south of Bonita Springs, on U.S. 41.

Poised between the Gulf of Mexico and the Everglades, Naples belies its wild setting and Indian past with the trappings of wealth—neo-Mediterranean-style mansions, neatly manicured golfing developments, revitalized downtown streets lined with galleries and one-of-a-kind shops, and a reputation for lively and eclectic dining. Visitors come for its luxury hotels—including two Ritz-Carltons—its fabulous white-sand beaches, fishing, shopping, theater and arts, and a lofty reputation for golf. Yet with all the highfalutin living, Naples still appeals to families, especially with its water park and the Golisano Children's Museum of Naples.

Old Naples, the historic downtown section, has two main commercial areas, 5th Avenue South and 3rd Street South, and there's also a small cluster of restaurants right by City Dock on Naples Bay. Farther north on U.S. 41 (the Tamiami Trail, or 9th Street here), hotels, shopping centers, and developments have fast been filling in the area around and south of Vanderbilt Beach, including the dining and shopping meccas Waterside Shops, and the Village on Venetian Bay.

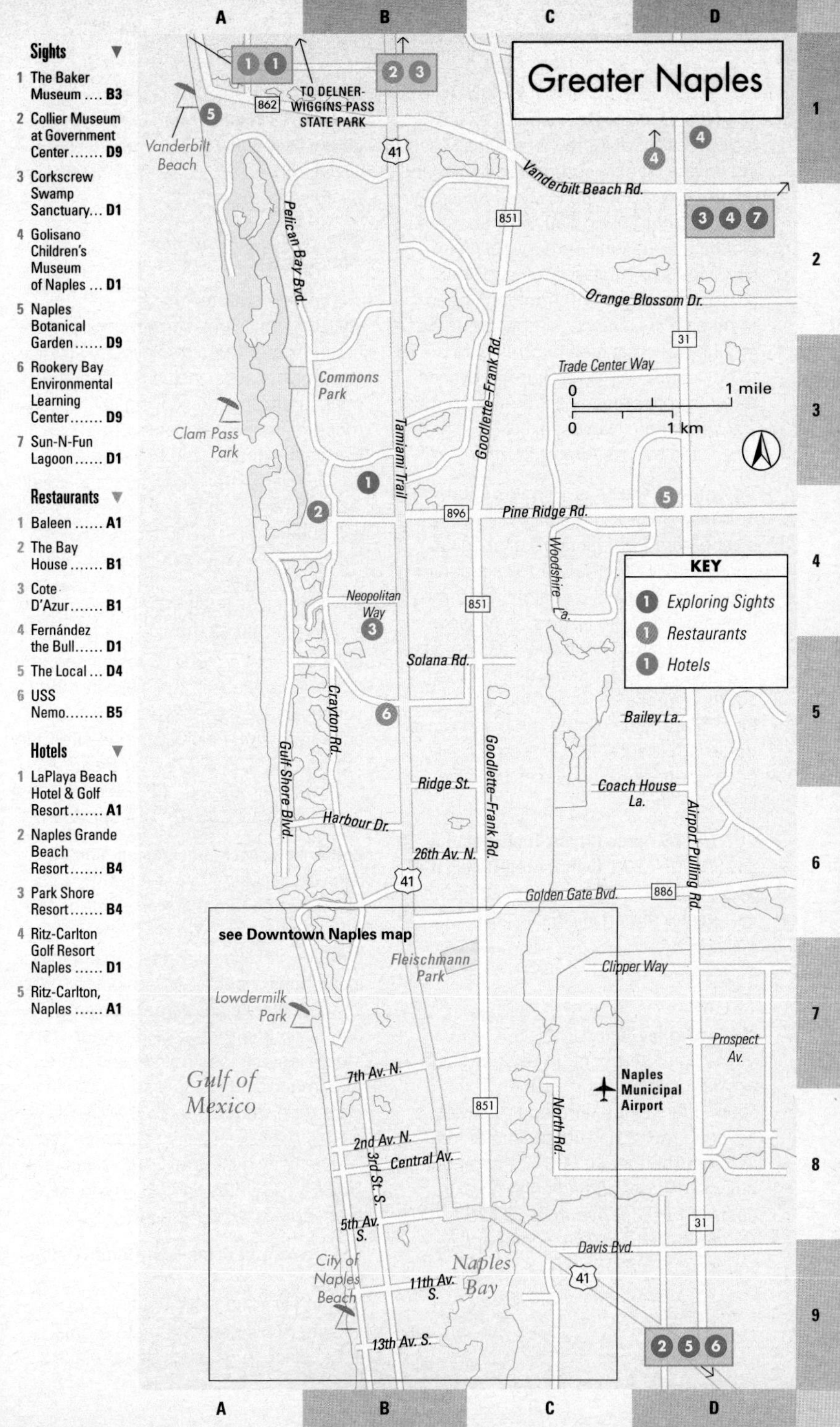

Sights
1 The Baker Museum B3
2 Collier Museum at Government Center....... D9
3 Corkscrew Swamp Sanctuary... D1
4 Golisano Children's Museum of Naples ... D1
5 Naples Botanical Garden...... D9
6 Rookery Bay Environmental Learning Center....... D9
7 Sun-N-Fun Lagoon...... D1
Restaurants
1 Baleen A1
2 The Bay House B1
3 Cote D'Azur....... B1
4 Fernández the Bull...... D1
5 The Local ... D4
6 USS Nemo........ B5
Hotels
1 LaPlaya Beach Hotel & Golf Resort....... A1
2 Naples Grande Beach Resort....... B4
3 Park Shore Resort....... B4
4 Ritz-Carlton Golf Resort Naples D1
5 Ritz-Carlton, Naples A1
Greater Naples
A
B
C
D
1
2
3
4
5
6
7
8
9
TO DELNER-WIGGINS PASS STATE PARK
862
41
Vanderbilt Beach
Vanderbilt Beach Rd.
851
Pelican Bay Blvd.
Orange Blossom Dr.
31
Trade Center Way
0
1 mile
0
1 km
Commons Park
Clam Pass Park
Tamiami Trail
Goodlette-Frank Rd.
896
Pine Ridge Rd.
Woodshire La.
KEY
Exploring Sights
Restaurants
Hotels
Neopolitan Way
Solana Rd.
Crayton Rd.
Gulf Shore Blvd.
Bailey La.
Ridge St.
Coach House La.
Harbour Dr.
26th Av. N.
Airport Pulling Rd.
Golden Gate Bvd.
886
see Downtown Naples map
Fleischmann Park
Clipper Way
Lowdermilk Park
Prospect Av.
Gulf of Mexico
7th Av. N.
Naples Municipal Airport
North Rd.
2nd Av. N.
Central Av.
3rd St. S.
5th Av. S.
Davis Bvd.
City of Naples Beach
11th Av. S.
Naples Bay
13th Av. S.

GETTING HERE AND AROUND

The Naples Municipal Airport is a small facility east of downtown principally serving private planes, commuter flights, and charters. A taxi for up to three passengers is about $60 to $90 from Southwest Florida International Airport (RSW) in Fort Myers to Naples; each additional person is charged $10. You don't need to reserve in advance; simply go to the ground-transportation booth. If you prefer to book a car or limo pickup in advance, three major companies are Aaron Airport Transportation, Naples Taxi & Limo Services, and Naples Airport Shuttle.

Downtown Naples is 15 miles south of Bonita Springs, on U.S. 41. If you're driving here from Florida's east coast, consider Alligator Alley, a toll section of Interstate 75 that's a straight shot from Fort Lauderdale to Naples. In Naples, east–west county highways exiting off Interstate 75 include, from north to south, Immokalee Road (Route 846), Pine Ridge Road (Route 896), and Collier Boulevard (Route 951), which actually goes north–south and takes you also to Marco Island.

CONTACTS Aaron Airport Transportation. ☎ *239/768–1898.* **Collier Area Transit (CAT).** ☎ *239/252–7777* 🌐 *www.colliergov.net/cat.* **Naples Airport Shuttle.** ☎ *239/430–4747, 888/569–2227* 🌐 *www.naplesairportshuttle.com.*

TOURS

Naples Trolley Tours

If you want someone to be your guide as you go about town, Naples Trolley Tours offers eight narrated tours daily, covering more than 100 points of interest in town. The tour lasts about two hours, but you can get off and on at no extra cost. ✉ *1010 6th Ave. S* ☎ *239/262–7300, 800/592–0848* 🌐 *www.naplestrolleytours.com* ☞ *$27.*

VISITOR INFORMATION

CONTACTS Naples, Marco Island, Everglades Convention and Visitors Bureau. ☎ *800/688–3600, 239/225–1013* 🌐 *www.paradisecoast.com.*

★ The Baker Museum

MUSEUM | This cool, contemporary museum at Artis–Naples displays provocative, innovative pieces, including renowned miniatures, antique walking sticks, modern and contemporary American and Mexican masters, and traveling exhibits. Dazzling installations by glass artist Dale Chihuly include a fiery cascade of a chandelier and an illuminated ceiling layered with many-hued glass bubbles, glass corkscrews, and other shapes that suggest the sea; alone, this warrants a visit, but with three floors and 15 galleries, your cultural curiosity is sure to pique, perhaps in the glass-domed conservatory. Reward your visual arts adventure with lunch at the on-site Cafe Intermezzo. ✉ *5833 Pelican Bay Blvd.* ☎ *239/597–1900, 800/597–1900* 🌐 *www.artisnaples.org* 🎟 *$10* ⏲ *Closed Mon.*

Collier Museum at Government Center

MUSEUM | **FAMILY** | To get a feel for local history, stroll the nicely presented indoor vignettes and traveling exhibits and outdoor parklike displays at this newly expanded museum. A Seminole *chickee* village, native plant garden, swamp buggy, reconstructed 19th-century fort, steam logging locomotive, and more capture important Naples-area developments from prehistoric times to the World War II era. You can even pack a lunch and picnic in the shady backyard. ✉ *3331 Tamiami Trail E* ☎ *239/252–8476* 🌐 *www.colliermuseums.com* 🎟 *Free.*

Conservancy of Southwest Florida Nature Center

NATURE PRESERVE | **FAMILY** | If you're looking to connect with nature, this is the place, regardless of age. Take a

A raccoon wades through Corkscrew Swamp Sanctuary.

45-minute electric boat tour (ages two+) along the Gordon River, rent a kayak, or go on a guided nature walk. The Dalton Discovery Center features interactive exhibits on six Florida ecosystems, including a touch tank where you can learn about many of the same animals you find on the local beaches, and meet the area's only loggerhead sea turtle living in a spectacular aquarium. Preschoolers can have hands-on fun at the Little Explorer Play Zone. The on-site wildlife hospital's viewing area gives you a peek at staff working on any number of animals. Check out Cinema Sunday and other events in their Nature Center. ■ **TIP→ The electric boat tours are free, and you don't have to pay the admission fee for the center to ride.** ✉ *1495 Smith Preserve Way* ☎ *239/262–0304* 🌐 *www.conservancy.org* 🎟 *$14.95.*

★ **Corkscrew Swamp Sanctuary**

NATURE PRESERVE | To get a feel for what this part of Florida was like before civil engineers began draining the swamps, drive 17 miles east of North Naples to these 13,000 acres of pine flatwood and cypress, grass-and-sedge "wet prairie," saw-grass marshland, and lakes and sloughs filled with water lettuce. Managed by the National Audubon Society, the sanctuary protects North America's largest remaining stand of ancient bald cypress, 600-year-old trees as tall as 130 feet, as well as endangered birds, such as wood storks, which often nest here. This is a favorite destination for serious birders and is the gateway to the Great Florida Birding and Wildlife Trail. If you spend a couple of hours to take the 2¼-mile self-guided tour along the boardwalk, you'll spot ferns, orchids, and air plants, as well as wading birds and possibly alligators and river otters. A nature center educates you about this precious, unusual habitat with a dramatic re-creation of the preserve and its creatures in the Swamp Theater. ■ **TIP→ The boardwalks are completely wheelchair-accessible.** ✉ *375 Sanctuary Rd. W* ✣ *17 miles east of I–75 on Rte. 846* ☎ *239/348–9151* 🌐 *corkscrew.audubon.org* 🎟 *$14.*

Golisano Children's Museum of Naples

MUSEUM | FAMILY | This bright, cheery 30,000-square-foot ode to playful learning burst onto Naples's cultural scene in 2012 after a decade of much-anticipated planning, and its 12 state-of-the-art permanent galleries do not disappoint. Kids of many ages and abilities (exhibits were designed to be accessible for children with special needs, too) will love the gigantic Banyan Tree, a focal point at 45 feet tall and a climbing obstacle of sorts; the Farm & Market, a cooperative playground where roles are assigned (a harvester or cashier, for example) to subtly enforce team building and math skills; and the Green Construction zone, where hard hats and eco-friendly building materials will inspire future architects. **■ TIP→ It's in the same park as Sun-n-Fun Lagoon, and it's possible to do both in one day.** ✉ *North Collier Regional Park, 15080 Livingston Rd.* ☎ *239/514–0084* 🌐 *www.cmon.org* 🎟 *$10* ⏲ *Closed Wed.*

Naples Botanical Garden

GARDEN | One of Naples's most culturally exciting attractions, the botanical "gardens with latitude" flourish with plants and architectural and decorative elements from Florida and other subtropical locales including Asia, Brazil, and the Caribbean. Highlights of the 170 acres include a Children's Garden with a butterfly house, tree house, waterfall, cave, Florida Cracker house, and hidden garden; an infinity water lily pool; an aromatic Enabling Garden with a how-to theme; and a dramatic waterfall feature. A visitor center offers a café, restaurant, and three gardens, including an orchid garden with more than 1,000 species and cultivars. ✉ *4820 Bayshore Dr.* ☎ *239/643–7275* 🌐 *www.naplesgarden.org* 🎟 *$19.95* ☞ *Complimentary wheelchairs; fee for scooters.*

Naples Zoo at Caribbean Gardens

ZOO | FAMILY | The lush 44-acre zoo got its start as a botanical garden in 1919 and has since drawn visitors curious to see lions, cheetahs, bears, leopards, gazelles—and a wildly popular giraffe herd. Other exhibits include the rare mountain bongos (approximately 100 left in the wild), an endangered Florida panther (as few as 180 cats left in the wild), and a *Reptile Rendezvous* show; a giant anteater and critically endangered cotton-top tamarins in the South American exhibits; and the Primate Expedition Cruise that sails past islands populated with monkeys, apes, and lemurs. Kids can amuse themselves in two play zones, and there are daily meet-the-keeper times, alligator feedings, and a live educational Safari animal presentation. Newer exhibits include critically endangered red-ruffed lemurs, rare juvenile clouded leopards, and francois langur primates. **■ TIP→ Purchase tickets online for a $1 discount per ticket.** ✉ *1590 Goodlette-Frank Rd.* ☎ *239/262–5409* 🌐 *www.napleszoo.org* 🎟 *$22.95.*

Palm Cottage

HOUSE | Houses in 19th-century South Florida were often built of a concrete-like material made of sand and seashells called tabby mortar. For a fine example of such construction, stop by Palm Cottage, built in 1895 and one of the Lower Gulf Coast's few surviving tabby homes. The historically accurate interior contains simple furnishings typical of the period. Next door to the cottage, Norris Gardens was designed to reflect turn-of-the-last-century garden trends. Docent tours of the home are included with admission; for an extra $10, join the weekly two-hour walking tour of the garden and historic district on Wednesday mornings (reservations required). ✉ *137 12th Ave. S* ☎ *239/261–8164, 800/979–3370 historic district reservations* 🌐 *www.napleshistoricalsociety.org* 🎟 *$13.*

Rookery Bay Environmental Learning Center

NATURE PRESERVE | FAMILY | In the midst of 110,000-acre Rookery Bay National

Marine Estuary, the center dramatically interprets the Everglades environment and local history with interactive models, aquariums, an art gallery, a film, tours, and "coastal connections" programs (45 minutes, at 11 and 2 daily). It's on the edge of the estuary, about five minutes east of Marco's north bridge on Collier Boulevard. Take a walk along Observation Bridge, a 440-foot pedestrian bridge that spans the reserve's creek from the center's second floor, and connects with 1½ miles of nature trails and leads to a creekside viewing platform. Guided and self-guided walks are available. Kayak and boat tours are also available through advance registration. Exhibits include an interactive research boat, a display on the importance of the Gulf of Mexico to coastal communities, and another on global climate change. Geocaches can be found on the trail and parking area. ■**TIP→ Kids go free on Friday in June and July. Also, visit the website for a printable coupon for admission.** ✉ *300 Tower Rd.* ☎ *239/530–5940* 🌐 *www.rookerybay.org* 🎫 *$5.*

Sun-N-Fun Lagoon

AMUSEMENT PARK/WATER PARK | FAMILY | This is a splashy water park across from the children's museum along the eastern edge of town. Interactive water features throughout, such as dumping buckets and spray guns, will delight younger kids, and there's a Tadpole Pool geared to those age six and under. The whole family will go for the diving pool, a Sunny's Lazy River, and five waterslides. The park is generally closed from October to President's Day weekend (except during some local school breaks). ✉ *North Collier Regional Park, 15000 Livingston Rd.* ☎ *239/252–4021* 🌐 *www.napleswaterpark.com* 🎫 *$13.*

Beaches

City of Naples Beach

BEACH—SIGHT | FAMILY | There's something here for everyone just west of the 3rd Street South shopping area, but what gets the most attention by far is the historic pier that extends deep into the Gulf and has the best free dolphin-viewing seats around. Sunsets are a nightly ritual, and dodging anglers' poles is par for the course. The concession stand sells food for humans as well as for fishy friends, and on the sand below, teenagers hold court at the volleyball nets and families picnic on blankets, while a handful of people can always be seen swooping up cockles, fighting conchs, and coquinas. For a charming landscape away from the commotion, head south on Gulf Shore Boulevard and take your pick of the public access points. They may not have the amenities of the pier—or amenities, period—but the solitude can't be beat. **Amenities:** food and drink; parking (fee); showers; toilets. **Best for:** sunsets; swimming. ✉ *12th Ave. S at Gulf Shore Blvd.* ☎ *239/213–3062* 🎫 *Parking $2.50 per hour, $1.50 minimum.*

Clam Pass Beach Park

BEACH—SIGHT | A quiet day at the beach gets an adventurous start when you board a tram and careen down a ¾-mile boardwalk through shaded mangroves and a network of canals. At the end is a pretty, secluded patch of sand that still has notable activities because of the family-vacation-magnet Naples Grande Beach Resort just a few steps from the public parking lot. The surf is calm, perfect for swimming, and aside from the usual lying out, shelling, and sand-castle building, you can spring for a kayak and meander around the marsh for a different kind of water experience. **Amenities:** food and drink; parking (fee); showers; toilets; water sports. **Best for:** solitude; swimming. ✉ *465 Seagate Dr.*

Did You Know?

Beaches are for so much more than sunning and sand-castle building. Many are used for fishing, weddings, and horseback riding. And come July 4, some, like the city of Naples Beach (shown here), draw people at night for viewing fireworks over the water.

☎ *239/252–4000* 🌐 *www.collierparks.com* 🎫 *Parking $8.*

★ **Delnor-Wiggins Pass State Park**

BEACH—SIGHT | This wide, virtually untouched expanse—about 166 acres—of open beach makes visitors feel transported from the bustling high-rises and resorts just a few blocks south. A full roster of eco-inclined features, like a designated fishing zone, hard-bottom reef (one of the few in the region and close enough to swim up to), boat dock, and observation tower hooks anglers, nature lovers, and water-sports enthusiasts drawn to the peaceful, laid-back vibe. Moms and dads love the educational displays on the local environment and the ranger-led sea turtle and birding programs, not to mention the picnic tables, grills, and plenty of shade offshore. A concession stand offers food, drinks, and beach gear easily accessible to those less inclined to self-catering. **Amenities:** food and drink; parking (fee); showers; toilets; water sports. **Best for:** snorkeling; solitude; walking. ✉ *11135 Gulf Shore Dr. N* ☎ *239/597–6196* 🌐 *www.floridastateparks.org/park/delnor-wiggins* 🎫 *$6 per vehicle with up to 8 people, $4 for single drivers, $2 for pedestrians and bicyclists.*

Lowdermilk Park

BEACH—SIGHT | **FAMILY** | Do you prefer your beach loud and active with a big dose of good old-fashioned fun? Kids running around in the surf, volleyballers hitting the sand, and tykes getting up close and personal with the park's most colorful residents, the red-throated Muscovy ducks, are all part of the Lowdermilk experience. Shallow waters and little-to-no wave action beg for a dip from even the most hesitant swimmer, and thatched umbrellas dotting the shoreline complete the happy tiki vibe and are yours for the taking—assuming you can snag one (they are strictly first-come-first-served). Even more, a food stand, two playgrounds, and some casual eateries down the strand at the Naples Beach Hotel make digging your feet into the sand a no-brainer. **Amenities:** food and drink; parking (fee); showers; toilets. **Best for:** swimming; walking. ✉ *1301 Gulf Shore Blvd. N* ☎ *239/213–3029* 🌐 *www.naplesgov.com* 🎫 *Parking $2.50 per hour, $1.50 minimum.*

Vanderbilt Beach

BEACH—SIGHT | If a day at the shore just doesn't seem quite complete without a piña colada and serious people-watching, this place is for you. The white powdery sand often looks like a kaleidoscope, with multihued towels and umbrellas dotting the landscape in front of the nearly 3 miles of tony north Naples condos and luxe resorts, including the Ritz-Carlton and LaPlaya. If you walk far enough—which many people do—you come across eye candy of a different kind: the architecturally stunning megamansions of Bay Colony perched up on the dunes. A covered public parking garage gives easy access, and the beach really comes alive at sunset with onlookers. **Amenities:** food and drink; parking (fee); showers; toilets; water sports. **Best for:** partiers; sunsets; walking. **■ TIP→ Stroll up to Gumbo Limbo at the Ritz for the best Floribbean, yet surprisingly not wallet-busting, lunches and panoramic views from a shaded deck.** ✉ *100 Vanderbilt Beach Rd.* ☎ *239/252–4000* 🌐 *www.collierparks.com* 🎫 *Parking $8.*

Restaurants

Baleen

$$$$ | **SEAFOOD** | The mood cast in this well-appointed dining room and the romantic Gulf-view patio that spills onto the sand feels like the perfect Florida restaurant experience. There's only one small problem: lighting is so low at dinner that you can't read the menu, even with its built-in flashlight. **Known for:** lobster frittata breakfast; signature blackened grouper; water views. ⓢ *Average main: $37* ✉ *La Playa Beach & Golf Resort, 9891 Gulf Shore Dr.* ☎ *239/598–5707, 800/237–6883* 🌐 *www.laplayaresort.com.*

Barbatella

$$ | ITALIAN | This trattoria with an edge is still just as popular as it was when it opened in 2012. The restaurant has three dining spaces to suit any whim: the wine bar, with sleek eclectic decor, has a communal table, green ceiling medallions, crystal chandeliers wrapped in birdcages, and a wine dispenser that allows guests to sip their way through 32 bottles (Italian, of course) by the 1-, 3-, or 6-ounce glass. **Known for:** pizzettes (small pizzas); Venetian-style meatballs; amazing gelato. ⓢ *Average main: $20* ✉ *1290 3rd St. S* ☎ *239/263–1955* 🌐 *www.barbatella-naples.com.*

The Bay House

$$$$ | SEAFOOD | Nestled in a hidden expanse of twisted mangrove trees and flowing canals is one of the area's best restaurants for casual fine dining—and beautifully natural scenery. Restored wooden rowboats and modern chandeliers hang from the ceiling of the main dining room, which is packed almost every night in season. **Known for:** crab bisque; coastal pan roast with fresh Gulf fish; live music. ⓢ *Average main: $32* ✉ *799 Walkerbilt Rd.* ☎ *239/591–3837* 🌐 *www.bayhousenaples.com* ⏲ *No lunch May–Nov.*

Bha! Bha! Persian Bistro

$$$ | MIDDLE EASTERN | Long considered one of Naples's best ethnic restaurants, loyal fans of Bha! Bha! have flocked to a tiny north Naples strip mall year in and year out to indulge in the restaurant's chic Persian atmosphere and cuisine. On the eve of its 15th birthday came a well-deserved present: a brand-new location on bustling Fifth Avenue South. **Known for:** authentic Persian cuisine; signature plum lamb; slow-braised duck. ⓢ *Average main: $25* ✉ *865 5th Ave. S* ☎ *239/594–5557* 🌐 *www.bhabhabistro.com.*

Chops City Grill

$$$$ | ECLECTIC | Count on high-quality cuisine that fuses Asian cuisine and steakhouse mainstays. It's sophisticated and popular, yet resort-wear casual, drawing everyone from young businesspeople to local retirees. **Known for:** succulent dry-aged steaks; region's best clam chowder; delicious side dishes. ⓢ *Average main: $32* ✉ *837 5th Ave. S* ☎ *239/262–4677* 🌐 *www.chopscitygrill.com* ⏲ *No lunch.*

Côte d'Azur

$$$$ | FRENCH | Capturing the essence of the French Riviera, Côte d'Azur offers a blend of country fare, exotic ingredients, and slow-cooked goodness with a menu that executes French technique with perfection and joie de vivre. The narrow dining room, with yellow-striped awnings and windows inset with mirrors and decorated with flower boxes, suggests a French provincial sidewalk café. **Known for:** whole fish of the day; crispy duck; authentic French experience. ⓢ *Average main: $40* ✉ *11224 Tamiami Trail N* ☎ *239/597–8867* 🌐 *www.cotedazurrestaurant.com.*

Fernández The Bull

$$ | CUBAN | Intrepid palates venture several miles inland to get a taste of the "Best Cuban Food in Naples," as voted by readers of *Gulfshore Life* magazine. You'll get authentic, home-cooked specialties, without pretension, at this simple storefront café. **Known for:** slow-roasted pork; old-school black beans and rice; Palomilla steak with onions. ⓢ *Average main: $19* ✉ *1201 Piper Blvd., Suite 10* ☎ *239/254–9855* 🌐 *www.fernandezthebull.com.*

★ The Local

$$ | CONTEMPORARY | You'll find an epicurean take on healthy eating at this farm-and-sea-to-table bistro that, as the name declares, looks almost exclusively to local suppliers to stock its kitchen. Though in a

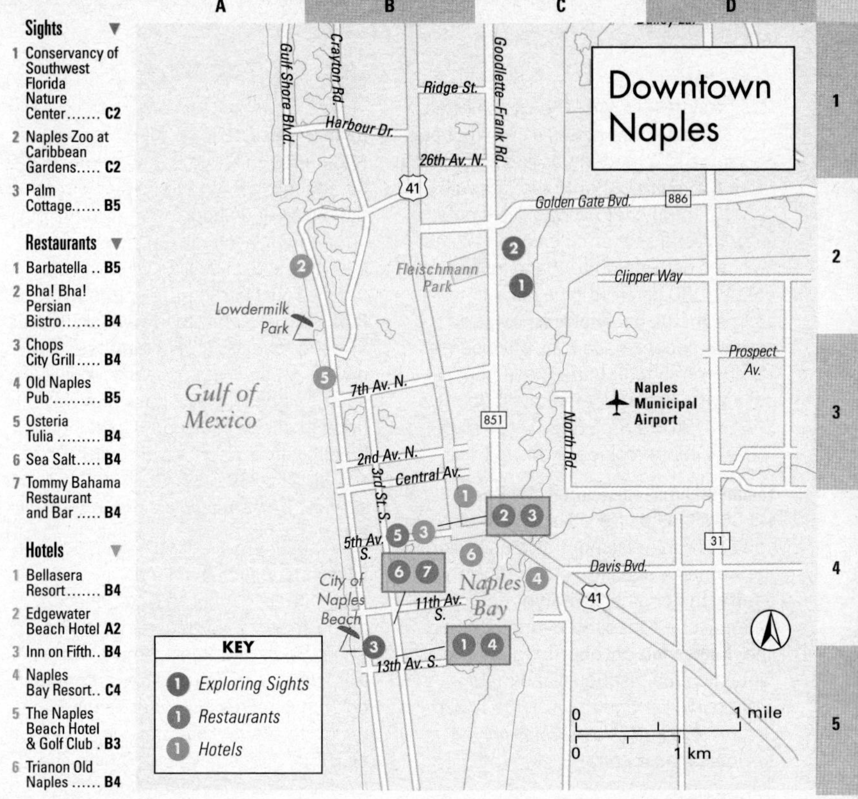

strip mall a few blocks inland, the setting is hip and polished with an interior that evokes both the beach and the farm, no doubt a reflection of the young and stylish owners' passion for nourishment. **Known for:** pot roast with grandma's veggies; flatbreads and pizzas; fresh ingredients. $ *Average main: $18* ✉ *5323 Airport Pulling Rd. N* ☎ *239/596–3276* 🌐 *www.thelocalnaples.com.*

Old Naples Pub

$$ | **AMERICAN** | Local blue- and white-collar workers gather with shoppers for affordable sandwiches and seafood in the vaulted, vine-twisted courtyard of this traditional pub, which has been tucked away from shopping traffic off upscale 3rd Street since 1990. It strikes one as an everybody-knows-your-name kind of place, with jars of pickles on the tables and friendly bartenders. **Known for:** casual, fun vibe; wide selection of beers; fresh fish platters. $ *Average main: $15* ✉ *255 13th Ave. S* ☎ *239/649–8200* 🌐 *www.naplespubs.com.*

★ Osteria Tulia

$$$ | **ITALIAN** | An ancestral air pervades at this intimate yet lively restaurant on 5th Avenue, where the Sicilian-born chef (and part owner) drives an authentic celebration of the Italian table. The concept is a refreshing departure from long, ornate menus and focuses on simple, finely produced, house-made Italian cuisine in a rustic, refined setting. **Known for:** homemade sausage and cheeses; freshly made pastas; rustic, family setting. $ *Average main: $25* ✉ *466 5th Ave. S* ☎ *239/213–2073* 🌐 *www.tulianaples.com.*

★ Sea Salt

$$$$ | **MEDITERRANEAN** | The city's hottest upscale restaurant draws a crowd of connoisseurs to a modern, coral-stone dining room that spills out onto the sidewalk. Venetian-born chef Fabrizio Aielli puts a New World spin on traditional Italian favorites on his nightly changing menu, utilizing 130 different types of salt from around the globe. **Known for:** charred octopus appetizer; daily prix-fixe sunset menu from 5 to 6; homemade pappardelle with Wagyu beef. *Average main: $40 ✉ 1186 3rd St. S ☎ 239/434–7258 🌐 www.seasaltnaples.com.*

Tommy Bahama Restaurant and Bar

$$$ | **CARIBBEAN** | Here Naples takes a youthful curve. Island music sounds on the umbrella-shaded courtyard at this eatery, the original prototype for a small national chain inspired by the clothing line. **Known for:** coconut fried shrimp; fantastic crab bisque; island-style setting. *Average main: $30 ✉ 1220 3rd St. S ☎ 239/643–6889 🌐 www.tommybahama.com.*

★ USS Nemo

$$$ | **SEAFOOD** | Don't be fooled by the tacky glowing sign from the highway: most Neapolitans swear this is *the* place for seafood in town, which is why you should still make a reservation even in the heat of summer. The food is in the vein of fine dining but served in a whimsical setting with portholes, antique bronze diving gear, and colorful sculptures of fish. **Known for:** miso-broiled sea bass; swordfish cioppino; fresh tuna with your choice of savory sauce. *Average main: $26 ✉ 3745 Tamiami Trail N ☎ 239/261–6366 🌐 www.ussnemorestaurant.com ⏲ No lunch weekends.*

Hotels

Bellasera Resort

$$$$ | **HOTEL** | This downtown hotel is just far enough "off 5th" to be away from the dining-and-shopping foot traffic but close enough for convenience, and it feels like a lovely Italian villa with its red-tile roofs and burnt-ocher stucco. **Pros:** spacious, full apartment units; free bikes for guests; first-come-first-served private cabanas at pool. **Cons:** must take shuttle to beach; on a busy highway (though surprisingly quiet); parking can be difficult. *Rooms from: $489 ✉ 221 9th St. S ☎ 239/649–7333, 888/612–1115 🌐 www.bellaseranaples.com 95 units No meals.*

Edgewater Beach Hotel

$$$$ | **HOTEL** | At this all-suite, beachfront property at the north end of scenic Gulf Shore Boulevard, the rooms are large and refreshing, exuding a relaxed, contemporary vibe. **Pros:** beautiful beach; quiet; exquisite views. **Cons:** far from shopping; surrounded closely by high-rises; pool area must be vacated at 10 pm. *Rooms from: $479 ✉ 1901 Gulf Shore Blvd. N ☎ 239/403–2000, 888/564–1308 🌐 www.edgewaternaples.com 125 suites No meals.*

Inn on Fifth

$$$$ | **HOTEL** | You can't top this luxe hotel if you want to plant yourself in the heart of Naples nightlife, dining, and shopping. **Pros:** central location; metro vibe; spa has free sauna for guests. **Cons:** pool is eye-level with power lines; beach is a long stroll or shuttle ride away. *Rooms from: $425 ✉ 699 5th Ave. S ☎ 239/403–8777, 888/403–8778 🌐 www.innonfifth.com 119 rooms No meals.*

★ LaPlaya Beach & Golf Resort

$$$$ | **RESORT** | Fresh off a $30 million renovation, LaPlaya bespeaks posh and panache down to the smallest detail—note the Balinese-style spa, marble bathrooms, and a stuffed sea turtle toy

to cuddle during your stay. **Pros:** right on the beach; high-end amenities; beautiful rooms renovated in 2018. **Cons:** golf course is off property; no locker rooms in spa; pricey resort and valet fee per night. *Rooms from: $619 9891 Gulf Shore Dr. 239/597–3123, 800/237–6883 www.laplayaresort.com 189 rooms No meals.*

Naples Bay Resort

$$$ | **RESORT** | **FAMILY** | Dual personalities are at work in this sprawling resort, and both are upscale and polished at every turn: at one end, a 97-slip marina with a luxury hotel (a boater's dream), and at the other a cottage resort with a busy, water-oriented recreation park. **Pros:** walk to downtown; $10 hop on/off all day water taxi to other bayside hot spots; five pools and a lazy river. **Cons:** no beach; some highway noise; sprawling property. *Rooms from: $389 1500 5th Ave. S 239/530–1199, 866/605–1199 www.naplesbayresort.com 193 units No meals 6-night minimum stay in cottages.*

The Naples Beach Hotel & Golf Club

$$$$ | **RESORT** | **FAMILY** | Family-owned and-managed since 1946, this art-deco resort is a piece of Naples history—and its stretch of powdery sand has lots of action at all times. **Pros:** terrific beach scene; golf course and driving range on property; complimentary kids' program. **Cons:** expensive nightly rates; have to cross street to reach spa and breakfast dining; though interiors are freshly renovated, signature old-school exterior may not appeal to sleek tastes. *Rooms from: $459 851 Gulf Shore Blvd. N 239/261–2222, 800/237–7600 www.naplesbeachhotel.com 319 rooms No meals.*

★ Naples Grande Beach Resort

$$$$ | **RESORT** | **FAMILY** | Beach access, a golf club, and top-shelf luxury are all yours at this ultramodern high-rise formerly known as the Waldorf Astoria Naples. **Pros:** indulgent spa; beach service with cabanas; attentive service. **Cons:** not directly on the beach; golf course is 6 miles away with no shuttle. *Rooms from: $729 475 Seagate Dr. 239/597–3232, 888/722–1267 www.naplesgrande.com 553 rooms No meals.*

Park Shore Resort

$$$ | **RENTAL** | Well situated near the beaches and shopping off Gulf Shore Boulevard, this hidden retreat is practical and comfortable. **Pros:** good value; tropical pool and shaded grounds; quiet. **Cons:** no restaurant; long walk to beach; no shuttle service. *Rooms from: $349 600 Neapolitan Way 800/548–2077 www.parkshorefl.com 156 rooms No meals.*

★ Ritz-Carlton Golf Resort, Naples

$$$$ | **RESORT** | Ardent golfers with a yen for luxury will find their dream vacation at Naples's most elegant golf resort where Ritz style prevails and service exceeds your wildest expectations. **Pros:** best golf academy in area; two championship courses at the front door; access to Ritz spa and beach via shuttle. **Cons:** 10-minute drive to beaches; expensive rates; farther inland than most properties. *Rooms from: $649 2600 Tiburón Dr. 239/593–2000 www.ritzcarlton.com 295 rooms No meals.*

★ Ritz-Carlton, Naples

$$$$ | **RESORT** | **FAMILY** | This is a regal Ritz-Carlton, with marble statues and antique furnishings blended with artistic modernity in the rooms and public spaces. **Pros:** flawless service; fun tiki bar and water-sports options; near north Naples shopping and restaurants; ultraindulgent spa. **Cons:** high price tag; hike to downtown; valet parking only; extra charge for beach umbrellas annoying at this nice a place. *Rooms from: $999 280 Vanderbilt Beach Rd. 239/598–3300 www.ritzcarlton.com 450 rooms No meals.*

Trianon Old Naples
$$$ | HOTEL | Refined ladies and gents will feel at home in this classy boutique hotel that's right smack in the central historic district, yet enrobed in an aura of privacy two quiet residential blocks south of 5th Avenue's bustle. **Pros:** can't-beat location for urbanites; large rooms; comfortable atmosphere. **Cons:** limited facilities; long walk (or short drive) to beach; no restaurant on-site. *Rooms from: $319* ✉ *955 7th Ave. S* ☎ *239/435–9600, 877/482–5228* 🌐 *www.trianonoldnaples.com* *58 rooms* *No meals.*

Nightlife

The heart of Old Naples, 5th Avenue South, already known for its scene of lively bars and sidewalk cafés, has undergone a renaissance of sorts.

Burn by Rocky Patel
DANCE CLUBS | At this part cigar bar, part dance club, you can expect a young crowd dancing to a house DJ. ✉ *9110 Strada Pl.* ☎ *239/653–9013* 🌐 *www.burnbyrockypatel.com.*

Naples Beach Brewery
BREWPUBS/BEER GARDENS | The Naples scene isn't only about fine wine anymore: This microbrewery's concoctions can be found in almost 50 local bars and restaurants including some of Naples's finest dining establishments. Twenty-plus house brews range from the straw-colored Weizen to the Naples Beach Stout. Look for a palm tree logo on bottles and taps signifying the local craft beers, or head directly to the brewery on Friday and Saturday afternoons for guided tours, tastings, and pizza made with their spent grain. There are also food trucks and live music most nights. Just don't expect to be wowed by a big gleaming factory, as this brewery is small and authentic, located in an industrial neighborhood sandwiched between hardware manufacturers—the real deal. ✉ *4110 Enterprise Ave., Suite 217* ☎ *239/304–8795* 🌐 *www.naplesbeachbrewery.com* *$15.*

The Pub
BARS/PUBS | Long lists of brews, flat-screens, and fun British decor attract a lively crowd to this popular outpost of a small, family-run chain. Brunch is served on weekends from 10 to 2. ✉ *9118 Strada Pl.* ☎ *239/594–2748* 🌐 *www.experiencethepub.com.*

Silverspot Cinema
CAFES—NIGHTLIFE | More than a plush movie theater, Silverspot offers a full evening's entertainment, including a lounge where you can sip specialty cocktails before showtime. You can even have dinner right in your comfy movie seat; just order, and it will be delivered to you while you're enjoying the show. ✉ *9118 Strada Pl., 2nd fl.* ☎ *239/592–0300* 🌐 *www.silverspot.net.*

Vergina
DANCE CLUBS | The mature crowd hits the dance floor for Gloria Gaynor and the Bee Gees. Upscale professionals gather here for daily happy-hour specials and the lighter bar menu. The restaurant serves a full menu for breakfast, lunch, and dinner. ✉ *700 5th Ave. S* ☎ *239/659–7008* 🌐 *www.verginarestaurant.com.*

Performing Arts

Naples is the cultural capital of this stretch of coast.

Naples Philharmonic
ARTS CENTERS | See the 85-piece Naples Philharmonic Orchestra perform more than 140 plays, ballets, orchestral, and chamber concerts each year at the Hayes Hall at Artis–Naples from September to June. The Miami City Ballet performs here during its winter season. ✉ *Artis–Naples, 5833 Pelican Bay Blvd.* ☎ *239/597–1900, 800/597–1900* 🌐 *www.artisnaples.org.*

Naples Players

THEATER | Musicals and dramas are performed year-round; winter shows often sell out well in advance. ✉ *Sugden Community Theatre, 701 5th Ave. S* ☎ *239/263–7990* 🌐 *www.naplesplayers.org.*

Shopping

Old Naples encompasses two distinct shopping areas marked by historic buildings and flowery landscaping: 5th Avenue South and 3rd Street South. Both are known for their abundance of fine-art galleries and monthly musical entertainment. Elsewhere, malls, outdoor plazas, and independent boutiques pepper the landscape, mostly on and around U.S. 41.

SHOPPING AREAS

Tin City

SHOPPING CENTERS/MALLS | Near 5th Avenue South, a collection of tin-roof former boat docks along Naples Bay has more than 30 boutiques, eateries, and souvenir shops, with everything from jewelry and T-shirts to Jet Ski rentals and seafood. ✉ *1200 5th Ave. S* 🌐 *www.tin-city.com.*

Waterside Shops

SHOPPING CENTERS/MALLS | Only in South Florida can you find more than four dozen upscale stores plus eateries wrapped around a series of waterfalls, waterways, and shaded open-air promenades. Saks 5th Avenue and Nordstrom are the main anchors; Tiffany & Company, De Beers, Ralph Lauren, and St. John are in the mix. ✉ *5415 Tamiami Trail N* ☎ *239/598–1605* 🌐 *www.watersideshops.com.*

SPECIALTY SHOPS

Gattle's

HOUSEHOLD ITEMS/FURNITURE | Started in 1904, this downtown shop stocks pricey-but-pretty linens. ✉ *1250 3rd St. S* ☎ *239/262–4791, 800/344–4552* 🌐 *www.gattles.com.*

Marissa Collections

CLOTHING | *The* destination in Naples for ultra-high-end designer women's wear. ✉ *1167 3rd St. S* ☎ *239/263–4333* 🌐 *www.marissacollections.com.*

Regatta

HOUSEHOLD ITEMS/FURNITURE | Among 5th Avenue South's selection with a decidedly local flair, this shop sells personal and home accessories with a sense of humor and style. ✉ *760 5th Ave. S* ☎ *239/262–3929* 🌐 *www.fifthavenuesouth.com/regatta.*

The Shelter Options Shoppe

OUTLET/DISCOUNT STORES | Naples's ladies who lunch often donate their year-old Armani cast-offs and fine collectibles to this terrific thrift shop whose proceeds benefit the Shelter for Abused Women & Children. ✉ *968 2nd Ave. N* ☎ *239/434–7115* 🌐 *www.optionsnaples.org.*

Activities

Lely Resort Golf and Country Club

GOLF | Flamingo Island (designed by Robert Trent Jones) and The Mustang (designed by Lee Trevino) are the two championship courses open to the public at Lely Resort. Flamingo Island features white-sand bunkers, hourglass fairways, and large greens, along with its signature 3200-yard hole 5 with a water-rimmed rolling fairway, bunkers, and two bridges providing the only access to the mainland. The Mustang features 12 lakes and rolling fairways. If you do more shanking than swinging, schedule time with their PGA teaching professional Charles Lostracco. ✉ *8004 Grand Lely Blvd.* ☎ *239/793–2600* 🌐 *www.lelyresortgolfandcountryclub.com* 🎫 *$169* 🏌 *Flamingo Island: 18 holes, 7171 yards, par 72; The Mustang: 18 holes, 7217 yards, par 72.*

Mangrove Outfitters

FISHING | Take a guided boat and learn to cast and tie flies. ✉ *4111 Tamiami Trail E* ☎ *239/793–3370, 888/319–9848* 🌐 *www.mangroveoutfitters.com.*

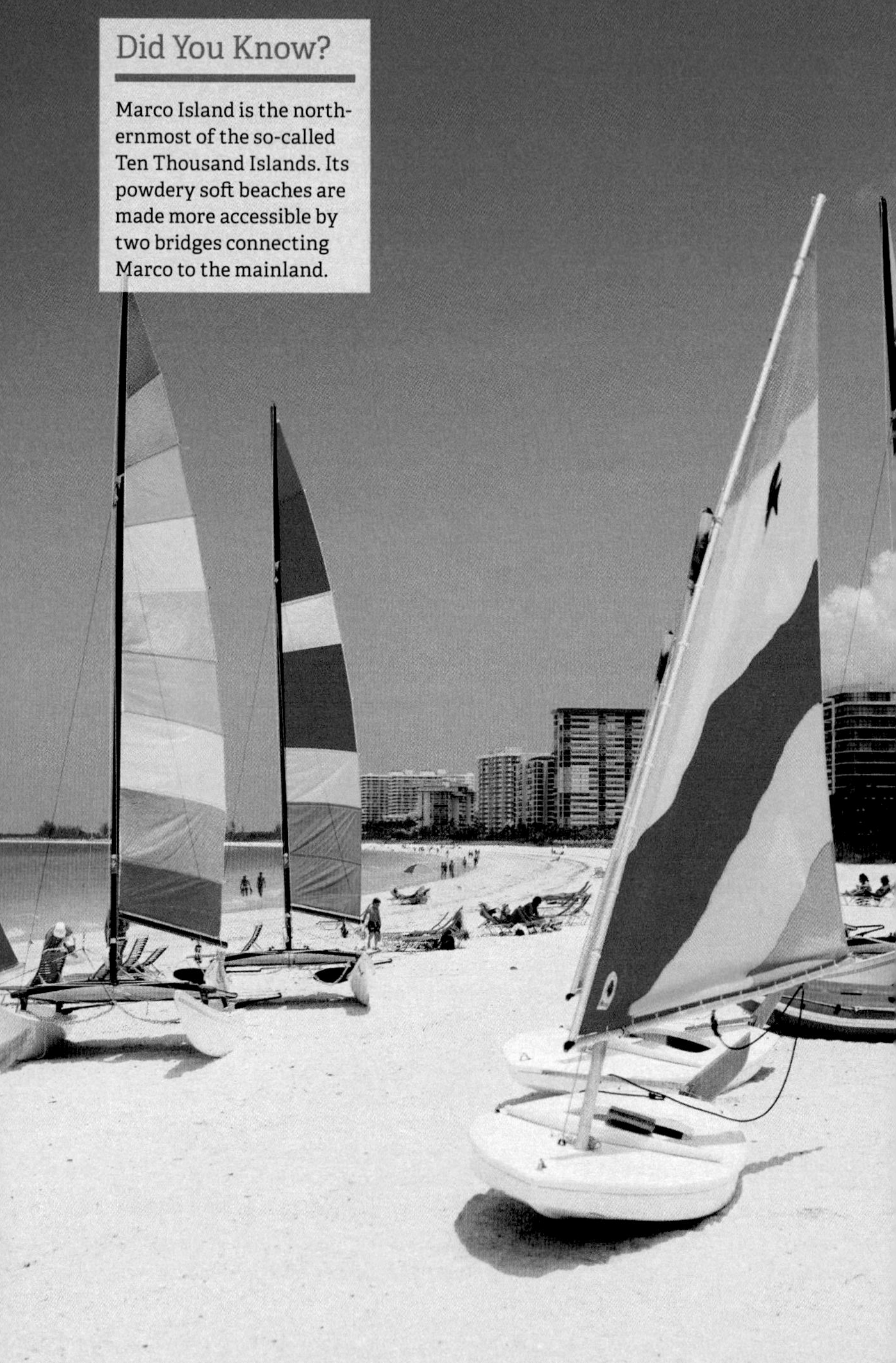

Did You Know?

Marco Island is the northernmost of the so-called Ten Thousand Islands. Its powdery soft beaches are made more accessible by two bridges connecting Marco to the mainland.

The Naples Beach Hotel & Golf Club

GOLF | This historic club has weekly clinics, a driving range, and a putting green and is replete with nostalgia as the region's oldest course, built in 1929. But lately, it's all about the "dramatic" $9-million renovations by acclaimed designer Jack Nicklaus and architect John Stanford. You'll find an all new, par-71 consisting of five tees, ranging from 4800 yards to over 6900 yards. **■ TIP→ It has been voted one of the "Top 50 Women-Friendly Golf Courses in the U.S." by the magazine** *Golf for Women.* ✉ *851 Gulf Shore Blvd. N* ☎ *239/435–2475* 🌐 *www.naplesbeachhotel.com* 🎫 *$55 for 9 holes, $99 for 18 holes* ⛳ *18 holes, 6488 yards, par 72.*

Naples Cyclery

BICYCLING | Daily or hourly rentals of two- and four-passenger surreys, tandems, and more are available at this convenient store in the Pavilion Shopping Center; weekly rentals are also available. **■ TIP→ If you need a little boost, have breakfast, lunch, or an espresso at the store's Fit & Fuel Café, where there's a serious fitting room if you're in the market for a custom-fit bike.** ✉ *Pavilion Shopping Center, 813 Vanderbilt Beach Rd.* ☎ *239/566–0600* 🌐 *www.naplescyclery.com* 🎫 *From $14.*

Port Of Naples Marina

BOATING | All new boats makes this the youngest fleet to rent. Choose pontoon or deck boats. ✉ *550 Port-O-Call Way* ☎ *239/774–0479* 🌐 *www.portofnaples-marina.com* 🎫 *From $249.*

Pure Naples

BOATING | **FAMILY** | Half-day deep-sea and backwater fishing trips depart twice daily. Sightseeing cruises and thrilling jet tours are also available, along with Jet Ski and boat rentals and private charters. ✉ *Tin City, 1200 5th Ave. S* ☎ *239/263–4949* 🌐 *www.purenaples.com.*

Tiburón Golf Club

GOLF | There are two 18-hole Greg Norman–designed courses, the Gold and the Black—an especially difficult course carved right out of a cypress preserve. Challenging and environmentally pristine, the links include narrow fairways, stacked sod wall bunkers, coquina sand, and no roughs. **■ TIP→ You cannot book months in advance unless you're staying at one of the Ritz-Carlton hotels. Nonguests can book 10 days out.** ✉ *Ritz-Carlton Golf Resort, 2620 Tiburón Dr.* ☎ *239/593–2201* 🌐 *www.tiburongcnaples.com* 🎫 *$99–$289* ⛳ *Tiburón Gold: 18 holes, 7271 yards, par 74.9; Tiburón Black: 18 holes, 6949 yards, par 75.01.*

Marco Island

20 miles south of Naples via Rte. 951.

High-rises dominate part of the shores of Marco Island, which is connected to the mainland by two bridges. Yet because of its distance from downtown Naples, it retains an isolated feeling much appreciated by those who love this corner of the world. Some natural areas have been preserved, and the down-home fishing village of Goodland, a 20-minute drive from historic Old Marco, resists change. Fishing, boating, sunning, swimming, and tennis are the primary activities here.

GETTING HERE AND AROUND

From Naples, Collier Boulevard (Route 951) takes you to Marco Island. If you're not renting a car, taxi rides cost about $100 from the regional airport in Fort Myers. Key West Express operates a ferry from Marco Island (from Christmas through Easter) and Fort Myers Beach (year-round) to Key West. The cost for the round-trip (less than four hours each way) is $147 from either Fort Myers Beach or Marco Island.

CONTACTS Collier Area Transit (CAT). ☎ *239/252–7777* 🌐 *www.colliergov.net/cat.* **Key West Express.** ✉ *951 Bald Eagle Dr.* ☎ *239/394–9700, 888/539–2628* 🌐 *www.keywestexpress.us.*

VISITOR INFORMATION

CONTACTS Naples, Marco Island, Everglades Convention and Visitors Bureau. ☎ *800/688–3600, 239/225–1013* 🌐 *www.paradisecoast.com.*

Marco Island Historical Museum

MUSEUM | Marco Island was once part of the ancient Calusa kingdom. The Key Marco Cat, a statue found in 1896 excavations, has become symbolic of the island's prehistoric significance. The original is part of the Smithsonian Institution's collection, but a replica of the Key Marco Cat is among displays illuminating the ancient past at this museum. Three rooms examine the island's history with dioramas, artifacts, and signage: the Calusa Room, Pioneer Room, and Modern Marco Room. A fourth hosts traveling exhibits focusing on the settlement history of the island. Outside, the yard was built to look like a Calusa village atop a shell mound with a water feature and *chickee* structure. ✉ *180 S. Heathwood Dr.* ☎ *239/642–1440* 🌐 *www.colliermuseums.com* 🎫 *Free.*

Tigertail Beach

BEACH—SIGHT | **FAMILY** | On the northwest side of the island is 2,500 feet of both developed and undeveloped areas. Once Gulf-front, in recent years a sand spit known as Sand Dollar Island has formed, which means the stretch especially at the north end has become mud flats—great for birding. There's plenty of powdery sand farther south and across the lagoon that draws a broad base of fans flocking there for its playgrounds, butterfly garden, volleyball nets, and kayak and umbrella rentals. Beach wheelchairs are also available for free use. ■ **TIP→ The Conservancy of Southwest Florida conducts free educational beach walks at Tigertail Beach every weekday from 8:30 to 9:30 from January to mid-April.** **Amenities:** food and drink; parking (fee); showers; toilets; water sports. **Best for:** sunset; swimming; walking. ✉ *490 Hernando Dr.* ☎ *239/252–4000* 🌐 *www.collierparks.com* 🎫 *Parking $8.*

Café de Marco

$$$ | **ECLECTIC** | This cozy little bistro with cheery pastel walls and stained-glass windows has served expertly prepared local fish since 1983. The jumbo prawns—an entire pound butterflied and broiled in their shell—are the signature dish, but grilled filet mignon on phyllo pastry proves the kitchen also knows how to do meat. **Known for:** jumbo prawns in the shell; shrimp Lenny with crab and bacon; oysters Rockefeller. $ *Average main: $30* ✉ *244 Palm St.* ☎ *239/394–6262* 🌐 *www.cafedemarco.com* ⊙ *Closed Sun. May–Dec. No lunch.*

Crazy Flamingo

$ | **AMERICAN** | Burgers, conch fritters, and chicken wings draw mostly locals to this neighborhood bar. Order at the counter, and take a seat indoors or outdoors on the sidewalk. **Known for:** fresh steamed and fried seafood; Uncle Vinny's steak sandwich; ultracasual atmosphere. $ *Average main: $12* ✉ *Marco Island Town Center, 1035 N. Collier Blvd.* ☎ *239/642–9600* 🌐 *www.thecrazyflamingo.com.*

Sale e Pepe

$$$$ | **ITALIAN** | Marco's best dining view comes also with some of its finest cuisine. The name means "salt and pepper," an indication that this palatial restaurant with terrace seating overlooking the beach adheres to the basics of southern Italian cuisine. **Known for:** beautiful Gulf views; homemade fresh pasta dishes; award-winning Italian cuisine. *Average main: $38* ✉ *Marco Beach Ocean Resort, 480 S. Collier Blvd.* ☎ *239/393–1400* 🌐 *www.sale-e-pepe.com.*

Snook Inn

$$$ | **SEAFOOD** | Situated on the water with live entertainment in the tiki bar and a loaded salad bar, it's no wonder this place has been a casual favorite for locals and visitors for decades. This is *the* place for good food, good music, and a fun crowd every day of the week on Marco. **Known for:** smoked-fish dip appetizer; lively atmosphere and good drinks under the chickee hut; expansive water views. *Average main: $21* ✉ *1215 Bald Eagle Dr.* ☎ *239/394–3313* 🌐 *www.snookinn.com.*

Sunset Grille

$$ | **AMERICAN** | Head to this popular spot for casual dining with a view of the beach and a menu of munchies, sandwiches, burgers, seafood, and steak. The lively sports-bar scene adds to the fun indoors; a porch accommodates alfresco diners—just beware if you leave your table that the porch has no screens, and the local gulls are thieves. **Known for:** seasonally inspired small plates; chef's loaded nachos; famous crab cake sandwich. *Average main: $19* ✉ *Apollo Condominiums, 900 S. Collier Blvd.* ☎ *239/389–0509* 🌐 *www.sunsetgrilleonmarcoisland.com.*

Verdi's American Bistro

$$$$ | **ECLECTIC** | There's a Zen feel to this intimate bistro built on creative American-Italian-Asian fusion cuisine. You'll feel as if you're dining in a home, and that's exactly how the owners want it to be: inviting, warm, and welcoming. **Known for:** incredible crispy duck; New Zealand rack of lamb; excellent service. *Average main: $32* ✉ *Sand Dollar Plaza, 241 N. Collier Blvd.* ☎ *239/394–5533* 🌐 *www.verdisbistro.com* *Closed Sept. No lunch.*

Hotels

The Boat House Motel

$$ | **HOTEL** | For a great location at a good price, check into this modest, but appealing, two-story motel at the north end of the island on the Marco River, close to the Gulf. **Pros:** away from busy beach traffic; affordable; boating docks and access. **Cons:** no beach; hard to find; tight parking area. *Rooms from: $250* ✉ *1180 Edington Pl.* ☎ *239/642–2400, 800/528–6345* 🌐 *www.theboathousemotel.com* *20 rooms* *No meals.*

Hilton Marco Island Beach Resort and Spa

$$$$ | **RESORT** | This 11-story hotel is smaller and more conservative than the Marriott—but it seems less busy and crowded. **Pros:** gorgeous, wide beach; large conference spaces; exclusive feel. **Cons:** a little stuffy; charges for self-parking; business focus. *Rooms from: $425* ✉ *560 S. Collier Blvd.* ☎ *239/394–5000, 800/445–8667* 🌐 *www.hiltonmarcoisland.com* *297 rooms* *No meals.*

JW Marriott Marco Island Beach Resort

$$$$ | **RESORT** | **FAMILY** | A grandiose circular drive with rock waterfalls front this hilltop, beachfront resort that has completed a $320-million makeover and rebranding journey to becoming the first-ever JW Marriott on the beach in the continental U.S. Made up of twin 11-story towers and villa-like suites, three on-site pools, and the widest stretch of sand on the island (over 3 miles), it's an island-seekers dream. **Pros:** great spa; 10 on-site restaurants; appeals to children and adults; two private golf courses. **Cons:** huge size; lots of convention business; paid parking across the street in an uncovered lot; $30 daily resort fee. *Rooms from: $579* ✉ *400 S. Collier Blvd.* ☎ *239/394–2511, 800/438–4373* 🌐 *www.jwmarco.com* *810 rooms* *No meals.*

★ Marco Beach Ocean Resort

$$$$ | **RESORT** | One of the island's first condo hotels, this 12-story beachfront class act has luxurious one- and two-bedroom suites decorated in elegant neutral tones with the finest fixtures. **Pros:** gourmet dining on-site; intimate atmosphere; sophisticated crowd. **Cons:** steep prices; squeezed between high-rises; near another busy resort. *Rooms from: $609 480 S. Collier Blvd. 239/393–1400, 800/715–8517 www.marcoresort.com 98 rooms No meals.*

Olde Marco Island Inn & Suites

$$$$ | **RENTAL** | This Victorian with tin roofs and royal-blue shutters and awnings in the heart of quieter Old Marco used to be the only place to stay on the island, and if you are looking for a property with some historic flair, it's still a good choice. **Pros:** full kitchen in every unit; free Wi-Fi; laundry facilities; free covered parking. **Cons:** must drive to beach; annexed to a shopping center; office closes at night. *Rooms from: $420 100 Palm St. 239/394–3131, 877/475–3466 www.oldemarcoinn.com 51 units No meals.*

Activities

BIKING

Scootertown Island Bike Shop

BICYCLING | Rentals are available at Scootertown Island Bike Shop for use on the island's bike path along beachfront condos, resorts, and residential areas. You can rent by the day or week. *1095 Bald Eagle Dr. 239/394–8400 www.islandbikeshops.com From $12.*

FISHING

Sunshine Tours

FISHING | Try a half-day deep-sea or three-hour backcountry fishing charter with this outfitter. *Rose Marina, 951 Bald Eagle Dr. 239/642–5415 www.sunshinetoursmarcoisland.com From $65.*

Chapter 10

ORLANDO AND ENVIRONS

Updated by
Joseph Hayes

Sights ★★★★☆ Restaurants ★★★★★ Hotels ★★★★☆ Shopping ★★★★★ Nightlife ★★★★☆

WELCOME TO ORLANDO AND ENVIRONS

TOP REASONS TO GO

★ **Quirky attractions:** The upside-down WonderWorks building, the oddball collection at Ripley's, and the adrenaline-filled Fun Spot America are all on the docket.

★ **Outdoor wonders:** From lakes and gardens in Orlando to natural springs in Wekiwa outside town, this area is home to outdoor beauties that extend far beyond the area's theme parks.

★ **Gateway to the parks:** Unleash your inner child at WDW's Magic Kingdom and Universal Orlando's Harry Potter. Visit Epcot's 11 countries, complete with perfect replicas of foreign monuments, unique crafts, themed rides, and traditional cuisine.

★ **Amazing animals:** Safari through Africa in Disney's Animal Kingdom, kiss a dolphin at Discovery Cove, and watch gators wrestle at Gatorland.

★ **Shopping ops:** Hit the national chains at Orlando's upscale malls, or browse Winter Park's unique Park Avenue boutiques.

1 **Orlando.** Thanks to Disney World, Orlando is the gateway for many visitors to Central Florida–but it offers much more than theme parks.

2 **Winter Park.** Looking for more laid-back local flavor? You'll find it just 10 miles northeast of Orlando in this charming suburb.

3 **Lake Buena Vista.** Lake Buena Vista offers a wide array of dining and lodging options adjacent to the area's biggest theme parks.

4 **Kissimmee.** Edging Orlando to the south is Kissimmee, with homegrown attractions like Gatorland and a historic downtown.

5 **Celebration.** Walt Disney World's planned residential community also has hotels and dining.

6 **Wekiwa Springs State Park.** A day trip away from Orlando, Wekiwa is great for hiking, picnicking, and swimming.

7 **LEGOLAND.** The larger-than-life park spans 150 acres, using millions of legos to inspire family fun.

8 **Bok Tower Gardens.** This beautiful outdoor sanctuary in Lake Wales is well worth a visit.

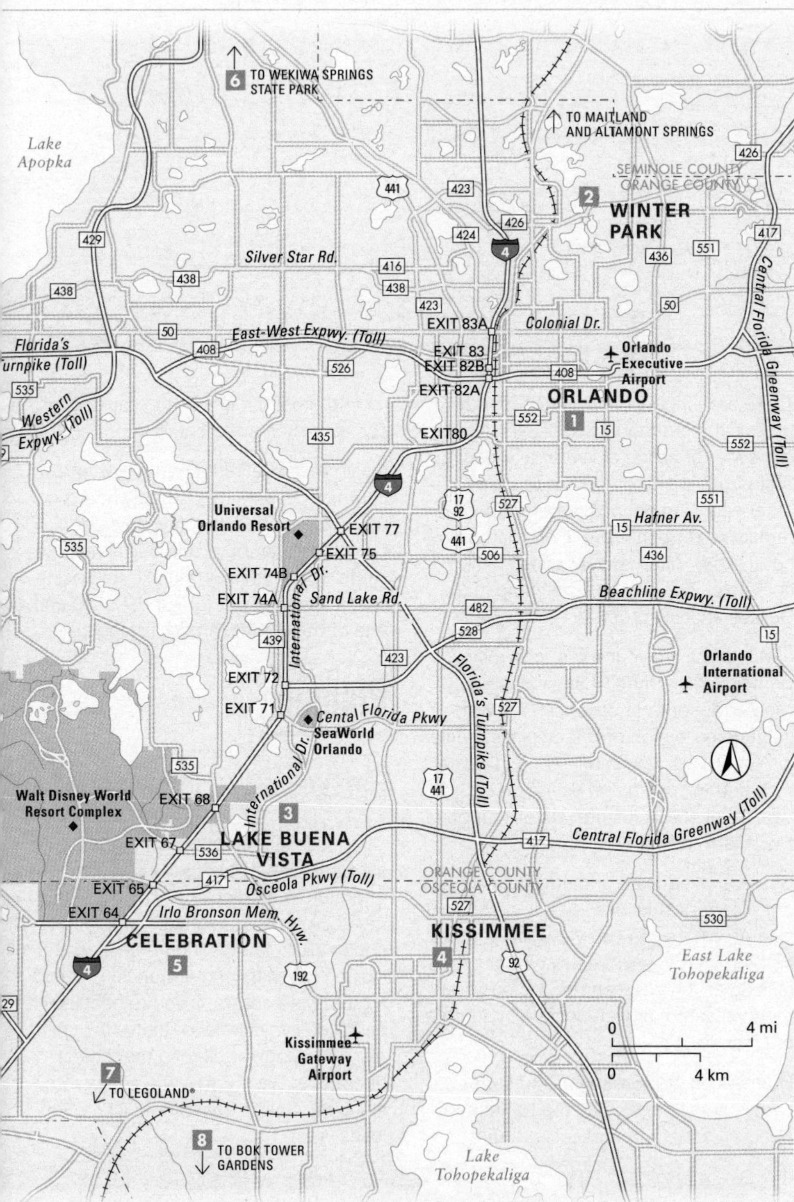
TO WEKIWA SPRINGS STATE PARK
TO MAITLAND AND ALTAMONT SPRINGS
Lake Apopka
SEMINOLE COUNTY
ORANGE COUNTY
WINTER PARK
Silver Star Rd.
Colonial Dr.
East-West Expwy. (Toll)
Florida's Turnpike (Toll)
Western Expwy. (Toll)
EXIT 83A
EXIT 83
EXIT 82B
EXIT 82A
EXIT80
Orlando Executive Airport
ORLANDO
Central Florida Greenway (Toll)
Universal Orlando Resort
EXIT 77
EXIT 75
EXIT 74B
EXIT 74A
International Dr.
Sand Lake Rd.
Hafner Av.
Beachline Expwy. (Toll)
Orlando International Airport
EXIT 72
EXIT 71
Cental Florida Pkwy
SeaWorld Orlando
Florida's Turnpike (Toll)
Walt Disney World Resort Complex
EXIT 68
EXIT 67
EXIT 65
EXIT 64
LAKE BUENA VISTA
Central Florida Greenway (Toll)
Osceola Pkwy (Toll)
ORANGE COUNTY
OSCEOLA COUNTY
Irlo Bronson Mem. Hyw.
CELEBRATION
KISSIMMEE
East Lake Tohopekaliga
Kissimmee Gateway Airport
0 4 mi
0 4 km
TO LEGOLAND®
TO BOK TOWER GARDENS
Lake Tohopekaliga

Most Orlando locals look at the theme parks as they would an unruly neighbor: it's big and loud, but it keeps a nice lawn (and they secretly love them). Central Florida's many theme parks can become overpowering for even the most enthusiastic visitor, and that's when an excursion into the "other" Orlando—the one the locals know and love—is in order.

There are ample opportunities for day trips. If the outdoors is your thing, you can swim or canoe at Wekiwa Springs State Park or one of the area's many other sparkling springs, where the water remains a refreshing 72°F no matter how hot the day. Alternatively, you can hike, horseback ride, canoe, and camp in the Ocala National Forest.

If museums are your thing, charming Winter Park has the Charles Hosmer Morse Museum of American Art with its huge collection of Tiffany glass. While in Winter Park, you can indulge in some high-end shopping and dining on Park Avenue or take a leisurely boat tour of the lakefront homes.

Got kids to educate and entertain? Check out WonderWorks or the Orlando Science Center, where you can view live gators and turtles. Even more live gators (some as long as 14 feet) can be viewed or fed (or even eaten) at Gatorland, just south of Orlando.

Do the kids prefer rockets and astronauts? Don't miss a day trip to Kennedy Space Center, where you can tour a rocket forest, sit in a space capsule, or see a space shuttle up close.

Kissimmee is a 19th-century cattle town south of Orlando that proudly hangs on to its roots with a twice-yearly rodeo where real cowboys ride bulls and rope cattle. The town sits on Lake Tohopekaliga, a favorite spot for airboat rides and one of the country's best fishing spots.

Planning

Getting Here and Around

Orlando is spread out. During rush hour, car traffic crawls along the often-crowded Interstate 4 (particularly now that the multibillion-dollar upgrade, expected to end in 2022, has begun, relocating and closing key exits and entrances), which runs to both coasts. If you're heading east, you can also take Route 528 (aka the Beachline), a toll road that heads directly for Cape Canaveral and points along the Space Coast; no such option leads west.

If you avoid rush-hour traffic, traveling to points of interest shouldn't take too much time out of your vacation. Winter Park is no more than 20 minutes from Downtown; International Drive and the theme parks are between 30 and 45 minutes away in heavier traffic. Orlando International Airport is only 9 miles south of Downtown, but it will take about 30 minutes via a circuitous network of highways (Interstate 4 west to Florida's Turnpike south to Route 528 east).

Sights

Orlando is a diverse and widely spread town. The Downtown area, though small, is dynamic, thanks to an ever-changing skyline of high-rises, sports venues, museums, restaurants, nightspots, a history museum, and several annual cultural events—including the country's largest performing and interactive arts festival, the IMMERSE Fest in October and the country's oldest Theater Fringe festival. Downtown also has a signature, central green, Lake Eola Park, which offers a respite from otherwise frantic touring.

Neighborhoods such as Thornton Park (great for dining) and Audubon Park (an outpost of quirky shopping) are fun to wander. Not too far to the north, you can come in contact with natural Florida—its manatees, gators, and crystal clear waters in spring-fed lakes.

Closer to the theme-park action, International Drive, the hub of resort and conference hotels, offers big restaurants and even bigger outlet-mall bargains. Sand Lake Road, between the two, is Orlando's Restaurant Row, with plenty of exciting dining prospects.

Restaurants

Dining in Orlando ranges from fast food and national chains to celebrity chefs—both international and local—serving locally sourced foods, creative preparations, and clever international influences. The theme parks now have some of the best restaurants in town, although you may opt for a rental car to seek out the local treasures.

The signs of Orlando's dining progress are most evident in the last place one would look: Disney's fast-food outlets. Every eatery on Disney property offers a tempting vegetarian option, and kiddie meals come with healthful sides and drinks unless you specifically request otherwise. Chefs at Disney's table-service restaurants consult face-to-face with guests about food allergies. And big-name chefs are now well represented in Disney Springs, though less so at Universal's CityWalk.

Orlando's destination restaurants can be found in the theme parks, as well as in the outlying towns. Sand Lake Road is now known as Restaurant Row for its eclectic collection of worthwhile tables. Here you'll find fashionable outlets for sushi and seafood, Italian and chops, Hawaiian fusion, and upscale Lebanese. Heading into the residential areas, the neighborhoods of Winter Park (actually its own city), Thornton Park, and Audubon Park are prime locales for chow. Scattered throughout Central Florida, low-key ethnic restaurants specialize in the fare of Turkey, India, Peru, Thailand, Vietnam—you name it. Prices in these family-owned finds are usually delightfully low.

MEAL PLANS

Disney Magic Your Way Plus Dining Plan allows you one table-service meal, one counter-service meal, and one snack per day of your trip at more than 100 theme-park and resort restaurants, provided you stay in a Disney hotel. You'll also receive a refillable drink mug for use at your hotel's fast fooderies. For more money you can upgrade the plan to include more; to save you can downgrade to a counter-service-only plan. Used wisely a Disney dining plan is a steal, but be careful to buy only the number of meals you'll want to eat. Moderate eaters can end up turning away appetizers and desserts to which they're entitled. Plan ahead, and use "extra" meals to your advantage by swapping two table-service meals for a Disney dinner show, say, or an evening at a high-end restaurant like California Grill.

Universal Dining Plan offers one sit-down and one quick-service meal at participating walk-up eateries inside Universal Studios and Islands of Adventure, plus a snack and soft drink. Meal plans can only be purchased with a resort stay. A quick-service-only arrangement, with one meal a day, can be purchased by anyone, as can all-you-can-drink soft drinks.

What it Costs

	$	$$	$$$	$$$$
AT DINNER	under $15	$15–$20	$21–$30	over $30

RESERVATIONS

Reservations are strongly recommended throughout the theme parks. Indeed, make reservations for Disney restaurants and character meals at both Universal and Disney at least 90 (and up to 180) days out. And be sure to ask about the cancellation policy—at a handful of Disney restaurants, for instance, you may be charged penalties if you don't give 24 to 48 hours' notice.

Unless otherwise noted, the restaurants listed are open daily for lunch and dinner. Restaurant reviews have been shortened. For full information, visit Fodors.com.

Nightlife

Outside of Downtown Disney and Universal's CityWalk, the focal point of adult Orlando nightlife is Downtown. If you stand on the corner of Orange Avenue and Church Street long enough, you can watch all types of gussied-up revelers walk by. The bars and music clubs here hop even after the 2 am last call.

Shopping

Visitors from as far away as Britain and Brazil often arrive in Orlando with empty suitcases for their purchases. Although shopping has all but disappeared from Downtown, the metro area is filled with options. There really is something for everyone—from high-end fashion to outlet-mall chic, from a mall filled with handmade crafts to a boutique-filled town, from an antique treasure to a hand-hewn Florida find.

The College Park area, once an antiques-hunter's dream, still has some treasures to be found along North Orange Avenue and Edgewater Drive, including Rock & Roll Heaven, the largest vinyl-record shop in Florida.

The simultaneously glitzy and kitschy International Drive has almost 500 designer outlet stores and odd, off-brand electronics shops. The factory outlets on the north end of I-Drive once consisted of shops with merchandise piled on tables; today the shops here are equal to their higher-priced first-run cousins. The strip also has plenty of massive restaurants and, for those in your group who don't feel like shopping, movie theaters.

Activities

There are many ways to enjoy the outdoors here, but a few activities stand out. You can keep your feet planted firmly on the ground and play golf (or miniature golf), or you can take to the "skies."

If golf is your passion, you already know that Gary Player, Annika Sorenstam, Nick Faldo, and the late Arnold Palmer—in fact, almost half the PGA tour—called Orlando their off-road home. It's not by accident that the Golf Channel originates from here. The Bay Hill Invitational and several LPGA tourneys (the headquarters is in Daytona) come to Orlando every year. And with more than 170 public and private courses, more than 20 golf academies, and dozens of mini golf putts, there's ample opportunity for you to play on world-class courses such as Grand Cypress or Champions Gate.

Hotels

With tens of thousands of lodging choices available in the Orlando area, from tents to deluxe villas, there is no lack of variety in price or amenities. In fact, narrowing down the possibilities is part of the fun.

More than 72 million visitors come to the Orlando area each year, making it the most popular tourism destination on the planet. More upscale hotels are opening as visitors demand more luxurious surroundings, such as luxe linens, tasteful and refined decor, organic toiletries, or ergonomic chairs and work desks. But no matter what your budget or desires, lodging comes in such a wide range of prices, themes, color schemes, brands, meal plans, and guest-room amenities, you will have no problem finding something that fits.

Resorts on and off Disney property combine function with fantasy, as befits visitor expectations. Characters in costume perform for the kids, pools are pirates' caves with waterfalls, and some, like the Gaylord Palms, go so far as to re-create Florida landmarks under a gargantuan glass roof, giving visitors the illusion of having visited more of the state than they expected.

International Drive's expanding attractions, including the Wheel at ICON Park (formerly the Orlando Eye), Madame Tussauds, and a widening array of eateries, are drawing more savvy conventioneers who bring their families along for the fun.

Many hotels have joined the trend toward green lodging, bringing recycling, water conservation, and other environmentally conscious practices to the table. Best of all, the sheer number and variety of hotel rooms means you can still find relative bargains throughout the Orlando area, even on Disney property, by researching your trip well, calling the lodgings directly, negotiating packages and prices, and shopping wisely.

About Our Reviews

Prices: Prices in the hotel reviews are the lowest cost of a standard double room in high season, excluding taxes, service charges, resort fees, and meal plans (except at all-inclusives). Prices for rentals are the lowest per-night cost for a one-bedroom unit in high season. Note that taxes in Central Florida can be as high as 12.5%.

Hotel reviews have been shortened. For full information, visit Fodors.com.

Reservations

Always book your lodging months in advance in Orlando, regardless of where you stay.

Walt Disney Travel Co

Packages can be arranged through the Walt Disney Travel Co., a service set up for UK and European travelers. Guests can find planning tools on the website that allow them to customize vacation itineraries based on interests as well as age, height restrictions, and medical needs. ⊠ *3 Queen Caroline St.* ☎ *800/2006–0809* 🌐 *www.disneyholidays.com.*

WDW Central Reservations Office
You can book many accommodations—Disney-owned hotels and some non-Disney-owned hotels—through the WDW Central Reservations Office. The website allows you to compare prices at the various on-site resorts.

People with disabilities can also use this number, as the representatives are all knowledgeable about services available at resorts and parks for guests with disabilities. All representatives have TTY ability. The website is also a valuable source for specific needs. Go to Guest Services and search the word *Disabilities.* ☎ *407/939–7838* 🌐 *disneyworld.disney.go.com.*

What It Costs

$	$$	$$$	$$$$
FOR TWO PEOPLE			
under $200	$200–$300	$301–$400	over $400

Visitor Information

CONTACTS Orlando Visitors Bureau. ⊠ *8102 International Dr., Orlando* ☎ *407/363–5872, 407/363–5872* 🌐 *www.visitorlando.com.*

Orlando

There's more to Orlando than theme parks: a thriving Downtown with ample opportunity to stay, eat, and play. Internationally recognized cultural events, theater, and the evolving music scene make Downtown more than just a stopping point.

Central Orlando

Sights

Crayola Experience
AMUSEMENT PARK/WATER PARK | FAMILY | One of the company's five "experiences" in the country, Crayola offers a 70,000-square-foot haven of color at the Florida Mall. An overwhelming 26 interactive stations extend throughout the two-floor center, including painting and modeling stations, where tykes can create animals out of clay and melted crayons. Don't miss the younger set's favorite: You Design, a virtual studio for coloring and digitally accessorizing a car or fashion wardrobe before watching the personal design make its debut on a large projected screen. Also be sure to make it a priority to check out the Crayon Factory, where live demonstrations show the crayon creation process from wax to wrapper. ⊠ *The Florida Mall, 8001 Orange Blossom Trail, Central Orlando* ☎ *407/757–1700* 🌐 *www.crayolaexperience.com* 🎫 *$24.99.*

★ Harry P. Leu Gardens
GARDEN | A few miles outside Downtown—on the former lakefront estate of a citrus entrepreneur—is this 50-acre garden. Among the highlights are a collection of historical blooms (many varieties of which were established before 1900), ancient oaks, a 50-foot floral clock, and one of the largest camellia collections in eastern North America (in bloom November–March). Mary Jane's Rose Garden, named after Leu's wife, is filled with more than 1,000 bushes; it's the largest formal rose garden south of Atlanta. The simple 19th-century Leu House Museum, once the Leu family home, preserves the furnishings and appointments of a well-to-do, turn-of-the-20th-century Florida family. Admission is free on the first Monday of the month from January through September. ⊠ *1920 N. Forest*

Where Should We Stay?

	VIBE	PROS	CONS
Disney	Thousands of rooms at every price; convenient to Disney parks; free transportation all over WDW complex.	Perks like early park entry, MagicBands or cards, and Magical Express, which lets you circumvent airport bag checks. Free Wi-Fi.	Without a rental car, you likely won't leave Disney. On-site buses, although free, can take a big bite of time out of your entertainment day; convenience comes at a price.
Universal	On-site hotels offer luxury, convenience, and value. Less expensive options are just outside the gates.	Central to Disney, Universal, SeaWorld, malls, and I–4; free water taxis to parks from on-site hotels.	Most on-site hotels are pricey; the Cabana Bay Beach, Aventura, and Endless Summer resorts are reasonable; expect heavy rush-hour traffic during drives to and from other parks.
I-Drive	A hotel, convention center, and activities bonanza. A trolley runs from one end to the other.	Outlet malls provide bargains; world-class restaurants; the Wheel at ICON Park lifts visitors up for a bird's-eye view; many hotels offer free park shuttles.	Transportation can be pricey, in cash and in time, as traffic is often heavy. Crime is up, especially after dark, although area hotels and businesses have increased security.
Kissimmee	It offers mom-and-pop motels and upscale choices, restaurants, and places to buy saltwater taffy.	It's just outside Disney, very close to Magic Kingdom. Lots of Old Florida charm and low prices.	Some of the older motels here are a little seedy. Petty crime in which tourists are victims is rare—but not unheard of.
Lake Buena Vista	Many hotel and restaurant chains here. Adjacent to WDW, which is where almost every guest in your hotel is headed.	Really close to WDW; plenty of dining and shopping options; easy access to I–4.	Heavy peak-hour traffic. As in all neighborhoods near Disney, a gallon of gas will cost 10%–15% more than elsewhere.
Central Orlando	Parts of town have the modern high-rises you'd expect. Other areas have oak tree–lined brick streets winding among small, cypress-ringed lakes.	Locally owned restaurants, trendy hotels, vibrant nightlife, and some quaint B&Bs. City buses serve the parks. There's good access to I–4.	You'll need to rent a car. And you will be part of the traffic headed to WDW. Expect the 25-mile drive to take at least 45 minutes.
Orlando International Airport	Mostly business and flight-crew hotels and car-rental outlets.	Great if you have an early flight or just want to shop in a mall. There's even a Hyatt on-site.	Watching planes, buses, taxis, and cars arrive and depart is all the entertainment you'll get.

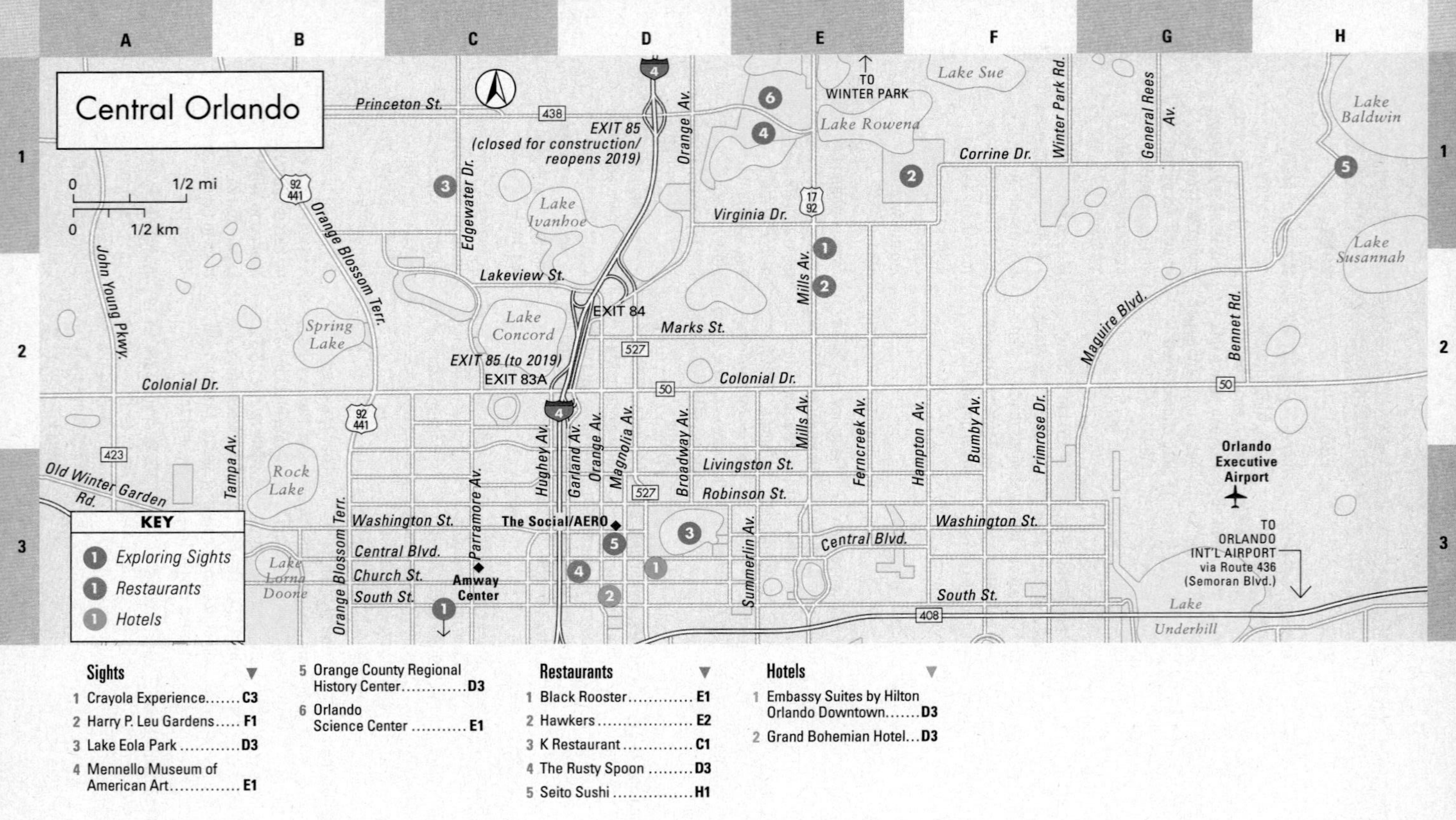
Central Orlando
0
1/2 mi
0
1/2 km
KEY
Exploring Sights
Restaurants
Hotels
A
B
C
D
E
F
G
H
1
2
3
TO WINTER PARK
Princeton St.
EXIT 85 (closed for construction/ reopens 2019)
EXIT 84
EXIT 85 (to 2019)
EXIT 83A
Lake Sue
Lake Rowena
Lake Baldwin
Lake Susannah
Lake Ivanhoe
Lake Concord
Spring Lake
Rock Lake
Lake Lorna Doone
Lake Underhill
Corrine Dr.
Winter Park Rd.
General Rees Av.
Edgewater Dr.
Orange Av.
Virginia Dr.
Lakeview St.
Mills Av.
Marks St.
John Young Pkwy.
Orange Blossom Terr.
Colonial Dr.
Maguire Blvd.
Bennet Rd.
Tampa Av.
Old Winter Garden Rd.
Hughey Av.
Garland Av.
Magnolia Av.
Broadway Av.
Ferncreek Av.
Hampton Av.
Bumby Av.
Primrose Dr.
Livingston St.
Robinson St.
Washington St.
Central Blvd.
Church St.
South St.
Parramore Av.
Summerlin Av.
The Social/AERO
Amway Center
Orlando Executive Airport
TO ORLANDO INT'L AIRPORT via Route 436 (Semoran Blvd.)
Sights
1 Crayola Experience....... C3
2 Harry P. Leu Gardens..... F1
3 Lake Eola Park D3
4 Mennello Museum of American Art.............. E1
5 Orange County Regional History Center............. D3
6 Orlando Science Center E1
Restaurants
1 Black Rooster............ E1
2 Hawkers.................. E2
3 K Restaurant............. C1
4 The Rusty Spoon D3
5 Seito Sushi H1
Hotels
1 Embassy Suites by Hilton Orlando Downtown....... D3
2 Grand Bohemian Hotel... D3

Ave., Audubon Park ☎ *407/246–2620* 🌐 *www.leugardens.org* 🎟 *$10.*

Lake Eola Park

FOUNTAIN | FAMILY | This beautifully landscaped 43-acre park is the verdant heart of Downtown Orlando, its mile-long walking path a gathering place for families, health enthusiasts out for a run, and culture mavens exploring area offerings. The well-lighted playground is alive with children; and ducks, swans, and native Florida birds call the lake home. A popular and expanded farmers' market takes up residence on Sunday morning and afternoon. The lakeside Walt Disney Amphitheater is a dramatic site for concerts, ethnic festivals, and spectacular Fourth of July fireworks. Don't resist the park's biggest draw: a ride in a swan-shaped pedal boat. Up to five adults can fit comfortably in each. (Children under 16 must be accompanied by an adult.) The Relax Grill, by the swan-boat launch, is a great place for a snack. The park is surrounded by great Downtown and Thornton Park restaurants and lounges. The ever-expanding skyline rings the lake with modern high-rises, making the peace of the park even more welcome. The landmark fountain features an LED-light-and-music show on summer evenings at 9:30. ✉ *195 N. Rosalind Ave., Downtown Orlando* ✣ *Center of Downtown Orlando* ☎ *407/246–4485 park, 407/246–4485* 🌐 *www.cityoforlando.net/parks/lake-eola-park* 🎟 *Swan boat rental $15 per ½ hr.*

★ Mennello Museum of American Art

MUSEUM | One of the few museums in the United States devoted to folk art has intimate galleries, some with lovely lakefront views. Look for the nation's most extensive permanent collection of Earl Cunningham paintings as well as works by many other self-taught artists. There's a wonderful video about Cunningham and his "curio shop" in St. Augustine, Florida. Temporary exhibitions have included the works of Wyeth, Cassatt, and Michael Eastman. At the museum shop you can purchase folk-art books, toys, and unusual gifts. The Marilyn L. Mennello Sculpture Garden is always open to the public. Oversized outdoor sculptures include works by Alice Aycock and Barbara Sorensen, shown alongside the 350-year-old live oak tree called "The Mayor." The Mennello is the site of the free annual Orlando Indie-Folk Festival, held the second weekend of February. ✉ *900 E. Princeton St., Lake Ivanhoe* ☎ *407/246–4278* 🌐 *www.mennellomuseum.org* 🎟 *$5* ⏲ *Closed Mon.*

Orange County Regional History Center

MUSEUM | FAMILY | Exhibits here take you on a journey back in time to discover how Florida's Paleo-Indians hunted and fished the land, what the Sunshine State was like when the Spaniards first arrived, and how life in Florida was different when citrus was king. Exhibitions cover the history of citrus-growing in Central Florida, samples of the work of the famed Highwaymen painters, and the advancement of the theme parks. Traveling exhibits bring modern technology and art to the museum. Free audio tours are available. **■ TIP→ Ticket holders get four hours free parking** ✉ *65 E. Central Blvd., Downtown Orlando* ☎ *407/836–8500, 800/965–2030* 🌐 *www.thehistorycenter.org* 🎟 *$8.*

★ Orlando Science Center

MUSEUM | FAMILY | The expanded, 11,000-square-foot Kids Town remains the center's most popular attraction. With exhibits about the human body, mechanics, computers, math, nature, the solar system, and optics, the science center has something for every child's inner geek. Traveling shows include an astronaut experience, the science of human anatomy, and the annual interactive technology expo called Otricon.

The four-story internal atrium is home to live gators and turtles and is a great spot for simply gazing at what Old Florida

The 300-seat Dr. Phillips CineDome, a movie theater with an eight-story screen at the Orlando Science Center, offers large-format Iwerks films.

once looked like. The 300-seat Dr. Phillips CineDome, a movie theater with a giant eight-story screen, offers large-format Iwerks films and planetarium programs. The Crosby Observatory and Florida's largest publicly accessible refractor telescope are here, as are several smaller telescopes; late-evening weekend date nights make the observatory a fun draw for adults, who can enjoy events like the annual Science of Wine and Cosmic Golf Challenge; and the very popular First Wednesdays wine-and-music gatherings. ✉ *777 E. Princeton St., Lake Ivanhoe* ☎ *407/514–2000* 🌐 *www.osc.org* 🎫 *$20.95; parking $5* 🕒 *Closed Wed. (except for First Wednesday evenings).*

Restaurants

★ Black Rooster

$ | **MEXICAN FUSION** | **FAMILY** | Nestled in the funky neighborhood of Mills 50, this small, casual taco place has everything from corn tortillas to guacamole that are made to order with every dish. Get the pulled roasted chicken tinga for sophisticated tastes, and the crispy fish for an unusual alternative to the Rooster's seared beef carne asada. **Known for:** inventive and flavorful tacos; chocolate chip spicy flan; made to order guacamole. $ *Average main: $4* ✉ *1323 N. Mills Ave., Central Orlando* ☎ *407/601–0994* 🌐 *www.blackroostertaqueria.com/* 🕒 *Closed Mon.*

★ Hawkers

$$ | **ASIAN FUSION** | **FAMILY** | Hipsters, families, and business groups dine side by side at this popular restaurant, a laid-back spot that specializes in Asian street food. Travel the continent with scratch-made family recipes from all around Southeast Asia. **Known for:** typical dishes like roti canai, sesame noodles, and stir-fried udon; hip and casual atmosphere; extensive and exotic beer selections. $ *Average main: $16* ✉ *1103 N. Mills Ave., Mills 50 District* ☎ *407/237–0606* 🌐 *eathawkers.com.*

★ K Restaurant

$$$$ | **AMERICAN** | At the forefront of Orlando's local and sustainable dining scene, K

is a hot spot for locals, serving upscale, eclectic American and Italian cuisine in an intimate setting. Besides happy-hour specials and dinner, K hosts wine tastings in the garden or on the patio and popular prix-fixe wine dinners. **Known for:** ever-changing seasonal menu; great local meeting spot away from Downtown Orlando; mac-and-cheese specials. *Average main: $34* *1710 Edgewater Dr., College Park* *407/872–2332* *www.krestaurantorlando.com* *Sun.*

★ The Rusty Spoon

$$$ | AMERICAN | Lovingly raised animals and locally grown produce are the menu foundation at this Downtown gastropub owned by chef Kathleen Blake, a multiple James Beard Award nominee. It's an ideal spot for a business lunch or dinner before a basketball game, theater, or concert. **Known for:** locally sourced and Florida-specific ingredients; "Lake Meadow" salad, with local greens and sautéed chicken livers; impressive service. *Average main: $25* *55 W. Church St., Downtown Orlando* *407/401–8811* *www.therustyspoon.com* *No lunch weekends.*

★ Seito Sushi

$$ | JAPANESE FUSION | The epitome of modern Japanese cuisine, Seito offers crowd-pleasing traditional ramen bowls as well as unique, handcrafted sushi combinations. The sophisticated and fun bar specializes in cask whiskey and multiple exclusive sake brands. **Known for:** hand-pulled ramen noodles; exclusively crafted sushi; boneless, fried whole snapper for two. *Average main: $18* *4898 New Broad St., Central Orlando* *407/898–8801* *seitosushi.com* *Baldwin Park.*

Hotels

Embassy Suites by Hilton Orlando Downtown

$$ | HOTEL | FAMILY | A short walk from a half-dozen cafés and restaurants, the Orange County History Center, and the performing arts center and sports venue, this hotel has numerous suites with views of nearby Lake Eola and its centerpiece fountain, swan boats, and jogging path. **Pros:** near Lake Eola and Downtown; free continental breakfast and afternoon beverages; free Wi-Fi. **Cons:** traffic can be heavy; on-street parking is hard to find, and there's a fee for on-site parking; Disney is at least 45 minutes away (an hour or more during rush hours). *Rooms from: $249* *191 E. Pine St., Downtown Orlando* *407/841–1000, 800/609–3339* *www.embassysuites.com* *167 suites* *Breakfast.*

Grand Bohemian Hotel

$$ | HOTEL | Located in the heart of Orlando, this European-style property is Downtown's only Four Diamond luxury hotel; it's adjacent to the performing arts center, a block from the sports venue, and it showcases hundreds of pieces of art, along with a rare Imperial Grand Bösendorfer piano, played by jazz pianists in the popular Bösendorfer Lounge. **Pros:** art gallery and sophisticated entertainment; free Wi-Fi; great restaurant; quiet, adult-friendly atmosphere. **Cons:** little to attract kids; meals are pricey; fees for parking, far from Disney and Universal. *Rooms from: $299* *325 S. Orange Ave., Downtown Orlando* *407/313–9000, 866/663–0024* *www.grandbohemianhotel.com* *212 rooms* *No meals.*

Nightlife

AERO

BARS/PUBS | On a starry, starry night it's a treat to escape the crowded street-level clubs of Downtown to this rooftop nightclub on top of The Social. Surrounded by some of Orlando's tallest buildings, it exudes hip, trendy vibes that are just right for those looking to dance to a DJ outdoors. Ladies' nights, themed events, and even yoga classes are offered. *60 N. Orange Ave.,*

Downtown Orlando ☎ *407/274–8452* 🌐 *www.aeroorlando.com.*

★ **The Social**

MUSIC CLUBS | Beloved by locals, The Social is a great place to see touring and area musicians. Up to seven nights a week, you can sip trademark martinis while listening to anything from indie rock to rockabilly to music mixed by DJs. Fans love the venue because the stage is low, the bands are close, and the enthusiasm is high. Several now-national acts got their start here, including Seven Mary Three (which released an album called *Orange Ave.* in honor of the venue's location), Matchbox Twenty, and other groups that don't have numbers in their names. Hours vary, and there is usually a cover. ✉ *54 N. Orange Ave., Downtown Orlando* ☎ *407/246–1419* 🌐 *www.thesocial.org.*

Florida Mall

SHOPPING CENTERS/MALLS | With more than 250 stores and 1.7 million square feet of shopping, this mall is large enough to vacation in (even easier since there's a 511-room hotel attached). Its location between the airport and International Drive makes it an easy stop for incoming and departing tourists hunting for a bargain. Exclusive shops include American Girl, the Crayola Experiences, and M&M World. Anchor stores include JC Penney, Dillard's, and Macy's, and dining is equally impressive, with two dozen restaurants and eateries. Stroller and wheelchair rentals are available, as are concierge services and currency exchange. ✉ *8001 S. Orange Blossom Trail, South Orlando* 🌐 *www.simon.com/mall/the-florida-mall.*

International Drive

Aquatica

AMUSEMENT PARK/WATER PARK | **FAMILY** | SeaWorld's water park offers a variety of both single-rider and family raft rides, fast and slow rivers, the enclosed body slide Dolphin Plunge, two massive wave pools and an extensive kids area. With 84,000 square feet of beaches and lagoons, pools and river rafting rides on 59 acres, Aquatica measures up comparably to Disney water parks and Universal's new Volcano Bay water theme park. And with more than 40 waterslides, from the gentle Kata's Kookaburra Cove to the freefall experience of Ihu's Breakaway Falls, Aquatica holds its own in water thrills. Kids are attracted to Walkabout Waters, a 60-foot-tall water-soaking jungle gym, where they can climb, slide, and get soaked. The new Ray Rush family raft ride offers multiple high-speed paths through enclosed tubes and transparent spheres. Teens and adults flock to the Dolphin Plunge, where two side-by-side transparent tubes allow you to join a pod of black-and-white dolphins underwater. Various mascot animals entertain throughout the park. Orcas, dolphins, and two entertaining sea lions, Clyde and Seamore, conduct comedy routines daily. There are height requirements of at least 42 inches for some rides, and all visitors need to know how to swim. ✉ *5800 Water Play Way, International Drive* ☎ *407/545–5500* 🌐 *aquaticabyseaworld.com/en/orlando* 🎟 *$59.99* ⏲ *Closed some days Jan.–Feb.*

Discovery Cove

AMUSEMENT PARK/WATER PARK | **FAMILY** | The only theme park in Orlando that may be called "exclusive," Discovery Cove offers you an uncrowded, daylong experience of animal encounters with dolphins, otters, sharks, and rays, as well as opportunities for relaxing swims and resort-style amenities. Lockers, wet suits, parking, breakfast, lunch, drinks, and snacks are all included in entry. Right next door to SeaWorld, the park has tropical landscaping, white-sand beaches, waterfalls, and vast freshwater lagoons to tempt waterbabies. The Explorer's Aviary houses hundreds of tropical birds. People come for the Atlantic bottlenose dolphin swimming experiences (which are included with park admission but which have been criticized by some animal rights activists), and you can snorkel with tropical fish and rays at the Grand Reef, hand-feed exotic birds, or just float on the Wind Away lazy river. Add-on experiences, such as using a diving helmet in the Grand Reef, or swimming with sharks, are available for an additional cost, and they often sell out. Prices vary wildly depending on day and package options (there are many). Visitors to Discovery Cove get unlimited admission to SeaWorld and Aquatica for 14 consecutive days around the reservation date. ✉ *6000 Discovery Cove Way, International Drive* ☎ *407/513–4600* 🌐 *discoverycove.com* 🎫 *From $230; package options can add up to another $185.*

★ The Wheel at ICON Park

LOCAL INTEREST | FAMILY | The Wheel (formerly called the Orlando Eye) is a 400-foot-tall observation wheel offering an almost unobstructed view of theme parks, lush green landscape, and the soaring buildings of the City Beautiful. Only 15 miles from Walt Disney World and near to Universal Studios Orlando, the massive Ferris wheel anchors ICON Park and its attractions, including Madame Tussauds, SEA LIFE Orlando aquarium, the 450-foot tall Starflyer drop tower, and the Skeletons: Museum of Osteology exhibit. The wheel's 30 high-tech capsules complete a rotation every 30 minutes. Apple iPad Air tablets on board help to locate points of interest throughout the trip, including the nearby theme parks, scenic landscapes, and even the Atlantic coast. Visibility on clear days can be more than 50 miles, reaching all the way east to Cape Canaveral. Rent a private capsule for up to 15 people, with champagne, for a sky-high experience. ✉ *I-Drive 360, 8401 International Dr., International Drive* ☎ *407/270–8644* 🌐 *iconparkorlando.com* 🎫 *$27.99.*

Fun Spot America

AMUSEMENT PARK/WATER PARK | FAMILY | Virtual reality met real excitement when Fun Spot added a VR system to its Freedom Flyer coaster, a high-tech element to a park known for wooden roller coasters, go-karts, and twirling teacups. You can see the neon-lit rides from miles away as you approach International Drive. Four go-kart tracks offer a variety of driving experiences. Though drivers must be at least 10 years old and meet height requirements, parents can drive younger children in two-seater cars on several of the tracks, including the Conquest Track. Nineteen rides range from the dizzying Paratrooper to an old-fashioned Revolver Ferris Wheel to the twirling toddler Teacups. Fun Spot features Central Florida's only wooden roller coaster as well as the Freedom Flyer steel suspension family coaster, a kiddie coaster, and SkyCoaster—part skydive, part hang-glide. There's also an arcade. The park's newest addition is the Gator Spot, in partnership with the iconic Gatorland and starring several live alligators and other Florida wildlife; it's a throwback to the old days of Orlando roadside attractions. ✉ *5700 Fun Spot Way, International Drive* ✥ *From Exit 75A, turn left onto International Dr., then left on Fun Spot Way* ☎ *407/363–3867* 🌐 *www.funspotattractions.com* 🎫 *$44.95 for all rides (online discounts available); some rides extra; admission for nonriders free.*

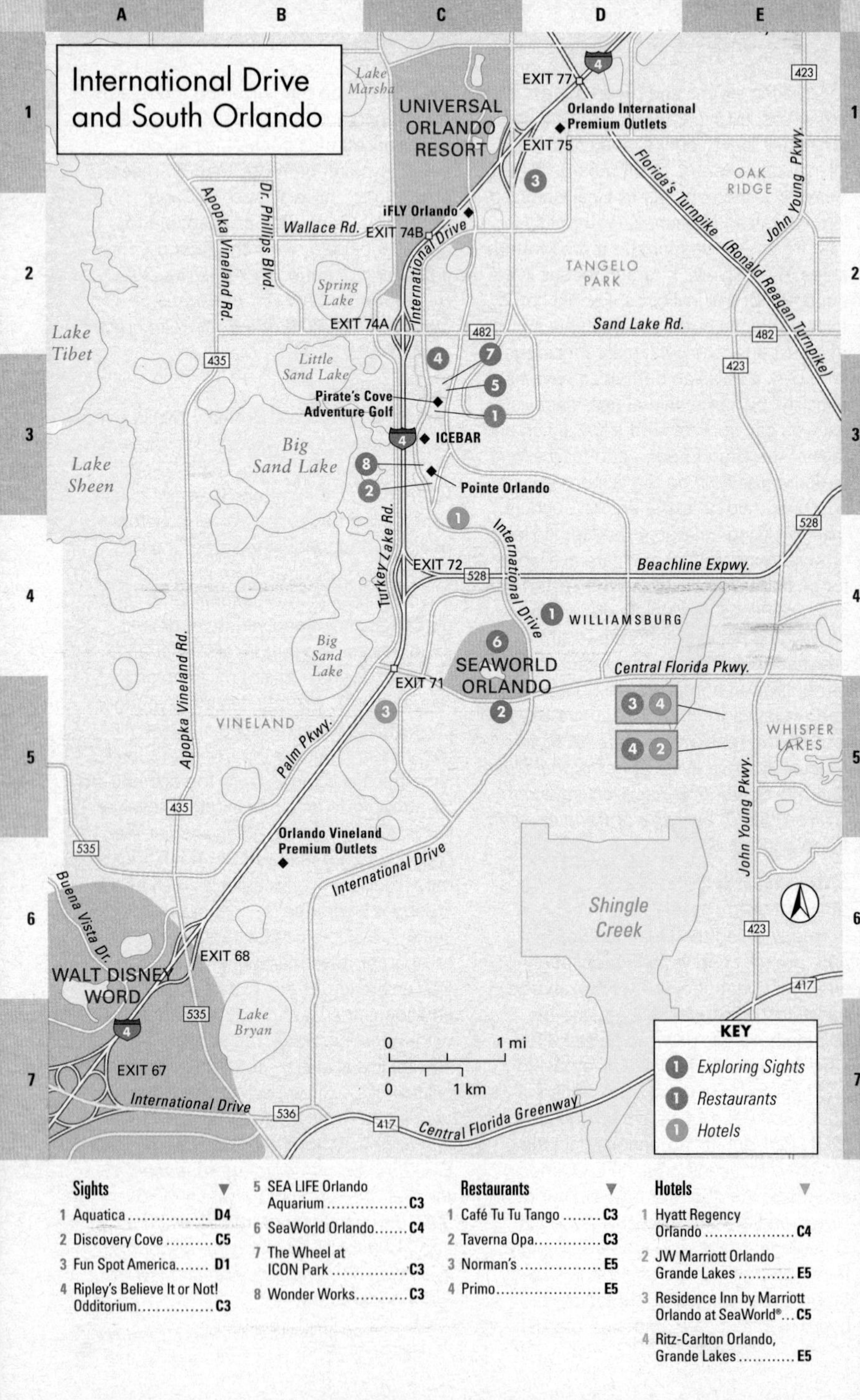

Sights

1 Aquatica D4
2 Discovery Cove C5
3 Fun Spot America....... D1
4 Ripley's Believe It or Not! Odditorium................ C3
5 SEA LIFE Orlando Aquarium C3
6 SeaWorld Orlando....... C4
7 The Wheel at ICON Park C3
8 Wonder Works.......... C3

Restaurants

1 Café Tu Tu Tango C3
2 Taverna Opa............. C3
3 Norman's E5
4 Primo..................... E5

Hotels

1 Hyatt Regency Orlando C4
2 JW Marriott Orlando Grande Lakes E5
3 Residence Inn by Marriott Orlando at SeaWorld®... C5
4 Ritz-Carlton Orlando, Grande Lakes E5

Ripley's Believe It or Not! Odditorium

MUSEUM | A 10-foot-square section of the Berlin Wall, a pain and torture chamber, two African fertility statues that women swear have helped them conceive—these and almost 200 other oddities (shrunken heads included) speak for themselves in this museum-cum-attraction in the heart of tourist territory on International Drive. The building itself is designed to appear as if it's sliding into one of Florida's notorious sinkholes. Give yourself an hour or two to soak up the weirdness, but remember: this is a looking, not touching, experience; it might drive antsy youngsters—and their parents—crazy. **■TIP→ Buy tickets online ahead of time, and you can get discounts.** ✉ *I-Drive 360, 8201 International Dr., International Drive* ☎ *407/351–5803* 🌐 *www.ripleysorlando.com* 🎟 *$21.99; parking free; online discounts.*

★ SEA LIFE Orlando Aquarium

ZOO | **FAMILY** | In the shadow of a 400-foot observation wheel and within the ICON Orlando 360 entertainment complex stands a kaleidoscope of underwater colors, where you can see some 5,000 sea creatures and explore various habitats. Plan to spend the better part of an afternoon exploring the attraction, as all ages delight at the close encounters with the aquarium's sharks, green sea turtles, and jellyfish. With an emphasis on education and conservation, exhibits are playful and informative, with fun features that include a 360-degree ocean tunnel and a children's soft play area. Combo tickets are available for SEA LIFE, the ICON Orlando wheel, and Madame Tussauds. ✉ *I-Drive 360, 8449 International Dr., International Drive* ☎ *866/622–0607* 🌐 *iconorlando.com/venues/attractions/sea-life-orlando-aquarium* 🎟 *$28.*

SeaWorld Orlando

AMUSEMENT PARK/WATER PARK | The oldest operating, biggest, and perhaps most controversial marine mammal park in the country, SeaWorld has been anchoring the Orlando Disney–alternative theme park business since 1964. Much has been made of the company's handling of animals, and they've been in "rebuild and repair" mode for several years after attendance and stock prices plummeted. But rumors of a sale haven't kept the park from introducing new, water-themed attractions: the birth of two walrus calves, Ginger and Aku, garnered a lot of attention, as did the virtual reality–augmented Kraken Unleashed coaster, and the world's tallest river raft drop, the Infinity Falls River Rapids. Coaster rides and literal spills are the order of the day, with more swirling, looping, and very wet coasters than just about anywhere. The 400-foot Sky Tower offers a bird's-eye view of the park, while the Mako and Manta coasters skim tantalizingly close to the water; SeaWorld proclaims Mako as Orlando's tallest, fastest, and longest roller coaster. Kraken Unleashed soars to 150 feet while riders dangle their feet from the floorless track and experience a virtual reality, headset-driven, sea-floor experience. The continuing animal attractions focus more on education than performance, but dolphin and orca stadium shows are still a big draw. You can visit the ice-filled home of Puck the penguin in Antarctica: Empire of the Penguin, while Clyde and Seamore's Sea Lion High brings out playful sea lions, walruses, and otters. Shark Encounter leads parkgoers through one of the world's largest underwater viewing tunnels to be surrounded by sharks, while the Stingray Lagoon offers hands-on encounters with stingrays and mantas. Much heralded by the park, marine animal rehab is the focus of the Manatee Rehabilitation Area, where visitors can see an up-close view of rescue operations; Pelican Preserve with bird rescue; and Pacific Point Preserve, which focuses on rehabilitating injured sea lions. ✉ *7007 SeaWorld Dr., International Drive* ☎ *407/545–5550* 🌐 *seaworld.com* 🎟 *$79.99, $20 parking.*

WonderWorks

AMUSEMENT PARK/WATER PARK | FAMILY | The building seems to be sinking into the ground—at a precarious angle and upside down. Many people stop to take pictures in front of the topsy-turvy facade, complete with upended palm trees and broken skyward-facing sidewalks. Inside the upside-down theme continues only as far as the lobby. After that it's a playground of 100 interactive experiences—some incorporating virtual reality, others educational (similar to those at a science museum), and still others pure entertainment. You can experience an earthquake or a hurricane, land a space shuttle using simulator controls, make giant bubbles in the Bubble Lab, play laser tag in the enormous laser-tag arena and arcade, design and ride your own roller coaster, lie on a bed of real nails, and play baseball with a virtual Major League batter. An *Outta Control Magic Comedy Dinner Show* is held here nightly. ✉ *9067 International Dr., International Drive* ☎ *407/351–8800* 🌐 *www.wonderworksonline.com/orlando* 🎫 *$33.99; Outta Control Magic Comedy Dinner Show $31.99 (online discounts available); parking $4–$10.*

Restaurants

Café Tu Tu Tango

$$$ | ECLECTIC | The food here is served tapas-style—everything is appetizer-size but plentiful, and relatively inexpensive. The restaurant is designed to resemble an artist's loft; artists paint at easels while diners take a culinary trip around the world. **Known for:** small plates ideal for sharing; live entertainment and artists; "Wine Down Wednesday" drink specials. $ *Average main: $23* ✉ *8625 International Dr., International Drive* ☎ *407/248–2222* 🌐 *www.cafetututango.com.*

Taverna Opa

$$$ | GREEK | FAMILY | This high-energy Greek restaurant offers a fun evening in a lively environment to supplement excellent Greek staples and a nice selection of *meze* (small plate) appetizers. Here the ouzo flows like a mountain stream, the Greek (and global) music almost reaches the level of a rock concert, and the roaming belly dancers actively encourage diners to join in. **Known for:** traditional Greek taverna food; live entertainment; large selection of meze, with vegetarian options. $ *Average main: $27* ✉ *Pointe Orlando, 9101 International Dr., International Drive* ☎ *407/351–8660* 🌐 *www.opaorlando.com.*

Hotels

Hyatt Regency Orlando

$ | RESORT | FAMILY | This deluxe high-rise conference hotel on International Drive offers anything a resort customer could want, with richly appointed rooms, two pools with cabanas, a full-service spa and fitness center the size of your local Y, two large restaurants, and a 360-seat, glass-walled lounge overlooking the pool. **Pros:** good spa; walk to more shops and restaurants; on the I-Ride Trolley route. **Cons:** check-in can take a while if a convention is arriving; long walk from end to end; daily resort and parking fees. $ *Rooms from: $194* ✉ *9801 International Dr., International Drive* ☎ *407/284–1234* 🌐 *www.orlando.regency.hyatt.com* *1,641 rooms* 🍴 *No meals.*

★ Residence Inn by Marriott Orlando at SeaWorld

$$ | HOTEL | FAMILY | From the welcoming lobby to the well-appointed suites (including dishwasher, microwave, pots, pans, dishes) and the parklike atmosphere around the pool, this hotel is a great choice if SeaWorld, Aquatica, I-Drive shopping, Universal, or the Convention Center are on your to-do list; a huge laundry is a boon for families. **Pros:** free shuttles to all theme parks; well-equipped kitchens; free breakfast, Wi-Fi, and parking. **Cons:** not much within walking distance; right next to busy Interstate 4;

it's a long way to Disney. $ *Rooms from: $259* ✉ *11000 Westwood Blvd., International Drive* ☎ *407/313–3600, 800/889–9728* 🌐 *www.residenceinnseaworld.com* *350 suites* 🍽 *Breakfast.*

Nightlife

B.B. King's Blues Club

MUSIC CLUBS | The blues legend-turned-entrepreneur lent his name to a string of blues clubs across America, including this one in Orlando. Like the others, this club has music at its heart. There's a dance floor and stage for live performances by the B.B. King All-Star Band and touring musicians seven nights a week. The variety is impressive, with a wide range of tunes inspired by everyone from the King of Blues (B.B.) to the Queen of Motown (Aretha), and the Soul of Funk (take your pick). Since you can't really experience Delta blues without Delta dining, the club doubles as a restaurant with fried dill pickles, catfish bites, po' boys, ribs, and other comfort foods. Wash it all down with a drink from the full bar. ✉ *Pointe Orlando, 9101 International Dr., International Drive* ☎ *407/370–4550* 🌐 *www.bbkingclubs.com/orlando.*

ICEBAR

BARS/PUBS | Thanks to the miracle of refrigeration, this is Orlando's coolest bar—literally and figuratively. Fifty tons of pure ice are kept at a constant 27°F and have been cut and sculpted by world-class carvers into a cozy (or as cozy as ice can be) sanctuary of tables, sofas, chairs, and a bar. The staff loans you a thermal cape and gloves (upgrade to a faux fur coat for an extra $10), and when you enter the frozen hall your drink is served in a glass made of crystal clear ice. There's no cover charge if you just want to hang out in the Fire Lounge or outdoor Polar Patio, but you will pay a cover to spend as much time as you can handle in the subfreezing ICEBAR. There's no beer or wine inside; it's simply too cold. **TIP→ For a non-frozen evening, visit the attached Fire Lounge** ✉ *Pointe Orlando, 8967 International Dr., International Drive* ☎ *407/426–7555* 🌐 *www.icebarorlando.com* 🎟 *$19.95; upgrade packages available.*

Shopping

Orlando International Premium Outlets

OUTLET/DISCOUNT STORES | Just a short drive from Universal Orlando, the city's largest outlet mall is a prime destination for international shoppers, who can find shoes, clothing, cosmetics, electronics, and household goods at a fraction of their home-country prices. The massive complex at the north tip of International Drive includes hot brands such as Armani, 7 for All Mankind, Bebe, Janie and Jack, Boss, and Skagen, along with Saks OFF 5th, Brooks Brothers, Coach, Kate Spade, and Disney. Searching for bargains works up an appetite, and there are plenty of places to eat here, too, either in the well-lit food court or in one of several sit-down and highly regarded restaurants. ✉ *International Drive, 4951 International Dr., International Drive* ☎ *407/352–9611* 🌐 *www.premiumoutlets.com/outlet/orlando-international.*

Orlando Vineland Premium Outlets

OUTLET/DISCOUNT STORES | This outlet capitalizes on its proximity to Disney (it's at the confluence of Interstate 4, State Road 535, and International Drive). Although it's easier to see from the highway than to enter (and parking is tedious and scarce), some smart shoppers have lunch on International Drive and take the I-Ride Trolley right to the front entrance (it runs every 15 minutes). The center's design makes this almost an open-air market, so walking can be pleasant on a nice day. You'll find Bottega Veneta, Burberry, Calvin Klein, Prada, Adidas, Tory Burch, Tommy Hilfiger, and Salvatore Ferragamo, among more than 160 stores. ✉ *8200 Vineland Ave., International Drive* ☎ *407/238–7787* 🌐 *www.premiumoutlets.com/outlet/orlando-vineland.*

Pointe Orlando

SHOPPING CENTERS/MALLS | **FAMILY** | This dining, shopping, and entertainment spot is conveniently located within walking distance of five top hotels and the Orange County Convention Center. Note that it costs to park. In addition to WonderWorks (an indoor hands-on science center) and the enormous Regal IMAX theater, the complex has specialty shops such as Hollister, Charming Charlie, Moondance, and Victoria's Secret. Restaurants have become a reason to visit, with the very high-end Capital Grille, the Oceanaire Seafood Room, Cuba Libre Restaurant and Rum Bar, The Pub, Marlow's Tavern, the popular Itta Bene, B.B. King's Blues Club, and Taverna Opa. Blue Martini and Lafayette's provide after-hours entertainment and adult beverages, Main Event is a restaurant/bowling alley, and The Improv features nationally recognized comedians. ✉ *9101 International Dr., International Drive* ☎ *407/248–2838* 🌐 *www.pointeorlando.com.*

South Orlando

Restaurants

★ Norman's

$$$$ | **ECLECTIC** | Legendary Florida chef Norman Van Aken brings impressive credentials to the restaurant that bears his name: he's credited with creating Floribbean cuisine and coining the term *fusion cooking.* The resort operation is a formal, sleek restaurant with marble floors, starched tablecloths, servers in ties and vests, eight certified sommeliers, and a creative, if expensive, menu. **Known for:** legendary James Beard Award–winning chef; exceptional seafood and Wagyu beef; extensive wine list. $ *Average main: $49* ✉ *Ritz-Carlton Orlando Grande Lakes, 4000 Central Florida Pkwy., South Orlando* ☎ *407/393–4333* 🌐 *www.normans.com* ⏲ *No lunch.*

★ Primo

$$$$ | **ITALIAN** | Chef Melissa Kelly cloned her Italian-organic Maine restaurant in an upscale Orlando hotel and brought her farm-to-table sensibilities with her. Here the daily dinner menu pays tribute to Italian cuisine utilizing produce grown in the hotel's organic garden. **Known for:** constantly changing menu using locally sourced ingredients; award-winning celebrity chef; homemade pastas. $ *Average main: $43* ✉ *JW Marriott Orlando Grande Lakes, 4040 Central Florida Pkwy., South Orlando* ☎ *407/393–4444* 🌐 *www.primorestaurant.com* ⏲ *No lunch.*

Hotels

JW Marriott Orlando Grande Lakes

$$ | **RESORT** | **FAMILY** | This lush resort, set in 500 acres of natural beauty, offers amenities galore, including a European-style spa, a Greg Norman–designed golf course, a lazy river–style pool complex, and kids' programs; rooms have ergonomic workstations and flat-screen TVs, and the restaurants are supplied from the property's organic farm. **Pros:** pool is great for kids and adults; shares amenities with the Ritz Carlton, including huge spa; free shuttle to SeaWorld and Universal. **Cons:** steep daily resort fee for parking and in-room Wi-Fi; the resort is huge and spread out; need a car to reach Disney or shopping. $ *Rooms from: $289* ✉ *4040 Central Florida Pkwy., South Orlando* ☎ *407/206–2300, 800/576–5750* 🌐 *www.grandelakes.com* *1,000 rooms* *No meals.*

★ Ritz-Carlton Orlando, Grande Lakes

$$$$ | **RESORT** | **FAMILY** | Orlando's only Ritz-Carlton is a particularly extravagant link in the luxury chain: it shares a lush 500-acre campus with the JW Marriott, and offers exemplary service, excellent restaurants, children's programs, a golf course, and 40-room spa; suites have balconies, decadent white-marble baths, and deluxe bedding, and a Royal Suite

Did You Know?

Walt Disney World has 27 holes of golf on three championship courses, as well as two miniature golf courses and a 9-hole walking course. Golfers who stay at a Disney property get free cabs from the hotel to the course and back.

satisfies even the most noble guest. **Pros:** truly luxurious; impeccable service; transportation to theme parks. **Cons:** remote from theme parks, attractions; lots of convention and meeting traffic; daily resort fee and parking fee. $ *Rooms from: $569* ✉ *4012 Central Florida Pkwy., South Orlando* ☎ *407/206–2400, 800/576–5760* 🌐 *www.ritzcarlton.com* *582 rooms* 🍽 *Breakfast; Some meals.*

Sand Lake Road

Restaurants

★ Peperoncino

$$$ | **ITALIAN** | You'll be transported to Calabria at this comfortable Italian restaurant. Divided into trattoria and pizzeria, chef-owners Barbara Alfano and Danilo Martorano put out a fresh menu of Italian specialties every evening. **Known for:** Southern Italian cuisine; duck breast and mushroom risotto; classic Italian pizza. $ *Average main: $25* ✉ *Dellagio, 7988 Via Dellagio Way, Ste. 108, Sand Lake Rd. Area* ☎ *407/440–2856* 🌐 *www.peperoncinocucina.com.*

Seasons 52

$$$ | **AMERICAN** | **FAMILY** | Parts of the menu change every week at this innovative restaurant that serves different foods at different times of year, depending on what's in season. It's hard to believe that a chain restaurant can continue to serve healthful yet hearty and very flavorful food, yet it does. **Known for:** waits for tables, even when you have a reservation; $5 plates and wines during the daily happy hour; flatbread starters that are big enough to share. $ *Average main: $21* ✉ *Plaza Venezia, 7700 Sand Lake Rd., Sand Lake Rd. Area* ✣ *I–4 Exit 75A* ☎ *407/354–5212* 🌐 *www.seasons52.com.*

★ Urbain 40

$$$ | **ECLECTIC** | Headed by James Beard–nominee Tim Keating, this American brasserie takes cues from classic French and Italian cuisine while adding a decidedly American spin. The simple elegant styling might recall a jazz club of the 1940s (hence the name) with live jazz piano during the evening, but people come for the food. **Known for:** inventive combinations of French, Italian, and Asian influences on American cuisine; perfectly prepared steak dishes; jazz lounge atmosphere during the evening. $ *Average main: $30* ✉ *8000 Via Dellagio Way, Sand Lake Rd. Area* ☎ *407/872–2640* 🌐 *urbain40.com/.*

Vines Grille & Wine Bar

$$$$ | **STEAKHOUSE** | Live jazz and blues music fills the night at the bar section of this dramatically designed restaurant, but the food and drink in the snazzy main dining room are headliners in their own right. The kitchen bills itself as a steak house, but it really is far more than that. **Known for:** extensive wine selection and cocktails; prime steaks cooked on a wood-fired grill; live jazz performances. $ *Average main: $62* ✉ *The Fountains, 7533 W. Sand Lake Rd., Sand Lake Rd. Area* ☎ *407/351–1227* 🌐 *www.seasons52.com* ⏲ *No lunch.*

Activities

★ Bob's Balloons

BALLOONING | **FAMILY** | After meeting in the pre-dawn hours at the ChampionsGate golf resort, you'll drive to one of several popular launch sites and watch as your balloon is prepared to go up, up, and away. For about an hour you'll float between the treetop level and as high as 1,000 feet, with views of farms and forest land, along with horses, deer, wild boar, cattle, and birds flying *below* you. You may be able to see Disney landmarks like the Animal Kingdom's Expedition Everest and Epcot's Spaceship Earth. Several other balloons are likely to go up near you so you'll view these colorful sky ornaments from an unparalleled sight line. There are seats in the basket, but you'll probably be too thrilled to sit down since this is an adventure that definitely surpasses the Magic Kingdom's Peter Pan's Flight. ✉ *Orlando* ☎ *407/466–6380, 877/824–4606* 🌐 *www.bobsballoons.com* 🎫 *From $175 per person.*

★ **Hollywood Drive-In Golf at Universal CityWalk**

MINIATURE GOLF | FAMILY | With a science-fiction alien invasion course paired with a 1950s horror movie monster course, there's something for kids and fun-loving adults alike. Spectacular lighting and sound effects mean that the play is different day and night. A 36-hole Double Feature package is available, and the course is open until 2 am for after theme-park romping. ✉ *6000 Universal Blvd., CityWalk* ☎ *407/802–4848* 🌐 *hollywooddriveingolf.com* 🎫 *From $15.99.*

★ **iFLY Orlando**

FLYING/SKYDIVING/SOARING | Okay, so technically you aren't really skydiving, but you come pretty close as you float atop a cushion of air in this 12-foot-high, 1,000-horsepower wind tunnel. Letting you experience everything skydivers do but closer to the ground, the experience starts with instruction, after which you suit up and hit the wind tunnel, where you soar like a bird (or try to) under your instructor's watchful eye. It's all so realistic that skydiving clubs come to hone their skills. It's also pretty surreal as you look through the window and see people floating in midair. The attraction is safe for anyone under 250 pounds and older than three. The 90-minute introductory experience includes two flights. You can purchase a video of your "jump" at the end. ✉ *8969 International Dr., International Drive* ☎ *407/337–4359* 🌐 *www.iflyworld.com/orlando/* 🎫 *From $69.95.*

Pirate's Cove Adventure Golf

MINIATURE GOLF | FAMILY | Two 18-hole miniature golf courses with a buccaneer theme wind around artificial mountains, through caves, beside waterfalls, and into lush foliage. The beginner's course is called Captain Kidd's Adventure; the more advanced course is Blackbeard's Challenge. In addition to this location at Lake Buena Vista (near Disney), there's a second Pirate's Cove on International Drive. ✉ *Crossroads Shopping Center, 12545 State Rd. 535, Lake Buena Vista* ☎ *407/827–1242* 🌐 *www.piratescove.net* 🎫 *From $13.50 to $22.50.*

Winter Park

6 miles northeast of Orlando, 20 miles northeast of WDW.

This peaceful, upscale community may be just outside the hustle and bustle of Orlando, but it feels like a different country. The town's name reflects its early role as a warm-weather haven for those escaping the frigid blasts of Northeast winters. From the late 1880s until the early 1930s, wealthy industrialists and their families would travel to Florida by rail on vacation, and many stayed, establishing grand homes and cultural institutions. The lovely, 8-square-mile village retains its charm with brick-paved streets, historic buildings, and well-maintained lakes and parkland. Even the town's bucolic 9-hole golf course (open to the public) is on the National Register of Historic Places.

On Park Avenue you can spend a few hours sightseeing, shopping, or both. The street is lined with small boutiques and fine restaurants and bookended by world-class museums: the Charles Hosmer Morse Museum of American Art, with the world's largest collection of artwork by Louis Comfort Tiffany, and the Cornell Fine Arts Museum on the Rollins College campus (the oldest college in Florida).

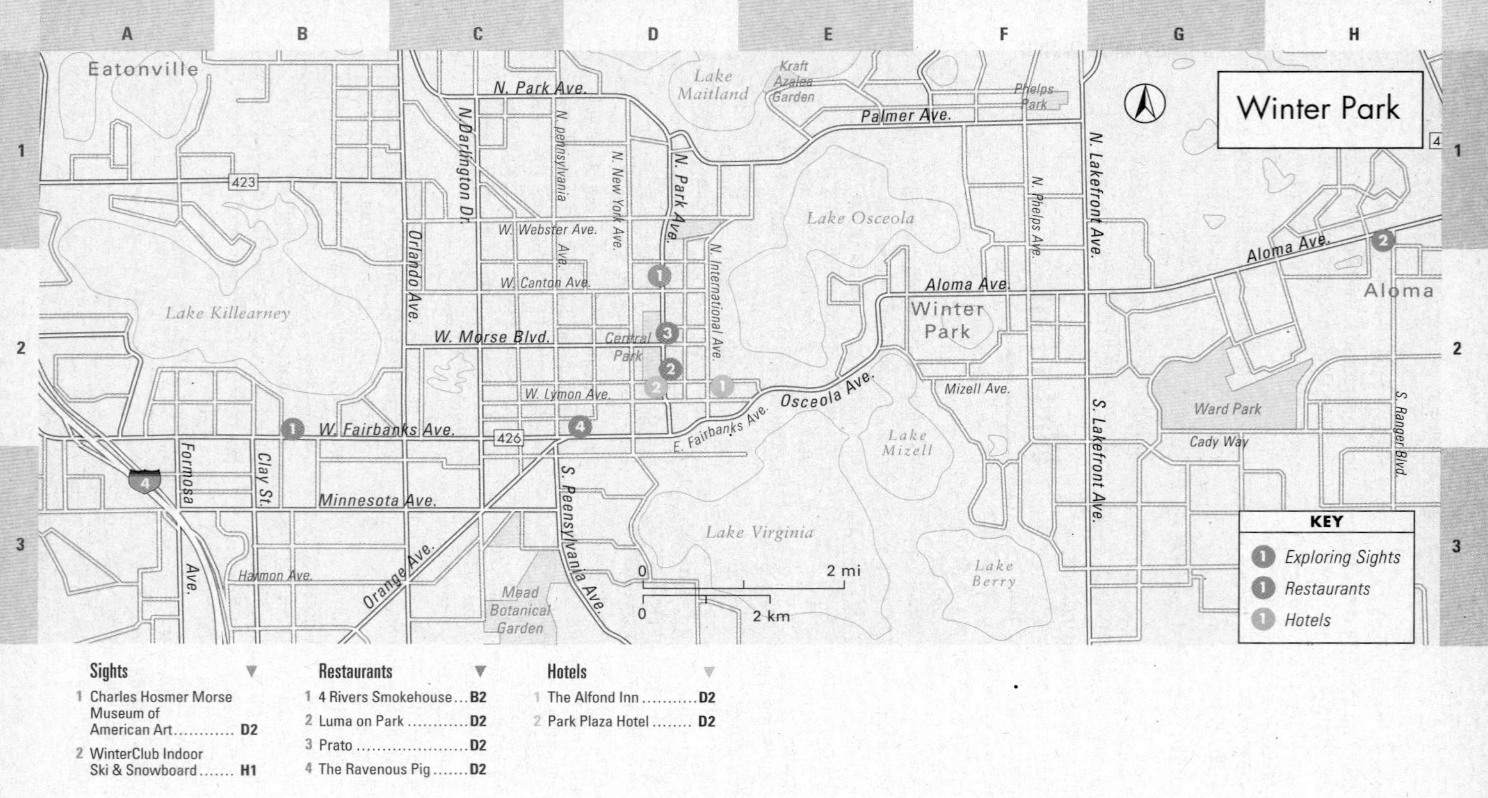

Sights

1 Charles Hosmer Morse Museum of American Art D2

2 WinterClub Indoor Ski & Snowboard H1

Restaurants

1 4 Rivers Smokehouse ... B2

2 Luma on Park D2

3 Prato D2

4 The Ravenous Pig D2

Hotels

1 The Alfond Inn D2

2 Park Plaza Hotel D2

TOURS

Scenic Boat Tour

BOAT TOURS | FAMILY | Head east from Park Avenue and, at the end of Morse Boulevard, you'll find the launching point for this tour, a Winter Park tradition since 1938. The one-hour cruise takes in 12 miles of waterways, including three lakes and narrow, oak- and cypress-shaded canals built in the 1800s as a transportation system for the logging industry. A well-schooled skipper shares stories about the moguls who built their mansions along the shore and points out wildlife and remnants of natural Florida still surrounding the expensive houses. Cash or check only is accepted. ✉ *312 E. Morse Blvd., Winter Park* ☎ *407/644–4056* 🌐 *www.scenicboattours.com* 🎫 *$14; children two–11, $7.*

Sights

★ Charles Hosmer Morse Museum of American Art

MUSEUM | The world's most comprehensive and important collection of work by Louis Comfort Tiffany—including immense stained-glass windows, lamps, watercolors, and desk sets—is in this museum, which also contains American decorative art and paintings from the mid-19th to the early 20th century. Among the draws is the 1,082-square-foot Tiffany Chapel, originally built for the 1893 World's Fair in Chicago. It took craftsmen two and a half years to painstakingly reassemble the chapel here. Many of the works were rescued from Tiffany's Long Island estate, Laurelton Hall, after a 1957 fire destroyed much of the property. The 12,000-square-foot Laurelton Hall wing allows for much more of the estate's collection to be displayed at one time. Exhibits in the wing include architectural and decorative elements from Laurelton's dining room, living room, and Fountain Court reception hall. There's also a re-creation of the striking Daffodil Terrace, so named for the glass daffodils that serve as the capitals for the terrace's marble columns. ✉ *445 N. Park Ave., Winter Park* ☎ *407/645–5311* 🌐 *www.morsemuseum.org* 🎫 *$6; free Fri., Nov.–Apr.* 🕒 *Closed Mon.*

WinterClub Indoor Ski & Snowboard

SPORTS VENUE | FAMILY | Snow enthusiasts can opt for the truly unique experience of skiing and snowboarding in shorts and a T-shirt at Orlando's WinterClub Indoor Ski & Snowboard, proving that heading south doesn't necessarily cancel out winter sports. The region's first indoor ski center welcomes participants at all levels to come practice and play on these high-tech "endless slopes." WinterClub's interactive Ski Simulator fuses high-definition, large video wall ski runs with a unique chassis that allows skiers to experience the same g-force effects as they would skiing in real life. ✉ *2950 Aloma Ave., Winter Park* ☎ *407/618–1123* 🌐 *www.winterclubski.com* 🎫 *From $49, packages available.*

Restaurants

★ 4 Rivers Smokehouse

$ | BARBECUE | FAMILY | What started as a tiny business in a former tire repair shop has turned into a multistate dynasty. The popular 4 Rivers, now with 14 locations and more on the way, turns out slow-cooked barbecue standards like pulled pork and Texas-style brisket. **Known for:** slow-smoked ribs, brisket, and chicken; Sweet Shop bakeries; bacon-wrapped smoked jalapeños. 💲 *Average main: $13* ✉ *1600 W. Fairbanks Ave., Winter Park* ☎ *855/368–7748* 🌐 *4rsmokehouse.com* 🕒 *Closed Sun.*

★ Luma on Park

$$$ | MODERN AMERICAN | One of the Orlando area's best restaurants, Luma on Park is a popular spot for progressive American cuisine served in a fashionable setting, run by award-winning chef Brandon McGlammery. Every ingredient is carefully sourced from local producers when possible, and scratch preparation—from pastas to sausages to pickled rhubarb—is the mantra. **Known for:** North Carolina flounder and Snake River flank steak; extensive wine list; attention to detail. [$] *Average main: $30* ✉ *290 S. Park Ave., Winter Park* ☎ *407/599–4111* 🌐 *www.lumaonpark.com.*

★ Prato

$$$ | **ITALIAN** | Progressive Italian cuisine in a casual, bustling wood-and-brick setting immediately made Prato a local favorite. Every item from the pancetta to the amaretti is crafted from scratch. **Known for:** young, hip clientele; outdoor curbside dining; Neapolitan pizzas. [$] *Average main: $23* ✉ *124 N. Park Ave., Winter Park* ☎ *407/262–0050* 🌐 *www.prato-wp.com* ⏲ *No lunch Mon. and Tues.*

★ The Ravenous Pig

$$$$ | **MODERN AMERICAN** | The first local restaurant to break into the "gastropub" category, the Pig is arguably Orlando's most popular foodie destination and has spawned several offshoots. Run by multiple James Beard–nominees James and Julie Petrakis, this husband-and-wife chef team dispenses delicacies like pork porterhouse or the pub burger. **Known for:** merged with Cask & Larder brewery; open until midnight Thursday–Saturday; house-made charcuterie. [$] *Average main: $31* ✉ *565 W. Fairbanks Ave., Winter Park* ☎ *407/628–2333* 🌐 *www.theravenouspig.com.*

Hotels

The Alfond Inn

$$$$ | **HOTEL** | This serenely sophisticated building in the heart of Winter Park, just steps from the shops and restaurants of Park Avenue, combines an upscale hotel with an art gallery; owned by neighboring Rollins College, rooms are decorated in cool grays with touches of the iconic Winter Park peacock blue, and have work stations and flat-screen TVs. **Pros:** five-minute walk to Park Avenue for pleasant strolls and dining; restaurant on property; free Wi-Fi. **Cons:** at least an hour's drive to the theme parks; valet parking only at $18 a night; traffic passing on the brick streets can be a bit noisy at night. [$] *Rooms from: $399* ✉ *300 E. New England Ave., Winter Park* ☎ *407/998–8090* 🌐 *www.thealfondinn.com* *112 rooms* 🍽 *No meals.*

Park Plaza Hotel

$ | **HOTEL** | Small and intimate, this beautifully updated 1922 establishment in tony Winter Park offers the charm of fern-bedecked wrought-iron balconies, along with free Wi-Fi and free breakfast in bed; the best accommodations are suites that open onto a flower-filled balcony over the street. **Pros:** valet parking; romantic atmosphere; view of Park Avenue shops and restaurants. **Cons:** railroad tracks are close, making for train noise at night; small rooms; a long way from theme parks. [$] *Rooms from: $169* ✉ *307 Park Ave. S, Winter Park* ☎ *407/647–1072, 800/228–7220* 🌐 *www.parkplazahotel.com* *28 rooms* 🍽 *Breakfast.*

Kissimmee

18 miles south of Orlando, 10 miles southeast of Walt Disney World (WDW).

Although Kissimmee is primarily known as the gateway to Disney (technically, the vast Disney property of theme parks and resorts lies in both Osceola and Orange counties), its non-WDW attractions just might tickle your fancy. They range from throwbacks to old-time Florida to dinner shows for you and 2,000 of your closest friends. Orlando is still one of the country's prime cattle producers, and the best sampling of Florida cowboy life is here during the Silver Springs Rodeo in February and June.

With at least 100,000 acres of freshwater lakes, the Kissimmee area brings anglers and boaters to national fishing tournaments and speedboat races. A

Kissimmee's Lake Tohopekaliga (affectionately known as Lake Toho) is famous with fishers the world over. It's also great for wildlife spotting—an especially exhilarating experience when done from an airboat.

50-mile-long series of lakes, the Kissimmee Waterway, connects Lake Tohopekaliga—a Native American name that means "Sleeping Tiger"—with huge Lake Okeechobee in South Florida, and from there, to both the Atlantic Ocean and the Gulf of Mexico.

Sights

Gatorland

AMUSEMENT PARK/WATER PARK | FAMILY | This campy attraction near the Orlando–Kissimmee border on U.S. 441 has endured since 1949 without much change, despite competition from the major parks. Over the years the theme park and registered conservancy has retained its gator-rasslin' spirit. Kids get a kick out of this unmanufactured, old-timey thrill ride.

The Gator Gulley Splash Park is complete with giant "egrets" spilling water from their beaks, dueling water guns mounted atop giant gators, and other water-park splash areas. There's also a small petting zoo and an aviary. A free train ride is a high point, taking you through an alligator breeding marsh and a natural swamp setting where you can spot gators, birds, and turtles. A three-story observation tower overlooks the breeding marsh, swamped with gator grunts, especially come sundown during mating season.

For a glimpse of 37 giant, rare, and deadly crocodiles, check out the *Jungle Crocs of the World* exhibit. To see eager gators leaping out of the water to catch their food, come on cool days for the *Gator Jumparoo Show* (summer heat just puts them to sleep). The most thrilling is the first one in the morning, when the gators are hungriest. There's also a *Gator Wrestlin' Show*, and although there's no doubt who's going to win the match, it's still fun to see the handlers take on those tough guys with the beady eyes. In the educational *Upclose Encounters* show, the show's host handles a variety of snakes. Recent park additions include Panther Springs, featuring brother-and-sister endangered panthers, and the wheelchair-accessible Screamin' Gator Zip Line (additional cost). The park's newest offering is the Stompin' Gator Off-Road Adventure, a cross between a pontoon boat and an off-road monster truck that tours untamed Florida. This is a genuine experience, and you leave knowing the difference between a gator and a croc. ■ **TIP→ Discount coupons are available online.** ✉ *14501 S. Orange Blossom Trail, Kissimmee* ✣ *Between Orlando and Kissimmee* ☎ *407/855–5496, 800/393–5297* 🌐 *www.gatorland.com* 🎫 *$29.99; $36.99 all extras; $10 off-road tours.*

Restaurants

Old Hickory Steakhouse

$$$$ | STEAKHOUSE | This upscale steak house in the Gaylord Palms resort is designed to look like rustic cabins in the Everglades. Beyond the playful facade is a polished restaurant with a classic steak-house menu of steaks and chops. **Known for:** particularly good steaks; free valet parking; consistently good service. 💲 *Average main: $47* ✉ *Gaylord Palms Resort, 6000 W. Osceola Pkwy., Kissimmee* ✣ *I–4 Exit 65* ☎ *407/586–1600* 🌐 *www.gaylordpalms.com* ⏲ *No lunch.*

★ Savion's Place

$ | CARIBBEAN | FAMILY | A melding of island cuisine with American down-home dishes, Savion's independently owned atmosphere extends to the menu. Prince Edward Island mussels share space with lobster mac-and-cheese, while mushroom Marsala meatloaf can appear on the table with "Grandma's recipe" jambalaya. **Known for:** home cooking with a Haitian flair; seafood gumbo and jambalaya; patio dining. 💲 *Average main: $12* ✉ *16 E. Dakin Ave., Kissimmee* ☎ *407/572–8719* 🌐 *savionsplace.com/.*

Hotels

Gaylord Palms Resort and Convention Center

$$ | RESORT | FAMILY | Built in the style of a grand turn-of-the-20th-century Florida resort, this huge building is meant to inspire awe, with an enormous glass-roofed atrium, and re-creations of Florida destination icons such as the Everglades, Key West, and Old St. Augustine; there's also a water park and movie events. **Pros:** you could have a great vacation without ever leaving the grounds; free shuttle to Disney; excellent on-site dining. **Cons:** daily resort and parking fee; distant from Universal or Downtown Orlando; hotel is so big that you will get your exercise walking within the building. 💲 *Rooms from: $239* ✉ *6000 W. Osceola Pkwy., Kissimmee* ☎ *407/586–0000* 🌐 *www.gaylordpalms.com* 🛏 *1,406 rooms* 🍽 *No meals.*

Celebration

Hotels

Meliá Orlando Suite Hotel at Celebration

$ | HOTEL | FAMILY | Much like a European boutique hotel, the Meliá Orlando is very human in scale, minimalist in decor. **Pros:** shuttle to Celebration and Disney parks; spa privileges at Celebration Day Spa; free parking. **Cons:** busy U.S. 192 is close by; daily resort fee; need a car to visit Universal, SeaWorld, or Downtown Orlando. 💲 *Rooms from: $132* ✉ *225 Celebration Pl., Celebration* ☎ *407/964–7000, 888/956–3542* 🌐 *www.melia.com* 🛏 *240 rooms* 🍽 *No meals; Free Breakfast; All-inclusive.*

Lake Buena Vista

Restaurants

★ Capa

$$$$ | **STEAKHOUSE** | Billed as a Spanish steak house, Capa is a concept cleverly executed in a chic, modern dining area. Clean lines are the palette for ancient-looking coins creatively arranged and a decor element of red ruffles reminiscent of a matador's red flag. **Known for:** superb steaks and seafood; grilled duck, lamb, and pork chops; enviable view of fireworks from the outdoor patio. *Average main: $52 ✉ Four Seasons Resort, 10100 Dream Tree Blvd., Lake Buena Vista ☎ 407/313–7777 🌐 www.fourseasons.com/orlando/dining/ ⌚ No lunch.*

La Luce

$$$ | **ITALIAN** | Originated by the late California restaurateur and chef Donna Scala, La Luce brings Italian cuisine with a Napa Valley farm-fresh flair to this upscale Hilton at the edge of Walt Disney World. Pastas are made fresh, steaks are handled with Italian care, and the cocktail bar is second to none. **Known for:** upscale and authentic Italian cuisine; "silk handkerchief" pasta; cocktail bar. *Average main: $30 ✉ Hilton Orlando Bonnet Creek, 14100 Bonnet Creek Resort La., Bonnet Creek ☎ 407/597–3600 🌐 www.laluceorlando.com ⌚ No lunch.*

Hotels

Holiday Inn Resorts Orlando Suites—Waterpark

$ | **RESORT** | **FAMILY** | The six-story resort, formerly the Nickelodeon Hotel, is built around a colorful water park with slides, splash bucket, and climbing zones. **Pros:** kids eat breakfast and dinner free; Disney shuttles included in resort fee; mini golf course. **Cons:** daily resort fee of $30; way too frenetic for folks without kids; poolside rooms can be noisy. *Rooms from: $159 ✉ 14500 Continental Gateway, Lake Buena Vista ☎ 407/387–5437, 866/462–6425 🌐 www.ihg.com/holidayinnresorts/hotels/us/en/orlando/disfs/hoteldetail ⇨ 777 rooms 🍴 Free Breakfast.*

★ Hyatt Regency Grand Cypress Resort

$$ | **RESORT** | **FAMILY** | Sitting amid 1,500 palm-filled acres just outside Disney's gate, this huge luxury resort has a private lake with watercraft, four golf courses, and miles of trails. **Pros:** elaborate spa; lots of recreation options, including huge pool and equestrian center; good on-site restaurants; the resort's Grand Cypress Golf Club has four courses. **Cons:** need a car or taxi to get to Downtown Orlando or Universal; pricey daily resort and parking fees; lots of conventioneers. *Rooms from: $239 ✉ 1 Grand Cypress Blvd., Lake Buena Vista ☎ 407/239–1234, 800/233–1234 🌐 www.hyattgrandcypress.com ⇨ 779 rooms 🍴 No meals.*

Staybridge Suites Lake Buena Vista

$ | **HOTEL** | **FAMILY** | Close to Disney, this pleasant all-suites hotel is perfect for a big family on a small budget who wants a home away from home; it's only a few miles along Palm Parkway from SeaWorld, Universal, and even the airport, so the frenzy of Interstate 4 can be avoided altogether. **Pros:** free scheduled shuttle service to WDW; free hot breakfast; free Wi-Fi and parking. **Cons:** no restaurant; no shuttles to Universal and SeaWorld; pool and dining areas can be crowded. *Rooms from: $172 ✉ 8751 Suiteside Dr., Lake Buena Vista ☎ 407/238–0777 🌐 www.ihg.com/staybridge/hotels/us/en/orlando/mcobv ⇨ 150 rooms 🍴 Breakfast.*

★ Waldorf Astoria Orlando

$$$$ | **RESORT** | Although it can't duplicate the famed original in New York City, this Waldorf echoes it with imagination and flair. **Pros:** lavish and luxurious hotel; free transportation to Disney parks; great spa and Rees Jones–designed golf course. **Cons:** pricey, but you knew that; if you can bear to leave your cabana, you'll need

Wildlife-rich Wekiwa Springs State Park is a great place to camp, hike, picnic, canoe, fish, swim, or snorkel.

a car to see anything else in the area; steep daily resort fee. $ *Rooms from: $489* ✉ *14200 Bonnet Creek Resort Ln., Bonnet Creek* ☎ *407/597–5500* 🌐 *www.waldorfastoriaorlando.com* *328 rooms* 🍽 *No meals.*

Day-Trips From Orlando

Wekiwa Springs State Park

13 miles northwest of Orlando, 28 miles north of WDW.

Sights

★ Wekiwa Springs State Park

NATIONAL/STATE PARK | **FAMILY** | *Wekiva* is a Creek Indian word meaning "flowing water"; *wekiwa* means "spring of water." The river, springs, and surrounding 6,400-acre Wekiwa Springs State Park are well suited to camping, hiking, picnicking, swimming, canoeing, and fishing. The area is also full of Florida wildlife: otters, raccoons, alligators, bobcats, deer, turtles, and birds.

Canoe trips can range from a simple hour-long paddle around the lagoon to observe a colony of water turtles to a full-day excursion through the less congested parts of the river, which haven't changed much since the area was inhabited by the Timacuan Indians. You can rent canoes in the town of Apopka, near the park's southern entrance.

The park has 60 campsites: some are "canoe sites" that you can reach only via the river, and others are "trail sites," meaning you must hike a good bit of the park's 13½-mile trail to reach them. Most, however, are for the less hardy—you can drive right up to them. Sites have electric and water hookups.

✉ *1800 Wekiva Circle, Apopka* ✣ *Take Interstate 4 Exit 94 (Longwood) and turn left on Route 434. Go 1¼ miles to Wekiwa Springs Road; turn right and go 4½ miles to the entrance, on the* *right ☎ 407/884–2008, 407/884–2009 🌐 floridastateparks.org/parks-and-trails/wekiwa-springs-state-park 🎟 $2 per pedestrian or bicycle; $6 per vehicle ⏱ Closes at sundown.*

Legoland

50 miles southwest of Orlando.

Sights

★ LEGOLAND Florida

AMUSEMENT PARK/WATER PARK | FAMILY | In addition to its 1:20-scale LEGO miniature reproductions of U.S. cities, the park features more than 50 rides, shows, and attractions throughout 10 different zones, as well as the marvelous botanical gardens from the original park.

The Danish toy company's philosophy is to help children "play well." And play they do, as LEGOLAND attractions are very hands-on. Kids can hoist themselves to the top of a tower, power a fire truck, or navigate a LEGO robot. Sights include huge LEGO dragons, wizards, knights, pirates, castles, roller coasters, race-tracks, villages, and cities.

The cityscapes in Miniland USA fascinate children and adults, who delight in discovering what's possible when you have enough bricks. Miniland opens with Kennedy Space Center, where a six-foot shuttle waits on the launch pad. Miami Beach features bikini-clad bathers and art deco hotels; St. Augustine and its ancient fort play into LEGO's pirate theme; Key West's Mallory Square is accurate right down to the trained cats leaping through rings of fire. The rest of the United States is not ignored: New York City, Las Vegas, San Francisco, and Washington, D.C., appear in intricate detail. Visitors spend hours looking for amusing details hidden in each city, like New York's purse snatcher.

Among other highlights are Ninjago, where kids battle computer-generated bad guys; LEGO Kingdoms, whose castle towers over a jousting area and a roller coaster where knights, damsels, dragons, and ogres are found; Land of Adventure, where you can explore hidden tombs and hunt for treasure; and the Imagination Zone, showcasing LEGO Mindstorms robots, where a giant head of Albert Einstein invites kids to explore and invent. Things get wild in LEGO Technic, the most active of the park's zones, where Test Track, Aquazone Wave Racers, and Technicycle let the family expend some energy. And the live Pirates' Cove show, where seafaring sailors wearing LEGO suits defend a huge ship from attacking pirates on water skis. LEGO Movie World replaces the former World of Chima park with rides and attractions from the blockbuster, including Splash Battle, Emmet's Triple Decker Flying Couch, and Unikitty's Disco Drop, taking riders to the top of Cloud Cuckoo Land.

LEGOLAND Water Park features a wave pool; Build-a-Raft, where families construct a LEGO vessel and float down a lazy river; a 375-foot pair of intertwined waterslides that plunge riders into a pool; and a DUPLO toddler water play area. Not to be forgotten, Cypress Gardens, at the heart of the park, preserves one of Florida's treasures. Families can wander the lush, tropical foliage and gasp at one of the world's largest banyan trees. Three on-site hotels offer LEGO-themed accommodations and park packages. *✉ 1 LEGOLAND Way, Winter Haven ☎ 877/350–5346 🌐 www.legoland.com 🎟 $94; parking $15; water park $22.50 additional ⏱ Closed Tues. and Wed. during Jan. and Feb.*

Bok Tower Gardens

57 miles southwest of Orlando, 42 miles southwest of WDW.

Sights

★ Bok Tower Gardens

GARDEN | FAMILY | You'll see citrus groves as you ride south along U.S. 27 to the small town of Lake Wales and the Bok Tower Gardens. This appealing sanctuary of plants, flowers, trees, and wildlife has been something of a local secret for years. Shady paths meander through pine forests with silvery moats, mockingbirds and swans, blooming thickets, and hidden sundials. The majestic, 200-foot Bok Tower is constructed of coquina—from seashells—and pink, white, and gray marble. The tower houses a carillon with 60 bronze bells that ring out each day at 1 and 3 pm during 30-minute recitals that might include Early American folk songs, Appalachian tunes, Irish ballads, or Latin hymns. The bells are also featured in recordings every half hour after 10 am, and sometimes even moonlight recitals. The landscape was designed in 1928 by Frederick Law Olmsted Jr., son of the planner of New York's Central Park. The grounds include the 20-room, Mediterranean-style Pinewood Estate, built in 1930 and open for self-guided touring. From January through April, guides lead you on a 60-minute tour of the gardens (included in the admission price); tours of the inside of the tower are a benefit of membership. ✉ *1151 Tower Blvd., Lake Wales* ☎ *863/676–1408* 🌐 *boktowergardens.org* 🎫 *From $15* 🕒 *Hours and access to Pinewood Estate vary seasonally.*

Chapter 11

WALT DISNEY WORLD

Updated by
Joseph Hayes

Sights ★★★★★ | Restaurants ★★★★★ | Hotels ★★★★★ | Shopping ★★★★☆ | Nightlife ★★★★☆

WELCOME TO WALT DISNEY WORLD

TOP REASONS TO GO

★ **Nostalgia:** Face it—Mickey and Company are old friends. And you probably have childhood pictures of yourself in front of Cinderella Castle. Even if you don't, nobody does yesteryear better: head to Main Street, U.S.A., and see.

★ **Memories in the making:** Who doesn't want to snap selfies on the Dumbo ride or of Junior after his Splash Mountain experience? The urge to pass that Disney nostalgia on to the next generation is strong.

★ **The thrills:** For some this means roller coasting to an Aerosmith sound track or simulating space flight; for others it's about cascading down a waterslide, venturing to a Star Wars–themed outer space, or going on safari.

★ **The chills:** If the Pirates of the Caribbean cave doesn't give you goose bumps, try the Haunted Mansion.

★ **The spectacle:** The list is long—fireworks, laser-light displays, arcade games, parades....

Walt Disney World straddles Orange and Osceola counties to the west of Interstate 4. Five exits will get you to the parks and resort areas: 62, 64AB, 65, 67, and 68. To reach hotels along I-Drive, use Exit 71, 72, 74A, or 75A and B.

1 Magic Kingdom. Disney's emblematic park is home to Space Mountain, Pirates of the Caribbean, and an expanded Fantasyland full of experiences.

2 Epcot. Future World's focus is science, technology, and hands-on experiences. In the World Showcase, you can tour 11 countries without getting jet-lagged and ride Frozen Ever After in Norway.

3 Disney's Hollywood Studios. Attractions at this re-creation of old-time Hollywood include Rock 'n' Roller Coaster Starring Aerosmith, Twilight Zone Tower of Terror, and the new Star Wars and Toy Story–related rides and shows.

4 Disney's Animal Kingdom. Amid a 403-acre wildlife preserve are an Asian-themed water ride, an African safari ride, a runaway-train coaster, and the Avatar-inspired land, Pandora.

5 Blizzard Beach. Water thrills range from steep flume rides to tubing expeditions in the midst of a park that you'd swear is a slowly melting ski resort. There's plenty for little ones, too.

6 Typhoon Lagoon. Sandy beaches, oceanlike waves, and a themed water coaster invite castaways to enjoy a day of fun and relaxation. Take the kids on Bay Slides and don snorkels to explore Shark Reef.

7 Disney Springs. Disney Springs is the place to go for shopping, dining, and great entertainment.

8 Disney's BoardWalk. The boardwalk is a nostalgia trip, with bicycles built for two, surreys with fringe on top, pizza, bars, and a dance hall.

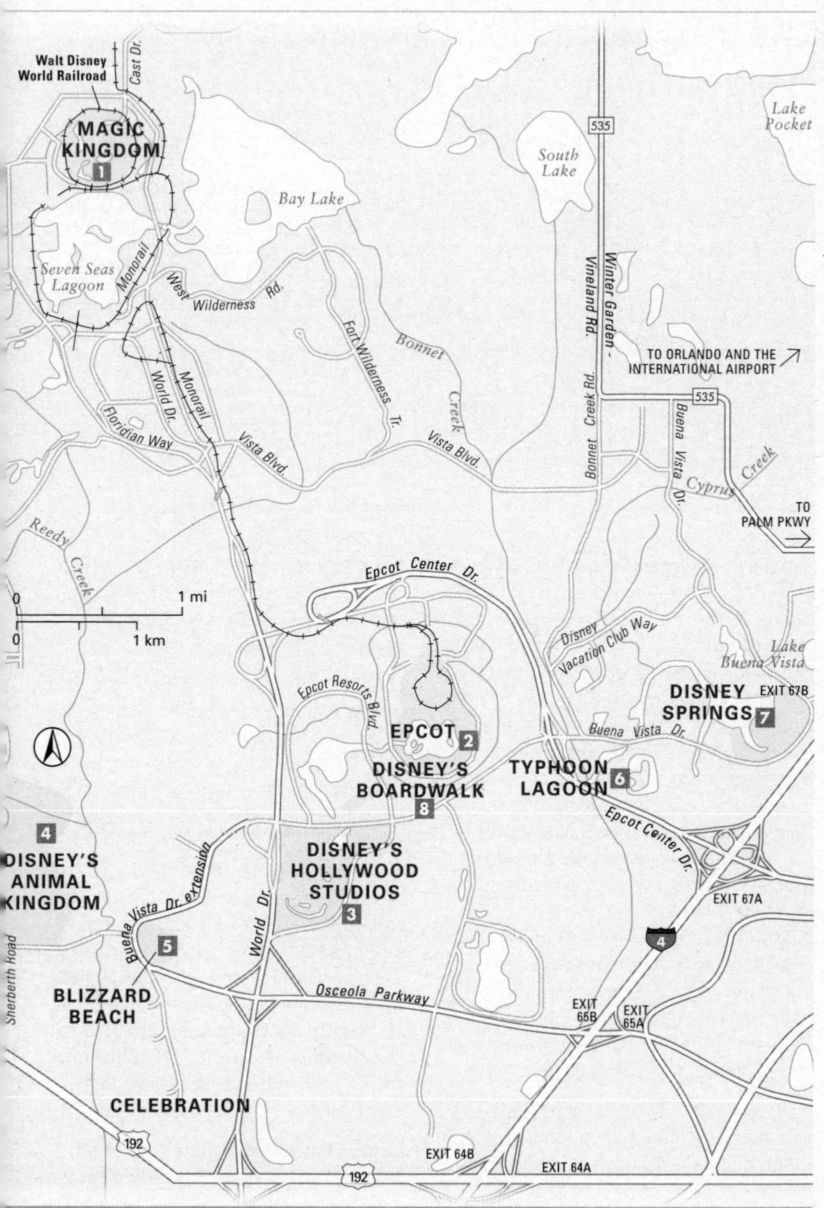
Walt Disney World Railroad
Cast Dr.
MAGIC KINGDOM
1
Bay Lake
South Lake
535
Lake Pocket
Seven Seas Lagoon
Monorail
West Wilderness Rd.
Fort Wilderness Tr.
Bonnet Creek
Vineland Rd.
Winter Garden -
Bonnet Creek Rd.
TO ORLANDO AND THE INTERNATIONAL AIRPORT
535
Buena Vista Dr.
Cypress Creek
TO PALM PKWY
World Dr.
Monorail
Floridian Way
Vista Blvd.
Vista Blvd.
Reedy Creek
0
1 mi
0
1 km
Epcot Center Dr.
Disney Vacation Club Way
Lake Buena Vista
Epcot Resorts Blvd.
DISNEY SPRINGS
7
EXIT 67B
EPCOT
2
Buena Vista Dr.
DISNEY'S BOARDWALK
8
TYPHOON LAGOON
6
Epcot Center Dr.
4
DISNEY'S ANIMAL KINGDOM
DISNEY'S HOLLYWOOD STUDIOS
3
Buena Vista Dr. extension
EXIT 67A
4
5
World Dr.
Sherberth Road
Osceola Parkway
BLIZZARD BEACH
EXIT 65B
EXIT 65A
CELEBRATION
192
EXIT 64B
EXIT 64A
192

Mickey Mouse. Tinker Bell. Cinderella. What would childhood be like without the magic of Disney? When kids and adults want to go to the theme park, they're heading to Disney. Here you're walking amid people from around the world and meeting characters like Snow White and Donald Duck while rides whirl nonstop and the irrepressible "It's a Small World" tune and lyrics run through your head. You can't help but believe dreams really do come true here.

The **Magic Kingdom** is the heart and soul of the Walt Disney World empire. It was the first Disney outpost in Florida when it opened in 1971, and it's the park that launched Disney's presence in France, Japan, Hong Kong, and Shanghai. For a landmark that wields such worldwide influence, the 142-acre Magic Kingdom may seem small—indeed, Epcot is more than double the size of the Magic Kingdom, and Animal Kingdom is almost triple the size when including the park's expansive animal habitats. But looks can be deceiving. Packed into six different "lands" are more than 50 major crowd-pleasers, and that's not counting all the ancillary attractions: shops, eateries, live entertainment, character meet-and-greet spots, fireworks shows, and parades.

Nowhere but at **Epcot** can you explore and experience the native food, entertainment, culture, and arts and crafts of countries in Europe, Asia, North Africa, and the Americas. What's more, employees at the World Showcase pavilions actually hail from the countries the pavilions represent.

Epcot, or "Experimental Prototype Community of Tomorrow," was the original inspiration for Walt Disney World. Walt envisioned a future in which nations coexisted in peace and harmony, reaping the miraculous harvest of technological achievement. The Epcot of today is both more and less than his original dream. Less, because the World Showcase presents views of its countries that are, as an Epcot guide once put it, "as Americans perceive them"—highly idealized. But this is a minor quibble in the face of the major achievement: Epcot is that rare paradox—a successful educational theme park that excels at entertainment, too.

Disney's Hollywood Studios was initially designed to be a trip back to Tinseltown's golden age, but the park is undergoing changes as it morphs into a future populated by characters and experiences from the *Star Wars* juggernaut, Pixar favorites and *Toy Story*.

The result is a theme park that blends movie-themed shows and attractions and high-tech wonders with breathtaking rides but that still retains a bit of Hollywood nostalgia. The park's old-time Hollywood atmosphere includes a rosy-hued view of the moviemaking business from the 1930s and '40s, amid sleek art-moderne buildings in pastel colors, funky diners, kitschy decorations, and sculptured gardens. But the future includes the dynamic 14-acre Star Wars land and an 11-acre Toy Story area.

Thanks to a rich library of film scores, the park is permeated with music—all familiar, all evoking the magic of the movies, and all constantly streaming from the camouflaged loudspeakers at a volume just right for humming along. Breaking through this musical background on a disconcertingly regular basis are the screams of fear from riders of the dropping elevator on the iconic Tower of Terror.

Disney's Animal Kingdom explores the stories of all animals—real, imaginary, and extinct. Enter through the Oasis, where you hear exotic background music and find yourself surrounded by gentle waterfalls and gardens alive with exotic birds, reptiles, and mammals. And the park now transforms as it opens at night.

At 403 acres and several times the size of the Magic Kingdom, Animal Kingdom is the largest in area of all Disney theme parks. Animal habitats take up much of that acreage. Creatures here thrive in careful re-creations of landscapes from Asia and Africa. Throughout the park, you'll also learn about conservation in a low-key way.

Amid all the nature are thrill rides, a 3-D show (housed in the "root system" of the iconic Tree of Life), two first-rate musicals, and character meet-and-greets. Cast members are as likely to hail from Kenya or South Africa as they are from Kentucky or South Carolina. It's all part of the charm. A mesmerizing park area based on the movie *Avatar* opened in 2017, with unique after-dark attractions and thrilling rides.

Typhoon Lagoon and **Blizzard Beach** are two of the world's best water parks. What sets them apart? It's the same thing that differentiates all Disney parks—the detailed themes. Whether you're cast away on a balmy island at Typhoon Lagoon or washed up on a ski-resort-turned-seaside-playground at Blizzard Beach, the landscaping and clever architecture will add to the fun of flume and raft rides, wave pools, and splash areas. Another plus: the vegetation has matured enough to create shade. The Disney water parks give you that lost-in-paradise feeling on top of all those high-speed, wedgie-inducing waterslides. They're so popular that crowds often reach overflow capacity in summer. If you're going to Disney for four days or more between April and October, add the Water Park Fun & More option to your Magic Your Way ticket.

Planning

Admission

At the gate, the per-person, per-day price for Magic Kingdom, Epcot, Hollywood Studios, and Animal Kingdom varies by season, day, and crowd levels, ranging from $109 to $159 for adults (ages 10 and older) and $104 to $124 for children (ages three–nine). You can buy tickets at the Ticket and Transportation Center (TTC) in the Magic Kingdom, from booths at other park entrances, in all on-site resorts if you're a guest, at the Disney store in the airport, and at various other sites around Orlando. You can also buy them in advance online—the best way to save time and money.

If you opt for a multiday ticket, you'll be issued a nontransferable pass that uses your fingerprint for ID. Hold your pass up to the reader, just like people with single-day tickets, and also slip your finger into the V-shaped reader. If you're staying at a Walt Disney World resort (or if you choose to buy one), a MagicBand wristband serves as park ticket, attraction FastPass+ ticket, and even hotel room key.

Operating Hours

Walt Disney World operates 365 days a year. Opening and closing times vary by park and by season, with the longest hours during prime summer months and year-end holidays. The parking lots open at least an hour before the parks do.

In general, openings hover around 9 am, though certain attractions might not start up till 10 or 11. Closings range between 5 and 8 pm in the off-season and between 8 and 10, 11, or even midnight in high season. Downtown Disney/Disney Springs and BoardWalk shops stay open as late as 11 pm.

EXTRA MAGIC HOURS

The Extra Magic Hours program gives Disney resort guests free early and late-night admission to certain parks on specified days—check ahead (🌐 *www.disneyworld.disney.go.com/calendars*) for information about each park's "magic hours" days to plan your early- and late-visit strategies.

Parking and In-Park Transport

Parking at Disney parks is free to resort guests (there is a parking charge at the resorts between $13 and $24 per night; guests with disabilities self-park free and valet free); all others pay $25 for cars (preferred parking, $50) and $30 for RVs and campers. Self-parking is free for everyone at Typhoon Lagoon, Blizzard Beach, Disney Springs, and the BoardWalk. Trams take you between the theme-park lots (*note your parking location!*) and turnstiles. Disney's buses, boats, monorails, and the new Skyliner gondolas (not to mention the premium, behind-the-scenes Minnie Van service at $25 per ride) whisk you from resort to park and park to park. Either take a Disney bus or drive to Typhoon Lagoon and Blizzard Beach. Once inside the water parks, you can walk, swim, slide, or chill out. Allow up to an hour for travel between parks and hotels on Disney transportation.

FastPass+

FastPass+ helps you avoid lines, and it's included in regular park admission. Using the new My Disney Experience app or FastPass+ kiosks in each park, you can select up to three attractions at one time; each appointment will give you a one-hour window within which you can experience each attraction. The FastPass+ appointments are loaded directly to your MagicBand or card. It's best to make appointments only for the most popular attractions and to stick with the standby queue for attractions that aren't in such demand. Strategy is everything.

Guests can get FastPass+ reservations for some designated character greetings, parades, and shows. These "experience" FastPass+ reservations count just the same as those for the rides. You get three to start with (in a single park) and can add as many more as you have time for (and these can be in a different park if you have the Park Hopper option). Best FastPass+ practices are explained by the program. It will direct you to the attractions where FastPass+ is most helpful. If these attractions don't meet your family's specific needs—your kids are too young to ride coasters, for example—the program will also help you customize your FastPass+ selections.

Disney Strategies

Keep in mind these essential strategies, tried and tested by generations of Disney fans.

Buy tickets before leaving home. It saves money and gives you time to look into all the ticket options. It also offers an opportunity for you to consider vacation packages and meal plans and to register with the My Disney Experience program and mobile app for vacation planning.

Make dining reservations before leaving home. If you don't, you might find yourself eating fast food (again) or leaving Disney for dinner. On-site restaurants, especially those featuring character appearances, book up months ahead, but be aware that last-minute cancellations or no shows will incur a fee.

Arrive at least 30 minutes before the parks open. We know it's your vacation and you want to sleep in. But you probably want to make the most of your time and money, too. Plan to be up by 7:30 am each day to get the most out of your park visits. After transit time it'll take you 15–20 minutes to park, get to the gates, and pick up your park guide maps and *Times Guide*.

See top attractions in the morning. And we mean *first thing.* Decide in advance on your can't-miss attractions, find their locations, and hotfoot it to them before 10 am.

Use FastPass+. The system is free, easy, more streamlined than ever with the new FastPass+ online prebooking system, and it's your ticket to the top attractions with little or no waiting in line. Even if you wait to book once you're in the park, you can now schedule up to three FastPasses at one time; paper FastPass tickets are obsolete. Instead your attraction appointments are loaded onto your MagicBand or plastic ticket, whichever you choose to use.

Use Baby Swap. Disney has a theme-park "rider switch" policy that works like this: one parent waits with the baby or toddler while the other parent rides the attraction. When the ride ends, they switch places with minimal wait.

Build in rest time. Start early and then leave the parks around 1 or 2 pm, thus avoiding the hottest and often most crowded period. After a couple of hours' rest at your hotel, head back for an evening spectacle or to ride a big-ticket ride (lines often are shorter around closing time).

Create an itinerary, but leave room for spontaneity. Don't try to plot your trip hour by hour. If you're staying at a Disney resort, find out which parks have Extra Magic Hours on which days.

Eat at off-hours. To avoid the mealtime rush hours, have a quick, light breakfast at 7 or 8 am, lunch at 11, and dinner at 5 or 6.

Hotels

Disney-operated hotels are fantasies unto themselves. Each is designed according to a theme (quaint New England, the relaxed culture of the Polynesian Islands, an African safari village, and so on), and each offers the same perks: free transportation from the airport and to the parks, the option to charge all of your purchases to your room, special guest-only park-visiting times, and much more. If you stay on-site, you'll have better access to the parks and be more immersed in the Disney experience.

Disney Resort Perks

Extra Magic Hours. You get special early and late-night admission to certain Disney parks on specified days. Call ahead for details so you can plan your early- and late-visit strategies.

Free Parking. Parking is free for Disney hotel guests at Disney hotel and theme-park lots.

Magical Express. If you're staying at a select Disney hotel, this free airport service means you don't need to rent a car or think about finding a shuttle or taxi or worry about baggage handling. You check your bags with special Disney tags, and they will be picked up and delivered to your room (though this can take a while). If your flight arrives before 5 am or after 10 pm, you will have to pick up your luggage and deliver it to the coach.

On departure the process works in reverse (though only on some participating airlines, so check in advance). You get your boarding pass and check your bags at the hotel. At the airport you go directly to your gate, skipping check-in. You won't see your bags until you're in your hometown airport. Participating airlines include Alaska, American, Delta, JetBlue, Southwest, and United.

Charging Privileges. You can charge most meals and purchases throughout Disney to your hotel room, using your MagicBands or cards.

Package Delivery. Anything you purchase at Disney—at a park, a hotel, or in Downtown Disney—can be delivered to your Disney hotel for free.

Priority Reservations. Disney hotel guests get priority reservations at Disney restaurants and choice tee times at Disney golf courses up to 30 days in advance, using your MagicBand or card.

Guaranteed Entry. Disney theme parks sometimes reach capacity, but on-site guests can enter even when others would be turned away.

ON-SITE NON-DISNEY HOTELS

Although not operated by the Disney organization, the Swan and the Dolphin, just outside Epcot; the Armed Services-exclusive Shades of Green, near the Magic Kingdom; and the hotels along Hotel Plaza Boulevard near Disney Springs call themselves "official" Walt Disney World hotels. Whereas the Swan, Dolphin, and Shades of Green have the special privileges of on-site Disney hotels, such as free transportation to and from the parks and early park entry, the Disney Springs resorts may use Disney transportation, but don't have all the same perks.

Other Disney Services

If you can shell out \$360–\$500 an hour (with a six-hour minimum), you can take a customized **VIP Tour** with guides who help you park-hop and get good seats at parades and shows. These tours include expedited entry to attractions, and they make navigating easy. Groups can have up to 10 people; book up to three months ahead.

WDW Tours

Reserve with WDW Tours up to 180 days in advance for behind-the-scenes tours that can run as long as 7 hours. Participant age requirements vary, so be sure to check before you book. ✉ *Walt*

Disney World ☎ *407/939–8687* 🌐 *www.disneyworld.com.*

Disney Contacts

Cruise Line: ☎ *800/370–0097* 🌐 *www.disneycruise.com*

Dining Reservations: ☎ *407/939–3463*

Extra Magic Hours: 🌐 *www.disneyworld.disney.go.com/calendars*

Fairy-Tale Weddings: ☎ *321/939–4610* 🌐 *www.disneyweddings.disney.go.com*

Golf Reservations: ☎ *407/939–4653*

Guest Info: ☎ *407/824–4321*

VIP Tours: ☎ *407/560–4033*

WDW Travel Company: ☎ *407/828–8101*

Web: 🌐 *www.disneyworld.disney.go.com*

The Magic Kingdom

Whether you arrive at the Magic Kingdom via monorail, boat, or bus, it's hard to escape that surge of excitement or suppress that smile upon sighting the towers of Cinderella Castle or the spires of Space Mountain. So what if it's a cliché by now? There's magic beyond the turnstiles, and you aren't going to miss one memorable moment.

Most visitors have some idea of what they'd like to see and do during their day in the Magic Kingdom. Popular attractions like Space Mountain and Splash Mountain are on the lists of any thrill seeker, and Fantasyland is Destination One for parents of small children and seekers of moderate thrills like the Seven Dwarfs Mine Train. Visitors who steer away from wilder rides are first in line at the Jungle Cruise or Pirates of the Caribbean in Adventureland.

It's great to have a strategy for seeing the park's attractions, grabbing a bite to eat, or scouring the shops for souvenir gold. But don't forget that Disney Imagineers—the creative pros behind every themed land and attraction—are famous for their attention to detail. Your experience will be richer if you take time to notice the extra touches—from the architecture to the music and the costumes. The same genius is evident even in the landscape, from the tropical setting of Adventureland to the red-stone slopes of Frontierland's Big Thunder Mountain Railroad.

Wherever you go, watch for hidden Mickeys—silhouettes and abstract images of Mickey Mouse—tucked by Imagineers into every corner of the Kingdom. For instance, at the Haunted Mansion look for him in the place settings in the banquet scene.

Much of the Magic Kingdom's pixie dust is spread by the people who work here, the costumed cast members who do their part to create fond memories for each guest who crosses their path. Maybe the grim ghoul who greets you solemnly at the Haunted Mansion will cause you to break down and giggle. Or the sunny shop assistant will help your daughter find the perfect sparkly shoes to match her princess dress. You get the feeling that everyone's in on the fun.

GETTING ORIENTED

The park is laid out on a north–south axis, with Cinderella Castle at the center and the various lands surrounding it in a broad circle.

As you pass underneath the railroad tracks, symbolically leaving behind the world of reality and entering a world of fantasy, you'll immediately notice the charming buildings lining Town Square and Main Street, U.S.A., which runs due north and ends at the Hub (also called Central Plaza), in front of Cinderella Castle. If you're lost or have questions, cast members are available at almost every turn to help you.

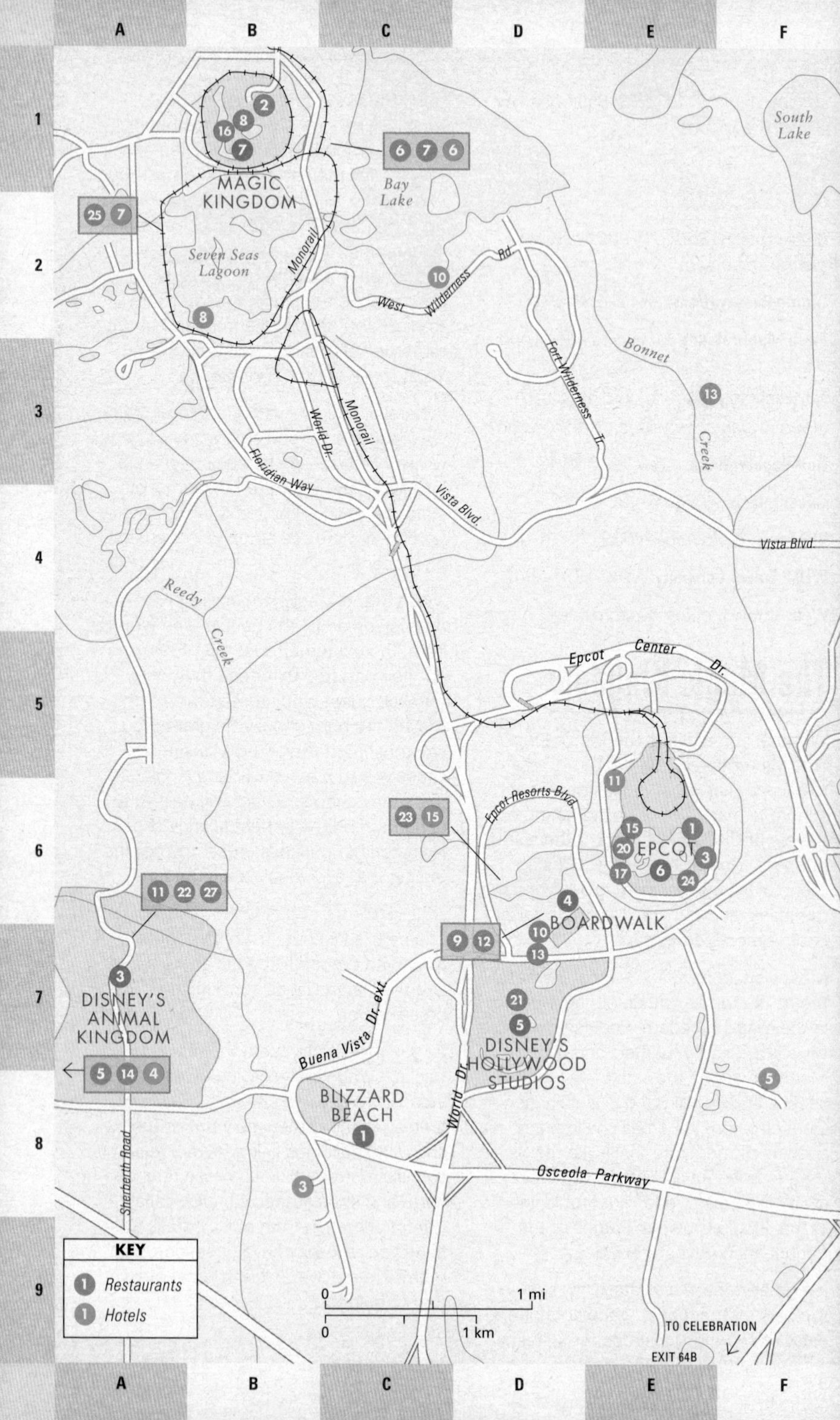

A
B
C
D
E
F
1
2
3
4
5
6
7
8
9
MAGIC KINGDOM
Seven Seas Lagoon
Bay Lake
South Lake
Monorail
West Wilderness Rd.
Fort Wilderness Tr.
Bonnet Creek
World Dr.
Floridian Way
Vista Blvd.
Reedy Creek
Epcot Center Dr.
Epcot Resorts Blvd.
EPCOT
BOARDWALK
DISNEY'S ANIMAL KINGDOM
Buena Vista Dr. ext.
DISNEY'S HOLLYWOOD STUDIOS
BLIZZARD BEACH
Osceola Parkway
Sherberth Road
KEY
Restaurants
Hotels
0
1 mi
0
1 km
TO CELEBRATION
EXIT 64B

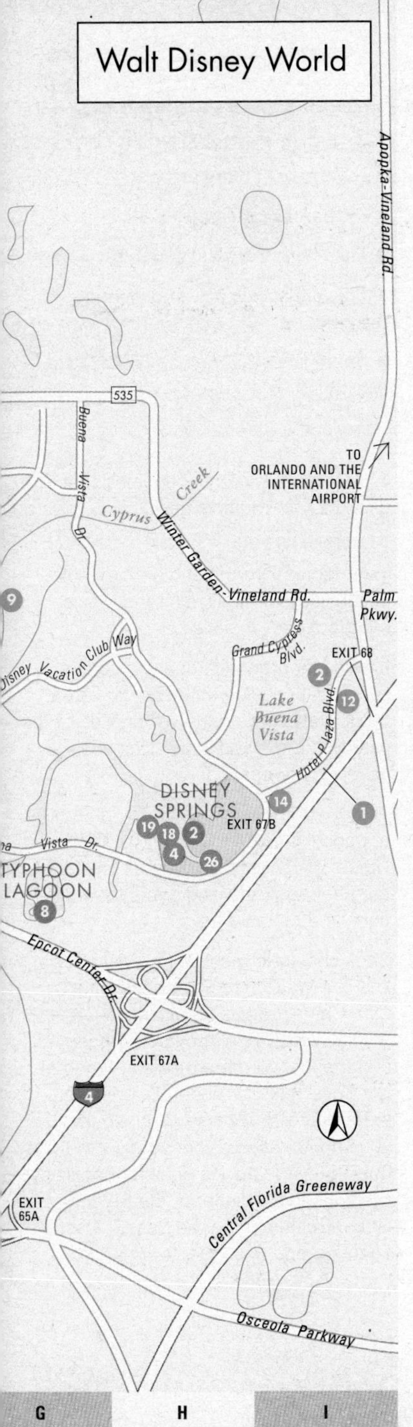

Sights

1 Blizzard Beach C8
2 Disney Springs H6
3 Disney's Animal Kingdom A7
4 Disney's BoardWalk D6
5 Disney's Hollywood Studios D7
6 EPCOT E6
7 The Magic Kingdom B1
8 Typhoon Lagoon G6

Restaurants

1 Akershus Royal Banquet Hall E6
2 Be Our Guest B1
3 Biergarten Restaurant .. E6
4 The BOATHOUSE H6
5 Boma–Flavors of Africa A7
6 California Grill C1
7 Chef Mickey's C1
8 Cinderella's Royal Table B1
9 ESPN Club D6
10 '50s Prime Time Café ... D7
11 Flame Tree Barbecue A7
12 Flying Fish D6
13 Hollywood Brown Derby D7
14 Jiko A7
15 Le Cellier Steakhouse ... E6
16 Liberty Tree Tavern B1
17 Monsieur Paul E6
18 Morimoto Asia H6
19 Raglan Road Irish Pub H6
20 Rose & Crown Pub & Dining Room E6
21 Sci-Fi Dine-In Theater Restaurant D7
22 Tiffins A7
23 Todd English's bluezoo D6
24 Via Napoli Ristorante e Pizzeria E6
25 Victoria & Albert's A2
26 Wolfgang Puck Bar & Grill H6
27 Yak & Yeti A7

Hotels

1 B Resort & Spa Disney Springs Resort Area I6
2 Best Western Lake Buena Vista Resort I5
3 Disney's All-Star Sports Resort B8
4 Disney's Animal Kingdom Lodge A7
5 Disney's Art of Animation Resort F8
6 Disney's Contemporary Resort C1
7 Disney's Grand Floridan Resort & Spa A2
8 Disney's Polynesian Village Resort B2
9 Disney's Port Orleans Resort-French Quarter G4
10 Disney's Wilderness Lodge C2
11 Disney's Yacht Club and Beach Club Resorts E6
12 DoubleTree Suites by Hilton Orlando Disney Springs Area I5
13 Four Seasons Orlando at Walt Disney World E3
14 Hilton Orlando Buena Vista Palace Disney Springs Area I6
15 Walt Disney World Dolphin D6

Top Attractions

For Ages 7 and Up

- Big Thunder Mountain Railroad
- Buzz Lightyear's Space Ranger Spin
- Haunted Mansion
- Pirates of the Caribbean
- Seven Dwarfs Mine Train
- Space Mountain

For Ages 6 and Under

- Dumbo the Flying Elephant
- Enchanted Tales with Belle
- The Magic Carpets of Aladdin
- The Many Adventures of Winnie the Pooh
- Under the Sea: Journey of the Little Mermaid

PARK AMENITIES

Guest Relations. To the left in Town Square as you face Main Street, **City Hall** houses Guest Relations (aka Guest Services), the Magic Kingdom's principal information center (☎ *407/824–4521*). Here you can search for misplaced belongings or companions, ask questions of staffers, and pick up a guide map and a *Times Guide* with schedules of events and character-greeting information. **■TIP→ If you're trying for a last-minute lunch or dinner reservation, you may be able to book it at City Hall.**

Lockers: Lockers ($10 or $15 plus $5 deposit) are in an arcade under the Main Street railroad station. If you're park-hopping, use your locker receipt to get a free locker at the next park.

Lost People and Things: Make plans for a place to meet in case of emergency or a lost member before you go any further. Instruct your kids to talk to anyone with a Disney name tag if they lose you. **City Hall** also has a lost-and-found and a computerized message center, where you can leave notes for your companions in the Magic Kingdom and other parks.

Stroller Rentals: You can rent strollers near the main entrance. Singles are $15 daily, $13 for multiday rental; doubles cost $31 daily, $27 for multiple days.

VISITING TIPS

Try to go toward the end of the week, because most families hit the Magic Kingdom early in a visit.

Ride a star attraction during a parade; lines ease considerably. (But be careful not to get stuck on the wrong side of the parade route when it starts, or you may never get across.)

At City Hall near the park's Town Square entrance, pick up a map and a *Times Guide,* which lists showtimes, character-greeting times, and hours for attractions and restaurants.

Book character meals early. Main Street, U.S.A.'s The Crystal Palace, A Buffet with Character has breakfast, lunch, and dinner with Winnie the Pooh, Tigger, and friends. All three meals at Cinderella's Royal Table in Cinderella Castle are extremely popular—so much so that you should reserve your spot six months out. The same advice goes for booking the full-service dinner at the Be Our Guest Restaurant in the Beast's Castle in Fantasyland.

Parades are a part of the Walt Disney World experience. Most are held daily.

Sights

MAIN STREET, U.S.A.

With its pastel Victorian-style buildings, antique automobiles ahoohga-oohga-ing, sparkling sidewalks, and an atmosphere of what one writer has called "almost hysterical joy," Main Street is more than a mere conduit to the other enchantments of the Magic Kingdom. It's where the spell is first cast.

You emerge from beneath the Walt Disney World Railroad Station (under construction at the time of updating, with a completion date before 2021) into a realization of one of the most tenacious American dreams. The perfect street in the perfect small town in a perfect moment of time is burnished to jewel-like quality, thanks to a four-fifths-scale reduction, nightly cleanings with high-pressure hoses, and constant repainting. And it's a very sunny world, thanks to an outpouring of welcoming entertainment: live bands, barbershop quartets, and background music from Disney films and American musicals played over loudspeakers. Horse-drawn trolleys and omnibuses with their horns tooting chug along the street. Vendors in Victorian costumes sell balloons and popcorn. And Cinderella's famous castle floats whimsically in the distance where Main Street disappears.

Although attractions with a capital A are minimal on Main Street, there are plenty of inducements—namely, shops and eateries—to while away your time and part you from your money. The largest of these, the Emporium, is often the last stop for souvenir hunters at day's end. At the Main Street Bakery, you can find your favorite latte (courtesy of Starbucks) and a sandwich or baked treats like cupcakes and brownies. If you can't resist an interactive challenge while making your way through the park, head first to the Firehouse, next to City Hall, to join the legendary wizard Merlin in the Sorcerers of the Magic Kingdom

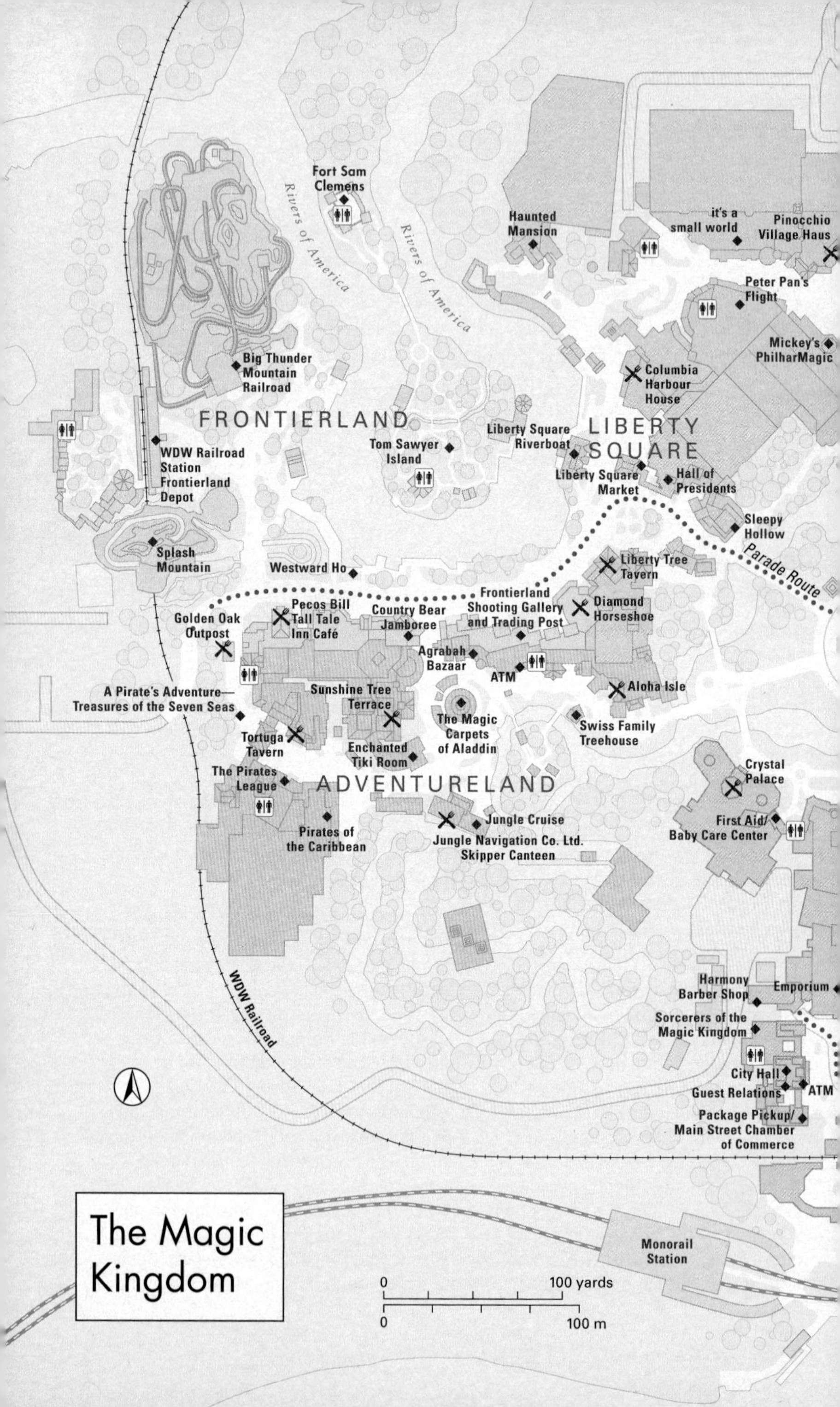

The Magic Kingdom
FRONTIERLAND
LIBERTY SQUARE
ADVENTURELAND
Rivers of America
Rivers of America
Fort Sam Clemens
Haunted Mansion
it's a small world
Pinocchio Village Haus
Peter Pan's Flight
Mickey's PhilharMagic
Columbia Harbour House
Big Thunder Mountain Railroad
Liberty Square Riverboat
Tom Sawyer Island
WDW Railroad Station Frontierland Depot
Liberty Square Market
Hall of Presidents
Sleepy Hollow
Parade Route
Splash Mountain
Westward Ho
Liberty Tree Tavern
Pecos Bill Tall Tale Inn Café
Country Bear Jamboree
Frontierland Shooting Gallery and Trading Post
Diamond Horseshoe
Golden Oak Outpost
Agrabah Bazaar
ATM
Aloha Isle
A Pirate's Adventure—Treasures of the Seven Seas
Sunshine Tree Terrace
The Magic Carpets of Aladdin
Swiss Family Treehouse
Tortuga Tavern
Enchanted Tiki Room
Crystal Palace
The Pirates League
Jungle Cruise
First Aid/ Baby Care Center
Pirates of the Caribbean
Jungle Navigation Co. Ltd. Skipper Canteen
WDW Railroad
Harmony Barber Shop
Emporium
Sorcerers of the Magic Kingdom
City Hall
Guest Relations
ATM
Package Pickup/ Main Street Chamber of Commerce
Monorail Station
0
100 yards
0
100 m

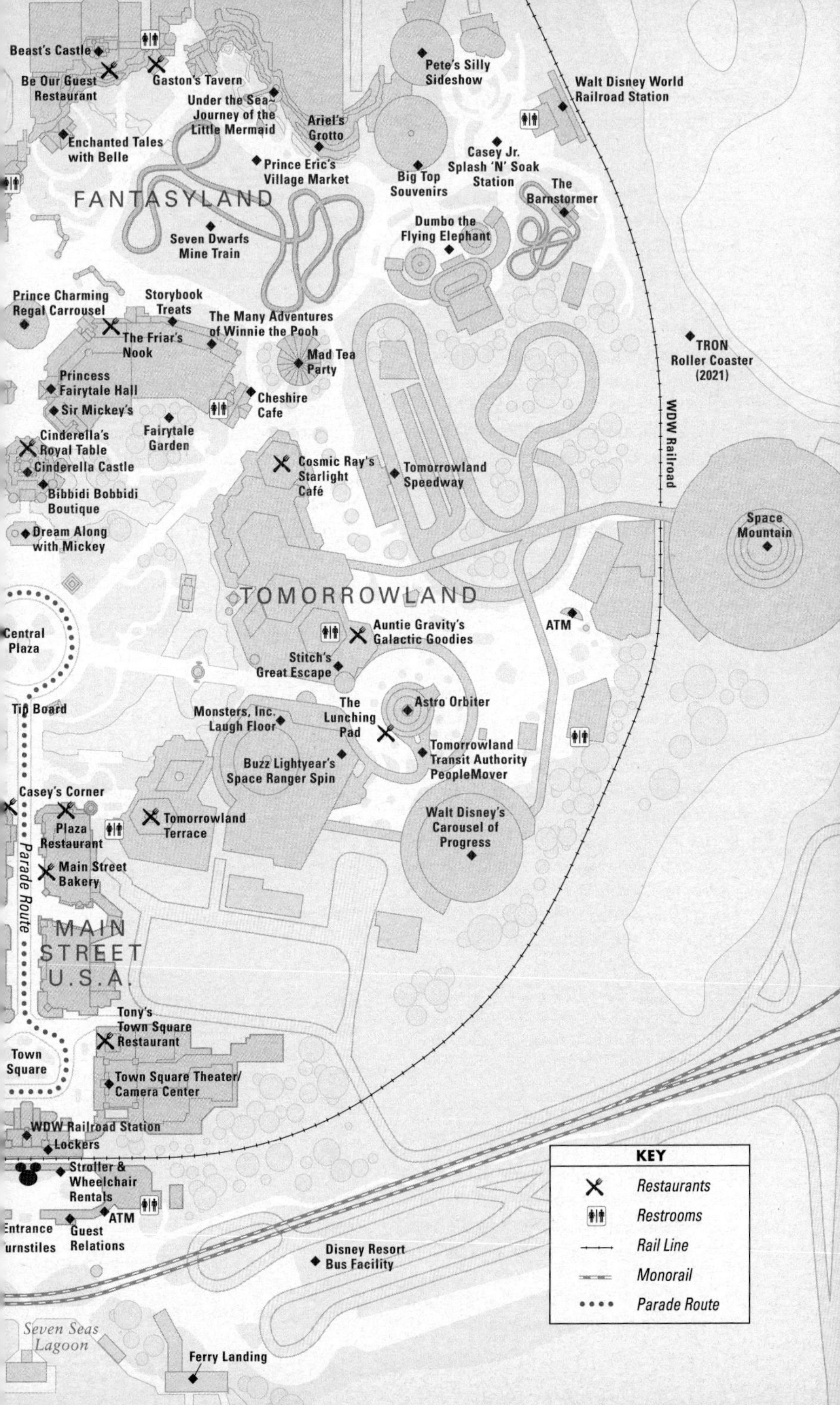
Beast's Castle
Be Our Guest Restaurant
Gaston's Tavern
Under the Sea~ Journey of the Little Mermaid
Pete's Silly Sideshow
Walt Disney World Railroad Station
Ariel's Grotto
Enchanted Tales with Belle
Prince Eric's Village Market
Big Top Souvenirs
Casey Jr. Splash 'N' Soak Station
The Barnstormer
FANTASYLAND
Seven Dwarfs Mine Train
Dumbo the Flying Elephant
Prince Charming Regal Carrousel
Storybook Treats
The Many Adventures of Winnie the Pooh
The Friar's Nook
Mad Tea Party
TRON Roller Coaster (2021)
Princess Fairytale Hall
Sir Mickey's
Cheshire Cafe
Fairytale Garden
Cinderella's Royal Table
Cinderella Castle
Cosmic Ray's Starlight Café
Tomorrowland Speedway
Bibbidi Bobbidi Boutique
WDW Railroad
Dream Along with Mickey
Space Mountain
TOMORROWLAND
Central Plaza
Auntie Gravity's Galactic Goodies
ATM
Stitch's Great Escape
Tip Board
The Lunching Pad
Astro Orbiter
Monsters, Inc. Laugh Floor
Tomorrowland Transit Authority PeopleMover
Buzz Lightyear's Space Ranger Spin
Casey's Corner
Walt Disney's Carousel of Progress
Plaza Restaurant
Tomorrowland Terrace
Main Street Bakery
Parade Route
MAIN STREET U.S.A.
Tony's Town Square Restaurant
Town Square
Town Square Theater/ Camera Center
WDW Railroad Station
Lockers
Stroller & Wheelchair Rentals
ATM
Entrance
urnstiles
Guest Relations
Disney Resort Bus Facility
Seven Seas Lagoon
Ferry Landing
KEY
Restaurants
Restrooms
Rail Line
Monorail
Parade Route

role-playing game. For no extra charge, you can take ownership of special cards with "magic spells" that help you search for symbols and bring down Disney villains like Yzma, Cruella, Scar, Jafar, and Maleficent. Don't worry—you'll have time between fireball battles and cyclone spells to ride Space Mountain.

The Harmony Barber Shop lets you step back in time for a haircut ($18 for children 12 and under, $19 for anyone older; appointments necessary). Babies or tots get Mickey Ears, a souvenir lock of hair, and a certificate if it's their first haircut ever, but you pay $25 for the experience. At the Town Square Theater, presented by Kodak, Mickey Mouse meets you for photos and autographs. And you can pick up a FastPass+ appointment for such meet-and-greets. While you're here, stock up on batteries and memory cards.

ADVENTURELAND

From the scrubbed brick, manicured lawns, and meticulously pruned trees of the Central Plaza, an artfully dilapidated wooden bridge leads to the jungles of Adventureland. Here South African cape honeysuckle droops, Brazilian bougainvillea drapes, Mexican flame vines cling, spider plants clone, and three varieties of palm trees sway. The bright, all-American sing-along tunes that fill the air along Main Street and Central Plaza are replaced by the recorded repetitions of trumpeting elephants, pounding drums, and squawking parrots. Nestled in this adventure book jungle is the hokey but cute Enchanted Tiki Room, Magic Carpets of Aladdin ride, and delighful Jungle Cruise riverboat.

Once contained within the Pirates of the Caribbean attraction, Captain Jack Sparrow and the crew of the Black Pearl are brazenly recruiting new hearties at the Pirates League, adjacent to the ride entrance. You can get pirate and mermaid makeovers (for lots of doubloons) here. On a nearby stage furnished with pirate booty, the captain instructs scurvy dog recruits on brandishing a sword at Captain Jack Sparrow's Pirate Tutorial (several shows a day). And that's not all! At A Pirate's Adventure: Treasures of the Seven Seas park, guests embark on an interactive quest with a pirate map and talisman to complete "raids" through Adventureland as they fight off pirate enemies along the way. Shiver me timbers—it's a pirate's life for ye!

FRONTIERLAND

Frontierland evokes the American frontier and is planted with mesquite, twisted Peruvian pepper trees, slash pines, and cacti. The period seems to be the latter half of the 19th century, and the West is being won by Disney cast members dressed in checked shirts, leather vests, cowboy hats, and brightly colored neckerchiefs. Banjo and fiddle music twangs from tree to tree and in the Country Bear Jamboree, and every once in a while a flash-mob country-dance party breaks out.

The screams that sometimes intrude into the jolly string music come from two of the Magic Kingdom's more thrilling rides: Splash Mountain, an elaborate flume ride, and Big Thunder Mountain Railroad, a roller coaster. The Walt Disney World Railroad tunnels past a colorful scene in Splash Mountain and drops you off between it and Thunder Mountain.

LIBERTY SQUARE

The rough-and-tumble Western frontier gently transforms into Colonial America as Liberty Square picks up where Frontierland leaves off. The weathered siding gives way to solid brick and neat clapboard. The mesquite and cactus are replaced by stately oaks and masses of azaleas. The theme is Colonial history, and the buildings, topped with weather vanes and exuding prosperity, are pure New England.

A replica of the Liberty Bell, crack and all, seems an appropriate prop to separate Liberty Square from Frontierland. There's

Coasting down Splash Mountain in Frontierland will put some zip in your doo-dah and some water on your clothes.

even a Liberty Tree, a more-than-150-year-old live oak, transported here from elsewhere on Disney property. Around the square are tree-shaded tables for an alfresco lunch and plenty of carts, fast-food eateries, and the Liberty Tree Tavern to supply the goods. You can also see the graveyard of the Haunted Mansion and the placid Liberty Square Riverboat.

FANTASYLAND

Walt Disney called this "a timeless land of enchantment," and Fantasyland does conjure pixie dust. Perhaps that's because the fanciful gingerbread houses, gleaming gold turrets, and, of course, the rides, are based on Disney-animated movies.

Many of these rides, which could ostensibly be classified as rides for children, are packed with enough delightful detail to engage the adults who accompany them. Fantasyland has always been the most heavily trafficked area in the park, and its rides and shows are almost always crowded.

Fantasyland is home to rides as well as the towering Beast's Castle. The Dumbo the Flying Elephant ride (double its original size), flying above circus-themed grounds that also include the Great Goofini coaster, starring Goofy as stuntman. A circus-themed Casey Jr. Splash 'N' Soak Station provides water-play respite for kids. Ariel of *The Little Mermaid* invites you to her own state-of-the-art attraction, Under the Sea: Journey of the Little Mermaid. Disney princesses welcome you for a photo op in the glittering Princess Fairytale Hall. You can be part of the show when you join Belle, Lumière, and Madame Wardrobe of *Beauty and the Beast* at the Enchanted Tales with Belle attraction for a story performance. Meanwhile, Beast may be brooding in his castle, where the Be Our Guest dining room beckons to lunch and dinner guests. And the musical Seven Dwarfs Mine Train family coaster hurtles guests into the bejeweled depths of the earth to the tune of, what else, *Heigh Ho*.

You can enter Fantasyland on foot from Liberty Square, Tomorrowland, or via the Walt Disney World Railroad, but the classic introduction is through Cinderella Castle. As you exit the castle's archway, look left to discover a charming and often overlooked touch: Cinderella Fountain, with its lovely bronze casting of the castle's namesake, who's dressed in her peasant togs and surrounded by her beloved mice and bird friends.

From the southern end of Liberty Square, head toward the park hub and stop at the Disney PhotoPass picture spot for one of the park's best, unobstructed ground-level views of Cinderella Castle. It's a great spot for that family photo.

TOMORROWLAND

The "future that never was" spins boldly into view as you enter Tomorrowland, where Disney Imagineers paint the landscape with whirling spaceships, flashy neon lights, and gleaming robots. This is the future as envisioned by early-20th-century sci-fi writers and moviemakers, when space flight, laser beams, and home computers were fiction, not fact. Retro Jetsonesque styling lends the area lasting chic.

Gamers who want to relive old thrills can ride the cutting-edge Tron Lightcycle, take a spin on the Tomorrowland Speedway, and battle alongside Buzz Lightyear's Astro Blasters. Though Tomorrowland Transit Authority (TTA) PeopleMover isn't a big-ticket ride, it's a great way to check out the landscape from above as it zooms in and out of Space Mountain and curves around the entire land.

Restaurants

★ Be Our Guest

$$$$ | **FRENCH** | This massive restaurant offers a *Beauty and the Beast* theme, French flair, and the Magic Kingdom's first wine and beer served at dinner; breakfast and lunch remain a fast-casual affair. Prix-fixe menus are served for breakfast and dinner (lunch is à la carte). **Known for:** the best French dip sandwich in town; dessert platter; character appearances. $ *Average main: $55* ✉ *Fantasyland, Magic Kingdom* ✣ *North end of Fantasyland* ☎ *407/939–3463* 🌐 *disneyworld.disney.go.com/dining.*

★ California Grill

$$$$ | **AMERICAN** | The view of the surrounding Disney parks from this 15th-floor restaurant—the World's signature dining establishment since 1995—is as stunning as the food, especially after dark, when you can watch the nightly Magic Kingdom fireworks from an outdoor viewing area. The space has stylish midcentury modern furnishings and chandeliers, while the exhibition kitchen is so well equipped that it has a cast-iron flat grill designed specifically for cooking fish. **Known for:** stunning views of the parks and fireworks; wild game charcuterie and fresh sushi; Sunday brunch. $ *Average main: $47* ✉ *Contemporary Resort, 4600 N. World Dr., Magic Kingdom Resort Area* ☎ *407/939–3463* 🌐 *disneyworld.disney.go.com/dining* ⊙ *No lunch.*

Chef Mickey's

$$$$ | **AMERICAN** | **FAMILY** | The fact that the Disney monorail zooms overhead right through the Contemporary Resort, and that Mickey, Minnie, or Goofy hang around for breakfast and dinner, would be enough to make it popular, but the food at Chef Mickey's is surprisingly good. Chef Mickey's is shiny and bright, still offering a breakfast buffet and brunch that includes French toast, mountains of specialty pancakes, and even a breakfast pizza. **Known for:** character meals and Storybook Moments; family-fare buffet and lots of it; specialty cocktails for the grown-ups. $ *Average main: $47* ✉ *Contemporary Resort, 4600 N. World Dr., Magic Kingdom Resort Area* ☎ *407/939–3463* 🌐 *disneyworld.disney.go.com/dining* ⊙ *No lunch.*

Cinderella's Royal Table
$$$$ | **AMERICAN** | **FAMILY** | Cinderella and other Disney princesses appear at this eatery in the castle's old mead hall, offering prix-fixe Fairyland dining as only Disney can supply. The Fairytale Breakfast offers all-you-can-eat options such as beef tenderloin and eggs and caramel apple–stuffed French toast. **Known for:** breakfasts from oatmeal to shrimp and grits; character appearances and autograph signings; distinctive medieval castle decor. *Average main: $59* *Cinderella Castle, Magic Kingdom* *407/939–3463* *disneyworld.disney.go.com/dining.*

★ Liberty Tree Tavern
$$$$ | **AMERICAN** | **FAMILY** | Now serving beer and wine, this formerly dry tavern holds a prime spot on the parade route, so you can catch a good meal while you wait. Each of the six dining rooms commemorates a historical U.S. figure, like Betsy Ross or Benjamin Franklin. **Known for:** Patriot's Platter of roast turkey, sliced pot roast, and carved pork roast; multiroom, authentic-looking colonial decor; Samuel Adams Boston Lager and wine. *Average main: $36* *Liberty Square, Magic Kingdom* *407/939–3463* *disneyworld.disney.go.com/dining.*

★ Victoria & Albert's
$$$$ | **MODERN AMERICAN** | At this ultraposh Disney restaurant, a well-polished service team will anticipate your every need, providing one of the plushest fine-dining experiences in Florida; the setting is so sophisticated that children under 10 aren't on the guest list. There's nothing quick about sitting down for dinner in the the seven- and 10-course main dining room, the 10-course intimate Queen Victoria's Room, or the over-the-top Chef's Table, which is actually in the restaurant's kitchen, but service is impeccable. **Known for:** highest-priced restaurant at WDW; enormous and expensive wine list; exclusive additions like Osetra caviar and Miyazaki beef. *Average main: $200* *Grand Floridian, 4401 Floridian Way, Magic Kingdom Resort Area* *407/939–3862* *www.victoria-alberts.com* *No lunch* *Jacket required.*

Hotels

Disney's Contemporary Resort
$$$$ | **RESORT** | You're paying for location at this sleek, modern, luxury resort next to the Magic Kingdom that despite being nearly 50 years old, still lives up to its name; park hopping is a breeze, as the monorail runs through the lobby. **Pros:** monorail access; Chef Mickey's, the epicenter of character-meal world; health and wellness suites. **Cons:** the mix of conventioneers and vacationers can make for chaos in the lobby; fee for self-parking; lobby eateries can be crowded and noisy. *Rooms from: $534* *4600 N. World Dr., Magic Kingdom Resort Area* *407/824–1000* *www.disneyworld.com* *1,028 rooms* *No meals; Free Breakfast.*

★ Disney's Grand Floridian Resort & Spa
$$$$ | **RESORT** | So close to the Magic Kingdom you can see the colors change on the Cinderella Castle, this red-roofed Victorian-style resort emulates the look of the great railroad resorts of the past with beautifully appointed rooms, rambling verandas, delicate, white-painted woodwork, and brick chimneys. **Pros:** one monorail stop from the Magic Kingdom; Victoria & Albert's offers an evening-long experience in fine dining; if you're a couple with no kids, this is definitely the most romantic on-property hotel. **Cons:** pricey; draws a large convention clientele; vacationing couples may be more comfortable than families with young children. *Rooms from: $708* *4401 Floridian Way, Magic Kingdom Resort Area* *407/824–3000* *www.disneyworld.com* *867 rooms* *No meals.*

Disney's Polynesian Village Resort
$$$$ | **RESORT** | **FAMILY** | This South Pacific–themed resort with its tropical backdrop

of orchids, ferns, and palms, lies directly across the lagoon from the Magic Kingdom, on the monorail and water taxi routes, and has lots of kids activities, making it a good family choice. **Pros:** on the monorail line; great atmosphere; kids' activities. **Cons:** pricey; lots of loud children; Magic Kingdom ferry noise affects some bungalows. *Rooms from: $703 1600 Seven Seas Dr., Magic Kingdom Resort Area 407/824–2000 www.disneyworld.disney.go.com/resorts 844 rooms No meals.*

Disney's Wilderness Lodge
$$$$ | RESORT | FAMILY | The architects designed this seven-story luxury resort to mimic the majestic turn-of-the-20th-century lodges of the American West. **Pros:** boarding point for romantic cruises or free water taxi to Magic Kingdom; elegant dining options; children's activity center. **Cons:** no direct bus to Magic Kingdom; no monorail access; noise from the antics at Whispering Canyon Cafe can be annoying. *Rooms from: $508 901 Timberline Dr., Magic Kingdom Resort Area 407/824–3200 www.disneyworld.com 716 rooms No meals.*

EPCOT

Walt Disney said that Epcot would "take its cue from the new ideas and new technologies that are now emerging from the creative centers of American industry." He wrote that Epcot—never completed, always improving—"will never cease to be a living blueprint of the future, a showcase to the world for the ingenuity of American free enterprise." That statement has never been more true than now, as so much in Epcot is undergoing big changes. Several attractions have closed, and Disney officials have announced new, and often more kid-friendly, attractions to be open by 2021.

The permanent settlement that Disney envisioned wasn't to be. Epcot opened in 1982—16 years after his death—as a showcase, ostensibly, for the concepts that would be incorporated into the real-life Epcots of the future. (Disney's vision *has* taken an altered shape in the self-contained city of Celebration, an urban-planner's dream opened in 1996 on Disney property near Kissimmee.)

Epcot, the theme park, has two key areas: Future World, where most pavilions are collaborations between Walt Disney Imagineering and U.S. corporations and are designed to demonstrate technological advances through innovative shows and attractions; and the World Showcase, where shops, restaurants, attractions, and live entertainment create microcosms of 11 countries from four continents.

For years Epcot was considered the more staid park, a place geared toward adults. But after its 10th anniversary, Epcot began to evolve into a livelier, more child-friendly park, with such "wow" attractions as Future World's Test Track, Mission: SPACE, Soarin', and in 2021 the Guardians of the Galaxy mega-ride.

There's something for everyone here. The World Showcase appeals to younger children with the Kidcot Fun Stop craft stations and the Norway pavilion's Frozen Ever After ride. Soarin', in the Land Pavilion, is a family favorite. The Seas with Nemo & Friends—with one of the world's largest saltwater aquariums and a Nemo-themed ride—is a must-see for all. Adrenaline junkie? Don't miss Test Track presented by Chevrolet, where you can design your own custom concept car, then put it through its high-speed paces.

Wear comfortable shoes—there's *a lot* of territory to cover here. Arrive early, and try to stay all day, squeezing in extras like high-tech games at Innoventions and a relaxing meal. If you enter through International Gateway before 11 am, cast members will direct you to Future World, which usually opens two hours before World Showcase, or you can indulge in a latte and éclair at the France bakery, the sole quick-service eatery open early in World Showcase.

Top Attractions

- Frozen Ever After
- Mission: SPACE
- Phineas and Ferb: Agent P's World Showcase Adventure
- Soarin'
- Test Track

GETTING ORIENTED

Epcot is composed of two areas: Future World and the World Showcase. The inner core of Future World's pavilions has the Spaceship Earth geosphere (which will be closing for extensive renovations in 2020) and a plaza anchored by the computer-animated Fountain of Nations.

Six pavilions compose Future World's outer ring. Each of the three east pavilions has a ride and the occasional postride showcase; a visit rarely takes more than 30 minutes. The blockbuster exhibits on the west side contain rides and interactive displays; each exhibit can take up to 90 minutes for the complete experience.

World Showcase pavilions are on the promenade that circles the World Showcase Lagoon. Each houses shops, restaurants, and friendly international staffers; some have films or displays. Mexico offers a tame ride. Live entertainment is scheduled at every pavilion except Norway. Disney's monorail and buses drop you off at the main entrance in front of Future World. But if you're staying at one of the Epcot resorts (the BoardWalk, Yacht Club, Beach Club, Dolphin, or Swan), you can use the International Gateway entrance between World Showcase's France and U.K. pavilions, which will be a station stop for the Skyliner gondolas.

PARK AMENITIES

Guest Relations: To the right of the ticket windows at the park entrance and to the left of Spaceship Earth inside the park, this is the place to pick up schedules and maps. You also can get maps at the park's International Gateway entrance and most shops. Guest Relations will also assist with dining reservations, ticket upgrades, and services for guests with disabilities.

Lockers: Lockers ($10 and $15, with $5 refundable deposit) are at the International Gateway and to the west of Spaceship Earth. Coin-operated lockers also are at the bus information center by the bus parking lot.

Lost People and Things: Make a plan for a meeting place if your group gets separated. Instruct children to speak to someone with a Disney name tag if you become separated. Guest Relations has a computerized message center for contacting companions in any of the parks.

Stroller Rentals: You can rent strollers on the east side of the Entrance Plaza and at the International Gateway. Singles are $15 daily, $13 for multiday rental; doubles cost $31 daily, $27 for multiple days. Even preschoolers will be glad for a stroller in this large park.

VISITING TIPS

Epcot is so vast and varied that you really need two days to explore. With just one day, you'll have to be highly selective.

Go early in the week, when others are at Magic Kingdom.

If you like a good festival, visit during the **International Flower & Garden Festival** (March through May) or the **International**

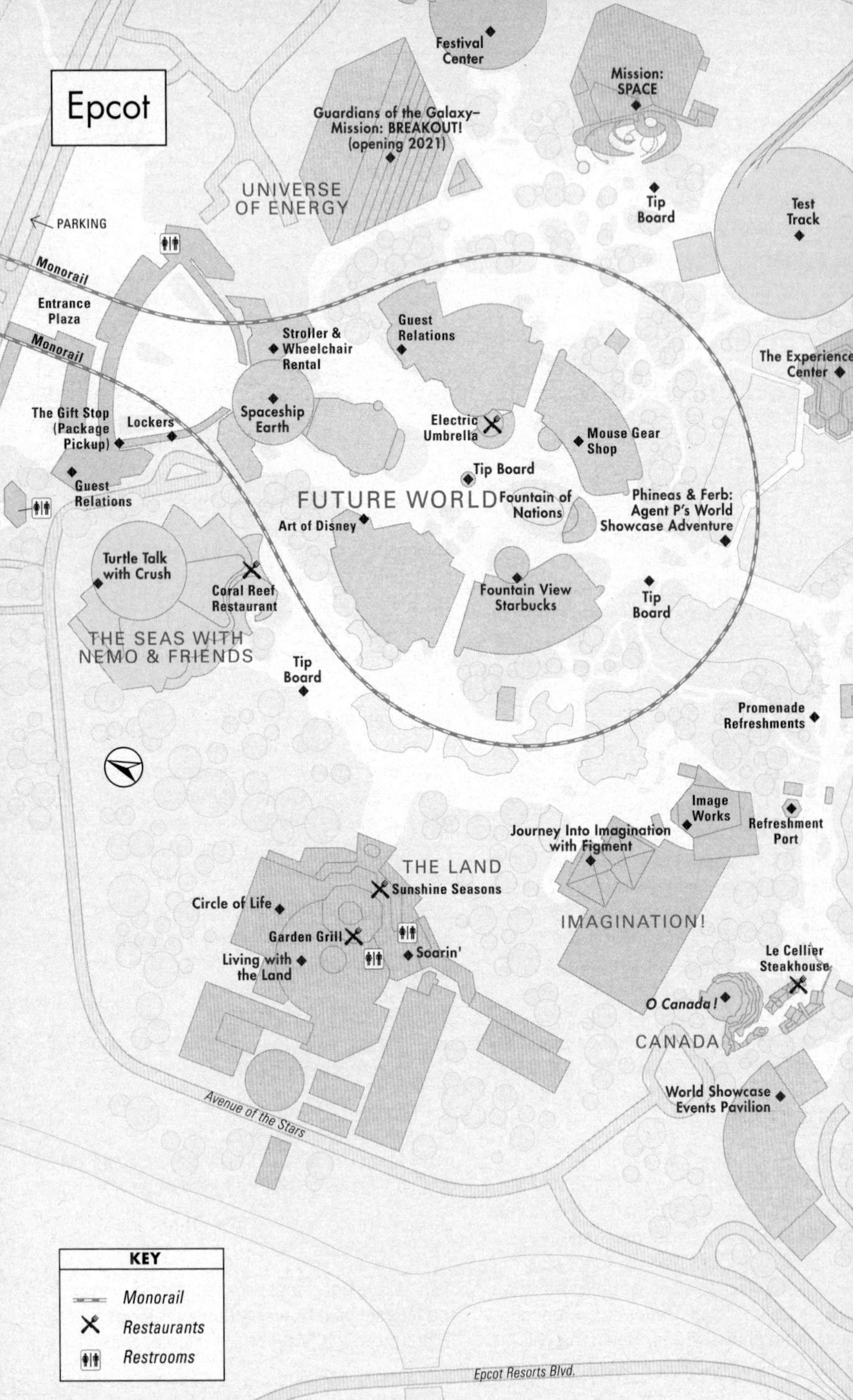

Epcot
Festival Center
Mission: SPACE
Guardians of the Galaxy–Mission: BREAKOUT! (opening 2021)
UNIVERSE OF ENERGY
Tip Board
Test Track
PARKING
Monorail
Entrance Plaza
Monorail
Stroller & Wheelchair Rental
Guest Relations
The Experience Center
Spaceship Earth
The Gift Stop (Package Pickup)
Lockers
Electric Umbrella
Mouse Gear Shop
Tip Board
Guest Relations
FUTURE WORLD
Fountain of Nations
Phineas & Ferb: Agent P's World Showcase Adventure
Art of Disney
Turtle Talk with Crush
Coral Reef Restaurant
Fountain View Starbucks
Tip Board
THE SEAS WITH NEMO & FRIENDS
Tip Board
Promenade Refreshments
Image Works
Refreshment Port
Journey Into Imagination with Figment
THE LAND
Sunshine Seasons
Circle of Life
IMAGINATION!
Garden Grill
Soarin'
Living with the Land
Le Cellier Steakhouse
O Canada!
CANADA
Avenue of the Stars
World Showcase Events Pavilion
KEY
Monorail
Restaurants
Restrooms
Epcot Resorts Blvd.

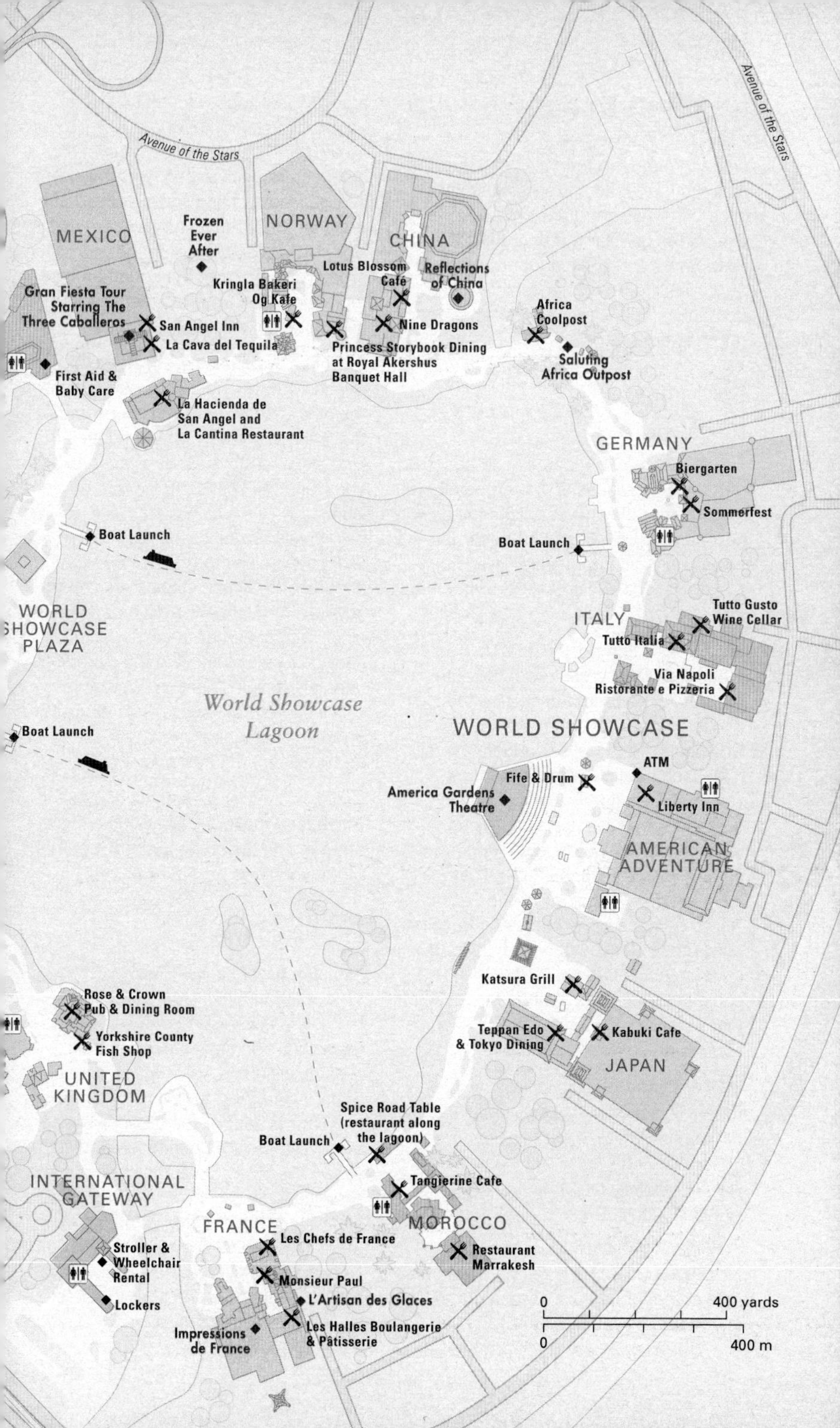

Avenue of the Stars
Avenue of the Stars
MEXICO
Frozen Ever After
NORWAY
CHINA
Lotus Blossom Café
Reflections of China
Kringla Bakeri Og Kafe
Gran Fiesta Tour Starring The Three Caballeros
San Angel Inn
La Cava del Tequila
Nine Dragons
Princess Storybook Dining at Royal Akershus Banquet Hall
Africa Coolpost
Saluting Africa Outpost
First Aid & Baby Care
La Hacienda de San Angel and La Cantina Restaurant
GERMANY
Biergarten
Sommerfest
Boat Launch
Boat Launch
WORLD SHOWCASE PLAZA
ITALY
Tutto Gusto Wine Cellar
Tutto Italia
Via Napoli Ristorante e Pizzeria
World Showcase Lagoon
WORLD SHOWCASE
Boat Launch
ATM
Fife & Drum
America Gardens Theatre
Liberty Inn
AMERICAN ADVENTURE
Katsura Grill
Rose & Crown Pub & Dining Room
Teppan Edo & Tokyo Dining
Kabuki Cafe
Yorkshire County Fish Shop
JAPAN
UNITED KINGDOM
Spice Road Table (restaurant along the lagoon)
Boat Launch
INTERNATIONAL GATEWAY
Tangierine Cafe
FRANCE
MOROCCO
Les Chefs de France
Stroller & Wheelchair Rental
Restaurant Marrakesh
Monsieur Paul
L'Artisan des Glaces
Lockers
0
400 yards
Impressions de France
Les Halles Boulangerie & Pâtisserie
0
400 m

Food & Wine Festival (September through mid-November).

Once through the turnstiles at either the main Future World entrance or the back World Showcase entrance, make a beeline for the popular Mission: SPACE and Test Track (for fast-paced thrills) or the Seas with Nemo & Friends and Soarin' (for family fun). Or get a FastPass+ and return later.

Sights

FUTURE WORLD

Future World's inner core is composed of the iconic Spaceship Earth geosphere (closing for renovations in 2020) and, beyond it, a plaza anchored by the awe-inspiring computer-animated Fountain of Nations, which shoots water 150 feet skyward.

Six pavilions compose Future World's outer ring. On the east side, they are Mission: SPACE, Test Track, and the location (under construction) of a massive Guardians of the Galaxy indoor coaster ride. Each pavilion presents a single, self-contained ride and an occasional postride showcase; a visit rarely takes more than 30 minutes, but it depends on how long you spend in the postride area. On the west side are the Seas with Nemo & Friends, The Land, and Imagination! These blockbuster exhibits contain both rides and interactive displays; you could spend at least 1½ hours at each of these pavilions, but there aren't enough hours in the day, so prioritize.

■ **TIP→ Before setting out, look into the Disney PhotoPass at the Camera Center in the Entrance Plaza. It tracks photos of your group shot by Disney photographers, which you can view and purchase later at the center or online.**

WORLD SHOWCASE

Nowhere but at Epcot can you explore a little corner of nearly a dozen countries in one day. As you stroll the 1.3 miles around the 40-acre World Showcase Lagoon, you circumnavigate the globe-according-to-Disney by experiencing the architecture, native food, entertainment, culture, and arts and crafts at pavilions representing countries in Europe, Asia, North Africa, and the Americas. Pavilion employees are from the countries they represent—Disney hires them as part of its international college program.

Solid film attractions are featured at the Canada, China, and France pavilions; the new Ratatouille ride rises behind the France Pavilion; Norway houses the Frozen Ever After ride; several art exhibitions; and the chance to try your foreign language skills with the staff. Each pavilion also has a designated Kidcot Fun Stop, open daily from 11 or noon until about 8 or 9, where youngsters can try a cultural crafts project. Live entertainment is an integral part of the experience, and you'll enjoy watching the incredibly talented Jeweled Dragon Acrobats in China and the Matsuriza Taiko drummers in Japan or laughing along with the mime and juggler in the Italy courtyard.

Dining is another favorite pastime at Epcot, and the World Showcase offers tempting tastes of the authentic cuisines of the countries here.

Restaurants

Akershus Royal Banquet Hall

$$$$ | **SCANDINAVIAN** | **FAMILY** | This restaurant has character buffets at all three meals, with an array of Disney princesses, including Ariel, Belle, Jasmine, Snow White, Aurora, Mary Poppins, and even an occasional cameo appearance by Cinderella. The breakfast menu is American, but lunch and dinner find an ever-changing assortment of Norwegian specialties, which may be foreign to children. **Known for:** an expansive buffet of Nordic specialties; Scandinavian appeal; scallops, mussels, and shrimp casserole. $ *Average main: $50* ✉ *Norway Pavilion,*

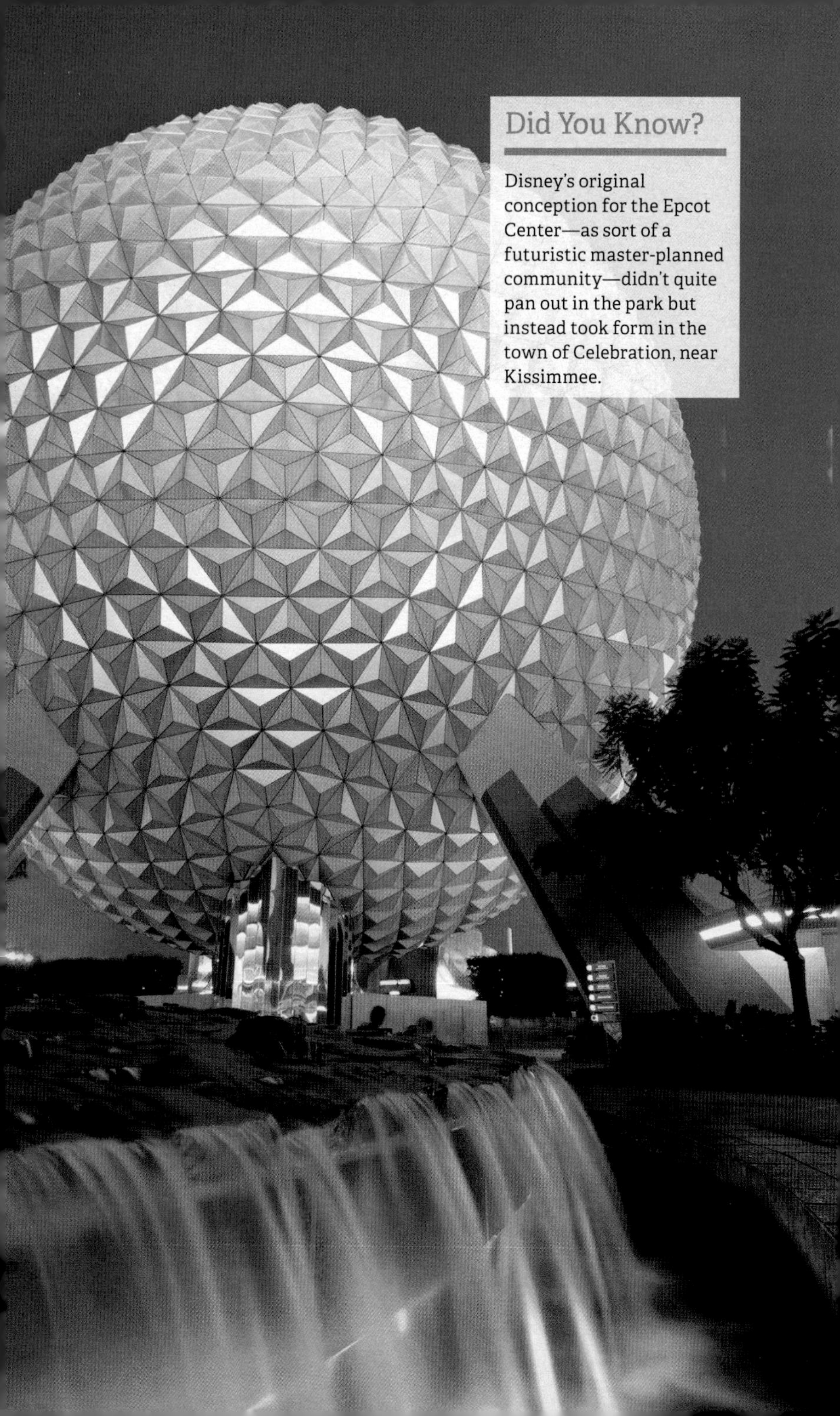

Did You Know?

Disney's original conception for the Epcot Center—as sort of a futuristic master-planned community—didn't quite pan out in the park but instead took form in the town of Celebration, near Kissimmee.

One of Epcot's most popular rides is Mission: Space, which simulates a shuttle launch.

World Showcase, Epcot ☎ *407/939–3463* 🌐 *disneyworld.disney.go.com/dining.*

Biergarten Restaurant

$$$$ | **GERMAN** | Oktoberfest runs 365 days a year here, where cheerful crowds and an oompah band set the stage for a buffet of German specialties. The menu and level of frivolity are the same at lunch and dinner. **Known for:** bratwurst, sausages, and other German specialties; lively oompah band music; buffet-style servings, including dessert bar. 💲 *Average main: $47* ✉ *Germany Pavilion, World Showcase, Epcot* ☎ *407/939–3463* 🌐 *disneyworld.disney.go.com/dining.*

★ **Flying Fish**

$$$$ | **SEAFOOD** | Flying Fish has maintained its place as one of Disney World's finest restaurants, with a menu heavy on the freshest seasonal seafood as well as steaks. The menu includes such options as wild Alaskan King salmon, Wagyu beef, and even exotic fare like bison and Hokkaido scallops. **Known for:** sophisticated dining on the Disney Boardwalk; fresh daily local and international seafood; AbracadaBAR cocktail lounge next door. 💲 *Average main: $48* ✉ *Disney's Boardwalk, 2101 Epcot Resorts Blvd., Epcot Resort Area* ☎ *407/939–2359* 🌐 *disneyworld.disney.go.com/dining* ⊗ *No lunch.*

Le Cellier Steakhouse

$$$$ | **CANADIAN** | This popular, charming eatery with stone arches and dark woods transports diners to a well-heeled setting similar to a cozy Canadian château, offering a menu heavy on meat and a good selection of wines and Canadian beer. The à la carte menu includes signature Canadian specialties such as Prince Edward Island mussels, the mandatory cheddar cheese soup, and an extraordinary Black Angus rib eye with butternut squash. **Known for:** Le Cellier signature coffee-rubbed black Angus rib eye; bouillabaise with Canadian lobster; exceptional personalized service. 💲 *Average main: $45* ✉ *Canada Pavilion, World Showcase, Epcot* ☎ *407/939–3463* 🌐 *disneyworld.disney.go.com/dining.*

★ Monsieur Paul

$$$$ | FRENCH | A mere staircase away from Epcot's busy World Showcase, Monsieur Paul is a subdued and sophisticated fine French restaurant. Make a reservation here if you are looking for an expensive, sophisticated, and delightful diversion from the theme park's bustle that is not particularly kid-friendly. **Known for:** the service is so good you'll think you're at a Michelin-starred restaurant; magret de canard (roasted duck breast); an extensive wine list. $ *Average main: $42 ✉ France Pavilion, World Showcase, Epcot ☎ 407/939–3463 🌐 disneyworld.disney.go.com/dining.*

Rose & Crown Pub & Dining Room

$$$ | BRITISH | FAMILY | If you're an Anglophile and you love a beer so thick you could stand a spoon up in your mug, this is the place to soak up both the suds and British street culture and get the best fish-and-chips in town. Try the traditional English fare—cottage or shepherd's pie, and, at times, the ever-popular bangers-and-mash (sausage over mashed potatoes). **Known for:** beer-battered fish-and-chips; Angus beef burger with Welsh rarebit sauce; wide selection of beers and ciders from the pub. $ *Average main: $24 ✉ United Kingdom Pavilion, World Showcase, Epcot ☎ 407/939–3463 🌐 disneyworld.disney.go.com/dining.*

Todd English's bluezoo

$$$$ | SEAFOOD | Celebrity chef Todd English designed the menu for this upscale seafood eatery, known perhaps more for style than substance. The sleek, modern restaurant resembles an underwater dining hall, with blue walls and carpeting, aluminum fish along the wall behind the bar, and bubblelike lighting fixtures. **Known for:** variety of seafood; celebrity chef dining; two hours of complimentary child care while dining. $ *Average main: $44 ✉ Walt Disney World Dolphin Hotel, 1500 Epcot Resorts Blvd., Epcot Resort Area ☎ 407/934–1111 🌐 www.thebluezoo.com ⏲ No lunch.*

Via Napoli Ristorante e Pizzeria

$$$ | PIZZA | FAMILY | Loud, mad, bustling, and chaotic, this casual, family-friendly restaurant in the Italy Pavilion features a menu of authentic, thin-crust Neapolitan-style pizzas from massive ovens named after Italian volcanoes that's supplemented by a large selection of southern Italian favorites. Pizzas come topped with pepperoni, mushrooms, or eggplant, artichokes, cotto ham, cheese, and even prosciutto and melon. **Known for:** pizzas from wood-fired ovens; spaghetti with veal meatballs; generous kid portions. $ *Average main: $30 ✉ Italy Pavilion, World Showcase, Epcot ☎ 407/939–3463 🌐 disneyworld.disney.go.com/dining.*

Hotels

Disney's Art of Animation Resort

$ | RESORT | FAMILY | This brightly colored, three-story resort is a kid's version of paradise: each of its four wings features images from *Finding Nemo, Cars, The Lion King*, or *The Little Mermaid*, and in-room linens and carpeting match the wing's theme. **Pros:** direct transportation to airport; free parking; images that kids adore. **Cons:** can be crowded; standard rooms fill up fast; the only on-site dining options are quick-service. $ *Rooms from: $195 ✉ 1850 Animation Way, Epcot Resort Area ☎ 407/938–7000 🌐 www.disneyworld.disney.go.com/resorts 🛏 1,984 rooms 🍽 No meals.*

Disney's Yacht Club and Beach Club Resorts

$$$$ | RESORT | FAMILY | These big Crescent Lake inns adjacent to Epcot and Hollywood Studios seem straight out of a Cape Cod summer, with their nautical decor, waterfront locale, light-filled rooms, rocking-chair porches, and family-friendly water-based activities. **Pros:** it's easy to walk or hop a ferry to Epcot or Hollywood Studios; gracious atmosphere; adjacent to Boardwalk entertainment and dining. **Cons:** distances within the resort can seem vast; remote from other parks; bus transportation is slow. $ *Rooms* *from: $593 ✉ 1700 Epcot Resorts Blvd., Epcot Resort Area ☎ 407/934–8000 Beach Club, 407/934–7000 Yacht Club 🌐 www.disneyworld.disney.go.com/resorts ⇆ 1,200 rooms 🍽 No meals.*

Four Seasons Orlando at Walt Disney World Resort

$$$$ | **RESORT** | The award-winning Four Seasons presides majestically over Disney's exclusive Golden Oak community, and its luxurious amenities and dedication to service are clear from the moment you step into the marble, flower-bedecked lobby and head for your room. **Pros:** free transportation to Disney parks; lots of on-site kids' entertainment; no resort fee; exclusive golf course for guests. **Cons:** pricey, but then, it is the Four Seasons; a long way from Universal or SeaWorld; remote from Disney parks. $ *Rooms from: $769 ✉ 10100 Dream Tree Blvd., Epcot Resort Area ☎ 407/313–7777 🌐 www.fourseasons.com/orlando ⇆ 444 rooms 🍽 No meals.*

Walt Disney World Dolphin

$$$$ | **RESORT** | A pair of 56-foot-tall sea creatures bookends this 25-story glass pyramid, a luxe resort designed, like the adjoining Swan (which is also on Disney property but not a Disney-owned resort), by world-renowned architect Michael Graves, and close enough to the parks that you can escape the midday heat for a dip in the pool. **Pros:** character meals available; access to all facilities at the Swan; free boat to BoardWalk, Epcot, and Hollywood Studios, buses to other parks. **Cons:** daily self-parking fee; a daily resort fee; no charging to room key at parks. $ *Rooms from: $635 ✉ 1500 Epcot Resorts Blvd., Epcot Resort Area ☎ 407/934–4000, 800/227–1500 🌐 www.swandolphin.com ⇆ 1,509 rooms 🍽 No meals.*

Nightlife

BARS

La Cava del Tequila

BARS/PUBS | Set inside the Mexico pavilion, this intimate bar serves more than 200 tequilas along with Mexican beers, wines, top-shelf cocktails, and a colorful array of margaritas. Try a tequila flight while snacking on tapas, chips, guacamole, and queso. ✉ *World Showcase Mexico pavilion, Epcot 🌐 www.disneyworld.disney.go.com/dining/epcot/cava-del-tequila.*

Rose & Crown Pub

BARS/PUBS | In this rollicking pub in the United Kingdom, patrons come to hear The Hat Lady (legendary local musician Carol Stein), the resident piano player who knows every sing-along song ever written and possesses an impressive knack for improvising personalized tunes on the spot. On busy nights, people stand four-to-six-deep at the bar. The fish-and-chips are first-rate, as are the bangers and mash, cottage pie, and other dishes from across the pond. Grab a pint and let the fun begin! ✉ *World Showcase United Kingdom pavilion, Epcot 🌐 www.disneyworld.disney.go.com/dining/epcot/rose-and-crown-pub.*

Tutto Gusto

BARS/PUBS | In Italy this cool and cozy wine cellar adjoining Tutto Italia is an ideal place to escape the crowds. You can order from among 200 varieties of wine, switch things up with a cold beer, and complement either with a small-plate selection of meats, cheeses, panini, pastas, and desserts. ✉ *World Showcase Italy pavilion, Epcot 🌐 www.disneyworld.disney.go.com/dining/epcot/tutto-gusto-wine-cellar.*

Top Attractions

For Ages 8 and Up

- Lightning McQueen's Racing Academy
- Rock 'n' Roller Coaster Starring Aerosmith
- Star Wars, Galaxy's Edge
- Toy Story Mania!
- Twilight Zone Tower of Terror
- Walt Disney: One Man's Dream

For Ages 7 and Under

- For the First Time in Forever: A "Frozen" Sing-Along Celebration
- Disney Junior Dance Party
- Mickey and Minnie's Runaway Railway
- Muppet*Vision 3-D
- Slinky Dog Dash

Disney's Hollywood Studios

The first thing you notice when you pass through the Hollywood Studios turnstiles is the laid-back California attitude. Palm-lined Hollywood Boulevard exudes glamour—but in a casual way that makes you feel as if you belong. The second thing you notice is the growing presence of *Star Wars*, with a land called Star Wars: Galaxy's Edge open in August 2019.

When the park opened in May 1989 its name was Disney-MGM Studios. Disney changed the name to Disney Hollywood Studios in 2008. Another name change in the near future is not outside the realm of possibility. But no matter the name, the inspiration springs from the same place: America's love affair with movies.

Though production has mostly halted at the park, you can enjoy plenty of attractions that showcase how filmmakers practice their craft. If you're wowed by action-film stunts, you can learn the tricks of the trade at the Indiana Jones Epic Stunt Spectacular! Then you can take a close look at the legend himself, at Walt Disney Presents, where sketches, artwork, and early animation join previews of what's coming next.

In a savvy effort to grab a bigger piece of the pop-culture pie, Disney is turning to new and exciting properties, as the *Star Wars* attractions take over more space at the park. Add in the expanding *Toy Story*, Incredibles, and Mickey and Minnie's Runaway Railway attractions and the park is sure to keep the whole family happy.

GETTING ORIENTED

The park is divided into sightseeing clusters. **Hollywood Boulevard** is the main artery to the heart of the park, and is where you find the glistening replica of Graumann's Chinese Theater.

Encircling it are **Sunset Boulevard,** the **Animation Courtyard, Mickey Avenue, The Incredibles' Metroville and Pixar Place, Commissary Lane, Toy Story Land, the Streets of America area,** and **Echo Lake**.

The entire park is smaller than Epcot, but the additions of Star Wars Galaxy's Edge, Toy Story Land, and Mickey & Minnie's Runaway Railway in 2019 mean there will be lots of excited visitors.

If you're staying at one of the Epcot resorts (BoardWalk, Yacht or Beach Club, Swan, or Dolphin), getting to the

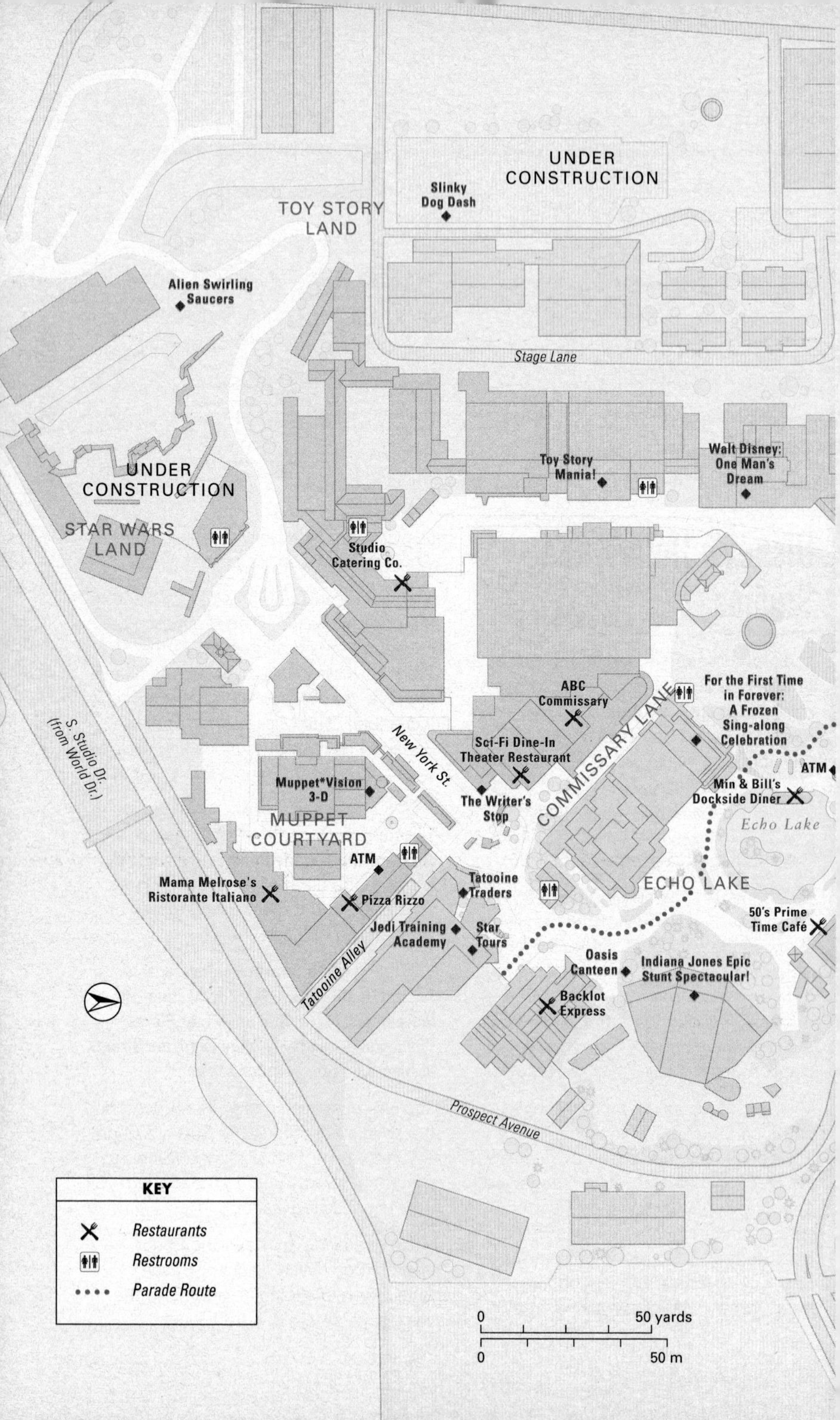

UNDER CONSTRUCTION
Slinky Dog Dash
TOY STORY LAND
Alien Swirling Saucers
Stage Lane
UNDER CONSTRUCTION
STAR WARS LAND
Toy Story Mania!
Walt Disney: One Man's Dream
Studio Catering Co.
S. Studio Dr. (from World Dr.)
ABC Commissary
For the First Time in Forever: A Frozen Sing-along Celebration
New York St.
Sci-Fi Dine-In Theater Restaurant
COMMISSARY LANE
ATM
Muppet*Vision 3-D
The Writer's Stop
Min & Bill's Dockside Diner
MUPPET COURTYARD
Echo Lake
ATM
Mama Melrose's Ristorante Italiano
Tatooine Traders
ECHO LAKE
Pizza Rizzo
Jedi Training Academy
Star Tours
50's Prime Time Café
Tatooine Alley
Oasis Canteen
Indiana Jones Epic Stunt Spectacular!
Backlot Express
Prospect Avenue
KEY
Restaurants
Restrooms
Parade Route
0
50 yards
0
50 m

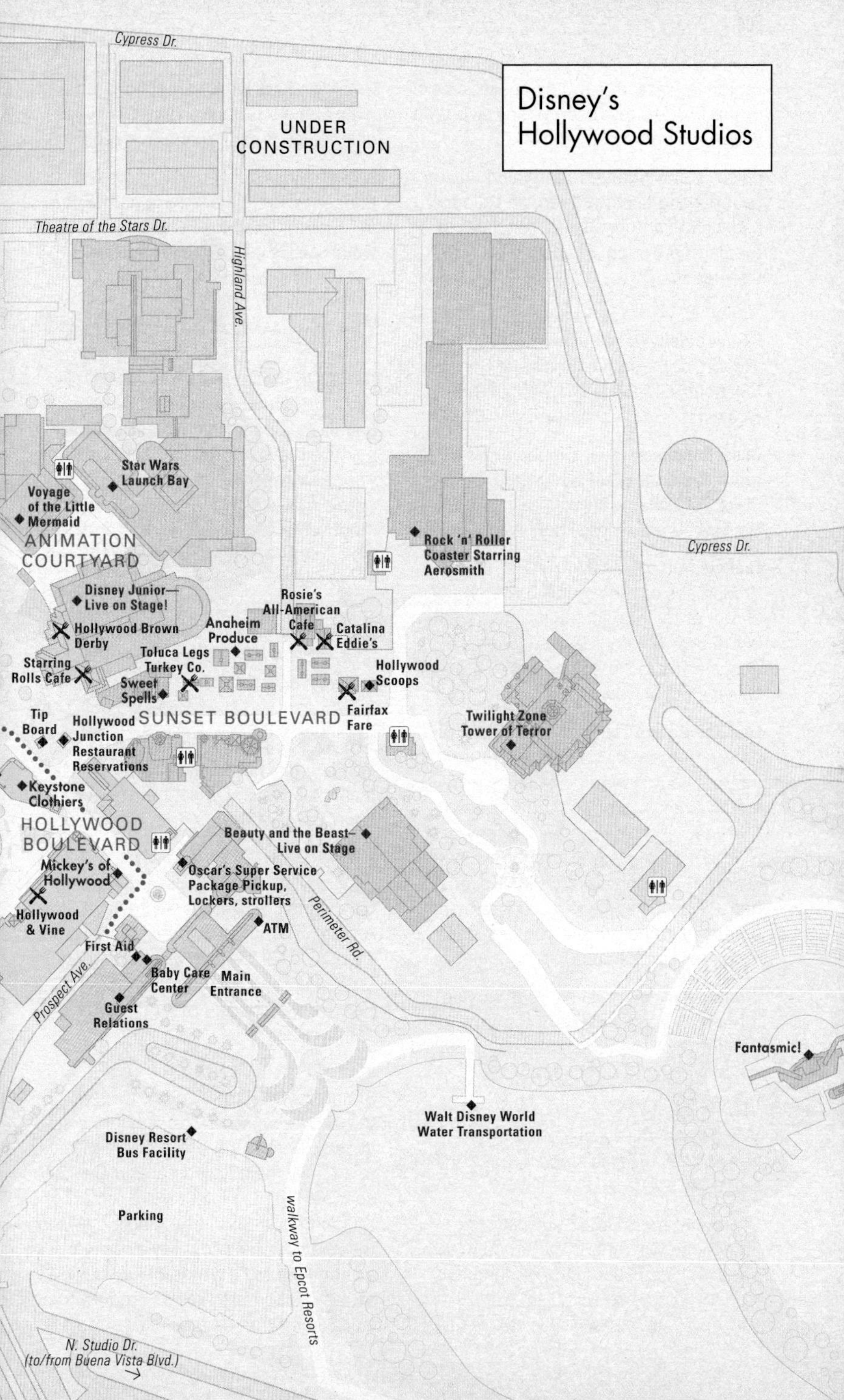
Disney's Hollywood Studios
Cypress Dr.
UNDER CONSTRUCTION
Theatre of the Stars Dr.
Highland Ave.
Star Wars Launch Bay
Voyage of the Little Mermaid
ANIMATION COURTYARD
Rock 'n' Roller Coaster Starring Aerosmith
Cypress Dr.
Disney Junior—Live on Stage!
Rosie's All-American Cafe
Anaheim Produce
Catalina Eddie's
Hollywood Brown Derby
Toluca Legs Turkey Co.
Starring Rolls Cafe
Sweet Spells
Hollywood Scoops
Fairfax Fare
Tip Board
Hollywood Junction Restaurant Reservations
SUNSET BOULEVARD
Twilight Zone Tower of Terror
Keystone Clothiers
HOLLYWOOD BOULEVARD
Beauty and the Beast–Live on Stage
Mickey's of Hollywood
Oscar's Super Service Package Pickup, Lockers, strollers
Hollywood & Vine
Perimeter Rd.
ATM
First Aid
Baby Care Center
Main Entrance
Prospect Ave.
Guest Relations
Fantasmic!
Walt Disney World Water Transportation
Disney Resort Bus Facility
Parking
walkway to Epcot Resorts
N. Studio Dr. (to/from Buena Vista Blvd.)

Entrance Plaza on a motor launch is part of the fun. Disney resort buses also drop you at the entrance.

If you're staying off-property and driving, your parking ticket will remain valid for parking at another Disney park later in the day—provided, of course, you have the stamina.

PARK AMENITIES

Disney's Hollywood Studios Lost and Found Report lost or found articles at Guest Relations. ✉ *Hollywood Blvd., Disney's Hollywood Studios* ☎ *407/560–4666*.

Guest Relations: You'll find it just inside the turnstiles on the left side of the Entrance Plaza. **A FastPass+ kiosk** is at the corner of Hollywood and Sunset boulevards.

Lockers: You can rent lockers at the Crossroads of the World kiosk in the center of the Entrance Plaza. The cost is $10 or $15 with a $5 refundable key deposit. The lockers themselves are at Oscar's Super Service.

Lost People and Things: Make plans for where to meet if you get separated. Instruct your kids to go to a Disney staffer with a name tag if they can't find you. If you lose them, ask any cast member for assistance; logbooks of lost children's names are kept at Guest Relations, which also has a computerized message center where you can leave notes for companions.

Stroller Rentals: Oscar's Super Service rents strollers. Single strollers are $15 daily, $13 for more than one day; doubles are $31 daily, $27 multiday.

VISITING TIPS

Visit early in the week, when most people are at Magic Kingdom and Animal Kingdom.

Check the Tip Board periodically for attractions with short wait times to visit between FastPass+ appointments.

Be at the Fantasmic! amphitheater at least an hour before showtime if you didn't book the VIP dinner package.

Need a burst of energy? On-the-run hunger pangs? Grab a slice at **PizzeRizzo** at Muppet Courtyard. Alternatively, **Hollywood Scoops** ice cream on Sunset is the place to be on a hot day.

 Sights

HOLLYWOOD BOULEVARD

With its palm trees, pastel buildings, and flashy neon, Hollywood Boulevard paints a rosy picture of 1930s Tinseltown. There's a sense of having walked right onto a movie set of old, with art-deco storefronts and roving starlets and nefarious agents—actually costumed actors known as the Citizens of Hollywood. Throughout the park, characters from *Star Wars* and other Disney movies—such as *The Incredibles*—pose for photos and sign autographs.

SUNSET BOULEVARD

This avenue honors Hollywood with facades derived from City of Angels landmarks, and leads straight to The Twilight Zone Tower of Terror.

ANIMATION COURTYARD

As you exit Sunset Boulevard, veer right through the high-arched gateway to the Animation Courtyard. Straight ahead are *Disney Junior Dance Party*, *Voyage of the Little Mermaid,* and the Star Wars Launch Bay, where fans can meet Chewbacca and Kylo Ren.

TOY STORY LAND

Shrink down to toy size and explore the 11-acre world of Buzz Lightyear and Woody. Troops of green army men lead to a family-friendly coaster and alien saucer ride. Opened in 2019 and replacing Studio Backlot Tour, the 11-acre playland transports visitors to Andy's backyard as honorary toys, where giant Popsicle sticks and Scrabble letters are furniture and Wheezy the penguin sings into a

Playskool mic. Home to one of the park's biggest attractions, Toy Story Mania! (a holdover from the now-absorbed Pixar Place), there's also the new Slinky Dog Dash. Alien Swirling Saucers is filled with toy rockets, space music, and the three-eyed aliens from Pizza Planet. Eat at Woody's Lunch Box, meet Woody, Jessie, and Buzz, and march to the sound of the Green Army Drum Corps.

STAR WARS LAND

Much of the southwest corner of the park has been behind walls and fences for the past two years, but 2019 is the year that *Star Wars Galaxy's Edge* takes over Hollywood Studios. The franchise, including characters and scenes from *Rogue One,* have already affected much of the entertainment and direction in the larger park. At 14 acres Star Wars Land will be the largest single-themed expansion ever added to a Disney theme park. Visitors will be transported to a galaxy far, far away, to a planet on the outer rim of civilization, one of the last stops before wild space, and right into a battle between the dark and light sides of the Force. One of the signature attractions puts you behind the controls of the Millennium Falcon; and Star Tours—the Adventures Continue will include a new mission based on elements from the upcoming *Star Wars Episode VIII*. The food, entertainment, and attractions are all part of the story, including the Cantina and a massive supper club with alien entertainment.

ECHO LAKE

In the center of the park is a cool, blue lake—an oasis fringed with trees, benches, and things like pink-and-aqua, chrome-trimmed restaurants with sassy waitresses and black-and-white TVs at the tables; the shipshape Min & Bill's Dockside Diner; and Tatooine Traders, where kids can build their own lightsabers and browse a trove of *Star Wars*–inspired goods.

Restaurants

50's Prime Time Café

$$ | **AMERICAN** | **FAMILY** | If you grew up in middle America in the 1950s—or if you're just a fan of classic TV shows like *I Love Lucy* and *The Donna Reed Show*—you'll appreciate the vintage atmosphere and all-American classic menu at this diner-style restaurant. Clips of old TV shows will welcome you as you feast on meat loaf, pot roast, or fried chicken, all served on a Formica tabletop. **Known for:** showing clips of classic TV shows during dinner; "Mom" wandering around tables telling kids to eat their veggies; golden-fried chicken, pot roast, and meat loaf sampler. *Average main: $18* *Echo Lake, Disney's Hollywood Studios* *407/939–3463* *disneyworld.disney.go.com/dining.*

Hollywood Brown Derby

$$$$ | **AMERICAN** | At this reproduction of the famous 1940s Hollywood favorite, the walls are lined with caricatures of older movie stars. The specialty is a Cobb salad, which was invented by Brown Derby founder Robert Cobb and still tossed table-side. **Known for:** old-Hollywood atmosphere; the Cobb Salad; duck two ways. *Average main: $40* *Hollywood Blvd., Disney's Hollywood Studios* *407/939–3463* *disneyworld.disney.go.com/dining.*

Sci-Fi Dine-In Theater Restaurant

$$$ | **AMERICAN** | **FAMILY** | If you don't mind zombies leering at you while you eat, then head to this enclosed faux drive-in, where you can eat in a booth that looks like a candy-colored 1950s convertible while watching clips from classics like *Attack of the Fifty-Foot Woman* and *Teenagers from Outer Space*. The menu includes choices like steak and garlic mashed potatoes, an Angus or veggie burger, shrimp with whole-grain pasta, and a huge Reuben sandwich with fries or cucumber salad. End with a hot-fudge sundae. **Known for:** menu of American

classics like steak and Reuben sandwich; build-your-own Angus burger; wine, sangria, and fun cocktails. [$] *Average main: $25* ✉ *Commissary La., Disney's Hollywood Studios* ☎ *407/939–3463* 🌐 *disneyworld.disney.go.com/dining.*

Disney's Animal Kingdom

If you're thinking, "Oh, it's just another zoo, let's skip it," think again. Walt Disney World's fourth theme park, opened in 1998, takes its inspiration from humankind's enduring love for animals and pulls out all the stops. Your day will be packed with unusual animal encounters, enchanting entertainment, themed rides that will leave you breathless, and Pandora—The World of Avatar, which takes visitors inside the culture and sights of James Cameron's film.

A large chunk of the park is devoted to animal habitats, especially the forest and savanna of Africa's Kilimanjaro Safaris. Towering acacia trees and tall grasses sweep across the land where antelopes, giraffes, and wildebeests roam. A lion kopje, warthog burrows, a zebra habitat, and an elephant watering hole provide ample space for inhabitants.

About 94 acres contain foliage like hibiscus and mulberry, perfect for antelope and many other species. The largest groups of Nile hippos and African elephants in North America live along the winding waterway that leads to the savanna. The generously landscaped Pangani Forest Exploration Trail provides roaming grounds for troops of gorillas and authentic habitats for meerkats, birds, fish, and other creatures.

Beyond the park's Africa territory, similar large spaces are set aside for the homes of Asian animals like tigers and giant fruit bats, as well as for creatures such as Galápagos tortoises and a giant anteater. Disney Imagineers didn't forget to include their trademark thrills, from the Kali River Rapids ride in Asia to the fast-paced DINOSAUR journey in DinoLand U.S.A. Expedition Everest, the park's current big thrill attraction, is a "runaway" train ride on a faux rugged mountain complete with icy ledges, dark caves, and a yeti legend. Of special interest are the glow-in-the-dark plants, flying banshees, floating mountains, and Na'vi culture of *Avatar* and its coming sequels.

Every evening the Tree of Life Awakenings bathes the central icon with color, and several live entertainment ensembles perform, including the Discovery Island Carnivale and the popular Tam Tam Drummers of Harambe. A lazer and fountain-filled evening show *Rivers of Light* is a dazzling way to end the night.

The only downside to the Animal Kingdom layout is that walking paths and spaces can get very crowded and hot in the warmest months. Your best bet is to arrive very early and see the animals first before the heat makes them (and you) woozy.

Just before the park opens, Minnie Mouse, Pluto, and other characters arrive at Trader's Outpost to welcome early guests into the park.

GETTING ORIENTED

Animal Kingdom's hub is the Tree of Life, in the middle of Discovery Island. The park's lands, each with a distinct personality, radiate from Discovery Island. To the southwest lies the very popular land of Pandora, based on the *Avatar* film and upcoming sequels. North of the hub is Africa, where Kilimanjaro Safaris travel across extensive savanna. In the northeast corner is Rafiki's Planet Watch with conservation activities.

Asia, with thrills like Expedition Everest and Kali River Rapids, is east of the hub, and DinoLand U.S.A. brings *T. rex* and other prehistoric creatures to life in the park's southeast corner.

If you're staying on-site, you can take a Disney bus to the Entrance Plaza. If you drive, the $20 parking fee allows you to park at other Disney lots throughout the day.

Although this is technically Disney's largest theme park, most of the land is reserved for the animals. Pedestrian areas are actually quite compact, with relatively narrow passageways. The only way to get around is on foot or in a wheelchair or electronic convenience vehicle (ECV).

PARK AMENITIES

Guest Relations: This office will help with tickets at a window to the left just before you pass through the turnstile. Once you've entered, Guest Relations staffers in the Oasis can provide park maps, schedules, and answers to questions. They can also assist with dining reservations, ticket upgrades, and services for guests with disabilities.

Lockers: Lockers are in Guest Relations in the Oasis. Rental fees are $10 to $15 (depending on size) for a day plus a $5 key deposit.

Lost People and Things: Instruct your kids to speak to someone with a Disney name tag if you become separated. Lost children are taken to the baby-care center, where they can watch Disney movies, or to Guest Relations, whichever is closer. If you do lose your child, contact any cast member immediately and Disney security personnel will be notified.

Animal Kingdom Lost and Found

To retrieve lost articles on the same day, visit or call Lost and Found, which is in the lobby of Guest Relations, just inside the park. ✉ *Oasis, Animal Kingdom* ☎ *407/938–2785.*

Stroller Rentals: Garden Gate Gifts in the Oasis rents strollers. Singles are $15 daily, $13 multiday; doubles run $31 daily, $27 multiday.

Top Attractions

Africa

- Festival of the Lion King
- Kilimanjaro Safaris

Asia

- Expedition Everest

DinoLand U.S.A.

- DINOSAUR
- Finding Nemo: The Musical

Discovery Island

- Tree of Life: It's Tough to Be a Bug!

Pandora—The World of Avatar

- Avatar Flight of Passage

VISITING TIPS

Try to visit during the week. Pedestrian areas are compact, and the park can feel uncomfortably packed on weekends.

The land of Pandora is a very popular draw, and with hours into evening, remains busy until the park closes.

Plan on a full day here. That way, while exploring Africa's Pangani Forest Exploration Trail, say, you can spend 10 minutes (rather than just 2) watching vigilant meerkats stand sentry or tracking a mama gorilla as she cares for her youngster.

Arrive a half hour before the park opens as much to see the wild animals at their friskiest (morning is a good time to do the safari ride) as to get a jump on the crowds. Evening safaris are popular.

For updates on line lengths, check the Tip Board, just after crossing the bridge into Discovery Island.

Good places to rendezvous include the outdoor Dawa Bar or Tamu Tamu Refreshments areas in Africa, in front of DinoLand U.S.A.'s Boneyard, or on

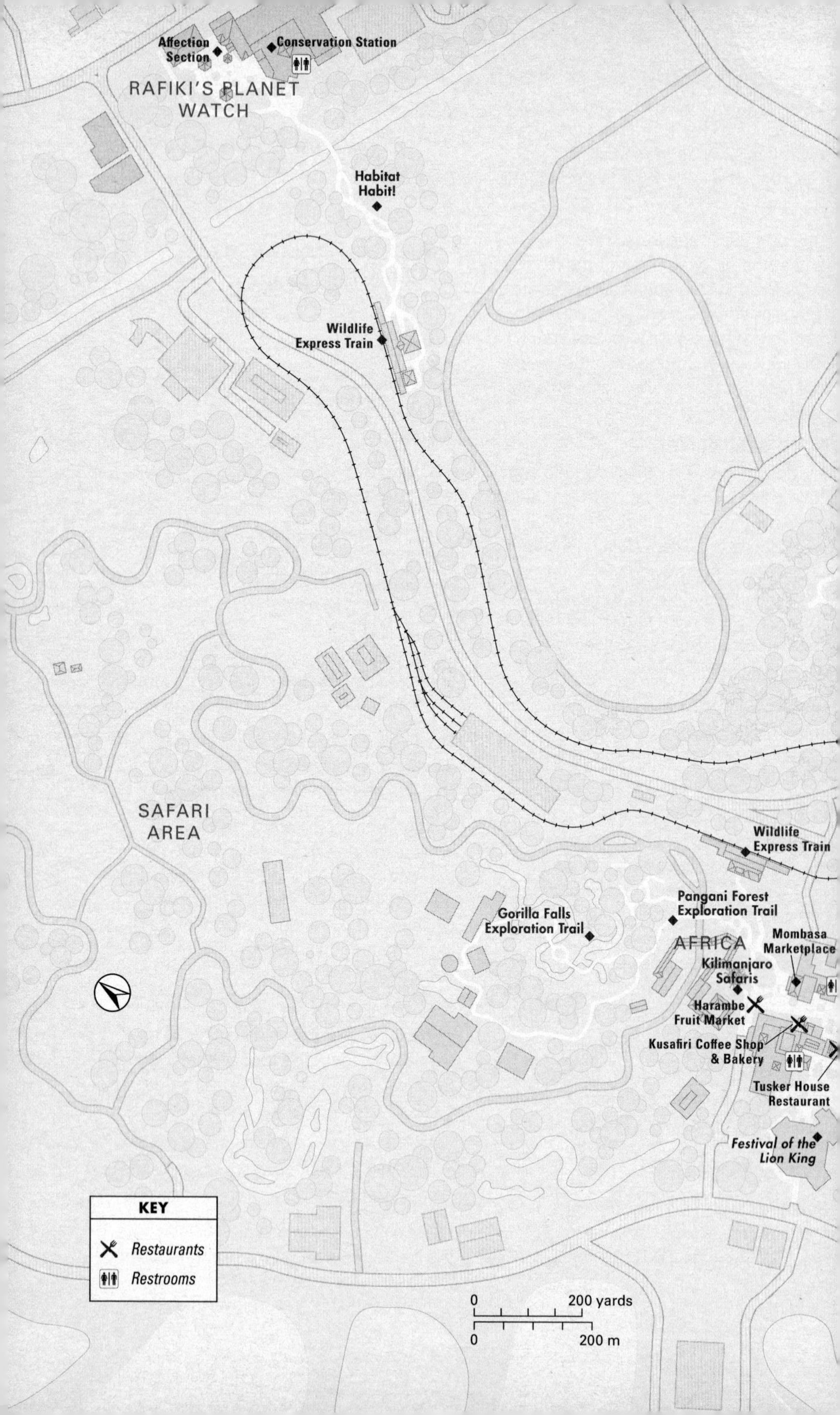
Affection Section
Conservation Station
RAFIKI'S PLANET WATCH
Habitat Habit!
Wildlife Express Train
SAFARI AREA
Wildlife Express Train
Pangani Forest Exploration Trail
Gorilla Falls Exploration Trail
AFRICA
Mombasa Marketplace
Kilimanjaro Safaris
Harambe Fruit Market
Kusafiri Coffee Shop & Bakery
Tusker House Restaurant
Festival of the Lion King
KEY
Restaurants
Restrooms
0
200 yards
0
200 m

Disney's Animal Kingdom

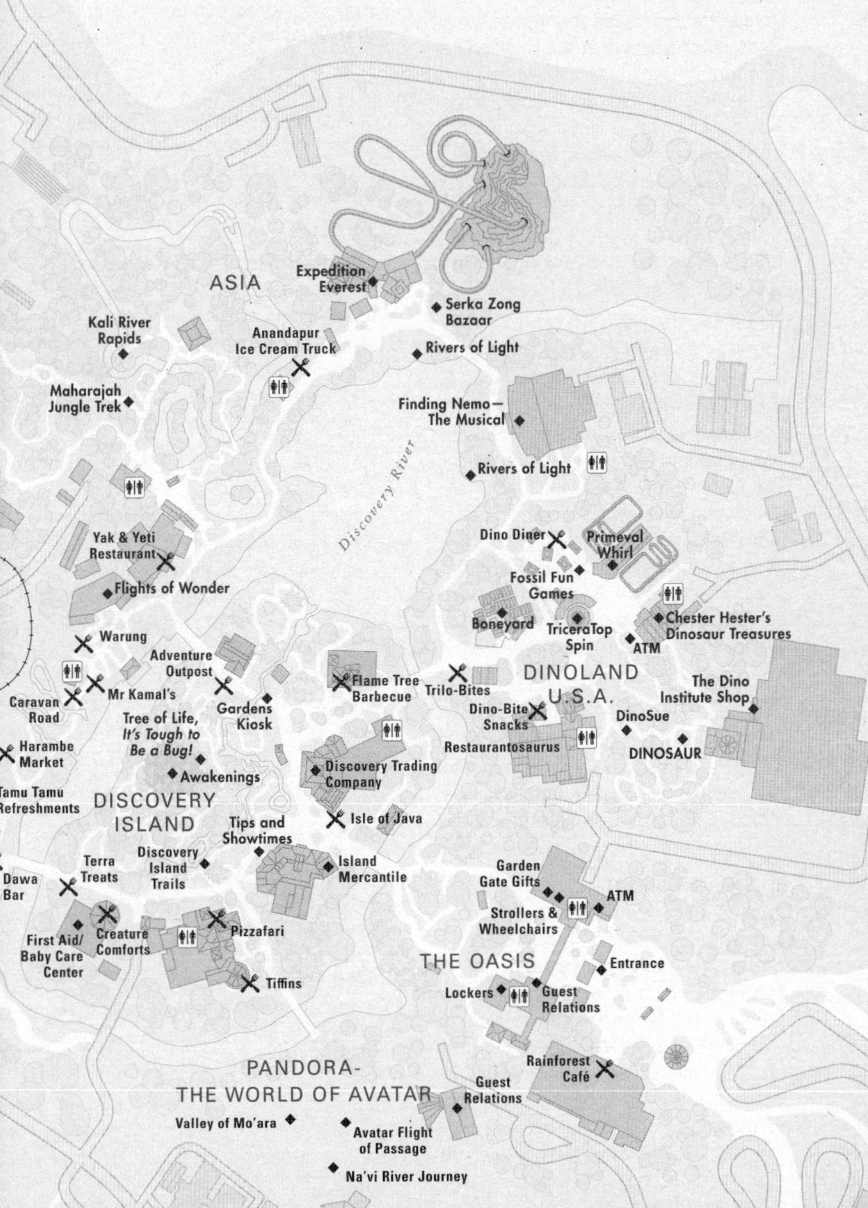

ASIA
Expedition Everest
Serka Zong Bazaar
Kali River Rapids
Anandapur Ice Cream Truck
Rivers of Light
Maharajah Jungle Trek
Finding Nemo—The Musical
Discovery River
Rivers of Light
Yak & Yeti Restaurant
Dino Diner
Primeval Whirl
Fossil Fun Games
Flights of Wonder
Boneyard
TriceraTop Spin
Chester Hester's Dinosaur Treasures
ATM
Warung
Adventure Outpost
Flame Tree Barbecue
Trilo-Bites
DINOLAND U.S.A.
The Dino Institute Shop
Mr Kamal's
Caravan Road
Gardens Kiosk
Dino-Bite Snacks
DinoSue
Tree of Life, It's Tough to Be a Bug!
Restaurantosaurus
DINOSAUR
Harambe Market
Discovery Trading Company
Awakenings
Tamu Tamu Refreshments
DISCOVERY ISLAND
Isle of Java
Tips and Showtimes
Terra Treats
Discovery Island Trails
Island Mercantile
Garden Gate Gifts
Dawa Bar
ATM
Strollers & Wheelchairs
First Aid/ Baby Care Center
Creature Comforts
Pizzafari
THE OASIS
Entrance
Tiffins
Lockers
Guest Relations
PANDORA- THE WORLD OF AVATAR
Rainforest Café
Guest Relations
Valley of Mo'ara
Avatar Flight of Passage
Na'vi River Journey

one of the benches outside Expedition Everest in Asia.

Sights

THE OASIS

This entrance makes you feel as if you've been plunked down in the middle of a rain forest. Cool mist, the aroma of flowers, playful animals, and colorful birds enliven a miniature landscape of streams and grottoes, waterfalls, and glades fringed with banana leaves and jacaranda. It's also where you can take care of essentials before entering. Here you'll find guide maps, stroller and wheelchair rentals, Guest Relations, and an ATM.

DISCOVERY ISLAND

The park hub and site of the Tree of Life, this island is encircled by Discovery River, which isn't an actual attraction but makes for attractive views from the bridge to Harambe and another between Asia and DinoLand U.S.A. The island's whimsical architecture, with wood carvings from Bali, lends charm and a touch of fantasy. The Discovery Island Trails that lead to the Tree of Life provide habitats for African crested porcupines, lemurs, Galápagos tortoises, and other creatures you won't want to miss.

You'll discover some great shops and good counter-service eateries here. Visitor services that aren't in the Oasis are here, on the border with Harambe, including the baby-care center and the first-aid center.

DINOLAND U.S.A.

Just as it sounds, this is the place to come in contact with re-created prehistoric creatures, including the fear-inspiring carnotaurus and the gentle iguanodon. The landscaping includes live plants that have evolved over the last 65 million years. In collaboration with Chicago's Field Museum, Disney displays a complete, full-scale skeleton cast of Dino-Sue—also known as "Sue"—the 65-million-year-old *Tyrannosaurus rex* discovered near the Black Hills of South Dakota.

After admiring Sue, you can go on the thrilling DINOSAUR ride, play in the Boneyard, or take in the *Finding Nemo: The Musical* show at the Theater in the Wild. Kids will want to try the TriceraTop Spin and the Primeval Whirl family coaster, which has spinning "time machines." There's no need to dig for souvenirs at Chester and Hester's Dinosaur Treasures gift shop—all you need is your wallet.

ASIA

Meant to resemble an Asian village, this land is full of remarkable rain-forest scenery and ruins. Groupings of trees grow from a crumbling tiger shrine, and massive towers—representing Thailand and Nepal—are the habitat for gibbons, whose hooting fills the air.

AFRICA

The largest of the lands is an area of forests and grasslands, predominantly an enclave for wildlife from the continent. Harambe, on the northern bank of Discovery River, is Africa's starting point. Inspired by several East African villages, this Disney town has so much detail that it's mind-boggling to try to soak it all up. Signs on the apparently peeling stucco walls are faded, as if bleached by the sun, and everything has a hot, dusty look. For souvenirs with Disney and African themes, browse through the Mombasa Marketplace and Ziwani Traders.

RAFIKI'S PLANET WATCH

While in the Harambe, Africa, section, board the 250-passenger rustic Wildlife Express steam train for a ride to a unique center of eco-awareness named for the wise baboon from *The Lion King*. Young children especially enjoy the chance to explore these three animal-friendly areas.

On Asia's Expedition Everest, you'll chug, twist, turn, and plunge up, through, and down Mt. Everest on nearly a mile of track. Oh, yeah, and beware of the yeti!

PANDORA—THE WORLD OF AVATAR

Inspired by the film *Avatar*, the land has floating mountains, bioluminescent plants, and flying inhabitants, and it brims with dazzling high-tech effects that are particularly resonant by night. Visitors are greeted by members of Alpha Centauri Expeditions, an ecotour group preparing Pandora for explorers and adventure seekers. The land contains two major attractions: the family-friendly Na'vi River Journey travels along a river through a rain forest with glow-in-the dark flowers to a meeting with a shaman. The more thrilling Avatar Flight of Passage allows guests to ride a Banshee over the world of Pandora, past the astonishing sight of giant, vine-covered mountains that seem to float in the air.

Restaurants

★ Boma—Flavors of Africa

$$$$ | AFRICAN | FAMILY | Boma takes Western-style ingredients and prepares them with an African twist. Guests walk through an African marketplace–style dining room to help themselves at counters piled high with flavor from an upscale buffet like no other. **Known for:** superb food both the timid and adventurous will like; African flavors and dishes; endless buffet with wonderful service that appeals to kids. *Average main: $43* ✉ *Animal Kingdom Lodge, 2901 Osceola Pkwy., Animal Kingdom Resort Area* ☎ *407/939–3463* 🌐 *disneyworld.disney.go.com/dining* ⏲ *No lunch.*

Flame Tree Barbecue

$ | FAST FOOD | FAMILY | This quick-service eatery is one of the relatively undiscovered gems of Disney's culinary offerings; there's nothing fancy here, but you can dig into ribs, chicken, and pulled-pork sandwiches. And yes, you can still get those giant turkey legs. **Known for:** reasonably priced barbecue in an Animal Kingdom setting; ribs, chicken, and pulled-pork sampler; variety of beer and wine. *Average main: $12 Discovery Island, Animal Kingdom disneyworld. disney.go.com/dining.*

★ Jiko

$$$$ | **AFRICAN** | The name of this restaurant means "the cooking place" in Swahili, and it is certainly that, offering a menu that is more African-inspired than purely African, as well as a strong selection of South African wines. The dining area surrounds two big, wood-burning ovens and a grill area where you can watch cooks in North African–style caps working on your meal. **Known for:** African cuisine with an American flair and Indonesian accents; sophisticated surroundings and decor; Wagyu beef and Moroccan lamb. *Average main: $45 Animal Kingdom Lodge, 2901 Osceola Pkwy., Animal Kingdom Resort Area 407/939–3463 disneyworld.disney.go.com/dining No lunch.*

★ Tiffins

$$$$ | **INTERNATIONAL** | **FAMILY** | Inspired by the worldwide journeys of Disney Imagineers, Tiffins is the theme parks' newest upscale sit-down restaurant and possibly the best theme park eatery, period. Serving a wide-ranging international menu that changes constantly, this gateway to Pandora has become intensely popular. **Known for:** superbly cooked, changing menu with Asian, Latin, and African flavors; elaborate decor; kids meals that aren't dumbed down. *Average main: $41 Discovery Island, Animal Kingdom 407/939–1947 disneyworld.disney.go.com/dining.*

Yak & Yeti

$$$ | **ASIAN** | This large, pan-Asian restaurant offers sit-down service in a two-story, 250-seat venue in the Asia section, offering everything from a variety of noodles to curries to Korean barbecued ribs. The decor is pleasantly faux-Asian, with cracked plaster walls, wood carvings, and tile mosaic tabletops. **Known for:** large menu with Indian, Japanese, Chinese, and Korean influences; welcoming lounge for escaping the weather; shareable dim sum and appetizer baskets. *Average main: $22 Asia, Animal Kingdom 407/939–3463 disneyworld.disney.go.com/dining.*

Hotels

Disney's All-Star Sports Resort

$ | **RESORT** | **FAMILY** | Stay here if you want the All-American, sports-mad, quintessential Disney-with-your-kids experience, or if you're a couple to whom all that pitter-pattering of little feet is a reasonable trade-off for a good deal on a room, albeit a small one. **Pros:** unbeatable price for a Disney property; kids love sports themes; close to Disney's ESPN Wide World of Sports Complex. **Cons:** no kids clubs or programs; distances between rooms and on-site amenities can seem vast; farthest resort from Magic Kingdom means you'll spend time on the bus. *Rooms from: $139 1701 W. Buena Vista Dr., Animal Kingdom Resort Area 407/939–5000 www.disneyworld.disney.go.com/resorts 1,704 rooms No meals.*

★ Disney's Animal Kingdom Lodge

$$$$ | **RESORT** | **FAMILY** | Entering the vast atrium lobby of this African-inspired lodge is like entering a cathedral with a roof formed of thatch instead of stone; giraffes, zebras, and other wildlife roam just outside the windows of the resort, designed to resemble a *kraal* (animal enclosure) in Africa. **Pros:** extraordinary wildlife and cultural experiences on-site; excellent restaurants; breakfast buffet in Boma is a bargain. **Cons:** shuttle to parks other than Animal Kingdom can take more than an hour; concierge-level rooms have $100-plus surcharge; long

corridors. $ *Rooms from: $436* ✉ *2901 Osceola Pkwy., Animal Kingdom Resort Area* ☎ *407/938–3000* 🌐 *www.disneyworld.disney.go.com/resorts* ⇄ *1,404 rooms* 🍽 *No meals.*

Walt Disney World Water Parks

The beauty of Disney's water parks is that you can make either experience fit your mood. Like crowds? Head for the lounge chairs along the Surf Pool at Typhoon Lagoon or Melt-Away Bay at Blizzard Beach. Prefer peace? Walk past lush foliage along each park's circular path until you spot a secluded lean-to or tree-shaded patch of sand.

Typhoon Lagoon

According to Disney legend, Typhoon Lagoon was created when the lush Placid Palms Resort was struck by a cataclysmic storm. It left a different world in its wake: surfboard-sundered trees, once-upright palms imitated the Leaning Tower of Pisa, and part of the original lagoon was cut off, trapping thousands of tropical fish—and a few sharks. Nothing, however, topped the fate of *Miss Tilly*, a shrimp boat from "Safen Sound, Florida," which was hurled high in the air and became impaled on Mt. Mayday, a magical volcano that periodically tries to dislodge *Miss Tilly* with huge geysers.

Ordinary folks, the legend continues, would have been crushed by such devastation. But the resourceful residents of Placid Palms were made of hardier stuff—and from the wreckage they created 56-acre Typhoon Lagoon, the self-proclaimed "world's ultimate water park."

Top Attractions

Typhoon Lagoon

- Crush 'n' Gusher
- Humunga Kowabunga
- Typhoon Lagoon Surf Pool

Blizzard Beach

- Slush Gusher
- Summit Plummet
- Tike's Peak

GETTING ORIENTED

The layout is so simple. The wave and swimming lagoon is at the park's center. Note that the waves are born in the Mt. Mayday side and break on the beaches closest to the entrance. Any attraction requiring a gravitational plunge starts around the summit of Mt. Mayday. Shark Reef and Ketchakiddee Creek flank the head of the lagoon, to Mt. Mayday's right and left, respectively, as you enter. The Crush 'n' Gusher water coaster is due right of Singapore Sal's.

You can take WDW bus transportation or drive to Typhoon Lagoon. There's no parking charge. Once inside, your options are to walk, swim, or slide.

WDW Information

Disney water parks close during off season for maintenance. Call WDW Information or check 🌐 *www.disneyworld.com*'s park calendars for days of operation. ✉ *1534 Blizzard Beach Dr., Blizzard Beach* ☎ *407/824–4321*.

WHAT TO EXPECT

You can speed down waterslides with names like Crush 'n' Gusher and Humunga Kowabunga or bump through rapids and falls at Mt. Mayday. You can also bob along in 5-foot waves in a surf pool the size of two football fields or, for a mellow break, float in inner tubes along the 2,100-foot Castaway Creek. Go snorkeling in Shark Reef, rubberneck as fellow human cannonballs are ejected from the Storm Slides, or hunker down in a hammock or lounge chair and read a book. Ketchakiddee Creek, for young children, replicates adult rides on a smaller scale. It's Disney's version of a day at the beach—complete with friendly Disney lifeguards. Most people agree that kids under seven and older adults prefer Typhoon Lagoon. Bigger kids and teens like Blizzard Beach.

During the off-season between October and April, Typhoon Lagoon closes for several weeks for routine maintenance and refurbishment.

PARK AMENITIES

Dressing Rooms and Lockers: There are thatched-roof dressing rooms and keyless lockers to the right on your way into the park. It costs $10 a day to rent a small locker and $15 for a large one. There are restrooms in every nook and cranny. Most have showers and are much less crowded than the dressing rooms. If you forgot your towel, rent ($2) or buy one at Singapore Sal's.

Guest Services: The staff at Typhoon Lagoon's Guest Services window outside the entrance turnstiles, to your left, can answer many questions. **■ TIP→ A chalkboard inside gives water temperature and surfing information.**

Lost People and Things: Ask about your misplaced people and things at the Guest Services window near the entrance turnstiles. Lost children are taken to an area by the Tip Board near the front of the park, where Disney cast members entertain them with games.

Private Cabanas: The park has a dozen premium, roped-off Beachcomber Shacks (patios, really) that groups of as many as six can rent. They generally offer shade and sun as well as plush loungers and other chairs, a table with an umbrella, and an ice chest with two bottles of water per guest (up to six). Each guest also gets two beach towels and a refillable soft-drink mug. The whole group gets a locker to share and an attendant to take and deliver food orders (cost of meals not included). The patios cost about $340 during peak season (usually March through late August), between $230 and $300 the rest of the year. Reserve (☎ *407/939–8687*) well in advance or arrive very early to book one at High 'N Dry. In summer, any patio that isn't prebooked sells out within a half hour of the park opening.

VISITING TIPS

- In summer come first thing in the morning (early birds can ride several times before the lines get long), late in the afternoon when park hours run later, or when the weather clears after a thundershower (rainstorms drive away crowds). Afternoons are also good in cooler weather, as the water is a bit warmer. To make a whole day of it, avoid weekends, when locals and visitors pack in.

- Women and girls should wear one-piece swimsuits unless they want to find their tops somewhere around their ears at the bottom of the waterslide.

- Invest in sunscreen and water shoes. Plan to slather sunscreen on several times throughout the day. An inexpensive pair of water shoes will save tootsies from hot sand and walkways and from restroom floors.

- Arrive 30 minutes before opening so you can park, buy tickets, rent towels, and snag inner tubes before the crowds descend, and, trust us, it gets very crowded.

From the wreckage—like that shown here—in the wake of a storm, Placid Palms Resort residents created 56-acre Typhoon Lagoon, or so the story goes....

Blizzard Beach

With its oxymoronic name, Blizzard Beach promises the seemingly impossible—a seaside playground with an alpine theme. As with its older cousin, Typhoon Lagoon, Disney Imagineers have created a legend to explain the park's origin.

The story goes that after a freak winter storm dropped snow over the western side of Walt Disney World, entrepreneurs created Florida's first downhill ski resort. Saunalike temperatures soon returned. But as the 66-acre resort's operators were ready to close up shop, they spotted a playful alligator sliding down the 120-foot-tall "liquid ice" slopes. The realization that the melting snow had created the world's tallest, fastest, and most exhilarating water-filled ski and toboggan runs gave birth to the ski resort–water park.

From its imposing ski-jump tower to its 1,200-foot series of rushing waterfalls, Blizzard Beach delivers cool fun even in the hot summertime. Where else can you wear your swimsuit on the slopes?

GETTING ORIENTED

The park layout makes it fairly simple to navigate. Once you enter and rent a locker, you'll cross a small bridge over Cross Country Creek before choosing a spot to park your towels and cooler. To the left is the Melt-Away Bay wave pool. Dead ahead you can see Mt. Gushmore, a chairlift to the top, and the park's many slopes and slides.

If thrills are your game, come early and line up for Summit Plummet, Slush Gusher, and Downhill Double Dipper before wait times go from light to moderate (or heavy). Anytime is a good time for a dip in Melt-Away Bay or a tube trip around Cross Country Creek. Parents with young children should claim their spot early at Tike's Peak, to the park's right even before you cross the bridge.

You can take WDW bus transportation or drive to Blizzard Beach. There's no charge for parking. Once inside, your options are to walk, swim, or slide.

WHAT TO EXPECT

Disney Imagineers have gone all out here to create the paradox of a ski resort in the midst of a tropical lagoon. Lots of verbal puns and sight gags play with the snow-in-Florida motif. The centerpiece is Mt. Gushmore, with its 120-foot-high Summit Plummet. Attractions have names like Teamboat Springs, a white-water raft ride. Themed speed slides include Toboggan Racers, Slush Gusher, and Snow Stormers. Between Mt. Gushmore's base and its summit, swim-skiers can also ride a chairlift converted from ski-resort to beach-resort use—with multihued umbrellas and snow skis on their undersides. Older kids and devoted waterslide enthusiasts generally prefer Blizzard Beach to other water parks.

PARK AMENITIES

Dressing Rooms and Lockers: Dressing rooms, showers, and restrooms are in the village area, just inside the main entrance. There are other restrooms in Lottawatta Lodge, at the Ski Patrol Training Camp, and just past the Melt-Away Bay beach area. Lockers are near the entrance, next to Snowless Joe's Rentals, and near Tike's Peak (the children's area and the most convenient if you have little swim-skiers in tow). It costs $10 to rent a small locker and $15 for a large one. Lockers are keyless, and require you to select a four-digit pin number. Note that there are only small lockers at Tike's Peak. The towels for rent ($2) at Snowless Joe's are tiny. If you forgot yours, you're better off buying a proper one at the Beach Haus.

Guest Services: Disney staffers at Blizzard Beach's Guest Services window, to the left of the ticket booth as you enter the park, can answer most of your questions. Get free life vests or rent towels and lockers at **Snowless Joe's**. Inner tubes, rafts, and slide mats are provided at the rides. Buy beach gear or rent towels or lockers at **Beach Haus. Shade Shack** is the place for a new pair of sunglasses.

Lost People and Things: Instruct youngsters to let a lifeguard know if they get lost. The lost-children station is beneath a large beach umbrella near the front of the park. And don't worry about the kids—a Disney cast member will keep them busy with activities.

Private Patios: The park has 14 Polar Patios to rent to groups of as many as six people. For $340 a day in peak season (usually March through late August) and between $225 and $300 other times of year, you get plush loungers, chairs, a table with umbrella, refillable beverage mugs, an ice chest with two water bottles per person, a group locker, and an attendant who will take your orders for and deliver lunch and snacks (food costs extra). It's best to book a patio far ahead of time (*407/939–8687*). If you arrive early enough, there might be an open patio; check at the Shade Shack.

Disney Springs

Sights

This sprawling shopping, dining, and entertainment complex has four areas: the Marketplace, West Side, The Landing, and Town Center. The large number of new shops, high-end, celebrity-chef run restaurants, and promenades continually expands, along with three huge parking garages. You can rent lockers, strollers, or wheelchairs, and there are two Guest Relations centers.

The Landing

PEDESTRIAN MALL | FAMILY | A family-oriented dining and entertainment district, this part of Disney Springs has nearly a dozen eateries, some run by celebrity chefs such as Morimoto, Art Smith, and Rick Bayless. The restaurants all offer indoor and patio dining, and some, such as Raglan Road, also offer entertainment, in this case music and traditional Irish step-dance performances every night and during weekend brunch. A massive entertainment complex, The Edison, offers daytime dining and nightime cabaret (and acrobats), while the adjoining Maria & Enzo's serves high-end Italian cuisine. The Boathouse features attractive waterfront dining, with views of the water taxis delivering folks across the lake, and the tiny, colorful boat-cars tootling up and down the ramp. Paddlefish, a three-story eatery inspired by a Mississippi paddle steamer, serves seafood, and the view from the top-floor lounge includes the erupting volcano at Rainforest Cafe across the water. ✉ *Disney Springs.*

Marketplace

ARTS VENUE | In the Marketplace, the easternmost Disney Springs area, you can meander along winding sidewalks and explore hidden alcoves. Children love to splash in fountains that spring from the pavement and ride the miniature train and old-time carousel. Toy stores entice with creation-stations and too many treasures to comprehend. There are plenty of spots to grab a bite, sip a cappuccino, or enjoy an ice cream along the lakefront (Ghirardelli's) while watching the volcano atop the Rainforest Cafe erupt or visit dinos at T-Rex. Most Marketplace shops, boutiques, and eateries begin opening at 9:30 am and stay open through 11 pm to midnight. ✉ *Disney Springs.*

Town Center

CLOTHING | Once a parking lot, this newest area of Disney Springs is home to upscale shopping and dining, along meandering pathways, and through squares and plazas surrounded with architecturally interesting buildings. There's something for all tastes (and most budgets): from Lilly Pulitzer to Ugg Boots, from Uniqlo's trendy Japanese-designs to Zara's Spanish-influenced clothing and accessories. Even if you are just looking, Town Center offers a rich window-shopping experience. Celebrity chef Rick Bayless has a waterfront eatery where he serves his take on Mexican, and the independently owned, local-chef-driven Polite Pig dishes up Southern charm and lots of pork-based dishes, while celeb chef Guy Fieri crafts the menu at Planet Hollywood. ✉ *1486 Buena Vista Dr., Orlando* ☎ *407/939–6244* 🌐 *www.disneysprings.com.*

West Side

MARINA | Big changes are still under way at the West Side. The main attractions are the House of Blues music hall, Cirque du Soleil, and Splitsville Luxury Lanes, a modern take on the American classic bowling alley, with 30 bowling lanes on two floors, weekend DJs, and upscale eats like fillet sliders and sushi at indoor and outdoor tables. DisneyQuest, the long-time virtual-reality indoor attraction, was bulldozed in 2017 to make way for The NBA Experience, a basketball-focused attraction expected to open in summer 2019, Cirque du Soleil's *La Nouba* show gave its final performance at the end of 2017, and the new show, an original creation by Cirque du Soleil that will pay homage to Disney's rich history of animation, is expected to open in 2019. You can take a ride in the Aéro30 helium balloon tethered here ($20 ages 10 and up, $15 ages three–nine), shop in boutiques, or dine in such restaurants as Jaleo by José Andres or City Works Eatery & Pour House, or hop on the water taxi at the dock and head across the lagoon to the Marketplace. Shops open at 9:30 or 10:30 am, and closing time is between 11 pm and 2 am. ✉ *Disney Springs.*

Restaurants

The BOATHOUSE

$$$$ | **SEAFOOD** | Contemporary and upscale, The BOATHOUSE sits directly on the Disney Springs waterfront, offering a menu of primarily fresh seafood and views of the restaurant's main attraction, so-called Amphicar tours. Boats that look like vintage, retrofitted vehicles offer the chance for a one-of-a-kind tour of Disney Springs as each vessel's four wheels submerge underwater, and a propeller jet glides riders throughout the lake. **Known for:** fresh seafood; lobster bake for two with whole Maine lobster and clams; "Amphicars" for rent. *Average main: $35* *Disney Springs, The Landing, Disney Springs* *407/939–2628* *disneyworld.disney.go.com/dining* *No credit cards.*

Morimoto Asia

$$$$ | **ASIAN FUSION** | Created by the Iron Chef himself, Masaharu Morimoto, this is Morimoto's first restaurant that moves outside the sushi realm. The Pan-Asian menu includes interesting variations on Chinese duck, Korean noodles, Singaporean laksa, and more. **Known for:** high-end sushi and Pan-Asian cuisine; late-night hours until 1 am on weekends; best views of the Disney Springs lagoon from the upstairs patio. *Average main: $35* *Disney Springs, The Landing, Lake Buena Vista* *407/939–6686* *www.patinagroup.com/morimoto-asia.*

★ Raglan Road Irish Pub

$$$ | **IRISH** | **FAMILY** | If an authentic Irish pub—actually transported from the Old Country plank by plank—is your thing, Raglan Road is the place to go, for both superb traditional dishes and inventive twists. In addition to excellent fish-and-chips and shepherd's pie, the chefs twist Irish cuisine to include Gulf shrimp and risotto with buffalo mozzarella and fresh peas. **Known for:** first-rate dining and special chef-driven events; extensive beer and ale selections, including exclusive brews; nightly, sometimes hourly, entertainment. *Average main: $25* *Disney Springs, The Landing, Disney Springs* *407/938–0300* *www.raglanroadirishpub.com.*

Wolfgang Puck Bar & Grill

$$$$ | **AMERICAN** | **FAMILY** | Celebrity chef Wolfgang Puck returns to Disney Springs after closing the Grand Café. His new California-crafted eatery serves signature pizzas, whole grilled fish and steaks, and gooey desserts for lunch and dinner service. **Known for:** name-brand dining in familiar surroundings; a California ranch-style atmosphere; world-famous pizza. *Average main: $35* *Disney Springs, Westside, Disney Springs* *407/938–9653* *www.wolfgangpuckcafeorlando.com.*

Hotels

B Resort & Spa Disney Springs Resort Area

$ | **RESORT** | **FAMILY** | The white-and-blue tower of the B Resort on Hotel Plaza Boulevard is just outside Disney Springs, and a stay there combines an excellent location with a reasonable price and whimsical design. **Pros:** walk to Disney Springs; kids' activities; park shuttles. **Cons:** resort fee; parking fee; need a car to get to Universal or Downtown Orlando. *Rooms from: $159* *1905 Hotel Plaza Blvd., Disney Springs Resort Area* *407/828–2828* *www.bhotelsandresorts.com/b-walt-disney-world* *394 rooms* *No meals.*

★ Best Western Lake Buena Vista Resort

$ | **RESORT** | **FAMILY** | Only a few minutes' walk from Disney Springs' wide range of shops and restaurants, this towering resort with its airy lobby offers luxury linens, flat-screen TVs, and, in many rooms, a bird's-eye view of the fireworks, all for a bargain price. **Pros:** a quick walk to shopping and restaurants; free transportation to parks, Magic Hours access to parks; kids eat free. **Cons:** inconvenient to Universal and Downtown

Orlando; transportation to the parks can be slow and crowded; resort and parking fees. $ *Rooms from: $152* ✉ *2000 Hotel Plaza Blvd., Disney Springs Resort Area* ☎ *407/828–2424, 800/780–7234* 🌐 *www.lakebuenavistaresorthotel.com* *325 rooms* 🍴 *No meals.*

Disney's Port Orleans Resort–French Quarter

$$ | **HOTEL** | Renovated in 2018, the Big Easy–style row houses with wrought-iron balconies clustered around magnolia- and oak-shaded squares in this relatively quiet resort are sharper than ever. **Pros:** authentic—or as authentic as Disney can make it—fun, New Orleans–style; moderate price; lots of recreation options, including boat rentals and carriage rides. **Cons:** even though there are fewer kids here, public areas can still be quite noisy; shuttle service is slow; food court is the only on-site dining option. $ *Rooms from: $257* ✉ *2201 Orleans Dr., Disney Springs Resort Area* ☎ *407/934–5000* 🌐 *www.disneyworld.disney.go.com/resorts* *1,008 rooms* 🍴 *No meals.*

DoubleTree Suites by Hilton Orlando Disney Springs Area

$ | **HOTEL** | **FAMILY** | Price and location make this all-suites, Hilton-owned hotel a good choice for families and business travelers, as there are amenities for both, and it's a quick, free bus ride to any of the Disney parks (with Extra Magic Hours access) and within walkable distance to Disney Springs. **Pros:** within walking distance to Disney Springs; access to Disney golf courses and early access to parks; free shuttle to Disney attractions. **Cons:** daily fee for Wi-Fi; inconvenient to Universal and Downtown Orlando; daily fee for parking. $ *Rooms from: $175* ✉ *2305 Hotel Plaza Blvd., Disney Springs Resort Area* ☎ *407/934–1000, 800/222–8733* 🌐 *www.doubletreeguestsuites.com* *229 units* 🍴 *No meals.*

Hilton Orlando Buena Vista Palace Disney Springs Area

$$ | **RESORT** | **FAMILY** | This towering hotel is just yards from Disney Springs and caters to business and leisure guests, offering many on-site amenities and recreational options, in addition to free shuttles to Disney parks, character breakfasts, and access to Disney golf courses. **Pros:** good restaurants and bars on-site; kids' activities and on-site water park; across the street from Disney Springs. **Cons:** inconvenient to Universal and Downtown Orlando; steep daily resort fee for Wi-Fi and fitness center; parking fee. $ *Rooms from: $209* ✉ *1900 E. Buena Vista Dr., Disney Springs Resort Area* ☎ *407/827–2727* 🌐 *www.buenavistapalace.com* *1,012 rooms* 🍴 *No meals; Free Breakfast.*

Nightlife

House of Blues

BARS/PUBS | The restaurant serves up live blues performances and rib-sticking Mississippi Delta cooking all week long, and there's often a jam session on the front porch. The attached concert hall has showcased such artists as Aretha Franklin, David Byrne, Steve Miller, and Willie Nelson, but check the calendar in advance since large acts like these are rare. Come hungry (and with an admission ticket) for the popular Sunday Gospel Brunch, where there's always a show and all-you-can-eat Southern food. ✉ *West Side, Disney Springs* ☎ *407/934–2583* 🌐 *www.disneyworld.disney.go.com/entertainment/disney-springs/house-of-blues-shows.*

Disney's BoardWalk

In the good ol' days, Americans escaped their city routines for breezy seaside boardwalks. Disney's BoardWalk is within walking distance of Epcot, across Crescent Lake from Disney's Yacht and

Beach Club Resorts, and fronting a hotel of the same name. You may be drawn to its good restaurants, bars, shops, surreys, and performers. After sunset, the mood is festive. **■TIP→ If you're here when Epcot is ready to close, you can watch the park fireworks from the bridge that connects BoardWalk to the Yacht and Beach Club resorts.**

Restaurants

ESPN Club

$$ | AMERICAN | Not only can you watch every possible televised sporting event on a big-screen TV here (the restaurant has about 100 monitors), but you can also periodically see ESPN programs being taped in the club itself. Food ranges from a variety of half-pound burgers, made with Angus chuck (and one topped with peanut butter and jelly), to Philly cheesesteaks and *char siu* sliders. **Known for:** gigantic space that still fills up on game days; pub food: nachos, chicken and waffles, big burgers; wine and regional beers. *Average main: $17 ✉ Disney's Boardwalk, 2101 Epcot Resorts Blvd., Epcot Resort Area ☎ 407/939–3463 ⊕ disneyworld.disney.go.com/dining.*

Nightlife

Atlantic Dance Hall

DANCE CLUBS | This popular, high-energy dance club plays music from the '80s onward, with a huge screen showing videos requested by the crowd. The parquet dance floor is set off by furnishings of deep blue, maroon, and gold, and the ceiling glows with stars and twinkling lights. Signature cocktails are in demand, and you can sip a cognac or choose from a selection of popular beers to inspire your dance floor moves. *✉ BoardWalk, Epcot Resort Area ☎ 407/939–2444 ⊕ www.disneyworld.disney.go.com/entertainment/boardwalk/atlantic-dance-hall.*

Big River Grille & Brewing Works

BARS/PUBS | The Boardwalk's only brewpub welcomes families with intimate tables and a waterfront patio; either is a splendid place to sample craft brews and upscale American pub grub like barbecued ribs or blackened Creole salmon. House brews on tap may include Southern Flyer Light Lager, Rocket Red Ale, and the seasonal Sweet Magnolia American Brown Ale. *✉ BoardWalk, Epcot Resort Area ☎ 407/560–0253 ⊕ www.disneyworld.disney.go.com/dining/boardwalk/big-river-grille-and-brewing-works.*

Jellyrolls

BARS/PUBS | In this rockin', boisterous piano bar, comedians double as emcees as they play dueling grand pianos nonstop. Their speed and intricacy is impressive, as is the depth of their playlist. The steady stream of conventions at Disney makes this the place to catch CEOs doing the conga to Barry Manilow's "Copacabana" (if that's your idea of a good time) and young Disney cast members checking in after they clock out. *✉ BoardWalk, Epcot Resort Area ☎ 407/560–8770 ⊕ www.disneyworld.disney.go.com/entertainment/boardwalk/jellyrolls $12 cover ☞ Guests must be 21 and over.*

Chapter 12

UNIVERSAL ORLANDO RESORT

12

Updated by
Joseph Hayes

Sights ★★★★★ | Restaurants ★★★★☆ | Hotels ★★★★☆ | Shopping ★★★★☆ | Nightlife ★★★★☆

WELCOME TO UNIVERSAL ORLANDO RESORT

TOP REASONS TO GO

★ **Harry Potter:** For die-hard fans, there's no other place to head in Florida than The Wizarding World of Harry Potter.

★ **The variety:** Universal Orlando Resort consists of two complete theme parks, the CityWalk entertainment complex, and seven on-site resorts. Universal's Volcano Bay Water Theme Park is the region's newest and most exciting water park.

★ **Theme-park powerhouse:** No other Orlando theme park can match the collective energy at Universal Studios, Islands of Adventure, and Volcano Bay. Wild rides, clever shows, constantly updated attractions, and an edgy attitude all push the envelope here.

★ **Party central:** Throughout the year, Universal hosts festive parkwide events such as Mardi Gras, Halloween Horror Nights, Grinchmas, the Summer Concert Series, and the Rock the Universe Christian-music celebration. And CityWalk is busy year-round.

Universal Orlando Resort is tucked into a corner created by the intersection of Interstate 4 and Kirkman Road (Highway 435), midway between Downtown Orlando and the Walt Disney World Resort. Here you'll be about 25 minutes from each.

1 Universal Studios Florida. The centerpiece of Universal Orlando is a creative and quirky tribute to Hollywood past, present, and future. Overall, the collection of wild rides, quiet retreats, live shows, street characters, and clever movies (both 3-D and 4-D) are as entertaining as the motion pictures they celebrate. Another plus is The Wizarding World of Harry Potter: Diagon Alley.

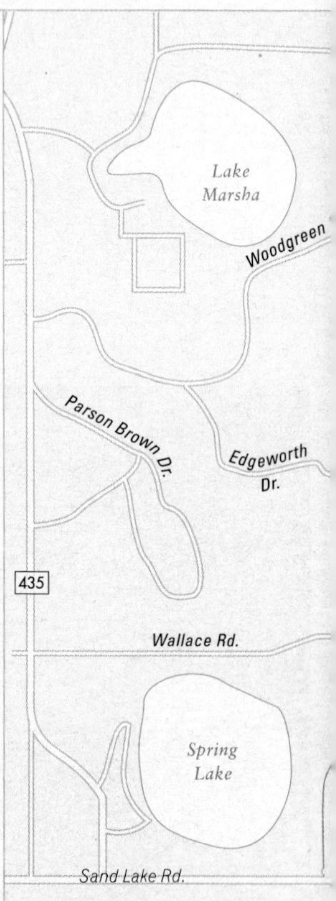

2 Islands of Adventure. Although The Wizarding World of Harry Potter: Hogsmeade may top visitors' to-do lists, the park also is home to Spider-Man, the Hulk, velociraptors, the Cat in the Hat, and dozens of other characters that give guests every reason to head to the islands.

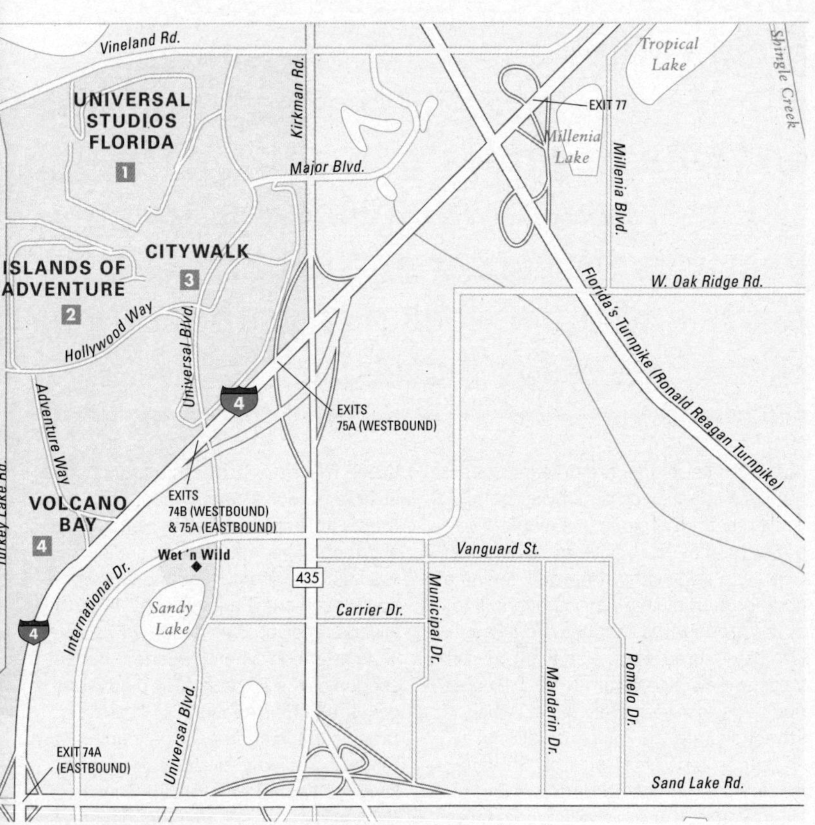

3 CityWalk. Even when the parks are closed (*especially* when the parks are closed), locals and visitors come to this sprawling entertainment and retail complex to watch movies; dine at theme restaurants; shop for everything from cigars to surf wear; and stay up late at nightclubs celebrating the French Quarter, Jamaica, and the coolest clubs of NYC.

4 Volcano Bay. A water park built around an "erupting" volcano, this park's wild rides and wave pool offer a very cool way to chill out.

Universal Orlando's personality is revealed the moment you arrive on property. Mood music, cartoonish architecture, abundant eye candy, subtle and overt sound effects, whirling and whizzing rides, plus a throng of fellow travelers will follow you to nearly every corner of the park. For peace and quiet, seek out a sanctuary at one of the resort hotels.

If you can keep up a breathless pace, there's a chance you could visit both big Universal theme parks in a single day, but to do that you'll have to invest in an Express Pass. Without it, you'll spend a good portion of that day waiting in line at the premium attractions. So allow two days, three if you also want to visit Volcano Bay or to return to your favorite rides at a more leisurely pace. Which attractions are the main attractions? At both Islands and Universal Studios, it's definitely The Wizarding World of Harry Potter. But the thrilling coasters and theme rides like Revenge of the Mummy and The Simpsons attractions are always popular.

Universal Studios appeals primarily to those who like loud, fast, high-energy attractions—generally teens and adults. Covering 444 acres, it's a rambling montage of sets, shops, and soundstages housing themed attractions, reproductions of New York and San Francisco and London, and some genuine moviemaking paraphernalia.

When Islands of Adventure first opened in 1999, it took attractions to a new level. Most—from Marvel Super Hero Island and Toon Lagoon to Seuss Landing and the Lost Continent—are impressive; some even out-Disney Disney. In 2010 Islands received well-deserved worldwide attention when it opened the first section of the 20-acre Wizarding World of Harry Potter. And in 2014 Universal Studios made another huge leap forward when it opened a full-scale version of Diagon Alley, complete with Gringotts Bank and a magical train that departs for Islands from Platform 9¾.

Planning

Getting Here and Around

East on Interstate 4 (from WDW and Tampa), exit at Universal Boulevard (75A); take a left into Universal Orlando Resort, and follow the signs. Heading west on Interstate 4 (from Downtown or Daytona), exit at Universal Boulevard (74B), turn right, and follow Hollywood Way.

Both Universal Studios and Islands require a lot of walking—a whole lot of walking, starting with the massive parking garage. Start off by using the parking area's moving walkways as much as possible. Arrive early at either park, and you may be able to complete a single lap that will get you to the main attractions.

Operating Hours

The parks are open 365 days a year, from 9 am to 7 pm, with hours as late as 10 pm in summer and at holidays. Universal's Volcano Bay will be open year-round, weather permitting, but with varying hours. Always call for exact hours since those at all three parks change seasonally.

Parking

Universal's two main garages total 3.4 million square feet, so *note your parking space.* The cost is $25 for cars and motorcycles, $30 for RVs and buses, and $40 for preferred parking. Although moving walkways get you partway, you could walk up to a half mile to reach the gates. Valet parking ($25 for up to two hours, $50 for more than two hours) is much closer. Parking in the CityWalk-centered main garages is free after 6 pm, and a special validated pass allows free parking for lunch at CityWalk. All on-site resort hotels have separate entrances and parking.

Admission

The at-the-gate, per-person, per-day rate for either Universal Studios Florida or Islands of Adventure varies by schedule and day (much like Disney), ranging from $114 to $129 (ages 10 and up) and starting at $109 for children (ages three–nine). Tip: To ride the Hogwart's Express and enjoy both Harry Potter experiences on the same day, you *must* have a park-to-park ticket, which starts at $169 (ages 10 and up) and $164 for children (ages three–nine). Multiday passes that include the two main parks offer a far less expensive per-day price. Also available is a three-park ticket, which includes Volcano Bay. Volcano Bay has a single-day admission price of $80, $75 for children.

Express Passes

The Express Pass ranges in price from about $89 to $159 for 29 locations at all three parks and CityWalk, per person. This pass gets you to the front of the line and saves a tremendous amount of time. Keep in mind, the pass is for one use only at each attraction—a $189 "unlimited" pass takes you to the head of the line for repeat visits. If you're a guest at a Universal hotel, this perk is free; your room key is your pass.

Universal Orlando Resort Dining Plan

If you prefer to pay in advance, Quick Service meals include one meal, two snacks, and a nonalcoholic beverage ($24–$30). Quick Service for kids starts at $15.99 Universal Studios locations include Mel's Drive-In, Louie's Italian, The Leaky Cauldron, and the Classic Monsters Café. At Islands of Adventure, your choices are the Comic Strip Café, Croissant Moon, Three Broomsticks, and Café 4. For vacation package guests, a full-service plan adds sit-down restaurants and snacks in dozens of places.

Hotels

Universal Orlando's on-site hotels were built in a little luxury enclave that has everything you need, so you never have to leave Universal property. In minutes you can walk from any hotel to CityWalk, Universal's dining and entertainment district, or take a water taxi that carries guests along a pleasant river ride to the parks.

The two newest Universal Orlando Resort hotels, Sapphire Falls and Aventura, join the more affordable Cabana Bay Beach Resort—with the new budget Endless Summer resort projected for completion in 2020. All on-site hotels offer free transportation to the Universal parks, as well as to SeaWorld and Aquatica.

A burgeoning hotel district across Kirkman Road and down to Sand Lake Road offers convenient accommodations and some even-less-expensive rates. Although these off-property hotels don't have the perks of the on-site places, you'll probably be smiling when you see your hotel bill.

Universal Orlando Resort Strategies

Arrive early. Come as early as 8 am if the parks open at 9. Seriously. Better to share them with hundreds of people than with thousands.

Visit on a weekday. Crowds are lighter, especially fall through spring, when kids are in school.

Don't forget anything in your car. Universal's parking areas are at least a half mile from park entrances, and a round-trip hike will eat up valuable time. Consider valet parking. It costs $50 for longer than two hours before 6 pm (twice as much as regular parking), but it puts you much closer to Universal's park entrances and just steps from CityWalk.

Know the restrictions. A few things aren't allowed in the parks: alcohol and glass containers; hard-sided coolers; soft-sided coolers larger than 8½ inches wide by 6 inches high by 6 inches deep; and coolers, suitcases, and other bags with wheels. But if your flight's leaving later, you can check your luggage at the parks (unless you just leave them in your car).

Look into the Express Pass. Jumping to the front of the line with this pass really is worth the extra cost on busy days—unless you stay at a resort hotel, in which case front-of-line access is one of the perks.

Ride solo. At Universal some rides have a single-rider line that moves much faster than regular lines.

Get expert advice. The folks at Guest Services (aka Guest Relations) have great insight. The reps can even create a custom itinerary free of charge.

Check out Child Swap. At certain Universal attractions, one parent can enter the attraction, take a spin, and then return to take care of the baby while the other parent rides without having to wait in line again.

Tours

VIP Tours

Universal has several VIP tours that are worthwhile if you're in a hurry, if crowds are heavy, if you're with a large group—and if you have the money to burn. The tours include extras like front-of-the-line access (that is, the right to jump to the head of the line), plus breakfast and lunch. You can also arrange for extras like priority restaurant seating, bilingual guides, gift bags, refreshments at check-in, wheelchairs, strollers, and valet

Universal Resort Perks

Head-of-the-Line Access. Your hotel key (except Cabana Bay) lets you go directly to the head of the line for most Universal Orlando attractions. Unlike Disney's FastPass+ program, you don't need to use this at a specific time; it's always good. Hotel guests also get early admission to the often-crowded Harry Potter attractions.

Priority Seating. Many of Universal's restaurants offer priority seating to those staying at on-site hotels.

Charging Privileges. You can charge most meals and purchases throughout Universal to your hotel room.

Delivery Services. If you buy something in the theme parks, you can have it sent directly to your room, so you don't have to carry it around.

Free Loaners. Some on-site hotels have a "Did You Forget?" closet that offers everything from kids' strollers to dog leashes to computer accessories. There's no fee for using this service.

parking. You'll need to arrange the tour at least 48 hours in advance by calling ahead or setting it up online. Prices cited here do not include sales tax or, more important, park admission; and tour prices vary by season, so consider these just estimated costs.

Nonexclusive one-day tours (i.e., you'll tour with other park guests) cost $189 per person for one park (five hours) and visit a minimum of eight major attractions. The cost goes up to $199 per person for a two-park, seven-hour tour. Then there are exclusive tours for your group only. If you're traveling with up to 10 people, consider splitting the cost of an eight-hour tour customized to your interests, which includes a sit-down breakfast, lunch, and dinner at the park of your choice. The private VIP tour starts at $3,099 plus tax for a group of five, with an extra $350 for each additional person. ✉ *Orlando* ☎ *866/346–9350* 🌐 *www.universalorlando.com.*

Contacts

Universal Orland Resort ☎ *407/363–8000* 🌐 *www.universalorlando.com*

Universal Dining and Tickets ☎ *407/224–7840*

Universal (Loews Resorts) Room Reservations ☎ *877/819–7884*

Universal Vacation Packages ☎ *800/407–4275*

Universal Studios

Inspired by the California original, Universal Studios celebrates the movies. The park is a jumble of areas and attractions. But the same is true of back-lot sets at a film studio. Suspend any disbelief you might have, and just enjoy the motion-picture magic.

At Production Central large soundstages house attractions based on films like *Shrek, Despicable Me,* and *Fast & Furious.* Because it's right near the entrance it can be the park's most crowded area.

Universal Studios

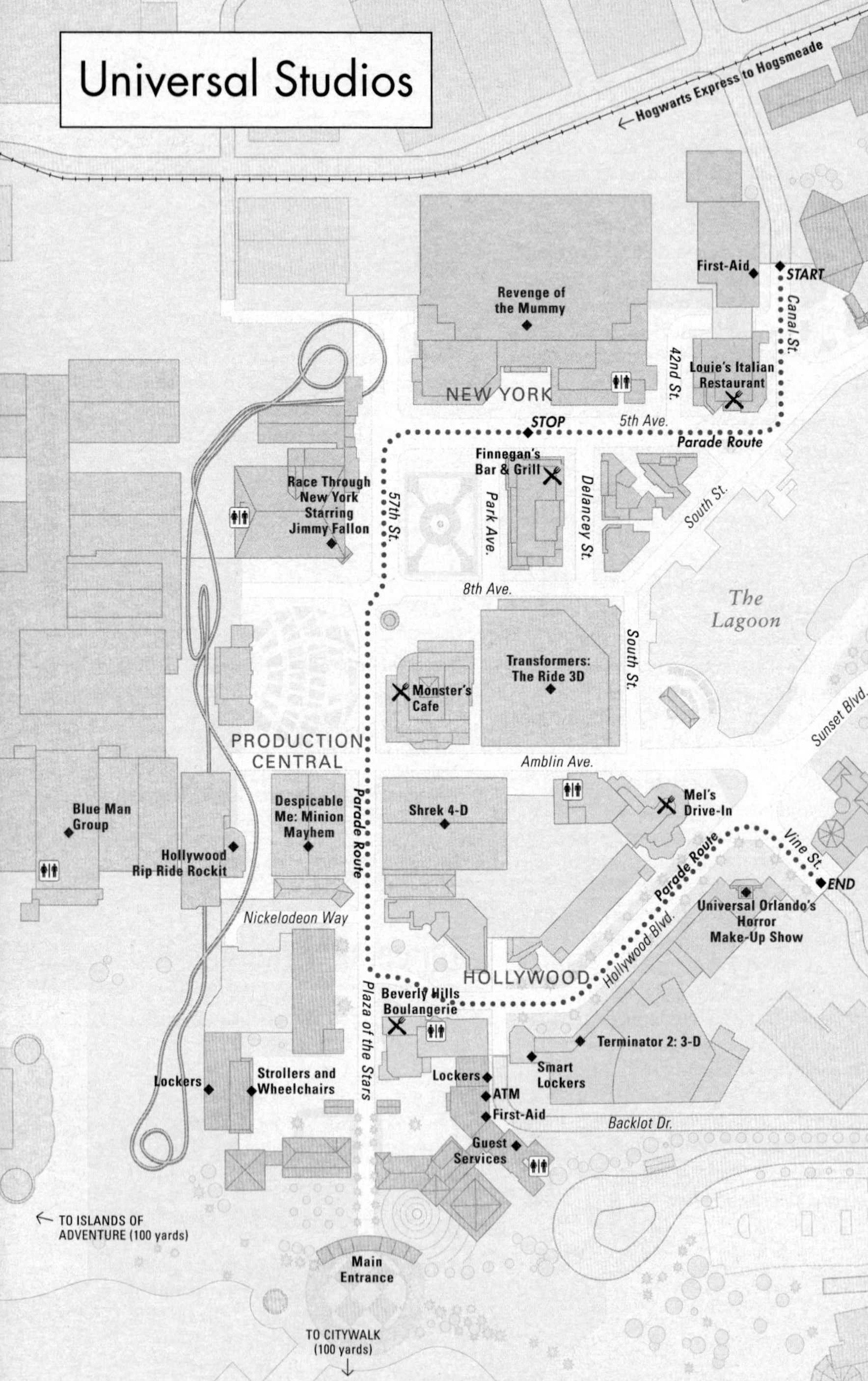

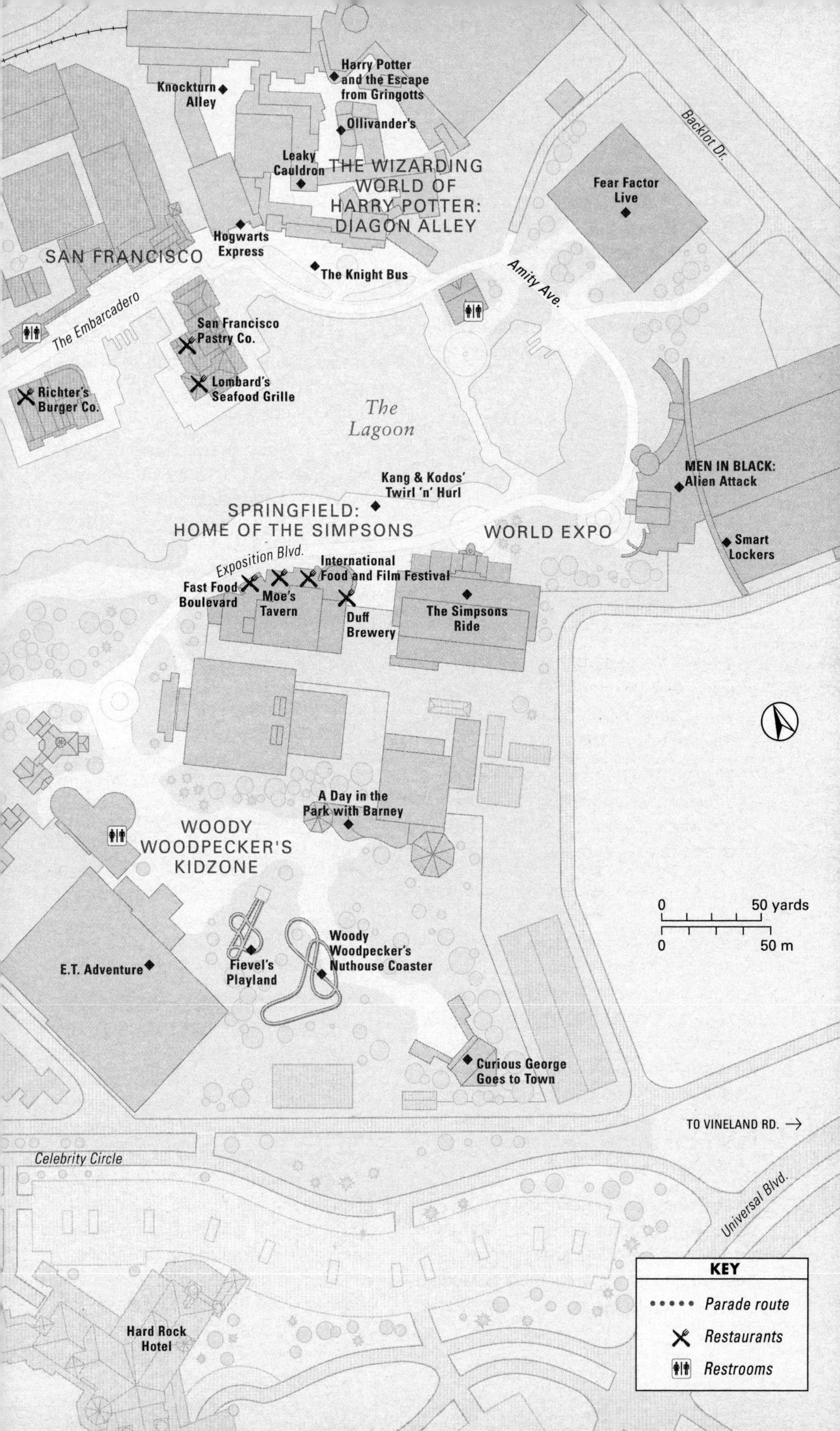

Harry Potter and the Escape from Gringotts
Knockturn Alley
Ollivander's
Leaky Cauldron
THE WIZARDING WORLD OF HARRY POTTER: DIAGON ALLEY
Backlot Dr.
Fear Factor Live
Hogwarts Express
SAN FRANCISCO
The Knight Bus
Amity Ave.
The Embarcadero
San Francisco Pastry Co.
Lombard's Seafood Grille
Richter's Burger Co.
The Lagoon
MEN IN BLACK: Alien Attack
Kang & Kodos' Twirl 'n' Hurl
SPRINGFIELD: HOME OF THE SIMPSONS
WORLD EXPO
Smart Lockers
Exposition Blvd.
International Food and Film Festival
Fast Food Boulevard
Moe's Tavern
Duff Brewery
The Simpsons Ride
A Day in the Park with Barney
WOODY WOODPECKER'S KIDZONE
0
50 yards
0
50 m
Woody Woodpecker's Nuthouse Coaster
Fievel's Playland
E.T. Adventure
Curious George Goes to Town
TO VINELAND RD. →
Celebrity Circle
Universal Blvd.
KEY
Parade route
Restaurants
Restrooms
Hard Rock Hotel

Top Attractions

Ages 7 and Up

Harry Potter and the Escape from Gringotts. Getting into the vault at Gringotts Bank can be a challenge, but it's also a first-class adventure thanks to technology similar to that of The Transformers and IOA's Spider-Man and Harry Potter and the Forbidden Journey.

Hollywood Rip Ride Rockit. On this superwild coaster, you select the sound track.

MEN IN BLACK: Alien Attack. The "world's first ride-through video game" gives you a chance to compete for points by plugging away at an endless swarm of aliens.

Revenge of the Mummy. It's a jarring, rocketing indoor coaster that takes you past scary mummies and billowing balls of fire (really).

Shrek 4-D. The 3-D film with sensory effects picks up where the original film left off—and adds some creepy extras in the process.

The Simpsons Ride. It puts you in the heart of Springfield on a wild-and-crazy virtual-reality experience.

Transformers: The Ride 3-D. Universal Studios' version of IOA's fantastic Spider-Man experience, but this one features a rough-and-tumble encounter with the mechanical stars of the film franchise.

Fast & Furious: Supercharged Its wild car chases and high-speed action are based on the hot movie series.

Ages 6 and Under

Animal Actors on Location! It's a perfect family show starring a menagerie of animals whose unusually high IQs are surpassed only by their cuteness and cuddle-ability.

Curious George Goes to Town. The celebrated simian visits the Man with the Yellow Hat in a small-scale water park.

A Day in the Park with Barney. Young children love the big purple dinosaur in his interactive home.

Here you see firsthand that not every film or program based in New York is actually shot in New York. Cleverly constructed sets mean that nearly every film studio can own its own Big Apple. Universal is no exception. As you explore Production Central, a collection of sparkling public buildings, well-worn neighborhoods, and back alleys are the next-best thing to Manhattan itself.

As you enter the area known as San Francisco, you're roughly one-third of the way through the park. The area is home to the Fast & Furious: Supercharged attraction. You can stop to take in the view across the lake and have a snack, or dine at the waterfront Lombard's Seafood Grille.

After passing scenes from San Francisco, you'll reach the Wizarding World of Harry Potter: Diagon Alley. What the books suggest and what filmmakers created, Universal has replicated—putting you in the middle of a fantastic fantasyland. Just ahead, World Expo features a single attraction—MEN IN BLACK: Alien Attack, a futuristic experience that's the polar opposite of neighboring Springfield: Home of the Simpsons, which is perhaps the park's most visually dynamic area. Its next door neighbor, Woody Woodpecker's KidZone, offers colorful attractions designed for toddlers and the under-10 crowd with diversions that include a junior-size roller coaster, a mini–water park, and a chance to meet E.T. and Barney the dinosaur.

Although the quiet parks, themed restaurants, and facades of flashy Rodeo Drive are truly an attraction in themselves, Hollywood has a few standout attractions, including Universal Orlando's Horror Make Up Show. By the time you've circled the park, you really will feel that Universal has put you in the movies.

GETTING ORIENTED

On a map, the park appears neatly divided into eight areas positioned around a huge lagoon. There's Production Central, which covers the entire left side of the Plaza of the Stars; New York, with street performances at 70 Delancey; San Francisco; the Wizarding World of Harry Potter: Diagon Alley; the futuristic World Expo; Springfield: Home of the Simpsons; Woody Woodpecker's KidZone; and Hollywood.

What's tricky is that—because it's designed like a series of movie sets—there's no straightforward way to tackle the park. You'll probably make some detours and do some backtracking. To save time and shoe leather, ask theme park hosts for itinerary suggestions and time-saving tips. Here are a few of our own suggestions.

TOURING TIPS

We highly recommend you purchase your tickets online because it gives you plenty of time to consider your many options and includes a discount. Entering Universal Studios can be overwhelming as you and thousands of others flood through the turnstiles at once. Study the map online before you go, then pick up a map in the entryway to CityWalk or by the park turnstiles and spend a few minutes reviewing it. Map out a route, find show schedules, and select restaurants. If a host is nearby, ask for insider advice on what to see first.

The "right" way. Upon entering, avoid the temptation to go left toward the towering soundstages, looping the park clockwise. Instead head right—bypassing shops, restaurants, and some crowds to primary attractions like The Simpsons Ride and MEN IN BLACK: Alien Attack.

Photo ops. Universal Studios posts signs that indicate photo spots and show how best to frame your shot.

Rendezvous. Good meeting spots include the Hello Kitty shop, near the entrance; Mel's Drive-In, midway through the park on the right; and the purple Knight Bus, just outside Diagon Alley, at the far end of the park.

PARK AMENITIES

Guest Services: Get strategy advice *before* visiting by calling Guest Services (☎ *407/224–4233*).

Lockers: Daily rates for lockers near the park entrance are $10 for a small unit and $12 for a larger one. Small, free lockers are near the entrances to many high-speed attractions (such as MEN IN BLACK: Alien Attack, Harry Potter: Escape from Gringotts, and Revenge of the Mummy), where you can stash your stuff before your ride; they're available to you for up to 90 minutes total. Larger lockers cost $2.

Lost People and Things: If you plan to split up, be sure everyone knows where and when to reconnect. Staffers take lost children to Guest Services near the main entrance. This is also where you might find lost personal items.

Stroller Rentals: Just inside the main entrance, there are strollers for $15 (single) and $25 (double) a day. You can also rent small kiddie cars ($18) or large ones ($28) by the day.

Sights

PRODUCTION CENTRAL

Expect plenty of loud, flashy, rollicking rides that appeal to tweens, teens, and adults. Clear the turnstiles and go straight. You can use Express Pass at all attractions.

NEW YORK

Universal has gone all out to re-create New York's skyscrapers, commercial districts, ethnic neighborhoods, and back alleys—right down to the cracked concrete. Hidden within these structures are restaurants, arcades, gift shops, and key attractions. And, although they're from Chicago, the Blues Brothers drive from the Second City to New York City in their Bluesmobile for free performances at 70 Delancey. Here you can use Express Pass at Revenge of the Mummy and Race Through New York Starring Jimmy Fallon.

SAN FRANCISCO

This area celebrates the West Coast with the wharves and warehouses of San Francisco's Embarcadero and Fisherman's Wharf districts, and speeds through the streets with the new-in-2018 Fast & Furious ride.

SPRINGFIELD: HOME OF THE SIMPSONS

One of television's longest-running shows inspired one of the park's most enjoyable lands; a strangely surreal yet familiar small town filled with landmarks you'd recognize, from Moe's Tavern to the towering Lard Lad of doughnut fame. The two primary attractions—The Simpsons Ride and Kang & Kodos' Twirl 'n' Hurl—offer fast admission with Universal Express Pass.

WORLD EXPO

At the far end of the park is a futuristic set of buildings containing one of Universal Studios' most popular attractions, MEN IN BLACK: Alien Attack.

WOODY WOODPECKER'S KIDZONE

With its colorful compilation of rides, shows, and play areas, this entire section caters to preschoolers. It's a pint-size Promised Land, where kids can try out a roller coaster and get sprayed, splashed, and soaked in a water-park area. It's also a great place for parents, since it gives them a needed break after nearly circling the park. All shows and attractions except Curious George and Fievel accept Universal Express Pass.

HOLLYWOOD

The quintessential tribute to the golden age of the silver screen, this area to the right of the park entrance celebrates icons like the Brown Derby, Schwab's Pharmacy, and art deco Hollywood. There are only a few attractions here, and all accept Universal Express Pass.

THE WIZARDING WORLD OF HARRY POTTER: DIAGON ALLEY

Don't think the facade of London row homes is all there is to see here. On the contrary, as in the Harry Potter movies, the good stuff remains hidden to mere muggles. When you spy an opening through a broken brick wall and step into Diagon Alley, the world changes as you see what an incredible blueprint J.K. Rowling created through her words. You can literally spend hours in this one district looking at the complete range of Potter-centric places: Universal Studios' version of Ollivanders wand shop; Weasleys' Wizard Wheezes (magical jokes and novelty items); the Magical Menagerie (all creatures furry, feathered, or scaly); Madam Malkin's Robes for All Occasions (wizard wear); Wiseacre's Wizarding Equipment; and Quality Quidditch Supplies. For practitioners of the Dark Arts, venture down Knockturn Alley and step inside Borgin and Burkes. For an appetizing break, stop at the Leaky Cauldron, the land's signature restaurant, or cool off at Florean Fortescue's Ice-Cream Parlour.

And when you're ready to head to Hogsmeade (conveniently located at the neighboring Islands of Adventure), make sure you have a park-to-park pass before stepping aboard the wonderful, magical Hogwarts Express—now departing to Islands of Adventure from Platform 9¾. Be sure to get a photo of friends and family disappearing through the brick wall.

Restaurants

Finnegan's Bar & Grill

$$ | **IRISH** | This Irish pub would look just right in Downtown Manhattan during the Ellis Island era. The menu offers classic Irish comfort food like shepherd's pie, corned beef and cabbage, bangers and mash, and fish-and-chips, plus Guinness on tap and a five-beer sampler. **Known for:** live music; classic Irish comfort food like shepherd's pie and beef stew; good place for a quick, filling sandwich. *Average main: $16 New York, Universal Studios 407/363–8757 www.universalorlando.com.*

Leaky Cauldron

$ | **BRITISH** | **FAMILY** | British pub staples are fitting fare for Diagon Alley's restaurant. The drinks menu complements those hearty meals with kooky-sounding beverages from the Harry Potter books like Tongue-Tying Lemon Squash, Otter's Fizzy Orange Juice, and Fishy Green Ale (it's minty, with blueberry-flavored boba). **Known for:** quick service; Potter-inspired meals; plowman's lunch of meats, cheeses, and salad; Butterbeer, of course. *Average main: $14 The Wizarding World of Harry Potter: Diagon Alley, Universal Studios 407/224–9716 www.universalorlando.com.*

Mama Della's Ristorante

$$$ | **ITALIAN** | Like stepping into Mama Della's dining room, this playfully themed Italian restaurant happens to have excellent food. The premise is that you're eating at a home-turned-restaurant—there's an actual "Mama Della" who appears nightly—and that warmth enhances the experience (as does the serenade by an accordionist, guitar player, and vocalist). **Known for:** intimate New York/Neapolitan environment; better-than-usual Italian cuisine; homemade gnocchi. *Average main: $30 Loews Portofino Bay Hotel, 5601 Universal Blvd., Universal Orlando Resort 407/503–3463 www.loewshotels.com No lunch.*

Mel's Drive-In

$ | **AMERICAN** | **FAMILY** | At the corner of Hollywood and Vine is a flashy 1950s-style eatery with a pink-and-white 1956 Ford Crown Victoria parked out in front. For burgers and fries, this is one of the best choices in the park, and it comes complete with a roving doo-wop group during peak seasons. **Known for:** drive-in styling; live entertainment; frosty milk shakes and grilled burgers. *Average main: $11 Hollywood, Universal Studios 407/363–8766 www.universalorlando.com.*

Hotels

★ Drury Inn & Suites Orlando

$ | **HOTEL** | **FAMILY** | This reasonably priced hotel, less than a mile from Universal, offers free Wi-Fi, free parking, free shuttle to Universal, free hot breakfast, free long-distance and local phone calls, and free hot food and cold beverages in the late afternoon. **Pros:** free everything; central location; reasonable price. **Cons:** if Disney is your destination, this might be a little far afield; next to two busy roadways; pool and gym are small. *Rooms from: $119 7301 W. Sand Lake Rd., at I–4, Universal Studios 407/354–1101 www.druryhotels.com 238 rooms Free Breakfast.*

Hard Rock Hotel at Universal Orlando
$$$ | **HOTEL** | Music rules in this mission-style building, from public areas decorated with rock memorabilia—Elvis's pajamas, Lady Gaga's latex gown, and Elton John's boots—to stylishly modern rooms, with deluxe bed linens, an entertainment center with flat-panel TV, and lots of accessible media device plugs. **Pros:** shuttle, water taxi, or short walk to Universal Parks and CityWalk; Universal Express Unlimited pass included; charge privileges extend to the other on-property Universal hotels. **Cons:** rooms and meals are pricey; fee for parking; loud rock music in public areas, even the pool. *Rooms from: $349 5800 Universal Blvd., CityWalk 407/503–7625, 800/232–7827 www.hardrockhotelorlando.com 650 rooms No meals.*

Loews Aventura Hotel
$$ | **RESORT** | **FAMILY** | New in 2018, Aventura has a clean, modern look and tech-driven atmosphere, with in-room touchpads that control everything (including ordering park tickets and room service). **Pros:** walking distance to Volcano Bay and Sapphire Falls; exceptional rooftop restaurant; fast service food court. **Cons:** parking can be a problem; no Express pass access; basic pool area without slides or activities. *Rooms from: $290 6725 Adventure Way, Universal Orlando Resort 407/503–6000 www.loewshotels.com/universals-aventura-hotel 600 rooms No meals.*

★ **Loews Portofino Bay Hotel at Universal Orlando**
$$$ | **HOTEL** | The charm and romance of Portofino, Italy, are conjured up at this lovely luxury resort, where part of the fun is exploring the waterfront Italian "village" from end to end; the other part is relaxing in well-appointed rooms that are decorated in aqua and cream, with deluxe beds and flat-screen TVs, and three pools that offer aquatic fun or peaceful sunning. **Pros:** large spa; short walk or ferry ride to CityWalk, Universal; Universal Express Unlimited pass included. **Cons:** rooms and meals are pricey; daily fee for parking; not convenient to Disney parks. *Rooms from: $359 5601 Universal Blvd., Universal Orlando Resort 407/503–1000, 800/232–7827 www.loewshotels.com/portofino-bay-hotel 750 rooms No meals.*

Loews Royal Pacific Resort at Universal Orlando
$$$ | **RESORT** | **FAMILY** | This Pacific Rim-themed hotel lies amid 53 serene acres of lush shrubs, soaring bamboo, orchids, and palms and features lots of amenities including a weekly Polynesian-style luau, daily character breakfasts, a 12,000-square-foot lagoon-style pool, an interactive water-play area, and kid-friendly activities. **Pros:** Universal Express Unlimited pass included; character dining; shuttle to CityWalk and parks. **Cons:** rooms can feel smallish; steep parking fee; can be busy with conventioneers. *Rooms from: $304 6300 Hollywood Way, Universal Orlando Resort 407/503–3000, 800/232–7827 www.universalorlando.com 1,000 rooms No meals.*

★ **Loews Sapphire Falls Resort**
$$ | **RESORT** | **FAMILY** | Waterfalls cascade into aqua pools, and lush gardens fill the grounds at this resort, which opened in 2016. **Pros:** reasonable rates; biggest pool of any Universal resort; excellent restaurant. **Cons:** pricey parking; early entry to Universal but no Express pass; thin walls. *Rooms from: $225 6601 Adventure Way, Orlando 888/430–4999, 888/430–4999 www.loewshotels.com/sapphire-falls-resort 1,000 rooms No meals.*

★ **Universal's Cabana Bay Beach Resort**
$ | **RESORT** | **FAMILY** | Universal's Cabana Bay Beach Resort takes guests back in time to a 1950s Florida beach town with a modern twist, and offers families a less expensive option to staying on-site

at Universal, with loads of benefits that include a 10-lane bowling alley, a Jack LaLanne fitness studio, early park admission, two pools, one with slide, lazy river, poolside activities, and complimentary shuttle buses to and from Universal parks and CityWalk and to nearby SeaWorld and Aquatica. **Pros:** early access to Universal; bowling alley; two swimming pools. **Cons:** very expensive parking fee; Disney is not close by; some rooms open onto outdoor passageways. *$ Rooms from: $164 ✉ 6550 Adventure Way, Universal Orlando Resort ☎ 407/503–4000 🌐 www.loewshotels.com/cabana-bay ⟹ 1,800 rooms 🍽 No meals.*

Islands of Adventure

More so than just about any other theme park, Islands of Adventure has gone all out to create settings and attractions that transport you from reality into the surreal. What's more, no one island here has much in common with any other, so in a way a visit here is almost like a visit to half a dozen different parks.

The park's unique nature is first revealed when you arrive at the Port of Entry and are greeted by a kaleidoscope of sights and a cacophony of sounds. It's all designed to put you in the frame of mind for adventure.

When you reach the central lagoon, your clockwise journey commences with Marvel Super Hero Island and its tightly packed concentration of roller coasters and thrill rides. Of special note is the amazingly high-tech and dazzling Amazing Adventures of Spider-Man. In just minutes you'll have experienced a day's worth of sensations—and you've only just begun.

Stepping into Toon Lagoon is like stepping into the pages of a comic book; which is the exact opposite feeling you'll get at neighboring Skull Island, where you'll find the high-intensity attraction Skull Island: Reign of Kong. The prehistoric battles here set the tone for several attractions in the upcoming island, Jurassic Park, where you'll come face-to-face with dozens of dinosaurs.

Top Attractions

Ages 7 and Up

- Amazing Adventures of Spider-Man
- Harry Potter and the Forbidden Journey
- Incredible Hulk Coaster

Ages 6 and Under

- The Cat in the Hat
- Flight of the Hippogriff
- Popeye & Bluto's Bilge-Rat Barges

You move from the world of science into the world of magic when you segue into the Wizarding World of Harry Potter. You can wander through the magnificently fictional—yet very realistic—realm of the young wizard and his Hogwarts classmates and tutors, including the village of Hogsmeade, with its snow-topped roofs, and the halls of Hogwarts Castle itself.

But that's not the end of it. In the Lost Continent the mood is that of a Renaissance fair, where crafters work inside colorful tents. It's as pronounced an atmosphere as that of the final island, Seuss Landing, which presents the incredible, topsy-turvy world of Dr. Seuss. It's a riot of colors and shapes and fantastic wildlife that pay tribute to the good doctor's vivid imagination.

GETTING ORIENTED

Getting your bearings at IOA is far easier than at its sister park, Universal Studios. Brochures in a multitude of languages are in a rack a few steps beyond the turnstiles. The brochures include a

You never know who might be waiting around the next corner in Jurassic Park.

foldout map that will acquaint you with the park's simple layout (it's a circle). And, ahead by the lagoon, boards are posted with up-to-the-minute ride and show information—including the length of lines at the major attractions.

You pass through the turnstiles and into the Port of Entry plaza, a bazaar that brings together bits and pieces of architecture, landscaping, music, and wares from many lands—Dutch windmills, Indonesian pedicabs, African masks, restrooms marked "Loo's Landing," and Egyptian figurines that adorn a massive archway inscribed with the notice "The Adventure Begins." From here, themed islands—arranged around a large lagoon—are connected by walkways that make navigation easy. When you've done the full circuit, you'll recall the fantastic range of sights, sounds, and experiences and realize there can be truth in advertising. This park really *is* an adventure.

TOURING TIPS

Hosts. Just about any employee is a host, whether they're at a kiosk or attraction or turnstile. Ask them about their favorite experiences—and for suggestions for saving time.

Photo ops. Islands of Adventure posts signs that indicate picture spots and show how best to frame your shot.

Retreat. Explore little-used sidewalks and quiet alcoves to counter the park's manic energy.

Split the difference. If the park's open late, split the day in half. See part of it in the morning, head off-site to a restaurant for lunch (your parking ticket is good all day) then head to your hotel for a swim or a nap (or both). Return in the cooler, less crowded evening.

ISLANDS OF ADVENTURES PLANNER

PARK AMENITIES

Guest Services: Guest Services (☎ *407/224–6350*) is right near the turnstiles, both before and after you enter Islands of Adventure.

Lockers: There are $10-a-day lockers across from Guest Services at the entrance; for $12 a day you can rent a family-size model. You have unlimited access to both types throughout the day—although it's a hike back to retrieve things. Scattered strategically throughout the park—notably at the Incredible Hulk Coaster, Jurassic Park River Adventure, and Forbidden Journey—are so-called Smart Lockers. These are free for the first 45 to 75 minutes, $2 per hour afterward, and max out at $14 per day. Stash backpacks and cameras here while you're being drenched on a watery ride or going through the spin cycle on a twisty one.

Lost People and Things: If you've misplaced something, head to Guest Services in the Port of Entry. This is also where park staffers take lost children.

Stroller Rentals: You can rent strollers ($15 per day for singles, $25 for doubles) at the Port of Entry to your left after the turnstiles. You can also rent kiddie cars—small ones for $18, and large ones for $28.

 Sights

MARVEL SUPER HERO ISLAND

The facades on Stanley Boulevard (named for Marvel's late co-creator Stan Lee) put you smack in the middle of an alternatively pleasant and apocalyptic comic-book world—complete with heroes, villains, and cartoony colors and flourishes. Although the spiky, horrific towers of Doctor Doom's Fearfall and the vivid green of the Hulk's coaster are focal points, the Amazing Adventures of Spider-Man is the must-see attraction. At various times Doctor Doom, Spider-Man, and the Incredible Hulk are available for photos, and sidewalk artists are on hand to paint your face like your favorite hero (or villain). All rides here accept Universal Express Pass.

TOON LAGOON

The main street, Comic Strip Lane, makes use of cartoon characters that are recognizable to anyone—anyone born before 1940, that is. Pert little Betty Boop, gangly Olive Oyl, muscle-bound Popeye, Krazy Kat, Pogo, and Alley Oop are all here, as are the relatively more contemporary Dudley Do-Right, Rocky, Bullwinkle, Beetle Bailey, Cathy, and Hagar the Horrible. With its colorful backdrops, chirpy music, hidden alcoves, squirting fountains, and highly animated scenery, Toon Town is a natural for younger kids (even if they don't know who these characters are). All attractions here accept Universal Express Pass except Me Ship, The Olive.

SKULL ISLAND

If you've ever seen the 1933 classic King Kong, you may recall that for its time (and ours) it was an intensely thrilling presentation of special effects and incredible characters. The same is true of this present-day incarnation, which recreates the mood and settings found in the original. Tucked in an area between Toon Lagoon and Jurassic Park, Skull Island presents a singular attraction—and what an attraction it is: an ongoing battle between King Kong and a host of oversized adversaries. Parents should note that this is the only attraction where there's a warning that the pre-show area may be too intense for kids.

JURASSIC PARK

Pass through the towering gates of Jurassic Park and the music becomes slightly ominous, the vegetation tropical and junglelike. All of this, plus the high-tension wires and warning signs, does a great job of re-creating

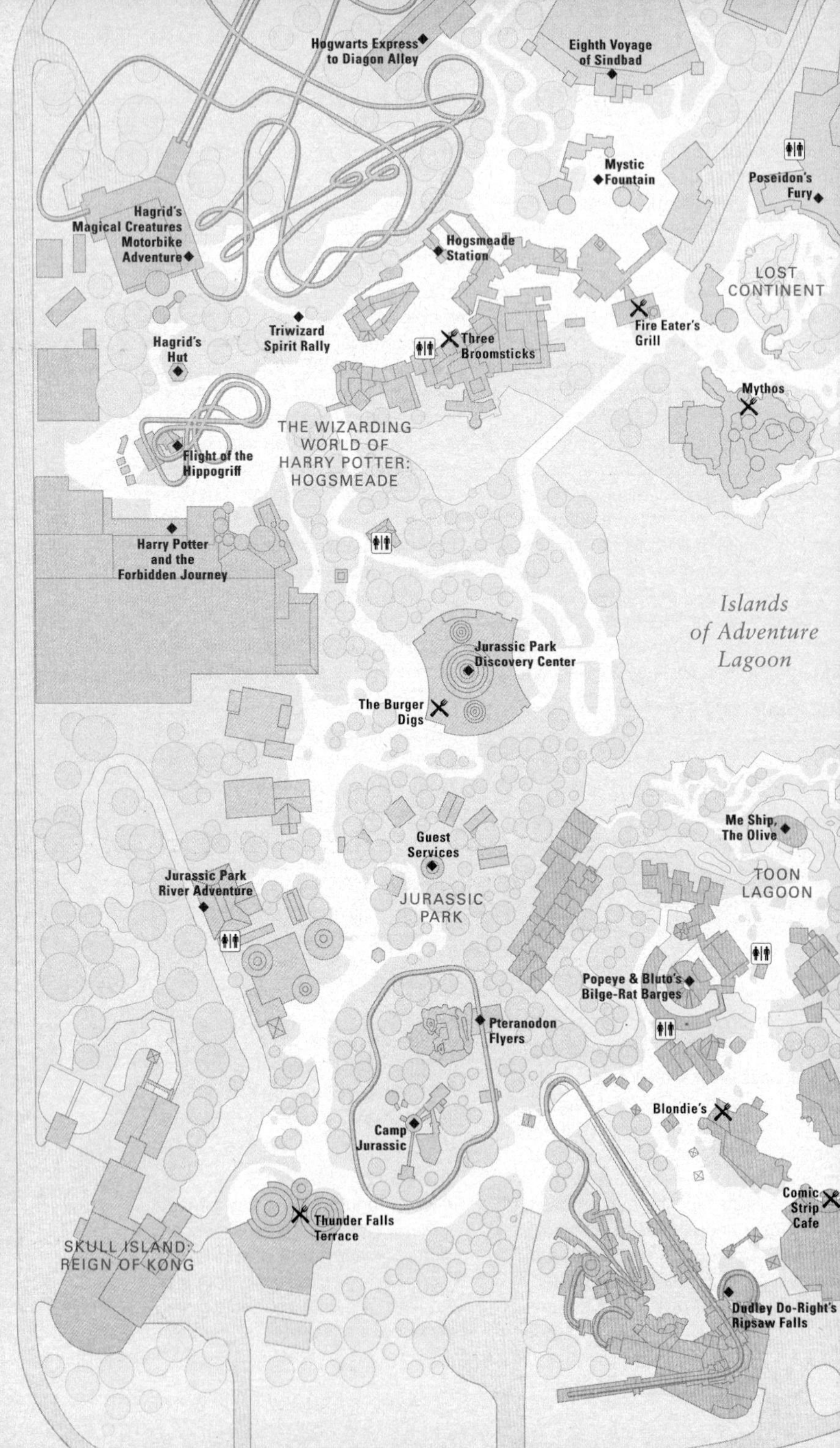

Hogwarts Express to Diagon Alley
Eighth Voyage of Sindbad
Mystic Fountain
Poseidon's Fury
Hagrid's Magical Creatures Motorbike Adventure
Hogsmeade Station
LOST CONTINENT
Fire Eater's Grill
Triwizard Spirit Rally
Three Broomsticks
Hagrid's Hut
Mythos
THE WIZARDING WORLD OF HARRY POTTER: HOGSMEADE
Flight of the Hippogriff
Harry Potter and the Forbidden Journey
Islands of Adventure Lagoon
Jurassic Park Discovery Center
The Burger Digs
Me Ship, The Olive
Guest Services
TOON LAGOON
Jurassic Park River Adventure
JURASSIC PARK
Popeye & Bluto's Bilge-Rat Barges
Pteranodon Flyers
Blondie's
Camp Jurassic
Comic Strip Cafe
Thunder Falls Terrace
SKULL ISLAND: REIGN OF KONG
Dudley Do-Right's Ripsaw Falls

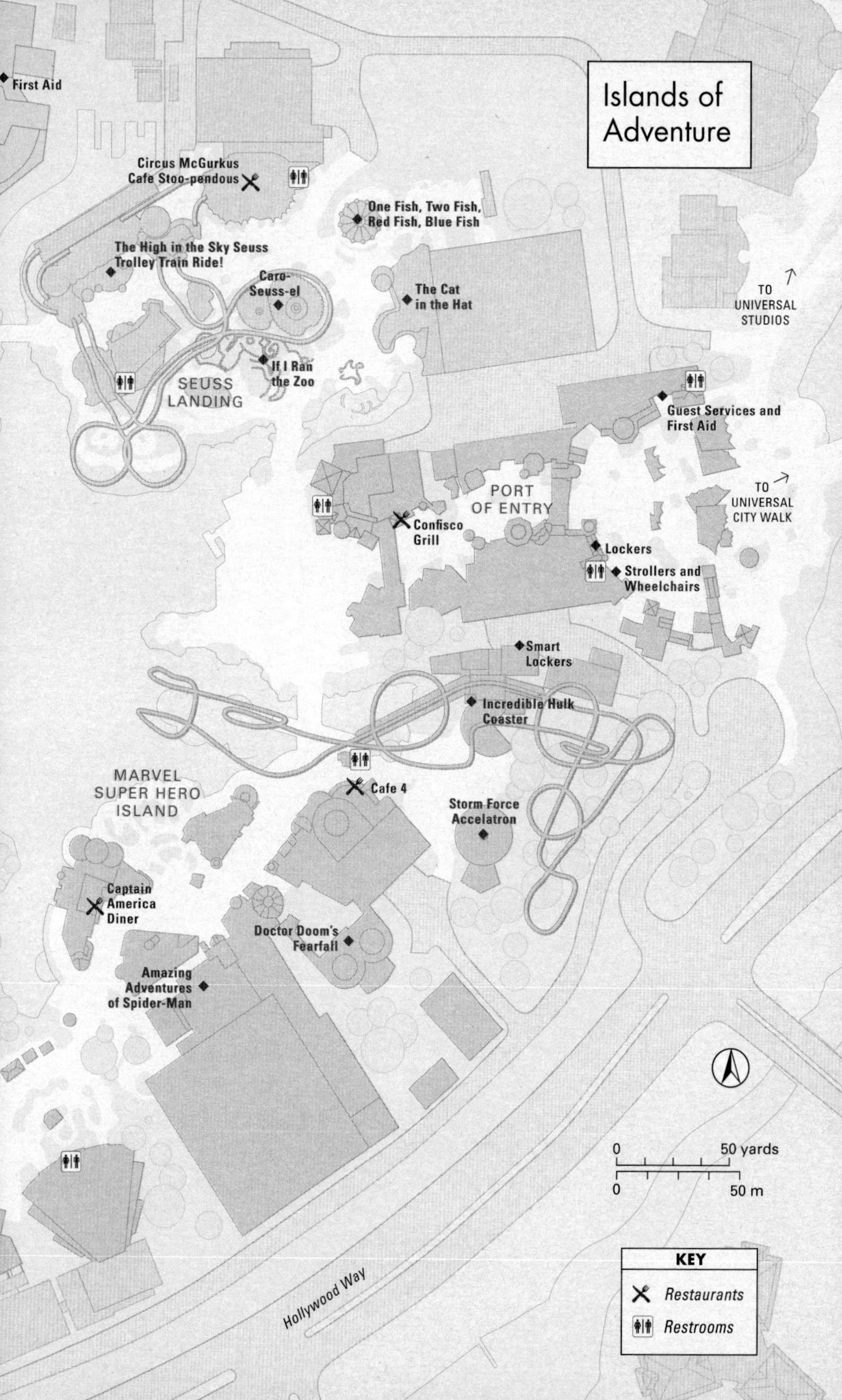

Islands of Adventure
First Aid
Circus McGurkus Cafe Stoo-pendous
One Fish, Two Fish, Red Fish, Blue Fish
The High in the Sky Seuss Trolley Train Ride!
Caro-Seuss-el
The Cat in the Hat
TO UNIVERSAL STUDIOS
If I Ran the Zoo
SEUSS LANDING
Guest Services and First Aid
PORT OF ENTRY
TO UNIVERSAL CITY WALK
Confisco Grill
Lockers
Strollers and Wheelchairs
Smart Lockers
Incredible Hulk Coaster
MARVEL SUPER HERO ISLAND
Cafe 4
Storm Force Accelatron
Captain America Diner
Doctor Doom's Fearfall
Amazing Adventures of Spider-Man
0
50 yards
0
50 m
KEY
Restaurants
Restrooms
Hollywood Way

Did You Know?

The Wizarding World of Harry Potter has been the most popular section of Universal Orlando since the Hogsmeade section debuted in Islands of Adventure in 2009. It was joined by a Diagon Alley section in Universal Studios in 2014.

the Jurassic Park of Steven Spielberg's blockbuster movie (and its sequels). The half-fun, half-frightening Jurassic Park River Adventure (the only attraction here that uses Universal Express Pass) is the standout, bringing to life key segments of the movie's climax.

THE WIZARDING WORLD OF HARRY POTTER: HOGSMEADE

In 2010 Islands of Adventure fulfilled the fantasy of Harry Potter devotees when it unveiled the biggest theme-park addition since the arrival of Disney's Animal Kingdom in 1998. At the highly publicized premiere, even the actors from the Potter film franchise were amazed. Having performed their roles largely before a green screen, they had never seen anything like this. Neither have you. The movie-magic-perfect re-creations of mythical locales such as Hogwarts and Hogsmeade Village are here, while playing supporting roles are a handful of candy shops, souvenir stores, and restaurants expertly and exquisitely themed to make you believe you've actually arrived in the incredible fantasy world of J.K. Rowling. Wands, Bertie Bott's Every-Flavour Beans™, Chocolate Frogs™, and best of all, Butterbeer are available for you to try. Expect to be impressed—and to wait in line. Even if you owned a wand and were a real wizard, the only attractions that accept the Universal Express Pass are Flight of the Hippogriff and the Harry Potter and the Forbidden Forest roller coaster. In fact, in peak season it sometimes reaches capacity, and you have to wait for others to leave before you can enter. If you have a two-park pass, you can board the Hogwarts Express for a delightful train journey to Diagon Alley at Universal Studios. A new roller coaster, Hagrid's Magical Creatures Motorbike Adventure, opened in June 2019.

LOST CONTINENT

Just beyond a wooden bridge, huge mythical birds guard the entrance to a land where trees are hung with weathered metal lanterns, and booming thunder mixes with chimes and vaguely Celtic melodies. Farther along the path, the scene looks similar to a Renaissance fair. Seers and fortune-tellers practice their trade in tents, and in a huge theater, wizards battle in Poseidon's Fury.

SEUSS LANDING

This 10-acre tribute to Dr. Seuss puts you in the midst of his classic children's books. This means spending quality time with the Cat, Things 1 and 2, Horton, the Lorax, and the Grinch. From topiary sculptures to lurching lampposts to curvy fences (there was never a straight line in any of the books) to buildings that glow in lavenders, pinks, peaches, and oranges, everything seems surreal. It's a wonderful place to wrap up a day. Even the Cat would approve. All rides here except If I Ran the Zoo accept Express Pass.

Restaurants

Confisco Grille

$ | **AMERICAN** | You could walk right past this full-service restaurant without noticing it, but if you want a good meal and sit-down service, don't pass by too quickly. The menu is American with international influences. **Known for:** Italian, Greek, Asian, and Mexican dishes; overlooked location means better chance of seating; Backwater Bar next door. *Average main: $13* ✉ *Port of Entry, Islands of Adventure* ☎ *407/224–4404* 🌐 *www.universalorlando.com.*

Mythos

$$$ | **ECLECTIC** | **FAMILY** | Built into a rock cliff, this enchanting eatery has a menu that includes such mainstays as pad Thai and pan-seared salmon with lemon-basil butter and sandwiches like crab-cake sliders and roast beef panini with caramelized yellow onions, roasted red peppers, and pepperoncini. The building itself—which looks like a giant rock formation from the outside and a huge

The Cat and his Hat, McGurkus and the Circus, and fish both red and blue are among the attractions geared to the under-seven set at Seuss Landing.

cave (albeit one with plush upholstered seating) from the inside—is enough to grab your attention, but so does the waterfront view of the big lagoon in the center of the theme park. **Known for:** spectacular decor; one of the best theme park restaurants; lamb burgers, crab cake sandwiches. $ *Average main: $22* *The Lost Continent, Islands of Adventure* *407/224–4533* *www.universalorlando.com* *No dinner.*

Three Broomsticks

$ | BRITISH | FAMILY | Harry Potter fans flock here to taste pumpkin juice (with hints of honey and vanilla) and Butterbeer (sort of like bubbly butterscotch cream soda, or maybe shortbread cookies). They're on the menu along with barbecue and traditional British foods at this Hogsmeade restaurant. **Known for:** quirky Harry Potter atmosphere; quick and courteous service; full English breakfast daily. $ *Average main: $12* *The Wizarding World of Harry Potter: Hogsmeade, Islands of Adventure* *407/224–4233* *www.universalorlando.com.*

CityWalk

With an attitude that's distinctly non-Disney, Universal has created nightlife for adults who want to party. The epicenter is CityWalk, a 30-acre entertainment and retail complex at the hub of promenades that lead to two Universal parks.

When it comes to retail, much of the merchandise includes things you can find elsewhere—and most likely for less. But when you're swept up in the energy of CityWalk and dazzled by the degree of window-shopping (not to mention the fact that you're on vacation and you're more inclined to spend), chances are you'll want to drop into stores selling everything from surf wear and cigars to tattoos and timepieces.

In addition to stores, the open and airy gathering place includes an over-the-top discotheque, a theater for the fabulous and extremely popular Blue Man Group, and a huge hall where karaoke's king. There's a New York pizza parlor, a Jamaican reggae lounge, a casual Key West hangout, and Hollywood Drive-In Golf, a pair of fun-filled 1950s sci-fi movie–themed miniature golf courses. On weeknights you find families and conventioneers; weekends a decidedly younger crowd parties until the wee hours.

Clubs have individual cover charges, but it's far more economical to pay for the whole kit and much of the caboodle. Choose a Party Pass (a one-price-all-clubs admission) for $11.99, or upgrade to a Party Pass-and-a-Movie for $15; a Party Pass-and-a-Meal for $21; a Movie-and-a-Meal for $21.95; or a Meal and a Mini-Golf Deal for $23.95.

At AMC Universal Cineplex, with its 20 screens (including IMAX), there's certain to be something you like—including nightly midnight movies. Meals (tax and gratuity included) are served at Jimmy Buffett's Margaritaville, the Hard Rock Cafe, and others. Nevertheless, it's a long haul from the garage to CityWalk—if you prefer, simply call Uber. ☎ *407/354–3374, 407/363–8000 Universal main line* 🌐 *www.citywalkorlando.com.*

Nightlife

With the wide range of nightlife you'll find at Universal, you may get the feeling that you're vacationing not in Orlando but in New York City. CityWalk's stores open by midmorning, and its restaurants come to life between lunchtime and late afternoon. Eateries that double as nightclubs (such as Pat O'Brien's, Bob Marley's, and the Red Coconut Club) start charging a cover sometime in the evening and apply age restrictions (usually 21) around 9. For details on a particular establishment, check with Guest Services.

Blue Man Group

THEATER | FAMILY | At their own venue, the ever-innovative Blue Man Group continues to pound out new music, sketches, and audience interaction. Attempting to understand the apps on a GiPad (a gigantic iPad), they may appear clueless and perplexed about cutting-edge technology (which for them can be as basic as a can of paint), but they're always excited when they can drum out rhythms on lengths of PVC pipes and throw a rave party finale for all in attendance. The show is a surreal comic masterpiece. Three levels of admission (Poncho, Tier 1, and Tier 2) hint at how messy things can get when the Blue Men cut loose. ✉ *CityWalk* ☎ *407/258–3626* 🌐 *www.universalorlando.com* 🎟 *$60–$110; VIP $200+.*

Bob Marley—A Tribute to Freedom

BARS/PUBS | Modeled after the King of Reggae's home in Kingston, Jamaica (even down to the air-conditioning window units), in a way this nightclub is also part museum, with more than 100 photographs and paintings showing pivotal moments in Marley's life. Though the place does serve Jamaican-influenced meals, most patrons are at the cozy bar or by the patio, where they can be jammin' to a (loud) live band that plays nightly. For a nice souvenir, pose by the wonderful Marley statue outside the club. Sunday is ladies' night from 10 pm to 2 am. ✉ *CityWalk* ☎ *407/224–2692* 🌐 *www.universalorlando.com/web/en/us/things-to-do/dining/bob-marley-a-tribute-to-freedom/index.html.*

CityWalk's Rising Star

BARS/PUBS | Here you and other hopeful (and hopeless) singers can really let loose in front of a live audience. Singers croon to recorded tracks on Sunday and Monday, but between Tuesday and Saturday you're accompanied by a live band complete with backup singers. A full bar is always on tap. Friday and Saturday are reserved for an over-21 crowd. ✉ *6000 Universal Blvd., CityWalk* ☎ *407/224–2961* 🌐 *www.universalorlando.com/web/en/us/things-to-do/entertainment/rising-star-karaoke/index.html* 🎟 *$7 cover charge.*

the groove

BARS/PUBS | In this cavernous multilevel hall, images flicker rapidly on several screens, with the lights, music, and mayhem appealing to a mostly under-30 crowd. Prepare for lots of fog, swirling lights, and sweaty bodies. The '70s-style Green Room is filled with beanbag chairs and everything you threw out when Duran Duran hit the charts. The Blue Room is sci-fi Jetson-y, and the Red Room is hot and romantic in a bordello sort of way. The music is equally diverse: Top 40, hip-hop, R&B, techno, and the occasional live band. ✉ *6000 Universal Blvd., CityWalk* ☎ *407/224–2692* 🌐 *www.universalorlando.com/web/en/us/things-to-do/entertainment/the-groove/index.html* 🎫 *$7 cover charge after 10 pm.*

Jimmy Buffett's Margaritaville

BARS/PUBS | Buffett tunes fill the air at the restaurant here and at the Volcano, Land Shark, and 12 Volt bars. Inside there's a miniature Pan Am Clipper suspended from the ceiling, music videos projected onto sails, limbo and hula-hoop contests, a huge margarita blender that erupts "when the volcano blows," and live music nightly—everything that Parrot-heads need to roost. Across the promenade, another full-size seaplane (emblazoned with "Jimmy Buffett, Captain") is the setting for the Lone Palm Airport, a pleasing and surprisingly popular outdoor waterfront bar. ✉ *6000 Universal Studios Plaza, Suite 704, CityWalk* ☎ *407/224–2155* 🌐 *www.universalorlando.com/web/en/us/things-to-do/dining/jimmy-buffetts-margaritaville/index.html.*

Pat O'Brien's

BARS/PUBS | An exact reproduction of the legendary New Orleans original, this comes complete with flaming fountain and dueling pianists who are playing for highly entertained regulars and visitors—even on weekday afternoons. Outside, the cozy and welcoming Patio Bar has a wealth of tables and chairs, allowing you to do nothing but enjoy the outdoors and your potent, rum-based Hurricanes in Orlando's version of the Big Easy. ✉ *6000 Universal Blvd., CityWalk* ☎ *407/224–2692* 🌐 *www.universalorlando.com/web/en/us/things-to-do/dining/pat-o-briens/index.html.*

Red Coconut Club

BARS/PUBS | Paying tribute to kitsch design of the 1950s, the interior here is part Vegas lounge, part Cuban club, and part Polynesian tiki bar. It's "where tropical meets trendy." There are three full bars on two levels, signature martinis, an extensive wine list, and VIP bottle service. Hang out in the lounge, on the balcony, or at the bar. On a budget? Take advantage of the daily happy hours and gourmet appetizer menu. Latin music takes over from 8 pm to midnight, then a DJ from midnight until 2 am. Thursday is ladies' night. ✉ *6000 Universal Blvd., CityWalk* ☎ *407/224–2425* 🌐 *www.universalorlando.com/web/en/us/things-to-do/entertainment/red-coconut-club/index.html* 🎫 *$7 cover charge after 10 pm.*

Shopping

This 30-acre entertainment and retail complex is at the hub of promenades that lead to Universal Studios and Islands of Adventure. Shops here sell fine jewelry, cool beachwear, fashionable clothing, and stylish accessories. The best stores are near the entrance/exit of the complex.

Fresh Produce

CLOTHING | Featuring fashions that look right at home in sunny Florida, this boutique showcases comfortable and colorful swimwear, blouses, Capri slacks, dresses, footwear, beach gear, and accessories designed for coastal comfort. ✉ *CityWalk* ☎ *407/363–9363* 🌐 *www.universalorlando.com/web/en/us/things-to-do/shopping/fresh-produce/index.html.*

Quiet Flight

CLOTHING | Granted the closest beach is about 60 miles east, but you can still get outfitted like a surfer at this shop, which sports an inventory featuring brand names such as Billabong, Quicksilver, Hurley, and Oakley. In addition to shorts and shirts, Quiet Flight also sells sandals, watches, sunglasses (Ray-Ban, Prada, and D&G among the featured names)—and surfboards! ✉ *CityWalk* ☎ *407/224–2125* 🌐 *www.universalorlando.com/web/en/us/things-to-do/shopping/quiet-flight-surf-shop/index.html.*

Volcano Bay

When you were a kid, chances are that the only thing you needed for cool summer fun was an inflatable pool and a garden hose. Well, you've grown up, and so have water parks. The choices for cool summer fun get no cooler than Universal's Volcano Bay, a theme park all on its own.

Built around a central, fire-spewing volcano, the park offers numerous high-energy slides and drops for adults; lots of slides and fountains where the little ones can frolic; an area for older kids with bubbling geysers, water guns, slides, and dump cups. There's also a white-water rapids ride, a lazy-river ride, a surf pool, and some quiet, sandy beaches on which you can stretch out and get a tan.

Speaking of high energy, this is a park that requires a lot of it. A day here is often a marathon of climbing steps, sliding, swimming, and splashing, though you may not notice just how much your stamina is being drained as you scamper from slide to slide. Plan to take breaks: laze in a beach chair and eat high-protein meals and snacks to maintain your strength.

If you're not a strong swimmer, don't worry. There are plenty of low-key attractions, and all the ride entrances are marked with warnings to let you know which ones are safe for you. Plus, during peak season, there are always lifeguards on duty daily. Also note that all the pools (if not the rides) are ADA-compliant and are heated in cooler weather. This, combined with Orlando's temperate climate, means that Volcano Bay is one of the few water parks in the country to stay open year-round.

Planning

TOURING TIPS

Skip the lines at the water with Volcano Bay's TapuTapu wristband system, which puts guests on a virtual line.

When you arrive, it's a good idea to pick up a map, scan the park layout, and stake out a spot on the beach before heading on or in. To claim a prime beach spot, arrive at least 15 minutes before the park opens, or visit on a cloudy day. If it looks like rain all day, though, head elsewhere. Universal Resort guests get early admission one hour before the general public.

Men should wear a true bathing suit, and women should opt for a one-piece rather than a bikini. Cutoff shorts and garments with rivets, metal buttons, buckles, or zippers aren't allowed.

Wading slippers are a good idea—hot sidewalks and sandpaper-like pool bottoms can do a number on your feet—but put them in a locker or carry them when taking a plunge, since they can catch on slides.

Items too large to carry should be stashed in a locker.

For extra privacy, a quiet oasis in the middle of the lazy river features cabanas with a fan, chaise longues, and a fridge stocked with a dozen bottles of water. It's a nice base for stowing your things, but the privilege costs some bucks. Depending on the time of the year, cabanas start at $199 to a high of $599 in the peak summer season for the whole family. Don't want to get up? Servers will bring food to you.

To bypass lines at the popular rides, get an Express Pass (available seasonally), accepted at most rides. Prices change based on park attendance and time of day, starting at $19.99. A limited number of passes are sold each day—all the more reason to get here early.

Okay. So you remembered your swimsuit and towel. But what about sunscreen? You can buy it and other necessities or souvenirs at Krakatoa Katy's gift shop. And if you did forget a towel, renting one here costs $4.99.

PARK AMENITIES

Guest Services: Get maps and other information at Guest Services located at the main entrance. ☎ *407/363–8000*

Lockers: There are dressing rooms with lockers in Wave Village, Rainforest Village, and River Village.

First Aid Station: left of main entrance.

Restrooms: throughout the park and at locker rooms.

Lost People and Things: Guest Services

★ Volcano Bay

Universal's newest park (at the moment) replaces the beloved Wet 'n' Wild with a tropically themed mountain oasis, with rides from the harrowing Krakatau Aqua Coaster and its four-person canoes plunging down the volcano to the relaxing Kopiko Wai Winding River. Raft rides, high-speed drop slides, and one-on-one water racing through underground caverns are some of the attractions. Six restaurants and bars are scattered throughout the thatch-covered villages. The innovative TapuTapu wristband reserves a virtual spot on any ride line, unlocks special features, and triggers selfies at designated spots. At $80, Volcano Bay is a bit more expensive than the Disney water parks, but the state-of-the-art technology might be worth it. ■ **TIP→ The area behind the massive volcano offers waterslides, lockers, and food options that many guests might overlook.** ✉ *6560 Adventure Way, Orlando, FL, Universal Orlando Resort* ☎ *407/363–8000* 🌐 *www.universalorlando.com.*

Chapter 13

NORTHEAST FLORIDA

Updated by Steve Master and Jennifer Greenhill-Taylor

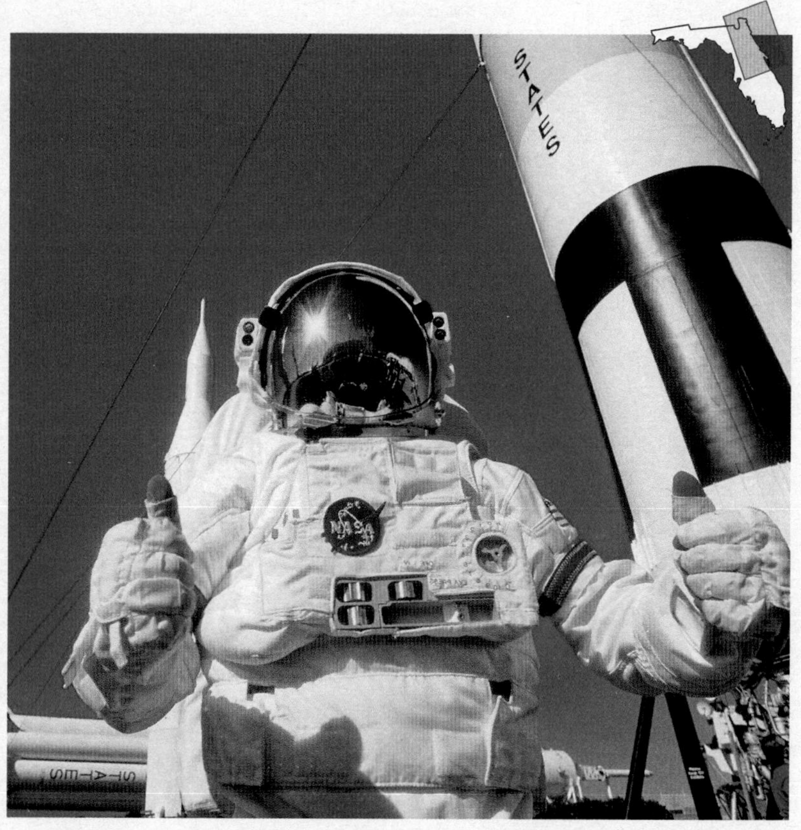

Sights ★★★★☆ | Restaurants ★★★★☆ | Hotels ★★★★☆ | Shopping ★★★★☆ | Nightlife ★★★★☆

WELCOME TO NORTHEAST FLORIDA

TOP REASONS TO GO

★ **Get out and play:** Beautiful beaches and a wealth of state and national parks mean swimming, sunbathing, kayaking, fishing, hiking, bird-watching, and camping opportunities are all nearby.

★ **Golfer's paradise:** "Above par" describes the golf scene, from award-winning courses to THE PLAYERS Championship to the World Golf Hall of Fame.

★ **Start your engines:** Few things get racing fans as revved up as tours of Daytona International Speedway, home of the Daytona 500, Coke Zero 400, and Rolex 24 at Daytona.

★ **Be in the now:** Whether you want a yoga retreat or the ultimate in sybaritic pampering, the oceanfront spas at Amelia Island and Ponte Vedra Beach make this region the place to be.

★ **The rest is history:** The nation's oldest city, St. Augustine, is a must-see for anyone interested in history.

1 **Jacksonville.** A big city with the down-to-earth charm of a small town.

2 **Atlantic Beach.** Beautiful sand and plentiful activities keep tourists coming back to this beach community.

3 **Neptune Beach.** Escape to Neptune from the more crowded sands to the north and south.

4 **Jacksonville Beach.** A popular family-friendly destination, this beach community has blossomed in recent years.

5 **Ponta Vedra Beach.** This upscale coastal community is known for its golf courses and swanky homes.

6 **Mayport.** Dating back more than 300 years, this fishing village has excellent, casual seafood restaurants and markets.

7 **Fort George Island.** The island is lush with foliage, natural vegetation, and wildlife.

8 **Amelia Island/Fernandina Beach.** There's a historic downtown, beautiful beaches, and two superlative resorts.

9 **St. Augustine.** You don't have to be a history buff to enjoy America's oldest city, founded in 1565.

10 **Daytona Beach.** The Daytona 500 and spring break put it on the map, but the region is popular with vacationing families, too.

11 **New Smyrna Beach.** Artists and surfers flock to the dune-lined beaches of this small town.

12 **Ocala National Forest.** This breathtaking national forest has lakes, springs, rivers, hiking trails, campgrounds, and historic sites.

13 **Gainesville.** Football fans must catch a Gator game at the University of Florida.

14 **Titusville.** Home to Merritt Island National Wildlife Refuge and the entrance to the Kennedy Space Center.

15 **Cocoa.** Not to be confused with Cocoa Beach, the quiet, small town is on the mainland.

16 **Cape Canaveral.** Watch rocket launches or catch a cruise ship from Port Canaveral.

17 **Cocoa Beach.** The town and its lovely beach are a mecca to Florida's surfing community.

18 **Melbourne.** Come here for golf, beaches, and The USSSA Space Coast Complex.

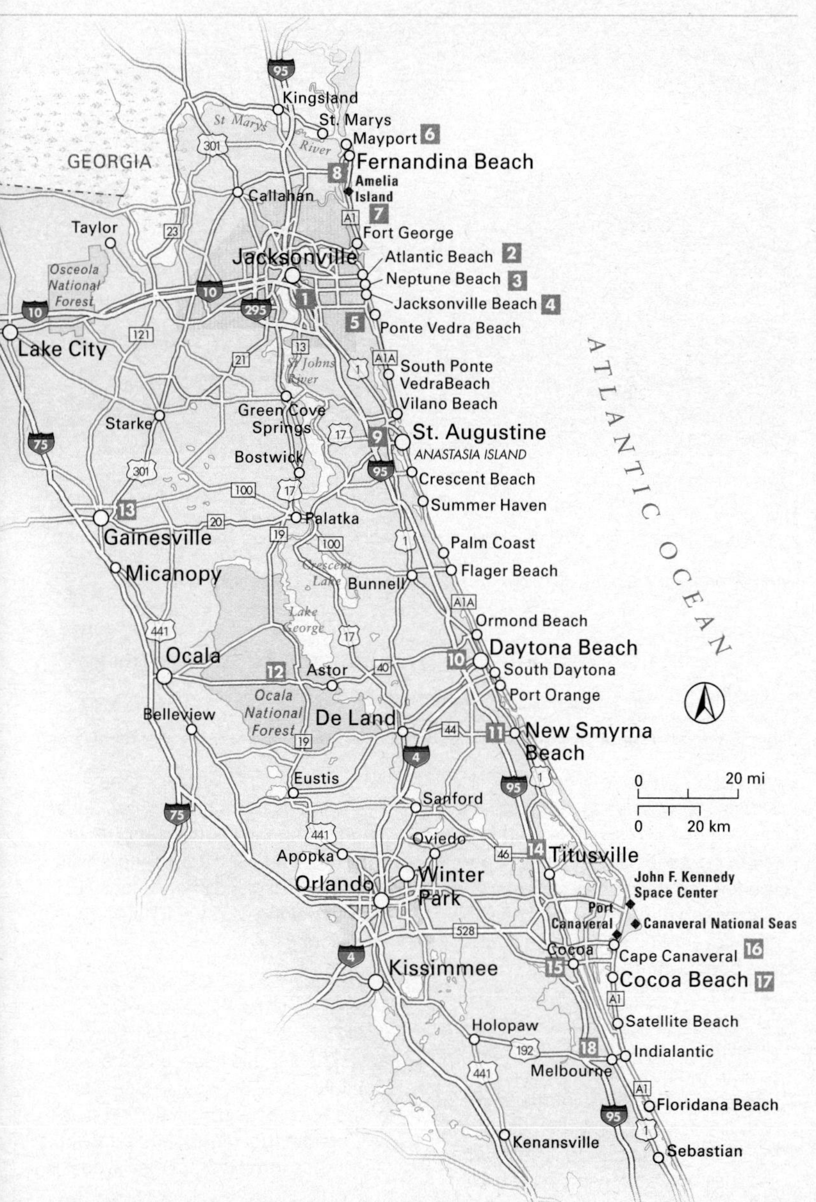
GEORGIA
Kingsland
St. Marys
St Marys River
Mayport 6
Fernandina Beach
8
Amelia Island
7
Callahan
Taylor
Fort George
Jacksonville
Atlantic Beach 2
Neptune Beach 3
Jacksonville Beach 4
Osceola National Forest
1
5
Ponte Vedra Beach
Lake City
St Johns River
South Ponte VedraBeach
Vilano Beach
Starke
Green Cove Springs
9
St. Augustine
ANASTASIA ISLAND
Bostwick
Crescent Beach
Summer Haven
13
Palatka
Gainesville
Palm Coast
Micanopy
Crescent Lake
Bunnell
Flager Beach
Lake George
Ormond Beach
Ocala
10
Daytona Beach
South Daytona
12
Astor
Port Orange
Ocala National Forest
Belleview
De Land
11
New Smyrna Beach
ATLANTIC OCEAN
Eustis
Sanford
0
20 mi
20 km
Oviedo
Apopka
14
Titusville
Winter Park
Orlando
John F. Kennedy Space Center
Port Canaveral
Canaveral National Seas
Cocoa
Cape Canaveral 16
15
Kissimmee
Cocoa Beach 17
Satellite Beach
Holopaw
18
Indialantic
Melbourne
Floridana Beach
Kenansville
Sebastian

THE SPACE SHUTTLE ATLANTIS

Even if you have never had the inclination to strap into a rocket or live in zero gravity, no trip to Florida would be complete without a visit to the Kennedy Space Center's Space Shuttle Atlantis exhibit. A full day can be spent experiencing the educational and emotional life and history of the American space shuttle program.

More than a mere exhibit, the *Space Shuttle Atlantis* defies stereotypes with a hands-on approach that enables you to not only see and hear, but also touch and feel, so that you *experience* rather than observe. There are no fingerprint-covered glass cases separating you from getting up close and personal with the symbolic passageways, 60-plus interactive displays, games, simulators, and even a slide to get you back to the ground level (adults are allowed). The *Atlantis* shuttle, complete with tile damage from the heat of reentry, never fails to amaze visitors who see it as only astronauts have before.

The walk-through replicas of the shuttle's living quarters help visitors understand life on the shuttle. The *Atlantis* exhibit has an open atmosphere with an enthusiastic and knowledgeable staff that brings out the inner-astronaut in everyone.

THE EXPERIENCE

The *Space Shuttle Atlantis* exhibit is easily located from the moment you enter the Kennedy Space Center Visitor Complex; the 184-foot life-size replica of the twin rocket boosters and massive orange fuel tank used to transport the shuttle into orbit are displayed just outside the main entry. The *Shuttle Launch Experience* begins with a dual-theater screening that showcases the history of the shuttle development. The motion-picturesque films provide a background and understanding of the necessity and evolution of the shuttle program. Passing through the theater and onto the upper level reveals *Atlantis*, appearing to float, as if in space, with cargo doors open and robotic Canada arm extended.

Even for the space novice, it is easy to see the amount of thought, planning, and insight that went into the design and construction of the *Atlantis* facility, not to mention the engineering and transportation challenges overcome in order to display a real-life shuttle. Rotated 43.21 degrees and almost close enough to touch, this experience is the closest that many non-astronauts will ever come to something that has actually been into space. The staff gladly answer any questions and provide an array of information regarding the facility, design, and interactive displays available for use. Touring *Atlantis* is an exploration in and of itself.

ACTIVITIES

The interactive games and displays are fun for children and parents alike, sometimes sparking fierce competition.

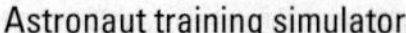
Astronaut training simulator

United States Astronaut Hall of Fame

Try your hand on the shuttle crane simulator and experience the complex task of attaching the Shuttle *Atlantis* to the 58,500-pound fuel tank. Features like this shed light on the often unheard engineering and physical obstacles encountered and conquered in order to prepare a shuttle for safe transport to the launch pad.

If you've ever wondered what it would be like to experience a shuttle liftoff, look no further. The *Shuttle Launch Experience* is the only place on Earth (and perhaps the galaxy) allowing non-astronauts to partake in a thrill only a select few Americans have known. After a series of informative videos, future astronauts are guided into the mock shuttle.

Once your safety belts have been fastened, the motion-based platform comes alive with specialized, interactive seating and high-fidelity video and audio to amaze the visitors with what astronauts call the most realistic simulation of a launch. After pushing through the high G-forces and separating from the rocket boosters and fuel tank, the simulation climaxes with a sense of weightlessness, along with a breathtaking view of the distant planet Earth.

For many travelers, Florida is about fantasy, thanks in no small part to Central Florida's make-believe kingdoms. But the northeastern part of the state—you could call it "authentic Florida"—has its own allure, with unspoiled beaches and rivers, historic small towns, and urban arts and culture.

Northeastern Florida's beaches have wide, shell-strewn expanses of sand, in some places firm enough to ride bikes on, and breakers just the right height for kids to jump. Thanks to the temperate climate and waters warmed by the Gulf Stream, these beaches are a year-round playground—when it's too cold to swim, you can still enjoy surf-fishing or just riding on the beach, or strolling the shoreline looking for shells and sharks' teeth.

Sun and surf aren't the only reasons to explore northeastern Florida, though. There's historic St. Augustine and its horse-drawn carriages, Daytona and its classic spring-break flavor, and the Space Coast and its sense of discovery. Along the way is an array of little towns—from Fernandina and its shrimp fleets to Micanopy and its antiques stores—that invite quiet exploration.

There's city life in the northeast, too. In the last decade or so, Jacksonville has revitalized its institutions and infrastructure. And with the revitalization has come an arts renaissance—from virtuoso productions in the theaters of the Times-Union Center for the Performing Arts and the Florida Theatre, to world-class exhibitions in the Museum of Contemporary Art.

So even if the ultimate reason for your Florida sojourn is Mickey and his friends, there's no reason to miss the northeast. Indeed, you'll find some authentic benefits—among them, a dearth of crowds and lines and an abundance of Southern hospitality, plus good value for the money.

Planning

When to Go

It's not 90°F and sunny here every day. In winter the weather is fair, averaging in the low 50s in Jacksonville and low 60s in Cocoa Beach, but the temperature sometimes dips below freezing for a day or two. Summer temperatures hover around 90°F, but the humidity makes it seem hotter, and late-afternoon thunderstorms are frequent. April and May are good months to visit, because the ocean is beginning to warm up and the beaches aren't yet packed. Fall is usually pleasant, too, but September is still hurricane season.

FESTIVALS AND ANNUAL EVENTS

Daytona Speed Weeks

Daytona pulls out all the stops with this auto extravaganza in late January and February. It starts with the Rolex 24-Hour Race and culminates with the famed Daytona 500. ☎ *800/748–7467* 🌐 *www.daytonainternationalspeedway.com.*

Rhythm and Ribs Festival

Champion barbecuers fire up the grill in March or April at this St. Augustine event. 🌐 *www.rhythmandribs.net.*

Space Coast Birding and Wildlife Festival

Birders flock to Titusville for five days of field trips, seminars, and workshops by leading ornithologists each January. ☎ *800/460–2664, 321/268–5224* 🌐 *www.spacecoastbirdingandwildlifefestival.org.*

Springing the Blues Festival

Nationally recognized performers and local talent entertain blues lovers during this free three-day affair at the SeaWalk Pavilion on Jacksonville Beach the first full weekend of April. 🌐 *www.springingtheblues.com.*

Getting Here and Around

AIR TRAVEL

Jacksonville International Airport (JAX) is the region's air hub. A welcome center with information on local attractions, including St. Augustine and Amelia Island, is on the ground floor at the foot of the escalator near baggage claim. It's open daily 9 am–10 pm.

Daytona Beach International (DAB) and Gainesville Regional (GNV) are smaller operations with fewer flights; that said, they may be more convenient in certain travel situations.

Although Orlando isn't part of the area, visitors to northeastern Florida often choose to arrive at Orlando International Airport (MCO), because cheaper flights are usually available. Driving east from Orlando on toll road 528 (aka the Beachline Expressway) brings you to Cocoa Beach in about an hour. To reach Daytona from Orlando, take Interstate 4 or the Beachline Expressway to Interstate 95 and drive north for an hour or so.

CAR TRAVEL

East–west traffic travels the northern part of the state on Interstate 10, a cross-country highway stretching from Jacksonville, Florida, to Santa Monica, California. Farther south, Interstate 4 connects Florida's west and east coasts. Signs on Interstate 4 designate it an east–west route, but actually the road rambles northeast from Tampa to Orlando, then heads north–northeast to Daytona. Two interstates head north–south on Florida's peninsula: Interstate 95 on the east coast and Interstate 75 on the west.

If you want to drive as close to the Atlantic as possible, choose Route A1A, but accept the fact that it will add considerably to your drive time. It runs along the barrier islands, changing its name several times along the way.

The Buccaneer Trail, which overlaps part of Route A1A, goes from St. Augustine north to Mayport, through marshlands and beaches, crosses the St. Johns via Ferry, and then proceeds north into Fort Clinch State Park. The extremely scenic Route 13, also known as the William Bartram Trail, runs from Jacksonville to East Palatka along the east side of St. Johns River through tiny hamlets. U.S. 17 travels the west side of the river, passing through Green Cove Springs and Palatka. Route 40 runs east–west through the Ocala National Forest, giving a nonstop view of stately pines and bold wildlife.

Hotels

For the busy seasons—during summer in and around Jacksonville and during spring, summer, winter, and holiday weekends all over Florida—reserve well ahead for top properties. Jacksonville's beach hotels fill up quickly for PGA's The Players Championship in mid-May. Daytona Beach presents similar problems during the Daytona 500 (late February), Bike Week (late February–early March), spring break (March), and the Coke Zero 400 (early July).

St. Augustine stays busy all year. In late summer and fall rates are low and availability is high, but it's also hurricane season. Although northeast Florida hasn't been hit directly since 1964, it's possible for threatening storms to disrupt plans.

Restaurants

The ocean, St. Johns River, and numerous lakes and smaller rivers teem with fish, and so, naturally, seafood dominates local menus. Northeast Florida also has fine-dining restaurants, and its ethnic eateries include some excellent Middle Eastern places. And then there are the barbecue joints—more of them than you can shake a hickory chip at.

Hotel and restaurant reviews have been shortened. For full information, visit Fodors.com.

What It Costs

$	$$	$$$	$$$$
RESTAURANTS			
under $15	$15–$20	$21–$30	over $30
HOTELS			
under $200	$200–$300	$301–$400	over $400

Tours

TourTime, Inc.
BUS TOURS | This company offers custom group and individual motor-coach tours of Jacksonville, Amelia Island, Jekyll Island, and St. Augustine, as well as river cruises and trips to Silver Springs, Kennedy Space Center, Orlando, Okefenokee Swamp, and Savannah. Advance reservations are required. ☎ *904/282–8500* 🌐 *www.tourtimeinc.com.*

Jacksonville

399 miles north of Miami, on I–95.

Jacksonville is an underrated vacation spot. It offers appealing downtown riverside areas, handsome residential neighborhoods, a thriving arts scene, spectacular beaches, craft breweries, inventive eateries, and, for football fans, the NFL's Jaguars and the NCAA Gator Bowl.

Although the city is the largest in area in the continental United States (841 square miles), its Old South flavor remains, especially in the Riverside Avondale Historic District. Here moss-draped oak trees frame prairie-style bungalows and Tudor Revival mansions, and palm trees, Spanish bayonet, and azaleas populate the landscape.

GETTING HERE AND AROUND

The main airport for the region is Jacksonville International Airport. Free shuttles run from the terminal to all parking lots (except the garage) around the clock, and transportation service into the city is available from numerous companies in vehicles that range from taxis to vans to elegant limousines. Check beforehand on prices, which vary widely, and on which credit cards are accepted. The average cost per person from airport to downtown is $35 to $45; it's $45 to $55 for trips to the beaches. The larger companies usually operate 24/7. Both Uber and Lyft can serve passengers at the airport.

Connecting the north and south banks of the St. Johns River, the St. Johns River Taxi runs between several locations, including Southbank Riverwalk at Friendship Park, the Doubletree Hotel, Lexington Hotel, TIAA Bank Field/Metro Park, and the Jacksonville Landing. The one-way trip takes about five minutes. The water taxis run Sunday through Thursday, 11 to 9, and Friday and Saturday from 11 to 11 (except during rain or other bad weather), with special hours on game days and for special events. The fare is $10 (cash only) for one day. Special ticketed tours are available to the Zoo, the Arts Fair, and other spots.

Jacksonville Transportation Authority buses and shuttles serve the city and its beaches. The city also operates a small monorail system that links the convention center and a few downtown areas to several other stations across the river on the Southbank and San Marco. It is free and runs weekdays from 6 am to 9 pm and Saturday and Sunday during special events only. JTA also operates the Mayport Ferry, which transports cars and pedestrians across the mouth of the St. Johns River.

AIRPORT Jacksonville International Airport (*JAX*). ✉ *14201 Pecan Park Rd.* ☎ *904/741–4902* 🌐 *www.flyjacksonville.com.*

AIRPORT TRANSFERS Dana's Limousine & Transportation. ☎ *904/744–3333* 🌐 *www.danaslimo.com.*

FERRIES St. Johns River Taxi. ✉ *Friendship Park, 1015 Museum Cir., Downtown* ☎ *904/860–8294* 🌐 *www.jaxrivertaxi.com.*

PUBLIC TRANSPORTATION Jacksonville Transportation Authority (*JTA*). ☎ *904/630–3100* 🌐 *www.jtafla.com.*

TAXIS Checker Cab–Jacksonville. ☎ *904/999–9999.* **Coastal Cab.** ☎ *904/246–9999* 🌐 *www.coastalcab-jax.com.*

VISITOR INFORMATION

CONTACTS Visit Jacksonville. ☎ *800/733–2668* 🌐 *www.visitjacksonville.com.*

Sights

Jacksonville was settled along both sides of the twisting St. Johns River, and a number of attractions are on or near its banks. Both sides of the river, which is spanned by myriad bridges and crossed by water taxis and ferries, have downtown areas and waterfront complexes of shops, restaurants, craft breweries, parks, and museums.

You can reach some attractions by water taxi or Skyway Express monorail system—scenic alternatives to driving back and forth across the bridges. That said, a car is generally necessary.

In addition to the visitor information center at the airport, there are two downtown (one at the Jacksonville Landing marketplace and one at Hemming Plaza), and another in Jacksonville Beach at the Beaches Historical Museum (✉ *381 Beach Blvd.*) that is open Tuesday through Saturday 9–5:30 and Sunday and Monday, 11–4.

★ Cummer Museum of Art & Gardens
GARDEN | The Wark Collection of early-18th-century Meissen porcelain is just one reason to visit this former estate on the St. Johns River, which includes 13 permanent galleries with more than 5,500 items spanning more than 4,000 years, and 3 acres of riverfront gardens that form a showcase for northeast Florida's blooming seasons and indigenous fauna. Art Connections allows kids of all ages to experience art through hands-on, interactive exhibits. The Thomas H. Jacobsen Gallery of American Art focuses on works by American artists,

On the Ale Trail

Once known for its huge, commercial Anheuser-Busch brewery, Jacksonville has become North Florida's mecca for craft beer. Two dozen small-batch producers have opened in the past decade, including the first locally owned brewery downtown, **Bold City Brewery**—and the number is growing. The gritty warehouse area where it all began has been transformed, and more than 15 breweries now comprise what's known as the Jax Ale Trail. Some of the breweries offer tours, most offer food, and all offer a wide variety of inventive beers and ales, in tasting flights and full pints. Participating breweries include **Aardwolf Brewing Company**, **Hyperion Brewing Company**, **Intuition Ale Works**, and **Main & Sixth Brewing**; you can pick up passports for the trail at any location. If oceanside imbibing is more to your liking, the scene has expanded to the beaches. Try **Atlantic Beach Brewing Company**.

including Max Weber, N.C. Wyeth, and Paul Manship. Complimentary tour guide brochures at the front desk help visitors navigate the galleries, as do podcasts. ✉ *829 Riverside Ave., Riverside* ☎ *904/356–6857* 🌐 *www.cummermuseum.org* 🎫 *$10, free Tues. 4–9* ⏲ *Closed Mon.*

Fort Caroline National Memorial

ARCHAEOLOGICAL SITE | Spread over 130 acres along the St. Johns River 13 miles northeast of downtown Jacksonville (via Route 113), this site is part of the vast Timucuan Ecological and Historic Preserve, holding both historical and recreational interest. Exhibits explore first contact between the Timucua people and Europeans, and the waterways and shady paths offer hikes and pristine beaches. The original fort was built in the 1560s by French Huguenots, who held what may have been the original Thanksgiving on the site. They were later slaughtered by the Spanish in the first major clash between European powers for control of what would become the United States. An oak-wood pathway leads to a replica of the original fort—a great, sunny place to picnic (bring your own food and drink), stretch your legs, and explore a small museum. The fort itself isn't all that impressive, but the area does have a colorful history. There's a 1-mile self-guided nature trail and wayside exhibits between the Visitor Center and the fort. ✉ *12713 Fort Caroline Rd.* ☎ *904/641–7155* 🌐 *www.nps.gov/foca* 🎫 *Free.*

Jacksonville Landing

MARINA | During the week, this riverfront market caters to locals (who sometimes arrive by boat) and tourists alike, with specialty shops, full-service restaurants—including an Irish pub, a steak house, a Mexican eatery, and a couple of sports bars—all of which look out over the boat traffic on the St. Johns River. Water taxis shuttle across the river between the Landing and the Southbank. The Landing hosts many weekend events each year, ranging from the good clean fun of the Lighted Boat Parade and Christmas Tree Lighting to the more raucous Florida/Georgia game after-party, as well as live music (usually of the local cover-band variety) in the courtyard.

A rainbow lorikeet might pop by and say hello while you're touring the Jacksonville Zoo.

✉ 2 W. Independent Dr., Downtown ☎ 904/353–1188 🌐 www.jacksonvillelanding.com 🎫 Free.

★ Jacksonville Zoo and Gardens

ZOO | FAMILY | The highly regarded zoo offers visitors the chance to hop on a train and explore different countries through the animals that live there, from the Land of the Tiger, a 2½-acre Asian attraction featuring Sumatran and Malayan tigers, to the African Plains area, which houses elephants, white rhinos, and two highly endangered leopards, in addition to other species of African birds and mammals. The Range of the Jaguar takes visitors to a 4-acre Central and South American exhibit, with exotic big cats as well as 20 other species native to the region. Among the other highlights are rare waterfowl and the Reptile House in Wild Florida, which showcases some of the world's most venomous snakes. Wild Florida is a 2½-acre area with black bears, bald eagles, white-tailed deer, and other animals native to Florida, while RiverQuest reveals the ecology of the adjacent Trout River. Play Park contains a Splash Ground, a forest play area, two mazes, and a discovery building; Stingray Bay has a 17,000-gallon pool where visitors can pet and feed the mysterious creatures; and DinoTrek's life-size dinosaurs offer a glimpse into the past. The zoo opened a Manatee Critical Care Center in 2016. Parking is free. *✉ 370 Zoo Pkwy. ✣ Off Heckscher Dr. E ☎ 904/757–4463 🌐 www.jacksonvillezoo.org 🎫 $19.95.*

★ MOCA Jacksonville

MUSEUM | In this loftlike, five-story downtown building, the former headquarters of the Western Union Telegraph Company, a permanent collection of 20th-century art shares space with traveling exhibitions and a theater space. The museum, owned and managed by the University of North Florida, encompasses five galleries and ArtExplorium, a highly interactive educational exhibit for kids, as well as a funky gift shop and Nola MOCA, open for lunch on weekdays and for dinner on Thursdays. MOCA Jacksonville also hosts film series, theater performances, and workshops throughout the year, and packs a big art-wallop into a relatively small 14,000 square feet. A once-a-month Art Walk is free to all. ✉ *Hemming Plaza, 333 N. Laura St., Downtown* ☎ *904/366–6911* 🌐 *www.mocajacksonville.unf.edu* 🎟 *$8* ⏲ *Closed Mon.*

Museum of Science & History

MUSEUM | **FAMILY** | Known locally as MOSH, this museum is home to the Bryan-Gooding Planetarium. As a next-generation planetarium, it can project 3-D laser shows that accompany the ever-popular First Friday Cosmic Concerts. For those taking in the planetarium shows, the resolution is significantly sharper than that of the biggest HDTV on the market. Whether you're a kid taking in Sesame Street's *One World, One Sky*, or an adult star-gazing in the *Skies over Jacksonville* tour of the night sky, the experience is awesome. MOSH also has a wide variety of interactive exhibits and programs that include Health in Motion: Discover What Moves You; JEA PowerPlay: Understanding our Energy Choices, where you can energize the future city of MOSHtopia as you learn about alternative energy resources and the science of energy; the Florida Naturalist's Center, where you can interact with northeast Florida wildlife; and the Currents of Time, where you'll navigate 12,000 years of northeast Florida history, from the region's earliest Native American settlers to modern-day events. Nationally acclaimed traveling exhibits are featured along with signature exhibits on local history. ✉ *1025 Museum Circle* ☎ *904/396–6674* 🌐 *www.themosh.org* 🎟 *$15.*

The Biggest City?

It's nearly impossible to visit or read about Jacksonville without hearing that it's the largest city in the United States. In fact, the River City's 841 square miles pale in comparison to the actual title holder: 4,710-square-mile Sitka, Alaska. More accurately, Jacksonville is the largest city in the continental United States, and that's due to the consolidation of Duval County and the city.

Restaurants

bb's

$$$ | **AMERICAN** | Sleek yet cozy, this hip bistro is popular with all types. The concrete floors and a stainless-steel wine bar provide an interesting backdrop for comfort-food-inspired entrées, but they also create a dining room that is uncommonly loud, especially on weekends. **Known for:** signature grilled pizzas; extensive selection of desserts from b the bakery; nightly entrée specials. [$] *Average main: $24* ✉ *1019 Hendricks Ave., San Marco* ☎ *904/306–0100* 🌐 *www.bbsrestaurant.com* ⏲ *Closed Sun.*

★ **Biscottis**

$$$ | **AMERICAN** | The local artwork on the redbrick walls is a mild distraction from the crowds jockeying for tables here for brunch, lunch, and dinner. The wide-ranging and locally sourced menus offer many unexpected delights, including a three-onion campanelle pasta and a blue fin tuna poke bowl. **Known for:** weekend brunch served until 3; decadent desserts from the bakery; ever-changing nightly entrée specials. [$] *Average main: $26* ✉ *3556 St. Johns Ave.* ☎ *904/387–2060* 🌐 *www.biscottis.net.*

Bistro Aix

$$$ | **FRENCH** | Named after the French city (and pronounced simply "X"), this sophisticated bistro-bar's leather booths, 1940s brickwork, and intricate marbled globes provide a perfect home for well-prepared French food. Regulars can't get enough of the classic bistro menu items, including creamy onion soup and escargot, entrées such as duck cassoulet, along with a variety of wood-fired pizzas and delectable desserts. **Known for:** steak frites au poivre; smaller options for some menu items; attentive service. *Average main: $28 1440 San Marco Blvd., San Marco 904/398–1949 www.bistrox.com.*

Clark's Fish Camp

$$ | **SEAFOOD** | It's out of the way, but every mile will be forgotten once you step inside this former bait shop overlooking Julington Creek. Clark's has more than 160 appetizers and entrées, including the usual—shrimp, catfish, and oysters—and the unusual—ostrich, rattlesnake, and kangaroo. **Known for:** exotic meats; waterfront location; extensive taxidermy collection. *Average main: $20 12903 Hood Landing Rd., Mandarin 904/268–3474 www.clarksfishcamp.net.*

European Street Café

$ | **EUROPEAN** | Wicker baskets and lofty shelves brimming with European confections and groceries fill practically every inch of space not occupied by café tables. The menu is similarly overloaded, with nearly 100 deli sandwiches and salads, including raspberry-almond chicken salad and the Blue Max, with pastrami, corned beef, Swiss cheese, sauerkraut, hot mustard, and blue-cheese dressing. **Known for:** raspberry-almond chicken salad; wide selection of beers on tap and in bottles; outdoor seating. *Average main: $9 2753 Park St. 904/384–9999 www.europeanstreet.com.*

★ Hawkers Asian Street Fare

$ | **ASIAN FUSION** | Fans of Asian street food hit the jackpot here, as Hawkers replicates the small, varied, often spicy, dishes sold by street vendors in Asia, using recipes passed down for generations. Sharing bowls of noodles, steamed buns, small plates, soups, and more makes for a convivial atmosphere. **Known for:** roti canai with curry sauce; small plates; hip vibe. *Average main: $8 1001 Park St. 904/508–0342 www.eathawkers.com.*

★ Matthew's

$$$$ | **ECLECTIC** | No one can accuse chef Matthew Medure of resting on his laurels, of which there are many. Widely praised for culinary creativity and dazzling presentation at his signature San Marco restaurant, Medure's French- and Italian-inspired cuisine offers a wide range of choices, from caviar to sweets. **Known for:** create-your-own charcuterie platters; huge wine list; six-course Chef's Adventure Menu. *Average main: $32 2107 Hendricks Ave., San Marco 904/396–9922 www.matthewsrestaurant.com Closed Sun. No lunch.*

Taste of Thai

$$ | **THAI** | Ravenous regulars dominate the tightly packed tables at this warm family-owned restaurant in a nondescript strip mall. Since 1997 chef–owner Aurathai Sellas, who might just be the most cheerful person in the entire restaurant business, has prepared the exotic dishes of her homeland, including *pla lad prig* (hot and spicy fish), *goog thod* (crispy shrimp), and chicken in peanut sauce, as well as pad Thai. **Known for:** pla lad prig (whole hot and spicy fried fish); always a friendly welcome; great service. *Average main: $15 4317 University Blvd. S, San Jose 904/737–9009 www.tasteofthaijax.com Closed Sun.*

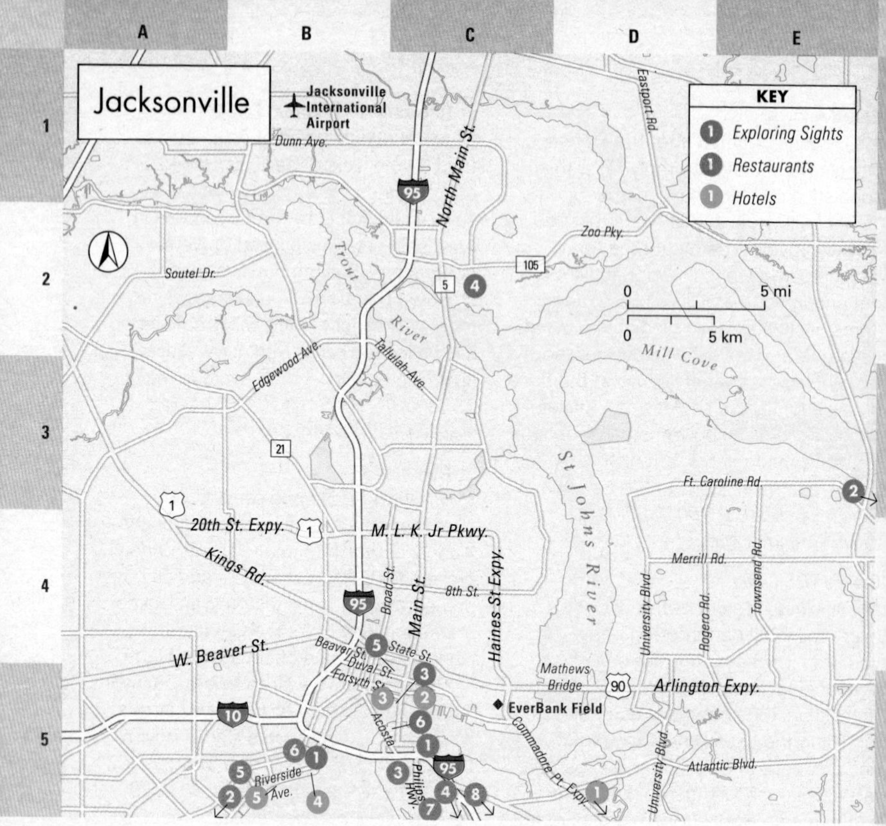

Sights

1 Cummer Museum of Art & Gardens **B5**

2 Fort Caroline National Memorial....... **E3**

3 Jacksonville Landing... **B5**

4 Jacksonville Zoo and Gardens.................. **C2**

5 MOCA Jacksonville **B4**

6 Museum of Science & History **C5**

Restaurants

1 bb's **C5**

2 Biscottis **B5**

3 Bistro Aix **C5**

4 Clark's Fish Camp........ **C5**

5 European Street Café .. **B5**

6 Hawkers Asian Street Fare............... **B5**

7 Matthew's **C5**

8 Taste of Thai............. **C5**

Hotels

1 Hotel Indigo Jacksonville–Deerwood Park **D5**

2 Hyatt Regency Jacksonville Riverfront.................. **C5**

3 Omni Jacksonville Hotel...................... **B5**

4 Riverdale Inn **B5**

5 St. Johns House **B5**

Hotels

Hotel Indigo Jacksonville-Deerwood Park

$ | **HOTEL** | Bright, bold, and visually different from any other Jacksonville property, this contemporary boutique hotel—albeit a chain—makes you feel more like you're staying in a hip apartment rather than a by-the-night lodging. **Pros:** free Wi-Fi throughout; all rooms have kitchenettes; pet-friendly. **Cons:** wood floors can be noisy; convenient to business parks but not downtown and its sights; lots of traffic at rush hour. *Rooms from: $140* *9840 Tapestry Park Cir., Southside* *904/996–7199, 877/846–3446* *www.hoteldeerwoodpark.com* *96 rooms* *No meals.*

Hyatt Regency Jacksonville Riverfront

$ | **HOTEL** | It doesn't get much more convenient than this 19-story, downtown, waterfront hotel within walking distance of Jacksonville Landing, TIAA Bank Field, Florida Theatre, Times-Union Center, MOCA, and all things downtown. **Pros:** rooftop pool and hot tub; free Wi-Fi; 24-hour gym and business center. **Cons:** not all rooms are riverfront; packed with meetings; huge, with a chain hotel feel. *Rooms from: $165* *225 E. Coastline Dr., Downtown* *904/588–1234* *www.jacksonville.regency.hyatt.com* *963 rooms* *No meals.*

Omni Jacksonville Hotel

$ | **HOTEL** | **FAMILY** | Jacksonville's most luxurious and glamorous downtown hotel offers across-the-street convenience to the big theatrical or musical shows at the Times-Union Center. **Pros:** excellent on-site restaurant; pet-friendly; kids receive special backpack, milk, and cookies. **Cons:** fee for Wi-Fi and parking; restaurant pricey; can be chaotic when there's a show across the street. *Rooms from: $180* *245 Water St.* *904/355–6664, 800/843–6664* *www.omnijacksonville.com* *354 rooms* *No meals.*

Riverdale Inn

$ | **B&B/INN** | In the early 1900s, Jacksonville's wealthiest residents built mansions along Riverside Avenue—dubbed the Row—and the three-story Riverdale Inn is one of only two such homes remaining. **Pros:** close to area restaurants and shops; private baths; charming, walkable neighborhood. **Cons:** small rooms; limited parking; strict cancellation policy. *Rooms from: $185* *1521 Riverside Ave., Riverside* *904/354–5080* *www.riverdaleinn.com* *11 rooms* *Breakfast.*

St. Johns House

$ | **B&B/INN** | You can enjoy the grace and elegance of the past and all the modern amenities at this surprisingly inexpensive B&B. **Pros:** historic home; beautiful Riverside location near parks, restaurants, and river; elegant antique furnishings. **Cons:** open only six months a year; no business center; strict cancellation policy. *Rooms from: $125* *1718 Osceola St., Riverside* *904/384–3724* *www.stjohnshouse.com* *Closed Mar. and June–Oct.* *2 rooms* *Breakfast.*

Nightlife

Comedy Zone

COMEDY CLUBS | The area's premier comedy club is inside the Ramada Inn Mandarin, offering full food and bar service, in addition to laughs. It's closed Mondays and has a varying cover charge based on the night's headliner. *Ramada Inn Mandarin, 3130 Hartley Rd.* *904/292–4242* *www.comedyzone.com.*

Jack Rabbits

MUSIC CLUBS | It's the place to catch the latest and greatest indie bands and budding rock stars, with a cover that varies by the headliner. *1528 Hendricks Ave.* *904/398–7496.*

Did You Know?

The Jacksonville Jazz Festival takes place in a five-block area centered on Laura Street in the heart of downtown. Highlights of the three-decade-old festival include performances by renowned jazz musicians, and jazz piano and youth jazz talent competitions.

Metro

BARS/PUBS | It's more than just a gay bar: it's like eight gay bars rolled into one, including a piano bar, dance club, lounge, and drag-show cabaret. ✉ *859 Willow Branch Ave., Riverside* ☎ *904/388–8719* 🌐 *www.metrojax.com.*

Murray Hill Theatre

MUSIC CLUBS | Fans of Christian music flock to this no-smoking, no-alcohol, drug-free club where national touring Christian artists perform. ✉ *932 Edgewood Ave. S, Westside* ☎ *904/388–3179* 🌐 *www.murrayhilltheatre.com.*

The Volstead

GATHERING PLACES | Named after the act that brought about Prohibition, this popular speakeasy-style bar in the heart of downtown has live music and swing dance lessons on Sunday nights. The elegant spot is known for its inventive cocktails, often made with local spirits and ingredients. ✉ *115 W. Adams St.* ☎ *904/414–3171* 🌐 *www.thevolsteadjax.com.*

Shopping

Five Points

SHOPPING NEIGHBORHOODS | This small shopping district less than a mile southwest of downtown has new and vintage-clothing boutiques, shoe stores, and antiques shops. It also has a growing collection of inventive and offbeat eateries and bars, not to mention some of the city's most colorful characters. ✉ *Intersection of Park, Margaret, and Lomax Sts., Riverside* 🌐 *www.5pointsjax.com.*

Riverside Arts Market

OUTDOOR/FLEA/GREEN MARKETS | The unique location—tucked under the soaring bridge that carries I-95 over the St. Johns River, a block from the Cummer Museum of Art & Gardens and a healthy walk along the RiverWalk from downtown—might be as much of a draw as the merchandise for this Saturday-only market. RAM attracts larger and larger crowds of singles, couples, families, and their dogs. They all come to shop for locally created art and crafts, sample food from vendors that include some excellent area restaurants, and check out street performers or the live music shows on the riverfront stage. Quality is high in every aspect—artists and vendors all go through a fairly rigorous application/audition process—and what there is to see or hear or eat varies from week to week. Sometimes there's also a farmers' market, with licensed farmers and growers selling everything from just-laid eggs and local honey to salad greens that were still in the earth the day before. Because it's sheltered by the bridge, RAM goes on rain or shine. Free parking is available at adjacent businesses, and a "bike valet" service encourages people to travel on two wheels. ✉ *715 Riverside Ave., Riverside* ☎ *904/389–2449* 🌐 *www.riversideartsmarket.com* 🎫 *Free.*

St. Johns Town Center

SHOPPING CENTERS/MALLS | Some of the shops at this huge outdoor "lifestyle center" aren't found anywhere else in northeast Florida, including Anthropologie, Apple, Lucky Brand Jeans, Lululemon, and Sephora, as well as a wide variety of dining choices, from fast-food to sit- down options such as the Cheesecake Factory, P.F. Chang's China Bistro, The Capital Grille, and Maggiano's Little Italy. ✉ *4663 River City Dr., Southside* ☎ *904/998–7156* 🌐 *www.simon.com/mall/st-johns-town-center.*

San Marco Square

SHOPPING CENTERS/MALLS | More than a dozen interesting apparel, home, and jewelry stores and upscale restaurants surround the open square in 1920s Mediterranean Revival–style buildings. ✉ *San Marco Blvd. at Atlantic Blvd., San Marco* 🌐 *mysanmarco.com.*

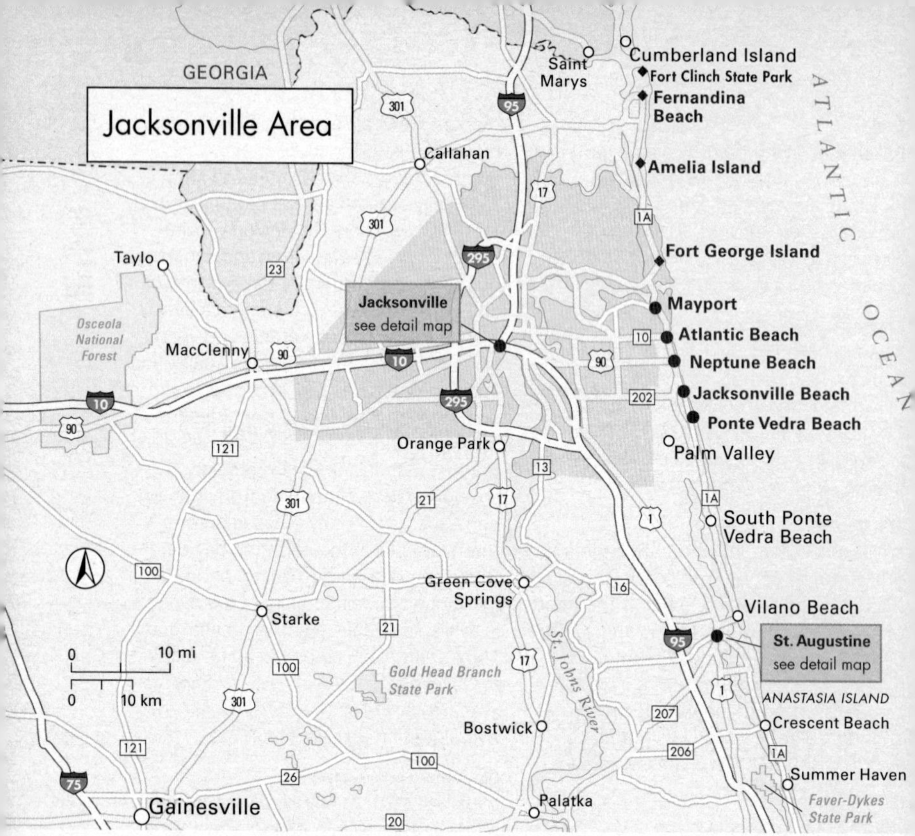

Jacksonville Area

GEORGIA
Cumberland Island
Saint Marys
Fort Clinch State Park
Fernandina Beach
Callahan
Amelia Island
Fort George Island
Taylo
Jacksonville
see detail map
Mayport
Atlantic Beach
Osceola National Forest
MacClenny
Neptune Beach
Jacksonville Beach
Ponte Vedra Beach
Palm Valley
Orange Park
South Ponte Vedra Beach
Green Cove Springs
Starke
Vilano Beach
St. Augustine
see detail map
Gold Head Branch State Park
St. Johns River
ANASTASIA ISLAND
Bostwick
Crescent Beach
Summer Haven
Gainesville
Palatka
Faver-Dykes State Park
ATLANTIC OCEAN
0 10 mi
0 10 km

The Shoppes of Avondale

SHOPPING CENTERS/MALLS | The highlights here include upscale clothing and accessories boutiques, art galleries, home-furnishings shops, a chocolatier, and trendy restaurants. ✉ *St. Johns Ave., Avondale* ✣ *Between Talbot Ave. and Dancy St.* 🌐 *www.shoppesofavondale.com.*

Activities

Jacksonville Jumbo Shrimp

BASEBALL/SOFTBALL | **FAMILY** | Formerly known as the Jacksonville Suns, this renamed AA minor-league affiliate of the Miami Marlins plays at the $34-million Baseball Grounds of Jacksonville. The city has a long history with baseball, as the site of the first Major League Spring Training in 1888, and forming its first professional team in 1904. Seeing the team play is a good way to have family fun at an affordable price. ✉ *Baseball Grounds of Jacksonville, 301 A. Philip Randolph Blvd., Downtown* ☎ *904/358–2846* 🌐 *www.jaxshrimp.com.*

TIAA Bank Field

FOOTBALL | The home of the NFL's Jacksonville Jaguars also kicks off each year with a New Year's Day bowl game, which usually features NCAA teams from the SEC and Big Ten conferences. Billed as the "World's Largest Outdoor Cocktail Party," the Florida versus Georgia Football Classic, or the "Florida–Georgia game," as it's better known, celebrates one of college football's most heated rivalries—between the Florida Gators and Georgia Bulldogs—every fall. ✉ *1 TIAA Bank Field Dr.* ☎ *904/633–6100* 🌐 *www.tiaabankfield.com.*

Atlantic Beach

20 miles east of Jacksonville, on U.S. 90 (Beach Blvd.).

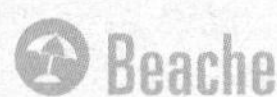

Beaches

Atlantic Beach

BEACH—SIGHT | If you're looking for sun-soaked relaxation, head for Atlantic Beach, where you can sink your feet into white, sugary sands or catch some waves in the warm surf. Beachgoers with canine companions are welcome at Atlantic Beach during the day and evening as long as the dog is leashed. Atlantic Beach and next-door Neptune Beach share the trendy Town Center, which has lots of tempting dining and shopping within a block of the beach. **Amenities:** food and drink; lifeguards (seasonal); showers; water sports. **Best for:** sunrise; surfing; swimming; walking. ✉ *Beach Ave., between 18th and 20th Sts.; Dewees Ave., between 1st and 16th Sts.; Ahern St. at Atlantic Blvd.* ☎ *904/247–5800* 🌐 *www.coab.us.*

Restaurants

The Fish Company Restaurant and Oyster Bar

$$ | **SEAFOOD** | If you want fresh fish, this is the place, and the owners, Bill and Ann Pinner, have lots of local street cred. And there are plenty of offerings for meat lovers in the family, too. **Known for:** oyster happy hour on Tues. and Weds.; fresh, local seafood; shrimp and grits. $ *Average main: $20* ✉ *725-12 Atlantic Blvd.* ☎ *904/246–0123* 🌐 *www.thefishcojax.com.*

★ Ocean 60

$$$ | **ECLECTIC** | Only a block from the Atlantic Ocean, this lively restaurant, wine bar, and martini room mixes fine dining and a laid-back, beachy atmosphere. The eclectic seasonal menu (which changes according to the fish available from the nearby Mayport docks) is quite sophisticated, including whole fried fish, pan-seared wild salmon, and locally caught shrimp. **Known for:** local, fresh-caught seafood; popular happy hour; live music on select weeknights. $ *Average main: $26* ✉ *60 Ocean Blvd.* ☎ *904/247–0060* 🌐 *www.ocean60.com* ⏲ *Closed Sun. No lunch.*

Ragtime Tavern Seafood & Grill

$$ | **CAJUN** | A New Orleans theme prevails at this lively venue, a longtime favorite with locals and visitors alike. The crowd ranges in age from 21 to midlife-crisis, and they come to sample the craft beer and eat the seafood-based fare, including Ragtime shrimp po'boy sandwiches, grilled fish, and shrimp and grits. **Known for:** shrimp po'boys; large craft beer selection; popular Sunday brunch. $ *Average main: $20* ✉ *207 Atlantic Blvd.* ☎ *904/241–7877* 🌐 *www.ragtimetavern.com.*

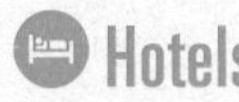

Hotels

One Ocean

$ | **RESORT** | Atlantic Beach's only high-rise oceanfront hotel captures the serenity of the sea through a color palette of translucent green, sand, and sky blue, and reflective materials such as glass and marble. **Pros:** exceptional service; walking distance to restaurants, shops, and the beach; all rooms have ocean view; 24-hour room service. **Cons:** tiny bathrooms; no self-parking on property; steep resort fee and separate parking fee. $ *Rooms from: $199* ✉ *1 Ocean Blvd.* ☎ *904/249–7402* 🌐 *www.oneocean-resort.com* *190 rooms* *No meals.*

Neptune Beach

1.7 miles south of Atlantic Beach.

Jacksonville Beaches

Perhaps because the Intracoastal Waterway isn't all that wide where it separates mainland Jacksonville from the beaches, people here aren't likely to think of themselves as "islanders." But they are, indeed, living on a barrier island, functioning with its own rhythms and led by its own elected officials. And, although there's only one island, there are four beach communities deemed "Jacksonville Beaches," each with its own mayor and city officials, tax base, and local legislation. They are, from north to south, Atlantic Beach, Neptune Beach, Jacksonville Beach, and Ponte Vedra Beach.

Beaches

Neptune Beach

BEACH—SIGHT | **FAMILY** | Between Atlantic and Jacksonville beaches, this is a great family spot. It's an excellent destination for those wishing to combine a day at the beach with other activities. Because Neptune and Atlantic beaches share Atlantic Avenue's Town Center, with its assortment of restaurants, galleries, stores, and boutiques, beachgoers can escape the sun when they're ready for great food, shopping, and live entertainment. **Amenities:** food and drink; lifeguards (seasonal); showers. **Best for:** sunrise; swimming; walking. ✉ *Strand St., between Atlantic Blvd. and Gaillardia Pl.; Oak St. at Rose Pl.; North St. at 20th Ave.* 🌐 *ci.neptune-beach.fl.us.*

Restaurants

Ellen's Kitchen

$ | **AMERICAN** | **FAMILY** | Ellen's kitchen has been an institution in the area for years, and probably will be for generations despite several moves, the most recent of which was from Jacksonville Beach to Neptune Beach. It's a great place to salve your hangover on a Sunday morning, but it also welcomes families thanks to the kid-friendly menu, very reasonable prices, and relaxed atmosphere. **Known for:** early-bird specials; friendly staff; grilled biscuits. *$ Average main: $9* ✉ *241 3rd St.* ☎ *904/372–4099* *No dinner.*

Hotels

★ Sea Horse Oceanfront Inn

$ | **HOTEL** | **FAMILY** | This coral-and-blue 1950s-era throwback caters to budget-minded guests seeking an ultracasual, laid-back oceanfront experience. **Pros:** beach access with private dune walk-over; popular bar on-site; free breakfast baskets at the front desk. **Cons:** no-frills decor; no room service; no elevator. *$ Rooms from: $199* ✉ *120 Atlantic Blvd.* ☎ *904/246–2175, 800/881–2330* 🌐 *www.jacksonvilleoceanfronthotel.com* *38 rooms* *Breakfast.*

Nightlife

Pete's Bar

BARS/PUBS | The oldest bar in the Jacksonville area (it's been around since 1933) is also notable for the cheapest drinks, cheapest pool tables, and most colorful clientele. It's also one of the only bars in the country where you can still smoke, so be warned. Serving locals and tourists for more than eight decades, Pete's has been written about by authors such as John Grisham and James W. Hall, probably because it's practically across the street from The BookMark, a great independent bookstore where writers love to give readings. ✉ *117 1st St.* ☎ *904/249–9158.*

Shopping

BookMark

BOOKS/STATIONERY | It may be small in size, but this book shop is big in prestige. Thanks to its knowledgeable owners, many famous authors love this place and always include it on their publicity tours. Once you've bought books here a time or two, the staff will be able to recommend ones you'll like with amazing accuracy. ✉ *220 1st St.* ☎ *904/241–9026* 🌐 *www.bookmarkbeach.com.*

Jacksonville Beach

2.2 miles south of Neptune Beach.

Sights

Adventure Landing and Shipwreck Island Water Park

AMUSEMENT PARK/WATER PARK | **FAMILY** | With go-karts, two miniature-golf courses, laser tag, batting cages, kiddie rides, and an arcade, Adventure Landing is more like an old-time boardwalk than a high-tech amusement park. But when the closest theme park is more than two hours away, you make do. The largest indoor/outdoor family-entertainment center in northeast Florida also encompasses Shipwreck Island Water Park, which features a lazy river for tubing, a 500,000-gallon wave pool, and four extreme slides—the Rage, HydroHalfpipe, Eye of the Storm, and Undertow. ✉ *1944 Beach Blvd.* ☎ *904/246–4386* 🌐 *www.adventurelanding.com* 🎟 *Adventure Landing free (fees for rides and games), Shipwreck Island $32.99.*

Beaches Museum & History Park

MUSEUM | **FAMILY** | This charming museum has exhibitions on the history of the beach communities, the St. Johns River, the fishing and shrimping industry, and the area's early settlers. Its gift shop is a good place to find Florida souvenirs of every variety, from tasteful histories of the local area to pure kitsch. Admission includes a guided tour of the adjacent historical park with its 1911 steam locomotive, railroad foreman's house, and the Mayport Depot. ✉ *381 Beach Blvd.* ☎ *904/241–5657* 🌐 *www.beachesmuseum.org* 🎟 *Free (donations accepted)* 🕓 *Closed Mon.*

Beaches

Jacksonville Beach

BEACH—SIGHT | Enjoy the waves at one of Jacksonville's busier beaches, which stretches along the coast for 4.1 miles. A boardwalk and a bevy of beachfront restaurants and shops are also draws, so expect moderate crowds during spring and summer school breaks. **Amenities:** food and drink; lifeguards (seasonal); parking (no fee); showers; toilets. **Best for:** partiers; sunrise; surfing; swimming. ✉ *1st St.* ✣ *Between Seagate and S. 16th Aves.* ☎ *904/247–6100* 🌐 *www.jacksonvillebeach.org.*

Restaurants

European Street Café

$ | **EUROPEAN** | This colorful, quirky, beer-hall inspired, family-owned eatery is part of a local chain and has a menu with an ambitious list of sandwiches, salads, and soups. There's also an overflowing gourmet-food section; a mind-boggling beer list; cookies big enough to knock someone unconscious; and a range of other generous desserts. **Known for:** generous sandwiches; extensive beer list; giant cookies. $ *Average main: $9* ✉ *992 Beach Blvd.* ☎ *904/249–3001* 🌐 *www.europeanstreet.com.*

Mojo Kitchen BBQ Pit & Blues Bar
$ | **BARBECUE** | True barbecue aficionados know that the country's really divided into four territories: North Carolina, Memphis, Kansas City, and Texas, each renowned for its own barbecue style. Owner Todd Lineberry did some serious research into each region before deciding his restaurants would honor all four traditions—along with some Deep South sides like cheese grits and fried green tomatoes as well as sweet tea and banana pudding. **Known for:** The Whole Hawg sampler with a bit of everything; homemade sides; burnt ends. *Average main: $14 1500 Beach Blvd. 904/247–6636 www.mojobbq.com.*

Hotels

Casa Marina Hotel
$ | **HOTEL** | Compared with nearby oceanfront hotels, it's small, and showing its age, but Casa Marina's rich history—it opened in 1925 and hosted Franklin Delano Roosevelt and Al Capone in its early days—make it a hit with those looking for a characterful retreat. **Pros:** oceanfront location; comfortable beds; quirky old hotel. **Cons:** no pool; noise from lounge; limited accessibility to upstairs bar. *Rooms from: $159 691 1st St. N 904/270–0025 www.casamarinahotel.com 23 rooms Breakfast.*

Nightlife

Lynch's Irish Pub
BARS/PUBS | Hoist a pint o' Guinness and enjoy live local music. This popular Irish eatery also offers traditional fare, along with pub grub. *514 N. 1st St. 904/249–5181 www.lynchsirishpub.com.*

Penthouse Lounge
BARS/PUBS | This oceanfront spot, perched atop the historic Casa Marina Hotel, offers beautiful views of the night sky or the moonrise over the ocean, in addition to a wide range of martinis and other cocktails. A full dinner is offered until 10 pm. *Casa Marina Hotel, 691 N. 1st St. 904/270–0025 www.casamarinahotel.com.*

Activities

Champion Cycling
BICYCLING | **FAMILY** | You can rent beach cruisers by the hour or the day—or get your high-end racing bike repaired—at this full-service bike shop. *1303 N. 3rd St. 904/241–0900 www.championcycling.net Bike rental: $10 an hour.*

Ponte Vedra Beach

3.9 miles south of Jacksonville Beach.

Beaches

Ponte Vedra Beach
BEACH—SIGHT | **FAMILY** | Public beach access for non–resort guests is minimal in most areas because of heavily restricted parking. But thanks to its free public parking, Mickler's Landing, south of most residences, is the most popular beach access point. It's also famous as a great place to find fossilized sharks' teeth. **Amenities:** lifeguards (seasonal); parking (no fee); showers; toilets. **Best for:** solitude; sunrise; walking. *Ponte Vedra Beach East of intersection of A1A S and Ponte Vedra Blvd.*

Restaurants

Aqua Grill
$$$ | **ECLECTIC** | Eclectic preparation of seafood is what Aqua Grill does best. The constantly changing menu might include Vidalia-crusted grouper, oysters Rockefeller, and locally caught snapper cooked as you like it. **Known for:** local snapper; lively bar scene that draws locals; lakefront dining. *Average main: $27 395 Front St. 904/285–3017 www.aquagrill.net.*

Hotels

★ The Lodge & Club

$$$ | **RESORT** | **FAMILY** | This Mediterranean revival oceanfront resort is luxury lodging at its best. **Pros:** access to facilities at Ponte Vedra Inn & Club; accommodating service; private beach. **Cons:** most recreation facilities off-site; auto gratuity charge added to bill nightly; remote location. *Rooms from: $399* ✉ *607 Ponte Vedra Blvd.* ☎ *904/273–9500, 866/330–9775* *www.pontevedra.com* *66 rooms* *No meals.*

★ Ponte Vedra Inn & Club

$$ | **RESORT** | **FAMILY** | Considered northeast Florida's premier resort for decades, this award-winning 1928 landmark continues to wow guests with its stellar service and large guest rooms housed in white-brick, red-tile-roof buildings lining the beach. **Pros:** accommodating, friendly staff; private beach; adults-only pool. **Cons:** charge for umbrellas and chaises on the beach; crowded pools at some times of year; remote location. *Rooms from: $299* ✉ *200 Ponte Vedra Blvd.* ☎ *904/285–1111, 800/234–7842* *www.pontevedra.com* *250 rooms, 33 suites* *No meals.*

Sawgrass Marriott Golf Resort & Spa

$$ | **RESORT** | **FAMILY** | Golf is at the heart of this luxurious resort, but there's no lack of opportunity for other recreation or for sheer indulgent relaxation, if that's what you're after. **Pros:** beautiful surroundings; readily available shuttle; efficient staff. **Cons:** beach requires a shuttle; steep resort fee; some rooms are noisy. *Rooms from: $239* ✉ *1000 PGA Tour Blvd.* ☎ *904/285–7777, 800/457–4653* *www.sawgrassmarriott.com* *514 rooms* *No meals.*

Activities

BIKING

Ponte Vedra Bikes

BICYCLING | This outfitter rents beach bikes by the hour, day or week, in addition to selling bike-related merchandise. ✉ *250 Solana Rd.* ☎ *904/373-0717.*

GOLF

Every May millions of golf fans watch golf's most elite competitors vie for the prestige of winning THE PLAYERS Championship. The event—considered by many to be the sport's "unofficial fifth major"—takes place each year at the Tournament Players Club (TPC) Sawgrass in Ponte Vedra Beach, 20 miles southeast of Jacksonville. Designed and built for major tournament golf, TPC has elevated seating areas that give more than 40,000 fans a great view of the action. And while you're in the area, be sure to visit the World Golf Hall of Fame a few miles down the road in St. Augustine.

Tournament Players Club Sawgrass

GOLF | There are two golf courses here: the Stadium Course (with its world-renowned Island Green), which hosts THE PLAYERS Championship each year, and the Pete Dye–designed Valley Course. In conjunction with the Sawgrass Marriott, TPC offers a wide variety of golf experiences. The Stadium Course underwent an extensive renovation in 2016, including resurfaced greens and some restructured holes. Though not as lauded as the Stadium Course, the Valley Course has hosted its share of major golf events, such as the Senior Players Championship and the NFL Golf Classic. Though challenging, it has wider fairways and more expansive greens than the Stadium Course, which was designed to test the world's best players. ✉ *110 Championship Way* ☎ *904/273–3235, 800/457–4653* *www.tpc.com/sawgrass* *Stadium Course $500; Dye's Valley Course $195* *Stadium Course: 18 holes, 7215 yards, par 72; Dye's Valley Course: 18 holes, 6864 yards, par 72.*

Mayport

20 miles northeast of downtown Jacksonville, on Rte. A1A/105.

Dating back more than 300 years, this fishing village has several excellent and very casual seafood restaurants and markets, and a commercial shrimping fleet. It's also home to one of the largest naval facilities in the country, Naval Station Mayport.

GETTING HERE AND AROUND

St. Johns River Ferry

The arrival of the *Jean Ribault* ferry in 1948 made everyday life here more convenient, as it connects the north and south ends of Florida State Road A1A, allowing easy access to and from the islands to the north of Jacksonville. Since then, the ferry, known locally as the Mayport Ferry, continues to delight passengers young and old as they embark on the 10-minute cruise across the river between Mayport and Fort George Island. The cost is $5 per motorcycle, $6 per car. Pedestrians enjoy the ride for just $1 each way. Check the web or call for departure times, but the ferry generally runs every half hour. ✉ *Ferry Landing, Hwy. A1A* ☎ *904/241–9969* 🌐 *stjohnsriverferry.com.*

Sights

★ Kathryn Abbey Hanna Park

BEACH—SIGHT | **FAMILY** | This 450-acre oceanfront city park and campground just north of Atlantic Beach is beloved by surfers, swimmers, campers, hikers, and especially bikers, who regularly hit the many off-road bike trails from novice right up to those named Grunt and Misery. You can rent canoes, kayaks, or paddleboats to go out on the 60-acre freshwater lake. Younger kids delight in the lakefront playground and a water park with fountains and squirting hoses. There are restrooms, picnic areas, and grills throughout, and from Memorial Day to Labor Day lifeguards supervise all water activities. Camping is available for tents and RVs, and there are cabins to rent. ✉ *500 Wonderwood Dr.* ☎ *904/249–4700* 🎫 *$5 per vehicle (cash only).*

Fort George Island

25 miles northeast of Jacksonville, on Rte. A1A/105.

One of the oldest inhabited areas of Florida, Fort George Island is lush with foliage, natural vegetation, and wildlife. A 4-mile nature and bike trail meanders across the island, revealing shell mounds dating as far back as 5,000 years.

Sights

Kingsley Plantation

ARCHAEOLOGICAL SITE | Built in 1792 by Zephaniah Kingsley, a landowner who produced Sea Island cotton, citrus, sugarcane, and corn with the aid of about 60 slaves, this is the oldest remaining cotton plantation in the state. The ruins of 23 tabby (a concretelike mixture of sand and crushed shells) slave houses, a barn, and the modest Kingsley home are open to the public via self-guided tours and reachable by bridge. ✉ *11676 Palmetto Ave.* ☎ *904/251–3537* 🌐 *www.nps.gov/timu* 🎫 *Free* 🕒 *Plantation house closed weekdays.*

Talbot Island State Parks

BEACH—SIGHT | These parks, including Big and Little Talbot islands, have 17 miles of gorgeous beaches, sand dunes, and golden marshes that hum with migratory birds and native waterfowl. Come to picnic, fish, swim, snorkel, or camp. Little Talbot Island, one of the few undeveloped barrier islands in Florida, has river otters, marsh rabbits, raccoons, alligators, and gopher tortoises. Canoe and kayak rentals are available, and the north area is considered the best surfing spot in northeast Florida. A 4-mile nature trail winds across Little Talbot, and there are several smaller trails on Big Talbot. ✉ *12157 Heckscher Dr.* ☎ *904/251–2320* 🌐 *www.floridastateparks.org/park/big-talbot-island* 🎫 *$5 per vehicle, up to 8 people.*

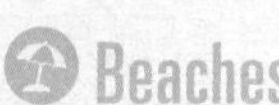

Beaches

Huguenot Memorial Park

BEACH—SIGHT | Though it's officially a Jacksonville city park, this popular spot on the northern side of the St. Johns River is often grouped with Amelia's beaches. Rough campsites are available. Among a handful of places where driving on the beach is permitted, it's unusual in that no special permit is required. Families with lots of beach equipment like the option of parking close to the water, but it takes vigilance to avoid soft sand and incoming tides. The ocean side offers good surfing, bodyboarding, and surf fishing. On the northwestern side is a shallow, sheltered lagoon that's a favorite with windsurfers, paddleboarders, and parents of small children. The southeastern side offers views of the aircraft carriers and destroyers at Mayport Naval Station. The park is also an important stop for migrating birds, so at certain times of the year, some areas are closed to vehicles. **Amenities:** lifeguards (seasonal); parking (no fee); showers; toilets. **Best for:** surfing; swimming; windsurfing. ✉ *10980 Heckscher Dr.* ☎ *904/251–3335* 🎫 *$3 per person, $4 per car.*

Amelia Island and Fernandina Beach

35 miles northeast of Jacksonville.

At the northeasternmost reach of Florida, Amelia Island has beautiful beaches with enormous sand dunes along its eastern flank, a state park with a Civil War fort, sophisticated restaurants, interesting shops, and accommodations that range from bed-and-breakfasts to luxury resorts. The town of Fernandina Beach is on the island's northern end; a century ago casinos and brothels thrived here, but those are gone. Today there's little reminder of the town's wild days, though one event comes close: the Isle of Eight Flags Shrimp Festival, held during the first weekend of May.

TOURS

Amelia River Cruises and Charters

BOAT TOURS | Narrated tours in shaded pontoon boats that explore the area's marshes, rivers, and wilderness beaches, from American Beach and Fernandina on Amelia Island to Cumberland Island in Georgia. ✉ *1 N. Front St., Fernandina Beach* ☎ *904/261–9972, 877/264–9972* 🌐 *www.ameliarivercruises.com* 🎫 *From $22.*

VISITOR INFORMATION

CONTACT Amelia Island Convention and Visitors Bureau. ☎ *904/277–0717* 🌐 *www.ameliaisland.com.*

Sights

Fernandina Historic District

HISTORIC SITE | This district in Fernandina Beach, which is home to Florida's oldest existing lighthouse, oldest bar, and oldest hotel, has more than 50 blocks of buildings listed on the National Register of Historic Places. Its 450 ornate structures built before 1927 offer some of the nation's finest examples of Queen Anne,

Word of Mouth

"On this particular day, the beach was strewn with starfish. They were everywhere. And they were still alive. I took a quick picture and then proceeded to run up and down the beach trying to save every one of them. I hope that I succeeded." —photo by funinthetub, Fodors.com member

Victorian, and Italianate homes. Many date from the haven's mid-19th-century glory days. Pick up a self-guided-tour map at the chamber of commerce, in the old train depot—once a stopping point on the first cross-state railroad—and take your time exploring the quaint shops, restaurants, and boutiques that populate the district, especially along Centre Street. ✉ *Fernandina Beach.*

★ Fort Clinch State Park

BEACH—SIGHT | FAMILY | One of the country's best-preserved and most complete 19th-century brick forts, Fort Clinch was built to discourage further British intrusion after the War of 1812 and was occupied in 1863 by the Confederacy; a year later it was retaken by the Union. During the Spanish-American War it was reactivated for a brief time, but no battles were ever fought on its grounds (which explains why it's so well preserved). Wander through restored buildings, including furnished barracks, a kitchen, and a repair shop. Living-history reenactments of Civil War garrison life are scheduled throughout the year. The 1,086-acre park surrounding the fort has full-facility camping, nature trails, carriage rides, a swimming beach, and surf and pier fishing. Nature buffs enjoy the variety of flora and fauna, especially since Fort Clinch is the only state park in northeast Florida designated by the Florida Fish and Wildlife Conservation Commission as a viewing destination for the eastern brown pelican, green sea turtle, and loggerhead sea turtle. ✉ *2601 Atlantic Ave., Fernandina Beach* ☎ *904/277–7274* 🌐 *www.floridastateparks.org/fortclinch* 🎟 *$6 per vehicle, up to 8 people; $4 motorcycles; $2.50 per person entry to fort.*

Beaches

There are a number of places on Amelia Island where driving on the beach is allowed in designated areas, Peters Point, Burney Park, and Amelia Island State Park. If you have a four-wheel-drive vehicle (and a lot of beach equipment to haul), you may want to try this. Be warned, though: it's easier to get stuck than you might think, and towing is expensive. You also need to watch the tides carefully if you don't want your car floating out to sea. And unless you're a county resident or disabled, you must buy a permit, which is available at the **Nassau County Historic Courthouse** (✉ *416 Centre St., Fernandina Beach* ☎ *904/491–6430*), **Flash Foods** (✉ *5518 S. Fletcher Ave., Fernandina Beach* ☎ *904/261–3113*), and several other locations. All city beaches have free admission.

Main Beach Park

BEACH—SIGHT | Of all Fernandina Beach beach access points, this is likely to be the most crowded—but also the most fun for kids and teens. Not only are there shaded playgrounds, sand volleyball courts, a beachfront playground, picnic tables, and a multipurpose court at the park itself, but there's old-school fun to be had at the adjacent skate park and vintage miniature-golf course, whose

A Banner Beach

Fernandina Beach is also known as the "Isle of Eight Flags," derived from the fact that it's the only American site to have been under eight different flags (French, Spanish, British, Patriots, Green Cross of Florida, Mexican Revolutionary, National Flag of the Confederacy, and United States). Every May the Isle of Eight Flags Shrimp Festival celebrates another of Fernandina's claims to fame: birthplace of the modern shrimping industry.

concession stand sells cold drinks, ice cream, and snow cones. A casual restaurant and bar are right on the beach. **Amenities:** food and drink; lifeguards (seasonal); parking (no fee); showers; toilets. **Best for:** swimming. ✉ *32 N. Fletcher Ave., Fernandina Beach* 🌐 *www.fbfl.us/298/Parks.*

Peters Point Beach

BEACH—SIGHT | At the south end of the island, this beach allows you free access to the same gorgeous sands used by vacationers at the Ritz-Carlton. It has a large parking area, a picnic area, barbecue grills, and three lifeguard towers. **Amenities:** lifeguards (seasonal); parking (no fee); showers; toilets. **Best for:** sunrise; surfing; swimming; walking. ✉ *1974 S. Fletcher Ave., Fernandina Beach* 🌐 *www.fbfl.us/298/Parks.*

Seaside Park Beach

BEACH—SIGHT | Like Main Beach to the north and Peters Point to the south, Seaside Park allows limited beach driving if you have a permit, but beware—vehicles here frequently get stuck and have to be towed. There are several pavilions with picnic tables and dune walkovers to the beach. It's a great place to fish or to ride bikes at low tide. Bikes and other beach equipment can be rented at Beach Rentals and More, right across from the park (*2021 S. Fletcher Ave.*). Also nearby, Sliders Seaside Grill is a venerable oceanfront restaurant where you can enjoy food and drinks inside or at the tiki bar overlooking the beach, often with live music. **Amenities:** food and drink; lifeguards (seasonal); parking (no fee); showers; toilets. **Best for:** surfing; swimming; walking. ✉ *Sadler Rd. at S. Fletcher Ave., Fernandina Beach* 🌐 *www.fbfl.us.*

★ Talbot Islands State Parks Beaches

BEACH—SIGHT | A few miles south of Fernandina Beach, the Talbot Islands State Parks system consists of seven parks, three of which have beach settings. All of the oceanfront parks have picnic areas and a small admission charge but free parking. **Little Talbot** is popular for swimming and beachcombing; however, swimming is restricted on parts of the beach because of swift currents. Sand dollars are often found at the far north end. **Big Talbot,** with its Boneyard Beach of wind-twisted trees, is not recommended for swimming but is a photographer's paradise. **Amelia Island State Park** is best known for letting you horseback ride on the beach as well as for the adjacent George Crady fishing pier. Kayak and canoe tours can be booked through the parks system's vendor, Kayak Amelia. **Amenities:** lifeguards (seasonal); parking (no fee); showers; toilets. **Best for:** solitude; sunrise; swimming; walking. ✉ *Rte. A1A, Fernandina Beach* ✣ *South of Fernandina Beach* 🌐 *www.floridastateparks.org* 🎫 *Little Talbot, $5 per vehicle; Big Talbot, $3 per vehicle for The Bluffs picnic area; Amelia Island, $2 per person.*

 Restaurants

Gilbert's Underground Kitchen

$$ | BARBECUE | FAMILY | Celebrity chef Kenny Gilbert opened this eclectic Fernandina Beach eatery after a stint on "Top Chef" brought him national fame. The menu is laden with authentic Old South recipes prepared with skill and flair and often with an individual twist. **Known for:** a wide variety of smoked meats; gator ribs; Brunswick stew. 💲 *Average main: $16* ✉ *510 S. 8th St., Fernandina Beach* ☎ *904/310–6374* 🌐 *www.undergroundkitchen.co* 🕒 *Closed Sun.*

★ Salt

$$$$ | ECLECTIC | The Ritz-Carlton's oceanfront restaurant serves inventive cuisine that utilizes seasonal ingredients. The signature dish is beef tenderloin served on a block of Himalayan salt. **Known for:** elegant oceanfront dining; beautifully prepared food; cooking classes. 💲 *Average main: $56* ✉ *The Ritz-Carlton, Amelia Island, 4750 Amelia Island Pkwy., Amelia Island* ☎ *904/277–1100* 🌐 *www.ritzcarlton.com.*

Sliders Seaside Grill

$$ | **SEAFOOD** | **FAMILY** | After the condo-building boom of the last decade or so, not many oceanfront restaurants remain in the area, but thankfully this is one of them. Indeed there aren't many places where you can enjoy an ocean view like this—a surf break offshore makes it a good place to watch surfers do their thing. **Known for:** moderately priced and family-friendly; fresh Florida seafood; live music year-round. *Average main: $18* ✉ *1998 S. Fletcher Ave., Fernandina Beach* ☎ *904/277–6652* 🌐 *www.slidersseaside.com.*

Verandah Restaurant

$$$$ | **SEAFOOD** | Although it's at the Omni Amelia Island Plantation Resort, this family-friendly restaurant is open to non–resort guests, many of whom drive in from Jacksonville. The dining room has a casual vibe, with plush, roomy booths and tables overlooking the tennis courts, but the menu is all business, with a focus on Southern and local food. **Known for:** she-crab soup in season; Mayport shrimp and clams; excellent service. *Average main: $39* ✉ *Omni Amelia Island Plantation, 142 Raquet Park Dr., Amelia Island* ☎ *904/277–5958* 🌐 *www.omnihotels.com* ⊙ *No lunch.*

Hotels

Amelia Hotel at the Beach

$ | **HOTEL** | **FAMILY** | Across the street from the beach, this midsize inn is not only convenient but an economical and family-friendly alternative to the area's luxury resorts and romantic and kid-unfriendly B&Bs. **Pros:** complimentary breakfast; free Wi-Fi; walk to the beach. **Cons:** small pool; not all rooms have balconies; no shade at the pool. *Rooms from: $125* ✉ *1997 S. Fletcher Ave., Fernandina Beach* ☎ *904/206–5200,* 🌐 *www.ameliahotel.com* *86 rooms* *Breakfast.*

Elizabeth Pointe Lodge

$$$ | **B&B/INN** | Guests at this beachfront inn, which resembles a Victorian-era beach cottage, can't say enough about the impeccable personal service, legendary breakfasts, and enjoyable evening social hour. **Pros:** hospitable staff; 24-hour desk attendant; free Wi-Fi. **Cons:** pricey for a B&B; not all rooms are oceanfront; must reserve well in advance in high season. *Rooms from: $309* ✉ *98 S. Fletcher Ave., Fernandina Beach* ☎ *904/277–4851,* 🌐 *www.elizabethpointelodge.com* *25 rooms* *Breakfast.*

Florida House Inn

$ | **B&B/INN** | This charming inn, which dates to the late 19th century, was once used by guests of the Vanderbilt, DuPont, and Carnegie families, who built "cottages" nearby on Cumberland and Jekyll islands. **Pros:** outstanding service; walk to Fernandina restaurants and shops; free Wi-Fi. **Cons:** Mermaid Bar can be noisy; rooms are small; not on the beach and no pool. *Rooms from: $198* ✉ *22 S. 3rd St., Fernandina Beach* ☎ *904/491–3322, 800/258–3301* 🌐 *www.floridahouseinn.com* *16 rooms* *Breakfast.*

★ **Omni Amelia Island Plantation Resort and the Villas of Amelia Island Plantation**

$$$$ | **RESORT** | **FAMILY** | This huge resort (1,350 acres) focuses on family-oriented accommodations and activities, including golf courses (54 holes, some oceanfront), 23 Har-Tru tennis courts, and expansive spa facilities. **Pros:** all rooms oceanfront with private outdoor space; extensive kids' programs; largest poolscape in northern Florida. **Cons:** some facilities require a golf cart or shuttle ride; $30 a day resort fee for Wi-Fi, parking, golf access and more; remote from town. *Rooms from: $409* ✉ *39 Beach Lagoon Rd., Amelia Island* ☎ *904/261–6161, 800/843–6664* 🌐 *www.omnihotels.com* *404 rooms, more than 300 villas* *No meals.*

Residence Inn Amelia Island

$$ | **HOTEL** | Travelers love this all-suites property for its great location, modern design features, and family-friendly amenities. **Pros:** complimentary island-wide shuttle; bike rental on property; pet-friendly (hefty fee, restrictions). **Cons:** no on-site restaurant or room service; historic district not within walking distance; not directly on the beach. *Rooms from: $260* *2301 Sadler Rd., Fernandina Beach* *904/277–2440* *www.residenceinnameliaisland.com* *133 suites* *Free Breakfast.*

★ The Ritz-Carlton, Amelia Island

$$$$ | **RESORT** | **FAMILY** | Guests know what to expect from the Ritz—elegance, superb comfort, excellent service—and the Amelia Island location is no exception. **Pros:** world-class spa; private beach access; great programs, activities, and amenities for kids, teens, and families. **Cons:** $33 daily resort fee; no self-parking ($20 per day valet); a drive to sights and other restaurants. *Rooms from: $519* *4750 Amelia Island Pkwy., Fernandina Beach* *904/277–1100* *www.ritz-carlton.com/ameliaisland* *496 rooms* *No meals.*

Nightlife

Falcon's Nest

BARS/PUBS | **FAMILY** | The 7,000-square-foot, aviation-themed club at the Omni Amelia Island Plantation is family-friendly, with games, sports on TV, drinks and food, in a tree-lined aerie with an outdoor deck. *Omni Amelia Island Plantation, 36 Amelia Village Circle, Amelia Island* *904/277–5166* *www.omnihotels.com/ameliaisland.*

Palace Saloon

BARS/PUBS | Florida's oldest continuously operating saloon entertained the Rockefellers and Carnegies at the turn of the 20th century but now caters to us common folk. When you enter the swinging doors and see the massive mahogany bar, tiled floors, and classic mural-adorned walls, you may feel as if you've gone back in time. The Palace also operates a package store, the only one in downtown Fernandina. *117 Centre St., Fernandina Beach* *844/441–2444* *www.thepalacesaloon.com.*

The Surf Restaurant & Bar

BARS/PUBS | Locals like to congregate on the outdoor deck here for drinks and good old-fashioned bar food (burgers, wings, nachos). The restaurant has an extensive menu, and the bar and deck offer live music throughout the week *3199 S. Fletcher Ave., Fernandina Beach* *904/261–5711* *www.thesurfonline.com.*

Shopping

Within the Fernandina Beach Historic District, a 50-block area on the National Register of Historic Places, are numerous shops, art galleries, and boutiques, many clustered along Centre Street, including the Palace Saloon, the oldest continuously operating drinking establishment (since 1903) in the state. An entirely separate Old Town, which is more than 200 years old, is considered the last town established under the 16th-century "Laws of the Indies" by the Spanish in the Americas. Old Town is located off North 14th Street.

Book Loft

BOOKS/STATIONERY | Popular for its readings and book signings, this old-fashioned, independent bookstore fits perfectly in an old-fashioned town. The owners say the upstairs loft, where used books are sold, even comes with a resident ghost named Catherine. The shop's staff are always ready to recommend a book, whether you're looking for local history or a quick summer read to enjoy by the pool. *214 Centre St., Fernandina Beach* *904/261–8991* *www.thebookloftamelia.com.*

Celtic Charm
CLOTHING | While the shop does offer a few quirky and slightly tacky items, its true charm is in the lovely clothing, jewelry, and ceramics from Ireland and Scotland. ✉ *310 Centre St., Fernandina Beach* ☎ *904/277–8009* 🌐 *www.ameliaisland.com/shopping/celtic-charm.*

Fantastic Fudge
FOOD/CANDY | **FAMILY** | Right there in the window, resting in splendor on several marble-topped tables, are huge blocks of fudge just calling your name—enough fudge to put every citizen of the town into a coma—not to mention ice cream (with house-made waffle cones), hand-dipped chocolates, caramel corn, and so on. Indeed, if you hang out at one of the tables in front of this confectionery/ice cream shop, you'll see just about every kind of person imaginable pause by the door, sigh, and give in to temptation. The service is fast and friendly, and the ice cream is excellent, too. ✉ *218 Centre St., Fernandina Beach* ☎ *904/277–4801* 🌐 *www.fantasticfudge.com.*

Gallery C
ART GALLERIES | Up a wildly painted staircase, this gallery owned by artist Carol Winner (the *C* in the gallery's name) displays and sells one-of-a-kind semiprecious jewelry and mixed-media creations, as well as paintings of local nature scenes. ✉ *218-B Ash St., Fernandina Beach* ☎ *904/583–4676* 🌐 *www.carolwinnerart.com.*

Island Art Association
ART GALLERIES | This cooperative gallery, run by volunteers, features the works of at least 50 local artists, working in a wide variety of media, including paint, wood, fiber, mixed media, photography, and glass. ✉ *18 N. 2nd St., Fernandina Beach* ☎ *904/261-7020* 🌐 *www.islandart.org.*

Lindy's Jewelry
JEWELRY/ACCESSORIES | For tasteful jewelry that reflects beach life, Lindy's is a good place to shop. Those who wish to commemorate their vacations in jewelry may be charmed by the fossilized shark teeth set into earrings and necklaces, along with beach-inspired jewelry from local smiths. ✉ *110 Centre St., Fernandina Beach* ☎ *904/277–4880* 🌐 *www.lindysjewelry.com.*

Slightly Off Centre Gallery & Gifts
ART GALLERIES | Just a block off the main drag, this store sells artistic ceramics as well as vivid photographs, paintings, pottery, and metalwork. ✉ *218-C Ash St., Fernandina Beach* ☎ *904/277–1147.*

Activities

Kayak Amelia
KAYAKING | **FAMILY** | This outfitter takes adventurous types on guided kayak tours of salt marshes and the Fort George River and also rents equipment for those looking to create their own adventures, whether on land or water. Reservations are required. There is also a Kayak Amelia shop on Centre Street, across from the Palace Saloon, in downtown Fernandina, but to rent a kayak or bike, you must contact the Talbot Island location. ✉ *13030 Heckscher Dr., Jacksonville* ☎ *904/251–0016* 🌐 *www.kayakamelia.com.*

Kelly Seahorse Ranch
HORSEBACK RIDING | At this family-owned ranch concession within the Amelia Island State Park, you can arrange horseback rides on the beach. It's closed on Monday. ✉ *Amelia Island State Park, 9500 1st Coast Hwy., Amelia Island* ☎ *904/491–5166* 🌐 *www.kellyranchinc.net* 💵 *$75 per person per hour for horse rental.*

St. Augustine

35 miles south of Jacksonville, on U.S. 1.

Along the banks of the shining Matanzas River lies St. Augustine, the nation's oldest city. It shows its age with charm,

Built to protect Spain's St. Augustine, the Castillo de San Marcos still stands along the shore.

its history revealed in the narrow cobblestone streets, the horse-drawn carriages festooned with flowers, and the coquina bastions of the Spanish fort that guard the bay like sentinels. Founded in 1565 by Spanish explorers, St. Augustine is the site of the fabled Fountain of Youth, but travelers find additional treasures in the Historic District, which was built in the Spanish Renaissance Revival style. Terra-cotta roofs and narrow balconies overhang a wonderful hodgepodge of shops and eateries that can be happily explored for weeks.

St. Augustine also has miles of beaches on Anastasia Island to the east. From the idyllic, unspoiled beaches of Anastasia State Park to the more boisterous St. Augustine Beach, travelers have a full range of options when it comes to enjoying an ocean outing.

VISITOR INFORMATION

Centrally located between the south and north ends of St. Augustine's Historic District, the St. Augustine & St. Johns County Visitor Information Center is a smart place to start your day. You can park in the multistoried garage here ($15 per vehicle per entry), as well as pick up maps, get information on and advice about attractions and restaurants, and hop aboard the sightseeing trolley.

CONTACTS St. Augustine, Ponte Vedra & the Beaches Visitors and Convention Bureau. ☎ *904/829–1711, 800/418–7529* 🌐 *www.floridashistoriccoast.com.* **St. Augustine & St. Johns County Visitor Information Center.** ✉ *10 W. Castillo Dr.* ☎ *904/825–1000.*

TOURS

Old Town Trolley Tour

GUIDED TOURS | These fully narrated tours cover more than 100 points of interest and are, perhaps, the best way to take in the Historic District. With parking at a premium and meters closely watched, it's nice to be able to park at one of the main stations (free) and get on and off at any of 23 stops throughout town. There are even shuttles to the beach. In the evening a macabre slant is added on the Ghosts and Gravestones Tour, which includes visits to the Old Jail and two cemeteries. ✉ *167 San Marco Ave.* ☎ *904/829–3800, 888/910–8687* 🌐 *www.trolleytours.com/staugustine* 🎫 *From $25.*

St. Augustine Gold Tours

DRIVING TOURS | This intimate tour, for a maximum of six people, takes you to all the historic downtown buildings, with expert, enthusiastic, and humorous narration. The 75-minute tour in an open-air electric vehicle is a crash course in the city's history and architecture. ✉ *6 Cordova St.* ✣ *Tour starts at driveway alongside Love Tree Cottage* ☎ *904/325–0574* 🌐 *staugustinegoldtours.com* 🎫 *$25.*

Sights

St. Augustine's neighborhoods are fairly compact. Most include a stretch of waterfront—whether ocean, river, or creek—which, along with Mediterranean architectural details like curves, archways, and red-tile roofs, gives the city its relaxed semitropical aura. Neighborhoods range from centuries old to mere decades, but all have sights worthy of attention.

It can be confusing to see references to the "Old City," "Old Town," and "Historic District." The Old City, like the Big Apple, refers not to a neighborhood but to the entire city of St. Augustine. Old Town is a small neighborhood, with the Plaza de la Constitución at its northern border, a row of shops and restaurants along King Street, many award-winning bed-and-breakfasts, and the Oldest House museum toward the south. Old Town is actually within a larger neighborhood, the Historic District, a 144-block area filled with many of the city's most popular attractions, including museums, parks, restaurants, nightspots, shops, and historic buildings.

St. Augustine's Uptown is filled with the shops, restaurants, and galleries along San Marco Boulevard, as well as museums, parks, and historic structures, all of which attract crowds. The narrow streets and hustle and bustle make for a vibrant atmosphere.

Heading east across the Bridge of Lions, you enter Anastasia Island, much of which is within city limits. In the 1920s real estate developer D. P. Davis had big plans for a Mediterranean-style development here, but the Florida land boom went bust. Today Davis Shores has a mélange of styles and a casual beach vibe.

★ Castillo de San Marcos National Monument

HISTORIC SITE | FAMILY | The focal point of St. Augustine, this massive and commanding structure was completed by the Spaniards in 1695 (English pirates were handy with a torch back then), and it looks every day of its three centuries. The fort was constructed of coquina, a soft limestone made of broken shells and coral that, unexpectedly, could absorb the impact of British cannonballs. (Unlike solid stone, the softer coquina wouldn't shatter when hit by large munitions.) The fort was also used as a prison during the Revolutionary and Civil wars.

Park rangers provide an introductory narration, after which you're on your own to explore the moat, turrets, and 16-foot-thick walls. Garrison rooms depict the life of the era, and special cannon-firing demonstrations are held several times a day Friday through Sunday year-round. Children 15 and under are admitted free and must be accompanied by an adult. Save the receipt, since admission is valid for seven consecutive days. ✉ *1 S. Castillo Dr.* ☎ *904/829–6506* 🌐 *www.nps.gov/casa* 🎫 *$15.*

Cathedral Basilica of St. Augustine

RELIGIOUS SITE | This cathedral has the country's oldest written parish records, dating from 1594. The circa-1797 structure underwent changes after a fire in 1887 as well as restoration work in the mid-1960s. If you're around for the

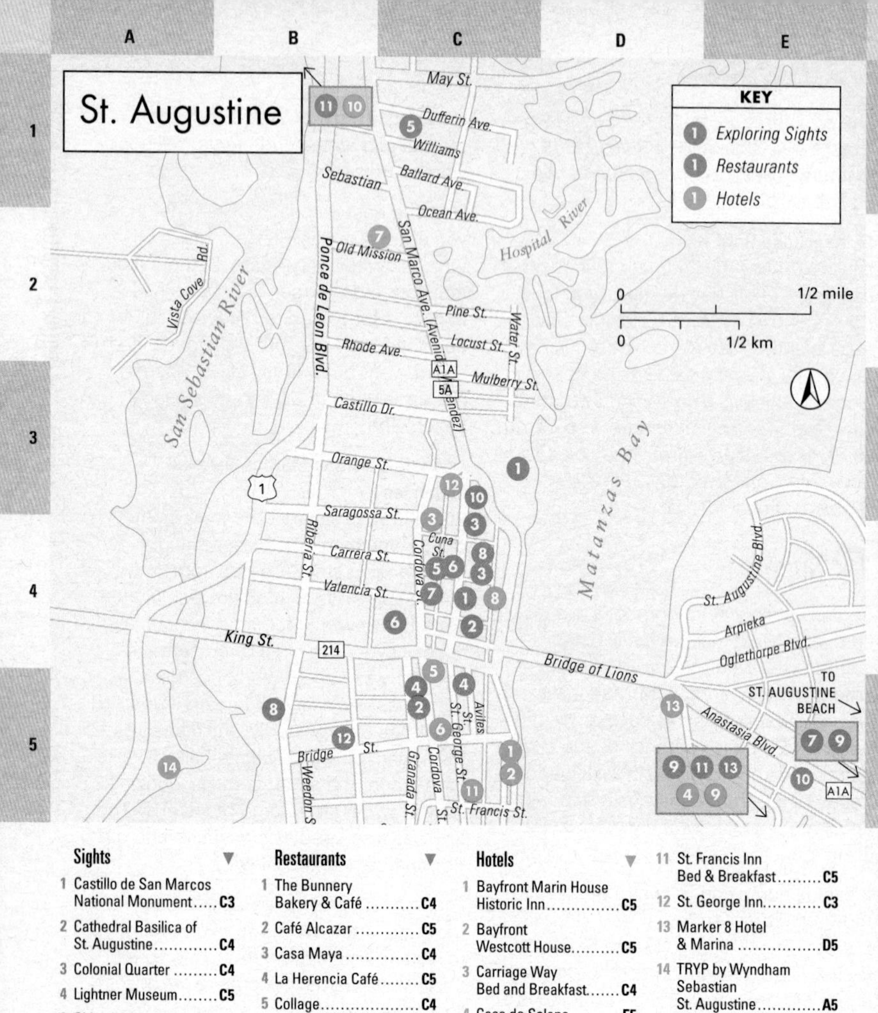

Sights

1 Castillo de San Marcos National Monument **C3**

2 Cathedral Basilica of St. Augustine **C4**

3 Colonial Quarter **C4**

4 Lightner Museum **C5**

5 Old Jail Museum **C1**

6 Ponce De Leon Hall, Flagler College **C4**

7 St. Augustine Alligator Farm Zoological Park.... **E5**

8 Saint Augustine Distillery **B5**

9 St. Augustine Lighthouse & Maritime Museum **E5**

10 St. Augustine Pirate & Treasure Museum **C3**

11 World Golf Hall of Fame **B1**

Restaurants

1 The Bunnery Bakery & Café **C4**

2 Café Alcazar **C5**

3 Casa Maya **C4**

4 La Herencia Café **C5**

5 Collage **C4**

6 Columbia.................. **C4**

7 The Floridian **C4**

8 Michael's Tasting Room............. **C4**

9 O.C. White's Seafood & Spirits........ **E5**

10 O'Steen's **E5**

11 Sunset Grille **E5**

12 Preserved **B5**

13 Terra & Acqua **E5**

Hotels

1 Bayfront Marin House Historic Inn............... **C5**

2 Bayfront Westcott House.......... **C5**

3 Carriage Way Bed and Breakfast....... **C4**

4 Casa de Solana **E5**

5 Casa Monica Resort & Spa **C5**

6 The Collector Luxury Inn & Gardens **C5**

7 DoubleTree by Hilton Historic District **C2**

8 Hilton St. Augustine Historic Bayfront......... **C4**

9 La Fiesta Ocean Inn & Suites................... **E5**

10 Renaissance Resort at World Golf Village ... **B1**

11 St. Francis Inn Bed & Breakfast......... **C5**

12 St. George Inn............ **C3**

13 Marker 8 Hotel & Marina **D5**

14 TRYP by Wyndham Sebastian St. Augustine............. **A5**

holidays, stop in for Christmas Eve's gorgeous Midnight Mass, conducted amid banks of flickering candles that reflect off gilded walls. Regular Sunday masses are held throughout the year at 7, 9, 11, and 5. ✉ *38 Cathedral Pl.* ☎ *904/824–2806* 🌐 *www.thefirstparish.org* 🎟 *Donations welcome.*

Colonial Quarter

MUSEUM VILLAGE | **FAMILY** | This 2-acre living-history museum gives visitors a vivid sense of life in 16th-, 17th-, and 18th-century St. Augustine. The De Mesa–Sanchez House dates from the 1740s and the other buildings—including a soldier's home, print shop, blacksmith's shop, and gunsmith—are replicas, mostly built on the original foundations. Costumed reenactors help make the history come alive. New additions to the complex include a 35-foot watchtower from which you have a panoramic view of the city. You can also dig for replica artifacts, create a leather medallion, take part in a musket drill, watch a 16th-century ship being built, and more. Tours start at 10:30, noon, 1:30, and 3. The complex also includes three restaurants: the Taberna del Caballo, St. Augustine Seafood Company and Bull & Crown. ✉ *33 St. George St.* ☎ *888/991–0933* 🌐 *colonialquarter.com* 🎟 *$12.99.*

Lightner Museum

MUSEUM | In his quest to turn Florida into an American Riviera, Henry Flagler built two fancy hotels in 1888: the Ponce de León, which became Flagler College, and the Alcazar, which closed during the Great Depression, was purchased by publisher Otto Lightner in 1946, and was donated to the city in 1948. It's now a museum with three floors of furnishings, costumes, Victorian art glass, not-to-be-missed ornate antique music boxes, and even an early 20th-century-era shrunken head from the Jivaro Indians of Ecuador. ✉ *75 King St.* ☎ *904/824–2874* 🌐 *www.lightnermuseum.org* 🎟 *$15.*

Old Jail Museum

MUSEUM | At this 19th-century prison, felons were detained and released or detained and hanged from the gallows in back. A knowledgeable "inmate" will guide you through the men's, women's, and maximum- security cells, relaying tales of executions and the less-than-appealing sanitary conditions of the jail in its heyday. After learning the history of local crime and punishment and seeing displays of weapons and other artifacts, you can browse the surfeit of souvenirs in Cracker Bob's Trading Post and the adjacent Old Store Museum. Note that the museum is at the starting point for the Old Town Trolley Tour. ✉ *167 San Marco Ave.* ☎ *904/829–3800* 🎟 *$10.*

Ponce de León Hall, Flagler College

BUILDING | Originally one of two posh hotels Henry Flagler built in the 1880s, this building—which is now part of a small liberal-arts college—is a riveting Spanish Renaissance Revival structure with towers, turrets, and stained glass by Louis Comfort Tiffany. The former Hotel Ponce de León is a National Historic Landmark, having hosted U.S. presidents Grover Cleveland, Theodore Roosevelt, and Warren Harding. Visitors can view the building free or take a guided tour offered daily through Flagler's Legacy Tours. ✉ *74 King St.* ☎ *904/829–6481, 904/823–3378 tour information* 🌐 *legacy.flagler.edu* 🎟 *Tours $12.*

St. Augustine Alligator Farm Zoological Park

ZOO | **FAMILY** | Founded in 1893, the Alligator Farm is one of Florida's oldest (and, at times, smelliest) zoological attractions and is credited with popularizing the alligator in the national consciousness and helping to fashion an image for the state. In addition to oddities like Maximo, a 15-foot, 1,250-pound saltwater crocodile, and a collection of rare albino alligators, the park is also home to Land of Crocodiles, the only place in the world to see all 26 species of living crocodilians.

Traversing the treetops in Crocodile Crossing is an inventive, ambitious, and expensive zip-line/rope course with more than 50 challenges and nine zip lines. In many places, a thin cable is all that keeps you from becoming croc cuisine. The shorter Sepik River course (three zip lines) is cheaper. Reptiles are the main attraction, but there's also a wading-bird rookery, an exotic-birds and mammals exhibit, a python cave, and nature trails. Educational presentations are held throughout the day, and kids love the wild-animal shows. ✉ *999 Anastasia Blvd.* ☎ *904/824–3337* 🌐 *www.alligatorfarm.com* 🎟 *$24.99; zip lines $37–$67.*

St. Augustine Distillery

WINERY/DISTILLERY | The first commercial block ice in Florida was made in this building over 100 years ago. Today the historic structure has been restored into a small-batch, craft distillery that makes whiskey, rum, gin, and vodka using ingredients sourced from local farms. A free tour orients visitors to the building's rich history, partnerships with local farms, and the spirit-making process. Visitors are asked to punch a time card to enter the working distillery; they are "paid" at the end with samples of cocktails such as the Florida Mule and New World gin and tonic. A gift shop sells an assortment of bar gadgets and accessories, along with bottles of the spirits. ✉ *112 Riberia St.* ☎ *904/825–4962* 🌐 *www.staugustinedistillery.com* 🎟 *Free.*

St. Augustine Lighthouse & Maritime Museum

HISTORIC SITE | It's unusual to find a lighthouse tucked into a residential neighborhood. This 1874 version replaced an earlier one built when the city was founded in 1565. Although its beacon no longer guides ships, it does draw thousands of visitors each year, in part because it has a reputation for being haunted. The visitor center has a museum featuring an exhibit called *Wrecked*, which displays artifacts from an 1872 British loyalist shipwreck discovered off the shores of St. Augustine. You can also see exhibits on the U.S. Coast Guard, historic boatbuilding, maritime archaeology, and the life of a lighthouse keeper—whose work involved far more than light housekeeping. You have to climb 219 steps to reach the peak, 140 feet up, but the wonderful view and fresh ocean breeze are well worth it. Children must be at least 44 inches tall to make the ascent. The museum also conducts evening Dark of the Moon Paranormal tours ($25) and Sunset-Moonrise tours ($30) that include a champagne toast and light hors d'oeuvres. ✉ *81 Lighthouse Ave.* ☎ *904/829–0745* 🌐 *www.staugustinelighthouse.org* 🎟 *$12.95.*

St. Augustine Pirate & Treasure Museum

MUSEUM | **FAMILY** | Inside this small museum established by entrepreneur and motivational speaker Pat Croce is a collection of more than 800 pirate artifacts, including one of only two Jolly Rogers (skull-and-crossbone flags) known to have actually flown above a ship. Exhibits include a mock-up of a tavern, a captain's quarters, and a ship's deck. You'll learn about the lives of everyday and famous pirates, their navigation techniques, their weaponry, and the concoctions they drank (including something called Kill Devil, which is rum mixed with gunpowder). You'll get to touch an actual treasure chest; see piles of gold, jade, emeralds, and pearls; and leave knowing full well that there were pirates before Captain Jack Sparrow. ✉ *12 S. Castillo Dr.* ☎ *877/467–5863, 904/819–1444* 🌐 *www.thepiratemuseum.com* 🎟 *$13.99.*

World Golf Hall of Fame

MUSEUM | This stunning tribute to the game of golf is the centerpiece of World Golf Village, an extraordinary complex that includes 36 holes of golf, a golf academy, several accommodations options, a convention center, spa, and a variety of restaurants, including Murray Bros. Caddyshack. The Hall of Fame features an adjacent IMAX theater and houses a variety of exhibits combining historical artifacts and personal memorabilia with the latest in interactive technology. Stand up to the pressures of the TV camera and crowd noise as you try to sink a final putt, take a swing on the museum's simulator, or snap a photo as you walk across a replica of St. Andrews's Swilcan Burn Bridge. The *Major Moments* exhibit on golf's four major men's championships allows you to place your name atop a star-studded leaderboard. Once you're sufficiently inspired, see how you fare on the 18-hole natural-grass putting course. Admission includes a chance to score a hole-in-one on the 132-yard Challenge Hole, which has an island green modeled after the famous 17th at TPC Sawgrass. If you do, you win a prize, such as admission to The Players Championship. ✉ *1 World Golf Pl.* ☎ *904/940–4123* 🌐 *www.worldgolfhalloffame.org* 🎟 *$20.95 (includes museum, round on 18-hole putting course, and shot at hole-in-one challenge); IMAX $8.50–$14.*

Beaches

Anastasia State Park Beach

BEACH—SIGHT | If you don't mind paying a bit for beach access, this park offers some outstanding choices. At one end of the beach, there's a playground and snack bar, where you can order sandwiches and cold drinks or rent a beach chair, umbrella, surfboard, or other beach paraphernalia. If you walk north along the beach, however, all traces of civilization seem to vanish. An offshore break makes the park a good surfing spot, there's a boat launch, and canoes and kayaks can be rented. The campgrounds are very popular, too. **Amenities:** food and drink; lifeguards (seasonal); parking (no fee); showers; toilets; water sports. **Best for:** solitude; surfing; swimming; walking. ✉ *1340-A Rte. A1A S* ☎ *904/461–2033* 🌐 *www.floridastateparks.org/park/anastasia* 🎟 *$8 per vehicle; $2 pedestrians.*

Butler Park Beach

BEACH—SIGHT | This quiet beach, located south of St. Augustine and north of Crescent Beach, once played a role in the civil rights movement of the 1960s. It attracted national attention for a "wade-in" that later led to Martin Luther King Jr. visiting St. Augustine. Today it is a county park that still provides access to the beachfront. **Amenities:** lifeguards (seasonal); parking (no fee); showers; toilets. **Best for:** swimming; walking. ✉ *Rte. A1A, south of St. Augustine Beach, 5860 A1A S.*

North Beach

BEACH—SIGHT | Just five minutes from St. Augustine, this site (aka Usina Beach) includes boat ramps, two campsites, and a picnic area with grills. If you'd rather opt for a restaurant than a picnic, you're in the right spot—a variety of eateries overlook the ocean or the Intracoastal Waterway. **Amenities:** lifeguards (seasonal); parking (no fee); showers; toilets. **Best for:** solitude; walking. ✉ *Rte. A1A, north of Vilano Beach.*

St. Augustine Beach

BEACH—SIGHT | Just south of Anastasia State Park, this beach has a livelier setting, thanks to the restaurants, bars, and shops along Beachfront Avenue and the 4-acre St. Johns County Ocean Pier Park. The park includes a playground, small splash park, sand volleyball courts, and a covered pavilion, where from May to September a series of Music by the Sea concerts are offered free. Speaking of free, the beach doesn't charge a fee, but the popular fishing pier does ($6). In addition, there are some areas designated for driving on the beach. **Amenities:** lifeguards (seasonal); parking (no fee); showers; toilets. **Best for:** swimming. ✉ *Old A1A/ Beach Blvd., south of Rte. 312.*

Vilano Beach

BEACH—SIGHT | This beach, just 2 miles north of St. Augustine, is sandwiched between the Tolomato River and the

Atlantic. In the 1920s it was home to the Grand Vilano Casino, but that was destroyed by a hurricane in 1937. Until recently Vilano Beach had deteriorated into a small, somewhat run-down area, though with a nice, laid-back '60s surf vibe. That's changed rapidly, however. Now it's home to new stores and restaurants, the Vilano Beach Fishing Pier, and other community improvements. A Hampton Inn & Suites is within a few minutes' walk. The beach has some nice breakers for surfing—skimboarding is also popular—but strong currents sometimes make it dangerous for swimming. It's also one of the few beaches on which you can still drive a car. **Amenities:** lifeguards (seasonal); showers; toilets. **Best for:** solitude; surfing; walking. ✉ *3400 Coastal Hwy., Vilano Beach.*

Restaurants

The Bunnery Bakery & Café
$ | **CAFÉ** | Hidden among the art galleries and trinket shops of St. George Street is this cozy little restaurant, which is very popular at breakfast and nearly as popular during lunch. There's nothing fancy—just high-back booths and a menu of pancakes, bacon, eggs, cinnamon buns, salads, and hot and cold sandwiches. **Known for:** all breads and buns made in-house; large selection of panini and grilled sandwiches; good omelets for breakfast. *$ Average main: $7* ✉ *121 St. George St.* ☎ *904/829–6166.*

Café Alcazar
$$ | **CAFÉ** | Housed in the magnificent Lightner Museum—formerly the luxurious Hotel Alcazar in its 1890s incarnation—this lovely little lunch spot sits where wealthy winter tourists once frolicked in the nation's largest indoor pool. Curried chicken salad, panini, and artichokes "Giovanni"—an addictive dish of baked artichokes with cheese and mushrooms on linguine—are among the many favorites here. **Known for:** elegant dining room; pastas; soups. *$ Average main: $15* ✉ *25 Granada St.* ☎ *904/825–9948* 🌐 *thealcazarcafe.com.*

Casa Maya
$$$ | **LATIN AMERICAN** | Everything is made from scratch here, from the sauces and marinades to the mixers for unique cocktails such as the cucumber jalapeño margarita. Daily specials might include pork and chicken tamales (prepared at home by chef-owner Karla Barrera), or fresh local cobia with tequila-marinated shrimp, mango corn salsa, and chipotle sauce. **Known for:** fresh seafood; Mayan soup with avocado and crispy tortillas; weekend breakfast. *$ Average main: $22* ✉ *22 Hypolita St.* ☎ *904/823–0787.*

★ Collage
$$$$ | **ECLECTIC** | Tucked away on Hypolita Street in the Historic District, the 48-seat restaurant highlights local seafood, which, depending on the success of the fishermen, will include several fish entrées each day. The ever-changing menu also often has steak, lamb, or veal selections, all served in an intimate setting that is a tad more upscale than most area restaurants. **Known for:** locally caught seafood and lobster ravioli; beef tenderloin with a variety of sauces; large, reasonably priced wine list. *$ Average main: $35* ✉ *60 Hypolita St.* ☎ *904/829–0055* 🌐 *www.collagestaug.com* ⏲ *No lunch.*

Le Herencia Cafe
$ | **CUBAN** | Cuban-style slow-roasted pork is the star at this übercasual café—and you can have it for breakfast, lunch, and dinner. Favorites include classic dishes like *ropa vieja*, empanadas, and a traditional Cuban sandwich that rivals any you'll find in Miami. **Known for:** all-day breakfast; Cuban sandwich; empanadas. *$ Average main: $13* ✉ *4 Aviles St.* ☎ *904/829–9487.*

Columbia
$$$ | **SPANISH** | Befitting its Cuban and Spanish cuisine, the historic restaurant

is decorated like an airy Spanish villa. You'll see many archival family photos; a white-stucco exterior; and an atrium dining room full of palm trees, hand-painted tiles, and decorative arches. **Known for:** paella Valenciana with seafood, chicken, and pork; tapas; 1905 salad with ham, cheese, tomatoes, and olives. *Average main: $28 ✉ 98 St. George St. ☎ 904/824–3341 🌐 www.columbiarestaurant.com.*

★ The Floridian

$$ | **MODERN AMERICAN** | **FAMILY** | Although vegetarians flock to this artsy and inspired eatery for the veggie-centric menu, there's plenty to tantalize omnivores as well. Delicious Southern food with flair ranges from braised pork belly biscuits to toast du jour, a rotating bruschetta inspired by the freshest produce from local farms. **Known for:** farm-to-table approach; vegetarian-friendly menu; entrée salads. *Average main: $20 ✉ 72 Spanish St. ☎ 904/829–0655 🌐 www.thefloridianstaug.com ⏲ Closed Tues.*

Michael's Tasting Room

$$$$ | **MEDITERRANEAN** | Mediterranean-style tapas are the specialty here, highlighted by dishes such as grilled oysters and goat cheese terrine layered with sun-dried tomatoes, olives, and pesto. Large plates include braised short ribs and the chef's daily fresh catch preparation. **Known for:** tapas; fresh seafood; large selection of Spanish wines. *Average main: $31 ✉ 25 Cuna St. ☎ 904/810–2400 🌐 www.tastetapas.com.*

O.C. White's Seafood & Spirits

$$$ | **SEAFOOD** | In the circa-1791 General Worth house across from the marina, this bustling little spot has a homey feel with a balanced clientele of locals, students, and visitors. Favorites include coconut shrimp, blue-crab cakes, and fresh local grouper. **Known for:** steamed shrimp; blue-crab cakes; shrimp and grits. *Average main: $27 ✉ 118 Ave. Menendez ☎ 904/824–0808 🌐 www.ocwhitesrestaurant.com.*

O'Steen's

$$ | **SEAFOOD** | Across the Bridge of Lions from downtown, this hole-in-the-wall restaurant is recognizable for the line of customers who wait patiently for fried shrimp (the specialty), seafood, and fried chicken. Needless to say it's been a popular local eatery for generations. **Known for:** fried shrimp with hush puppies; pies (particularly banana cream); cash only. *Average main: $16 ✉ 205 Anastasia Blvd. ☎ 904/829–6974 🌐 www.osteensrestaurant.com 💳 No credit cards ⏲ Closed Sun. and Mon.*

★ Preserved

$$$ | **SOUTHERN** | Local foodies rejoiced when James Beard–nominated chef Brian Whittington brought his eclectic Southern cuisine to a city thin on upscale dining. As you dig into fresh fish with crawfish étouffée or the Cheshire pork chop (many have declared it the best they've ever eaten), delight in the fact that this charmingly "preserved" Victorian home once belonged to Thomas Jefferson's great granddaughter, Maria Jefferson Shine. **Known for:** historic setting; pork chop; Sunday brunch. *Average main: $27 ✉ 102 Bridge St. ☎ 904/679–4940 🌐 preservedrestaurant.com ⏲ Closed Mon.*

Sunset Grille

$$ | **SEAFOOD** | They take their chowders seriously in St. Augustine, and many will tell you Sunset Grille's is the best—so good that it's poured over french fries as an appetizer. If you prefer a lighter version, a cup of the award-winning chowder works as a perfect prelude to the fresh fish dinners featuring Caribbean snapper and macadamia-crusted grouper. **Known for:** clam chowder (either creamy New England or tomato-based Minorcan); seared or blackened fresh fish; no-reservations policy. *Average main: $18 ✉ 421 A1A Beach Blvd., St. Augustine Beach ☎ 904/471–5555 🌐 www.sunsetgrillea1a.com.*

Terra & Acqua

$$ | **ITALIAN** | Homemade pasta, fresh seafood, and brick-oven pizzas are just some of the delights attracting locals and tourists alike to this casual Italian gem a few blocks from the beach. Giant chalkboards signal the fresh fish creations of the day, but it's tough to resist the pasta dishes such as papardelle *cinghiale* (handmade papardelle with wild boar, plum tomatoes, and fresh herbs). **Known for:** handmade pasta; freshly caught seafood; brick-oven pizza. *Average main: $20* *134 Sea Grove Main St., St. Augustine Beach* *904/429–9647* *www.terraacquarestaurant.com* *Closed Sun.*

Hotels

Bayfront Marin House Historic Inn

$$ | **B&B/INN** | **FAMILY** | This romantic waterfront inn has gorgeous antiques and contemporary conveniences, such as plush beds, double Jacuzzis, bay views, and flat-screen TVs. **Pros:** personal service; child- and pet-friendly; riverfront location. **Cons:** parking a block away; dining area small if weather forces breakfast indoors; some smallish rooms. *Rooms from: $239* *142 Ave. Menendez* *904/824–4301* *www.bayfrontmarinhouse.com* *15 rooms* *Breakfast.*

Bayfront Westcott House

$$ | **B&B/INN** | A bit more elegant and formal than the average B&B, this inn wows guests with a combination of English and American antiques and a wealth of complimentary food, from extravagant breakfasts to wine and canapés in the early evening. **Pros:** great views, most from private balconies; romantic rooms; free Wi-Fi. **Cons:** parking a short distance away; carriage house rooms not as elegant as main house; bathrooms tight for taller guests. *Rooms from: $210* *146 Ave. Menendez* *904/825–4602, 800/513–9814* *www.westcotthouse.com* *16 rooms* *Breakfast.*

Carriage Way Bed and Breakfast

$ | **B&B/INN** | When it comes to location, the Victorian-era Carriage Way has the best of both worlds; it's far enough from the Historic District to avoid tourist noise but close enough to have easy access to excellent restaurants (try the nearby Floridian) and shops. **Pros:** great location; personal attention; excellent breakfasts. **Cons:** some small rooms; street can get loud with traffic; limited time window for breakfast. *Rooms from: $179* *70 Cuna St.* *904/829–2467, 800/908–9832* *www.carriageway.com* *15 rooms* *Breakfast.*

Casa de Solana

$ | **B&B/INN** | There's a reason you feel like you're stepping back in time when you enter this 1820s-era inn made of coquina and handmade bricks: It's on the oldest street in the oldest European-settled city in the country. **Pros:** excellent service; delicious breakfast; convenient location. **Cons:** some small rooms; free parking is three blocks away; "forced" socialization. *Rooms from: $169* *21 Aviles St.* *904/824–3555* *www.casadesolana.com* *10 rooms* *Breakfast.*

★ **Casa Monica Resort & Spa**

$$ | **HOTEL** | Hand-stenciled Moorish columns and arches, handcrafted chandeliers, and gilded iron tables decorate the lobby of this late-1800s Flagler-era masterpiece. **Pros:** downtown location near attractions; luxurious spa; TVs in all rooms. **Cons:** busy lobby; expensive ($24) parking; small rooms. *Rooms from: $224* *95 Cordova St.* *904/827–1888, 800/648–1888* *www.casamonica.com* *138 rooms* *No meals.*

★ **The Collector Luxury Inn & Gardens**

$$ | **B&B/INN** | Few hotels in Florida reflect their city quite like The Collector: Consisting of nine buildings dating back to the late 1700s, this luxury, adults-only property occupies an entire city block in the Historic District, the product of a painstaking and imaginative restoration of some of

the city's most historic homes, which have been revived with modern luxuries. **Pros:** heated pool; kitchenettes in rooms; great location. **Cons:** no on-site restaurant; $30 amenity fee; valet parking only. *Rooms from: $229* *149 Cordova St.* *904/209–5800* *www.thecollectorinn.com* *30 rooms* *Free Breakfast.*

DoubleTree by Hilton Historic District
$ | **HOTEL** | Despite being one of the newer additions to the St. Augustine lodging scene, the DoubleTree blends seamlessly into the city's Old World Spanish ethos. **Pros:** free shuttle service to downtown; charming outdoor space with pool; comfortable beds. **Cons:** several-block walk to central tourist area; small lobby; $12 parking fee. *Rooms from: $159* *116 San Marco Ave.* *904/825–1923* *www.staugustinehistoricdistrict.doubletree.com* *97 rooms* *No meals.*

Hilton St. Augustine Historic Bayfront
$$ | **HOTEL** | **FAMILY** | In the heart of historic St. Augustine, this Spanish-colonial-inspired hotel overlooking Matanzas Bay has 19 separate buildings in a village setting, and most rooms have water or city-attraction views. **Pros:** good location for tourist sights; comfortable beds; great for families. **Cons:** expensive valet parking only ($25); late-night noise at street level; not all rooms have bay views. *Rooms from: $246* *32 Ave. Menendez* *904/829–2277, 800/445–8667* *www.hilton.com* *72 rooms* *No meals.*

La Fiesta Ocean Inn & Suites
$ | **HOTEL** | Chains have since taken over St. Augustine Beach, but this longtime favorite—the only remaining "Mom and Pop" on the beach—is still doing business (lots of it) and remains as beloved as ever. **Pros:** on the beach; breakfast delivered to rooms; refrigerators and microwaves in rooms. **Cons:** tiny lobby; resort fee; strict cancellation policy. *Rooms from: $140* *810 A1A Beach Blvd., St. Augustine Beach* *904/471–2220* *www.lafiestainn.com* *46 rooms* *Breakfast.*

Marker 8 Hotel & Marina
$ | **HOTEL** | The nautical theme at this boutique hotel is no gimmick, as the charming 26-room establishment also serves as a working marina. **Pros:** bay views; made-to-order breakfast; comfortable beds. **Cons:** small pool; tiny elevator; 10-minute walk over bridge to downtown. *Rooms from: $184* *1 Dolphin Dr.* *904/829–9042* *www.marker8hotel.com* *26 rooms* *Free Breakfast.*

★ Renaissance Resort at World Golf Village
$ | **RESORT** | If you want to be within walking distance of all World Golf Village has to offer, this resort is an excellent choice. **Pros:** excellent restaurant and bar; large bathrooms; free shuttle to golf courses, spa, and downtown St. Augustine. **Cons:** small pool; daily fee for Internet/phone; 25 minutes from downtown. *Rooms from: $140* *500 S. Legacy Trail* *904/940–8000, 888/740–7020* *www.worldgolfrenaissance.com* *301 rooms* *No meals.*

St. Francis Inn Bed & Breakfast
$$ | **B&B/INN** | This late-18th-century inn in the Historic District, a guesthouse since 1845, offers main-house rooms and suites, a room in the former carriage house, and a five-room cottage, all with a serene vibe and a delicious Southern breakfast buffet included. **Pros:** warm hospitality; lots of extras; short walk to Historic District attractions. **Cons:** small rooms; small pool; small bathrooms. *Rooms from: $204* *279 St. George St.* *904/824–6068, 800/824–6062* *www.stfrancisinn.com* *17 rooms* *Breakfast.*

St. George Inn
$$ | **B&B/INN** | You can't be any closer to the St. George Street bustle than this 25-room inn nestled in the City Gate Plaza. **Pros:** convenient downtown location; balconies have views; comfortable beds. **Cons:** some street noise; parking

two blocks away; shared balconies. *Rooms from: $209* *4 St. George St.* *904/827–5740, 888/827–5740* *www.stgeorge-inn.com* *25 rooms* *Breakfast.*

TRYP by Wyndham Sebastian St. Augustine
$ | **HOTEL** | It's easy to mistake this colorful hotel, about a mile from the Historic District, for an upscale condominium complex. **Pros:** large rooms; on-site café and bar; inviting public areas. **Cons:** outside the Historic District; few rooms have balconies; some noise in rooms facing main road. *Rooms from: $179* *333 S. Ponce de Leon Blvd.* *904/209–5580* *www.wyndhamhotels.com* *95 rooms* *No meals.*

Nightlife

A1A Aleworks
BREWPUBS/BEER GARDENS | The Aleworks always seems to be filled with students and visitors taste-driving the microbrews and other selections from the full bar. Seats on the second-story balcony provide a great view of the marina and bay across the street. It's a little like being on Bourbon Street—but clean. *1 King St.* *904/829–2977* *www.a1aaleworks.com.*

Odd Birds Bar
BARS/PUBS | You can catch live music under the stars here, or chill on a couch with a craft cocktail at the cozy upstairs bar. If you're lucky, you'll visit on a "Bartender Diplomacy Night" featuring a guest bartender from another city. For a late-night bite, the Venezuelan arepas hit the spot. *33 Charlotte St.* *904/679–4933* *www.oddbirdsbar.com.*

Prohibition Kitchen
MUSIC CLUBS | This Prohibition-era themed gastropub boasts the longest bar in the city and offers live music six nights a week. A late-night food menu is available until midnight on weekends. *119 St. George St.* *904/209–5704* *www.pkstaug.com.*

Scarlett O'Hara's
BARS/PUBS | It's a popular and convenient spot to stop for lunch or dinner (preferably enjoyed on the front porch); later in the evening it turns up the volume with blues, jazz, disco, Top 40, or karaoke. Whatever's playing, it's always packed. *70 Hypolita St.* *904/824–6535* *www.scarlettoharas.net.*

Tini Martini Bar
BARS/PUBS | The veranda overlooking Matanzas Bay at this Casablanca Inn bar is the perfect place to enjoy a cocktail, people-watch, and listen to live music. *Casablanca Inn, 24 Ave. Menendez* *904/829–0928* *www.tini-martini-bar.com.*

Tradewinds
MUSIC CLUBS | It's been showcasing bands—from country to rock and roll—since 1964. Thanks to the music, beer, and margaritas, you may feel as if you're in Key West. *124 Charlotte St.* *904/826–1590* *www.tradewindslounge.com.*

The World Famous Oasis Deck and Restaurant
BARS/PUBS | If you're staying on Anastasia Island, this is your best nightlife bet. It has more than 20 draft beer selections, beach access, and what many locals consider the best burgers in town. *4000 Rte. A1A S, at Ocean Trace Rd.* *904/471–3424* *www.worldfamousoasis.com.*

Shopping

One of the most pleasing pastimes in St. Augustine is a stroll along St. George Street, a pedestrian mall with shoulder-to-shoulder art galleries and one-of-a-kind shops selling candles, home accents, handmade jewelry, aromatherapy products, pottery, books, and clothing. There are also restaurants, clubs, and a veritable orchestra of street musicians.

Several blocks north of the Castillo and the popular St. George Street, a string of shops—galleries, antiques, a bookstore—line both sides of San Marco Avenue. Although this strip isn't as eclectic as it used to be, you'll still find some interesting independent stores.

MALLS

St. Augustine Outlets
SHOPPING CENTERS/MALLS | Several miles outside the city, Prime Outlets has almost 60 name-brand stores including Old Navy, Saks 5th Avenue's OFF 5TH, Cole Haan, and Michael Kors. ✉ *500 Outlet Mall Blvd.* ☎ *904/826–1311* 🌐 *www.staugoutlets.com.*

Uptown Shops
ANTIQUES/COLLECTIBLES | Locally owned boutiques, galleries, antique shops, and a cupcake bakery are among the attractions of this five-block shopping district just a few blocks north of downtown. ✉ *North San Marco Ave.*

St. Augustine Premium Outlets
OUTLET/DISCOUNT STORES | Just north of St. Augustine, off Interstate 95, is this collection of 85 designer and brand-name outlet stores. ✉ *2700 State Rd. 16* ☎ *904/825–1555* 🌐 *www.premiumoutlets.com.*

Activities

EcoTours
TOUR—SPORTS | Amid America's most enduring human history, EcoTours investigates St. Augustine's natural history. Scenic cruises, kayak tours, and catamaran excursions on Matanzas Bay offer a chance to see bottlenose dolphins, bird habitats, lakes, creeks, and saltwater marshes. Along the way are incredible photo ops of the city and the Castillo from the water. ✉ *111 Ave. Menendez* ☎ *904/377–7245* 🌐 *www.staugustineecotours.com.*

Florida Water Tours
BOATING | Watch the dolphins frolic and the osprey and pelicans feed from aboard the *Osprey*, a 45-foot pontoon boat. Tours include a dolphin and wildlife adventure, sunset cruise, and wine-tasting cruise. ✉ *107 Yacht Club Dr., Dock A-19* ☎ *904/827–7728* 🌐 *www.floridawatertour.com.*

Ripple Effect Ecotours
BOATING | Rent a kayak or take a boat or kayak tour at this outfitter south of St. Augustine. ✉ *Town of Marineland Marina, 101 Tolstoy La.* ☎ *904/347–1565* 🌐 *www.rippleeffectecotours.com.*

Schooner *Freedom*
TOUR—SPORTS | Cutting a sharp profile, this 76-foot replica of a 19th-century blockade-runner sails from the marina for excursions across Matanzas Bay. You can relax and savor the breeze, or you can help the crew prepare to set sail. There are two-hour day and sunset sails as well as a 75-minute moonlight tour. Precise times vary by season. Reservations are advised. ✉ *St. Augustine Municipal Marina, 111 Ave. Menendez, Slip 86* ☎ *904/810–1010* 🌐 *www.schoonerfreedom.com* 🎟 *From $40.*

Sea Love Charters
FISHING | Tackle and bait are included on this outfit's half- or full-day deep-sea fishing trips. ✉ *Cat's Paw Marina, 220 Nix Boat Yard Rd.* ☎ *904/824–3328* 🌐 *www.sealovefishing.com.*

Solano Cycle
BICYCLING | Here you can rent bicycles, scooters, and "scoot coups," which look like the offspring of a scooter and a bumper car and are $49 for the first hour (one-hour minimum) and $69 for two hours. ✉ *32 San Marco Ave.* ☎ *904/825–6766* 🌐 *www.solanocycle.com.*

St. Augustine Bike Rentals
BICYCLING | In addition to renting bicycles, scooters, and "scoot coups," you can catch a guided bicycle or Segway tour

here. ✉ *125A King St.* ☎ *904/547–2074* 🌐 *www.staugustinebikerentals.com* 🎟 *Rentals from $7; tours from $30.*

Surf Station

WATER SPORTS | Here you can rent surfboards, skimboards, and bodyboards. ✉ *1020 Anastasia Blvd.* ☎ *904/471–9463, 800/460–6394* 🌐 *www.surf-station.com.*

World Golf Village

GOLF | The World Golf Hall of Fame complex has two 18-hole layouts named for and partially designed by golf legends Sam Snead, Gene Sarazen, Arnold Palmer, and Jack Nicklaus. The King & Bear course, a collaboration of Palmer and Nicklaus, features a design that symbolizes the styles of both golfing legends, including holes that especially reward outstanding power of the tees. Palmer chose the par-4 15th as one of his "Dream 18" in a *Sports Illustrated* report. It's the most picturesque hole on the course, with a dramatic rock wall surrounding the green. Snead and Sarazen consulted with designer Bobby Weed in creating The Slammer & Squire course, which features generous fairways and lots of water hazards. Amenities for both courses include complimentary range balls and fresh chilled apples on the 1st and 10th tees. ✉ *1 World Golf Pl.* ☎ *904/940–6100 Slammer & Squire, 904/940–6200 King & Bear* 🌐 *www.worldgolfvillage.com* 🎟 *King & Bear, $129; Slammer & Squire, $109* 🏌 *King & Bear Course: 18 holes, 7279 yards, par 72; Slammer & Squire Course: 18 holes, 6939 yards, par 72.*

Daytona Beach

65 miles south of St. Augustine.

Best known for the Daytona 500, Daytona has been the center of automobile racing since cars were first raced along the beach here in 1902. February is the biggest month for race enthusiasts, and there are weekly events at the International Speedway. During race weeks, bike weeks, spring-break periods, and summer holidays, expect extremely heavy traffic. On the mainland, near the inland waterway, several blocks of Beach Street have been "streetscaped," and shops and restaurants open onto an inviting, broad, brick sidewalk.

GETTING HERE AND AROUND

Several airlines have regular service to Daytona Beach International Airport, which is next to Daytona International Speedway on International Speedway Boulevard, an east–west artery that stretches from Interstate 95 to the beaches. The average drive time from the airport to beachside hotels is 20 minutes; Yellow Cab–Daytona Beach makes the trip for $15–$36.

DOTS Transit Service has scheduled service ($36 one-way, $67 round-trip) connecting Daytona Beach, DeLand, Deltona, and the Orlando International Airport, which serves more airlines and has more direct flights but is about a 70-mile commute via Interstate 4 and State Road 417 (allow at least 90 minutes).

Daytona Beach has an excellent bus network, Votran, which serves the beach area, airport, shopping malls, and major arteries, including service to DeLand and New Smyrna Beach and the DeBary SunRail station, where passengers can connect to various Orlando area locales. Exact fare is required for Votran ($1.75) if using cash.

CONTACTS Daytona Beach International Airport (*DAB*). ✉ *700 Catalina Dr.* ☎ *386/248–8069* 🌐 *www.flydaytonafirst.com.* **DOTS Transit Service.** ☎ *386/257–5411, 800/231–1965* 🌐 *www.dots-daytonabeach.com.* **Votran.** ☎ *386/761–7700* 🌐 *www.votran.org.* **Yellow Cab–Daytona Beach.** ☎ *386/255–5555, 888/333–3356* 🌐 *www.daytonataxi.com.*

VISITOR INFORMATION

CONTACTS Daytona Beach Area Convention and Visitors Bureau. *800/544–0415* *www.daytonabeach.com.*

Sights

★ Blue Spring State Park

WILDLIFE-WATCHING | January and February are the top months for sighting sea cows at this designated manatee refuge, but they begin to head here in November, as soon as the water gets cold enough (below 68°F). Your best bet for spotting a manatee is to walk along the boardwalk. The park, which is 30 miles southwest of Daytona Beach on Interstate 4, was once a river port where paddle wheelers stopped to take on cargoes of oranges. Home to the largest spring on the St. Johns River, the park offers hiking, camping, picnicking facilities, and two-bedroom cabins (two-night minimum weekends and holidays). It also contains a historic homestead that's open to the public. *2100 W. French Ave., Orange City* *386/775–3663* *www.floridastateparks.org/bluespring* *$6 per vehicle, up to 8 people; $2 pedestrians, bicyclists.*

★ Daytona International Speedway

AUTO RACING | If the beach is the main attraction in town, this iconic sports venue—home to the Daytona 500—is a close second. The massive speedway, which opened in 1959, completed a $400-million renovation in 2015 that transformed the aging structure into a bona fide "motorsports stadium." Now it's part racetrack, part sports stadium, and it seats more than 100,000 fans. Major racing events include the IMSA Rolex 24 at Daytona in January, Daytona 500 in February, Daytona 200 motorcycle race in March, and Coke Zero 400 in July. The venue hosts a multitude of other events throughout the year, including the Daytona Turkey Run car show on Thanksgiving weekend, but racing is the focus. Those visiting on non-race days can enjoy one of the various tours. The three-hour VIP Tour (the most expensive option) includes having your photo taken in Victory Lane, a visit to the speedway's Archives and Research Center (home to Sir Malcolm Campbell's Bluebird III), and a close-up look at the most recent Daytona 500 winning car. *1801 W. International Speedway Blvd.* *800/748–7467* *www.daytonainternationalspeedway.com* *Guided tours $18–$55.*

Daytona Lagoon

AMUSEMENT PARK/WATER PARK | **FAMILY** | Parents looking for a nonsandy way to occupy the kids for a few hours or a whole day may find their salvation at this colorful complex that features go-kart racing, an 18-hole miniature golf course, a 3,000-square-foot laser tag arena, a 25-foot rock wall, a "Sky Maze" ropes course and zip line, a video arcade with 80 games, and a water park featuring slides galore and seven different water attractions. There's a bar for adults, and an eatery, Oasis Cafe. *601 Earl St.* *386/254–5020* *www.daytonalagoon.com* *$27.99.*

Halifax Historical Museum

MUSEUM | Memorabilia from the early days of beach automobile racing are on display here, as are historic photographs, Native American and Civil War artifacts, a postcard exhibit, and a video that details city history. There's a shop for gifts and antiques, too. Admission is by donation on Thursday and on Saturday, kids 12 and under are free. *252 S. Beach St.* *386/255–6976* *www.halifaxhistorical.org* *$7* *Closed Sun. and Mon.*

Museum of Arts & Sciences

MUSEUM | **FAMILY** | This behemoth museum has displays of Chinese art and an eye-popping complete skeleton of a giant ground sloth that's 130,000 years old. The museum also boasts a new Visible Storage Building, one of the most significant collections of Cuban art outside of

Cuba, a large Coca-Cola and Americana collection, a rare Napoleonic exhibit, and one of the more expansive collections of American art in the southeast. Kids love the Charles and Linda Williams Children's Museum, which features interactive science, engineering, and physics exhibits; a nature preserve with half a mile of boardwalks and nature trails; and a state-of-the-art planetarium with daily shows. Florida art dating back to the 18th century is featured in the Cici and Hyatt Brown Museum of Art, a freestanding, 26,000-square-foot Florida Cracker–style addition opened in 2015. Artists represented include John James Audubon, Thomas Hart Benton, and N.C. Wyeth. ✉ *352 S. Nova Rd.* ☎ *386/255–0285* 🌐 *www.moas.org* 🎫 *$12.95 for science museum; $10.95 for art museum; $18.95 combo ticket for both museums.*

Ponce de León Inlet Lighthouse and Museum

LIGHTHOUSE | At the southern tip of the barrier island that includes Daytona Beach is the sleepy town of Ponce Inlet, with a small marina, a few bars, and casual seafood restaurants. Boardwalks traverse delicate dunes and provide easy access to the beach, although storms have caused serious erosion. Marking this prime spot is the bright-red, century-old Ponce de León Inlet Light Station, a National Historic Monument and museum, the tallest lighthouse in the state and the third tallest in the country. Climb to the top of the 175-foot-tall lighthouse tower for a bird's-eye view of Ponce Inlet. ✉ *4931 S. Peninsula Dr., Ponce Inlet* ☎ *386/761–1821* 🌐 *www.ponceinlet.org* 🎫 *$6.95.*

Beaches

★ Daytona Beach

BEACH—SIGHT | At the World's Most Famous Beach you can drive right onto the sand (at least from one hour after sunrise to one hour before sunset), spread out a blanket, and have all your belongings at hand (with the exception of alcohol, which is prohibited). All that said, heavy traffic during summer and holidays makes it dangerous for children, and families should be extra careful or stay in the designated car-free zones. The speed limit is 10 mph, and there's a $20 fee, collected at the beach ramps.

The wide, 23-mile-long beach can get crowded in the "strip" area (between International Speedway Boulevard and Seabreeze Boulevard) with its food vendors, beachfront bars, volleyball matches, and motorized-water-sports enthusiasts. Those seeking a quieter experience can head either north or south toward car-free zones in more residential areas. The hard-packed sand that makes the beach suitable for driving is also perfect for running and cycling. There's also excellent surf fishing directly from the beach. **Amenities:** food and drink; lifeguards; parking (some with fee); showers; toilets; water sports. **Best for:** sunrise; surfing; swimming; walking. **■ TIP→ Signs on Route A1A indicate car access via beach ramps. Sand traps aren't limited to the golf course, though—cars can get stuck.** ✉ *Rte. A1A* 🌐 *www.daytonabeach.com.*

Restaurants

Aunt Catfish's on the River

$$$ | **SEAFOOD** | **FAMILY** | Don't be surprised if your server introduces herself as your cousin, though you've never seen her before in your life. The silly Southern hospitality is only one of the draws at this wildly popular restaurant specializing in mouthwatering plates of fresh seafood and other Southern favorites. **Known for:** Southern-style seafood; Sunday brunch; hot cinnamon rolls. $ *Average main: $23* ✉ *4009 Halifax Dr., Port Orange* ☎ *386/767–4768* 🌐 *www.auntcatfishontheriver.com.*

Daytona Brickyard

$$ | **AMERICAN** | It's not just the locals who swear that the Brickyard's charbroiled sirloin burgers are the best they've ever tasted—devotees have been known to drive from Georgia just for lunch. Given its name and location in the heart of NASCAR country, the popular bar and grill is covered in racing memorabilia. **Known for:** giant sirloin burgers; wings with various sauces; racing memorabilia decor. *Average main: $15* *747 International Speedway Blvd.* *386/253–2270* *www.brickyardlounge.com.*

Hyde Park Prime Steakhouse

$$$$ | **STEAKHOUSE** | This chophouse provides an upscale alternative to Daytona's more prevalent shorts-and-flip-flop joints. Steaks, especially the cuts named after race-car drivers, and mouthwatering sides (don't miss the potatoes Gruyère gratin) are the main attractions. **Known for:** wide selection of steaks; Gruyère gratin potatoes; happy hour on weekdays. *Average main: $40* *Hilton Daytona Beach Resort/Ocean Walk Village, 100 N. Atlantic Ave.* *386/226–9844* *www.hydeparkrestaurants.com* *No lunch.*

★ **Martini's Organic**

$$$ | **CONTEMPORARY** | The local beautiful people seem to flock to this trendy south Daytona eatery and lounge as much for the scene as for the food. The rotating menu emphasizes organic, locally sourced, seasonal ingredients, which owner–chef Clay Butters uses to create beef, seafood, and poultry dishes as appealing to the eye as the taste buds. **Known for:** fresh, organic ingredients; Bahamian lobster sauté; chic setting. *Average main: $28* *1815 S. Ridgewood Ave.* *386/763–1090* *www.martinisorganic.com.*

Tia Cori's Tacos

$ | **MEXICAN** | Mexican street food is the specialty at this tiny, counter-service eatery in the downtown riverfront shopping district. The namesake tacos come Mexican style (with onion, cilantro, and lime), but for 50¢ more you can get an Americanized version with cheese. **Known for:** authentic Mexican-style tacos; $5 margaritas; long lines. *Average main: $7* *214 N. Beach St.* *386/947–4333* *www.tiacoristacos.com* *Closed Sun.*

Zen Bistro

$ | **THAI** | Rich curries and spicy noodle dishes are the attractions at this family-owned Thai restaurant, which grew so popular that it vacated its 30-seat original location and moved a few blocks away. Start with the fresh rolls or mussels cooked in Thai basil, then sample the *pad see ew* (stir-fried noodles) or the red curry with shrimp. **Known for:** pumpkin curry; noodle dishes; fresh rolls. *Average main: $14* *223 Magnolia Ave.* *386/248–0453* *www.zenbistrodaytona.com* *Closed Sun.*

Hotels

Courtyard Daytona Beach Speedway/Airport

$ | **HOTEL** | For those visiting Daytona Beach for something other than surf and sand (a certain iconic racing facility comes to mind), this smartly located Marriott is the perfect base. **Pros:** proximity to speedway; welcoming indoor and outdoor public areas; dining on property. **Cons:** some noise from nearby airport; 15-minute drive to the beach; Bistro closes early. *Rooms from: $109* *1605 Richard Petty Blvd.* *386/255–3388* *www.marriott.com* *122 rooms* *No meals.*

Hard Rock Hotel Daytona Beach

$ | **RESORT** | Worth a visit for the rock-n-roll memorabilia alone, the Hard Rock Daytona Beach marries the traditional music-themed brand with the city's passions—auto racing, motorcycles, and the beach. **Pros:** on the beach; cool music memorabilia; live music daily. **Cons:** not all rooms have balconies; overpriced bar drinks; noise in rooms facing concert stage. $ *Rooms from: $129* ✉ *918 N. Atlantic Ave.* ☎ *844/745–1502* 🌐 *www.hardrockhoteldaytonabeach.com* 🛏 *200 rooms* 🍽 *No meals.*

Hilton Daytona Beach Resort/Ocean Walk Village

$ | RESORT | Perched on one of the few traffic-free strips of beach in Daytona, this high-rise is as popular with families as it is with couples. **Pros:** direct beach access; proximity to shops and restaurants; pool scene. **Cons:** inconvenient self-parking; resort fee; not all rooms have balconies. $ *Rooms from: $160* ✉ *100 N. Atlantic Ave.* ☎ *386/254–8200, 866/536–8477* 🌐 *www.daytonahilton.com* 🛏 *744 rooms* 🍽 *No meals.*

★ **The Shores Resort & Spa**

$ | RESORT | Rustic furniture and beds swathed in mosquito netting are a nod to Old Florida at this 11-story beachfront resort, but there's nothing rustic about the amenities, including a luxury four-poster bed, doorless Italian marble showers, and a 42-inch plasma TV in every room. **Pros:** beachfront; spa; 24-hour room service. **Cons:** expensive restaurant; overcrowding during special events; self-parking charge. $ *Rooms from: $199* ✉ *2637 S. Atlantic Ave., Daytona Beach Shores* ☎ *386/767–7350, 866/934–7467* 🌐 *www.shoresresort.com* 🛏 *212 rooms* 🍽 *No meals.*

Nightlife

Boot Hill Saloon

BARS/PUBS | Despite its reputation as a biker bar, this place welcomes nonbikers and even nonbiker tourists! ✉ *310 Main St.* ☎ *386/258–9506* 🌐 *www.boothillsaloon.com.*

Ocean Walk Village

BARS/PUBS | Lively and always hopping, Ocean Walk is a cluster of shops, restaurants, and bars (the Mai Tai Bar is a good bet) stretching along Atlantic Avenue and the ocean. ✉ *250 N. Atlantic Ave.* ☎ *386/258–9544* 🌐 *www.oceanwalkvillage.com.*

Tomoka Brewing Company

BREWPUBS/BEER GARDENS | Port Orange gastropub offers a rotating selection of seasonal beers to go along with its signature brews such as Hazy Sunrise Wheat Ale and Lunar Eclipse Stout. There's an eclectic food menu with highlights including pulled pork tacos and smoked wings with a variety of sauces. ✉ *4647 S. Clyde Morris Blvd* ☎ *386/256-4979* 🌐 *www.tomokabrewingco.com.*

The Oyster Pub

BARS/PUBS | Sports fans and oyster lovers congregate by the thousands here. ✉ *555 Seabreeze Blvd.* ☎ *386/255–6348* 🌐 *www.oysterpub.com.*

Shopping

Daytona Flea and Farmers' Market

OUTDOOR/FLEA/GREEN MARKETS | One of the largest flea markets in the South draws residents from all over the state as well as visitors to the state. It's open weekends, including Friday, from 9 to 5. ✉ *2987 Bellevue Ave.* ☎ *386/253–3330* 🌐 *www.daytonafleamarket.com.*

Destination Daytona

SHOPPING CENTERS/MALLS | This 100-acre biker enclave is complete with an expansive Harley-Davidson dealership; retail shops; a restaurant; bars; a tattoo parlor; a hotel; and a pavilion used for concerts, conventions—even biker-inspired weddings. ✉ *1635 N. U.S. 1, Ormond Beach* 🌐 *www.brucerossmeyer.com.*

One Daytona

FOOD/CANDY | A massive shopping, dining, and entertainment complex across the street from Daytona International Speedway, One Daytona is anchored by luxury Cobb Theaters mulitplex and Bass Pro Shops Outpost. The complex also includes Oklahoma Joe's Bar-B-Cue, Kilwin's Confections, Game Time, and two hotels. ✉ *1 Daytona Blvd.* 🌐 *www.onedaytona.com.*

TangerOutlets

OUTLET/DISCOUNT STORES | The 70-plus outlets here include Nike, Michael Kors, Polo Ralph Lauren, and Under Armour. ✉ *1100 Cornerstone Blvd.* ☎ *386/843–7459* 🌐 *www.tangeroutlet.com/daytona.*

Activities

Cracker Creek

BIRD WATCHING | At this eco-adventure park you can rent kayaks, canoes, and hydrobikes, or take ecotours on scenic Spruce Creek. There are also on-site picnic facilities. ✉ *1795 Taylor Rd., Port Orange* ☎ *386/304–0778* 🌐 *www.crackercreek.com.*

LPGA International

GOLF | This is where aspiring women professionals compete to earn a place on the LPGA Tour. The qualifying tournament—Q-school—is held every January, but the meticulously maintained courses are open to the public year-round. The Jones Course, designed by Rees Jones, is a links-style course with large, fast, undulating greens. Fairways are tighter on the Hills Course, designed by Arthur Hills, with long, difficult par-5s due to long carries and well-guarded greens. Wildlife is abundant, with bald eagles, owls, and deer as well as rattlesnakes and gators (some quite large). The course has driving, putting, and short-game practice areas, and an excellent restaurant, Malcolm's. ✉ *1000 Champions Dr.* ☎ *386/523–2001* 🌐 *www.lpgainternational.com* *$74* *Jones Course: 18 holes, 7088 yards, par 72; Hills Course: 18 holes, 6984 yards, par 72.*

Manatee Scenic Boat Tours

WILDLIFE-WATCHING | **FAMILY** | This Ponce Inlet operator takes you on narrated cruises of the Intracoastal Waterway. Kids will love looking for the creatures also known as sea cows, and your guide might tell you how (sun-delirious?) sailors may have mistaken them for mermaids. ✉ *4884 Front St., Ponce Inlet* ☎ *386/267–4972,* 🌐 *www.manateecruise.com* *$25.*

Maui Nix

WATER SPORTS | This is one of several outfitters that rent surfboards and bodyboards. ✉ *635 N. Atlantic Ave.* ☎ *386/253–1234* 🌐 *www.mauinix.com/store.*

Salty Dog Surf Shop

WATER SPORTS | You can rent surfboards or paddleboards here. ✉ *201 E. Granada Blvd., Ormond Beach* ☎ *386/673–5277* 🌐 *www.saltydogsurfshop.com.*

Sea Spirit Fishing

FISHING | Five- to nine-hour private and group charters are options with this operator. ✉ *SeaLove Marina, 4884 Front St., Ponce Inlet* ☎ *386/763–4388* 🌐 *www.seaspiritfishing.com.*

Tomoka State Park

BIRD WATCHING | With more than 160 species to see, this scenic park is perfect for bird-watching. It also has wooded campsites, bicycle and walking paths, and kayak and canoe rentals on the Tomoka and Halifax rivers. It's on the site of a Timucuan Indian settlement discovered in 1605 by Spanish explorer Alvaro Mexia. ✉ *2099 N. Beach St., Ormond Beach* ✣ *3 miles north of Ormond Beach* ☎ *386/676–4050* 🌐 *www.floridastateparks.org/tomoka* *$5 per vehicle, up to 8 people; $2 pedestrians.*

New Smyrna Beach

19 miles south of Daytona Beach, 56 miles northeast of Orlando.

The long, dune-lined beach of this small town abuts the Canaveral National Seashore. Behind the dunes sit beach houses, small motels, and an occasional high-rise (except at the extreme northern tip, where none is higher than seven stories). Canal Street, on the mainland, and Flagler Avenue, with many beach-side shops and restaurants, have both been "streetscaped" with wide brick sidewalks and stately palm trees. The town is also known for its internationally recognized artists' workshop and some of the best surfing on the East Coast.

Sights

Arts on Douglas

MUSEUM | In a warehouse that has been converted into a stunning 5,000-square-foot, high-ceiling art gallery, Arts on Douglas has a new exhibit of works by a Florida artist every month. Representing more than 50 Florida artists, the gallery holds an opening reception every first Saturday of the month from 4 to 7 pm. ✉ *123 Douglas St.* ☎ *386/428–1133* 🌐 *www.artsondouglas.net* 🎫 *Free* 🕑 *Closed Sun. and Mon.*

Atlantic Center for the Arts

MUSEUM | With exhibits that change every two months, the Atlantic Center for the Arts has works of internationally known artists. Mediums include sculpture, mixed materials, video, drawings, prints, and paintings. Intensive three-week residencies are periodically run by visual-, literary-, and performing-master artists. ✉ *1414 Art Center Ave.* ☎ *386/427–6975* 🌐 *www.atlanticcenterforthearts.org* 🎫 *Free* 🕑 *Closed Sun. and Mon.*

Canaveral National Seashore

NATIONAL/STATE PARK | Miles of grassy windswept dunes and a virtually empty beach await you at this remarkable 57,000-acre park on a barrier island with 24 miles of undeveloped coastline spanning from New Smyrna to Titusville. The unspoiled area of hilly sand dunes, grassy marshes, and seashell-sprinkled beaches is a large part of NASA's buffer zone and is home to more than 1,000 species of plants and 300 species of birds and other animals. Surf and lagoon fishing are available, and a hiking trail leads to the top of an American Indian shell midden at Turtle Mound. For an additional charge, visitors can take a pontoon-boat tour ($20) or participate in the turtle-watch interpretive program ($14). Reservations are required. A visitor center is on Route A1A at Apollo Beach. Weekends are busy, and parts of the park are closed when mandated by launch operations at the Kennedy Space Center, so call ahead. ✉ *Visitor Information Center, 7611 S. Atlantic Ave.* ☎ *386/428–3384* 🌐 *www.nps.gov/cana* 🎫 *$10 cars; $1 pedestrians, bicycles.*

Smyrna Dunes Park

NATIONAL/STATE PARK | In this park, on a barrier island at the northernmost tip of New Smyrna Beach peninsula, 1½ miles of boardwalks crisscross sand dunes and delicate dune vegetation to lead to beaches and a fishing jetty. Botanical signs identify the flora, and there are picnic tables and an information center. It's also one of the few county parks where pets are allowed (on leashes, that is). ✉ *2995 N. Peninsula Ave.* ☎ *386/424–2935* 🌐 *www.volusia.org/services/public-works/coastal-division/coastal-parks/smyrna-dunes-park.stml* 🎫 *$10 per vehicle, up to 8 people.*

Beaches

Apollo Beach

BEACH—SIGHT | In addition to typical beach activities, visitors to this beach on the northern end of Canaveral National Seashore can also ride horses here (with a permit), hike self-guided trails, and tour the historic Eldora Statehouse. From Interstate 95, take Exit 220 and head east. **Amenities:** lifeguards (seasonal); parking (fee); toilets. **Best for:** solitude; swimming; walking. ✉ *Rte. A1A, at the southern end of New Smyrna Beach* ☎ *386/428–3384* 🎫 *$10 per vehicle for national seashore.*

New Smyrna Beach

BEACH—SIGHT | This public beach extends 7 miles from the northernmost part of New Smyrna's barrier island south to the Canaveral National Seashore. It's mostly hard-packed white sand, and at low tide can be stunningly wide in some areas. The beach is lined with heaps of sandy dunes, but because they're endangered, it's against the law to walk on or play in them or to pick the sea grass, which helps to stabilize the dunes. From sunrise to sunset cars are allowed on certain sections of the beach (speed limit: 10 mph). In season there's a $20 beach-access fee for cars. **Amenities:** food and drink; lifeguards; parking (some with fee); showers; toilets; water sports. **Best for:** sunrise; surfing; swimming; walking. ✉ *Rte. A1A.*

Restaurants

CorkScrew Bar & Grille

$$ | **AMERICAN** | It's worth venturing inland from the beach to this popular spot in the Canal Street shopping district. The lively, beachy-casual dining room is decorated with tropical plants, exposed brick walls, and umbrellas (yes, umbrellas indoors). **Known for:** goat cheese bites; margaritas; crab cakes. [$] *Average main: $19* ✉ *235 Canal St.* ☎ *386/957–3955* 🌐 *www.corkscrewbarandgrille.com* 🕒 *Closed Mon.*

J.B.'s Fish Camp and Restaurant

$$ | **SEAFOOD** | Better known simply as J.B.'s, this local landmark is on the eastern shore of the Indian River (i.e., the middle of nowhere). Crowds gather around the picnic-style tables inside and out, or belly up to the bar to dine on mounds of spicy seafood, Cajun alligator, J.B.'s famous crab cakes, and rock shrimp by the dozen. **Known for:** spicy steamed rock shrimp; fresh fish and crabcake sandwiches; delicious hush puppies. [$] *Average main: $17* ✉ *859 Pompano Ave.* ☎ *386/427–5747* 🌐 *www.jbsfishcamp.com.*

Norwood's Restaurant & Wine Shop

$$$ | **SEAFOOD** | Fresh local fish and shrimp are the specialties at this bustling New Smyrna Beach landmark, open since 1946. Built as a gas station, the building later served as a general store and piggy-bank factory, but the remodeled interior belies this backstory; the place is replete with wood, from the chairs and booths to the walls and rafters. **Known for:** she-crab soup; vast wine selection; unique tree-house bar. [$] *Average main: $22* ✉ *400 2nd Ave.* ☎ *386/428–4621* 🌐 *www.norwoods.com.*

Hotels

★ **Black Dolphin Inn**

$$ | **B&B/INN** | On a quaint residential street, this Spanish-style, three-story inn combines the charm and hospitality of a B&B with modern sensibilities and a chic, coastal-casual vibe. **Pros:** hospitable staff; river views; comfy beds. **Cons:** no pool; must drive to the beach; occasional noise in lower-floor rooms. [$] *Rooms from: $239* ✉ *916 S. Riverside Dr.* ☎ *386/410–4868, 855/410–4868* 🌐 *www.blackdolphininn.com* *14 rooms* *Breakfast.*

Riverview Hotel and Spa

$ | **B&B/INN** | A landmark since 1885, this former bridge tender's home is set back from the Intracoastal Waterway at the edge of the north causeway, which still has an operating drawbridge. **Pros:** on-site spa and dining; hospitable staff; homey feel. **Cons:** small rooms in main house; strict cancellation policy; blocks from the beach. [$] *Rooms from: $178* ✉ *103 Flagler Ave.* ☎ *386/428–5858, 800/945–7416* 🌐 *www.riverviewhotel.com* *18 rooms* *Breakfast.*

Ocala National Forest

Eastern entrance 40 miles west of Daytona Beach, northern entrance 52 miles south of Jacksonville.

This breathtaking 383,000-acre national forest off Route 40 has lakes, springs, rivers, hiking trails, campgrounds, and historic sites. It also has the largest off-highway vehicle trail system in the southeast and three major recreational areas: Alexander Springs, Salt Springs, and Juniper Springs. To get here, take Interstate 4 east to Exit 92, and head west on Route 436 to U.S. 441, which you take north to Route 19 north.

Sights

Alexander Springs Recreation Area
BODY OF WATER | In this recreation area you'll find a stream for swimming, canoeing, and kayaking and a campground. ✉ *49525 Rte. 445 S, off Rte. 40, Altoona* 🌐 *www.fs.usda.gov/recarea/ocala* 🎫 *$5.50.*

Juniper Springs Recreation Area
BODY OF WATER | Here you'll find a stone waterwheel house, a campground, a natural-spring swimming pool, and hiking trails. The 7-mile Juniper Springs run is a narrow, twisting, and winding canoe ride, which, although exhilarating, isn't for the novice. ✉ *14100 Rte. 40 N, Silver Springs* 🌐 *www.fs.usda.gov/recarea/ocala* 🎫 *$5.50.*

Salt Springs Recreation Area
BODY OF WATER | The draw here is a natural saltwater spring where Atlantic blue crabs come to spawn each summer. ✉ *Visitor Center, 14100 Rte. 19, Fort McCoy* ☎ *352/685–3070* 🎫 *$6.*

Later, Gators

Depending on what time of year you visit, Gainesville's population could be plus or minus 50,000. Home to one of the largest colleges in the country, the University of Florida, Gainesville, takes on a different personality during the summer, when most students return home. During the fall and spring terms, the downtown streets are teeming with students on bikes, scooters, and foot, but in summer it's much more laid-back.

Activities

Juniper Springs Canoe Rentals
CANOEING/ROWING/SKULLING | This operator inside the national forest offers canoe rentals. ✉ *Juniper Springs Recreation Area, 26701 Florida 40, Silver Springs* ☎ *877/444–6777* 🎫 *$42 (includes shuttle transports at end of run); $47 tandem kayak.*

Gainesville

98 miles northwest of Daytona Beach.

The University of Florida (UF) anchors this sprawling town. Visitors are mostly Gator football fans and parents of students, so the styles and costs of accommodations are aimed at budget-minded travelers rather than luxury-seeking vacationers. The surrounding area encompasses several state parks and interesting gardens and geological sites.

GETTING HERE AND AROUND

Gainesville Regional Airport is served by American and Delta. From the airport, taxi fare to the center of Gainesville is about $20; some hotels provide free airport pickup.

CONTACT Gainesville Regional Airport (*GNV*). *3880 N.E. 39th Ave. 352/373–0249 www.gra-gnv.com.*

VISITOR INFORMATION

CONTACT Gainesville/Alachua County Visitors and Convention Bureau. *352/374–5260, 866/778–5002 www.visitgainesville.com.*

Sights

Devil's Millhopper Geological State Park

NATURE SITE | Scientists surmise that thousands of years ago an underground cavern collapsed and created this geological wonder that is designated as a National Natural Landmark. You pass a dozen small waterfalls as you head down 236 steps to the bottom of this botanical wonderland: exotic subtropical ferns and trees growing in a 500-foot-wide, 120-foot-deep sinkhole. You can pack a lunch to enjoy in one of the park's picnic areas. And bring Spot, too; just keep him on a leash. Guided walks with a park ranger are offered Saturday mornings at 10. *4732 Millhopper Rd., off U.S. 441 352/955–2008 www.floridastateparks.org/devilsmillhopper $4 per vehicle, up to 8 people; $2 pedestrians and bicyclists Closed Mon. and Tues.*

Florida Museum of Natural History

MUSEUM | **FAMILY** | On the campus of the University of Florida, the state's official museum of natural history, and the largest natural history museum in the Southeast, has holdings of more than 40 million specimens of amphibians, birds, butterflies, fish, mammals, mollusks, reptiles, vertebrate and invertebrate fossils, recent and fossil plants, and archaeology and anthropology artifacts. It also holds one of the world's largest collections of butterflies and moths. Permanent exhibits include information on Florida's geological and fossil history, its early native peoples, and biodiversity of flora and fauna. Visitors can enjoy live butterflies, witness a Calusa Indian welcoming ceremony, experience a life-size limestone cave, and see fossil skeletons of a mammoth and mastodon from the last ice age. The museum features changing temporary exhibits, and kids eight and under will love the interactive Discovery Room. Butterfly releases take place weekdays at 2, and weekends at 2, 3, and 4, weather permitting. *University of Florida Cultural Plaza, S.W. 34th St. at Hull Rd. 352/846–2000 www.flmnh.ufl.edu Free; Butterfly Rainforest $14; parking $4.*

Marjorie Kinnan Rawlings Historic State Park

HISTORIC SITE | **FAMILY** | One of America's most cherished authors found inspiration in this out-of-the-way hamlet about 20 miles outside of Gainesville. The 90-acre park, set amid aromatic citrus groves, has a playground for kids and short hiking trails, where you might see owls, deer, or Rawlings' beloved "red birds." But the main attraction is the restored Florida Cracker–style home, where Rawlings wrote classics such as *The Yearling* and *Cross Creek* and entertained the likes of poet Robert Frost, author Thornton Wilder, and actor Gregory Peck. Although the house is guarded closely by spirited roosters, guided tours are offered seasonally. *18700 S. County Rd. 325, Hawthorne 352/466–3672 www.floridastateparks.org/marjoriekinnanrawlings $3 per car; house tour (Thurs.–Sun.) is an additional $3 No house tours Aug. and Sept.*

Samuel P. Harn Museum of Art

MUSEUM | This 112,800-square-foot museum has five main collections: Asian, with works dating back to the Neolithic era; African, encompassing costumes, domestic wares, and personal adornments; Modern, featuring the works of Georgia O'Keeffe, William

Morris Hunt, Claude Monet, and George Bellows; Contemporary, with original pieces by Yayoi Kusama and El Anatsui; and Photography, including the work of Jerry N. Uelsmann, a retired University of Florida professor. *3259 Hull Rd. 352/392–9826 www.harn.ufl.edu Free; parking $4 weekdays before 3:30 pm Closed Mon.*

Restaurants

Civilization
$$ | **ECLECTIC** | *Eclectic* only begins to describe this wildly popular restaurant with the funny name, throwback policies (cash only), and inventive dishes representing all regions of the globe. The menu contains nods to any cuisine you might imagine—from Ethiopia to Greece to Thailand, and points in between. **Known for:** very vegetarian- and vegan-friendly; Sheba plate (Ethiopian sampler); weekend brunch. *Average main: $15 1511 N.W. 2nd St. 352/380–0544 welcometocivilization.com No credit cards.*

Emiliano's Café
$$ | **LATIN AMERICAN** | Linen tablecloths and art deco–style artwork create a casual, elegant feel at this Gainesville institution that has been serving Pan-Latin cuisine since 1984. Start with the Spanish stew (a family recipe) and then move on to one of the chef's signature dishes such as mofongo or paella (Spanish saffron rice with shrimp, clams, mussels, fresh fish, chicken, artichoke hearts, peas, asparagus, and pimientos). **Known for:** seafood and chicken paella; mofongo; weekend brunch. *Average main: $18 7 S.E. 1st Ave. 352/375–7381 www.emilianoscafe.com.*

★ Paramount Grill
$$$$ | **EUROPEAN** | This tiny, fine-dining restaurant may have single-handedly changed the perception of Gainesville from a college town fueled by pizza, chicken wings, and pitchers of beer to an up-and-coming culinary destination with imaginative menus driven by fresh Florida produce. The ever-changing menu might include such items as an organic beet salad, grilled salmon over sweet potato and Cotija cheese enchiladas, or pan-roasted Angus fillet over chive-mashed Yukon Golds. **Known for:** filet mignon; grilled duck breast; Sunday brunch. *Average main: $31 12 S.W. 1st Ave. 352/378–3398 www.paramountgrill.com.*

Hotels

Hilton University of Florida Conference Center Gainesville
$ | **HOTEL** | With 25,000 square feet of meeting space, the University of Florida's flagship hotel caters most obviously to business travelers, but its location on the southwest corner of campus also makes it a good choice for UF visitors. **Pros:** proximity to college; spacious rooms; free use of business center. **Cons:** spotty service; rates skyrocket on football weekends; charge for Wi-Fi. *Rooms from: $179 1714 S.W. 34th St. 352/371–3600 www.hilton.com 248 rooms No meals.*

Laurel Oak Inn
$ | **B&B/INN** | Guests at this 1885 Queen Anne–style dwelling say they're so comfortable and at ease they feel that they're in a home, not an inn. **Pros:** delicious breakfast; location; hospitable staff. **Cons:** processing fee for cancellations; no pool; two-night minimum on weekends. *Rooms from: $159 221 S.E. 7th St. 352/373–4535 www.laureloakinn.com 5 roms Free Breakfast.*

★ The Magnolia Plantation
$ | **B&B/INN** | Among only a handful of French Second Empire buildings in the southeastern United States, this inn consists of a main house, built in 1885, and nine adorable cottages. **Pros:** friendly service; breakfast; nightly social hour. **Cons:** some small rooms; seven-day

cancellation policy; cottages may require minimum stays. *Rooms from: $189* *309 S.E. 7th St.* *352/375–6653, 800/201–2379* *www.magnoliabnb.com* *9 cottages* *Breakfast.*

Sweetwater Branch Inn Bed & Breakfast
$ | **B&B/INN** | Modern conveniences such as hair dryers, complimentary Wi-Fi, a new pool, and business services mix with Southern charm and hospitality, all wrapped up in two grand Victorian homes surrounded by lush tropical gardens. **Pros:** Southern-style breakfast; Jacuzzi suites; walking distance to town. **Cons:** occasional noise issues; frequent on-site weddings; strict cancellation policy. *Rooms from: $144* *625 E. University Ave.* *352/373–6760, 800/595–7760* *www.sweetwaterinn.com* *20 rooms* *Free Breakfast.*

Activities

Ben Hill Griffin Stadium
FOOTBALL | The University of Florida Gators play their home games in the largest stadium in the state, also referred to as The Swamp. *Lemerand Dr., at Stadium Rd.* *352/375–4683.*

Gainesville Raceway
AUTO RACING | The site of professional and amateur auto and motorcycle races, including Gatornationals in March, is also home to Frank Hawley's Drag Racing School (*frankhawley.com*). *11211 N. County Rd. 225* *352/377–0046 Raceway, 866/480–7223 Drag Racing School* *www.gainesvilleraceway.com.*

Titusville

34 miles south of New Smyrna Beach, 67 miles east of Orlando.

It's unusual that such a small, easily overlooked community could accommodate what it does, namely the magnificent Merritt Island National Wildlife Refuge and the entrance to the Kennedy Space Center, the nerve center of the U.S. space program.

The Space Coast

South of the Daytona Beach area and Canaveral National Seashore are Merritt Island National Wildlife Refuge, the John F. Kennedy Space Center, and Cape Canaveral—giving this area the name "Space Coast." This area is also home to a popular cruise-ship port, Port Canaveral, and the laid-back town of Cocoa Beach, which attracts visitors on weekends year-round because of its proximity to Orlando, 50 miles to the west.

Sights

American Police Hall of Fame & Museum
MUSEUM | Police officers deserve our respect, and you'll be reminded why at this intriguing attraction. In addition to movie memorabilia like the *Robocop* costume and *Blade Runner* car , informative displays offer insight into the dangers officers face every day: drugs, homicides, and criminals who can create knives from dental putty and guns from a bicycle spoke. Other exhibits spotlight the gory history of capital punishment (from hangings to the guillotine to the electric chair) and crime scene investigation, terrorism, and a rotunda where more than 9,000 names are etched in marble to honor police officers who have died in the line of duty. A 24-stall shooting range provides rental guns. *6350 Horizon Dr.* *321/264–0911* *www.aphf.org* *$13, children 4–12 $8.*

★ Kennedy Space Center Visitor Complex
HISTORIC SITE | FAMILY | America's space program—past, present, and future—is the star at this must-see attraction, just 45 minutes east of Orlando, where visitors are treated to a multitude of interactive experiences. Located on a 140,000-acre barrier island, Kennedy Space Center was NASA's launch headquarters from the beginning of the space program in the 1960s until the final shuttle launch in 2012. Thanks to an invigorated NASA program and to high-tech entrepreneurs who have turned their interests to space, visitors to the complex can once again view live rocket launches from the Cape. In fact, there were 20 launches in 2018, and even more expected in 2019 (check the website for launch schedule).

The visitor center is divided into Mission Zones, with tours and attractions organized chronologically, beginning with the Heroes & Legends attraction, which celebrates the men and women who've journeyed to space, and features the relocated U.S. Astronaut Hall of Fame. The original *Mercury 7* team and the later *Gemini, Apollo, Skylab,* and shuttle astronauts have contributed artifacts and memorabilia to make it the world's premium archive of astronauts' personal stories. You can watch videos of historic moments in the space program and see one-of-a-kind items such as Wally Schirra's *Sigma 7* Mercury space capsule, Gus Grissom's space suit (colored silver only because NASA thought silver looked more "spacey"), and a flag that made it to the moon. The exhibit *First on the Moon* focuses on crew selection for *Apollo 11* and the Soviet Union's role in the space race. Throughout the visitor center, a wide range of hands-on interactive exhibits teach about space travel. One of the more challenging activities is a space-shuttle simulator that lets you try your hand at landing the craft—and afterward replays a side view of your rolling and pitching descent.

The IMAX film, *Journey to Space*, narrated by *Star Trek* legend Sir Patrick Stewart, fills a five-story movie screen with dramatic footage shot by NASA astronauts during missions, accentuating the bravery of all space travelers while capturing the spirit of the human desire to explore and expand. The film honors the milestones of the Space Shuttle Program—deploying and repairing the Hubble Space Telescope, assembling the International Space Station—and then looks forward to the deep-space exploration missions to come, offering a glimpse of the Space Launch System rocket that will send the *Orion* crew capsule toward Mars.

The drama of the IMAX films gives you great background for the many interactive programs available at the complex. The bus tour included with admission (buses depart every 15 minutes) takes you past iconic spots, including the 525-foot-tall Vehicle Assembly Building and launch pads, where rockets once more await departure. Stops include the Apollo/Saturn V Center, where you can look up in awe at one of three remaining Saturn V moon rockets, the largest rocket ever built. Exhibits include artifacts in the Treasure Gallery, and the Lunar Theater, which shows the first moon landing. Visitors can dine next to a genuine moon rock at the cleverly named Moon Rock Café.

Several in-depth tours (extra charge) offer more intimate views of the VAB, and the Cape Canaveral launch pads, where NASA, SpaceX, and the United Launch Alliance rockets await takeoff. Other iconic images include the countdown clock at NASA's Press Site, a giant crawler transporter that carried Apollo moon rockets and space shuttles to the launch pad, and the Launch Control Center.

The space shuttle *Atlantis* attraction offers views of this historic spacecraft as only astronauts have seen it—suspended as if in space, rotated 43.21

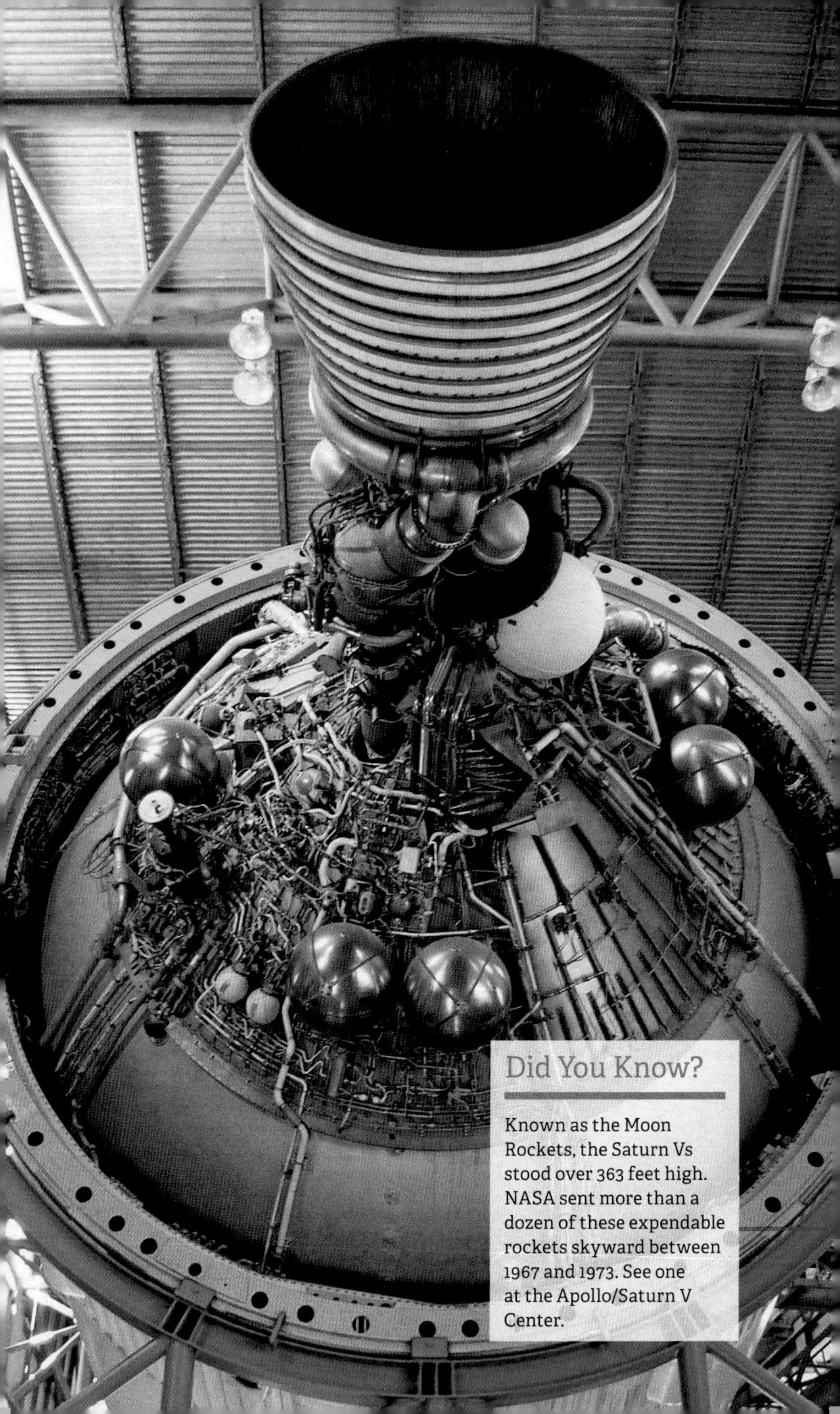

Did You Know?

Known as the Moon Rockets, the Saturn Vs stood over 363 feet high. NASA sent more than a dozen of these expendable rockets skyward between 1967 and 1973. See one at the Apollo/Saturn V Center.

degrees with payload bay doors open and its robotic arm extended, as if it has just undocked from the International Space Station. The attraction includes a variety of interactive highlights, including opportunities to perform an Extravehicular Activity (EVA), train like an astronaut, and create sonic booms while piloting *Atlantis* to a safe landing.

Don't miss the outdoor Rocket Garden, with walkways winding beside a group of historic vintage rockets, from early Atlas spacecraft to a *Saturn IB*. The Children's Playdome enables kids to play among the next generation of spacecraft, climb a moon-rock wall, and crawl through rocket tunnels. Astronaut Encounter Theater has two daily programs where retired NASA astronauts share their adventures in space travel and show a short film.

More befitting a theme park (complete with the health warnings), the Shuttle Launch Experience is the center's most spectacular attraction. Designed by a team of astronauts, NASA experts, and renowned attraction engineers, the 44,000-square-foot structure uses a sophisticated motion-based platform, special-effects seats, and high-fidelity visual and audio components to simulate the sensations experienced in an actual space-shuttle launch, including MaxQ, Solid Rocker Booster separation, main engine cutoff, and External Tank separation. The journey culminates with a breathtaking view of Earth from space.

A fitting way to end the day is a stop at the black-granite Astronaut Memorial, which honors those who lost their lives in the name of space exploration.

Other add-ons include Lunch with an Astronaut, where astronauts talk about their experiences and engage in a good-natured Q&A; the typical line of questioning from kids: "How do you eat/sleep/relieve yourself in space?" ✉ *Kennedy Space Center Visitor Complex, Rte. 405* ☎ *877/313–2610* 🌐 *www.kennedyspacecenter.com* 🎟 *$57 (includes bus tour, IMAX movies, visitor complex shows and exhibits); specialty tours $25; Lunch with an Astronaut $29.99.*

Valiant Air Command Warbird Museum & Tico Airshow

HISTORIC SITE | Don't judge a book by its cover: what's inside this very ordinary-looking building is extraordinary. Operated mostly through the efforts of an enthusiastic team of volunteers, the museum is a treasure trove of aviation history, with memorabilia from World Wars I and II, Korea, and Vietnam, as well as extensive displays of vintage military flying gear and uniforms. There are posters that were used to help identify Japanese planes, plus a Huey helicopter and the cockpit of an F-106 that you can sit in. In the north hangar a group of dedicated aviation volunteers busily restores old planes. It's an inspiring sight, and a good place to hear some war stories. In the spring the museum puts on the Tico Warbird Airshow, featuring fighter and bomber aircraft that formerly flew in combat around the world. The lobby gift shop sells real flight suits, old flight magazines, bomber jackets, books, models, and T-shirts. ✉ *6600 Tico Rd.* ☎ *321/268–1941* 🌐 *www.vacwarbirds.org* 🎟 *$20.*

Beaches

Playalinda Beach

BEACH—SIGHT | The southern access for the Canaveral National Seashore, remote Playalinda Beach has pristine sands and is the longest stretch of undeveloped coast on Florida's Atlantic seaboard. You can, however, see the launch pads at Cape Kennedy from the beach. Hundreds of giant sea turtles come ashore here from May through August to lay their eggs. Fourteen parking lots anchor the beach at 1-mile intervals. From Interstate 95, take Exit

The sun sets over Merritt Island National Wildlife Refuge.

249 and head east. Bring bug repellent in case of horseflies, and note that you may see some unauthorized clothing-optional activity. **Amenities:** lifeguards (seasonal); parking (fee); toilets. **Best for:** solitude; swimming; walking. ✉ *Rte. 402* ⊕ *At the northern end of Beach Rd.* ☎ *321/267–1110* 🌐 *www.nps.gov/cana* 🎟 *$10 per vehicle for national seashore.*

Restaurants

Dixie Crossroads
$$$ | **SEAFOOD** | **FAMILY** | This sprawling restaurant is always crowded and festive, but it's not just the rustic setting that draws the throngs—it's the seafood. The specialty is rock shrimp, which are served fried, broiled, or steamed. **Known for:** locally caught rock shrimp; corn fritters dusted with powdered sugar; long waits for tables at peak hours. $ *Average main: $24* ✉ *1475 Garden St.* ⊕ *2 miles east of I–95 Exit 220* ☎ *321/268–5000* 🌐 *www.dixiecrossroads.com.*

Hotels

Hampton Inn Titusville
$$ | **HOTEL** | **FAMILY** | Proximity to the Kennedy Space Center and reasonable rates make this four-story hotel a top pick for an overnight near the center. **Pros:** free Wi-Fi; extra-comfy beds; convenient to Interstate 95. **Cons:** thin walls; no restaurant on-site; no room service. $ *Rooms from: $236* ✉ *4760 Helen Hauser Blvd.* ☎ *321/383–9191* 🌐 *www.hamptoninn.com* 🛏 *90 rooms* 🍽 *Breakfast.*

Activities

★ Merritt Island National Wildlife Refuge
HIKING/WALKING | Owned by NASA, but part of the National Wildlife Refuge System, this 140,000-acre refuge, which adjoins the Canaveral National Seashore, acts as a buffer around Kennedy Space Center while protecting 1,000 species of plants and 500 species of wildlife, including 15 federally considered threatened or endangered. It's an immense

area dotted by brackish estuaries and marshes, coastal dunes, hardwood hammocks, and pine forests. You can borrow field guides and binoculars at the visitor center (5 miles east of U.S. 1 in Titusville on State Road 402) to track down falcons, ospreys, eagles, turkeys, doves, cuckoos, owls, and woodpeckers, as well as loggerhead turtles, alligators, wild boar, and otters. A 20-minute video about refuge wildlife and accessibility—only 10,000 acres are developed—can help orient you. This is a wild, natural area, not a zoo or theme park. Visitors should use appropriate caution, as this is home to snakes, alligators, and stinging insects.

You might take a self-guided driving tour along the 7-mile Black Point Wildlife Drive. Several roads and trails are vulnerable to hurricane damage, and may be closed if there has been a strong storm. Check the website or call 321/861–2352 for updates on closures. If you exit the north end of the refuge, look for the Manatee Observation Area just north of the Haulover Canal (maps are at the visitor center). They usually show up in spring and fall. There are also fishing camps, fishing boat ramps, and six hiking trails scattered throughout the area. If you do want to fish, a free, downloadable permit is required. The refuge does not close when there is a rocket launch. ✉ *Visitor Center, Rte. 402* ✣ *5 miles east of U.S. 1 across Titusville Causeway* ☏ *321/861–0667, 321/861–0669 visitor center* 🌐 *www.fws.gov/refuge/merritt_island* 🎟 *$10 daily fee per vehicle to use Black Point Wildlife drive.*

Cocoa

17 miles south of Titusville.

Not to be confused with the seaside community of Cocoa Beach, the small town of Cocoa sits smack-dab on mainland Florida and faces the Intracoastal Waterway, known locally as Indian River. There's a museum as well as a rustic fish camp along the St. Johns River, a few miles inland.

Folks in a rush to get to the beach tend to overlook Cocoa's Victorian-style village, but it's worth a stop and is perhaps Cocoa's most interesting feature. Within the cluster of restored turn-of-the-20th-century buildings and cobblestone walkways you can enjoy several restaurants, indoor and outdoor cafés, snack and ice-cream shops, and more than 50 specialty shops and art galleries. The area hosts music performances in the gazebo, arts-and-crafts shows, and other family-friendly events throughout the year. To get to Cocoa Village, head east on Route 520—named King Street in Cocoa—and when the streets get narrow and the road curves, make a right onto Brevard Avenue; follow the signs for the free municipal parking lot.

Sights

Brevard Museum of History & Natural Science

MUSEUM | FAMILY | This is the place to come to see what the lay of the local land looked like in other eras. Hands-on activities draw children, who especially migrate toward the Imagination Center, where they can act out history or reenact a rocket flight. Not to be missed are Ice Age–era creatures such as a fully articulated mastodon, giant ground sloth, and saber-tooth cat, all of which lived in the area. The Windover Archaeological Exhibit features 7,000-year-old artifacts indigenous to the region. In 1984, a shallow pond revealed the burial ground of more than 200 native people who lived in the area about 7,000 years ago. Preserved in the muck were bones and, to the archaeologists' surprise, the brains of these ancient people. Nature lovers appreciate the museum's butterfly garden and the nature center with 22 acres of trails encompassing three distinct ecosystems—sand pine hills, lake lands,

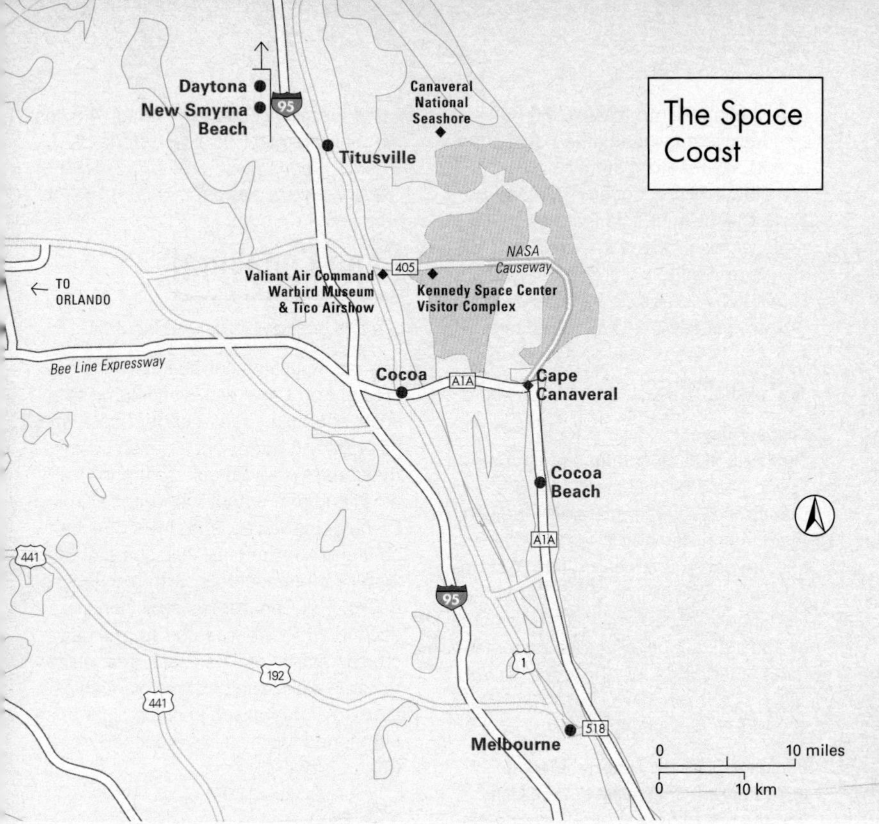

and marshlands. ✉ *2201 Michigan Ave.* ☎ *321/632–1830* 🌐 *www.myfloridahistory.org* 🎟 *$9* 🕐 *Closed Sun.–Wed.*

Restaurants

★ Café Margaux

$$$ | EUROPEAN | Eclectic, creative, and international is the best way to describe the cuisine and decor at this charming Cocoa Village spot, featured on the Food Network. The menu blends French, Italian, and Asian influences with dishes such as walnut-and-fig-stuffed quail over Brie-whipped purple potatoes, penne and pheasant breast in Manchego garlic Madeira cream, or an astronomically priced 14 oz. **Known for:** great steaks; outdoor seating under umbrellas; vast wine list. 💲 *Average main: $29* ✉ *220 Brevard Ave.* ☎ *321/639–8343* 🌐 *www.margaux.com* 🕐 *Closed Sun.*

Lone Cabbage Fish Camp

$ | ECLECTIC | The word rustic doesn't even begin to describe this down-home, no-nonsense fish camp restaurant (translation: you eat off paper plates with plastic forks) housed in a weathered, old, clapboard shack along with a bait shop and airboat-tour company. Set your calorie counter on stun, as you peruse the plates of fried fish, frogs' legs, turtle, and alligator (as well as burgers and hot dogs). **Known for:** fried fish; frogs' legs and gator; airboat rides. 💲 *Average main: $14* ✉ *8199 Rte. 520* ✥ *At St. Johns River* ☎ *321/632–4199.*

Performing Arts

The Historic Cocoa Village Playhouse

THEATER | FAMILY | In 1918 the building that now holds this theater was a Ford dealership that sold Model Ts. After that, it evolved into the Aladdin Theater, a vaudeville house, and then did a turn as a movie theater before returning to live theatrical productions in 1989. The performance schedule features touring professional productions, concerts, and shows geared to children on vacation. *300 Brevard Ave.* *321/636–5050* *www.cocoavillageplayhouse.com.*

Shopping

Cocoa Village

SHOPPING NEIGHBORHOODS | You could spend hours browsing in the more than 50 boutiques here, along Brevard Avenue and Harrison Street (the latter has the densest concentration of shops). Although most stores are of the gift and clothing variety, the village is also home to antiques shops, art galleries, restaurants, a tattoo parlor, and a spa. *Rte. 520* *At Brevard Ave.* *321/631–9075* *www.visitcocoavillage.com.*

Renninger's Flea & Farmers' Market

OUTDOOR/FLEA/GREEN MARKETS | **FAMILY** | You're sure to find a bargain at one of the 800+ booths at this market, which is held every Friday, Saturday, and Sunday from 9 to 4. *4835 W. Eau Gallie Blvd., Melbourne* *321/242–9124* *renningers.net* *Closed Mon.–Thurs.*

Twister Airboat Rides

BOATING | **FAMILY** | If you haven't seen the swampy, alligator-ridden waters of Florida, then you haven't really seen Florida. This thrilling wildlife tour goes where eagles and wading birds coexist with water moccasins and gators. The Coast Guard–certified deluxe airboats hit speeds of up to 45 mph and offer unparalleled opportunities to photograph native species. The basic tour lasts 30 minutes, but 60- and 90-minute ecotours are also available at an additional cost by reservation only. Twister Airboat Rides is inside the Lone Cabbage Fish Camp, about 9 miles west of Cocoa's city limits, 4 miles west of Interstate 95. *8199 Rte. 520* *At St. Johns River* *321/632–4199* *www.twisterairboatrides.com* *$24.*

Cape Canaveral

5 miles east of Cocoa via Rte. A1A.

The once-bustling commercial fishing area of Port Canaveral is still home to a small shrimping fleet, charter boats, and party fishing boats, but its main business these days is as a cruise-ship port. The north end of the port, where the Carnival, Disney, Norwegian, and Royal Caribbean cruise lines set sail, has some good waterfront restaurants, with big viewing decks. Port Canaveral is now Florida's second-busiest cruise port for multiday cruises, which makes this a great place to catch a glimpse of these giant ships. It's also a great place to catch sight of an unmanned rocket being launched from Cape Canaveral.

Exploration Tower

LOCAL INTEREST | **FAMILY** | The best view at Port Canaveral is no longer from the top of a cruise ship. In fact, the view from atop this towering seven-story structure makes the cruise ships look—well, not so massive after all. The tower, a short walk from the cruise port, is equal parts museum and scenic overlook. The seventh-floor observation deck offers impressive views of the cruise port, the Atlantic Ocean, the Banana River, and even the Vehicle Assembly Building at Kennedy Space Center. Other floors house exhibits highlighting the cultural history of the area, from space flight to surfing, bird and sea life to the rich maritime history. Kids will enjoy interactive exhibits, including a virtual ship's bridge that allows you to pilot a boat through the Canaveral Channel and into the Atlantic. A theater shows a 20-minute film dedicated to the history of Brevard County, and a small café sells refreshments and baked goods. The ground floor houses a visitor information center. ✉ *670 Dave Nisbet Dr.* ☎ *321/394–3408* 🌐 *www.explorationtower.com* 🎫 *$6.50.*

Restaurants

Seafood Atlantic
$$ | SEAFOOD | Locals think of this casual waterfront seafood market/eatery as a well-kept secret, but more and more cruise patrons are making their way here for a pre- or post-cruise treat. The market is connected to the restaurant, guaranteeing not only freshness but an array of choices. **Known for:** variety of shrimp; crab cakes; views of departing and arriving cruise ships. 💲 *Average main: $19* ✉ *520 Glen Cheek Dr.* ☎ *321/784–1963* 🌐 *www.seafoodatlantic.org* 🕒 *Closed Mon. and Tues.*

Thai Thai III
$$ | ASIAN FUSION | The mouthwatering photos on the menu don't do the real stuff justice. Locals and cruise-ship vacationers frequent this casual Thai/Japanese eatery within walking distance of cruise-port hotels. **Known for:** pad Thai and curries; bento box lunches; great takeout. 💲 *Average main: $20* ✉ *8660 Astronaut Blvd.* ☎ *321/784–1561.*

Hotels

Radisson Resort at the Port
$ | HOTEL | For cruise-ship passengers who can't wait to get under way, this splashy resort, done up in pink and turquoise, already feels like the Caribbean. **Pros:** tropical landscaping in pool area; on-site eateries; free Wi-Fi. **Cons:** rooms around the pool can be noisy; loud air-conditioning in some rooms; no complimentary breakfast. 💲 *Rooms from: $124* ✉ *8701 Astronaut Blvd.* ☎ *321/784–0000, 888/201–1718* 🌐 *www.radisson.com/capecanaveralfl* 🛏 *356 rooms* 🍽 *No meals.*

Residence Inn by Marriott Cape Canaveral Cocoa Beach
$$ | HOTEL | Billing itself as the closest all-suites hotel to the Kennedy Space Center is this four-story Residence Inn, painted cheery yellow. **Pros:** helpful staff; free breakfast buffet; free Wi-Fi. **Cons:** less than picturesque views; street noise in some rooms; fee for parking. 💲 *Rooms from: $279* ✉ *8959 Astronaut Blvd.* ☎ *321/323–1100, 800/331–3131* 🌐 *www.marriott.com* 🛏 *150 suites* 🍽 *Breakfast.*

Shopping

Cove Marketplace
SHOPPING CENTERS/MALLS | Whether you're at Port Canaveral for a cruise or are just passing through, this area on the south side of the harbor has shops, restaurants, and entertainment venues, including the seven-story Exploration Tower. Since most of the bars and eateries are located on the public waterfront area, you'll have a great view of the cruise ships. ✉ *Glen Cheek Dr., at Scallop Dr., Port Canaveral* 🌐 *www.visitspacecoast.com* 🎫 *Free.*

Cocoa Beach

5 miles south of Cape Canaveral, 58 miles southeast of Orlando.

After crossing a long and high bridge just east of Cocoa Village, you drop down upon a barrier island. A few miles farther and you'll reach the Atlantic Ocean and picture-perfect Cocoa Beach at Route A1A.

In the early 1960s Cocoa Beach was a sleepy, little-known town. But in 1965 the sitcom *I Dream of Jeannie* premiered. The endearing show featured an astronaut, played by Larry Hagman, and his "Jeannie" in a bottle, Barbara Eden, and was set in Cocoa Beach. Though the series was never shot in Florida, creator Sidney Sheldon paid homage to the town with local references to Cape Kennedy (now known as the Kennedy Space Center) and Bernard's Surf restaurant. Today the town and its lovely beach are a mecca to Florida's surfing community.

VISITOR INFORMATION

CONTACTS Cocoa Beach Convention and Visitors Bureau. ☎ *321/784–6444* 🌐 *www.visitcocoabeach.com.*

Sights

Westgate Cocoa Beach Pier

MARINA | By day this historic pier is a good place to stroll—if you don't mind weatherworn wood and sandy, watery paths. Although most of the pier is free to walk on, there's a small charge to enter the fishing area at the end of the 800-foot-long boardwalk (even to look around), and a separate fishing fee. You can rent rods and reels here for an additional $20. Surf competitions can be viewed from the pier, as it's a popular surf spot. By night visitors and locals—beach bums and surfers among them—head here to party. Weekends see live music. ■ **TIP→ The pier is a great place to watch launches from Kennedy Space Center or Cape Canaveral.** ✉ *401 Meade Ave.* ☎ *321/783–7549* 🌐 *www.cocoabeachpier.com* 🎫 *$2, or free with receipt from parking or shop; $7 to fish; $15 parking.*

Beaches

Cocoa Beach

BEACH—SIGHT | This is one of the Space Coast's nicest beaches—and the place where the great professional surfer Kelly Slater got his start. The beach boasts one of the steadiest surf breaks on the East Coast and has wide stretches of hard sand that are excellent for biking, jogging, power walking, and strolling. In some places there are dressing rooms, showers, playgrounds, picnic areas with grills, snack shops, and surfside parking lots. Beach vendors offer necessities, and lifeguards are on duty in the summer. A popular entry road, Route 520 crosses the Banana River into Cocoa Beach. At its east end, 5-acre **Alan Shepard Park,** named for the famous astronaut, aptly provides excellent views of launches from Kennedy Space Center and Cape Canaveral. Facilities here include 10 picnic pavilions, shower and restroom facilities, and more than 300 parking spaces. Beach vendors carry necessities for sunning and swimming. Parking is $15. Shops and restaurants are within walking distance. Another enticing Cocoa Beach entry point is 10-acre **Sidney Fischer Park,** in the 2100 block of Route A1A in the central beach area. It has showers, playgrounds, changing areas, picnic areas with grills, snack shops, and plenty of well-maintained, inexpensive parking lots ($5 for cars). **Amenities:** food and drink; lifeguards (seasonal); parking (fee); showers; toilets; water sports. **Best for:** sunrise; surfing; swimming; walking. ✉ *401 Meade Ave.* ✥ *Rte. A1A from Cape Canaveral to Patrick Air Force Base.*

Restaurants

Heidelberg

$$$ | **GERMAN** | As the name suggests, the cuisine here is definitely German, from the sauerbraten served with potato dumplings and red cabbage to the beef Stroganoff and spaetzle to the classically prepared Wiener schnitzel. All the soups and desserts are homemade; try the Viennese-style apple strudel and the rum-zapped almond-cream tortes. **Known for:** classic Wiener schnitzel; delicious apple strudel; live music Wednesday through Saturday. 💲 *Average main: $29* ✉ *7 N. Orlando Ave.* ✥ *Opposite city hall* ☎ *321/783–6806* 🌐 *www.heidelbergcocoabeach.com* ⏲ *Closed Mon. and Tues. No lunch Sun.*

Keith's Oyster Bar

$ | **SEAFOOD** | This open-air seafood bar on the beach, at the entrance of the Cocoa Beach Pier, serves oysters on the half shell. You can also grab a fish sandwich

The Cocoa Beach Pier is a magnet for nightlife in Cocoa Beach.

or burger here, crab legs by the pound, or one of the popular buckets of steamed shrimp or coconut shrimp. **Known for:** oysters on the half shell; pretty good cocktails; oceanfront dining. *Average main: $14 Cocoa Beach Pier, 401 Meade Ave. 321/783–7549 www.cocoabeachpier.com.*

Hotels

Best Western Cocoa Beach Hotel & Suites

$$ | HOTEL | FAMILY | Families love this Best Western for its affordable suites, and everyone loves it for its oceanfront location (just a half block from the Cocoa Beach Pier), the great views of launches from Kennedy Space Center and Cape Canaveral, and its proximity to Port Canaveral. **Pros:** free Wi-Fi and HBO; good location; cruise terminal shuttle $14 round trip. **Cons:** parking fee $5; small bathrooms; noise from the pier. *Rooms from: $209 5600 N. Atlantic Ave. 321/783–7621 www.best-westerncocoabeach.com 292 rooms Free Breakfast.*

Hampton Inn Cocoa Beach

$$ | HOTEL | FAMILY | Centrally located between Cocoa Beach and Canaveral, this convenient hotel is only minutes from most attractions in the area, including the cruise port. **Pros:** free hot breakfast; free parking; free Wi-Fi. **Cons:** no full-service restaurant on-site; ocean view is limited; breakfast can be crowded. *Rooms from: $256 3425 N. Atlantic Ave. 321/799–4099 www.hamptoninn3.hilton.com 150 rooms Free Breakfast.*

Hilton Cocoa Beach Oceanfront

$$ | HOTEL | FAMILY | You can't get any closer to the beach than this seven-story oceanfront hotel, where most rooms have ocean views. **Pros:** beachfront; friendly staff; on-site eateries. **Cons:** fees for Wi-Fi and parking; small pool and bathrooms; no balconies. *Rooms from: $277 1550 N. Atlantic Ave. 321/799–0003 www.hiltoncocoabeach.com 296 rooms No meals.*

Inn at Cocoa Beach

$ | **B&B/INN** | This charming oceanfront inn has spacious, individually decorated rooms, some with four-poster beds, upholstered chairs, and balconies or patios; most have ocean views. **Pros:** quiet; romantic; honor bar. **Cons:** no on-site restaurant; tiny bathrooms; thin walls. *Rooms from: $155 ✉ 4300 Ocean Beach Blvd. ☎ 321/799–3460, 800/343–5307 outside Florida 🌐 www.theinnatcocoabeach.com 50 rooms 🍴 Breakfast.*

★ The Resort on Cocoa Beach

$$ | **RESORT** | **FAMILY** | Even if the beach weren't in its backyard, this family-friendly, oceanfront property offers enough activities and amenities—from tennis and basketball courts to a game room, pool, and 50-seat movie theater—to keep everyone entertained. **Pros:** kids' activities; full kitchens; in-room washers and dryers; large balconies; free Wi-Fi. **Cons:** weekend check-ins can be crowded; not all rooms are oceanfront; slow elevators. *Rooms from: $250 ✉ 1600 N. Atlantic Ave. ☎ 321/783–4000, 866/469–8222 🌐 www.theresortoncocoabeach.com 124 suites 🍴 No meals.*

Westgate Cocoa Beach Resort

$$ | **HOTEL** | Despite its dated Tiki-torch exterior, this totally renovated resort offers spacious, upscale accommodations and beachfront amenities, just a mile from the pier and handy to the cruise port. **Pros:** well-equipped kitchen; luxury linens; free shuttle to pier and restaurants. **Cons:** no sea views; pool music can be intrusive; no full-service restaurant on-site. *Rooms from: $250 ✉ 3550 N. Atlantic Ave. ☎ 321/783–2230 🌐 www.westgateresorts.com 120 rooms 🍴 No meals.*

Shopping

Merritt Square Mall

SHOPPING CENTERS/MALLS | The area's only major shopping mall is about a 20-minute ride from the beach. Stores include Macy's, Dillard's, JCPenney, Sears, Foot Locker, Island Surf and Skate, and roughly 100 others. It's an indoor mall, a rapidly diminishing fixture in the Florida landscape, making for comfortable shopping in the heat of summer. There's a 16-screen multiplex, along with a food court and several restaurant chains. *✉ 777 E. Merritt Island Causeway, Merritt Island ☎ 321/452–3270 🌐 www.merrittsquaremall.com.*

Activities

Adventure Kayak of Cocoa Beach

KAYAKING | Specializing in manatee encounters, this outfitter organizes one- and two-person kayak tours of mangroves, channels, and islands. Tours launch from various locations in the Cocoa Beach area. *✉ 599 Ramp Rd. ☎ 321/480–8632 🌐 www.kayakcocoabeach.com From $35.*

Cocoa Beach Surf Company

SURFING | This huge surf complex sits inside the Four Points by Sheraton resort, and has three floors of boards, apparel, sunglasses, and anything else a surfer, wannabe-surfer, or souvenir-seeker could need. Also on-site are a 5,600-gallon fish and shark tank and the Shark Pit Bar and Grill. You can rent surfboards, bodyboards, and wet suits, as well as umbrellas, chairs, and bikes. And staffers teach wannabes—from kids to seniors—how to surf. There are group, semiprivate, and private lessons available in one-, two-, and three-hour sessions. All gear is provided. *✉ Four Points by Sheraton, 4001 N. Atlantic Ave. ☎ 321/799–9930 🌐 www.cocoabeachsurf.com From $40.*

★ **Ron Jon Surf Shop**

SPORTING GOODS | It's impossible to miss the flagship and original Ron Jon: it takes up nearly two blocks along Route A1A and has a giant surfboard and an art-deco facade painted orange, blue, yellow, and turquoise. What started in 1963 as a small T-shirt and bathing-suit shop has evolved into a 52,000-square-foot superstore that's open every day 'round the clock. The shop rents water-sports gear as well as chairs and umbrellas, and it sells every kind of beachwear, surf wax, plus the requisite T-shirts and flip-flops. ✉ *4151 N. Atlantic Ave., Rte. A1A* ☎ *321/799–8888* 🌐 *www.ronjonsurfshop.com.*

Melbourne

20 miles south of Cocoa Beach.

Despite its dependence on the high-tech space industry, this town is decidedly laid-back. Most of the city is on the mainland, but a small portion trickles onto a barrier island, separated by the Indian River Lagoon and accessible by several inlets, including the Sebastian.

Sights

★ **Brevard Zoo**

ZOO | **FAMILY** | At this Association of Zoo and Aquariums–accredited zoo you can stroll along the shaded boardwalks and get a close-up look at rhinos, giraffes, cheetahs, alligators, crocodiles, lemurs, jaguars, eagles, river otters, kangaroos, and exotic birds. Keeper chats are held throughout the day in which zookeepers feed and highlight various animals. Stop by Paws-On, an interactive learning playground with a petting zone, wildlife detective training academy, and the Indian River Play Lagoon. Hand-feed a giraffe in Expedition Africa or a lorikeet in the aviary; and step up to the Wetlands Outpost, an elevated pavilion that's a gateway to 22 acres of wetlands through which you can paddle kayaks and keep an eye open for the 4,000 species of wildlife that live in these waters and woods. Adventurers seeking a chimp's-eye view can zip-line through the zoo on Treetop Trek. ✉ *8225 N. Wickham Rd.* ☎ *321/254–9453* 🌐 *www.brevardzoo.org* 🎫 *$19.95.*

Beaches

Paradise Beach

BEACH—SIGHT | Small and scenic, this 1,600-foot stretch of sand is part of a 10-acre park north of Indialantic, about 20 miles south of Cocoa Beach on Route A1A. It has a refreshment stand, volleyball courts, outdoor showers, a beachfront park with pavilions, grills, picnic tables, and lifeguards in summer. **Amenities:** food and drink; lifeguards (seasonal); parking; showers; toilets. **Best for**: sunrise; surfing; swimming; walking. ✉ *2301 N. Rte. A1A* 🌐 *www.brevardcounty.us/parksrecreation/south/howardfutch.*

Satellite Beach

BEACH—SIGHT | This sleepy little community just south of Patrick Air Force Base, about 15 miles south of Cocoa Beach on Route A1A, sits on a narrow barrier island with the Atlantic Ocean on one side and the Indian River lagoon on the other. Its beach is protected by dunes, and sea turtles flock there to lay their eggs. A popular spot for family vacations because of its slow pace and lack of crowds, Satellite Beach has several beachfront parks with playgrounds, pavilions, and picnic facilities. One park, which teaches visitors about the importance of the dune system, has boardwalks that meander over the dunes to the beach. **Amenities:** food and drink; lifeguards; parking; showers; toilets; water sports. **Best for:** sunrise; surfing; swimming; walking. ✉ *Rte. A1A, Satellite Beach* 🌐 *www.satellitebeachfl.org.*

Activities

Baytree National Golf Links

GOLF | "Challenging but fair" is how golfers describe this award-winning, links-style course, designed by PGA legend Gary Player (aka "The Black Knight."). This semiprivate course, built in 1992, is known for its unique red shale coquina waste areas. A round can be something of a roller coaster ride, with an easy hole or two followed by a perplexingly challenging one. The 454-yard, par-4 18th, for instance, is rated among the toughest in Brevard County. It plays into the wind and requires an imposing carry over wetlands, followed by an approach into a green guarded by water on all sides. The club has a restaurant and full practice facility. ✉ *8207 National Dr.* ☎ *321/259–9060* 🌐 *www.baytreenational.com* *$46 for 9 holes* *18 holes, 7043 yards, par 72.*

USSSA Space Coast Complex

BASEBALL/SOFTBALL | **FAMILY** | Formerly Space Coast Stadium, spring-training home to several major league baseball teams, this 85-acre, multisport complex with 15 fields, and three championship-style stadiums is now operated by the United States Specialty Sports Association, and is an international center for amateur baseball and softball. It's also home to a National Pro Fastpitch professional women's softball team, USSSA Pride. ✉ *5800 Stadium Pkwy., Viera* ☎ *800/741–3014 Stadium* 🌐 *www.usssaspacecoast.com.*

Viera East Golf Club

GOLF | Rated among the best public courses—and values—on the Space Coast, Viera East reflects course architect Joe Lee's credo that "golf should be enjoyable, not a chore." Novices appreciate the forgiving, open layout with generous landing areas; more advanced players embrace the challenge of Lee's strategically placed bunkers (there are 66), water hazards, and expansive, undulating greens. The coastal breezes can make club selection tricky at times. Opened in 1994, the course is framed by marshlands, lakes, ponds, and pine and cypress trees. The par-5 14th is among the more picturesque and challenging holes, with a green surrounded by water. ✉ *2300 Clubhouse Dr., Viera* ☎ *321/639–6500* 🌐 *www.vieragolf.com* *$47.50 weekdays; $51.50 weekends* *18 holes, 6720 yards, par 72.*

Chapter 14

NORTHWEST FLORIDA

Updated by
Rosanne Dunkelberger

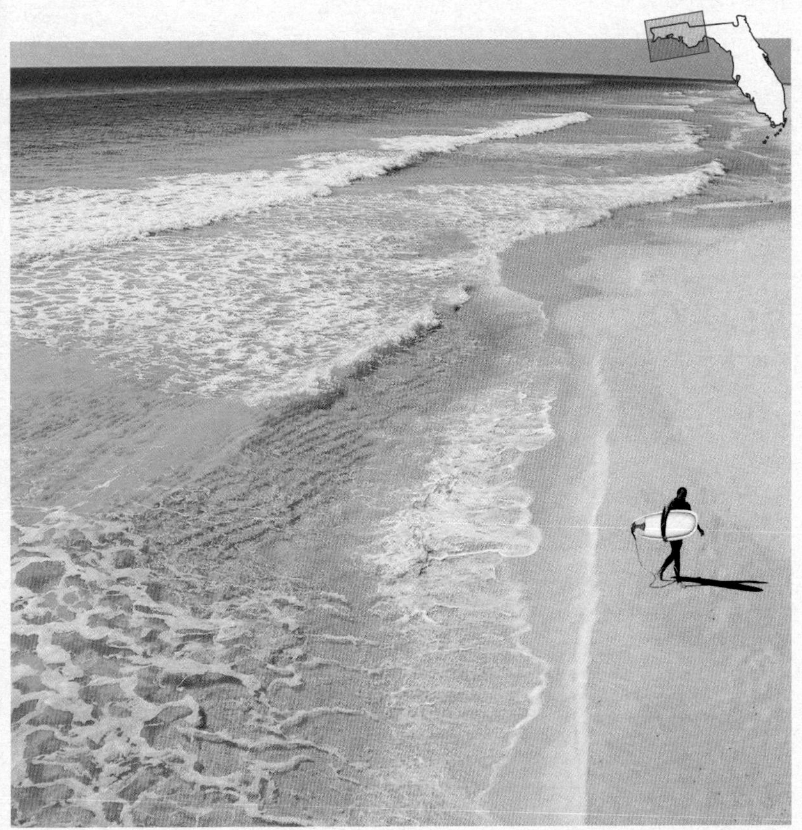

Sights ★★★★☆ Restaurants ★★★☆☆ Hotels ★★★☆☆ Shopping ★★★☆☆ Nightlife ★★★☆☆

WELCOME TO NORTHWEST FLORIDA

TOP REASONS TO GO

★ **Snowy-white beaches:** Much of the Gulf Coast shoreline is relatively unobstructed by high-rise condos and hotels, and the white-powder sand is alluring.

★ **Lots of history:** Spanish, Native American, and, later, French and English influences shaped the direction of this region and are well represented in its architecture, historic sites, and museums.

★ **Easygoing and exciting:** Northwest Florida, aka The Panhandle, used to have a reputation as being Southern and slow as molasses. But nowadays, the region is growing, giving visitors a wide choice of activities on the beaches and beyond. The Southern hospitality can still be found in abundance, and chances are very good you will be called "hon" by a waitress.

★ **Capital sights:** As the state capital (chosen because it was midway between the two earlier Spanish headquarters of St. Augustine and Pensacola), Tallahassee has historical museums, two major universities, and plenty of outdoor activities and natural beauty.

1 **Pensacola.** By preserving architecture from early Spanish settlements, Pensacola earns points for retaining the influence of these early explorers.

2 **Pensacola Beach.** One of the longest barrier islands in the world, Pensacola Beach has a low-key, family-friendly feel and many local hangouts, fishing galore, and historic Ft. Pickens.

3 **DeFuniak Springs.** Visit an up-and-coming winery or poke around small-town America here.

4 **Falling Waters State Park.** Florida's highest waterfall is just a day trip away from Pensacola.

5 **Florida Caverns State Park.** Explore underground caverns where aeons-old rock formations create bizarre scenes.

6 **Fort Walton Beach.** Between Pensacola and Panama City Beach, Fort Walton is home to a marine park, white sand, and emerald waters.

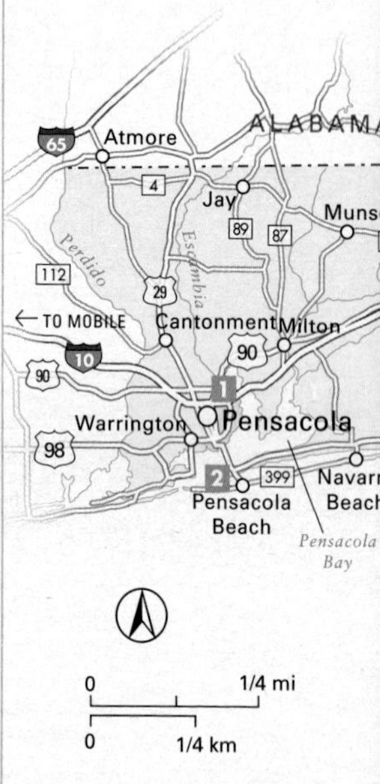

7 **Destin.** Known for its blue-green waters and sugarlike sand beaches made of Appalachian quartz crystals, this city on the Emerald Coast is great for fishing, paddleboarding, and setting up on the sand.

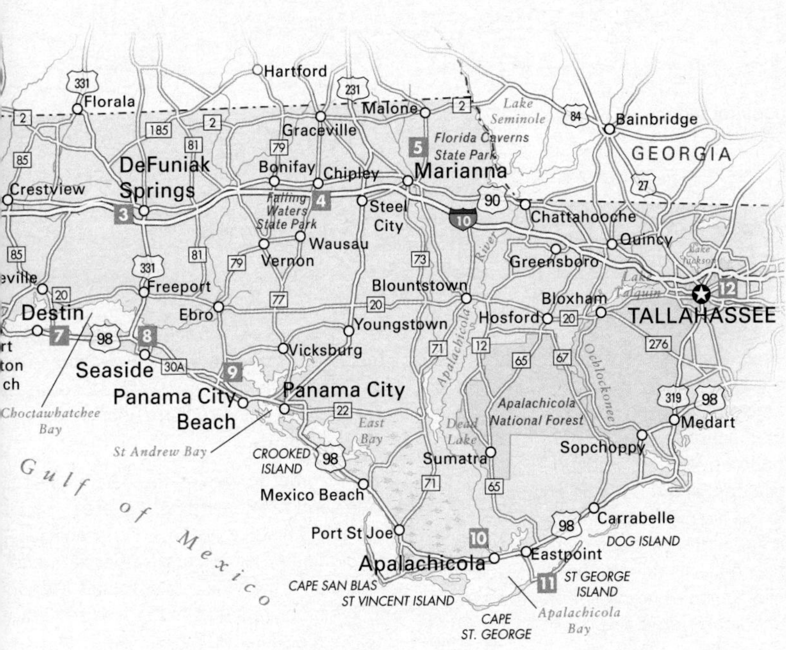

8 South Walton. Running along 30A is a group of 16 beach communities—all with their own unique flavor—and the best-kept secret of Florida. They're idyllic and blissfully devoid of high-rises.

9 Panama City Beach. Once spring break central, this beach town has transformed into a top family-friendly destination.

10 Apalachicola. Known for its oysters, this sleepy Old Florida town is a nostalgic slice of the Forgotten Coast.

11 St. George Island. Uncrowded white sand, a beautiful state park, and a landmark lighthouse make this locally loved beach a must-see in the Panhandle.

12 Tallahassee. In the state capital you can see the historic and new capitols, visit the state's historical museum, attend an FSU football game, explore 600 miles of trails, and go for a country ride down canopied roads.

The sugar-white sands of the Panhandle's beaches stretch 227 miles from Pensacola east to Apalachicola. Sprinkle in clear emerald waters, towering dunes, and laid-back small towns where the fish are always biting and the folks are friendly, and you have a region with local color that's beloved by Floridians and visitors alike.

There are sights in the Panhandle, but sightseeing isn't the principal activity. The region is better known for its rich history, ample fishing and diving, and its opportunities for relaxation. Here it's about Southern drawls, a gentle pace, fresh seafood, and more grits and old-fashioned hospitality than anywhere else in the state. Sleepy (and not so sleepy) beach towns offer world-class golf, deep-sea fishing, relaxing spa treatments, and unbeatable shopping.

There's glamour here, too. Look for it in winning resorts throughout the region and in the abundance of nightlife, arts, and culture—from local symphonies to boutique art galleries—particularly in the more metropolitan areas. And then there's the food: from fresh catches of the day to some of the nation's finest oysters to mom-and-pop favorites offering fried seafood goodness.

Jump in a car, rent a bike, or buy a spot on a charter boat—you're never too far from outdoor adventure, with more miles of preserved coastline than anywhere else in the state. Destin is, after all, dubbed "The World's Luckiest Fishing Village," and the sport of YOLO Boarding (this region's term for the popular paddle-boarding craze) has invaded the area in full force, offering a unique waterborne view of the entire region's unspoiled, natural beauty.

Don't forget to veer off the beach roads and venture into some of the area's picturesque historic districts. Pensacola is known as America's first settlement, and the rest of the region follows suit with rich history dating from the first settlers. The state's capital, Tallahassee, has its own unique history woven of politics, varying cultures, and innovation. Between the local charm, natural splendor, outdoor adventures, and miles of coastline, it's no wonder that the Panhandle is so beloved.

Planning

When to Go

At the beach, peak season is Memorial Day to Labor Day, with another spike during spring break. Vendors, attractions, and other activities are in full swing in the summer. In-the-know travelers plan their beach trips during the "secret season" from mid-September through November. Crowds and traffic (which can be brutal on the beachfront highways) quiet down after students go back to school. Hotel prices drop, the weather is less hot (but still warm enough to swim and enjoy the beach) and many communities plan festivals—most celebrating food, wine, and music. Inland, especially in Tallahassee, high season is during the weekends of the fall football season and weekdays when the Legislature is in session (January–February on even years, March–April on odd years.

TOP FESTIVALS

Destin Fishing Rodeo

Anglers young and old can compete in offshore and inshore categories in the month-long competition in October. All events are free and open to the public. ✉ *Destin* ☎ *850/837–6734* 🌐 *www.destinfishingrodeo.org.*

Florida Seafood Festival

In November Apalachicola celebrates the oyster harvest with oyster-shucking and -eating contests, as well as blue-crab races, a 5K, carnival midway and entertainment. ✉ *Apalachicola* ☎ *850/653–4720* 🌐 *www.floridaseafoodfestival.com.*

Sandestin Wine Festival

Sandestin's Village of Baytowne Wharf becomes an oenophile's delight during this weekend-long tasting (and eating) event. It kicks off with the Grand Wine Tasting, where hundreds of domestic and international wines will be poured. Representatives from vineyards are on hand to teach about the finest appellations from wine-producing countries around the world. And if you find something you like, you can buy it on-site. Other events include a champagne-and-seafood cruise, a Sunday brunch, wine dinners throughout the weekend, and gourmet food and wine pairings. ✉ *The Village of Baytowne Wharf, 9100 Baytowne Blvd., Sandestin* 🌐 *www.sandestinwinefestival.com.*

30A Songwriters Festival

This festival, held over the Martin Luther King Jr. holiday weekend in January, attracts music lovers to 30A for more than 250 performances. Many musical genres—country, Americana and folk, blues and soul—are represented by more than 175 songwriters and musicians performing in 30 venues, from 75 to 200 seats indoors to 5,000 outdoors. Past performers have included Emmylou Harris, John Prine, Rosanne Cash, Graham Nash, and Jackson Browne. For a preview check out the 2019 30ASWF Playlist on Spotify. ✉ *105 Hogtown Bayou Ln., Santa Rosa Beach* ☎ *850/622–5970* 🌐 *www.30asongwritersfestival.com.*

Word of South

This relatively new festival celebrates a unique blend of writers and musicians with a weeked full of performances, readings, and author appearances. Most of the events take place outdoors on several stages spread throughout Cascades Park in downtown Tallahassee. There are ticketed shows, but most of the events are free and many are created with kids in mind. ✉ *Cascades Park, 1001 S. Gadsden St., Tallahassee* 🌐 *www.wordofsouthfestival.com.*

Getting Here and Around

AIR TRAVEL

The region is home to two primary airports—Northwest Florida Beaches International Airport (ECP) and Pensacola International Airport (VPS)—which offer flights from a number of major airlines. In addition, there are airports with regularly scheduled passenger service at Tallahassee International Airport, as well as a public airport—Northwest Florida Regional Airport—in Fort Walton Beach on the Eglin Air Force Base.

CONTACTS Northwest Florida Beaches International Airport (*ECP*). ✉ *6300 W. Bay Pkwy., Panama City* ☎ *850/763–6751* 🌐 *www.iflybeaches.com.* **Northwest**

Florida Regional Airport (*VPS*). ✉ *1701 FL-85 Eglin AFB, Fort Walton Beach* ☎ *850/651–7160* 🌐 *www.flyvps.com*. **Pensacola International Airport** (*PNS*). ✉ *2430 Airport Blvd., Pensacola* ☎ *850/436–5000* 🌐 *www.flypensacola.com*. **Tallahassee International Airport** (*TLH*). ✉ *3300 Capital Circle SW, Tallahassee* ☎ *850/891–7800* 🌐 *www.flytallahassee.com*.

CAR TRAVEL

The main east–west arteries across the top of the state are Interstate 10 and U.S. 90. Interstate 10 can be faster but monotonous, while U.S. 90 routes you along the main streets of several county seats. U.S. 98 snakes eastward along the coast, splitting into 98 and 98A at Inlet Beach before rejoining at Panama City and continuing on to Port St. Joe and Apalachicola. The view of the Gulf from U.S. 98 can be breathtaking, especially at sunset.

If you need to get from one end of the Panhandle to the other in a timely manner, drive inland to Interstate 10, where the speed limit runs as high as 70 mph in places. Major north–south highways that weave through the Panhandle are (from east to west) U.S. 231, U.S. 331, Route 85, and U.S. 29. From U.S. 331, which runs over a causeway at the east end of Choctawhatchee Bay between Route 20 and U.S. 98, the panorama of barge traffic and cabin cruisers on the twinkling waters of the Intracoastal Waterway will get your attention.

Hotels

Many of the lodging selections here revolve around extended-stay options: resorts, condos, and time-shares that allow for a week or more in simple efficiencies, as well as fully furnished homes. There are also cabins, RV parking, and camping at many of the region's state parks. In any case, these are great for families and get-togethers, allowing you to do your own housekeeping and cooking, while exploring the area.

Local visitors' bureaus often act as clearinghouses for these types of properties, and you can also search online for vacation rentals. On the coast, but especially inland, the choices seem geared more toward mom-and-pop motels in addition to the usual line of chain hotels. **■ TIP→ During the summer and over holiday weekends, always reserve well ahead for top properties.**

Restaurants

An abundance of seafood is served at coastal restaurants: oysters, crab, shrimp, scallops, and a variety of fish. Of course, that's not all there is on the menu. This part of Florida still impresses diners with old-fashioned comfort foods such as meat loaf, fried chicken, beans and corn bread, okra, and fried green tomatoes. You'll also find small-town seafood shacks where you can dine on local favorites such as fried mullet, cheese grits, coleslaw, and hush puppies. Restaurants, like resorts, vary their operating hours off-season, so call first if visiting during winter months.

Hotel and restaurant reviews have been shortened. For full information, visit Fodors.com.

What It Costs

$	$$	$$$	$$$$
RESTAURANTS			
under $15	$15–$20	$21–$30	over $30
HOTELS			
under $200	$200–$300	$301–$400	over $400

Pensacola

59 miles east of Mobile, Alabama, via I–10.

Pensacola consists of four distinct districts—Seville, Palafox, East Hill, and North Hill—though they're easy to explore as a unit. Stroll down streets mapped out by the British and renamed by the Spanish, such as Cervantes, Palafox, Intendencia, and Tarragona.

An influx of restaurants and bars has brought new nightlife to the historic districts, especially Palafox Street, which is now home to a thriving entertainment scene. Taste buds water over fresh coastal cuisine from a number of award-winning, locally owned and operated restaurants, and the downtown entertainment district offers fun for any age throughout the year—festivals, events at bars and concert venues, and a growing Mardi Gras celebration.

At the southern terminus of Palafox Street is Plaza DeLuna, a two-acre park with open grounds, interactive water fountains, and concessions. It's a quiet place to sit and watch the bay, fish, or enjoy an evening sunset.

GETTING HERE AND AROUND

Pensacola International Airport has dozens of daily flights and is served by American Airlines (American Eagle), Delta, Southwest, Silver Airways, United, and US Airways. From Pensacola International Airport via Yellow Cab, it costs about $14 to get downtown or about $32 to reach Pensacola Beach.

In Pensacola and Pensacola Beach, Escambia County Area Transit provides regular citywide bus service ($1.75), downtown trolley routes, tours through the historic districts, and free trolley service to the beach from mid-May to Labor Day on Friday, Saturday, and Sunday evenings as well as Saturday afternoon.

CONTACTS Escambia County Area Transit *(ECAT). ☎ 850/595–3228 ⊕ www.goecat.com.* **Yellow Cab.** *☎ 850/433–3333.*

VISITOR INFORMATION

CONTACTS Pensacola Visitor Information Center. *✉ 1401 E. Gregory St. ☎ 850/434–1234, 800/874–1234 toll free ⊕ www.visitpensacola.com.*

Sights

Historic Pensacola Village

HISTORIC SITE | Within the Seville Square Historic District is this complex of several museums and historic homes whose indoor and outdoor exhibits trace the area's history back 450 years. The Museum of Industry (*200 E. Zaragoza St.*), in a late-19th-century warehouse, is home to permanent exhibits dedicated to the lumber, maritime, and shipping industries—once mainstays of Pensacola's economy. A reproduction of a 19th-century streetscape is displayed in the Museum of Commerce (*201 E. Zaragoza St.*).

Strolling through the area gives you a good (and free) look at many architectural styles, but to enter some of the buildings you must purchase an all-inclusive ticket online or at Tivoli High House, T. T. Wentworth Museum, or Pensacola Children's Museum. Guided tours lasting 60–90 minutes—available Tuesday through Saturday at 11 am and 1 pm—allow you to experience the history of Pensacola as you traverse the village. Ask about seasonal options, like Victorian Holiday Traditions and Haunted Ghost tours. *✉ Tivoli High House, 205 E. Zaragoza St. ⊕ www.historicpensacola.org 🎫 $8 ⏲ Closed Mon.*

★ National Museum of Naval Aviation

LOCAL INTEREST | Within the Pensacola Naval Air Station (widely considered to be the must-see attraction in Pensacola), this 300,000-square-foot museum has more than 140 aircraft representing more than 100 years of Naval Aviation. Among them are the NC-4, which in

1919 became the first plane to cross the Atlantic; the famous World War II fighter the F-6 *Hellcat;* and the Skylab Command Module.

Other attractions include an atomic bomb (it's defused, we promise), and the restored Cubi Bar Café—a very cool former airmen's club transplanted here from the Philippines. Relive the morning's maneuvers in the 14-seat motion-based simulator as well as an IMAX theater playing *Fighter Pilot, The Magic of Flight,* and other educational films.

The museum also offers two Max-Flight Simulators that takes users on a high-definition adventure in air-to-air combat and stunt flying in an interactive 360-degree pitch-and-roll technology experience. The $20 experience is for one or two. There's also two HD Motion-Based Simulators that offer a larger group of up to 15 people a five-minute, multisensory experience combining a high-definition projection screen and surround-sound, with the motion of the ride compartment. Riders can choose their own adventure, either a ride with the Blue Angels or take off from an aircraft carrier and do battle in the Iraqi desert in the Desert Storm Simulation.

While at the museum you may hear the Navy's Blue Angels aerobatic squadron buzzing overhead. This is their home base, and they practice maneuvers here on most Tuesday and Wednesday mornings at 11:30 from March to November. The pilots usually stick around after the show to shake hands and sign autographs. During the show, cover your ears as the six F/A 18s blast off in unison for 45 minutes of thrills and skill. Watching the Blue Angels practice their aerobatics is one of the best free shows in all of Florida. ✉ *Pensacola Naval Air Station, 1750 Radford Blvd.* ☎ *800/327–5002* 🌐 *www.navalaviationmuseum.org* 🎫 *Museum free; IMAX film $6.50; flight simulators $6 or $20.*

Palafox Historic District

HISTORIC SITE | Palafox Street is the main stem of historic downtown Pensacola and the center of the Palafox Historic District. The commercial and government hub of Old Pensacola is now an active cultural and entertainment district, where locally owned and operated bars and restaurants attract flocks of locals and visitors. The opulent, renovated Spanish Renaissance–style Saenger Theater, Pensacola's 1925 movie palace, hosts performances by the local symphony and opera, as well as national acts.

On Palafox between Government and Zaragoza streets is a statue of Andrew Jackson, which commemorates the formal transfer of Florida from Spain to the United States in 1821. While in the area, stop by Veterans Memorial Park, just off Bayfront Parkway near 9th Avenue. The ¾-scale replica of the Vietnam Memorial in Washington, D.C., honors the more than 58,000 Americans who lost their lives in the Vietnam War. ✉ *Palafox St.* 🌐 *downtownpensacola.com.*

Pensacola Children's Museum

MUSEUM VILLAGE | **FAMILY** | The Pensacola Children's Museum is the newest museum in the West Florida Historic Preservation, Inc. complex. The museum offers a variety of programs for children of all ages, including story time, art projects, and a plethora of interactive historical exhibits from maritime to multicultural themes. ✉ *115 E. Zaragoza St.* ☎ *850/595–5985* 🌐 *www.historicpensacola.org* 🎫 *$5 adults; $3 children* 🕓 *Closed Mon.*

Pensacola Museum of Art

HISTORIC SITE | Pensacola's city jail once occupied the 1906 Spanish Revival–style building that is now the secure home for the museum's permanent collection of paintings, sculptures, and works on paper by 20th- and 21st-century artists—and we do mean secure: you can still see the actual cells with their huge iron doors. Traveling exhibits have focused on photography (Wegman, Leibovitz, Ansel Adams), Dutch masters, regional artists, and the occasional art-world icon, such as Andy Warhol or Salvador Dalí. ✉ *407 S. Jefferson St.* ☎ *850/432–6247* 🌐 *www.pensacolamuseum.org* 🎫 *$7* ⏲ *Closed Mon.*

Seville Square Historic District
HISTORIC SITE | Established in 1559, this is the site of Pensacola's first permanent Spanish settlement (it beat St. Augustine's by six years). Its center is Seville Square, a live oak–shaded park bounded by Alcaniz, Adams, Zaragoza, and Government streets. Roam 14 brick streets past honeymoon cottages and homes set in a parklike setting. Many buildings have been converted into restaurants, bars, offices, and shops that overlook broad Pensacola Bay and coastal road U.S. 98, which provides access to the Gulf Coast and beaches. ✉ *Pensacola* ☎ *850/595–5985.*

T. T. Wentworth Jr. Florida State Museum
BUILDING | FAMILY | Even if you don't like museums, this one is worth a look. Housed in the elaborate, Renaissance Revival–style former city hall, it has an interesting mix of exhibits illustrating life in the Florida Panhandle over the centuries. One of these, the *City of Five Flags*, provides a good introduction to Pensacola's history. Mr. Wentworth was quite a collector (as well as a politician and salesman), and his eccentric collection includes a mummified cat (creepy) and the size 37 left shoe of Robert Wadlow, the world's tallest man (not creepy, but a really big shoe). A wide range of both permanent and traveling exhibits can be found here, as well as a child-size interactive area with a ship and fort where kids can play and pretend to be colonial Pensacolans. A popular new exhibit gives a look inside the infamous Trader Jon's bar, where young flight students mingled with celebrities and local politicians. ✉ *330 S. Jefferson St.* ☎ *850/595–5985* 🌐 *www.historicpensacola.org* 🎫 *$8 for seven-day pass to all historic Pensacola sites* ⏲ *Closed Mon.*

Time Zones

Northwest Florida is split between two time zones, eastern and central. The zones are mostly delineated by the Apalachicola River. In the western Panhandle, Pensacola, Destin, and Panama City are in the central time zone while the area from Port St. Joe and Apalachicola eastward to Tallahassee is in the eastern time zone. Even natives can get confused by the switch from "fast time" (eastern, the same time as New York), to "slow time" (central, which is an hour behind).

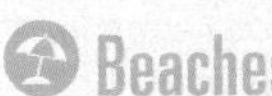

Beaches

Perdido Key State Park
BEACH—SIGHT | FAMILY | Part of Gulf Islands National Seashore, this state park is on Perdido Key, a 247-acre barrier island. Its beach, now referred to as Johnson Beach, was one of the few beaches open to African-Americans during segregation. Today the park offers primitive camping year-round, but it's also ideal for a day of swimming, shelling, birding and surf fishing. It is within walking distance of dining and nightlife on the key and is a short drive from Alabama. **Amenities:** picnic pavilion; showers; toilets. **Best for:** sunsets; swimming; walking. ✉ *15301 Perdido Key Dr., Perdido Key* ✣ *5 miles southwest of Pensacola off Rte. 292* 🌐 *www.floridastateparks.org/perdidokey* 🎫 *$3 per vehicle.*

Restaurants

Fish House
$$$ | SEAFOOD | Come one, come all, come hungry, and come at 11 am to witness the calm before the lunch storm. The

wide-ranging menu of fish dishes is the bait, and each can be served in a variety of ways: ginger-crusted, grilled, blackened, pecan-crusted, or Pacific-grilled, which puts any dish over the top. **Known for:** "Grits a Ya-Ya" (shrimp and cheese grits); large wine list; great water views. *Average main: $28 600 S. Barracks St. 850/470–0003 fishhousepensacola.com.*

Jackson's Steakhouse

$$$$ | AMERICAN | A favorite among the downtown crowd for business lunches and intimate dinners, Jackson's has received the Florida Trend Golden Spoon Hall of Fame Award for its superb steaks and local seafood. The setting's not bad, either: Housed in an 1860s-era mercantile building, the restaurant overlooks Plaza Ferdinand, where General Andrew Jackson first raised the American flag in Pensacola. **Known for:** upscale menu; wine pairings; local celebrity chef, Irv Miller. *Average main: $35 400 S. Palafox St. 850/469–9898 for reservations www.jacksonsrestaurant.com.*

★ McGuire's Irish Pub

$$ | IRISH | Since 1977 this authentic Irish pub has promised its patrons "feasting, imbibery, and debauchery" seven nights a week. A sense of humor pervades the place, evidenced by the range of prices on hamburgers—$10–$100 depending on whether you want it topped with cheddar or served with caviar and champagne. **Known for:** large menu, including both meat and seafood; extensive wine cellar and cocktail list; home-brewed beer. *Average main: $20 600 E. Gregory St. 850/433–6789 www.mcguiresirishpub.com.*

Restaurant IRON

$$$$ | SOUTHERN | Contemporary Southern treats—in both the food and cocktail varieties—abound at this hip, sleek gem on Pensacola's hottest downtown strip. The modern menu takes its cue from Southern and seafood favorites prepared with modern methods and artistic plating (chicken and dumplings is a cheese-stuffed organic chicken served with gnocchi). **Known for:** modern twists on Southern favorites; extensive, ambitious cocktail menu; elegant setting. *Average main: $36 22 N. Palafox St. 850/476–7776 www.restaurantiron.com.*

The Wine Bar on Palafox

$$ | MODERN AMERICAN | The Wine Bar on Palafox has become the place to see and be seen in downtown Pensacola. Choose from dozens of wines by the glass or bottle, or visit during happy hour for many selections featured two-for-one. **Known for:** hip downtown vibe; extensive wine selection; cheese boards and innovative main courses. *Average main: $18 16 Palafox Pl. 850/607–2089 thewinebaronpalafox.com Closed Sun.*

Hotels

New World Inn

$ | B&B/INN | If you like your inns small, warm, and cozy, with the bay on one side and a short two-block walk to the downtown historic area on the other, this is the one for you. **Pros:** steps away from downtown hot spots and attractions; historically inspired property; quiet and intimate. **Cons:** not family-friendly; lacks amenities of larger properties; rooms have a very busy look. *Rooms from: $159 600 S. Palafox St. 850/432–4111 skopelosatnewworld.com 15 rooms Breakfast.*

Pensacola Grand Hotel

$ | HOTEL | On the site of the restored historic Louisville & Nashville (L&N) railroad passenger depot, the Pensacola Grand Hotel has a 15-story glass tower attached to the train depot by a glass atrium with incredible views of historic Pensacola. **Pros:** great location near downtown; amenities perfect for business travelers. **Cons:** standard chain hotel setting; there are more intimate choices closer to downtown.

Like an Old West town with a Victorian twist, historic Pensacola is eye candy for architecture buffs.

Rooms from: $188 *200 E. Gregory St.* *850/433–3336, 800/348–3336 toll free* *www.pensacolagrandhotel.com* *210 rooms* *No meals.*

Solé Inn and Suites

$ | **HOTEL** | If you want to stay in the middle of downtown action but within reasonable distance of Pensacola's beaches, this hotel offers a bit of style in a central location for a great price. **Pros:** upscale, fully renovated 1950s motel; complimentary happy hour; free Wi-Fi. **Cons:** small bathrooms; location can be loud in peak season; rooms open directly to the outdoors. *Rooms from: $109* *200 N. Palafox St.* *850/470–9298, 888/470–9298* *www.soleinnandsuites.com* *45 rooms* *Breakfast.*

Nightlife

Pensacola offers a wide variety of lively places to enjoy once the sun goes down, from Irish pubs to local watering holes that were once the haunts of old naval heroes. You can sample homegrown concoctions at upscale martini bars and the tunes of local and national music acts at numerous live-music venues.

Old Hickory Whiskey Bar

BARS/PUBS | With a prohibition-era feel (think dark mahogany and industrial touches), this bar will take you back in time with its 375 whiskeys—and counting. If you're not interested in sipping yours straight, modern seasonal cocktails are sure to please even the most sophisticated palate. Fun fact: the bar's name was inspired by Andrew Jackson, the first Territorial Governor of Florida, who was called "Old Hickory" for his fierceness in battle. *123 S. Palafox* *850/332–5916* *www.oldhickorywhiskeybar.com.*

Seville Quarter

BARS/PUBS | In the heart of the Historic District is Pensacola's equivalent of New Orleans's French Quarter. In fact, you may think you've traveled to Louisiana when you enter any of its seven bars and two courtyards offering an eclectic mix of live music. College students pack the place on Thursday, tourists come on the weekend, and military men and women from six nearby bases are stationed here nearly all the time. This is a classic Pensacola nightspot, and on most nights there's a small cover after 8 pm. ✉ *130 E. Government St.* ☎ *850/434–6211* 🌐 *www.sevillequarter.com* 🎫.

Vinyl Music Hall

BARS/PUBS | Music now fills the space of this 112-year-old former Masonic lodge. An impressive variety of bands and acts have floated through the intimate music venue, which offers mostly standing room. It's also home to 5½ bar, where mixologists create unique, handcrafted drinks from the classic to the contemporary in a swanky, downtown loft atmosphere. The box office is open weekdays between noon and 5 as well as before all events (one hour before start time). ✉ *2 S. Palafox Pl.* ☎ *877/435–9849* 🌐 *www.vinylmusichall.com.*

World of Beer

BARS/PUBS | Two Pensacola-area natives dreamed up this watering hole while in college in Tampa, where the original location is still operating. They brought the business home and plopped it right on bustling Palafox. It's hard not to find a beer you like here, so saddle up to the bar and pick from dozens of drafts on tap or bottled brews. World of Beer also serves bar fare, like German pretzels and chimichurri meatballs. ✉ *200 S. Palafox* ☎ *850/332–7952* 🌐 *www.worldofbeer.com/pensacola.*

Shopping

The Pensacola area is home to a variety of shopping options. The Palafox and Seville Historic Districts are enjoyable areas for browsing or buying; here boutiques sell trendy clothing and imported and eclectic home furnishings. Meanwhile, the area's main shopping staple, Cordova Mall, contains national chain stores.

Cordova Mall

SHOPPING CENTERS/MALLS | Ten miles north of the Historic Districts, this mall is anchored by department stores Dillard's and Belk. There are also more than 125 specialty shops, including the usual mall suspects like Victoria's Secret and Bath & Body Works, and a food court. ✉ *5100 N. 9th Ave.* ☎ *850/477–5355* 🌐 *www.simon.com/mall/cordova-mall.*

Activities

BASEBALL

Pensacola Blue Wahoos

BASEBALL/SOFTBALL | **FAMILY** | The latest gem of the city sits on Pensacola's waterfront and offers a multiuse, public-private park development with a 5,038-seat multipurpose stadium and Randall K. and Marth A. Hunter Amphitheater that overlooks beautiful Pensacola Bay. The stadium is home to the Pensacola Blue Wahoos, the Double A minor league affiliate of the Minnesota Twins. Keep an eye out for tickets—they sell out fast—as well as a variety of other events that fill the stadium and surrounding park year-round. ✉ *Vince J. Whibbs Sr. Community Maritime Park, 301 W. Main St.* ☎ *850/934–8444* 🌐 *bluewahoos.com* 🎫 *Tickets $7–$9 SRO, $10–14 seats.*

CANOEING AND KAYAKING

The Pensacola Bay area is known as the "Canoe Capital of Florida," and the pure sand-bottom Blackwater River is a particularly nice place to paddle. You can rent canoes and kayaks from a number of local companies as well as from outfits on nearby Perdido Key, home to the picturesque Perdido Watershed.

Adventures Unlimited

CANOEING/ROWING/SKULLING | If you want to get away from it all (cell service is spotty) and have outdoor fun, drive about an hour north of Pensacola to Adventures Unlimited. This outfitter on Coldwater Creek rents canoes, kayaks, tubes, and stand-up paddleboards for adventurers to explore the Coldwater and Blackwater rivers in the Blackwater State Forest. Though prime canoe season lasts roughly from March through mid-November, Adventures Unlimited rents year-round. There are also nearly a mile of zip lines, some reaching 65 feet in the air. There are campsites and unique cabins, including the "Lorax Loft," a treehouse cabin with a branch running right through the kitchen. ✉ *8974 Tomahawk Landing Rd., Milton* ☎ *850/623–6197, 800/239–6864* 🌐 *www.adventuresunlimited.com.*

Blackwater Canoe Rental

CAMPING—SPORTS-OUTDOORS | Canoe, kayak, and tube rentals for exploring the Blackwater River are available from this outfitter in Milton, located northeast of Pensacola off Interstate 10 Exit 31. ✉ *6974 Deaton Bridge Rd., Milton* ☎ *850/623–0235* 🌐 *www.blackwatercanoe.com.*

FISHING

With 52 miles of coastline and a number of inland waterways, the Pensacola area is a great place to drop a line. Bottom fishing is best for amberjack and grouper; offshore trolling trips search for tuna, wahoo, and sailfish; and inshore charters are out to hook redfish, cobia, and pompano. For a complete list of local fishing charters, visit 🌐 *www.pensacolafishing.com.*

Pensacola Beach Marina and Charters

FISHING | For a full- or half-day deep-sea charter, try the Pensacola Beach Marina, which represents several charter outfits. ✉ *655 Pensacola Beach Blvd., Pensacola Beach* ☎ *850/932–0304* 🌐 *www.pensacolabeachmarina.com.*

GOLF

The bay area has a number of award-winning and picturesque golf courses. Some offer beach views, and others are local haunts.

Club at Hidden Creek

GOLF | Hidden Creek is known for its lush landscape, rolling terrain, and scenic layout. The public course, designed by Ron Garl, offers challenging play for all levels of golfers with water throughout and well-guarded greens. It's rated one of the "Top 201 Courses to Play in North America" by *Golf Digest.* A natural grass practice facility with driving, putting, and chipping areas offers another unique feature. ✉ *3070 PGA Blvd., Navarre* ☎ *850/939–4604* 🌐 *theclubathiddencreek.com* 🎫 *$25–$45* ⛳ *18 holes, 6805 yards, par 72.*

Lost Key Golf Club

GOLF | Framed by the natural beauty of Perdido Key, Lost Key is a short drive from downtown Pensacola, near the Florida/Alabama border. This Arnold Palmer Signature Design Course was the first golf course in the world to be certified as an Audubon International Silver Signature Sanctuary. Each hole of this course, which is open to the public, has five sets of tees to challenge all skill levels. The clubhouse has a full-service golf shop, men's and ladies' locker room facilities with lounge areas, and a restaurant and bar with indoor and outdoor seating and panoramic views of the golf course. ✉ *625 Lost Key Dr.* ☎ *850/549–2161, 888/256–7853* 🌐 *www.lostkey.com* 🎫 *$39–$79* ⛳ *18 holes, 6801 yards, par 71.*

Pensacola Beach

5 miles south of Pensacola via U.S. 98 to Rte. 399 (Bob Sikes) Bridge.

Connected to Pensacola by two long bridges, the island offers both a Gulf-front and "sound" side for those seeking a calmer seaside experience. Public beaches abound in the area, including Casino Beach at the tip of Pensacola Beach Road, which offers live entertainment at its pavilion in the summer, as well as showers and bathrooms. Quietwater Beach Boardwalk, across the street from

Casino Beach, also offers boutique shopping, eateries, and nightlife.

Long home to chain hotels as well as locally owned motels, the beach has opened a number of condominiums and resorts in recent years. Don't miss renting a bike or taking a drive to explore both Fort Pickens Road and J. Earle Bowden Way (connecting Pensacola Beach to the Navarre Beach area), which have reopened after many years of being closed to vehicular traffic. They offer breathtaking, unobstructed views of the Gulf.

GETTING HERE

Pensacola Beach is a short drive (just 5 miles) from Pensacola across the Bob Sikes Bridge (Route 399).

Sights

Ft. Pickens

ARCHAEOLOGICAL SITE | Constructed of more than 21 million locally made bricks, this fort, dating back to 1834, once served as a prison for Apache chief Geronimo. A National Park Service plaque describes the complex as a "confusing jumble of fortifications," but the real attractions here are the beach, nature exhibits, a large campground, an excellent gift shop, and breathtaking views of Pensacola Bay and the lighthouse across the inlet. It's the perfect place for a picnic lunch and a bit of history, too. ✉ *Fort Pickens Rd.* ✥ *At the western tip of the island* ☎ *850/934–2600* 🎫 *$7 per person, $20 per vehicle for 7-day pass to all areas of the Gulf Islands National Seashore.*

Beaches

Casino Beach

BEACH—SIGHT | Named for the Casino Resort, the island's first tourist spot when it opened in 1931 (the same day as the first Pensacola Beach Bridge), this beach offers everything from seasonal live entertainment to public restrooms and showers. You can also lounge in the shade of the Pensacola Beach Gulf Pier. Casino Beach has the most parking for beach access on the island and is just a short stroll from dining, entertainment, and major hotels such as the Margaritaville Beach Hotel and Holiday Inn Resort Beachfront Hotel. **Amenities:** food and drink; lifeguards (seasonal); parking (free); showers; toilets. **Best for:** swimming; walking. ✉ *735 Pensacola Beach Blvd.*

Langdon Beach

BEACH—SIGHT | The Panhandle is home to the Florida District of the Gulf Islands National Seashore, the longest tract of protected seashore in the United States. At the Ft. Pickens area of the park on the Gulf-side tip of Santa Rosa Island, this beach is one of the top spots to experience the unspoiled beauty and snow-white beaches for which this area is known. Keep an eye out for wildlife of the flying variety; the Ft. Pickens area is known for its nesting shorebirds. A large covered pavilion is great for picnicking and a few minutes of shade. **Amenities:** lifeguards; parking (no fee); showers; toilets; water sports. **Best for:** snorkeling; solitude; sunrise; sunset; walking. ✉ *Fort Pickens Rd.* ✥ *3 miles west of Pensacola Beach on west end of Santa Rosa Island* 🌐 *www.nps.gov/guis/index.htm.*

Restaurants

Casino Beach Bar & Grille

$$ | **ECLECTIC** | One of the newer hot spots for drinking and dining, this restaurant and bar benefits from its location directly on the Gulf of Mexico. Eat in the covered open-air bar, or pick a spot under an umbrella on the Gulf-front patio and dig into island-inspired fare featuring plantains and beans, along with favorites like fish tacos, poke bowls, and gumbo. **Known for:** handcrafted cocktails; unsurpassed views; fish tacos. $ *Average main: $18*

41 Ft. Pickens Rd. 850/932–6313 *www.casinobeachbar.com.*

Flounder's Chowder and Ale House
$$ | **SEAFOOD** | The wide and peaceful Gulf spreads out before you at this casual restaurant where, armed with a fruity libation, you're all set for a night of "floundering" at its best. Funkiness comes courtesy of an eclectic collection of objets d'art; tastiness is served in specialties such as seafood nachos and the shrimp-boat platter. **Known for:** flounder chowder; live entertainment nightly in season; Gulf-inspired cocktails. *Average main: $16 800 Quietwater Beach Blvd., Gulf Breeze 850/932–2003 www.flounderschowderhouse.com.*

Grand Marlin Restaurant and Oyster Bar
$$$ | **SEAFOOD** | This restaurant offers unforgettable views of Santa Rosa Sound and Pensacola Bay along with mouth-watering fresh local cuisine. Top-notch seafood shares the menu—printed daily—with specials. **Known for:** fresh seafood and Apalachicola oysters; breathtaking views; sophisticated atmosphere. *Average main: $21 400 Pensacola Beach Blvd. 850/677–9153 www.thegrandmarlin.com.*

Peg Leg Pete's
$$ | **SEAFOOD** | **FAMILY** | Prepare for long lines during the summertime at this local favorite. Dig into seafood favorites at one of three dining areas—indoors, outdoors on the covered deck, or at picnic tables downstairs, near the aptly named Under Where Bar, where there's often live music. **Known for:** lively, family-friendly atmosphere; big portions; fried fish and shrimp. *Average main: $15 1010 Ft. Pickens Rd., Gulf Breeze 850/932–4139 www.peglegpetes.com.*

Hotels

Hilton Pensacola Beach Hotel
$ | **HOTEL** | Right on the Gulf, this hotel offers incredible views at one of the beach's most affordable prices. **Pros:** impeccably well kept; great on-site dining; water views from all rooms. **Cons:** chain hotel feel; high price during season. *Rooms from: $179 12 Via De Luna 850/916–2999, 866/916–2999 www.hiltonpensacolabeach.com 272 rooms No meals.*

Holiday Inn Resort Pensacola Beach
$$ | **RESORT** | **FAMILY** | Known for its 250-foot lazy river and cascading waterfall, this Gulf-front hotel is one of the most family-friendly on the beach. **Pros:** indoor pool and large outdoor pool; beach-view fitness center; seasonal kids' programs. **Cons:** some rooms have parking-lot views; pool area very crowded during peak season. *Rooms from: $200 14 Via de Luna 850/932–5331 holidayinnresortpensacolabeach.com 206 rooms No meals.*

Margaritaville Beach Hotel
$$ | **HOTEL** | This tropical getaway, inspired by the lyrics of Jimmy Buffett, gives you the relaxed, fun Margaritaville experience with the amenities of a top-notch hotel. **Pros:** clean, inviting atmosphere; lots of dining options; local spa services available. **Cons:** somewhat off the beaten path. *Rooms from: $299 165 Fort Pickens Rd. 850/916–9755 www.margaritavillehotel.com 162 rooms No meals.*

Activities

Chase-N-Fins
WILDLIFE-WATCHING | **FAMILY** | Climb aboard this 50-foot navy utility launch, which cruises Pensacola Bay along Ft. Pickens, Pensacola Pass, and the Lighthouse at Pensacola Naval Air Station in search of friendly dolphins. *655 Pensacola Beach Blvd. 850/492–6337 www.chase-n-fins.com From $25.*

Pensacola Beach Gulf Pier
FISHING | The 1,471-foot-long pier touts itself as "the most friendly pier around." It hosts serious anglers who find everything they'll need here—from pole

rentals to bait—to land that big one, but those looking to catch only a beautiful sunset are welcome, too. Check the pier's website for the latest reports on what's biting. ✉ *41 Fort Pickens Rd.* ☎ *850/934–7200* 🌐 *www.fishpensacolabeachpier.com* 🎟 *$7.50 fishers, $1.25 observers.*

Premier Dolphin Cruises

WILDLIFE-WATCHING | **FAMILY** | Operated by Portofino Island Resort, this 63-foot open-air covered catamaran sets sail from the Portofino Boardwalk on Pensacola Beach. The boat includes bar and food sales and private restrooms. Morning and midday cruises are the best time to view dolphins, but the sunset cruise is something spectacular. ✉ *400 Quietwater Beach Rd.* ☎ *855/393–7783* 🌐 *www.pensacoladolphincruise.com* ☞ *$27.*

Day Trips from Pensacola

Inland, where the northern reaches of the Panhandle butt up against the back porches of Alabama and Georgia, you'll find a part of Florida that is definitely more Dixie than Sunshine State, with few lodging options other than the chain motels that flank the Interstate 10 exits and a decidedly slower pace of life than you'll find on the tourist-heavy Gulf Coast.

But the area's natural attractions—hills and farmland, untouched small towns, and state parks—make for great day trips from the coast should the sky turn gray or the skin red. Explore underground caverns where aeons-old rock formations create bizarre scenes, visit one of Florida's up-and-coming wineries, or poke around small-town America in DeFuniak Springs. Altogether, the inland area of the Panhandle is one of the state's most satisfyingly soothing regions.

DeFuniak Springs

77 miles northeast of Pensacola on U.S. 90 off I–10.

This scenic spot has a rather unusual claim to fame: at its center lies a nearly perfectly symmetrical spring-fed lake, one of only two such naturally circular bodies of water in the world (the other is in Switzerland). A sidewalk encircles Lake DeFuniak (also called Circle Lake), which is dotted by pine and shade trees, creating a very pleasing atmosphere for a long-distance mosey.

In 1885 the town was chosen as the location for the New York Chautauqua educational society's winter assembly. The Chautauqua programs were discontinued in 1922, but DeFuniak Springs attempts to revive them, in spirit at least, by sponsoring a countywide Chautauqua Festival in April. Christmas is a particularly festive time, when the sprawling Victorian houses surrounding the lake are decorated to the nines.

There's not a tremendous amount to see here, but if you have the good sense to travel U.S. 90 to discover Old Florida, at least take the time to travel Circle Drive to see its beautiful Victorian homes and walk around the small downtown area and drop in its bookstores, cafés, and small shops.

Sights

Britton Hill

HIKING/WALKING | **FAMILY** | Britton Hill is the high point in Florida, located just south of the Florida–Alabama state line off County Road 285 in the town of Lakewood. At 334 feet above sea level, it is the lowest high point in the United States, so it's an easy one to check off the list for highpointers. ✉ *2759 North County Highway 285, DeFuniak Springs.*

Chautauqua Winery

WINERY/DISTILLERY | Open since 1989, the winery has won honors in national and international competitions, with most wines crafted from two varieties of sweet muscadine grapes, the white Carlos and red Noble. Take a free tour to see how ancient art blends with modern technology. Keep in mind, most of the action takes place during harvest season, from late August through September, when the owners invite visitors to pick and eat some grapes from their on-site preview vineyard (the 50-acre vineyard is about 12 miles north of Defuniak Springs). Wine tastings are held daily throughout the year, and the under-21 set is invited to sample muscadine grape juice. ✉ *364 Hugh Adams Rd., DeFuniak Springs* ☎ *850/892–5887* 🌐 *www.chautauquawinery.com* 🎟 *Free.*

Falling Waters State Park

35 miles east of DeFuniak Springs via U.S. 90 and Rte. 77.

Falling Waters State Park

NATIONAL/STATE PARK | This site of a Civil War–era whiskey distillery and, later, an exotic plant nursery (some species still thrive in the wild) is best known for also being the site of the Falling Waters Sink. The 100-foot-deep cylindrical pit provides the background for a waterfall, and there's an observation deck for viewing this natural phenomenon. The water free-falls 67 feet to the bottom of the sink, but where it goes after that is a mystery. ✉ *1130 State Park Rd., Chipley* ☎ *850/638–6130* 🌐 *www.floridastateparks.org/fallingwaters* 🎟 *$5 per vehicle, up to eight people.*

Florida Caverns State Park

13 miles northeast of Falling Waters off U.S. 90 on Rte. 166.

A short drive from the center of Marianna, a cute and pristine community, you can see what's behind or—more accurately—what's beneath it all.

Florida Caverns State Park

CAVE | In October 2018 Florida Caverns State Park was devastated by Hurricane Michael. More than 90 percent of the park's trees were felled, and it is not expected to reopen until some time in 2019 or 2020. Check the park website or call the office for the latest information on what parts of the park are operational. When operational, the park includes hiking trails, campsites, and areas for swimming, horseback riding, and canoeing on the Chipola River. You won't want to miss the ranger-led cave tours revealing stalactites, stalagmites, soda straws, columns, rim stones, flowstones, and "waterfalls" of solid rock at these underground caverns, where the temperature hovers at an oh-so-pleasant 68°F year-round. ✉ *3345 Caverns Rd., Marianna* ✣ *Off U.S. 90 on Rte. 166* ☎ *850/482–1228* 🌐 *https://www.floridastateparks.org/parks-and-trails/florida-caverns-state-park* 🎟 *Park $5 per vehicle, up to eight people; caverns $8.*

Fort Walton Beach

46 miles east of Pensacola via U.S. 98.

This coastal town dates from the Civil War but had to wait more than 75 years to come into its own. Patriots loyal to the Confederate cause organized Walton's Guard (named in honor of Colonel George Walton, onetime acting territorial governor of West Florida) and camped at a site on Santa Rosa Sound, later known

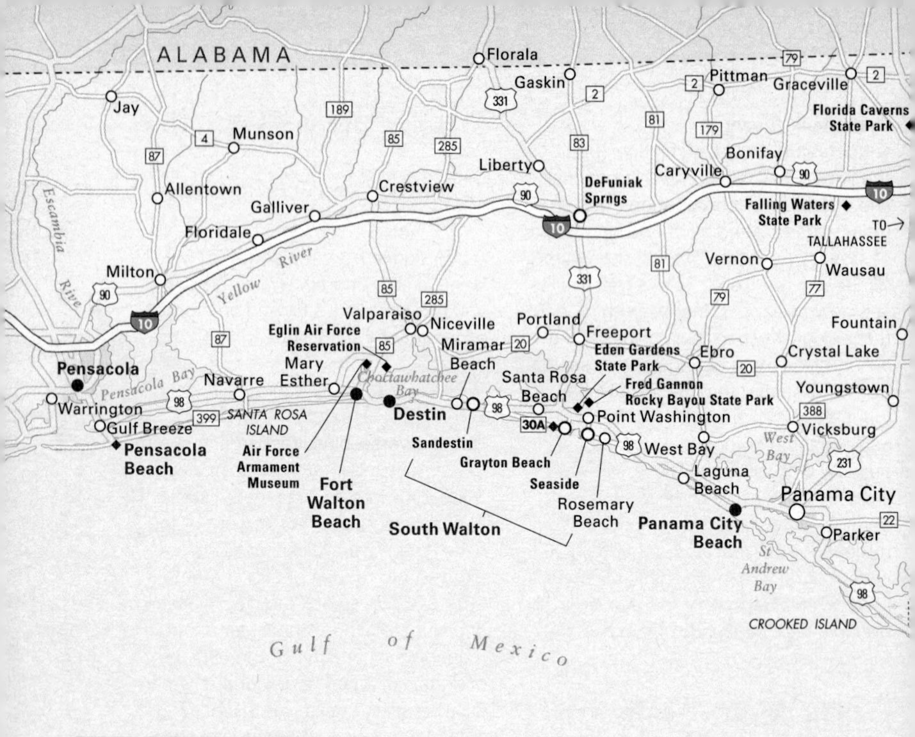

Pensacola Bay and the Emerald Coast

as Camp Walton. In 1940 fewer than 90 people lived in Fort Walton Beach, but within a decade the city became a boomtown, thanks to New Deal money for roads and bridges and the development of Eglin Field during World War II.

Although off-limits to civilians, Eglin Air Force Base, which encompasses 724 square miles of land with 10 auxiliary fields and 21 runways, is Fort Walton Beach's main source of income. Tourism runs a close second. Despite inland sprawl, the town has a cute little shopping district with independent merchants along U.S. 98.

GETTING HERE AND AROUND

Northwest Florida Regional Airport (VPS), on Highway 85 in North Eglin, is served by American Airlines, Delta, United Airlines, and Allegiant. There is no public transportation from the airport, but it is serviced by several national car-rental agencies and more than 30 ground transportation companies. For a complete list, visit *www.flyvps.com* and click on Taxis & Shuttles.

Sights

Air Force Armament Museum

MUSEUM | The collection at this museum just outside the Eglin Air Force Base's main gate contains more than 5,000 armaments (e.g., missiles, bombs, and aircraft) from World Wars I and II and the Korean, Vietnam, and Gulf wars. Included are uniforms, engines, weapons, aircraft, and flight simulators. You can't miss the museum—there's a squadron of aircraft including a B-17 Flying Fortress, an SR-71 Blackbird, a B-52, a B-25, and helicopters parked on the grounds in front. A continuously playing 32-minute movie, *Arming* *the Future*, features current weapons and Eglin's history and its role in their development. The self-guided tour includes interactive displays. Visitors are encouraged to take photos. ✉ *Eglin Air Force Base, 100 Museum Dr. (Rte. 85)* ☎ *850/882–4062* 🌐 *www.afarmament-museum.com* 🎫 *Free* ⏲ *Closed Sun.*

Eglin Air Force Base Reservation
MILITARY SITE | The 250,000 acres of the Eglin reservation conditionally open to the public include 21 ponds and plenty of challenging, twisting wooded trails that are all open to exploration. The area appeals to outdoors enthusiasts who want to hunt, fish, canoe, and swim. You can buy a day pass to hike or mountain bike on the Timberlake Trail. In order to gain access to the areas of the reservation that are open to the public (and many areas are closed all the time, others just some of the time), you must obtain a permit from the Natural Resource Division (also known locally as the Jackson Guard). ✉ *Jackson Guard, 107 Rte. 85 N, Niceville* ☎ *850/882–4165* 🌐 *eglin.isportsman.net* ⏲ *Closed Sun.*

Gulfarium
ZOO | FAMILY | This marine adventure park has been a beloved attraction for locals and visitors alike for more than 60 years. Species exhibited here include dolphins, otters, penguins, alligators, harbor seals, and sharks. Meander through a range of exhibits and get up close and personal with marine life thanks to several new interactive experiences, from swimming with our watery friends to feedings. For the not-so faint of heart, the Stingray Bay Snorkel offers a chance to swim with the creatures as well as sharks, but for an even more intensive (and expensive) experience, there's a five-hour one-on-one with a marine-mammal trainer. The Gulfarium is also home to the C.A.R.E. Center, which rescues and rehabilitates injured sea turtles and, when possible, releases them back into the wild. ✉ *1010 Miracle Strip Pkwy.* ☎ *850/243–9046, 800/247–8575* 🌐 *www.gulfarium.com* 🎫 *$23.95, animal encounters extra.*

John Beasley Park
BEACH—SIGHT | This tranquil seaside county park rests among the rolling dunes on Okaloosa Island. Two dune walkovers lead to the beach, where there are a dozen covered picnic tables, pavilions, changing rooms, and freshwater showers—plus lifeguards in summer. The city's hottest nightlife is just down the road, but families can enjoy the scenic beauty. There is also an emphasis on wheelchair beach access. **Amenities:** lifeguards; ample parking; showers; toilets. **Best for:** sunset; unobstructed views; walking. ✉ *1550 Miracle Strip Parkway* 🌐 *www.emeraldcoastfl.com/listing/john-c-beasley-park/84/.*

Angler's Beachside Grill and Sports Bar
$$ | AMERICAN | FAMILY | Unless you sit in the water, you can't dine any closer to the Gulf than at this casual beachside bar and grill next to the Gulfarium. Located at the entrance to Okaloosa Island Pier (and within a complex of other nightclubs and restaurants), Angler's houses the requisite sports bar with TVs broadcasting sports events, including in the elevators and bathrooms. **Known for:** sports bar fare plus fresh fish; warm smoked tuna dip; excellent Gulf views. $ *Average main: $19* ✉ *1030 Miracle Strip Pkwy.* ☎ *850/796–0260.*

Holiday Inn Resort Fort Walton Beach Hotel
$$ | HOTEL | FAMILY | Located directly on the beach facing the Gulf of Mexico, this family-friendly resort has enough activities to keep all ages entertained—including one of the best pools in the area. **Pros:** steps from the beach; supervised

The Emerald Coast

On U.S. 98, several towns, each with its own personality, are strung along the shoreline from Pensacola southeast to St. George Island, their waters so strikingly green against the white sand that the area is called the Emerald Coast. The side-by-side cities of Destin and Fort Walton Beach seemingly merge into one sprawling destination and continue to spread as more condominiums, resort developments, shopping centers, and restaurants crowd the skyline each year. The view changes drastically—and for the better—farther along the coast as you veer off 98 and enter Scenic Route 30A, the main coastal road that leads to a more quiet stretch known as South Walton. Route 30A was developed later and more mindfully than the resorts along U.S. 98, and the road is much closer to the water. There aren't high-rise developments, and the majority of dwellings are privately owned homes and condominiums, many available to vacationers.

Continuing southeast on U.S. 98, you come to Panama City Beach. Front Beach Road, once crammed with carnival-like amusement parks and other attractions that earned it the not-so-complimentary nickname "Redneck Riviera," is now home to up-to-date shopping and entertainment complexes and new condos that have given the area a much-needed face-lift. Sadly, much of the up-and-coming sleeper cities of Port St. Joe and Mexico Beach were devastated by Hurricane Michael in 2018 and face years of reconstruction. Farther east is the quiet blue-collar town of Apalachicola. Once Florida's main oyster fishery, the town features a quaint, historic downtown filled with eateries and shops. Cross the Apalachicola Bay via the Bryant Patton Bridge to St. George Island. This unspoiled 28-mile-long barrier island offers some of America's most scenic beaches, including St. George Island State Park, which has the longest beachfront of any state park in Florida.

kids' programs; number of rooms with Gulf views. **Cons:** pay extra for beach services; some features unavailable in off-season because of routine maintenance. *$ Rooms from: $278 ✉ 1299 Miracle Strip Pkwy. SE ☎ 850/301–9000 🌐 holidayinnresortfortwaltonbeach.com 152 rooms No meals.*

The Island, by Hotel RL

$ | **RESORT** | **FAMILY** | At this family-friendly, beachside resort—recently renovated and upgraded—activity revolves around a 194,000-gallon pool (allegedly the area's largest) with a spectacular swim-through waterfall and a bar in the Grotto's rock wall. **Pros:** very family-friendly; walking distance to Island Time entertainment venue; private beach. **Cons:** renovations might be still under way; ask for a renovated room; attracts spring-break crowd. *$ Rooms from: $172 ✉ 1500 Miracle Strip Pkwy. SE ☎ 850/243–9161, 850/874–8962 for reservations 🌐 www.redlion.com/hotel-rl/fl/fort-walton/island-hotel-rl 335 rooms No meals.*

The Boardwalk

BARS/PUBS | This massive dining-and-entertainment complex at the entrance to the Okaloosa Island Pier includes several restaurants (Rockin Tacos, The Crab Trap, Floyd's Shrimp House, Al's Beach Club and Burger Bar, Lobster Tail, and Pino Gelato) as well as an assortment of live entertainment and shops. ✉ *1450 Miracle Strip Pkwy.* 🌐 *www.theboardwalkoi.com.*

Activities

Discovery Dive World
DIVING/SNORKELING | Run by military veterans, this full-service shop offers a variety of gear and lessons in snorkeling and diving, but its specialty is spear-fishing. Professional Association of Diving Instructors–certified courses are offered. ✉ *92 S. John Sims Pkwy. (SR 20), Valparaiso* ☎ *850/678–5001* 🌐 *www.discoverydiveworld.com* ☞ *Gear rental from $5 to $84 for a full set. Charter rates vary.*

Okaloosa Island Fishing Pier
FISHING | **FAMILY** | Don't miss a chance to go out to the end of this quarter-mile-long pier. Operators brag that it's possible to snag large tarpon, tuna, king mackerel and cobia from the octagon-shaped end of the pier. There's an admission fee (and a fee to fish), and you can buy bait and tackle, and rent poles as well. ✉ *1030 Miracle Strip Pkwy. E* ☎ *850/244–1023* 🌐 *www.okaloosaislandpier.net* 🎫 *$2; $8 to fish.*

Destin

8 miles east of Fort Walton Beach via U.S. 98.

Fort Walton Beach's "neighbor" lies on the other side of the strait connecting Choctawhatchee Bay with the Gulf of Mexico. The drive on Okaloosa Island between Fort Walton Beach and Destin is unique. The skinny island is largely undeveloped, so you'll get a great sense of the original coastline, with water views peeking through the massive dune line on one side and the estuarine waters of Choctawhatchee Bay on the other. Destin takes its name from its founder, Leonard A. Destin, a Connecticut sea captain who settled his family here sometime in the 1830s. For the next 100 years, Destin remained a sleepy little fishing village until the strait, or East Pass, was bridged in 1935. Then recreational anglers discovered its white sands, blue-green waters, and abundance of some of the most sought-after sport fish in the world. More billfish are hauled in around Destin each year than from all other Gulf ports combined, giving credence to its nickname, the World's Luckiest Fishing Village.

But you don't have to be the rod-and-reel type to love Destin. There's plenty to entertain everyone, from the sand-pail set to senior citizens, and there are many nice restaurants, which you'll have an easier time finding if you remember that the main drag through town is referred to as both U.S. 98 and Emerald Coast Parkway. The name makes sense, but part of what makes the Gulf look so emerald in these parts is the contrasting whiteness of the sand on the beach. Actually, it's pure, powder-soft Appalachian quartz, dropped off by a glacier a few thousand years back. Since quartz doesn't compress (and crews clean and rake the beach each evening), your feet get the sole-satisfying benefit of soft, sugary "sand" so pure it squeaks.

VISITOR INFORMATION

CONTACTS Destin Chamber of Commerce. ☎ *850/837–6241* 🌐 *www.destinchamber.com.*

Sights

Big Kahuna's Water & Adventure Park
AMUSEMENT PARK/WATER PARK | **FAMILY** | The water park is the big draw here, with a half dozen thrilling slides, raging (and lazy) rivers, a giant wave pool and areas just for little kids—more than 40 activities that will provide a day of freshwater fun. This complex has additional dry family-friendly attractions: 54 holes of miniature golf on three courses and aerial thrill rides. ✉ *1007 U.S. 98 E* ☎ *850/837–8319* 🌐 *www.bigkahunas.com* 🎫 *Grounds free, water park (based*

Live oaks draped with Spanish moss are most common in Northwest Florida.

on height) $35.99–$45.99, children under 2 free; miniature golf $6.99, Sky Coaster or Cyclone $14.99 ⏲ Water Park closed Labor Day–Apr. Adventure Park closed Labor Day–late Mar.

Beaches

Crab Island

BEACH—SIGHT | Not really an island, nor a beach, Crab Island is actually a sandbar in Destin's East Pass, just north of the Destin (aka Marler) Bridge. A favorite with locals, Crab Island draws water lovers and boaters, who wade to the sandbar or drop anchor in droves on fair-weather days, especially weekends. Several businesses in the area offer boat and jet ski rentals. People are friendly, so it's a great place to make new friends, and the shallow waters are good for families. A food barge as well as slides and other water activities are provided on the "island" seasonally. **Amenities:** food and drink; water sports. **Best for:** partiers; snorkeling; swimming. ✉ *Destin* ✣ *North side of East Pass and Marler Bridge.*

Henderson Park Beach State Park

BEACH—SIGHT | **FAMILY** | When Burney Henderson sold his family's land to the state to become a park, it preserved the last remaining coastal scrub area in Destin. The park has more than a mile of undisturbed beachfront, campsites, and a boardwalk overtop 30-foot snow-white sand dunes. Make a day of it: Walk the nature trail early in the morning, spend the afternoon at the beach, and hang around to enjoy a spectacular sunset. ✉ *17000 Emerald Coast Pkwy.* ☎ *850/837–7550* 🌐 *www.floridastateparks.org/parks-and trails/henderson-beach-state-park* 🎫 *$6 per vehicle.*

Restaurants

Harbor Docks

$$$ | **SEAFOOD** | **FAMILY** | Harbor Docks' casual feel is marked by picnic tables and hibachi grills and a beautiful view of Destin Harbor. Seafood is the star of the menu, and the restaurant, which has been around since 1979, has its own seafood market next door. **Known**

for: popular sushi bar; locally sourced seafood and produce; homemade fish dip. *Average main: $25* *538 Harbor Blvd.* *850/837–2506* *www.harbordocks.com.*

Marina Café

$$$ | **SEAFOOD** | A harbor view, impeccable service, and sophisticated fare create one of the finest dining experiences on the Emerald Coast. Call the creations contemporary Continental, offering diners a choice of Gulf seafood, USDA steaks, gourmet pizzas, classic creole, Mediterranean, or Pan-Asian dishes. **Known for:** fresh-caught seafood; extensive wine list; attentive service. *Average main: $24* *404 Harbor Blvd.* *850/837–7960* *www.marinacafe.com.*

Hotels

Emerald Grande at HarborWalk Village

$$$$ | **RESORT** | Even locals seek out the views at this harbor-front destination-within-a-destination, with luxurious accommodations and a full menu of amenities, including a full-service spa, marina, health club, and indoor/outdoor pools. **Pros:** great for larger families and groups; many top-rated amenities are part of the complex; steps away from HarborWalk Village. **Cons:** very busy and family-oriented, so it's not ideal for a romantic couple's getaway; must water-taxi to the beach. *Rooms from: $487* *10 Harbor Blvd.* *800/676–0091* *www.emeraldgrande.com* *269 rooms* *No meals.*

★ The Henderson Beach Resort & Spa

$$$$ | **RESORT** | No detail in style and service has been overlooked at Destin's newest resort hotel, which opened in 2016; from the grand foyer to the beautifully appointed rooms decorated in soothing coastal shades, The Henderson resort exudes luxury and tranquility. **Pros:** exceptional service; beautiful coastal decor; full-service spa. **Cons:** pricey; not directly on the beach; some rooms have better views than others. *Rooms from: $475* *200 Henderson Resort Way* *855/741–2777* *hendersonbeachresort.com* *170 rooms* *No meals.*

Shopping

Banana Bart's

GIFTS/SOUVENIRS | There are tourist shops up and down the Emerald Coast Parkway selling suntan lotion, swimsuits, floats, and gator heads, but there's nothing quite like Banana Bart's. In a sea of newness, this brightly painted store is a standout, situated in one of Destin's original 1930s-era fishing shacks. Inside there really is a Banana Bart, who opened his store more than 30 years ago. Every square inch of this rabbit warren of a store is jam-packed with baubles, jewelry, and stuff appealing to all ages. Bart has a great selection of bespoke T-shirts with graphics extolling the virtues of the beach life. And the parking lot offers a lovely view of Destin Harbor. *620 Harbor Blvd.* *850/837–4355.*

Destin Commons

SHOPPING CENTERS/MALLS | This open-air lifestyle center features more than 90 high-end specialty shops and dining options, as well as a 14-screen theater, miniature train, and nautical theme park for kids. You can't miss the mega-sized, Bass Pro Shops, a two-story outdoor extravaganza that includes an aquarium and a massive selection of outdoor gear, from boats to clothes to fishing hooks. Also on-site is Uncle Buck's FishBowl & Grill, which includes an underwater-themed bowling alley and restaurant. *4100 Legendary Dr.* *850/337–8700* *www.destincommons.com.*

Activities

Destin has the largest charter-boat fishing fleet in the state. You can also pier-fish from the 3,000-foot-long Destin Catwalk and along East Pass Bridge. Paddleboarding, as well as scuba diving are also popular. Although visibility here (about 50 feet) isn't on par with the reefs of the Atlantic Coast, divers can explore artificial reefs, wrecks, and a limestone shelf at depths of up to 90 feet.

Dockside Watersports & Parasailing

FISHING | While a great place to pick up bait, tackle, and most anything else you need for a day of fishing, Dockside's claim to fame is renting pontoon boats and personal watercraft to tourists, providing detailed instructions on operating the vessel, and Pmaking recommendations for and providing directions to the best places to enjoy a day on the water, including Crab Island in Choctawhatchee Bay just north of the bridge. Be warned: Changes in Coast Guard regulations limit the number of passengers on vessels, depending on size. Confirm before booking. ✉ *390 Harbor Blvd.* ☏ *850/428–3313* 🌐 *www.boatrentalsindestin.com.*

Emerald Coast Paddleboard

WATER SPORTS | Combining stand-up paddleboarding (SUP) with yoga classes, Emerald Coast Paddleboard provides healthy adventurists a way to connect nature and fitness, focusing on balance, wellness and bliss, seasonally from May to October. SUP Yoga is great fun for small groups such as bachelorette parties, bridal parties, and family or college reunions. They cater to all levels, from those with no yoga or SUP experience to serious practitioners of both. Paddling excursions and private SUP Yoga group classes start at $10 per person, if you bring your own board. ✉ *Twin Cities Park, N. John Sims Pkwy, Valparaiso* ☏ *850/376–3966* 🌐 *emeraldcoastpaddleboard.com.*

Emerald Coast Scuba

SCUBA DIVING | A full-service dive shop with top-of-the-line equipment and accessories for sale or rent, Emerald Coast Scuba has been in business more than 30 years. Climb aboard the Aquanaut for excursions to snorkel, swim or lounge in the shallows of the Destin Jetty, or explore the reefs and wrecks off the Emerald Coast. Professional Association of Diving Instructors-certified courses and swimming lessons are offered. ✉ *503-B Harbor Blvd.* ☏ *850/837–0955* 🌐 *www.divedestin.com* 🎫 *Dive trips from $65, snorkel cruises from $30.*

GUSU Paddlesports

WATER SPORTS | Get Up Stand Up (GUSU) Paddlesports rents paddleboards, surfboards, skateboards, beach chairs, beach umbrellas, and lounge sets along the Emerald Coast from Destin to South Walton. It manufactures its own boards and sells clothing and accessories. ✉ *219 Mountain Dr.* ☏ *850/460–7300* 🌐 *www.gusupaddlesports.com* 🎫 *Paddleboard rentals from $30 for 1½ hours to $90 for a full day; multiday rentals from $75 per day.*

HarborWalk Marina

FISHING | At this rustic-looking waterfront complex you can get bait, gas, tackle, and food before heading out in search of the 20 species of edible game fish in Destin's waters. Regularly scheduled party-boat fishing excursions offer a cheaper alternative to chartering or renting your own boat. All are available here, for a price. ✉ *66 Harbor Blvd. (U.S. 98 E)* ☏ *850/650–2400* 🌐 *harborwalkmarina.net.*

Indian Bayou Golf Club

GOLF | The 18-hole Indian Bayou Golf Club, a semi-private course that opened in 1978, features four sets of tees for different skill levels. Greens and fairways are Bermuda grass. This is one of the more affordable courses in the area. ✉ *1 Country Club Dr. E* ✥ *Off Airport Rd., off U.S. 98* ☏ *850/837–6191* 🌐 *www.indianbayougolf.com* 🎫 *From $30* ⛳ *Choctaw Course: 9 holes, 3464 yards, par 36. Seminole Course: 9 holes, 3614 yards, par 36.*

Kelly Plantation Golf Club

GOLF | Designed by Fred Couples and Gene Bates, this semiprivate course is rated 4.5 stars by *Golf Digest*. The overall layout is encouraging for novice golfers from the forward tees, with hardly any forced carries; however, from the back tees, it's an entirely different game. Stretching 7,099 yards, the course offers a serious driving test for long hitters. Greens are unique on almost every hole. Keep an eye out for hole 4's spectacular, panoramic view of Choctawhatchee Bay, and take in the scents and sights of magnolias and palmettos, native to Northwest Florida. The Grille at Kelly Plantation Golf Club is open to the public and features classic clubhouse fare. ✉ *307 Kelly Plantation Dr.* ☎ *850/650–7600* 🌐 *www.kellyplantationgolf.com* *$69–$145* *18 holes, 7099 yards, par 72.*

Regatta Bay Golf and Country Club

GOLF | One of the top-ranked courses in Northwest Florida, semiprivate Regatta Bay is open to the public and also home to Destin's only Golf Academy. The par-72 course, designed by Robert C. Walker, former lead architect for Arnold Palmer, is nestled in almost 120 acres of nature preserve along Choctawhatchee Bay and offers challenges to players of all skill levels. Amenities include GPS-enabled golf carts, mango-scented iced towels, on-course circulating beverage carts, and a full-service restaurant. ✉ *465 Regatta Bay Blvd.* ☎ *850/337–8080* 🌐 *www.regattabay.com* *$69–$95* *18 holes, 6894 yards, par 72.*

SUP Express

WATER SPORTS | Offering paddleboard and kayak rentals with free delivery, SUP Express also offers guided sunrise, sunset, and glow-in-the-dark night paddling tours. Safety equipment is included. Call for availability and rates for guided tours, multiple-day rentals, and weekly and group discounts. ✉ *Destin* ☎ *850/290–3787* 🌐 *www.supexpress.com* ☞ *Half-day rental (4 hours) $45; full-day $75.*

South Walton

The 16 beach communities of Miramar, Sandestin, Dune Allen, Gulf Place, Santa Rosa Beach, Blue Mountain Beach, Grayton Beach, WaterColor, Seaside, Seagrove, WaterSound, Seacrest, Seascape, Alys Beach, Rosemary Beach, and Inlet Beach are spread out along the 26-mile stretch of coastline between Destin and Panama City Beach in South Walton County, or SoWal, if you want to sound hip and local. Though you see the taller structures of Destin and Panama City Beach on either side in the distance, much of the area's buildings are low-slung, less imposing structures. A decidedly laid-back, refined mood prevails in these parts, where vacation homes go for millions and selecting a dinner spot is usually the day's most challenging decision. You're sure to find a town to fit your vacationing personality—from sprawling mega-resorts like Sandestin or Watercolor to sophisticated, new communities like Alys Beach to Old Florida cabins found in places originally discovered by locals like Grayton Beach and Inlet Beach.

Accommodations consist primarily of private-home rentals, the majority of which are managed by local real-estate firms. But there are also resorts and boutique hotels for a more hotel-like experience. Pretty much every community along Scenic Route 30A has a walkable town center with restaurants, bars, and a growing number of boutiques selling everything from fine art and unique hand-painted furniture to jewelry, gifts, and clothes. And the entire stretch of small communities is connected by a bike, walking, and running path, so you can see them all in a day or explore at your leisure.

VISITOR INFORMATION

CONTACTS South Walton Visitor Center. ✉ *25777 U.S. Highway 331 S, Santa Rosa Beach* ✣ *At the intersection of*

Attractions Below the Surface

Although sand and surf are the main attractions along the Gulf beaches, much more goes on beneath those emerald-green waters. The South Walton Artificial Reef Association (SWARA) recently created four snorkel-able reefs in whimsical shapes in South Walton that are 12 to 21 feet below the water's surface. Located 250 to 300 yards offshore, you'll need a kayak, paddleboard, or personal flotation device to reach them, but the steel, concrete, and limestone structures are already attracting fish and other sea life. The reef shaped like a dolphin is off the coast of Miramar Beach, the seahorse off Topsail Hill State Preserve, the sea turtle off Grayton Beach, and the cobia off Inlet Beach. SWARA also has created a dozen other reefs in deeper water along the coastline for fishing and diving. The group's website (🌐 *www.swarareefs.org*) includes GPS locations and a listing of tour services, dive shops, and fishing charters that visit the reefs.

U.S. Highways 331 and 98 ☎ *850/267–1216, 800/822–6877* 🌐 *www.visitsouthwalton.com.*

Miramar Beach/Sandestin

Much of the Miramar Beach community is consumed by the Sandestin Golf and Beach Resort, which sprawls over 2,400 acres from the beach to the Choctawhatchee Bay. Park the car here and you may never have to leave the resort property for your entire visit. It's a one-stop shop for family fun or a quiet getaway, offering everything from stunning golf courses to exceptional spa services. The Village of Baytowne Wharf in Sandestin offers a plethora of restaurants and nightlife options for those seeking entertainment. This is one of the areas in South Walton where you can also enjoy views of both the Gulf of Mexico and Choctawhatchee Bay, mere minutes from each other. Miramar Beach also is home to the popular and more compact Sandestin Hilton Beach Golf Resort & Spa. Year-round events and abundant shopping, including a massive outlet mall, also make the area a draw for guests all four seasons.

Hotels

Hilton Sandestin Beach Golf Resort & Spa
$$$ | **HOTEL** | **FAMILY** | While it adheres to the Hilton standards of comfort and service, this family-friendly hotel, which has been run by the same owners for more than 30 years, is constantly refreshing and expanding the resort's amenities, and it shows. **Pros:** plethora of on-site dining options; every room has Gulf views; three pools, including one indoors. **Cons:** additional resort fee; can get busy during conference events; beach can get congested in season. *Rooms from: $369* ✉ *4000 Sandestin Blvd. S, Destin* ☎ *850/267–9500, 800/559–1805 reservations* 🌐 *www.hiltonsandestinbeach.com* *602 rooms* *No meals.*

Sandestin Bayside
$$ | **RENTAL** | The Bayside Inn offers the best value on the Sandestin resort, with the lowest cost per night combined with amenities including free bicycle, body-board and kayak rentals, fitness center access, and tennis court time. **Pros:** good value; book through the resort and several amenities are included; great views of the Choctawhatchee Bay. **Cons:**

you could end up with a parking lot view; the inn has a chain hotel sensibility; perhaps too much privacy. *$ Rooms from: $249 ✉ 9300 Emerald Coast Pkwy, Sandestin ☎ 800/622–1623 reservations 🌐 www.sandestin.com 🛏 1,300 rooms 🍽 No meals.*

Sandestin Beachside

$$$ | RENTAL | FAMILY | The beachside includes tower properties directly on the beach, Westwinds and Beachside 1 and 2; the Luau tower and low-rise villas are a short walk (golf carts are available at some units) to the beach. **Pros:** right on the beach; Gulf views; large units with kitchens available are great for families. **Cons:** hectic during summer season; units are individually owned and design quality can vary; it's a hike or a car/tram ride to get to The Village of Baytowne Wharf. *$ Rooms from: $350 ✉ 9300 Emerald Coast Pkwy., Sandestin ☎ 800/622–1623 reservations 🌐 www.sandestin.com 🛏 1,300 rooms 🍽 No meals.*

Sandestin Lakeside

$$$ | RENTAL | The lakes that make Sandestin's four golf courses a challenge offer ample opportunity for visitors to enjoy serene water views in a variety of locations around the resort. **Pros:** close to golf courses; more-homelike accommodations; choices with up to five bedrooms. **Cons:** can be three miles from the beach; not where the action is; no hotel-style amenities. *$ Rooms from: $329 ✉ 9300 Emerald Coast Pkwy., Sandestin ☎ 800/622–1623 reservations 🌐 www.sandestin.com 🛏 1,300 rooms 🍽 No meals.*

The Village of Baytowne Wharf and Grand Sandestin

$$ | RESORT | All the accommodations here are just a short walk away from the resort's bayside offerings, including The Village of Baytowne Wharf (and its shops, entertainment, and special events), The Baytowne Marina (featuring rentals for bayside fun), Sandestin's Tennis Center, and the kid-friendly Jolee Island Nature Park. **Pros:** close to The Village of Baytowne Wharf and other bayside activities; views of the Choctawhatchee Bay; beautiful sunsets. **Cons:** beach is a 20-minute tram ride away; special events can draw large crowds; access to portions of the property can be closed off due to weddings, etc.. *$ Rooms from: $249 ✉ 9300 Emerald Coast Pkwy., Sandestin ☎ 800 /622–1623 reservations 🌐 www.sandestin.com 🛏 1,300 rooms 🍽 No meals.*

Nightlife

Sandestin Village of Baytowne Wharf

NIGHTLIFE OVERVIEW | When the sun goes down and you have spectacular sunset views from Baytowne Wharf's boardwalks, restaurants, and fishing pier, the fun revs up. Live music venues include John Wehner's Village Door Nightclub and Rum Runners, home of the "World Famous" dueling pianos. Fat Tuesday Daiquiri Bar adds to a "spirited" evening, and Hammerhead's Bar & Grille promises to stay open "until the fun stops." In many ways the beating heart of the Sandestin Resort, Baytowne Wharf hosts a jam-packed schedule of events, festivals, and entertainment, especially during holidays, day and night. *✉ Sandestin Resort, 9300 Emerald Coast Pkwy. W, Sandestin ☎ 800/622–1038 🌐 www.baytownewharf.com.*

Shopping

Silver Sands Premium Outlets

OUTLET/DISCOUNT STORES | Put on your eight-hour shoes if you want to explore all the outlet stores at this mega-outdoor mall. There are 110 of them, representing just about every household name in fashion, accessories, home goods, and beauty. Saks Fifth Avenue Off 5th anchors one end, and in between you'll find quality merchandise for bargain prices in stores like Nike, Tommy Hilfiger, Coach, Polo Ralph Lauren, J Crew, and Waterford Wedgwood. There are several freestanding restaurants, including Panera Bread and Carrabba's Italian Grill to revive your spirits for another round of shopping. ✉ *10562 Emerald Coast Pkwy. W, Miramar Beach* ☎ *850/654–9771* 🌐 *www.premiumoutlets.com/outlet/silver-sands.*

The Market Shops

SHOPPING CENTERS/MALLS | There aren't many shops left in this complex at the entrance to Sandestin, but all are locally owned, so you'll get a good sense of the casually elegant style that defines the Emerald Coast. One of the oldest and largest shops is Sunset Shoes. They carry a huge inventory of comfort shoe brands like Mephisto, Ugg, and Birkenstock and have added clothing and high-end accessories to the mix. There also is a nice collection of casual eateries and snack shops. The complex features a greenspace that hosts frequent concerts, festivals, and other entertainment. ✉ *Sandestin Resort, 9300 Emerald Coast Pkwy. W, Sandestin* ☎ *850/837–3077* 🌐 *www.themarketshops.com.*

Grand Boulevard at Sandestin Town Center

SHOPPING CENTERS/MALLS | This town center–style shopping and dining complex is on the area's main thoroughfare, just a hop, skip, and jump from the Sandestin Resort. For the high-end shopper, the center offers favorite national brands like Chicos, J.Jill, Orvis, and Tommy Bahama. Magnolia House and Zoo Gallery are unique local shops worthy of a visit. Dining options include Mitchell's Fish Market, P. F. Chang's China Bistro, and Vin'tij. Grand Boulevard is also home to Emeril's Coastal Italian, his first restaurant in his new hometown. The center includes the Boulevard 10, a state-of-the-art movie theater, and Ovation Dining Club, which brings a whole new meaning to the phrase "dinner and a movie." ✉ *495 Grand Blvd., Miramar Beach* ☎ *850/654–5929* 🌐 *www.grandboulevard.com.*

Activities

For sheer number of holes, Sandestin tops the list with 72 (four courses): Baytowne Golf Club at Sandestin, the Burnt Pines Course, and the Raven Golf Club. For more information, see 🌐 *www.sandestin.com/golfers.*

Baytowne Golf Club

GOLF | FAMILY | The only course on the Emerald Coast that runs from "beach to bay," Baytowne also has elevation changes not usually found in the area and multiple teeing areas that can be challenging for scratch golfers and forgiving for beginners, kids, and others wanting to play a quick round. ✉ *1199 Troon Dr., Sandestin* ☎ *850/267–8155* 🌐 *www.baytownegolf.com* *18 holes, 6804 yards, par 71* ☞ *$65–$95.*

Raven Golf Club

GOLF | This picturesque course is a two-time home to the Boeing Championship—a stop on the PGA Champions Tour—and is carved through the marshes and pine trees of Sandestin Resort. Robert Trent Jones Jr. crafted the course as what he calls "a true modern traditional." The Raven Golf Club requires strategy on every tee, as golfers are presented with a variety of shot options accompanied by changes in color and texture throughout the course. It will require almost every club and trick in your bag. ✉ *9300 Emerald Coast Pkwy. W, Sandestin* ☎ *850/267–8155* 🌐 *www.sandestin.com/golfers* *$88–$135* *18 holes, 6931 yards, par 71.*

★ Topsail Hill Preserve State Park

BEACHES | FAMILY | Named for its towering dunes that look like ship's sails, Topsail Hill has three miles of pristine beaches, 1,600 acres, and 10 miles of trails—a natural environment that offers hikers, bikers, bird-watchers, paddlers, and other outdoors people an unparalleled opportunity to experience the original Florida. Hidden in those dunes are a rare treat: two large dune lakes. There are 14 in Walton County, but they are found in only a few other places in the world. On occasion, the wind and water will create a "blowout," when a channel is formed, allowing the lake and Gulf waters to meet. Rangers lead guided hikes on Sundays and other educational events. Accommodations include sites for tents and RVs, as well as bungalows and cabins. ✉ *7525 West County Highway 30A, Santa Rosa Beach* ☎ *850/267–8330* 🌐 *www.floridastateparks.org/parks-and-trails/topsail-hill-preserve-state-park* ☞ *Admission $6 per vehicle.*

Elsewhere in South Walton

18 miles east of Destin via U.S. 98 on Rte. 30A (Exit 85).

The South Walton area continues along Scenic Highway 30A, the route that hugs the coastline of eastern Walton County. Locals sometimes refer to the area as 30A, and generally, the pace is slower than neighboring Destin and Sandestin. During the summer season, when traffic along 30A can slow to a crawl, it's probably faster to get from Point A to Point B by biking along the 19-mile-long Timpoochee Trail. The evolution of the area over the past few decades has made 30A a magnet for creative and talented artists, purveyors of food and drink, and retailers. While the white sand is a given, there are many other natural wonders, including towering dunes and dune lakes, to be explored and enjoyed.

Alys Beach

NEIGHBORHOOD | With a palette of blazing-white buildings and bright-green grass, it's impossible to miss Alys Beach, one of 30A's newest communities. From a distance, the community looks very simple, but Alys Beach is the result of painstaking planning, including walkways oriented to capture the coastal breezes. It's fun to peek through open doorways to see colorful island-style courtyards reminiscent of Bermuda or Antigua. Homeowners there participate in a particularly charming tradition: Outside of most homes is a "gift" to the community. It might be a small fountain, a vine-covered pot, or even a whimsical stone divan. During Digital Graffiti, a two-day event held in the summer, digital artists project their work onto the "canvas" of Alys Beach's white walls. ✉ *9581 E. County Hwy 30A, Panama City Beach* ✣ *6 miles east of Seaside* ☎ *850/213–5500* 🌐 *www.alysbeach.com.*

Eden Gardens State Park

HOUSE | Scarlett O'Hara could be at home here on the lawn of an antebellum mansion amid an arcade of moss-draped live oaks. Tours of the mansion are given every hour on the hour, and furnishings inside the spacious rooms date as far back as the 17th century. The surrounding grounds—the perfect setting for a picnic lunch—are beautiful year-round, but they're nothing short of spectacular in mid-March, when the azaleas and dogwoods are in full bloom. ✉ *181 Eden Gardens Road, Santa Rosa Beach* ☎ *850/267–8320* 🌐 *www.floridastateparks.org/parks-and-trails/eden-gardens-state-park* 🎫 *$4 per vehicle, $2 pedestrians and bicyclists (it's on the honor system), house tours $4* ⏲ *House closed Tues. and Wed.*

Seaside

BEACH—SIGHT | In the early 1980s, husband-and-wife team of Robert and Daryl Davis created the community of their dreams on 80 acres of beachfront scrubland. Instead of the high-rises that were popular at the time, the couple envisioned a simpler place, with walkable paths and houses built off the ground with porches with deep roof overhangs and southern exposure to catch the breezes. The little town boomed and its style was dubbed "New Urbanism," which inspired other 30A communities

Planned Perfection in Seaside

The thriving planned community of Seaside, with old-fashioned Victorian architecture, brick streets, restaurants, retail stores, and a surfeit of art galleries, kicked off the trend of "new urbanism." The development style was designed to promote a neighborly, old-fashioned lifestyle. There's much to be said for an attractive, billboard-free village where you can park your car and walk everywhere you need to go. Pastel-colored homes with white-picket fences, front-porch rockers, and captain's walks are set along redbrick streets, and all are within walking distance of the town center and its unusual cafés and shops. The community is so reminiscent of a storybook town that producers chose it for the set of the 1998 film *The Truman Show*, starring Jim Carrey.

The community has come into its own in the last few years, achieving a comfortable, lived-in look and feel that had escaped it since its founding in the late 1970s. Some of the once-shiny tin roofs are starting to rust around the edges and the foliage has matured, creating pockets of privacy and shade. There are also more signs of a real neighborhood with bars and bookstores added to the mix. Still, although Seaside's popularity continues to soar, it retains a suspicious sense of *Twilight Zone* perfection that can weird out some visitors.

Other planned neighborhoods, variations on the theme pioneered by Seaside's founders, have carved out niches along the dozen miles of Route 30A east to Rosemary Beach. The focus in the 107-acre planned community is on preserving the local environment (the landscape is completely made up of indigenous plants) and maintaining its small-town appeal. A nascent sense of community is sprouting at the Town Green, a perfect patch of manicured lawn fronting the beach, where locals gather with their wineglasses to toast the sunset. In total South Walton touts 16 of these new urbanism–style beach communities and resorts.

such as WaterColor and Rosemary Beach, but has also spread well across the globe. The town center, also carefully curated, has become a magnet for visitors, with unique shops and eating opportunities such as Bud & Alleys restaurant and "Airstream Row," a funky lineup of the vintage iconic trailers offering everything from grilled cheese to organic smoothies. ✉ *Scenic Route 30A, Seaside* 🌐 *www.seasidefl.com.*

Underwater Museum of Art

LOCAL INTEREST | Art galleries abound along the coast, but the most unique is the new Underwater Museum of Art, a sculpture garden located 60 feet below the surface off the coast of Grayton Beach State Park. Seven pieces were installed in 2018—a deer, pineapple, octopus, skull, and other abstract shapes—and the organizations partnering to create the exhibit plan to add sculptures in the future. Note that you must have diving certification to visit the dive site. ✉ *357 Main Park Rd., Grayton Beach* ☎ *850/622–5970* 🌐 *umafl.org.*

Beaches

★ Grayton Beach State Park

BEACH—SIGHT | This is the place to see what Florida looked like when only Native Americans lived here. One of the most scenic spots along the Gulf Coast, this 2,220-acre park is composed primarily of untouched Florida woodlands within the Coastal Lowlands region. It also has salt marshes, rolling dunes covered with sea oats, crystal-white sand, and contrasting blue-green waters. The park has facilities for swimming, fishing, and snorkeling, and there's an elevated boardwalk that winds over the dunes to the beach, as well as walking trails around the marsh and into the piney woods. Notice that the "bushes" you see are actually the tops of full-size slash pines and Southern magnolias, an effect created by the frequent shifting of the dunes. Even if you're just passing by, the beach here is worth a stop. Thirty fully equipped cabins and a campground provide overnight options. **Amenities:** fishing; parking (fee); showers; toilets; water sports. **Best for:** snorkeling; sunrise; swimming; walking. ✉ *357 Main Park Rd., Grayton Beach* ✣ *Off Rte. 30A* ☎ *850/267–8300* 🌐 *www.floridastateparks.org/grayton-beach* 🎫 *$5 per vehicle, up to 8 people; $2 pedestrians/cyclists.*

Restaurants

Bud & Alley's

$$$ | EUROPEAN | This down-to-earth beachside bistro (named for a pet cat and dog) has been a local favorite since 1986. Tucked in the dunes by the Gulf, the rooftop Tarpon Club bar makes a great perch for a sunset toast (guess the exact moment the sun will disappear and win a drink). **Known for:** Southern classics like gumbo and barbecue pork shank; fresh, seasonal fish and vegetables; sunset views. [$] *Average main: $30* ✉ *2236 E. Rte. 30A, Seaside* ☎ *850/231–5900* 🌐 *www.budandalleys.com.*

Café Thirty-A

$$$$ | EUROPEAN | About a mile and half east of Seaside in a beautiful Florida-style home with high ceilings and a wide veranda, this restaurant has an elegant look—bolstered by white linen tablecloths—and impeccable service. The menu changes nightly and might include such entrées as wood-oven-roasted wild king salmon, sesame-crusted rare yellowfin tuna, and grilled filet mignon. **Known for:** excellent personal service; grilled quail with creamy grits appetizer; large martini and cocktail menu. [$] *Average main: $32* ✉ *3899 E. Rte. 30A, Seagrove Beach* ☎ *850/231–2166* 🌐 *www.cafethirtya.com* ⏲ *No lunch.*

Chanticleer Eatery

$$ | CAJUN | FAMILY | A little off the beaten path, but very much worth looking for, Chanticleer has colorful decor featuring giant rooster paintings, but it's the food that will have you crowing. Much of the menu is homemade, including the bread, soups, and to-die-for cookies. **Known for:** Krioyo (cree-yo-yo) pasta; $2 off every drink happy hour; fresh-baked cookies. [$] *Average main: $20* ✉ *55 Clayton Ln., Santa Rosa Beach* ☎ *850/213–9065* 🌐 *www.chanticleereatery.com* ⏲ *Lunch, closed Sun.; Dinner, closed Sat.–Sun.*

Cuvee 30A

$$$$ | AMERICAN | When he migrated from Louisiana to Northwest Florida, chef Tim Creehan became a culinary celebrity, known for his creative takes on steak and seafood. He's helmed restaurants up and down the coast and now showcases his award-winning talents as chef–owner of Cuvee 30A, where entrées include black pepper–crusted yellowfin tuna and pecan-crusted grouper Vince. **Known for:** extensive wine list; high-profile, highly lauded chef Creehan; steak. [$] *Average main: $36* ✉ *30 Avenue, 12805 Hwy. 98, Rosemary Beach* ✣ *At the junction of Scenic 30A and Hwy. 98* ☎ *850/909–0111* 🌐 *www.Cuvee30A.com.*

★ FOOW

$$$ | ECLECTIC | For years the award-winning Fish Out of Water restaurant in the resort town of WaterColor was a favorite fine-dining experience for visitors and locals alike. After a major renovation, the restaurant has returned under its acronym name, and the look is more sleek and casual (covered-up swimsuits are allowed) and more family-friendly, but the menu and service are still exceptional and the Gulf views are even better. **Known for:** small seasonal menus utilizing mostly local produce, meat, and fish; water views from every seat; outdoor bar and patio. *Average main: $22* *WaterColor Inn, 34 Goldenrod Cir., 2nd fl., Santa Rosa Beach* *850/534–5050* *www.watercolorresort.com* *Closed Mon. and winter.*

Great Southern Cafe

$$$ | **SEAFOOD** | Jim Shirley, founder of Pensacola's very popular Fish House, has brought his Grits a Ya-Ya to this restaurant on Seaside's town square. Breakfast is served from 8 to 11, when the menu segues to regional fare, including Gulf shrimp, Apalachicola oysters, and fresh sides such as collards, okra, black-eyed peas, fried green tomatoes, and sweet potatoes. **Known for:** Grits a Ya-Ya (blackened shrimp on cheese grits); shrimp po'boys; breakfast. *Average main: $24* *83 Central Sq., Seaside* *850/231–7327* *www.thegreatsoutherncafe.com.*

Hotels

Cottage Rental Agency

When residents aren't using their pricey one- to six- bedroom porticoed, neo-Victorian cottages, they rent them out. Homes have fully equipped kitchens, TV/DVDs and vacuum cleaners and are a perfect option for a family vacation or a large group. It features a hotel-style check-in and concierge services. And the rental agency helps by throwing in a bottle of wine, golf discounts, bicycles, free DVD checkout (with popcorn!) and other perks. There are more than 200 different properties in Seaside and along 30A sleeping from 2 to 14 people. What you won't find are the services and amenities of a full-service hotel. *2311 E. Rte. 30A, Santa Rosa Beach* *850/231–2222, 866/966–2565 reservations* *www.cottagerentalagency.com* *275 units* *No meals.*

The Pearl Hotel

$$$$ | **HOTEL** | No detail was overlooked in the creation of one of the area's newest and most sophisticated hotels, which offers luxury, elegance, and comfort. **Pros:** on-site spa; access to private beach club at WaterSound; unparalelled service. **Cons:** hotel has a small footprint; expensive. *Rooms from: $559* *63 Main Street, Rosemary Beach* *850/588–2881, 877/935–6114 reservations* *www.thepearlrb.com* *55 rooms* *No meals.*

The Rosemary Beach Inn

$$ | **B&B/INN** | European style is combined with understated chic beauty with Gulf-front views in this intimate inn in the small community of Rosemary Beach. **Pros:** caring owners; near activities and dining; beach chairs and umbrella included. **Cons:** most rooms fairly small; very limited parking (most is on-street); two-night minimum stay Thursday–Saturday. *Rooms from: $300* *78 Main St., Rosemary Beach* *866/348–8952* *www.therosemarybeachinn.com* *11 rooms* *Breakfast.*

★ WaterColor Inn and Resort

$$$ | **HOTEL** | Nature meets seaside chic at this boutique property, the crown jewel of the area's latest—and largest—planned communities. **Pros:** upscale and fancy; free Wi-Fi included; canoe use and tennis included in rates. **Cons:** clientele can be standoffish; you have to pay extra for beach gear. *Rooms from: $333* *34 Goldenrod Circle, Santa Rosa Beach* *850/534–5000* *www.watercolorresort.com* *60 rooms* *Breakfast.*

Shopping

The neighborhoods of 30A are a shopper's paradise, with small stores and boutiques offering a variety of merchandise you won't see elsewhere. There's plenty of beach casual clothes and accessories, and the area's many talented artists offer

If you saw *The Truman Show,* you may recognize several places in Seaside, where the movie was filmed.

their creative takes in galleries situated up and down the coast.

Cabana by The Seaside Style

CLOTHING | This beachside bazaar of open-air "huts" sells clothing and accessories with a beachy boho style. The offerings include straw hats, sandals and other casual footwear, totes, sunglasses, sarongs, handmade jewelry, and more. The fashionable clothes they carry are all made from natural fabrics. ✉ *Seaside* ✥ *In Seaside, next to Bud & Alley's restaurant* ☏ *850/231–5829* 🌐 *www.seasidefl.com/community/cabana-by-the-seaside-style.*

Rosemary Beach

SHOPPING NEIGHBORHOODS | This neighborhood's "downtown" has great shops clustered mostly on Barrett Square and Main Street. It's easy to stroll from boutique to toy store to gift shop to home decor showroom—and take a coffee break at Amavida Coffee & Tea or stop at a restaurant if you're in need of greater revivification. ✉ *Rosemary Beach* 🌐 *www.rosemarybeach.com/merchant-directory.*

Shops of Grayton

SHOPPING CENTERS/MALLS | This quaint shopping area offers eight colorful cottages in a colorful complex where you can buy gifts, artwork, and antiques. Or grab a bite and a loaf at the Black Bear Bread Co. café and bakery. ✉ *26 Logan Ln., Grayton Beach* ✥ *2 miles south of U.S. 98.*

Sundog Books

BOOKS/STATIONERY | This independent bookstore in Seaside will have just the beach read for you to while away the hours in the sand or on the porch. It's crammed full and can get very busy, but the staff is knowledgable and helpful. There's also a record store upstairs. ✉ *89 Central Sq., Seaside* ☏ *850/231–5481* 🌐 *www.sundogbooks.com.*

Butterfly Bike & Kayak

BOATING | A few miles from Seaside in Seagrove Beach, this outfitter rents bikes, kayaks, scooters, beach set-ups, and golf carts and has free delivery and pickup. Bike rentals run from $20 per day to $50 per week. Kayak and paddleboard rentals start at $75 a day. ✉ *3657 E. Rte. 30A, Seagrove Beach* ☎ *850/231–2826* 🌐 *www.mybikerental.net* 💵 *From $20 per day, from $45 per wk.*

LDV

WATER SPORTS | With a service area from Navarre Beach to the communities of Scenic 30A, LDV (short for La Dolce Vita) will bring the beach necessities to you, including beach setups, bikes, golf carts, kayaks and paddleboards, to you. Their services also include pontoon boat and jet ski rentals and bonfires. ☎ *866/651–1869* 🌐 *www.ldvbeach.com.*

Panama City Beach

21 miles southeast of Seaside off U.S. 98.

Although Front Beach Road is lined by high-rises (about two dozen in total) built mostly during the early 2000s, Panama City Beach's ample 27-mile coastline still gives you opportunities to avoid the crowds and congestion. Tighter restrictions have pretty much eliminated the shenanigans of college spring break, making PCB more attractive to families seeking a PG-rated spring vacation for their school-aged children. The one constant in this ever-changing cityscape is the area's natural beauty, which, in many areas, helps you forget the commercialization in others.

There's definitely a busy section of Front Beach Road, but there also are two undeveloped and fully protected state parks and their equally beautiful beaches. The shoreline is so long that even when a mile is packed, there are 26 more where you can toss a beach blanket and find the old motels that have managed to survive. Or you travel inland toward West Bay and find even quieter quarters, including expanses of undeveloped pinelands and a city park with ample biking trails. What's more, the beaches along what used to be called the Miracle Strip, with their powder-soft sand and translucent emerald waters, are some of the finest in the state, so it's easy to understand why developers wanted to build here.

The busiest season stretches from spring (when college students descend en masse from neighboring states for spring break and a lot of raucous partying) to summer (when families and others come for the warm Gulf waters and beautiful beaches). Come before mid-March, when the temperatures can still be chilly and definitely not conducive to water activities, or after Labor Day through October, when the water is still warm and inviting, and you will find a much quieter vacation destination.

Cabanas, umbrellas, sailboats, personal watercraft, and floats are available from any of dozens of vendors along the beach. St. Andrews State Park, on the southeast end of the beaches, is treasured by locals and visitors alike. Camp Helen State Park, on the northwest end of the beaches, is a popular wedding venue with an incredible beach. In the 18 mile-stretch in between, there are nearly 100 public beach access points. The beautiful white sands, navigable waterways, and plentiful marine life that once attracted Spanish explorers today draw invaders of the vacationing kind—namely families, the vast majority of whom hail from nearby Georgia and Alabama. **■ TIP→ When coming here, be sure to set your sights—and your GPS—for Panama City Beach. Panama City is its beachless inland cousin.**

If you're lucky, you may see a great blue heron foraging on Shell Island in St. Andrews State Park.

GETTING HERE AND AROUND

The Northwest Florida Beaches International Airport on the east shore of Panama City's West Bay has routes operated by Delta, American Airlines, United, and Southwest. From the airport to the beach area, depending on the location of your hotel, it's about $15 to $27 by taxi. Try Yellow Cab or Beach Boy's Shuttle, Taxi, and Limo.

When navigating Panama City Beach by car, don't limit yourself to Front Beach Road—the stop-and-go traffic will drive you nuts. You can avoid the congestion by following parallel roads like Back Beach Road and U.S. 98, although they can get busy during the summer, too. Bay Town Trolley serves Bay County, including downtown Panama City and the beaches ($1.50, $4 for an all-day pass); Panama City Beach is served by Route 7.

CONTACTS Bay Town Trolley. ☏ *850/960–1084* 🌐 *www.baytowntrolley.org.* **Beach Boys Shuttle, Taxi and Limo.** ☏ *850/236–6234.* **Yellow Cab.** ☏ *850/763–4691.*

VISITOR INFORMATION

CONTACTS Panama City Beach Convention and Visitors Bureau. ☏ *850/233–5070, 800/722–3224* 🌐 *www.visitpanamacitybeach.com.*

Sights

Conservation Park

BICYCLING | If you want something different from the beach, Conservation Park offers a more woodland experience for hikers, bikers, birders, and nature lovers. The park itself is 2,900 acres and features 12 different trails from 0.6 to 11 miles long—24 miles total. The trails include a mile of boardwalks through cypress domes. Leashed dogs are allowed. Guided Audubon bird walks and other programs are offered seasonally. ✉ *100 Conservation Dr.* ☏ *850/233–5045* 🌐 *www.panamacitybeachparksandrecreation.com/conservation-park.*

Gulf World Marine Park

AMUSEMENT PARK/WATER PARK | **FAMILY** | With educational shows and chats featuring dolphins, sharks, birds, and more, plus a tropical garden, and alligator and otter exhibits, the park is a winner with kids. The stingray-petting pool and the shark-feeding and scuba demonstrations are big crowd pleasers, and the old favorites—performing sea lions, otters, and bottlenose dolphins—still hold their own. You might consider an interactive program, such as Trainer for a Day, which takes you behind the scenes to assist in food preparation and training sessions and lets you make an on-stage appearance in the Dolphin Show. The $250, six-hour program includes a souvenir photo, lunch, and trainer T-shirt. Gulf World is also home to the Gulf World Marine Institute, dedicated to sea turtle and marine mammal rescue, rehabilitation, and release. ✉ *15412 Front Beach Rd.* ☎ *850/234–5271* 🌐 *www.gulfworldmarinepark.com* 🎫 *$29.*

Shipwreck Island Waterpark

AMUSEMENT PARK/WATER PARK | FAMILY | This 20-acre water park has everything from speedy slides and tubes to a giant wave pool to the slow-moving Lazy River. There are attractions to please any family member all day long. Oddly enough, admission is based on height (whether you are over or under 50 inches), with under 35 inches free. Wear water shoes or flip-flops to protect your feet on the hot pavement. ✉ *12201 Hutchison Blvd.* ☎ *850/234–3333* 🌐 *www.shipwreckisland.com* 🎫 *$35.98* ⏲ *Closed Oct.–Mar.*

★ St. Andrews State Park

BEACH—SIGHT | FAMILY | At the southeastern tip of Panama City Beach, the hotels and condos and traffic stop, and there suddenly appears a pristine 1,260-acre park that offers a peek at what the entire beach area looked like before development arrived. Although swimming is one of the most popular activities, the waters around the park also are ideal for fishing, snorkeling, paddling, and surfing. A rock jetty creates a calm, shallow play area that is perfect for young children. The pinewoods took a hit from Hurricane Michael in 2018, but visitors can still hike on clearly marked nature trails. There are also camping facilities, a snack bar, and rental concessions. During tourist season, board a shuttle to Shell Island, a 700-acre barrier island in the Gulf of Mexico. There's not so much shelling these days, but dolphin and other wildlife are abundant. ✉ *4607 State Park La.* ☎ *850/708–6100* 🌐 *www.floridastateparks.org/parks-and-trails/st-andrews-state-park* 🎫 *$8 per vehicle, up to eight people.*

 Beaches

Camp Helen State Park

BEACH—SIGHT | Next to Panama City Beach's coastal dune lake, this former getaway for employees of Avondale Textile Mills still has a few of the original cabins and a lodge that is popular for weddings and meetings. The bucolic surroundings are good for bird-watching, but the main draw may be the beautiful, powdery beach and the remnants of a pier, featured in Luke Bryan's music video for his song "Roller Coaster." It's a half-mile hike down to the beach, but you're almost guaranteed to find some peace. **Amenities:** parking. **Best for:** solitude; swimming; walking. ✉ *23937 Panama City Beach Pkwy.* ☎ *850/233–5059* 🌐 *www.floridastateparks.org/park/camp-helen* 🎫 *$4 per vehicle; $2 per person for pedestrians or bicyclists.*

Mexico Beach

BEACH—SIGHT | Just over 30 miles east of Panama City along scenic U.S. 98, what was a jewel of a beach was practically destroyed in 2018 after a direct hit from Category 4 Hurricane Michael. It's known for seclusion and a slower pace than its neighbor to the west, Panama City Beach. Efforts to rebuild have begun in earnest, with some restaurants and vacation rentals now open. It's worth checking in to see if the community is ready to welcome visitors again. ✉ *U.S.*

98, Mexico Beach ↔ 35 miles east of Panama City Beach ☎ 888/723–2546 🌐 mexicobeach.com.

Panama City Beach

BEACH—SIGHT | FAMILY | With 27 miles of shoreline, Panama City Beach offers the sugar-white sand and emerald-green waters the Emerald Coast is known for, and lots of high-rises. There are plenty of places to stay, play, swim, splash, and feast, so there's no excuse for getting bored or hungry. Because of the way the coastline curves in this section of the Florida Panhandle, Panama City Beach actually lies west of Panama City, not south of it. As a result, PCB was on the edge of Hurricane Michael's impact zone and spared much of the damage seen just to its east. And while it still attracts the spring-break crowd, it's far less rowdy and much more family-focused these days. **Amenities:** lifeguards; parking; showers; toilets; water sports. **Best for:** partiers; swimming; walking. ✉ *Front Beach Rd.* ↔ *Between U.S. 98 and St. Andrews State Park* ☎ *800/722–3224.*

Restaurants

Although you'll find an almost endless array of chain restaurants in Panama City Beach, the city does have some extremely good locally owned restaurants as well if you are willing to look beyond Pier Park and Front Beach Road.

Billy's Steamed Seafood Restaurant, Oyster Bar, and Crab House

$$ | SEAFOOD | Join the throng of locals who really know their seafood. Then roll up your sleeves and dig into some of the Gulf's finest blue crabs and shrimp seasoned to perfection with Billy's special recipe. **Known for:** no-frills local hangout; fresh Gulf seafood; Billy's special spice blend. 💲 *Average main: $16* ✉ *3000 Thomas Dr.* ☎ *850/235–2349* 🌐 *www.billysoysterbar.com.*

Capt. Anderson's

$$$ | SEAFOOD | Come early to watch the boats unload the catch of the day on the docks and to beat the long line that forms each afternoon at this noted restaurant with a real family feel. Since 1967, Capt. **Known for:** views of fishing fleet; large selection of fresh seafood and steaks; Greek specialties. 💲 *Average main: $30* ✉ *5551 N. Lagoon Dr.* ☎ *850/234–2225* 🌐 *captanderson.com.*

Firefly

$$$$ | AMERICAN | This local gem offers a fine-dining experience in a casual atmosphere. The white-light adorned oak tree in the center of the room creates a warm, wistful, and romantic feeling. **Known for:** upscale Southern feel-good staples and fresh seafood; romantic atmosphere; excellent service. 💲 *Average main: $34* ✉ *535 N. Richard Jackson Blvd.* ☎ *850/249–3359* 🌐 *fireflypcb.com.*

Schooners

$$ | SEAFOOD | FAMILY | This beachfront spot—which is really tucked away down a small avenue—bills itself as the "last local beach club," and more boldly, "the best place on Earth." Drawing a mix of locals and tourists, it's actually a perfect spot for a casual family lunch or early dinner: kids can have burgers and play on the beach while Mom and Dad enjoy grown-up drinks and simple fare such as homemade gumbo, steak, a burger, or seafood like crab-stuffed shrimp, fresh grouper, and grilled tuna steaks. **Known for:** basic burgers and seafood menu; lively, especially at sunset; family-friendly atmosphere. 💲 *Average main: $17* ✉ *5121 Gulf Dr.* ☎ *850/235–3555* 🌐 *www.schooners.com.*

Hotels

If you want a quieter experience, look for lodging on the bayside of Panama City Beach. You'll have a bit more traveling to get to the beaches, but the quieter surroundings can be very pleasant, especially during the high season.

Carillon Beach Resort Inn

$$ | RENTAL | FAMILY | Old-world charm and lovely architecture make perfect partners at this resort in a unique "planned village community" with lots of amenities, including four swimming pools, two hot tubs, two tennis courts, children's playground, and a full-service spa and salon. **Pros:** showcases local wildlife and beauty; pet-friendly suites available for additional fee; all rooms have kitchenettes; beach shuttle available. **Cons:** must walk to the closest access to the resort's private beach; not on the beach. *Rooms from: $250 114 Carillon Market St. 850/334–9100, 877/300–3220 for reservations www.carillonbeachresortinn.com 46 units No meals.*

Edgewater Beach Resort

$$ | RENTAL | This high-rise resort on the beach bills itself as the only full-service resort in Panama City Beach and offers a variety of activities and amenities. **Pros:** variety of lodging options; 110 acres of beautiful beachfront property; activities director can help guests get the most from their vacations. **Cons:** can get busy and noisy in season; units are owned and operated by several different management companies, so quality and service standards can vary. *Rooms from: $219 11212 Front Beach Rd. 855/874–8686 for information, 877/278–0544 for reservations www.edgewaterbeachresort.com 520 units No meals.*

Legacy by the Sea

$ | HOTEL | FAMILY | One of six hotels in the "By the Sea" resort group in Panama City Beach, Legacy's 14 stories ensure stunning views from almost every room's balcony. **Pros:** everything is within walking distance; plenty of resort amenities; suites have kitchenettes, rooms have microwave and mini-refrigerator. **Cons:** located in a crowded and congested area; lots of traffic in the area during peak season. *Rooms from: $179 15325 Front Beach Rd. 850/249–8601, 888/627–0625 bythesearesorts.com/resorts/legacy 139 rooms Breakfast.*

Nightlife

Club La Vela

BARS/PUBS | Remember all that stuff we said about Panama City Beach being more family-friendly? Toss it right out the window at Club La Vela. Here you party hard with concerts (acts have included Aerosmith and Ludacris), international DJs, 48 bar stations, 50,000 watts of sound, swimming pools, a tropical waterfall, and dance halls like The Thunderdome. Though there are a few quiet spaces, drunk, loud, and crowded is the name of the game. *8813 Thomas Dr. 850/234–1061, 850/234–3866 www.clublavela.com.*

Pineapple Willy's

BARS/PUBS | The total beach bar experience, this eatery and bar is geared to families and tourists—as well as sports fans—and is a hot spot for live music. The signature rum drink, the Pineapple Willy, was the inspiration for its full slate of tropical and frozen drinks and the hangout's tiki attitude. *9875 S. Thomas Dr. 850/235–0928 www.pwillys.com.*

Tootsie's Orchid House

BARS/PUBS | A little bit of Nashville honky tonk has been transplanted to PCB's Pier Park at Tootsie's, which features country music acts on a regular basis. It's a lively atmosphere with cocktails and bar bites that tantalize a variety of palates. *700 S. Pier Park Dr. 850/236-3459 www.tootsies.net.*

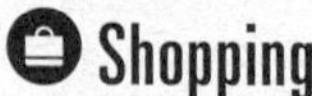

Shopping

Pier Park

SHOPPING CENTERS/MALLS | FAMILY | Occupying a huge swath of land that was once an amusement park, this outdoor 900,000-square-foot entertainment/

shopping/dining complex creates the downtown feel that Panama City Beach otherwise lacks. Anchor stores including Dillard's and Target keep things active during the day, along with a number of specialty shops, and clubs like Jimmy Buffett's Margaritaville and the 16-screen Grand Theatre keep things hopping after dark. Other venues, such as Ron Jon Surf Shop and Dave & Buster's, offer even more reason to see this vibrant and enjoyable complex. Pier Park is a venue for fun festivals and special events at festivals and holiday celebrations throughout the year. One of its newest additions is the SkyWheel, a 200-foot tall Ferris wheel with 30 gondolas to give "flyers" a 360-degree view of the Gulf Coast day and night. ✉ *600 Pier Park Dr.* ☎ *850/236–9974* 🌐 *www.shoppierpark.com.*

Activities

Airboat Adventures

TOUR—SPORTS | For a fun, fast, and exciting eco-tour, check out the backwaters of West Bay—rivers, creeks, and marshland that are full of native Florida wildlife, including American bald eagles, ospreys, heron, dolphins, and alligators. Enjoy the beautiful scenery while gliding on water in a real, Everglades-style airboat. Prices vary depending on cruise but start at $33. ✉ *6523 Highway 79* ☎ *850/230–3822* 🌐 *www.swampvette.com.*

★ Dolphin and Snorkel Tours

BOATING | Cruise around the bay to see dolphins with stops for snorkeling and (on longer tours) lunch, as well as stops around Andrews State Park and Shell Island. Trips are educational and eco-friendly without causing undue disturbance to wildlife. ✉ *Pirates Cove Marina, 3901 Thomas Dr.* ☎ *850/866–8815* 🌐 *www.dolphinandsnorkeltours.com* 🎫 *From $68.*

Holiday Golf Club

GOLF | Located 2.5 miles east of Pier Park, Holiday Golf Club is an 18-hole par-72 championship golf course. It also has Bay County's only lighted 9-hole par-3 course. Greens fees start at $45 for 18 holes and $25 for nine holes. ✉ *100 Fairway Blvd.* ☎ *850/234–1800* 🌐 *www.holidaygolfclub.com* ⛳ *18 holes, 6859 yards, par 72.*

Panama City Dive Center

SCUBA DIVING | At the full-service PCDC, you can arrange for instruction, gear purchase or rental, and charters. Boat charters are available for scuba diving and snorkeling. ✉ *4823 Thomas Dr.* ☎ *850/235–3390* 🌐 *www.pcdivecenter.com* 🎫 *From $34.*

Paradise Adventures

BOATING | Known for an array of dolphin tours, sunset sails, and half-day sightseeing cruises, Paradise Adventures' catamaran cruises have showcased the natural beauty of the area for visitors and locals alike. They also offer a Shell Island Adventure Tour. ✉ *3901 Thomas Dr.* ☎ *850/769–3866* 🌐 *paradiseadventurespcb.com* 🎫 *From $45.*

Signal Hill

GOLF | The oldest golf course in the area, built in 1963, presents breathtaking scenery. This is an older-style course with fairways running parallel, so you can end up with players from other holes in your fairway. The back nine are much more challenging than the front nine. Greens fees start at $25 for nine holes. ✉ *9615 Thomas Dr.* ☎ *850/234–5051* 🌐 *signalhillgolfcourse.com* ⛳ *18 holes, 5617 yards, par 71.*

Apalachicola

65 miles southeast of Panama City Beach on U.S. 98.

It feels like a long haul between Panama City Beach and here. Add an odd name and a town's below-the-radar reputation to that long drive and you may be tempted to skip Apalachicola. But you shouldn't. It's an interesting town with a rich history complemented by a growing cosmopolitan veneer. And that makes it worth a visit.

Meaning "land of the friendly people" in the language of its original Native American inhabitants, Apalachicola—known in these parts as simply Apalach—lies on the Panhandle's southernmost bulge. European settlers began arriving in 1821, and by 1847 the southern terminus of the Apalachicola River steamboat route was a bustling port town. Although the town is now known as the Oyster Capital of the World, oystering became king only after the local cotton industry flagged—the city's extra-wide streets, built to accommodate bales of cotton awaiting transport, are a remnant of that trade—and the sponge industry moved down the coast after depleting local sponge colonies.

But the newest industry here is tourism, and visitors have begun discovering the Forgotten Coast, as the area is known, flocking to its intimate hotels and bed-and-breakfasts and dining at excellent restaurants. The downtown area is compact, easily walkable, and full of unique local shops selling maritime artifacts, souvenirs, and art. If you like oysters or want to go back in time to the Old South of Gothic churches and spooky graveyards, Apalachicola is a good place to start.

VISITOR INFORMATION

CONTACTS Apalachicola Bay Chamber of Commerce and Visitor Center. ✉ *17 Ave. E* ☎ *850/653–9419* 🌐 *www.apalachicolabay.org.*

Apalachicola Seafood Grill & Steakhouse
$$ | **SEAFOOD** | Where will you find the world's largest fish sandwich? Right here in downtown Apalachicola, where the portion is way too big for the bun. **Known for:** "world's largest" fish sandwich; blue-crab cakes; diner atmosphere and reasonable prices, especially at lunch. $ *Average main: $18* ✉ *100 Market St.* ☎ *850/653–9510* ⏲ *Closed Sun.*

★ Owl Café
$$$ | **AMERICAN** | Located in a behemoth clapboard building on a prime corner in the heart of downtown Apalachicola, this old-fashioned, charming lunch-and-dinner spot pleases modern palates, both in the white-linen elegance of the dining room and in the colorful garden terrace. The food is an artful blend of old and new as well: the chicken wrap seems as much at home on the lunch menu as the gator and pork sausage creole. **Known for:** varied menu, heavy on seafood selections; large wine selection; weekend brunch. $ *Average main: $23* ✉ *15 Ave. D* ☎ *850/653–9888* 🌐 *www.owlcafeflorida.com.*

Tamara's Café
$$$ | **LATIN AMERICAN** | Mixing Florida flavors with South American flair, Tamara, a native Venezuelan, opened this colorful bistro in a 1920s-era building in the 1990s, and it has been a local staple ever since. Now owned by her daughter and son-in-law, it continues to serve a menu of reliable, Latin-accented Florida cuisine, especially seafood. **Known for:** Latin-influenced cuisine, especially seafood; tapas menu; small but excellent dessert menu. $ *Average main: $23* ✉ *71 Market St.* ☎ *850/653–4111* 🌐 *www.tamarascafe.com* ⏲ *Closed Mon.*

Up the Creek Raw Bar
$$ | **SEAFOOD** | **FAMILY** | Come for the oysters, stay for the view. Oysters are the star of the menu, served raw, baked, steamed or covered with a creative array of toppings, like the Southern Fella, a lightly cooked oyster dressed with collard greens, butter, Parmesan cheese, bread crumbs, and crispy bacon. **Known for:** oysters; serene natural views; pet-friendly on the patio. $ *Average main: $15* ✉ *313*

Water St. ☎ *850/653–2525* 🌐 *www.upthecreekrawbar.com.*

Hotels

The Consulate
$$ | **RENTAL** | These four elegant suites, on the second story of the former offices of the French consul, range in size from 650 to 1,650 square feet and combine a 19th-century feel with 21st-century luxury. **Pros:** large rooms; more character than you'd find in a chain hotel; pets allowed with deposit. **Cons:** a bit pricey for Apalachicola; balcony for front units is shared space. *Rooms from: $275* ✉ *76 Water St.* ☎ *850/653–1515* 🌐 *www.consulatesuites.com* *4 suites* *No meals.*

Coombs Inn & Suites
$ | **B&B/INN** | A combination of neighboring homes and a carriage house, this entire complex was created with Victorian flair. **Pros:** clean and comfortable; on-site, friendly owner who's happy to assist with travel tips and suggestions; complimentary bikes. **Cons:** be prepared to meet and greet other guests at the inn; if you favor complete privacy, a hotel may suit you better. *Rooms from: $159* ✉ *80 6th St.* ☎ *850/653–9199, 888/224–8320 for reservations* 🌐 *www.coombshouseinn.com* *23 rooms* *Breakfast.*

Gibson Inn
$ | **B&B/INN** | One of a few inns on the National Register of Historic Places still operating as a full-service facility, this turn-of-the-20th-century hostelry in the heart of downtown is easily identified by its wraparound porches, intricate fretwork, and widow's walk. **Pros:** smack-dab in the center of town; peaceful veranda; on-site restaurant. **Cons:** may get a little busy when weddings take place in the main lobby; hotel will remain open during renovations. *Rooms from: $120* ✉ *51 Ave. C* ☎ *850/653–2191* 🌐 *www.gibson-inn.com* *30 rooms* *Free Breakfast.*

Shopping

The best way to shop in Apalachicola is just to stroll around the tiny downtown area. There are always new stores joining old favorites, and somewhere along the way you'll find something that'll pique your interest.

Grady Market
CLOTHING | On the first floor of The Consulate inn is a collection of antiques and home decor as well as clothing and accessories. There is also a selection of T-shirts and souvenirs, so you'll remember your visit to the Forgotten Coast. ✉ *The Consulate, 76 Water St.* ☎ *850/653–4099* 🌐 *www.downtownapalachicola.com/business/grady-market.*

St. George Island

8 miles southeast of Apalachicola via Bryant Patton Bridge off U.S. 98.

Cross the long, long bridge leading east out of Apalachicola and then look to your right for another lengthy span that takes you south to pristine St. George Island. Sitting 5 miles out in the Gulf of Mexico, the island is bordered by Apalachicola Bay and the Gulf, offering the best of both to create a laid-back seaside retreat.

The rich bay is an angler's dream, while the snowy-white beaches and clear Gulf waters satisfy even the most finicky beachgoer. Indulge in bicycling, hiking, canoeing, and snorkeling, or find a secluded spot for reading, gathering shells, or bird-watching. Accommodations mostly take the form of privately owned, fully furnished condos and single-family homes.

Sights

Cape St. George Lighthouse
MUSEUM | As you descend into St. George Island after crossing the Bryant Patton Memorial Bridge, you can't miss the St.

George Lighthouse, located front and center. It has a long and storied history; it was felled by hurricanes and beach erosion and rebuilt several times. After its last collapse in 2005, concerned citizens picked up the pieces (literally) and rebuilt the lighthouse on its current site along with a museum and a gift shop. Those who make it to the top have earned that fabulous view by climbing 92 spiral stairs and a ladder. ✉ *2B East Gulf Beach Dr.* ☎ *850/927–7745* 🌐 *www.stgeorgelight.org* 🎫 *To climb, $5 adults; entrance to the museum is free* ⏲ *Closed Thurs.*

Beaches

★ Dr. Julian G. Bruce St. George Island State Park

BEACH—SIGHT | This is Old Florida at its undisturbed best. On the east end of the island are 9 miles of undeveloped beaches and dunes—the longest beachfront of any state park in Florida. Sandy coves, salt marshes, oak forests, and pines provide shelter for many birds, including bald eagles and ospreys on the bay side. On the Gulf side, there's plenty of room to spread out and make a day of it sunning, swimming, picnicking, and watching shorebirds dart about as you walk at the waterline. Pavilions located throughout the park offer potless restrooms and plentiful parking. Campers and boaters are also welcome. Hurricane Michael caused great damage to the park in 2018, and certain amenities may be closed. Visit the park website for updated information. **Amenities:** parking; showers; toilets. **Best for:** swimming; walking. ✉ *1900 E. Gulf Beach Dr.* ☎ *850/927–2111, 800/326–3521 for camping reservations* 🌐 *www.floridastateparks.org/parks-and-trails/dr-julian-g-bruce-st-george-island-state-park* 🎫 *$6 per vehicle, up to 8 people.*

Restaurants

BJ's Pizza and Subs

$ | **PIZZA** | This simple beach shack near the bridge serves solid, if predictable, fare. The menu includes sandwiches and wraps, salads, and appetizers, but the pizza is definitely worth stopping for. **Known for:** good casual fare, but really good pizza; owned by the same family since 1990; family- and pet- (on the porch) friendly. 💲 *Average main: $7* ✉ *105 W. Gulf Beach Dr.* ☎ *850/927–2805* 🌐 *www.sgipizza.com.*

The Blue Parrot Oceanfront Cafe

$$ | **SEAFOOD** | You'll feel as if you're sneaking in the back door as you climb the side stairs leading to an outdoor deck overlooking the Gulf (this is the island's only restaurant on the beach). Or if you can, grab a table indoors. **Known for:** good basic fried and grilled seafood; good frozen drinks; busy on the weekends. 💲 *Average main: $20* ✉ *68 W. Gorrie Dr.* ☎ *850/927–2987* 🌐 *www.blueparrotsgi.com.*

Tallahassee

103 miles east of Panama City, 78 miles northeast of Apalachicola.

Tallahassee is quite different from the sun-and-surf coastal towns. The only Southern capital spared in the Civil War, Tallahassee has preserved its history. Vestiges of the city's colorful past are found throughout. For example, in the Capitol complex, the Historic Capitol building is strikingly paired with the New Capitol skyscraper.

The canopies of ancient oaks and spring bowers of azaleas line many streets; among the best "canopy roads" are St. Augustine, Miccosukee, Meridian, Old Bainbridge, and Centerville. Between March and April, flowers bloom, and the Springtime Tallahassee festival is in full swing.

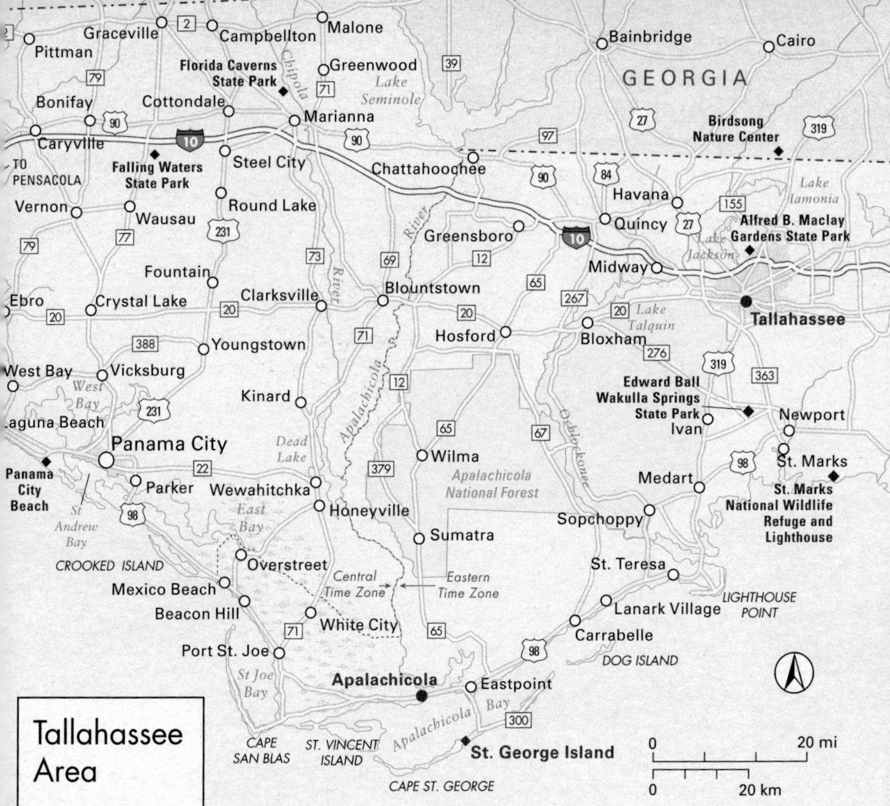

GETTING HERE AND AROUND

Just 14 miles south of the Georgia border and nearer to Atlanta than Miami, Tallahassee is midway between Jacksonville and Pensacola. Tallahassee International Airport is served by American, Delta, United Express, and US Airways. From the airport to downtown is around $20 via City Taxi or Yellow Cab.

CONTACTS City Taxi. ☎ *850/575–7575.* **Yellow Cab.** ☎ *850/999–9999* 🌐 *www.tallahasseeyellowcab.com.*

VISITOR INFORMATION

CONTACTS Visit Tallahassee. ✉ *106 E. Jefferson St.* ☎ *850/606–2305, 800/628–2866 toll-free* 🌐 *www.visittallahassee.com.*

Sights

★ Alfred B. Maclay Gardens State Park

GARDEN | Starting in December, the grounds at this 1,200-acre estate, one of Florida's most stunning ornamental gardens, are afire with azaleas, dogwood, Oriental magnolias, spring bulbs of tulips and irises, banana shrubs, honeysuckle, silverbell trees, pansies, and camellias. Wander past the reflecting pool into the tiny walled garden and around the lakes and woodlands. See if you can find the secret garden. Once the winter home of Alfred Maclay, a banker and financier from New York, the Maclay residence (open January through April) is furnished as it was in the 1920s. Picnic areas and a playground, as well as swimming, kayaking, and boating facilities are open to the public. Outer portions of the park include 11 miles of trails used for walking,

Did You Know?

Just south of Tallahassee, the St. Marks National Wildlife Refuge is home to the second oldest lighthouse in Florida.

running, bicycling, and horseback riding. ✉ *3540 Thomasville Rd.* ☎ *850/487–4556* 🌐 *www.floridastateparks.org/maclay-gardens* 🎫 *$6 per vehicle, up to 8 people; garden extra $6 per person Jan.–Apr. (blooming season), free rest of year.*

★ Cascades Park

ARTS VENUE | History tells us that Territorial Governor William Pope Duval was so entranced by a lovely cascading waterfall, he chose a nearby hill to build Florida's first Capitol. History was not kind to the site, which became a dump and later a water retention area. It was only recently that the city planned a remarkable transformation, and Cascades Park has become one of Tallahassee's newest and most beloved parks. In addition to the two lakes that hold and channel storm water downstream, the 24-acre park includes an ampitheater, dancing water fountains, a playground, a historical self tour and wide, and meandering sidewalks. A concrete waterfall was installed as a nod to the long-gone original. A brick building that housed the electric utility has been repurposed into a restaurant, where diners can enjoy a water, sound, and light show with their dinner. It attracts hundreds of locals daily and is a hub for festivals celebrating Shakespeare and books and music. The ampitheater hosts free concerts as well as appearances by nationally known acts. ✉ *1001 S. Gadsden St.* ☎ *850/891–3866* 🌐 *www.discovercascades.com* 🎫 *Free.*

Challenger Learning Center

OBSERVATORY | **FAMILY** | Visitors of all ages can't help but get excited about math and science exploration at this "edutainment" center featuring a space mission simulator, an IMAX 3D theater, and the Downtown Digital Dome Theatre & Planetarium. Kids and kids at heart can reenact a space mission with the Space Mission Simulator. The next best thing to actual space flight, the simulator features a Mission Control room designed after NASA Johnson Space Center and an orbiting space station modeled after the laboratory on the International Space Station. The Downtown Digital Dome Theatre & Planetarium is 50-foot-high, high-definition theater with a booming surround sound system and state-of-the-art projectors. It offers educational programs as well as musical odysseys. Also on site is an IMAX 3-D theater, showing documentaries and popular movies. ✉ *200 S. Duval St.* ☎ *850/645–7827 business office and show times* 🌐 *www.challengertlh.com* 🎫 *Planetarium $5, IMAX $8–$10.*

★ Edward Ball Wakulla Springs State Park

NATIONAL/STATE PARK | Known for having one of the largest and deepest springs in the world, this very picturesque and highly recommended park remains relatively untouched, retaining the wild and exotic look it had in the mid-20th century, when two *Tarzan* movies and *Creature from the Black Lagoon* were shot here. Beyond the 1930s-era Spanish Mediterranean-style lodge (open to overnight guests) is the spring where river boats set off deep into the lush, jungle-lined waterway to catch glimpses of alligators, snakes, and waterfowl. Because of decreased visibility, glass-bottom boat tours are a rare treat (usually in the late winter or early spring) allowing you to peer into the springs' mysterious waters. In the summer, an observation tower offers a chance to plunge into the springs' heart-stopping 70-degree water. In winter a climb to the top affords a great opportunity to see visiting manatees. ✉ *465 Wakulla Park Dr., Wakulla Springs* ✥ *15 miles south of Tallahassee on State Road 61.* ☎ *850/561–7276* 🌐 *www.floridastateparks.org/parks-and-trails/edward-ball-wakulla-springs-state-park* 🎫 *$6 per vehicle, up to eight people; boat tour $8.*

Florida Historic Capitol Museum

GOVERNMENT BUILDING | **FAMILY** | In front of the modern, 22-story tower that serves as Florida's state Capitol sits a domed, classical-styled building with whimsical candy-striped awnings—the "old" Capitol it replaced. As the "new" Capitol was being constructed in the 1970s, there was much conversation about what to do with the old one, including tearing it down completely. It was finally decided the Historic Capitol would evolve into a museum of Florida's political history and a four-year-long restoration would commence, bringing back the structure with its stained glass interior dome to how it appeared in 1902. The hallways, governor's suite and chambers of the House, Senate, and Supreme Court were restored. Other rooms have been filled with artifacts that trace Florida's political history from territorial days to the present. Docents will provide information for self-guided tours, and you can download a free audio tour from the museum's website. ✉ *400 S. Monroe St.* ✣ *At the intersection of Apalachee Pkwy. and S. Monroe St.* ☎ *850/487–1902* 🌐 *www.flhistoriccapitol.gov* 🎫 *Free.*

Mission San Luis Archaeological and Historic Site

ARCHAEOLOGICAL SITE | FAMILY | On the site of a 17th-century Spanish mission and Apalachee Indian town, this museum focuses on the archaeology of the late 1600s, when this and three nearby villages had a population of more than 1,400. Threatened by Creek Indians and British forces, the locals burned the village and fled in 1704. Researchers continue to conduct digs and analyze their findings. Although it is surrounded by homes and shopping centers, this re-creation of a 17th-century Spanish village and its living-history guides will take visitors far away from the modern day. Several buildings have been restored or rebuilt to give a sense of how the Spaniards and Apalachee coexisted and assimilated each other's foods and traditions. Particularly impressive is a Native American Council House. With a palm-thatched roof, the "city hall," the cavernous structure stands five stories tall and 140 feet in diameter. A 24,000-square-foot, state-of-the-art visitor center offers an expanded exhibit hall and gift shop. ✉ *2100 W. Tennessee St.* ☎ *850/245–6406* 🌐 *www.missionsanluis.org* 🎫 *$5* ⏲ *Closed Mon.*

Museum of Florida History

MUSEUM | If you thought Florida was founded by Walt Disney, stop in here. The displays explain the state's past by highlighting the unique geological and historical events that have shaped the state. Exhibits include a mammoth armadillo grazing in a savanna, the remains of a giant mastodon found in nearby Wakulla Springs, and a dugout canoe that once carried Native Americans into Florida's backwaters. Florida's history also includes settlements by the Spanish, British, French, and Confederates who fought for possession of the state.

Gold bars, weapons, flags, maps, furniture, a steamboat, and other artifacts underscore the fact that although most Americans date the nation to 1776, Florida's residents were building settlements hundreds of years earlier. If this intrigues you, one floor up is the Florida State Archives and Library, where there's a treasure trove of government records, manuscripts, photographs, genealogical records, and other materials. ■ **TIP→ It was in these archives that researchers found footage of a young Jim Morrison appearing in a promotional film for Florida's universities.** ✉ *500 S. Bronough St.* ☎ *850/245–6400, 850/245–6600 library, 850/245–6700 archives* 🌐 *www.museumoffloridahistory.com* 🎫 *Free.*

New Capitol

GOVERNMENT BUILDING | Although it's known as the "New" Capitol, the 22-story modern skyscraper flanked by lower-slung House and Senate offices is actually more than 40 years old. In the 1960s, when there was talk of relocating the seat of the state's business to a more central location like Orlando, Panhandle legislators got to work and approved the construction of a sorely needed capitol

Guided tours are given daily at Florida's Old Capitol in Tallahassee. It sits in front of the 22-story New Capitol.

complex that would anchor the capital right where it was. It's perfectly placed at the crest of a hill, sitting prominently behind the classical revival-styled Historic Capitol. After going through security, pick up a brochure for a self-guided tour at the Florida Visitors Center, located on the plaza level. The governor's office is on the first floor, along with galleries including the Florida Artists Hall of Fame, a series of plaques that pay tribute to Floridians such as Ray Charles, Burt Reynolds, Tennessee Williams, Ernest Hemingway, and Marjorie Kinnan Rawlings.

The Italian marble-lined rotunda area is abuzz when the state legislature meets for its annual 60-day session (January and February in even years, March through April in odd years) and the census grows from 1,500 workers to 5,000. The House and Senate chambers on the fifth floor provide viewer galleries for watching lawmaking in action. To get away from the crowds, spend a few contemplative moments in the Heritage Chapel, constructed of Florida materials including coquina and cypress. Another don't-miss is "Stormsong" outside of the west entrance to the Capitol. The steel sculpture of dolphins cavorting in a cascade of water celebrates the state's wildlife. ✉ *400 S. Monroe St.* ☎ *850/488–6167* 🌐 *www.floridacapitol.myflorida.com* 🎟 *Free* 🕓 *Closed weekends and holidays.*

★ St. Marks National Wildlife Refuge and Lighthouse

ARCHAEOLOGICAL SITE | FAMILY | Natural salt marshes, tidal flats, and freshwater pools used by early natives set the stage for the once-powerful Ft. San Marcos de Apalache, which was built nearby in 1639. Stones salvaged from the fort were used in the lighthouse, which is still in operation. In winter the 100,000-acre-plus refuge on the shores of Apalachee Bay is the resting place for thousands of migratory birds of more than 300 species, but the alligators seem to like it year-round (keep your camera ready). The visitor center has information on more than 75 miles of marked trails. One of the most

African American History

From the Knott House, where the Emancipation Proclamation was first read in Florida, to HBCU Florida A&M University to civil rights to the blues, Tallahassee has an abundance of historical sites significant to African American history. Start on the Civil Rights Heritage Walk, 16 sidewalk panels commemorating those who participated in the 1956 bus boycott and lunch counter sit-ins. It will lead you to Tallahassee's visitor center, where you can map out a route to several spots of interest, including the nearby John G. Riley House and Museum, the Union Bank Museum, and commemorations of the Smokey Hollow community. Farther afield is the Black Archives Research Center & Museum, on the FAMU campus, as well as several other sites.

popular times to visit is in October, when Monarch butterflies flock to the refuge for a little R&R during their winter migration to Mexico. Twenty-five miles south of Tallahassee, the refuge can be reached via Route 363. ✉ *1255 Lighthouse Rd., St. Marks* ☎ *850/925–6121* 🌐 *saintmarks.fws.gov* 🎟 *$5 per vehicle.*

Tallahassee Museum

MUSEUM VILLAGE | **FAMILY** | Not exactly a museum, this is really an expansive, bucolic park showcasing a peaceful and intriguing look at Old Florida, located about 20 minutes from downtown. Historic 19th-century buildings are on-site, including an 1880s pioneer farm, a one-room schoolhouse, and a Southern plantation manor. On weekends, the village comes alive with living history demonstrations, including cooking, blacksmithing, quilting, and other activities of the day. A boardwalk meanders through the 52 acres of natural habitat that make up the zoo, which has such varied animals as panthers, bobcats, white-tailed deer, bald eagles, red wolves, hawks, owls, otters, and black bears. Guest animals drop in for visits and close-up-and-personal animal encounters are scheduled daily. You can get a bird's-eye view of the museum at Tree-to-Tree Adventures. The area (additional admission required) features sky-high zip lines and an aerial obstacle course. Don't miss the nature walk featuring the colorful dinosaur sculptures of Jim Gary, created entirely from recycled car parts. ✉ *3945 Museum Dr.* ✥ *Turn off Orange Ave. at Rankin Rd.* ☎ *850/575–8684* 🌐 *www.tallahasseemuseum.org* 🎟 *$12.*

Restaurants

★ Cypress Restaurant

$$$$ | **SOUTHERN** | Since 2000 (when the reporters, attorneys, and assorted bigwigs put the restaurant on the map during the presidential election recount), Cypress has endured as one of Tallahassee's most popular special-occasion restaurants. Chef-owner David Gwynn prides himself on his gourmet takes on Southern specialities such as Cypress Oysters & Biscuits and Basil, Ginger & Orange Shrimp & Grits. **Known for:** refined, but casual atmosphere; elevated Southern cuisine; regional craft beer and spirits. $ *Average main: $31* ✉ *320 E. Tennessee St.* ☎ *850/513–1000* 🌐 *www.cypressrestaurant.com.*

Hopkins' Eatery

$ | **AMERICAN** | Locals in the know flock here for superb salads, homemade soups, and sandwiches—expect a short wait at lunchtime—via simple counter service. Opt for a chunky chicken melt, smothered beef, or garden vegetarian sub. **Known for:** good salads and sandwiches; spearmint iced tea; cakes and pies. *Average main: $7 1415 Market St. 850/668–0311 www.hopkinseatery.com Closed Sun., no dinner Sat.*

Kool Beanz Café

$$ | **FUSION** | The cuisine is as eclectic and cozy as the atmosphere at this Tallahassee staple, loved by locals and visitors alike. The decor is part of the charm, with a vibrant array of paintings by local artists. **Known for:** fine food with a casual vibe; creative and colorful dishes; long lines, especially on weekends. *Average main: $20 921 Thomasville Rd. 850/224–2466 www.koolbeanz-cafe.com.*

Savour

$$$ | **CONTEMPORARY** | Savour embraces elegance and comfort, with billowy curtains, French-chic furnishings, upholstered seats, and gold accents. It provides the perfect backdrop for its food, which includes a short seasonal menu of traditional offerings of steak, seafood, pork, and chicken creatively prepared and beautifully presented. **Known for:** elegant presentations; friendly, knowledgeable servers; steak and seafood. *Average main: $28 115 E. Park Ave. 850/765–6966 www.savourtallahassee.com.*

Hotels

Aloft Tallahassee Downtown

$$ | **HOTEL** | This urban-chic hotel provides the tree-lined downtown district with a bit of trendy fun courtesy of loft-style rooms with bright, minimalist decor. **Pros:** convenient to downtown, universities, and nightlife/restaurants; free Wi-Fi. **Cons:** small, utilitarian rooms; because it's pet-friendly, there can be a lot of animals in the hotel. *Rooms from: $283 200 N. Monroe St. 850/513–0313, 866/513–0313 162 rooms No meals.*

Governors Inn

$$ | **B&B/INN** | Only a block from the capitol, this plushly restored historic livery stable is abuzz during the week with politicians, press, lobbyists, and business travelers; on weekends, it's a perfect jumping-off point for tourists who want to visit downtown or couples looking for a romantic getaway. **Pros:** good service; well-appointed rooms, some suites have fireplaces; near museums, restaurants, and the Capitol. **Cons:** in a very busy area; hotel can be busy with events and meetings; parking is valet-only. *Rooms from: $239 Governors Inn, 209 S. Adams St. In the middle of downtown, a block from the Capitol buildings 850/681–6855 thegovinn.org 49 rooms Breakfast.*

★ Hotel Duval

$$ | **HOTEL** | This boutique hotel, a renovated version of the landmark built in 1951, sets a high standard for small luxury hotels in the capital. **Pros:** top-level amenities; good restaurants; unique suites. **Cons:** not suited to families; small rooms; valet parking (for an additional fee) required. *Rooms from: $260 415 N. Monroe St. 850/224–6000 www.hotelduval.com 117 rooms No meals.*

Nightlife

Bradfordville Blues Club

MUSIC CLUBS | You'll have to break out the GPS to find this cinder-block juke joint on a dirt road in rural Leon County, but it's worth the trip if you love world-class blues music and ice-cold beer. Open Friday and Saturday nights, the 120-seat ultracasual venue also features nightly bonfires and fried catfish. The walls and tabletops are covered with more than 50 autographed portraits of the blues greats who have passed through the BBC, as it's known locally. *7152 Moses Ln. 850/906–0766 www.bradfordvilleblues.com.*

CollegeTown/Gaines Street

NIGHTLIFE OVERVIEW | In the shadow of Florida State University's Doak Campbell Stadium and within sight of Florida A&M University, CollegeTown was built as an entertainment hub for college students. Contiguous with a rapidly redeveloping Gaines Street, the area offers shopping during the day and is lively after dark. From the gastropub **Madison Social,** to the casual beer bar **Township,** to the Miami-vibe of **Recess,** with its rooftop swimming pool, anyone can find their fun within a few blocks. Gaines Street has live music venues like **The Wilbury,** and whiskey aficionados have their choice of 170 bottles at **Warhorse** (which conveniently has a walk-through to **Gaines Street Pies** next door). ✉ *S. Woodward Ave.* ☎ *850/765–9925* 🌐 *www.fsucollegetown.net.*

Level 8 Lounge

PIANO BARS/LOUNGES | This rooftop lounge has a sleek, chic sophistication that matches the boutique hotel to which it's attached. Enjoy panoramic views of the capital city while you sip a drink from the custom drink menu or nibble on small bites from the bar menu. ✉ *Hotel Duval, 415 N. Monroe St.* ☎ *850/224–6000* 🌐 *hotelduval.com.*

★ **Proof Brewing Company**

BARS/PUBS | Tallahassee's first entry into the local craft brewing movement was Proof, which opened a brewery, tasting room and hangout spot in the funky arts community of Railroad Square. Its brews have become so popular that Proof moved to a much larger facility in what used to be Tallahassee's Coca-Cola bottling plant that will allow it to expand production from 6,000 to 30,000 barrels per year. The new site also allowed them to expand their tasting room and beer garden with a collection of indoor and outdoor games. They also added a restaurant, Proper–the Brewpub at Proof. Proper offers pub-grub favorities including burgers, sandwiches, and dogs as well as a pretty extensive choice of fries. Well-behaved, leashed dogs and children with their parents are allowed. ✉ *1320 S. Monroe St.* ☎ *850/320–6775* 🌐 *www.proofbrewingco.com.*

Waterworks

MUSIC CLUBS | With its retro-chic tiki-bar fittings and waterfall windows, Waterworks is quirky, fun, and a true Tallahassee institution (the funky bar has been in Midtown since before there was a Midtown). In addition to its tiki cocktails, Waterworks also offers a menu of sandwiches, salads, apps and small plates for lunch and dinner. A ✉ *1133 Thomasville Rd.* ☎ *850/224–1887.*

Performing Arts

Tallahassee Symphony Orchestra

MUSIC | You can expect an exceptional symphony experience because this orchestra includes music faculty from Florida State University as well as talented local artists. Concerts are held in FSU's beautiful and acoustically superb Ruby Diamond Concert Hall. Look up to see the owl sculpture winging along above the audience. A special treat are free open rehearsals before the performances, where you can watch Conductor Darko Butorac interact with the musicians. ✉ *Ruby Diamond Concert Hall, 222 S. Copeland St.* ☎ *850/644–5541* 🌐 *www.tallahasseesymphony.org.*

Theatre Tallahassee

THEATER | This theater featuring local talent has an eight-production season that runs from August through June, featuring everything from musicals in its Mainstage theater to more adult-themed shows in the intimate black-box style Studio theater. ✉ *1861 Thomasville Rd.* ☎ *850/224–8474* 🌐 *theatretallahassee.org.*

Shopping

Market District

SHOPPING NEIGHBORHOODS | Hop off Interstate 10 at Exit 203 to head to this shopping and dining district filled with more than 50 locally owned specialty shops, salons, cafés, and restaurants. Hearth & Soul, Narcissus, and Coton Colors are popular, as are many other stores scattered around the area in smaller enclaves. Not to worry, though—most are within walking distance of one another. The Market District is the place for a taste of true local culture. It's slightly west of Thomasville Road at the intersection of Timberlane Road and Market Street. ✉ *Timberlane Rd. at Market St.* 🌐 *www.themarketdistrict.net.*

Midtown District

SHOPPING NEIGHBORHOODS | This area mixes a little bit of Southern charm with city chic, offering everything from the stylish fashions of Sparkle and Divas and Devils, to luxury beauty and spa services at Kanvas, to the independent bookstore Midtown Reader. Shops can be found along North Monroe Street heading toward downtown, as well as some of the side streets. If you get hungry picking up purchases, revive yourself with the simple but tasty fare at Paisley Cafe, or relax and enjoy Japanese pub food at Izzy Pub and Sushi. ✉ *Tallahassee* ✣ *Between North Moore St. and Thomasville Rd., between W. 7th Ave. and W. 4th Ave.*

Activities

Tallahassee Trails

BICYCLING | Hike, bike, bird, run, or paddle; there are more than 600 miles of trails in and around Tallahassee to help you enjoy the outdoors. All have been compiled into one website: 🌐 *trailahassee.com*. It features interactive maps and GPS technology as well as a "Find a Trail" function that helps users find the best trails based on the surface, their skill level, and activities. Beginning paddlers might enjoy a four-hour excursion on the Lafayette Passage Paddle Trail, while hard-core mountain bikers have their choice of five challenging unpaved trails, including the twisty-turny and dauntingly named Red Bug. ✉ *Tallahassee* 🌐 *www.trailahassee.com.*

Index

A

B

T

Photo Credits

Front Cover: Aurora Photos, USA [Description: Beach at sunrise at Moorings Village Resort, Florida Keys, USA.] **Back cover, from left to right:** Jaimie Tuchman/istockphoto, littleny/ istockphoto, dosecreative/istockphoto. **Spine:** kyletperry/istockphoto. **Interior, from left to right:** Coraline M/shutterstock (1). Sean Pavone/shutterstock (2). FloridaStock/Shutterstock (5). **Chapter 1: Experience Florida:** Zhukova Valentyna,shutterstock (8). Sean Pavone/Shutterstock (10). CK Ma/Shutterstock (11). Art Deco Tours (11). Pola Damonte/Shutterstock (12). William Rodrigues Dos Santos/Dreamstime.com (12). Juneisy Q. Hawkins/Shutterstock (13). Courtesy of Hemingway Home (14). Ball & Chain/Michael Strader Marko (14). Romrodphoto/Shutterstock (14). Courtesy Miami Design District (14). Sean Pavone/Shutterstock (15). Courtesy of Miami Dolphins (15). Courtesy of Visit South Walton (16). Joost van Uffelen/shutterstock (16). Wangkun Jia/Dreamstime.com (16). NaughtyNut/shutterstock (17). Jon Bilous/shutterstock (18). Courtesy of Funky Buddha Brewery (18). Casey Crandall/shutterstock (18). travelview/shutterstock (18). Courtesy The John and Mable Ringling Museum of Art (19). Florida's Historic Coast (20). Courtesy of Daytona International Speedway (20). Steve Bower/shutterstock (20). Steven Diaz (21). voloshin311/Shutterstock (26). bonchan/shutterstock (26). comeirrez/Shutterstock (26). Olyina/Shutterstock (27). Andrew Meade (27). Alexander Demyanenko/Shutterstock (28). Luke Popwell/Dreamstime.com (28). Kamira/Shutterstock (28). Simon Dannhauer/Shutterstock (29). Dmitry Vinogradov/Dreamstime.com (29). VISIT FLORIDA (30). Rob Hainer/shutterstock (30). Nicholas A Collura-Gehrt (30). Susanne Pommer/shutterstock (31). Parick Farrell and Peter W. Cross (31). Zachary Balber/Courtesy of The Bass, Miami Beach (32). Wangkun Jia/Shutterstock (32). Richard Goldberg/Shutterstock (32). Courteesy of Art Basel (32). Felix Mizioznikov/Dreamstime.com (33). Oriol Tarridas Photography (33). Comayagua99/Wikimedia.org (33). Daniel Bock/Courtesy of Museum of Contemporary Art North Miami (MOCA) (33). **Chapter 3: Miami and Miami Beach:** iStockphoto (53). Roxana Gonzalez/ Shutterstock (56). Alena Haurylik/Shutterstock (57). JUPITERIMAGES/ Brand X /Alamy (57). dk/Alamy (85). Nicholas Pitt/Alamy (85). Copyright 2013 Ryan Forbes/AVABLU (87). Nicholas Pitt/Alamy (87). Tinamou/Dreamstime.com (87). Laura Paresky (87). Ian Patrick/Alamy (87). INTERFOTO Pressebildagentur/Alamy (88). culliganphoto/Alamy (88). Ian Patrick/Alamy (88). Garth Aikens/Miami Beach Convention Center (89). Robert Harding Picture Library Ltd/Alamy (100). John Tunney/Dreamstime.com (110). **Chapter 4: Everglades:** jo Crebbin/shutterstock (123). tbkmedia.de / Alamy (128-129). Andrewtappert (132). David R. Frazier Photolibrary, Inc./Alamy (132). andrewtappert/wikimedia.org (132). FloridaStock/Shutterstock (132). inga spence / Alamy (132). umar faruq/Shutterstock (133). mlorenz/Shutterstock (133). Peter Arnold, Inc. / Alamy (133). Caleb Foster/Shutterstock (133). Larsek/Shutterstock (133). FloridaStock/Shutterstock (134). John A. Anderson/Shutterstock (134). FloridaStock/Shutterstock (134). Norman Bateman/Shutterstock (134). Krzysztof Slusarczyk/Shutterstock (135). David Drake & Deborah Jaffe (135). Norman Bateman/Shutterstock (135). Jerry Zitterman/Shutterstock (135). Steven Widoff/Alamy (142). Marc Muench/ Alamy (146). jimfeng (150). VISIT FLORIDA. (155). **Chapter 5: The Florida Keys:** ventdusud/shutterstock (159). Gregory Wrona/Alamy (162). Michael Ventura/Alamy (163). Claudio Lovo/Shutterstock (163). Stephen Frink/ Florida Keys News Bureau. No Sales (171). flasporty/ flickr [CC BY-NC 2.0] (178). Korzeniewski/Dreamstime.com (183). PBorowka/Shutterstock (185). Melissa Schalke/iStockphoto (187). Henryk Sadura/Alamy (195). CedarBendDrive/Flickr [CC BY-NC 2.0] (207). Visit Florida (209). John P Franzis (211). Starwood Hotels & Resorts (222). Daniel Korzeniewski/Shutterstock (224). **Chapter 6: Fort Lauderdale:** Sean Pavone/shutterstock (231). Eric Gevaert/Shutterstock (247). Terrance Klassen/age fotostock (250). Lago Mar Resort & Club-Fort Lauderdale (252). **Chapter 7: Palm Beach and the Treasure Coast:** Sean Pavone/shutterstock (267). Sargent Photography (273). mrk_photo/flickr [CC BY-NC 2.0] (285). FloridaStock/Shutterstock (292). Morikami Museum and Japanese Gardens (296). VISIT FLORIDA. (308). VISIT FLORIDA. (321). **Chapter 8: The Tampa Bay Area:** Sayran/Dreamstime.com (325). Photosounds/Dreamstime.com (333). Seymour Levy (351). Watland (361). Richard T. Nowitz/age fotostock (369). Larry Porges/ shutterstock (371). P00381 TIPTON DONALD/age fotostock (377). cogito ergo imago/Flickr [CC BY-SA 2.0] (381). **Chapter 9: The Lower Gulf Coast:** Dan Leffel/agefotostock (387). VISIT FLORIDA. (396). Walter Bibikow/age fotostock (403). blewisphotography/Shutterstock (407). Mitch Aunger/Shutterstock (408). Don Mammoser/shutterstock.com (425). Dennis Guyitt/iStockphoto (428). World Pictures/age fotostock (436). **Chapter 10: Orlando and Environs:** Rabbit75/Dreamstime.com (441). Orlando CVB (452). VISIT FLORIDA. (461). Kissimmee - The Heart of Florida/Flickr [CC BY-SA 2.0] (467). spakattacks/Flickr [CC BY-SA 2.0] (470). **Chapter 11: Walt Disney World:** Sunflower6000/ Dreamstime.com (473). Lequint/Dreamstime.com (485). JoshMcConnell/Flickr [CC BY-SA 2.0] (489). Disney (497). Berniephillips/Dreamstime.com (498). tom.arthur/Flickr [CC BY-SA 2.0] (511). PrincessAshley/Flickr [CC BY-SA 2.0] (515). **Chapter 12: Universal Orlando Resort:** 2007 Universal Orlando Resort. All rights reserved. (521). Grandmaisonc/Dreamstime.com (536). 2014 Universal Orlando Resort. All rights reserved. (540). Kmiragaya/Dreamstime.com (542). **Chapter 13: Northeast Florida:** FRILET Patrick (547). Kennedy Space Center (550-551) (All). Karel Gallas/Shutterstock (557). Jeff Greenberg/age fotostock (562). Funinthetube, Fodors.com (572). Arkorn/Dreamstime.com (578). yeowatzup/flickr [CC BY-SA 2.0] (603). Dimitris Timpilis/shutterstock.com (605). Louishenault/Dreamstime.com (611). **Chapter 14: Northwest Florida:** Cheryl Casey/Shutterstock (615). Kathy Hicks/iStockphoto (625). Judykennamer/Dreamstime.com (636). geishaboy500/flickr [CC BY-SA 2.0] (647). JNB Photography/Shutterstock (649). Wilsilver77/Dreamstime (658-659). Dennis MacDonald/age fotostock (662).

*About Our Writers: All photos are courtesy of the writers except for the following.

*Every effort has been made to trace the copyright holders, and we apologize in advance for any accidental errors. We would be happy to apply the corrections in the following edition of this publication.

Notes

Notes

Notes

Notes

Notes

Notes

Notes

Notes

Notes

Notes

Notes